Highly Recommended

OSWAAL BOOKS®

LEARNING MADE SIMPLE

OBJECTIVE Quantitative Aptitude

For All Competitive Examinations

SSC/Defence/Banking/LIC/RRB/CAT & other Important Examinations

1 **100% Updated** with Latest Questions of different examinations

2 **Chapter-wise Segregation** with concise revision notes & learning objectives

3 **Crisp Revision** with smart mind maps and important formulae & tricks

4 **Extensive Practice** with fully solved 1500+ practice questions with 3 levels of difficulty

5 **Valuable Exam Insights** with chapter-wise & Exam-wise trend analysis

3rd EDITION, YEAR 2025

ISBN "9789367474204"

SYLLABUS COVERED

Objective Quantitative Aptitude

PUBLISHED BY

OSWAAL BOOKS & LEARNING PVT. LTD.

1/11, Sahitya Kunj, M.G. Road,
Agra - 282002, (UP) India

1010, Cambourne Business Centre
Cambridge, Cambridgeshire
CB 236DP, United kingdom

0562-2857671

contact@oswaalbooks.com

www.OswaalBooks.com

Printed at Sahitya Bhawan, Agra

Contents

- Deciphering Quantitative Aptitude & Its Importance 4 - 4
- Preface 5 - 5
- Tips to Crack Quantitative Aptitude in first Attempt 6 - 6
- Syllabus for major competitive Examinations 7 - 11
- Chapter-wise & Exam-wise Trend Analysis 12 - 12
- Important Formulae & Tricks 15 - 24

Section - 1 : Arithmetic

1. Percentage	1 - 12
2. Profit, Loss & Discount	13 - 24
3. Simple Interest	25 - 37
4. Compound Interest	38 - 55
5. Ratio and Proportion	56 - 65
6. Partnership	66 - 72
7. Average	73 - 86
8. Mixture & Allegation	87 - 96
9. Speed, Time & Distance	97 - 114
10. Time and Work	115 - 129
11. Pipes and Cisterns	130 - 144

Section - 2: Advance Maths

12. Geometry	145 - 178
13. Mensuration	179 - 201
14. Algebra	202 - 222
15. Trigonometry	223 - 248
16. Height & Distance	249 - 262
17. Co-ordinate Geometry	263 - 278

Section - 3: Number System

18. Number System	279 - 293
19. Power Indices & Surds	294 - 309
20. Simplification	310 - 327

Section - 4: Data Interpretation

21. Bar & Line Graph	328 - 343
22. Pie-Chart	344 - 354
23. Data Tabulation	355 - 368
24. Caselets	369 - 378

Section - 5: Modern Mathematics

25. Permutation & Combination	379 - 384
26. Probability	385 - 390
27. Set Theory	391 - 399

❑❑

Deciphering Quantitative Aptitude & Its Importance

Quantitative aptitude refers to the ability to understand and solve mathematical problems quickly and accurately. It involves the application of basic arithmetic, algebra, geometry, and other mathematical concepts to solve problems related to quantitative analysis, data interpretation, and logical reasoning.

Some common topics included in quantitative aptitude assessments are:

1. *Arithmetic:* This involves solving problems related to addition, subtraction, multiplication, division, percentages, ratio, and proportion.
2. *Algebra:* This includes solving problems related to linear and quadratic equations, inequalities, and simultaneous equations.
3. *Geometry:* This includes problems related to lines, angles, triangles, circles, and polygons.
4. *Trigonometry:* This involves solving problems related to trigonometric functions such as sine, cosine, and tangent.
5. ***Data Interpretation:*** This involves analysing and interpreting data presented in graphs, charts, and tables.

   To improve your quantitative aptitude skills, you can practice solving mathematical problems regularly, familiarize yourself with different formulas and concepts, and improve your mental calculation speed.

   Quantitative Aptitude, also known as mathematical aptitude, is a vital component of most competitive exams in India. It tests a candidate's ability to solve numerical problems accurately and quickly. Here are some of the competitive exams where Quantitative Aptitude plays a significant role:

6. ***Bank Exams:*** Quantitative Aptitude is an essential component of bank exams like IBPS PO, IBPS Clerk, SBI PO, SBI Clerk, etc. The section includes questions on topics like arithmetic, algebra, geometry, trigonometry, and data interpretation.
7. ***SSC Exams:*** Quantitative Aptitude is also an important section of various Staff Selection Commission (SSC) exams, including SSC CGL, SSC CHSL, etc. The section includes questions on topics like time and distance, profit and loss, percentage, ratio and proportion, etc.
8. ***Railway Exams:*** Quantitative Aptitude is a crucial section in railway exams like RRB NTPC, RRB JE, etc. The section includes questions on topics like number system, simplification, geometry, data interpretation, etc.
9. ***MBA Entrance Exams:*** Quantitative Aptitude is a crucial section in MBA entrance exams like CAT, XAT, MAT, etc. The section includes questions on topics like arithmetic, algebra, geometry, trigonometry, and data interpretation.
10. ***UPSC Civil Services Exam:*** Quantitative Aptitude is a part of the CSAT (Civil Services Aptitude Test) paper in the UPSC Civil Services Exam. The section includes questions on topics like data interpretation, simplification, and arithmetic.

In conclusion, Quantitative Aptitude is a critical component of various competitive exams in India, and it is essential to have a good understanding of mathematical concepts to perform well in these exams.

Preface

Welcome to the revised edition of "Objective Quantitative Aptitude"! This book aims to equip readers with a comprehensive understanding of quantitative aptitude concepts essential for various competitive exams and entrance tests such as Banking, SSC, Railways, UPSC, and various other State Level Exams.

The objective of this book is to provide a comprehensive understanding of the concepts of Quantitative Aptitude and their applications to the readers. The book covers all essential topics of Quantitative Aptitude such as Simplification, Number System, Ratio & Proportion, Percentage, Profit & Loss, Time & Distance, Time & Work, Data Interpretation, etc.

This book is meticulously crafted to cater to the diverse needs of aspirants preparing for competitive exams. Whether you are a beginner looking to build a strong foundation or an experienced candidate aiming to refine your skills, "Objective Quantitative Aptitude" provides a structured approach to mastering quantitative aptitude concepts.

Some unique features of this book are:

- ***100% Updated:*** with latest questions asked in different examinations.
- ***Crisp Revision:*** Concepts Review, Important Formulae & Tricks and Mind Maps offer bite-sized and just-in-time revision tools.
- ***Extensive Practice:*** with More than 1500 Previous year questions from various competitive exams segregated based on difficulty level.
- ***Concept Clarity:*** Easy to Grasp , concepts through Solved examples.
- ***Expert Tips:*** Helps you get expert knowledge to master the Quantitative Aptitude Concepts on your first attempt.
- ***Learning Objectives:*** Outlines what aspirant should understand or be able to achieve after the course
- ***To-the-point theory:*** The book provides concise and clear explanations of quantitative aptitude concepts without overwhelming readers with too much information.
- ***Quick and easy techniques:*** The book offers shortcuts and easy-to-follow techniques to help readers solve typical exam questions quickly and efficiently.

In conclusion, this book aims to provide a one-stop solution for all the aspirants who are preparing for competitive exams.

It is hoped that the book will be immensely useful to the readers and will help them to achieve their desired goals.

Our books have always been well received by our readers and this is a testament to our research-oriented approach. Our learning pedagogy supplements our editorial research and makes our book current and relevant. We hope our resources will help students to supplement their examination preparation strategy and help them secure high scores.

We wish our readers great success ahead!

Happy learning!

Team Oswaal

Tips to Crack Quantitative Aptitude in the First Attempt

The Quantitative Aptitude is a crucial section in many competitive exams in India, such as bank exams, UPSC, SSC, CAT, and other MBA entrance exams. Quantitative Aptitude has a major role in competitive exams in India as it tests essential knowledge and skills required for various fields & evaluates analytical and problem-solving skills. Cracking the quantitative aptitude section of a competitive exam in the first attempt requires hard work, dedication, and a strategic approach. Here are some tips that can help you achieve success in your first attempt:

1 Think Right

Calming yourself and thinking positive is the first and the best course of action that one is required to take. Think and believe that the exam goal is achievable if worked upon smartly.

2 Start studying from the beginning

All the aspirants are aware of how vast, comprehensive and detailed the syllabus of the Quantitative section is. To crack the exam in the first attempt you have to start preparing for the exam from the beginning of your 12th class. It is only then that you will be able to complete the entire syllabus. Following this approach will also allow you plenty of time to revise.

3 Respect the syllabus and arrange the materials accordingly

While preparing for the Quantitative Aptitude nothing can be labelled as less important. Questions can come from the most unexpected topics too. Laying down your whole syllabus in front of you will help you to decide on the study material you require.

4 Get the right tools and study material

Gathering and preparing from the appropriate study material is something you cannot be ignorant towards. You can refer to Oswaal 'Objective Quantitative Aptitude' to enhance your preparation. the is on the lines of the current syllabus and can be entrusted upon before the examination.

5 Schedule total me for each subject

Creating a schedule which gives due time to all the subjects is a must. Giving proper time to all the subjects daily will help you cover the syllabus on time, giving you enough time for revision.

6 Understand the concepts

No one can crack the Quantitative Aptitude exam just by mugging up all the concepts and topics. The syllabus of the exam is in-depth such that you need to understand every concept.

7 Practice a lot of Sample Papers

Oswaal 'Objective Quantitative Aptitude' will not only help you in understanding the examination pattern, but they will also help you in figuring out the questons that come up every year and this might give you an edge over other students. The includes all the typologies of Questons asked in the Examination, Previous Years Papers with solutions, Mind Maps, etc. Referring to various sample papers might also help you in comprehending the areas which require more work.

8 Revise whenever you get me

Make sure you revise as much as possible. The revision will help you in keeping the concepts fresh in your mind.

9 Analysing your performance

While you are solving papers, make sure you keep a track of time i.e. how much time does it take to solve one section or one question? Make a report of the sections and type of questions which take minimum and maximum me.

Syllabus for major Competitive Examinations

CHSL (Combined Higher Secondary Level)
➢ **Number Systems:** Computation of Whole Number, Decimal and Fractions, Relationship between numbers.
➢ **Fundamental arithmetical operations:** Percentages, Ratio and Proportion, Square roots, Averages, Interest (Simple and Compound), Profit and Loss, Discount, Partnership Business, Mixture and Allegation, Time and distance, Time and work.
➢ **Mensuration:** Triangle, Quadrilaterals, Regular Polygons, Circle, Right Prism, Right Circular Cone, Right Circular Cylinder, Sphere, Hemispheres, Rectangular Parallelepiped, Regular Right Pyramid with triangular or square Base.
➢ **Algebra:** Basic algebraic identities of School Algebra and Elementary surds (simple problems) and Graphs of Linear Equations.
➢ **Geometry:** Familiarity with elementary geometric figures and facts: Triangle and its various kinds of centres, Congruence and similarity of triangles, Circle and its chords, tangents, angles subtended by chords of a circle, common tangents to two or more circles.
➢ **Trigonometry:** Trigonometry, Trigonometric ratios, Complementary angles, Height and distances (simple problems only) Standard Identities like sin2 θ + Cos2 θ = 1 etc.
➢ **Statistical Charts:** Use of Tables and Graphs: Histogram, Frequency polygon, Bar-diagram, Pie-chart.

SSC - CGL (Combined Graduate Level)	
➢ Computation of whole numbers	➢ Circle and its chords, tangents, angles subtended by chords of a circle, common tangents to two or more circles
➢ Decimals	➢ Triangle
➢ Fractions	➢ Quadrilaterals
➢ Relationships between numbers	➢ Regular Polygons
➢ Profit and Loss	➢ Right Prism
➢ Discount	➢ Right Circular Cone
➢ Partnership Business	➢ Right Circular Cylinder
➢ Mixture and Alligation	➢ Sphere
➢ Time and distance	➢ Heights and Distances
➢ Time & Work	➢ Histogram
➢ Percentage	➢ Frequency polygon
➢ Ratio & Proportion	➢ Bar diagram & Pie chart
➢ Square roots	➢ Hemispheres
➢ Averages	➢ Rectangular Parallelepiped
➢ Interest	➢ Regular Right Pyramid with triangular or square base
➢ Basic algebraic identities of School Algebra & Elementary surds	➢ Trigonometric ratio
➢ Graphs of Linear Equations	➢ Degree and Radian Measures
➢ Triangle and its various kinds of centres	➢ Standard Identities
➢ Congruence and similarity of triangles	➢ Complementary angles

Contd....

LIC - AAO (Assistant Administrative Officer)	
➢ Simplification ➢ Simple and Compound Interest ➢ Problem on Ages ➢ Probability ➢ Cistern and Pipe ➢ Mensuration ➢ Percentage ➢ Data Sufficiency ➢ Number Series ➢ Profit and Loss ➢ Work and Time ➢ Average	➢ Quadratic Equations ➢ Ratio and Proportion ➢ Surds and Indices ➢ Data Interpretation (Bar Graph, Line Chart, Tabular, Radar/Web, Pie Chart) ➢ HCF and LCM ➢ Permutation and Combination ➢ Speed, Distance and Time ➢ Boats and Streams ➢ Approximation ➢ Partnership ➢ Mixtures & Alligations

IBPS PO – Probationary Officer	IBPS – Clerk
➢ Data Interpretation ➢ Mensuration ➢ Profit ➢ Discount ➢ Probability ➢ Simple and Compound Interest ➢ Logarithms, ➢ Volume and Surface Area ➢ Partnership, Stocks and Shares ➢ Distance and Time ➢ Time and Work ➢ Ratio and Proportion ➢ Elements of Algebra ➢ Discount ➢ Trigonometry ➢ Equations ➢ Permutation and Combinations ➢ Height and Distances ➢ Clocks ➢ Percentages ➢ Mixture and Allegation ➢ Speed.	➢ NNumber Series ➢ Simplification/ Approximation ➢ Data Sufficiency ➢ Average ➢ Ratio and Proportion ➢ Time and Distance ➢ Relations ➢ Permutation and Combination ➢ Data Interpretation ➢ Quadratic Equation ➢ Mensuration ➢ Profit and Loss ➢ Work, Time, and Energy ➢ Probability ➢ Simple and Compound Interest

Contd....

NDA/NA - National Defence Academy/Naval Academy	
Topic	**Topic-wise**
Algebra	Sets, Venn diagrams, De Morgan laws, Cartesian product, relation, equivalence relation. Real numbers, Complex numbers, Modulus, Cube roots, Conversion of a number in Binary system to Decimals, and vice-versa. Arithmetic, Geometric and Harmonic progressions. Quadratic equations, Linear inequations, Permutation and Combination, Binomial theorem, and Logarithms.
Calculus	Concept of a real-valued function, domain, range, and graph of a function. Composite functions, one-to-one, onto, and inverse functions. The notion of limit, Standard limits, Continuity of functions, algebraic operations on continuous functions. Derivative of function at a point, geometrical and physical interpretation of a derivative-application. Derivatives of sum, product, and quotient of functions, a derivative of a function concerning another function, the derivative of a composite function. Second-order derivatives. Increasing and decreasing functions. Application of derivatives in problems of maxima and minima
Matrices and Determinants	Types of matrices, operations on matrices. Determinant of a matrix, basic properties of determinants. Adjoint and inverse of a square matrix, Applications-Solution of a system of linear equations in two or three unknowns by Cramer's rule and by Matrix Method.
Integral Calculus and Differential Equations	Integration as inverse of differentiation, integration by substitution and by parts, standard integrals involving algebraic expressions, trigonometric, exponential, and hyperbolic functions. Evaluation of definite integrals—determination of areas of plane regions bounded by curves—applications.Definition of order and degree of a differential equation, formation of a differential equation by examples. General and particular solution of differential equations, solution of the first order, and first-degree differential equations of various types—examples. Application in problems of growth and decay.
Trigonometry	Angles and their measures in degrees and radians. Trigonometric ratios. Trigonometric identities Sum and difference formulae. Multiple and Sub-multiple angles. Inverse trigonometric functions. Applications-Height and distance, properties of triangles.
Vector Algebra	Vectors in two and three dimensions, magnitude, and direction of a vector. Unit and null vectors, the addition of vectors, scalar multiplication of a vector, scalar product, or dot product of two vectors. Vector product or cross product of two vectors. Applications—work done by a force and moment of a force and in geometrical problems.
Analytical Geometry Of Two and Three Dimension	Rectangular Cartesian Coordinate system. Distance formula. Equation of a line in various forms. The angle between two lines. Distance of a point from a line. Equation of a circle in standard and a general form. Standard forms of parabola, ellipse, and hyperbola. Eccentricity and axis of a conic. Point in a three-dimensional space, the distance between two points. Direction Cosines and direction ratios. Equation two points. Direction Cosines and direction ratios. Equation of a plane and a line in various forms. The angle between two lines and the angle between two planes. Equation of a sphere.
Statistics and Probability	Probability: Random experiment, outcomes, and associated sample space, events, mutually exclusive and exhaustive events, impossible and certain events. Union and Intersection of events. Complementary, elementary, and composite events. Definition of probability—classical and statistical—examples. Elementary theorems on probability—simple problems. Conditional probability, Bayes' theorem—simple problems. Random variable as function on a sample space. Binomial distribution, examples of random experiments giving rise to Binomial distribution.

Contd....

CDS-Cobined Defence Services	
Algebra	✶ Basic Operations ✶ simple factors ✶ Remainder Theorem ✶ H.C.F. ✶ L.C.M. ✶ Theory of polynomials ✶ solutions of quadratic equations ✶ relation between its roots and coefficients (Only real roots to be considered) ✶ Simultaneous linear equations in two unknowns—analytical and graphical solutions ✶ Simultaneous linear inequations in two variables and their solutions ✶ Practical problems leading to two simultaneous linear equations or inequations in two variables or quadratic equations in one variable & their solutions ✶ Set language and set notation ✶ Rational expressions and conditional identities ✶ Laws of indices
Arithematic	✶ Number System: Natural numbers, Integers, Rational and Real numbers. ✶ Fundamental operations: addition, substraction, multiplication, division, Square roots, Decimal fractions ✶ Unitary method ✶ time and distance ✶ time and work ✶ percentages ✶ applications to simple and compound interest ✶ profit and loss ✶ ratio and proportion ✶ variation ✶ Elementary Number Theory: Division algorithm ✶ Prime and composite numbers ✶ Tests of divisibility by 2, 3, 4, 5, 9 and 11 ✶ Multiples and factors. Factorisation Theorem ✶ H.C.F and L.C.M. ✶ Euclidean algorithm ✶ Logarithms to base 10 ✶ laws of logarithms ✶ use of logarithmic tables
Trigonometry	✶ sine ×, cosine ×, tangent × when 0° < × < 90° ✶ Values of sin ×, cos × and tan ×, for × = 0°, 30°, 45°, 60° and 90° ✶ Simple trigonometric identities ✶ Use of trigonometric tables ✶ Simple cases of heights and distances
Geometry	✶ Lines and angles ✶ Plane and plane figures ✶ Theorems on Properties of angles at a point ✶ Parallel lines ✶ Sides and angles of a triangle ✶ Congruency of triangles ✶ Similar triangles

	✶ Concurrence of medians and altitudes ✶ Properties of angles ✶ sides and diagonals of a Parallelogram ✶ rectangle and square ✶ Circles and its properties including tangents and normals ✶ Loci
Mensuration	✶ Areas of squares ✶ rectangles ✶ parallelograms ✶ triangle and circle ✶ Areas of figures which can be split up into these figures (Field Book) ✶ Surface area and volume of cuboids ✶ lateral surface and volume of right circular cones and cylinders ✶ surface area and volume of spheres
Statistics	✶ Collection and tabulation of statistical data ✶ Graphical representation frequency polygons ✶ histograms ✶ bar charts ✶ pie charts etc ✶ Measures of central tendency

Common Admission Test (CAT)				
Arithmetic	**Algebra**	**Number system**	**Modern Maths**	**Geometry**
Mixtures & Alligations	Higher Order Equation	LCM & HCF	Permutations	Circles
Averages	Graphs	Base System	Combinations	Quadrilaterals
Percentages	Linear Equations	Factors	Probability	Mensuration
Races	Inequalities	Divisibility	Functions	Trigonometry
Profits and Loss	Logarithms	Digits	Sequences & Series	Triangles
Pipers and Cisterns	Maxima and MInima	Complex Numbers	Progressions	Polygons
Ratio & Proportion	Quadratic Equations	Higher Powers	Set Theory	Coordinate Geometry
Time & Work		Remainder Theorem	Venn Diagram	
Speed, Time & Distance		Trailing Zeroes		
Trains and Boats		Surds and Indicies		
Simple & Compound Interest				

Chapter-wise & Exam-wise Trend Analysis

Chapters & Topics	Exam - wise Weightage Analysis							
	SSC - CHSL	SSC - CGL	IBPS PO	IBPS Clerk	NDA	CDS	CAT	LIC AAO
Percentage	1	1	-	1-2	-		-	-
Profit, Loss, and Discount	1	2	1-2	1-3	-			-
Simple Interest and Compound Interest	2	1	1-2	1-3	-		4	-
Ratio and Proportion	-	1	3-4	1-3	-		3	-
Partnership	-	-	-	-	-		-	-
Average	1	1	-	1-3	-		2	-
Mixture and Alligation	-	-	-	0-2	-	14	-	-
Time , Speed & Distance	1	1	1-2	1-4	-		1	-
Boat and Stream	-	-	-	-	-		-	-
Time and Work	1	1	-	1-2	-		-	-
Pipes and Cisterns	-	-	-	-	-		-	-
Quadratic Equations	-	-	-	-	-		-	-
Derivatives	-	-	-	-	18		-	-
Age Problems	-	-	2-3	-	-		-	-
Geometry	1	5	-	-	-	13	3	-
Mensuration	1	2	-	2-4	-	23	-	-
Algebra	-	4	5-6	3-5	31	11	4	-
Trigonometry	2-3	3	-	-	21	11	-	-
Height and distance	-	-	-	-	-	-	-	-
Co–Ordinate Geometry	-	-	-	-	20	-	-	-
Matrices and Determinants	-	-	-	-	9	-	-	-
Number system	-	-	-	0-1	-	18	1	-
Number Series	-	-	-	3-5	-	-	-	5
Divisibility Rules		-	2-5	-	-	-	-	-
Unit digit		-	-	-	-	-	-	-
Number of zeroes		-	-	-	-	-	-	-
Factors	1	-	1-2	-	-	-	-	-
Remainder theorem		-	-	-	-	-	-	-
A.P and G.P		-	-	-	-	-	-	-
Power Indices and Surds		-	-	-	-	-	-	-
Simplification		1	5-6	10-15	-	-	-	5
Data Interpretation	3	4	3-4	5-10	-	-	3	11
Modern Mathematics	-	-	-	0-1	-	-	1	-
Miscellaneous	10-12	-	10-15	-	13	10	4	14
Total	**25**	**25**	**35**	**50**	**150**	**100**	**26**	**35**

Exclusive School Books Suppliers

	ANDHRA PRADESH
VIJAYAWADA	Sri Vikas Book Centre, 9848571114, 9440715700,
	MAHARASHTRA
PUNE	Madhusheela Books & Stationery, 7875899892, Pravin Sales, 8888038889
	TAMIL NADU
CHENNAI	Bookmark-IT, 7305151653
	TELANGANA
HYDERABAD	Sri Balaji Book Depot , 9676996199, (040) 27613300
	WEST BENGAL
KOLKATA	United Book House, 9831344622

Our Distributors

	ANDHRA PRADESH
TIRUPATI	Sree Aditya Book Centre, 7013300914, 8332972720
VISAKHAPATHAM	JBD Educational, 9246632691, 9246633693, Sri Rajeshwari Book Link, 9848036014,
	Gupta Brothers Books, 0891- 2754454
NANDYAL	Madhu Traders, 9490516655
KAKINADA	Sudhita Book Centre, 9848241369
VIJAYAWADA	Sree Vidya Book Depot, 9491830839
KADAPA	Uday Book Links, 8562222977
	ANDAMAN & NICOBAR ISLAND
PORTBLAIR	Krishna Book Centre, 9474205570
	ARUNACHAL PRADESH
NAHARLAGUN	New Pothi Ghar, 8731832947
	ASSAM
SILCHAR	Book Emporium, 9675972993, 6000763186, Ashok Publication, 7896141127,
	New Book Stall, 9435712617
GUWAHATI	Kayaan Enterprises, (0361) 2630443, Orchid Book house, 9864624209,
TINSUKIA	Kamakhya Book Stall, 8404047765
	BIHAR
PATNA	Nova Publisher & Distributors, (0612) 2666404
	Vikas Book Depot, 9504780402, Alka Book Agency, 9835655005,
	Gyan Ganga Limited, 9304826651, Rishu Pustak Bhandar, 8294576789,
	Sri Durga Pustak Mandir, 9334477386
	Bokaro Student Friends Pvt. Ltd, 7277931285
BIHAR SHARIF	Good Books , 8210685462
MUZAFFARPUR	Pustak Bhandar, 7870834225
	CHATTISGARH
AMBIKAPUR	M.P Department Stores, 9425254264
BOKARO	Bokaro Student Friends Pvt. Ltd, Bokaro, 7277931285
DURG	Bhagwati Bhawani Book Depot, 0788-2327620, 9827473100
RAIPUR	Shri Ramdev Traders, 9981761797, Gupta Pustak Mandir, 7974220323,
BILASPUR	Pustak Bhawan, 9300667909
	DELHI
DELHI	Mittal Books, (011) 23288887, 9899037390, A One Books, New Delhi, 8800497047,
	Batheja Super Store, 9871833924, 9811182352, Zombozone, 9871274082,
	LDS Marketing, 9811182352/9999353491, R.D. Chawla & Sons, 9810045752,
	Janta Book Depot, 9313046321
	Bokaro Student Friends Pvt. Ltd, 7004074900
	GUJARAT
AHMEDABAD	Patel Book Agencies, 9898184248, 9824386112, 9825900335,
	Shalibhadra Stationers, 9904477855
VAPI	Goutam Book Sellers, 9081790813
VALSAD	Mahavir Stationers, 9429474177
VADODARA	Shree ji Book Depot, 9824649375, Nilesh Book Centre, 9924458748
	Umakant Book Sellers & Stationer, 6359396370
AHMEDNAGAR	Hira Stationers, 9970150300
	HARYANA
ROHTAK	Swami Kitab Ghar, 9355611088, Babu Ram Pradeep Kumar, 9813214692
BALLABGARH	Kashi Ram Kishan lal, 9289504004, 8920567245
HISAR	Natraj Book Distributors, 7988917452
KAITHAL	Naveen Book Depot, 9466421630
GURGAON	Book Care Centre Venture, 9654564783
REWARI	Repro Books Ltd, 8657315914, Annu book depot, 9053246268
	JAMMU & Kashmir
JAMMU	Black And White, 9906668028
	JHARKHAND
BOKARO	Bokaro Student Friends Pvt. Ltd. (0654) 2233094, 7360021503,
	Bharati Bhawan Agencies, 06542-265302, 9431740797
HAZARIBAGH	Khandelwal Book Depot, 9708607489
DEOGHAR	Navyug Sahitya Mandir, 9031917035
RANCHI	Crown Book Distributor & Publishers, (0651) 2213735, 9431173904,
	Pustak Mandir, 9431115138, Agarwal Book Depot, 9334869210, Jayshree Book House, 8434430311
	Bokaro Student Friends Pvt. Ltd, 7360021508
DHANBAD	Bokaro Student Friends Pvt. Ltd, 6202834756
DUMKA	Vidyarthi Pustak Bhandar, 9431310228
	KARNATAKA
HUBLI	Renuka Book Distributor, (0836) 2244124,
	Vidyamandir Book Distributors, 9980773976
BANGLORE	Krishna book house, 9739847334,
	Sapna Book House Pvt. Ltd., 9980513242,
	Sree Sai Ram Book Traders, 9738881088
BELLERI	Hema Book World, (Chamrajpet) () 080-40905110, 9945731121
	MADHYA PRADESH
INDORE	Pustak Bhawan, 8982150100, Akruti Publishing House, 9826015516, Bhaiya Industries, Indore, 9109120101
GWALIOR	Agarwal Book Depot, 9425116210
NEEMUCH	Old & New Book Centre, 9827075062
INDORE	Sushil Prakashan, (0731) 2503333, 2535892, 9425322330,
	Bhaiya Store, 9425318103, Arun Prakashan, 9424890785,
	Bhaiya Book Centre, 9424081874, S.P. & Publication, 7000025933
JABALPUR	Vinay Pustak Sadan, 8962362667, Akash Book Distributor, 8989111444
	Anand Books and Stationers, 9425323508
KATNI	Shri Mahavir Agency, 9425363412
REWA	Goyal Book & Stationery, 9893892450
SATNA	Shree Abhay Pustak Bhandar, 9826145077
	MAHARASHTRA
AMRAVATI	Delta Pen House, 9890350073
PUNE	Natraj Book Depot, (020) 24485054, 9890054092, Vikas Book House, 9921331187,
	Vardhman Educational, 9860574354,
	Pravin Sales, 9890683475,
	New Saraswati Granth Bhandar, 9422323859,
	Yash Agencies, 9850956542,
	Sai Book Collection, 9623224343
AURANGABAD	Aarti Book Centre, 9422203836
BEED	Adarsh Book Depot, 9860374645
MUMBAI	Vidyarthi Sales Agencies, 9819776110, New Student Agencies, 7045065799,
	Shivam Books & Stationery, 8619805332
LATUR	Yash Book House, 9637936999
NAGPUR	Laxmi Pustakalay and Stationers, (0712) 2727354, Vijay Book Depot, 9860122094
	Renuka Book Distributor, 9765406133, Novelty Book Depot, 9657690220,
	Shree Mahalaxmi Pustakalaya, 7507099360
NANDED	Unique Book Depot, 7507448655
NASHIK	New India Book House, 9623123458
DHULE	Navjeevan Book Stall, 7020525561
YAVATMAL	Shri Ganesh Pustkalaya, 9423131275
VASAI	Prime Book Centre, Vasai, 9890293662
	ODISHA
CUTTACK	A. K. Mishra Agencies, 9437025991, 9437081319
SAMBALPUR	Maa Saraswati Pustak Bhandar, 9776597739
BHUBANESHWAR	M/s Pragnya, 8847888616, 9437943777, Padmalaya, 9437026922,
	Bidyashree, 9937017070, Books Godown, 7894281110
BARIPADA	Trimurti Book World, 9437034735
KORAPUT	Ambica Book Centre, 7008585008
	PUNJAB
AMBALA	Bharat Book Depot, 7988455354
PATIALA	Goel Sons, 9463619978,
	Adarsh Enterprises, 9814347613
JALANDHAR	Cheap Book Store, 9872223458, 9878258592, City Book Shop, 9417440753,
	Subhash Book Depot, 9876453625,
	Gaurav Book world, 9478821183
NABHA	Khanna Book Depot, 9814309320
LUDHIANA	Amit Book, 9815807871,
	Gupta Brothers, 9888200206,
	Bhatia Book Centre, 9815277131, Amit Book Depot, 9815807871
CHANDIGARH	Mohindra Book Depot, 9814920226, Manchanda Book House, 9464777470
BATHINDA	Goyal Sons , 9464478362
	RAJASTHAN
AJMER	Laxmi General Store, Ajmer, 0145- 2428942 9460652197
KOTA	Raj Traders, 9309232829
BHILWARA	Nakoda Book Depot, (01482) 243653, 9214983594,
BHIWADI	Alankar Book Depot, 9414707462
JAIPUR	Saraswati Book House, (0141) 2610823, 9829811155,
	Goyal Book Distt., 9460983939, 9414782130
UDAIPUR	OP Book Stall, 9887955068
JODHPUR	Kitab Mahal, 9460957875
	TRIPURA
AGARTALA	Books Corner, 8794894165, 8984657146
	TAMIL NADU
VILLUPURAM	Book Park, 9994445135
COIMBATORE	Majestic Book House, (0422) 2384333, CBSE Book Shop, 9585979752

2/1/2025

Exclusive School Books Suppliers

	KERALA
ERNAKULAM	Academic Book House, (0484) 2376613, H & C Store, 9864196344
KOTTAYAM	Asad Book Centre, (0481) 2566992
TRIVANDRUM	Academic Book House, (0471) 2333349, 9447063349
CALICUT	Aman Book Stall, (0495) 2721282,
KOZHIKODE	T.B.S. Publishers Distributors, 7559822223
	TAMIL NADU
PUDUCHERRY	Sri Lakshmi Book Stall, 7871555145
SALEM	Pattu book centre, 9894816280
TRICHY	Rasi Publication, 9894816280
MADURAI	Selvi Book Shoppe, 9843057435, Jayam Book Centre, 9894658036
CHENNAI	Arraba Book Traders, (044) 25387868, 9841459105, M.R. Book Store (044) 25364596,
	Kalaimagal Store, (044) 5544072, 9940619404, Vijaya Stores, 9381037417,
	Bookmark It-Books & Stat. Store, 7305151653,
	M.K. Stores, 9840030099, Tiger Books Pvt. Ltd., 9710447000,
	Prince Book House, Chennai, 0444-2053926, 9952068491,
	S K Publishers & Distributors, 9789865544,
	TELANGANA
HYDERABAD	Sri Balaji Book Depot, (040) 27613300, 9866355473, Shah Book House, 9849564564
	Vishal Book Distributors, 9246333166
	UTTARAKHAND
DEHRADUN	Inder Book Agencies, 9634045280, Amar Book Depot, 8130491477,
	New Nationai Book House, 9897830283/9720590054
	Brothers Pustak Bhandar, 9897833882, Goyal Book Store, 9897318047,
KASHIPUR	Neelam Book Depot, 9927305987
	UTTAR PRADESH
AGRA	Sparsh Book Agency, 9412257817,
	Sanjay Publication, 8126699922 Arti book centre, 8630128856,
	Om Pustak Mandir, (0562) 2464014, 9319117771
	Panchsheel Books, 9412257962, 9412257961
	Manav Book World, 9760316933
AMROHA	Sonu Book Depot, 7983784443
MATHURA	Sapra Traders, 9410076716
LAKHIMPUR KHERI	Universal Book Centre, 9838681025
ALLAHABAD	Mehrotra Book Agency, (0532) 2266865, 9415636890
AZAMGARH	Sasta Sahitya Bhandar, 9450029674
ALIGARH	K.B.C.L. Agarwal, 9897124960,
	Shaligram Agencies, 9412317800
BALRAMPUR	Universal Book Center, 8933826726

BAREILLY	Shiksha Prakashan Grih, 9837829284,
	Deepak Book Depot 9837027416, Saraswati Sadan, 9997779670
UJJAIN	Shreenath Book Depot, 9827544045
HARDOI	Mittal Pustak Kendra, 9838201466
GOLAGOKARNNATH	Halan Book Depot, 8400894545
BALIA	Vidya Kendra, 9415281234
DHAMPUR	Ramkumar Mahaveer Prasad, 9411942550
NAJIBABAD	Gupta News Agency, 8868932500
KANPUR	Radha News Agency, 8957247427,
	Raj Book Dist., 9235616506,
	H K Book Distributors, 9506033137/9935146730
GORAKHPUR	Central Book House, 9935454590, Friends & Co., 9450277154,
	Dinesh book depot, 9125818274,
	Vidyarthi Sahitya Bhandar, 6394026706
LUCKNOW	Vyapar Sadan, 7607102462, Om Book Depot, 7705871398, Azad Book Depot Pvt. Ltd., 7317000250, Book Sadan, 9839487327, Rama Book Depot (Retail), 7355078254
	Ashirwad Book Depot, 9235501197, Book.com, 7458922755, Universal Books, 9450302161, Sheetla Book Agency, 9235832418, Vidyarthi Kendra Publisher & Distributor Pvt Ltd, 9554967415, Tripathi Book House, 9415425943,
	Navyug Book Agencies, 8073564410, Asha Books Pvt. Ltd., 9415002443
	Universal Book Distributing Co, 0522-2324909, Pustak Vatika, 7905317119
MEERUT	Ideal Book Depot, (0121) 4059252, 9837066307
NOIDA	Prozo Distribution Pvt. Ltd., 9318395520, Goyal Books Overseas Pvt.Ltd., 1204655555, 9873387003
	Crackon India Private Limited, 8447301092
PRAYAGRAJ	Kanhaiya Pustak Bhawan, 9415317109
MAWANA	Subhash Book Depot, 9760262264
RENUKOOT	Om Stationers, 7007326732
VARANASI	Bokaro Student Friends Pvt. Ltd , 9798050654
	WEST BENGAL
KOLKATA	Oriental Publishers & Distributor (033) 40628367, Katha 'O' Kahini, (033) 22196313, 22419071, Saha Book House, (033), 22193671, 9333416484,
	United Book House, 9831344622, Bijay Pustak Bhandar, 8961260603,
	Shawan Books Distributors, 8336820363
	Krishna Book House, 9123083874
DAVANGERE	Lakshmi Agencies, 9844168836
NORTH DINAJPUR	Sarkar Book Suppliers, 9830949359
COOCH BEHAR	S.B. Book Distributor, Cooch behar, 9002670771
KHARAGPUR	Subhani Book Store, 9046891334
SILIGURI	Agarwal Book House, 9832038727,
DINAJPUR	Krishna Book House, 9434394212
MURSHIDABAD	New Book House, 8944876176, 9434013126

2/1/2025

Important Formulae and Tricks

Percentage

Concept of Percentage: A percentage is a relative value which denotes the hundredth part of any term.

- If x is R% more than y, then y is less than x by $\left(\frac{R}{100+R}\times 100\right)\%$
- If x is R% less than y, then y is more than x by $\left(\frac{R}{100-R}\times 100\right)\%$

Percentage increase/decrease: If the price of an item increases by $x\%$, then the reduction in the consumptions expenditure is:

$$\left(\frac{x}{100+x}\times 100\right)\%$$

If the price of an item decreases by $x\%$, then the increase in the consumption decrease the expenditure is:

$$\left(\frac{x}{100-x}\times 100\right)\%$$

Percentage change result on population: Assuming the population of a city is x now and it increases at the rate of $y\%$ per annum,

- Population after n years = $x\left(1+\frac{y}{100}\right)^n$
- Population n years ago = $\frac{x}{\left(1+\frac{y}{100}\right)^n}$

Depreciation: Assuming the current value of an article is x and it depreciates at the rate of $y\%$ per year;

- Value of the article after n years = $x\left(1-\frac{y}{100}\right)^n$ Value of the article n years ago = $\frac{x}{\left(1-\frac{y}{100}\right)^n}$

PERCENTAGE FRACTION TABLE

Fractions	% Values
1	100%
1/2	50%
1/3	33.33%
1/4	25%
1/5	20%
1/6	16.66%
1/7	14.28%
1/8	12.5%
1/9	11.11%
1/10	10%
1/11	9.09%
1/12	8.33%
1/13	7.69%
1/14	7.14%
1/15	6.66%
1/16	6.25%
1/17	5.88%
1/18	5.55%
1/19	5.26%
1/20	5%

Profit and Loss

- Profit = Selling Price – Cost Price.
- Profit percentage (P%) = (Profit /Cost Price) × 100
- Loss = Cost Price – Selling Price
- Loss percentage (L%) = (Loss /Cost Price) × 100
- Marked price = Discount + Selling price
- Discount = Marked Price – Selling Price
- Discount Percentage = (Discount/Marked price) × 100
- Successive discount percentage = $\frac{x+y-(xy)}{100}$

Simple Interest

- If a certain sum P in T years at R% per annum amounts to A , then the simple interest will be:

  A–P = $\left(\frac{P\times R\times T}{100}\right)$ ....[where A–P = simple interest(SI)]

  OR

  $$SI=\frac{(P\times R\times T)}{100}$$

- The annual payment that will discharge a debt of Rs. A due in T years at R% per annum is .

  $$\text{Annual payment}=\frac{100A}{100T+\frac{RT(T-1)}{2}}$$

- If a certain sum is invested in n types of investments in such a manner that an equal amount is obtained on each investment where interest rates are R_1, R_2, R_3 ......, R_n, respectively and time periods are T_1, T_2, T_3, ..., T_n, respectively, then the ratio in which the amounts are invested is

$$\frac{1}{100+R_1T_1}:\frac{1}{100+R_2T_2}:\frac{1}{100+R_3T_3}:\frac{1}{100+R_nT_n}$$

- If a certain sum of money becomes n times itself in T years at simple interest, then the rate of interest per annum is

$$R=\frac{100(n-1)}{T}$$

- If a certain sum of money becomes n times itself at R% per annum simple interest in T years, then

$$T=\left(\frac{n-1}{R}\right)\times 100 \text{ years}$$

- If a certain sum of money becomes n times itself in T years at simple interest, then the time T in which it will become m times itself is given by

$$T'=\left(\frac{m-1}{n-1}\right)\times T \text{ years}$$

- Effect of change of P, R, and T on simple interest is given by the following formula:

$$=\frac{\text{Product of fixed parameter}}{100}\times$$

[difference of product of variable parameters]

For example, if rate (R) changes from R_1 to R_2 and P, T are fixed, then

$$\text{Change in SI}=\frac{PT}{100}\times(R_1-R_2)$$

Similarly, if principal (P) changes from P_1 to P_2 and R, T are fixed, then change in SI $=\frac{RT}{100}\times(P_1-P_2)$

Also, if rate (R) changes from R_1 to R_2 and time (T) changes from T_1 to T_2 but principal (P) is fixed, then change in

$$SI=\frac{P}{100}\times(R_1T_1-R_2T_2)$$

- If a certain sum of money P lent out at SI amounts to A_1 in T_1 years and to A_2 in T_2 years, then

$$P=\frac{A_1T_2-A_2T_1}{T_2-T_1} \text{ and } R=\frac{A_1-A_2}{A_1T_2-A_2T_1}\times 100\%$$

- If a certain sum of money P lent out for a certain time T amounts to A_1 at R_1 % per annum and to A_2 at R_2 % per annum, then

$$P=\frac{A_2R_1-A_1R_2}{R_1-R_2} \text{ and } T=\frac{A_1-A_2}{A_2R_1-A_1R_2}\times 100 \text{ years}$$

- If an amount P_1 is lent at the simple interest rate of R_1 % per annum and another amount P_2 at the simple interest rate of R_2 % per annum, then the rate of interest for the whole sum is

$$R=\left(\frac{P_1R_1-P_2R_2}{P_1+P_2}\right)$$

Compound Interest

- The amount A due after t years, when a principal P is given on compound interest at the rate R% per annum is given by

$$A=P\left(1+\frac{R}{100}\right)^t$$

  - Compound interest (CI) = A – P

$$=P\left[\left(1+\frac{R}{100}\right)^t-1\right]$$

  - Rate of interest (R)

$$=\left[\left(\frac{A}{P}\right)^{\frac{1}{t}}-1\right]\% \text{ p.a.}$$

NOTE: Simple interest and compound interest for 1 year at a given rate of interest per annum are always equal.

- When interest is compounded half-yearly, then

$$\text{Amount (A)}=P\left(1+\frac{R}{100\times 2}\right)^{2t}$$

- If the interest is compounded quarterly, then

$$\text{Amount (A)}=P\left(1+\frac{R}{100\times 4}\right)^{4t}$$

- When the rates of interest are different for different years, say R_1, R_2, R_3 percent for the first, second and third year, respectively, then

$$\text{Amount}=P\left(1+\frac{R_1}{100}\right)\left(1+\frac{R_2}{100}\right)\left(1+\frac{R_3}{100}\right)$$

- When the time is given in the form of a fraction, say 2 3/4 years, then,

$$\text{Amount}=P\left(1+\frac{R_1}{100}\right)^2\times\left(1+\frac{\frac{3}{4}R}{100}\right)$$

- (a) The difference between the compound interest and the simple interest on a certain sum of money for 3 years at R% per annum is given by

$$CI-SI=P\left(\frac{R}{100}\right)^2 \text{ [in terms of P and R]}$$

and, $CI-SI=\frac{R\times SI}{2\times 100}$ [in terms of SI and R]

(b) The difference between the compound interest and the simple interest on a certain sum of money for 2 years at R% per annum is given by

$$CI-SI=P\left[\left(\frac{R}{100}\right)^3+\left(\frac{R}{100}\right)^2\right]$$

[in terms of P and R]

$$\text{And } CI-SI=\frac{SI}{3}\left[\left(\frac{R}{100}\right)^3+3\left(\frac{R}{100}\right)\right]$$

- If a certain sum becomes n times in t years at compound interest, then the same sum becomes nm times in mt years.
- If a certain sum becomes n times in t years, then the rate of compound interest is given by

$$R = 100\left[(n)^{\frac{1}{t}} - 1\right]$$

- If a certain sum of money at compound interest amounts to Rs. x in A years and to Rs. y in B years, then the rate of interest per annum is

$$R = \left[\left(\frac{y}{x}\right)^{\frac{1}{B-A}} - 1\right] \times 100$$

- If a loan of Rs. P at R% compound interest per annum is to be repaid in n equal yearly installments, then the value of each installment is given by

$$\text{Rs. } \frac{P}{\left(\frac{100}{100+R}\right) + \left(\frac{100}{100+R}\right)^2 + \ldots \left(\frac{100}{100+R}\right)^n}$$

Time and Work

- Total Work Done = Time Taken × Rate of Work
- Rate of Work = 1 / Time Taken
- Time Taken = 1 / Rate of Work
- If a piece of work is done in x number of days, then the work done in one day $= \frac{1}{x}$
- Total work done = Number of Days × Efficiency

IMPORTANT POINTS

1. Efficiency and Time are inversely proportional to each other.
2. $x : y$ is the ratio of the number of men which are required to complete a piece of work, then the ratio of the time taken by them to complete the work will be $y : x$.
3. If x number of people can do W1 work in D1 days, working T1 hours each day and the number of people can do W2 work in D2 days, working T2 hours each day, then the relation between them will be

$$\frac{M1 \times D1 \times T1}{W1} = \frac{M2 \times D2 \times T2}{W2}$$

Pipe and Cistern

- If a pipe can fill a tank in x hours, then the part filled in 1 hour $= \frac{1}{x}$
- If a pipe can fill a tank in x hours and another pipe can empty the full tank in y hours, then the net part filled in 1 hour, when both the pipes are opened:

$$\left(\frac{1}{x} - \frac{1}{y}\right)$$

- Time taken to fill the tank, when both the pipes are opened:

$$\left(\frac{x \times y}{y - x}\right)$$

- If a pipe can fill a tank in x hours and another pipe can fill the same tank in y hours, then the net part filled in 1 hr, when both pipes are opened:

$$\left(\frac{1}{x} + \frac{1}{y}\right)$$

- So, time to fill the tank will be:

$$\left[\frac{x \times y}{(x+y)}\right]$$

- If a pipe fills a tank in x hrs and another fills the same tank in y hrs, but a third empties the full tank in z hrs and all of them are opened together, the net part filled in 1 hr:

$$\left(\frac{1}{x} + \frac{1}{y} - \frac{1}{z}\right)$$

- So, time taken to fill the tank:

$$\frac{xyz}{(yz + xz - xy)}$$

Speed, Time and Distance

- Speed = Distance/Time
- Time = Distance/Speed
- Distance = (Speed × Time)
- Average Speed = Total Distance / Total Time
- 1 km/hr $= \frac{5}{18}$ m/sec
- 1 m/sec $= \frac{18}{5}$ km/hr
- If the ratio of the speeds of A and B is $a : b$, then the ratio of the time taken by them to cover the same distance is $\frac{1}{a} : \frac{1}{b} = b : a$.
- Suppose a man covers a certain distance at x km/hr and an equal distance at y km/hr. Then, the average speed during the whole journey is $\left(\frac{2xy}{x+y}\right)$ km/hr.
- If two people A and B set out from two points P and Q at the same time and cross paths after spending T1 and T2 hours getting to P and Q, respectively, then (A's speed) / (B's speed) equals $\sqrt{\left(\frac{T2}{T1}\right)}$

TRAINS

1. If the speed of the two trains is S_1 and S_2, respectively and lengths are L_1 and L_2
   While moving in the opposite direction
   Relative speed = $S_1 + S_2$
   Time taken = $[(L_1 + L_2)/(S_1 + S_2)]$
   While moving in the same direction
   Relative speed = $S_1 - S_2$
   Time taken = $[(L_1 + L_2)/(S_1 - S_2)]$

2. When two trains of lengths l_1 and l_2 cross each other at speeds of S_1 and S_2, respectively, in time t, the equation is given as $S_1 + S_2 = \frac{(l_1 + l_2)}{t}$.
3. When a train of length l_1 passes another train of length l_2 at a speed, the formula is expressed as $S_1 - S_2 = \frac{(l_1 + l_2)}{t}$.
4. When a train of length l_1 travelling at a speed of S_1 traverses a platform, bridge, or tunnel of length l_2 in time t, the equation is stated as $S_1 = \frac{(l_1 + l_2)}{t}$.
5. If the train passes an electric pole then
   Length of the Train= Train's speed × Time
   Time = Length of the Train/speed
   Speed = Length of the Train / Time

Boats and Streams

BASIC CONCEPT OF BOATS AND STREAM

Still water: If the water is not moving, then it is called still water.

Speed of boat in still water is
= ½ (Downstream Speed + Upstream Speed)

Stream: Moving water of the river is called a stream.

Upstream: If a boat moves in the opposite direction as of the stream.

Downstream: When the boat moves in the direction of the stream.

Cyclist and wind: Cyclist analogous to boat and wind analogous to stream.

Swimmer and stream: Swimmer analogous to boat

If the speed of boat in still water is 'b' km/hr and speed of the stream is 's' km/hr,

Speed of boat downstream = $(b + s)$ km/hr, since the boat goes with the stream of water and hence its speed increase.

Speed of boat upstream = $(b - s)$ km/hr, since the boat goes against the stream of water and hence, its speed gets reduced.

Distance = Speed × Time

D = ST

Ratio and Proportion

Ratio: Ratio is the comparison between two quantities in terms of their magnitudes. The ratio of two quantities a and b in some units is the fraction a/b and we write it as $a : b$. In the ratio $a : b$, we call 'a' as the first term or antecedent and 'b', the second term or consequent.

RULE

- The multiplication or division of each term of a ratio by the same non-zero number does not affect the ratio.
- The comparison should always be done of the same quantity (of length, of weight, etc.)

Proportion: When two ratios are equal, then the four quantities involved in the two ratios are said to be proportional.

When a, b, c, d are in proportion, then a and d are called EXTREMES and b and c are called MEANS.

If $a : b = c : d$, we write, $a : b :: c : d$ and say that a, b, c, d are in proportion. Here a and b are called extremes, and b and c are called means terms.

Thus, $a : b :: c : d \Rightarrow (a \times d) = (b \times c)$

Fourth proportional: If 2 : 3 :: 5 : 7, then 7 is called the fourth proportional to 2, 3, 5.

$$a : b : c : d : e = 4 : 10 : 6 : 9 : 15$$

Third proportional: If 2 : 3 :: 5 : 7, then 5 is called the third proportional to 2 and 3.

Mean proportional: Mean proportional between a and b is $\sqrt{ab}$.

Compounded ratio: The compound ratio of the ratios $(a : b), (c : d), (e : f)$ is $(ace : bdf)$

Duplicate ratio of $(a : b)$ is $(a^2 : b^2)$

Sub-duplicate ratio of $(a : b)$is $(\sqrt{a} : \sqrt{b})$

Triplicate Ratio of $(a : b)$ is $(a^3 : b^3)$

Sub-triplicate ratio of $(a : b)$ is $\left(a^{\frac{1}{3}} : b^{\frac{1}{3}}\right)$.

Average

- Average = Sum of quantities/ Number of quantities
- Sum of quantities = Average × Number of quantities
- The average of the first n natural numbers is $\frac{(n+1)}{2}$.
- The average of the squares of the first n natural numbers is $\frac{(n+1)(2n+1)}{6}$.
- The average of cubes of the first n natural numbers is $\frac{n(n+1)^2}{4}$.
- The average of the first n odd numbers is given by (last odd number +1) / 2
- The average of the first n even numbers is given by (last even number + 2) / 2
- The average of squares of first n consecutive even numbers is $\frac{2(n+1)(2n+1)}{3}$.
- The average of squares of consecutive even numbers till n is $\frac{(n+1)(n+2)}{3}$.
- The average of squares of squares of consecutive odd numbers till n is $\frac{n(n+2)}{3}$.
- If the average of n consecutive numbers is m, then the difference between the smallest and the largest number is $2(m - 1)$.
- If the number of quantities in two groups is n_1 and n_2 and their average is x and y, respectively, the combined average is $\frac{(n_1x + n_2y)}{(n_1 + n_2)}$.

- The average of n quantities is equal to x. When a quantity is removed, the average becomes y. The value of the removed quantity is $n(x - y) + y$.
- The average of n quantities is equal to x. When a quantity is added, the average becomes y. The value of the new quantity is $n(y - x) + y$.

Partnership

If P and Q contributed Rs. a and b, respectively for one year in business, then their profit or loss at that time will be:

P's benefit (or misfortune) : Q's profit (or misfortune) $= a : b$.

Compound Partnership: In a compound partnership, the money is invested during different periods of time by multiple investors. The benefit-sharing proportion is ascertained by duplicating the capital contributed with the unit of time (generally months).

- P1: P2 = C1 × T1: C2 × T2
- P1 = Partner 1's Profit.
- C1 = Partner 1's Capital.
- T1 = Time period for which Partner 1 contributed his capital.
- P2 = Partner 2's Profit.
- C2 = Partner 2's Capital.
- T2 = Time period for which Partner 2 contributed his capital.

Mensuration

Mensuration Formula of 2D Shapes

Check out the formula for area and perimeter of some of the 2D shapes:

Shape	Area (Square units)	Perimeter (units)
Square	a^2	$4a$
Rectangle	$l \times b$	$2(l + b)$
Circle	πr^2	$2\pi r$
Scalene Triangle	$\sqrt{[s(s-a)(s-b)(s-c)]}$ where, $s = \frac{(a+b+c)}{2}$	$a + b + c$
Isosceles Triangle	½ × $b \times h$	$2a + b$
Equilateral Triangle	$\left(\frac{\sqrt{3}}{4}\right) \times a^2$	$3a$
Right Angle Triangle	½ × $b \times h$	b + hypotenuse + h
Rhombus	½ × $d_1 \times d_2$	4 × side
Parallelogram	$b \times h$	2(l+b)
Trapezium	½ $h(a+b)$	$a+b+c+d$

Mensuration Formula of 3D Shapes

Shape	Volume (Cubic units)	Curved Surface Area (CSA) or Lateral Surface Area (LSA) (Square units)	Total Surface Area (TSA) (Square units)
Cube	a^3	$4a^2$	$6a^2$
Cuboid	$l \times b \times h$	$2h(l + b)$	$2(lb + bh + hl)$
Sphere	$\left(\frac{4}{3}\right)\pi r^3$	$4\pi r^2$	$4\pi r^2$
Hemisphere	$\left(\frac{2}{3}\right)\pi r^3$	$2\pi r^2$	$3\pi r^2$
Cylinder	$\pi r^2 h$	$2\pi rh$	$2\pi rh + 2\pi r^2$
Cone	$\left(\frac{1}{3}\right)\pi r^2 h$	$\pi r l$	$\pi r(r + l)$

Mensuration Formulas in Detail

- **Scalene Triangle:**

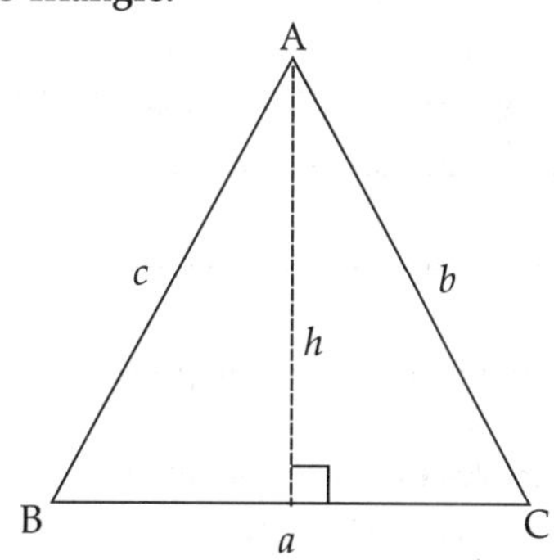

$$\text{Area} = \frac{1}{2}\text{ base} \times \text{height}$$

$$\text{Area} = \sqrt{s(s-a)(s-b)(s-c)}$$

$$\text{where } s = \frac{a+b+c}{2}$$

$$\text{Area} = \frac{1}{2} \times a \times c \sin B$$

$$= \frac{1}{2} \times a \times b \times \sin C = \frac{1}{2} \times a \times b \times \sin C$$

- **Isosceles Triangle:**

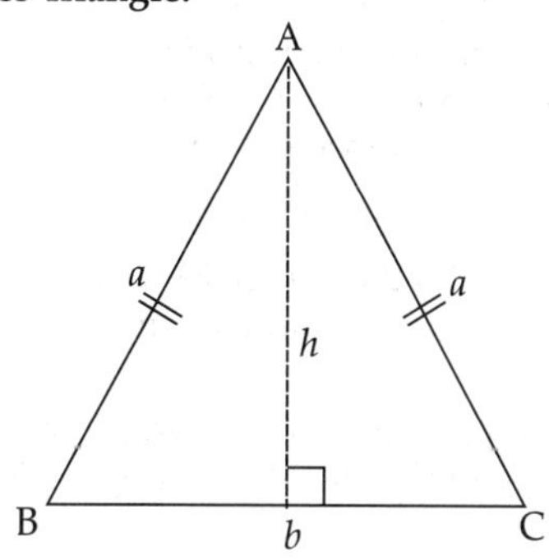

Height (h) $= \frac{1}{2}\sqrt{4a^2 - b^2}$

Area $= \frac{1}{2} \times$ base $\times$ height

Area $= \frac{1}{2} b\sqrt{4a^2 - b^2}$

➢ **Equilateral Triangle:**

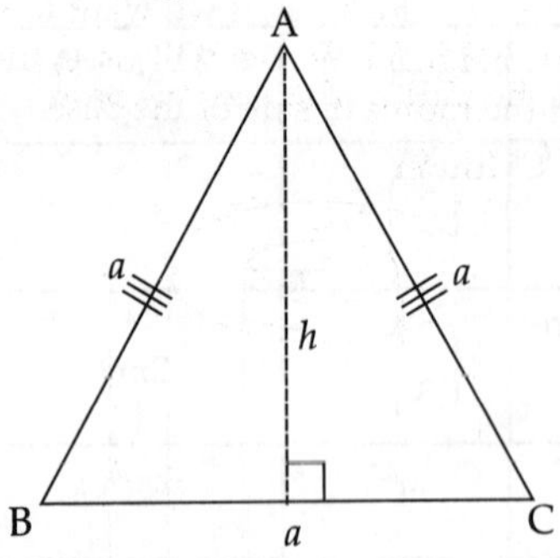

Area $= \frac{\sqrt{3}}{4} a^2$

$h = \frac{\sqrt{3}}{2} a$

1. Cuboid

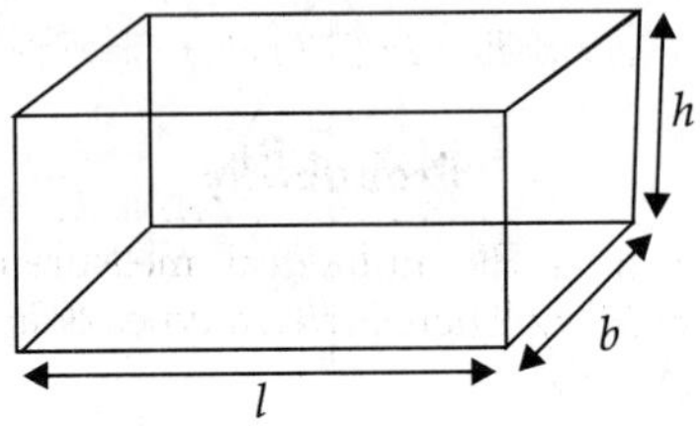

➢ Volume of cuboid = l × b × h

➢ Lateral surface Area = Perimeter of Base × Height Base = 2(l + b) × h

➢ Total surface area = Lateral surface Area + 2 × Area of base = 2 (lh + bh + lb)

➢ Diagonal = $\sqrt{l^2 + b^2 + h^2}$

➢ $V = \sqrt{A_1 \times A_2 \times A_2}$

$A_1 \Rightarrow$ Area of base or top = lb

$A_2 \Rightarrow$ Area of one side face = bh

$A_3 \Rightarrow$ Area of another side face = hl

➢ To find the total surface area of a cuboid if the sum of all three sides and diagonals are given. Total surface area = (sum of all three side)^2 – (Diagonal)^2

➢ For painting the surface area of a box or to know how much tin sheet is required, we will use total surface area.

➢ To find the length of the longest pole to be placed is a room, we will calculate diagonal, i.e., $\sqrt{l^2 + b^2 + h^2}$.

2. Cube

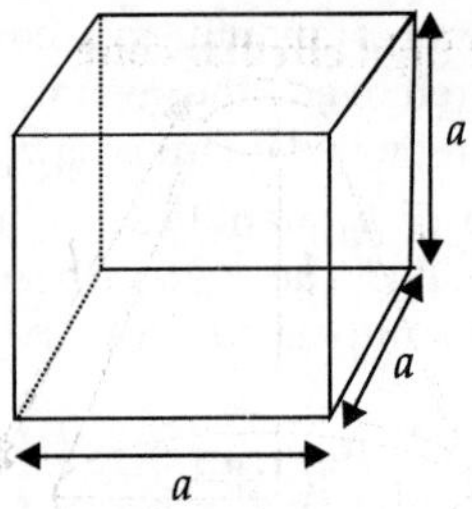

➢ Volume = (side)^3 $= a^3$

➢ Lateral surface area = $4a^2$

➢ Total surface area = $6a^2$

➢ Diagonal of the cube = $\sqrt{3}a$

➢ Face diagonal of the cube = $\sqrt{2}a$

➢ Volume of cube = $\left(\sqrt{\frac{\text{total surface area}}{6}}\right)^3$

➢ In Radius of cube = $\frac{a}{2}$

➢ Circumradius of cube = $\frac{\sqrt{3}}{2} a$

3. Right circular cone

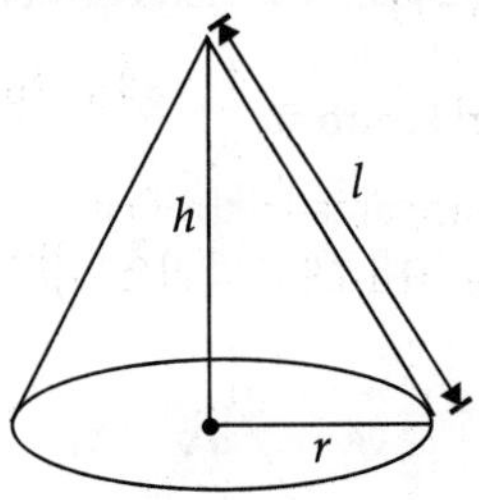

➢ Slant height, $l = \sqrt{r^2 + h^2}$

➢ Volume $= \frac{1}{3} \times$ area of base $\times$ height $= \frac{1}{3}\pi r^2 h$

➢ Curved surface area $= \frac{1}{2}$ (Perimeter of base) × slant height $= \frac{1}{2} \times 2\pi r \times l = \pi r\sqrt{r^2 + h^2}$

➢ Total surface area = C.S.A + Area of base $= \pi rl + \pi r^2 = \pi r\,(l + r)$

➢ If cone is formed by sector of a circle, then.

(a) Slant height = radius of circle

(b) circumference of base of cone = length of arc of sector

➢ Radius of maximum size sphere in a cone $= (h \times r)/(l + r)$

$$= \frac{h \times r}{l + r} \begin{bmatrix} r \to \text{radius of cone} \\ l \to \text{slant height of cone} \\ h \to \text{height of cone} \end{bmatrix}$$

➢ If cone is cut parallel to its base and ratio of heights, radius or slant height of both parts is given as $\to x : y$. Then, Ratio of their volume = $x^3 : y^3$

4. **Frustum of a right circular cone**

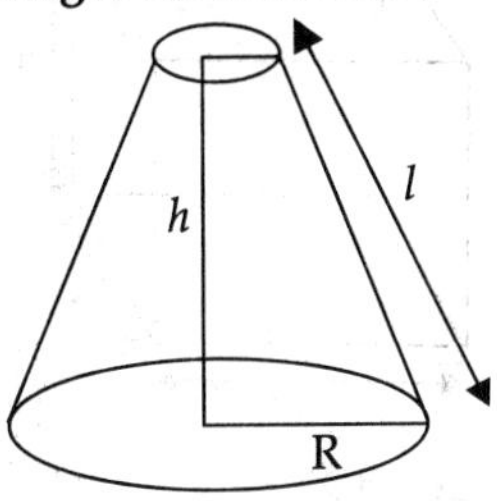

➢ Slant height

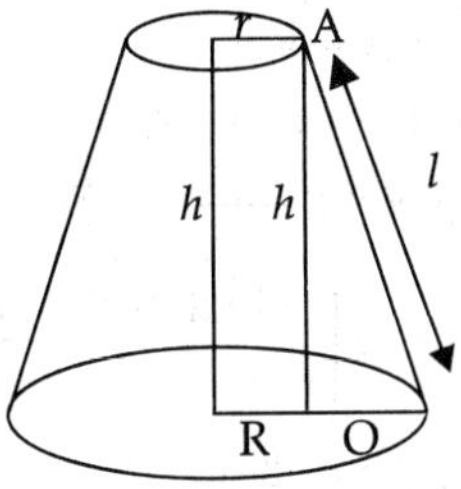

AC = l, AB = h, BC = R – r

Applying Pythagorean theorem in ΔABC

$L=\sqrt{h^2+(\text{R}-r)}$

➢ Volume of frustrum = $\frac{1}{3}\pi(\text{R}^2+r^2\text{R}r)h$

➢ Curved surface area = $\pi(\text{R}+r)l$

➢ Total surface area T.S.A = $\pi(\text{R}+r)l+\pi\ (\text{R}^2 + r^2)$

5. **Prism**

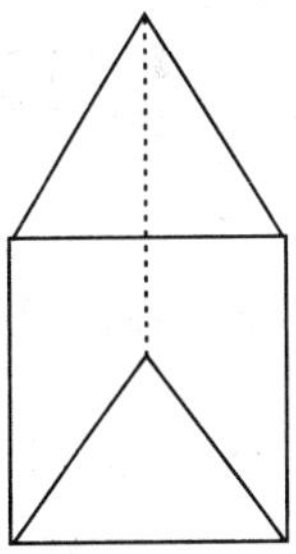

➢ A prism a solid object with:
   (a) Identical Ends
   (b) Flat faces

➢ Volume of Prism = Area of base × height

➢ Lateral surface area of prism
   = perimeter of base × height

➢ Total surface area of prism
   = Perimeter of base × height +2 × area of base

6. **Pyramids**

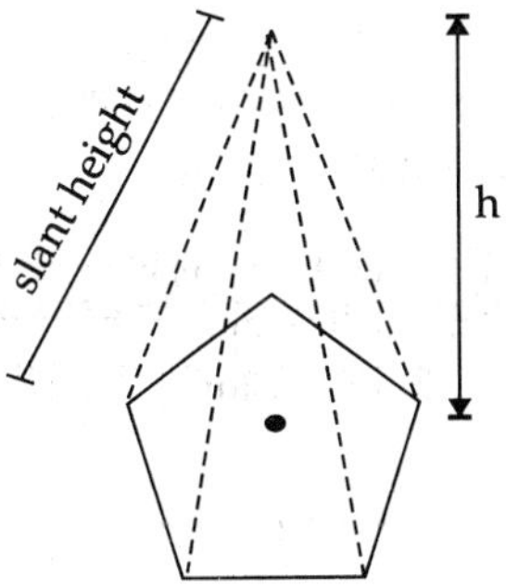

➢ Volume = $\frac{1}{3}$ (area of base) × height

➢ Curve surface area = $\frac{1}{2}$ ×(perimeter of base) × slant height.

➢ Total surface area = curved surface area + area of the base.

➢ Whenever in a question, if we want to find the slant height or height, then we will used inradius of the base not the radius of side of the base.

7. **Hollow Cylinder**

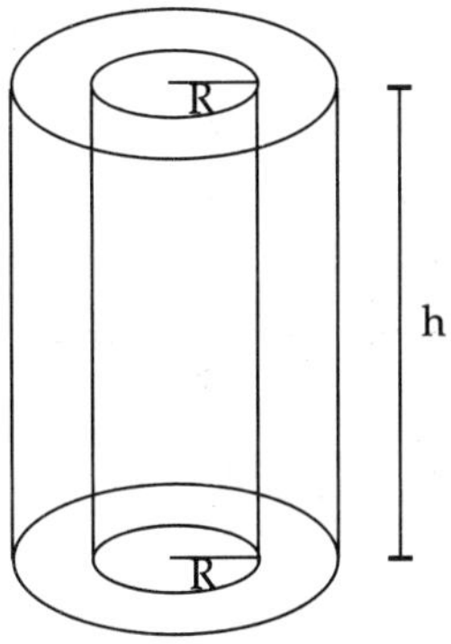

➢ Volume = $\pi(\text{R}^2 - r^2)h$

➢ Curved Surface Area = $2\pi\ (\text{R} + r)h$

➢ Total surface area = $2\pi\ (\text{R}+r)\ h + 2\pi\ (\text{R}^2 - r^2)$

Probability

Probability: It is the numerical measurement of the degree of certainty. There are two types of approaches to study probability:

Experimental or Empirical Probability: The result of probability based on the actual experiment is called experimental probability. In this case, the results could be different if we do the same experiment again.

Probability of Occurrence of an Event:

$$\text{P((E)}=\frac{\text{(Number of Outcomes of Favourable to E)}}{\text{(Total number of possible outcomes)}}$$

Theoretical probability: Associated with an event E, it is defined as "If there are 'n' elementary events associated with a random experiment and m of these are favourable to the event E, then the probability of occurrence of an event is defined by P(E) as the ratio mn."

If P(E) = 1, then it is called a 'Certain Event'.

If P(E) = 0, then it is called an 'Impossible Event'.

The probability of an event E is a number P(E) such that: 0 ≤ P(E) ≤ 1.

An event having only one outcome is called an elementary event. The sum of the probabilities of all the elementary events of an experiment is 1.

For any event E, P(E) + P(E⁻) = 1, where E⁻ stands for 'not E'. E and E⁻ are called complementary events.

Favourable outcomes are those outcomes in the sample space that are favourable to the occurrence of an event.

Sample Space: A collection of all possible outcomes of an experiment is known as a sample space. It is denoted by 'S' and represented in curly brackets.

Trigonometry

Trigonometric Ratios: To study different trigonometric ratio functions, we will use a right-angled triangle. Suppose ABC is a right-angled triangle with angle A = 90°.

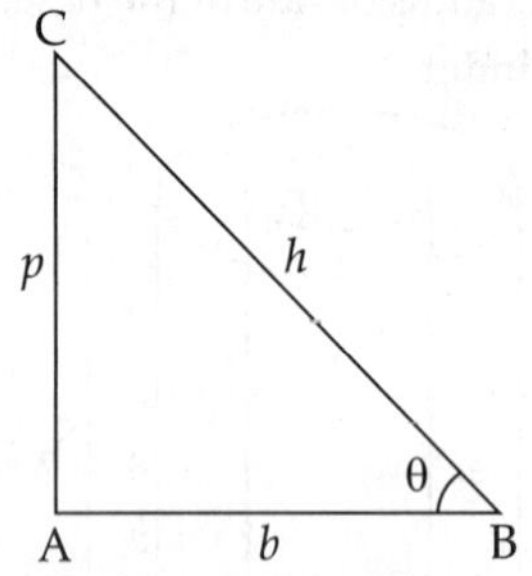

$$\sin\theta = \frac{AC}{BC} = \frac{p}{h} = \frac{\text{Perpendicular}}{\text{Hypotenuse}}$$

$$\cos\theta = \frac{AB}{BC} = \frac{b}{h} = \frac{\text{Base}}{\text{Hypotenuse}}$$

$$\tan\theta = \frac{AC}{BC} = \frac{p}{h} = \frac{\text{Perpendicular}}{\text{Base}}$$

Relations between Trigonometric Ratios

(i) $\text{cosec}\theta = \dfrac{1}{\sin\theta}$ or $\text{cosec}\,\theta \times \sin\theta = 1$

(ii) $\sec\theta = \dfrac{1}{\cos\theta}$ or $\sec\theta \times \cos\theta = 1$

(iii) $\cot\theta = \dfrac{1}{\tan\theta}$ or $\cot\theta \times \tan\theta = 1$

(iv) $\tan\theta = \dfrac{\sin\theta}{\cos\theta}$

(v) $\cot\theta = \dfrac{\cos\theta}{\sin\theta}$

Value of Trigonometric Ratios in Different Quadrants

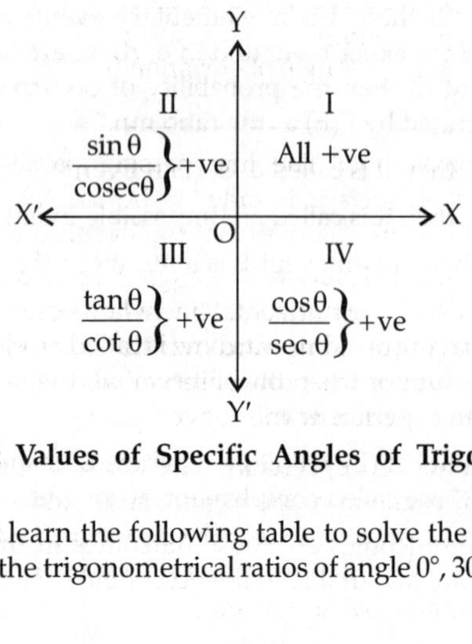

Different Values of Specific Angles of Trigonometric Ratio

You must learn the following table to solve the questions based on the trigonometrical ratios of angle 0°, 30°, 45°, 60°.

0°	0°	30°	45°	60°	90°
sin	0	$\frac{1}{2}$	$\frac{1}{\sqrt{2}}$	$\frac{\sqrt{3}}{2}$	1
cos	1	$\frac{\sqrt{3}}{2}$	$\frac{1}{\sqrt{2}}$	$\frac{1}{2}$	0
tan	0	$\frac{1}{\sqrt{3}}$	1	$\sqrt{3}$	∞
cot	∞	$\sqrt{3}$	1	$\frac{1}{\sqrt{3}}$	0
sec	1	$\frac{2}{\sqrt{3}}$	$\sqrt{2}$	2	∞
cosec	∞	2	$\sqrt{2}$	$\frac{2}{\sqrt{3}}$	1

Relation between squares of different types of trigonometric ratios

(i) $\sin^2\theta + \cos^2\theta = 1$ or $\sin^2\theta = 1 - \cos^2\theta$ or $\cos^2\theta = 1 - \sin^2\theta$

(ii) $1 + \tan^2\theta = \sec^2\theta$ or $\tan^2\theta = \sec^2\theta - 1$ or $\sec^2\theta - \tan^2\theta = 1$

(iii) $1 + \cot^2\theta = \text{cosec}^2\theta$ or $\text{cosec}^2\theta - 1 = \cot^2\theta$ or $\text{cosec}^2\theta - \cot^2\theta = 1$

Important concept to solve a specific type of question

If A + B = 90°

Results that are true always:

(i) sin A. sec B = 1 or sin A = cos B

(ii) cos A. cosec B = 1 or sec A = cosec B

(iii) tan A. tan B = 1 or tan A = cot B

(iv) cot A. cot B = 1

(v) $\sin^2 A + \sin^2 B = 1$

(vi) $\cos^2 A + \cos^2 B = 1$

Important Trigonometry Formula for Sum and Difference of Two Angles

(1) sin (A+B) = sinA. cosB + cosA sinB

(2) sin(A – B) = sinA. cosB – cosA sinB

(3) cos(A+B) = cosA. cosB – sinA sinB

(4) cos(A–B) = cosA. cosB + sinA sinB

(5) 2sinA.cosB = sin(A+B) + sin (A–B)

(6) 2 cosA. sinB = sin(A+B) – sin (A–B)

(7) 2 sinA. sinB = cos(A–B) – cos(A+B)

(8) 2 cosA.cosB = cos(A+B) + cos(A–B)

(9) $\sin^2A - \sin^2B = \sin(A+B).\sin(A-B)$

(10) $\cos^2A - \cos^2B = \cos(A+B).\cos(A-B)$

Trigonometry Formulas For Tangent

(i) $\tan(A+B) = \dfrac{\tan A + \tan B}{1 - \tan A.\tan B}$

(ii) $\tan(A-B) = \dfrac{\tan A - \tan B}{1 + \tan A.\tan B}$

(iii) $\cot(A+B) = \dfrac{\cot A.\cot B - 1}{\cot A + \cot B}$

(iv) $\cot(A-B) = \dfrac{\cot A.\cot B + 1}{\cot A - \cot B}$

(v) $\tan(45+\theta) = \dfrac{1+\tan\theta}{1-\tan\theta} = \dfrac{\cos\theta + \sin\theta}{\cos\theta - \sin\theta}$

(vi) $\tan(45-\theta) = \dfrac{1-\tan\theta}{1+\tan\theta} = \dfrac{\cos\theta - \sin\theta}{\cos\theta + \sin\theta}$

FORMULAS LIST

- If $A + B + C = 180°$
  Then, $\tan A + \tan B + \tan C = \tan A.\tan B.\tan C$
- If $A + B + C = 90°$
  Then, $\cot A + \cot B + \cot C = \cot A \cot B \cot C$
- (a) If $\sin\theta + \text{cosec}\,\theta = 2$
  $\sin^m\theta + \text{cosec}^m\,\theta = 2$

(b) $\cos\theta + \sec\theta = 2$
Then, $\cos^m\theta + \sec^m\theta = 2$

(c) $\tan\theta + \cot\theta = 2$
Then, $\tan^m\theta + \cot^m\theta = 2$

(d) $\sin 15° = \dfrac{\sqrt{3}-1}{2\sqrt{2}}$

$\cos 15° = \dfrac{\sqrt{3}+1}{2\sqrt{2}}$

$\tan 15° = 2 - \sqrt{3}$

$\tan 75° = 2 + \sqrt{3}$

$\tan 22\frac{1}{2} = \sqrt{2} - 1$

$\cos 22\frac{1}{2} = \sqrt{2} + 1$

$\sin 18° = \cos 72° = \dfrac{\sqrt{5}-1}{4}$

$\sin 54° = \cos 36° = \dfrac{\sqrt{5}+1}{4}$

$\sin 22\frac{1}{2}° = \dfrac{\sqrt{2-\sqrt{2}}}{2}$

$\cos 22\frac{1}{2}° = \dfrac{\sqrt{2-\sqrt{2}}}{2}$

Trigonometry Maximum & Minimum Value

Maximum & Minimum Value

	Minimum	Maximum
➢ sinθ, cos θ [odd power]	–1	+1
➢ sinθ, cos θ [even power]	0	+1
➢ tanθ, cot θ [odd power]	–∞	+∞
➢ tanθ, cot θ [even power]	0	+∞
➢ secθ, cosec θ [odd power]	–∞	+∞
➢ secθ, cosec θ [even power]	+1	+∞

$a \sin^2\theta + \cos^2\theta$

if $a > b$	if $b > a$
Max $\rightarrow a$	Max $\rightarrow b$
Min $\rightarrow b$	Min $\rightarrow b$

θ.θ

$\text{Max} \Rightarrow \dfrac{1}{2^n}$ | Min $\rightarrow n \rightarrow$ odd $\rightarrow -\dfrac{1}{2^n}$
Min $\rightarrow n \rightarrow$ even $\rightarrow 0$

θ+θ

Maximum $\rightarrow 1$

Min $\Rightarrow$ Pθ = 45°

$a \sin\theta + b\cos\theta$

$\text{Max} \Rightarrow +\sqrt{a^2+b^2}$

$\text{Min} \Rightarrow -\sqrt{a^2+b^2}$

$a \sin^2\theta + b\,\text{cosec}^2\theta$	$a\cos^2\theta + b\sec^2\theta$
if $a < b$	if $a < b$
Min $= a + b$	Min $= a + b$
if $b > a$	if $b > a$
Min $= 2\sqrt{ab}$	Min $= \sqrt{ab}$

$a\,\text{cosec}^2\theta + b\sec^2\theta$

Min $= (\sqrt{a}+\sqrt{b})^2$

$a\tan^2\theta + b\cot^2\theta$

Min $= 2\sqrt{ab}$

Height and Distance

- **Line of Sight:** The imaginary horizontal straight line drawn from the observer's eye to the objects to be viewed. It gives an accurate idea of where the observers view.

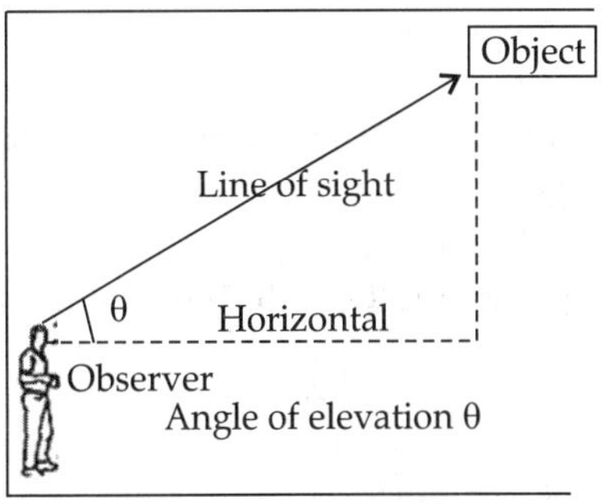

- **Horizontal line:** The line passing parallel to the ground or surface is called a horizontal line. The horizontal line is shown in the above figure.
- **The angle of elevation:** The angle formed by the light of sight with the horizontal line when observers view the object situated upward over the horizontal line. It is formed only when the observer views the upward-placed object. (Refer the above figure.)
- **The angle of depression:** The angle of depression is the inclination of the light of sight and horizontal line when observers view the downward object. It is formed only when the observer views the object at the ground from any height.

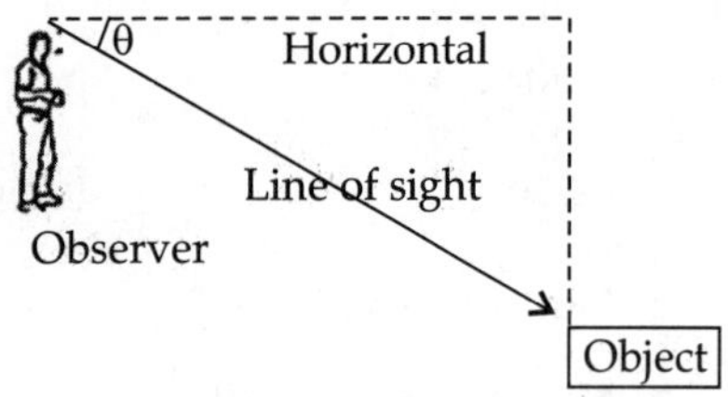

Angle of elevation θ

FORMULA

The height and distance can be simply calculated using trigonometric ratios. Generally, the Tan trigonometric function is used to get the height and distance accurately.

We know that the ratio of the Tan function is tan = Height/ Distance = Perpendicular/Base

You know the values of the tan function at different angles for this. The trigonometric values are mentioned in the table given below. You can refer to the table for this.

NOTE: $\tan 0° = 0$, $\tan 30° = \frac{1}{\sqrt{3}}$, $\tan 45° = 1$

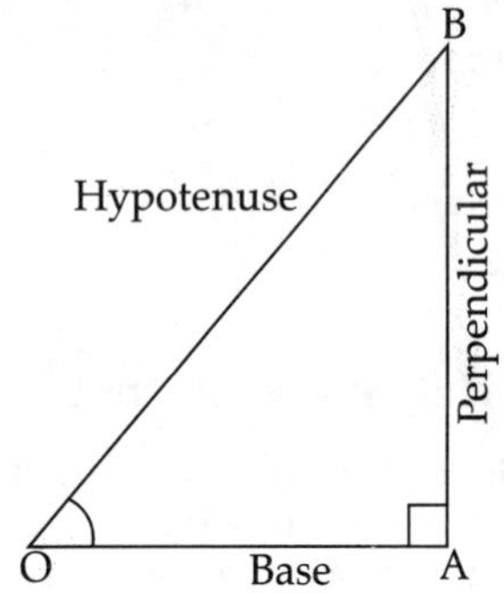

Trigonometric Ratios

The trigonometric ratios and formulas are mentioned below:

- sinθ = perpendicular/hypotenuse = AB/OB
- cosθ = base/hypotenuse = OA/OB
- tanθ = perpendicular/base = AB/OA
- cosecθ = 1/sinθ = OB/AB
- secθ = 1/cosθ = OB/OA
- cotθ = 1/tanθ = OA/AB

Trigonometric Identities

1. $\sin^2\theta + \cos^2\theta = 1$
2. $1 + \tan^2\theta = \sec^2\theta$
3. $1 + \cot^2\theta = \mathrm{cosec}^2\theta$

Algebra

- $a^2 - b^2 = (a - b)(a + b)$
- $(a + b)^2 = a^2 + 2ab + b^2$
- $a^2 + b^2 = (a + b)^2 - 2ab$
- $(a - b)^2 = a^2 - 2ab + b^2$
- $(a + b + c)^2 = a^2 + b^2 + c^2 + 2ab + 2bc + 2ca$
- $(a - b - c)^2 = a^2 + b^2 + c^2 - 2ab + 2bc - 2ca$
- $(a + b)^3 = a^3 + 3a^2b + 3ab^2 + b^3$
- $(a + b)^3 = a^3 + b^3 + 3ab(a + b)$
- $(a - b)^3 = a^3 - 3a^2b + 3ab^2 - b^3$
- $(a - b)^3 = a^3 - b^3 - 3ab(a - b)$
- $a^3 - b^3 = (a - b)(a^2 + ab + b^2)$
- $a^3 + b^3 = (a + b)(a^2 - ab + b^2)$
- $(a + b)^4 = a^4 + 4a^3b + 6a^2b^2 + 4ab^3 + b^2$
- $(a - b)^4 = a^4 - 4a^3b + 6a^2b^2 - 4ab^3 + b^4$
- $a^4 - b^4 = (a - b)(a + b)(a^2 + b^2)$
- $a^5 - b^5 = (a - b)(a^4 + a^3b + a^2b^2 + ab^3 + b^4)$

Algebraic Formulas-Laws of Exponents

Multiplication Rule	$a^x \times a^y = a^{x+y}$
Division Rule	$a^x \div a^y = a^{x-y}$
Power of a Power Rule	$(a^x)^y = a^{xy}$
Power of a Product Rule	$(ab)^x = a^x b^x$
Power of a Fraction Rule	$\left(\frac{a}{b}\right)^x = \frac{a^x}{b^x}$
Zero Exponent	$a^0 = 1$
Negative Exponent	$a^{-x} = \frac{1}{a^x}$
Fractional Exponent	$a^{\frac{x}{y}} = \sqrt[y]{a^x}$

Algebra Formulas for Irrational Numbers: The Algebra formulas used to solve equations based on irrational numbers are as follows:

1. $\sqrt{ab} = \sqrt{a}\sqrt{b}$
2. $\sqrt{\frac{a}{b}} = \frac{\sqrt{a}}{\sqrt{b}}$
3. $(\sqrt{a} + \sqrt{b})(\sqrt{a} - \sqrt{b}) = a - b$
4. $(\sqrt{a} + \sqrt{b})^2 = a + 2\sqrt{ab} + b$
5. $(a + \sqrt{b})(a - \sqrt{b}) = a^2 - b$

Percentage

A percentage is a fraction of 100 denoted by "%"

Percentage $= \frac{\text{Value}}{\text{Total value}} \times 100$

Percentage decrement

$= \frac{(\text{Initial value} - \text{Final value})}{\text{Initial value}} \times 100$

Percentage increment

$= \frac{(\text{Final value} - \text{Initial value})}{\text{Initial value}} \times 100$

Value of machine after n years $= P\left(1 - \frac{R}{100}\right)^n$

Value of machine before n years $= \frac{P}{\left(1 - \frac{R}{100}\right)^n}$

Successive percentage change

$= \left(a + b + \frac{ab}{100}\right)\%$

Population of town is P and increases by R% per annum then population 'x' years ago $= \frac{P}{\left(1 + \frac{R}{100}\right)^x}$

Population x years ago

$P\left(1 + \frac{R}{100}\right)^x$

Population of town is P and decreases by R% per year, then population after x years

$= P\left(1 - \frac{R}{100}\right)^x$

Population x year ago

$= \frac{P}{\left(1 - \frac{R}{100}\right)^x}$

Section-1 : Arithmetic

Chapter 1

Percentage

LEARNING OBJECTIVES:

- Percentage and fractional value of different numbers.
- Concepts related to election based questions, expenditure based question.
- Different types of questions that are covered in different competitive exams such as SSC, bank, railway, CAT, etc.
- Method of solving questions related to percentage.

SOME IMPORTANT CONCEPTS RELATED TO PERCENTAGE

- **Percentage:** A percentage is a fraction of 100. It is denoted by the symbol %.
- **Percentage change:** Percentage change is the difference between the new value and the old value, expressed as a percentage of the old value.
  i.e., percentage change, if value changes from 25 to 30 $= \frac{30-25}{25} \times 100 = 20\%$
- **Fraction to percentage conversion:** To convert a fraction to a percentage, multiply the fraction by 100.
  i.e., percentage value of $\frac{1}{5} = \frac{1}{5} \times 100 = 20\%$
- **Percentage to fraction conversion:** To convert a percentage to a fraction, divide the percentage by 100 and simplify the fraction.
  i.e., fraction value of 30% $= \frac{30}{100} = \frac{3}{10}$
- **Percentage to decimal conversion:** To convert a percentage to a decimal, divide the percentage by 100.
  i.e., decimal value of 30% $= \frac{30}{100} = 0.3$
- **Decimal to percentage conversion:** To convert a decimal to a percentage, multiply the decimal by 100.
  i.e., percentage value of 0.3 = 0.3 × 100 = 30%
- **Percentage of a number:** To calculate the percentage of a number, multiply the number by the percentage and divide by 100.
  i.e., 20% of 50 $= 50 \times \frac{20}{100} = 10$
- **Successive percentage change:** When a value changes by successive percentage changes, the net percentage change is calculated by multiplying the individual percentage changes.
  i.e., two successive changes of 20% and 25% in 100
  $= 100 \times \frac{120}{100} \times \frac{125}{100} = 150$

So, net percentage change = (150-100)/100 × 100 = 50%

FORMULAE:

- Percentage increase = [(new value – old value)/old value] × 100%
- Percentage decrease = [(old value – new value)/old value] × 100%
- Percentage change = [(new value – old value)/old value] × 100%
- Percentage to fraction $= \left(\frac{\text{percentage}}{100}\right)$
- Fraction to percentage = (fraction × 100)
- Percentage to decimal $= \left(\frac{\text{percentage}}{100}\right)$
- Decimal to percentage = (decimal × 100)
- Percentage of a number = (percentage/100) × number
- Net percentage change $= a + b + \left(\frac{ab}{100}\right)$
  where a and b are the successive percentage changes.
- If the price of an item decreases, a person can buy a few kg more in A rupees, the actual price of that item.
  Actual Price = Rate × $\frac{A}{100}$ – Rate × X Per kg
- If the population of a city is P and it increases at the rate of R% perannum, then population after 'n' years:
  Population $= P \times \left(1 + \frac{R}{100}\right)^n$
- If the population of a city is P and it decreases at the rate of R% perannum, then population after 'n' years:
  Population $= P \times \left(1 - \frac{R}{100}\right)^n$

- If the population of a city is P and it increases at the rate of R% per annum, then population of the city 'n' years ago :

$$\text{Population } n \text{ years ago} = \frac{P}{\left(1+\frac{R}{100}\right)^n}$$

- If the city's population is P and it decreases at the rate of R% per annum, then city's population 'n' years ago:

$$\text{Population } n \text{ years ago} = \frac{P}{\left(1-\frac{R}{100}\right)^n}$$

Percentage – Fraction Table

1% = 1/100	25% = 1/4	80% = 4/5
2% = 1/50	33.33% = 1/3	83.33% = 5/6
4% = 1/25	37.50% = 3/8	87.50% = 7/8
5% = 1/20	40% = 2/5	100% = 1
8.33% = 1/12	50% = 1/2	120% = 6/5
10% = 1/10	60% = 3/5	125% = 5/4
12.50% = 1/8	62.50% = 5/8	133.33% = 4/3
16.67% = 1/6	66.67% = 2/3	150% = 3/2
20% = 1/5	75% = 3/4	175% = 7/4

Example 1: Radha saves x% of her income. If her expenditure increases by 20% and her income increases by 28%, then her savings increase by 40%. Find x.

(a) 56 (b) 40
(c) 60 (d) 70

Sol. (b) Expenditure : Saving

20% : 40%

28%

12% : 8%

$\therefore$ Savings $= \frac{2}{5} \times 100 = 40\%$

$x = 40\%$

Example 2: The population of a town increased by 15% in 2018 and 10% in 2019. Due to pandemic, it decreased by 10% in 2020. What was the percentage increase in population of town in 3 years?

(a) 12.5% (b) 17.5%
(c) 13.85% (d) 15%

Sol. (c) Let population = 100

$\Rightarrow$ Population after 3 years

$= 100 \times \frac{115}{100} \times \frac{110}{100} \times \frac{90}{100} = 113.85$

Percentage increase $= \frac{113.85 - 100}{100} \times 100$

$= 13.85\%$

Example 3: A number P is 20% more than a number Q but 10% less than a number R. What percentage is number Q of number R?

(a) 80% (b) 85%
(c) 75% (d) 90%

Sol. (c)

P	:	Q	:	R
6	:	5		
9		:		10
18	:	15	:	20

$\Rightarrow$ Required percentage $= \frac{15}{20} \times 100 = 75\%$

Example 4: If each side of a triangle is increased by 13%, then its area will increase by:

(a) 21.69% (b) 13%
(c) 27.69% (d) 26%

Sol. (c) 100 $\longrightarrow$ 113

$\downarrow$ $\downarrow$

10000 $\longrightarrow$ 12769

Percentage increase $= \frac{12769 - 10000}{10000} \times 100$

$= 27.69\%$

Example 5: Rita's income is 15% less than Richa's income. By what per cent Richa's income is more than Rita's income?

(a) $15\frac{11}{17}\%$ (b) $17\frac{11}{17}\%$

(c) $16\frac{11}{17}\%$ (d) $14\frac{11}{17}\%$

Sol. (b) Rita : Richa = 17 : 20

So, required% $= \frac{3}{17} \times 100 = 17\frac{11}{17}\%$

Example 6: A person's salary has increased from ₹ 7,000 to ₹ 12,000. What is the percentage increase in his salary?

(a) $71\frac{3}{7}\%$ (b) $61\frac{1}{7}\%$

(c) $69\frac{1}{7}\%$ (d) $76\frac{4}{7}\%$

Sol. (a) Increase in salary is ₹ 5,000 i.e., 7,000 $\rightarrow$ 12,000

So, percentage increase $= \frac{5,000}{7,000} \times 100 = 71\frac{3}{7}\%$

Example 7: If 49% of $x = y$, they y% of 50 is:

(a) 40% of y (b) 50% of x
(c) 50% of y (d) 24.5% of x

Sol. (d) $\frac{x}{y} = \frac{100}{49}$

$y\%$ of $50 = \frac{50 \times 49}{100} = 24.5$

i.e., 24.5% of x.

Level 1 Beginner

1. A team played 40 games in a season and won 24 of them. What per cent of games played did the team win? **[SSC 10+2 2012]**
(A) 70% (B) 40% (C) 60% (D) 35%

2. 1% of 1% of 25% of 1,000 is: **[SSC 10+2 2014]**
(A) .025 (B) .0025
(C) .25 (D) .00025

3. Ram's income is greater than Shyam's income by 20%. Then, the per cent by which Shyam's income is less than Ram's income is: **[SSC 10+2 2013]**
(A) $16\frac{2}{3}$ % (B) $18\frac{2}{5}$ %
(C) $10\frac{1}{5}$ % (D) $12\frac{1}{3}$ %

4. If 125% of x is 100, then x is: **[SSC 2012]**
(A) 80 (B) 150 (C) 400 (D) 125

5. If 40% of $\frac{4}{5}$ of $\frac{3}{4}$ of a number is 48, then what is 1% of the same number? **[SSC Sub Inspector 2014]**
(A) 20 (B) 2 (C) 10 (D) 1

6. In an examination, 75% candidates passed in English and 60% passed in Mathematics. 25% failed in both and 240 passed in the examination. Find the total number of candidates. **[SSC Sub Inspector 2014]**
(A) 492 (B) 300 (C) 500 (D) 400

7. A shopkeeper purchased 200 bulbs for ₹ 10 each. However, 5 bulbs were fused and had to be thrown away. The remaining were sold at ₹ 12 each. What will be the percentage profit? **[SSC Clerk 2014]**
(A) 25% (B) 15% (C) 13% (D) 17%

8. A person's salary increased from ₹ 8,100 to ₹ 9,000. What is the percentage increase in his salary? **[SSC CGL 2019]**
(A) $6\frac{1}{9}$% (B) $13\frac{7}{9}$% (C) $11\frac{1}{9}$% (D) $9\frac{1}{9}$%

9. In an examination, 92% of the students passed and 480 students failed. If so, how many students appeared in the examination? **[SSC CGL 2019]**
(A) 6,200 (B) 5,000 (C) 6,000 (D) 5,800

10. The value of 18% of 15% of $\frac{25}{9}$ of 3,800 is: **[SSC CGL 2019]**
(A) 285 (B) 582 (C) 583 (D) 385

11. Convert $\frac{9}{40}$ into percentage: **[SSC CPO 2018]**
(A) $2\frac{1}{2}$ % (B) 2%
(C) 22% (D) $22\frac{1}{2}$ %

12. 8% of 5 litres is: **[SSC CPO 2018]**
(A) 0.4 ml (B) 400 ml (C) 40 ml (D) 4 ml

13. What percentage of ₹ 124 is ₹ 49.60? **[SSC CPO 2018]**
(A) 250 (B) 16 (C) 123 (D) 40

14. A saves 12% of her income. If she spends ₹ 2,16,128, then her total income is: **[SSC CPO 2018]**
(A) ₹ 2,42,063 (B) ₹ 2,45,600
(C) ₹ 2,48,000 (D) ₹ 2,43,560

15. If A's salary is 60% more than B's salary, then by what percentage is B's salary is less than that of A? **[SSC CGL 2019]**
(A) 47.7% (B) 33.3% (C) 37.5% (D) 45%

16. Radha saves 25% of her income. If her expenditure increases by 20% and her income increases by 29%, then her savings increase by: **[SSC CGL 2021]**
(A) 56% (B) 52% (C) 65% (D) 70%

17. The value of a motorcycle depreciates every year by 4%. What will be its value after 2 years, if its present value is ₹ 75,000? **[SSC CGL 2019]**
(A) ₹ 72,000 (B) ₹ 70,120
(C) ₹ 69,120 (D) ₹ 69,000

18. Ajay spends 25% of his salary on house rent, 5% on food, 15% on travel, 10% on clothes and the remaining amount of ₹ 27,000 is saved. What is Ajay's income? **[SBI 2014]**
(A) ₹ 60,000 (B) ₹ 80,500
(C) ₹ 60,700 (D) ₹ 70,500

19. In 2021, Sam received an annual increment in his salary by 40% but due to recession in 2022, company started taking cost cutting measures and his salary was reduced by 15%. What was the net change in his salary? **[SSC CHSL 2023]**
(A) 17% increase (B) 19% increase
(C) 9% decrease (D) 11% increase

20. 72% of the students of a certain class took biology and 44% took mathematics. If each student took biology or mathematics and 40 took both, then the total number of students in the class was: **[SSC Sub Inspector 2012]**
(A) 200 (B) 230 (C) 250 (D) 320

21. Roma spends 25% of her income on food, 15% on children's books and 75% of the remaining income on uniforms. What is the percentage of income she is left with? **[SSC CHSL 2023]**
(A) 35% (B) 20% (C) 15% (D) 19%

22. Two persons contested on election of parliament. The winning candidate secured 57% of the total votes polled and won by a majority of 42,000 votes. The number of total votes polled is: **[SSC MT 2013]**
(A) 4,00,000 (B) 5,00,000
(C) 6,00,000 (D) 3,00,000

23. If each side of a cube is decreased by 12%, then the percentage decrease in its surface area is: **[SSC CHSL 2023]**

(A) 25.66% **(B)** 28.23%
(C) 22.56% **(D)** 26.54%

24. In a class, if 60% of the students are boys & the number of girls is 36, then the number of boys is: **[SSC CGL 2019]**

(A) 65 **(B)** 54 **(C)** 60 **(D)** 58

25. Mohan's income is 40% more than Shyam's income. Shyam's income is what per cent less than Mohan's income? **[SSC CHSL 2021]**

(A) $28\frac{2}{7}\%$ **(B)** $28\frac{5}{7}\%$

(C) $28\frac{3}{7}\%$ **(D)** $28\frac{4}{7}\%$

2 Level Intermediate

1. One litre of water is evaporated from 6 litres of a solution containing 5% salt. The percentage of salt in the remaining solution is: **[SSC CGL 2014]**

(A) $4\frac{4}{9}\%$ **(B)** $5\frac{5}{7}\%$ **(C)** 5% **(D)** 6%

2. Raghav spends 80% of his income. If his income increases by 12% and his expenditure increases by 17.5%, then what is the percentage decrease in his savings? **[SSC CHSL 2021]**

(A) 15% **(B)** 10% **(C)** 12% **(D)** 8%

3. A number is mistakely multiplied by $\frac{7}{5}$ instead of being multiplied by $\frac{3}{2}$. What is the percentage change in the result due to this mistake? **[SSC CHSL 2021]**

(A) $6\frac{2}{3}\%$ **(B)** $7\frac{2}{3}\%$ **(C)** $3\frac{2}{3}\%$ **(D)** $5\frac{2}{3}\%$

4. The price of sugar is increased by 24%. A person wants to increase his expenditure by 18% only. By approximately what per cent should he decrease his consumption? **[SSC CGL 2018]**

(A) 5.3% **(B)** 5.1% **(C)** 4.6% **(D)** 4.8%

5. A reduction of 20% in the price of sugar enables a purchases to obtain 4 kg more for ₹ 160. The original price of sugar per kg is: **[SSC CGL 2019]**

(A) ₹ 12 **(B)** ₹ 10 **(C)** ₹ 14 **(D)** ₹ 15

6. The monthly salaries of A and B together amount to ₹ 40,000. A spends 85% of his salary and B spends 95% of his salary. If now their savings are the same, then the salary of A is: **[SSC CGL 2014]**

(A) ₹ 10,000 **(B)** ₹ 12,000
(C) ₹ 16,000 **(D)** ₹ 18,000

7. Rakesh got 273 marks in an examination and scored 5% more than the pass %. If Lokesh got 312 marks, then by what % above the pass mark did he pass the examination? **[SSC CGL 2013]**

(A) 20% **(B)** 27% **(C)** 25% **(D)** 15%

8. The price of sugar is increased by 17%. A person wants to increase his expenditure by 5% only. By approximately what percent should he decrease his consumption? **[SSC CGL 2018]**

(A) 10.3% **(B)** 10.7% **(C)** 10.9% **(D)** 9.9%

9. The radius of a sphere is reduced by 40%. By what per cent will its volume decrease? **[SSC CGL 2019]**

(A) 60% **(B)** 64%
(C) 72.5% **(D)** 78.4%

10. The salaries of P and Q together amount to ₹ 1,20,000. P spends 95% of his salary and Q 85% of his. If their savings are the same, then what is P's salary? **[SSC CHSL 2022]**

(A) ₹ 80,000 **(B)** ₹ 72,000
(C) ₹ 90,000 **(D)** ₹ 60,000

11. The price of a TV has been reduced by 20%. In order to restore the original price, the new price must be increased by: **[SSC CHSL 2022]**

(A) 20% **(B)** 28% **(C)** 31% **(D)** 25%

12. The monthly income of Manisha was ₹ 1,20,000 and her monthly expenditure was ₹ 55,000. Next year, her income increased by 22% and her expenditure increase by 10%. Find the percentage increase in her savings (correct to 2 decimal places). **[SSC CHSL 2022]**

(A) 28.16% **(B)** 26.25%
(C) 32.15% **(D)** 30.08%

13. If A is 28% more than B and C's 25% less than the sum of A and B, then by what per cent will C be more than A? **[SSC CGL 2018]**

(A) 32.2% **(B)** 28%
(C) 43% **(D)** 33.6%

14. A spends 65% of his income. His income is increased by 20.1% and his expenditure increased by 25%. His savings: **[SSC CGL 2018]**

(A) increase by 11% **(B)** increase by 5%
(C) decrease by 5% **(D)** decrease by 11%

15. If 25% of half of x is equal to 2.5 times the value of 30% of one-fourth of y, then x is what per cent more or less than y? **[SSC 2018]**

(A) $33\frac{1}{3}\%$ more **(B)** 50% more

(C) $33\frac{1}{3}\%$ less **(D)** 50% less

16. The income of A is 24% more than the income of B. By what per cent is the income of B is less than income of A? [SSC CPO 2018]

(A) $\frac{600}{31}\%$ (B) $\frac{150}{7}\%$

(C) $\frac{600}{29}\%$ (D) $\frac{500}{31}\%$

17. If $\left[3\frac{6}{7} \div \frac{54}{7} - \left\{3 - \left(2\frac{3}{4} - \frac{3}{2}\right)\right\}\right] + A \div 4 = 0$, then what is the value of A? [SSC CHSL 2022]

(A) 9 (B) 6 (C) 5 (D) 4

18. A's salary is 35% more than B's salary. How much per cent in B's salary less than that of A's? [SSC CGL 2019]

(A) 20% (B) 35%

(C) 26% (D) 17.5%

19. Amrya owns $66\frac{2}{3}\%$ of a property. If 30% of the property that she owns is ₹ 1,25,000, then 45% of the value of property is: [SSC 2019]

(A) ₹ 2,70,000 (B) ₹ 2,81,250

(C) ₹ 2,25,000 (D) ₹ 2,62,500

Level 3 Expert

1. If $(x + 20)\%$ of 250 is 25% more than $x\%$ of 220, then 10% of $(x + 50)$ is what % less than 15% of x? [SSC CGL 2019]

(A) $16\frac{2}{3}$ (B) $8\frac{1}{3}$ (C) $13\frac{1}{3}$ (D) $33\frac{1}{3}$

2. Bushan's monthly income is ₹45,000 and his monthly expenditure is ₹33,000. If his monthly income is increased by 22% while monthly expenditure is increased by 11%, then what is his new monthly savings (in ₹)? [SSC CHSL 2023]

(A) 18,270 (B) 18,690

(C) 18,000 (D) 19,000

3. During his entire school life, John's average marks in science was 80% and his average marks in mathematics was 90%. If his combined average marks in science and mathematics was 84%, while the total marks obtained by him in science was 54,000, what was John's total marks obtained in mathematics? [SSC CHSL 2022]

(A) 90000 (B) 81000 (C) 36000 (D) 60000

4. Lucky spends 85% of her income. If her expenditure increases by $x\%$, savings increase by 60% income increases by 26%, then what is the value of x? [SSC CGL 2021]

(A) 30% (B) 34% (C) 26% (D) 20%

5. The price of a commodity increases by 28%. However, the expenditure of it increases by 12%. What is the percentage increase or decrease in consumption? [SSC CHSL 2021]

(A) 16% increase (B) 12.5% decrease

(C) 12.5% increase (D) 16% decrease

6. By mistake, the reciprocal of a positive fraction got typed in place of itself and there by, its value got reduced by $\frac{175}{4}\%$. What was the value of fraction? [SSC CGL 2021]

(A) $\frac{1}{2}$ (B) $\frac{4}{3}$ (C) $\frac{3}{4}$ (D) $\frac{1}{4}$

7. Two students A and B appeared for an examination. A secured 8 marks more than B and the marks of the former was 55% of the sum of their marks. The marks obtained by A and B, respectively, are: [SSC CHSL 2021]

(A) 44, 36 (B) 36, 28 (C) 38, 30 (D) 40, 32

8. If decreasing 180 by $x\%$ gives the same result as increasing 60 by $x\%$, then $x\%$ of 410 will be more than $(x + 20)\%$ of 210 by: [SSC CHSL 2021]

(A) 36.57% (B) 31.67%

(C) 33.33% (D) 39.46%

9. The income of A is 25% more than that of B and the income of C is 65% less than the sum of the income of A and B. Income of C is what per cent less than the income of A? [SSC CGL 2019]

(A) 28% (B) 32% (C) 32% (D) 37%

10. If 60% of $(x - y)$ = 45% of $(x + y)$ and $y = k\%$ of x, then 21% of k is equal to: [SSC CGL 2019]

(A) 1 (B) 6 (C) 7 (D) 3

11. If A is 48% more than B and C is 60% less than the sum of A and B, then A is what % more than C? [SSC CGL 2019]

(A) 50.2% (B) 49.8%

(C) 49.2% (D) 50.8%

12. In an election between Ram and Shyamal, one got 30% of the total votes and thus lost by 900 votes. If 90% of the voters voted and no invalid or illegal votes were cast, then what was the numbers of voters in the voting list? [SSC CHSL 2022]

(A) 2800 (B) 2500 (C) 2700 (D) 2300

13. Rajiv scored 20 percent marks in an exam and failed by 25 marks. If he scores 50 percent marks, then he gets 20 marks more than passing marks. What is the passing marks for the exam? [SSC CHSL 2023]

(A) 40 (B) 35 (C) 55 (D) 45

14. The sum of salaries of A and B together is ₹ 43,000. A spends 95% of his salary and B spends 80% of his salary. If now their savings are the same, what is B's salary? [SSC CGL 2019]

(A) ₹ 8,000 (B) ₹ 34,400

(C) ₹ 10,600 (D) ₹ 8,600

15. Sudha spends 80% of her income. When her income is increased by 30%, she increases her expenditure by 25%. Her savings: [SSC CHSL 2018]

(A) increased by 5% (B) decreased by 30%
(C) decreased by 5% (D) increased by 50%

16. The price of an article increases by 20% every year. If the difference between the price at the end of third and fourth years is ₹ 259.20, then 40% of the price at the end of 2nd year is: [SSC CHSL 2018]

(A) 484 (B) 432
(C) 384 (D) 472

17. The ratio of the income of A to that of B is 5 : 7. A and B save ₹ 4,000 and ₹ 5,000, respectively. If the expenditure of A is equal to $66\frac{2}{3}\%$ of the expenditure of B, then the total income of A and B is: [SSC CGL 2018]

(A) ₹ 25,200 (B) ₹ 24,000
(C) ₹ 26,400 (D) ₹ 28,800

18. A is 25% more than B and B is 40% less than C. If C is 30% more than D, then by what per cent is A less than D? [SSC CGL 2018]

(A) 1.5% (B) 2.5% (C) 4% (D) 5%

19. If decreasing 110 by $x\%$ gives the same result as increasing 50 by $x\%$, then $x\%$ of 650 is what percentage more than $(x - 10)\%$ of 780? [SSC CGL 2019]

(A) 17% (B) 12% (C) 18% (D) 14%

20. A man spends $10\frac{1}{2}\%$ of his salary on items of daily use and 30% of the remainder on house rent; after that, he is left with ₹ 12,000. How much is his salary (consider the round-up value)? [SSC CHSL 2022]

(A) ₹ 18,050 (B) ₹ 19,154
(C) ₹ 10,054 (D) ₹ 19,000

ANSWER KEY

Level-1: Beginner

1.	(C)	2.	(A)	3.	(A)	4.	(A)	5.	(B)	6.	(D)	7.	(D)	8.	(C)	9.	(C)	10.	(A)
11.	(D)	12.	(B)	13.	(D)	14.	(B)	15.	(C)	16.	(A)	17.	(C)	18.	(A)	19.	(B)	20.	(C)
21.	(C)	22.	(D)	23.	(C)	24.	(B)	25.	(D)										

Level-2: Intermediate

1.	(D)	2.	(B)	3.	(A)	4.	(D)	5.	(B)	6.	(A)	7.	(A)	8.	(A)	9.	(D)	10.	(C)
11.	(D)	12.	(C)	13.	(D)	14.	(A)	15.	(B)	16.	(A)	17.	(C)	18.	(C)	19.	(B)		

Level-3: Expert

1.	(A)	2.	(A)	3.	(C)	4.	(D)	5.	(B)	6.	(B)	7.	(A)	8.	(D)	9.	(D)	10.	(D)
11.	(C)	12.	(B)	13.	(C)	14.	(D)	15.	(D)	16.	(B)	17.	(B)	18.	(B)	19.	(D)	20.	(B)

Solutions with Detailed Explanations

Level-1: BEGINNER

1. Option (C) is correct.

Explanation: Required percentage $= \frac{24}{40} \times 100 = 60\%$

2. Option (A) is correct.

Explanation: $\frac{1}{100} \times \frac{1}{100} \times \frac{25}{100} \times 1,000 = 0.025$

3. Option (A) is correct.

Explanation:

$$R = S + 0.2S - 1.2S$$

$$\text{Required\%} = \left(\frac{R-S}{R}\right)\times 100 = \left(1-\frac{S}{R}\right)\times 100$$

$$= \left(1-\frac{1}{1.2}\right)\times 100 = \frac{100}{6} = 16\frac{2}{3}\%$$

4. Option (A) is correct.

Explanation:

$$\frac{125}{100}\times x = 100$$

$$\Rightarrow \quad x = \frac{100\times 100}{125} \Rightarrow 80$$

5. **Option (B) is correct.**

Explanation:

Let the number = x

$$\frac{40}{100}\times\frac{4}{5}\times\frac{3}{4}\times x = 48$$

$$\frac{6}{25}x = 48$$

$$x = \frac{48\times 25}{6} = 200$$

$\Rightarrow$ 1% of 200 = 2

6. **Option (D) is correct.**

Explanation: Let the total number of students be x.

Let A and B represent the sets of students who passed in English and Mathematics, respectively.

$$\Rightarrow n(A\cup B) = n(A) + n(B) - n(A\cap B)$$

$$= 75\% \text{ of } x + 60\% \text{ of } x - (x - 25\% \text{ of } x)$$

$$= \frac{3}{4}x + \frac{3}{5}x - \frac{3}{4}x = \frac{3}{5}x$$

So, $\frac{3}{5}x = 240$

$$x = 400$$

7. **Option (D) is correct.**

Explanation:

Total C.P. = 200 × 10 = ₹ 2,000

Total S.P. = 12 × 195 = ₹ 2,340

$$\% \text{ profit} = \frac{2{,}340 - 2{,}000}{2{,}000}\times 100 = 17\%$$

8. **Option (C) is correct.**

Explanation: Increase in salary = ₹ 900. i.e.,

$8{,}100 \rightarrow 9{,}000$

$$\text{Percentage increase} = \frac{900}{8{,}100}\times 100 = 11\frac{1}{9}\%$$

9. **Option (C) is correct.**

Explanation: Let total number of students who appeared in an examination be x.

According to the question,

$$x\times\frac{8}{100} = 480$$

$$\Rightarrow x = 6{,}000$$

10. **Option (A) is correct.**

Explanation: $\frac{18}{100}\times\frac{15}{100}\times\frac{25}{9}\times 3{,}800 = 285$

11. **Option (D) is correct.**

Explanation: $\frac{9}{40}\times 100 = \frac{45}{2}\% = 22\frac{1}{2}\%$

12. **Option (B) is correct.**

Explanation:

5 litres = 5,000 ml

$$8\% \text{ of 5 litres} = 5{,}000\times\frac{8}{100}$$

$$= 400 \text{ ml}$$

13. **Option (D) is correct.**

Explanation:

According to the question,

$$124 \times x\% = 49.60$$

$$\Rightarrow x = \frac{4{,}960}{124} = 40$$

14. **Option (B) is correct.**

Explanation:

$$12\% = \frac{3 \rightarrow \text{Saving}}{25 \rightarrow \text{Income}}$$

Expenditure = 22 units = 2,16,128

1 unit = 9824

25 units = 245600

So, total income = ₹ 2,45,600

15. **Option (C) is correct.**

Explanation:

Let salary of A and B are A and B, respectively.

So, according to the question,

A : B = 160 : 100

$$\text{Required}\% = \frac{60}{160}\times 100 = 37.5\%$$

16. **Option (A) is correct.**

Explanation:

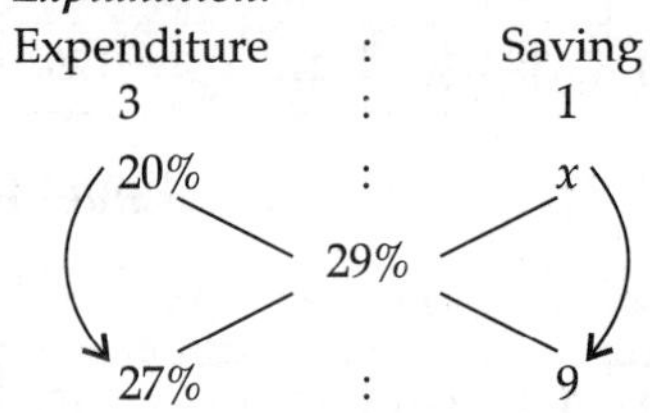

$$x - 29 = 27 \Rightarrow x = 56\%$$

17. **Option (C) is correct.**

Explanation: Value after two years

$$= 75{,}000\times\frac{96}{100}\times\frac{96}{100} = ₹\ 69{,}120$$

18. **Option (A) is correct.**

Explanation:

Saving percentage = (100 – 55)% = 45%

If the income of Ajay be ₹x, then,

$$\frac{45\times x}{100} = 27{,}000$$

$$\Rightarrow x = ₹\ 60{,}000$$

19. **Option (B) is correct.**

Explanation: Let salary of Som = ₹100

∴ His salary after 40% increment = ₹140

$$\text{His salary after 15\% reduction} = \left[\frac{100-15}{100}\right]\times 140$$

$$= \frac{85\times 14}{10} = 119$$

∴ Net change in his salary is 19% increase.

20. Option (C) is correct.

Explanation: Let the total number of students in class be x.

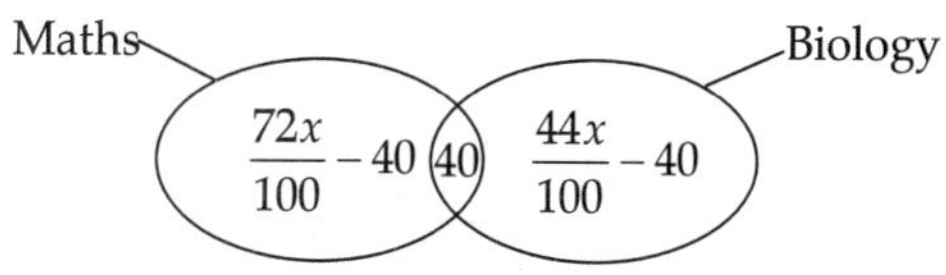

$$\frac{72x}{100}-40+40+\frac{44x}{100}-40=x$$

$$\Rightarrow \frac{72x}{100}x+\frac{44x}{100}-x=40$$

$$\Rightarrow \quad x=\frac{40\times100}{16}\Rightarrow x=250$$

21. Option (C) is correct.

Explanation: Let her income = ₹100

Expenditure on food = ₹25

Expenditure on children's book = ₹15

Expenditure on uniform = $\frac{75}{100}$ [100 – 40] = ₹45

∴ Remaining amount = ₹15

⇒ Remaining percentage of income = 15%

22. Option (D) is correct.

Explanation: % of votes secured by the second candidate = (100 – 57)% = 43%

Let total votes polled be x.

According to question,

$$(57-43)\ \%\text{ of }x = 42{,}000$$

$$\Rightarrow 14\%\text{ of }x = 42{,}000$$

$$\Rightarrow x = 3{,}00{,}000$$

23. Option (C) is correct.

Explanation: Let the side of cube = a units

∴ Surface area of cube = $6a^2$ sq. units

New side of cube = $6\times\left(\frac{22}{25}a\right)^2$ sq. units

∴ Decrease in the surface area

$$=\frac{6a^2-6\times\left(\frac{22}{25}a\right)^2}{6a^2}\times100$$

$$=22.56\%$$

24. Option (B) is correct.

Explanation: According to the question,

Number of girls = (100 – 60)% = 40%

⇒ 40% = 36

So, 60% = 54

Number of boys = 54

25. Option (D) is correct.

Explanation:

Mohan : Shyam = 7 : 5

Shyam's income is less by = $\frac{2}{7}\times100\% = 28\frac{4}{7}\%$

Level-2: INTERMEDIATE

1. Option (D) is correct.

Explanation: Quantity of salt = 5% of 6 litres = 300 ml

Quantity of water = 6,000 ml – 300 ml = 5,700 ml

Quantity of water left after evaporation

= (5,700 – 1000) ml = 4,700 ml

$$\%\text{ of salt} = \frac{300\text{ ml}}{(4{,}700+300)\text{ml}}\times100 = 6\%$$

2. Option (B) is correct.

Explanation:

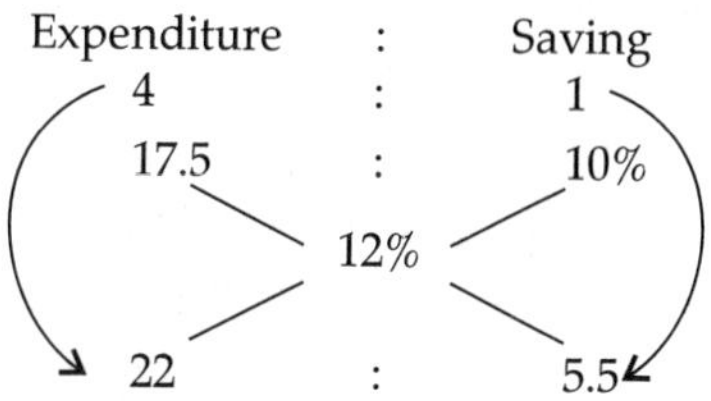

10% decrease in savings.

3. Option (A) is correct.

Explanation: Required percentage change

$$=\frac{\frac{3}{2}-\frac{7}{5}}{\frac{3}{2}}\times100\% = \frac{20\%}{3}\Rightarrow 6\frac{2}{3}\%$$

4. Option (D) is correct.

Explanation:

P = 100 — 124

C = 124 — 100 118

Consumption decrease = $\frac{6}{124}\times100 = 4.8\%$

5. Option (B) is correct.

Explanation: As price is reduced by 20% or $\frac{1}{5}$ factor.

Then consumption will increase by a factor of $\frac{1}{4}$, as expenditure is constant.

According to question,

$$\frac{1}{4}\times x = 4\text{ kg}$$

$$\therefore\quad x = 16\text{ kg}$$

Price of 16 kg = 160

$$\therefore\quad \text{Price of 1 kg} = \frac{160}{16} = ₹\,10$$

So, price of sugar is ₹ 10/ kg

6. Option (A) is correct.

Explanation: Let the monthly salary of A be x, monthly salary of B is (40,000 – x)

Savings of A = (100 – 85)% of x = 0.15 x

Savings of B = (100 – 95)% of (40,000 – x)

= 0.05 (40,000 – x)

0.15x = 0.05 (40,000 – x)

⇒ 0.15x + 0.05x = 40,000 × 0.05

$$\Rightarrow \quad 0.2x = 2{,}000$$
$$\Rightarrow \quad x = ₹\,10{,}000$$

7. **Option (A) is correct.**

Explanation:

Let passing marks = p

$$p \times 1.05 = 273$$
$$p = 260$$

$$\text{Lokesh passing\%} = \frac{312-260}{260} \times 100 = 20\%$$

8. **Option (A) is correct.**

Explanation:

100 ⟶ 117 ; 100 ⟶ 105 ; 117 → 105 : −12

$$\%\text{ decrease} = \frac{12}{117} \times 100 = 10.3\%$$

9. **Option (D) is correct.**

Explanation:

$$\frac{R_1}{R_2} = \frac{60}{100} = \frac{3}{5}$$

$$\text{Volume} = V_1 : V_2 = 27 : 125$$

$$\text{Volume decrease} = \frac{98}{125} \times 100 = 78.4\%$$

10. **Option (C) is correct.**

Explanation: Given,

Total salary of P and Q = ₹ 120000

Let salary of P = ₹ x

And salary of Q = ₹ 120000 – x

According to the question,

$$x \times \frac{5}{100} = (120000 - x) \times \frac{15}{100}$$

$$\Rightarrow \quad 5x = 1800000 - 15x$$
$$\Rightarrow \quad x = 90000$$

So, salary of P = ₹ 90000

11. **Option (D) is correct.**

Explanation: Let the price of T.V = ₹ 100

After decreasing price by 20%, new price = ₹ 80

Required percentage increase in price

$$= \frac{100-80}{80} \times 100 = 25\%$$

12. **Option (C) is correct.**

Explanation: Given,

Monthly income of Manisha = ₹ 120000

And monthly expenditure = ₹ 55000

So, savings = 120000 – 55000 = ₹ 65000

According to the question,

$$\text{Next year her salary} = 120000 \times \frac{122}{100} = ₹\,146400$$

$$\text{And the new expenditure} = 55000 \times \frac{110}{100} = ₹\,60500$$

So, new savings = 146400 – 60500 = ₹ 85900

Now, required percentage increase

$$= \frac{85900-65000}{65000} \times 100 = 32.15\%$$

13. **Option (D) is correct.**

Explanation:

Suppose B = 100, then A = 128,

$$C = \frac{3}{4}(A+B) = \frac{3}{4} \times 228 = 171$$

128 : 100 : 171 (128 → 171 : +43)

$$\text{Required percentage} = \frac{43}{128} \times 100$$

$$= \frac{1{,}075}{32} = 33.59 \approx 33.6\%$$

14. **Option (A) is correct.**

Explanation:

I = E : S

400 = 260 : 140

480.4 = 325 : 155.4

(400 → 480.4 : +20.1% ; 140 → 155.4 : +15.4)

$$\Rightarrow \quad \text{Savings\%} = \frac{15.4}{140} \times 100 = 11\%$$

15. **Option (B) is correct.**

Explanation: According to the question,

$$\frac{1}{4} \times \frac{1}{2} \times x = \frac{5}{2} \times \frac{3}{10} \times \frac{1}{4} \times y$$

$$\frac{x}{y} = \frac{3}{2}$$

Required% = 3 – 2/2 × 100 = 50%

$x \rightarrow$ 50% more than y

16. **Option (A) is correct.**

Explanation: According to the question,

A : B = 124 : 100 = 31 : 25

$$\text{So, required\%} = \frac{6}{31} \times 100 = \frac{600}{31}\%$$

17. **Option (C) is correct.**

Explanation:

Value of expression

$$\left[3\frac{6}{7} \div \frac{54}{7} - \left\{3 - \left(2\frac{3}{4} - \frac{3}{2}\right)\right\}\right] + A \div 4 = 0$$

$$\Rightarrow \quad \left[\frac{27}{7} \div \frac{54}{7} - \left\{3 - \left(\frac{5}{4}\right)\right\}\right] + A \div 4 = 0$$

$$\Rightarrow \quad \left[\frac{27}{7} \div \frac{54}{7} - \frac{7}{4}\right] + A \div 4 = 0$$

$$\Rightarrow \quad \left[\frac{1}{2} - \frac{7}{4}\right] + A \div 4 = 0$$

$$\Rightarrow \quad \left[\frac{-5}{4}\right] + A \div 4 = 0$$

$$\Rightarrow \quad A \div 4 = \frac{5}{4}$$

$$\Rightarrow \quad A = 5$$

18. **Option (C) is correct.**

Explanation: A : B = 135 : 100

$$\text{Required\%} = \frac{35}{135} \times 100 \approx 26\%$$

19. Option (B) is correct.

Explanation: Let total property be x.

$$x \times \frac{2}{3} \times \frac{3}{10} = 12{,}500$$

$$\Rightarrow \quad x = 6{,}25{,}000$$

$$x \times \frac{45}{100} = ₹\ 2{,}81{,}250$$

Level-3: EXPERT

1. Option (A) is correct.

Explanation:

$$\frac{(x+20)}{100} \times 250 = \frac{125}{100} \times \frac{x}{100} \times 220$$

$$x = 200$$

$$\Rightarrow 10\% \text{ of } (x + 50) = \frac{10}{100} \times 250 = 25$$

$$\Rightarrow \quad 15\% \text{ of } x = \frac{15}{100} \times 200 = 30$$

$$\Rightarrow \quad \text{Required\%} = \frac{30 - 25}{30} \times 100$$

$$= \frac{5}{30} \times 100 = 16\frac{2}{3}\%$$

2. Option (A) is correct.

Explanation:

Monthly income = ₹45000 and monthly expenditure = ₹33000

New saving after increment

$$= \frac{122}{100} \times 45000 - \frac{111}{100} \times 33000$$

$$= 122 \times 450 - 111 \times 330 = ₹18270$$

3. Option (C) is correct.

Explanation: Using mixture formula:

Science 80% Maths 90%

84%

Ratio ⇒ 6 : 4

or 3 : 2

Given that total marks obtained in Science = 54000

$\therefore$ Marks obtained in Maths $= \frac{54000}{3} \times 2 = 36000$

4. Option (D) is correct.

Explanation:

Income	Expenditure	Saving
200	170	30
↓ 26% Increase		↓ 60%
252		48

As, $252 - 48 = 204$

$$\% \text{ Expenditure increase} = \frac{204-170}{170} = \frac{34}{170} = 20\%$$

5. Option (B) is correct.

Explanation: Let price, consumption and expenditure are P, C and E, respectively.

$$P \times C = E$$

Let, $25 \times 4 = 100$

Then, after changes new expenditure

$= 32 \times 3.5 = 112$

So, percentage decrease $= \frac{0.5}{4} \times 100$

= 12.5% (decrease)

6. Option (B) is correct.

Explanation:

Correct $\rightarrow \frac{4}{3} \times 12 \longrightarrow 16$

Wrong $\rightarrow \frac{3}{4} \times 12 \longrightarrow 9$

-7 (By option)

$$\% \text{ reduction} = \frac{7}{16} \times 100 = \frac{175}{4}\%$$

7. Option (A) is correct.

Explanation:

$$A - B = 8$$

$$A = (A + B) \times \frac{55}{100}$$

$$\frac{A}{A+B} = \frac{11}{20} \Rightarrow \frac{A}{B} = \frac{11 \rightarrow 44}{9 \rightarrow 36}$$

8. Option (D) is correct.

Explanation:

$$\frac{180}{60} = \frac{(100+x)\%}{(100-x)\%}$$

$$\Rightarrow \quad x = 50$$

$$50\% \text{ of } 410 = 205$$

$$70\% \text{ of } 210 = 147$$

So, $\text{required\%} = \frac{205-147}{147} \times 100 = 39.46\%$

9. Option (D) is correct.

Explanation:

$$25\% \text{ more} = \frac{5}{4}$$

$$C = 35\% \text{ of } (A + B)$$

A : B : C

500 400 315

-185

$$\text{Required\%} = \frac{185}{500} \times 100 = 37\%$$

10. Option (D) is correct.

Explanation:

$$60\% \text{ of } (x - y) = 45\% \text{ of } (x + y)$$

$$\Rightarrow \quad \frac{3}{5}(x-y) = \frac{9}{20}(x+y)$$

$$\Rightarrow \quad 4(x - y) = 3x + 3y$$

$$\Rightarrow \quad x = 7y$$

$$\Rightarrow \quad x : y = 7 : 1$$

$$7 \times \frac{k}{100} = 1 \Rightarrow k = \frac{100}{7}$$

$$\Rightarrow \quad 21\% \text{ of } k = \frac{21}{100} \times \frac{100}{7} = 3$$

11. Option (C) is correct.

Explanation:

$$A : B : C = 148 : 100 : \frac{248 \times 40}{100}$$

$$= 148 : 100 : 99.2$$

$$\text{Required\%} = \frac{48.8}{99.2} \times 100 = 49.2\%$$

12. Option (B) is correct.

Explanation: Let the total number of voters = x

So, number of voters voted in the election = $0.9x$

According to the question,

$$\Rightarrow 0.9x \times \frac{30}{100} + 900 = 0.9x \times \frac{70}{100}$$

$$\Rightarrow 0.9x \times \frac{40}{100} = 900$$

$$\Rightarrow x = 2500$$

So, total number of voters = 2500

13. Option (C) is correct.

Explanation: Let the total marks = x

According to the question,

$$\Rightarrow \frac{20}{100}x + 25 = \frac{50}{100}x - 20$$

$$\Rightarrow \frac{1}{5}x + 45 = \frac{1}{2}x \Rightarrow \frac{3}{10}x = 45$$

$$\Rightarrow \quad x = 150$$

So, the passing marks = $\frac{20}{100} \times 150 + 25 = 55$

14. Option (D) is correct.

Explanation:

$$5\% \text{ of A} = 20\% \text{ of B}$$

$$\frac{A}{B} = \frac{4}{1}$$

$$\Rightarrow \quad 5 \text{ units} = 43{,}000$$

$$\therefore \quad \text{B's salary} = 8{,}600$$

15. Option (D) is correct.

Explanation:

I	=	E	S
100	=	80	20
130	=	100	30

Savings increased by 50%

16. Option (B) is correct.

Explanation:

We know, $\quad 20\% = \frac{1}{5}$

Let price = 625

end of 1st year = 750

2nd year = 900

3rd year = 1,080

4th year = 1,296

Difference = 216 = 259.20

40% of 900 = 360 = 432

17. Option (B) is correct.

Explanation:

$$66\frac{2}{3}\% = \frac{2}{3}$$

I = 5 : 7

E → 2 : 3

S → 4,000 : 5,000

12,000 : 10,000

15 – 14 unit = 12,000 – 10,000

1 unit – 2,000

12 units → 24,000

18. Option (B) is correct.

Explanation: According to the question,

A : B : C : D = 195 : 156 : 260 : 200

$$\text{Required\%} = \frac{5}{200} \times 100 = 2.5\%$$

19. Option (D) is correct.

Explanation:

$$110\left(\frac{100 - x}{100}\right) = 50\left(\frac{100 + x}{100}\right)$$

$$x = \frac{75}{2}\%$$

$$x\% \text{ of } 650 = 243.75$$

$$(x - 10)\% \text{ of } 780 = 214.50$$

$$\text{Required more\%} = \frac{29.25}{214.5} \times 100 = 13.63\% \approx 14\%$$

20. Option (B) is correct.

Explanation: Let the salary of the person = ₹ x

So, amount left after his daily use items spendings

$$= x - \frac{21}{200}x = \frac{179}{200}x$$

According to the question,

$$\Rightarrow \frac{179}{200} \times \frac{70}{100}x = 12000$$

$$\Rightarrow \quad x = 19154$$

So, the salary of the person = ₹ 19154

Profit, Loss and Discount

Cost Price (CP) →

Price at someone bought an item

Selling Price (SP) →

Price at someone sells an item

Profit →

When SP > CP

Loss →

When CP > SP

Marked Price →

Price printed on product

Discount →

Rebate provided by shopkeeper to the customer on marked price

If Profit% and Loss% are equal then, Profit = Loss

Profit = Selling Price – Cost Price

$$\text{Profit\%} = \frac{\text{Profit}}{\text{CP}} \times 100$$

Loss = Cost Price – Selling Price

$$\text{Loss\%} = \frac{\text{Loss}}{\text{CP}} \times 100$$

Discount = Marked Price – Selling Price

When Discount % = zero then, Marked Price = Selling Price

$$\text{Discount\%} = \frac{\text{Discount}}{\text{Marked Price}} \times 100$$

When two discounts d_1 and d_2 are given, then equivalent discount $= d_1 + d_2 - \frac{(d_1 \times d_2)}{100}$

Chapter 2

Profit, Loss and Discount

LEARNING OBJECTIVES:

- Method of calculating profit and loss while selling an article.
- Concepts related to marked price, discount, cost price and selling price.
- Concept of dishonest shopkeeper.
- Various types of questions asked in competitive exams related to profit, loss and discount.

When we buy a thing, in the market for a given price and subsequently sell it for a different price, we can make a profit or a loss. It is one of the most useful mathematical notions. Several forms of transactions occur in every day life, and they all incorporate the concept of profit and loss. Profit and loss concepts are deal with using numerous phrases such as cost price, selling price, discount, marked price, profit and loss.

- **Cost price:** The price at which someone bought an item.
- **Selling price:** The price at which someone sells the article.
- **Profit:** When the selling price of an article is more than its cost price.
- **Loss:** When the cost price of an article is more than its selling price.
- **Marked price:** The price printed on the product.
- **Discount:** The rebate provided by a shopkeeper to the customer when the customer buys a product.

IMPORTANT FORMULA

- Profit = Selling Price (SP) – Cost Price (CP)
- Loss = Cost Price (CP) – Selling Price (SP)
- $\text{Profit\%} = \dfrac{\text{Profit}}{\text{Cost price}} \times 100$
- $\text{Loss\%} = \dfrac{\text{Loss}}{\text{Cost price}} \times 100$
- Discount = Marked price – Selling price
- $\text{Discount\%} = \dfrac{\text{Discount}}{\text{Marked price}} \times 100$

  When two discounts d_1 and d_2 are given, then equivalent discount $= d_1 + d_1 - \dfrac{(d_1 \times d_2)}{100}$

Example 1: Rahul bought an article for ₹ 500 and sells it at 10% profit. Find the selling price of the article.

(a) ₹ 550 (b) ₹ 600
(c) ₹ 750 (d) ₹ 450

Sol. (a) Using, selling price $= \dfrac{\text{CP}(100 + \text{Profit\%})}{100}$

$$= \frac{500(100+10)}{100}$$

$$= \frac{500 \times 110}{100} = ₹\,550$$

Example 2: Two successive discounts of 10% and 5% is equivalent to single discount of:

(a) 12% (b) 14.5%
(c) 15% (d) 18%

Sol. (b) Using, equivalent single discount

$$= d_1 + d_2 - \frac{(d_1 \times d_2)}{100} = 10 + 5 - \frac{(10 \times 5)}{100}$$

$$= 15 - \frac{50}{100} = \frac{29}{2} = 14.5\%$$

Example 3: The ratio of cost price to selling price is 5:4. Find loss or profit per cent.

(a) 20% loss (b) 10% profit
(c) 20% profit (d) 10% loss

Sol. (a) Since, $\dfrac{\text{CP}}{\text{SP}} = \dfrac{5}{4}$

Assuming, CP = $5x$

and SP = $4x$

Here, CP > SP, so in this case, loss is occured.

Using, $\text{loss\%} = \dfrac{(\text{CP} - \text{SP})}{\text{CP}} \times 100$

$$= \frac{(5x - 4x)}{5x} \times 100$$

$$= 20\%$$

Example 4: A man bought an article for ₹ 700. At what price should he sell the article to gain 10%?

(a) ₹ 870 (b) ₹ 850
(c) ₹ 770 (d) ₹780

Sol. (c) Using, SP = CP + profit% of CP

SP = 700 + 10% of 700

= 700 + 70 = ₹ 770

Example 5: By selling an article for ₹ 550, Rahul gains 10% of profit. To get a profit of 20%, Rahul should sell the article for:

(a) ₹ 600 (b) ₹ 500
(c) ₹ 400 (d) ₹ 300

Sol. (a) SP = ₹ 550

Profit% = 10%

Let, CP = x

$\Rightarrow$ x + 10% of x = 550

$$\Rightarrow \quad x + \frac{x}{10} = 550$$

$\Rightarrow$ $11x$ = 5,500

$\Rightarrow$ x = ₹ 500

Now, to get 20% profit, the article should be sold at 120% value of cost price.

So, new selling price = 120% of cost price = $\frac{120}{100} \times 500$

= ₹ 600

Example 6: A sells an article to B on 10% profit, B sold the article to C on 5% profit. If C pays ₹ 1,155, then find the cost price of article for A.

(a) ₹ 900 (b) ₹ 800
(c) ₹ 1,200 (d) ₹ 1,000

Sol. (d) Assuming CP for A = ₹ x

According to the question,

$$x \times \frac{110}{100} \times \frac{105}{100} = 1155$$

$$x = 1000$$

Example 7: An article is sold for 10% profit. If it was sold for 5% loss, then the shopkeeper got ₹ 75 less as compared to 10% profit. Find the cost price of the article.

(a) ₹ 500 (b) ₹ 700
(c) ₹ 1000 (d) ₹ 300

Sol. (a) We know that, CP = 100%

When sold for 10% profit

SP = 110%

When sold for 5% loss

SP = 95%

According to the question,

110% – 95% = 75

15% = 75

100% = (75/15)100 = ₹ 500

Example 8: An article is marked 10% above CP, then 10% discount is given by the shopkeeper. Find profit or loss per cent in the whole transaction.

(a) 1% loss (b) No loss, no profit
(c) 1% profit (d) 2% loss

Sol. (a) Assuming, CP = 100%

Marked price = 110%

SP = 110% – [10% of 110%]

= 99%

Hence, loss = 100% – 99% [CP – SP]

= 1% loss

Level 1 Beginner

1. If the ratio of cost price and selling price of an article is 10:11, the percentage of profit is: [SSC CGL 2021]
(A) 8 (B) 10 (C) 11 (D) 15

2. By selling an article, a man makes a profit of 25% of its selling price. His profit per cent is: [SSC CGL 2012]
(A) 20 (B) 25 (C) $16\frac{2}{3}$ (D) $33\frac{1}{3}$

3. If the cost price of 15 books is equal to the selling price of 20 books, then the loss per cent is: [SSC CGL 2011]
(A) 16 (B) 20 (C) 24 (D) 25

4. If a tradesman marks his goods 25% above the costprice and allows his customers a 12% reduction on their bill, then the percentage profit he makes is: [SSC CHSL 2022]
(A) 30% (B) 20% (C) 40% (D) 10%

5. Sucessive discounts of 10%, 20% and 30% is equivalent to single discount of: [SSC CGL 2010]
(A) 60% (B) 49.6% (C) 40.5% (D) 36%

6. What single discount is equivalent to two successive discount of 20% and 15%? [SSC 2011]
(A) 35% (B) 32% (C) 34% (D) 30%

7. If the selling price of 10 articles is equal to the cost price of 11 articles, then the gain per cent is: [SSC CGL 2011]
(A) 10 (B) 11 (C) 15 (D) 25

8. The cost price of an article is 40% of its selling price. What per cent of the cost price is the selling price? [SSC CGL 2011]
(A) 140% (B) 200% (C) 220% (D) 250%

9. There is a 20% discount on a dozen pairs of shoes marked at ₹ 7,200. How many pair of shoes can be bought with ₹ 1,440? [SSC CHSL 2022]
(A) 3 (B) 5 (C) 2 (D) 4

10. A fruit seller purchased 300 bananas at the rate of ₹ 18 per dozen and sold 200 bananas at the rate of ₹ 24 per dozen and the remaining bananas at the rate of ₹ 21 per dozen. What is his net profit percentage? [SSC CHSL 2022]
(A) 28% (B) 26%
(C) 27% (D) $27\frac{7}{9}\%$

11. By selling an article for ₹ 21,000, a man gains 5% of profit. To get a profit of 15%, he has to sell it for: **[SSC Sub. Inspector 2012]**

(A) ₹ 19,800 (B) ₹ 20,700
(C) ₹ 23,000 (D) ₹ 25,000

12. The profit% of a bookseller if he sells a book at marked price after enjoying a commisison of 25% on marked price will be: **[SSC CHSL 2012]**

(A) 30% (B) 25%
(C) 20% (D) 33.33%

13. A sells an article to B at a gain of 10%, B sells it to C at a gain of 5%. If C pays ₹ 462 for it, what did it cost to A? **[SSC CHSL 2012]**

(A) ₹ 500 (B) ₹ 450
(C) ₹ 600 (D) ₹ 400

14. A seller gives 4 toys free of cost on buying 14 toys. What percent does the customer get as a discount? **[SSC CHSL 2022]**

(A) $21\frac{2}{9}\%$ (B) $22\frac{2}{9}\%$
(C) $24\frac{2}{9}\%$ (D) $23\frac{2}{9}\%$

15. A watch is sold at a profit of 30%. Had it been sold for ₹ 80 less, there would have been a loss of 10%. What is the cost price of the watch? **[SSC CGL 2012]**

(A) ₹ 150 (B) ₹ 200 (C) ₹ 400 (D) ₹ 800

16. A dealer offered a machine for sale for ₹ 27,500 but even if he had charged 10% less, he would have made a profit of 10%. The actual cost of the machine is: **[SSC CGL 2012]**

(A) ₹ 22,000 (B) ₹ 24,250
(C) ₹ 22,500 (D) ₹ 22,275

17. A man sold an article at a loss of 20%. If he sells the article for ₹ 12 more, he would have gained 10%. The cost price of the article is: **[SSC CGL 2012]**

(A) ₹ 60 (B) ₹ 40 (C) ₹ 30 (D) ₹ 22

18. An article is sold for ₹ 300 at a profit of 20%. Had it been sold ₹ 235, the loss percentage would have been: **[SSC CGL 2013]**

(A) 5 (B) 6 (C) 16 (D) 3

19. The marked price of a table is ₹ 12,000. If it was sold for ₹ 10,500 after allowing a certain discount, then the rate of discount is: **[SSC CGL 2013]**

(A) 12.5% (B) 15% (C) 17.5% (D) 10%

20. On the eve of Gandhi Jayanti, Gandhi Ashram declared a 25% discount on silk. If the selling price of a silk saree is ₹ 525, then what is its marked price? **[SSC CGL 2013]**

(A) ₹ 700 (B) ₹ 725
(C) ₹ 750 (D) ₹ 775

21. A shopkeeper marks his goods 20% above his cost price and gives 15% discount on the marked price. His gain per cent is: **[SSC CGL 2014]**

(A) 5% (B) 4% (C) 2% (D) 1%

22. If a shopkeeper purchases cashew nut at ₹ 250/kg and sells it at ₹ 10 per 50 grams, then he will have: **[SSC Sub. Inspector 2015]**

(A) 25% profit (B) 20% profit
(C) 20% loss (D) 25% loss

23. By selling an article for ₹ 450. I lose 20%. For what amount, should I sell it to gain 20%? **[SSC CHSL 2015]**

(A) ₹ 490 (B) ₹ 470
(C) ₹ 562.50 (D) ₹ 675

24. A fruit seller buys oranges at the rate of ₹ 10/dozen and sells at the rate of ₹ 12/dozen. His gain per cent is : **[SSC CHSL 2015]**

(A) 15% (B) 20% (C) $8\frac{1}{3}\%$ (D) 12%

25. 10% discount and then 20% discount in succession is equivalent to the total discount of: **[SSC CGL 2016]**

(A) 15% (B) 30% (C) 24% (D) 28%

Level 2 Intermediate

1. A manufacturer marked an article at Rs. 50 and sold it allowing 20% discount. If his profit was 25%, then the cost price of the article was: **[SSC CGL 2010]**

(A) ₹ 40 (B) ₹ 35 (C) ₹ 32 (D) ₹ 30

2. A person sells wheat at a profit of 25 percent. If he reduces its selling price by Rs. 40, then he suffers a loss of 25 percent. What was the initial selling price of the wheat? **[SSC CHSL 2023]**

(A) ₹ 80 (B) ₹ 120 (C) ₹ 60 (D) ₹ 100

3. By selling a bicycle fo ₹ 2,850, a shopkeeper gains 14%. If the profit is reduced to 8%, then the selling price will be: **[SSC CGL 2011]**

(A) ₹ 2,600 (B) ₹ 2,700
(C) ₹ 2,800 (D) ₹ 3,000

4. While selling a watch, a shopkeeper gives a discount of 5%. If he gives a discount of 6%, he earns ₹ 15 less as profit. What is the marked price of the watch? **[SSC CGL 2011]**

(A) ₹ 1,250 (B) ₹ 1,400
(C) ₹ 1,500 (D) ₹ 750

5. Krishna purchased a number of articles at ₹ 10 for each and the same number for ₹ 14 each. He mixed them together and sold them for ₹ 13 each. Then, his gain or loss per cent is: **[SSC CGL 2011]**

(A) Loss $8\frac{1}{3}\%$ (B) Gain $8\frac{2}{3}\%$
(C) Loss $8\frac{2}{3}\%$ (D) Gain $8\frac{1}{3}\%$

6. X sells two articles for ₹ 4,000 each with no loss and no gain in the transaction. If one was sold at a gain of 25%, the other is sold at a loss of: [SSC CGL 2012]

(A) 2.5% (B) $18\frac{2}{9}\%$

(C) $16\frac{2}{3}\%$ (D) 20%

7. After allowing 15% discount, a dealer wishes to sell a machine for ₹1,22,700. At what price must the machine be marked? (Consider up to two decimals) [SSC CHSL 2022]

(A) ₹1,22,352.94 (B) ₹1,44,352.94

(C) ₹1,48,352.94 (D) ₹1,36,352.94

8. A businessman allows a discount of 10% on the written price. How much above the cost price must he mark on his goods to make a profit of 17%? [SSC CGL 2012]

(A) 30% (B) 20% (C) 27% (D) 18%

9. The price of an original article is first decreased by 20% and then increased by 30%. If the resultant price is ₹ 416, then the original price of the article is: [SSC CGL 2013]

(A) ₹ 350 (B) ₹ 450

(C) ₹ 405 (D) ₹ 400

10. A bookseller sells a book at a profit of 10%. If he had bought it at 4% less and sold it for ₹ 6 more, he would have gained $18\frac{3}{4}\%$ profit. The cost price of the book is: [MTS 2014]

(A) ₹ 160 (B) ₹ 170

(C) ₹ 150 (D) ₹ 155

11. A man sells two watches at ₹ 99 each. On one, he gets 10% profit and on the other, he loses 10%. His net gain or loss per cent is: [MTS 2014]

(A) 1% loss (B) no loss no profit

(C) 1% gain (D) 10% loss

12. A shopkeeper makes a profit of 12.5% after allowing a discount of 10% on the marked price of an article. Find his profit percentage if the article is sold at the marked price, allowing no discount. [SSC CHSL 2022]

(A) 25% (B) 30% (C) 22.5% (D) 27%

13. A shopkeeper sold an item for ₹ 1,800 at a discount of 10% and gained ₹ 200. He had not given the discount, his gain would be: [SSC MTS 2014]

(A) ₹ 300 (B) ₹ 400

(C) ₹ 180 (D) ₹ 200

14. A tea merchant professes to sell tea at the cost price but uses a false weight of 900 gram for a kilogram. The profit per cent in his transaction is: [SSC Sub. Inspector 2014]

(A) $11\frac{1}{9}\%$ (B) 10%

(C) $9\frac{1}{11}\%$ (D) 15%

15. A shopkeeper allows 10% discount on goods when he sells without credit. Cost price of his goods is 80% of his selling price. If he sells his goods by cash, then his profit is: [SSC CGL 2015]

(A) 50% (B) 70%

(C) 25% (D) 40%

16. Ram bought a T.V. with 20% discount on the labelled price. If he had bought it with 30% discount, he would have saved ₹ 800. The value of the T.V. set that he bought is: [SSC CGL 2014]

(A) ₹ 5,000 (B) ₹ 8,000

(C) ₹ 9,000 (D) ₹ 1,000

17. A trader marks his goods 20% above C.P but allows his customers a discount of ₹ 10%. The C.P. of a black board, which is sold for ₹ 216 is: [SSC Sub. Inspector 2015]

(A) ₹ 200 (B) ₹ 180

(C) ₹ 108 (D) ₹ 196

18. A fan is listed at ₹ 150/- with a discount of 20%. What additional discount must be offered to the customer to bring the net price to ₹ 108/-? [SSC MTS 2017]

(A) 15% (B) 5% (C) 10% (D) 20%

19. At what per cent above the cost price must a person mark the price of an article so that he can enjoy 20% profit after allowing 20% discount? [SSC MTS 2017]

(A) 60% (B) 30% (C) 50% (D) 40%

20. A man bought 15 mangoes for a rupee. How many mangoes were sold for a rupee so that there is a loss of 25%? [SSC Sub. Inspector 2017]

(A) 10 (B) 12 (C) 18 (D) 20

21. A merchant allows a discount of 20 percent on marked price. If he wants to earn a profit of 20 percent. then marked price will be how much percentage more than the cost price? [SSC CHSL 2023]

(A) 50% (B) 40% (C) 45% (D) 37.5%

22. The difference between successive discounts of 40% followed by 30% and 45% followed by 20% on the marked price of an article is ₹ 12. The marked price of the article is: [SSC CGL 2015]

(A) ₹ 400 (B) ₹ 200

(C) ₹ 800 (D) ₹ 600

23. A man purchased an article for ₹ 1,500 and sold it at 25% above the cost price. If he has to pay Rs. 75 as tax on it, his net profit percentage will be: [SSC CHSL 2015]

(A) 25% (B) 30% (C) 15% (D) 20%

24. A man sold his watch at a loss of 5%. Had he sold it for ₹ 56.25 more, he would have gained 10%. What is the cost price of the watch (in Rs)? [SSC CHSL 2014]

(A) ₹ 370 (B) ₹ 365 (C) ₹ 375 (D) ₹ 390

Level 3 Expert

1. If on a marked price, the difference of selling prices with a discount of 30% and two successive discounts of 20% and 10% is Rs. 72, then the marked price (in rupees) is: [SSC CGL 2011]
(A) 3,600 (B) 3,000 (C) 2,500 (D) 2,400

2. If P : Q = 10 : 11 and Q : R = 11 : 12, then P + Q : Q + R : R + P is: [SSC CHSL 2022]
(A) 21 : 23 : 22 (B) 22 : 21 : 23
(C) 11 : 12 : 10 (D) 23 : 22 : 21

3. A trader bought two horses for ₹ 19,500. He sold one at a loss of 20% and other at a profit of 15%. If the selling prices of each horse is the same, then their C.P. are respectively. [SSC CGL 2011]
(A) ₹ 10,000 and ₹ 9,500 (B) ₹ 11,500 and ₹ 8,000
(C) ₹ 12,000 and ₹ 7,500 (D) ₹ 10,500 and ₹ 9,000

4. Under a sale offer, Tanvir was offered a 32% discount on the part of the marked price that was paid in cash, but had to add 1.2% on the part of the marked price paid through a credit card. If Tanvir paid 75% of the marked price in cash and the rest through a credit card, what percentage of the marked price was his total final payment? [SSC CHSL 2022]
(A) 76.6% (B) 75.9% (C) 76.1% (D) 76.3%

5. If the price of sugar is raised by 25%. Find how much per cent a householder must reduce his consumption of sugar so as not to increase his expenditure? [SSC CGL 2011]
(A) 10% (B) 20% (C) 18% (D) 25%

6. Vijay sells bananas at the rate of Rs. 14 per dozen and earns a profit of 40 percent. The cost price of the bananas increases by 30 percent. If the selling price remains the same, then what is his new profit percent? [SSC CHSL 2023]
(A) 7.69% (B) 9.09% (C) 7.14% (D) 8.83%

7. The price of a commodity rises from ₹ 6 per kg to ₹ 7.50 per kg. If the expenditure cannot increase, the percentage of reduction in consumption is: [SSC CGL 2011]
(A) 15% (B) 20% (C) 25% (D) 30%

8. The difference between a discount of 40% on ₹ 500 and two successive discounts of 36%, 4% on the same amount is: [SSC CHSL 2011]
(A) ₹ 0 (B) ₹ 2
(C) ₹ 1.93 (D) ₹ 7.20

9. A man purchased some eggs at 3 for ₹ 5 and sold them at 5 for ₹ 12. Thus, he gained ₹ 143 in all. The number of eggs he bought is: [SSC CGL 2012]
(A) 210 (B) 200 (C) 195 (D) 190

10. Rahul bought two cycles for a total sum of ₹ 1,500. He sold one cycle at 20% loss and the other cycle at 20% gain. If the selling price of both the cycles is the same, find the cost price of two cycles (in ₹). [SSC Sub. Inspector 2012]
(A) ₹ 500, 1000 (B) ₹ 600, 900
(C) ₹ 750, 750 (D) ₹ 550, 950

11. A man sold two articles at ₹ 375 each. On one, he gains 25% and on the other, he loses 25%. The gain or loss % in the whole transaction is: [SSC CHSL 2012]
(A) 6% (B) $4\frac{1}{6}\%$ (C) 50% (D) $6\frac{1}{4}\%$

12. A shopkeeper blends to varieties of tea costing ₹ 18 and ₹ 13 per 100 gram in the ratio 7:3. He sells the blended variety at the rate of ₹ 18.15 per 100 gm. His percentage gain in the transaction is: [SSC CHSL 2013]
(A) 8% (B) 10% (C) 12% (D) 14%

13. If books bought at prices ranging from ₹ 150 to ₹ 300 are sold at prices ranging from ₹ 250 to ₹ 350, then what is the greatest possible profit that might be made in selling 15 books? [SSC CHSL 2013]
(A) Cannot be determined (B) ₹ 3,000
(C) ₹ 750 (D) ₹ 4,250

14. The marked price of a mixie is ₹ 1600. The shopkeeper gives successive discount of 10% and x% of the customers. If the customer pays ₹ 1,224 for the mixie, then find the value of x. [SSC CGL 2013]
(A) 8% (B) 10% (C) 12% (D) 15%

15. A reduction in the price of apples enables a person to purchase 3 apples for ₹ 1 instead of ₹ 1.25. What is the % reduction in price (approx.)? [SSC CGL Tier-II 2013]
(A) 20 (B) 25 (C) 30 (D) 33

ANSWER KEY

Level-1: Beginner

1.	(B)	2.	(D)	3.	(D)	4.	(D)	5.	(B)	6.	(B)	7.	(A)	8.	(D)	9.	(A)	10.	(D)
11.	(C)	12.	(D)	13.	(D)	14.	(B)	15.	(B)	16.	(C)	17.	(B)	18.	(B)	19.	(A)	20.	(A)
21.	(C)	22.	(C)	23.	(D)	24.	(B)	25.	(D)										

Level-2: Intermediate

1.	(C)	2.	(D)	3.	(B)	4.	(C)	5.	(D)	6.	(C)	7.	(B)	8.	(A)	9.	(D)	10.	(C)
11.	(A)	12.	(A)	13.	(B)	14.	(A)	15.	(C)	16.	(B)	17.	(A)	18.	(C)	19.	(C)	20.	(D)
21.	(A)	22.	(D)	23.	(D)	24.	(C)												

Level-3: Expert

1.	(A)	2.	(A)	3.	(B)	4.	(D)	5.	(B)	6.	(A)	7.	(B)	8.	(D)	9.	(C)	10.	(B)
11.	(D)	12.	(B)	13.	(B)	14.	(D)	15.	(A)										

Solutions with Detailed Explanations

Level-1: BEGINNER

1. **Option (B) is correct.**

Explanation: Cost Price/Selling Price = 10/11

Let Cost Price = ₹ $10x$

and Selling Price = ₹ $11x$

$$\therefore \quad \text{Profit\%} = \left(\frac{\text{SP}-\text{CP}}{\text{CP}}\right)\times 100$$

$$= \frac{(11x-10x)}{10x}\times 100 = 10\%$$

2. **Option (D) is correct.**

Explanation:

Assuming SP = ₹ 100

Then profit will be ₹ 25

So, CP = 100 – 25 = ₹ 75

Using; CP = SP – Profit

$$\text{Hence, profit \% on CP} = \frac{\text{Profit}}{\text{CP}}\times 100$$

$$= \frac{25}{75}\times 100 = 33\frac{1}{3}\%$$

3. **Option (D) is correct.**

Explanation: According to question,

$$15\text{ CP} = 20\text{ SP}$$

$$\frac{\text{CP}}{\text{SP}} = \frac{20}{15} = \frac{4}{3}$$

Let CP = ₹ $4x$

and SP = ₹ $3x$

$$\therefore \text{ Loss percentage} = \frac{(4x-3x)}{4x}\times 100$$

$$= \frac{1}{4}\times 100 = 25\%$$

4. **Option (D) is correct.**

Explanation: Let the cost price of article = ₹ 100

So, marked price = ₹ 125

$$\text{Now selling price} = 125\times\frac{100-12}{100} = \text{Rs. } 110$$

$$\text{So, profit percentage} = \frac{110-100}{100}\times 100 = 10\%$$

5. **Option (B) is correct.**

Explanation: Successive discount [10%, 20%, 30%]

$$= 100 - \left[100\times\frac{90}{100}\times\frac{80}{100}\times\frac{70}{100}\right] = 49.6\%$$

6. **Option (B) is correct.**

Explanation: Using; successive discount = $a+b-\frac{ab}{100}$

[Here, a and b are two discounts]

$$= 20+15-\frac{20\times 15}{100} = 32\%$$

7. **Option (A) is correct.**

Explanation: According to question,

$$10.\text{SP} = 11.\text{CP}$$

$$\frac{\text{SP}}{\text{CP}} = \frac{11}{10}$$

$$\text{Hence,} \quad \text{Profit\%} = \frac{(11-10)}{10}\times 100 = 10\%$$

8. **Option (D) is correct.**

Explanation:

Assuming, SP = ₹ 100

40% of SP = ₹ 40

So, CP = ₹ 40

$$\text{Hence, required\%} = \frac{100}{40}\times 100 = 250\%$$

9. **Option (A) is correct.**

Explanation: Given,

Marked price of a dozen pairs of shoes = ₹ 7200

So, marked price of one pairs of shoes

$$= \frac{7200}{12} = ₹600$$

So, selling price of one pairs of shoes

$$= 600\times\frac{80}{100} = ₹480$$

Required number of pairs of shoes

$$= \frac{1440}{480} = 3$$

10. Option (D) is correct.

Explanation: The cost price of 300 bananas

$$= \frac{18}{12} \times 300 = ₹450$$

And selling price of 300 bananas

$$= \frac{24}{12} \times 200 + \frac{21}{12} \times 100 = 400 + 175 = 575$$

So, the net profit percentage

$$= \frac{575 - 450}{450} \times 100 = 27\frac{7}{9}\%$$

11. Option (C) is correct.

Explanation: According to question,

$$105\% = 21{,}000$$

$$100\% = 21{,}000 \times \frac{100}{105} = 20{,}000$$

[CP = 100% = 20,000]

Hence, SP with 15% profit = $20{,}000 \times \frac{115}{100} = ₹\,23{,}000$

12. Option (D) is correct.

Explanation: Assuming price of book = ₹ 100

25% of 100 = 25 [Commission amount]

Actual rate = 100 – 25 = ₹ 75

Profit = 100 – 75 = ₹ 25

Hence, profit% = $\frac{25}{75} \times 100 = 33.33\%$

13. Option (D) is correct.

Explanation: According to question,

Assuming, CP to A = ₹ x

$$x \times \frac{110}{100} \times \frac{105}{100} = 462$$

$\Rightarrow$ $x = 400$

Hence, cost to A = ₹ 400

14. Option (B) is correct.

Explanation: Given: A seller gives 4 toys free of cost on buying 14 toys.

So, profit percentage = $\frac{4}{18} \times 100 = 22\frac{2}{9}\%$

15. Option (B) is correct.

Explanation:

Assuming CP = 100%

According to question,

130% = 90% + 80

40% = 80

1% = 2

Hence, 100% = 200

So, the CP is Rs. 200

16. Option (C) is correct.

Explanation:

Assuming CP = ₹ x

According to question,

$$110\% \text{ of } x = 27{,}500 \times \left(\frac{100-10}{100}\right)$$

Hence, $x = 27{,}500 \times \frac{9}{10} \times \frac{10}{11} = 22{,}500$

17. Option (B) is correct.

Explanation:

Assuming CP = 100%

According to question,

80% = 110% – 12

30% = 12

Hence, 100% = $\frac{12}{30} \times 100 = 40$

So, the CP of article = Rs. 40

18. Option (B) is correct.

Explanation:

Actual price = 300 [Selling price]

Profit = 20%

120% of CP = 300

CP = (300/120)100 = ₹ 250

According to question,

New selling price = Rs. 235

So, loss percentage = [(250 - 235)/250]100 = 6%

Hence, loss% = 6%

19. Option (A) is correct.

Explanation: Assuming discount = d%

According to question,

$$\frac{d}{100} \times 12{,}000 = 12{,}000 - 10{,}500$$

$$\frac{d}{100} \times 12{,}000 = 1{,}500$$

Hence, $d = 12.5\%$

20. Option (A) is correct.

Explanation:

SP = ₹ 525

Assuming marked price = x

SP after 25% discount = $x - 0.25\,x = 0.75\,x$

According to question,

$525 = 0.75\,x$

Hence, x = ₹ 700

21. Option (C) is correct.

Explanation:

Let CP = ₹ 100

Then, MP = ₹ 120

Discount = 15% of MP

$$= \frac{15 \times 120}{100} = ₹\,18$$

Selling Price = MP – Discount

= 120 – 18 = ₹ 102

Hence, gain% = $\frac{(102 - 100)}{100} \times 100\% = 2\%$

22. Option (C) is correct.

Explanation: SP = ₹ 10/50 grams

$$\text{SP of 1 gm} = ₹\ \frac{10}{50}$$

$$\text{SP of 1000 gm} = \frac{10}{50}\times 1000 = \text{Rs.}200$$

$$\text{So,}\quad \text{loss\%} = \frac{(250-200)}{250}\times 100 = 20\%$$

23. Option (D) is correct.

Explanation: According to question,

$$\frac{450}{100-20} = \frac{SP_2}{100+20}$$

$$SP_2 = 450\times\frac{120}{80} = \text{Rs. } 675$$

24. Option (B) is correct.

Explanation: Cost price of 1 dozen oranges = Rs. 10

Selling price of 1 dozen oranges = Rs. 12

$$\text{So, gain percentage} = \frac{(12-10)}{10}\times 100 = 20\%$$

25. Option (D) is correct.

Explanation: Using, successive discount formula

$$\text{Discount} = a+b-\frac{ab}{100} = 10+20-\frac{(10\times 20)}{100} = 28\%$$

Level-2: INTERMEDIATE

1. Option (C) is correct.

Explanation:

Marked price = ₹ 50 (Given)

$$\text{So,}\quad SP = \frac{50\times 80}{100} = ₹\ 40$$

$$\text{Hence,}\quad CP = \frac{40\times 100}{125} = ₹\ 32$$

2. Option (D) is correct.

Explanation:

Let the cost price of wheat = ₹ x per kg

Then selling price of wheat = ₹ $1.25x$ per kg

According to the question,

$\Rightarrow 1.25x - 40 = .75x$

$\Rightarrow .50x = 40$

$\Rightarrow x = 80$

So, the cost price of wheat = ₹ 80 per kg

And selling price of wheat = 1.25 × 80

= ₹ 100 per kg

3. Option (B) is correct.

Explanation: According to the question,

$$CP = \frac{100}{114}\times 2{,}850 = ₹\ 2{,}500$$

$$\text{So, SP [Profit of 8\%]} = \frac{108}{100}\times 2{,}500 = ₹\ 2{,}700$$

4. Option (C) is correct.

Explanation:

Discount 1 = 5%

Discount 2 = 6%

Assuming marked price = ₹ P

$$d_2 - d_1 = (6\% - 5\%) = 1\%$$

$$1\% \text{ of P} = 15$$

Hence, 100% of P = ₹ 1,500

5. Option (D) is correct.

Explanation: Let Krishna bought two articles, one for ₹ 10 and other for ₹ 14.

CP of both = 10 + 14 = ₹ 24

SP of both = 13 × 2 = ₹ 26

$$\text{Hence,}\quad \text{profit\%} = \frac{(26-24)}{24}\times 100 = 8\frac{1}{3}\%$$

6. Option (C) is correct.

Explanation:

SP of 1[st] = ₹ 4,000

Gain% = 25%

$$\text{CP of 1}^{st} = \frac{100}{125}\times 4{,}000 = ₹\ 3{,}200$$

So, 2nd article's CP = 8,000 – 3,200 = ₹ 4800

2nd article's SP = ₹ 4,000

Hence, loss percentage for 2nd article

$$= \frac{800}{4800}\times 100 = 16\frac{2}{3}\%$$

7. Option (B) is correct.

Explanation: Given:

Selling price of machine = ₹ 122700

And discount percentage = 15%

Let the marked price of machine = ₹ x

According to the question,

$$\Rightarrow x\times\frac{100-15}{100} = 122700$$

$$\Rightarrow x = 122700\times\frac{100}{85}$$

$$\Rightarrow x = 144352.94$$

So, the marked price of machine = ₹ 144352.94

8. Option (A) is correct.

Explanation: Assuming CP = ₹ 100

Let marked or written price = ₹ x

According to question,

$$x\times\frac{90}{100} = 117$$

$$\text{Hence,}\quad x = \frac{117\times 100}{90} = 130$$

i.e., 30% above CP.

9. Option (D) is correct.

Explanation: Assuming original price = ₹ P

According to question,

$$P\times\frac{80}{100}\times\frac{130}{100} = 416$$

$$\text{Hence,}\quad P = \frac{416\times 100\times 100}{80\times 130} = ₹400$$

10. Option (C) is correct.

Explanation:

Assuming CP = ₹ 100

Profit = 10%

New CP = ₹ 96 [4% less]

If, gain = $18\frac{3}{4}\%$

SP = $118\frac{3}{4}\%$ of ₹ 96 = ₹ 114

According to question,

Difference (in SP) = 114 – 110 = ₹ 4

CP = ₹ 100

So, if difference in SP = ₹ 6

then, CP = $\frac{100}{4} \times 6$ = ₹ 150

11. Option (A) is correct.

Explanation: Given that, the selling price of each watch = ₹ 99

For 10% loss, CP = (99/90)100 = ₹ 110

For 10% profit, CP = (99/110)100 = ₹ 90

Total CP = (110 + 90) = ₹ 200

SP = 99 + 99 = ₹ 198

So, Loss% = $\frac{(200-198)}{200} \times 100 = 1\%$

12. Option (A) is correct.

Explanation: Let the marked price of article = ₹ 100

According to the question,

$$C.P. \times \frac{112.5}{100} = 100 \times \frac{90}{100}$$

⇒ C.P. = ₹ 80

So, profit percentage when the article sold at marked price

$$= \frac{100-80}{80} \times 100 = 25\%$$

13. Option (B) is correct.

Explanation: CP = 1,800 – 200 = ₹ 1,600

Marked price = $\frac{1,800}{100-10} \times 100$ = ₹ 2,000

Hence, if no discount given

Profit = 2,000 – 1,600 = ₹ 400

14. Option (A) is correct.

Explanation:

Profit = 1000 – 900 = 100

Profit% = $\frac{100}{900} \times 100 = 11\frac{1}{9}\%$

15. Option (C) is correct.

Explanation: Assuming marked price = ₹ x

⇒ SP = $\frac{90x}{100}$ = ₹ $\frac{9x}{10}$

⇒ CP = $\frac{80 \times 9x}{100 \times 10}$ = ₹ $\frac{36}{50}x$

So, gain = $\frac{45x - 36x}{50}$ = ₹ $\frac{9x}{50}$

Hence, Gain% = $\frac{9x/50}{36x/50} \times 100 = 25\%$

16. Option (B) is correct.

Explanation: According to question,[x = MRP of T.V.]

$$\frac{x \times 80}{100} - \frac{x \times 70}{100} = 800$$

$$\frac{10x}{100} = 800$$

Hence, $x = \frac{800 \times 100}{10}$ = ₹ 8,000

17. Option (A) is correct.

Explanation:

Assuming CP = ₹ x

⇒ Marked price = ₹ 1.2 x

According to question,

$1.2x = 12x - 2,160$

$10.8x = 2,160$

$x = 2,160 / 10.8 = 200$

Hence, CP of blackboard = ₹ 200

18. Option (C) is correct.

Explanation: SP (after 20% discount)

= $150 \times \frac{80}{100}$ = ₹ 120

So, $x \times \frac{120}{100} = 108$

⇒ x = ₹ 90

Hence, required discount = (100 – 90)% = 10%

19. Option (C) is correct.

Explanation:

Assuming CP = ₹ 100

⇒ SP = ₹ 120

Assuming marked price = ₹ x

⇒ 80% of x = 120

⇒ $x = \frac{120}{0.8} = 150$

Hence, required% = $\frac{150-100}{100} \times 100 = 50\%$

20. Option (D) is correct.

Explanation:

Loss% = $\frac{(CP - SP)}{CP} \times 100$

SP = $\frac{3CP}{4}$

CP of 1 mango = $\frac{1}{15}$

So, SP of 1 mango = $\frac{1}{20}$

Hence, he sold 20 mangoes for a rupee.

21. Option (A) is correct.

Explanation:

Let the marked price of article = ₹ 100

So, selling price = ₹ 80

According to the question:

Cost price of article $= 80 \times \frac{100}{120} = ₹\ \frac{200}{3}$

Required percentage

$$= \frac{100 - \frac{200}{3}}{\frac{200}{3}} \times 100 = \frac{\frac{100}{3}}{\frac{200}{3}} \times 100 = 50\%$$

22. Option (D) is correct.

Explanation: For 40% and 30%

$$\text{Single discount} = \left[40 + 30 - \frac{40 \times 30}{100}\right] = 58\%$$

For 45% and 20%

$$\text{Single discount} = \left(45 + 20 - \frac{45 \times 20}{100}\right) = 56\%$$

Assuming marked price = ₹ P

According to question,

$$P \times (58 - 56)\% = 12$$

$$\Rightarrow \frac{P \times 2}{100} = 12$$

Hence, $P = \frac{1,200}{2} = ₹\ 600$

23. Option (D) is correct.

Explanation: CP = ₹ 1,500

25% of 1500 = 375

So, SP = 1,500 + 375 = ₹ 1,875

Profit = 1,875 – 1,500 – 75 [75 = tax]

= 300

Hence, required profit% $= 300 \times \frac{100}{1500} = 20\%$

24. Option (C) is correct.

Explanation:

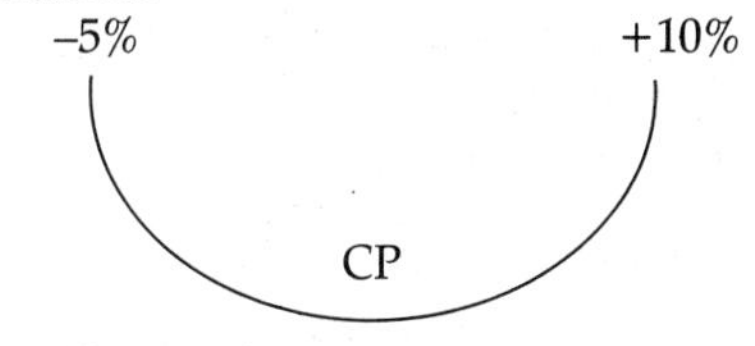

10% – (–5%) = 56.25

15% → 56.25

1% → 3.75

Hence, 100% = 375

So, cost price of watch = ₹ 375

Level-3: EXPERT

1. Option (A) is correct.

Explanation:

$$\text{Successive discount} = 20 + 10 - \frac{(20 \times 10)}{100} = 28\%$$

Difference in discount = (30 – 28)% = 2%

Given

(30% – 28%) = 72

So, 2% = 72

⇒ 1% = 36

Hence, 100% = ₹ 3,600

2. Option (A) is correct.

Explanation: Given, P : Q = 10 : 11

And Q : R = 11 : 12

So, P : Q : R = 10 : 11 : 12

So, P+Q : Q+R : R+P = (10+11) : (11+12) : (12+10)

⇒ P+Q : Q+R : R+P = 21 : 23 : 22

3. Option (B) is correct.

Explanation:

Assuming CP of first = ₹ P

CP of second = ₹ (19,500 – P)

According to the question,

$$\frac{80}{100}P = (19,500 - P) \times \frac{115}{100}$$

$$\Rightarrow P = \frac{4,48,500}{39} = ₹\ 11,500$$

⇒ CP of second horse = 19,500 – 11,500 = ₹ 8,000

4. Option (D) is correct.

Explanation: Let the marked price = ₹ 100

According to the question,

Amount paid by Tanvir

$$= 75 \times \frac{100 - 32}{100} + 25 + 25 \times \frac{1.2}{100} = ₹\ 76.3$$

So, required percentage = 76.3%

5. Option (B) is correct.

Explanation:

25%↑ ⇒ 125

x%↓ ⇒ 100

Hence, $x = \frac{25}{125} \times 100 = 20\%$

6. Option (A) is correct.

Explanation:

Selling price of banana $= ₹\ \frac{14}{12}$

So, cost price $= \frac{14 \times 100}{12 \times 140} = ₹\ \frac{5}{6}$

New cost price of banana $= \frac{5}{6} \times \frac{130}{100} = ₹\ \frac{13}{12}$

So, profit percentage

$$= \frac{\frac{14}{12} - \frac{13}{12}}{\frac{13}{12}} \times 100 = \frac{\frac{1}{12}}{\frac{13}{12}} \times 100 = \frac{100}{13} = 7.69\%$$

7. Option (B) is correct.

Explanation: Assuming consumption = 100 kg

New consumption = x kg

According to the question,

$$100 \times 6 = x \times 7.5$$

$$x = 80 \text{ kg}$$

Hence, reduction is consumption

$$= (100 - 80) \times \frac{100}{100} = 20\%$$

8. Option (D) is correct.

Explanation:

$$\text{Marked price} = ₹\,500$$
$$\text{Discount} = 40\%$$
$$\text{SP} = 500 - 40\% \text{ of } 500$$
$$= ₹\,300 \quad ...(1)$$

36% and 4% successive discount

$$\text{SP after 36\% discount} = 500 - \frac{36}{100} \times 500 = ₹\,320$$

$$\text{SP after 4\% discount} = 320 - \frac{4}{100} \times 320$$
$$= ₹\,307.20 \quad ...(2)$$

From (2) and (1), we get

$$307.20 - 300 = ₹\,7.20$$

9. Option (C) is correct.

Explanation: Cost price of each egg = ₹ $\frac{5}{3}$

Selling price of each egg = ₹ $\frac{12}{5}$

So, profit on each egg = $\frac{12}{5} - \frac{5}{3} = ₹\frac{11}{15}$

Given that total profit = ₹ 143

Let number of eggs he bought = x

$$\text{So,} \quad \frac{11}{15} \times x = 143$$
$$x = 195$$

Hence, he bought 195 eggs.

10. Option (B) is correct.

Explanation: Assuming CP of 1st cycle = ₹ C

CP of other = ₹ (1,500 – C)

According to the question,

$$C + \frac{20}{100}C = (1{,}500 - C) - \frac{20}{100}(1{,}500 - C)$$
$$2C = 1{,}200$$

Hence, C = ₹ 600

and CP of other cycle = 1,500 – 600 = ₹ 900

11. Option (D) is correct.

Explanation:

$$\text{1st article} \quad CP = \frac{100 \times 375}{125} = ₹\,300$$

$$\text{IInd article} \quad CP = \frac{100 \times 375}{75} = ₹\,500$$

$$\text{Total CP} = 500 + 300 = ₹\,800$$
$$\text{Total SP} = 375 + 375 = ₹\,750$$

$$\text{Hence,} \quad \text{loss\%} = \frac{800 - 750}{800} \times 100$$
$$= 6.25\% \text{ i.e., } 6\frac{1}{4}\%$$

12. Option (B) is correct.

Explanation: $CP = 18 \times \frac{7}{10} + 13 \times \frac{3}{10}$

$$= \frac{165}{10} = ₹\,16.5$$

$$SP = ₹\,18.15 \quad \text{[Given]}$$

$$\text{Hence,} \quad \text{Gain\%} = \frac{1.65}{16.5} \times 100 = 10\%$$

13. Option (B) is correct.

Explanation: For maximum profit

CP must be minimum i.e., 150

SP must be maximum = 350

$$\text{Profit} = SP - CP$$
$$= 350 - 150 = ₹\,200\text{/book}$$

Hence, profit on 15 books = 200 × 15 = ₹ 3,000

14. Option (D) is correct.

Explanation: MP = ₹ 1,600

After 1st discount (10%) = $1{,}600 \times \frac{90}{100} = ₹\,1{,}440$

$$\text{Final SP} = ₹\,1{,}224 \quad \text{[Given]}$$

$$\text{So,} \quad \frac{x}{100} \times 1{,}440 = 1{,}440 - 1{,}224$$

$$\text{Hence,} \quad x = 15\%$$

15. Option (A) is correct.

Explanation: Required % reduction

$$= \frac{0.25}{1.25} \times 100 = 20\%$$

■■■

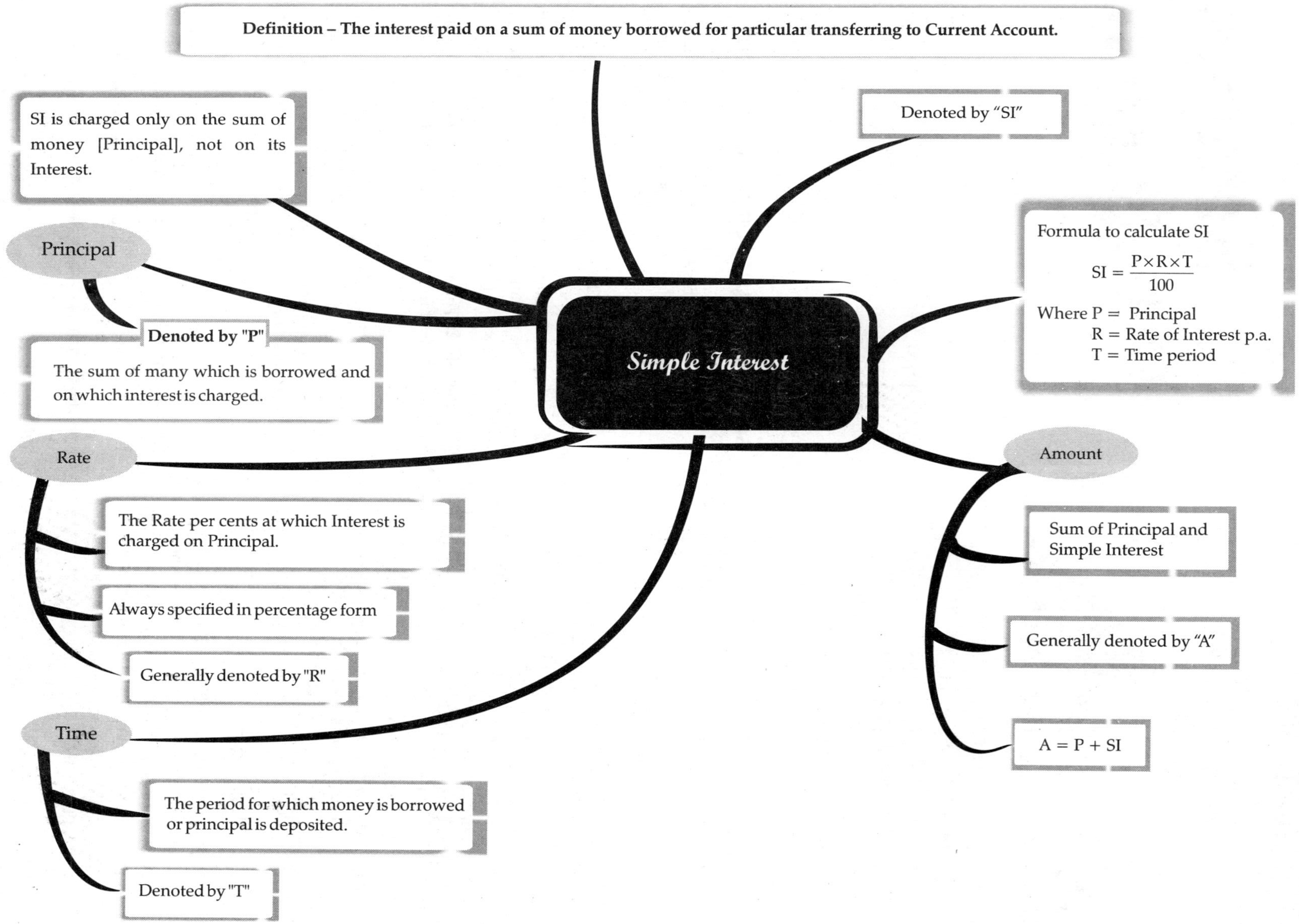
Definition – The interest paid on a sum of money borrowed for particular transferring to Current Account.
Simple Interest
SI is charged only on the sum of money [Principal], not on its Interest.
Principal
Denoted by "P"
The sum of many which is borrowed and on which interest is charged.
Rate
The Rate per cents at which Interest is charged on Principal.
Always specified in percentage form
Generally denoted by "R"
Time
The period for which money is borrowed or principal is deposited.
Denoted by "T"
Denoted by "SI"
Formula to calculate SI
$SI = \frac{P \times R \times T}{100}$
Where P = Principal
R = Rate of Interest p.a.
T = Time period
Amount
Sum of Principal and Simple Interest
Generally denoted by "A"
A = P + SI

CHAPTER 3

Simple Interest

LEARNING OBJECTIVES:

- Interest is applied while taking or giving certain amount of money.
- Method of calculating simple interest.
- Method to know principal amount, time and rate per cent.
- Different types of question asked in competitive exams.
- Real life application related to borrowing or lending money.

- **Interest:** When a person or organisation borrows some money from another person or organisation (bank, other financial institutes), then the borrower pays some extra amount of money at the time of repayment. That extra amount of money during repayment is called interest.
- **Principal (P):** Generally denoted by "P". It is the amount of money borrowed for a certain time.
- **Amount:** The sum of interest and principal is known as amount and denoted by "A".

$$A = I + P \quad \text{[where, I is the interest]}$$

- **Rate of Interest:** Denoted by "R". It is the rate at which interest is charged on principal and always specified in percentage form.
- **Time (T):** The period for which money is borrowed.
- **Simple Interest (SI):** Interest is calculated on the principal amount for any length of time. In simple interest, the interest is always calculated on the original principal.

$$SI = \frac{P \times R \times T}{100}$$

Example 1: What would be the simple interest obtained on an amount of ₹ 5,760 at the rate of 6% p.a. after 3 years?

Sol. Here, Time = 3 years

Rate of Interest = 6% p.a. (per annum)

Principal (P) = ₹ 5,760

Using: $SI = \frac{PRT}{100}$

$= \frac{5,760 \times 6 \times 3}{100} = 1,036.80$

Hence, SI = 1,036.80

SOME IMPORTANT FORMULAE AND TRICKS

- $A = P + SI$

[where, A is amount and P is principal]

We can calculate the amount directly by using [If SI is not given]

$$A = P\left[1 + \frac{R \times T}{100}\right]$$

- When an amount becomes n times of itself in y years at rate of interest $r\%$ per annum, then

$$r \times y = (n - 1) \times 100$$

Example 2: The rate at which a sum becomes four times of itself in 15 years, the SI will be:

Sol. Using SI = (P×R×T)/100

3P = (P×R×15)/100

R = 20% per annum

- If rate of interest (R) becomes $R_2\%$ from $R_1\%$ and ₹ y is earned more in T years, then

$$P = \frac{y \times 100}{(R_2 - R_1) \times T}$$

[where P = Principal]

Example 3: If annual rate of simple interest increases from 10% to $12\frac{1}{2}\%$, a man's yearly income increases by ₹ 1,250. His principal (in ₹) is:

Sol. Using $P = \frac{y \times 100}{(R_2 - R_1) \times T}$

y = ₹ 1,250

$R_2 - R_1 = 12\frac{1}{2}\% - 10\% = \frac{5}{2}\%$

$$T = 1 \text{ years}$$

$$P = \frac{1250 \times 100}{\left(\frac{5}{2}\right) \times 1}$$

Hence, $P = 50,000$

- If a certain amount of money amounts to ₹ y in t_1 year and ₹ z in t_2 year, then

$$P = \frac{yt_2 - zt_1}{t_2 - t_1}$$

$$R = \frac{(z-y) \times 100}{yt_2 - zt_1}$$

- If principal becomes n times of itself in y_1 years at the rate of $r\%$ p.a. and z times in y_2 years at the rate of $r_2\%$ per annum, then

$$\frac{n-1}{y_1} = \frac{z-1}{y_2} \text{ and } \frac{n-1}{r_1} = \frac{z-1}{r_2}$$

Example 4: A sum of money at simple interest i_1 becomes double in 5 years. At another rate of simple interest i_2, it becomes three times in 12 years. Then, the two rates of interest i_1 and i_2, respectively are :

Sol. In case 1 : Assuming

Sum = x

SI = x

$$\text{Rate} = \left(\frac{100 \times x}{x \times 5}\right) = \left(\frac{100 \times SI}{P \times T}\right)\% = 20\%$$

$$\left[\text{Using SI} = \frac{PRT}{100}\right]$$

In case 2:

Sum = y, SI = $2y$

Hence Rate = $\left(\frac{100 \times 2y}{y \times 12}\right)\% = 16\frac{2}{3}\%$

Example 5: The simple interest on a sum of money is $\frac{4}{9}$ of the principal. Find the rate per cent and time if both are numerically equal.

Sol. If Sum = y

Then, $SI = \frac{4y}{9}$

Using $SI = \frac{P \times R \times T}{100}$

$$\frac{4y}{9} = \frac{y \times R \times R}{100}$$

$$R^2 = \frac{400}{9}$$

Hence, $R = 6\frac{2}{3}\%$

and Time = R = $6\frac{2}{3}$ = 6 years 8 months

1 Level Beginner

1. In how much time will a sum of ₹ 5,000 invested at the rate of 15% simple interest per annum amount to ₹ 6,500? [SSC CGL 2021]
(A) 2.5 years (B) 1 year
(C) 1.5 years (D) 2 years

2. The difference between the simple interest on a fixed amount for 7 years and on the same amount for 12 years is ₹ 2,500. If rate of interest is 10% p.a., then the amount is : [SSC CGL 2021]
(A) ₹ 6,000 (B) ₹ 5,000
(C) ₹ 4,500 (D) ₹ 5,500

3. What is the simple interest on a sum of ₹ 99,000 at $12\frac{1}{2}\%$ per annum for a period of 9 months? [SSC CGL 2021]
(A) ₹ 9,282.25 (B) ₹ 8,281.25
(C) ₹ 7,281.25 (D) ₹ 9,281.25

4. If simple interest for 9 years is equal to 45% of the principal, then the rate of interest per annum is equal to: [SSC CGL 2021]
(A) 5% (B) 8% (C) 9% (D) 6%

5. ₹ 4,300 becomes ₹ 4,644 in 2 years at simple interest and the principal amount that will become ₹ 10,104 in 5 years at the same rate of interest is: [SSC CGL 2019]
(A) 8,420 (B) 9,260 (C) 5,710 (D) 7,200

6. At a certain annual rate (rounded off to the nearest integer) of simple interest, a sum of money becomes nine times its original value in 21 years. By how much does the rate of interest change if the same sum of money has to become 12 times its original value in 25 years? [SSC CHSL 2023]
(A) Decreases by 6% (B) Increases by 6%
(C) Increases by 8% (D) Decreases by 8%

7. A sum lent out at compound interest amounts to ₹ 1,250 in one year and ₹ 1,458 in 3 years at a certain rate percentage p.a. What is the simple interest on the same sum for $5\frac{2}{5}$ years at the same rate of interest? [SSC CGL 2019]
(A) ₹ 520 (B) ₹ 600 (C) ₹ 500 (D) ₹ 480

8. If in 13 years, a fixed sum doubles at simple interest. What will be the interest rate per year? [SSC CGL 2019]
(A) 7.69% (B) 7.92% (C) 8.69% (D) 7.9%

9. A sum of ₹ x amount to ₹ 9,246 in 4 years and to ₹ 11,298.75 in $7\frac{1}{2}$ years, at $y\%$ p.a. simple interest. The value of x and y are respectively. [SSC CHSL 2021]
(A) 6900 and 8.5 (B) 6800 and 8.5
(C) 6500 and 8 (D) 7200 and 7.5

10. Sunita invested ₹ 12,000 on simple interest at the rate of 10% p.a. to obtain a total amount of ₹ 20,400 after a certain period. For how many years did she invest to obtain the above amount? [SSC CPO 2020]

(A) 6 (B) 7 (C) 9 (D) 8

11. At what rate of interest will a sum of ₹ 4,500 amount of ₹ 6,525 at simple interest for 5 years? [CHSL 2020]

(A) 10% (B) 12% (C) 9% (D) 8%

12. The difference of simple interest on a sum of money for 8 years and 10 years is ₹ 200. If the rate of interest is 10% p.a., then what is the sum? [CHSL 2020]

(A) 1,000 (B) 1,400 (C) 1,600 (D) 1,200

13. Latha deposited an amount of ₹ 35,000 in a bank with simple interest 11% per annum. How much interest will she earn after one year? [CHSL 2019]

(A) ₹ 3,370 (B) ₹ 3,500
(C) ₹ 3,850 (D) ₹ 3,220

14. If the present amount is ₹ 87,750 with 8% rate of interest in 4 years, then what was the principal amount. [CHSL 2020]

(A) ₹ 78,456.34 (B) ₹ 66,477.2
(C) ₹ 56,896.98 (D) ₹ 69,345.6

15. A person borrows ₹ 7,000 for 3 years at 5% p.a. simple interest. He immediately lends it to another person at $6\frac{1}{3}\%$ p.a. for 3 years. Find his gain in the transaction per year. [CHSL 2020]

(A) ₹ 90 (B) ₹ 93.33
(C) ₹ 92 (D) ₹ 95.33

16. In a certain time, a sum of money becomes five times itself if the rate of interest is 16% p.a. Then, the certain time (in years) is : [CHSL 2019]

(A) 32 (B) 28 (C) 25 (D) 30

17. In how many years shall ₹ 3,500 invested at the rate of 10% simple interest per annum, amount to ₹ 4,500? [CHSL 2020]

(A) $2\frac{5}{7}$ years (B) $2\frac{3}{7}$ years
(C) $2\frac{6}{7}$ years (D) $2\frac{4}{7}$ years

18. In how many years will the simple interest on a sum of money be equal to the principal at the rate of $12\frac{2}{4}\%$ p.a.? [CHSL 2020]

(A) 7 years (B) 5 years
(C) 8 years (D) 6 years

19. A person deposits ₹ 8,000 in a bank which pays 8% p.a. simple interest. The amount after 8 years will be: [SSC CPO 2019]

(A) ₹ 12,600 (B) ₹ 13,140
(C) ₹ 13,120 (D) ₹ 12,545

20. Find the simple interest on ₹ 74,000 at $18\frac{2}{3}\%$ per annum for a period of 8 months. [CHSL 2019]

(A) ₹ 9,486.32 (B) ₹ 8,956.74
(C) ₹ 8,458.96 (D) ₹ 9,208.88

21. In how many years and month will a sum of ₹ 24 become ₹ 56 at 16% simple interest per annum? [CHSL 2020]

(A) 7 years 8 months (B) 8 years 4 months
(C) 6 years 11 months (D) 6 years 5 months

22. In how many years will a sum of ₹ 5,000 yield a simple interest of ₹ 2,000 at an interest rate of 10% p.a.? [CHSL 2020]

(A) 5 years (B) 3 years
(C) 4 years (D) 6 years

23. What amount a man would have received on a principal of Rs.7,500 after two years at simple interest at the rate of 7 per cent per annum? [SSC CHSL 2023]

(A) ₹ 8,400 (B) ₹ 8,550
(C) ₹ 7,600 (D) ₹ 7,400

Level 2 Intermediate

1. A sum lent at simple interest amount to ₹ 6,240.80 in 1 year and to ₹ 7,563.20 in 4 years. The sum (in ₹) and rate of interest per annum, respectively, are:[CGL 2021]

(A) 6,200, 8.5% (B) 5,800, 8.5%
(C) 5,800, 7.6% (D) 6,200, 7.6%

2. The rate of simple interest for first 2 years is 8% p.a., for next 4 years, it is 10% p.a. and for beyond 6 years, it is 12% p.a. If a person gets ₹ 18,358.60 as simple interest for 9 years, then how much money (in ₹) did he invest? [SSC CGL 2020]

(A) 21,075 (B) 20,087
(C) 19,674 (D) 19,955

3. A sum at simple interest becomes ₹ 14,880 after 3 years and ₹ 16,800 after 5 years. Find the simple interest on the same sum at 10% per annum for 4 years (in ₹). [SSC CGL 2020]

(A) 4,740 (B) 4,800 (C) 4,860 (D) 5,184

4. A certain sum amounts to ₹ 81,840 in 3 years and to ₹ 92,400 in 5 years at x% p.a. under simple interest. If the rate of interest becomes $(x+2)$%, then in how many years will the same sum become double itself? [SSC CGL 2020]

(A) $12\frac{1}{2}$ (B) 8 (C) 10 (D) 20

5. A sum of ₹ 25,600 is invested on simple interest partly at 7% per annum and remaining at 9% per annum. The total interest at the end of 3 years is ₹ 5,832. How much money (in ₹) was invested at 9% per annum? [CGL 2020]

(A) 18,000 (B) 7,700
(C) 9,600 (D) 16,000

6. A person lent ₹ 12,000 to B for 3 years and ₹ 10,000 to C for 4 years on simple interest at the same rate of interest and received ₹ 6,080 in all from both of them as interest. What is the annual rate of interest?[CGL 2023]

(A) 15 percent (B) 8 percent
(C) 11 percent (D) 5 percent

7. The rate of simple interest on a sum of money is 5% p.a. for the first 4 years, 8% p.a. for the next 3 years and 10% p.a. for the period beyond 7 years. If the simple interest accrued by the sum over a period of 10 years is ₹ 1,850, then the sum is: [CGL 2019]
(A) ₹ 1,500 (B) ₹ 2,750
(C) ₹ 1,650 (D) ₹ 2,500

8. Amit borrowed a sum of 25,000 rupees on simple interest. Bhola borrowed the same amount on compound interest. At the end of 2 years, Bhola had to pay 160 rupees more interest than Amit. The rate of interest charged per annum is: [CGL 2019]
(A) $\frac{16}{25}\%$ (B) 8% (C) $\frac{8}{25}\%$ (D) $3\frac{1}{8}\%$

9. When two equal amounts are deposited for 5 years and 3 years at the rate of 7% and 9% per annum, respectively and the difference of their interest is 475. Find the deposited amount.[CGL 2019]
(A) ₹ 5,937.5 (B) ₹ 5,837.5
(C) ₹ 6,037.5 (D) ₹ 5,992.5

10. If the annual rate of simple interest increases from 11% to $17\frac{1}{2}\%$, a person's yearly income increases by ₹ 1,071.20. The principal amount invested (in ₹) is: [CPO 2020]
(A) ₹ 19,120 (B) ₹ 17,250
(C) ₹ 10,710 (D) ₹ 16,480

11. A sum of ₹ 27,000 is divided into two parts A and B such that the simple interest at the rate of 15% p.a. on A and B after 2 years and 4 years, respectively, is equal. The total interest (in ₹) received together from A and B is: [CPO 2020]
(A) 9,600 (B) 5,400
(C) 18,000 (D) 10,800

12. A sum of ₹ 36,000 is divided into two parts, A and B such that the simple interest at the rate of 15% p.a. on A and B after 2 years and 4 years, respectively is equal. The total interest (in ₹) received from A is: [CPO 2020]
(A) 7,200 (B) 5,400 (C) 3,600 (D) 1,800

13. In how much time will the simple interest on a certain sum of money be $\frac{6}{5}$ times the sum at 20% per annum? [CHSL 2020]
(A) 6 years (B) 8 years
(C) 7 years (D) 5 years

14. Suresh lent out a sum of money to Rakesh for 5 years at simple interest. At the end of 5 years, Rakesh paid $\frac{9}{8}$ of the sum to Suresh to clear out the amount. Find the rate of simple interest per annum. [CHSL 2020]
(A) 3% p.a. (B) 2% p.a.
(C) 3.5% p.a. (D) 2.5% p.a.

15. The amount of ₹ 12,000 is taken at a certain rate of simple interest. After four months of borrowing in amount of ₹ 6,000 has been added to the principal. And the rate of interest was doubled against the previous rate to receive total 2,880 as interest at the end of the year. Calculate the interest rate initially paid. [CHSL 2019]
(A) 14% (B) 16% (C) 12% (D) 10%

16. A person lent Rs. 12,000 to B for 3 years and Rs. 10,000 to C for 4 years on simple interest at the same rate of interest and received Rs. 6,080 in all from both of them as interest. What is the annual rate of interest? [SSC CHSL 2023]
(A) 15% (B) 8% (C) 11% (D) 5%

17. A sum of money amounts to ₹ 7,500 in 5 years and to ₹ 8500 in 7 years at simple interest at the same rate of interest. The rate of interest per annum is: [CHSL 2020]
(A) 12% (B) 9% (C) 11% (D) 10%

18. A sum of ₹ 8,400 amounts to ₹ 11,046 at 8.75% p.a. simple interest in a certain time. What is the simple interest on the sum of ₹ 9,600 at the same rate for the same time? [CPO 2019]
(A) ₹ 2990 (B) ₹ 3012
(C) ₹ 2686 (D) ₹ 3024

19. A sum amounts to ₹ 14,395.20 at 9.25% p.a. simple interest in 5.4 years. What will be the simple interest on the same sum at 8.6% p.a. in 4.5 years?[CPO 2019]
(A) 3,715.20 (B) 3,627 (C) 3,797.76 (D) 3,672

20. A sum of ₹ 10,500 amounts to ₹ 13,825 in $3\frac{4}{5}$ years at a certain rate per cent per annum simple interest. What will be the simple interest on the same sum for 5 years at double the earlier rate? [CPO 2020]
(A) 8,470 (B) 8,750 (C) 8,670 (D) 8,560

21. A sum of ₹ 15,000 is invested partly at 12% per annum and the remaining at 10% per annum simple interest. If the total interest at the end of 2 years is ₹ 3,344, how much money was invested at 10% per annum? [CPO 2019]
(A) ₹ 6,600 (B) ₹ 6,400
(C) ₹ 6,200 (D) ₹ 6,500

22. A sum of ₹ 10,200 is invested partly at 8% p.a. and remaining at 6% p.a. for 3 years at simple interest. If the total interest is ₹ 2,124, how much money was invested at 6% p.a.? [CPO 2019]
(A) ₹ 4,800 (B) ₹ 4,900
(C) ₹ 5,200 (D) ₹ 5,400

23. A man invested an equal sum at the same rate of interest on simple interest for T and T + 4 years and the respective ratio of interest is 1 : 2, respectively. Find T? [IBPS CLERK 2020]
(A) 6 (B) 2 (C) 5 (D) 4

3 Expert Level

1. The 12% interest earned on a sum of money of ₹ 2,60,000 is to be used for awarding 24 scholarships of equal value every year in a school. What is the value (in ₹) of each scholarship? [CGL 2021]
(A) 1,300 (B) 1,150 (C) 1,200 (D) 1,250

2. If the simple interest on a certain sum of money borrowed for 4 years at 9.5% per annum exceeds the simple interest on the same sum for 3 years at 12.5% per annum by ₹ 225, then the sum borrowed is: [CGL 2021]
(A) ₹ 3,50,000 (B) ₹ 4,50,000
(C) ₹ 4,80,000 (D) ₹ 4,20,000

3. A sum of ₹ x amounts to ₹ 9,246 in 4 years and ₹ 11,298.75 in $7\frac{1}{2}$ years, at y% p.a. simple interest. The values of x and y are respectively, are: [CGL 2021]
(A) 6,900, 8.5 (B) 6,800, 8.5
(C) 6,500, 8 (D) 7,200, 7.5

4. A sum of ₹ x amounts to ₹ 8,563.50 in $3\frac{1}{2}$ years and to ₹ 10,527 in 7 years at y% p.a. simple interest. The values of x and y, respectively, are: [SSC CGL 2021]
(A) 6,600 and 8 (B) 6,800 and $8\frac{1}{2}$
(C) 6,600 and $8\frac{1}{2}$ (D) 7,000 and 8

5. A sum of ₹ 4,000 amounts to ₹ 5,008 in 3 years at simple interest at the ratio of x% per annum. If the interest rate becomes $(x + 2.6)$%, then the revised maturity amount will be: [SSC CGL 2021]
(A) ₹ 5,320 (B) ₹ 5,420
(C) ₹ 5,330 (D) ₹ 5,200

6. Two equal sums were lent on simple interest at 6% and 10% per annum, respectively. The first sum was recovered 2 years later than the second sum and the amount in each case was ₹ 1,105. What was the sum (in ₹) lent in each scheme? [SSC CGL 2020]
(A) 900 (B) 850 (C) 936 (D) 891

7. A sum of money was lent in two parts in the ratio 4:5 for 4 years and 5 years, respectively, both at the rate of 8% per annum simple interest. If the difference between the interests earned from the two parts is ₹ 4,680, then what was the total sum lent (in ₹)? [CGL 2020]
(A) 58,500 (B) 46,800
(C) 65,000 (D) 42,120

8. ₹ 4,000 is given at 5% per annum for 1 year and interest is compounded half yearly. ₹ 2,000 is given at 40% per annum compounded quarterly for 1 year. The total interest received is nearest to: [CHSL 2020]
(A) ₹ 1,440.40 (B) ₹ 1,888.80
(C) ₹ 1,130.70 (D) ₹ 1,333.30

9. A man takes a loan of some amount at some rate of simple interest. After 3 years, the amount is doubled and the rate of interest is decreased by 2%. After 5 years, if the total interest paid on the whole is ₹ 13,600 which is equal to the same when the first amount was taken for $11\frac{1}{3}$ years, then the loan taken initially was: [CHSL 2021]
(A) ₹ 13,600 (B) ₹ 12,500
(C) ₹ 10,000 (D) ₹ 12,000

10. A person invested a total of ₹ 9,000 in three parts at 3%, 4% and 6% per annum on simple interest. At the end of the year, he received equal interest in all the three cases. The amount invested at 6% is: [CHSL 2020]
(A) ₹ 2,000 (B) ₹ 3,000
(C) ₹ 4,000 (D) ₹ 5,000

11. Sundeep invested $\frac{1}{8}$ of a certain sum at 5% p.a. for 2 years and $\frac{3}{5}$ of the sum at 6% p.a. for 2 years and the remaining at 10% p.a. for 2 years. If the total interest received is ₹ 1,674, then the total sum invested is: [CPO 2019]
(A) ₹ 10,500 (B) ₹ 12,500
(C) ₹ 12,000 (D) ₹ 13,000

12. A certain sum (in ₹) is invested at simple interest at y% per annum for $3\frac{1}{2}$ years. If it had been invested at $(y + 4)$% per annum at simple interest, it would have fetched ₹ 4,452 more as interest. What is the sum? [CPO 2019]
(A) ₹ 30,400 (B) ₹ 31,800
(C) ₹ 42,800 (D) ₹ 42,400

13. A person invested a sum of ₹ 18,600 at x% p.a. and another sum that is twice the former at $(x + 2)$% p.a. both at simple interest. If the total interest earned on both investments for $3\frac{1}{2}$ years is ₹ 23,110.50, then the rate of interest p.a. on the second investment is: [CPO 2019]
(A) 11% (B) 10.5%
(C) 13% (D) 12.5%

14. A person invested one fourth of the sum of Rs 25,000 at a certain rate of simple interest and rest at 4% p.a. higher rate. If the total interest received for 2 years is 4,125, then what is the rate at which second sum was invested? [CPO 2019]
(A) 9.5% (B) 9.25% (C) 5.25% (D) 7.5%

15. The price of a TV set worth ₹ 20,000 is to be paid in 20 installments of ₹ 1,000 each. If the rate of interest be 6% per annum, and the first installment to be paid at the time of purchase, the value of the last installment covering the interest as well will be: [CPO 2020]
(A) ₹ 1,050 (B) ₹ 2,050
(C) ₹ 3,000 (D) None of these

16. The sum invested in Scheme B is thrice the sum invested in Scheme A. The investment in Scheme A is made for 4 years at 8% p.a. simple interest and in Scheme B for 2 years at 13% p.a. simple interest. The total interest earned from both the schemes is ₹ 1,320. Find the amount invested in Scheme A.**[IBPS PO 2015]**

(A) 1,200 **(B)** 1,140 **(C)** 960 **(D)** 1,500

ANSWER KEY

Level-1: Beginner

1.	(D)	2.	(B)	3.	(D)	4.	(A)	5.	(A)	6.	(B)	7.	(C)	8.	(A)	9.	(A)	10.	(B)
11.	(C)	12.	(A)	13.	(C)	14.	(B)	15.	(B)	16.	(C)	17.	(C)	18.	(C)	19.	(C)	20.	(D)
21.	(B)	22.	(C)	23.	(B)														

Level-2: Intermediate

1.	(C)	2.	(D)	3.	(B)	4.	(C)	5.	(B)	6.	(C)	7.	(D)	8.	(B)	9.	(A)	10.	(D)
11.	(D)	12.	(A)	13.	(A)	14.	(D)	15.	(D)	16.	(B)	17.	(D)	18.	(D)	19.	(A)	20.	(B)
21.	(B)	22.	(D)	23.	(D)														

Level-3: Expert

1.	(A)	2.	(B)	3.	(A)	4.	(C)	5.	(A)	6.	(B)	7.	(A)	8.	(C)	9.	(C)	10.	(A)
11.	(C)	12.	(B)	13.	(D)	14.	(B)	15.	(D)	16.	(A)								

Solutions with Detailed Explanations

Level-1: BEGINNER

1. Option (D) is correct.

Explanation:

Using:

$$\text{Simple Interest} = \frac{\text{Principal} \times \text{Rate} \times \text{Time}}{100}$$

$$\text{Time} = \frac{\text{Simple Interest} \times 100}{\text{Principal} \times \text{Rate}}$$

$$= \frac{1,500 \times 100}{5,000 \times 15}$$

Hence, Time = 2 years.

2. Option (B) is correct.

Explanation:

Given: SI for 12 years – SI for 7 years = 2,500

SI for 5 years = 2,500

SI for 1 year = ₹ 500

Rate of interest = 10% p.a.

Using, $SI = \frac{P \times R \times T}{100}$

$$500 = \frac{P \times 10 \times 1}{100}$$

P = 5,000

Hence, principal amount = ₹ 5,000

3. Option (D) is correct.

Explanation:

Using, $SI = \frac{P \times R \times T}{100}$

$$= \frac{99,000}{100} \times \frac{25}{2} \times \frac{9}{12} = 9,281.25$$

4. Option (A) is correct.

Explanation: SI for 9 years = 45% of principal

So, SI for 1 year = $\frac{45}{9} = 5\%$

Hence, rate of interest = 5%

5. Option (A) is correct.

Explanation: We know that

SI = Total amount – Principal

= 4,644 – 4,300 = ₹ 344

Using $SI = \frac{P \times R \times T}{100}$

$$344 = \frac{4,300\text{ ´ }R\text{ ´ }2}{100}$$

R = 4%

Now,

Total Amount = ₹ 10,104

R = 4%

Using

Total amount = P + SI

$$10,104 = P + \frac{P \times 4 \times 5}{100}$$

120P = 10,104 × 100

Hence, P = ₹ 8,420

6. **Option (B) is correct.**
Explanation:
Let principal amount = ₹P
and rate of simple interest = r%
According to question:
$$8P = \frac{P \times r \times 21}{100}$$
$$\Rightarrow \quad r = \frac{800}{21}\% = 38.1\% \cong 38\%$$
Let new rate of interest = r'
According to question
$$11P = \frac{P \times r' \times 25}{100}$$
$$\Rightarrow \quad r' = 44\%$$
Increase in rate of interest:
$$= (44 - 38)\%$$
$$= 6\%$$

7. **Option (C) is correct.**
Explanation: Interest for two years (on 1,250)
$$= 1{,}458 - 1{,}250 = ₹\ 208$$
$$\text{Principal} = 1{,}250$$
$$\text{Amount} = 1{,}250 + 208 = 1{,}458$$
$$\text{Principal : Amount} = 1{,}250 : 1{,}458$$
After simplification
$$P : A = 625 : 729 = 25 : 27$$
$$\text{Rate of interest} = \left[\frac{(27-25)}{25}\right] \times 100 = 8\%$$
$$\text{So,} \quad P \times \frac{27}{50} = 1{,}250$$
$$\text{Principal} = \frac{1{,}250 \times 50}{27}$$
$$\text{S.I.} = \frac{P \times R \times T}{100}$$
$$= \frac{1{,}250 \times 50}{27} \times \frac{8}{100} \times \frac{27}{5}$$
Hence, SI = ₹ 500

8. **Option (A) is correct.**
Explanation: Assuming Principal = ₹ 100
It becomes double in 13 years, i.e., 200
It is clear that ₹ 100 is the interest amount in 13 years.
$$\text{Using} \quad SI = \frac{P \times R \times T}{100}$$
$$100 = \frac{100 \times R \times 13}{100}$$
Hence, rate of interest = 7.69%

9. **Option (A) is correct.**
Explanation: Given:
A sum of ₹ x becomes ₹ 9246 in 4 years and ₹ 11298.75 in 7.5 years at y% per annum simple rate.
SI earned in these 3.5 years = 11298.75 – 9246 = ₹ 2052.75
$$\text{So, SI earned in 1 year} = \frac{2025.75}{3.5} = ₹\ 586.5$$
SI earned in 4 years = 586.5 × 4 = ₹ 2346
So, principal amount = 9246 – 2346 = ₹ 6900
$$\text{And rate of interest} = \frac{586.5}{6900} \times 100 = 8.5\%$$

10. **Option (B) is correct.**
Explanation:
$$\text{Using} \quad SI = \frac{P \times R \times T}{100}$$
$$SI = \text{Amount} - \text{Principal}$$
$$= 20{,}400 - 12{,}000 = 8{,}400$$
$$8400 = \frac{12{,}000 \times 10 \times T}{100}$$
Hence, T = 7 years

11. **Option (C) is correct.**
Explanation:
$$\text{Using,} \quad SI = \frac{P \times R \times T}{100}$$
$$\frac{4{,}500\ ´\ R\ ´\ 5}{100} = 2{,}025$$
[SI = Amount – Principal]
Hence, R = 9%

12. **Option (A) is correct.**
Explanation:
$$\text{Using,} \quad SI = \frac{P \times R \times T}{100}$$
Given,
SI for 10 years – SI for 8 years = 200
$$\frac{P \times 10 \times 10}{100} - \frac{P \times 10 \times 8}{100} = 200$$
Hence, P = 1,000

13. **Option (C) is correct.**
Explanation:
Using,
$$SI = \frac{P \times R \times T}{100}$$
$$= \frac{35{,}000 \times 11 \times 1}{100}$$
Hence SI = ₹ 3,850

14. **Option (B) is correct.**
Explanation: In four years, total rate of interest = 8% × 4 = 32%
According to question
132% of principal = 87,750
100% of principal = 66,477.2
Hence, P = 66,477.2

15. **Option (B) is correct.**
$$\textit{Explanation:} \quad \text{Gain\%} = 6\frac{1}{3}\% - 5\% = \frac{4}{3}\%$$
$$\text{per year gain} = \frac{4}{3}\% \text{ of } 7{,}000 = ₹\ 93.33$$

16. Option (C) is correct.

Explanation:

Using, $SI = \frac{P \times R \times T}{100}$

Given sum of money becomes five times itself

So, $SI = 4P$

$4P = \frac{P \times 16 \times T}{100}$

Hence, $T = 25$ years

17. Option (C) is correct.

Explanation:

Using, $SI = \frac{P \times R \times T}{100}$

$SI = 4{,}500 - 3{,}500 = 1{,}000$

$1{,}000 = \frac{3{,}500 \times t \times 10}{100}$

Hence, $T = 2\frac{6}{7}$ years.

18. Option (C) is correct.

Explanation: Using

$SI = \frac{P \times R \times T}{100}$

$P = \frac{P \times R \times T}{100}$

$T \times \frac{25}{2} = 100$

Hence, $T = 8$ years

19. Option (C) is correct.

Explanation: Using

$SI = \frac{P \times R \times T}{100}$

$SI = \frac{8{,}000\ ´\ 8\ ´\ 8}{100}$

$SI = 5{,}120$

Hence, Amount = SI + P

= 8,000 + 5,120 = ₹ 13,120

20. Option (D) is correct.

Explanation: Using

$SI = \frac{P \times R \times T}{100}$

$= \frac{74{,}000 \times 56 \times 8}{3 \times 12 \times 100} = 9{,}208.88$

21. Option (B) is correct.

Explanation: $SI = \frac{P \times R \times T}{100}$

$32 = \frac{16 \times 24 \times T}{100}$

[As SI = 56 – 24 = 32]

Hence $T = \frac{25}{3}$

i.e., 8 years 4 months

22. Option (C) is correct.

Explanation: Using

$SI = \frac{P \times R \times T}{100}$

$\frac{5{,}000 \times 10 \times T}{100} = 2{,}000$

Hence, $T = 4$ years

23. Option (B) is correct.

Explanation:

Given, P = ₹ 7500

R = 7% per annum

T = 2 years

We have, $SI = \frac{P \times R \times T}{100} = \frac{7500 \times 7 \times 2}{100} = 1050$

So, amount after 2 years = 7500 + 1050 = 8550

Level-2: INTERMEDIATE

1. Option (C) is correct.

Explanation:

SI for 3 years = 7,563.20 – 6,240.80 = 1,322.4

P = 6,240.80 – 440.80 = ₹ 5,800

SI for 1 year = 1322.4/3 = 440.8

P = 6,240.80 – 440.80 = ₹ 5,800

Using $SI = \frac{P \times R \times T}{100}$

$440.8 = \frac{P \times R \times 1}{100}$

$PR = 440.8 \times 100$

[R = (440.8/5,800) × 100 = 7.6%]

2. Option (D) is correct.

Explanation:

Total time = 9 years

Rate for first 2 years = 8% × 2 = 16%

Rate for the next 4 years = 10% × 4 = 40%

for the next 3 years

Rate = 12% × 3 = 36%

Total rate of interest = 92%

92% of Principal = 18,358.6

Hence, 100% of Principal = 19,955

3. Option (B) is correct.

Explanation:

P + SI after 3 years = 14,880

P + SI after 5 years = 16,800

SI for 2 years [between 5th and 3rd year] = 1,920

SI for 1 year = 960

SI for 3 years = 960 × 3 = 2,880

Amount (Principal) = Amount after 3 years – SI for 3 years = 12,000

Rate of interest = 40%

Hence, SI = 40% of 12,000 = ₹ 4,800

4. Option (C) is correct.

Explanation:

Principal $\xrightarrow[\text{3 years}]{}$ 81,840 $\xrightarrow[\text{2 years}]{}$ 92,400

SI for 2 years = 10,560

$$\text{for 3 years} = 5{,}280 \times 3 = 15{,}840$$

$$P = 81{,}840 - 15{,}840 = 66{,}000$$

$$\text{Rate \%} = \frac{5{,}280}{66{,}000} \times 100 = 8\%$$

Using
$$SI = \frac{P \times R \times T}{100}$$

$$66000 = \frac{66{,}000 \times (8+2) \times t}{100}$$

Hence $T = 10$ years.

5. **Option (B) is correct.**
Explanation: Using alligation method

9% ↘ ↙ 7%

$\frac{973}{128}\%$

↙ ↘

77 179

$$\left[5{,}832 = \frac{25{,}600\% r \times 3}{100}, r = \frac{973}{128}\right]$$

$$179 + 77 = 256 \rightarrow 25{,}600$$

Hence $77 = 7{,}700$

6. **Option (C) is correct.**
Explanation:
Given,
P_1 = ₹ 12000
T_1 = 3 years
P_2 = ₹ 10000
T_2 = 4 years

Let the rate of interest = R% per annum

We have, $SI = \frac{PTR}{100}$

According to the question,

$\Rightarrow (SI)_1 + (SI)_2 = 6080$

$\Rightarrow \frac{12000 \times 3 \times R}{100} + \frac{10000 \times 4 \times R}{100} = 6080$

$\Rightarrow 360R + 400R = 6080$

$\Rightarrow R = 8\%$

So, the rate of interest = 8% per annum

7. **Option (D) is correct.**
Explanation: According to question

$$\text{Total rate} = 4 \times 5\% + 3 \times 8\% + 3 \times 10\% = 74\%$$

74% of principal = 1,850 [Given]

Hence, principal = $\frac{1{,}850}{74\%}$ = ₹ 2,500

8. **Option (B) is correct.**
Explanation: As given, Amit borrowed on SI while Bhola at CI.

$$25{,}000 \xrightarrow{R\%} x$$

$$25{,}000 \xrightarrow{R\%} x \xrightarrow{R\%} z$$

$$25{,}000 \times \frac{R}{100} \times \frac{R}{100} = 160$$

Hence, $R = 8\%$

9. **Option (A) is correct.**
Explanation: Total interest for 1st amount
= 5 × 7% = 35%
Total interest for 2nd amount = 3 × 9% = 27%
Difference of interest = 8% = 475
8% of P = 475
Hence, P = 5,937.5

10. **Option (D) is correct.**
Explanation: Total increase in annual rate of SI

$$\Rightarrow 17\frac{1}{2}\% - 11\% = 6\frac{1}{2}\%$$

According to question

$$6\frac{1}{2}\% = 1{,}071.20$$

$$100\% = 16{,}480$$

Hence, Principal = 16,480

11. **Option (D) is correct.**
Explanation: Total interest on A after 2 years
= 15% × 2 = 30%
Total interest on B after 4 years = 15% × 4 = 60%
According to question

30% A = 60% of B
30A = 60B
A : B = 2 : 1

$$A = \frac{2}{3} \times 27000 = 18{,}000$$

B = 27,000 – 18,000 = 9,000
R = 15%
T for A = 2 years
(A) SI = (18,000× 15× 2)/100 = 5,400
[It is given that SI is equal for A and B]
SI for B = 5,400

Hence, total interest = ₹ 10,800

12. **Option (A) is correct.**
Explanation: According to question
Total interest of A = Total Interest of B

15% × 2 of A = 15% × 4 of B
30A = 60B
A : B = 2 : 1
R = 15%
for A – Time = 2 years

Hence, SI from A = $\frac{PRT}{100}$

$$\left[\text{Principal for A} = \frac{2}{3} \times 36{,}000 = 24{,}000\right]$$

= ₹ 7,200

13. **Option (A) is correct.**
Explanation: Using

$$SI = \frac{P \times R \times T}{100}$$

$$\frac{6}{5}P = \frac{20 \times P \times t}{100} \quad \left[SI = \frac{6}{5}P \rightarrow \text{Given}\right]$$

Hence, $t = 6$ years

14. Option (D) is correct.

Explanation:

Using $SI = \frac{P \times R \times T}{100}$

$$\frac{P \times R \times 5}{100} = \frac{1}{8}P\left[SI = \frac{1}{8}P\right]$$

Hence, $R = 2.5\%$

15. Option (D) is correct.

Explanation:

Using $SI = \frac{P \times R \times T}{100}$

According to question

$$\frac{18,000 \times 2R \times 8}{100 \times 12} + \frac{12,000 \times R \times 4}{100 \times 12} = 2,800$$

$$280R = 2,800$$

Hence, $R = 10\%$

16. Option (B) is correct.

Explanation: Given,

P_1 = ₹ 12000

T_1 = 3 years

P_2 = ₹ 10000

T_2 = 4 years

Let the rate of interest = R% per annum

We have, $SI = \frac{P \times R \times T}{100}$,

According to the question,

$$\Rightarrow \frac{P_1 \times R_1 \times T_1}{100} + \frac{P_2 \times R_2 \times T_2}{100} = 6080$$

$$\Rightarrow \frac{12000 \times R \times 3}{100} + \frac{10000 \times R \times 4}{100} = 6080$$

$\Rightarrow 360R + 400R = 6080$

$\Rightarrow \quad R = 8\%$

So, the rate of interest = 8% per annum

17. Option (D) is correct.

Explanation:

In two years, amount becomes 8,500 from 7,500

Interest in two years = 1,000

Interest in one year = 500 (S.I.)

Principal = 7,500 – 5 × 500 = 5,000

Hence, $R\% = \frac{500}{5,000} \times 100 = 10\%$

18. Option (D) is correct.

Explanation:

Using $SI = \frac{P \times R \times T}{100}$

$$11,046 - 8,400 = \frac{8,400 \times 8.75 \times T}{100}$$

$$2,646 = \frac{73,500 \times T}{100}$$

$$T = 3.6 \text{ years}$$

Now, again using

$$SI = \frac{P \times R \times T}{100}$$

$$SI = \frac{9,600 \times 8.75 \times 3.6}{100}$$

Hence, SI = 3,024

19. Option (A) is correct.

9.25% × 5.4 = Total interest

= 50% [approximate value]

Given: 150% of P = 14,395.20

P = 9,600 [approximate value]

Hence, $SI = \frac{9600 \times 8.6 \times 4.5}{100} = 3,715.20$

20. Option (B) is correct.

Explanation:

Interest in $3\frac{4}{5}$ years = 13,825 – 10,500 = 3,325

Interest in 5 years = $3,325 \times \frac{5}{10} \times 5 = 4,375$

After the rate is doubled, the interest

= 2 × 4,375 = 8,750

21. Option (B) is correct.

Explanation:

Average rate of interest = $\frac{3,34,400}{15000 \times 2} = \frac{3,344}{300}$

12% 10%

3,600 3,000

$\frac{3344}{300}$

344 256

Given 600 = 15,000

Hence, 256 = 6,400 [Money interest at 10%]

22. Option (D) is correct.

Explanation: Interest for 3 years = 2,124

for 1 year = 2,124/3 = 708

Using Alligation method

612 (6%) 816 (8%)

$\frac{708}{102}$

108 96

9 8

Sum interest at 8% = 10,200

8 = 10,200

1 = 600

Hence, the sum invested 6% = 9 i.e. 9 × 600 = ₹ 5,400

23. Option (D) is correct.

Explanation: Assuming money interest = ₹ y

Rate of interest = R%

According to question

$$\frac{1}{2} = \frac{y \times R \times T}{y \times R \times (T+4)} \quad \left[\text{using } SI = \frac{P \times R \times T}{100}\right]$$

Hence, T = 4 years

Level-3: EXPERT

1. **Option (A) is correct.**
Explanation:
Using $SI = \frac{PRT}{100} = \frac{2,60,000 \times 12}{100}$
If awarded for 24 students, then each scholarship
$= \frac{2,60,000 \times 12}{100 \times 24} = ₹\ 1,300$

2. **Option (B) is correct.**
Explanation: According to question,
$\frac{P \times 9.5 \times 4}{100} - \frac{P \times 12.5}{100} \times 3 = 225 \quad \left[\text{Using S.I.} = \frac{PRT}{100}\right]$
Hence, $P = 4,50,000$

3. **Option (A) is correct.**
Explanation: According to question:
Interest between $7\frac{1}{2}$ years and 4 years
$= 11,298.75 - 9,246$
Interest for $3\frac{1}{2}$ years $= 2,052.75$
Interest for 4 years = 2,346
Hence amount, i.e., "x" = 9,246 – 2,346 = 6900
Rate of interest $(y) = \frac{2,346}{6,900 \times 4} \times 100\% = 8.5\%$

4. **Option (C) is correct.**
Explanation: According to question:
Interest for 3.5 years = 8,963.50
Hence, sum = 8,563.50 – 1,963.50
$x = 6,600$
Rate $= 8\frac{1}{2}\% \quad \left[\text{Using SI} = \frac{P \times R \times T}{100}\right]$

5. **Option (A) is correct.**
Explanation:
Total increment in SI $= \frac{4,000 \times 2.6\% \times 3}{100} = 312$
Hence, new amount = 5,008 + 312 = 5,320

6. **Option (B) is correct.**
Explanation: According to question:
$(t + 2) \times 6\% = 10\% \times t$
$t = 3$
Using : Amount = P + SI
$P + \frac{P \times 6 \times 5}{100} = 1,105$
Hence, $P = 850$

7. **Option (A) is correct.**
Explanation:
SI on 1st part $= \frac{4x \times 8 \times 4}{100} \quad \left[\text{Using SI} = \frac{PRT}{100}\right]$
$= \frac{128}{100}x$
SI for 2nd part $= \frac{5x \times 8 \times 5}{100} = 2x$
Difference of interest $= \frac{72x}{100}$
According to question:
$\frac{72x}{100} = 4,680$
$x = ₹\ 6,500$
Hence, total sum $= 4x + 5x = 9x$
$= 9 \times 6,500 = 58,500$

8. **Option (C) is correct.**
Explanation: If interest is compounded half yearly
$R = \frac{R}{2}\% = \frac{5}{2}\%$
Now $\frac{5}{2}\%$ of $4,000 = 100$
for second half interest is 100 + 2.5 = 102.5
Total interest = 100 + 102.5 = 202.5
Now $r = \frac{R}{4}$ [Compounded quarterly]
Hence, interest on 2,000 at $\frac{R}{4}\%$ rate = 1,130.70

9. **Option (C) is correct.**
Explanation:
Using $SI = \frac{P \times R \times T}{100}$
$13,600 = \frac{P \times R \times 34}{300}$
$PR = 1,20,000$ ...(1)
$\frac{2P \times 5 \times (R-2)}{100} + \frac{3PR}{100} = 13,600$
$13PR - 20P = 13,60,000$
[Putting value of PR from (1)]
Hence, $P = 10,000$

10. **Option (A) is correct.**
Explanation: According to question:
$3A = 4B = 6C$
$A : B : C = 4 : 3 : 2$
If $9x = 9,000$
$x = 1,000$
Hence, $2x = 2 \times 1,000 = 2,000$

11. **Option (C) is correct.**
Explanation: According to question:
$1674 = \frac{11}{40} \times 20 + \frac{1}{8} \times 2 \times 5 + \frac{3}{5} \times 6 \times 2$
$100\% = 12,000$
Hence, total sum = ₹ 12,000

12. **Option (B) is correct.**
Explanation: 4% increase in rate, so
$4 \times \frac{7}{2} = 14\%$
Now, 14% of x = 44,52
Hence, $x = ₹\ 31,800$

13. Option (D) is correct.

Explanation:

$$\text{Total interest} = \left(\frac{7x}{2}\right) + 2\left[\left(\frac{7}{2}\right) \times (x+2)\right]\% \text{ of } 18,600$$

$$(21x + 28) = \frac{23,110.50}{93}$$

$$x = 10.5$$

Hence, for second investment

$$\text{Rate} = 10.5 + 2 = 12.5\%$$

14. Option (B) is correct.

Explanation: According to question:

$$t_1 \times r\% + \frac{3}{4} \times (r+4)\% = 8.25\%$$

$$r = 5.25\%$$

Hence, second rate of interest at which sum was invested = 5.25 + 4 = 9.25%

15. Option (D) is correct.

Explanation: According to question

Money paid at time of purchase = ₹ 1,000

Remaining payment = 20,000 – 1,000 = ₹ 19,000

$$\text{Using} \quad SI = \frac{PRT}{100}$$

Principal decreases ₹ 1,000/month as every month installment.

Duration of each principal = 1 month

$$\text{Rate} = 6\%$$

$$\begin{aligned}\text{Principal} &= (19,000 + 18,000 + ... + 1,000) \\ &= 1,000 \times (19 + 18 + ... + 1) \\ &= (1 + ... + 18 + 19)\end{aligned}$$

[A.P. with $a = 1, d = 1$]

Sum of AP = No. of terms/2 (first term + last term)

$$\text{So,} \quad \text{Principal} = 1,000 \times \frac{19}{2} \times (1+19) = 1,90,000$$

$$\text{Now} \quad SI = 1,90,000 \times \frac{6}{100} \times \frac{1}{12} = 950$$

$$\left[\text{Using } SI = \frac{PRT}{100}\right]$$

So, the last installment will be 1,000 + 950 = 1,950

16. Option (A) is correct.

Explanation: Assuming, amount invested in Scheme A = Z and Scheme B = 3Z

$$\text{Now,} \quad \frac{Z \times 4 \times 8}{100} + \frac{3Z \times 2 \times 13}{100} = 1,320$$

$$\frac{11Z}{10} = 1,320$$

Hence, Z = ₹ 1,200

[Amount invested in Scheme A]

■■■

Compound Interest

Interest calculated on Principal as well as Interest accumulated over previous period

Principal value changes for every period

$CI = P\left(1+\frac{R}{100}\right)^T - P$

Where P is Principal amount
T is time period
R is Rate of Interest p.a.
CI = Compound Interest

Amount = Principal + Interest
(A) (P) (I)

$A = P\left(1+\frac{R}{100}\right)^T$ – Annually

$A = P\left(1+\frac{R}{200}\right)^{2T}$ – Half yearly

$A = P\left(1+\frac{R}{400}\right)^{4T}$ – Quarterly

For 1st year CI and SI is same
Where SI = Simple Interest

Difference between SI and CI when Rate of Interest is same for two years

$$\text{Difference} = P\left(\frac{R}{100}\right)^2$$

For three years

$$\text{Difference} = P\left(\frac{R}{100}\right)^2\left(\frac{300+R}{100}\right)$$

If R_1, R_2 and R_3 are Interest for 1st, 2nd and 3rd year, respectively then,

$$\text{Amount} = P\left(1+\frac{R_1}{100}\right)\left(1+\frac{R_2}{100}\right)\left(1+\frac{R_3}{100}\right)$$

When Amount A_1 in n years and A_2 in $(n + 1)$ years then,

$$P = A_1\left(\frac{A_1}{A_2}\right)^n$$

When CI becomes m times in T years

$$R = \left[(m)^{1/T} - 1\right] \times 100$$

If sum of money becomes "x" times in y years at CI then it becomes "x^n" times in 'ny' years

Chapter 4

Compound Interest

LEARNING OBJECTIVES:

- ❖ Methods to solve questions related to compound interest.
- ❖ To better understand compounding of money.
- ❖ Questions asked in various competitive exams such as SSC, Bank, Railway, UPSC, CAT, etc.
- ❖ Real life application (related to compounding of interest when money is borrowed or lenter).
- ❖ To calculate principal amount, rate per cent or time while giving or taking loan @ CI.

➢ Interest we earn on interest is known as compound interest. For first year compound interest is same as simple interest.

Compound interest = Amount – Principal

$$\text{Amount (A)} = P\left(1+\frac{r}{n}\right)^{tn}$$

where, A = amount

P = principal

r = rate of interest

t = time in years

n = number of times interest is compounded in one year

$$\text{Compound interest (CI)} = P\left(1+\frac{r}{n}\right)^{tn} - P$$

IMPORTANT CONCEPTS AND FORMULAS

➲ To calculate CI at any sum of money lended for T years at R% p.a. compounded annually. Use,

$$CI = P\left(1+\frac{R}{100}\right)^{T} - P$$

➲ When rate of interest is same and we have to calculate difference (D) between SI and CI.

(i) If time period = 2 years

$$D = P\left(\frac{R}{100}\right)^{2}$$

(ii) When time period = 3 years

$$D = \frac{PR^2(300+R)}{(100)^3}$$

➲ When interest is compounded half yearly, yearly and quarterly.

	Yearly	Half-yearly	Quarterly
Time period	T	2T	4T
Rate of interest	R	$\frac{R}{2}$	$\frac{R}{4}$

➲ If sum of money at CI amounts to 'x' times in 'y' years, then it will become 'x^n' times in 'ny' year.

➲ If compound interest become 'x' times in 'y' years then

$$\text{Rate of Interest} = [x^{1/y} - 1] \times 100$$

CONCEPT-1

➢ To calculate compound interest (CI) of any sum of money lended for T years at R% p.a. compounded annually. Use:

$$CI = P\left(1+\frac{R}{100}\right)^{T} - P$$

where, P = Principal amount

Total amount = CI + P

Example 1: Find the compound interest on ₹ 1,700 for 2 years at 10% p.a.c.a.

(a) 357 (b) 452 (c) 376 (d) 673

Sol. (a) Traditional Approach :

$$CI = P\left(1+\frac{R}{100}\right)^{T} - P$$

$$= 1{,}700\left(1+\frac{10}{100}\right)^{2} - 1{,}700$$

$$= 17[121] - 1{,}700$$

$$= 17 \times 21 = ₹\ 357$$

Hence, option (a) is correct.

SHORTCUT METHOD:

We know that rate of interest increases successively in compound interest.

Effective rate of interest (R) after two years

$$= R + R + \frac{R \times R}{100}$$

$$= 10 + 10 + \frac{10 \times 10}{100} = 21\%$$

Hence CI = 21% of Principal

= 21% of 1,700 = ₹ 357

CONCEPT-2

Calculate the difference between SI and CI when rate of interest is the same.

➤ When time period of 2 years is given:

$$\text{Difference (D)} = P\left(\frac{R}{100}\right)^2$$

Example 2: Find difference between SI and CI @ 10% p.a. compounded annually for 2 years on ₹2,000.

(a) 18 (b) 20 (c) 10 (d) 15

Sol. (b) Using, $D = P\left(\frac{R}{100}\right)^2$

$$D = 2000 \times \left(\frac{10}{100}\right)^2$$

$$D = 20$$

Hence, option (b) is correct.

➤ When time period of 3 years is given

$$\text{Difference (D)} = PR^2\left(\frac{300 + R}{100^3}\right)$$

Example 3: Find the difference between SI and CI @ 20% p.a. for 3 years on a sum of ₹ 8,800.

(a) 1,126.4 (b) 2,634

(c) 1,152 (d) 3,624.5

Sol. (a) Using: $D = \frac{PR^2(300 + R)}{100^3}$

$$D = \frac{8{,}800 \times 400 \times 320}{10{,}00{,}000}$$

$$D = 1{,}126.4$$

Hence, option (a) is correct.

CONCEPT-3

➤ When interest is compounded half yearly, yearly and quarterly:

	Yearly	Half-yearly	Quarterly
Time Period	T	2T	4T
Rate of Interest	R	$\frac{R}{2}$	$\frac{R}{4}$

Example 4: A sum of money 16,000 is invested for 18 months at 10% on CI. If the interest is compounded half yearly, what will be the interest to be earned?

(a) 4,518 (b) 2,252 (c) 2,522 (d) 4,194

Sol. (c) Using, $CI = P\left(1 + \frac{R}{100}\right)^T - P$

but for half yearly

$$R = \frac{R}{2}$$

Time period = 3

[there are three half years in 18 months]

$$CI + P = 16{,}000\left(1 + \frac{5}{100}\right)^3 - 16{,}000$$

$$\text{Total amount} = 16{,}000 \times \frac{105}{100} \times \frac{105}{100} \times \frac{105}{100} - 16{,}000$$

$$= 2{,}522$$

Hence, option (c) is correct.

For annually

$$A = P\left(1 + \frac{R}{100}\right)^T$$

For half yearly

$$A = P\left(1 + \frac{R}{200}\right)^{2T}$$

For quarterly

$$A = P\left(1 + \frac{R}{400}\right)^{4T}$$

Where A = Amount, P = Principal

T = Time period, R = Rate of Interest

CONCEPT-4

➤ If the sum of money at CI amounts to x times in y years then it will become x^n times in ny years.

Example 5: Sum of money at CI amounts to twice in 3 years. In how many years will it become 4 times of itself.

(a) 6 years (b) 4 years

(c) 2 years (d) 3 years

Sol. (a) Using, $x^n = ny$

$$2^n = n \times 3$$

$$4 = 6 \text{ years}$$

[Here, x is no. of times and y is no. of years]

Hence, it will become 4 times in 6 years.

CONCEPT-5

➤ To find the rate per cent if compound interest becomes "x" times in "y" years

$$R = \left[x^{\frac{1}{y}} - 1\right] \times 100$$

Example 6: At what rate per cent CI will become $\frac{25}{4}$ times in 2 years?

(a) 75% (b) 150% (c) 50% (d) 125%

Sol. (b) Using, $R = \left[x^{\frac{1}{y}} - 1\right] \times 100$

$= \left[\left(\frac{25}{4}\right)^{\frac{1}{2}} - 1\right] \times 100$

$= \left(\frac{5}{2} - 1\right) \times 100 = \frac{3}{2} \times 100 = 150\%$

Hence option (b) is correct.

Level 1 Beginner

1. Find the compound interest on a sum of ₹ 8,000 at the rate of 5% per annum for 2 years, the interest is calculated annually. [NTPC Tier-I 2021]
(A) ₹ 820 (B) ₹ 630
(C) ₹ 780 (D) ₹ 920

2. A sum of ₹ 7,500 amounts to ₹ 9,075 at 10% p.a. interest being compounded yearly in a certain time. The simple interest (in ₹) on the same sum for the same time and the same rate is:[SSC CGL Tier-I 2021]
(A) 1,500 (B) 1,480
(C) 1,520 (D) 1,530

3. The interest (in ₹) to be paid on a sum of ₹ 30,000 at 15% p.a. after $2\frac{2}{3}$ years, if interest is compounded yearly is: [SSC CGL Tier-I 2021]
(A) 12,364.50 (B) 13,642.50
(C) 16,342.50 (D) 14,362.50

4. At what rate per cent p.a. will ₹ 7,200 amount to ₹ 7,938 in one year, if the interest is compounded half yearly. [SSC CGL Tier-I 2022]
(A) 5 (B) 12
(C) 8 (D) 10

5. If the difference between compound interest compounded annually and simple interest on a certain sum of money for 3 years at 10% p.a. is ₹ 279, then the sum is: [SSC CGL Tier-I 2021]
(A) ₹ 10,000 (B) ₹ 8,000
(C) ₹ 7,500 (D) ₹ 9,000

6. On a sum of money for 2 years compound interest and simple interest are ₹550 and ₹500. Find the rate of interest (in per annum). [SSC CHSL 2023]
(A) 40% (B) 10%
(C) 20% (D) 30%

7. In what time will a sum of ₹ 1,25,000 amounts to ₹ 1,48,877 at 12% p.a., if the interest is being compounded half yearly? [SSC CHSL Tier-I 2021]
(A) $1\frac{1}{2}$ years (B) $2\frac{1}{2}$ years
(C) 1 year (D) 3 years

8. The simple interest on a certain sum for 3 years at 12% p.a. is ₹ 6,750. What is the compound interest (in ₹) on the same sum for 2 years at 20% p.a., if the interest is compounded half-yearly? (Approx value) [SSC CHSL Tier-I 2021]
(A) 8,000 (B) 8,702
(C) 7,729 (D) 6,750

9. A man invested ₹ P at 12% p.a. on compound interest for 2 years. If at the end of the second year, he gets ₹ 1,200 as an interest, then find ₹ P. [IBPS RRB PO PRELIMS 2020]
(A) 4,865 (B) 4,985.50
(C) 4,716.98 (D) 4,656.62

10. At what rate will a sum of ₹ 1,000 amount to ₹ 1,102.50 in 2 years at compound interest? [IBPS RRB PO CLERK 2018]
(A) 6.5% (B) 6%
(C) 5% (D) 5.5%

11. What is the compound interest (in ₹) on a sum of ₹ 46,000 for $2\frac{2}{5}$ years at 15% p.a. interest being compounded annually (interest to a ₹)? [SSC CHSL Tier-I 2020]
(A) 18,458 (B) 18,485
(C) 19,854 (D) 19,458

12. A sum of money amounts to ₹ 28,224 in 2 years and ₹ 29,635.20 in 3 years when invested on compound interest, compounded annually. What is the sum of money (in ₹) ? [SSC CHSL Tier-I 2019]
(A) 26,880 (B) 26,095
(C) 26,000 (D) 25,600

13. Simple interest and compound interest (Compounding annually) on a principal at a certain rate of interest for 2 years is ₹ 1600 and ₹ 1760 respectively. What is the principal? [SSC CHSL 2023]
(A) ₹ 10000 (B) ₹ 7000
(C) ₹ 6000 (D) ₹ 4000

14. The simple interest on a sum of money at 10% per annum for 2 years is ₹ 8,100. What will be the compound interest (in ₹) on the same sum for the same period at same rate of interest? [SSC CGL Tier-I 2019]
(A) 8,100 (B) 8,505
(C) 8,715 (D) 9,000

15. The compound interest on ₹ 4000 after 3 years is ₹ 630.50. Then, the rate of interest compounded yearly is : [SSC MTS Tier-I 2019]
(A) 7% (B) 5%
(C) 8% (D) 6%

16. If the difference between the compound interest and simple interest on a certain sum of money for 3 years at 10% p.a. is ₹ 558, then the sum is: **[SSC CGL Tier-I 2019]**
(A) ₹ 18,500 (B) ₹ 18,000
(C) ₹ 16,000 (D) ₹ 15,000

17. The interest occurred on a sum of money at the rate of 10% p.a. compound interest in 2 years is ₹ 630. Find the simple interest (in ₹) of the same sum for 3 years at the same rate. **[NTPC Tier-I 2019]**
(A) 850 (B) 950
(C) 900 (D) 650

18. What would be the compound interest occured on an amount of ₹ 8,000 at the rate of 15 p.c.p.a. in 3 years? **[IBPS PRE 2017]**
(A) ₹ 4,051 (B) ₹ 4,167
(C) ₹ 4,283 (D) ₹ 4,325

19. At what rate of compound interest per annum will a sum of ₹ 1,200 become ₹ 13,48.32 in 2 years? **[SSC CHSL Tier-I 2017]**
(A) 7.5% (B) 6.5%
(C) 7% (D) 6%

20. The difference between CI and SI on a certain sum of money for 3 years at 5% p.a. is ₹122. Find the sum invested. **[IBPS RRB Office Assistant 2017]**
(A) ₹ 10,000 (B) ₹ 12,000
(C) ₹ 16,000 (D) ₹ 20,000

21. What is the difference between the compound interest on ₹ 5,000 for $1\frac{1}{2}$ year at 4% per annum compounded yearly and half yearly? **[SSC Junior Associate Pre 2017]**
(A) 2 (B) 3
(C) 4 (D) None of these

22. The difference between total SI earned on Rs 'P' at 12% p.a. for 3 years and total CI earned on same sum at 15% p.a. for 2 years when compounded annually is ₹ 375. Find P? (in ₹) **[RBI Assistant PRE 2020]**
(A) 10,000 (B) 15,000
(C) 20,000 (D) 14,000

23. Difference between CI and SI on a sum for 3 years at 20% p.a. is 176. Find the simple interest on the sum after 2 years at 10% p.a. **[RBI Assistant PRE 2018]**
(A) 225 (B) 250
(C) 300 (D) 550

24. The compound interest obtained on an amount in 2 years at the rate of interest of 10% p.a. is ₹ 1,932. What will be the simple interest for same sum in three years at 6% p.a.? **[ESIC DC Clerk Pre 2019]**
(A) ₹ 1,656 (B) ₹ 1,452
(C) ₹ 1,810 (D) ₹ 1,920

25. The simple interest accrued on a certain principal is ₹ 1200 in 3 years at the rate of 8% per annum. What would be the compound interest (compounding annually) accrued on twice of that principal at the rate of 10% per annum in 2 years? **[SSC CHSL 2023]**
(A) ₹ 1,050 (B) ₹ 2,150
(C) ₹ 2,100 (D) ₹ 1,100

26. A sum of ₹ 10,500 amounts to ₹ 13,650 in 2 years at a certain rate per cent per annum simple interest. The same sum will amount to what in 1 year at the same rate, if the interest is compounded half yearly? **[CHSL 2020]**
(A) ₹ 12,124 (B) ₹ 12,134
(C) ₹ 12,143 (D) ₹ 12,314

27. The simple interest on a sum of Rs. 12,000 at the end of 5 years is Rs. 6,000. What would have been the compound interest on the same sum at the same rate for 3 years when compounded annually? **[CHSL 2021]**
(A) ₹ 3,972 **2.** ₹ 3,970 **3.** ₹ 2,520 **4.** ₹ 3,600

Level 2 Intermediate

1. What is the compound interest (in ₹) on a sum of ₹ 8,192 for $1\frac{1}{4}$ years at 15% per annum, if interest is compounded 5-monthly? **[SSC CGL 2021]**
(A) 1,640 (B) 1,740
(C) 1,634 (D) 1,735

2. A certain sum amounts to ₹ 2,91,600 in 2 years and to ₹ 3,14,928 in 3 years on compound interest compounded annually. How much will be the simple interest (in₹) on ₹ 40,000 at the same rate for 2 years? **[SSC CGL Tier-II 2021]**
(A) 7,500 (B) 6,400
(C) 8,000 (D) 9,600

3. A certain sum becomes ₹ 13,650 at 15% p.a. simple interest after 2 years. What will be the amount (in ₹) of the same sum after 1 year at the same rate of interest, if the interest is compounded half yearly? **[SSC CGL Tier-I 2021]**
(A) 13,625 (B) 11,000
(C) 12,134 (D) 10,500

4. The simple interest on a certain sum of money for 5 years at the rate of 10% p.a. is half the compound interest on ₹ 5,000 for 2 years at the rate of 10% p.a., interest compounded yearly. The sum on simple interest is: **[SSC CHSL Tier-II 2020]**
(A) ₹ 1,450 (B) ₹ 1,050
(C) ₹ 1,500 (D) ₹ 1,540

5. Find the compound interest (in ₹) on a sum of ₹ 7,500 for 4 years if the rate of interest is 20% p.a. for the first two years and 10% p.a. for the next two years. The interest is compounded annually. **[SSC CHSL Tier-II 2020]**
(A) 5,658 (B) 5,586
(C) 6,558 (D) 5,568

6. Anamika paid ₹ 4,965 as CI on a loan of ₹ 15,000 after 3 years when compounded annually. Suman took a loan of ₹ 10,000 at the same rate on simple interest. How much interest did Suman pay after 3 years? [SSC CHSL Tier-II 2020]

(A) ₹ 4,500 (B) ₹ 4,000
(C) ₹ 3,000 (D) ₹ 3,500

7. A sum of ₹ 2,432 amounts to ₹ 2,681.28 in 2 years at a certain rate per annum, interest compounded yearly. What will be the simple interest (in ₹) on the same sum for $4\frac{3}{8}$ years at double the same rate? [SSC CHSL Tier-II 2021]

(A) 1,276.80 (B) 1,094.40
(C) 1,064 (D) 1,368

8. Surekha borrowed a sum of money and returned it in two equal annual installments of ₹ 5,547 each. If the rate of interest was $7\frac{1}{2}\%$ p.a. compounded yearly, then the total interest paid by her was: [SSC CGL Tier-I 2019]

(A) ₹ 1,444 (B) ₹ 1,096
(C) ₹ 1,126 (D) ₹ 1,134

9. A loan is to be returned in two equal installments. If the rate of interest is 10% p.a.c.a. and each installment is ₹ 5,808, then total interest charged in this scheme is: [SSC CGL Tier-II 2019]

(A) ₹ 1,563 (B) ₹ 1,536
(C) ₹ 1,632 (D) ₹ 1,602

10. Ram deposited an amount of ₹ 8,000 in a bank's saving account with 6.5% interest compounded monthly. What amount will he get at the end of 18 months? [SSC CGL Tier-I 2019]

(A) ₹ 8,816.97 (B) ₹ 8,788.98
(C) ₹ 8,790.4 (D) ₹ 8,907.56

11. The simple interest accrued on a certain principal is ₹ 1200 in 3 years at the rate of 8% per annum. What would be the compound interest (compounding annually) accrued on twice of that principal at the rate of 10% per annum in 2 years? [SSC CHSL 2023]

(A) ₹ 1,050 (B) ₹ 2,150
(C) ₹ 2,100 (D) ₹ 1,100

12. The difference between CI and SI on ₹ x at 9% p.a. for 2 years is ₹ 2,025. What is the value of x? [SSC CGL Tier-I 2019]

(A) 2,500 (B) 2,400
(C) 2,800 (D) 2,200

13. The simple interest on a sum of money for 3 years at an interest rate of 6% p.a. is ₹ 6,750. What will be the compound interest on the same sum at the same rate for the same period, compounded annually? [SSC CHSL Tier-II 2019]

(A) ₹ 7,163 (B) ₹ 7,103
(C) ₹ 7,133 (D) ₹ 7,663

14. A certain sum amounts to ₹15,500 in 2 years at 12% p.a. simple interest. The sum will amount to what in $1\frac{1}{2}$ years at 10% p.a., if the interest is compounded half yearly. [SSC CHSL Tier-II 2020]

(A) ₹ 14,470 (B) ₹ 15,125
(C) ₹ 14,360 (D) ₹ 13,460

15. The simple interest on a sum of ₹8,000 at a certain rate per cent per .annum for 3 years is ₹3,600. What will be the amount (in ₹) of the same sum after 2 years at the same rate, if the interest is compounded 8-monthly? [SSC CHSL 2021]

(A) 10,580 (B) 10,450
(C) 10,648 (D) 11,239

16. If a person invested 6,000 at T% SI for 3 years and the same amount at (T + 5)% CI for 2 years and the difference between both interests is ₹ 60. Then, find T. [IBPS RRB PO Pre 2019]

(A) 15% (B) 18%
(C) 12% (D) 20%

17. A person invested two equal amounts in two different schemes. In first scheme, amount is invested at 8% p.a. on SI for T years and SI received is ₹ 20,000 while in the second scheme, amount is invested at 10% p.a. for 2 years at CI and CI received is ₹ 1,050. Find T. [IBPS PO Pre 2019]

(A) 4 years (B) 8 years
(C) 5 years (D) 3 years

18. A certain amount of money was lent for a period of 1 year 9 months at a rate of 10% per annum compounded annually. If the compound interest is ₹1,460, find the amount of money lent. [SSC CHSL 2023]

(A) ₹ 8,200 (B) ₹ 7,500
(C) ₹ 6,000 (D) ₹ 8,000

19. The simple interest on a certain sum for 3 years at 12% p.a. is ₹ 6,750. What is the compound interest (in ₹) on the same sum for 2 years at 20% p.a., if interest is compounded half-yearly?[SSC CHSL Tier-II 2019]

(A) 8,000 (B) 8,702
(C) 7,729 (D) 6,750

20. A sum of money amounts to ₹ 28,224 in 2 years and to ₹ 29,635.20 in 3 years when invested on compound interest, compounded annually. What is the sum of money? [SSC CHSL Tier-I 2019]

(A) ₹ 26,880 (B) ₹ 26,095
(C) ₹ 26,000 (D) ₹ 25,600

21. The simple interest on a certain sum for 2 years at 8% p.a. is ₹ 225 less than the compound interest on the same sum for 2 years at 10% per annum. The sum is: [IBPS RRB CLERK 2018]

(A) ₹ 3,200 (B) ₹ 4,200
(C) ₹ 4,000 (D) ₹ 4,500

3 Level Expert

1. A man invested a certain sum in Scheme A at 15% p.a. for 2 years and earned ₹ 1,950 simple interest. He increased his sum by ₹ 'x' and invested in another Scheme B at 10% p.a. CI for 2 years and received ₹ 1,680 as compound interest. Find value of 'x'. **[IBPS PO Pre 2020]**
   (A) 1,750 (B) 1,500
   (C) 1,250 (D) None of these
2. A certain amount invested at a certain rate, compounds annually. grows to an amount in five years, which is a factor of 1.1881 more than to what it would have grown in 3 years. What is the rate per cent? **[SSC CHSL Tier-II 2019]**
   (A) 9 (B) 8.1
   (C) 8 (D) 9.2
3. A person borrowed a certain sum at 10% p.a. for three years interest being compounded annually. At the end of 2 years, he repaid a sum of ₹ 6,634 and at the end of third year, he cleared off the debt by paying ₹ 13,200. What was the sum borrowed by him. **[SSC CHSL Tier-II 2019]**
   (A) ₹ 16,400 (B) ₹ 15,400
   (C) ₹ 15,600 (D) ₹ 16,500
4. A sum of ₹ x was borroed and paid back in two equal yearly installments, each of ₹ 35,280. If the rate of interest was 5% compounded annually, then value of x is: **[SSC CGL Tier-II 2019]**
   (A) 64,400 (B) 65,600
   (C) 64,800 (D) 65,400
5. What sum of money at compound interest will amount to ₹ 4,630.08 in 3 years if the rate of interest is 4% for the first year, 5% for the second year and 6% for the third year? **[SSC CGL Tier-I 2019]**
   (A) 4,500 (B) 4,800
   (C) 4,000 (D) 3,500
6. There is a 60% increase in an amount in 5 years at simple interest. What will be the compound interest on ₹ 6,250 for 2 years at the same rate of interest, when the interest is compounded yearly? **[SSC CGL 2019]**
   (A) ₹ 1,590 (B) ₹ 1,560
   (C) ₹ 1,500 (D) ₹ 1,480
7. What is the compound interest (in Rs.) on a sum of Rs. 46,000 for $2\frac{2}{5}$ years at 15% per annum, interest being compounded annually (nearest to a Rs.)? **[SSC CHSL 2021]**
   (A) 18,458 (B) 19,458
   (C) 19,485 (D) 18,485
8. Rahul invested equal sum of money at CI under Scheme A and B; under Scheme A, rate was 10% where it is 12% in Scheme B. The CI after 2 years on the sum invested in scheme A was ₹ 1,050. How much is the interest earned under Scheme B after two years, if the interest is compounded annually in both Schemes? **[SSC CGL 2019]**
   (A) ₹ 1,722 (B) ₹ 1,372
   (C) ₹ 1,270 (D) ₹ 1,272
9. A sum of ₹ 8,000 invested at 10% p.a. amounts to ₹ 9,261 in certain time, interest compounded half yearly. What will be the compound interest (in ₹) on the same sum for the same time at double the earlier rate of interest, when interest is compounded annually? **[SSC CHSL Tier-I 2020]**
   (A) 2,520 (B) 2,480
   (C) 2,560 (D) 2,500
10. A and B together borrowed a sum of ₹ 51,750 at an interest rate of 7% p.a. compound interest in such a way that to settle the loan A paid as much amount after 3 years as paid by B after 4 years from the day of borrowing. The sum borrowed by A was: **[SSC CGL 2018]**
    (A) 25,650 (B) 26,750
    (C) 25,000 (D) 24,860
11. The mobile phone is available for ₹ 79,860 by cash payment or by paying ₹ 60,000 as down payment and the remaining amount in three equal installments. If the shopkeeper charges interest at the rate of 10% per annum compounded annually, then the amount of each installment (in ₹) will be: **[SSC CHSL 2019]**
    (A) 7,986 (B) 6,689
    (C) 6,789 (D) 6,000
12. A man invested a total of ₹ 12,050 in two parts: one at 10% SI for 2 years and the other at the same rate at CI compounded annually for the same time. The amount he received from both the parts are equal. The sum (in ₹) invested at CI is: **[SSC CHSL 2019]**
    (A) 5,780 (B) 5,850
    (C) 6,000 (D) 5,800
13. Krishan invested a sum of ₹ 25,000 in two parts. He earned 11% p.a. on part 1 and 10% p.a. compound interest compounded annually on part 2. If the total interest received by him after 2 years is ₹ 5,370, then find the sum invested on simple interest (Part 1). **[SSC CGL 2021]**
    (A) ₹ 11,000 (B) ₹ 12,000
    (C) ₹ 12,500 (D) ₹ 13,000
14. The SI on a sum of ₹ 8,000 at a certain rate per cent per annum for 3 years is ₹ 3,600. What will be the amount (in ₹) of the same sum after 2 years at the same rate, if the interest is compounded 8-monthly? **[SSC CHSL 2021]**
    (A) 11,239 (B) 10,450
    (C) 10,580 (D) 10,648
15. Atul borrowed a sum of 12,000 and agreed to repay it by paying 4,800 at the end of first year and ₹ 9,240 at the end of second year. What is the rate of compound interest compounded annually? **[SSC CGL Tier-I 2021]**

(A) 10% (B) 12%
(C) 8.5% (D) 8%

16. A person borrowed a sum of ₹ 30,800 at 10% p.a. for 3 years, compounded annually. At the end of two years, he paid ₹ 13,268. At the end of 3rd year, he paid ₹ x to clear the debt. Find x. [SSC MTS 2019]
(A) 26,200 (B) 26,620
(C) 26,400 (D) 26,510

17. A man borrowed a certain sum and agreed to repay it by paying ₹ 4,000 at the end of first year and ₹ 7,700 at the end of second year. If rate of CI compounded annually is 10% per annum, find the sum he borrowed. [SSC CGL Tier-I 2021]
(A) 11,500 (B) 11,000
(C) 9,000 (D) 10,000

18. A borrowed a sum of ₹ 1,60,000 from B at 10% p.a. simple interest. At the same time, he lent the same sum to C at the same rate on CI compounded semi-annually for 2 years. Find the amount earned by A in the whole transaction. [SSC CGL 2021]
(A) 4,280 (B) 2,840
(C) 4,281 (D) 2,481

19. A person invested two equal amounts in two different schemes. In the first scheme, the amount is invested at 8% p.a. on SI for T years and SI received is ₹ 2,000 while in the second scheme, the amount invested at 10% p.a. for 2 years at CI and CI received is ₹ 1050. Find T. [IBPS RRB PO Pre 2018]
(A) 5 years (B) 4 years
(C) 8 years (D) 6 years

20. A father left a will of ₹ 16,400 for his two sons aged 17 and 18 years. They must get equal amounts when they are 20 years, at 5% compound interest. Find the present share of the younger son. [RRB 2017]
(A) ₹ 8,000 (B) ₹ 8,200
(C) ₹ 8,400 (D) ₹ 8,800

21. Anamika paid ₹ 4,965 as compound interest on a loan of ₹ 15,000 after 3 years. When compounded annually. Suman took a loan of ₹ 10,000 at the same rate of simple interest. How much interest did Suman pay after 3 years? [SSC CPO 2021]
(A) ₹ 4,500 (B) ₹ 4,000
(C) ₹ 3,000 (D) ₹ 3,500

22. A sum of ₹ 3,125 amounts to ₹ 3,515.20 in 3 years at x% p.a., interest being compounded yearly. What will be the simple interest (in ₹) on the same sum and for same time at $(x + 2)$% p.a.? [CGL 2020]
(A) 554 (B) 562.50 (C) 550 (D) 500

ANSWER KEY

Level-1: Beginner

1.	(A)	2.	(A)	3.	(B)	4.	(D)	5.	(D)	6.	(C)	7.	(A)	8.	(B)	9.	(C)	10.	(C)
11.	(B)	12.	(D)	13.	(D)	14.	(B)	15.	(B)	16.	(B)	17.	(C)	18.	(B)	19.	(D)	20.	(C)
21.	(A)	22.	(A)	23.	(D)	24.	(A)	25.	(C)	26.	(B)	27.	(A)						

Level-2: Intermediate

1.	(C)	2.	(B)	3.	(C)	4.	(B)	5.	(D)	6.	(C)	7.	(C)	8.	(D)	9.	(B)	10.	(A)
11.	(C)	12.	(A)	13.	(A)	14.	(A)	15.	(C)	16.	(A)	17.	(C)	18.	(D)	19.	(B)	20.	(D)
21.	(D)																		

Level-3: Expert

1.	(B)	2.	(A)	3.	(B)	4.	(B)	5.	(C)	6.	(A)	7.	(D)	8.	(D)	9.	(C)	10.	(B)
11.	(A)	12.	(C)	13.	(B)	14.	(D)	15.	(D)	16.	(C)	17.	(D)	18.	(D)	19.	(A)	20.	(A)
21.	(C)	22.	(B)																

Solutions with Detailed Explanations

Level-1: BEGINNER

1. **Option (A) is correct.**

Explanation:

Traditional method

Using, $$CI = P\left(1+\frac{R}{100}\right)^T - P$$

$$= 8,000\left[1+\frac{5}{100}\right]^2 - 8,000$$

$$= 8,000\left[\frac{21}{20}\right]^2 - 8,000$$

$$= 8,820 - 8,000 = 820$$

Alternate Method:

Rate of interest = 5% p.a.

Time = 2 years

We know that the rate of interest increases successively in case of compound interest.

Using : $A + B + \frac{AB}{100}$ successive percentage change

Rate after 2 years

$$\left[5+5+\frac{5\times5}{100}\right]\% = 10.25\%$$

$$CI = 10.25\% \text{ of principal}$$
$$= 10.25\% \text{ of } 8,000 = 820$$

2. **Option (A) is correct.**

Explanation:

Using, $\text{Amount} = \text{Principal}\left(1+\frac{\text{Rate}}{100}\right)^{\text{Time period}}$

$$9,075 = 7,500\left(1+\frac{10}{100}\right)^T$$

$$\frac{121}{100} = \left(\frac{11}{10}\right)^T$$

$$T = 2 \text{ years}$$

$$SI = \frac{\text{Principal}\times\text{Time}\times\text{Rate}}{100}$$

$$= \frac{7,500\times10\times2}{100} = ₹\,1,500$$

3. **Option (B) is correct.**

Explanation: (Traditional Approach)

Using, $\text{Amount} = \text{Principal}\left(1+\frac{R_1}{100}\right)\left(1+\frac{R_2}{100}\right)\left(1+\frac{R_3}{100}\right)$

For the first 2 years, R = 15%

For $\frac{2}{3}$ years, R becomes $15\times\frac{2}{3} = 10\%$

R_1 = 15% (for 1st year)

R_2 = 15% (for 2nd year)

R_3 = 10% (for $\frac{2}{3}$ years)

$$A = 30,000\times\left(1+\frac{15}{100}\right)\left(1+\frac{15}{100}\right)\left(1+\frac{10}{100}\right)$$

$$= 30,000\times\frac{23}{20}\times\frac{23}{20}\times\frac{11}{10}$$

$$A = 43,642.5$$

$$CI = 43,642.5 - 30,000$$

[Using CI = Amount – Principal]

$$= ₹\,13,642.5$$

Alternate Approach:

Amount after 2 + 2/3 years

$$= 30,000\times\frac{115}{100}\times\frac{115}{100}\times\frac{110}{100} = ₹\,43,642.5$$

Hence, CI = Amount – Principal

$= 43,642.5 - 30,000 = ₹\,13,642.5$

4. **Option (D) is correct.**

Explanation: For half yearly, time becomes double and rate of interest becomes half.

Using, $A = P\left(1+\frac{R}{2\times100}\right)^{2T}$

$$7,938 = 7,200\left(1+\frac{R}{2\times100}\right)^{2T}$$

$$\frac{441}{400} = \left(1+\frac{R}{200}\right)^2$$

$$\left(\frac{21}{20}\right)^2 = \left[\frac{(200+R)}{200}\right]^2$$

$$R = 10\%$$

5. **Option (D) is correct.**

Explanation: Traditional approach

Assuming Principal = P

$$SI = \frac{P\times10\times3}{100} \quad \left[\text{Using } SI = \frac{PRT}{100}\right]$$

$$= \frac{3P}{10} \quad \text{...(1)}$$

Now, $CI = P\left(1+\frac{10}{100}\right)^3 - P$

$$\left[\text{Using } CI = P\left(1+\frac{R}{100}\right)^T - P\right]$$

$$= P\left(\frac{11}{10}\right)^3 - P$$

$$= \frac{1,331}{1,000}P - P \quad \text{...(2)}$$

Given CI – SI = 279

From (1) and (2)

$$\frac{1,331}{1,000}P - P - \frac{3P}{10} = 279$$

$$\frac{31P}{1,000} = 279$$

$$P = ₹\,9,000$$

Alternate approach:

Assuming P = 1,000

$$SI = \frac{1,000\times10\times3}{100} = 300$$

$$CI = 1,000\left[1+\frac{10}{100}\right]^3 - 1,000 = 331$$

$$CI - SI = 31$$

But according to the question,

$$CI - SI = 279$$

So, $31 = 279$

$$1,000 = \frac{279}{31}\times1000 = ₹\,9,000$$

6. **Option (C) is correct.**

Explanation:

Let the principal = ₹P

$\therefore$ Simple interest $= \dfrac{P \times R \times 2}{100}$

[R → rate of interest, T = 2 years]

$\Rightarrow \dfrac{50000}{2} = PR$

$\Rightarrow P = \dfrac{25000}{R}$ ...(i)

Difference between S.I. & C.I. for 2 years

$$C.I. - S.I. = P\left[\frac{R}{100}\right]^2$$

$\Rightarrow 550 - 500 = \dfrac{25000}{R} \times \dfrac{R^2}{1000}$ [Using eqn (i)]

$\Rightarrow \dfrac{50 \times 10}{25} = R$

$\Rightarrow R = 20$

So rate of interest = 20%

7. **Option (A) is correct.**

Explanation:

Using, $A = P\left(1+\dfrac{R}{200}\right)^{2T}$

When interest compounded half yearly

$$1,48,877 = 1,25,000\left(1+\frac{12}{200}\right)^{2T}$$

$$\left(\frac{53}{50}\right)^3 = \left(\frac{53}{50}\right)^{2T}$$

$2T = 3$

$T = 1.5$ years

8. **Option (B) is correct.**

Explanation: $SI = \dfrac{P \times 3 \times 12}{100}$ $\left[\text{Using } SI = \dfrac{P \times R \times T}{100}\right]$

$6,750 = \dfrac{36P}{100}$

$P = \dfrac{6,750 \times 100}{36} = 18,750$

New for CI compounded half yearly

Using $A = P\left(1+\dfrac{R}{200}\right)^{2n}$

$A = 18,750 \times \left(1+\dfrac{20}{200}\right)^4$

$A = 18,750 \times \dfrac{11}{10} \times \dfrac{11}{10} \times \dfrac{11}{10} \times \dfrac{11}{10}$

$= 27,452$

CI = Amount – Principal

CI = 27,452 – 18,750 = ₹ 8,702

9. **Option (C) is correct.**

Explanation: Traditional way

Using, $CI = P\left(1+\dfrac{R}{100}\right)^T - P$

$1,200 = P\left(1+\dfrac{12}{100}\right)^2 - P$

$1,200 = P \times \dfrac{112}{100} \times \dfrac{112}{100} - P$

$1,200 = P\left[\dfrac{112}{100} \times \dfrac{112}{100} - 1\right]$

$1,200 = P \times 1.2544$

$P = 4,716.98$

Alternate way:

Rate = 12% per annum for 2 years

Rate of interest after 2 year $= \left(12+12+\dfrac{12 \times 12}{100}\right)\%$

$\left[\text{Using } A+B+\dfrac{AB}{100}\right]$

$= \left[24+\dfrac{144}{100}\right]\% = 25.44\%$

CI = 25.44% of principal

$1200 = \dfrac{25.44}{100} \times \text{Principal}$

Principal = 4,716.98

10. **Option (C) is correct.**

Explanation:

Using $A = P\left(1+\dfrac{r}{100}\right)^t$

$1,102.50 = 1,000\left(1+\dfrac{r}{100}\right)^2$

$100 + r = 105$

$r = 5\%$

11. **Option (B) is correct.**

Explanation:

Using $CI = P\left(1+\dfrac{R}{100}\right)^t - P$

for 2 years total amount $= 46,000 \times \left(1+\dfrac{15}{100}\right)^2$

= ₹ 60,835

for $\dfrac{2}{5}$ years rate of interest = 15% of $\dfrac{2}{5}$ = 6%

So, total amount becomes

$= 60,835 \times \left(1+\dfrac{6}{100}\right)^1$ = ₹ 64,485.1

Hence, Interest = Amount – Principal

= 64,485.1 – 46,000 = ₹ 18,485.

12. **Option (D) is correct.**

Explanation:

Total rate of interest for 2 years

$= r + r + \dfrac{r \times r}{100}$ ...(1)

$$\text{Rate of interest} = \text{percentage change}$$

$$= \frac{\text{Amount} - \text{Principal}}{\text{Principal}} \times 100$$

$$= \frac{29{,}635.20 - 28{,}224}{100} = 5\%$$

Total rate of interest for 2 years

Using (1)

$$5 + 5 + \frac{(5 \times 5)}{100} = 10.25\%$$

$$110.25\% \text{ Principal} = 28{,}224$$

$$\text{Principle} = \frac{28{,}224}{11{,}025} \times 10{,}000 = ₹\,25{,}600$$

13. Option (D) is correct.

Explanation:

Given that the SI for 2 years = ₹ 1600

And CI for two years = ₹ 1760

Let the principal amount = ₹ P

Using, $SI = \frac{PRT}{100}$

$$\Rightarrow \quad 1600 = \frac{2PR}{100}$$

$$\Rightarrow \quad PR = 80000 \qquad \ldots(1)$$

We have, CI – SI for two years $= \frac{PR^2}{10000}$

$$\Rightarrow \quad 1760 - 1600 = \frac{PR \times R}{10000}$$

$$\Rightarrow \quad 160 = \frac{80000 \times R}{10000}$$

(PR = 80000 from eq. (1))

$$\Rightarrow \quad R = 20\%$$

From eq. (1),

$$P \times 20 = 80000$$

$$P = 4000$$

So, the principal amount = ₹ 4000

14. Option (B) is correct.

Explanation:

Using $SI = \frac{PRT}{100}$

$$8{,}100 = \frac{P \times 10 \times 2}{100}$$

$$P = 8{,}100 \times 5 = 40{,}500$$

CI for 2 years at 10%, per annum

$$\text{Total interest at CI} = 10 + 10 + \frac{10 \times 10}{100} = 21\%$$

$$CI = 21\% \text{ of } P$$

$$= 21\% \text{ of } 40{,}500 = ₹\,8{,}505$$

15. Option (B) is correct.

Explanation:

Using $A = P\left(1 + \frac{R}{100}\right)^T$

$$\text{Amount (A)} = \text{Principal} + \text{Interest}$$

$$= 4{,}000 + 630.50 = 4{,}630.50$$

$$4{,}630.50 = 4{,}000\left(1 + \frac{R}{100}\right)^3$$

$$\frac{21}{20} - 1 = \frac{R}{100}$$

$$\frac{1}{20} = \frac{R}{100}$$

$$R = 5\%$$

16. Option (B) is correct.

Explanation: Using:

Difference between SI and CI for 3 years at the same rate of interest $= P\left(\frac{R}{100}\right)^2 \times \frac{300 + R}{100}$

$$558 = P\left(\frac{10}{100}\right)^2 \times \frac{300 + 10}{100}$$

$$P = 558 \times 100 \times \frac{100}{310}$$

Hence, $P = ₹\,18{,}000$

17. Option (C) is correct.

Explanation:

Using $CI = P\left(1 + \frac{R}{100}\right)^T - P$

$$630 = P\left(\frac{121}{100}\right) - P$$

$$P = ₹\,3{,}000$$

Putting value of P in calculating SI for 3 years

$$SI = \frac{P \times R \times T}{100} = \frac{3{,}000 \times 10 \times 3}{100} = ₹\,900$$

18. Option (B) is correct.

Explanation:

Using $CI = P\left(1 + \frac{R}{100}\right)^T - P$

$$= 8{,}000\left(1 + \frac{15}{100}\right)^3 - 8{,}000$$

$$= 8{,}000 \times \frac{115}{100} \times \frac{115}{100} \times \frac{115}{100} - 8{,}000$$

$$= 12{,}167 - 8{,}000 = ₹\,4{,}167$$

19. Option (D) is correct.

Explanation:

Using $\text{Amount} = P\left(1 + \frac{R}{100}\right)^T$

$$1{,}348.32 = 1{,}200\left(1 + \frac{R}{100}\right)^2$$

$$1.1236 = \frac{(100 + R)^2}{10{,}000}$$

$$11{,}236 = (100 + R)^2$$

$$106 = 100 + R$$

Hence, $R = 6\%$

20. Option (C) is correct.

Explanation:

Using $P = D\left(\frac{100}{R}\right)^2 \times \frac{100}{300 + R}$

Where D is the difference between SI and for 3 years.

$$P = 122\left(\frac{100}{5}\right)^2 \times \frac{100}{305}$$

$$P = 122 \times 400 \times \frac{100}{305}$$

$$P = ₹\ 16,000$$

21. Option (A) is correct.

Explanation: CI when interest is compounded yearly

$$= 5000 \times \left(1+\frac{4}{100}\right) \times \left(1+\frac{\frac{1}{2}\times 4}{100}\right) = ₹\ 5,304$$

When compounded half yearly

$$CI = 5000 \times \left(1+\frac{2}{100}\right)^3$$

$$= 5,000 \times \frac{51}{50} \times \frac{51}{50} \times \frac{51}{50} = ₹\ 5,306.04$$

$$\text{Difference} = 5,306.04 - 5,304 = 2.04 \approx 2$$

22. Option (A) is correct.

Explanation: $SI = \frac{PRT}{100} = \frac{P \times 12 \times 3}{100}$

$$SI = \frac{36}{100}P = 36\% \text{ of } P$$

Total rate of interest at CI for 2 years

$$= r + r + \frac{r \times r}{100} = 30 + 2.25 = 32.25$$

36% of P – 32.25% of P = 375

$$P = \frac{375}{3.75} \times 100 = ₹\ 10,000$$

23. Option (D) is correct.

Explanation:

Using $P = D\left(\frac{100}{R}\right)^2 \times \frac{100}{300+R}$

$$P = 176 \times \left(\frac{100}{20}\right)^2 \times \frac{100}{320}$$

$$P = 1,375 \quad \text{...(1)}$$

Using (1) calculate SI

$$SI = \frac{PRT}{100}$$

$$= \frac{1,375 \times 20 \times 2}{100} = ₹\ 550$$

24. Option (A) is correct.

Explanation: Total rate of interest after 2 years

$$= 10 + 10 + \frac{10 \times 10}{100} = 21\%$$

21% of Principal (P) = CI

21% of P = 1,932

P = 9,200

Using value of P to calculate SI

$$SI = \frac{PRT}{100} = \frac{3,125 \times 6 \times 3}{100}$$

$$= 1,656$$

25. Option (C) is correct.

Explanation:

Given,

Simple interest in 3 years = ₹ 1200

Let the principal amount = ₹ P

Rate of interest = 8%

Using, $SI = \frac{PRT}{100}$

$$\Rightarrow \quad 1200 = \frac{P \times 8 \times 3}{100}$$

$$\Rightarrow \quad P = 5000$$

Now, rate of interest = 10% annum

Time = 2 years

Using, $A = P\left(1+\frac{r}{100}\right)^2$

$$\Rightarrow A = 10000\left(1+\frac{10}{100}\right)^2 \Rightarrow A = 10000 \times \frac{11}{10} \times \frac{11}{10} = 12100$$

So, compound interest = 12100 – 10000 = ₹ 2100

26. Option (B) is correct.

Explanation:

Using, $SI = \frac{P \times R \times T}{100}$

$$13,650 - 10,500 = \frac{10,500 \times 2 \times r}{100}$$

$$r = 15\%$$

If compounded half yearly, then $r = \frac{15}{2}\% = 7.5\%$

Now,

$$\text{Total amount} = \frac{10,500 \times 107.5 \times 107.5}{100 \times 100} = ₹\ 12,134$$

27. Option (A) is correct.

Explanation:

Given,

Principal amount (P) = ₹ 12000

Time (T) = 5 years

SI = ₹ 600/0

Let, the rate of interest = R% per annum

We have, $SI = \frac{P \times R \times T}{100}$

$$₹\ 6000 = \frac{12000 \times R \times 5}{100}$$

$$₹\ 6000 = 600\ R$$

$$₹\ R = 10\%$$

Now time = 3 years

By compound interest formula,

$$A = P\left(1+\frac{R}{100}\right)^3$$

$$\Rightarrow \quad A = 12000\left(1+\frac{10}{100}\right)^3$$

$$\Rightarrow \quad A = 12000 \times \frac{11}{10} \times \frac{11}{10} \times \frac{11}{10}$$

$$\Rightarrow \quad A = 15972$$

So, compound interest = 15972 – 12000 = ₹ 3972

Level-2: INTERMEDIATE

1. **Option (C) is correct.**

Explanation: Using amount = $P\left(1+\frac{R}{100}\right)^T$

$$1\frac{1}{4} = 15 \text{ months}$$

When interest is compounded 5 monthly

Time period becomes 3

Rate becomes $\frac{5}{12}$ of rate of interest

$$\frac{5}{12}\times 15 = \frac{25}{4}\%$$

$$CI = P\left(1+\frac{R}{100}\right)^T - P$$

$$= 8{,}192\times\frac{817}{4{,}096} = ₹\,1{,}634$$

2. **Option (B) is correct.**

Explanation:

Using $$A = P\left(1+\frac{R}{100}\right)^T$$

$$2{,}91{,}600 = P\left(1+\frac{R}{100}\right)^2 \quad ...(1)$$

$$3{,}14{,}928 = P\left(1+\frac{R}{100}\right)^3 \quad ...(2)$$

Solving (1) and (2)

$$1+\frac{R}{100} = 1.08$$

$$R = 8\%$$

Using the value of R to calculate SI

$$SI = \frac{PRT}{100}$$

$$= \frac{40{,}000\times 8\times 2}{100} = ₹\,6{,}400$$

3. **Option (C) is correct.**

Explanation:

Using SI = Amount – Principal

Assuming Principal = P

SI = 13,650 – P

According to question

$$\frac{P\times 15\times 2}{100} = 13{,}650 - P$$

$$13P = 1{,}36{,}500$$

$$P = 10{,}500$$

Using the value of P to calculate amount after 1 year.

We know that for half yearly, time becomes twice and interest becomes half.

Now, amount after 1 year = $10{,}500\times\left(1+\frac{R}{100}\right)^T$

$$= 10{,}500\times\left(1+\frac{7.5}{100}\right)^2$$

$$= 12{,}134.0625 \approx 12{,}134$$

4. **Option (B) is correct.**

Explanation:

Using $$CI = P\left(1+\frac{R}{100}\right)^n - P$$

$$= 5{,}000\left(1+\frac{10}{100}\right)^2 - 500$$

$$= 5{,}000\times\frac{11}{10}\times\frac{11}{10} - 5{,}000$$

$$= ₹\,1{,}050$$

Given that $$SI = \frac{1}{2} \text{ of } CI$$

$$SI = \frac{1}{2}\times 1030 = 525$$

Using

$$SI = \frac{PRT}{100}$$

$$525 = \frac{5\times P\times 10}{100}$$

$$\frac{50P}{100} = 525$$

$$P = ₹\,1{,}050$$

5. **Option (D) is correct.**

Explanation: CI for the first two years

$$CI = P\left[1+\frac{R}{100}\right]^T - P$$

$$= 7{,}500\left(1+\frac{20}{100}\right)^2 - 7{,}500$$

$$= 7{,}500\times\frac{36}{25} = ₹\,3{,}300$$

CI for the next two years

Principal becomes = 7,500 + 3,300 = 10,800

$$CI' = P\left[1+\frac{R}{100}\right]^T - P$$

$$CI' = 10{,}800\left(1+\frac{10}{100}\right)^2 - 10{,}800$$

$$= 10{,}800\times\frac{121}{100} = 2268$$

Total interest = CI + CI'

= 3,300 + 2,268 = ₹ 5,568

6. **Option (C) is correct.**

Explanation: Principal for Anamika (loan of Anamika) = 15,000

Principal for Suman = 10,000

According to question

Amount paid by Anamika = 15,000 + 4,965 = 19,965

Using $$A = P\left(1+\frac{R}{100}\right)^T$$

$$19{,}965 = 15{,}000\left(1+\frac{R}{100}\right)^3$$

$$\frac{11}{10} = 1+\frac{r}{100}$$

$$r = 10\%$$

Rate of interest is the same for Suman and Anamika, i.e., 10%

$$\text{SI paid by Suman} = \frac{10{,}000 \times 3 \times 10}{100} = ₹\,3{,}000$$

7. **Option (C) is correct.**

Explanation:

Using $$A = P\left(1+\frac{r}{100}\right)^T$$

$$2{,}681.28 = 2{,}432\left(1+\frac{r}{100}\right)^2$$

$$\frac{441}{400} = \left(\frac{100+r}{100}\right)^2 \Rightarrow \frac{21}{20} = \frac{100+r}{100}$$

$$105 = 100 + r$$

$$r = 5\%$$

Now, SI on 2,432 at double the interest, i.e.,

$$(5 \times 2)\% = 10\%$$

$$SI = 2{,}432 \times \frac{10}{100} \times \frac{35}{8} = ₹\,1{,}064$$

8. **Option (D) is correct.**

Explanation:

$$\text{Installment} = P\left(1+\frac{R}{100}\right)^1 \quad ...(1)$$

$$\text{Installment} = P\left(1+\frac{R}{100}\right)^2 \text{ for 2 years} \quad ...(2)$$

From (1) and (2)

$$P = \frac{5{,}547}{\left(\frac{43}{40}\right)^1} + \frac{5{,}547}{\left(\frac{43}{40}\right)^2}$$

$$P = 5{,}547\ (3{,}320/1{,}830) = 9{,}960$$

$$\text{Total installment} = 11{,}094\ [\text{as } 5547 \times 2]$$

$$\text{Interest} = 11{,}094 - 9{,}960 = ₹\,1{,}134$$

9. **Option (B) is correct.**

Explanation:

Using $$P = A\left(1+\frac{R}{100}\right)^T$$

$$\text{Interest} = [\text{Installment} + \text{Installment}] - P$$

where P = loan amount

According to question

$$P = \frac{5{,}808}{\left(1+\frac{1}{10}\right)} + \frac{5{,}808}{\left(1+\frac{1}{10}\right)^2}$$

$$P = 5{,}280 + 4{,}800 = 10{,}080$$

$$\text{Interest} = [5{,}808 + 5{,}808] - 10{,}080$$

$$= 11{,}616 - 10{,}080 = ₹\,1{,}536$$

10. **Option (A) is correct.**

Explanation:

Using $$\text{Amount} = P\left(1+\frac{R}{100}\right)^T$$

$$A = 8{,}000\left[1+\frac{6.5}{12 \times 100}\right]^{18}$$

$$= ₹\,8{,}816.97$$

11. **Option (C) is correct.**

Explanation: Given,

Simple interest in 3 years = ₹ 1200

Let the principal amount = ₹ P

Rate of interest = 8%

Using, $$SI = \frac{PRT}{100} \Rightarrow 1200 = \frac{P \times 8 \times 3}{100}$$

$$\Rightarrow P = 5000$$

Now, rate of interest = 10% annum

Time = 2 years

Using, $$A = P\left(1+\frac{r}{100}\right)^2$$

$$\Rightarrow A = 10000\left(1+\frac{10}{100}\right)^2 \Rightarrow A = 10000 \times \frac{11}{10} \times \frac{11}{10} = 12100$$

So, compound interest = 12100 – 10000 = ₹ 2100

12. **Option (A) is correct.**

Explanation:

Using $$D = P\left(\frac{R}{100}\right)^2$$

Where, D is the difference between CI and SI with same rate of interest and two years time

$$20.25 = \frac{P \times 81}{10{,}000}$$

$$P = ₹\,2{,}500$$

13. **Option (A) is correct.**

Explanation:

Using $$CI = P\left(1+\frac{R}{100}\right)^T - P$$

$$CI = P\left[1+\frac{6}{100}\right]^3 - P \quad ...(1)$$

Finding value of P

$$SI = 6{,}750 = \frac{6 \times 3 \times P}{100}$$

$$P = 37{,}500$$

Using value of P in (1)

$$CI = 37{,}500\left[\left(1+\frac{6}{100}\right)^3 - 1\right] = ₹\,7{,}163.12$$

14. **Option (A) is correct.**

Explanation: $$SI = \frac{P \times R \times T}{100}$$

$$= \frac{2 \times 12P}{100} = 24\,P/100$$

$$\text{Amount} = SI + \text{Principal} = \frac{124P}{100}$$

According to question

$$\frac{124P}{100} = 15{,}500$$

$$P = 12{,}500$$

$$\text{Time} = 1.5 \text{ year}$$

$$R = 10\%$$

Using, $A = P\left(1+\frac{R}{100}\right)^T$

for half yearly R becomes $\frac{R}{2}$ while T becomes 2 × T

$$= 12{,}500 \times \left(1+\frac{10}{200}\right)^{1.5\times 2}$$

$$= 12{,}500 \times \left(\frac{210}{200}\right)^3$$

$$= 14{,}470.315 = ₹\ 14{,}470$$

15. Option (C) is correct.

Explanation:

Given: Principal amount = ₹ 8000

Time = 3 years

SI = ₹ 3600

Let rate of interest = R% per annum

We have,

$$\Rightarrow \quad SI = \frac{P \times R \times T}{100}$$

$$\Rightarrow \quad 3600 = \frac{8000 \times R \times 3}{100}$$

$$\Rightarrow \quad R = 15\% \text{ per annum}$$

So, rate of interest for 8 months = $15 \times \frac{8}{12}$

= 10% per 8 months

Time = 2 year

Number of cycles for compound interest

= 24/8 = 3

We have, $A = P\,(1 + \frac{r}{100})^n$

$$\Rightarrow \quad A = 8000\,(1 + \frac{10}{100})^3$$

$$\Rightarrow \quad A = 8000 \times \frac{11}{10} \times \frac{11}{10} \times \frac{11}{10}$$

= 10648

So, total amount after 2 years = 10648

16. Option (A) is correct.

Explanation:

Let T = 15%

$$\text{Simple interest} = \frac{P \times R \times T}{100}$$

$$= \frac{6{,}000 \times 3 \times 15}{100} = ₹\ 2{,}700$$

Giving through options

T + 5 = 20%

$$\text{CI after two years} = 6{,}000 \times \frac{44}{100} = 2{,}640$$

Difference = 2,700 – 2,640 = ₹ 60

So,value of T = 15% is correct.

17. Option (C) is correct.

Explanation: Total rate of interest after 2 years

$$= 10 + 10 + \frac{10 \times 10}{100} = 21\%$$

[Using successive percentage change]

21% of P = 1,050

P = 5,000

Using the value of P to calculate time in simple interest

$$2{,}000 = \frac{3{,}125 \times 6 \times 3}{100}$$

T = 5 years

18. Option (D) is correct.

Explanation:

Let principal amount tent = ₹x

Rate of interest, R = 10% per annum

Time period = 1 year 9 months

Amount after 1 year

$$= x + \frac{x \times 10 \times 1}{100} = \frac{11}{10}x$$

Amount after next 9 months

$$= \frac{11}{10}x + \frac{\frac{11}{10}x \times 10 \times \frac{9}{12}}{100}$$

[9 months = $\frac{9}{12}$ years]

$$= \frac{11}{10}x + \frac{33x}{400} = \frac{473}{400}x$$

Compound interest = Amount – Principal

$$1460 = \frac{473}{400}x - x$$

$$1460 = \frac{73x}{400}$$

$$x = \frac{1460 \times 400}{73} = 8000$$

∴ Amount lent = ₹8000

19. Option (B) is correct.

Explanation:

Using $A = P\left(1+\frac{R}{100}\right)^T$

and $SI = \frac{PRT}{100}$

$$6{,}750 = \frac{P \times 3 \times 12}{100}$$

P = 18,750

Using the value of P to calculate CI

We know that, Rate become half in case of CI compounded half yearly and time period becomes double.

New rate = 10%, Time period = 4

$$A = 18{,}750 \times \left(1+\frac{10}{100}\right)^4$$

$$= 18{,}750 \times \left(\frac{110}{100}\right)^4$$

A = 27,451.8 ≈ ₹ 27,452

CI = Amount – Principal

27,452 – 18,750 = ₹ 8702

20. Option (D) is correct.

Explanation: Using amount after 1 year formula = $\frac{b^2}{a}$

[b = amount in n+1 years; a = amount in years]

$$= \frac{29,635.2 \times 29,635.2}{a} = 26,880$$

Rate of interest = Percentage change in initial amount with respect to final amount

$$= \frac{(28,224 - 26,880)}{26,880} \times 100 = 5\%$$

Amount after 1 year = Principal amount + 5% of Principal

$$1.05\text{ P} = 26,880$$

$$\text{P} = ₹\ 25,600$$

21. Option (D) is correct.

Explanation: According to question

$$\text{P}\left[\frac{11}{10} \times \frac{11}{10} - 1\right] - \frac{\text{P} \times 2 \times 8}{100} = 225$$

$$\text{P} = \frac{22,500}{5}$$

Hence, P = ₹4,500 [P = Principal amount]

Level-3: EXPERT

1. Option (B) is correct.

Explanation:

Using $\text{SI} = \frac{\text{P} \times \text{R} \times \text{T}}{100}$ - (Scheme A)

$$1,950 = \frac{15 \times 2 \times \text{P}}{100}$$

$$\text{P} = ₹\ 6,500$$

Scheme (B) P = 6,500 + x

R = 10% p.a.

Total rate of interest for 2 years $= 10 + 10 + \frac{10 \times 10}{100}$

[Using successive percentage]

= 21%

CI = 21% of (6,500 + x)

$$1,680 = \frac{21}{100} \times (6,500 + x)$$

Hence, x = 8,000 – 6,500 = ₹ 1,500

2. Option (A) is correct.

Explanation: Assuming principal = 100

At the end of 3 years

$$\text{Amount} = 100 \times \left(1 + \frac{\text{R}}{100}\right)^3 \quad ...(1)$$

$$\left[\text{Using A} = \text{P}\left(1 + \frac{\text{R}}{100}\right)^{\text{T}}\right]$$

At the end of five years

$$\text{A} = 100 \times \left(1 + \frac{\text{R}}{100}\right)^5 \quad ...(2)$$

Dividing (2) by (1)

$$2 \div 1 = \left(1 + \frac{\text{R}}{100}\right)^2 = 1.1881$$

$$\frac{\text{R}}{100} = 0.09$$

$$\text{R} = 9\%$$

3. Option (B) is correct.

Explanation: Assuming Principal = 100 P

After 2 years, Amount $= 100\text{P} \times \frac{11}{10} \times \frac{11}{10} = 121\text{P}$

$$\left[\text{Using A=P}\left(1+\frac{\text{R}}{100}\right)^{\text{T}}\right]$$

$$121\text{P} = 18,634$$

$$100\text{P} = \frac{18,634}{121} \times 100 = ₹\ 15,400$$

4. Option (B) is correct.

Explanation:

Using

$$\text{P} = \frac{\text{Amount}}{\left(1+\frac{\text{r}}{100}\right)} + \frac{\text{Amount}}{\left(1+\frac{\text{r}}{100}\right)^2} \; .... \frac{\text{Amount}}{\left(1+\frac{\text{r}}{100}\right)^n}$$

Formula for installments

where Amount = installment

$$\text{P} = \frac{35,280}{\left(1+\frac{5}{100}\right)} + \frac{35,280}{\left(1+\frac{5}{100}\right)^2}$$

P = 33,600 + 32,000 = 65,600

5. Option (C) is correct.

Explanation:

Using

$$\text{Amount} = \text{P}\left(1+\frac{\text{R}_1}{100}\right)\left(1+\frac{\text{R}_2}{100}\right)\left(1+\frac{\text{R}_3}{100}\right)$$

$$4,630.08 = \text{P} \times \left(1+\frac{4}{100}\right) \times \left(1+\frac{5}{100}\right) \times \left(1+\frac{6}{100}\right)$$

P = 4,630.08 × 25 × 20 × 100/(21 × 26 × 106)

= ₹ 4,000

6. Option (A) is correct.

Explanation:

SI for 5 years = 60% of principal $= \frac{\text{P} \times \text{R} \times 5}{100}$

R% = 12%

$$\text{CI} = \text{P}\left(1+\frac{\text{R}}{100}\right)^2 - \text{P}$$

$$= 6,250\left(1+\frac{12}{100}\right)^2 - 6,250$$

$$= 6,250\left(\frac{28}{25}\right)^2 - 6,250 = ₹\ 1,590$$

7. Option (D) is correct.

Explanation:

Given:

Principal amount = ₹ 46000

Rate of interest = 15% per annum

And time $= 2\frac{2}{5}$ years

We have, total amount $= \text{P}\left(1+\frac{r}{100}\right)^n$

So, total amount after 2 years $= P\left(1+\frac{15}{100}\right)^n$

$= 46000 \times \frac{23}{20} \times \frac{23}{20} = ₹\,60835$

Now for 2/5 years, the rate of interest $= 15 \times \frac{2}{5} = 6\%$

And principal amount = ₹ 60835

So total amount $= 60835\left(1 + \frac{6}{100}\right) = ₹\,64485.1$

So, compound interest $= 64485.1 - 46000 \approx ₹\,18485$

8. **Option (D) is correct.**
Explanation: Rate for Scheme A = 10%
Effective Rate of Interest for 2 years

$= 10 + 10 + \frac{10 \times 10}{100} = 21\%$

Rate for Scheme B = 12%

Effective Rate $= 12 + 12 + \frac{(12 \times 12)}{100} = 25.44\%$

According to question

21% = 1,050

$25.44\% = \frac{1,050}{21} \times 25.44 = ₹\,1,272$

9. **Option (C) is correct.**
Explanation:

Using $A = P\left(1+\frac{r}{100}\right)^t$

$6,261 = 8,000\left(1+\frac{5}{100}\right)^t$

$\left[R = \frac{R}{2} \text{ for half yearly}\right]$

$\left(\frac{21}{20}\right)^t = \left(\frac{21}{20}\right)^3$

t = 3 half year = one and half year

Now, $A = P\left(1+\frac{r}{100}\right)^t$

$= 8,000\left(1+\frac{20}{100}\right)\left(1+\frac{10}{100}\right)$

$= 8,000 \times \frac{120}{100} \times \frac{11}{10} = 10,560$

CI = 10,560 – 8,000 = 2,560
(CI = Amount – Principal)

10. **Option (B) is correct.**
Explanation: Difference between years is 1.

A : B = 107 : 100
Total unit = $107x + 100x = 207x$
Given $207x = 51,750$
$x = 250$
$107x = 26,750$ [Sum borrowed by A]

11. **Option (A) is correct.**
Explanation: Using amount to be paid in installment
= 79,860 – 60,000 = Rs 19,860
Assuming installment be I

$$19,860 = \frac{I}{\left(1+\frac{10}{100}\right)} + \frac{I}{\left(1+\frac{10}{100}\right)^2} + \frac{I}{\left(1+\frac{10}{100}\right)^3}$$

[Using formula for installments]

$I = 19,860 \times \frac{1,331}{3,310} = 7,986$

12. **Option (C) is correct.**
Explanation: Effective rate for 2 years in CI

$= 10 + 10 + \frac{10 \times 10}{100} = 21\%$

Assuming x and y be the principal amount on SI and CI, respectively

$x + \frac{(2 \times x \times 10)}{100} = y + \frac{(21y)}{100}$

$\frac{x}{y} = \frac{121}{120}$

Given

(121 + 120) 241 = 12,050
1 = 50
Principal on CI = 120 = 50 × 120 = ₹ 6,000

13. **Option (B) is correct.**
Explanation: Assuming he invested "L" in part 1 and (25,000 – L) in part 2.
According to question

$\frac{(L \times 11 \times 2)}{100} + (25,000 - L) \times \frac{11}{10} \times \frac{11}{10} - (25,000 - L)$

= 5,370

L = 5,37,000 – 30,25,000 + 25,00,000
= 12,000

Hence, he invested "L", i.e., ₹12,000 in simple interest.

14. **Option (D) is correct.**
Explanation: According to question

$\frac{P \times R \times T}{100} = 3,600$

$\frac{3,125 \times 6 \times 3}{100} = 3,600$

R = 15%

Now, for 8 monthly compounded

$\left[\text{R becomes } R \times \frac{8}{12}\right]$

$\text{Amount} = 8,000 \times \left(1+\frac{10}{100}\right)^{\frac{24}{8}} = 10,648$

$\left[\text{Using, } A = P\left(1+\frac{R}{100}\right)^T\right]$

15. **Option (D) is correct.**
Explanation: Money borrowed = 12,000
Total amount repaid = 4,800 + 9,240 = 14,040
Interest = total amount paid – money borrowed
= 2,040

$\text{Amount} = 12,000\left(1+\frac{R}{100}\right)^2 \left[\text{Using } A = P\left(1+\frac{R}{100}\right)^T\right]$

$R = 8.2\% \approx 8\%$

16. Option (C) is correct.

Explanation: Amount after 2 years

$$= 30,800 \times \left(1+\frac{10}{100}\right)^2 \quad \left[\text{Using } A = P\left(1+\frac{R}{100}\right)^T\right]$$

= ₹ 37,268

But he paid 13,268

Remaining amount = 37,268 – 13,268 = 24,000

$$\text{Amount after one year} = 24,000 \times \frac{11}{10} = 26,400$$

17. Option (D) is correct.

Explanation:

$$\text{Using} \quad A = P\left(1+\frac{R}{100}\right)^t$$

$$= P\left(1+\frac{10}{100}\right)^1 = \frac{11}{10}P$$

But he paid 7,700

$$\text{So,} \quad P = 7,700 \times \frac{10}{11} = ₹\ 7,000$$

Using

Total amount = Principal + interest

i.e. 7,000 + 4,000 = ₹ 11,000

$$\text{So,} \quad P = 11,000 \times \frac{10}{11} = ₹\ 10,000$$

18. Option (D) is correct.

Explanation:

$$\text{Using} \quad SI = \frac{PRT}{100}$$

$$= \frac{1,60,000 \times 2 \times 10}{100} = ₹\ 32,000$$

When compounded half yearly

$$r' = \frac{r}{2}$$

$$t' = 2t$$

$$\text{Amount} = P\left(1+\frac{r}{200}\right)^{2t}$$

Compounded half yearly/semi quarterly

$$A = 160000\left[1+\frac{10}{200}\right]^4 = ₹\ 194481$$

Amount = CI + Principal

1,94,481 = CI + 1,60,000

CI = 34,481

Amount / Profit gained by A = CI – SI

= 34,481 – 32,000 = ₹ 2,481

19. Option (A) is correct.

Explanation: Compound interest at 10% p.a. in 2 years

$$\text{Effective rate of interest} = 10 + 10 + \frac{10 \times 10}{100} = 21\%$$

According to question

21% of principal = 1,050

Principal (P) = 5,000

$$\text{Now} \quad 2,000 = \frac{5,000 \times 8 \times t}{100}$$

$$\left[\text{Using } SI = \frac{P \times R \times T}{100}\right]$$

t = 5 years

20. Option (A) is correct.

Explanation: Assuming share of younger and elder sons be ₹ P and (16,400 – P)

According to question

Amount of ₹ P after 3 years

= Amount of ₹ (16,400 – P) after 2 years

$$P\left(1+\frac{5}{100}\right)^3 = (16,400 - P)\left(1+\frac{5}{100}\right)^2$$

$$\left[\text{Using } A=P\left(1+\frac{R}{100}\right)^T\right]$$

$$\frac{21}{20}P + P = 16,400$$

$$P = \frac{16,400 \times 20}{41}$$

P = 8,000

21. Option (C) is correct.

$$\textit{Explanation:} \quad \frac{A}{P} = \frac{19,965}{15,000} = \left(\frac{11}{10}\right)^3$$

Hence, Rate = 10%

$$\text{Hence,} \quad SI = 10,000 \times \frac{1}{100} \times 3$$

$$\left[\text{Using } SI=\frac{P \times R \times T}{100}\right]$$

= 3,000

22. Option (B) is correct.

Explanation:

$$\text{Using} \quad A = P\left(1+\frac{R}{100}\right)^t$$

$$3,515.20 = 3,125\left(1+\frac{x}{100}\right)^3$$

x = 4%

According to question:

Rate = $(x + 2)\%$ = 6%

$$\text{Using} \quad SI = \frac{PRT}{100}$$

$$\frac{3,125 \times 6 \times 3}{100} = 562.50$$

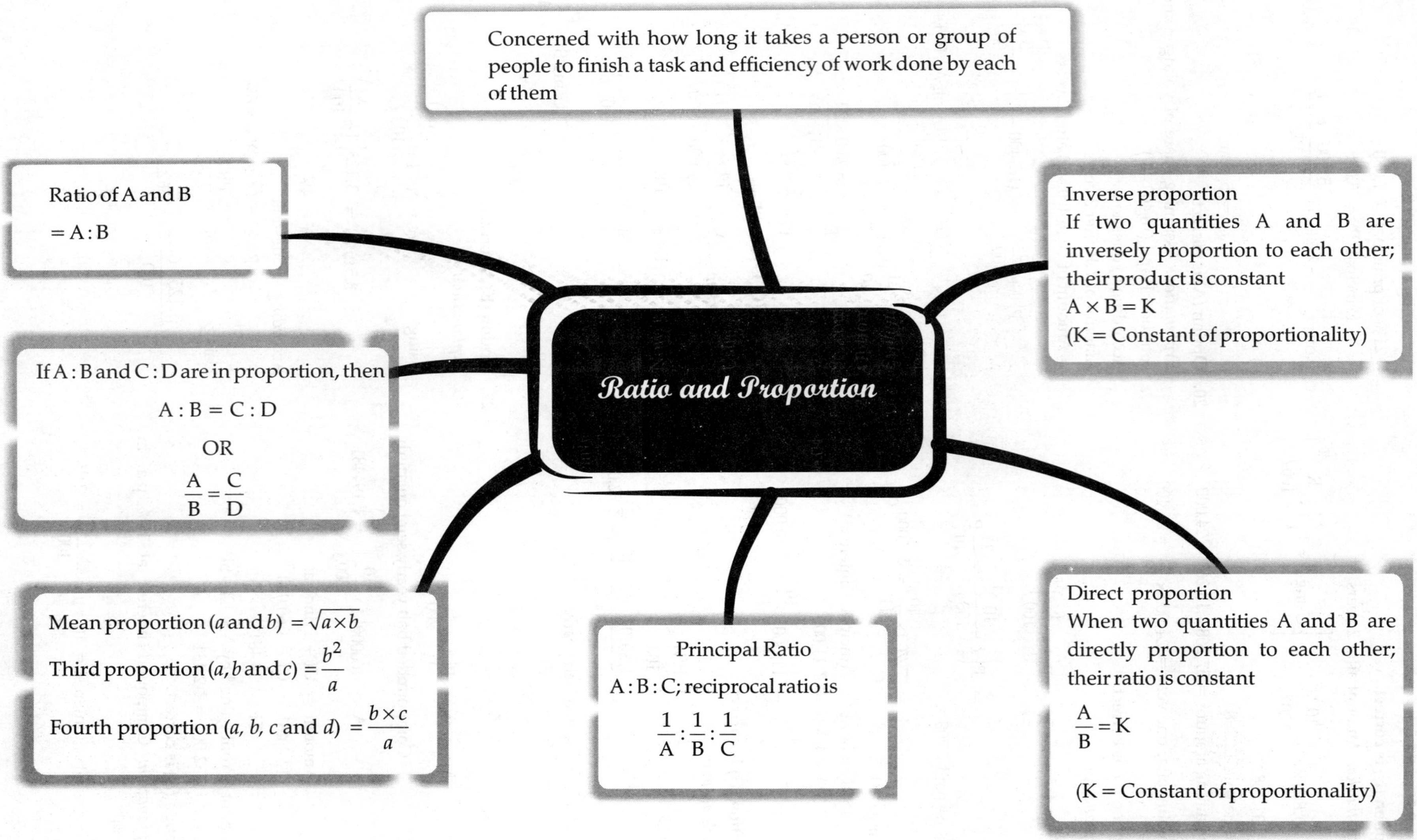
Ratio and Proportion
Concerned with how long it takes a person or group of people to finish a task and efficiency of work done by each of them
Ratio of A and B
= A : B
If A : B and C : D are in proportion, then
A : B = C : D
OR
$\frac{A}{B} = \frac{C}{D}$
Mean proportion (a and b) = $\sqrt{a \times b}$
Third proportion (a, b and c) = $\frac{b^2}{a}$
Fourth proportion (a, b, c and d) = $\frac{b \times c}{a}$
Principal Ratio
A : B : C; reciprocal ratio is
$\frac{1}{A} : \frac{1}{B} : \frac{1}{C}$
Inverse proportion
If two quantities A and B are inversely proportion to each other; their product is constant
A × B = K
(K = Constant of proportionality)
Direct proportion
When two quantities A and B are directly proportion to each other; their ratio is constant
$\frac{A}{B} = K$
(K = Constant of proportionality)

Chapter 5

Ratio and Proportion

LEARNING OBJECTIVES:

- Methods to solve questions related to ratio and proportions.
- Equivalent ratio, means, extreme.
- Method to compare two quantities.
- Questions asked in various competitive exams such as SSC, Bank, Railway, UPSC, CSAT, etc.
- Application of ratio–proportion in other topics of quantitative aptitude.

IMPORTANT FORMULA

- Ratio and proportion are two important mathematical concepts that are used to compare quantities and establish relationships between them.
- A ratio is a comparison of two or more quantities in terms of their size. Ratios can be expressed in different forms, such as fractions, decimals, or percentages. For example, if we have two quantities A and B, then their ratio is expressed as A:B, A/B, or A to B.
- Proportion, on the other hand, is a statement of equality between two or more ratios. If two ratios are equal, they are said to be in proportion. Proportions can be represented in various forms, such as fractions, decimals, or percentages. For example, if we have two ratios A:B and C:D, then we can express them as A/B = C/D or A:B::C:D, where the symbol "::" means "is to" or "as".
- In practical terms, ratios and proportions are used in a variety of settings, such as in finance, cooking, and construction. For instance, in finance, ratios are used to compare a company's financial performance to its peers or to its own historical data. In cooking, ratios are used to determine the right proportions of ingredients in a recipe. In construction, ratios and proportions are used to ensure that structures are built with the correct dimensions and proportions.
- In addition to their practical applications, ratios and proportions also have important theoretical properties. For example, they can be used to solve various types of problems, such as scaling, indirect proportion, and mixture problems. Furthermore, they are closely related to other mathematical concepts, such as fractions, decimals, and percentages, as well as to algebraic concepts, such as equations and inequalities.
- Overall, the concepts of ratio and proportion are fundamental to many fields of study and have broad applications in real-world settings. A strong understanding of these concepts is essential for success in many areas of academic and professional life.

- There are several important formulas for ratio and proportion that are commonly used in various mathematical applications. Here are some of the most important ones:

1. **Ratio Formula:** The formula for calculating the ratio between two quantities A and B is:

   Ratio of A and B = $\frac{A}{B}$
2. **Proportion Formula:** The formula for calculating the proportion between two ratios A : B and C : D is:
   A : B = C : D, or A/B = C/D, or A/C = B/D
3. **Mean Proportional Formula:** The mean proportional of two numbers a and b is the square root of their product, i.e.,
   Mean proportional of a and b = $\sqrt{(a \times b)}$
4. **Third Proportional Formula:** If three numbers a, b, and c are in proportion, then the third proportional is given by:
   Third proportional of a, b, and c = $(b^2) / a$
5. **Fourth Proportional Formula:** If four numbers a, b, c, and d are in proportion, then the fourth proportional is given by:

   Fourth proportional of a, b, c, and d = $\frac{(b \times c)}{a}$
6. **Direct Proportion Formula:** When two quantities A and B are directly proportional to each other, their ratio is constant. The formula for direct proportion is:

   $\frac{A}{B} = k$, where k is the constant of proportionality.

7. **Inverse Proportion Formula:** When two quantities A and B are inversely proportional to each other, their product is constant. The formula for inverse proportion is:
$A \times B = k$, where k is the constant of proportionality.
These formulas can be used to solve various types of problems involving ratio and proportion, such as scaling, indirect proportion, and mixture problems.

Example 1: The ratio of two numbers A and B is 5 : 8. If 5 is added to each of A and B, then the ratio of A and B becomes 2 : 3. The sum of A and B is:

(a) 42 (b) 78
(c) 65 (d) 91

Sol. (c) $A : B = 5x : 8x$

$$\frac{5x+5}{8x+5} = \frac{2}{3}$$

$$x = 5$$

$$A + B = 13x \Rightarrow 65$$

Example 2: Fourth proportion to 12, 18 and 6 is the same as the third proportion to k and 6. What is the value of k?

(a) $3\sqrt{6}$ (b) 13.4
(c) 4 (d) 3

Sol. (c) Fourth proportion $= \frac{18 \times 6}{12} = 9$

Third proportion $= \frac{36}{k}$

According to the question,

$$9 = \frac{36}{k} \Rightarrow k = 4$$

Example 3: The ratio of present ages of A and B is 7 : 8. After 6 years from now, the ratio of their ages will be 8 : 9. If C's present age is 10 years more than the present age of A, find the present age of C.

(a) 56 (b) 52
(c) 59 (d) 45

Sol. (b)

7 : 8
X
8 : 9

1 unit → 6
7 → 42 years
Present age of A = 42
Present age of C = 52

Example 4: A, B and C are partners. They share profits in the ratio of 5 : 3 : 6. If A earns ₹ 1,92,380 as his share of profit, then the share of C is:

(a) ₹ 82,448 (b) ₹ 1,15,428
(c) ₹ 1,60,317 (d) ₹ 2,30,856

Sol. (d) A : B : C
5 : 3 : 6
5 unit = 1,92,380
Then 6 unit = 2,30,856

Example 5: What is the ratio between the fourth proportional of 3, 4, 9 and the mean proportional of 2 and 98?

(a) 7 : 8 (b) 7 : 6
(c) 6 : 7 (d) 8 : 5

Sol. (c) Required ratio $= \frac{9 \times 4}{3} : \sqrt{9 \times 98}$

$= 12 : 14 = 6 : 7$

Example 6: Divide Rs 8,288 between A, B and C such that the proportion of their shares is 5 : 7 : 9. The share of C is :

(a) ₹ 2,032 (b) ₹ 3,552
(c) ₹ 3,872 (d) ₹ 2,612

Sol. (b) C's share $= 8{,}288 \times \frac{9}{21} =$ ₹ 3,552

Example 7: If $a : b : c = \frac{1}{4} : \frac{1}{3} : \frac{1}{2}$, then $\frac{a}{b} : \frac{b}{c} : \frac{c}{a} = ?$

(a) 12 : 9 : 8 (b) 9 : 8 : 24
(c) 8 : 9 : 24 (d) 9 : 12 : 8

Sol. (b) $a : b : c = 3 : 4 : 6$

So, $\frac{3}{4} : \frac{4}{6} : \frac{6}{3} = 9 : 8 : 24$

Level 1 Beginner

1. What is the difference in the mean proportional between 1.8 and 3.2 and the third proportional to 5 and 3? [SSC CGL 2021]
(A) 0.6 (B) 0.4 (C) 0.5 (D) 0.7
2. If $x : y = 4 : 5$, then the value of $(8x - 6y) : (9x - 7y)$ is: [SSC CHSL 2021]
(A) 2 : 1 (B) 7 : 2 (C) 2 : 3 (D) 1 : 3
3. What is the ratio of the mean proportional between 1.2 and 10.8 to the third proportional to 0.2 and 1.2? [SSC CHSL 2021]
(A) 1 : 3 (B) 1 : 2 (C) 2 : 1 (D) 3 : 1
4. If x is the mean proportional between 12.8 and 64.8 and y is the third proportional to 38.4 and 57.6, then $2x : y$ is equal to : [SSC CGL 2019]
(A) 2 : 3 (B) 1 : 2 (C) 3 : 4 (D) 4 : 5
5. If the average price of three chairs is Rs 14,014 and their prices are in the ratio of 3 : 4 : 7, then the highest price of chair is : [SSC CPO 2020]
(A) 3,003 (B) 1,001 (C) 21,021 (D) 5,005
6. If A is $\frac{1}{6}$ of C and B is twice of A, and the average of A, B and C is 30, find the difference between A and C. [SSC CPO 2020]
(A) 60 (B) 40 (C) 80 (D) 50
7. ₹ 7,80,516 is divided among A, B, C and D in the proportion of 2 : 3 : 4 : 3. The share of C is: [SSC CGL 2020]
(A) ₹ 1,3,0086 (B) ₹ 2,24,562
(C) ₹ 2,60,172 (D) ₹ 1,95,129

8. If $x : y = 3 : 2$ and $x + y = 90$, then the value $(x - y)$ is: [SSC CHSL 2020]
(A) 12 (B) 18 (C) 16 (D) 14

9. Two numbers are respectively 25% and 60% more than a third number. The ratio of the two numbers is: [SSC CHSL 2020]
(A) 20 : 30 (B) 20 : 35
(C) 25 : 32 (D) 21 : 31

10. Twice the salary of A is five times the salary of B, and four times the salary of B is equal to twice the salary of C. If the salary of C is ₹ 1,600, then the salary of A is: [SSC CPO 2019]
(A) ₹ 2,000 (B) ₹ 3,000
(C) ₹ 2,500 (D) ₹ 2,600

11. What is the ratio of the mean proportional between 4.8 and 10.8 and the third proportional to 0.4 and 2.4? [SSC CGL 2018]
(A) 2 : 1 (B) 3 : 2 (C) 1 : 2 (D) 2:3

12. Three partners P, Q and R invest ₹ 1,000, ₹ 1,200 and ₹ 1,500, respectively, in a business. What should be the share of Q if the total profit is ₹ 666? [SSC 2023]
(A) ₹ 216 (B) ₹ 275 (C) ₹ 252 (D) ₹ 284

13. Eight years ago, the ratio of ages of A and B was 9 : 10. The ratio of their ages 4 years from now will be 12 : 13. What is the age of C now, if his age is 6 years more than that of A? [SSC CHSL 2018]
(A) 56 (B) 42 (C) 50 (D) 48

14. If the radius of a sphere is thrice than the radius of a hemisphere, then what will be the respective ratio of their volumes? [SSC CHSL 2023]
(A) 27 : 1 (B) 16 : 1 (C) 54 : 1 (D) 18 : 1

15. Two numbers are in the ratio 3 : 4. On increasing each of them by 30, the ratio becomes 9 : 10. The numbers are: [SSC CHSL 2019]
(A) 30,40 (B) 15, 20 (C) 12, 16 (D) 18, 24

16. ₹ 40,06,736 is divided among A, B and C such that the ratio between A and B is 2 : 3 and B and C is 1 : 2. The share of C is: [SSC CPO 2019]
(A) ₹ 73,952 (B) ₹ 1,10,928
(C) ₹ 2,64,796 (D) ₹ 2,21,856

17. If $x : y : z = 3 : 4 : 5$ and $x + y + z = 96$, then what is the value of z? [SSC MTS 2019]
(A) 42 (B) 36 (C) 32 (D) 40

18. The expenditure and savings of a person are in ratio of 4 : 3. His savings increase by 1/5 of his income and income remains the same. What is the new ratio of his expenditure and savings? [SSC CHSL 2023]
(A) 12 : 17 (B) 14 : 17 (C) 13 : 22 (D) 15 : 13

19. Two numbers are in the ratio 5 : 7. If the first number is 20, then the second number will be : [SSC CGL 2020]
(A) 18 (B) 28 (C) 8 (D) 32

20. A certain amount is divided among Sunita, Amit and Vibha in the ratio of 2 : 3 : 4. If Vibha gets ₹ 14,416, then the total amount is : [SSC CGL 2021]
(A) ₹ 43,248 (B) ₹ 3,664
(C) ₹ 32,436 (D) ₹ 16,219

Level 2 Intermediate

1. If 2,145 : x :: 3,003 : 42, then the value of y so that x : 2,508 :: y : 11,704, is: [SSC CHSL 2020]
(A) 212 (B) 156 (C) 140 (D) 96

2. If $p/q = r/s = t/u = 2/5$, then what is the value of $(4p + 3r + 7t) : (4q + 3s + 7u)$? [SSC CHSL 2023]
(A) 4 : 11 (B) 3 : 7
(C) 2 : 5 (D) 5 : 9

3. A sum of ₹ 8,200 was divided among A, B and C in such a way that A had ₹ 500 more than B and C had ₹ 300 more than A. How much was C's alone share? [SSC CPO 2020]
(A) 2,000 (B) 2,300 (C) 3,100 (D) 2,800

4. Seven years ago, the ratio of ages of A and b was 4 : 5. Eight years hence, the ratio of the ages of A and B will be 9 : 10. What is the difference between their present ages? [SSC CPO 2020]
(A) 3 (B) 6 (C) 2 (D) 4

5. A certain sum was to be divided between A and B in the ratio 8 : 5. However, be mistake, it was divided in the ratio 5 : 8. Thus, A gets ₹300 less than his original share. Find the sum. [SSC CHSL 2023]
(A) ₹2,600 (B) ₹1,500 (C) ₹1,300 (D) ₹600

6. If x is subtracted from each of 24, 40, 33 and 57, the numbers obtained are in proportion. The ratio of $(5x + 12)$ to $(4x + 15)$ is: [SSC CGL 2021]
(A) 4 : 3 (B) 14 : 13 (C) 7 : 4 (D) 7 : 5

7. Two numbers are in the ratio 7 : 5. On diminishing each of them by 40, the ratio becomes 27 : 17. The sum of the numbers is: [SSC CHSL 2018]
(A) 300 (B) 240 (C) 325 (D) 275

8. The ages of A and B are in the ratio 5 : 7. Five years ago, their ages were in the ratio 5 : 8. The respective present ages are: [SSC CPO 2018]
(A) 20, 28 (B) 15, 21 (C) 10, 14 (D) 25, 40

9. What is the sum of mean proportional between 10.8 and 4.8 and the third proportional of 2 and 4? [SSC CPO 2018]
(A) 10.2 (B) 11.2 (C) 8.2 (D) 15.2

10. If $a : b : c = 1 : 3 : 5$, what is the value of $\frac{4a-b+2c}{3(a+b+c)}$? [SSC CHSL 2019]
(A) $\frac{8}{27}$ (B) $\frac{10}{27}$ (C) $\frac{11}{27}$ (D) $\frac{1}{3}$

11. What is the ratio between the fourth proportional of 3, 4, 9 and the mean proportional between 2 and 98? [SSC CHSL 2019]
(A) 7 : 8 (B) 7 : 6
(C) 8 : 7 (D) 6 : 7

12. ₹ 15,000 was invested by A and B together to start a small business. They got a profit of ₹ 2,000 at the end of the year. B took his profit share of ₹ 600. How much did A invest? [SSC CPO 2019]
(A) 9,000 (B) 2,000
(C) 10,500 (D) 10,000

13. The ratio of present ages of A and B is 8 : 9. After 9 years, the ratio will become 19 : 21. C is 3 years younger to B. What is the present age of C? [SSC CGL 2019]

(A) 49 (B) 48
(C) 51 (D) 52

14. The ratio of the present ages of A and B is 6 : 5. Four years ago, this ratio was 5 : 4. What will be the ratio of ages of A and B after 12 years from now? [SSC CHSL 2019]

(A) 3 : 2 (B) 8 : 7
(C) 9 : 8 (D) 7 : 6

15. The sum of three numbers is 777. The ratio between the first two numbers is 7 : 9 and the ratio between the second and third number is 8 : 7. The second number is: [SSC CPO 2018]

(A) 252 (B) 147
(C) 63 (D) 189

3 Level Expert

1. The salary of Mahesh is ₹ 12,000 more than Sumit. If the ratio of Mahesh's salary to a Sumit's salary is 7 : 4, then what is the salary of Sumit? [SSC MTS 2019]

(A) 13,000 (B) 14,000
(C) 15,000 (D) 16,000

2. There are 150 students in a school. If the ratio between the number of boys and girls is 4 : 1, then find the mean proportional between the number of boys and girls. [SSC MTS 2019]

(A) 50 (B) 40 (C) 30 (D) 60

3. In a right circular cylinder, the ratio of the curved surface to the total surface area is 3:7. Find the ratio of the height of the cylinder to the radius of its base. [SSC CHSL 2022]

(A) 3 : 4 (B) 2 : 3 (C) 3 : 2 (D) 4 : 3

4. If $x + y = 52$ and $x - y = 20$, then find the value of $x : y$? [SSC MTS 2019]

(A) 3 : 2 (B) 3 : 4 (C) 9 : 4 (D) 7 : 5

5. If a sum of ₹1,180 is to be divided among A, B and C, such that 2 times A's share, 5 times B's share and 7 times C's share, are equal, then A's share is: [SSC CGL 2020]

(A) ₹ 650 (B) ₹ 500
(C) ₹ 750 (D) ₹ 700

6. In a wallet, there are notes of the denominations of ₹ 10 and ₹ 50. The total notes is 12. The number of ₹ 10 and ₹ 50 notes are in the ratio of 1 : 2. Total money in the wallet is: [SSC CGL 2020]

(A) ₹ 280 (B) ₹ 360
(C) ₹ 440 (D) ₹ 110

7. ₹ 3,600 is divided between Seema, Komal and Rita, such that the ratios of the shares of Seema : Komal = 1.5 : 2 and Komal : Rita = 2 : 2.5. Find Rita's share. [SSC CHSL 2020]

(A) ₹ 1,500 (B) ₹ 1,300
(C) ₹ 1,400 (D) ₹ 1,200

8. The sum of 3 natural numbers is 280. If the ratio between the first number and second number is 2 : 3 and the ratio between the second & third number is 4 : 5, find the second number. [SSC CGL 2019]

(A) 90 (B) 86
(C) 96 (D) 80

9. A, B, C subscribe a sum of ₹ 75,500 for a business. A subscribes ₹ 3,500 more than B and B, subscribes ₹ 4,500 more than C. Out of a total profit of ₹ 45,300, how much does A receive? [SSC CPO 2020]

(A) 12,600 (B) 15,000
(C) 17,400 (D) 14,700

10. A solid cylinder has a radius of 9 cm and a height of 25 cm. What is the ratio of its total surface area to its curved surface area? [SSC CHSL 2022]

(A) 9 : 25 (B) 25 : 9 (C) 25 : 34 (D) 34 : 25

11. If $(a + b) : (b + c) : (c + a) = 7 : 6 : 5$ and $a + b + c = 27$, then what will be the value of $\frac{1}{a} : \frac{1}{b} : \frac{1}{c}$? [SSC CGL 2018]

(A) 3 : 6 : 4 (B) 3 : 2 : 4
(C) 4 : 3 : 6 (D) 3 : 4 : 2

12. The sum of three numbers is 280. If the ratio between the first and second numbers is 2 : 3 and the ratio between second and third number is 4 : 5, then the second number is: [SSC CGL 2020]

(A) 96 (B) 86 (C) 90 (D) 80

13. A sum of Rs. 11,236 is divided among A, B and C such that the ratio of the share of A and B is 3 : 5 and the ratio of the shares of A and C is 4 : 7. the share of B is: [SSC CHSL 2021]

(A) Rs. 3,392 (B) Rs. 2,544
(C) Rs. 4,452 (D) Rs. 4,240

14. Three numbers are in the ratio $\frac{1}{2} : \frac{2}{3} : \frac{3}{4}$. The difference between the greatest and smallest no. is 27. The smallest number is: [SSC CHSL 2018]

(A) 81 (B) 40
(C) 72 (D) 54

15. Two numbers are in the ratio 4 : 9. If both the numbers are increased by 12, the ratio becomes 11 : 21. The sum of the original numbers is: [SSC CPO 2018]

(A) 128 (B) 64
(C) 52 (D) 104

ANSWER KEY

Level-1: Beginner

1.	(A)	2.	(A)	3.	(B)	4.	(A)	5.	(C)	6.	(D)	7.	(C)	8.	(B)	9.	(C)	10.	(A)
11.	(C)	12.	(A)	13.	(C)	14.	(C)	15.	(B)	16.	(D)	17.	(D)	18.	(C)	19.	(B)	20.	(C)

Level-2: Intermediate

1.	(C)	2.	(C)	3.	(C)	4.	(A)	5.	(C)	6.	(B)	7.	(A)	8.	(B)	9.	(D)	10.	(C)
11.	(D)	12.	(C)	13.	(C)	14.	(C)	15.	(D)										

Level-3: Expert

1.	(D)	2.	(D)	3.	(A)	4.	(C)	5.	(D)	6.	(C)	7.	(A)	8.	(C)	9.	(D)	10.	(D)
11.	(C)	12.	(A)	13.	(D)	14.	(D)	15.	(D)										

Solutions with Detailed Explanations

Level-1: BEGINNER

1. **Option (A) is correct.**

Explanation:

Third proportional = $\frac{9}{5} = 1.8$

Mean proportional = $\sqrt{3.2 \times 1.8} = 2.4$

Difference = 0.6

2. **Option (A) is correct.**

Explanation: $x : y = 4 : 5$

$$\Rightarrow \frac{(8x-6y)}{9x-7y} = \frac{8(4)-6(5)}{9(4)-7(5)} = \frac{32-30}{36-35}$$

$\Rightarrow 2 : 1$

3. **Option (B) is correct.**

Explanation: Mean proportional between 1.2 and 10.8

$= \sqrt{1.2 \times 10.8} = 3.6$

Third proportional to 0.2 and 1.2

$= \frac{1.2 \times 1.2}{0.2} = 7.2$

$\Rightarrow$ Ratio = 1 : 2

4. **Option (A) is correct.**

Explanation:

Mean proportional $(x) = \sqrt{12.8 \times 64.8}$

$= \frac{8 \times 36}{10}$

Third proportional = $\frac{(57.6)^2}{38.4}$

$$\Rightarrow \quad 2x : y = \frac{2 \times 8 \times 36}{10} : \frac{864}{10} \Rightarrow 2 : 3$$

5. **Option (C) is correct.**

Explanation: 3 : 4 : 7

$$14k = 14{,}014 \times 3$$
$$k = 3{,}003$$
$$7k = 21{,}021$$

So, price of the highest price of chair = ₹ 21,021

6. **Option (D) is correct.**

Explanation:

$$A : C = 1 : 6$$
$$B : A = 2 : 1$$
$$A : B : C = 1 : 2 : 6$$
$$9k = 90 \Rightarrow k = 10$$
$$A - C = 5k = 50$$

7. **Option (C) is correct.**

Explanation: A : B : C : D

$$2 : 3 : 4 : 3 = 12$$
$$4 = \frac{7{,}80{,}516}{12} \times 4 = 2{,}60{,}172$$

8. **Option (B) is correct.**

Explanation:

$$x : y = 3 : 2, \; x + y = 90$$
$$5 \text{ unit} = 90 \quad \Rightarrow 1 = 18$$

9. **Option (C) is correct.**

Explanation:

125 : 160 : 100

125 : 160

25 : 32

10. **Option (A) is correct.**

Explanation: Let their salaries are A, B and C, respectively.

According to the question,

A : B and B : C

5 : 2 1 : 2

So, A : B : C = 5 : 2 : 4

4 unit = 1,600

1 unit = 4,00

5 unit = 2,000

So, the salary of A = ₹ 2,000

11. Option (C) is correct.

Explanation: Mean proportional of 4.8 and 10.8

$$= \sqrt{4.8\times10.8} = \sqrt{\frac{16\times3\times12\times9}{100}} = 7.2$$

3rd proportional of 0.4 and 2.4

$$= 0.4 \xrightarrow{\times6} 2.4 \xrightarrow{\times6} 14.4$$

$$\text{Ratio} = \frac{7.2}{14.4} = 1:2$$

12. Option (A) is correct.

Explanation:

Ratio of profit of P, Q and R = 1000:1200:1500

= 10:12:15

Share of Q in profit of ₹660 = 12 37

× 666 = ₹216

13. Option (C) is correct.

Explanation:

A : B

9 : 10

12 : 13

3 units = 12

1 unit = 4

So, Age of A = 48 – 4 = 44

Age of C = 44 + 6 = 50

14. Option (C) is correct.

Explanation:

Given that the radius of sphere is thrice than the radius of hemisphere.

Let the radius of hemisphere = x

Then the radius of sphere = $3x$

We have, volume of sphere = $\frac{4}{3}\neq r^3$

So, volume of the given sphere = $\frac{4}{3}\pi(3x)^3 = 36\pi x^3$

we have, volume of hemisphere = $\frac{2}{3}\pi r^3$

So, volume of the given hemisphere = $\frac{2}{3}\pi x^3$

$$\text{Required ratio} = \frac{36\pi x^3}{\frac{2}{3}\pi x^3} = \frac{54}{1}$$

15. Option (B) is correct.

Explanation: Let the numbers be $3k$ and $4k$.

$$\frac{3k+30}{4k+30} = \frac{9}{10}$$

$\Rightarrow$ $30k + 300 = 36k + 270$

$\Rightarrow$ $6k = 30$

$k = 5$

So, the numbers are 3 × 5 = 15 and 4 × 5 = 20

16. Option (D) is correct.

Explanation:

A : B = 2 : 3 B : C = 1 : 2

Balancing the ratio for B

A : B : C = 2 : 3 : 6

$$\text{Share of C} = 4{,}06{,}736 \times \frac{6}{11} = ₹\,2{,}21{,}856$$

17. Option (D) is correct.

Explanation: Let x = 3 units, y = 4 units, z = 5 units

According to question,

(3 + 4 + 5) units = 96

1 unit = 8

So, z = 5 units = 40

18. Option (C) is correct.

Explanation:

Given that the ratio of expenditure and savings = 4 : 3

Let the expenditure and savings are $4x$ and $3x$ respectively.

So, income = $4x + 3x = 7x$

According to the question,

$$\text{New saving} = 3x + 7x\times\frac{1}{5} = \frac{22x}{5}$$

$$\text{So, expenditure} = 7x - \frac{22x}{5} = \frac{13x}{5}$$

$$\text{Required ratio} = \frac{13x}{5} : \frac{22x}{5} = 13:22$$

19. Option (B) is correct.

Explanation: Ratio of two numbers is 5 : 7

First no. = $5a$

Second no. = $7a$

$5a = 20 \Rightarrow a = 4$

Second no. = 7 × 4 = 28

20. Option (C) is correct.

Explanation: Ratio of amount of Sunita, Amit and Vibha = $2x : 3x : 4x$

Total amount = $9x$

According to the question,

$4x$ = ₹ 14,416

Then, $9x = \frac{14{,}416}{4}\times 9$ = ₹ 32,436

Level-2: INTERMEDIATE

1. Option (C) is correct.

Explanation: 2,145 : x : : 3,003 : 42

$$\frac{2{,}145}{x} = \frac{3{,}003}{42}$$

$x = 30$

x : 2,508 : y : 11,704

$y = 140$

2. Option (C) is correct.

Explanation:

Given that $\frac{p}{q} = \frac{r}{s} = \frac{t}{u} = \frac{2}{5}$

So, $p = \frac{2}{5}q,\ r = \frac{2}{5}s,\ t = \frac{2}{5}u$

$$\text{So, value of } \frac{4p+3r+7t}{4q+3s+7u} = \frac{4\times\frac{2}{5}q+3\times\frac{2}{5}s+7\times\frac{2}{5}u}{4q+3s+7u}$$

$$= \frac{\frac{2}{5}(4q+3s+7u)}{4q+3s+7u} = \frac{2}{5}$$

3. **Option (C) is correct.**

Explanation: Let the share of A = x

Then, the share of B = $x - 500$

$$\text{Share of C} = x + 300$$
$$A + B + C = 3x - 200 = 8{,}200$$
$$3x = 8{,}400$$
$$x = 2{,}800$$

So, share of C = 3,100

4. **Option (A) is correct.**

Explanation: Ratio of A and B 7 years ago = 4 : 5

Ratio of A and B 8 years hence = 9 : 10

Total difference in time = 8 + 7 = 15 years

5 units = 15 years

1 unit = 3 years

5. **Option (C) is correct.**

Explanation:

Let the amount to be divided = ₹$13x$

A's original share = $\frac{8}{13} \times 13x$ = ₹$8x$

A's wrongly given share = $\frac{5}{13} \times 13x$ = ₹$5x$

According to question

$$8x - 5x = 300$$
$$\Rightarrow \quad 3x = 300$$
$$\Rightarrow \quad x = 100$$

∴ Amount = 13 × 100 = ₹1300

6. **Option (B) is correct.**

Explanation:

$$\frac{(24-x)}{(40-x)} = \frac{(33-x)}{(57-x)}$$
$$\frac{64-2x}{16} = \frac{90-2x}{24}$$
$$192 - 6x = 180 - 4x$$
$$x = 6$$
$$\frac{5x+12}{4x+15} \Rightarrow \frac{43}{39} \Rightarrow \left(\frac{14}{13}\right)$$

7. **Option (A) is correct.**

Explanation:

$$\frac{7x-40}{5x-40} = \frac{27}{17}$$
$$16x = 40 \times 10$$
$$x = 25$$
$$\text{Sum} = 12x = 12 \times 25 = 300$$

8. **Option (B) is correct.**

Explanation:

	A		B
Before	5	:	8

Difference: 3

Now	5	:	7

Difference: 2

A		B
5 × 2	:	8 × 2
5 × 3	:	7 × 3

	A	:	B	
=	10		16	5 = 5
	15		21	1 = 1

⇒ Present age = 15 and 21

9. **Option (D) is correct.**

Explanation:

$$\text{Mean proportion} = \sqrt{ab}$$
$$= \sqrt{10.8 \times 4.8} \Rightarrow 7.2$$
$$\text{Third proportional} = \frac{b^2}{a} \Rightarrow \frac{4 \times 4}{2} = 8$$
$$\text{Sum} = 7.2 + 8 = 15.2$$

10. **Option (C) is correct.**

Explanation:

$$a : b : c = 1 : 3 : 5$$

Let $a = k, b = 3k, c = 5k$

$$\frac{4a-b+2c}{3(a+b+c)} \Rightarrow \frac{4(k)-3k+2(5k)}{2(k+3k+5k)} = \frac{11k}{27k} = \frac{11}{27}$$

11. **Option (D) is correct.**

Explanation:

Fourth proportional of 3, 4, 9 = $\frac{9 \times 4}{3} = 12$

Mean proportional between 2 & 98 = $\sqrt{2 \times 98} = 14$

Required ratio = 12 : 14 = 6 : 7

12. **Option (C) is correct.**

Explanation:

Total profit = 2,000

Share of B = 600

Share of A = 2,000 – 600 = 1,400

Ratio of shares of A : B = 7 : 3

Amount invested by A = $15{,}000 \times \frac{7}{10} \Rightarrow 10{,}500$

13. **Option (C) is correct.**

Explanation: Let the present age of A and B be $8x$ and $9x$

Current age of C = $9x - 3$

According to question,

$$\frac{8x+9}{9x+9} = \frac{19}{21}$$
$$\Rightarrow \quad 168x + 189 = 171x + 171$$
$$\Rightarrow \quad 3x = 18$$
$$\Rightarrow \quad x = 6$$

So, the current age of C = 9 (6) – 3 = 51

14. **Option (C) is correct.**

Explanation: Let the age of A and B be $6k$ and $5k$, respectively.

According to question,

$$\frac{6k-4}{5k-4} = \frac{5}{4}$$
$$\Rightarrow \quad 24k - 16 = 25k - 20$$
$$\Rightarrow \quad k = 4$$

Required ratio = 6(4) + 12 : 5 (4) + 12

⇒ 9 : 8

15. Option (D) is correct.

Explanation:

$$A:B = 7:9$$
$$B:C = 3:7$$
$$A:B:C = 7:9:21$$

So, the second number $= 777 \times \frac{9}{37} = 189$

Level-3: EXPERT

1. Option (D) is correct.

Explanation:

Let the salary of Mahesh = 7 units

And salary of Sumit = 4 units

According to question

$$(7-4) \text{ units} = 12{,}000$$
$$1 \text{ unit} = 4{,}000$$
$$\text{Salary of Sumit} = 4 \text{ units} = 4x$$
$$= 4{,}000 = 16{,}000$$

2. Option (D) is correct.

Explanation: Let the total number of boys = 4 units and the total number of girls = 1 unit

According to question,

$$(4+1) \text{ units} = 150$$
$$1 \text{ unit} = 30$$
$$\text{Number of boys} = 4 \text{ units} = 4 \times 30 = 120$$
$$\text{Number of girls} = 1 \text{ unit} = 30$$

Mean proportion of number of boys & number of girls $= \sqrt{120 \times 30} = 60$

3. Option (A) is correct.

Explanation: Given that ratio between curved surface area to total surface area = 3 : 7

We know, curved surface area of a cylinder = $2\pi rh$

And the total surface area

$$= 2\pi rh + 2\pi r^2 = 2\pi r(h+r)$$

So, $\frac{2\pi rh}{2\pi r(h+r)} = \frac{3}{7}$

$\Rightarrow$ $7h = 3h + 3r$

$\Rightarrow$ $\frac{h}{r} = \frac{3}{4}$

4. Option (C) is correct.

Explanation:

$$x + y = 52 \quad ...(1)$$
$$x - y = 20 \quad ...(2)$$

Add (1) and (2)

$$2x = 72$$

$\Rightarrow$ $x = 36$

$$y = 52 - 36$$
$$= 36 - 20 = 16$$
$$\text{Ratio} = 36:16 = 9:4$$

5. Option (D) is correct.

Explanation: According to question,

$$2A = 5B = 7C$$
$$A:B:C = 35:14:10 = 59 \text{ units}$$
$$59 \text{ units} = ₹\,1{,}180$$
$$1 \text{ unit} = ₹\,20$$
$$\text{A's share} = ₹\,700$$

6. Option (C) is correct.

Explanation:

Notes of ₹ 10 and ₹ 50 are in the ratio = 1 : 2 = $3x$

$$3x = 12 \Rightarrow x = 4$$

There are 4 notes of ₹ 10 and 8 notes of ₹ 50

Total money in wallet = 40 + 400 = ₹ 440

7. Option (A) is correct.

Explanation:

Seema	:	Komal	:	Rita
1.5	:	2		
		2	:	2.5
3	:	4	:	5

$$\text{Total share} = 3 + 4 + 5 = 12 \text{ units}$$
$$\text{Rita's share} = \frac{5}{12} \times 3{,}600 = ₹\,1{,}500$$

8. Option (C) is correct.

Explanation: Let the three numbers be a, b, c

$$\frac{a}{b} = \frac{2}{3}, \frac{b}{c} = \frac{4}{5}$$

$a : b : c$

8 : 12 : 15

$$a = 8k, b = 12k, c = 15k$$
$$8k + 12k + 15k = 35k$$
$$35k = 280$$
$$k = 8$$
$$b = 96$$
$$\text{Second no.} = 96$$

9. Option (D) is correct.

Explanation: Total of A, B and C = 75,500

According to question,

$$A = B + 3{,}500$$
$$B = C + 4{,}500$$
$$A = C + 8{,}000$$
$$C + 800 + C + 4{,}500 + C = 75{,}000$$
$$3C + 12{,}500 = 75{,}000$$
$$C = 21{,}000$$
$$A = 24{,}500$$
$$\text{Share of A} = \frac{24{,}500}{75{,}500} \times 45{,}300 = 14{,}700$$

10. Option (D) is correct.

Explanation:

Given,

The radius of solid cylinder = 9 cm

And height = 25 cm

Using total surface area of cylinder = $2\pi rh + 2\pi r^2$

And curved surface area = $2\pi rh$

Required ratio $= \frac{2\pi rh + 2\pi r^2}{2\pi rh} = \frac{h+r}{h} = \frac{25+9}{25} = \frac{34}{25}$

11. Option (C) is correct.

Explanation:

$$2(a + b + c) = 18$$
$$a + b + c = 9 \text{ unit} \rightarrow 27$$
$$1 \text{ unit} \rightarrow 3$$

$$a = 27 - 6 \times 3 = 9$$
$$b = 27 - 5 \times 3 = 12$$
$$c = 27 - 7 \times 3 = 6$$
$$\frac{1}{a}:\frac{1}{b}:\frac{1}{c} = \frac{1}{9}:\frac{1}{12}:\frac{1}{6}$$

Required ratio after multiply by LCM 36 = 4 : 3 : 6

12. Option (A) is correct.

Explanation:

I : II : III = 8 : 12 : 15

35 unit → 280

12 unit → 96

13. Option (D) is correct.

Explanation:

Given amount = ₹ 11236

Ratio of the shares of A and B = 3 : 5

Ratio of the shares of A and C = 4 : 7

So, Ratio of the shares of A, B and C = 3×4 : 5×4 : 3×7
= 12 : 20 : 21

So, the share of B = $\frac{20}{12+20+21} \times 11236$ = ₹ 4240

14. Option (D) is correct.

Explanation: Ratio of numbers = 6 : 8 : 9

According to the question,

3 unit ⟶ 27

6 unit ⟶ 54

15. Option (D) is correct.

Explanation: Let numbers be $4x$, $9x$.

$$\frac{4x+12}{9x+12} = \frac{11}{21}$$
$$84x + 252 = 99x + 132$$
$$\text{Sum} = 13x = 13 \times 8 = 104$$

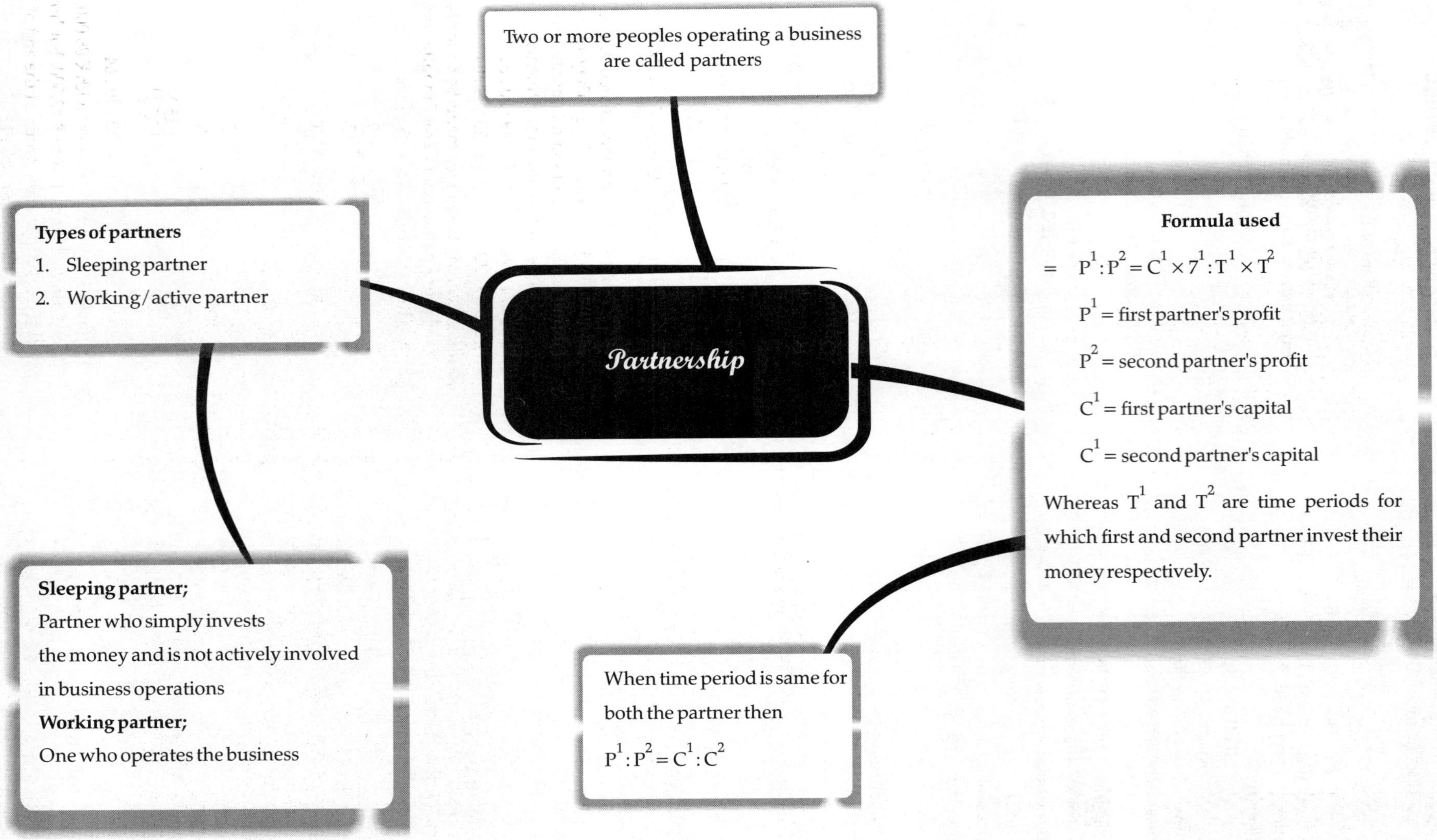
Partnership
Two or more peoples operating a business are called partners
Formula used
$= P^1 : P^2 = C^1 \times 7^1 : T^1 \times T^2$
P^1 = first partner's profit
P^2 = second partner's profit
C^1 = first partner's capital
C^1 = second partner's capital
Whereas T^1 and T^2 are time periods for which first and second partner invest their money respectively.
When time period is same for both the partner then
$P^1 : P^2 = C^1 : C^2$
Types of partners
1. Sleeping partner
2. Working/active partner
Sleeping partner;
Partner who simply invests the money and is not actively involved in business operations
Working partner;
One who operates the business

Chapter 6

Partnership

LEARNING OBJECTIVES:

- Partnership while starting a business or investing in scheme.
- Profit shares of different partners.
- Questions related to partnership, profit and shares of partners.
- Sleeping partner and active partner.
- Question asked in various competitive exams such as bank, SSC, railway, CSAT, CAT, etc.

➢ Two or more people operating a business together are referred to as partners, and the business arrangement is known as a partnership.

WORKING AND SLEEPING PARTNERS

➢ A partner who simply invests the money is referred to as a sleeping partner, whereas one who operates the business is known as a working partner.

FORMULA USED IN PARTNERSHIP

$P' : P'' = C' \times T' : C'' \times T''$

- P' = First partner's profit.
- C' = First partner's capital.
- T' = Period during which first partner contributed capital.
- P'' = Second partner's profit.
- C'' = Second partner's capital.
- T'' = Period during which second partner contributed capital.

I. When all of the partners' investments are for the same period of time, the gain or loss is distributed among the partners in proportion to their investments.

Suppose A and B invest ₹ a and ₹ b respectively for 12 months, i.e., one year, then at the end of the year:

(A's share of profit): (B's share of profit) = $a : b$.

II. When investments are for different time periods, equivalent capitals for a unit of time are calculated by taking (capital n number of units of time). The gain or loss is now divided by the capitals' ratio.

Suppose A invests ₹ n for k months and B invests ₹ m for l months then,

(A's share of profit): (B's share of profit)= $nk : ml$.

Example 1: A, B, C subscribe ₹ 50,000 for a business. A subscribes ₹ 4,000 more than B and B ₹ 5,000 more than C. Out of a total profit of ₹ 35,000, A receives:

(a) 8,400 (b) 14,700
(c) 2,500 (d) None of these

Sol. (b) Let C = x.

Then, B = $x + 5000$

and A = $x + 5000 + 4000$

= $x + 9000$

So, $x + x + 5000 + x + 9000 = 50{,}000$

$$3x = 36{,}000$$

$$x = 12{,}000$$

$$A : B : C = 21{,}000 : 17{,}000 : 12{,}000 = 21 : 17 : 12.$$

$$\text{So, A's share} = \left(35{,}000 \times \frac{21}{50}\right) = 14{,}700$$

Example 2: Three partners shared the profit in a business in the ratio 5 : 7 : 8. They had partnered for 14 months, 8 months and 7 months, respectively. What was the ratio of their investments?

(a) 5 : 71 : 80 (b) 49 : 20 : 64
(c) 10 : 9 : 30 (d) 20 : 49 : 64

Sol. (d) Assuming their investments be ₹ x for 14 months, ₹ y for 8 months and ₹ z for 7 months, respectively

Then, $14x : 8y : 7z = 5 : 7 : 8.$

$$\frac{14x}{8y} = \frac{5}{7}$$

$$98x = 40y$$

$$y = \left(\frac{49}{20}\right)x$$

and
$$\frac{14x}{7z} = \frac{5}{8}$$

$$z = \left(\frac{16}{5}\right)x$$

Hence, $x : y : z = 20 : 49 : 64$

Example 3: A began a business with ₹ 85,000. He was joined afterwards by B with ₹ 42,500. For how much period does B join, if the profits at the end of the year are divided in the ratio of 3 : 1?

(a) 4 months (b) 6 months
(c) 8 months (d) 5 months

Sol. (c) Assuming B joined for M months.

$$\left[\frac{(85,000 \times 12)}{(42,500 \times M)}\right] = \frac{3}{1}$$

$$M = \left(\frac{(85,000 \times 12)}{42,500 \times 3}\right) = 8$$

Example 4: Arun, Kamal and Vinay invested ₹ 8,000, ₹ 4,000 and ₹ 8,000, respectively in a business. Arun left after six months. If after eight months, there was a gain of ₹ 4,005, then what will be the share of Kamal?

(a) ₹ 890 (b) ₹ 1,335
(c) ₹ 990 (d) None of these

Sol. (a) Arun : Kamal : Vinay

$= (8,000 \times 6) : (4,000 \times 8) : (8,000 \times 8)$
$= 48 : 32 : 64 = 3 : 2 : 4$

Hence, Kamal's share $= 4,005 \times \left(\frac{2}{9}\right) =$ ₹ 890

Example 5: Moni started a software business by investing ₹ 50,000. After six months, Nalini joined her with a capital of ₹ 80,000. After 3 years, they earned a profit of ₹ 24,500. What was Moni's share in the profit?

(a) ₹ 10,000 (b) ₹ 10,500
(c) ₹ 7,000 (d) ₹ 11,000

Sol. (b) Moni : Nalini $= (50,000 \times 36) : (80,000 \times 30)$
$= 3 : 4$

Moni's share $= 24,500 \times \left(\frac{3}{7}\right) =$ ₹ 10,500

Level 1 Beginner

1. P invested Rs. 4000 for one year. Q joined him with an investment of Rs. 6000 after few months. If at the end of one year the ratio of profits of P and Q is 4: 3. then Q joined after how many months? **[SSC CHSL 2023]**
   (A) 4 months **(B)** 3 months
   (C) 8 months **(D)** 6 months
2. A invests ₹ 64,000 in a business. After few months B joined him with ₹ 48,000. At the end of year, the total profit was divided between them in the ratio 2:1. After how many months did B join ? **[SSC CHSL 2nd sitting 2013]**
   (A) 7 **(B)** 8 **(C)** 4 **(D)** 6
3. A and B invest ₹ 3,000 and ₹ 2,400 respectively in a business. If after one year there is a loss of ₹ 720, how much loss will B bear? (loss or profit is in proportion to their investments) **[SSC CGL 1st sitting 2016]**
   (A) 720 **(B)** 320 **(C)** 400 **(D)** 360
4. A, B and C invested amounts in the ratio 3:4:5, respectively. If the schemes offered compound interest at the rate of 20% per annum,15% per annum and 10% per annum, respectively, then what will be the ratio of their amounts after 1 year? **[SSC CGL 2017]**
   (A) 6:6:5 **(B)** 5:6:6
   (C) 6:5:6 **(D)** 5:6:5
5. Raman, Manan, and Kamal are partners and invest in a business such that Raman invests 2/5 th of total and Manan invest 3/8th of the total. What is the ratio of profit of Raman,Manan and Kamal, respectively? **[SSC Sub Inspector 2017]**
   (A) 16:9:15 **(B)** 16:15:9
   (C) 12:9:7 **(D)** None of these
6. Rohit started a business with Rs 75000 and after some months Simran joined him with Rs 60000. If the profit at the end of the year is divided in the ratio 3 : 1, then after how many months did Simran join Rohit? **[SSC CHSL 2017]**
   (A) 7 **(B)** 8 **(C)** 6 **(D)** 4
7. A started a business with a initial investment of ₹ 1,200. 'X' month after the start of business, B joined A with on initial investment of ₹ 1,500. If total profit was 1,950 at the end of year and B's share of profit was 750. Find 'X'. **[RRB PO 2017]**
   (A) 5 months **(B)** 6 months
   (C) 7 months **(D)** 8 months
8. A and B entered into a partnership by investing some amounts. The investment of A is twice of the investment of B. Another person C joined them after 4 months. At the end of a year, the profit share of A and C is equal. Then find the profit share of B is what percent of the profit share of C. **[RRB PO 2018]**
   (A) 50% **(B)** 60%
   (C) 66.66% **(D)** 80%

Level 2 Intermediate

1. If A invested ₹ 12,000 at some rate of interest of S.I and B joined him after 3 months investing 16,000 at same rate of interest if A leaves before 2 month of completion, then what will be the share of B's profit after 1 year if total profit is ₹ 22,000? **[RRB PO 2019]**
   (A) 10,000 **(B)** 14,000
   (C) 12,000 **(D)** 11,000
2. P invested 60% more than Q and R invested 20% more than Q. If ratio of investment time-period (P : Q : R) is 2 : 4 : 3 and the sum of profit shares of Q and R is ₹ 8,550 then find the profit share of P.
   (A) ₹ 3,200 **(B)** ₹ 4,000
   (C) ₹ 3,600 **(D)** ₹ 3,000

3. 'A' invested ₹ 4,000 and 'B' invested ₹ 1,000 more than A. After eight months 'C' invested ₹ 3,000. If at the end of the year 'C' gets profit of ₹ 700, then find the total profit. [IBPS RRB PO 2019]
(A) ₹ 7,000 (B) ₹ 3,600
(C) ₹ 3,200 (D) ₹ 2,500

4. A invests ₹ 12,000 for X months while B invests ₹ 16,000 for 9 months in a scheme. The profit share of B is ₹ 12,000 out of total profit ₹ 21,000. Then find the value of X ? [IBPS RRB PO 2020]
(A) 6 months (B) 7 months
(C) 8 months (D) 9 months

5. A started a business by investing ₹ 50,000. After 6 months B joined him by investing ₹ 75,000. After another 6 months C joined with ₹ 1,25,000. What is the ratio of profit shared after 2 years among A, B and C? [IBPS RRB Clerk 2017]
(A) 8:9:7 (B) 8:9:10 (C) 7:8:9 (D) 9:7:6

6. S, T and U started a business and their capitals are in the ratio of 3 : 4 : 6. At the end they receive the profit in the ratio of 1 : 2 : 3. What will be the respective ratio of time period for which they contributed their capitals? [SSC CHSL 2017]
(A) 3 : 2 : 2 (B) 2 : 3 : 3
(C) 2 : 2 : 3 (D) 4 : 5 : 3

7. A started a business, B and C joined him in the 1st year, they invested in the ratio of 5:4:7, respectively and the period for which they invested was in the ratio of 4:3:2, respectively. In the 2nd year, A doubled the investment, B and C continued with the same investment as they investor for the same number of month as they did in 1st year. The total profit in 2 years was 14,000. What is B's share of profit? [IBPS RRB Clerk 2019]
(A) 2,500 (B) 3,000 (C) 3,500 (D) 4,000

8. A, B and C started a business with their investments in the ratio 1 : 2 : 4. After 6 month A invested the half amount more as before and B invested same the amount as before while C withdrew 1/4th of his investment. Find the ratio of their profits at the end of the year. [IBPS RRB Clerk 2020]
(A) 5 : 12 : 14 (B) 12 : 5 : 14
(C) 5 : 11 : 13 (D) 7 : 13 : 23

3 Level Expert

1. A, B and C invested in a business in the ratio 6 : 8 : 9. If B invested for a period whose numerical value is 112.5% of B's investment but A and C invested for one year. If profit of B at the end of the year is 16,750 then what is the share of profit of C? [IBPS PO Mains 2016]
(A) 20,225 (B) 22,125
(C) 25,225 (D) 25,125

2. Three partners P, Q and R invested their amounts in ratio of 2 : 5 : 7. At the end of 6 months, 'P' added some more amount such that his investment become equals to half of sum of 'Q' and 'R' initial investment. If at the end of the year, Q's share in profit is ₹ 425, then find the total profit. [IBPS PO Mains 2018]
(A) 1,250 (B) 1,360 (C) 1,840 (D) 1,050

3. A invested ₹ X in a scheme. After 6 months, B joined with ₹ 4,000 more than that of A. After an year, ratio of profit of B to the total profit was 3 : 7. Find the value of X. [IBPS PO Mains 2019]
(A) 4,000 (B) 8,000
(C) 6,000 (D) 16,000

4. A and B started a business together with capital of ₹ 8,000 and ₹ 10,000, respectively. A left the business after 5 months while B continued. A gets 20% of total profit for managing business and remaining is distributed in ratio of their profit sharing. If after a year, A gets total profit of ₹ 2,500 then, find the total profit earned by 'A' and 'B' together. [IBPS PO 2016]
(A) 10,000 (B) 8,500 (C) 7,500 (D) 6,250

5. A, B and C entered into a partnership. A invested ₹ 2,560 and B ₹ 2,000. At the end of the year, they gained ₹ 1,105 out of which A got ₹ 320.C's capital was: [SSC CGL Tier II 2020]
(A) ₹ 4,280 (B) ₹ 2,480
(C) ₹ 4,820 (D) ₹ 2,840

6. A and B start an enterprise together, with A as active partner. A invest ₹ 4,000 and ₹ 2,000 after 8 months. B invest ₹ 5,000 and withdraws ₹ 2,000 after 9 months. Being the active partner, A takes ₹ 100 per month as allowance, from the profit. What is share of B if the profit for the year was is ₹ 6,700: [SSC CGL Tier-II 2017]
(A) ₹ 3,350 (B) ₹ 3,250
(C) ₹ 2,700 (D) ₹ 2,800

7. A and B started a business with ₹ 20,000 and ₹ 35,000, respectively. They agreed to share profit in the ratio of their capital. C joins the partnership with the condition that A, B and C will share profit equally and pays ₹ 2,20,000 as premium for this, to be shared between A and B. This is to be divided between A and B in the ratio: [SSC CGL 2010]
(A) 10 : 1 (B) 1 : 10 (C) 9 : 10 (D) 10 : 9

8. P, Q and R are partners and invest in a business. P invests 1/5th of total investments and Q invests 1/4th of the total investments. What is the ratio of investments of P, Q and R respectively? [SSC CHSL 2023]
(A) 4 : 8 : 11 (B) 4 : 5 : 11
(C) 4 : 7 : 11 (D) 4 : 5 : 9

ANSWER KEY

Level-1: Beginner

1.	(D)	2.	(C)	3.	(B)	4.	(A)	5.	(B)	6.	(A)	7.	(B)	8.	(C)

Level-2: Intermediate

1.	(C)	2.	(C)	3.	(A)	4.	(A)	5.	(B)	6.	(B)	7.	(B)	8.	(A)

Level-3: Expert

1.	(D)	2.	(B)	3.	(B)	4.	(D)	5.	(A)	6.	(C)	7.	(A)	8.	(B)

Solutions with Detailed Explanations

Level-1 : BEGINNER

1. **Option (D) is correct.**
Explanation: Given,
P invested ₹ 4000 for one year.
Let Q invested ₹ 6000 for x months.
According to the question,
$$\Rightarrow \frac{4000 \times 12}{6000 \times x} = \frac{4}{3}$$
$$\Rightarrow \quad x = 6$$
So, Q joined the business for 6 months.

2. **Option (C) is correct.**
Explanation: B entered after x months.
Ratio of equivalent capital for 1 year
$= 64,000 \times 12 : 48,000\ (12 - x)$
$= 16 : (12 - x)$
$$\frac{16}{12 - x} = \frac{2}{1}$$
$$x = 4 \text{ months}$$

3. **Option (B) is correct.**
Explanation: Loss will be divided according to their investment ratio.
$$A : B = 3,000 : 2,400, \text{ i.e., } 5 : 4$$
$$\text{Loss of B} = \left[\left(\frac{4}{(5+4)}\right)\right] \times 720 = ₹\ 320$$

4. **Option (A) is correct.**
Explanation: Let the amount invested = $3a$, $4a$, $5a$, respectively.
$\Rightarrow$ Compound interest for A = P(1 + 0.2) – P
$= 3a \times 1.2 - 3a = 0.6a$
$\Rightarrow$ Compound interest for B = P(1 + 0.15) – P
$= 4a \times 1.15 - 4a = 0.6a$
$\Rightarrow$ Compound interest for C = P(1 + 0.1) – P
$= 5a \times 1.1 - 5a = 0.5a$
$\Rightarrow$ Required ratio $= 0.6a : 0.6a : 0.5a = 6 : 6 : 5$

5. **Option (B) is correct.**
Explanation:
$$\text{Raman's share} = \frac{2}{5} = 40\%$$
$$\text{Manan's} = \frac{3}{8} = 37.5\%$$
$$\text{Kamal's share} = 100 - (40 + 37.5) = 22.5\%$$
$$\text{Required ratio} = 40 : 37.5 : 22.5 = 16 : 15 : 9$$

6. **Option (A) is correct.**
Explanation: Let Simran joined after 'n' months
$$\therefore \text{Share ratio} = \frac{75000 \times 12}{60000 \times (12 - n)} = \frac{3}{1}$$
$$\Rightarrow \frac{5 \times 12}{4 \times (12 - n)} = \frac{3}{1}$$
$$\Rightarrow 12 - n = 5 \Rightarrow n = 12 - 5 = 7 \text{ months}$$

7. **Option (B) is correct.**
Explanation: P's : Q' s
$1,200 \times 12 : 1,500 \times x$
$48 : 5x$
$$\text{Q's share} = 750 = \left[\frac{5x}{(48 + 5x)}\right] \times 1,950$$
$$x = 6 \text{ months}$$

8. **Option (C) is correct.**
Explanation: Lets take the investment of B be x
Therefore investment by A will be $2x$
$2x \times 12 : x \times 12 : C \times 8 = Pa : Pb : Pc$
$2x$ = A investment
12 = 12 months is the time period of A's investment.
We have taken C's investment as C and the time taken as 8 months because he joined after 4 months
$$\frac{2x \times 12}{C \times 8} = \frac{Pa}{Pc}$$
Taking this from the above equation formed.
We are given $Pa = Pc$
Therefore, $24x = 8C$
$C = 3x$

Now, we have the investment of all 3 (A, B and C)

B = x

A = $2x$

C = $3x$

$$\frac{C-B}{C} \times 100 = \frac{3x-x}{3x} \times 100 = 66.66\ \%$$

Level-2: INTERMEDIATE

1. **Option (C) is correct.**
Explanation: Ratio = 5 : 6

B's share = $22{,}000 \times \frac{6}{11}$ = ₹ 12,000

2. **Option (C) is correct.**
Explanation: Assuming the investment of Q = $100x$
Investment of P = $160x$
Investment of R = $120x$
Ratio of profit : P : Q : R
= $160x \times 2 : 100x \times 4 : 120x \times 3$
According to question,
19 unit = ₹ 8,550
So, 8 unit = 450 × 8 = ₹ 3,600

3. **Option (A) is correct.**
Explanation:
A : B : C = 4,000 : 5,000 : 3,000 (ratio of interest)
4 : 5 : 3
Rate of time = 12 : 12 : 4
Profit share ratio = 12 : 15 : 3
i.e., 4 : 5 : 1
1 unit = 700
So, 10 unit = 7,000 (total profit)

4. **Option (A) is correct.**
Explanation:
Profit of A = 21,000 – 12,000 = 9,000
Profit of A per month
= (12,000 ÷ 9,000) × 1,000 = 1,333.33
Value of x = 9,000 ÷ 1,333.33 = 6 months

5. **Option (B) is correct.**
Explanation:
The sums of money invested by A = ₹ 50,000 × 24
= ₹ 12,00,000
B = ₹ 75,000 × 18 = ₹ 13,50,000
C = ₹ 125,000 × 12 = ₹ 15,00,000
So, the ratio of profit share after 2 year among A, B and C is 12,00,000 : 13,50,000 : 15,00,000 or 12 : 13.5 : 15 or 24 : 27 : 30 or 8 : 9 : 10

6. **Option (B) is correct.**
Explanation:
Let capitals ratio of *S*, *T* and *U* are $3x$, $4x$ and $6x$
Let time period to contribute in business by *S*, *T* and *U* are n_1, n_2 and n_3 respectively
∴ Profit ratio = $3xn_1 : 4xn_2 : 6xn_3 = 1 : 2 : 3$
$3n_1 : 4n_2 : 6n_3 = 1 : 2 : 3$

$$\Rightarrow \frac{3n_1}{4n_2} = \frac{1}{2} \Rightarrow \frac{n_1}{n_2} = \frac{1}{2} \times \frac{4}{3} = \frac{2}{3} \quad \ldots \text{(i)}$$

and $\frac{n_2}{n_3} = \frac{3}{3}$ ... (ii)

from (i) and (ii)
$n_1 : n_2 : n_3 = 2 : 3 : 3$

7. **Option (B) is correct.**
Explanation: Let their investment in 1st year = $5x$, $4x$, $7x$

Time = 1 year, $\frac{3}{4}$ year, $\frac{1}{2}$ year

Investment in second year = $10x$, $4x$, $7x$

Time = 1 year, $\frac{3}{4}$ year, $\frac{1}{2}$ year

Ratio of profit = 15 : 6 : 7

Share of B = $\frac{6}{28} \times 14{,}000$ = ₹ 3,000

8. **Option (A) is correct.**
Explanation: Given in question, the ratio of investments of A , B and C = 1 : 2 : 4
Let the investments of A, B and C are P, 2P and 4P .
Ratio of equivalent capitals of A, B and C for 1 year
(P × 6 + 3P/2 × 6) : 2P × 6 + 4 P × 6 : 4P × 6 + 3P × 6
Ratio of equivalent capitals of A, B and C for 1 year
= 15P : 36P : 42P = 5 : 12 : 14

Level-3: EXPERT

1. **Option (D) is correct.**
Explanation: Investment ratio
$= 6 \times 12 : \frac{8 \times 8 \times 1{,}125}{100} : 9 \times 12$
2 : 2 : 3

Hence, C's profit = $16{,}750 \times \frac{3}{2}$ = 25,125

2. **Option (B) is correct.**
Explanation: Assuming the amount invested by P, Q and R be $2a$, $5a$ and $7a$, respectively and total profit be 'P'
⇒ Ratio of profit = $2a \times 6 + 6a \times 6 : 5a \times 12 : 7a \times 12$
⇒ Ratio of profit = 4 : 5 : 7

⇒ Q's share in profit = $\frac{5}{16}$ × P = 425

P = ₹ 1,360
Hence, total profit = ₹ 1,360

3. **Option (B) is correct.**
Explanation: A has invested ₹ X for 12 months and B has invested ₹X + 4,000 for 6 months only, then the profit share will also be for 6 months only.
The ratio of B's profit to that of total profit is 3:7,
Let B's profit is 3*x*
Then, A's profit will be 4*x*, as total profit is 7*x*.
So, A to B ratio will be 4 : 3

$$X : \frac{(X + 4,000)}{2} = 4 : 3$$

$$6x = 4x + 16,000$$

$$2x = 16,000$$

$$x = 8,000$$

4. **Option (D) is correct.**

Explanation: Assuming total profit = $100p$

A gets 20% profit = $20p$

Remaining profit shared in ratio

= 8,000 × 5 : 10,000×12

i.e., 1 : 3

$$A\text{'s profit} = 20p + 80p \times \frac{1}{4} = 40p$$

According to question

$$40p = 2,500$$

Hence, required profit = $100p$

$$= \left(\frac{2,500}{40}\right) \times 100 = 6,250.$$

5. **Option (A) is correct.**

Explanation: Let C's capital be ₹ p

Then, A : B : C = 2,560 : 2,000 : p

$$A\text{'s share} = 1105 \times \left(\frac{2,560}{(4,560 + p)}\right) = 320$$

$$320p + 14,59,200 = 28,28,800$$

$$p = 4,280$$

6. **Option (C) is correct.**

Explanation: Ratio of the equivalent capitals of A and B for 1 year

= (4,000 × 8 + 6,000 × 4) : (5,000 × 9 + 3,000 × 3)

= (32,000 + 24,000) : (45,000 + 9,000)

= 56,000 : 54,000 = 28 : 27

Sum of the terms of ratio = 28 + 27 = 55

A is an active partner.

Allowance got by A in 1 year = ₹ 1,200

Remaining profit = ₹ (6,700 – 1,200) = ₹ 5,500

$$\text{Hence, B's share} = ₹ \left(\frac{27}{55}\right) \times 5500 = ₹\ 2,700$$

7. **Option (A) is correct.**

Explanation: Ratio of total capital A and B

= 20,000 × 12 : 35,000 × 12 = 2,40,000 : 4,20,000

Now, C gives ₹2,20,000 to both to make the capital equal.

A's Capital = B's capital

= 2,40,000 : 4,20,000 + 2,00,000 : 2,00,000

= 44,000 : 4,40,000

If A takes ₹ 2,00,000 and B takes ₹ 20,000 from C then both have the equal capital

So required ratio of divided amount

= 2,00,000 : 20,000 = 20 : 2 = 10 : 1

8. **Option (B) is correct.**

Explanation: Let the total investment = x

$$\text{Investment of P} = \frac{x}{5}$$

$$\text{Investment of Q} = \frac{x}{4}$$

$$\text{So, investment of R} = x - \frac{x}{5} - \frac{x}{4} = \frac{11x}{20}$$

$$\text{Ratio of investment of P, Q and R} = \frac{x}{5} : \frac{x}{4} : \frac{11x}{20}$$

$$= 4 : 5 : 11$$

Average

Set: Collection of objects such as number, letter etc.

Average $= \dfrac{\text{Sum of data in a set}}{\text{No. of Data (observation)}}$

Average of 'n' consecutive natural number $= \dfrac{(n+1)}{2}$

Average of 1st n even consecutive natural numbers $= n(n+1)$

Average of 1st n odd consecutive natural numbers $= n^2$

Average of n consecutive odd numbers $= n$

Average of n consecutive odd numbers till $n = \dfrac{(n+1)}{2}$

'A' is the average and each of the number

	New Average
Added by a	A + a
Subtracted by a	A – a
Multiplied by a	A × a
Divided by a	$\dfrac{A}{a}$

Chapter 7

Average

LEARNING OBJECTIVES:

- Numbers and their mean values.
- Application in real life.
- Calculate run rate, bowling average in cricket match.
- Calculate problems related to weight, age, distribution of quantity.
- Questions asked in various competitive exams such as SSC, Bank, CSAT, Railway, etc.
- Problems based on ages.

- Averages are the most central values in a set of data. Simply divide the sum of all values in a set by the total number of values to calculate the average. In other words, an average value represents the data set's middle value. The data set can consist of anything, such as age, money, runs, etc.
- **Formula used to calculate average:** Average = [Sum of Data (or observations) in a set] / [Number of data (or observations) in that set]

  e.g., Average of numbers 5, 7, 8, 6, 12 will be:

  $$\frac{[5+7+8+6+12]}{5} = 7.6$$

- **Applications of average in real life:** In real life, the average formula has numerous applications. If we want to find the average age of men or women in a group, or the average male height in India, we add all the values and divide by the number of values.

  $$\text{Average} = \frac{\text{Sum of values}}{\text{Number of values}}$$

ARITHMETIC MEAN

- The most common type of Average is the Arithmetic mean. If n numbers are given, each denoted by a_i (where i = 1, 2, ..., n), then the arithmetic mean is the sum of the terms divided by n.

  $$\text{A.M.} = \frac{1}{n}\sum_{i=1}^{n} a_i = \frac{1}{n}(a_1 + a_2 + a_3 + a_4 + ... + a_n)$$

  n, is the number of observations

  i, represents the index of summation

  a_i = data value for the given index

GEOMETRIC MEAN

- The geometric mean is a method for determining a set's central tendency by taking the nth root of the product of n numbers. It is not the same as the arithmetic mean, in which we add the observations and divide the sum by the number of observations. However, in geometric mean, we find the product of all observations and then the nth root of the product, where n is the number of observations.

  $$\text{G.M.} = \sqrt[n]{x_1 x_2 ... x_n}$$

HARMONIC MEAN

- The reciprocal of the average of the reciprocals of the given data values is defined as the harmonic mean.
- The harmonic mean can be calculated using the following formula:

  Harmonic Mean, H.M.

  $$= \frac{n}{\left[\left(\frac{1}{x_1}\right) + \left(\frac{1}{x_2}\right) + \left(\frac{1}{x_3}\right) + ... + \left(\frac{1}{x_n}\right)\right]}$$

SOME IMPORTANT FORMULAE

- Average of 'n' consecutive natural numbers $= \frac{(n+1)}{2}$
- Average of the square of consecutive n natural numbers $= \frac{[(n+1)(2n+1)]}{6}$.
- Average of cubes of consecutive n natural numbers $= \frac{[n(n+1)^2]}{4}$
- Average of n consecutive even numbers = $(n+1)$
- Average of consecutive even numbers till n $= \left(\frac{n}{2}\right)+1$
- Average of n consecutive odd numbers = n
- Average of consecutive odd numbers till $n = \frac{(n+1)}{2}$

- Sum of 1st n even consecutive natural numbers is $= n(n + 1)$
- Sum of 1st n odd consecutive natural numbers is $= n^2$

Example 1: Two years ago, the average age of A and B was 26, and B is 5 years younger to C, then find the difference between the age of A and C?

(a) 8 (b) 10
(c) 9 (d) 12

Sol. (c) Total age of A and B = 2×26 (2 years ago)
= 52 years

Sum of present age of A and B = 52+2×2
= 52 + 4= 56 years

A's age after 5 years = 40 years
A's present age = 40 – 5 = 35 years
B's present age = 56 – 35 = 21 years
C's present age = 21 + 5 = 26 years

Hence, difference between the age of A and C
= 35 – 26 = 9 years

Example 2: The average weight of a class is 60 kg and average weight of boys in the class is 80 kg. The ratio of boys to girls in the class is 5:4. If there are 72 students in the class, then find the average weight of girls in the class?

(a) 53 kg (b) 54 kg
(c) 35 kg (d) 45 kg

Sol. (c) The average weight of the class = 60 kg
The average weight of boys in the class = 80 kg
The ratio of boys to girls in the class is 5:4
The number of students in the class = 72

The number of girls = $\frac{4}{9} \times 72 \Rightarrow 32$

The number of boys = $\frac{5}{9} \times 72 \Rightarrow 40$

Total weight of students in the class
= 72 × 60 ⇒ 4,320
The total weight of boy in class
= 40 × 80 ⇒ 3,200
The total weight of girls = total weight – total weight of boys ⇒ 4,320 – 3,200 = 1,120

The average weight of girls = $\frac{1120}{32} \Rightarrow 35$

Hence, the required answer is 35.

Example 3: There are 40 children in a class in which boys are 4 more than the girls. If the average weight of all the students is 42.5 kg and the average weight of all the girls is 48 kg, then find the average weight of all the boys?

(a) 53 kg (b) 32 kg
(c) 35 kg (d) 38 kg

Sol. (d) Assuming the number of girls = x
Then, number of boys = $x + 4$
Total number of children = 40 = $x + x + 4$
⇒ 36 = $2x$
⇒ x = 18
So, number of girls = 18
Number of boys = $x + 4 = 22$
Average weight of the students in the class
= 42.5 kg (given)
⇒ {Total weight of 18 girls
+ Total weight of 22 boys}/{40} = 42.5 ...(1)
If average weight of girls in the class is 48 kg

$\Rightarrow \frac{\{\text{Total weight of 18 girls}\}}{\{18\}} = 48$

⇒ Total weight of 18 girls = 864 ...(2)
Replacing value from (2) in (1),

$\frac{\{864 + \text{Total weight of 22 boys}\}}{\{40\}} = 42.5$

⇒ 864 + Total weight of 22 boys = 1,700
⇒ Total weight of 22 boys = 836
Hence, average weight of boys

$= \frac{\{\text{Total weight of 22 boys}\}}{\{22\}} = 38$

Example 4: The average weight of 60 students in a class was calculated as 40 kg. Later, it was found that the weight of one of the students was calculated as 36 kg, whereas his actual weight was 33 kg. What is the actual average weight of the students in the class?

(a) 53 kg (b) 39.95 kg
(c) 35.54 kg (d) 38.28 kg

Sol. (b) Total correct weight = (40 × 60) – 36 + 33
= 2,400 – 3 = 2,397 kg

Hence, required average weight = $\frac{2,397}{60}$
= 39.95 kg

Example 5: The average of 10 numbers is 23. If each number is increased by 4, what will the new average be?

(a) 27 (b) 39
(c) 54 (d) 28

Sol. (a) Average of 10 numbers = 23

$\frac{\text{Sum}}{\text{Total number}} = 23$

$\frac{\text{Sum}}{10} = 23$

Sum of the 10 numbers = 230
If each number is increased by 4, the total increase
= 4 × 10 = 40
New sum = 230 + 40 = 270

Hence, the new average = $\frac{270}{10} = 27$

SHORTCUT:
If each number is increased by 4, then the average will also increase by 4.
So, new average = 23 + 4 = 27

Example 6: The average weight of a team of seven players is 56 kg. The individual weights (in kg) of six of them are 52, 57, 55, 60, 59 and 55. Find the weight of the seventh player.

(a) 27 (b) 39
(c) 54 (d) 28

Sol. (c) Average weight of 7 players = 56 kg
Total weight of 7 players = (56 × 7) kg = 392 kg
Total weight of 6 players

$= (52 + 57 + 55 + 60 + 59 + 55)$ kg = 338 kg

Weight of the 7th boy = (total weight of 7 players) – (total weight of 6 players)

= (392 – 338) kg = 54 kg

Hence, the weight of the seventh player is 54 kg.

Example 7: A batsman makes a score of 64 runs in the 16th innings and thus increased his average by 3. Find his average after the 16th inning.

(a) 29 (b) 19
(c) 14 (d) 18

Sol. (b) Let the average after the 16th innings be A.

So, the average after the 15th innings will be (A – 3)

$$15(A - 3) + 64 = 16A$$
$$\Rightarrow A = 19$$

Hence, average after 16th innings is 19.

Example 8: The average age of the girls in a class is 16 years and that of the boys is 15 years. The average age for the whole class is:

(a) 25 years (b) 19 years
(c) 11 years (d) Data inadequate

Sol. (d) The number of boys, girls, or pupils in the class must be known in order to calculate the average, but neither quantity has been provided.

Therefore, the information is insufficient.

Example 9: In a family of 8, the boys eat on an average 72 kg of food and girls eat on an average 50 kg of food. The boys and girls are equal in number. A hungry girl named Neeru joined the family for dinner and the average consumption became 67. How much did Neeru eat (in kgs)?

(a) 112 kg (b) 119 kg
(c) 115 kg (d) None of these

Sol. (c) As boys and girls are equal so, there are 4 girls and 4 boys then, total consumption will be $72 \times 4 = 288$ (by boys) and $50 \times 4 = 200$ (by girls)

Total consumption = 288 + 200 = 488

But after including Neeru, the average consumption for 9 people is given to be 67.

So, the total consumption will be $67 \times 9 = 603$.

Hence, Neeru's consumption will be

= 603 – 488 = 115 kg

Example 10: In a match of 50 overs, team A's average runs for the first 30 overs was 4.5 runs/over while for the remaining 20 overs the average was 5.5 runs/over. Team B chased the target and lost by 10 runs.

Find the average runs per over scored by team B. (Team B played all the 50 overs).

(a) 4.7 (b) 5.2
(c) 8.3 (d) None of these

Sol. (a) Team A's average runs for the first 30 overs was 4.5 runs/over

$$\text{Run} = 30 \times 4.5 = 135$$

While for the remaining 20 overs the average was 5.5 runs/over

$$\text{Run} = 20 \times 5.5 = 110$$
$$\text{Total runs} = 135 + 110 = 245$$

Team B chased the target and lost by 10 runs.

$$\text{Total runs by B} = 245 - 10 = 235$$

Required average runs per over scored by team B

$$= \frac{235}{50} = 4.7$$

1 Beginner Level

1. The average of the first 100 positive integers is: [SSC CGL 1st Shift 2010]

(A) 50 (B) 50.5 (C) 51 (D) 55

2. In a family, the average of a father and a mother is 35 years. The average age of the father, mother and their only son is 27 years. What is the age of the son? [SSC CGL 1st Shift 2010]

(A) 12 years (B) 11 years
(C) 10.5 years (D) 10 years

3. The average of the first 1234 ________ numbers is equal to 1234. [SSC CHSL 2019]

(A) odd (B) even
(C) prime (D) natural

4. The average of odd numbers up to 100 is: [SSC CGL 2nd Shift 2010]

(A) 50.5 (B) 50 (C) 49.5 (D) 49

5. The average age of four boys, five years ago was 9 years. On including a new boy, the present average age of all the five is 15 years. The present age of the new boy is: [SSC CGL 1st Shift 2012]

(A) 14 years (B) 6 years
(C) 15 years (D) 19 years

6. The price of an article is raised by 45% and then two successive discounts of 15% each are allowed. Ultimately the price of the article is .... [SSC CHSL 2022]

(A) decreased by 7.7625%
(B) increased by 4.7625%
(C) decreased by 4.7625%
(D) increased by 7.7625%

7. The average temperature of Monday, Tuesday and Wednesday was 30°C and that of Tuesday, Wednesday and Thursday was 28°C. If the temperature on Monday was 35°C, then the temperature on Thursday was: [SSC CGL 2012]

(A) 33°C (B) 30°C (C) 29°C (D) 32°C

8. The mean of 19 observations is 24. If the mean of the first 10 observations is 17 and that of the last 10 observations is 24, find the 10th observation. [SSC CGL 1st Shift 2012]

(A) 65 (B) 37 (C) –46 (D) 53

9. The average age of a jury of 5 is 40. If a member aged 35 resigns and a man aged 25 becomes a member, then the average age of the new jury is: [SSC CGL 2nd Shift 2012]
(A) 30 (B) 38 (C) 40 (D) 42

10. The first number is one-third of the second number. The second number is 1.5 times of the third number. The third number is three times the fourth number. If the average of the four numbers is 10, find the largest of the number. [SSC CHSL 2022]
(A) 12 (B) 18 (C) 16 (D) 15

11. The average weight of 12 crewmen in a boat is increased by 1/3 kg, when one of the crewmen whose weight is 55 kg is replaced by a new man.What is the weight of that new men? [SSC CHSL 2012]
(A) 58 (B) 60 (C) 57 (D) 59

12. Out of 10 teachers of a school, one teacher retires and in his place, a new teacher of age 25 years joins. As a result, the average age of teachers is reduced by 3 years. The age (in years) of the retired teacher is: [SSC CGL 1st Shift 2013]
(A) 50 (B) 58 (C) 60 (D) 55

13. The average of 50 numbers is 38. If two numbers namely 45 and 55 are discarded, the average of the remaining numbers is: [SSC CGL 1st Shift 2013]
(A) 36 (B) 35 (C) 32.5 (D) 37.5

14. A cricket player after playing 10 tests scored 100 runs in the 11th test. As a result, the average of his runs is increased by 5. The present average of runs is: [SSC CGL 1st Shift 2013]
(A) 45 (B) 40 (C) 50 (D) 55

15. The average of nine numbers is 50. The average of the first five numbers is 54 and that of the last three numbers is 52. Then, the sixth number is: [SSC CGL 1st Shift 2013]
(A) 24 (B) 44 (C) 30 (D) 34

16. The average of the first nine integral multiples of 3 is [SSC CGL 1st Shift 2013]
(A) 15 (B) 18 (C) 21 (D) 12

17. Out of 40 boys in a class, the average weight of 30 boys is 60 kg and the average weight of the remaining is 56 kg.The average weight (in kg) of the whole class is: [SSC CGL 2nd Shift 2013]
(A) 58.5 (B) 58 (C) 57 (D) 59

18. The average of the first five multiples of 7 will be: [SSC CGL 2nd Shift 2013]
(A) 14 (B) 21 (C) 175 (D) 24.5

19. The average of 32, 34, 38, 21, 26 and x is 30. What will be the value of x? [SSC CHSL 2023]
(A) 31 (B) 29 (C) 27 (D) 28

20. The average of 20 numbers is 15 and the average of the first five is 12. The average of the rest is: [SSC CGL 2nd Shift 2013]
(A) 16 (B) 15 (C) 14 (D) 13

21. The average weight of 8 persons increased by 2.5 kg when a new person comes in place of one of them weighting 45 kg. What is the weight of the new person? [SSC CHSL 2022]
(A) 63 kg (B) 60 kg (C) 65 kg (D) 62 kg

22. The average of 30 numbers is 40 and that of the other 40 numbers is 30. The average of all the numbers is: [SSC CHSL 2013]
(A) 34.5 (B) $34\frac{2}{7}$ (C) 35 (D) 34

23. The average height of 8 students is 152 cm. Two more students of heights 144 cm and 155 cm join the group. What is the new average height? [SSC Multitasking 2014]
(A) 151.5 cm (B) 152.5 cm
(C) 151 cm (D) 150.5 cm

24. A boy found that the average of 20 numbers is 35 when he writes a number '61' instead of '16'. The correct average of 20 numbers is: [SSC Sub Inspector 2014]
(A) 32.75 (B) 37.25 (C) 34.75 (D) 34.25

25. The average salary of all the workers in a workshop is Rs 8,000. The average salary of 7 technicians is Rs 12,000 and the average salary of the rest is Rs 6,000. The total number of workers in the workshop is: [SSC CHSL 2014]
(A) 20 (B) 21 (C) 22 (D) 23

26. 3 years ago, the average age of a family of 5 members was 17 years. A baby having been born, the average age of the family is the same today. The present age of the baby is: [SSC CHSL 2014]
(A) 1 year (B) $1\frac{1}{2}$ years
(C) 2 years (D) 3 years

27. What is the arithmetic mean of the first 20 odd natural numbers? [SSC CGL 1st Sit. 2015]
(A) 17 (B) 19 (C) 22 (D) 20

28. The average of some natural numbers is 15. If 30 is added to the first number and 5 is subtracted from the last number, the average becomes 17.5. Then, the number of natural number is: [SSC Sub Inspector 2015]
(A) 20 (B) 30 (C) 15 (D) 10

29. The average of 13 results is 70. The average of the first seven is 65 and that of the last seven is 75, then the seventh result is : [SSC CHSL 2015]
(A) 70 (B) 70.5 (C) 68 (D) 67

30. The average of 100 observations was calculated as 35. It was found later that one of the observations was misread as 83 instead of 53. The correct average is: [SSC CGL 1st Shift 2016]
(A) 32.7 (B) 34.7 (C) 35.7 (D) 36.7

31. At an average of 80 km/h Shatabdi Express reaches Ranchi from Kolkata in 7 hours. Then, the distance between Kolkata and Ranchi is: [SSC CGL 1st Shift 2016]
(A) 560 km (B) 506 km (C) 560 m (D) 650 m

32. The average runs conceded by a bowler in 5 matches is 45 and 15.75 in other 4 matches. What is the average runs conceded by the bowler in 9 matches? [SSC CGL 2017]
(A) 15 (B) 32 (C) 35 (D) 53.5

33. The mean of marks secured by 60 students in division A of class X is 64, 40 students of division B is 60 and that of 60 students of division C is 58. Find the mean of marks of the students of three divisions of Class X. **[SSC CGL 2017]**
(A) 60.05 **(B)** 59.35 **(C)** 62.15 **(D)** 60.75

34. The average marks obtained by a class of 60 students is 65. The average mark of half of the students is found to be 85. The average mark of the remaining students is: **[SSC CGL 2nd Shift 2016]**
(A) 35 **(B)** 45 **(C)** 55 **(D)** 65

35. The average of 9 observations was found to be 35. Later on, it was detected that an observation 81 was misread as 18. The correct average of the observations is: **[SSC CGL 2nd Shift 2016]**
(A) 28 **(B)** 42 **(C)** 32 **(D)** 45

36. The average monthly income of A and B is Rs 15,050, the average monthly income of B and C is Rs 15,350 and the average income of A and C is Rs 15,200. The monthly income of A is: **[SSC Sub Inspector 2016]**
(A) Rs 15,900 **(B)** Rs 15,200
(C) Rs 14,900 **(D)** Rs 15,500

37. The average of 17 results is 60. If the average of the first 9 results is 57 and that of the last 9 results is 65, then what will be the value of the 9th result? **[SSC CGL 2017]**
(A) 39 **(B)** 78 **(C)** 117 **(D)** 156

38. What is the average of the squares of the first 19 natural numbers? **[SSC Sub Inspector 2017]**
(A) 124 **(B)** 127.5 **(C)** 130 **(D)** 133.5

39. In a match, average of runs scored by 5 players is 49. If the runs scored by four players are 75, 30, 62 and 21, respectively, then how many runs did the 5th player score? **[SSC Sub Inspector 2017]**
(A) 43 **(B)** 49 **(C)** 57 **(D)** 89

Level 2 Intermediate

1. The mean of 50 numbers is 30. Later, it was discovered that two entries were wrongly entered as 82 and 13 instead of 28 and 31. Find the correct mean. **[SSC CGL Ist Shift 2011]**
(A) 36.12 **(B)** 30.66 **(C)** 29.28 **(D)** 38.21

2. The average of three consecutive odd numbers is 12 more than one-third of the first of these numbers. What is the last of the three numbers? **[SSC CGL Ist Shift 2011]**
(A) 15 **(B)** 17 **(C)** 19 **(D)** 21

3. The average of 18 observations is recorded as 124. Later, it was found that two observations with values 64 and 28 were entered wrongly as 46 and 82. Find the correct average of the 18 observations. **[SSC CGL IInd Shift 2011]**
(A) $111\frac{7}{9}$ **(B)** 122 **(C)** 123 **(D)** $137\frac{3}{7}$

4. Average of the height of 286 students of a school is 50 unit. If the average of the height of the boys is 53 unit and the average of the height of the girls is 31 unit, then what will be the ratio of the total height of boys and the total height of girls respectively? **[SSC CHSL 2023]**
(A) 1004 : 91 **(B)** 530 : 31
(C) 1007 : 93 **(D)** 1111 : 62

5. A batsman in his 12th innings makes a score of 63 runs and there by increases his average scores by 2. What is his average after the 12th innings? **[SSC CHSL 2012]**
(A) 13 **(B)** 41 **(C)** 49 **(D)** 26

6. In a class, there are 39 students and their average weight is 51 kg. If we include the weight of the teacher, then the average weight becomes 51.2 kg. What is the weight of the teacher? **[SSC CHSL 2022]**
(A) 53 kg **(B)** 59 kg **(C)** 57 kg **(D)** 51 kg

7. Out of 20 boys, 6 are each of 1 m 15 cm in height, 8 are of 1 m 10 cm and rest are of 1 m 12 cm.The average height of all of them is: **[SSC Multitasking 2013]**
(A) 1 m 12 cm **(B)** 1 m 12.1 cm
(C) 1 m 21.1 cm **(D)** None of these

8. The average age of boys in the class is twice the number of girls in the class.The ratio of boys and girls in the class of 50 is 4:1. The total of the ages (in years) of the boys in the class is: **[SSC CGL 2014]**
(A) 2,000 **(B)** 2,500 **(C)** 800 **(D)** 400

9. There are 100 students in 3 sections A, B and C of a class. The average marks of all the 3 sections was 84. The average of B and C was 87.5 and the average marks of A is 70. The number of students in A was: **[SSC CGL 2014]**
(A) 30 **(B)** 35 **(C)** 20 **(D)** 25

10. The average weight of 15 oarsmen in a boat is increased by 1.6 kg when one of the crew, who weighs 42 kg is replaced by a new man. Find the weight of the new man (in kg). **[SSC CGL 1st Shift 2015]**
(A) 65 **(B)** 66 **(C)** 43 **(D)** 67

11. The batting average of a cricket player for 30 innings is 40 runs. His highest score exceeds his lowest score by 100 runs. If these two innings are not included, the average of the remaining 28 innings is 38 runs. The lowest score of the player is: **[SSC Multitasking 2014]**
(A) 18 **(B)** 20 **(C)** 12 **(D)** 15

12. Visitors to a show were charged ₹ 15 each on the first day, ₹ 7.50 on the second day, ₹ 2.50 on the third day and total attendance on three days was in the ratio 2:5:13, respectively. The average charge per person for the entire three days is: **[SSC CGL 2nd Shift 2016]**
(A) ₹ 5 **(B)** ₹ 5.50 **(C)** ₹ 6 **(D)** ₹ 7

13. The average of 5 members of a family is 24 years. If the youngest member is 8 years old, then what was the average age (in years) of the family at the time of the birth of the youngest member? **[SSC CGL 2017]**
(A) 16 **(B)** 20 **(C)** 24 **(D)** 32

14. The average age of 120 members of a society is 60.7 years. By addition of 30 new members, the average age becomes 56.3 years. What is the average age (in years) of newly joined members? [SSC CGL 2017]
(A) 36.5 (B) 37.2 (C) 38.3 (D) 38.7

15. Average of the marks of 132 students of a college is 50. If the average of the marks of the passed students is 55 and the average of the marks of the failed students is 35, then what will be the respective ratio of the total marks of passed students and the total marks of failed students? [SSC CHSL 2023]
(A) 1 : 3 (B) 11 : 7 (C) 33 : 7 (D) 21 : 8

16. The average age of 30 students is 20 years and average age of 20 other students is 30 years. The average age of the total number of students is: [SSC MTS 2017]
(A) 24 years (B) 48 years
(C) 25 years (D) 50 years

17. The average age of 30 students is 15 years. It was observed that while calculating the average age, the age of a student was taken as 15 years instead of 9 years. What will be the correct average age?
[SSC CHSL 2023]
(A) 14.2 years (B) 16.4 years
(C) 15.6 years (D) 14.8 years

18. In a class of 50 students, 46% are girls and the remaining are boys. The average of the boys' marks is 58 and that of the girls' is 62. What is the average marks of the whole class? [SSC CGL 2019]
(A) 59.84 (B) 60.65 (C) 60.38 (D) 60.12

19. In a class of 40 students, 60% are girls. The average of the girls' marks is 72 and that of the boys is 54. What is the average marks of the whole class?
[SSC CGL 2019]
(A) 65.4 (B) 65 (C) 64.8 (D) 52.2

20. In a class of 50 students, 60% are boys. The average marks of the boys is 62, and that of the girls is 68. What is the average marks of the whole class?
[SSC CGL 2020]
(A) 64.8 (B) 64.4 (C) 65.2 (D) 64.6

Level 3 Expert

1. There are 3 groups of person – male, female and children. There are 20 males and the number of females and children taken together is 4 more than that of the males. The average weight of males is 54 kg, that of females is 49 kg and that of children is 30 kg. If the average weight of the whole group is 48.25 kg, then what is the difference between the number of females and the number of children?
[SSC CHSL 2021]
(A) 17 (B) 14 (C) 10 (D) 7

2. The average weight of some students in a group is 58 kg. If students of average weight 54 kg leave the group, and 3 students weighing 53.6 kg, 54 kg and 57.4 kg join the group, then the average weight of the remaining students in the group will increase by 575 g. The number of students, initially, in the group is:
[SSC CHSL 2021]
(A) 40 (B) 45 (C) 35 (D) 50

3. In a class of 80 students, 60% participate in games and the rest do not. The average weight of the former group is 5% more than that of the latter. If the average weight of all the students is 51.5 kg, then what is the average weight (in kg) of the former group?
[SSC CHSL 2019]
(A) 57.6 (B) 54.5 (C) 60 (D) 52.5

4. The average weight of the students in a group was 75.4 kg. Later on, four students having weights, 72.9 kg, 73.8 kg, 79.5 kg and 87.4 kg joined the group. As a result, the average weight of all the students in the group increased by 0.24 kg. What was the number of students in the group initially? [SSC CHSL 2019]
(A) 46 (B) 36 (C) 50 (D) 48

5. The average of n numbers is 36. If each of 75% of the numbers is increased by 6 and each of the remaining numbers is decreased by 9, then the new average of the numbers is: [SSC CHSL 2020]
(A) 37.125 (B) 33.75 (C) 38.25 (D) 36.25

6. Set A contains seven numbers and the average of these numbers is 41. Set B contains five numbers and the average of these numbers is 44. The overall average of both the sets is: [SSC MTS 2019]
(A) 42.75 (B) 42.25 (C) 41.75 (D) 42.5

7. During his entire school life, John's average marks in science was 80% and his average marks in mathematics was 90%. If his combined average marks in science and mathematics was 84%, while the total marks obtained by him in science was 54,000, what was John's total marks obtained in mathematics?
[SSC CHSL 2022]
(A) 90000 (B) 81000 (C) 36000 (D) 60000

8. The daily average rainfall on 5 days of the week is 30 mm. If the rainfall on days 6th and 7th are 42 mm and 25 mm, respectively, then what is the average daily rainfall for the 7 days? [SSC MTS 2021]
(A) 31 (B) 29.5 (C) 33 (D) 28.5

9. A person was asked to guess his own weight. He estimated his weight to be over 70 kg but less than 80 kg. His friend estimated his weight to be more than 74 kg but less than 84 kg. His mother said that his weight is less than 78 kg. Assuming that the weights are a whole number and that the three had correctly guessed, then what is the average of the possible weights? [SSC CGL 2019]
(A) 76.5 (B) 76 (C) 77 (D) 75

10. The average weight of some students in a class was 58.4 kg. When 5 students having the average weight 62.8 kg joined the class, the average weight of all the

students in the class increased by 0.55 kg. The number of students initially in the class were: [SSC CGL 2021]
(A) 30 (B) 35 (C) 25 (D) 40

11. The average age of a number of persons in a group was calculated as 35 years, which was 2.5 years more than the correct average as there was an error in recording the age of two persons as 38.5 years and 40 years instead of 29 years and 22 years, respectively. The number of persons in the group was: [SSC CGL 2020]
(A) 11 (B) 12 (C) 15 (D) 16

12. The average of some numbers is 54.6. If 75% of the numbers are increased by 5.6 each and the rest are decreased by 8.4 each, then what is the average of the numbers so obtained? [SSC CGL 2020]
(A) 56.7 (B) 55.6 (C) 55.8 (D) 56.3

13. 24 students collected money for donation. The average contribution was ₹ 50. Later on, their teacher also contributed some money. Now, the contribution is ₹ 56. The teacher's contribution is: [SSC CGL 2021]
(A) 56 (B) 200 (C) 106 (D) 194

14. The average score in Mathematics of 90 students of sections A and B together is 49. The number of students in A was 25% more than that of B, and the average score of the students in B was 20% higher than that of the students in A. What is the average score of the students in A? [SSC CGL 2021]
(A) 44.5 (B) 44 (C) 45 (D) 45.5

15. The average marks of 30 boys is 88, and when the top scores were excluded, the average marks reduced to 87.5. If the top two scores differ by 2, then the highest marks is: [SSC CGL 2020]
(A) 94 (B) 96 (C) 92 (D) 90

ANSWER KEY

Level-1: Beginner

1.	(B)	2.	(B)	3.	(A)	4.	(B)	5.	(D)	6.	(B)	7.	(C)	8.	(C)	9.	(B)	10.	(B)
11.	(D)	12.	(D)	13.	(D)	14.	(C)	15.	(A)	16.	(A)	17.	(D)	18.	(B)	19.	(B)	20.	(A)
21.	(C)	22.	(B)	23.	(A)	24.	(A)	25.	(B)	26.	(C)	27.	(D)	28.	(D)	29.	(A)	30.	(B)
31.	(A)	32.	(B)	33.	(D)	34.	(B)	35.	(B)	36.	(C)	37.	(B)	38.	(C)	39.	(C)		

Level-2: Intermediate

1.	(C)	2.	(C)	3.	(B)	4.	(C)	5.	(B)	6.	(B)	7.	(B)	8.	(C)	9.	(C)	10.	(B)
11.	(A)	12.	(A)	13.	(B)	14.	(D)	15.	(C)	16.	(A)	17.	(D)	18.	(A)	19.	(C)	20.	(B)

Level-3: Expert

1.	(C)	2.	(B)	3.	(D)	4.	(A)	5.	(C)	6.	(B)	7.	(C)	8.	(A)	9.	(B)	10.	(B)
11.	(A)	12.	(A)	13.	(B)	14.	(C)	15.	(B)										

Solutions with Detailed Explanations

Level-1: BEGINNER

1. **Option (B) is correct.**

Explanation:

Average of first 'n' natural numbers $= \dfrac{(n+1)}{2}$

According to question,

First 100 natural (positive) integers

$= 1 + 2 + 3 + ... + 100$

So, average of first 100 positive integers

$$= \frac{(100+1)}{2} \quad \left[\text{Using } \frac{(n+1)}{2}\right]$$

$$= 50.5$$

2. **Option (B) is correct.**

Explanation: Assuming age of father $= x$ years

Age of mother $= y$ years

According to question,

$$\frac{x+y}{2} = 35$$

$$x + y = 70$$

$$x = 70 - y \qquad ...(1)$$

Assuming age of son = 'S' years

As given in the question,

$$\frac{(x+y+s)}{3} = 27$$

$$x + y + s = 81$$

Putting (1)

$$70 - y + y + s = 81$$

$$s = 81 - 70$$

i.e., 11

Hence, age of son = 11 years

3. **Option (A) is correct.**

Explanation: We know that the average of the first 'n' odd numbers is always 'n'. Hence, average of the first 1234 odd numbers is 1234.

4. **Option (B) is correct.**

Explanation: Odd numbers from 1 to 100

$$= 1 + 3 + 5 + ... + 99$$

$$\text{Average} = \frac{(\text{first term} + \text{last term})}{2}$$

$$= \frac{(1+99)}{2} = 50$$

5. **Option (D) is correct.**

Explanation: Present average age of 4 boys = 9 + 5 = 14 years.

Sum of present age of these four boys

= 14 + 14 + 14 + 14 = 56 years

Present age of 5 boys = 15 × 5 = 75 years

Hence, present age of new boy = 75 – 56 = 19 years

6. **Option (B) is correct.**

Explanation: Let the price of article = ₹ 100

After increasing price by increasing 45%,

new price = ₹ 145

$$\text{Total discount percentage} = 15 + 15 - \frac{15 \times 15}{100}$$

$$= 27.75\%$$

So, new price of article

$$= 145 \times \frac{100 - 27.75}{100} = \text{Rs. } 104.7625$$

Required percentage increase = 104.7625 – 100

= 4.7625%

7. **Option (C) is correct.**

Explanation: Assuming temperature of Tuesday be x and temperature of Wednesday be y.

According to question,

$$\frac{(35 + x + y)}{3} = 30$$

$$x + y = 55$$

i.e., sum of temperatures of Tuesday and Wednesday.

Assuming Thursday's temperature = z

$$\text{Now,} \quad \frac{x + y + z}{3} = 28$$

$$\frac{55 + z}{3} = 28$$

Hence, $z = 29°C$

i.e., Thursday's temperature

8. **Option (C) is correct.**

Explanation: Sum of 19 observations = 19 × 24 = 456

Sum of 1st 10 observations = 10 × 17 = 170

Sum of last 10 observations = 10 × 24 = 240

∴ 10th observation = 170 + 240 – 456 = –46

9. **Option (B) is correct.**

Explanation: According to the question,

Average age of new Jury is:

$$= \left(\frac{5 \times 40 - 35 + 25}{5}\right) = \left(\frac{200 - 10}{5}\right) = 38 \text{ years}$$

10. **Option (B) is correct.**

Explanation:

Let the fourth number = $2x$

Then third number = $6x$

And second number = $9x$

And first number = $3x$

According to the question,

$$\Rightarrow \quad \frac{2x + 6x + 9x + 3x}{4} = 10$$

$$\Rightarrow \quad 20x = 40$$

$$\Rightarrow \quad x = 2$$

So, the largest number = $9x$ = 18

11. **Option (D) is correct.**

Explanation: Increase in weight = $12 \times \frac{1}{3} = 4$

Hence, weight of new man

= weight of crewmen + total increase in weight

= 55 + 4 = 59 kg.

12. **Option (D) is correct.**

Explanation: Age of new teacher = 25 years

Total age decreased = 10 × 3 = 30 years

Hence, age of retired teacher

= Age of new teacher + total age decreased

= 25 + 30 = 55 years

13. **Option (D) is correct.**

Explanation: Average of remaining set of numbers

$$= \frac{50 \times 38 - (45 + 55)}{50 - 2} = \frac{1900 - 100}{48} = 37.5$$

14. **Option (C) is correct.**

Explanation: Assuming average of run till 10th test = r

According to question,

Sum of 10th innings = 10 r

Sum of 11th innings = 11 (r + 5)

Now,

$$11(r + 5) - 10r = 100$$

$$r = 100 - 55 = 45$$

Hence, present average = (r + 5) = (45 + 5) = 50 runs

15. **Option (A) is correct.**

Explanation: Sum of nine numbers = 50 × 9 = 450

Sum of the first five numbers = 54 × 5 = 270

Sum of the last three numbers = 3 × 52 = 156

Hence, sixth number = (450 – (270 + 156)] = 24

16. **Option (A) is correct.**

Explanation: First nine multiples of 3 ⇒ 3, 6, 9, 12, 15, 18, 21, 24, 27

Sum of first nine multiples of 3

$$\Rightarrow \quad 3(1 + 2 + 3 + ... + 9)$$

$$= 3 \times 9 \times \frac{10}{2} = 135$$

Hence, required average $= \frac{135}{9} = 15$

17. **Option (D) is correct.**

Explanation: Average weight of whole class

$$= \frac{\text{Sum of weight of all 40 boys}}{40}$$

$$= \frac{\{\text{Sum of weight of 30 boys + Sum of weight of remaining 10}\}}{40}$$

$$= \left\{\frac{1,800 + 560}{40}\right\} = 59 \text{ kg}$$

18. **Option (B) is correct.**

Explanation: First five multiples of 7 are 7, 14, 21, 28, 35 Hence, required average = 7 + 14 + 21 + 28 + 35/5 = 21

19. **Option (B) is correct.**

Explanation: Given that the average of 32, 34, 38, 21, 26 and x = 30

So, $\frac{32 + 34 + 38 + 21 + 26 + x}{6} = 30$

$$\Rightarrow \quad 151 + x = 180$$

$$\Rightarrow \quad x = 29$$

20. **Option (A) is correct.**

Explanation: Sum of 20 numbers = 15 × 20 = 300

Sum of first five numbers = 12 × 5 = 60

Sum of remaining numbers = 300 – 60 = 240

Hence, required average $= \frac{240}{15} = 16$

21. **Option (C) is correct.**

Explanation: Let the weight of new person = x kg

According to the question,

$$x - 45 = 8 \times 2.5$$

$$\Rightarrow \quad x = 65$$

So, the weight of new person = 65 kg

22. **Option (B) is correct.**

Explanation: Sum of 30 numbers = 40 × 30 = 1,200

Sum of 40 numbers = 40 × 30 = 1,200

Hence, required average $= \frac{(1,200 + 1,200)}{70} = 34\frac{2}{7}$

23. **Option (A) is correct.**

Explanation: Total height of 8 students

= 8 × 152 cm = 1,216 cm

Total height of 10 students

= 1,216 + 144 + 155 = 1,515 cm

Hence, new average $= \frac{1,515}{10} = 151.5$ cm

24. **Option (A) is correct.**

Explanation:

$$\text{Correct average} = 35 + \left(\frac{16 - 61}{20}\right)$$

$$= 35 - \frac{45}{20} = 32.75$$

25. **Option (B) is correct.**

Explanation: Assuming number of workers be x.

According to question,

$$\Rightarrow \quad 8,000 \times x = 12,000 \times 7 + 6,000 (x - 7)$$

$$2,000x = 6,000 \times 7$$

Here, $x = \frac{42,000}{2,000} = 21$

26. **Option (C) is correct.**

Explanation: Sum of ages of 5 members (3 years ago) = 17 × 5 = 85

Sum of present ages of 5 members = 20 × 5 = 100

After baby's birth

Sum of present ages of 6 members = 17 × 6 = 102

Hence, age of baby = 102 – 100 = 2 years.

27. **Option (D) is correct.**

Explanation:

Sum of the first 20 natural odd numbers = $(20)^2$ = 400

[Using sum of first n all natural numbers = n^2]

Hence, required average $= \frac{400}{20} = 20$

28. **Option (D) is correct.**

Explanation: Assuming number of natural numbers = n

Average = 15

So, sum of n natural numbers = $15n$

As given in question,

30 is added and 5 is subtracted

So, $15n + 30 - 5 = 15n + 25$

According to question,

$$\frac{15n + 25}{n} = 17.5$$

$$2.5n = 25$$

Hence, $n = \frac{25}{2.5} = 10$

29. **Option (A) is correct.**

Explanation: Sum of 13 observations = 13 × 70 = 910

Sum of first 7 = 65 × 7 = 455

Sum of last 7 = 75 × 7 = 525

Hence, 7th observation = 910 – (455 + 525) = 70

30. **Option (B) is correct.**

Explanation:

$$\text{Required average} = \frac{100 \times 35 - 83 + 53}{100}$$

$= \frac{3,470}{100} = 34.7$

31. Option (A) is correct.

Explanation: Using

$$\text{Speed} = \frac{\text{Distance}}{\text{Time}}$$

$$80 = \frac{\text{Distance}}{7}$$

Hence, Distance = 7 × 80 = 560 km

32. Option (B) is correct.

Explanation: Total runs by bowler
= 5 × 45 = 225 [in 5 matches]
Total runs by bowler in other 4 matches
= 4 × 15.75 = 63
Hence, average runs conceded by bowler in

9 matches = $\frac{225+63}{9} = 32$

33. Option (D) is correct.

Explanation: Total marks by 60 students in A
= 60 × 64 = 3,840
Total marks in B = 40 × 60 = 2,400
Total marks in C = 60 × 58 = 3,480

Hence, mean marks = $\frac{(3,840+2,400+3,480)}{60+40+60}$

= 60.75

34. Option (B) is correct.

Explanation: Average marks of remaining students

$= \frac{60\times 65 - 30\times 85}{30} = \frac{3,900-2,550}{30} = 45$

35. Option (B) is correct.

Explanation:

Incorrect mean = 35
Sum of 9 observations = 35 × 9 = 315
Correct sum = 315 – 18 + 81 = 378

Hence, required mean = $\frac{378}{9} = 42$

36. Option (C) is correct.

Explanation:
Total income of A and B = 2 × 15,050 = 30,100
Income of B and C = 2 × 15,350 = 30,700
Income of A and C = 2 × 15,200 = 30,400

Hence, total income = $\frac{30,100+30,700+30,400}{2}$

= ₹ 45,600

Income of A = 45,600 – 30,700 = ₹ 14,900

37. Option (B) is correct.

Explanation:

9th result = 9 × 57 + 9 × 65 – 17 × 60
= 513 + 585 – 1,020 = 78

38. Option (C) is correct.

Explanation: Using,
Sum of first n natural numbers

$= \frac{n(n+1)(2n+1)}{6}$

Sum of 19 natural numbers = $\frac{19\times 20\times 39}{6} = 2,470$

Hence, required average = $\frac{2,470}{19} = 130$

39. Option (C) is correct.

Explanation: Assuming runs scored by fifth player = x
According to question,

$$\text{Average runs} = \frac{75+30+62+21+x}{5}$$

= 49 (average runs)

Hence, x = 245 – 188 = 57

Level-2: INTERMEDIATE

1. Option (C) is correct.

Explanation: Sum of 50 numbers = 50 × 30 = 1,500 [Incorrect sum]

Correct sum of these 50 numbers
= 1,500 – 82 – 13 + 28 + 31 = 1,464

Hence, correct mean = $\frac{1,464}{50} = 29.28$

2. Option (C) is correct.

Explanation: Three consecutive odd numbers
= x, x + 2, x + 4

$$\frac{x+x+2+x+4}{3} = \frac{1}{3}x+12$$

$$\frac{3x+6}{3} = \frac{x+36}{3}$$

$3x + 6 = x + 36$

$2x = 30$

$x = 15$

Hence, last number = x + 4, i.e., 15 + 4 = 19

3. Option (B) is correct.

Explanation: According to question,
Difference in observations = 64 + 28 – 46 – 82 = –36

Hence, required (correct) average = $124 - \frac{36}{18} = 122$

4. Option (C) is correct.

Explanation:

Let the number of boys is x unit and the number of girls is (286 – x) unit.

Total height of all the 50 students = 286 × 50 = 14300 unit

Total height of boys = 53x unit
Total height of girls = (286 – x)31 unit
According to the question,
53x + (286 – x)31 = 14300
⇒ 22x = 13300 – 8866
⇒ x = 247
So, total height of boys = 53 × 247 = 13091 unit
Total height of girls = (286 – 247)31 = 1209 unit

So, required ratio = $\frac{13091}{1209} = \frac{1007}{93}$

5. **Option (B) is correct.**
Explanation: As given in the question,
Average increases by 2 runs
So, increased runs = 11 × 2 = 22 runs
Hence, his average after 12 innings = 63 – 22 = 41

6. **Option (B) is correct.**
Explanation:
The average weight of 39 students = 51 kg
So, total weight of 39 students = 51 × 39 – 1989
Let the weight of teacher = x kg
According to the question,
$$x + 1989 = 40 \times 51.2$$
$$\Rightarrow \quad x = 2048 - 1989$$
$$\Rightarrow \quad x = 59$$
So, the weight of teacher = 59 kg

7. **Option (B) is correct.**
Explanation:
Height of 6 = 6 × 1 m 15 cm = 6 m 90 cm
Height of 8 = 8 × 1 m 10 cm = 8 m 80 cm
Height of 6 = 6 × 1 m 12 cm = 6 m 72 cm
So, total height of 20 persons = 22 m 42 cm
$$\text{Hence, Average} = \frac{22\text{m } 42\text{cm}}{20} = 1\text{m } 12.1 \text{ cm}$$

8. **Option (C) is correct.**
Explanation:
$$\text{Boys in class} = \frac{4}{5} \times 50 = 40$$
$$\text{Girls in class} = \frac{1}{5} \times 500 = 10$$
Average age of boys = 10 × 2 = 20 years
Hence, total age of boys = 20 × 40 = 800 years.

9. **Option (C) is correct.**
Explanation: Assuming no. of students in section A = n
∴ Number of students in section B and C = 100 – n
According to question,
$$n \times 70 + (100 - n) \times 87.5 = 84 \times 100$$
$$8{,}750 - 17.5n = 8{,}400$$
$$17.5\, n = 8{,}750 - 8{,}400 = 350$$
$$\text{Hence,} \quad n = \frac{350}{17.5} = 20$$

10. **Option (B) is correct.**
Explanation:
Number of oarsmen = 15
Weight of one oarsman = 42 kg
Total weight increased after replacement = 1.6
Let, O = 15 W = 42 T = 1.6
So, weight of new oarsman = (W + O × T)
= (42 + 15 × 1.6) = 66 kg

11. **Option (A) is correct.**
Explanation:
40 × 30 = sum of 30 innings, i.e, 1,200
Assuming lowest score = T
Highest = T + 100
38 × 28 = 1,064 = Sum of 28 innings
Sum of 30 innings = Sum (28 innings) + T + T + 100
1,200 = 1,064 + 2T
Hence, T = 18

12. **Option (A) is correct.**
Explanation: Assuming attendence on first, second and third day is 2, 5 and 13
So, total visitors = 2 + 5 + 13 = 20
Total money collected
= 2 × 15 + 5 × 7.50 + 13 × 2.50
= 30 + 37.5 + 32.5 = 100
$$\text{Hence, average charge per person} = \frac{100}{20} = 5$$

13. **Option (B) is correct.**
Explanation: Total age of family = 5 × 24 = 120 years
Age 8 years ago = 120 – [5 × 8] = 80 years
$$\text{Hence, required average} = \frac{80}{4} = 20$$

14. **Option (D) is correct.**
Explanation:
Total age earlier = 120 × 60.7 = 7,284
Total age presently = 150 × 56.3 = 8,445
So, age of new members = 8,445 – 7,284 = 1,161
$$\text{Hence, required average} = \frac{1{,}161}{30} = 38.7$$

15. **Option (C) is correct.**
Explanation:
Total marks of 132 students = 132 × 50 = 6600
Let number of passed students = x
And number of failed students = 132 – x
Total marks of passed students = 55x
Total marks of failed students = (132 – x)35
According to the question,
$$\Rightarrow \quad 55x + (132 - x)35 = 6600$$
$$\Rightarrow \quad 20x + 4620 = 6600$$
$$\Rightarrow \quad x = 99$$
number of passed students = x = 99
and number of failed students = 132 – x = 132 – 99 = 33
required ratio = (55 × 99) : (33 × 35) = 33 : 7

16. **Option (A) is correct.**
Explanation: Age of 30 students = 30 × 20 = 600 years
Age of 20 students = 20 × 30 = 600 years
$$\text{Hence, required average} = \frac{1{,}200}{50} = 24 \text{ years}$$

17. **Option (D) is correct.**
Explanation: Given that,
The average age of 30 students = 15 years
So, total age of 30 students = 15 × 30 = 450 years
According to the question, new average
$$= \frac{450 - 15 + 9}{30} = 14.8 \text{ years}$$

18. Option (A) is correct.

Explanation:

No. of girls $= 50\times\frac{46}{100} = 23$

No. of boys $= 50 - 23 = 27$

Total marks of girls $= 62 \times 23 = 1{,}426$

Marks of boys $= 58 \times 27 = 1{,}566$

Hence, average marks of whole class $= \frac{1426+1566}{50}$

$= 59.84$

19. Option (C) is correct.

Explanation:

No. of girls $= 40\times\frac{60}{100} = 24$

So, boys $= 40 - 24 = 16$

Total marks of girls $= 72 \times 24 = 1{,}728$

Total marks of boys $= 54 \times 16 = 864$

Hence, required average $= \frac{2{,}592}{40} = 64.8$

20. Option (B) is correct.

Explanation:

No. of boys $= 50\times\frac{60}{100} = 30$

No. of girls $= 50 - 30 = 20$

Total marks of girls $= 68 \times 20 = 1{,}360$

Total marks of boys $= 62 \times 30 = 1{,}860$

Hence, required average $= \frac{3{,}220}{50} = 64.4$

Level-3: EXPERT

1. Option (C) is correct.

Explanation: Total number of males = 20

Let number of females $= x$

And the number of children $= 24 - x$

According to the question,

Total weight of males $= 54 \times 20 = 1080$ kg

And total weight of females $= 49x$ kg

Total weight of children $= (24 - x)\times 30$ kg

Total weight of whole group $= (20 + 24) \times 48.25 = 2123$ kg

According to the question,

$2123 = 1080 + 49x + (24 - x)\times 30$

$\Rightarrow 1043 = 49x + 720 - 30x$

$\Rightarrow 19x = 323$

$\Rightarrow x = 17$

So, number of females = 17

And number of children $= 24 - 17 = 7$

Required difference $= 17 - 7 = 10$

2. Option (B) is correct.

Explanation:

Let the number of students $= x$ kg

Total weight of x students $= 58x$ kg

8 students' total weight who left the group

$= 54 \times 8 = 432$ kg

Total weight of 3 students who joined the group

$= 53.6 + 54 + 57.4 = 165$ kg

According to the question,

$\Rightarrow \frac{58x+165-432}{x+3-8} = 58 + .575$

$\Rightarrow \frac{58x-267}{x-5} = 58.575$

$\Rightarrow 58x - 267 = 58.575x - 292.875$

$\Rightarrow 0.575x = 25.875$

$\Rightarrow x = 45$

So, the number of students = 45

3. Option (D) is correct.

Explanation: Total weight of 80 students

$= 80 \times 51.5 = 4{,}120$ kg, 60% participated in games

So, total participants = 60% of 80 = 48

No. of students who did not participate

$= 80 - 48 = 32$

Assuming weight of 32 students be w

So, weight of 48 students $= w + w \times 5\% = 1.05\,w$

According to question,

$1.05w \times 48 + w \times 32 = 4{,}120$

$w = 50$

Hence, weight of former group $= 1.05w \times 50$

$= 52.5$ kg

4. Option (A) is correct.

Explanation: Assuming number of students be N.

Total weight $= 75.4 \times N$

After joining of 4th student, average weight of group

$= 75.4 + 0.24 = 75.64$ kg.

Now, total weight $= 75.64 \times (N + 4)$

According to question,

$75.64 \times (N + 4) = 75.4\,N + 72.9 + 73.8 + 79.5 + 87.4$

$0.84\,N = 313.6 - 302.56$

Hence, $N = \frac{11.04}{0.24}$

$N = 46$

5. Option (C) is correct.

Explanation: Assuming total number = 100

Average = 36

Sum $= 36 \times 100 = 3{,}600$

75% of 100 = 75

Total increase $= 75 \times 6 = 450$ [75 numbers]

Total decrease $= 25 \times (-9) = -225$ [25 numbers]

So, increase in 100 numbers $= 450 - 225 = 225$

Now Total $= 3{,}600 + 225 = 3{,}825$

Hence, required average $= \frac{3{,}825}{100} = 38.25$

6. Option (B) is correct.

Explanation: Sum of all seven numbers of set A

$= 41 \times 7 = 287$

Sum of five of set B $= 44 \times 5 = 220$

Hence, required average = $\frac{287+220}{12} = 42.25$

7. **Option (C) is correct.**
Explanation: Using mixture formula:

Science 80%   Maths 90%

84%

Ratio ⇒ 6 : 4
or 3 : 2

Given that total marks obtained in Science = 54000

$\therefore$ Marks obtained in Maths = $\frac{54000}{3} \times 2 = 36000$

8. **Option (A) is correct.**
Explanation: Total rainfall in 5 days = 5 × 30
= 150 mm
Rainfalls in whole week = 150 + 42 + 25 = 217 mm
Hence, average rainfall = $\frac{217}{7} = 31$ mm

9. **Option (B) is correct.**
Explanation:
Person guessed = 71 to 79
Friend guessed = 75 to 83
Mother guessed = less than 78
So, possible weight = 75, 76, 77
Hence, required average = $\frac{75+76+77}{3} = 76$ kg

10. **Option (B) is correct.**
Explanation: Assuming total number of students be "T" after joining of 5 students
According to question,
$$0.55T = 5(62.8 - 58.4)$$
$$T = \frac{(5 \times 4.4)}{0.55}$$
$$T = 40$$
Hence, no. of students in class were = 40 – 5 = 35

11. **Option (A) is correct.**
Explanation: According to question,
Total number of persons = $\frac{(38.5+40-29-22)}{2.5} = 11$

12. **Option (A) is correct.**
Explanation: Assuming there are 4 numbers, each of 54.6 value
Sum of these 4 = 54.6 × 4 = 218.4
According to question,
75% of total increased by 5.6 each
i.e., $\frac{3}{4} \times 4 = 3(54.6 + 5.6)$
25% decreased by 8.4 each
i.e., $\frac{1}{4}$ of 4 = 1 (54.6 – 8.4)
No sum of these 4 = 3(54.6 + 5.6) + 1 (54.6 – 8.4)
= 3 × 60.2 + 46.2 = 226.8
Hence, new average = $\frac{226.8}{4} = 56.7$

13. **Option (B) is correct.**
Explanation: Contribution of teacher
= 24 × (56 – 50) + 56 = 144 + 56 = 200

14. **Option (C) is correct.**
Explanation: Assuming number of students in B = 4
No. of students in A = $4 \times \frac{5}{4} = 5$
Total students = 5 + 4 = 9
Average score of 9 = 49
Assuming average score of A be 5T
Average score of B = 5T × $\frac{6}{5}$ = 6T
According to question,
$$5T \times 5 + 6T \times 4 = 9 \times 49$$
$$25T + 24T = 9 \times 49$$
$$T = 9$$
Hence, average score of A = 5 × 9 = 45

15. **Option (B) is correct.**
Explanation: Average marks of 30 boys = 88
Deviation of marks of 28 boys = 0.5 × 30 = 15
Sum of marks of 2 boys = 87.5 + 87.5 + 15 = 190
Let higher marks be 'T' and lower be 'T – 2'
Hence, T + T – 2 = 190
T = 96

Mixture and Alligation

Mixture: Created by adding together two or more different sorts of quantities

Alligation: Method of solving arithmetic problems involvig ingredient mixtures

When a unit of liquid is replaced with equal volume of other liquid. Again b litres of mixture is replaced then

Final volume $= x\left(1-\frac{a}{x}\right)\left(1-\frac{b}{x}\right)$

[Hence x = initial quantity of first liquid]

If same volume of liquid replaced "n" time then:

Final volume $= x\left(1-\frac{a}{x}\right)^n$

[x = initial quantity of first liquid]

Alligation formula:

Quantity of cheaper

$$\frac{\text{Quantity of cheaper}}{\text{Quantity of dearer}} = \frac{\text{CP of dearer} - \text{Mean price}}{\text{Mean price} - \text{CP of cheaper}}$$

CP of cheaper   CP of dearer

Mean price

CP of cheaper – Mean price   Mean price – CP of cheaper

Chapter 8

Mixture and Alligation

LEARNING OBJECTIVES:

- Problems related to mixing of two or more than two quantities.
- Method of alligation.
- Application of alligation formula in other topics of quantitative aptitude.
- Question asked in various competitive exams such as SSC, bank, CSAT, railway, etc.

➢ **Mixture:** A mixture is created by adding together two or more different sorts of quantities.

➢ **Alligation:** Alligation is a method of solving arithmetic problems involving ingredient mixtures. This rule allows us to determine the ratio in which two or more ingredients at the given price must be mixed to produce the desired price mixture.

The fundamental formula for determining the ratio in which the ingredients are mixed is;

$$\frac{\text{Quantity of cheaper}}{\text{Quantity of dearer}} = \frac{\text{CP of dearer} - \text{Mean price}}{\text{Mean price} - \text{CP of cheaper}}$$

It is also known as the rule of alligation and can be written as:

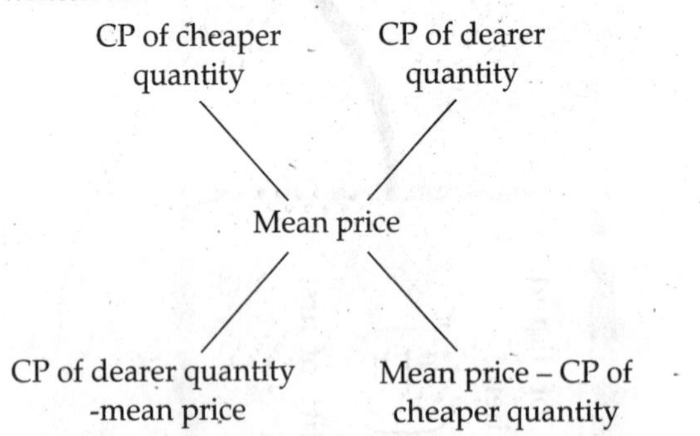

Example 1: The ratios of copper to zinc in alloys A and B are 3 : 4 and 5 : 9, respectively. A and B are taken in the ratio 2 : 3 and melted to from a new alloy C. What is the ratio of copper to zinc in C?

(a) 8 : 13 (b) 3 : 5

(c) 9 : 11 (d) 27 : 43

Sol. (d)

	Copper	:	Zinc	:	Total
A	3	:	4	:	7
B	5	:	9	:	14

Balancing the ratio for total quantity and the ratio in which mixtures are taken:

	Copper	:	Zinc	:	Total
A	12	:	16	:	$7 \times 2 \times 2$
B	15	:	27	:	$14 \times 1 \times 3$
	27	:	43		

Example 2: Alloy A contains copper and zinc in the ratio of 4 : 3 and alloy B contains copper and zinc in the ratio of 5 : 2. A and B are taken in the ratio of 5 : 6 and melted to form a new alloy. The percentage of zinc in the new alloy is closest to:

(a) 54 (b) 34.2

(c) 36.8 (d) 35

Sol. (d)

	Copper	:	Zinc	:	Total
A	4	:	3	:	7
B	5	:	2	:	7

Balancing the ratio for the ratios in which mixtures are taken.

	Copper	:	Zinc	:	Total
A	20	:	15	:	7×5
B	30	:	12	:	7×6
	50	:	27		

$$\text{Required \% age} = \frac{27}{50+27} \times 100 = 35$$

Example 3: A vessel contains a 32 litres solution of acid and water in which the ratio of acid and water is 5 : 3. If 12 litres of the solution are taken out and $7\frac{1}{2}$ litres of water are added to it, then what is the ratio of acid and water in the resulting solution?

(a) 4 : 7 (b) 5 : 6

(c) 4 : 9 (d) 8 : 11

Sol. (b) Let the quantity of acid = 5 units

and quantity of water = 3 units

According to the question,

$(5 + 3)$ units $= 32$

1 unit = 4
5 units = 20
3 units = 12

In 12 litres of solution are taken out from the mixture quantity of acid

$= 12\times\frac{5}{8}=7\frac{1}{2}$ litres

In 12 litres of solution are taken out from the mixture quantity of water

$= 12-7\frac{1}{2}=4\frac{1}{2}$ litres

$= 20-7\frac{1}{2}:12-4\frac{1}{2}+7\frac{1}{2}$

$= \frac{25}{2}:15 = 5:6$

Example 4: Fresh fruit contains 68% water and dry fruit contains 20% water. How much dry fruit can be obtained from 100 kg of fresh fruit?

(a) 80 (b) 60
(c) 40 (d) 20

Sol. (c) Pulp : Water

$68\% = \frac{17}{25}$ and $20\% = \frac{1}{5}$

Fresh fruit 8 : 17
Dry fruit 4 : 1

Balancing the ratio for pulp

	Pulp	Water
Fresh fruit	32	68
Dry fruit	32	8

According to the question,
From 100 kg fresh fruit, obtained dry fruits
= 32 + 8 = 40 kg
(32 + 68) units = 100 kg
y unit = 1 kg
400 units = 40 kg

Example 5: A milkman uses three containers for selling milk, their capacities for selling milk, their capacities being 40 L, 30 L and 20 L, respectively. He fills respectively 87.5%, 80% and 90% of the containers with a mix of milk and water in the ratio, 3 : 2, 5 : 1, and 7 : 2 respectively. What is the ratio of the total quantity of milk to that of water carried by him?

(a) 7 : 2 (b) 31 : 12
(c) 35 : 9 (d) 5 : 2

Sol. (d) 87.5% of 40 = 35 kg
80% of 30 = 24 kg
90% of 20 = 18 kg

$\text{Total milk} = 35\times\frac{3}{3+2}+24\times\frac{5}{5+1}+18\times\frac{7}{7+2} = 55 \text{ kg}$

Total water = [35 + 24 + 18 – 55] = 22
Required ratio = 55 : 22 = 5 : 2

Example 6: A mixture has milk and water in the ratio (by volume) of 8 : 3. If 3 litres of water is added to it, then the new ratio of milk and water be comes 2 : 1. What are the quantities of milk and water, respectively in the mixture initially?

(a) 24 litres and 9 litres
(b) 32 litres and 12 litres
(c) 40 litres and 15 litres
(d) 16 litres and 6 litres

Sol. (a)

	Milk	Water
Initial	8	3
New	8	4

Now,
(4 – 3) unit
Initial quantity of milk = 8 units
= 8 × 3 = 24 litres
Initial quantity of water= 3 units
= 3 × 3 = 9 litres

Example 7: The ratio of milk and water in a mixture is 4 : 3. If we add 2 litres of water, the ratio of milk and water becomes 8 : 7. What is the quantity of the final mixture?

(a) 18 litres (b) 30 litres
(c) 24 litres (d) 32 litres

Sol. (b)

	Milk	Water
Initial	4	3
New	8	7

Only water is added so quantity of milk in both cases will be the same. So, balance the ratio for milk.

	Milk	Water
Initial	8	6
New	8	7

Now,
(7 – 6) units = 2
Final quantity of mixture = (8 + 7) units
= 15 × 2 = 30 litres

Example 8: In the 60 litres mixture of milk and water, the quantities of milk and water are in the ratio of 3 : 2. If we want to make the ratio of the quantities of milk and water 1 : 1, then how much extra water should be put in the mixture?

(a) 10 litres (b) 16 litres
(c) 12 litres (d) 14 litres

Sol. (a)

	Milk	Water
Initial	3	2
New	1	1

Only water is added so the quantity of milk in both cases will be the same. So, balance the ratio for milk.

	Milk	Water
Initial	3	2
New	3	3

Now,
(3 + 2) units = 60
1 unit = 12
Required quantity of water = (3 – 2) units
1 unit = 12 litres

Level 1 Beginner

1. 5 litres of honey contains 80% sugar. 3 litres of water is added to this honey. What is the percentage of sugar in the new mixture? [SSC CHSL 2018]
   (A) 40 (B) 50 (C) 60 (D) 75
2. In what ratio should suger costing ₹ 40 per kg be mixed with sugar coasting ₹ 48 per kg so as to earn a profit of 20% by selling the mixture at ₹ 54 per kg? [SSC CHSL 2020]
   (A) 3 : 5 (B) 4 : 7 (C) 5 : 8 (D) 2 : 3
3. An alloy contains metals X and Y only in the ratio 5 : 2 and alloy B contains these metals in the ratio 3 : 4. Alloy C is prepared by mixing A and B in the ratio 4 : 5. The percentage of X in alloy C is: [SSC CGL 2021]
   (A) 45 (B) $55\frac{5}{9}$ (C) $44\frac{4}{9}$ (D) 56
4. A 40-litre mixture of milk and water contains milk and water in the ratio of 7 : 3. How many litres of water should be added to the mixture so that the resulting mixture has 60% of water in it? [SSC CHSL 2023]
   (A) 30 (B) 35 (C) 20 (D) 25
5. In what ratio, sugar costing ₹ 60 per kg be mixed with sugar costing ₹ 42 per kg such that by selling the mixture at ₹ 56 per kg there is a gain of 12%? [SSC CGL 2018]
   (A) 5 : 6 (B) 8 : 9 (C) 4 : 5 (D) 5 : 7
6. Fresh fruit contains 68% water and dry fruit contains 20% water. How much dry fruit can be obtained from 100 kg of fresh fruits? [SSC CPO 2018]
   (A) 80 (B) 60 (C) 40 (D) 20
7. 40 litres of 60% cocnentration of acid solution is added to 35 litres of 80% concentration of acid solution. What is the concentration of acid in the new solution? [SSC CGL Mains 2018]
   (A) 66% (B) $66\frac{2}{3}\%$ (C) $69\frac{1}{3}\%$ (D) 69%
8. A bought 38 kg rice @ ₹ 54.50 per kg, 45 kg rice @ ₹ 62 per kg and 55 per kg rice @ ₹ 48 per kg, He sold the mixture @ ₹ 65 per kg. His profit or loss percentage is: [SSC CPO 2018]
   (A) Loss 1.04 (B) Profit 16.8
   (C) Loss 1.7 (D) Profit 19.6
9. 5 kg of ₹ 18 per kg wheat is mixed with 2 kg of another type of wheat to get a mixture costing ₹ 20 per kg. Find the price (per kg) of the costlier wheat. [SSC CHSL 2022]
   (A) ₹ 27 (B) ₹ 25
   (C) ₹ 29 (D) ₹ 30
10. Alloy A contains copper and zinc in the ratio of 4 : 3 and alloy B contains copper and zinc in the ratio of 5 : 2. A and B are taken in the ratio of 5 : 6 and melted to form a new alloy. The percentage of zinc in the new alloy is closest to : [SSC CGL Mains 2018]
    (A) 54 (B) 34.2 (C) 36.8 (D) 35
11. A container contains 20 L mixture in which there is 10% sulphuric acid. Find the quantity of sulphuric acid to be added to make the solution to contain 25% sulphuric acid. [SSC CGL Tier-II 2020]
    (A) 3 L (B) 4 L (C) 2 L (D) 5 L
12. A vessel contains a 32-litre solution of acid and water in which the ratio of acid and water is 5 : 3. If 12 litres of the solution are taken out and $7\frac{1}{2}$ litres of water are added to it, then what is the ratio of acid and water in the resulting solution? [SSC CGL Mains 2018]
    (A) 4 : 7 (B) 5 : 6 (C) 4 : 9 (D) 8 : 11
13. A mixture contains alcohol and water in the ratio 4 : 3. If 5 litres of water is added to the mixture, the ratio becomes 4 : 5. The quantity of alcohol in the given mixture is: [SSC 2013]
    (A) 3 litres (B) 4 litres
    (C) 15 litres (D) 10 litres
14. How many kg of salt costing ₹ 28 per kg must be mixed with 39.6 kg of salt costing ₹ 16 per kg, so that selling the mixture at ₹ 29.90, there is a gain of 15%? [SSC CGL 2018]
    (A) 33 (B) 31 (C) 35 (D) 32
15. A vessel contains 60 litres of milk. First, 12 litres of milk are taken out from it and replaced by water. Afterward, another 12 litres are taken out from the mixture and replaced with water. The ratio of milk and water in the resultant mixture is :[SSC LDC 2015]
    (A) 16 : 9 (B) 15 : 10 (C) 16 : 10 (D) 9 : 5

Level 2 Intermediate

1. A can is full of a mixture of two liquids A and B in the ratio of 7 : 5. When 9 litres of mixture are drawn off from the can and replaced by the same quantity of liquid B, the ratio of A and B in the can becomes 7 : 9. The capacity of the can is: [SSC CPO 2016]
   (A) 21 litres (B) 20 litres
   (C) 10 litres (D) 36 litres
2. The proportion of acid and water in three samples is 2 : 1, 3 : 2, and 5 : 3. A mixture containing equal quantities of all three samples is made. The ratio of water and acid in the mixture is. [SSC 2013]
   (A) 120 : 133 (B) 227 : 133
   (C) 227 : 120 (D) 133 : 127
3. 60 kg of an alloy A is mixed with 100 kg of alloy B. If alloy A has lead and tin in the ratio 3 : 2 and alloy B

has tin and copper in the ratio 1 : 4, the amount of tin in the new alloy is. [SSC CGL 2015]
(A) 44 kg (B) 53 kg (C) 80 kg (D) 24 kg

4. In a mixture, the ratio of a chemical X and water is 15 : 9. When 48 litres of this mixture is replaced with water, the ratio becomes 11 : 13. Find the quantity of water after replacement. [SSC CHSL 2023]
(A) 97.5 litres (B) 99 litres
(C) 92 litres (D) 102.5 litres

5. 729 ml of a mixture contains milk and water in the ratio 7 : 2. How much more water is to be added to get a new mixture containing milk and water in the ratio 7 : 3? [SSC CGL 2015]
(A) 60 ml (B) 71 ml (C) 52 ml (D) 81 ml

6. In 2 kg mixture of copper and aluminium, 30% is copper. How much aluminium powder should be added to the mixture so that the quantity of copper becomes 20%. [SSC LDC 2015]
(A) 900 g (B) 800 g
(C) 1,000 g (D) 1,200 g

7. The ratio of the quantities of acid and water in a mixture is 1 : 3. If 5 litres of acid are further added to the mixture, the new ratio becomes 1 : 2. The quantity of the new mixture in litres is. [SSC 2011]
(A) 32 (B) 40 (C) 42 (D) 45

8. Three glasses of equal volume contain acid mixed with water. The ratio of acid and water is 2 : 3, 3 : 4 and 4 : 5, respectively. Contents of the glasses are poured in a large vessel. The ratio of acid and water in the large vessel is: [SSC CGL Mains 2015]
(A) 417 : 564 (B) 401 : 544
(C) 407 : 560 (D) 411 : 540

9. In 50 gm alloy of gold and silver, the gold is 80% by weight. How much gold should be mixed to this alloy so that the weight of gold becomes 95%? [SSC 2005]
(A) 200 g (B) 150 g
(C) 50 g (D) 10 g

10. A person has a chemical of Rs 25 per litre. In what ratio should water be mixed with the chemical the mixture at ₹ 20 litres he may get profit of 25%? [SSC 2007]
(A) 14 : 9 (B) 16 : 9 (C) 9 : 14 (D) 9 : 16

11. In what ratio must a mixture of 30% alcohol strength be mixed with that of 50% alcohol strength so as to get a mixture of 45% alcohol strength? [SSC 2008]
(A) 1 : 2 (B) 1 : 3 (C) 2 : 1 (D) 3 : 1

12. In one glass, milk and water are mixed in the ratio 3 : 5 and in another glass they are mixed in the ratio 6 : 1. In what ratio should the content of the two glasses be mixed together so that the new mixture contains milk and water in the ratio 1 : 1 ? [SSC 2009]
(A) 20 : 7 (B) 8 : 3 (C) 27 : 4 (D) 25 : 9

13. A mixture of 80 litres of wine and water contains 60 per cent wine. How much water must be added to make it 50 per cent wine in the new mixture? [SSC 2010]
(A) 16 litres (B) 18 litres
(C) 19 litres (D) 20 litres

14. The ratio of the volume of water and glycerine in 240 cc of mixture is 1 : 3. What is the quantity of water (in cc) that should be added to the mixture so that the volume of water and glycerine becomes 2 : 3? [SSC 2011]
(A) 55 (B) 60 (C) 62.5 (D) 64

15. Two vessels A and B contain milk and water mixed in the ratio 4:3 and 2:3, respectively. The ratio in which their mixtures are to be mixed to form a new mixture containing half milk and half water is: [SSC 2012]
(A) 7 : 5 (B) 6 : 5 (C) 5 : 6 (D) 4 : 3

Level 3 Expert

1. Two alloys are both made up of copper and tin. The ratio of copper and tin in the first alloy is 1 : 3 and in the second alloy is 2 : 5. In what ratio should the two alloys be mixed to obtain a new alloy in which the ratio of tin and copper is 8 : 3? [SSC 2013]
(A) 3 : 5 (B) 4 : 7 (C) 3 : 8 (D) 5 : 11

2. A goldsmith has two types of gold, one of 12 carats and the other of 16 carats, each with a different level of purity. In what proportion should he mix them to create an ornament with a purity of 15 carats? [SSC 2014]
(A) 1 : 3 (B) 2 : 3 (C) 3 : 2 (D) 3 : 1

3. Two vessels contain mixture of petrol and kirosene in the ratio 4 : 3 and 3 : 5, respectively. The ratio of the volumes of the quantities from the new mixture may contain same volume of petrol and kerosene is: [SSC LDC 2015]
(A) 7 : 4 (B) 9 : 6 (C) 3 : 2 (D) 7 : 8

4. From a cask filled with wine, 75 litres are first drawn and replaced with water. From this mixture, 60 litres are drawn and replaced with water. The ratio of wine to water in the cask is now 3 : 2. How many litres of wine did the cask initially hold? [SSC CHSL 2023]
(A) 225 (B) 250
(C) 375 (D) 300

5. In a 729-litre mixture of milk and water, the ratio of milk to water is 7 : 2. To get a new mixture containing milk and water in the ratio 7 : 3, the amount of water to be added is: [SSC 2008]
(A) 81 litres (B) 71 litres
(C) 56 litres (D) 50 litres

6. A mixture of 40% litres of milk and water contains 10% of water. How much water must be added to make the water 20% in the new mixture? [SSC 2010]
(A) 10 litres (B) 7 litres
(C) 5 litres (D) 3 litres

7. In a mixture of 25 litres, the ratio of acid to water is 4 : 1. Another 3 litres of waters are added to the mixture. The ratio of acid to water in the new mixture is: [SSC 2011]
(A) 5 : 2 (B) 2 : 5 (C) 3 : 5 (D) 5 : 3

8. A container contains 60 litres of milk. From this container, 6 litres of milk was taken out and replaced by water. This process was repeated further two times. The amount of milk left in the containers is: [SSC 2012]
(A) 34.24 litres (B) 39.64 litres
(C) 43.74 litres (D) 47.9 litres

ANSWER KEY

Level-1: Beginner

1.	(B)	2.	(A)	3.	(B)	4.	(A)	5.	(C)	6.	(C)	7.	(C)	8.	(D)	9.	(B)	10.	(D)
11.	(B)	12.	(B)	13.	(D)	14.	(A)	15.	(A)										

Level-2: Intermediate

1.	(D)	2.	(D)	3.	(A)	4.	(A)	5.	(D)	6.	(C)	7.	(D)	8.	(B)	9.	(B)	10.	(D)
11.	(B)	12.	(A)	13.	(A)	14.	(B)	15.	(A)										

Level-3: Expert

1.	(B)	2.	(A)	3.	(A)	4.	(D)	5.	(A)	6.	(C)	7.	(A)	8.	(C)				

Solutions with Detailed Explanations

Level-1: BEGINNER

1. **Option (B) is correct.**
Explanation:
Quantity of sugar $= 5 \times \frac{80}{100} = 4$
New total quantity = 5 + 3 = 8 L
Percentage of sugar in new mixture
$= \frac{4}{8} \times 100 = 50\%$

2. **Option (A) is correct.**
Explanation: Using mixture formula,
CP CP
CP
Q_1 Q_1
Cost price of mixture = (54/120)100 = ₹ 45 per kg
40 48
45
3 5
So, required ratio = 3 : 5

3. **Option (B) is correct.**
Explanation:
Ratio for metal A = 5 : 2 × 4 ⇒ 20 : 8
[Multiplied by 4 for balancing]
Ratio for metal B = 3 : 4 × 5 ⇒ 15 : 20
[Multiplied by 5 for balancing]
Required ratio = 35 : 28 = 5 : 4
Required percentage $= \frac{5}{9} = 55\frac{5}{9}\%$

4. **Option (A) is correct.**
Explanation:
Ratio of milk and water = 7:3
$\therefore$ Milk in mixture $= \frac{7}{10} \times 40 = 28$ litres
Water in mixture = 12 litres
Let we added x litre water in mixture.
$\therefore$ Percentage of water in mixture $= \frac{12+x}{40+x} \times 100$
According to the question,
$\Rightarrow 60 = \frac{12+x}{40+x} \times 100$
$\Rightarrow 240 + 6x = 120 + 10x$
$\Rightarrow 4x = 120$
$\Rightarrow x = 30$
We need to add 30 litre water in mixture.

5. **Option (C) is correct.**
Explanation:
Cost price of mixture = (56/112)100 = Rs. 50 /kg
60 42
50
8 : 10
4 : 5
Required ratio = 4 : 5

6. **Option (C) is correct.**
Explanation:
Fresh fruit $\xrightarrow{} \overset{W}{17} : \overset{S}{8} = 25 \xrightarrow{\times 4} 100$ kg

Dry Fruit $\rightarrow 2:8 = 10 \xrightarrow{\times 4} 40$ kg

7. Option (C) is correct.

Explanation:

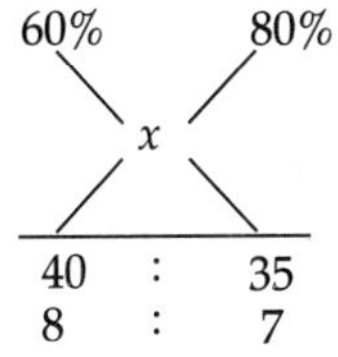

$$x = \frac{60 \times 8 + 80 \times 7}{8+7} = 69\frac{1}{3}\%$$

8. Option (D) is correct.

Explanation: According to question,

$$\text{Price of mixture} = \frac{38 \times 54.5 + 45 \times 62 + 55 \times 48}{38 + 45 + 55}$$

$$= \frac{2{,}071 + 2{,}790 + 2{,}840}{138} = ₹\,54.35 / \text{kg}$$

According to question,

$$\text{Profit percentage} = \frac{(65 - 54.35)}{54.35} \times 100 = 19.6\%$$

9. Option (B) is correct.

Explanation:

Let the price of costlier wheat = x/kg.

Using mixture formula:

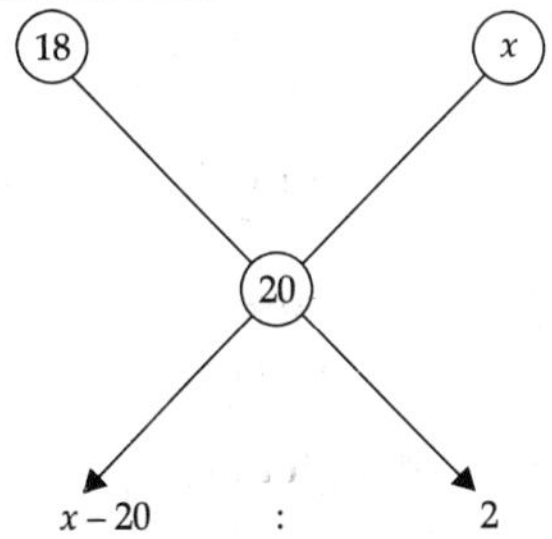

According to the question,

$$\frac{x - 20}{2} = \frac{5}{2}$$

$$\Rightarrow \quad 2x - 40 = 10$$

$$\Rightarrow \quad x = 25$$

$\therefore$ Price of costlier wheat = ₹ 25/kg.

10. Option (D) is correct.

Explanation:

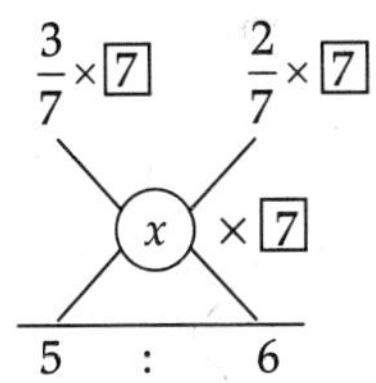

$$7x = \frac{3 \times 5 + 2 \times 6}{5+6} = \frac{27}{11}$$

$$x = \frac{27}{77} \times 100 = 35\%$$

11. Option (B) is correct.

Explanation:

$$10\% \text{ of } 20\,l = 2l$$

According to the question,

$$\frac{2+x}{18} = \frac{1}{3}, \text{ [Final ratio = 1 : 3]}$$

So, $x = 4\text{L}$

12. Option (B) is correct.

Explanation:

Given that the ratio of acid and water = 5 : 3

So, acid in solution = 32 × (5/8) = 20 L

and water in solution = 32 × (3/8) = 12 L

$$\text{Acid in 12 liters solution} = \frac{5}{8} \times 12 = 7.5 \text{ L}$$

$$\text{Water in 12 liters solution} = \frac{3}{8} \times 12 = 4.5 \text{ L}$$

Water added 20 – 7.5 : 12 – 4.5 + 7.5 = 5 : 6

13. Option (D) is correct.

Explanation: According to the question,

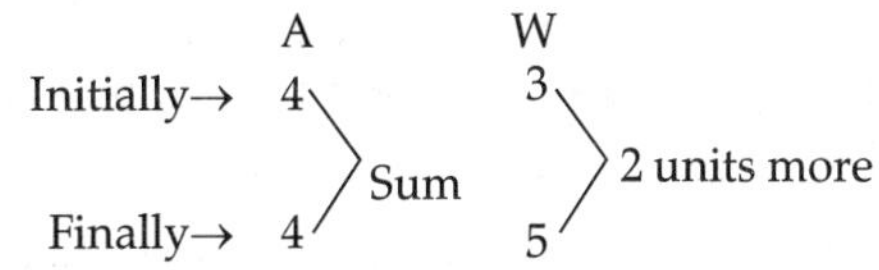

2 units → 5 litres

$$1 \text{ unit} \rightarrow \frac{5}{2} \text{ litres}$$

$$4 \text{ units} \rightarrow \frac{5}{2} \times 4 = 10 \text{ litres}$$

$\therefore$ Quantity of Alcohol = 10 litres

14. Option (A) is correct.

Explanation:

$$15\% \text{ profit} = \frac{23}{20} = \frac{SP}{CP}$$

$$\text{So,} \quad CP = \frac{29.9}{23} \times 20 = ₹\,26$$

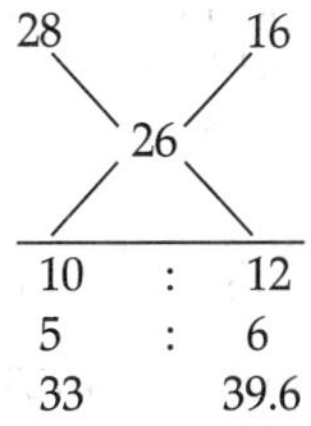

So, required quantity = 33 kg

15. Option (A) is correct.

Explanation:

Total milk = 60 litres

Drawn off = 12 litres

$$\frac{\text{Final quantity}}{\text{Initial quantity}} = \left(1 - \frac{x}{c}\right)^t$$

x = replaced of quantity

c = capacity

t = number of process

$$\frac{\text{Final quantity}}{\text{Initial quantity}} = \left(1 - \frac{12}{60}\right)^2 = \left(\frac{4}{5}\right)^2 = \frac{16}{25}$$

Ratio of milk and water in the resultant mixture = 16 : 9

Level-2: INTERMEDIATE

1. **Option (D) is correct.**

Explanation: According to the question,

A B

7 + 5 = 12 units

Final → 7 + 9= 16

4 units → 9

1 unit → $\frac{9}{4}$

16 units → $\frac{9}{4} \times 16 = 36$

The capacity of the can = 36 litres.

2. **Option (D) is correct.**

Explanation: According to the question,

	Acid	Water	Total	
Sample 1	2 × 40 = 80 :	1 × 40 = 40	3 × 40	
Sample 2	3 × 24 = 72 :	2 × 24 = 48	5 × 24	= 120
Sample 3	5 × 15 = 75 :	3 × 15 = 45	8 × 15	
Ratio of quantity	227 :	133		
Required ratio	133 :	227		

3. **Option (A) is correct.**

Explanation:

60 kg → 3 : 2 → 36 kg (Lead), 24 kg (Tin)

100 kg → 1 : 4 → 20 kg (Tin), 80 kg (Copper)

Total

Tin = 24 + 20 = 44 kg.

4. **Option (A) is correct.**

Explanation: Let the volume of mixture = 24*a* litres.

Volume of chemical X = 15*a l* and volume of water = 9*a l*

48 litres of mixture will have 30*l* chemical X and 18*l* water.

According to question

$$\frac{15a-30}{9a-18+48} = \frac{11}{13}$$

$\Rightarrow$ $195a - 390 = 99a + 330$

$\Rightarrow$ $96a = 720$

$\Rightarrow$ $a = 7.5$

Now, quantity of water after replacement

$= 9 \times 7.5 + 30$

$= 97.5$ litres

5. **Option (D) is correct.**

Explanation:

729 → milk : water = 7 : 2 ⇒ 9 units = 729

1 unit = 81

	M	:	W
Initial →	7	:	2
After adding water	7	:	3

(1 unit)

7 always milk will be same

1 unit of water will be added = 1

Unit = 81 ml

6. **Option (C) is correct.**

Explanation: According to the question

Mixture of copper and aluminium = 2,000 g

30% is copper means = $\frac{30}{100} \times 2{,}000$

= 600 g copper

$$\frac{600}{1{,}400 + x} = \frac{20\%}{80\%}$$

$1{,}400 + x = 2{,}400$

$x = 1000$ g

7. **Option (D) is correct.**

Explanation:

According to the question,

	Acid		Water
Initial Solution →	$1_{\times 2} = 2$		$3_{\times 2} = 6$
Final Solution →	$1_{\times 3} = 3$	:	$2 \times 3 = 6$

(1 unit Increase; Same)

Final solution

We know 5 litres acid is added,

1 unit = 5 litres

9 units → 5 × 9 = 45 litres

∵ Final mixture = 45 litres.

8. **Option (B) is correct.**

Explanation:

Acid : Water Mixture

Glass 1 $[2 : 3 = 5]_{\times 63}$

Glass 2 $[3 : 4 = 7]_{\times 45}$

Glass 3 $[4 : 5 = 9]_{\times 35}$

Glass 1 126 : 189 = 315

Glass 2 135 : 180 = 315

Glass 3 140 : 175 = 315

\+ \+

401 : 544

9. **Option (B) is correct.**

Explanation: By alligation rule

80% 100%

95%

(100 – 95) : (95 – 80) = 15

5 : 15

1 3 (This is the quantity of gold added in ratio)

↓ ×50 ↓

50 gm 150 gm

10. Option (D) is correct.

Explanation: Let the price of water be ₹ 0

According to the question,

S.P. of the mixture = ₹ 20

C.P. of the mixture = $20 \times \frac{100}{125} = \text{Rs}16$

Now, using alligation method

Chemical Water
25 0
16
(16 – 0) = 16 (25 – 16) = 9

Ratio of water to chemical = 9 : 16

11. Option (B) is correct.

Explanation: According ot the question,

By alligation :

Alcohol in first mixture — Alcohol in second mixture
30% 50%
45% (alcohol in final mixture)
5 15
1 : 3

12. Option (A) is correct.

Explanation: According to question

	Milk :	Water
One glass	3×7	5×7 = 8
Another glass	6×8	1×8 = 7
Final	1×28	1×28 = 2

(7, 8, 28 → 56)

One glass	21 :	35
Another glass	48 :	8
Final	28 :	28

Apply alligation:

21 48
28
20 7

⇒ Ratio → 20 : 7

13. Option (A) is correct.

Explanation: According to the question,

Water in initial mixture pure water

40% 100%
50% Water in mixture
50% 10%
5 1
↓× 16 ↓× 16
80 (litres) 16 (litres)

14. Option (B) is correct.

Explanation: According to the question,

Mixture = 240 cc

Rate of $\frac{\text{Water}}{\text{Glycerine}} = \frac{1}{3}$ > 4 unit

4 units → 240

1 unit → 60

$\therefore \frac{\text{Water}}{\text{Glycerine}} = \frac{1 \times 60}{3 \times 60} = \frac{60}{180}$

Water Glycerine
60 180
+ x
2 3 (×60)
×60↓
120

$\therefore$ 60 + x = 120

x = 60 cc

Quantity of water = 60

15. Option (A) is correct.

Explanation: According to the question,

	Milk	Water
Vessel A	4 :	3
Vessel B	2 :	3

Now, using alligation

A B
$\frac{4}{7}$ $\frac{2}{5}$
$\frac{1}{2}$
$\left(\frac{1}{2}-\frac{2}{5}\right)=\frac{1}{10}$ $\frac{1}{14}=\left(\frac{4}{7}-\frac{1}{2}\right)$

Final 14 : 10

Ratio 7 : 5

Level-3: EXPERT

1. Option (B) is correct.

Explanation: According to the question,

	Copper	Tin
Second alloy	1 :	3
Second alloy	2 :	5
Mix alloy	= 3 :	8

Now, using alligation

alloy - 1 alloy - 2
$\frac{1}{4}$ $\frac{2}{7}$
$\frac{3}{11}$
$\left(\frac{2}{7}-\frac{3}{11}\right)=\frac{1}{77}$ $\frac{1}{44}=\left(\frac{3}{11}-\frac{1}{4}\right)$

Required ratio = 1/77 : 1/44 → 4 : 7

2. **Option (A) is correct.**
Explanation: According to the question,
By using alligation method:

Gold 1 Gold 2
12 16
15
(16 – 15) = 1 (15 – 12) = 3

Ratio of quantity is 1 : 3.

3. **Option (A) is correct.**
Explanation: First vessel Second vessel
$\frac{4}{7}$ $\frac{3}{8}$
$\frac{1}{2}$
$\frac{1}{8}$ $\frac{1}{14}$

Petrol : Kerosene = $\frac{1}{8}:\frac{1}{14}$ = 14 : 8 = 7 : 4

4. **Option (D) is correct.**
Explanation:
Let capacity of the given cask full of wine = x litres
Ratio of wine to water after first replacement of 75 litres.
So, now ratio of wine and water in cask.

$$= \frac{x-75}{75} = (x-75) : 75$$

Water removed from this mixture of,

$$= \frac{75}{x} \times 60\text{ l}$$

After mixing 60 l water, Now water in the mixture

$$= 75 - \frac{75\times 60}{x} + 60$$

$$= \left(135 - \frac{4500}{x}\right)\text{l}$$

According to question,

$$\frac{x-\left(135-\frac{4500}{x}\right)}{135-\frac{4500}{x}} = \frac{3}{2}$$

$\Rightarrow$ $x = 300$ or $\frac{75}{2}$

$\because$ First replacement of 75 l. So capacity of cask cannot be $\frac{75}{2}$ litres

$\therefore$ Capacity of cask full of wine = 300 litres

5. **Option (A) is correct.**
Explanation: According to the question,

Milk : Water
7 : 2 } =9
7 : 3 } 1 unit

Remember, water is added not milk, to make equal.
Here, milk is already equal.
9 units = 729
1 unit = 81 litres
The amount of water added = 81 litres

6. **Option (C) is correct.**
Explanation: By alligation,

Initial Mixture Water
10% 100%
20%
80 : 10
8 : 1
↓×5 ↓×5
40 5 litres

7. **Option (A) is correct.**
Explanation: According to the question,
Mixture = 25 litres

Ratio of $\frac{\text{Acid}}{\text{water}} = \frac{4}{1}$ > 5 units

$\therefore$ 5 units → 25 litres
1 unit → 5 litres

$\therefore$ $\frac{\text{Acid}}{\text{water}} = \frac{4\times 5}{1\times 5} = \frac{20}{5}$

Initial Acid : Water
20 : 5
+
3
Final ratio = 20 : 8
= 5 : 2

8. **Option (C) is correct.**
Explanation: According to the question,
Initial quantity = 60 litres
As we know that,

$$\text{Final quantity} = \text{Initial quantity}\left(1-\frac{\text{Volume taken out}}{\text{Initial quantity}}\right)^n$$

Where 'n' = number of time taken for the volume to be taken out

$$\text{Final quantity} = 60\left(1-\frac{6}{60}\right)^3$$

$$= 60\times\frac{9}{10}\times\frac{9}{10}\times\frac{9}{10}$$

Final quantity of milk = 43.74 litres

Speed Time and Distance

$$\text{Speed} = \frac{\text{Distance}}{\text{Time}}$$

$$\text{Average speed} = \frac{\text{Total distance}}{\text{total time taken}}$$

When speed is given $\frac{2S_1S_2}{S_1+S_2} \rightarrow$ average speed

Unit Conversion

$$1 \text{ km/h} = \frac{5}{18} \text{ m/s}$$

$$1 \text{ m/s} = \frac{18}{5} \text{ km/h}$$

When Distance is same

If total time is given

$$D = \frac{S_1 \times S_2}{S_1 + S_2}(T_1 + T_2)$$

If difference of time is given

$$D = \frac{S_1 \times S_2}{S_1 - S_2}(T_1 - T_2)$$

Here S_1 and S_2 are different speeds T_1 and T_2 represents time

Trains

When moving in same direction relative speed = $|S_1 - S_2|$

When moving in opposite direction relative speed = $S_1 + S_2$

Boats and Stream

Upstream Speed
= Speed of boat – Speed of stream

Downstream speed
= Speed of boat + Speed of stream

Speed of still water
= Speed of boat

CHAPTER 9

Speed, Time and Distance

LEARNING OBJECTIVES:

- Problems related to trains.
- Problems related to boats and streams.
- Problems related to average speed.
- Methods of calculating time, speed and distance.
- Questions asked in various competitive exams such as SSC, Bank, CSAT, railway, etc.
- Application in real life.

FORMULA LIST:

$$\text{Speed} = \frac{\text{Distance}}{\text{Time}}$$

$$\text{Time} = \frac{\text{Distance}}{\text{Speed}}$$

$$\text{Distance} = (\text{Speed} \times \text{Time})$$

$$\text{Average Speed} = \frac{\text{Total Distance}}{\text{Total Time}}$$

$$1 \text{ km/h} = \frac{5}{18} \text{ m/s}$$

$$1 \text{ m/s} = \frac{18}{5} \text{ km/h}$$

- If the ratio of the speeds of A and B is $a{:}b$, then the ratio of the times taken by them to cover the same distance is $\frac{1}{a}:\frac{1}{b} = b{:}a$.
- Suppose a man covers a certain distance at x km/h and an equal distance at y km/h.
  Then, the average speed during the whole journey is $\left(\frac{2xy}{x+y}\right)$ km/h.
- If two people A and B set out from two points P and Q at the same time and cross paths after spending T_1 and T_2 hours getting to P and Q, respectively, then (A's speed) / (B's speed) equals $\sqrt{\left(\frac{T_2}{T_1}\right)}$.

TIME AND DISTANCE FORMULA- TRAINS:

- The time and distance formula can be implemented on the problems on trains. Although the basic concept of time and distance is the same, some changes are due to the train length. Let's take a look at the time and distance formula for trains.
- If the speed of the two trains is S_1 and S_2, respectively and lengths are L_1 and L_2, then,
  While moving in the opposite direction

  $$\text{Relative speed} = S_1+S_2$$

  $$\text{Time taken} = \left[\frac{(L_1+L_2)}{(S_1+S_2)}\right]$$

  While moving in the same direction

  $$\text{Relative speed} = S_1 - S_2$$

  $$\text{Time taken} = \left[\frac{(L_1+L_2)}{(S_1-S_2)}\right]$$

- When two trains of lengths L_1 and L_2 cross each other at speeds of S_1 and S_2, respectively, in time t, the equation is given as $S_1 + S_2 = \left(\frac{L_1+L_2}{t}\right)$
- When a train of length L_1 at a speed S_1 passing another train of length L_2 at a speed S_2 formula is expressed as $S_1 = \left(\frac{L_1+L_2}{t}\right)$
- When a train of length L_1 travelling at a speed of S_1 traverses a platform, bridge, or tunnel of length L_2 in time t, the equation is stated as $S_1 - S_2 = \left(\frac{L_1+L_2}{t}\right)$
- If the train passes an electric pole, then
  Length of the Train= Train's Speed × Time
  Time = Length of the Train/Speed
  Speed = Length of the Train / Time

SPEED, TIME AND DISTANCE CONVERSIONS:

- Here, we have given some speed, time and distance conversions which are very useful while solving numericals based on the time and distance formula.

1 kilometer = 1,000 meters
= 0.6214 mile
1 mile = 1.609 kilometer
1 hour = 60 minutes
= 60×60 seconds
= 3600 seconds
1 mile = 1,760 yards
1 yard = 3 feet
1 mile = 5,280 feet

$$1 \text{ km/h} = \frac{5}{18} \text{ m/s}$$

$$1 \text{ m/s} = \frac{18}{5} \text{ km/h} = 3.6 \text{ km/h}$$

$$1 \text{ km/h} = \frac{5}{8} \text{ miles/h}$$

$$1 \text{ mph} = \frac{(1 \times 1{,}760)}{(1 \times 3{,}600)} = \frac{22}{45} \text{ yards/s}$$

$$1 \text{ mph} = \frac{(1 \times 5{,}280)}{(1 \times 3{,}600)} = 22/15 \text{ ft/s}$$

BASIC CONCEPT OF BOATS AND STREAM

Still water:

- If the water is not moving, then it is called still water. Speed of boat in still water = ½ (Downstream Speed + Upstream Speed)

Stream:

- Moving water of the river is called stream.

Upstream:

- If a boat or a swimmer moves in the opposite direction of the stream, then it is called upstream movement. In this case, motion of the boat or swimmer is opposed by the motion of stream.

Downstream:

- If a boat or a swimmer moves in the same direction of the stream, then it is called downstream movement. In this case, motion of the boat or swimmer is supported by the motion of stream. When the speed of the boat or a swimmer is given, then it normally means speed in still water. Concepts and formulas of boats and streams are also applicable to problems involving:

Cyclist and wind:

- Cyclist analogous to boat and wind analogous to stream.

Swimmer and stream:

Swimmer analogous to boat

- If the speed of boat in still water is 'b' km/h and speed of stream is 's' km/h,
Speed of boat downstream = $(b + s)$ km/h, since the boat goes with the stream of water hence, its speed increases.
Speed of boat upstream = $(b - s)$ km/h, the boat goes against the stream of water and hence, its speed gets reduced.

Distance = Speed × Time

Example 1: Ratio of speed of boat in downstream and speed of stream is 9:1, if speed of the current is 3 km per h, then find the distance travelled (in km) upstream in 5 hours.

(a) 105 (b) 110
(c) 120 (d) 95

Sol. (a) Ratio of speed of boat downstream and speed of stream is 9:1
Given, speed of current = 3 km/ h
So, speed of boat downstream = $9 \times 3 = 27$ km/h
Speed of boat in still water = Speed of boat in downstream – Speed of current
= 27 – 3 = 24 km/h
Speed of boat upstream = 24 – 3 = 21 km/h
Distance travelled by boat upstream in 5 hours = $21 \times 5 = 105$ km

Example 2: The ratio of speed of boat in still water to speed of stream is 8:1. It takes 4 h to cover 54 km downstream and 42 km upstream. Find the downstream speed of boat.

(a) 25 kmph (b) 24 kmph
(c) 27 kmph (d) None of these

Sol. (c) Let speed of boat in still water stream be $8x$ kmph and x kmph, respectively.
According to question,

$$\frac{54}{(8x + x)} + \left(\frac{42}{8x - x}\right) = 4$$

$$\Rightarrow \left(\frac{6}{x}\right) + \left(\frac{6}{x}\right) = 4$$

$$\Rightarrow x = 3$$

$\Rightarrow$ Downstream speed = $8x + x = 27$ kmph

Example 3: Time taken to travel a certain distance of 'x' km at speed of 40 km/h is 2 h more than the time taken to travel $(x + 20)$ km at speed of 60 km/h. Find the time taken to travel $(x + 40)$ km at the speed of 40 km/h?

(a) 8 h (b) 9 h
(c) 5 h (d) 4 h

Sol. (a) Using, Time = Distance/Speed

$$\left(\frac{x}{40}\right) - \left(\frac{(x+20)}{60}\right) = 2$$

$$x - 40 = 240$$

$$x = 280 \text{ km}$$

Hence, required time = $\frac{(x+40)}{40} = \frac{320}{40} = 8$ h

Example 4: A man travels from Point P to Q with 90 km/h and from Q to R with 60 km/h. Total distance between P to R is 200 km. If his average speed is 75 km/h, then find the distance between P and Q?

(a) 80 km (b) 120 km
(c) 150 km (d) 90 km

Sol. (b) Assuming distance between P to Q be a km
And Q to R be b km
According to question,

$$75 = \frac{200}{\left[\left(\frac{a}{90}\right)+\left(\frac{b}{60}\right)\right]}$$

$$60a+90b = 200 \times 90 \times 60 \times \left(\frac{1}{75}\right)$$

$$2a+3b = 480 \quad ...(1)$$

Given that, $a+b = 200$ ...(2)
Solving (1) and (2),
Hence, $a = 120$ km

Example 5: The distance between the policeman and thief is 100 meters. Speed of policeman is 8 km/h whereas speed of thief is 10 km/h. How far will the thief have to run before the policeman catches him?
(a) 200 m (b) 500 m
(c) 100 m (d) None of these

Sol. (d) Policeman will never catch thief as speed of policeman is less than the thief.

Example 6: The distance between the policeman and their is 100 meters. Speed of policeman is 10 km/h where speed of thief is 8 km/h. How far will the thief have to run before policeman catches him?
(a) 100 m (b) 200 m
(c) 300 m (d) 400 m

Sol. (d) Distance between the policeman and thief = 100 m
If the thief covers x m distance, then the policeman have to cover $100+x$.
Here, running time is the same.
So, using $\frac{D_1}{D_2}$ = Speed of policemen/speed of thief

$$\Rightarrow \frac{(100+x)}{x} = \frac{10}{8}$$

$$\Rightarrow x = 400 \text{ m}$$

Example 7: Two trains of equal length are running on parallel lines in the same direction at 40 km/h and 30 km/h. The faster train passes the slower train in 18 seconds. The length of each train is:
(a) 100 m (b) 25 m
(c) 90 m (d) 110 m

Sol. (b) Assuming, length of each train = l
They are running in the same direction, then relative speed
= (speed of faster train – speed of slower train)
= (40 – 30) km/h
= 10 km/h

$$\because 10 \text{ km/h} = 10 \times \frac{5}{18} \text{ m/s} = \frac{25}{9} \text{ m/s}$$

Using, speed = distance/time

$$\frac{25}{9} = \frac{2l}{18}$$

$$2l = \frac{25 \times 18}{9}$$

or, $l = \frac{25 \times 8}{2 \times 9}$

or, $l = 25$ m

Example 8: Two stations A and B are 110 km apart on a straight line. One train P starts from A at 7 a.m. and travels towards B at 20 kmph. Another train Q starts from B at 8 a.m. and travels towards A at a speed of 25 kmph. At what time will they meet?
(a) 11 a.m. (b) 9 a.m.
(c) 12 noon (d) 10 a.m.

Sol. (d) Assuming they meet x h after start.
Distance covered by train P in x h = $20x$ km
Distance covered by Q in $(x – 1)$ h
= $25 (x – 1)$ km [As Q starts 1 h later than P.]
According to the question,

$$20x + 25(x – 1) = 110$$

$$\Rightarrow 45x = 135$$

$$\Rightarrow x = 3$$

So, they meet 3 h after 7 a.m., i.e., 10 a.m.

Example 9: Two trains one from Gurgaon to Pune and the other from Pune to Gurgaon, start simultaneously. After they meet, the trains reach their destinations after 9 h and 16 h, respectively. The ratio of their speeds is:
(a) 2:3 (b) 3:2
(c) 4:3 (d) 3:4

Sol. (c) Assuming the trains be G and P (G-train starting from Gurgaon, P- train starting from Pune)
Using,
Speed 1:Speed 2 = $\sqrt{\text{time}}$ after meet of 1: $\sqrt{\text{time}}$ after meet of 2
G's speed:P's speed = $\sqrt{16} : \sqrt{9}$
G's speed:P's speed = 4:3

Example 10: A man can row at 8 km/h in still water. If the velocity of current is 2 km/h and it takes him 4 h to row to a place and come back, how far is the place?
(a) 20 km (b) 18 km
(c) 15 km (d) 19 km

Sol. (c) Speed of boat in still water = 8 km/h
Speed of current = 2 km/h
Downstream speed = 8 + 2 = 10 km/h
Upstream speed = 8 – 2 = 6 km/h
Distance = D
Time taken = 4 h

$$\therefore \frac{D}{10}+\frac{D}{6} = 4$$

$$\Rightarrow \frac{3D+5D}{30} = 4$$

$$\Rightarrow 8D = 120$$

$$\Rightarrow D = 15 \text{ km}$$

Level 1 Beginner

1. A car covers four successive 6 km stretches at speeds of 25 kmph, 50 kmph, 75 kmph and 150 kmph respectively. Its average speed over this distance is: **[SSC CGL-II 2012]**
   (A) 25 km/h (B) 50 km/h
   (C) 45 km/h (D) None of these
2. A car covers a certain distance travelling at a speed of 60 km/h and returns to the starting point at a speed of 40 km/h. The average speed of the car for the entire journey is: **[SSC CHSL 2022]**
   (A) 20 km/h (B) 48 km/h
   (C) 120 km/h (D) 50 km/h
3. A train 100 metres long meets a man going in the opposite direction at 5 km/h and passes him in $7\frac{1}{5}$ seconds. What is the speed of the train in km/h ? **[SSC CHSL 2012]**
   (A) 45 km/h (B) 60 km/h
   (C) 55 km/h (D) 50 km/h
4. Walking at a speed of 5 km/h, a man reaches his office 6 min late. Walking at 6 km/h, he reaches there 2 min early. The distance of his office is: **[SSC Multitasking 2013]**
   (A) 2 km (B) 3 km (C) 4 km (D) 5 km
5. A boat can row 36 km upstream in 9 hours and the same distance downstream in 3 hours. What is the speed of the boat in still water? **[SSC CHSL 2023]**
   (A) 14 km/h (B) 8 km/h
   (C) 10 km/h (D) 6 km/h
6. By walking at $\frac{3}{4}$ of his usual speed, a man reaches his office 20 minutes later than his usual time. The usual time taken by him to reach his office is: **[SSC CGL-I 2010]**
   (A) 75 minutes (B) 60 minutes
   (C) 40 minutes (D) 30 minutes
7. A train, 300 m long, passed a man, walking along the line in the same direction at the rate of 3 km/h in 33 seconds. The speed of the train is: **[SSC CGL-I 2010]**
   (A) 30 km/h (B) 32 km/h
   (C) $32\frac{8}{11}$ km/h (D) $35\frac{8}{11}$ km/h
8. In a 100 m race, Kamal defeats Bimal by 5 seconds. If the speed of Kamal is 18 Kmph, then the speed of Bimal is: **[SSC CGL-II 2010]**
   (A) 12 m/s (B) 3 m/s
   (C) 5 m/s (D) 4 m/s
9. A train, 240 m long crosses a man walking along the line in the opposite direction at the rate of 3 kmph in 10 seconds. The speed of the train is: **[SSC CGL-II 2010]**
   (A) 63 km/h (B) 75 km/h
   (C) 83.4 km/h (D) 86.4 km/h
10. A boatman rows 1 km in 5 minutes, along the stream and 6 km in 1 hour against the stream. The speed of the stream is: **[SSC CGL-II 2010]**
   (A) 3 km/h (B) 6 km/h
   (C) 10 km/h (D) 12 km/h
11. A student goes to school at the rate of 2½ km/h and reaches 6 minutes late. If he travels at the speed of 3 km/h, he is 10 minutes early. The distance (in km) between the school and his house is: **[SSC CGL-I 2011]**
   (A) 4 (B) 3 (C) 6 (D) 5
12. Walking at 6/7th of his usual speed, a man is 25 minutes too late. His usual time to cover this distance is: **[SSC CGL-II 2011]**
   (A) 2 h 30 minutes (B) 2 h 15 minutes
   (C) 2 h 25 minutes (D) 2 h 10 minutes
13. Walking at 5 km/h, a student reaches his school from his house 15 minutes early and walking at 3 km/h, he is late by 9 minutes. What is the distance between his school and his house? **[SSC CGL-II 2011]**
   (A) 3 km (B) 5 km (C) 6 km (D) 4 km
14. A thief is noticed by a policeman from a distance of 200 m. The thief starts running and the policeman chases him. The thief and the policeman run at the rate of 10 km per hour and 11 km per hour, respectively. The distance (in metres) between them after 6 minutes is: **[SSC CGL-I 2012]**
   (A) 190 (B) 200 (C) 100 (D) 150
15. With average speed of 40 km/h, a train reaches its destination in time. If it goes with an average speed of 35 km/h, it is late by 15 minutes. The total journey is: **[SSC CGL-I 2012]**
   (A) 30 km (B) 40 km
   (C) 70 km (D) 80 km
16. A train 270 metre long is running at a speed of 36 km per hour, then it will cross a bridge of length 180 metres in: **[SSC Sub Inspector 2013]**
   (A) 40 s (B) 45 s (C) 50 s (D) 35 s
17. A train is moving at a speed of 80 km/h and covers a certain distance in 4.5 h. The speed of the train to cover the same distance in 4 h is: **[SSC CHSL 2013]**
   (A) 90 km/h (B) 100 km/h
   (C) 70 km/h (D) 85 km/h
18. Sanjana can row a boat at 9 km/h in the still water. It takes her twice as long to row up a certain distance as to row down the same distance in the river. What is the rate of the stream (in km/h)? **[SSC CHSL 2023]**
   (A) 4 (B) 1 (C) 3 (D) 2
19. A train moving at a rate of 36 km/h crosses a standing man in 10 seconds. It will cross a platform 55 metres long, in: **[SSC CGL-I 2013]**

(A) $\frac{160}{16}$ seconds (B) 6 seconds
(C) 8 seconds (D) 51/3 seconds

20. Speed of stream is 4 km/hr and the speed of boat is 11 km/hr. In how much time will the boat cover a distance of 21 km upstream and 45 km downstream? **[SSC CHSL 2023]**
(A) 6 hours (B) 3 hours
(C) 4 hours (D) 7 hours

21. Anil calculated that it will take 45 minutes to cover a distance using 60 km/h by his car. How long will it take to cover the same distance, if the speed of his car is reduced by 15 km/h? **[SSC CGL-I 2013]**
(A) 36 min (B) 55.38 min
(C) 48 min (D) 40 min

22. Two trains 320 m and 205 m in length are running towards each other on parallel lines. One train runs at the rate of 70 kmph and the other train runs at the rate of 56 kmph. Find the time they will take to cross each other (in seconds). **[SSC CHSL 2023]**
(A) 10 (B) 20
(C) 12 (D) 15

23. By walking at 3/4 of his usual speed, a man reaches his office 20 minutes later than usual. His usual time is: **[SSC CGL-I 2013]**
(A) 30 min. (B) 75 min.
(C) 90 min. (D) 60 min.

24. A railway train 100 metres long is running at the speed of 30 km/h. In what time does it pass a man standing near a line? **[SSC Multitasking 2014]**
(A) 10 seconds (B) 13 seconds
(C) 12 seconds (D) 15 seconds

25. A student goes to school at the rate of 5/2 km/h and reaches 6 minutes late. If he travels at the speed of 3 km/h, then he reaches 10 minutes earlier. The distance of the school is: **[SSC Sub Inspector 2014]**
(A) 45 km (B) 20 km (C) 10 km (D) 4 km

26. A train 50 metre long passes a platform 100 metre long in 10 s. The speed of the train in km/h is: **[SSC Sub Inspector 2014]**
(A) 50 km/h (B) 54 km/h
(C) 48 km/h (D) 40 km/h

27. A horse take 2 ½ seconds to complete a round around a circular field. If the speed of the horse was 66 m/s, then the radius of the field is:
(A) 25.62 m (B) 26.52 m
(C) 25.26 m (D) 26.25 m

28. If a train runs at 70 km/h, it reaches its destination late by 12 minutes. But if it runs at 80 km/h, it is late by 3 minutes. The correct time to cover the journey is: **[SSC CGL 2014]**
(A) 58 minutes (B) 2 h
(C) 1 h (D) 59 minutes

29. How many seconds will a train 120 metres long running at the rate of 36 km/h take to cross a bridge of 360 metres in length? **[SSC Sub Inspector 2015]**
(A) 48 s (B) 36 s (C) 40 s (D) 46 s

30. A train 150 m long passes a km stone in 30 seconds and another train of the same length travelling in the opposite direction in 10 seconds. The speed of the second train is: **[SSC CHSL 2015]**
(A) 125 km/h (B) 25 km/h
(C) 90 km/h (D) 75 km/h

31. Raju and Sohan started a car race from the same point, in the same direction and at the same circular track of length 1725 m with speeds of 72 km/h. and 90 km/h, respectively. After how much time (in seconds) will they meet again for the first time? **[SSC CHSL 2023]**
(A) 345 seconds (B) 335 seconds
(C) 340 seconds (D) 350 seconds

32. A farmer travelled a distance of 61 km in 9 h. He travelled partly on foot at the rate of 4 km/h and partly on a bicycle at the rate of 9 km/h. The distance travelled on foot is: **[SSC CGL-I 2015]**
(A) 17 km (B) 16 km (C) 15 km (D) 14 km

33. A train runs at an average speed of 75 km/h. If the distance to be covered is 1050 Kms. How long will the train take to cover it ? **[SSC CGL-I 2015]**
(A) 13 h (B) 12 h (C) 14 h (D) 15 h

34. A train 180 metre long is running at a speed of 90 km/h. How long will it take to pass a post? **[SSC CGL-I 2015]**
(A) 8.2 s (B) 7.8 s
(C) 8 s (D) 7.2 s

35. A train, 200 m long, is running at a speed of 54 km/h. The time in seconds that will be taken by train to cross a 175 m long bridge is: **[SSC CGL-I 2016]**
(A) 125 (B) 20 (C) 25 (D) 10

36. A man travelled a distance 72 km in 12 h. He travelled partly on foot at 5 km/h and partly on a bicycle at 10 km/h. The distance travelled by foot is **[SSC Sub Inspector 2016]**
(A) 46 km (B) 52 km (C) 50 km (D) 48 km

37. A bus starts running with the initial speed of 21 km/h and its speed increases every hour by 3 km/h. How many hours will it take to cover a distance of 252 km? **[SSC CGL 2017]**
(A) 3 (B) 5 (C) 8 (D) 10

38. Two cars travel from city A to city B at a speed of 36 km/h and 48 km/h, respectively. If one car takes 3 h lesser time than the other car for the journey, then the distance between City A and City B is: **[SSC CHSL 2017]**
(A) 518 km (B) 432 km
(C) 648 km (D) 346 km

39. A train covers a distance of 12 km in 10 minutes. If it takes 6 seconds to pass a telegraph post, then the length of the train is: **[SSC MTS 2017]**
(A) 120 m (B) 90 m (C) 100 m (D) 140 m

40. A bus moving at 40 km per hour covers a distance in 6 h 15 minutes. If it travels the same distance at 50 km per hour, then how long will it take to cover the distance? **[SSC Sub Inspector 2015]**
(A) 6 h (B) 2 h
(C) 4 h (D) 5 h

2 Level Intermediate

1. Buses start from a bus terminal with a speed of 20 km/h at intervals of 10 minutes. What is the speed of a man coming from the opposite direction towards the bus terminal, if he meets the buses at intervals of 8 minutes ? [SSC CGL-I 2010]
(A) 3 km/h (B) 4 km/h
(C) 5 km/h (D) 7 km/h

2. A man can row 6 km/h in still water. If the speed of the current is 2 km/h, it takes 3 h more in upstream than in downstream for the same distance. The distance is: [SSC CGL-I 2011]
(A) 30 km (B) 24 km (C) 20 km (D) 32km

3. A train overtakes two persons who are walking in the same direction in which the train is running, at the rate of 2 kmph and 4 kmph and passes them completely in 9 and 10 seconds, respectively. The length of the train (in metres): [SSC CGL-II 2012]
(A) 72 (B) 45 (C) 54 (D) 50

4. Ship is moving at a speed of 30 km/h. To know the depth of the ocean beneath it, it sends a radio wave which travels at a speed 200 m/s. The ship receives the signal after it has moved 500 m. The depth of the ocean is: [SSC CGL-I 2012]
(A) 6 km (B) 12 km (C) 4 km (D) 8 km

5. A car travels a distance of 60 km at uniform speed. If the speed of car is increased by 8 km/hr, then it takes 2 hours less to cover the same distance. What is the original speed of the car? [SSC CHSL 2023]
(A) 12 km/h (B) 16 km/h
(C) 10 km/h (D) 15 km/h

6. Zeenat and Nasreen participate in a circular race of 1.2 km. They start the race at a speed of 18 km/h and 27 km/h. respectively, from the same point at the same time. After how much time (in minutes) will they meet at the starting point for the first time, if they are running in the same direction? [SSC CHSL 2023]
(A) 9 (B) 7 (C) 10 (D) 8

7. A man rides at the rate of 18 km/h, but stops for 6 mins, to change horses at the end of every 7th km. The time that he will take to cover a distance of 90 km is: [SSC CGL-II 2013]
(A) 6 h (B) 6 h 12 min
(C) 6 h 18 min (D) 6 h 24 min

8. A certain distance is covered at a certain speed. If half of this distance is covered in double the time, the ratio of the two speeds is: [SSC CGL-II 2013]
(A) 1 : 4 (B) 2 : 1 (C) 1 : 2 (D) 4 : 1

9. Two cars X and Y start running towards each other from two places 216 km apart. The ratio of the speeds of X and Y is 5 : 7 and the speed of X is 60 km/h. After how many minutes will X and Y meet each other? [SSC CHSL 2021]
(A) 75 (B) 72 (C) 90 (D) 80

10. Raju has to cover a distance of 240 km in 4 h. If he covers one-third of the journey in $(2/7)^{th}$ time, what is his speed at the beginning of the journey ? [SSC Multitasking 2014]
(A) 70 km/h (B) 75 km/h
(C) 60 km/h (D) 65 km/h

11. A is twice as fast as B and B is thice as fast as C. The journey covered by C in 42 minutes will be covered by A in: [SSC CHSL 2014]
(A) 5 minutes (B) 7 minutes
(C) 3 minutes (D) 1 h

12. It takes 8 h for a 600 km journey, if 120 km is done by train and the rest by car. It takes 20 minutes more, if 200 km is down by train and the rest by car. The ratio of the speed of the train to that of the car is: [SSC CGL 2014]
(A) 2 : 3 (B) 3 : 2 (C) 3 : 4 (D) 4 : 3

13. A ship after sailing 12 km towards south from a particular place covered 5 km more towards east. Then, the straightway distance of the ship from that place is [SSC CGL-I 2015]
(A) 18 km (B) 15 km
(C) 13 km (D) 11 km

14. Walking at the rate of 4 kmph, a man covers certain distance in 2 h 45 min. Running at a speed of 16.5 kmph, the man will cover the same distance in how many minutes ? [SSC CGL-I 2015]
(A) 35 min (B) 40 min
(C) 45 min (D) 50 min

15. A man goes to a place on a bicycle at a speed of 16 km/h and comes back at lower speed. If the average speed is 6.4 km/h in total, then the return speed (in km/h) is: [SSC CGL-I 2016]
(A) 10 (B) 8 (C) 6 (D) 4

16. One third part of a certain journey is covered at the speed of 10 km/hr. one fourth part at the speed of 15 km/hr and the rest part at the speed of 20 km/hr. What will be the average speed for the whole journey? [SSC CHSL 2023]
(A) 15 km/h (B) $\frac{200}{17}$ km/h
(C) $\frac{240}{17}$ km/h (D) $\frac{280}{17}$ km/h

17. Points A and B are 100 km apart on a highway. One car starts from A and another from B at the same time. If the cars travel in the same direction, they meet in 5 h. If the cars travel towards each other, they meet in 1 hour. What is the speed of the faster car? [SSC Sub Inspector 2016]
(A) 70 km/h (B) 40 km/h
(C) 60 km/h (D) 80 km/h

18. A boat can go 15 km downstream and 8 km upstream in 2 h. It can go 20 km downstream and 12 upstream in 2 h 50 min. What is the speed (in km/h) of the boat while going downstream? **[SSC CHSL 2021]**

(A) 20 **(B)** 18 **(C)** 15 **(D)** 16

19. A train leaves Delhi at 10 a.m. and reaches Jaipur at 4 p.m. on the same day. Another train leaves Jaipur at 12 p.m. and reaches Delhi at 5 p.m. on the same day. What is the time of day (approximately) when the two trains will meet? **[SSC CGL 2017]**

(A) 1:42 p.m. **(B)** 1:27 p.m.
(C) 2:04 p.m. **(D)** 1:49 p.m.

20. A motorcyclist left $6\frac{6}{9}$ minutes later than the scheduled time but in order to reach its destination 21 km away in time, he had to increase his speed by 12 km/h from the usual speed. What is usual speed (in km/h) of the motorcyclist? **[SSC Sub Inspector 2017]**

(A) 28 **(B)** 35 **(C)** 42 **(D)** 64

21. A bus starts running with an initial speed of 33 km/h and its speed increases every hour by a certain amount. If it takes 7 h to cover a distance of 315 km, then what will be hourly increment (in km/h) in the speed of the bus? **[SSC Sub Inspector 2017]**

(A) 1 **(B)** 2 **(C)** 3 **(D)** 4

22. If a train maintains an average speed of 42 km per hour, it arrives at its destination at the right time, if however, the average speed is 40 km per hour, it arrives 15 minutes late. Find the length of the journey. **[SSC MTS 2017]**

(A) 210 km **(B)** 205 km
(C) 209 km **(D)** 200 km

3 Expert Level

1. On a journey across Kolkata, a taxi averages 50 km per hour for 50% of the distance 40 km per hour for 40% of it and 20 km per hour for the remaining. The average speed in km/h, for the whole journey is: **[SSC Sub Inspector 2013]**

(A) 42 **(B)** 40 **(C)** 35 **(D)** 45

2. Speed of a train is 30 percent more than the speed of a car. Both start from point P at the same time and reach point Q at the same time. P and Q are 130 km apart from each other. On the way train stops for 30 minutes at a station. What is the speed of the train? **[SSC CHSL 2023]**

(A) 78 km/h **(B)** 72 km/h
(C) 60 km/h **(D)** 70 km/h

3. The average marks scored by a student in 4 subjects is 75. But when the marks of English are added to it, the overall average became 70. How much did he score in English? **[SSC CHSL 2022]**

(A) 50 **(B)** 60 **(C)** 55 **(D)** 65

4. A train travels 40% faster than a car. Both start from point A at the same time and reach point B, 140 km away at the same time. On the way, the train takes 25 minutes for stopping at the stations. What is the speed (in km/h) of the train? **[SSC CGL 2017]**

(A) 135 **(B)** 150 **(C)** 134.4 **(D)** 143

5. A truck covers a distance of 384 km at a certain speed. If the speed is decreased by 16 km/h, it will take 2 h more to cover the same distance. 75% of its original speed (in km/h) is: **[SSC CGL 2019]**

(A) 45 **(B)** 54 **(C)** 48 **(D)** 42

6. A and B are travelling towards each other from the points P and Q, respectively. After crossing each other, A and B take $6\frac{1}{8}$ h and 8 h, respectively, to reach their destinations Q and P, respectively. If the speed of B is 16.8 km/h, then the speed (in km/h) of A is: **[SSC CGL 2019]**

(A) 20.8 **(B)** 19.8 **(C)** 19.2 **(D)** 20.4

7. A train travelling at 44 km/h crosses a man walking with a speed of 8 km/h in the same direction in 15 seconds. If the train crosses a woman coming from the opposite direction in 10 seconds, then what is the speed (in km/h) of the woman? **[SSC CHSL 2018]**

(A) 10.5 **(B)** 10 **(C)** 9 **(D)** 8.5

8. Two trains of the same length are running on parallel tracks in the same direction at 54 km/h and 42 km/h, respectively. The faster train passes the other train in 63 seconds. What is the length (in metres) of each train? **[SSC CHSL 2019]**

(A) 90 **(B)** 81 **(C)** 105 **(D)** 210

9. Given that the lengths of the paths of a ball thown with different speeds by two boys are the same, if they take 0.6 seconds and 1 second, respectively to cover the said length, what is the average speed of travel for the first thow, if the same for the second is 96 km/h? **[SSC CHSL 2020]**

(A) 100 kmph **(B)** 150 kmph
(C) 160 kmph **(D)** 200 kmph

10. A train travelling at the speed of x km/h crossed a 200 m long platform in 30 seconds and overtook a man walking in the same direction at the speed of 6 km/h in 20 seconds. What is the value of x? **[SSC CGL Tier-II 2019]**

(A) 50 **(B)** 54 **(C)** 56 **(D)** 60

11. A and B started their journeys from X to Y and Y to X, respectively. After crossing each other, A and B completed the remaining parts of their journey in 25 h and 36 h, respectively. If the speed of B is 35 km/h, then the speed (in km/h) of A is : **[SSC CGL Tier-II 2018]**

(A) 40 **(B)** 42 **(C)** 32 **(D)** 36

12. To cover a distance of 416 km, a train A takes $2\frac{2}{3}$ h more than train B. If the speed of A is doubled, it would take $1\frac{1}{3}$ h less than B. What is the speed (in km/h) of train A ? [SSC CGL Tier-II 2020]
(A) 56 (B) 54 (C) 52 (D) 65

13. A journey of 96 km takes one hour less by a fast train (A) than by a slow train (B). If the average speed of B is 16 km/h less than that of A, then the average speed (in km/h) of A is: [SSC CGL Tier-I 2019]
(A) 64 (B) 48 (C) 54 (D) 60

14. A person covers 40% of the distance from A to B at 8 km/h, 40% of the remaining distance at 9 km/h and the rest at 12 km/h. His average speed (in km/h) for the journey is : [SSC CGL 2018]
(A) $9\frac{5}{8}$ (B) $9\frac{2}{3}$ (C) $9\frac{3}{8}$ (D) $9\frac{1}{3}$

15. A thief is spotted by a policeman from a distance of 480 m. When the policeman starts the chase, the thief also starts running. If the speed of the thief is 19 km/h and that of the policeman is 23 km/h, then how far would the thief have to run before he is overtaken? [SSC CHSL 2022]
(A) 2080 m (B) 2280 m
(C) 2290 m (D) 2180 m

16. A travels a certain distance with thee different speeds; first covers 3 km with a speed of 9 km/h, the second 6 km with a speed of 15 km/h and the third 9 km with a speed of 18 km/h. What is the average speed (in kmph) of A's entire journey? [SSC MTS 2019]
(A) $\frac{660}{37}$ (B) $\frac{480}{37}$ (C) $\frac{460}{37}$ (D) $\frac{540}{37}$

17. A boat can go 3 km upstream and 5 km downstream in 55 minutes. It can also go 9 km downstream and 4 km upstream in 1 h 25 minutes. How much time (in h) will it take to go 43.2 km downstream ? [SSC CPO 2017]
(A) 3.0 (B) 3.6 (C) 4.5 (D) 3.2

18. The speed of a boat in still water is 15 km/h, and the speed of the current is 5 km/h. In how much time (in h) will the boat travel a distance of 60 km upstream and the same distance downstream? [SSC CPO 2020]
(A) 12 (B) 9 (C) 10 (D) 20

19. A boat can go 3.6 km upstream and 5.4 km downstream in 54 minutes, while it can go 5.4 km upstream and 3.6 km downstream in 58.5 minutes. The time (in minutes) taken by the boat in going 10 km downstream is: [SSC CGL 2020]
(A) 48 (B) 54 (C) 50 (D) 45

20. A delivery boy started from his office at 10 a.m. to deliver an article. He rode his scooter at a speed of 32 km/h. He delivered the article and waited for 15 minutes to get the payment. After the payment was made, he reached his office at 11.25 a.m., travelling at a speed of 24 km/h. Find the total distance travelled by the boy. [SSC CGL TIER-II 2020]
(A) 32 km (B) 30 km (C) 35 km (D) 40 km

ANSWER KEY

Level-1: Beginner

1.	(B)	2.	(B)	3.	(A)	4.	(C)	5.	(B)	6.	(B)	7.	(D)	8.	(D)	9.	(C)	10.	(A)
11.	(A)	12.	(A)	13.	(A)	14.	(C)	15.	(C)	16.	(B)	17.	(A)	18.	(C)	19.	(A)	20.	(A)
21.	(B)	22.	(D)	23.	(D)	24.	(C)	25.	(D)	26.	(B)	27.	(D)	28.	(C)	29.	(A)	30.	(C)
31.	(A)	32.	(B)	33.	(C)	34.	(D)	35.	(C)	36.	(D)	37.	(C)	38.	(B)	39.	(A)	40.	(D)

Level-2: Intermediate

1.	(C)	2.	(B)	3.	(D)	4.	(A)	5.	(A)	6.	(D)	7.	(B)	8.	(D)	9.	(C)	10.	(A)
11.	(B)	12.	(C)	13.	(C)	14.	(B)	15.	(D)	16.	(C)	17.	(C)	18.	(C)	19.	(D)	20.	(C)
21.	(D)	22.	(A)																

Level-3: Expert

1.	(B)	2.	(A)	3.	(A)	4.	(C)	5.	(C)	6.	(C)	7.	(B)	8.	(C)	9.	(C)	10.	(D)
11.	(B)	12.	(C)	13.	(B)	14.	(C)	15.	(B)	16.	(D)	17.	(B)	18.	(B)	19.	(C)	20.	(A)

Solutions with Detailed Explanation

Level-1 : BEGINNER

1. **Option (B) is correct.**

Explanation: When the distance is D same, then

average speed = $\frac{4 \times abcd}{[abc+bcd+abd+acd]}$

Here, *a*, *b*, *c* and *d* are different speeds.

So, average speed as asked in the question is;

$$\frac{4\times25\times50\times75\times150}{[(25\times50\times75)+(50\times75\times150)+(25\times50\times150)+(25\times75\times150)]}$$

= 50 kmph

2. **Option (B) is correct.**

Explanation:

Using, average speed = $\frac{2.S_1.S_2}{S_1+S_2}$

Where, S_1 and S_2 are speeds for to and fro journey respectively.

So, average speed = $\frac{2\times60\times40}{60+40}$ = 48 km/h

3. **Option (A) is correct.**

Explanation:

Speed of man = 5 km/h

Let speed of train = T km/h

$(T+5)\times\frac{5}{18}\times7.2 = 100$

(Speed adds if two things moving in opposite direction)

$\Rightarrow$ T = 45 kmph

4. **Option (C) is correct.**

Explanation:

Here $S_1 = 5, t_1 = 6$

$S_2 = 6, t_2 = 2$

Using, Distance = $\frac{(S_1\times S_2)(t_1+t_2)}{S_2-S_1}$

$= \frac{(6\times5)(6+2)}{6-5}$

$= 30\times\left(\frac{8}{60}\right) = 4$ km

5. **Option (B) is correct.**

Explanation:

Let the speed of boat = *a* km/h

Let the speed of stream = *b* km/h

Then downstream speed = (*a* + *b*) km/h

Then upstream speed = (*a* – *b*) km/h

Using, time = $\frac{\text{distance}}{\text{speed}}$

$\Rightarrow 9 = \frac{36}{a-b}$

$\Rightarrow a - b = 4$ ...(1)

And $3 = \frac{36}{a+b}$

$\Rightarrow a + b = 12$ ...(2)

After solving eq. (1) and (2),

a = 8 and *b* = 4

so, the speed of boat = 8 km/h

6. **Option (B) is correct.**

Explanation: At $\frac{3}{4}$ of the usual speed, the time taken is $\frac{4}{3}$ of the usual time.

Let usual time taken by him is *x* mins.

$\frac{4}{3}$ of usual time – usual time = 20 mins.

$\Rightarrow \frac{4x-3x}{3} = 20$

$\Rightarrow \frac{x}{3} = 20$

$x = 60$ mins.

7. **Option (D) is correct.**

Explanation: Assuming speed of train = *x* km/h

Length of train = 300 metres

They are in the same direction, then the relative speed = (*x* – 3) km/h

According to the question,

$\left[\frac{300}{(x-3)}\right]\times\frac{18}{5} = 33$

$\Rightarrow \frac{100\times18}{(5x-15)} = 11$

$\Rightarrow 1800 = 55x - 165$

$\Rightarrow 55x = 1965$

Hence, $x = \frac{1965}{55}$ i.e., $35\frac{8}{11}$ km/h

8. **Option (D) is correct.**

Explanation: Total distance travelled by both the players = 100 m

Speed of Kamal = 18 kmph = $18\times\frac{5}{18}$ = 5 m/s

Using, Time = Distance/Speed

$\Rightarrow$ Time = $\frac{100}{5}$

$\Rightarrow$ Time = 20 secs ...(1)

Kamal takes 20 secs to cover 100m.

So, Bimal takes (20+5)= 25 secs to cover 100 m.

Again, (in Bimal's case)

Using, Distance = speed × time

$\Rightarrow$ 100 = speed × 25

$\Rightarrow \frac{100}{25}$ = speed

Hence, required speed is 4 m/s.

9. **Option (C) is correct.**

Explanation:

Assuming, speed = s km/h

Using, Time = Distance/Speed

$\Rightarrow \frac{240\times18}{[(s+3)\times5]} = 10$

$\Rightarrow 432 = (5s + 15)$

$\Rightarrow s = \frac{417}{5} = 83.4$ km/h

10. **Option (A) is correct.**

Explanation: Assuming speed of boat is "*a*" and stream be "*b*".

Using, Speed = Distance/Time

When rows downstream,

$a + b = \frac{1}{\left(\frac{5}{60}\right)} = 12$ ...(1)

When rows upstream

$$a - b = \frac{6}{1} = 6 \quad ...(2)$$

Subtracting (1) and (2)

$$b = 3$$

Hence, speed of stream is 3 km/h.

11. Option (A) is correct.

Explanation: Assuming the distance = d

According to the question,

$$\left(\frac{d}{2.5}\right) - \left(\frac{d}{3}\right) = \frac{16}{60}$$

$$\Rightarrow \frac{(6d - 5d)}{15} = \frac{16}{60}$$

$$\Rightarrow d = \left(\frac{16}{60}\right) \times 15 = 4 \text{ km}$$

12. Option (A) is correct.

Explanation: Assuming a be the distance travelled and b be the original speed.

Time = Distance/Speed

The original time taken = $\frac{a}{b}$

Walking 6/7th of his usual speed.

i.e., new speed is $\frac{6}{7}b$

So, new time is $\frac{a}{\left(\frac{6}{7}\right)b}$

A man is 25 minutes too late.

So, New time – Original time = 25

$$\frac{7a}{6b} - \frac{a}{b} = 25$$

$$\Rightarrow \frac{a}{b}\left(\frac{7-6}{6}\right) = 25$$

$$\Rightarrow \frac{a}{b} = 25 \times 6$$

$$= 150 \text{ minutes i.e., 2 h 30 minutes}$$

13. Option (A) is correct.

Explanation:

Here, $S_1 = 3, t_1 = 9$

$S_2 = 5, t_2 = 15$

Using; Distance $= \frac{(S_1 \times S_2)(t_1 + t_2)}{S_2 - S_1}$

$$= \frac{(3 \times 5)(9 + 15)}{5 - 3} \times \left(\frac{1}{60}\right) = 3 \text{ km}$$

14. Option (C) is correct.

Explanation: Given that the initial distance between the policeman and thief = 200 m

Relative speed = (11 – 10)=1 km

Using; distance = speed × time

Distance covered by policeman in 6 mins.

$$= 1 \times \left(\frac{6}{60}\right) = \frac{1}{10} \text{ km} = 100 \text{ m}$$

Hence, the required distance i.e., after 6 mins.

$$= 200 - 100 = 100 \text{ m}$$

15. Option (C) is correct.

Explanation: Assuming total distance = d km

According to question,

$$\left(\frac{d}{35}\right) - \left(\frac{d}{40}\right) = \frac{15}{60}$$

$$\Rightarrow \frac{d}{280} = \frac{1}{4}$$

$$\Rightarrow d = \frac{280}{4} = 70 \text{ km}$$

16. Option (B) is correct.

Explanation:

$$36 \text{ km/h} = 36 \times \left(\frac{5}{18}\right) = 10 \text{ m/s}$$

Using; time $= \frac{\text{distance}}{\text{speed}}$

$$\text{Required time} = \frac{(270 + 180)}{10} = 45 \text{ s.}$$

17. Option (A) is correct.

Explanation: Distance covered by train = 80 × 4.5 = 360 km

Speed of train to cover 360 km in 4 h = $\frac{360}{4}$

= 90 km/h

18. Option (C) is correct.

Explanation: Speed of boat in still water = 9 km/h

Let speed of stream = x km/h and boat travel a distance km up-down in river.

According to question

$$2 \times \frac{y}{x+9} = \frac{y}{9-x}$$

$$\Rightarrow 18 - 2x = x + 9$$

$$\Rightarrow 3x = 9$$

$$\Rightarrow x = 3$$

∴ Speed of stream = 3 km/h

19. Option (A) is correct.

Explanation:

$$\text{Train's length} = 36 \times \left(\frac{5}{18}\right) \times 10 = 100 \text{ m}$$

So, time taken by train to cover 55 m platform

$$= \frac{(100 + 55)}{\left(\frac{36 \times 5}{18}\right)} = \frac{155}{10} \text{ s.}$$

20. Option (A) is correct.

Explanation:

Given,

The speed of stream = 4 km/h

Speed of boat = 11 km/h

So, upstream speed = 11 – 4 = 7 km/h

And downstream speed = 11 + 4 = 15 km/h

We have, Time = $\frac{\text{Distance}}{\text{Speed}}$

According to the question,

$$\Rightarrow \text{Total time taken} = \frac{21}{7} + \frac{45}{15} = 3 + 3 = 6 \text{ hr}$$

21. Option (B) is correct.

Explanation:

$$\text{Speed} = \frac{60}{45} \times 60 = 80 \text{ km/h}$$

If speed is 65 km/h, then

$$\text{Time} = \frac{60 \text{ km}}{65 \text{ km/hr}} \times 60 = 55.38$$

22. Option (D) is correct.

Explanation:

Total length of both trams, $d = 320 + 205 = 525$ m

Relative speed of both trams = (70+56) km/h

$$= 126 \times \frac{5}{18} \text{ m/s} = 35 \text{ m/s}$$

$$\text{Required time to cross each other} = \frac{525}{35} = 15 \text{ seconds.}$$

23. Option (D) is correct.

Explanation: At $\frac{3}{4}$ of the usual speed, the time taken is $\frac{4}{3}$ of the usual time.

Let usual time = a min

According to the question,

$$\left(\frac{4}{3}\right)a - a = 20 \text{ min}$$

$$\Rightarrow \frac{4a}{3} - a = 20$$

$$\Rightarrow \frac{a}{3} = 20$$

$$\Rightarrow a = 60 \text{ min.}$$

24. Option (C) is correct.

Explanation: Given, speed = 30 km/h = $\frac{25}{3}$ m/s.

$$\Rightarrow \text{Time} = \frac{\text{distance}}{\text{speed}}$$

$$= \frac{100}{\left(\frac{25}{3}\right)} = 12 \text{ s.}$$

25. Option (D) is correct.

Explanation: Let the distance be a km.

The time difference for the 2 speeds is 16 minutes.

$$\frac{a}{2.5} - \frac{a}{3} = \frac{16}{60} = \frac{4}{15}$$

$$\Rightarrow 6a - 5a = 4$$

$$\Rightarrow a = 4 \text{ km}$$

26. Option (B) is correct.

Explanation:

$$\text{Speed} = \frac{\text{distance}}{\text{time}}$$

$$= \frac{(100+50)}{10} = 15 \text{ m/s}$$

$$= 15 \times \left(\frac{18}{5}\right) = 54 \text{ km/h}$$

27. Option (D) is correct.

Explanation: Distance covered by horse

$$= 66 \times \left(\frac{5}{2}\right) = 165 \text{ m}$$

So, circumference of circle, $2\pi r = 165$

$$\Rightarrow 2 \times \frac{22}{7} \times r = 165$$

$$r = 26.25 \text{ meters}$$

28. Option (C) is correct.

Explanation: Let distance travelled be a km

Difference of time = 12 – 3 = 9 min

$$= \frac{9}{60} = \frac{3}{20} \text{h}$$

According to the question,

$$\left(\frac{a}{70}\right) - \left(\frac{a}{80}\right) = \frac{3}{20} \text{ h}$$

$$\Rightarrow \frac{(8a - 7a)}{56} = \frac{3}{2}$$

$$\Rightarrow a = 84 \text{ km}$$

$$\text{So, required time} = \left(\frac{84}{70}\right) \text{h} - 12 \text{ min}$$

$$= 72 \text{ min} - 12 \text{ min}$$

$$= 60 \text{ min i.e. } 1 \text{ h}$$

29. Option (A) is correct.

Explanation:

$$\text{Speed} = 36 \times \left(\frac{5}{18}\right) \text{kmph} = 10 \text{ m/s}$$

So, time = (train's length + bridge length) /speed of train

$$= \frac{(120+360)}{10} = 48 \text{ s}$$

30. Option (C) is correct.

Explanation:

$$\text{Speed of train} = \frac{150}{30} = 5 \text{m/s}$$

Assuming speed of train B = a m/s

Using, distance (length of both trains)

= speed × time

$$\Rightarrow 300 = (5 + a) \times 10$$

$$\Rightarrow a = 25 \text{ m/s} = 25 \times \frac{18}{5} = 90 \text{ km/h}$$

31. Option (A) is correct.

Explanation:

Relative speed of Raju and Sohan

$$= (90 - 72) \text{ km/h}$$

$$= 18 \text{ km/h} = 18 \times \frac{5}{18} \text{ m/s}$$

$$= 5 \text{ m/s}$$

$$\text{They will meet again for the first time} = \frac{1725}{5} \text{ sec}$$

$$= 345 \text{ sec}$$

32. Option (B) is correct.

Explanation: Let distance on foot = a km

and distance on bicycle = $(61 - a)$ km

According to question,

$$\left(\frac{a}{4}\right)+\left(\frac{(61-a)}{9}\right) = 9$$

$\Rightarrow$ $5a = 80$

$\Rightarrow$ $a = 16$ km

33. Option (C) is correct.

Explanation:

$$\text{Time} = \frac{\text{distance}}{\text{speed}} = \frac{1{,}050}{75} = 14 \text{ h}$$

34. Option (D) is correct.

Explanation:

Using, $\text{Time} = \frac{\text{distance}}{\text{speed}}$

$$= \frac{180}{\left(90\times\frac{5}{18}\right)} = 7.2 \text{ secs}$$

35. Option (C) is correct.

Explanation:

$$\text{Time} = \frac{\text{distance}}{\text{speed}}$$

where distance = 200 m + 175 m

$$= \frac{(200+175)}{\left(54\times\frac{5}{18}\right)} = 25 \text{ secs}$$

36. Option (D) is correct.

Explanation: Given, time taken to travel 72 km = 12 h.

Let d distance travelled by bicycle and $(72 - d)$ km on foot.

Using $\text{Time} = \frac{\text{distance}}{\text{speed}}$

$\Rightarrow$ $\frac{d}{10}+\frac{(72-d)}{5} = 12$

$\Rightarrow$ $d + 144 - 2d = 120$

$\Rightarrow$ $d = 24$

So, distance travelled on foot = 72 – 24 = 48 km

37. Option (C) is correct.

Explanation:

1st hour - 21 km/h - Total distance 21 km
2nd hour - 24 km/h - Total distance 45 km
3rd hour - 27 km/h - Total distance 72 km
4th hour - 30 km/h - Total distance 102 km
5th hour - 33 km/h - Total distance 135 km
6th hour - 36 km/h - Total distance 171 km
7th hour - 39 km/h - Total distance 210 km
8th hour - 42 km/h - Total Distance 252 km

So, required time = 8 h

38. Option (B) is correct.

Explanation: Let the distance be × and time taken be t.

Distance is same, so, distance = speed × time

$\Rightarrow$ $48(t-3) = 36 \times t$

$\Rightarrow$ $12t = 144 \Rightarrow t = 12$ h

$\therefore$ Distance $= 36 \times 12 = 432$ km

39. Option (A) is correct.

Explanation:

As it travels 12 km in 10 minutes.

So, speed = 12 km/10 min. = 12,000 m/600s

speed = 20 m/s

Let the length of the train be x,

So, train travels a distance x in 6 seconds,

We know that; speed = distance/time

$$20 \text{ m/s} = \frac{x}{6}\text{s}$$

$$20 \times 6 \text{ m} = x$$

$$x = 120 \text{ m}$$

40. Option (D) is correct.

Explanation:

Here, $S_1 = 40$ km/h, $t_1 = \frac{25}{4}$

$S_2 = 50$ km/h, $t_2 = ?$

According to the question,

$$S_1t_1 = S_2t_2$$

$\Rightarrow$ $40\times\frac{25}{4} = 50t_2$

$t_2 = 5$ h

Level-2: INTERMEDIATE

1. Option (C) is correct.

Explanation: Assuming speed of the man is S kmph.

Distance covered in 10 minutes at 20 kmph = distance covered in 8 minutes at (20 + S) kmph.

i.e. $20\times\frac{10}{60} = \frac{8}{60}\times(20+S)$

$\Rightarrow$ $200 = 160 + 8S$

$\Rightarrow$ $8S = 40$

$\Rightarrow$ $S = 5$ kmph

2. Option (B) is correct.

Explanation:

Downstream speed = 6 + 2 = 8 kmph

Upstream speed = 6 – 2 = 4 kmph

Assuming, space distance = d

According to the question,

$$\left(\frac{d}{4}\right)-\left(\frac{d}{8}\right) = 3$$

$\Rightarrow$ $\frac{2d-d}{8} = 3$

$\Rightarrow$ $d = 24$ km

3. Option (D) is correct.

Explanation: Assuming the train's speed = S kmph

Train's length = L kmph

Speed of 1st person = 2 kmph = $\frac{2\times5}{18}=\frac{5}{9}$ m/s

Speed of 2nd person = 4 kmph = $\frac{4\times5}{18}=\frac{10}{9}$ m/s

According to the question,

$$\frac{L}{S-\frac{5}{9}} = 9$$

and

$$\frac{L}{S-\frac{10}{9}} = 10$$

$$9S - L = 5 \quad ...(1)$$
$$90S - 9L = 100 \quad ...(2)$$
$$L = 50 \quad \text{[By solving eq. (1) and (2)]}$$

4. **Option (A) is correct.**

Explanation: Ship's speed = 30 kmph = 8.33 m/s

Distance travelled by ship = 500 m

So, from the above data, we can find the time taken to travel the distance = $\frac{500}{8.33}$ = 60 s

Now, also given,

Speed of radiowaves = 200 m/s

Let d = depth of the ocean

The time taken by the radiowave to reach the bottom = 60 s

Since the signal touches the bottom & reflects back to the ship, the distance travelled by the signal will be twice the depth of the ocean, i.e.,

Distance travelled = $2d$

Since, distance travelled = Speed x Time

So we have, $2d = 200 \times 60$

So the total distance travelled by the signal = 12,000 m & depth of the ocean,

$$d = \frac{12,000}{2} = 6000 \text{ m i.e., 6 km}$$

5. **Option (A) is correct.**

Explanation:

Given:

Distance = 60 km

Let the initial speed of car = x km/h

So, new speed = $x + 8$ km/h

We have, time = $\frac{\text{distance}}{\text{speed}}$

According to the question,

$\Rightarrow \frac{60}{x} - \frac{60}{x+8} = 2$

$\Rightarrow 30x + 240 - 30x = x^2 + 8x$

$\Rightarrow x^2 + 8x - 240 = 0$

$\Rightarrow (x - 12)(x + 20) = 0$

So, $x = 12, -20$

So, the initial speed of car = 12 km/h

6. **Option (D) is correct.**

Explanation:

Relative speed of both Zeenat and Nasreen,

$$= (27 - 18) \text{ km/h}$$
$$= 9 \times \frac{5}{18} \text{ m/s}$$
$$= 2.5 \text{ m/s}$$

Time taken by them to meet for the first time on the track while running in some direction

$$= \frac{\text{Length of track}}{\text{Relative speed}}$$
$$= \frac{1200}{2.5} = 480 \text{ s}$$
$$= \frac{480}{60} = 8 \text{ m}$$

7. **Option (B) is correct.**

Explanation:

Rider's speed = 18 kmph

Distance = 90 km

Stops for every 7th km

So, $90 = (12 \times 7) + 6$

i.e., he stops 12 times

Time taken by rider = 12×6 = 72 mins i.e., 1 h 12 mins

$$\text{Actual time} = \frac{90}{18} = 5 \text{ h}$$
$$\text{Required time} = 5 \text{ h} + 1 \text{ h } 12 \text{ mins} = 6 \text{ h } 12 \text{ mins}$$

8. **Option (D) is correct.**

Explanation: Speed 1 = $\frac{\text{distance}}{\text{time}}$

$$\text{Speed 2} = \frac{\left(\frac{\text{distance}}{2}\right)}{2 \times \text{time}} = \frac{\text{distance}}{4 \text{time}}$$

Required ratio = speed 1 : speed 2 = 4 : 1

9. **Option (C) is correct.**

Explanation:

Distance between the cars X and Y = 216km

The ratio of the speeds of X and Y = 5 : 7

Speed of car X = 60 km/h

So, speed of car Y = $7 \times \frac{60}{5}$ = 84 km/h

Both trains moving towards each other. So, their relative speed = 84 + 60 = 144 km/h

We have, time = $\frac{\text{distance}}{\text{speed}}$

$\Rightarrow$ time = $\frac{216}{144} = \frac{3}{2} \text{ h} = \frac{3}{2} \times 60 \text{ m} = 90 \text{ m}$

10. **Option (A) is correct.**

Explanation:

$$\text{Distance} = \frac{240 \times 1}{3} = 80 \text{ km}$$
$$\text{Time} = \frac{4 \times 2}{7} = \frac{8}{7} \text{ h}$$

Using, Speed = $\frac{\text{distance}}{\text{time}} = \frac{80}{\left(\frac{8}{7}\right)}$ = 70 kmph

11. **Option (B) is correct.**

Explanation: Assuming x be the speed of C.

So, the speed of B will be = $3(x)$

So, the speed of A will be = $2[3(x)] = 6x$

C: Speed = x

Time = 42 min

Distance travelled = Speed × Time = $42x$

A: Speed = $6x$

Time = ?

Distance = $42x$

Time = Distance ÷ Speed = $42x \div 6x$

= 7 min

12. Option (C) is correct.

Explanation: Assuming speed of train be t kmph and car be c kmph.

According to the question,

$$\left(\frac{120}{t}\right)+\left(\frac{480}{c}\right) = 8$$

$$\Rightarrow \quad \left(\frac{1}{t}\right)+\left(\frac{4}{c}\right) = \frac{1}{15} \quad ...(1)$$

and, $$\left(\frac{200}{t}\right)+\left(\frac{400}{c}\right) = \frac{25}{3}$$

$$\Rightarrow \quad \left(\frac{1}{t}\right)+\left(\frac{2}{c}\right) = \frac{1}{24} \quad ...(2)$$

Solving (1) and (2), $t = 60, c = 80$

Ratio of speeds $= 60 : 80 = 3 : 4$

13. Option (C) is correct.

Explanation:

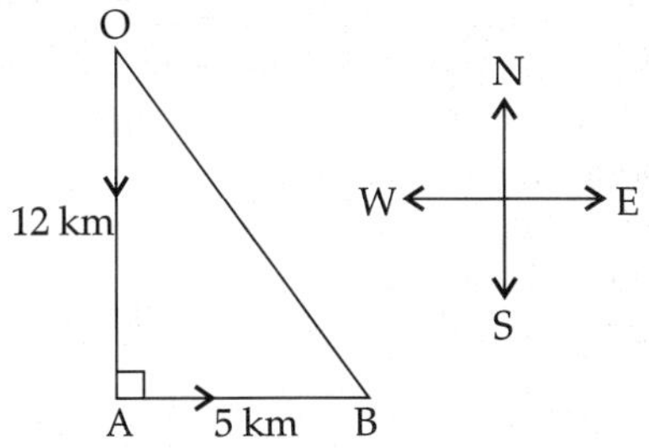

From right angle triangle, we have

$$\therefore \quad OB = \sqrt{OA^2 + AB^2}$$

$$\Rightarrow \quad OB = \sqrt{12^2 + 5^2}$$

$$\Rightarrow \quad OB = \sqrt{144 + 25}$$

$$\Rightarrow \quad OB = \sqrt{169} = 13 \text{ km}$$

14. Option (B) is correct.

Explanation:

$$\text{Distance} = \text{speed} \times \text{time}$$

$$= 4 \times \frac{11}{4} = 11 \text{ km}$$

$$\text{New speed} = 16.5 \text{ kmph}$$

$$\text{Time} = \frac{\text{distance}}{\text{speed}}$$

$$= \frac{11}{16.5} = 0.66 \text{ h i.e., 40 min.}$$

15. Option (D) is correct.

Explanation: Using average speed $= \dfrac{2xy}{(x+y)}$

$$6.4 = \frac{(2 \times 16 \times y)}{(16+y)} \Rightarrow 6.4 = \frac{32y}{(16+y)}$$

By solving, $y = 4$ kmph

16. Option (C) is correct.

Explanation:

We have, average speed $= \dfrac{\text{Total distance}}{\text{Total time}}$

According to the question,

Average speed

$$= \frac{D}{\frac{D}{3\times10}+\frac{D}{4\times15}+\frac{5D}{12\times20}} = \frac{D}{\frac{D}{30}+\frac{D}{60}+\frac{5D}{240}}$$

$$= \frac{240}{8+4+5} = \frac{240}{17} \text{ km/h}$$

17. Option (C) is correct.

Explanation: Assuming speed of two cars be a kmph and b kmph.

$$5a - 5b = 100$$

$$\Rightarrow \quad a - b = 20 \quad ...(1)$$

$$\text{and} \quad a + b = 100 \quad ...(2)$$

By adding (1) and (2),

$$2a = 120$$

$$\Rightarrow \quad a = 60$$

By subtracting (1) and (2)

$$b = 40$$

Hence, speed of faster car = 60 kmph

18. Option (C) is correct.

Explanation:

Let the downstream speed = X km/hr

And upstream speed = y km/hr

We know, time $= \dfrac{\text{distance}}{\text{speed}}$

According to the question,

$$\Rightarrow \quad \frac{15}{x}+\frac{8}{y}=2$$

Let $\dfrac{1}{x} = P$ and $\dfrac{1}{y} = Q$

$$\Rightarrow \quad 15P + 8Q = 2 \quad ...(1)$$

And $\dfrac{20}{x}+\dfrac{12}{y}=2\dfrac{5}{6}$

$$\Rightarrow \quad 120P + 72Q = 17 \quad ...(2)$$

By equation (1) and (2),

$$P = \frac{1}{15} \text{ and } Q = \frac{1}{8}$$

We have, $\dfrac{1}{x} = P$

So, $x = 15$

So, the downstream speed = 15 km/hr

19. Option (D) is correct.

Explanation:

Time of A : Time of B = 6 : 5

Speed A : Speed B = 5 : 6

Let speeds be 5K and 6K

Train A travels 2 h before Train B starts from Jaipur.

In remaining 4 h, it will cover 5K × 4= 20K km

= Distance between two trains at 12 p.m. = 20K

$$\text{Time to meet} = \frac{\text{Distance}}{\text{Relative speed}}$$

$$= \frac{20K}{(5K+6K)}$$

$$= \frac{20}{11} = 1\frac{9}{11} \text{ h}$$

$$= 1 \text{ hr} + \frac{9}{11} \times 60 \text{ min.}$$
$$= 1 \text{ hr } 49 \text{ minutes } 5 \text{ seconds.}$$

They meet at 12 pm + 1 hr 49 min 5 s
= 1 : 49 : 05 pm

20. Option (C) is correct.
Explanation: Let the original speed be x km/h.

Time taken $= t_1$
$$= \frac{\text{Distance}}{\text{Speed}} = \frac{21}{x} \text{ h}$$

When left late by $6\frac{6}{9}$ min.,

$$\text{Time} = t_2$$
$$= \text{travel time + waiting time}$$
$$= \frac{21}{(x+12)} + \frac{1}{9} \text{ h}$$

According to the question,
$$\because \quad t_1 = t_2$$
$$\frac{21}{x} = \frac{21}{(x+12)} + \frac{1}{9}$$
$$\Rightarrow \frac{(21x+252-21x)}{(x \times (x+12))} = \frac{1}{9}$$
$$\Rightarrow \frac{252}{(x^2+12x)} = \frac{1}{9}$$
$$\Rightarrow 2268 = x^2 + 12x$$
$$\Rightarrow x^2 + 12x - 2268 = 0$$
$$\Rightarrow x^2 + 54x - 42x - 2268 = 0$$
$$\Rightarrow x(x + 54) - 42(x + 54) = 0$$
$$\Rightarrow (x + 54)(x - 42) = 0$$
$$x = -54 \ \& \ x = 42 \text{ km/h}$$

Since speed cannot be negative, the original speed is 42 km/h.

21. Option (D) is correct.
Explanation: Assuming hourly increment be i
$$33 + (33 + i) + (33 + 2i) + (33 + 3i) + (33 + 4i) + (33 + 5i) + (33+6i) = 315$$
$$\Rightarrow 21i + 231 = 315$$
$$\Rightarrow i = 4 \text{ kmph}$$

22. Option (A) is correct.
Explanation: Suppose the length of the journey is 42 km and the average speed is 40 km, then it will be late by 3 minutes because the train runs 40 km in 1 h/60 minutes. i.e., 1 km in $\frac{60}{40} = 1.5$
and 2 km in 1.5 × 2 = 3
3 minutes late if length is 42 km
1 min that is $\frac{42}{3} = 14$ km
15 minute that is 14 × 15 = 210 km

Level-3: EXPERT

1. Option (B) is correct.
Explanation:
Let total distance = 100 km

Then, total time $= \left(\frac{50}{50}\right) + \left(\frac{40}{40}\right) + \left(\frac{10}{20}\right)$
$$= \frac{5}{2} \text{ h}$$

So, Average speed $= \frac{(100 \times 2)}{5} = 40$ kmph

2. Option (A) is correct.
Explanation:
Given that the distance between P and Q = 130 km
Let the speed of car = x km/h
Then speed of train = $1.3x$ km/h

Using, Time $= \frac{\text{Distance}}{\text{Speed}}$
$$\Rightarrow \frac{130}{x} - \frac{130}{1.3x} = \frac{1}{2}$$
$$\Rightarrow x = 60$$

So, the speed of train = 1.3 × 60 = 78 km/h

3. Option (A) is correct.
Explanation:
Average marks of four subject = 75
So, total marks = 75 × 4 = 300
After adding english, the average = 70
So, total marks of all five subjects = 70 × 5 = 350
So, english marks = 350 – 300 = 50 marks

4. Option (C) is correct.
Explanation: Let speed of car be 'x'.
So speed of train is $1.4x$.
Let time taken by car be 't'.

So, time taken by train is $\left(t - \frac{25}{60}\right)$

For train, distance = speed × time
$$140 = 1.4x\left(t - \frac{25}{60}\right)$$

For car, $140 = xt$
Subtracting both the equations, we get
$$xt = 1.4x\left(t - \frac{25}{60}\right)$$
$$t = \frac{35}{24}$$
$$\Rightarrow 140 = x \times \frac{35}{24}$$
or $$x = 96$$

So, speed of train = $1.4x$
$$= 1.4 \times 96 = 134.4 \text{ kmph}$$

5. Option (C) is correct.
Explanation: Let original speed be x.
$$\frac{384}{x} = T \quad \text{...(1)}$$
$$\frac{384}{(x-16)} = T + 2 \quad \text{...(2)}$$

Solving (1) and (2) we get, $x = 64$ kmph
75% of 64 is 48 kmph.

6. **Option (C) is correct.**

Explanation:

(i) A & B are travelling towards each other from the points P and Q, respectively.

(ii) Let R denote the crossing point of A & B.

(iii) After crossing each other at R, A & B take $6\frac{1}{8}$ h & 8 h, respectively to reach their destinations Q & P, respectively.

(iv) If the speed of B is 16.8 km/h, then let S denotes the speed (in km/h) of A.

Hence, we get the following relations,

$$\frac{PR}{S} = \frac{QR}{16.8} \quad ...(1)$$

$$\frac{RQ}{S} = 6\frac{1}{8} = \frac{49}{8} \quad ...(2a)$$

$$\frac{RP}{16.8} = 8 \text{ or } PR = 16.8 \times 8 \quad [\because RP = PR]$$

or $$PR = 16.8 \times 8 \quad ... (2b)$$

From (1) & (2a) we get,

$$\frac{PR}{S} = \frac{QR}{16.8} = S \times \frac{\frac{49}{8}}{16.8} \quad [\because RQ = QR]$$

or $$16.8 \times \frac{8}{S} = S \times \frac{\frac{49}{8}}{16.8} \text{ [from (2b)]}$$

or $$S = 16.8 \times \frac{8}{7} = 19.2 \text{ (km/h)}$$

7. **Option (B) is correct.**

Explanation: Let 'L' be the length of train and 'S' be woman's speed.

Speed of train relative to man

$$= 44 - 8 = 36 \text{ km/h}$$

or $$= \frac{36}{3.6} = 10 \text{ m/s}$$

$$\text{'L'} = 10 \times 15 = 150 \text{ m}$$

Speed of train relative to woman =(44+S) km/h

So $$\left(\frac{(44+S)}{3.6}\right) \times 10 = 150$$

$$S = 10 \text{ km/h}$$

8. **Option (C) is correct.**

Explanation: Let the length of each train be L metres. The distance travelled by them will be twice their length that is 2L metres.

The relative speed is (54 – 42) = 12 km/h

Converting into m/s, we get $12 \times \frac{5}{18}$ i.e., $\frac{10}{3}$ m/s

Therefore, to know the length of the train

$$\frac{2L}{63} = \frac{10}{3} \quad \text{(distance / time = speed)}$$

$$L = 105 \text{ m}$$

9. **Option (C) is correct.**

Explanation:

Ratio of time = 0.6 : 1 = 3 : 5

Length is equal.

So, ratio of speed = 5 : 3

3 units = 96

$$\Rightarrow \quad 5 \text{ units} = 96 \times \frac{5}{3} = 160 \text{ km/h}$$

10. **Option (D) is correct.**

Explanation: Let the length of the train be l metre

Speed of the train = s km/h

Speed of the man = 6 km/h

According to the question,

$$\Rightarrow \quad s \times \frac{5}{18} = (l + 200)/30$$

$$\Rightarrow \quad l = (30s \times \frac{5}{18}) - 200 \quad ...(1)$$

And $$(s-6) \times \frac{5}{18} = \frac{l}{20}$$

$$\Rightarrow \quad l = 20(s-6) \times \frac{5}{18} \quad ...(2)$$

Put the value of l in equation,

$$\Rightarrow 20(s-6) \times \frac{5}{18} = [30s \times \frac{5}{18}] - 200$$

$$\Rightarrow \quad 100s - 600 = 150s - 3600$$

$$\Rightarrow \quad 150s - 100s = 3600 - 600$$

$$\Rightarrow \quad 50s = 3000$$

$$\Rightarrow \quad s = \frac{3000}{50} = 60 \text{ km/h}$$

11. **Option (B) is correct.**

Explanation: Let the speed of A = x km/h and speed of B = 35 km/h

Let both A and B cross after t h

At the time of crossing:

Distance travelled by A in t h = $x.t$ and distance travelled by B in t h = $35.t$ kms

After crossing, A will travel $35.t$ kms. and B will travel $x.t$ kms.

$$35.t = x.25 \quad ...(1)$$

$$x.t = 35 \times 36 \quad ...(2)$$

Dividing eqn. (1) by eqn. (2).

$$35.t/x.t = \frac{x.25}{35 \times 36}$$

or, $$\frac{7}{x} = \frac{x}{7 \times 36}$$

or, $$x^2 = 7 \times 7 \times 36$$

or, $$x = \sqrt{\{7 \times 7 \times 2 \times 2 \times 3 \times 3\}}$$

$$= 42 \text{ km/h.}$$

12. **Option (C) is correct.**

Explanation: If speed is doubled, time taken is halved, if distance is constant.

⇒ If normal time taken to cover 416 km is t, then :

$$\frac{1}{2}t = \left(2\frac{2}{3} + 1\frac{1}{3}\right) \text{ h}$$

$$\Rightarrow \quad t = 8 \text{ h}$$

$$\Rightarrow \text{Speed of train A} = \frac{416}{8} = 52 \text{ kmph}$$

13. Option (B) is correct.

Explanation: Assuming speed of train A is 48 kmph.

$$\text{Speed of B} = 48 - 16 = 32 \text{ kmph}$$

According to question,

$$\left(\frac{96}{32}\right) - \left(\frac{96}{48}\right) = 1$$

$$3 - 2 = 1$$

$$1 = 1 \text{ satisfied}$$

So, average speed of train A = 48 kmph

14. Option (C) is correct.

Explanation: Assuming total distance = 100 km

Using,

$$\text{Average speed} = \frac{\text{total distance}}{\text{total time}}$$

$$= \frac{100}{\left(\frac{40}{8}+\frac{24}{9}+\frac{36}{12}\right)}$$

$$= \frac{300}{32} = 9\frac{3}{8} \text{ km/h}$$

15. Option (B) is correct.

Explanation:

Distance between policeman and thief = 480 m

Speed of policeman = 23 km/h

Speed of thief = 19 km/h

Relative speed = 23 – 19 = 4 km/h

$$= 4 \times \frac{5}{18} = \frac{10}{9} \text{ m/s}$$

Time taken by policeman to catch the thief

$$= \frac{480}{\frac{10}{9}} = 432 \text{ sec}$$

$$\text{So, required distance} = 19 \times \frac{5}{18} \times 432 = 2280 \text{ m}$$

16. Option (D) is correct.

Explanation:

$$\text{Average speed} = \frac{\text{Total distance}}{\text{Total time}}$$

$$= \frac{(3+6+9)}{\left[\left(\frac{3}{9}\right)+\left(\frac{6}{15}\right)+\left(\frac{9}{18}\right)\right]} = \frac{(18 \times 90)}{111}$$

$$= \frac{540}{37} \text{ kmph}$$

17. Option (B) is correct.

Explanation: Let b be the speed of the boat in still water and c be the speed of current. Then:

$$\left(\frac{3}{b-c}\right)+\left(\frac{5}{b+c}\right) = \frac{55}{60} \quad \text{...(1)}$$

$$\left(\frac{4}{b-c}\right)+\left(\frac{9}{b+c}\right) = \frac{85}{60} \quad \text{...(2)}$$

By eq.(1) × 4 and eq. (2) × 3,

$$\text{So, } \frac{12}{(b-c)}+\frac{27}{(b+c)} = \frac{255}{60}$$

$$\frac{12}{(b-c)}+\frac{20}{(b+c)} = \frac{220}{60}$$

$$\text{Then, } \frac{7}{(b+c)} = \frac{35}{60}$$

$$35b + 35c = 420$$

$$b + c = \frac{420}{35}$$

$$= 12 \text{ km/h downstream speed}$$

$$\text{Required time} = \frac{43.2}{12} = 3.6 \text{ h}$$

18. Option (B) is correct.

Explanation: Let the speed of boat is X km/h, and the speed of the stream is Y km/h, then, speed of boat upstream = (X – Y) km/h and speed of boat downstream = (X + Y) km/h

$$\because \quad \text{Time} = \frac{\text{Distance}}{\text{Time}}$$

According to the question:

$$\frac{D}{(X-Y)}+\frac{D}{(X+Y)} = T$$

$$\frac{60}{15-5}+\frac{60}{15+5} = T$$

$$\Rightarrow \quad T = \left(\frac{60}{10}+\frac{60}{20}\right) h$$

$$= (6 + 3) \text{ h} = 9 \text{ h}$$

19. Option (C) is correct.

Explanation: A = upstream speed,

B = downstream speed

$$3.6A+5.4B = 54 \quad \text{...(1)}$$

$$5.4A+3.6B = 58.5 \quad \text{...(2)}$$

Dividing by 1.8, we get

$$2A+3B = 30$$

$$3A+2B = 32.5$$

Solving both equations,

$$5B = 25 \text{ min}$$

So, required time = 10B = 50 min

20. Option (A) is correct.

Explanation: Assuming distance between office and delivery location = d

$$\text{Total time} = \frac{d}{32}+\frac{d}{24}+\frac{1}{4} = \frac{17}{12}$$

$$\left(\frac{d}{8}\right)\left(\frac{7}{12}\right) = \frac{7}{6}$$

$$d = 16$$

Hence, total distance covered by him = 2 × 16 = 32 km

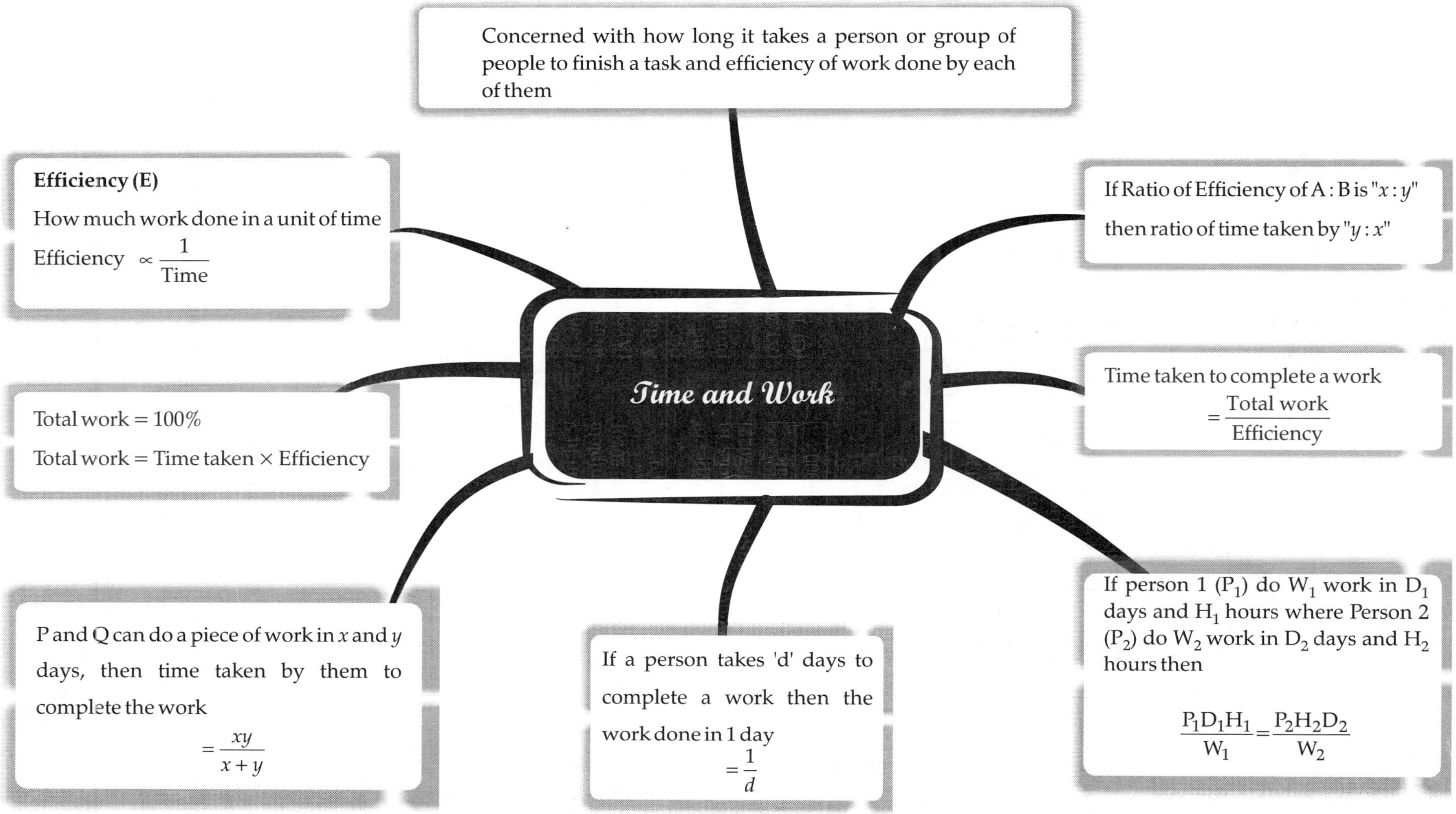
Time and Work
Concerned with how long it takes a person or group of people to finish a task and efficiency of work done by each of them
Efficiency (E)
How much work done in a unit of time
Efficiency $\propto \frac{1}{\text{Time}}$
Total work = 100%
Total work = Time taken × Efficiency
P and Q can do a piece of work in x and y days, then time taken by them to complete the work
$= \frac{xy}{x+y}$
If a person takes 'd' days to complete a work then the work done in 1 day
$= \frac{1}{d}$
If Ratio of Efficiency of A : B is "$x : y$" then ratio of time taken by "$y : x$"
Time taken to complete a work
$= \frac{\text{Total work}}{\text{Efficiency}}$
If person 1 (P_1) do W_1 work in D_1 days and H_1 hours where Person 2 (P_2) do W_2 work in D_2 days and H_2 hours then
$\frac{P_1D_1H_1}{W_1} = \frac{P_2H_2D_2}{W_2}$

Chapter 10

Time and Work

LEARNING OBJECTIVES:

- Questions related to time required for completing a work.
- Efficiency of different persons or group.
- Relation between time and efficiency.
- Real life application of time and work.
- Questions asked in various competitive exams such as SSC, railway, bank, CSAT, CAT, etc.
- Method of solving alternate work questions.

Time and work concepts deal with the time taken by a person or a group of people to finish a task and the efficiency of work done by each of them.

- **Efficiency:** It means how much work one person or a group of people can do in one day or one hour.
  Efficiency is always inversely proportional to time.

  $$\text{Efficiency} \propto \frac{1}{\text{Time}}$$

- **Time:** It denotes the total time taken to complete a task.
- **Total work:** It is 100% of work assigned to a person or a group of people. Total work is directly proportional to time taken.

  $$\text{Total work} \propto \text{Time}$$

- **Remaining work:** Remaining work is
  Total work – Completed work.
  We can calculate total work by using the formula given below:

  $$\boxed{\text{Total work} = \text{Time taken} \times \text{Efficiency}}$$

POINTS TO BE REMEMBER

- If a person takes '*d*' days to complete a work, then the work done in 1 day $= \frac{1}{d}$
- If a person can do $\frac{1}{d}$ work in 1 day, then he will complete the work in '*d*' days.
- If ratio of efficiency of A : B is $x : y$, then ratio of time of A : B will be $y : x$.
- If P_1 can do W_1 work in D_1 days and H_1 hours and P_2 can do W_2 work in D_2 days and H_2 hours
- Then, $\frac{P_1D_1H_1}{W_1} = \frac{P_2D_2H_2}{W_2}$
- If P and Q can do a piece of work in x and y days, then time taken by them to complete the work.

  $$= \frac{xy}{x+y}$$

Example 1: A can do a piece of work in 8 days and B can complete the same in 5 days. In how many days both will complete the work?

Sol.

$$\text{A's 1 day work} = \frac{1}{8}$$

$$\text{B's 1 day work} = \frac{1}{5}$$

$$\text{1 day work of A + B} = \frac{1}{8} + \frac{1}{5} = \frac{13}{40}$$

Hence, both will complete the work in $\frac{40}{13}$ days.

Alternate approach:

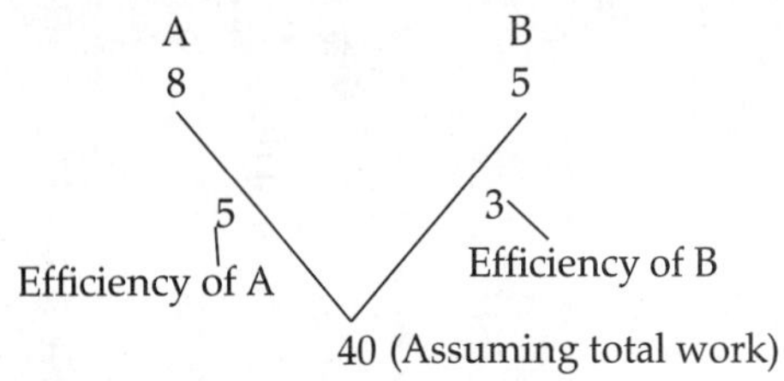

Using, $\text{Time taken} = \frac{\text{Total work}}{\text{Efficiency}}$

$$= \frac{40}{8+5} = \frac{40}{13}$$

Example 2: A takes twice as much time as B and thrice as much time as C to complete a job. If they work together, they can complete the job in 4 days. Find the time taken by A alone to complete the job.

Sol. Assuming A takes '*d*' days to complete the job.

B takes $\frac{d}{2}$ days and C take $\frac{d}{3}$ days.

$$\text{A's 1 day work} = \frac{1}{d}$$

$$\text{B's 1 day work} = \frac{2}{d}$$

$$\text{C's 1 day work} = \frac{3}{d}$$

$$4\left(\frac{1}{d}+\frac{2}{d}+\frac{3}{d}\right) = 1$$

$$d = 24$$

Hence, A takes 24 days to complete the work.

Alternate approach: Assuming A takes 6 days to complete the job

B takes 3 days and C take 2 days

Given they will complete the work in 4 days

Ratio of time taken by A : B : C = 6 : 3 : 2

$$\text{Ratio of Efficiency} = \frac{1}{6}:\frac{1}{3}:\frac{1}{2}$$

$$A:B:C = 1:2:3$$

$$\text{Total work} = \text{Efficiency} \times \text{Time}$$

$$(1 + 2 + 3) \times 4 = 24 \text{ unit}$$

Hence, time taken by A = $\frac{24}{1}$ = 24 days.

Example 3: 10 men working 5 hours/day earn ₹ 300. How much money will 15 men working 10 hours /day earn?

Sol. Using $\frac{M_1D_1H_1}{W_1} = \frac{M_2D_2H_2}{W_2}$

$$\frac{10 \times 5}{300} = \frac{15 \times 10}{x}$$

Hence, $x = 900$

Example 4: Amir and Akhbar can finish a task in 30 days and 15 days, respectively. Akhbar worked on the task for 8 days and left the job. In how many days can Amir alone finish the remaining work?

Sol.

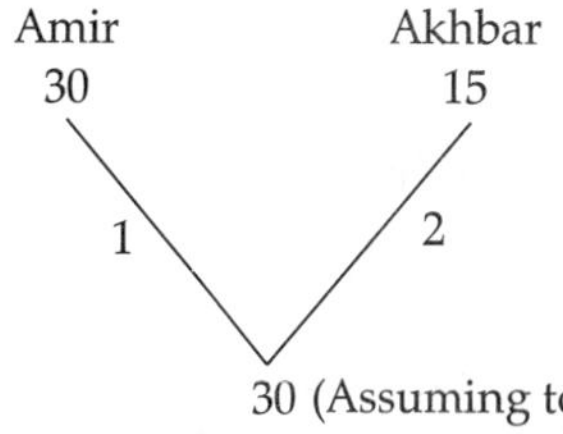

Work done by Akhbar in 8 days = 8 × 2 = 16

Remaining work = 30 – 16 = 14

Time taken by Amir to finish the remaining work

$$= \frac{14}{1} = 14 \text{ days}$$

$$\left[\text{Using Time} = \frac{\text{Total work}}{\text{Efficiency}}\right]$$

Example 5: 6 men or 5 women earn ₹ 14,820 in two days. How much will 4 women and 6 men earn in one day?

Sol. 6 men earn in one day = $\frac{14{,}820}{2} = 7{,}410$

5 women earn in 2 days = 14,820

5 women earn in 1 day = 7,410

1 woman earns in 1 day = 1,482

So, 4 women earn in 1 day = 1,482 × 4 = 5,928.

Hence, 4 women and 6 men earn in one day

= (7,410 + 5,928) = ₹ 13,338

Level 1 Beginner

1. If 18 men can cut a field in 35 days, then in how many days can 21 men cut the same field? [SSC CGL 2019]
   (A) 32 (B) 30 (C) 27 (D) 28
2. A can do a piece of work in 6 days. B can do it in 9 days. With the assistance of C, they can complete it in 3 days. In how many days can C alone do the work? [CGL Tier-I 2019]
   (A) 18 (B) 16 (C) 12 (D) 8
3. A is twice as good as B and together they finish the piece of work in 13 days. In how many days will B alone finish the work? [CPO 2019]
   (A) 18.5 (B) 42 (C) 21 (D) 39
4. A and B can do a piece of work in 36 days. B and C can do the same work in 60 days. A and C can do the same work in 45 days. In how many days can A alone complete the same work? [CPO 2020]
   (A) 90 (B) 45
   (C) 60 (D) 120
5. Avi and Bindu can complete a project in four and twelve hours, respectively. Avi begins project at 5 a.m., and they work alternately for one hour each. When will the project be completed? [SSC CHSL 2022]
   (A) 9 a.m. (B) 11 a.m.
   (C) 1 p.m. (D) 10 a.m.
6. A is twice as good as B and together they can finish a piece of work in 13 days. In how many days will A alone finish the work? [CPO 2020]
   (A) 41 (B) $19\frac{1}{2}$ (C) $9\frac{1}{4}$ (D) 39
7. 10 men or 15 women can complete a work in 30 days. In how many days can 15 men 27 women complete the work? [SSC CHSL 2021]
   (A) $6\frac{1}{11}$ (B) $11\frac{1}{11}$ (C) $5\frac{1}{11}$ (D) $9\frac{1}{11}$
8. A and B can work together in 18 days. A is three times as efficient as B. In how many days B alone can complete the work? [CGL 2020]
   (A) 54 (B) 60 (C) 64 (D) 72

9. A and B together can do a piece of work in 12 days. A alone can do it in 18 days. In how many days B alone can do the work? **[CGL Tier-II 2020]**

(A) 30 **(B)** 36 **(C)** 24 **(D)** 32

10. 6 men or 2 women or 4 boys can finish a work in 77 days. How many days will 1 man, 1 woman and 1 boy together take to finish the same work? **[SSC CHSL 2022]**

(A) 86 **(B)** 80 **(C)** 84 **(D)** 82

11. X and Y together can finish a piece of work in 15 days, while Y alone can finish it in 40 days. X alone can finish the work in: **[CHSL 2020]**

(A) 24 **(B)** 26 **(C)** 25 **(D)** 23

12. P and Q can finish a work in 10 days and 5 days, respectively. Q worked for 2 days and left. In how many days can P alone finish the work [remaining work]? **[SSC CHSL 2019]**

(A) 4 **(B)** 10 **(C)** 6 **(D)** 8

13. Smith and Ajit can complete a task in 12 days and 18 days, respectively. If they work together on the task for 4 days, then the fraction of task that will be left is: **[SSC CHSL 2020]**

(A) $\frac{5}{9}$ **(B)** $\frac{2}{9}$ **(C)** $\frac{1}{9}$ **(D)** $\frac{4}{9}$

14. P can do a work in 10 days while Q can do the same in 15 days. If they work on it together for 3 days, then the fraction of the work that is left is: **[CHSL 2020]**

(A) $\frac{1}{3}$ **(B)** $\frac{2}{3}$ **(C)** $\frac{1}{2}$ **(D)** $\frac{4}{3}$

15. Ravi, Mohan and Govinda can complete a task in 20, 10 and 15 days, respectively. In how many days can Ravi, Mohan and Govinda together complete the same task? **[CHSL 2018]**

(A) 8 **(B)** 4 **(C)** 2 **(D)** $\frac{60}{13}$

16. Kamal and Anil can dig a pond in 8 days and 14 days, respectively. If the total expense of digging is ₹ 4,400, then how much money will Anil earn? **[CHSL 2020]**

(A) 1,500 **(B)** 1,300 **(C)** 1,600 **(D)** 1,400

17. Ravi can complete a task in 6 days and Mohan in 9 days. In how many days can they together complete the same task? **[CHSL 2020]**

(A) 15 **(B)** $3\frac{2}{5}$ **(C)** $3\frac{3}{5}$ **(D)** 9

18. The table below gives the numbers of three types of trees that were planted by government agencies in six consecutive years. **[SSC CHSL 2022]**

Year	Banyan	Neem	Teak
2013	30000	25000	15000
2014	35000	30000	5000
2015	35000	45000	10000
2016	40000	40000	25000
2017	45000	55000	35000
2018	55000	50000	40000

What was the percentage increase in the number of teak trees that were planted by these agencies in 2017 compared to the number of teak trees that were planted by these agencies in 2016?

(A) 35% **(B)** 30% **(C)** 44% **(D)** 40%

19. 30 men working 8 hours per day can dig a pond in 16 days. By working for how many hours per day can 32 men dig the same pond in 20 days? **[CHSL 2020]**

(A) 6 hours **(B)** 5 hours
(C) 8 hours **(D)** 7 hours

20. If 10 men can complete a piece of work in 12 days by working 7 hours a day, then in how many days can in men do the same work by working 6 hours a day? **[CPO 2019]**

(A) 16 **(B)** 10 **(C)** 12 **(D)** 15

21. A, B and C can do a piece of work in 30 days, 45 days and 90 days, respectively. A starts the work and he is assisted by B and C together on every third day. In how many days will the work be completed? **[CPO Tier-I 2019]**

(A) 23 **(B)** $24\frac{2}{3}$ **(C)** 30 **(D)** $22\frac{1}{2}$

22. A can do $\frac{4}{5}$ of a work in 20 days and B can do $\frac{3}{4}$ of the same work in 15 days. They work for 10 days. C completes the remaining work in 1 day. B and C can complete $\frac{3}{4}$ of the same work in: **[CPO 2019]**

(A) 8 days **(B)** 5 days
(C) 4 days **(D)** 6 days

23. If 45 people can complete a work in 18 days, working 8 hours a day, then how many people are required to complete two-third of the same work in 20 days, working 9 hours a day? **[CPO 2018]**

(A) 36 **(B)** 40 **(C)** 30 **(D)** 24

24. A dealer sells two machines at the rate of Rs. 15000 per machine. On one he earns a profit of 20 percent and on the other he loses 40 percent. What is his profit/loss percentage in the whole transaction? **[SSC CHSL 2023]**

(A) 20% loss **(B)** 10% loss
(C) 10% profit **(D)** 20% profit

Level 2 Intermediate

1. A, B and C can individually complete a piece of work in 24, 15 and 12 days, respectively. B and C started the work and worked for 3 days and then left. The number of days required by A alone to complete the remaining work is: **[CGL Tier-I 2019]**

(A) 11 **(B)** 15.5 **(C)** 18 **(D)** 13.2

2. Tina alone can do a piece of work in 12 days and Meena alone can do the same work in 15 days. If Tina and Meena undertook to do this work for Rs. 18,000, then how much amount will Meena get, if they work together? [SSC CHSL 2023]

(A) Rs.10,000 **(B)** Rs.6,000
(C) Rs.12,000 **(D)** Rs.8,000

3. A can do a work in 30 days. B is 25% more efficient than A and C is 20% more efficient than B. They all worked together for 3 days. B will complete the remaining work in: [CGL 2018]

(A) 15 **(B)** 12 **(C)** 20 **(D)** 18

4. A, B and C can individually complete a task in 20 days, 16 days and 30 days, respectively. If A and B started working on the task and they worked for 4 days and left, then the no. of days required by C to complete the remaining task is: [CGL 2019]

(A) $16\frac{1}{2}$ **(B)** $12\frac{1}{2}$ **(C)** 13 **(D)** 10

5. A can complete a task in 12 days and B can complete the same task in 18 days. They start working together but A works for only 2 days. The remaining work is completed by B. If the total wage is ₹ 2,400, then what is B's share (in ₹)? [SSC CHSL 2022]

(A) 1600 **(B)** 1800 **(C)** 1200 **(D)** 2000

6. 10 men or 12 women can finish the same work in 10 days. If 5 men and 2 women undertake the work together, in how many days will they complete the work? [SSC CGL Tier-I 2019]

(A) 15 **(B)** 40 **(C)** 20 **(D)** 60

7. The ratio of time taken by Anamika and Bani to complete a work is 1 : 3, respectively.
Therefore, Anamika is able to finish a job in 40 days less than Bani. If they work together, they can complete the work in ______ days. [SSC CHSL 2022]

(A) 20 **(B)** 10 **(C)** 15 **(D)** 25

8. A, B and C can individually complete a task in 24, 16 and 32 days, respectively. If A and C started the work and worked for 6 days and left, then B can complete the remaining work in how many days? [SSC CGL Tier-I 2019]

(A) 9 **(B)** 12 **(C)** 10 **(D)** 12.5

9. X can do a work in 3 days, Y does 3 times of the same work in 8 days and Z does 5 times of the same work in 12 days. If they have to work together for 6 hours in a day, in how much time can they complete the work? [CPO 2020]

(A) 4 hours **(B)** 5 hours
(C) 5 hours 20 minutes **(D)** 4 hours 10 minutes

10. A and B can do a piece of work in 25 days. B alone can do $66\frac{2}{3}\%$ of the same work in 30 days. In how many days A alone can do $\frac{4}{15}$th of the same work? [CPO 2020]

(A) 15 **(B)** 20 **(C)** 18 **(D)** 12

11. A can complete a work in 20 days, while B can complete the same work in 25 days. Both worked together for 10 days and then C alone completed the remaining work in 10 days. In how many days will A, B and C together complete the same work? [SSC CHSL 2021]

(A) 5 days **(B)** 10 days **(C)** 12 days **(D)** 8 days

12. 3 men and 4 women can do a piece of work in 7 days, whereas 2 men and 1 woman can do it in 14 days. Seven women will complete the same work in: [CGL Tier-II 2020]

(A) 10 days **(B)** 8 days
(C) 9 days **(D)** 12 days

13. A and B can do a piece of work in 18 days. B and C can do it in 30 days. If A is twice as good as C, in how many days B alone can complete the work? [SSC CGL Tier-II 2020]

(A) 90 **(B)** 75 **(C)** 80 **(D)** 100

14. 25 men can complete a task in 16 days. 4 days after starting work, 5 more men join. How many days will be needed by all to complete the remaining task? [CHSL 2020]

(A) 12 **(B)** 10 **(C)** 15 **(D)** 18

15. P can work thrice as fast as Q. Working independently Q can complete the work in 24 days. In how many days can they together complete the same work? [CHSL 2020]

(A) 5 **(B)** 4 **(C)** 6 **(D)** 8

16. If 27 people, working 8 hours a day, can complete a task in 12 days, then in how many days will 18 people finish the task, working 9 hours a day? [SSC CHSL 2019]

(A) 18 **(B)** 15 **(C)** 16 **(D)** 20

17. Ramu works 4 times as fast as Sonu. Sonu can complete a work in 20 days. In how many days they together can complete the same work? [SSC CHSL 2020]

(A) 5 **(B)** 4 **(C)** 6 **(D)** 3

18. A, B and C together can complete a work in x, 30 and 45 days, respectively, B and C worked together for 6 days. The remaining work completed by A alone in 12 days. The value of x is. [SSC CHSL 2021]

(A) 18 **(B)** 20 **(C)** 24 **(D)** 15

19. A works twice as fast as B and B works twice as fast as C. All three working together can finish a task in 4 days with the help of D. If D alone can finish the same task in 16 days, in how many days will A alone finish 75% of the same task? [CPO Tier-I 2019]

(A) 6 **(B)** 9 **(C)** 8 **(D)** 7

20. 3 men and 5 women together can complete a work in 6 days, whereas 4 men and 9 women together can do it in 4 days. How many women are required to do the same work in 7 days? [CPO Tier-I 2019]

(A) 15 **(B)** 12 **(C)** 14 **(D)** 10

21. The ratio of efficiencies of A, B and C is 2:5:3 working together. If they can complete a work in 27 days, B and C together can complete $\frac{4}{9}$th part of that work in: [SSC CGL 2019]

(A) 27 days **(B)** 15 days
(C) $17\frac{1}{7}$ days **(D)** 24 days

3 Expert Level

1. A can do a certain piece of work in 40 days. B is 25% more efficient than A and C is 28% more efficient than B. They work together for 5 days. The remaining work will be completed by B alone in how many days? **[CGL Tier-I 2019]**
(A) $16\frac{3}{5}$ (B) $20\frac{1}{2}$ (C) $20\frac{3}{4}$ (D) $16\frac{1}{5}$

2. A and B working together can complete a work in d days, working along A takes $(8 + d)$ days and B takes $(18 + d)$ days to complete the same work. A works for 4 days. The remaining work will be completed by B alone in: **[SSC CGL 2019]**
(A) 24 days (B) 16 days
(C) 18 days (D) 20 days

3. 4 men and 6 women can complete a certain piece of work in 5 days whereas 3 men and 4 women can complete it in 7 days. How many men should assist 25 women to complete $2\frac{1}{2}$ times the same work in 5 days? **[CGL Tier-I 2019]**
(A) 8 (B) 10 (C) 4 (D) 5

4. A contract is to be completed in 75 days and 187 men work 15 hours per day. After 65 days, $\frac{3}{5}$ of the work is completed. How many additional men can be employed, so that the work can be completed on time, each man now working 17 hours a day? **[CGL 2018]**
(A) 514 (B) 532 (C) 528 (D) 495

5. A and B can do a job in 10 days and 5 days, respectively. They worked together for two days, after which B was replaced by C and the work was finished in the next 3 days. How long will C alone take to finish 60% of the job? **[CPO 2020]**
(A) 30 days (B) 25 days
(C) 18 days (D) 24 days

6. A can do a piece of work in 15 days, B is 25% more efficient than A and C is 40% more efficient than B. A and C worked for 3 days and then C leaves. A and B together will complete the remaining work in: **[SSC CGL Tier-II 2020]**
(A) 3 days (B) $2\frac{1}{2}$ days
(C) 4 days (D) $3\frac{1}{2}$ days

7. A can do 20% of a work in 4 days, B can do $33\frac{1}{3}$% of the same work in 10 days. They worked together for 9 days. C completed the remaining work in 6 days. B and C together will complete 7.5% of the same work in: **[CGL Tier-II 2020]**
(A) 9 (B) 15 (C) 10 (D) 12

8. A can finish a work in 15 days, B can finish the same work in 25 days. They work together for 5 days. The rest of the work is finished by A and C in 4 days. Then C alone can finish the work in: **[SSC CHSL 2023]**
(A) 18 days (B) 24 days
(C) 20 days (D) 21 days

9. A, B and C can do a work in 18, 36 and 54 days, repsectively. They started the work together, but B and C left 5 days and 10 days before completion of work. In how many days will the work be completed? **[CGL Tier-II 2019]**
(A) 14 (B) 15 (C) 13 (D) 12

10. A can finish a piece of work in a certain number of days. B takes 45% more number of days to finish the same work independently. They worked together for 58 days and then the remaining work was done by B alone in 29 days. In how many days can A alone complete the work? **[CHSL 2020]**
(A) 110 (B) 118 (C) 98 (D) 120

11. 4 boys from School A and 6 boys from School B can set up an exhibition in 5 days, where 5 boys from School A and 10 boys from School C together can do it in 4 days or 3 boys from School B and 4 boys from School C together can do in 10 days. Then, how many boys from School A can set up the exhibition in one day? **[CPO 2019]**
(A) 40 (B) 80 (C) 60 (D) 20

12. P can complete five-eights of a work in 15 days and Q can complete $\frac{3}{4}$ of the same work in 30 days. They worked together for 8 days and then P left. Q will complete the remaining work in how many days? **[CPO Tier-I 2019]**
(A) 15 days 16 hours (B) 18 days 16 hours
(C) 20 days 4 hours (D) 15 days 8 hours

13. X and Y can together do a work in $2\frac{2}{5}$ days, Y and Z in 3 days and X and Z can do it in 4 days. They all together can complete the same work in: **[CPO Tier-I 2019]**
(A) 1 day (B) 2 days
(C) $\frac{1}{2}$ day (D) $2\frac{1}{2}$ days

14. Raj alone can complete a work in 20 days and Pratap alone can complete the same work in half of the time taken by Raj. In how many days will both together complete 3/5 part of the total work? **[SSC CHSL 2023]**
(A) 10 days (B) 4 days
(C) 6 days (D) 8 days

15. A is as efficient as B and C together. A and B working together can complete a work in 36 days and C alone can complete it in 60 days. A and C work together for

10 days. B will complete the remaining work alone in: [CGL Mains 2018]

(A) 110 days (B) 88 days
(C) 84 days (D) 90 days

16. 25 people can complete a work in 60 days. They started the work. 10 people left the work after X days. If the whole work was completed in 80 days, then what is the value of X? [CGL Mains 2018]

(A) 9 (B) 8 (C) 12 (D) 15

17. A, B and C can finish a task in 42 days, 84 days and 28 days, respectively. A started the work. B joined him after 3 days. If C joined them after 5 days from the beginning, then for how many days did A work till the completion of task? [CHSL (10+2) 2018]

(A) 20 (B) 15 (C) 17 (D) 18

18. To do a certain work, A and B work on alternate days with B beginning the work on the first day. A alone can complete it in 24 days. If the work is completed in $11\frac{1}{3}$ days, then B alone can complete $\frac{7}{9}$th part of the original work in: [SSC CGL 2021]

(A) $5\frac{1}{2}$ days (B) 4 days
(C) $4\frac{1}{2}$ days (D) 6 days

19. A and B can complete a work in 15 days and 10 days, respectively. They started doing the work together but after 4 days, B had to leave. Then, A worked with a new work and C completed the work [remaining] in 3 days. If C works alone, in how many days can he do 40% of the same work? [CGL 2021]

(A) 9 (B) 8 (C) 10 (D) $8\frac{1}{3}$

20. To complete a certain task, X is 40% more efficient than Y and Z is 40% less efficient than Y. Working together, they can complete the task in 21 days. Y and Z together worked for 35 days. The remaining work will be completed by X alone in: [SSC CHSL 2021]

(A) 8 days (B) 4 days
(C) 6 days (D) 5 days

ANSWER KEY

Level-1: Beginner

1.	(B)	2.	(A)	3.	(D)	4.	(C)	5.	(B)	6.	(B)	7.	(D)	8.	(D)	9.	(B)	10.	(C)
11.	(A)	12.	(C)	13.	(D)	14.	(C)	15.	(D)	16.	(C)	17.	(C)	18.	(D)	19.	(A)	20.	(B)
21.	(A)	22.	(B)	23.	(D)	24.	(C)												

Level-2: Intermediate

1.	(D)	2.	(D)	3.	(D)	4.	(A)	5.	(D)	6.	(A)	7.	(C)	8.	(A)	9.	(C)	10.	(A)
11.	(B)	12.	(A)	13.	(A)	14.	(B)	15.	(C)	16.	(C)	17.	(B)	18.	(A)	19.	(D)	20.	(B)
21.	(B)																		

Level-3: Expert

1.	(A)	2.	(A)	3.	(D)	4.	(C)	5.	(C)	6.	(A)	7.	(C)	8.	(C)	9.	(C)	10.	(B)
11.	(A)	12.	(B)	13.	(B)	14.	(B)	15.	(A)	16.	(C)	17.	(C)	18.	(D)	19.	(A)	20.	(D)

Solutions with Detailed Explanations

Level-1: BEGINNER

1. Option (B) is correct.

Explanation:

Using,
$$m_1d_1 = m_2d_2$$
$$18 \times 35 = 21 \times x$$
$$x = 30 \text{ days}$$

2. Option (A) is correct.

Explanation:

$$A \times 6 = B \times 9 \quad [\text{Using } m_1d_1 = m_2d_2]$$
$$\frac{A}{B} = \frac{9}{6}$$

Ratio of efficiency of A and B = 3 : 2

So, total work is: A × 6 or B × 9

i.e. $3 \times 6 = 2 \times 9 = 18$

$$\text{Efficiency of A + B + C} = \frac{\text{Total work}}{\text{Time taken by A+B+C}}$$

i.e., $\frac{18}{3} = 6$

Now, efficiency of C = (Efficiency of A + B + C) − (Efficiency of A + B)

$= 6 - 5 = 1$

So, time taken by C $= \frac{18}{1} = 18$ days

3. **Option (D) is correct.**

Explanation: A is twice as good as B (Given)

So, efficiency of A is twice of B

A : B = 2 : 1 [Efficiency]

Hence, total work = Efficiency × Time taken

= 3 × 13 = 39 days

4. **Option (C) is correct.**

Explanation:

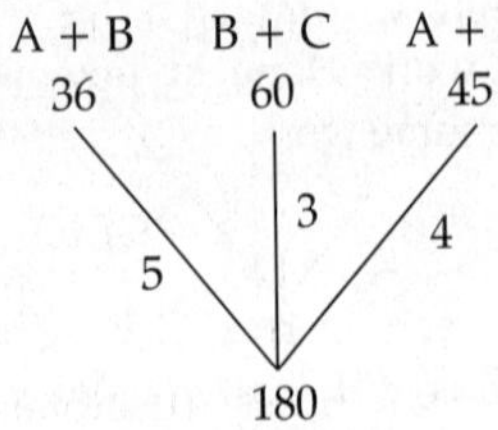

(Assume total work = 180 units)

Efficiency of A + B + C

= Efficiency (A + B + B + C + A + C)/2

$= \frac{(5+3+4)}{2} = 6$

Now, efficiency of A

= Efficiency of (A + B + C) – Efficiency of (B + C)

= 6 – 3 = 3

Hence, time taken by A = $\frac{\text{Total work}}{\text{Efficiency (A)}}$

$= \frac{180}{3} = 60$ days

5. **Option (B) is correct.**

Explanation:

Given:

Time taken by Avi to complete the project = 4 h

Time taken by Bindu to complete the project = 12 h

Let the project = LCM (4, 12) = 12 unit

Work done by Avi per hour = $\frac{12}{4} = 3$ unit/h

Work done by Bindu per hour = $\frac{12}{12} = 1$ unit/h

Work done by both of them in 2 hours = 3 + 1 = 4 unit

So, time taken by them to complete the project working alternately = $\frac{12}{4} \times 2 = 6$h

So, exact time when project will finish = 5:00 am + 6h = 11:00 am

6. **Option (B) is correct.**

Explanation: A : B = 2 : 1

[As A is 2 times as efficient as B]

Total work = Efficiency × Time taken

= 3 × 13 = 39

Now, time taken by A = $\frac{39}{2}$ i.e., $19\frac{1}{2}$days.

7. **Option (D) is correct.**

Explanation:

Given,

10 men can complete the work in = 30 days

15 women can complete the work in = 30 days

We have, $M_1D_1 = M_2D_2$

⇒ 10 M × 30 = 15 W × 30

⇒ MW =32

So, ratio of man's and woman's efficiency = 3:2

So, let the total work = 3 × 10 × 30 = 900 units

Per day work of 15 men and 27 women

= 15 × 3 + 27 × 2 = 99 unit/day

Required number of days = $\frac{900}{99} = 11\frac{1}{19}$ = days

8. **Option (D) is correct.**

Explanation: A is 3 times efficient as B, so,

A : B = 3 : 1 [Efficiency Ratio]

Total work = Efficiency × time taken

= 4 × 18 = 72

Hence, time taken by B to complete the work

$= \frac{72}{1} = 72$ days

9. **Option (B) is correct.**

Explanation:

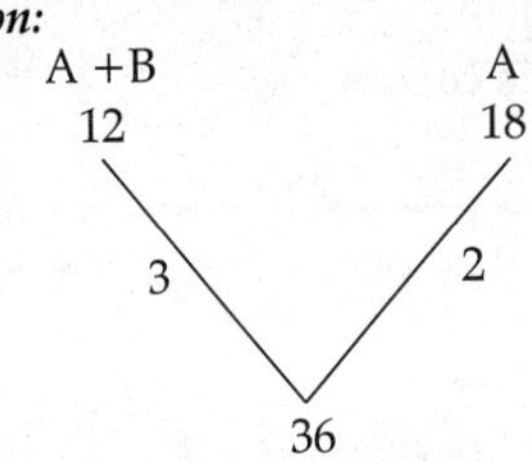

[Assuming total work = 36 unit]

Time taken by B = $\frac{\text{Total work}}{\text{Efficiency of B}}$

Where, efficiency of B = 3 – 2 = 1 unit/day

$= \frac{36}{1} = 36$

[B's efficiency = 3 – 2 = 1]

10. **Option (C) is correct.**

Explanation:

Given:

6 men can complete the work in = 77 days

So, total work done by 1 men = 77×6 days

2 women can complete the work in = 77 days

So, total work done by 1 women = 77×2 days

4 boys can complete the work in = 77 days

So, total work done by 1 boy = 77×4 days

Let the total work

$= \text{LCM}(77 \times 6, 77 \times 2, 77 \times 4) = 77 \times 12$ units

So, per day work of 1 man = $\frac{77 \times 12}{77 \times 6} = 2$ unit/day

And per day work of 1 woman = $\frac{77 \times 12}{77 \times 2} = 6$ unit/day

And per day work of 1 boy = $\frac{77 \times 12}{77 \times 4} = 3$ unit/day

So, time taken by 1 man, 1 woman and 1 boy together to finish the work $= \frac{77 \times 12}{2+6+3} = 84$ days

Shortcut:

A.T.Q.

Total work = $6M \times 77 = 2W \times 77 = 4B \times 77$

⇒ 3M = W = 2B = x

So, $M = x/3$, $W = x$, and $B = x/2$

So, time taken by 1 man, 1 woman and 1 boy to finish

$$\text{the work} = \frac{6M \times 77}{M + W + B} = \frac{6 \times \frac{x}{3} \times 77}{\frac{x}{3} + x + \frac{x}{2}} = \frac{2 \times x \times 77}{\frac{11x}{6}}$$

$$= 84 \text{ days}$$

11. Option (A) is correct.

Explanation:

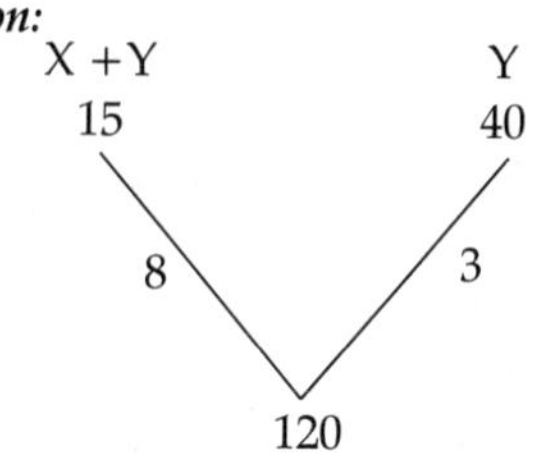

(Let total work = 120 unit)

Efficiency of X = 8 – 3 = 5 unit/day

$$\text{Hence, time taken by X alone} = \frac{120}{5} = 24 \text{ days}$$

12. Option (C) is correct.

Explanation:

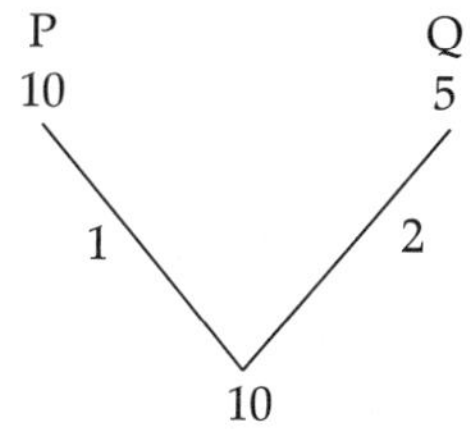

(Let total work = 10 unit)

2 days of work by Q = 2 × 2, i.e., 4 units

Remaining work = 10 – 4 = 6 unit

Hence, time taken by P (Remaining work)

$$= \frac{6}{1} = 6 \text{ days}$$

13. Option (D) is correct.

Explanation:

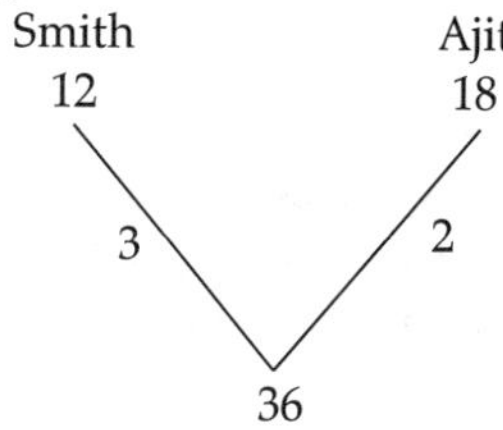

(Let total work = 36 unit)

4 days work of both = 5 × 4 = 20 units

Remaining work = 36 – 20 = 16

$$\text{Hence, required fraction of work} = \frac{16}{36} = \frac{4}{9}$$

14. Option (C) is correct.

Explanation:

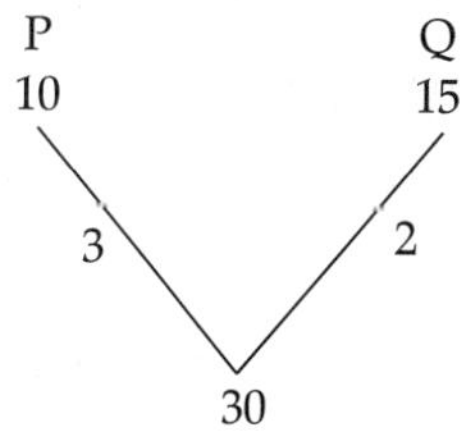

(Let total work = 30 unit)

3 days work of P + Q = 5 × 3 = 15 unit

remaining work = 30 – 15 = 15 unit

$$\text{Hence, fraction of remaining work} = \frac{15}{30} \text{ i.e., } \frac{1}{2}$$

15. Option (D) is correct.

Explanation:

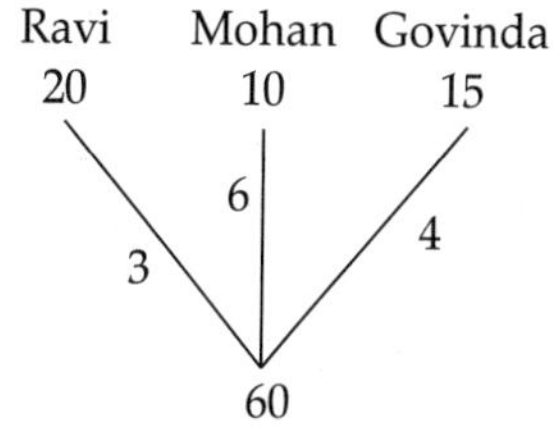

(Let total work = 60 unit)

$$\text{Hence, they together can complete it in } \frac{60}{4+6+3} \text{ days}$$

$$\text{i.e., } \frac{60}{13} \text{ days}$$

16. Option (C) is correct.

Explanation:

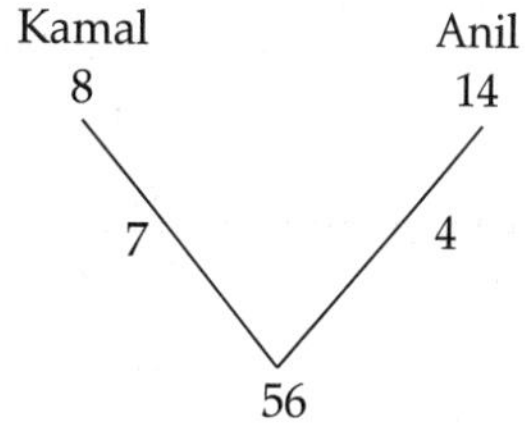

(Let total work = 56 unit)

Kamal : Anil = 7 : 4 [Ratio of Efficiency]

11 units → 4,400

So, 4 units → 1,600

Hence, Anil earns ₹ 1,600.

17. Option (C) is correct.

Explanation:

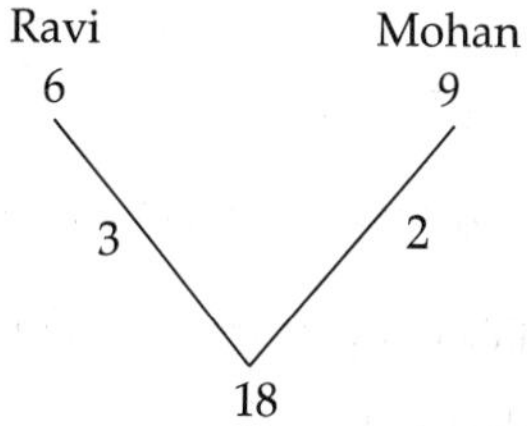

(Let total work = 18 unit)

Hence, time taken by Ravi + Mohan

$$= \frac{\text{Total work}}{\text{Efficiency (Ravi + Mohan)}}$$

$$= \frac{18}{5} \text{ i.e., } 3\frac{3}{5}$$

18. Option (D) is correct.

Explanation:

Given:

Number of teak trees planted in year 2017 = 35000

And number of teak trees planted in year 2016 = 25000

So, required percentage increase

$$= \frac{35000 - 25000}{25000} \times 100 = 40\%$$

19. Option (A) is correct.

Explanation:

Using, $\frac{m_1h_1d_1}{w_1} = \frac{m_2h_2d_2}{w_2}$

$30 \times 8 \times 16 = 32x \times 20$

Hence, $x = 6$ hours

20. Option (B) is correct.

Explanation:

Using, $m_1h_1d_1 = m_2d_2h_2$

$10 \times 12 \times 7 = 14 \times 6 \times x$

Hence, $x = 10$

21. Option (A) is correct.

Explanation:

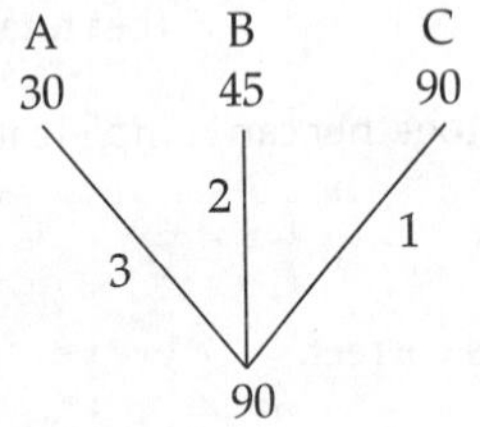

Let total work = 90 units (LCM of 30, 45, 90)

Hence, work done by A in 1 day = 3 units

Work done by B in 1 day = 2 units

Work done by C in 1 day = 1 unit

According to the question,

Work done in 3 days = 3 + 3 + (3+2+1) units = 12 units

So work done in 3 × 7 days = 12 × 7 = 84 units

And A working alone for next 2 days will complete the left 6 units of work.

Hence, total days needed to complete 90 units of work = 21 + 2 = 23 days

22. Option (B) is correct.

Explanation: Time taken by A to complete work

$= \frac{20 \times 5}{4} = 25$ days

B does it in $\frac{15 \times 4}{3} \rightarrow 20$ days

Now,

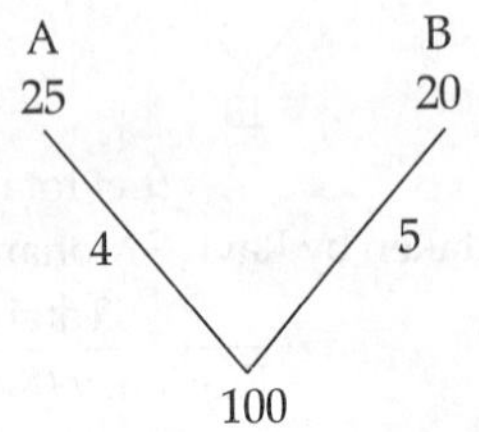

(Let total work = 100 unit)

10 days of (A + B) = 10 × 9 = 90 units

Remaining work = 10 units

C completes remaining work in 1 day

So, C's efficiency = 10

Now, time taken by B + C to complete $\frac{3}{4}$

Same work $= \frac{\frac{3}{4} \times 100}{5+10} = \frac{75}{15} = 5$ days

23. Option (D) is correct.

Explanation:

Using, $\frac{h_1m_1d_1}{w_1} = \frac{m_2d_2h_2}{w_1}$

$8 \times 45 \times 18 = \frac{x \times 20 \times 9 \times 3}{2} = 24$

So, $x = 24$ men

24. Option (C) is correct.

Explanation:

Ratio of the time taken by a man and a woman = 2 : 3

So, the ratio of the efficiency of a man and a woman = 3 : 2

Time taken by both to finish the work = 24 days

Let total work = 24 × (2 + 3) = 120 unit

So, time taken by a woman to finish the work alone

$= \frac{120}{2} = 60$ days

Level-2: INTERMEDIATE

1. Option (D) is correct.

Explanation:

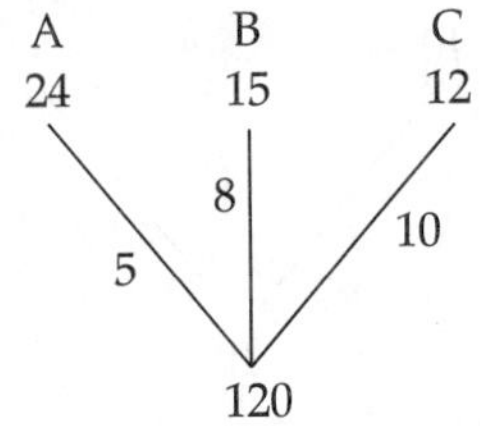

(Let total work = 120 unit)

3 day's work of B + C = 3 × (8 + 10) = 54 units

remaining work = 120 – 54 = 66

Hence, time taken by A to complete the remaining work $= \frac{66}{5}$ i.e., 13.2

2. Option (D) is correct.

Explanation: Given:

Teena can finish the work in = 12 days

Meena can finish the work in = 15 days

Ratio of time taken by them = 12 : 15 = 4 : 5

So, ratio of their efficiencies = 5 : 4

The amount which Meena will get

$= \frac{4}{9} \times 18000 =$ ₹ 8000

3. Option (D) is correct.

Explanation: Assuming efficiency of B is 100

So, efficiency of A = 80

[B is 25% more efficient than A]

efficiency of A be = 4

Efficiency of B $= 4 \times \frac{5}{4} = 5$

Efficiency of C $= 5 \times \frac{6}{5} = 6$

Total work= 30 ×4 = 120

Efficiency of C = 120 [Given]

Total work = 30 × 80

[Efficiency (A) × Time (A)]

= 2,400 unit

Now, 3 day's work of A + B + C

= (100 + 120 + 80) × 3 = 600 unit

Remaining work = 2,400 – 600 = 1,800 unit

work done by A, B and C in 3 day = (4 + 5 + 6) × 3 = 45

Remaining work 120 – 45 = 75

$\therefore$ B completes the remaining work in = $\frac{75}{5}$

= 15 days

Hence, time taken by B to complete the remaining work = $\left(\frac{1,800}{100} = 18 \text{ days}\right)$

4. Option (A) is correct.

Explanation:

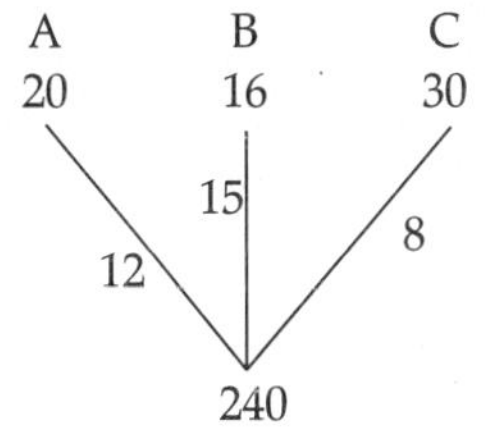

(Let total work = 240 unit)

4 day's work of A + B = (12 + 15) × 4 = 108

Remaining work = 240 – 108 = 132

Time taken by C to complete the remaining work

$= \frac{132}{8}$ i.e., $16\frac{1}{2}$

5. Option (D) is correct.

Explanation:

Given,

Time taken by A to finish the task = 12 days

Time taken by B to finish the task = 18 days

Let the total work = LCM (12, 18) = 36 units

So, A's per day work = $\frac{36}{12} = 3$ unit/day

B's per day work = $\frac{36}{18} = 2$ unit/day

Work done by A in two days = $3 \times 2 = 6$ units

So, remaining work done by B = 36 – 6 = 30 units

So, ratio of the amounts they received = 6 : 30 = 1 : 5

So, B's share = $\frac{5}{6} \times 2400 =$ ₹ 2000

6. Option (A) is correct.

Explanation:

10 men = 12 women

Men : women = 6 : 5 (Efficiency)

So, total work = 10 × 6 × 10 = 600 units

Now, time taken by 5 men + 2 women

$= \frac{600}{5 \times 6 + 2 \times 5}$

$= \frac{600}{40} = 15$ days

7. Option (C) is correct.

Explanation:

Ratio of time taken by Anamika and Bani = 1 : 3

According to the question,

$3x - x = 40$

$\Rightarrow \quad x = 20$

So, time taken by Anamika = 20 days

And time taken by Bani = 60 days

Let total work = LCM (20, 60) = 60 unit

So, efficiency of Anamika = $\frac{60}{20} = 3\frac{\text{unit}}{\text{day}}$

efficiency of Bani = $\frac{60}{60} = 1\frac{\text{unit}}{\text{day}}$

so, time taken by them together = $\frac{60}{3+1} = 15$ days

8. Option (A) is correct.

Explanation:

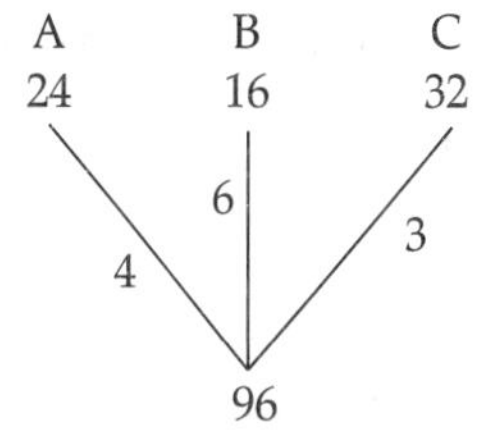

(Let total work = 96 unit)

6 day's work of A + C = (4 + 3) × 6 = 42 unit

Remaining = 96 – 42, i.e., 54 unit

Hence, time taken by B = $\frac{54}{6} = 9$ days

9. Option (C) is correct.

Explanation:

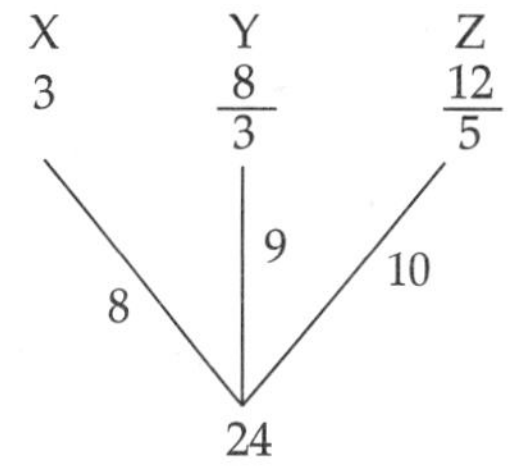

(Let total work = 24 unit)

Time taken by A + B + C = $\frac{24 \times 6}{21}$

[they works 6 hours in a day]

i.e., 5 hours 20 minutes

10. Option (A) is correct.

Explanation: B does $66\frac{2}{3}\%$ of work in 30 days.

So, B completes the work in 45 days.

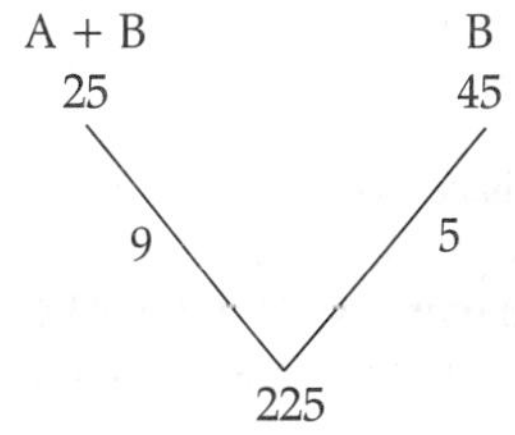

(Let total work = 225 unit)

Time taken by A to complete $\frac{4}{15}$ of work

$$= \frac{\frac{4}{15} \times 225}{4} \text{ i.e., 15 days.}$$

11. Option (B) is correct.

Explanation:

Given: A can complete the work in = 20 days

B can complete the work in = 25 days

Total work = LCM (20, 25) = 100 unit

A's per day work = 100/20 = 5 unit/day

B's per day work = 100/25 = 4 unit/day

Remaining work after 10 days = 100 – (5 + 4) × 10 = 10 unit

Time taken by C to finish 10 unit work = 10 days

So, C's per day work = 10/10 = 1 unit/day

Time taken by A, B and C together to finish the work

$$= \frac{100}{5+4+1} = 10 \text{ days}$$

12. Option (A) is correct.

Explanation:

$$(3m + 4w) \times 7 = (2m + w) \times 14$$

$$w : m = 1 : 2 \text{ [Efficiency]}$$

$$\text{Total work} = (3 \times 2 + 4 \times 1) \times 7 = 70 \text{ units}$$

Hence, time taken by 7 women $= \frac{70}{7} = 10$ days

13. Option (A) is correct.

Explanation:

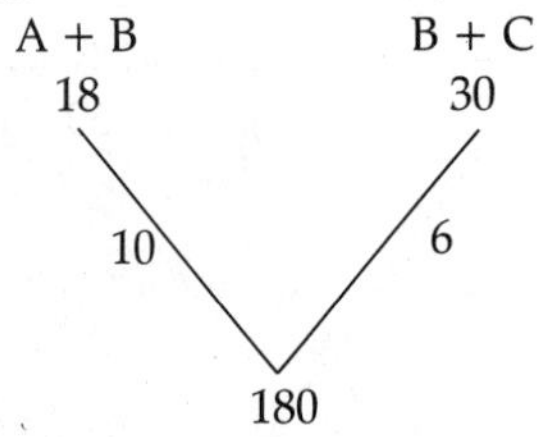

(Let total work = 180 unit)

$$A : C = 2 : 1 \text{ (Given)}$$

Efficiency (A + B) – Efficiency (B + C)

$$A - C = 4$$

$$2x - x = 4$$

$$x = 4$$

Efficiency of A is 8, so B's efficiency is 2

$$A + B = 10$$

Hence, time taken by B alone $= \frac{180}{2} = 90$ days

14. Option (B) is correct.

Explanation: Remaining days = 16 – 4 = 12 days

So, $12 \times 25 = 30 \times x$ [Using $m_1 d_1 = m_2 d_2$]

Hence, $x = 10$ days

15. Option (C) is correct.

Explanation: P : Q = 3 : 1

Total work = 24 × 1 = 24 units

Hence, time taken by P + Q to complete the work

$$= \frac{24}{4} = 6 \text{ days}$$

.16. Option (C) is correct.

Explanation:

$$27 \times 8 \times 12 = 18 \times 9 \times x$$

[Using $m_1 d_1 x_1 = m_2 d_2 x_2$]

Hence, $x = 16$ days

17. Option (B) is correct.

Explanation: R : S = 4 : 1

Total work = 20 × 1 = 20 units

Hence, time taken by both to complete the work

$$= \frac{20}{5} = 4 \text{ days}$$

18. Option (A) is correct.

Explanation: A can complete the work in = x days

B can complete the work in = 30 days

C can complete the work in = 45 days

Let total work = LCM (x, 30, 45) = $90x$ unit

So, A's per day work = 90 unit/day

B's per day work = $3x$ unit/day

C's per day work = $2x$ unit/day

Work done by B and C in 6 days = $6(3x + 2x) = 30x$

So, remaining work = $90x - 30x = 60x$

According to the question, $60x = 12 \times 90$

$$x = 18$$

19. Option (D) is correct.

Explanation: Let

Efficiency of C = 1

∴ Efficiency of B = 2

Efficiency of A = 4

Efficiency of D = x

According to question,

$$(1 + 2 + 4 + x) = 16 \times x$$

$$x = \frac{7}{3}$$

∴ Total work = 16 units

Now time taken by A alone to finish 75% of work

$$= 16 \times \frac{7}{3} \times \frac{3}{4} \times \frac{1}{4} = 7 \text{ days}$$

20. Option (B) is correct.

Explanation:

$$(3m + 5w) \times 6 = (4m + 9m) \times 4$$

$$(3m + 5w) \times 3 = (4m + 9m) \times 2$$

$$9m + 15w = 8m + 18w$$

$$9m - 8m = 18w - 15w$$

$$1m = 3w$$

$$m : w = 3 : 1$$

According to the question,

$$(3 \times 3 + 5 \times 1) \times 6 = 1 \times x \times 7$$

Hence, $x = 12$ [Using $m_1 d_1 h_1 = m_2 d_2 h_2$]

21. Option (B) is correct.

Explanation:

$$\text{Total work} = \text{Efficiency} \times \text{time}$$

$$= (2 + 5 + 3) \times 27 = 270 \text{ units}$$

Hence, time taken by B + C to complete $\frac{4}{9}$th of work

$$= \frac{270}{8} \times \frac{4}{9} = 15 \text{ days}$$

Level-3: EXPERT

1. **Option (A) is correct.**

Explanation:

Assuming efficiency of B = 100

Efficiency of A = 80

C's efficiency = 128

Total work = 80 × 40 = 3,200 units

5 day's work of A + B + C = (100 + 80 + 128) × 5

= 1,540 units

Remaining work = 3,200 – 1,540 = 1,660 units

Hence, time taken by B to complete 1,660 units of work = $\frac{1,660}{100}$ i.e., $16\frac{3}{5}$

2. **Option (A) is correct.**

Explanation:

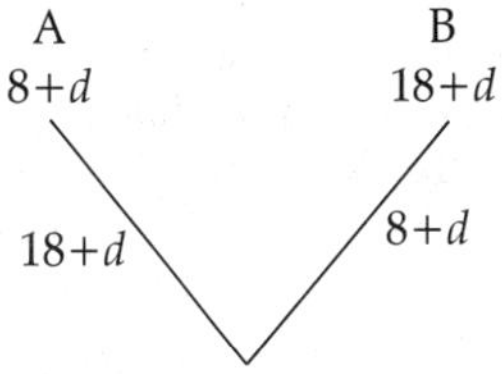

$(8 + d)(18 + d)$ i.e., total work

According to the question,

$$\frac{(8+d)(18+d)}{18+d+8+d} = d$$

$d = 12$

4 days of A's work = 4 × (18 + 12) = 120

Remaining work = Total work – 120

= [20 × 30] – 120

= 600 – 120 = 480 units

Hence, time taken by B = $\frac{480}{20}$ i.e., 24 days

3. **Option (D) is correct.**

Explanation:

$(4m + 6w) \times 5 = (3m + 4w) \times 7$

[Using $m_1d_1H_1 = m_2d_2H_2$]

$M = 2w$

$m : w = 2 : 1$

Assuming no. of men required to complete $2\frac{1}{2}$ times the same work in 5 days = T

$(T \times 2 + 25) \times 5 = \frac{5}{2} \times (4 \times 2 + 6 \times 1)$

$\Rightarrow$ 2T = 10

Hence, T = 5

4. **Option (C) is correct.**

Explanation:

Using, $\frac{m_1d_1H_1}{w_1} = \frac{m_2d_2H_2}{w_2}$

$$\frac{187 \times 65 \times 15}{3} = \frac{10 \times 17(187 + x)}{2}$$

Hence $x = 528$

5. **Option (C) is correct.**

Explanation:

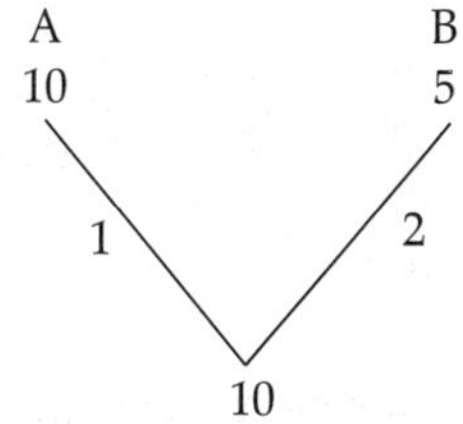

(Let total work = 10 unit)

two days of (A + B) work = 2 × 3 = 6 units

Remaining work = 4 units

Next 3 days A does 3 work where 1 unit of work is done by C in 3 days

C's efficiency = $\frac{1}{3}$

Now, 60% of total work, i.e., 10 = 6

Time taken by C = $\frac{6}{\frac{1}{3}}$ = 18 days

6. **Option (A) is correct.**

Explanation: According to question

A : B : C = 8 : 10 : 14

Total work = 15 × 8 = 120 units

3 days of A + C work = 3 × (8 + 14) = 66 units

Remaining work = 120 – 66 = 54 units

Hence, time taken by A + B to complete remaining work = $\frac{54}{18}$ = 3 days

7. **Option (C) is correct.**

Explanation: A can do 100% work → 4 × 5 = 20 days

B can do in 30 days

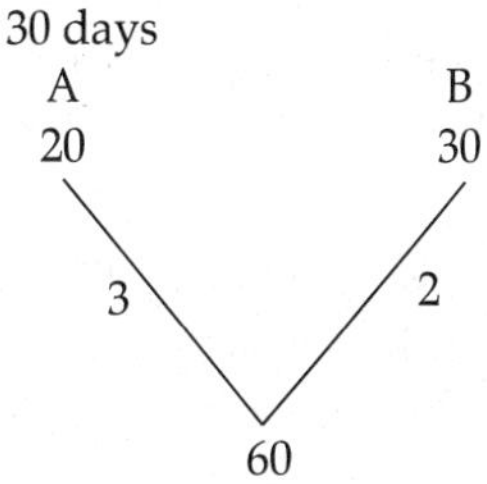

(Let total work = 60 unit)

9 days of (A + B) work = 9 × 4 = 45 units

Remaining = 15 units

C = $\frac{15}{6} = 2.5$

75% of total work = $\frac{3}{4} \times 60 = 45$

Hence, time taken by B and C = $\frac{45}{4.5} = 10$ days

8. **Option (C) is correct.**

Explanation:

Work can be finished by A in 15 days.

Work can be finished by B in 25 days.

Work can be finished by C in x days (Assumption).

According to question,

$$5\left[\frac{1}{15}+\frac{1}{25}\right]+4\left[\frac{1}{15}+\frac{1}{x}\right] = 1$$

$$\Rightarrow \frac{5}{15}+\frac{5}{25}+\frac{4}{15}+\frac{4}{x} = 1$$

$\Rightarrow \frac{4}{x} = 1 - \frac{120}{150} = \frac{1}{5}$

$\Rightarrow x = 20$

$\therefore$ C can finish the work in 20 days.

9. Option (C) is correct.

Explanation:

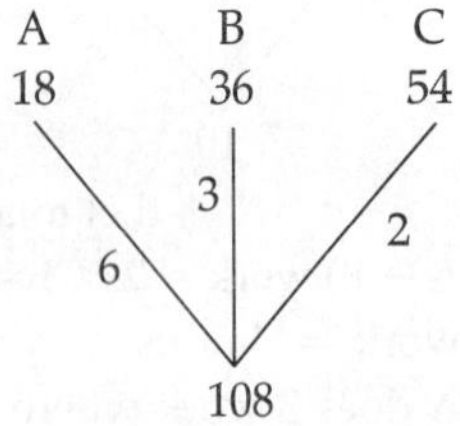

(Let total work = 108 unit)

Hence, B left 5 days before completion, So in 5 days B can do $\rightarrow 3 \times 5 = 15$ units of work

In 10 days, C can do $10 \times 2 \rightarrow 20$ units of work

Now total work will be $105 + 15 + 20 \Rightarrow 143$ units

Hence, time taken to complete total work.

$$= \frac{143}{11} = 13 \text{ days}$$

10. Option (B) is correct.

Explanation: B takes 45% max number of days to finish the work independently. So, ratio of time taken by A and B is 20 : 29.

We know that efficiency $\propto \frac{1}{\text{Time}}$

So $(A : B)_{\text{Efficiency}} = 29 : 20$

They work for 58 days and remaining work done by B alone in 29 days.

So, $49 \times 58 + 20 \times 29 = 3{,}422$ units $\rightarrow$ total work

Hence, time taken by A alone to complete the work

$$= \frac{3{,}422}{29} = 118 \text{ days}$$

11. Option (A) is correct.

Explanation:

Using, $m_1d_1H_1 = m_2d_2H_2$

$(4A + 6B) \times 5 = (5A + 10C) \times 4 = (3B + 4C) \times 10$

$= 2A = 3B$

$\frac{A}{B} = \frac{3}{2}$ (Ratio of efficiencies)

So, Total work $= (4 \times 3 + 6 \times 2) \times 5 = 120$ units

Hence, no. of boys that can set up the exhibition in one day from School A $= \frac{120}{3} = 40$

12. Option (B) is correct.

Explanation: P can do $\frac{5}{8}$ of work in 15 days

So, P can complete the work in 24 days

Q can complete in 40 days.

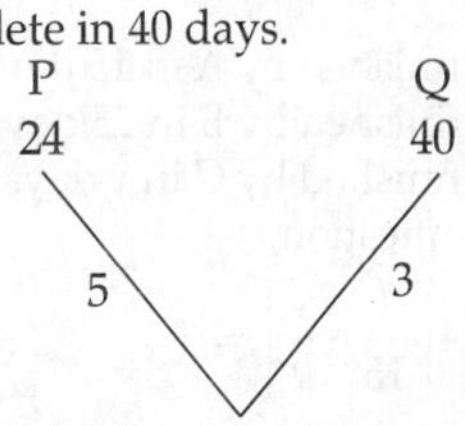

(Let total work = 120 unit)

8 days work of P and Q $= (5 + 3) \times 8 = 64$ units

Remaining work $= 120 - 64 = 56$ units

Hence, Q will complete the remaining work in $= \frac{56}{3}$

$= 18$ days 16 hours.

13. Option (B) is correct.

Explanation:

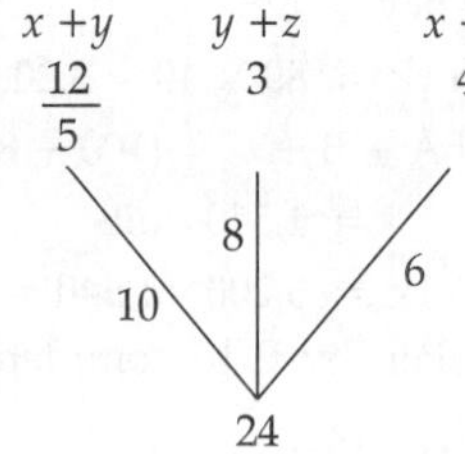

(Let total work = 24 unit)

So, efficiency by $x + y + z = \frac{10+8+6}{2} = 12$ units

Hence, time taken by $x + y + z = \frac{24}{12} = 2$ days

14. Option (B) is correct.

Explanation:

Given, Time taken by Raj = 20 days

So, time taken by Pratap = 10 days

Let the total work = LCM (20, 10) = 20 units

Efficiency of Raj $= \frac{20}{20} = 1$ unit per day

Efficiency of Pratap $= \frac{20}{10} = 2$ unit per day

So, time taken by them to complete 3/5th of the work

$$= \frac{3}{5} \times \frac{20}{(1+2)} = 4 \text{ days}$$

15. Option (A) is correct.

Explanation:

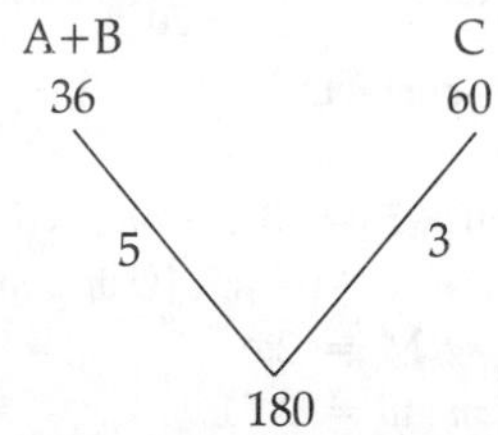

(Let total work = 180 unit)

It is given that efficiency of A = B + C

$A + B + C = 5 + 3 = 8$

$2A = 8$

$A = 4$

Efficiency of A = 4, Efficiency of B = 1

So, 10 days work of A + C $= (4 + 3) \times 10 = 70$ units

Remaining work $= 180 - 70 = 110$ units

Hence, the number of days taken by B to complete the remaining work $= \frac{110}{1} = 110$ days

16. Option (C) is correct.

Explanation:

Using, Total work = Time $\times$ Efficiency

$= 25 \times 60 = 1{,}500$ units

Work done by 15 people in 80 days

$= 15 \times 80 = 1{,}200$ units

[As 10 people left]

Remaining work = 300 units

It is done by 25 people.

Hence, time taken = $\frac{300}{25} = 12$ days

17. Option (C) is correct.

Explanation:

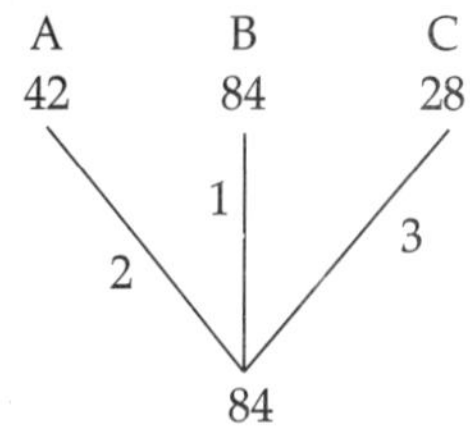

(Let total work = 84 unit)

A's 5 days of work = 5 × 2 = 10 units

B's 2 days of work = 1 × 2 = 2 units

Remaining work = 84 – 12 = 72 units

Time to work by A + B + C = $\frac{72}{6} = 12$ days

Hence, A did work for 12 + 5 = 17 days

18. Option (D) is correct.

Explanation: A's 1 day work = $\frac{1}{24}$ for $11\frac{1}{3}$ days, B begins the work.

So, B worked for 6 days and A for $5\frac{1}{3}$ days

A's $5\frac{1}{3}$ days work = $\frac{16}{3} \times \frac{1}{24} = \frac{2}{9}$

Hence, remaining work = $\frac{7}{9}$ and time taken by B to do $\frac{7}{9}$ work is 6 days.

19. Option (A) is correct.

Explanation:

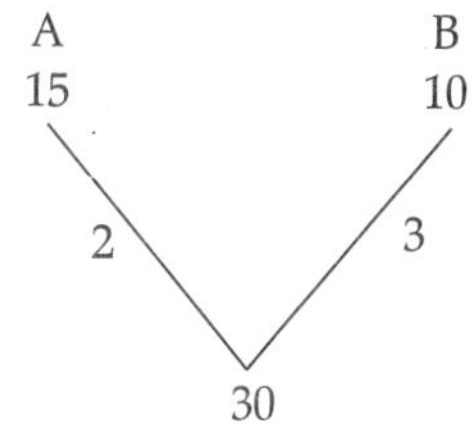

(Let total work = 30 unit)

4 days work of A + B = 4 × 5 = 20 units

Remaining work = 30 – 20 = 10 units

Time taken by A + C to complete remaining work = 3 days

So, efficiency of A + C = 3.33

Efficiency of C = 3.33 – 2 = 1.33

Hence, time taken by C to complete 40% of total work

$= \frac{\frac{40}{100} \times 30}{1.33} = 9$ days

20. Option (D) is correct.

Explanation: Assuming efficiency of

Y = 100

X = 140

Z = 60

Ratio of efficiency of X : Y : Z = 7 : 5 : 3

Total work = time × efficiency

= (7 + 5 + 3) × 21 = 315 units

Now, 35 days work of Y and Z = 8 × 35 = 280 units

Hence, remaining work i.e. 35 units to be completed by X in = $\frac{35}{7} = 5$ days

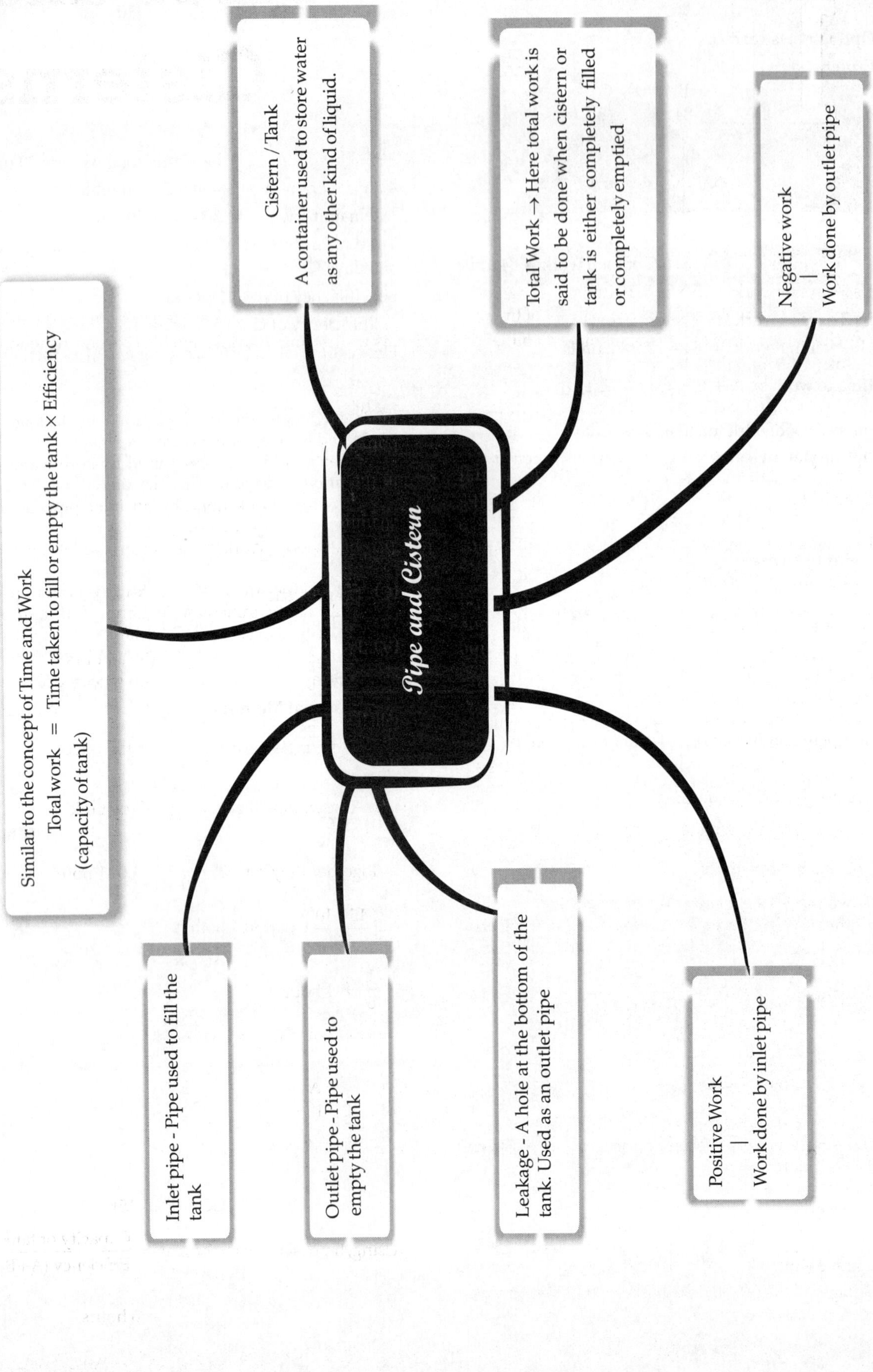

Pipe and Cistern
Cistern / Tank
A container used to store water as any other kind of liquid.
Total Work → Here total work is said to be done when cistern or tank is either completely filled or completely emptied
Negative work
Work done by outlet pipe
Similar to the concept of Time and Work
Total work = Time taken to fill or empty the tank × Efficiency (capacity of tank)
Inlet pipe - Pipe used to fill the tank
Outlet pipe - Pipe used to empty the tank
Leakage - A hole at the bottom of the tank. Used as an outlet pipe
Positive Work
Work done by inlet pipe

Chapter 11

Pipes and Cisterns

LEARNING OBJECTIVES:

- Pipe and cistern is similar to the concept of time and work or we can say that it is a sub topic of time and work. In this topic, we will learn about inlet and outlet pipe, capacity of tank and time taken to fill a part or the whole tank (cistern).

SOME IMPORTANT FORMULAE

- If 'h' hours are required to fill a cistern, then part filled in 1 hour $= \frac{1}{h}$
- If 'h' hours are required to empty a cistern, then part empty in 1 hour $= \frac{1}{h}$
- Net or total work done = total capacity of tank
- Total capacity of tank/total work done = Time taken to completely fill the tank × Efficiency of pipe.
- If pipe A is an inlet pipe and pipe B is an outlet pipe, then total efficiency = A – B, where A is efficiency of pipe A and B is efficiency of pipe B.
- If one inlet pipe can fill the tank in 'a' hours and the other inlet pipe can fill the same in 'b' hours, then the time taken to fill the tank completely $= \frac{ab}{a+b}$ [opened at same time]
- If two pipes take a and b hours, respectively, to fill a tank of water and a third pipe is opened which takes c hours to empty the tank, then the time taken to fill the tank $= \frac{1}{\left[\left(\frac{1}{a}\right)+\left(\frac{1}{b}\right)-\left(\frac{1}{c}\right)\right]}$ and the net part of the tank filled in 1 hour $= \left[\frac{1}{a}+\frac{1}{b}-\frac{1}{c}\right]$

- **Inlet pipe:** It is a pipe connected to a tank or a cistern and used to fill the tank or cistern. The work done by the inlet pipe is considered as positive work.
- **Outlet pipe:** It is a pipe connected to the tank or cistern and used to empty the tank or cistern. The work done by the outlet pipe is considered as negative work.
- **Leakage:** Leakage is a hole at the bottom of the tank and it is similar to an outlet pipe. It is used to empty a full filled tank where work done by leakage is considered to be negative work.
- **Cistern or tank:** It is a vessel used to store water or any other type of liquid.
- **Positive work:** Work done by an inlet pipe or the work done to fill the cistern.
- **Negative work:** Work done by an outlet pipe or leakage.

Example 1: Pipe A can fill a tank in 10 hours while pipe B can fill the same tank in 15 hours. If both the pipes are opened together, then the tank will be filled in:

(a) 6 hours (b) 8 hours
(c) 10 hours (d) 12 hours

Sol. (a) Traditional Method:

In 1 hour, pipe A can fill $\frac{1}{10}$ of the tank

In 1 hour, pipe B can fill $\frac{1}{15}$ of the tank

Together they can fill $\left[\frac{1}{10}+\frac{1}{15}\right]$ in 1 hour.

$\left(\frac{15+10}{150}\right)$ part in 1 hour

$\frac{1}{6} \rightarrow$ 1 hour

Hence, 1 or 100% in 6 hours.

Shortcut Approach:

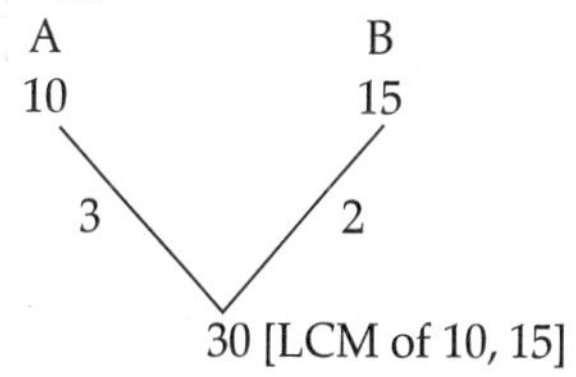

Using, time taken to fill the tank $= \frac{\text{Capacity of tank}}{\text{Efficiency (A+B)}}$

$= \frac{30}{5} = 6$ hours

Example 2: Pipe A can fill a tank in 10 hours where pipe B is an outlet pipe and can empty the completely filled tank in 20 hours. If both are opened together, in how much time will the tank be completely filled?

(a) 10 hours (b) 20 hours
(c) 40 hours (d) 30 hours

Sol. **(b)**

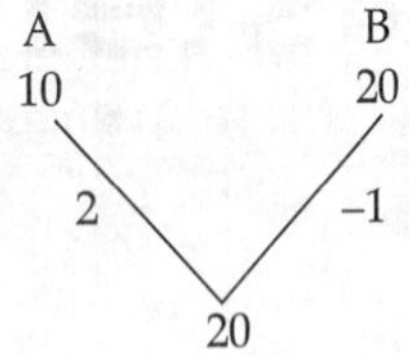

[B is an outlet pipe, so efficiency or work done by B will be negative]

Using, Time taken to fill the tank = $\frac{\text{Capacity of tank}}{\text{Total efficiency}}$

$= \frac{20}{2+(-1)} = 20$ hours.

Example 3: Three pipes A, B and C fill a tank in 6 hours. After working together for 2 hours, C is closed and A and B can fill the remaining part in 7 hours. The number of hours taken by C alone to fill the tank is:

(a) 13 hours (b) 8 hours
(c) 7 hours (d) 14 hours

Sol. **(d)** In 1 hour, (A + B + C) will fill $\frac{1}{6}$ part of tank

So in 2 hours, they [A + B + C] will fill $\frac{2}{6}$ i.e., $\frac{1}{3}$

Remaining part = $1-\frac{1}{3}=\frac{2}{3}$

Given, $\frac{2}{3}$ part is filled by A + B in 7 hours

So, 1 part is filled by A + B in $\frac{21}{2}$ hours.

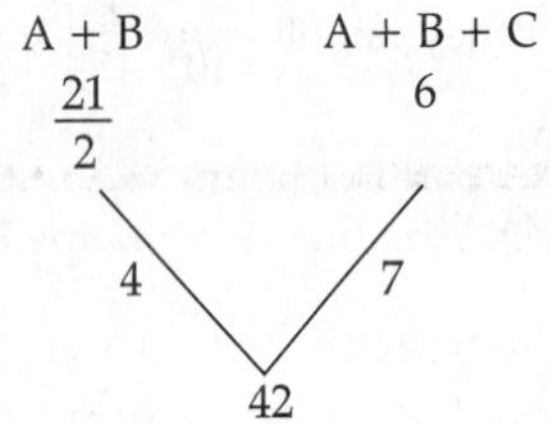

Now, Efficiency of C = Efficiency of (A + B + C) – Efficiency of (A + B)

$= 7 - 4 = 3$

Hence, C will fill the tank in = $\frac{42}{3}$ = 14 hours.

Example 4: Pipes A and B can fill a cistern in 10 hours and 15 hours, respectively. When a third pipe C which works as an outlet pipe is also opened, then the cistern can be filled in 18 hours.

The outlet pipe can empty a full cistern in:

(a) 5 hours (b) 9 hours
(c) 14 hours (d) 10 hours

Sol. **(b)**

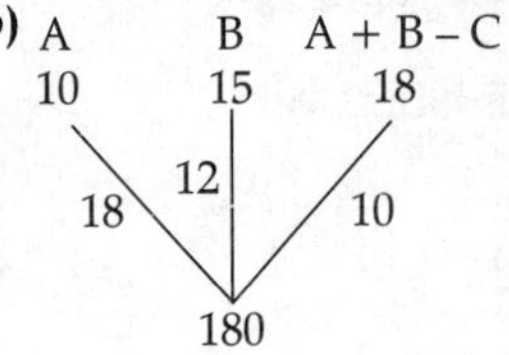

Efficiency of C = $(A + B - C)_{Efficiency} - (A + B)_{Efficiency}$

= 10 – (18 + 12) = –20 [C is outlet pipe]

Here, C will empty the cistern in $\frac{180}{20}$ = 9 hours.

Example 5: If one pipe A can fill a tank in 20 minutes, then 5 pipes, each of 20% efficiency of A, can fill the tank in:

(a) 20 min (b) 22 min
(c) 18 min (d) 25 min

Sol. **(a)** Efficiency of A = $\frac{1}{20}$

20% efficiency = 20% of $\frac{1}{20}=\frac{1}{100}$

Rate of efficiency [A : 20% of A] = $\frac{1}{20}:\frac{1}{100}=5:1$

We know that Time $\propto \frac{1}{\text{Efficiency}}$

Time ratio = 1 : 5
1 = 20 minutes
5 = 100 minutes

So, if one pipe takes 100 minutes, then 5 will take $\frac{100}{5}$ = 20 minutes.

Example 6: A, B and C are three taps that can fill a tank in 40 minutes, 60 minutes and 30 minutes, respectively. A is opened first and at every 3rd minute, B and C are opened. In how much time, can the tank be filled?

(a) 20 minutes (b) 24 minutes
(c) 10 minutes (d) 30 minutes

Sol. **(b)**

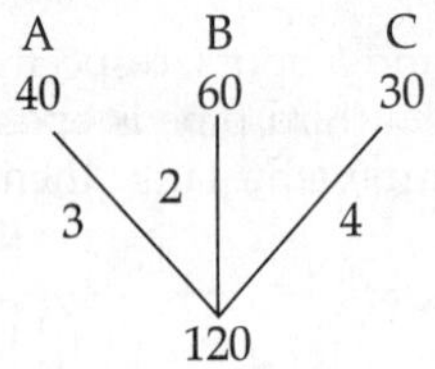

In 3 minutes, they fill → 3 + 3 + 3 + 2 + 4 = 15 units

Hence, in 24 minutes, they completely fill the tank, i.e., 120 units.

Example 7: Pipe A can fill an empty tank in 6 hours and pipe B in 8 hours. If both the pipes are opened and after 2 hours, pipe A is closed, how much time will B take to fill the remaining tank?

(a) 3 hours (b) $3\frac{1}{2}$ hours
(c) $4\frac{1}{3}$ hours (d) $3\frac{1}{3}$ hours

Sol. (d) Assuming B will take '*h*' hours to fill the remaining tank.

According to question,

$$\frac{2}{6}+\frac{h+2}{8} = 1$$

$$28 + 6h = 48$$

Hence, $h = \frac{20}{6} = 3\frac{1}{3}$ hours

Alter:

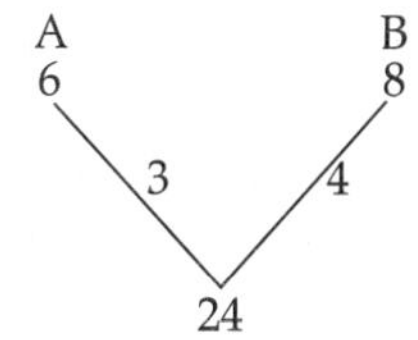

1 hour, A + B work = 7

2 hour, A + B work = 14

Remaining work = 24 – 14 = 10

Remaining work complete by B = $\frac{10}{3} = 3\frac{1}{3}$

Example 8: Having the same capacity, 9 taps fill up a water tank in 20 minutes. How many taps of the same capacity will be required to fill up the same water tank in 15 minutes.

(a) 10 (b) 12

(c) 13 (d) 14

Sol. (b) 1 minute work of 9 taps = $\frac{1}{20}$

1 tap 1 minute work = $\frac{1}{180}$

Assuming 'T' taps are used to fill the tank in 15 minutes

So, $T\times\frac{1}{180} = \frac{1}{15}$

$$T = \frac{180}{15} = 12$$

Alter: $m_1d_1 = m_2d_2$

$$9 \times 20 = 15 \times T$$

$$T = 12$$

Example 9: A water tank can be filled by a tap in 30 minutes and another tap can fill it in 60 minutes. If both the taps are kept open for 5 minutes and then the first tap is closed, how long will it take for the tank to be filled?

(a) 45 minutes (b) 42 minutes

(c) 30 minutes (d) 12 minutes

Sol. (a)

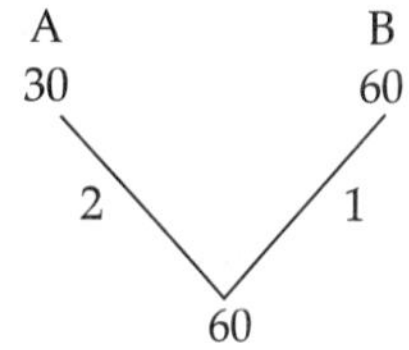

A and B's 5 minutes work = 5 × (2 + 1) = 15

Remaining = 60 – 15 = 45

Hence, 45 unit of work will be done by B in $\frac{45}{1}$ = 45 minutes.

Example 10: Two pipes can fill a tank in 18 hours and 15 hours, respectively. There is a hole at the bottom of the tank which can empty the completely filled tank in 45 hours. If both pipes are opened, then how many hours will it take to fill the tank?

(a) 5 hours (b) 10 hours

(c) 12 hours (d) 14 hours

Sol. (b)

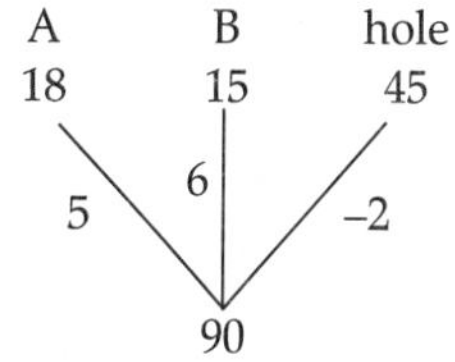

[Work done by leakage or hole is always negative]

Using, time taken = $\frac{\text{total work}}{\text{effective efficiency}}$

$$= \frac{90}{5+6-2} = 10 \text{ hours}$$

Level 1 Beginner

1. Two pipes A and B can fill a tank in 15 hours and 18 hours, respectively. Both pipes are opened simultaneously to fill the tank. In how many hours will the empty tank be filled? **[CPO 2020]**

   (A) $7\frac{2}{11}$ **(B)** $9\frac{2}{11}$ **(C)** $10\frac{2}{11}$ **(D)** $8\frac{2}{11}$

2. Two pipes can fill a tank in 15 hours and 4 hours, respectively, while a third pipe can empty it in 12 hours. How long (in hours) will it take to fill the empty tank if all the three pipes are open end simultaneously? **[CPO 2019]**

   (A) $\frac{20}{7}$ **(B)** $\frac{15}{7}$ **(C)** $\frac{50}{7}$ **(D)** $\frac{30}{7}$

3. When operated separately, pipe A takes 5 hours less than pipe B to fill a cistern and when both pipes are opened together, the cistern gets filled in 6 hours. In how much time (hours) will pipe B fill the cistern alone? **[CHSL 2020]**

   (A) 18 **(B)** 15 **(C)** 9 **(D)** 10

4. A pump can fill a tank with water in 3 hours. Because of a leak, it took $3\frac{1}{3}$ hours to fill the tank. In how many hours can the leak alone drain all the water of the tank when it is full? **[CPO 2020]**

   (A) 21 **(B)** 15 **(C)** 30 **(D)** 10

5. Pipes A and B can fill a tank in 16 hours and 24 hours, respectively, whereas pipe C can empty the full tank in 40 hours. If all three pipes one opened together but pipe C is closed after 10 hours, then after how many hours will the remaining part of the tank be filled? **[CPO 2020]**

   (A) $\frac{10}{7}$ **(B)** 2 **(C)** 5 **(D)** $5\frac{1}{2}$

6. Pipes A, B and C can fill a tank in 15, 30 and 40 hours, respectively. If pipes A, B and C are opened at 6 a.m., 8 a.m. and 10 a.m., respectively, on the same day, then when will the tank be full? **[CPO 2020]**

(A) 3:20 p.m. **(B)** 11:20 p.m.
(C) 7:20 p.m. **(D)** 5:20 p.m.

7. Tap A can fill a tank in 20 hours and tap B can fill the same in 30 hours. If both taps are opened together, then how much time will be taken to fill the tank? **[CHSL 2020]**

(A) 10 hours **(B)** 16 hours
(C) 12 hours **(D)** 24 hours

8. Tap A can fill a tank in 6 hours and tap B can empty the same tank in 10 hours. If both taps are opened together, then how much time (in hours) will be taken to fill the tank? **[CHSL 2020]**

(A) 15 **(B)** 18 **(C)** 20 **(D)** 16

9. Pipe A can fill the empty tank in 6 hours and pipe B can fill the same in 8 hours. If pipe C can empty the full tank in 10 hours, then in how much time will the tank get filled when all three pipes are opened together? **[CHSL 2019]**

(A) $4\frac{4}{23}$ hours **(B)** $5\frac{5}{23}$ hours
(C) $7\frac{1}{2}$ hours **(D)** $6\frac{1}{5}$ hours

10. Two pipes A and B can fill a tank in 18 and 24 minutes, respectively. If both pipes are opened together, then at what time should pipe B closed so that the tank is completely filled in 12 minutes. **[CPO Tier-I 2019]**

(A) 6 minutes **(B)** 9 minutes
(C) 5 minutes **(D)** 8 minutes

11. Pipes A and B can empty a full tank in 18 and 24 hours, respectively. Pipe C alone can fill the tank in 36 hours. If the tank is $\frac{5}{6}$ full and all the three pipes are opened together, then in how many hours will the tank be emptied? **[CPO Tier-I 2019]**

(A) $10\frac{1}{2}$ **(B)** $12\frac{1}{2}$ **(C)** 10 **(D)** 12

12. Pipes A and B can fill a tank in 18 minutes and $22\frac{1}{2}$ minutes, respectively while pipe C can empty the full tank in 12 minutes. A and B are opened together for 6 minutes and then closed. Now, C is opened, C alone will empty the tank in: **[CPO 2019]**

(A) 5 minutes **(B)** $8\frac{2}{5}$ minutes
(C) $7\frac{1}{5}$ minutes **(D)** 6 minutes

13. Pipes A and B are filling pipes where pipe C is an emptying pipe. A and B can fill a tank in 72 and 90 minutes, respectively. When all the three pipes are opened together, the tank gets filled in 2 hours. A and B are opened together for 12 minutes, then closed and C is opened. The tank will be empty after: **[CGL Mains 2018]**

(A) 15 minutes **(B)** 18 minutes
(C) 12 minutes **(D)** 16 minutes

14. A tap can fill a tank in 4 hours. Another tap can fill the same tank in 6 hours. If both the taps are opened at the same time, then in how much time will the empty tank be filled completely? **[SSC CHSL 2021]**

(A) 3 h **(B)** 2 h 24 min
(C) 2 h 30 min **(D)** 2 h

15. Pipes A and B can fill a tank in 6 hours and 9 hours, respectively and pipe C can empty the full tank in 12 hours. If all three pipes are opened together when a tank is empty, in how many hours will 35% of the tank be filled? **[CPO Tier-I 2018]**

(A) 1.9 **(B)** 1.6 **(C)** 1.1 **(D)** 1.8

16. Pipes A and B can fill a tank in 8 hours and 12 hours, respectively, pipe C can empty the full tank in 6 hours, A and B are opened for 3 hours and then closed and C is opened instantly. C will empty the tank in: **[CHSL (10+2) 2018]**

(A) $4\frac{1}{2}$ hours **(B)** $4\frac{1}{4}$ hours
(C) $3\frac{1}{2}$ hours **(D)** $3\frac{3}{4}$ hours

17. Two pipes can fill a cistern in 72 and 90 minutes, respectively. If both the pipes are left open, how long will it take for the cistern to be half full? **[CPO Tier-I 2019]**

(A) 40 minutes **(B)** 24 minutes
(C) 48 minutes **(D)** 20 minutes

18. A pipe can fill a tank in 3 hours and a leak can empty the tank in 5 hours. If the tap and the leak (which was half closed) were left open, how long will it take for the tank to fill? **[CPO 2018]**

(A) $4\frac{2}{7}$ hours **(B)** $7\frac{1}{2}$ hours
(C) $5\frac{1}{3}$ hours **(D)** $6\frac{2}{3}$ hours

19. An inlet pipe can fill a tank in 10 hours and an outlet pipe can empty the tank in 20 hours. Both pipes are opened at 6:30 a.m., then by when will the tank get filled? **[CHSL 2018]**

(A) 2:30 a.m. next day **(B)** 2 a.m. next day
(C) 1 a.m. next day **(D)** 12:00 midnight

20. Pipe A can fill a cistern in 4 hours and another pipe B is installed. Both pipes together fill the cistern in $2\frac{1}{2}$ hours. How long will it take for B alone to fill the cistern? **[CPO 2018]**

(A) $6\frac{2}{3}$ hours **(B)** 5 hours
(C) $5\frac{1}{6}$ hours **(D)** $6\frac{3}{8}$ hours

Level 2 Intermediate

1. Pipes A, B and C can fill an empty tank in $\frac{30}{7}$ hours, if all three pipes are opened simultaneously. A and B are filling pipes and C is an emptying pipe. Pipe A can fill the tank in 15 hours and pipes C can empty it in 12 hours. In how many hours can B alone fill the empty tank? [CPO 2020]
(A) 4 (B) 6 (C) 3 (D) 5

2. Pipe X can fill a tank in 20 hours and Pipe Y can fill the tank in 35 hours. Both the pipes are opened on alternate hours. Pipe Y is opened first, then in how much time (in hours) the tank will be full? [SSC CHSL 2017]
(A) 269/11 (B) 280/11 (C) 179/7 (D) 172/7

3. Tap A can fill a tank in 6 hours, tap B in 8 hours and tap C can empty it in 4 hours. How long will it take to fill the empty tank if all the pipes are opened together? [SSC CHSL 2020]
(A) 24 (B) 30 (C) 28 (D) 20

4. Three pipes, A, B and C can fill an empty cistern in 2, 3 and 6 hours, respectively. They are opened together. After how much time should B be closed, so that the cistern gets filled in exactly 1 h 15 min? [CPO 2019]
(A) 30 min (B) 15 min
(C) 20 min (D) 45 min

5. Pipes A, B and C together fill a tank in 12 hours. All the three pipes are opened together for 4 hours and pipe C is closed. A and B together takes 10 hours to fill the remaining part of the cistern. C alone will fill $\frac{2}{3}$rd of the cistern in: [CPO Tier-I 2019]
(A) 50 hours (B) 60 hours
(C) 40 hours (D) 48 hours

6. Pipes A and B together can fill an empty tank in $6\frac{2}{3}$ minutes. If A takes 3 minutes more than B to fill the tank, then the time (in minutes) in which A alone would fill one-third of the tank is: [CPO 2018]
(A) 4.5 (B) 6 (C) 5.5 (D) 5

7. Pipes A and B can fill a tank in 36 and 48 hours, respectively. If both are opened together for 9 hours and then A is closed, pipe B alone will fill the remaining part in: [CPO Tier-I 2019]
(A) $20\frac{1}{2}$ hours (B) 25 hours
(C) 24 hours (D) 27 hours

8. Pipes A and B can empty a tank in 6 hours and 16 hours, respectively. C is a filling pipe, all the three pipes were opened together. They took 80 minutes to empty $\frac{5}{18}$ of the tank. Pipe C alone can fill the tank in: [CGL 2019]
(A) 48 hours (B) 42 hours
(C) 40 hours (D) 36 hours

9. Pipes A and B together can fill a tank in 16 hours. Whereas pipe C alone can empty the full tank in 24 hours. A and B were opened together for 10 hours and then closed and pipe C was then opened. The tank was now emptied by C in: [CGL Tier-I 2019]
(A) 18 hours (B) 10 hours
(C) 15 hours (D) 12 hours

10. Pipes A and B can fill a tank in 12 hours and 16 hours, respectively and pipe C can empty the full tank in 24 hours. All three pipes are opened together, but after 4 hours, pipe A is closed. In how many hours from the beginning will the tank be filled? [CPO Tier-I 2018]
(A) 24 (B) 28 (C) 30 (D) 32

11. Two pipes A and B can fill a tank in 16 hours and 20 hours, respectively. They are opened alternatively for 1 hour each starting with pipe A first. In how many hours will the empty tank be filled? [SSC 2018]
(A) $17\frac{3}{4}$ (B) $17\frac{1}{5}$ (C) $17\frac{3}{5}$ (D) $17\frac{1}{4}$

12. A pipe can fill a tank in 32 minutes. Due to leakage, the tank gets filled in 48 minutes. In how much time will the leakage will take to empty the full tank is? [IBPS CLERK 2019]
(A) 1 hour 56 minutes (B) 1 hour 42 minutes
(C) 1 hour 42 minutes (D) 1 hour 36 minutes

13. A pipe can fill a tank in 30 minutes. Due to leakages A and B, the filled tank would be drained off in $1\frac{1}{2}$ hours and $1\frac{1}{4}$ hours, respectively. How much time will it take to fill the tank if pipe A and B are left open? [SSC CHSL 2018]
(A) $1\frac{7}{8}$ hours (B) $1\frac{1}{3}$ hours
(C) $1\frac{4}{5}$ hours (D) $1\frac{5}{6}$ hours

14. Two pipes A and B can fill a tank in 20 minutes and 30 minutes, respectively. If only pipe B was kept open in the beginning for $\frac{1}{5}$th of the total time and then both pipes A and B were kept open for the remaining time, how many minutes did it take for the pipes to fill the tank? [CPO Tier-I 2018]
(A) $13\frac{7}{11}$ (B) $16\frac{5}{23}$ (C) $16\frac{1}{23}$ (D) $11\frac{1}{25}$

15. Three pipes A, B and C can fill a cistern in 15, 24 and 36 minutes, respectively. If pipe D can drain a full tank in 1 hour, how long will it take for the tank to be filled if all the four pipes are kept open together? [SSC CPO 2019]

(A) $9\frac{1}{8}$ hours (B) $5\frac{12}{25}$ hours

(C) $7\frac{2}{3}$ hours (D) $8\frac{16}{43}$ hours

3 Level Expert

1. Pipes A and B can fill a tank in 10 and 40 hours, respectively. C is an outlet pipe attached to the tank. If all the three pipes are opened simultaneously, it takes 80 minutes more time than what A and B together take to fill the tank. A and B are kept open for 7 hours and then closed and C was opened. C will empty the tank [in hours]: [CGL Tier-I 2019]

(A) 42 (B) 45.5
(C) 49 (D) 38.5

2. Pipes A and B can fill a tank in 43.2 minutes and 108 minutes, respectively. Pipe C can empty it at 3 litres/minute. When all the three pipes are opened together, they fill the tank in 54 minutes. The capacity (in litres) of the tank is : [CGL Tier-II 2020]

(A) 200 (B) 160 (C) 180 (D) 216

3. Pipes A and B can fill a tank in 12 and 15 minutes, respectively. The tank when full can be emptied by pipe C in x minutes. When all the three pipes are opened, the tank is full in 10 minutes. The value of x is : [CGL Tier-II 2020]

(A) 18 (B) 15 (C) 20 (D) 24

4. Pipes A, B and C can fill a tank in 10, 15 and 30 hours, respectively. D is an emptying pipe which alone can empty the full tank in x hours. A, B and C are opened together for 3 hours and then closed. Now, D is opened which alone empties the tank in 30 hours. What is the value of x? [CPO Tier-I 2019]

(A) 40 (B) 60 (C) 50 (D) 45

5. Three pipes A, B and C can fill a cistern in 12, 18 and 24 minutes, respectively. If all the pipes are opened together for 7 minutes, what will be the volume of the water that overflows as the percentage of total volume of the cistern? [CPO 2019]

(A) $26\frac{7}{18}$ (B) $23\frac{1}{3}$

(C) $23\frac{2}{3}$ (D) $26\frac{5}{18}$

6. Three pipes A, B and C fill a tank in 4 hours. Pipe C can fill the tank at twice the speed of pipe B and pipe B can fill at thrice the speed of A. Find out the time taken by A to fill the tank? [CGL 2019]

(A) 25 hours (B) 40 hours
(C) 32 hours (D) 30 hours

7. Taps A and B can fill a tank in 15 and 10 minutes, respectively while tap C can empty the full tank in x minutes. If all the three taps are opened, the tank is filled in 8 minutes. Tap C alone will empty $\frac{3}{8}$ th of tank in: [CPO Tier-III 2019]

(A) 10 minutes (B) $10\frac{1}{2}$ minutes

(C) 9 minutes (D) $8\frac{1}{2}$ minutes

8. Pipe A can fill a tank of capacity 350 litres in $3\frac{1}{2}$ minutes. Pipe B can fill a tank of capacity 780 litres in $8\frac{2}{3}$ minutes. How long (in min) will it take to fill a tank of capacity 1615 litres, if both pipes are opened together? [CPO Tier-II 2019]

(A) $7\frac{1}{2}$ (B) $8\frac{1}{2}$ (C) 9 (D) 8

9. Pipes A and B can fill a tank in 1 and 2 hours, respectively while pipe C can empty it in 1 hour 15 minutes. A and C are turned on together 9 a.m. After 2 hours only A is closed and B is turned on. When will the tank be emptied? [CGL Tier-I 2018]

(A) 12:10 p.m. (B) 11:30 a.m.
(C) 10:30 a.m. (D) 12:20 p.m.

10. Pipes A and B can fill a tank in 16 and 24 hours, respectively and pipe C can empty it in x hours. All the pipes were opened at 10:30 a.m. but C was closed at 2:30 p.m. If the tank was full at 8:30 p.m. on the same day, find the value of x. [CGL Mains 2020]

(A) 64 (B) 48 (C) 45 (D) 96

11. $\frac{1}{4}$ of a tank can be filled in 3 hours by pipe A and $\frac{1}{3}$ of the same tank can be filled in 2 hours by pipe B. How long will it take for the tank to be filled if both the pipes are kept open? [CPO 2018]

(A) 5 hours (B) 4 hours

(C) $2\frac{1}{2}$ hours (D) 2 hours

12. Three pipes X, Y and Z discharge three different chemicals A, B and C. The pipes can fill the tank in 20, 25 and 40 minutes, respectively. What will be the proportion of chemical B in the tank, if all the pipes are open for 10 minutes? [CPO Tier-I 2018]

(A) $\frac{11}{15}$ (B) $\frac{13}{23}$ (C) $\frac{8}{23}$ (D) $\frac{4}{7}$

13. A pipe can fill a tank in 4 hours and the leak at the bottom can empty it in 6 hours. After the tank is $\frac{1}{3}$ full, the leak is completely closed. How much time will the tank take to get filled completely? [CPO 2019]

(A) 12 hours **(B)** 4 hours

(C) 9 hours **(D)** $\frac{20}{3}$ hours

14. Two pipes A and B can fill an empty tank in 8 and 12 hours, respectively. They are opened alternately for 1 hour each, starting with pipe A first. In how many hours will the empty tank be filled?[CGL Mains 2018]

(A) 9 **(B)** $9\frac{1}{4}$ **(C)** $9\frac{1}{2}$ **(D)** $9\frac{1}{3}$

15. Water flows through a cylindrical pipe of internal diameter 7 cm at the rate of 5 m/s. The time, in minutes, the pipe would take to fill an empty rectangular tank 4m × 3m × 2.31m is: [CDS 2016]

(A) 28 **(B)** 40 **(C)** 20 **(D)** 12

ANSWER KEY

Level-1: Beginner

1.	(D)	2.	(D)	3.	(B)	4.	(C)	5.	(B)	6.	(A)	7.	(C)	8.	(A)	9.	(B)	10.	(D)
11.	(D)	12.	(C)	13.	(B)	14.	(B)	15.	(D)	16.	(D)	17.	(D)	18.	(A)	19.	(A)	20.	(A)

Level-2: Intermediate

1.	(A)	2.	(C)	3.	(A)	4.	(A)	5.	(C)	6.	(D)	7.	(D)	8.	(A)	9.	(C)	10.	(D)
11.	(A)	12.	(D)	13.	(A)	14.	(A)	15.	(D)										

Level-3: Expert

1.	(C)	2.	(D)	3.	(C)	4.	(C)	5.	(A)	6.	(B)	7.	(C)	8.	(B)	9.	(D)	10.	(D)
11.	(B)	12.	(C)	13.	(D)	14.	(C)	15.	(B)										

Solutions with Detailed Explanations

Level-1: BEGINNER

1. Option (D) is correct.

Explanation:

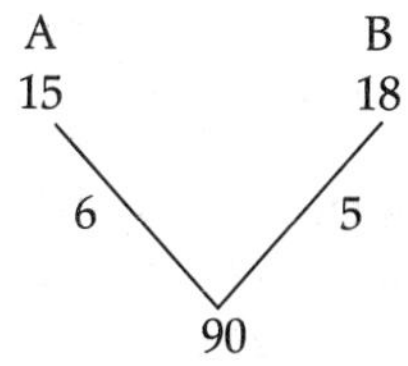

$$\text{Using Time taken} = \frac{\text{Capacity of tank}}{\text{Efficiency of pipes}}$$

$$= \frac{90}{6+5} = 8\frac{2}{11}$$

2. Option (D) is correct.

Explanation:

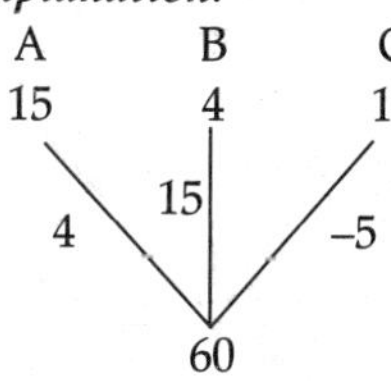

(as C is the outlet pipe)

Total efficiency = 4 + 15 + (–5) = 14 units

$$\text{Using, Time taken} = \frac{60}{14} = \frac{30}{7}$$

3. Option (B) is correct.

Explanation:

Assuming time taken by pipe B = x hours

Time taken by pipe A = $x - 5$ hours

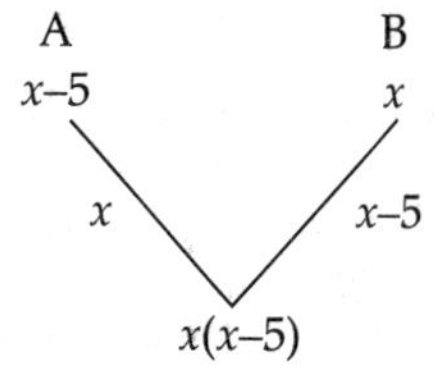

According to question,

$$\frac{x(x-5)}{x+x-5} = 6$$

$$x^2 - 5x = 6(2x - 5)$$

$$x^2 - 5x = 12x - 30$$

$$x^2 - 17x + 30 = 0$$

Solving quadratic equation

$$x = 15, 2$$

x cannot be 2 because A takes $(x - 5)$ hours to completely fill the tank. If we take 2 as the value of x,

then time taken by A will be –3 and as we know time cannot be negative.
Hence, $x = 15$ hours, i.e., time taken by B alone.

4. **Option (C) is correct.**

Explanation:

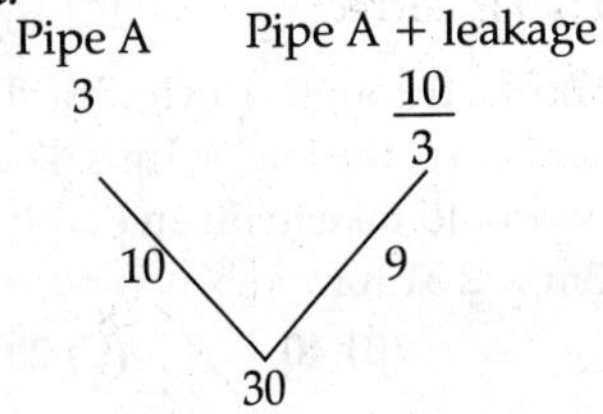

Efficiency of pipe A = 10 and with leakage it is 9.
Hence, efficiency of leakage = –1

$$\text{Using time taken by leakage} = \frac{\text{Total capacity}}{\text{Efficiency of leakage}}$$

$$= \frac{30}{1} = 30 \text{ hours}$$

5. **Option (B) is correct.**

Explanation:

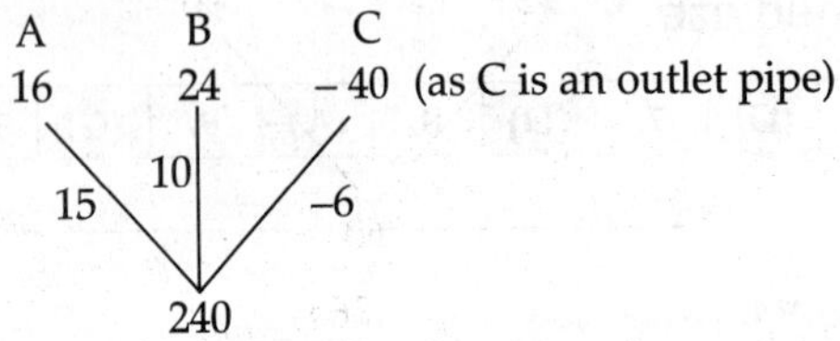

If all pipes are open, then they will fill (15 + 10 – 6) = 19 units in 1 hour.
In 10 hours, they fill 19 × 10 = 190 units
Remaining part = 240 – 190 = 50 units
Time taken by A and B to fill the remaining part, i.e.,

$$50 \text{ units} = \frac{50}{25} = 2 \text{ hours}$$

6. **Option (A) is correct.**

Explanation:

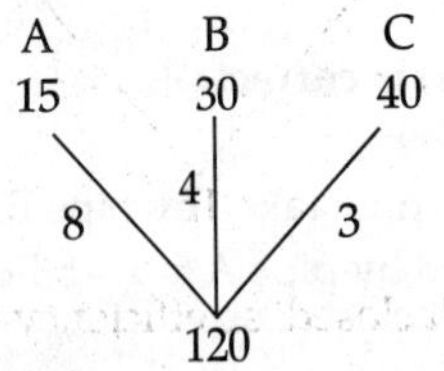

Pipe A opened at 6 a.m., so till 10 a.m., i.e., in 4 hours A will fill 8 × 4 = 32 units
Pipe B which opened at 8 a.m., so till 10 a.m., i.e., 2 hours, it will fill 4 × 2 = 8 units
Remaining part = 120 – (32 + 8) = 80 units
Now, at 10 a.m. all the three pipes are opened
So, time taken to fill remaining part, i.e., 80 units

$$= \frac{80}{8+4+3} = \frac{80}{15} \text{ hours} = 5 \text{ hours } 20 \text{ minutes}$$

So, the tank will be filled at 3:20 p.m.

7. **Option (C) is correct.**

Explanation:

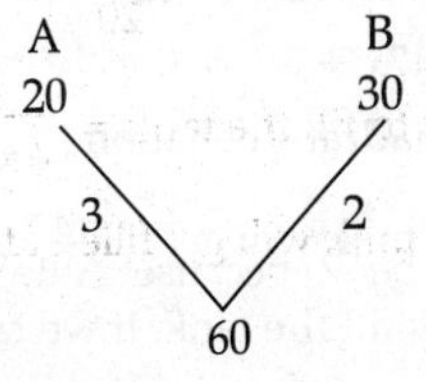

$$\text{Using time taken} = \frac{\text{Total capacity}}{\text{Efficiency}} = \frac{60}{5} = 12 \text{ hours}$$

8. **Option (A) is correct.**

Explanation:

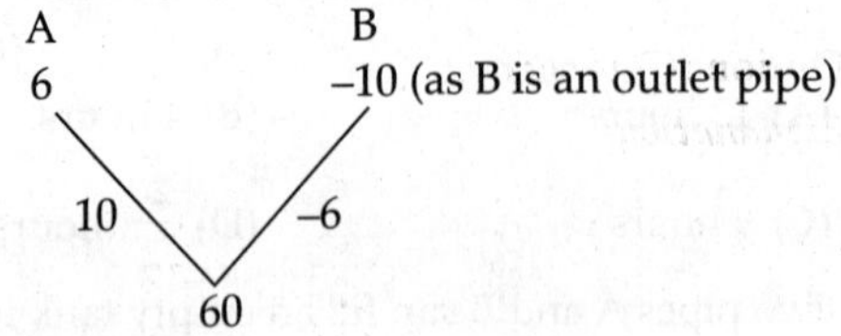

Total efficiency = 10 + (–6) = 4

$$\text{Hence, time taken} = \frac{60}{4} = 15 \text{ hours}$$

9. **Option (B) is correct.**

Explanation:

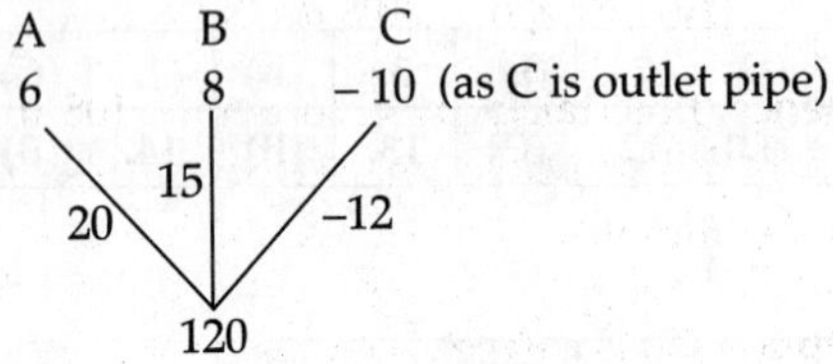

$$\text{Using, Time} = \frac{\text{Total capacity}}{\text{Total efficiency}}$$

$$= \frac{120}{20+15+(-12)}$$

$$= \frac{120}{23} = 5\frac{5}{23} \text{ hours}$$

Hence, the correct answer is $5\frac{5}{23}$ hours.

10. **Option (D) is correct.**

Explanation:

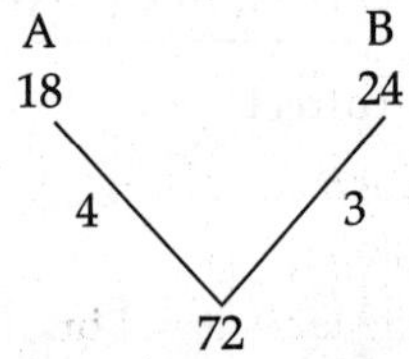

A worked 12 min = 12 × 4 = 48 units
Remaining work = 72 – 48 units
= 24 units

$$24 \text{ units filled by B} = \frac{24}{3} = 8 \text{ min}$$

11. **Option (D) is correct.**

Explanation:

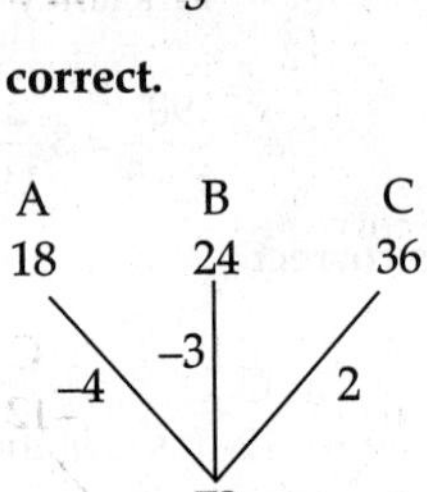

Total capacity = 72

$$\frac{5}{6} \text{ of total capacity} = \frac{5}{6} \times 72 = 60$$

Hence, if pipes are opened, then $\frac{5}{6}$ of tank, i.e.,

60 units will empty in $\frac{60}{(-4)+(-3)+2}$ = 12 hours

12. Option (C) is correct.

Explanation:

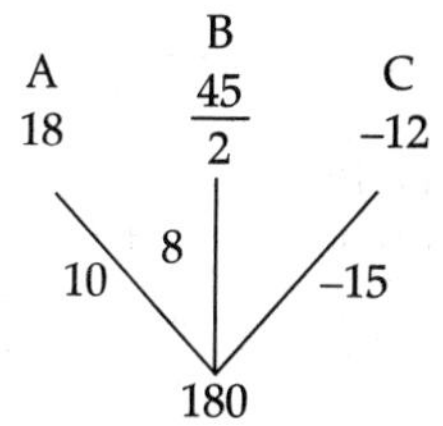

In 6 minutes, A and B will fill

$(10 + 8) \times 6 = 108$ units

Hence, time taken by C to empty 108 units = $\frac{108}{15}$

$= 7\frac{1}{5}$ minutes

13. Option (B) is correct.

Explanation:

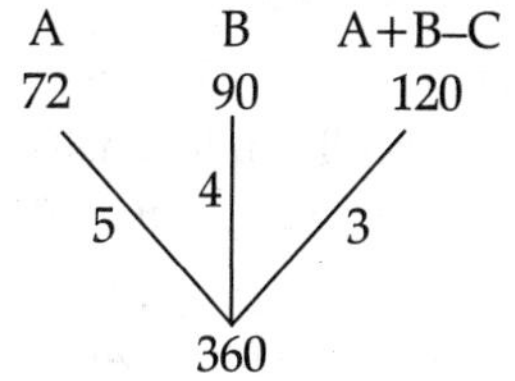

Efficiency of pipe C = 5 + 4 – 3 = 6

Total filled by A and B in 12 minutes

$= (5 + 4) \times 12 = 108$

Hence, time taken by C to empty it

$= \frac{108}{6} = 18$ mintues.

14. Option (B) is correct.

Explanation: Given:

Tap A can fill the tank in = 4 hr

Tap B can fill the tank in = 6 hr

Let the capacity of tank = LCM (4, 6) = 12

Filling capacity of tap A = 12/4 = 3 l/h

Filling capacity of tap B = 12/6 = 2 l/h

So, time taken by both tap to fill the tank

$= \frac{12}{3+2} = 2\frac{2}{5}$ hr = 2 hr 24 min

15. Option (D) is correct.

Explanation:

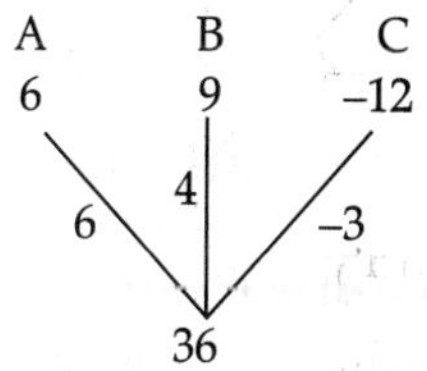

35% of tank $= \frac{35}{100} \times 36 = 12.6$

Hence, time taken to fill 12.6 units = $\frac{12.6}{6+4+(-3)}$

= 1.8 hours

16. Option (D) is correct.

Explanation:

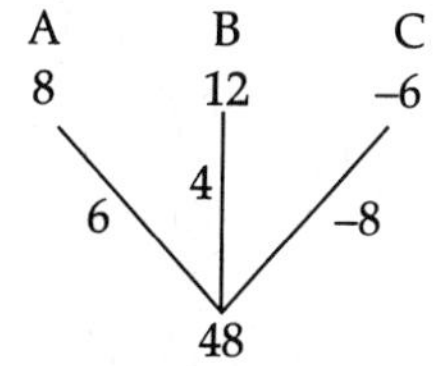

In 3 hours, A and B will fill $(6 + 4) \times 3 = 30$ units

Hence, time taken by C to empty 30 units

$= \frac{30}{8} = 3\frac{3}{4}$ hours

17. Option (D) is correct.

Explanation:

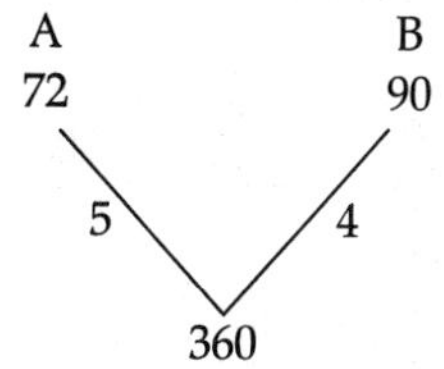

Half capacity of tank = $\frac{360}{2} = 180$

Hence, time taken by both pipes to half fill cistern.

$= \frac{180}{9} = 20$ minutes

18. Option (A) is correct.

Explanation:

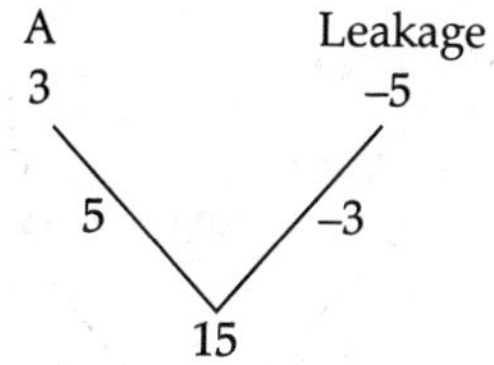

Leak is half closed, so efficiency of leak = $\frac{3}{2} = 1.5$

Hence, time taken to fill the tank

$= \frac{15}{5+(-1.5)} = \frac{15}{3.5} = 4\frac{2}{7}$ hours

19. Option (A) is correct.

Explanation:

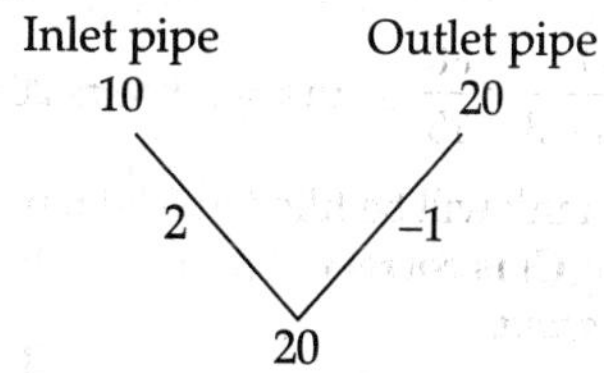

Time taken to fill the tank = $\frac{20}{2+(-1)}$ = 20 hours

Hence, the tank will get filled at 2:30 a.m. next day.

20. Option (A) is correct.

Explanation:

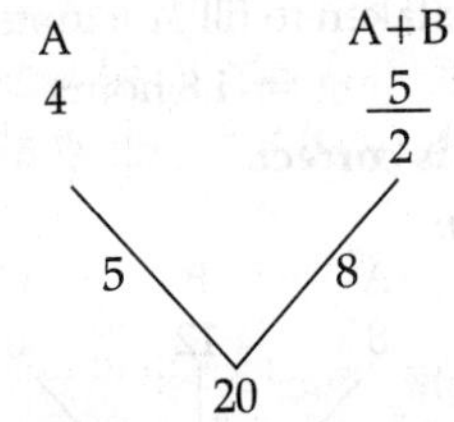

Efficiency of B = 8 – 5 = 3

Hence, time taken by B to fill the tank alone = $\frac{20}{3}$

$= 6\frac{2}{3}$ hours

Level-2: INTERMEDIATE

1. Option (A) is correct.

Explanation:

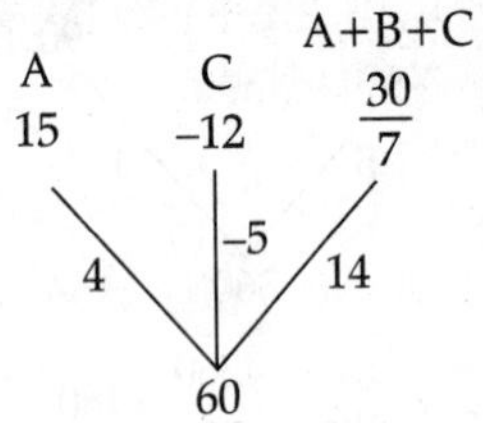

Efficiency of B = Total efficiency – Efficiency (A+C)
= 14 –(4 – 5) = 15

Hence, time taken by B = $\frac{60}{15}$ = 4 hours.

2. Option (C) is correct.

Explanation:

Given, time taken by pipe X to fill the tank
= 20 hours

Time taken by pipe Y to fill the tank = 35 hours

Total capacity of tank = L.C.M. of 20 and 35 = 140 units

Efficiency of pipe X = $\frac{140}{20}$ = 7 units/hour

Efficiency of pipe Y = $\frac{140}{35}$ =4 units/hour

Efficiency of pipe X and Y together = 7 + 4 = 11 units/2 hours

Now, 140 = 12 × 11 + 8

So both X and Y will work 2 hours and 12 times a day

∴ Remaining 8 units can be filled by both X and Y

Time taken by X to fill 4 units = $\frac{4}{7}$ hours

∴ Total time = $2 \times 12 + 1 + \frac{4}{7}$

$= 25 + \frac{4}{7} = \frac{179}{7}$ hours.

3. Option (A) is correct.

Explanation:

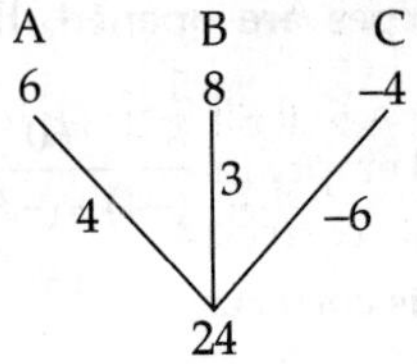

Hence, time taken = $\frac{24}{4+3+(-6)}$ = 24 hours

4. Option (A) is correct.

Explanation:

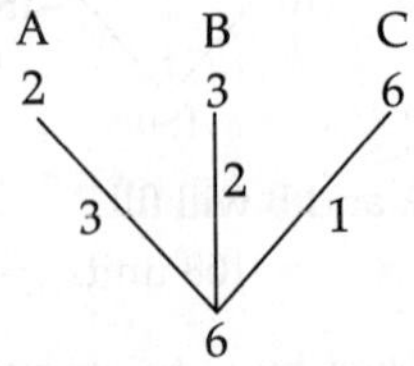

1 h 15 min. = $\frac{5}{4}$ hours

Cistern filled by A and C in $\frac{5}{4}$ hours = 5 units

Remaining = 6 – 5 = 1 unit

Pipe B can fill in 1 hour = 2 units

Hence, pipe B can fill 1 unit in half hour, i.e., 30 min.

So, Pipe B should be closed after 30 minutes.

5. Option (C) is correct.

Explanation: Assuming total capacity of tank = 60 units

So, efficiency of A + B + C= 5

In 4 hours, A + B + C will fill 5 × 4 = 20 units

Remaining = 60 – 20 = 40 units

A + B fill 40 units in 10 hours

So, efficiency of A + B = $\frac{40}{10}$ = 4

Efficiency of C = 5 – 4 = 1

Hence, time taken by C to fill $\frac{2}{3}$ of 60 i.e. 40 units

$= \frac{40}{1}$ = 40 hours

6. Option (D) is correct.

Explanation: Assuming pipe B can alone fill the tank in x min.

So, pipe A will fill it in $(x + 3)$ minutes.

According to question,

$$\frac{1}{(x+3)} + \frac{1}{x} = \frac{3}{20}$$

$$(2x + 3)\,20 = 3x^2 + 9x$$

$$40x + 60 = 3x^2 + 9x$$

$$3x^2 - 31x - 60 = 0$$

$$(x - 12)(3x + 5x) = 0$$

$$x - 12 = 0$$

$$x = 12$$

Time taken by A = $x + 3 = 12 + 3 = 15$ minutes

Hence, pipe A will fill $\frac{1}{3}$ tank in $15 \times \frac{1}{3}$ = 5 minutes

7. Option (D) is correct.

Explanation:

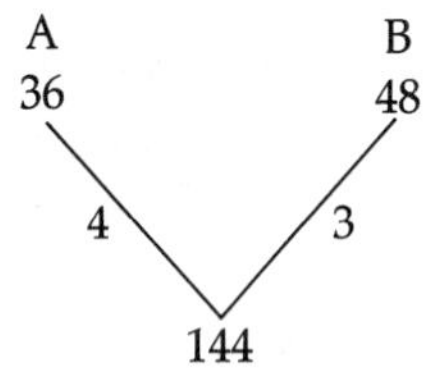

In 9 hours, A + B will fill = $(4 + 3) \times 9 = 63$ units

Remaining part = $144 - 63 = 81$ units

Hence, time taken by B alone to fill 81 units

$$= \frac{81}{3} = 27 \text{ hours}$$

8. Option (A) is correct.

Explanation:

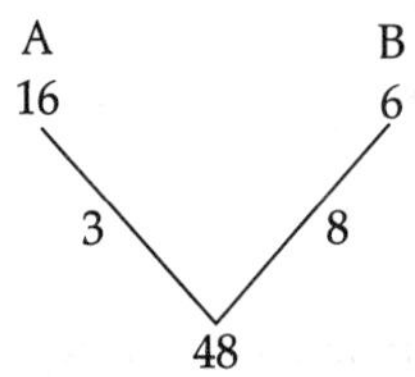

Assuming efficiency of C = x

$$(8+3-x)\times\frac{80}{60} = 48\times\frac{5}{18}$$

$$(11-x)\times\frac{4}{3} = \frac{40}{3}$$

$$x = 11 - 10$$

$$x = 1$$

Hence, time taken by pipe C = $\frac{48}{1}$ = 48 hours

9. Option (C) is correct.

Explanation:

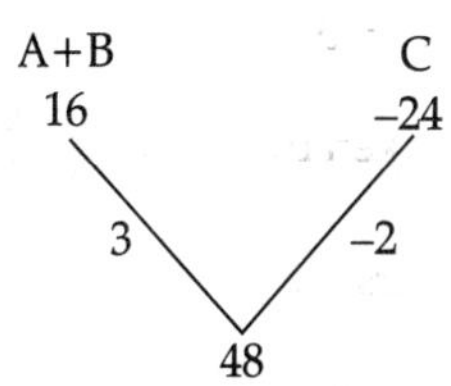

In 10 hours, A + B will fill $3 \times 10 = 30$ units

If pipe C is opened now,

then time taken by C to empty

$$30 \text{ units} = \frac{30}{2} = 15 \text{ hours}$$

Hence, 15 hours is the correct answer.

10. Option (D) is correct.

Explanation:

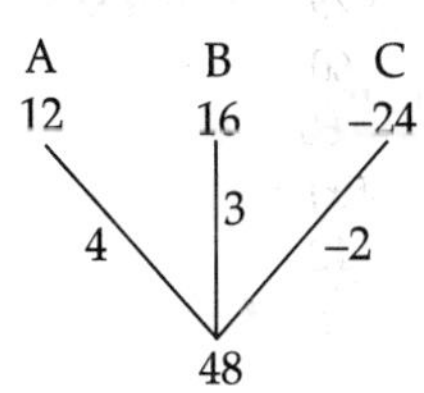

In 4 hours, A + B + C will fill

$[4 + 3 + (-2)] \times 4$ = 20 units

Remaining = $48 - 20 = 28$ units

Time taken by B and C to fill 28 units

$$= \frac{28}{3+(-2)} = 28 \text{ hours}$$

Hence, the total time taken to fill the tank

= (4 + 28) hours = 32 hours.

11. Option (A) is correct.

Explanation:

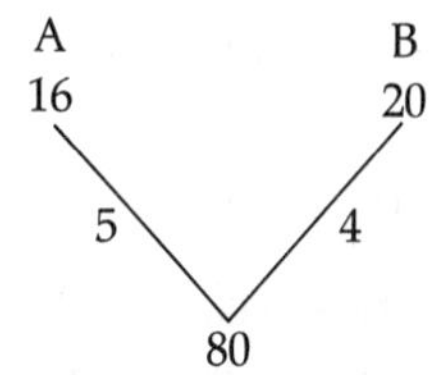

In the first hour, A will fill 5 units.

In the second hour, B will fill 4 units.

In 2 hours, they fill 9 units.

9 units in 2 hours

72 units in 16 hours

In the next hour, i.e., 17 hours, A will fill 5 units

77 units in 17 hours.

Remaining part = $80 - 77 = 3$ units

Now, B will fill units in $\frac{3}{4}$ hours

Hence, total time taken to fill the tank

$$= 17 + \frac{3}{4} = 17\frac{3}{4} \text{ hours.}$$

12. Option (D) is correct.

Explanation:

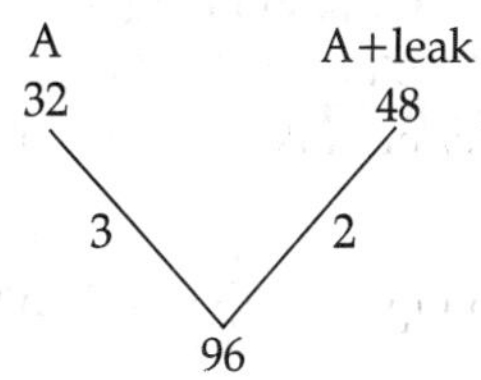

Efficiency of leak = $2 - 3 = -1$

Hence, time taken by leak to empty the full tank

$= \frac{96}{1}$ = 96 minutes which is 1 hour 36 minutes.

13. Option (A) is correct.

Explanation:

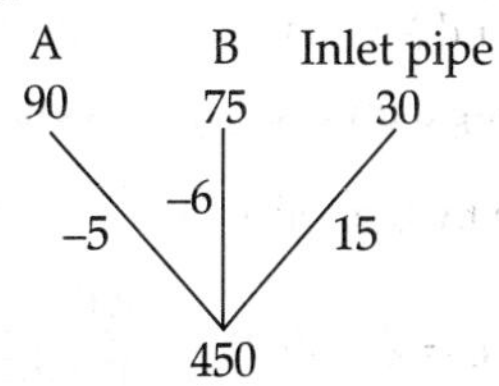

Hence, time taken to fill the cistern = $\frac{450}{15+[-5+(-6)]}$

$$= 1\frac{7}{8} \text{ h}$$

14. Option (A) is correct.

Explanation:

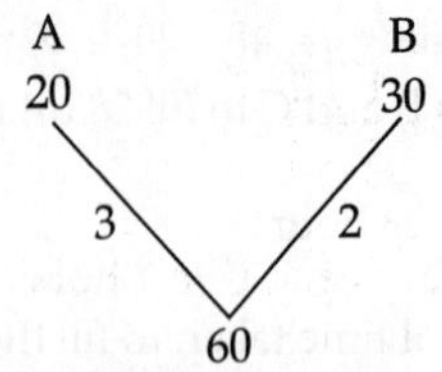

Assuming total time to fill the tank = x

According to question,

$$\left(\frac{x}{5}\right)\times 2+\left(x-\frac{x}{5}\right)\times(3+2) = 60$$

$$\frac{2x}{5}+4x = 60$$

$$22x = 300$$

Hence, $x = \frac{300}{22}=\frac{150}{11}=13\frac{7}{11}$ hours.

15. Option (D) is correct.

Explanation:

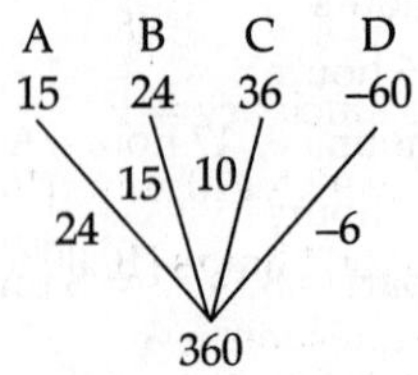

Hence, time taken by all the pipes to fill the tank

$$= \frac{360}{24+15+10+(-6)}$$

$$= \frac{360}{43\times 60}\text{hours} = 8\frac{16}{43}\text{ hours}$$

Level-3: EXPERT

1. Option (C) is correct.

Explanation:

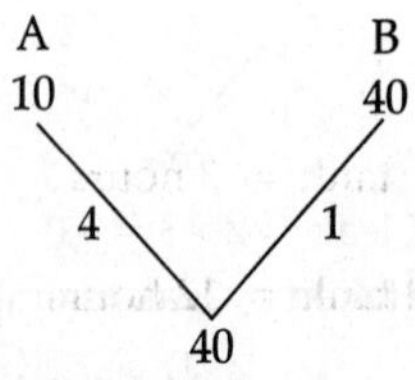

Assuming C's efficiency = x

Time taken by (A+B)'s to fill the tank

$$= \frac{40}{(1+4)} = 8 \text{ hours}$$

So, time taken by (A+B+C)'s together to fill the tank

$$= 8 + \frac{4}{3}=\frac{28}{3} \text{ hours}$$

$$\text{Efficiency of A + B + C} = \frac{\text{Total capacity of tank}}{\text{Time taken by A +B+C}}$$

$$= \frac{40}{\left(\frac{28}{3}\right)} = \frac{30}{7}$$

According to question,

$$4 + 1 + x = \frac{30}{7}$$

$$x = -\frac{5}{7}$$

Time taken by C to empty the filled tank by

$$\text{A and B in 7 hours} = \frac{(4+1)\times 7}{\frac{5}{7}} = 49 \text{ hours}$$

2. Option (D) is correct.

Explanation:

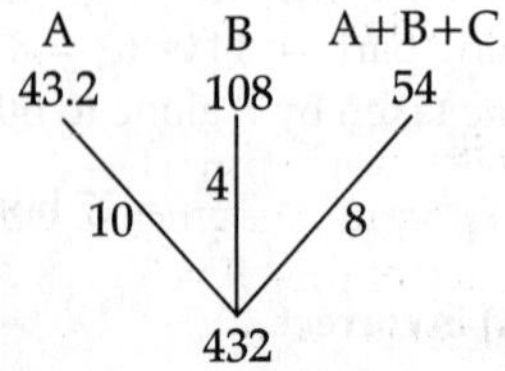

Efficiency of C = (10 + 4 – 8) = 6 units/min

Hence, capacity of tank = $\frac{432}{6}\times 3$ = 216 litres

3. Option (C) is correct.

Explanation:

Using, total capacity = Efficiency × Time

$$\frac{1}{\text{Capacity}} = \frac{1}{A}+\frac{1}{B}-\frac{1}{C}$$

$$\frac{1}{10} = \frac{1}{12}+\frac{1}{15}-\frac{1}{C}$$

$$\frac{1}{C} = \frac{(5+4-6)}{60}$$

$$\frac{1}{C} = \frac{1}{20}$$

Hence, C, i.e., x = 20

4. Option (C) is correct.

Explanation:

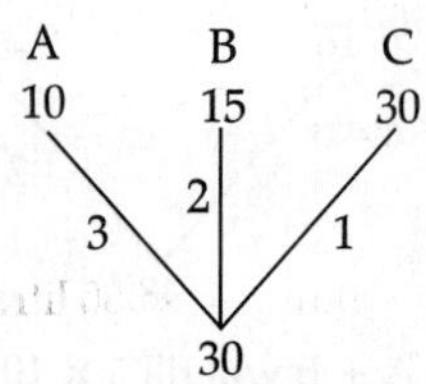

Work done by A, B and C in 3 hours

= (3 + 2 + 1) × 3 = 18

Assuming efficiency of pipe D = x

$$30 \times x = 18$$

$$x = \frac{18}{30}=\frac{3}{5}$$

Hence, pipe D alone can empty the filled tank in

$$= \frac{30}{\left(\frac{3}{5}\right)} = 50 \text{ hours}$$

5. Option (A) is correct.

Explanation:

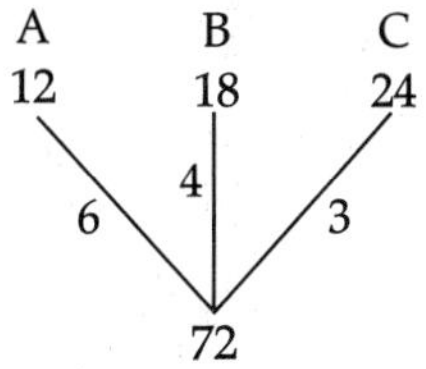

Total capacity = 72 units

Work done by A, B and C in 7 minutes

= (6 + 4 + 3) × 7 = 91

Volume of water overflows = 91 – 72 = 19

Hence, required percentage = $\left(\frac{19}{72}\right) \times 100 = 26\frac{7}{18}\%$

6. Option (B) is correct.

Explanation: Assuming efficiency of pipe A = 1

then efficiency of pipe B = 3

Pipe C's efficiency = 6

Using, total capacity = Time × efficiency

= 4 × (1 + 3 + 6) = 40 units

Hence, pipe A can fill the whole tank in $\frac{40}{1}$ = 40 hours

7. Option (C) is correct.

Explanation:

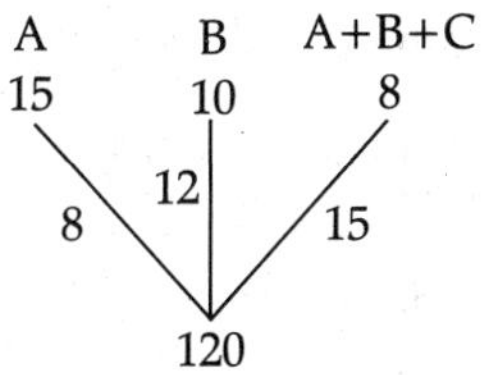

Efficiency of pipe C = $(A + B + C)_{Eff.} - (A + B)_{Eff.}$

= 15 – (12 + 8)

= – 5 [C is an outlet pipe]

$\frac{3}{8}$ of the tank = $120 \times \frac{3}{8} = 45$

Hence, tap C alone can empty the 45 units of tank in

$= \frac{45}{5} = 9$ minutes

8. Option (B) is correct.

Explanation:

Pipe A: In $3\frac{1}{2}$ minutes = 350 litres

In 1 minute = $350 \times \frac{2}{7}$ = 100 litres

Pipe B: In $8\frac{2}{3}$ minutes = 780 litres

In 1 minute = $780 \times \frac{3}{26}$ = 90 litres

Together (A + B) fill in 1 min = 100 + 90 = 190 litres

Hence, 1,615 litres filled by them in $\frac{1,615}{190} = 8\frac{1}{2}$ minutes

9. Option (D) is correct.

Explanation: Tank filled by A and C in 1 hour

$= \left(\frac{1}{1}\right) - \left(\frac{4}{5}\right) = \frac{1}{5}$

In 2 hours = $2 \times \frac{1}{5} = \frac{2}{5}$

Tank emptied by B and C in 1 hour = $\frac{4}{5} - \frac{1}{2} = \frac{3}{10}$

So, time taken by B and C to empty the tank

$= \frac{2}{5} \times \frac{10}{3} = \frac{4}{3}$ hours

Hence, the required time will be

9:00 + 2 hours + 1 hour 20 min = 12:20 p.m.

10. Option (D) is correct.

Explanation:

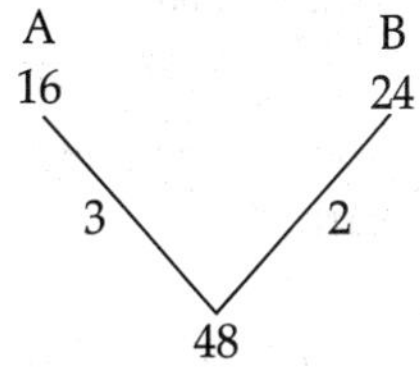

Assuming C's efficiency = P

Pipes A and B work for 10 hours [10 : 30 a.m. to 8:30 p.m.]

Pipe C works for 4 hours [10:30 to 2:30 p.m.]

According to question,

10 (3 + 2) – 4P = 48

4P = 50 – 48

P = $\frac{1}{2}$

Hence, pipe C alone can empty the tank in $\frac{48}{\frac{1}{2}}$

= 96 hours

11. Option (B) is correct.

Explanation:

Pipe A

$\frac{1}{4}$ tank = 3 hours

Full tank = 12 hours

In 1 hour = $\frac{1}{12}$ tank

Pipe B

$\frac{1}{3}$ tank = 2 hours

Full tank = 2 × 3 = 6 hours

In 1 hour = $\frac{1}{6}$ tank

Pipe (A + B) can fill in 1 hour = $\left(\frac{1}{12} + \frac{1}{6}\right) = \frac{1}{4}$

Hence, they together can fill the whole tank in 4 hours.

12. Option (C) is correct.

Explanation:

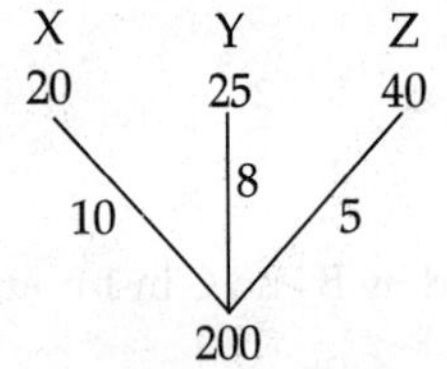

Pipe X can fill in 1 min = 10

Pipe X can fill in 10 min = 10 × 10 = 100

Pipe Y can fill in 10 min = 8 × 10 = 80

Pipe Z can fill in 10 min = 5 × 10 = 50

Hence, proportion of chemical B after 10 min.

$$= \frac{80}{100+80+50} = \frac{80}{230} \text{ i.e., } \frac{8}{23}$$

13. Option (D) is correct.

Explanation:

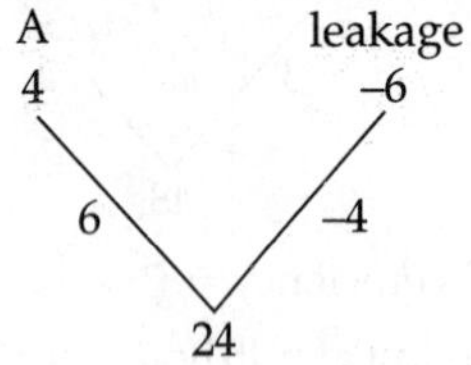

Time taken to fill $\frac{1}{3}$ of tank, i.e., $\frac{1}{3}\times 24$

$$= \frac{\frac{1}{3}\times 24}{6+(-4)} = \frac{8}{2} = 4 \text{ hours}$$

$$\text{Remaining} = \frac{2}{3}\times 24 = 16$$

Now, leak is closed

So, time taken to fill 16 units = $\frac{16}{6} = \frac{8}{3}$ hours

Hence, total time taken to fill the tank completely

$$= \left(4+\frac{8}{3}\right) \text{ hours} = \frac{20}{3} \text{ hours}$$

14. Option (C) is correct.

Explanation:

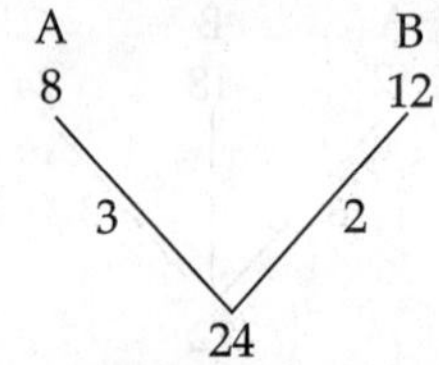

In the first hour, A will fill = 3 units

In the second hour, B will fill = 2 units

So, in 2 hours (A + B) will fill = 3 + 2 = 5 units

In 8 hours = 20 units

In 9th hour, A will fill 3 units

Here, 23 units are filled

Remaining = 24 – 23 = 1 unit

So, B will fill 1 unit in $\frac{1}{2}$ hour

Hence, total time taken to fill the tank completely

$$= \left(9+\frac{1}{2}\right) \text{ hour} = 9\frac{1}{2} \text{ hour}$$

15. Option (B) is correct.

Explanation:

$$\text{Radius} = \frac{7}{2} = 3.5 \text{ cm or } 0.00355 \text{ m}$$

Volume of water flow/sec = $\pi r^2 h$

$= 192.5 \times 10^{-6} \text{ m}^3$

So, water discharge/minute = $192.5 \times 10^{-6} \text{ m}^3 \times 60$

$= 11.55 \times 10^{-3} \text{ m}^3$

= 11.55 litres

Now, volume of tank = 4 × 3 × 2.31 = 27.72 m^3

= 27,720 litres

Hence, time taken to fill the tank = $\frac{27,720}{11.55}$

= 2,400 minutes or 40 hours.

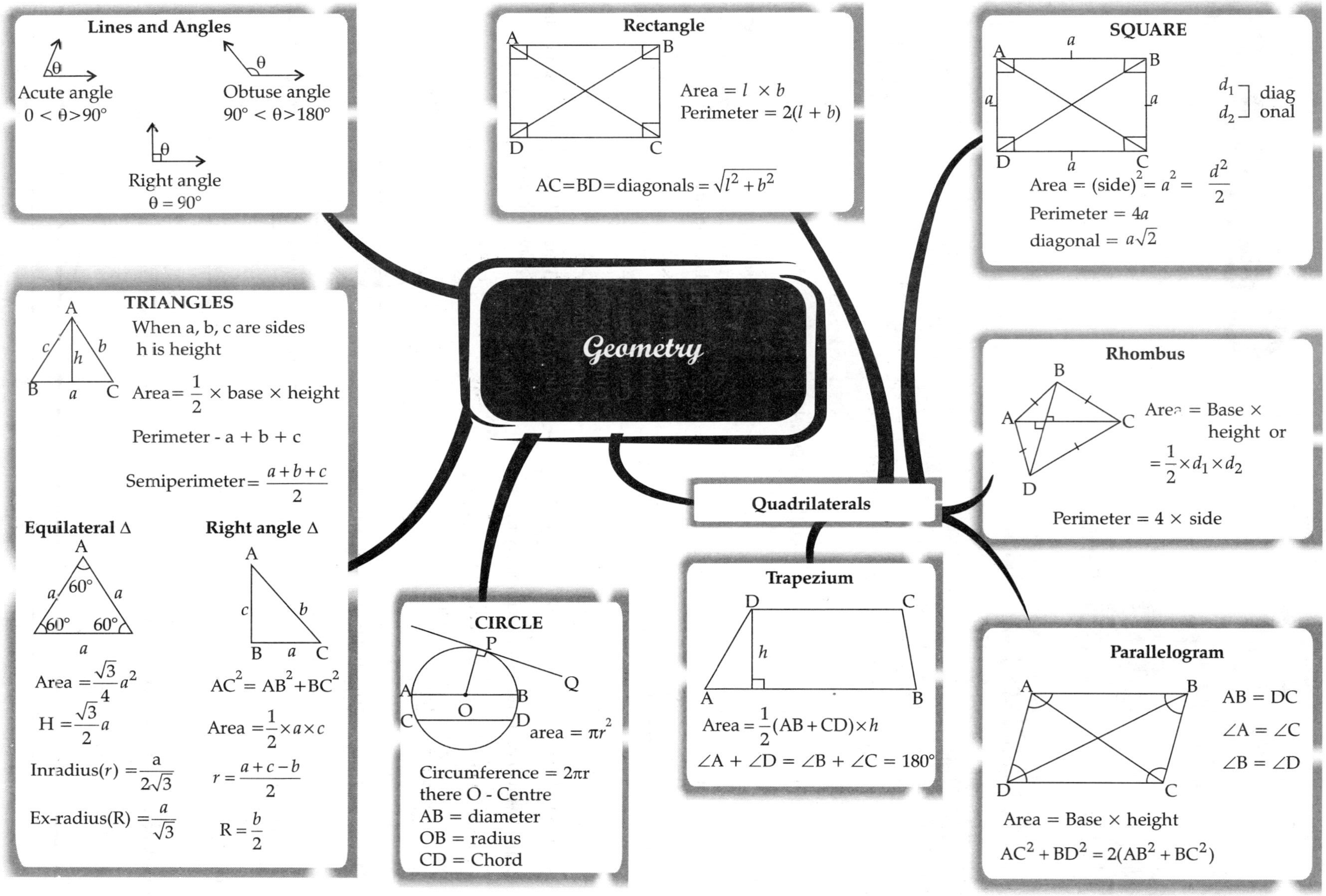
Geometry
Lines and Angles
Acute angle
0 < θ>90°
Obtuse angle
90° < θ>180°
Right angle
θ = 90°
Rectangle
Area = $l \times b$
Perimeter = $2(l + b)$
AC=BD=diagonals = $\sqrt{l^2 + b^2}$
SQUARE
d_1 d_2 diagonal
Area = $(\text{side})^2 = a^2 = \frac{d^2}{2}$
Perimeter = $4a$
diagonal = $a\sqrt{2}$
TRIANGLES
When a, b, c are sides
h is height
Area= $\frac{1}{2}$ × base × height
Perimeter - a + b + c
Semiperimeter= $\frac{a+b+c}{2}$
Equilateral Δ
Area = $\frac{\sqrt{3}}{4}a^2$
H = $\frac{\sqrt{3}}{2}a$
Inradius(r) = $\frac{a}{2\sqrt{3}}$
Ex-radius(R) = $\frac{a}{\sqrt{3}}$
Right angle Δ
$AC^2 = AB^2 + BC^2$
Area = $\frac{1}{2} \times a \times c$
$r = \frac{a+c-b}{2}$
R = $\frac{b}{2}$
Quadrilaterals
Rhombus
Area = Base × height or
= $\frac{1}{2} \times d_1 \times d_2$
Perimeter = 4 × side
CIRCLE
area = πr^2
Circumference = $2\pi r$
there O - Centre
AB = diameter
OB = radius
CD = Chord
Trapezium
Area = $\frac{1}{2}(AB + CD) \times h$
∠A + ∠D = ∠B + ∠C = 180°
Parallelogram
AB = DC
∠A = ∠C
∠B = ∠D
Area = Base × height
$AC^2 + BD^2 = 2(AB^2 + BC^2)$

Section-2 : Advance Maths

Chapter 12

Geometry

LEARNING OBJECTIVES:

- ❖ Basic concept of lines and angles.
- ❖ Triangles: Basic to high level.
- ❖ Congruency and similarity of triangles.
- ❖ Concepts of circle, chords and tangents.
- ❖ Different types of questions asked in various competitive exams.
- ❖ Method of solving questions.

LINES AND ANGLES

LINES

(a) A line is made up of an infinite number of points and it has only length.

(b) There are no end points of a line.

A⟷B denoted as $\overleftrightarrow{AB}$

➤ **Types:**

Straight line **Curved line**

Collinear points : Three or more points lying on a line are called collinear points.

➤ **Line segment:** A line segment has two end points. It cannot be extended in any direction.

denoted as $\overline{AB}$

➤ **Ray:** It can be extended in one direction, which is denoted by an arrow.

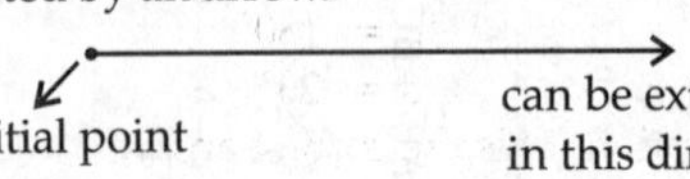

denoted as $\overrightarrow{AB}$

➤ **Parallel lines:** When two lines never intersect each other at any point and the distance between then is constant, they are said to be parallel.
Distance: (⊥) Perpendicular distance

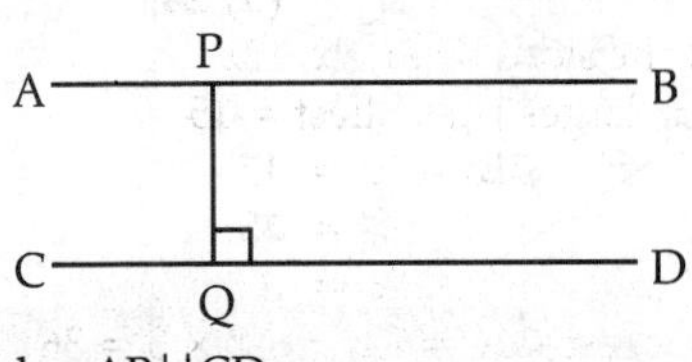

denoted as AB||CD

➤ **Concurrent lines:** When three or more lines intersect at one common point they are concurrent with each other and are called concurrent lines.

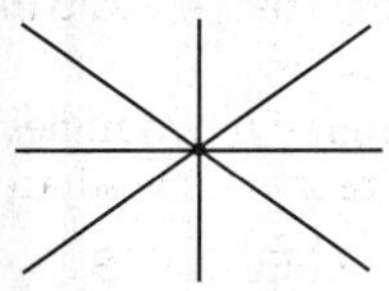

➤ **Coplanar lines:** When all lines lie in the same plane, they are called coplanar lines.

ANGLES

➤ Angle covered by full circle = 360°

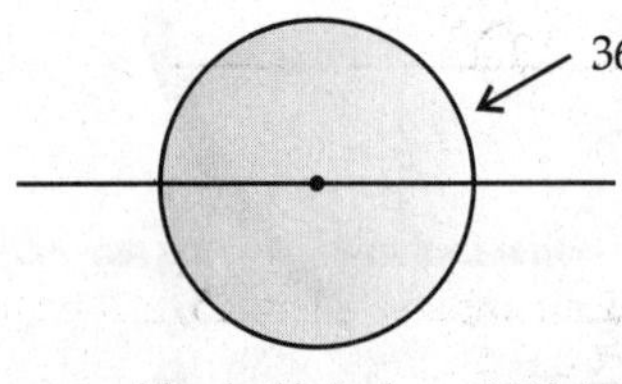

➤ Angle covered by half circle = 180° (straight angle)

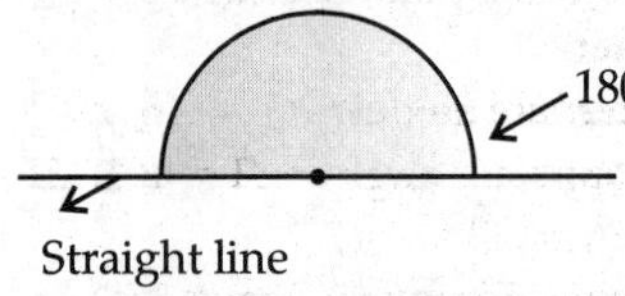

➤ Angles formed on an any straight line is 180°

(i)

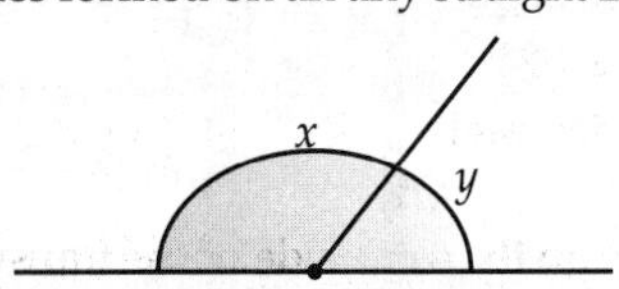

$x + y = 180°$ (linear pair)

(ii)

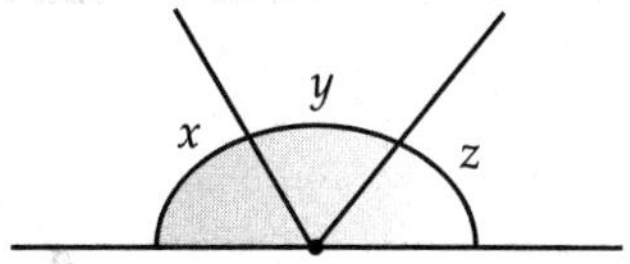

$x + y + z = 180°$ (linear triplet)

TYPES OF ANGLES

1. Acute ∠
$0° < \theta > 90°$

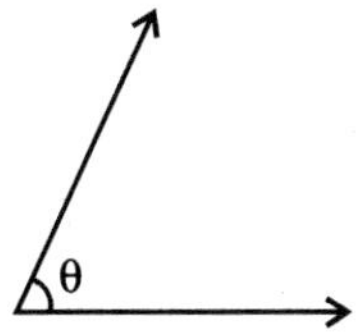

2. Obtuse ∠
$90° < \theta > 180°$

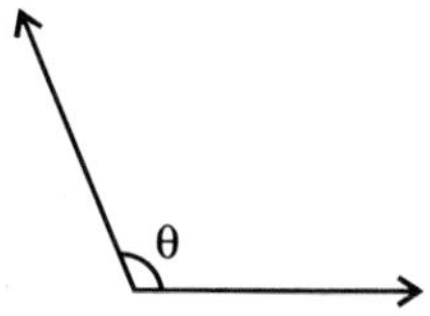

3. Right ∠
$\theta = 90°$

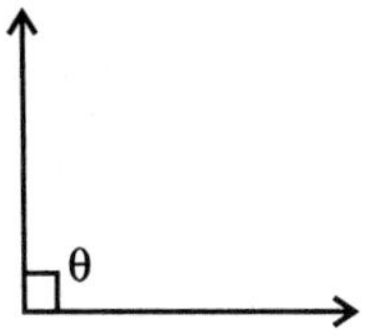

4. Reflex ∠
$180° < \theta > 360°$

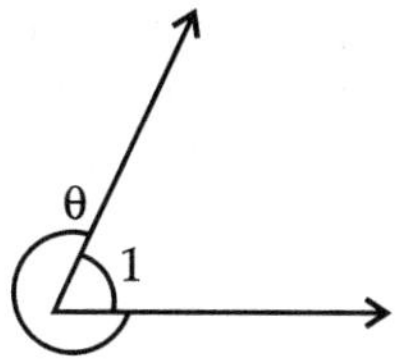

$\angle\theta = 360 - \angle 1$

➢ **Some other types of angles:**

1. **Complementary angles:** If the sum of two angles is equal to 90°, they are said to be complementary angles.
2. **Supplementary angles:** If the sum of two angles is equal to 180°, they are said to be supplementary angles.
3. **Adjacent angles:** If two angles have one common side, they are said to be adjacent angles..

CONCEPT OF PARALLEL LINES

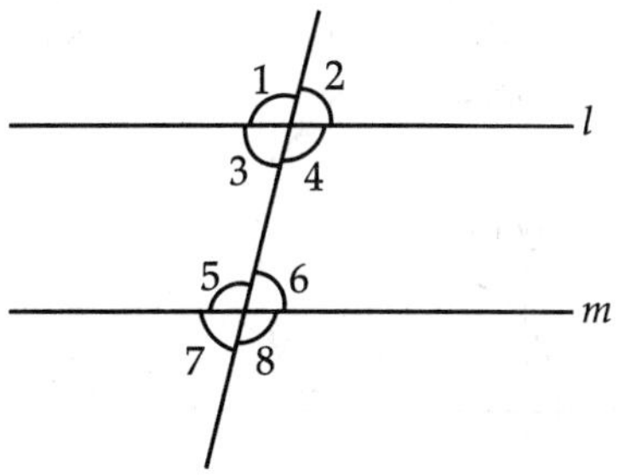

$l \parallel m$

➢ **Corresponding angles:** $\angle 1 = \angle 5, \angle 2 = \angle 6$
$\angle 4 = \angle 8, \angle 3 = \angle 7$
- Corresponding pairs of angles are always equal to each other.

➢ **Interior alternate angles:** $\angle 3 = \angle 6, \angle 4 = \angle 5$

➢ **Vertically opposite angles:** $\angle 1 = \angle 4, \angle 2 = \angle 3$, $\angle 5 = \angle 8, \angle 6 = \angle 7$

➢ **Opposite interior angles:** Sum is 180°
$\angle 3 + \angle 5 = 180°$
$\angle 4 + \angle 6 = 180°$

➢ Opposite exterior angles

OR

Exterior angles on the same side of the transversal
$\angle 1 + \angle 7 = 180°$
$\angle 2 + \angle 8 = 180°$

Example 1: If $\angle 1 = 50°$, find other angles.

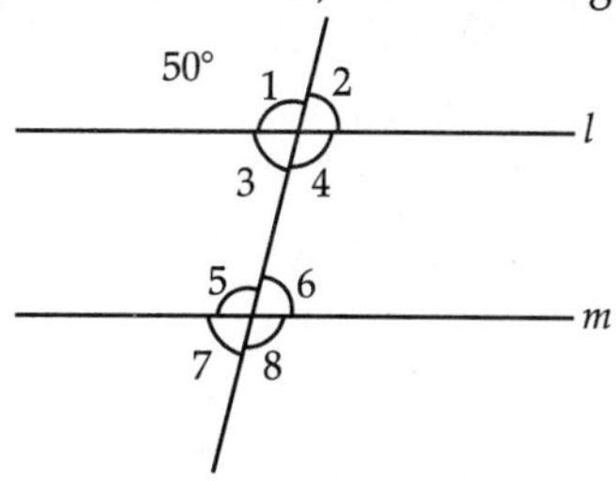

Sol.
$\angle 1 + \angle 2 = 180°$ (linear pair)
$50° + \angle 2 = 180°$
$\angle 2 = 130°$
So, $\angle 3 = \angle 2 = 130°$ (V.O.A.)
$\angle 4 = \angle 1 = 50°$ (V.O.A.)
Now, $\angle 3 + \angle 5 = 180°$ (Opposite int. angles)
$130° + \angle 5 = 180°$
$\angle 5 = 50°$
So, $\angle 5 + \angle 6 = 180°$
$50° + \angle 6 = 180°$
$\angle 6 = 130$

Example 2: The ratio of two supplementary angles is 3 : 2. The angles are:

(a) 40°, 65° (b) 72°, 108°
(c) 112°, 68° (d) 108°, 72°

Sol. (d) Let the angles be $3x, 2x$
$3x + 2x = 180°$
(Sum of supplementary angles is 180°)
$5x = 180°$
$x = 36°$
So, $3x = 3 \times 36 = 108°$
$2x = 2 \times 36 = 72°$
So, option (d) is the correct answer.

Example 3: What is the value of x in the given figure?

(a) 70° (b) 30°
(c) 20° (d) 45°

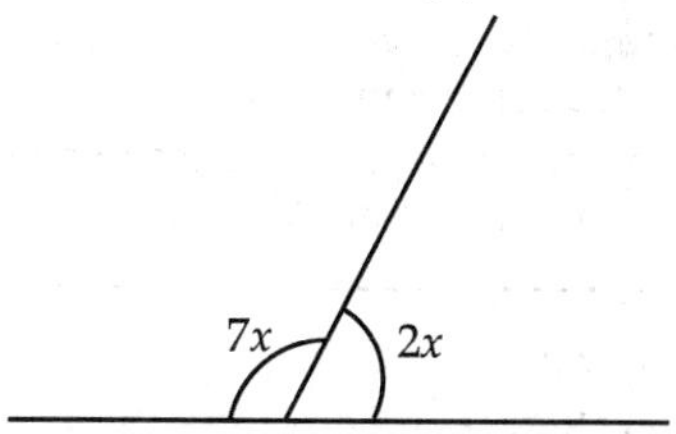

Sol. (c) $7x + 2x = 180°$ (straight angle or straight line)
$9x = 180°$
$x = 20°$
So, option (c) is the correct answer.

Example 4: The ratio of three sides of a triangle is 7 : 9 : 12. The difference between the length of the largest and smallest sides is 15 cm. Find the length of the largest side.

(a) 60 (b) 47
(c) 36 (d) 24

Sol. (c) Let the sides be $7x, 9x, 12x$
Also, largest – smallest = 15
So, $12x - 7x = 15$
$5x = 15$
$x = 3$
∴ largest side $= 12x \Rightarrow 12 \times 3 = 36$
So, option (c) is the correct answer.

TRIANGLES

- **Triangle:** A triangle is a closed figure with three sides.

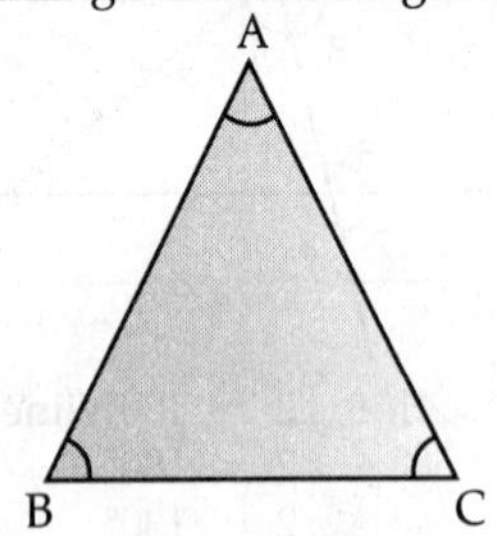

(1) Here, ABC is a triangle with sides AB, BC, CA.
(2) Three angles: $\angle A$, $\angle B$, $\angle C$.

Properties of a Triangle

- **Angle sum property:** It states that the sum of all three angles of a triangle is 180°.
  In the above figure, $\angle A + \angle B + \angle C = 180°$.
- **Exterior angle property:** It states that each exterior angle is equal to the sum of 2 interior opposite angles.

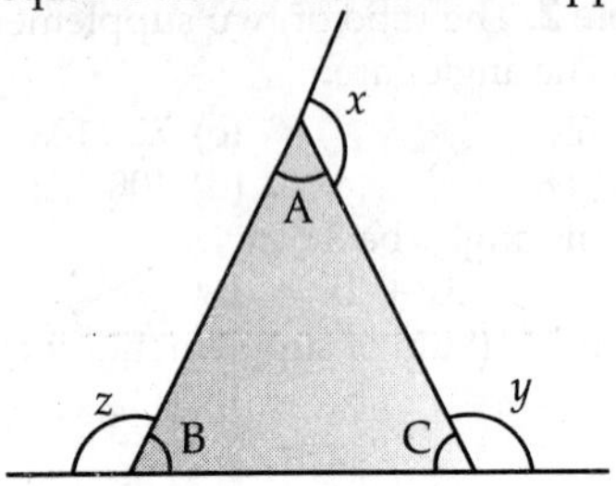

$\angle z = \angle A + \angle C$
$\angle y = \angle A + \angle B$
$\angle x = \angle B + \angle C$

- The sum of two sides is always greater than the third side.

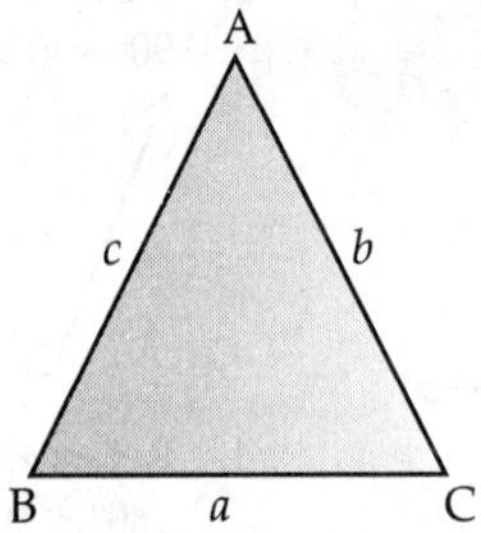

Let, a, b, c be the three sides.
Now, $a + b > c$
$b + c > a$
$c + a > b$

- **Types of Triangles**
1. **On the basis of angles.**

Acute ∠ Triangle	Obtuse ∠ Triangle	Right ∠ Triangle
• Each angle is less than 90° and more than 0°. 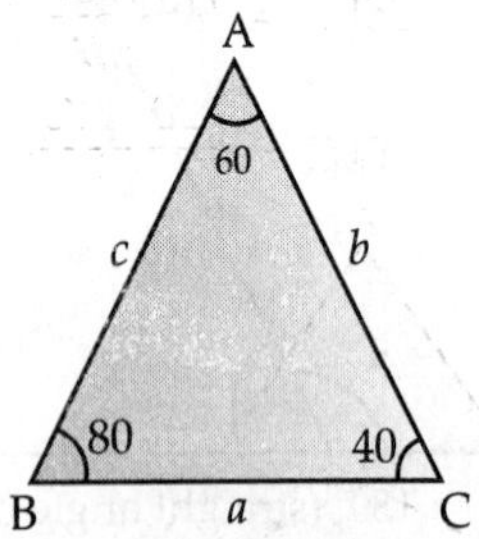 • Let a, b, c be the sides and b is the largest side. • If $a^2 < c^2 + b^2$, then Δ is an acute angle triangle.	• One angle is more than 90°. 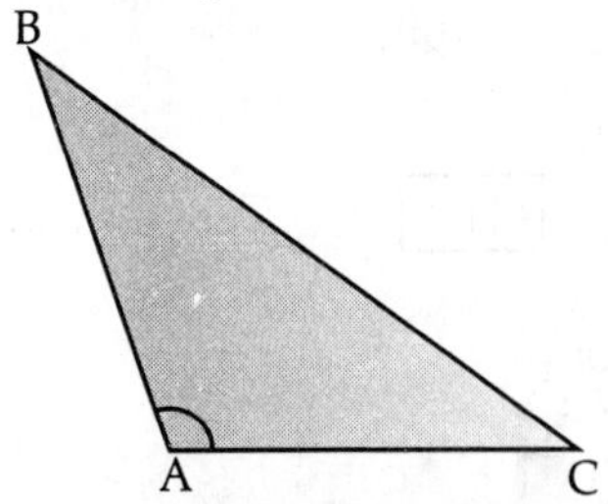 $\angle A$ = obtuse angle • Let a, b, c be the sides of the triangle. • If $a^2 > c^2 + b^2$, then Δ is obtuse angle triangle.	• One angle is 90°. 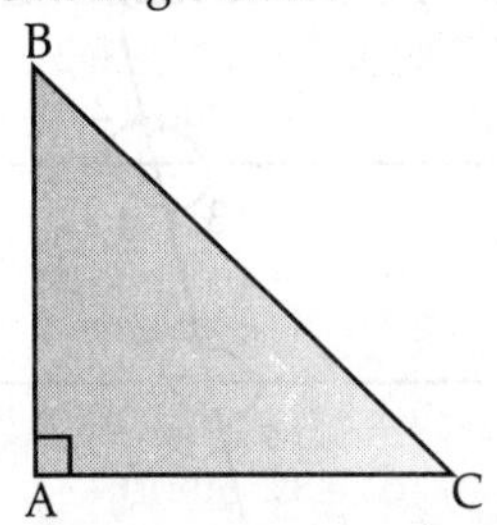 $\angle A = 90°$ • Let a, b, c be the sides of the triangle. • If $a^2 = c^2 + b^2$, then Δ is right angle triangle.

2. **On the basis of sides.**

1. Scalene	2. Isoceles	3. Equilateral
1. A triangle that has no equal sides.	1. A triangle that has two sides equal length and one different.	1. A triangle in which all sides have the same length.
2. AB ≠ BC ≠ CA	2. AB = AC ≠ BC	2. AB = BC = AC
3. Each angle is different.	3. The two angles opposite to equal sides are equal.	3. All angles are equal.

➢ Mid point, Median, Altitude of a triangle

1. **Mid point:** It is the middle point of a side. Thus, it divides the side in two equals parts.

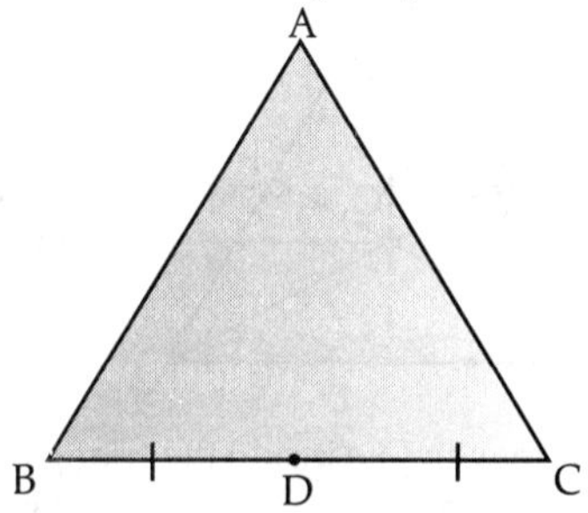

Let 'D' be the mid-point of BC

$\therefore$ BD = DC

2. **Median:** Median is the line drawn from the vertex to the midpoint of its opposite side. It also divides the side into two equal parts.

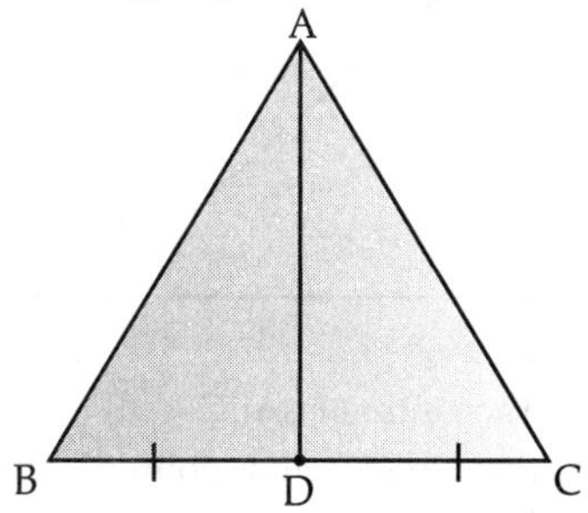

Here, 'D' is the midpoint of BC and 'AD' is the median.

> **NOTE:** It also divides the area of ΔABC into two equal parts.

$\therefore$ Area ΔABD = Area $\Delta ACD = \frac{1}{2}$ Area ΔABC

3. **Altitude:** It is the line drawn from the vertex to the opposite side being $\perp$ to it. It forms 90° angle to the opposite side.

> **NOTE:** It may or may not divide the side into equal parts.

➢ Angle bisector theorem (Interior angle)

If AD bisects interior $\angle A$, then

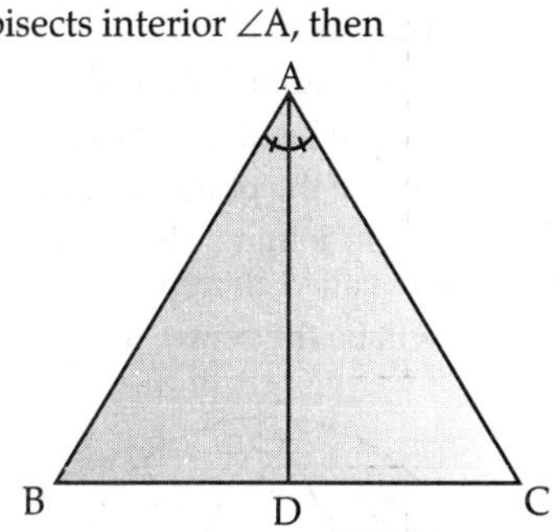

$$\frac{AB}{AC} = \frac{BD}{DC}$$

also $$\frac{AB}{BD} = \frac{AC}{DC}$$

➢ Angle Bisector Theorem (Exterior angle)

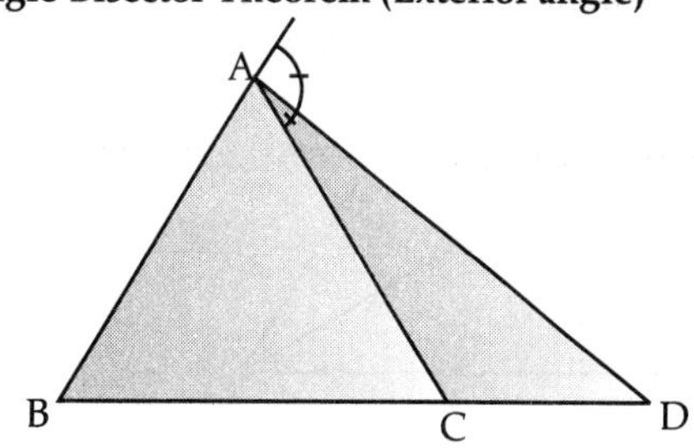

If AD is the exterior angle bisector, then

$$\frac{AB}{AC} = \frac{BD}{DC}$$

OTHER IMPORTANT POINTS

➢ If two line segments are drawn from two vertices to the incentre of a triangle, the angle formed between them $\theta = 90° + \frac{\angle A}{2}$

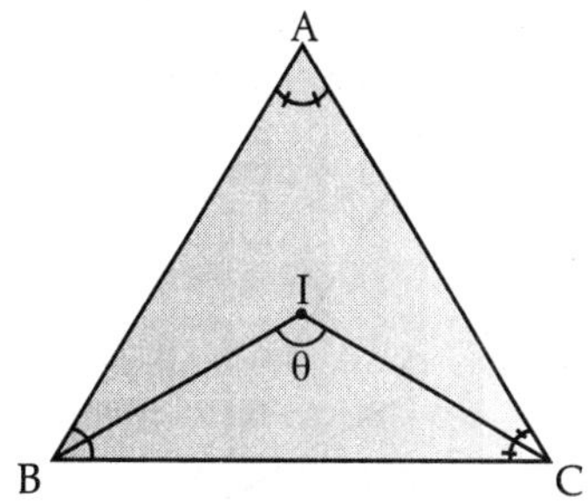

$$\angle BIC = 90 + \frac{\angle A}{2}$$

$$\angle BIC = 180 - \frac{\angle B + \angle C}{2}$$

➢ The angle between two exterior angle bisectors of the triangle is the diference between the right angle and half of the third angle.

$$\angle BI'C = 90 - \frac{\angle A}{2}$$

Also, $$\angle BI'C = \frac{\angle B + \angle C}{2}$$

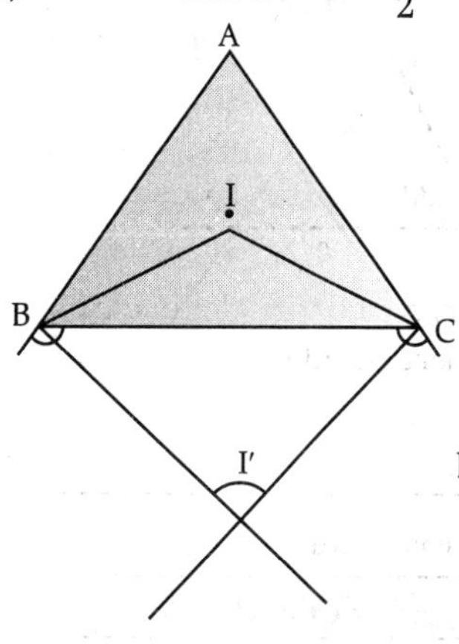

Ex-centre

Example 1: The internal bisectors of $\angle B$ and $\angle C$ of ΔABC intersect at O. If $\angle A = 100°$, then the measure of $\angle BOC$ is: **[SSC CGL Tier-I Exam]**

(a) 140° (b) 120°

(c) 110° (d) 130°

Sol. (a)

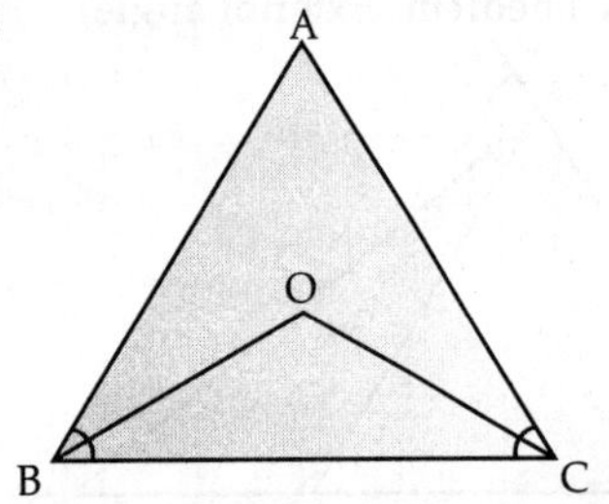

We know, $\angle BOC = 90 + \frac{\angle A}{2}$

So $= 90 + \frac{100}{2} = 90 + 50 = 140°$

So, option (a) is the correct answer.

Example 2: Let O be the incentre of a triangle ABC and 'D' be a point on the side BC of a triangle ABC, such that OD ⊥ BC. If ∠BOD = 15°, then ∠ABC = ?

(a) 75° (b) 45°
(c) 150° (d) 90°

Sol. (c)

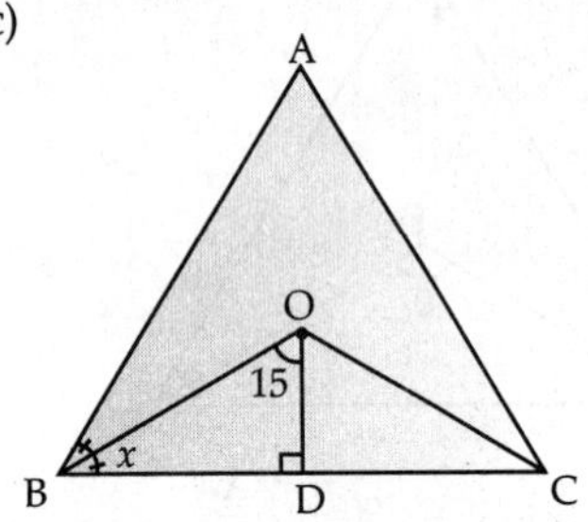

We know,

∠BDO + ∠BOD + ∠OBD = 180° [Angle sum property]

$90° + 15° + x = 180°$

$105° + x = 180°$

$x = 75°$

We also know ∠ABC $= 2x = 2 \times 75° = 150°$.

So, option (c) is the correct answer.

Example 3: In ΔABC, the external bisectors of angles ∠B and ∠C meet at the point I'. If ∠A = 70°, then find the measure of angle BI'C.

(a) 55° (b) 75°
(c) 160° (d) 50°

Sol. (a)

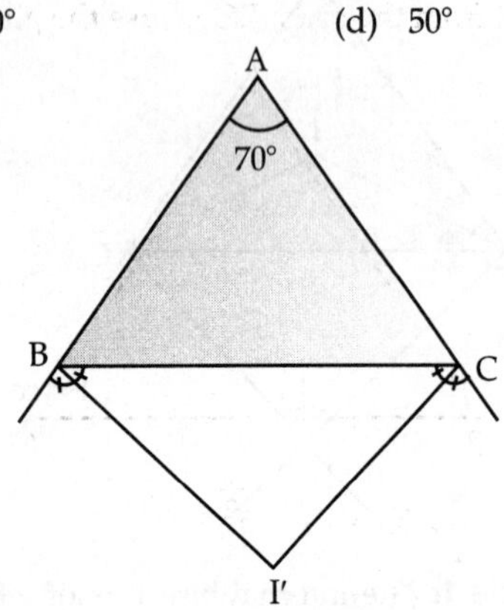

We know, $\angle BI'C = 90 - \frac{\angle A}{2}$

$= 90 - \frac{70}{2} = 90 - 35 = 55°$

So, option (a) is the correct answer.

2. **Orthocentre:** Intersection point of all three altitudes of a triangle.

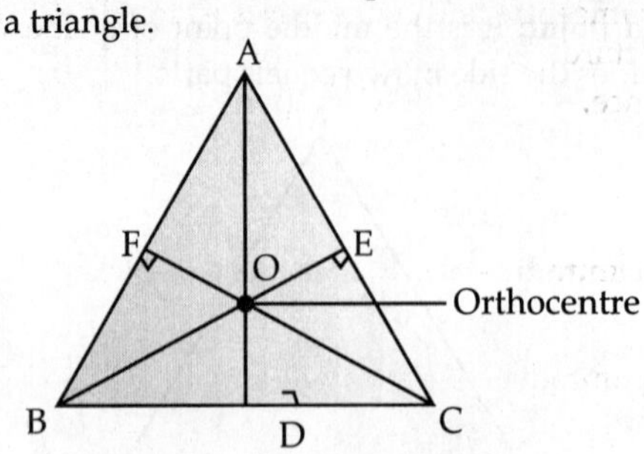

- It may or may not lie inside the triangle.
- In an obtuse angle triangle, it always lies outside the triangle.
- The orthocentre of a right angled triangle is found at the right angle of that triangle.

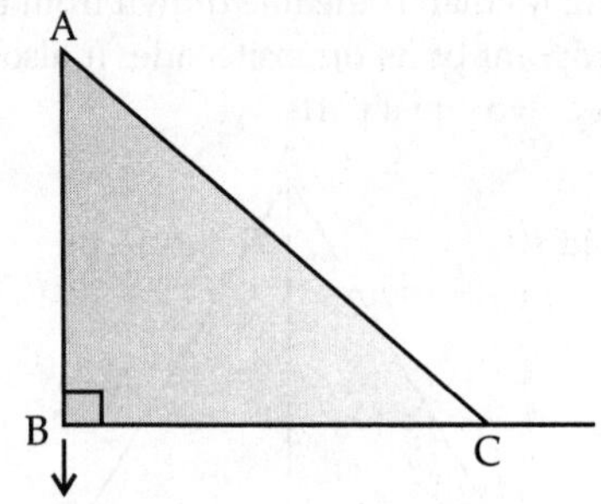

Orthocentre of ΔABC

3. **Circumcentre:** Intersection point of ⊥ bisectors. [⊥ – perpendicular]

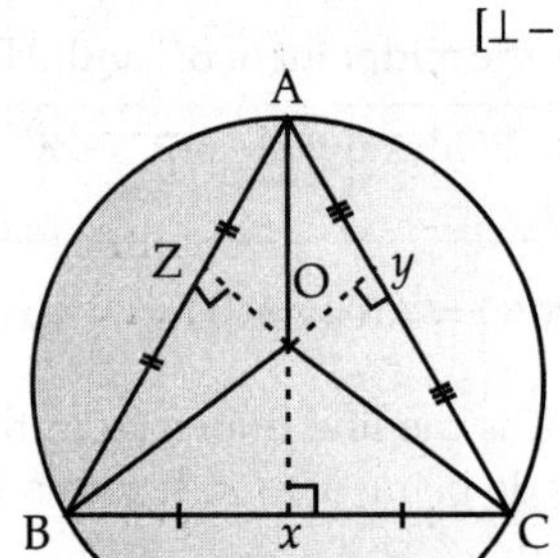

Here 'O' is circumcentre and AO, OB, OC are the radii.

- The perpendicular bisector is a line segment perpendicular to a segment that passes through the midpoint of the segment.
- AO = BO = CO = Radius [Always]
- It may or may not lie inside a triangle.
- It always lies outside the obtuse angled triangle.
- If we draw a circle joining all three vertices of the triangle, it will be called circumcircle.

Circumcentre will be the centre of that circumcircle.

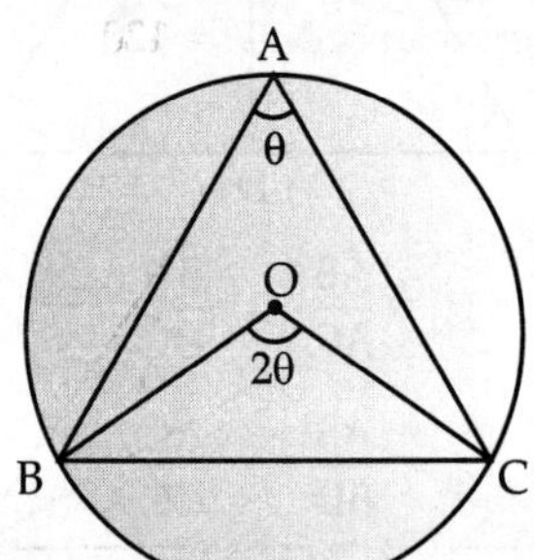

The angle between line segments joining the circumcentre and two vertices is double the angle of the third.

Hence, $\angle BOC = 2\angle A$

$\angle COA = 2\angle B$

$\angle AOB = 2\angle C$

- **Circumradius (R):** $\frac{abc}{4\Delta}$ area of a triangle
- Circumradius of right angled triangle

$R = \frac{H}{2}$ [H–Hypotenuse] or $R = \frac{C}{2}$ [biggest side]

- **Equilateral triangle's circumradius:**

$$R = \frac{a}{\sqrt{3}} = 2(r)\ [r \rightarrow \text{Inradius}]$$

- Ratio of inradius and circumradius of an equilateral triangle:

$r : R = 1 : 2$

4. **Centroid (G):** It is the intersection point of medians drawn from three vertices.

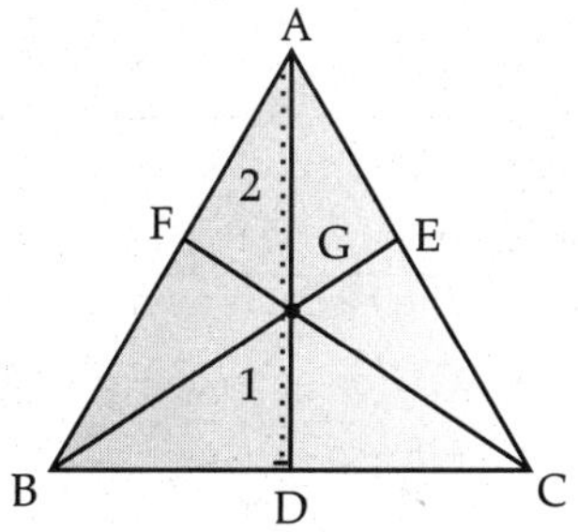

In triangle ΔABC, AD, CF and BE are medians.

- Each median is divided in 2 : 1 by centroid (G)

i.e., $\frac{AG}{GD} = \frac{CG}{GF} = \frac{BG}{GE} = \frac{2}{1}$

- It always lies inside the triangle.
- Medians divide the triangle into six small triangles of equal area.

Let area of ΔXYZ be 'A'

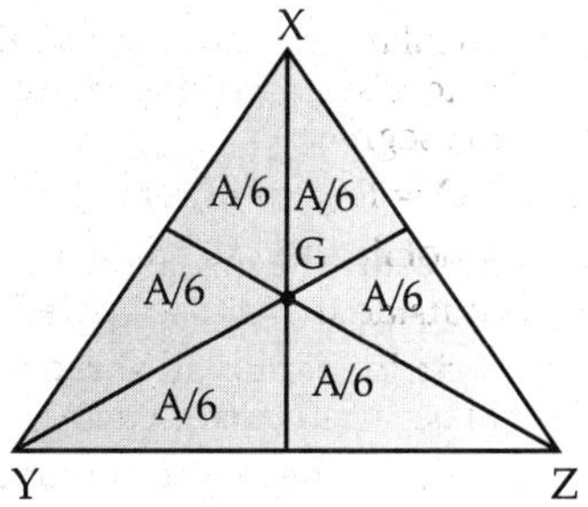

Example: Let area of ΔXYZ = 120

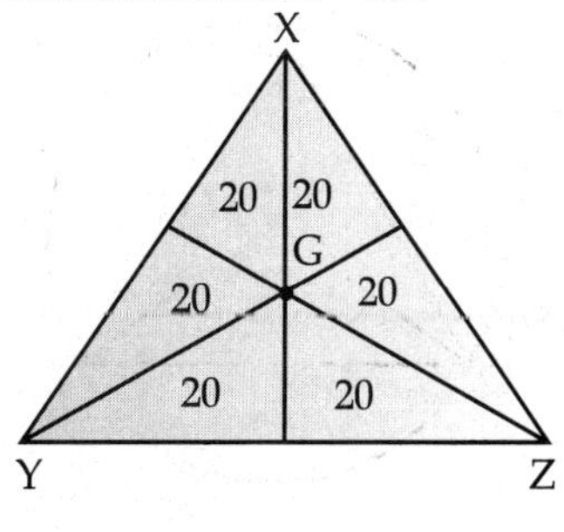

AREA AND PERIMETER

1. **Scalene triangle:**

Perimeter: Sum of all three sides = $a + b + c$

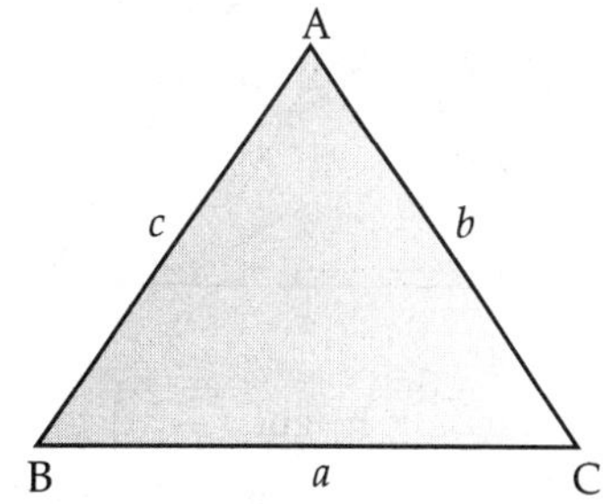

Semiperimeter (s) = $\frac{a+b+c}{2}$

Area = $\sqrt{s(s-a)(s-b)(s-c)} \rightarrow$ Heron's formula

s - semiperimeter
a - length of side BC
b - length of side AC
c - length of side AB

Note: If height is given,

Area of a $\Delta = \frac{1}{2} \times$ base $\times$ height

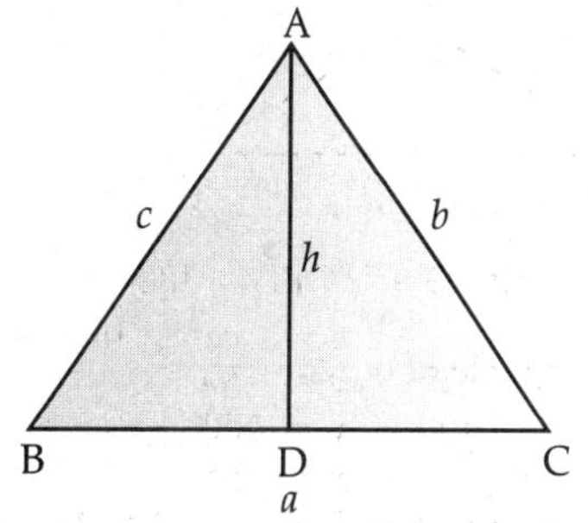

$$= \frac{1}{2} \times a \times h = \frac{1}{2} b \times h = \frac{1}{2} \times c \times h$$

- Heron's formula is applicable for all kinds of triangles.

2. **Isosceles Triangle:** Heron's formula is applicable here also but from the exam P.O.V., use the given formula:

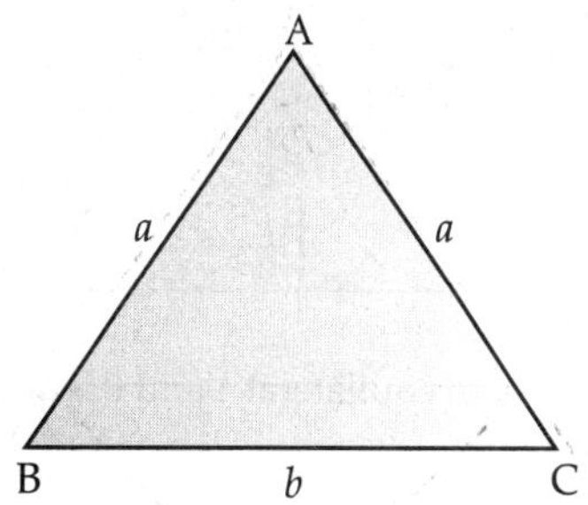

$$A = \frac{1}{4} \times b \times \sqrt{4a^2 - b^2}$$

Here, b = different side

a = similar sides

3. **Equilateral triangle**

- Perimeter = $a + b + c = 3 \times a$

ABC is an equilateral Δ.

where $a = b = c$

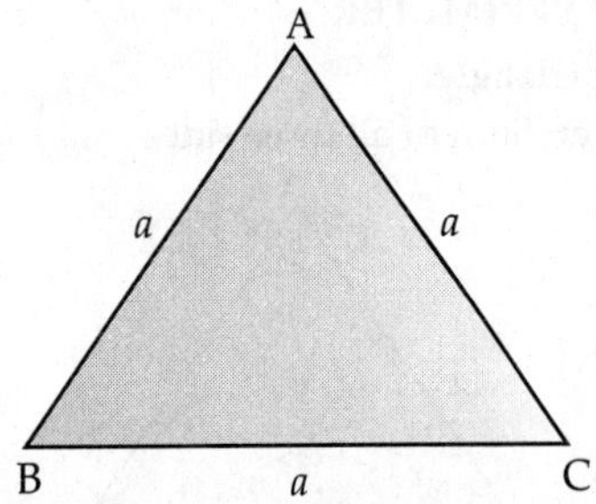

- Area = $\frac{1}{2}$ × base × height

$= \frac{1}{2} \times a \times \frac{\sqrt{3}}{2} a$ $\quad \because$ Height $= \frac{\sqrt{3}}{2} a$

$= \frac{\sqrt{3}}{4} a^2$

- Centroid, incentre and circumcentre all coincide is an equilateral triangle.
- Median, angle bisector and altitude are the same in an equilateral triangle.
- Inradius of eq. $\Delta = r = \frac{a}{2\sqrt{3}}$
- Circumradius of eq. $\Delta = R = \frac{a}{\sqrt{3}} = 2r$
- Area of circumcircle $= \frac{\pi a^2}{3}$
- Area of incircle of eq. $\Delta = \frac{\pi a^2}{12}$
- $R : r = 2 : 1$

SOME IMPORTANT RESULTS RELATED TO AN EQUILATERAL Δ.

(i)

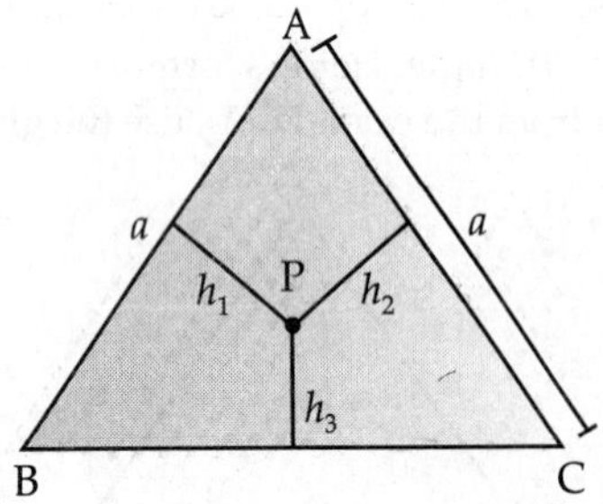

Here, ABC is an equilateral Δ and P is any point inside it. In this case,

Height of eq. Δ $\quad H = h_1 + h_2 + h_3$

Side - $\quad a = \frac{2}{\sqrt{3}}(h_1 + h_2 + h_3)$

$a = \frac{2}{\sqrt{3}}(H)$

Also, $\quad$ area $= \frac{\sqrt{3}}{3}(h_1 + h_2 + h_3)^2$

(ii)

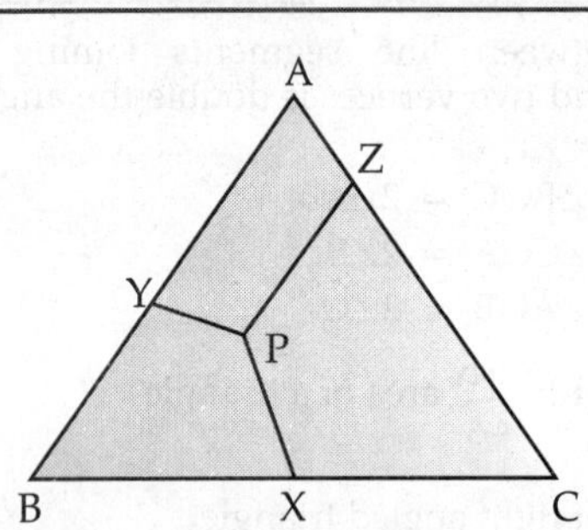

If P is any point inside the Δ such that PY||BC, PZ || AB and PX||AC, then PY + PZ + PX = AB = BC = AC

4. **Right angled triangle**

- One angle is 90°
- $(Hyp)^2 = (Base)^2 + (Perpendicular)^2$

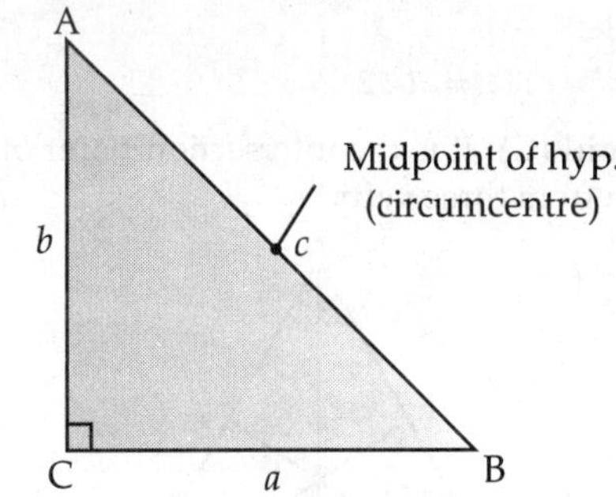

$AB^2 = BC^2 + AC^2$ or $c^2 = a^2 + b^2$

- Perimeter $= a + b + c$
- Area $= \frac{1}{2} \times a \times b$
- Inradius $= \frac{\Delta}{s} = \frac{ab}{a+b+c}$

where s is the semiperimeter

- Also, $r = \frac{a+b-c}{2}, R = \frac{c}{2}$

and $2(r + R) = a + b$

- Shortest median in right angled triangle is 'R'.
- Orthocentre lies on the right angle of the triangle.
- Circumcentre lies on the hypotenuse of right angled triangle.
- Centroid and incentre lie inside the triangle.

IMPORTANT RESULTS OF A RIGHT ANGLED TRIANGLE

1.

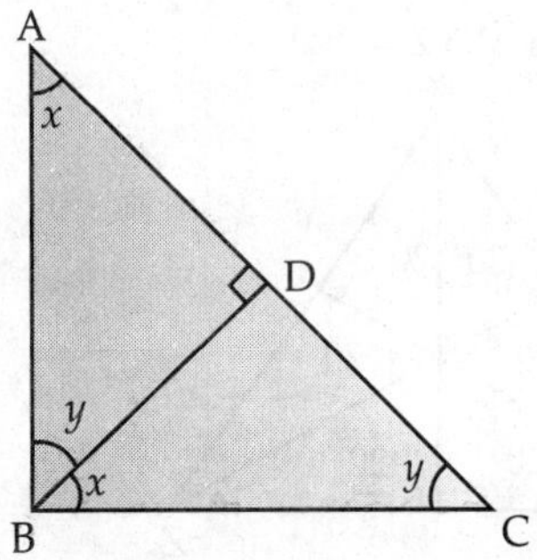

ΔABC is a right angled triangle with ∠B = 90°

Case 1 : ΔADB ~ ΔBDC

$$\frac{BD}{AD} = \frac{DC}{BD}$$

So, $BD^2 = AD \times DC$ ...(1)

Case 2: ΔABC ~ ΔADB

$$\frac{AB}{AC} = \frac{AD}{AB}$$

$$AB^2 = AD \times AC \quad ...(2)$$

Case 3: ΔABC ~ ΔBDC

$$\frac{BC}{AC} = \frac{DC}{BC}$$

$$BC^2 = DC \times AC \quad ...(3)$$

Now from Eq. (2) and (3)

$$\frac{AB^2}{BC^2} = \frac{AD}{CD}$$

IMPORTANT THEOREMS

➢ **Basic proportionality theorem.**

If DE||BC, then the other two sides are divided proportionally.

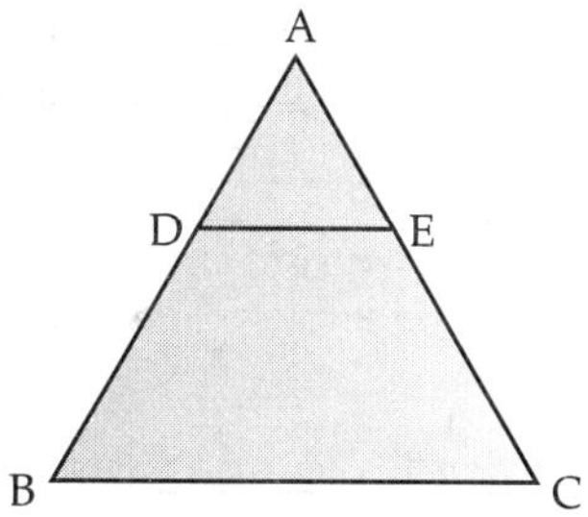

$$\frac{AD}{DB} = \frac{AE}{EC} \text{ or } \frac{AD}{AB} = \frac{AE}{AC}$$

$$\frac{AD}{DE} = \frac{AB}{BC} = \frac{AE}{DE} = \frac{AC}{BC}$$

➢ **Mid point theorem:** If mid points of two adjacent lines/sides are joined by a line segment, then this segment is || to the third side.

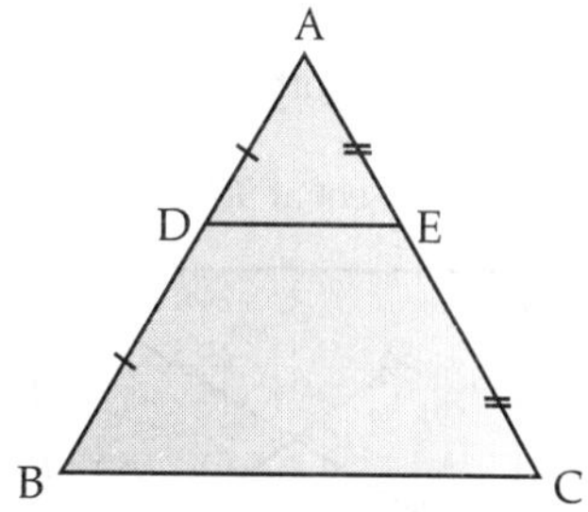

i.e., if AD = BD and AE = CE

then, DE || BC

3. **Apollonius theorem**

If AD = median, then

$$AB^2 + AC^2 = 2\,(AD^2 + BD^2)$$

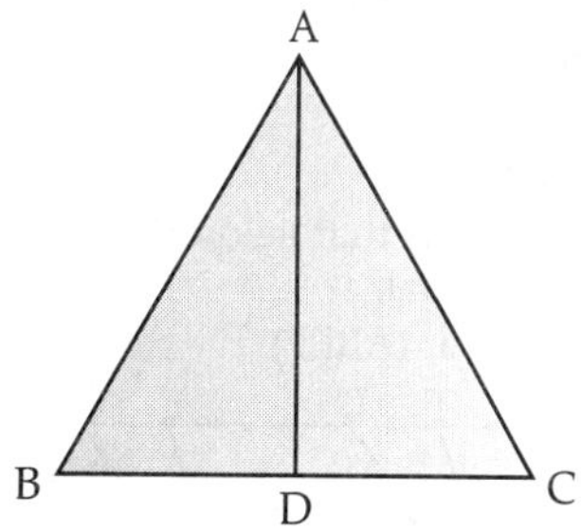

QUADRILATERALS

➢ A quadrilateral is a four-sided closed figure. It is denoted as '⏢' ABCD.

IMPORTANT FACTS

➲ $\angle A + \angle B + \angle C + \angle D = 360°$

Sum of all four angles is 360°

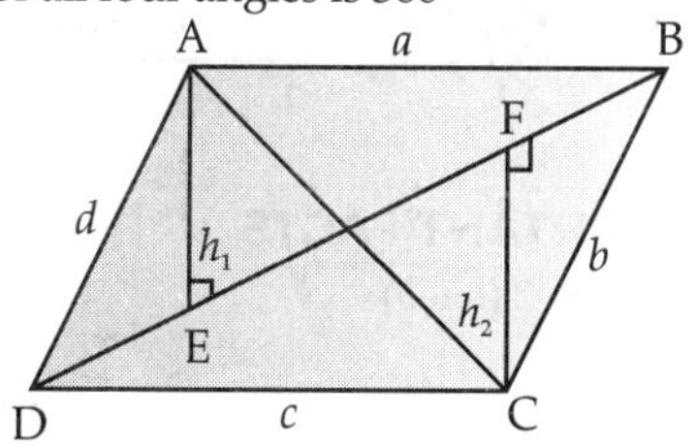

➲ Area of a quadrilateral ABCD = $\frac{1}{2}(BD)(h_1 + h_2)$

Here, h_1 and h_2 are heights BD – diagonal

or Area = $\frac{1}{2} \times d_1 \times d_2 \times \sin\theta$

Here, d_1 = diagonal

d_2 = diagonal

➲ If the diagonals intersect at 90°, then

$$a^2 + c^2 = b^2 + d^2$$

NOTE:

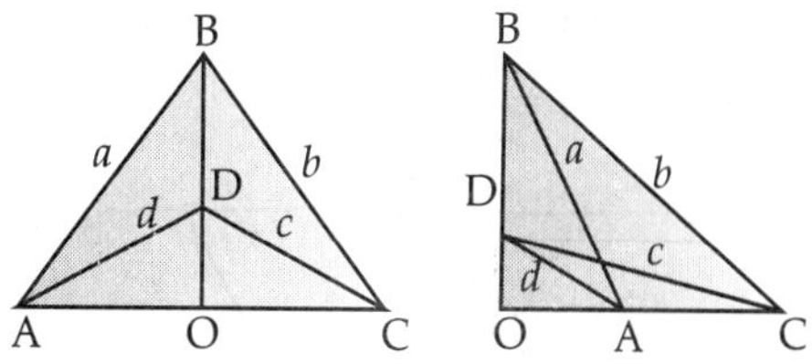

Here also,

$$a^2 + c^2 = b^2 + d^2$$

Quadrilaterals

1. Parallelogram 2. Square 3. Rectangle 4. Rhombus 5. Trapezium

1. **Parallelogram (|| gm)**

➢ It is a type of quadrilateral which has equal opposite sides and equal opposite angles.

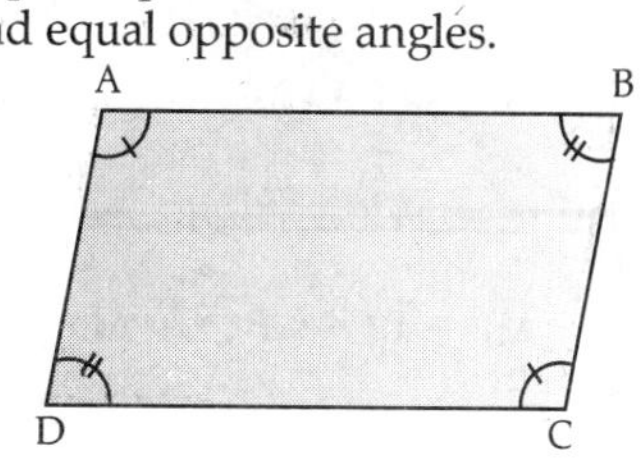

IMPORTANT FACTS

1. Opposite sides are equal
   So, AB = DC and AD = BC
2. Opposite angles are equal
   So, $\angle A = \angle C$
   $\angle B = \angle D$
3. Sum of two adjacent angle is 180°
   $\angle A + \angle B = 180°$, $\angle A + \angle D = 180$, $\angle D + \angle C = 180$,
   $\angle B + \angle C = 180°$.
4. Diagonals bisect each other. But diagonals need not be equal.
5. Diagonals do not bisect at 90°.

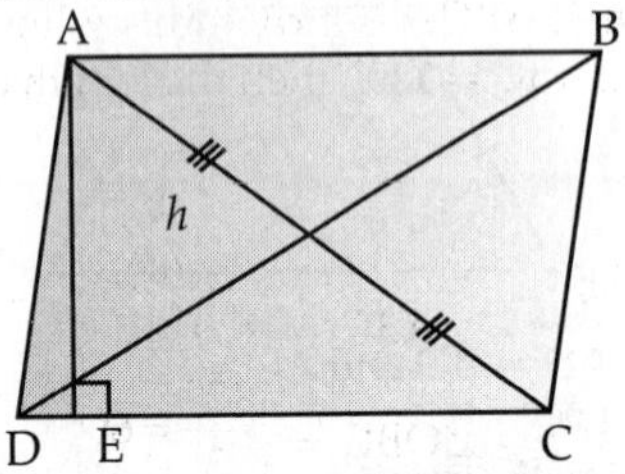

6. Area of || gm = base × height = CD × h
   or = $l \times b \times \sin\theta$ where l = length, b = breadth
7. Each diagonal of a ||gm divides it into two congruent triangles.
   So, $\Delta ABD \cong \Delta BCD$
   $\Delta ABC \cong \Delta ADC$
8. Area of the ||gms that lie on the same base and b/w are || lines is equal.
   So, ar ABCD = ar (ABEF)

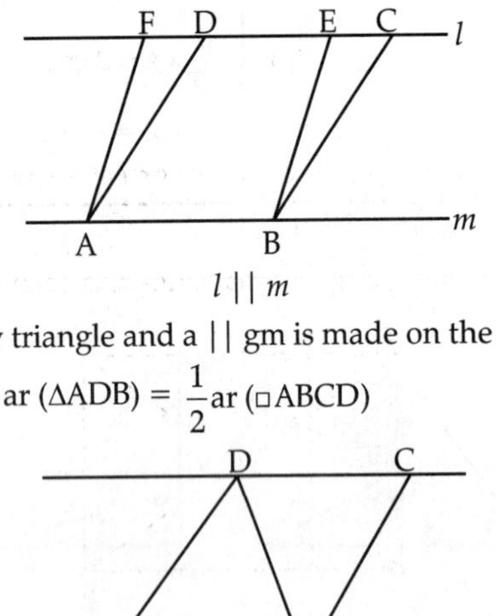

$l \parallel m$

9. If any triangle and a || gm is made on the same base then, ar (ΔADB) = $\frac{1}{2}$ar (□ABCD)

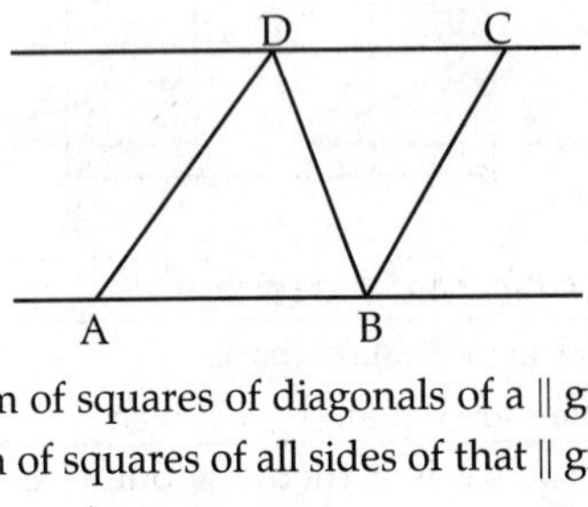

10. The sum of squares of diagonals of a || gm is equal to the sum of squares of all sides of that || gm.

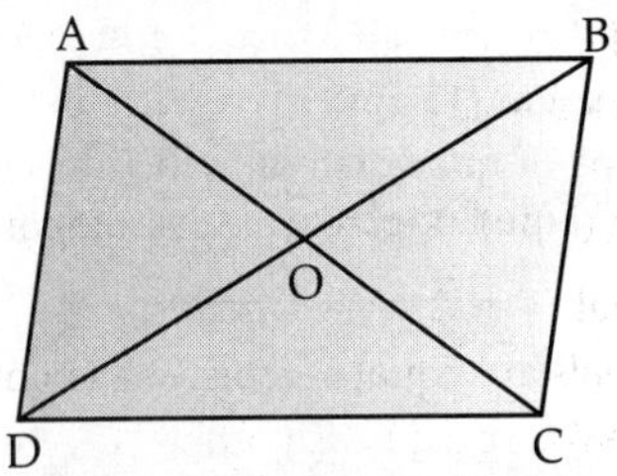

$AC^2 + BD^2 = AB^2 + BC^2 + BC^2 + AD^2$
$= 2(AB^2 + BC^2)$

Example 1: ABCD is a || gm in which diagonals intersect at 'O'. Find the area of ΔDOC, if area of || gm ABCD is 104 cm^2.

(a) 52 (b) 26
(c) 32 (d) 46

Sol. (b) We know

$$Ar(\Delta DOC) = \frac{1}{4} ar \ (\| \text{ gm ABCD})$$
$$= \frac{1}{4} \times 104 = 26$$

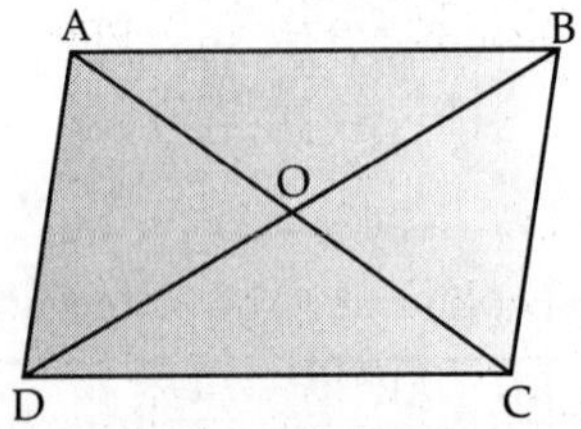

Example 2: ABCD is a || gm in which CD = 10 cm and AE = 5 cm. Find the area of || gm ABCD.

(a) 25 (b) 70
(c) 50 (d) 40

Sol. (c) Area of || gm = base × height
= 10 × 5 = 50 cm^2

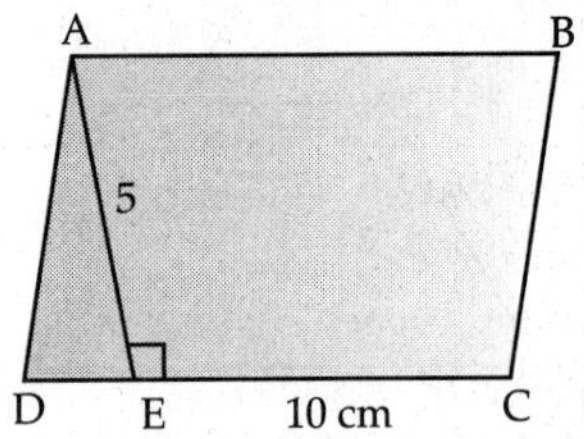

2. Rectangle

➤ A rectangle is a || gm with each angle of 90°.

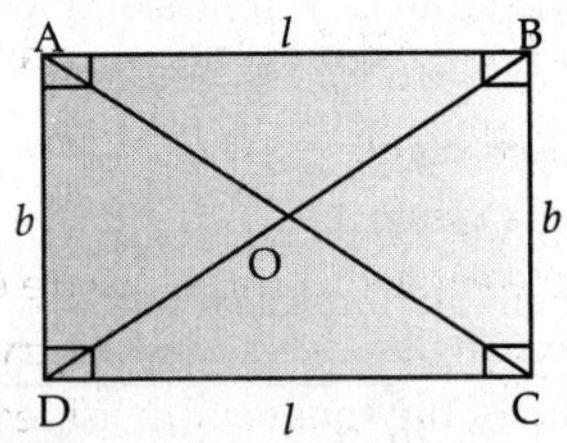

SOME IMPORTANT FACTS

- Perimeter = 2 (l + b)
- Area = $l \times b$
- Both diagonals are equal
  Diagonals, AC = BD = $\sqrt{l^2 + b^2}$
- Diagonals bisect each other but not at 90°

Example 3: In rectangle ABCD, PA = 6 cm, PB = 4 cm and PC = 3 cm. P is a point on the rectangle. Find PD (in cm)

(a) $\sqrt{31}$ (b) $\sqrt{45}$
(c) $\sqrt{29}$ (d) $\sqrt{51}$

Sol. (c) We know, (diagonals are equal)

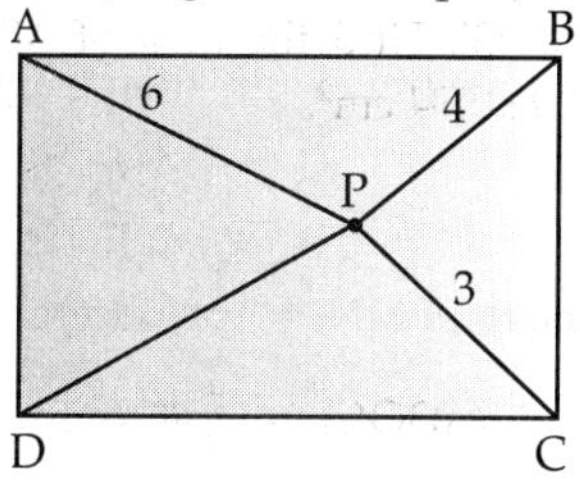

$$PA^2 + PC^2 = PB^2 + PD^2$$
$$6^2 + 3^2 = 4^2 + PD^2$$
$$36 + 9 = 16 + PD^2$$
$$45 - 16 = PD^2$$
$$29 = PD^2$$
$$\sqrt{29} = PD$$

Hence, option (c) is the correct answer.

3. Rhombus

➤ It is a || gm having all 4 sides equal.

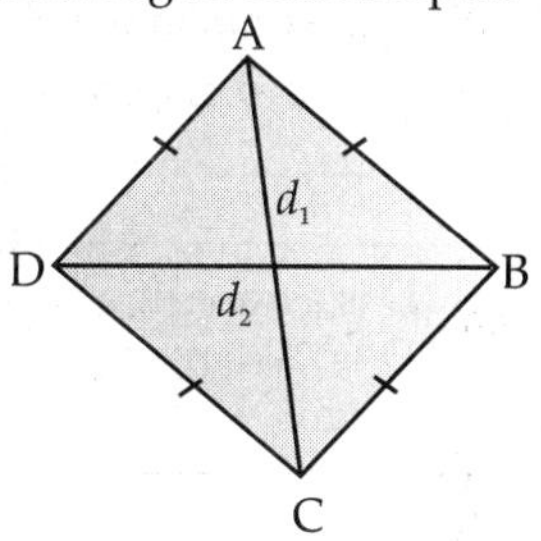

SOME IMPORTANT FACTS

- All sides are equal.
- Diagonals bisect each other at 90°.
- Diagonals are not equal.
- Diagonals are ⊥ to each other.
- Rhombus = Square (If diagonals are equal)
- Area of a Rhombus
  (a) $\frac{1}{2} \times d_1 \times d_2$ (If diagonals are given)
  (b) $(\text{Side})^2 \times \sin\theta$
  (c) base × height
- Opposite angle of a rhombus are equal.
- Adjacent angles are supplementry, i.e., 180°.
- The sum of the square of the sides of a Rhombus is equal to the sum of the squares of its diagonals.
  $d_1^2 + d_2^2 = 4a^2$ where, a = side

Example 4: If the perimeter of a rhombus is 150 cm and length of one diagonal is 50 cm. Then, find the area of the rhombus.

(a) 625 (b) $625\sqrt{5}$
(c) 400 (d) $320\sqrt{5}$

Sol. (b) Side (a) $= \frac{\text{Perimeter}}{4} = \frac{150}{4}$

$$2a \Rightarrow \frac{150}{\cancel{4}_2} \times \cancel{2}$$

$$2a = 75$$

So $$4a^2 = d_1^2 + d_2^2 \Rightarrow (2a)^2$$
$$= d_1^2 + (d_2)^2$$

$\Rightarrow$ $$(75)^2 = (50)^2 + d_2^2$$
$$d_2^2 = (75)^2 - (50)^2$$
$$= (75 + 50)(75 - 50)$$
$$= 125 \times 25 = 25 \times 5 \times 25$$
$$d_2 = 25\sqrt{5}$$

So, Area $= \frac{1}{2} d_1 d_2 = \frac{1}{\cancel{2}} \times \cancel{50}^{25} \times 25\sqrt{5} = 625\sqrt{5}$

Hence, option (b) is the correct answer.

Example 5: ABCD is a rhombus whose side AB = 4 cm and ∠ABC = 120°, then the length of diagonal BD is ?

(a) 1 (b) 2
(c) 3 (d) 4

Sol. (d) $$\angle ABC = 120°$$
$$\angle OBC = \frac{120}{2} = 60°$$

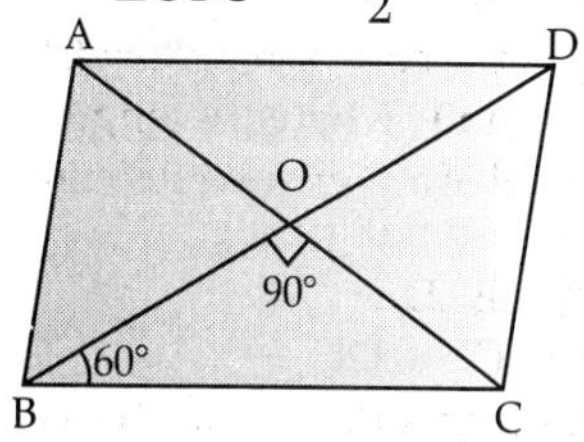

In ΔBOC, $$\cos 60° = \frac{BO}{4}$$
$$BO = \frac{1}{2} \times 4 = 2 \text{ cm}$$
$$BD = 2 \times 2 = 4 \text{ cm}$$

Hence, option (d) is the correct answer.

4. Square

➤ It is a rectangle with equal sides and each angle 90°.

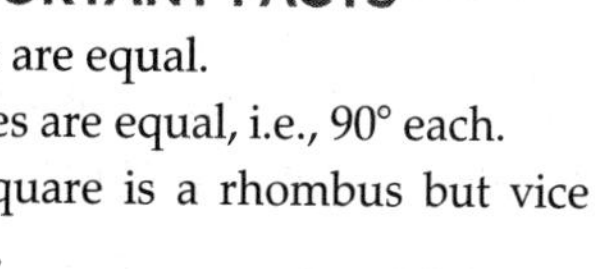

SOME IMPORTANT FACTS

- All sides are equal.
- All angles are equal, i.e., 90° each.
- Every square is a rhombus but vice versa is not possible.
- Perimeter = $4a$
- Area = $(\text{Side})^2 = a^2 = \frac{d^2}{2}$ [d = diagonal]
  diagonal = $a\sqrt{2}$
- Diagonals are equal and bisect each other.
- Diagonals are ⊥ to each other.
- After joining the mid points of adjacent sides, the figure obtained is a square.

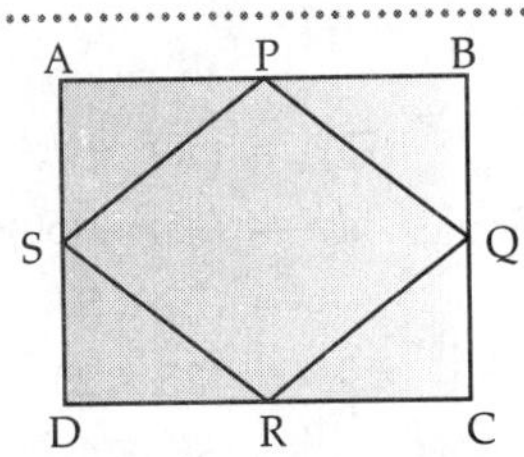

ABCD is a square and also, PQRS is a square.

5. Trapezium

➤ It is a quadrilateral with two parallels sides and two non-parallel sides.

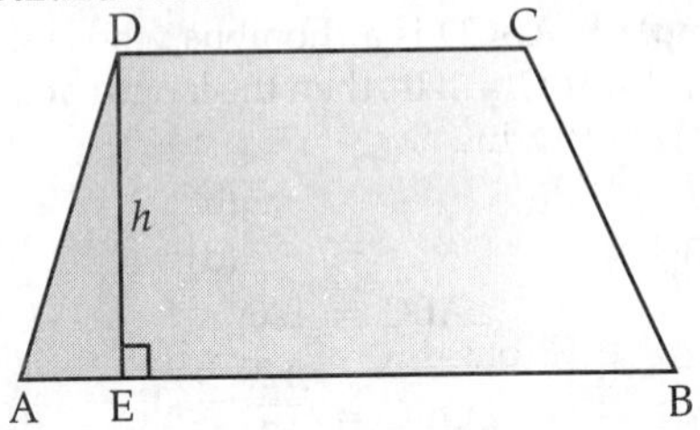

AD and CB are non-parallel sides. h is the height.

SOME IMPORTANT FACTS

- Area $= \frac{1}{2} \times$ (sum of parallel sides) $\times$ height

  $= \frac{1}{2} \times (AB+CD) \times DE = \frac{1}{2}(AB+CD) \times h$
- $\angle A + \angle D = \angle B + \angle C = 180°$
- If E and F are mid points, then EF (Median)

  $= \frac{1}{2}(AB+CD)$ Also, $\frac{AE}{ED} = \frac{BF}{FC}$

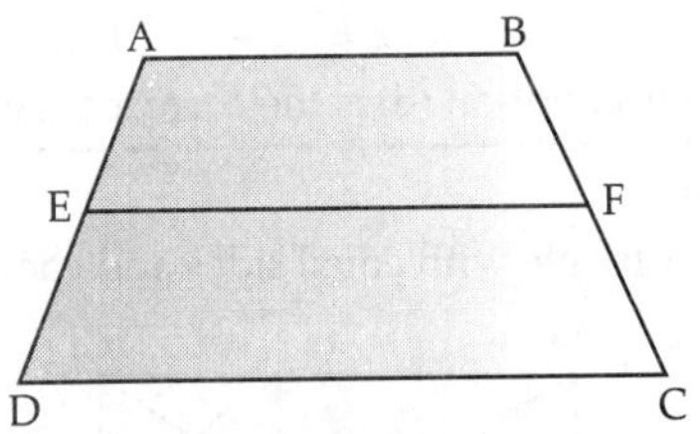

- After joining the mid points of adjacent sides of a trapezium, four similar triangles are obtained.
- $\frac{AO}{OC} = \frac{BO}{OD} = \frac{AB}{DC}$

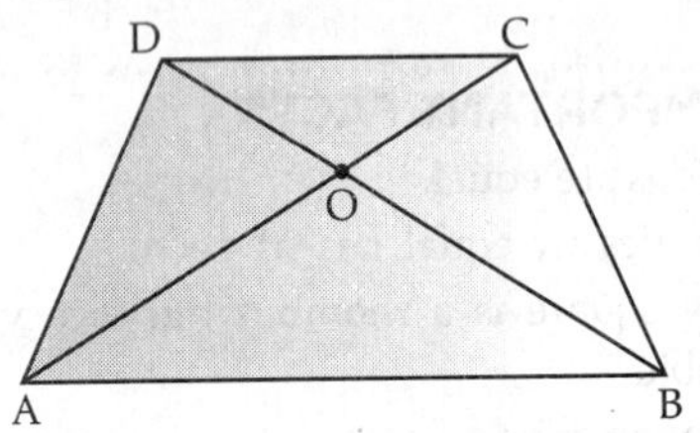

- $AC^2 + BD^2 = BC^2 + AD^2 + 2AB \cdot CD$

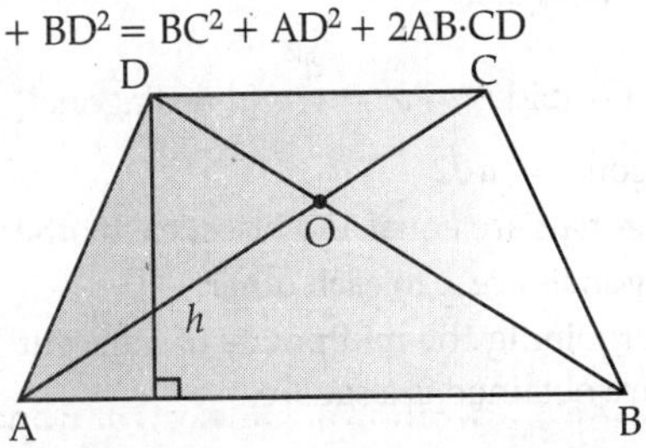

Example 13: If the parallel sides of a trapezium are 8 cm and 4 cm, M and N are mid points of the diagonals of the trapezium, then length of MN is :

(a) 12 (b) 6
(c) 20 (d) 2

Sol. (d) Length of MN $= \frac{1}{2}$ (difference of || sides)

$= \frac{1}{2}(8-4) = 2$ cm

Hence, option (d) is the correct answer.

NOTE:
If 'M' and 'N' are the mid points of diagonals AC and BD, then MN $= \frac{1}{2}$ [AB ~ DC]

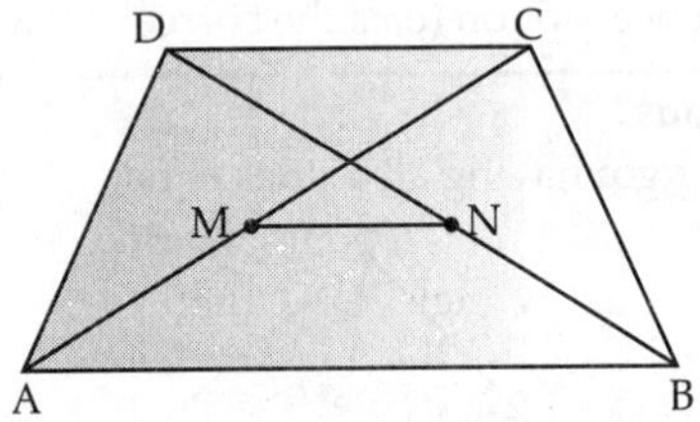

Example 6: ABCD is a trapezium, such that AB = CD and AD||BC. AD = 10 cm and BC = 18 cm. If the area of ABCD is 70 cm², what is the value of CD?

(a) 5 (b) $\sqrt{29}$
(c) $\sqrt{41}$ (d) 6

Sol. (c)

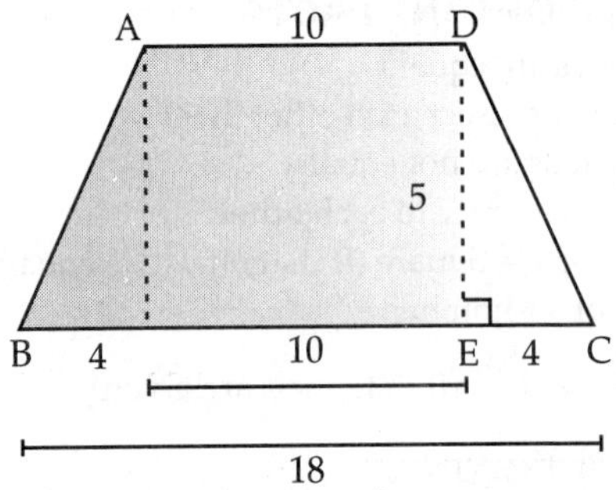

We know, Area $= \frac{1}{2}(AD+BC) \times DE$

$70 = \frac{1}{2} \times (10+18) \times DE$

$= \frac{1}{2} \times (28) \times DE$

$DE = 5$

Also, $CE = \frac{18-10}{2} = 4$

So, by pythagoras theorem

$CD^2 = (DE)^2 + (CE)^2$

$= (5)^2 + (4)^2$

$CD = \sqrt{41}$

Hence, option (c) is the correct answer.

POLYGONS

➤ Polygon is a closed figure bounded by three or more sides.

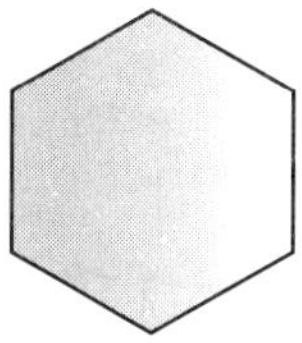

	Sides
➤ Triangle	- 3
Quadrilateral	- 4
Pentagon	- 5
Hexagon	- 6
Heptagon	- 7
Octagon	- 8
Nonagon	- 9
Decagon	- 10

Regular Polygon

➤ A regular polygon is a polygon which has equal sides and the interior angles are equal.

SOME IMPORTANT FACTS

- Sum of interior angles = $(n-2) \times 180°$, n = no. of sides.
- Each exterior angle = $\frac{360°}{n}$
- Sum of all exterior angles = 360°
- Each interior angle = 180° – Exterior angle

  $= \frac{180(n-2)}{n}$

  Also, interior angle + exterior angle = 180
- No. of diagonals = $\frac{n(n-3)}{2}$
- Area of a regular polygon = $\frac{na^2}{4} \times \cot\left(\frac{180}{n}\right)^{\circ}$
- Perimeter = $n \times l$ where l = length of side.

Example 1: Find the sum of all interior angles of a regular polygon whose one exterior angle is 20°.

(a) 3250 (b) 2550

(c) 2880 (d) 1995

Sol. (c) We know, int. angle + ext. angle = 180°

Int. angle = 180° – 20° = 160°

Now,

$$\text{No. of sides} = \frac{360}{20} = 18$$

∴ Sum of all int. angles = 160 × 18 = 2880

Hence, option (c) is the correct answer.

Example 2: If each interior angle of a regular polygon is three times its exterior angle, then the no. of sides of the polygon is:

(a) 6 (b) 5

(c) 8 (d) 9

Sol. (c)

$$I + E = 180 \qquad I = \text{Interior angle}$$
$$3x + x = 180 \qquad E = \text{Exterior angle}$$
$$x = 45°$$
$$\text{No. of sides} = \frac{360}{45} = 8$$

CIRCLE

➤ **Circle:** It is a set of points which are at a constant distance from its centre.

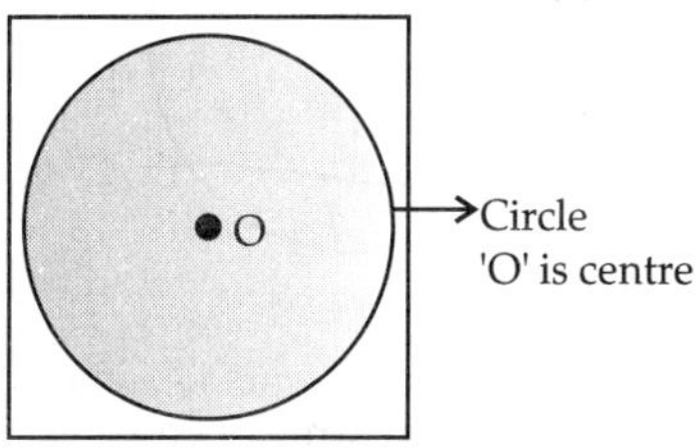

SOME IMPORTANTS TERMS RELATED TO A CIRCLE

➤ **Diameter:** A line segment passes through the centre and has its end points on the circumference of the circle. 'AB' is the diameter, $d = 2r$

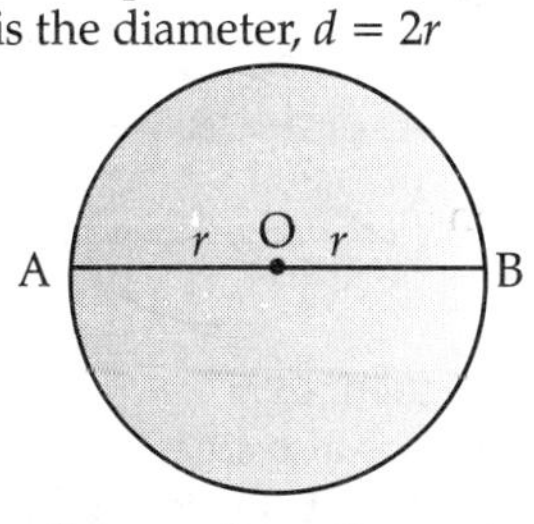

➤ **Radius:** The distance from the centre to the point on the circumference.

$\therefore r = \frac{d}{2}$

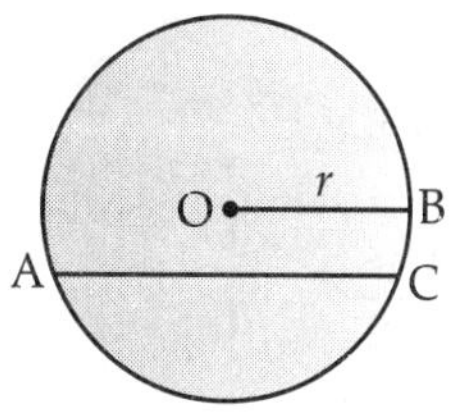

OB = radius

AC = chord

➤ **Chord:** It is a line segment whose end points lie on the circumference.

➤ **Secant:** It is a line segment which intersects a circle at two different pts.

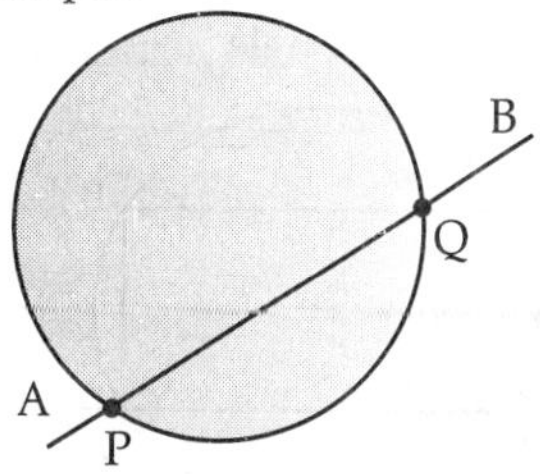

Here, AB is a secant that intersects at P and Q.

- **Tangent:** It is a line that meets the circle only at one point.

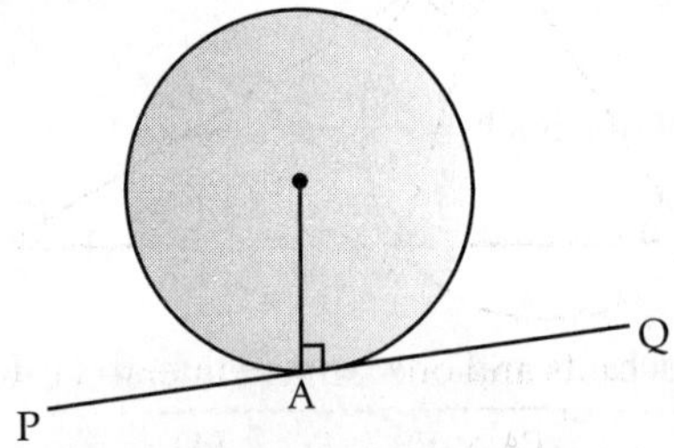

PQ = tangent meeting at point A.

NOTE: Radius is alwas ⊥ to a tangent.

- **Arc:** It is a part of circumference.
- **Sector:** Sector is made by an arc and two radii of a circle. Here, PAQ is the arc and OPAQ is the sector.

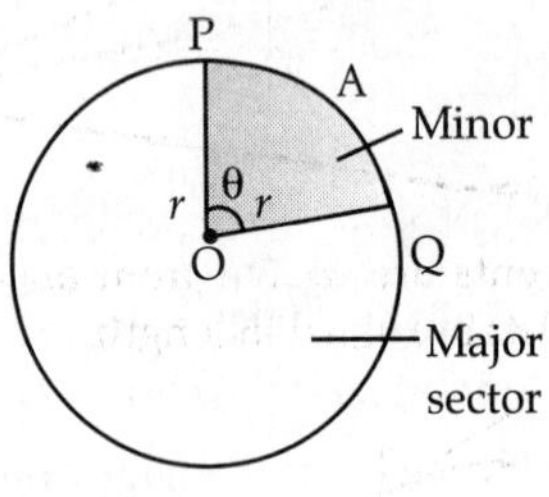

Area of sector $= \dfrac{\pi r^2\theta}{360°}$

- **Concentric circles:** When two circles have same centre, they are said to be concentric circles.

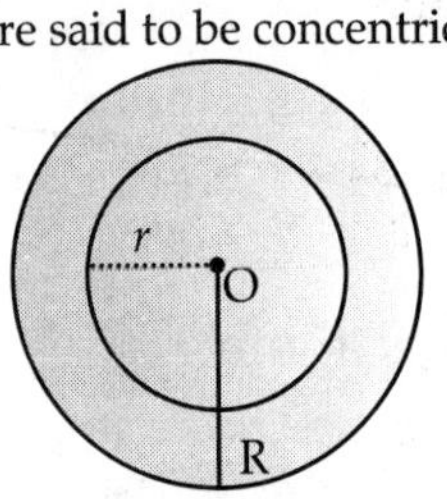

Here, r and R are the radii of two circles with the same centre 'O'.

- **Central angle:** Angle at the centre.

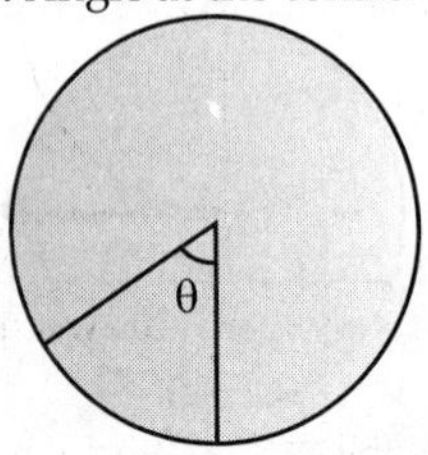

- **Cyclic Quadrilateral:** The quadrilateral which has all four vertices on the circle.

  Sum of opposite angles is supplementary

  $\angle 2 + \angle 1 = 180°$, $\angle 1 + \angle 3 = 180°$

  $\angle 2 = \angle 3$ ∵ In a cyclic quadrilateral, ext. angle = opp. int. angle

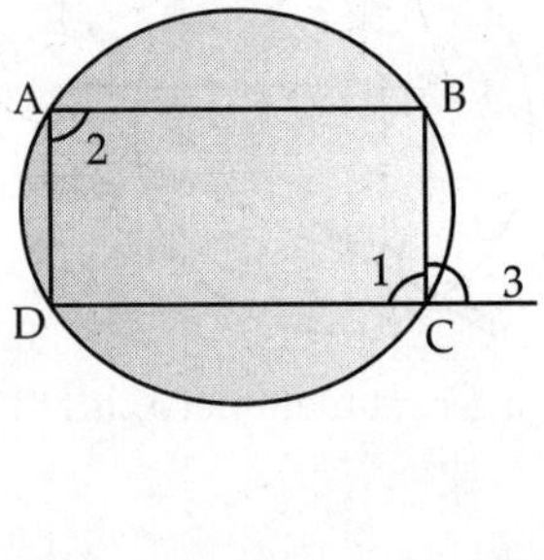

SOME IMPORTANT PROPERTIES OF A CIRCLE

1. Here, OM ⊥ AB

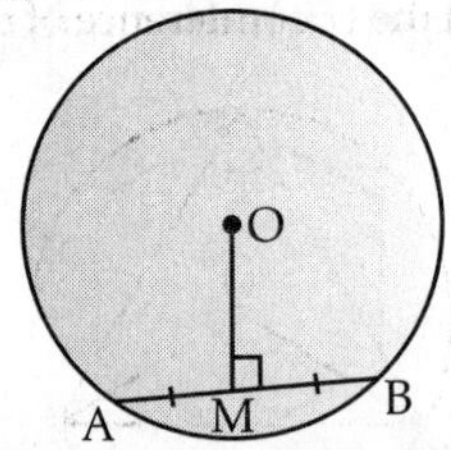

So, AM = MB (⊥ divides AB into two equal parts)

2. The above property can be said like this also

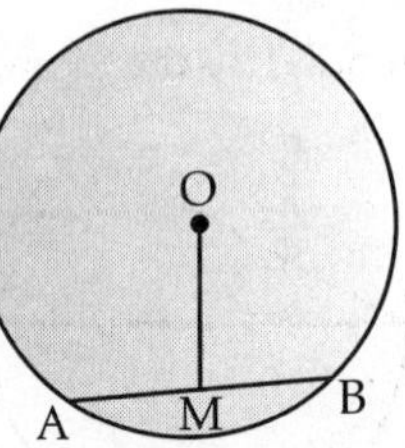

- Line joined from mid point of AD to the centre is ⊥ to AB. i.e., AM = MB, then OM ⊥ AB.

3. A line passing through the centre is a diameter and a chord also. Diameter is the longest chord.

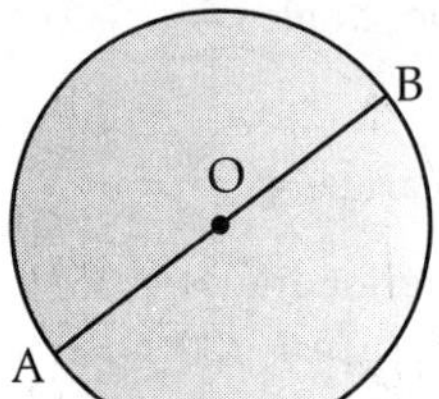

Note: A diameter can be chord but all chords cannot be the diameter.

4. If two chords are equal in length, then their ⊥ distance from the centre is also equal.

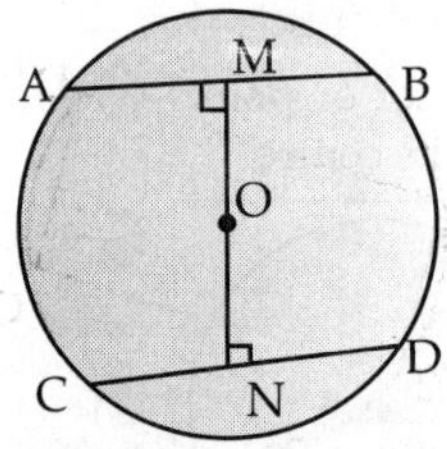

If AB = CD, then OM = ON

NOTE: Vice-versa is also true, i.e., chords which are equidistant from the centre are equal.

5. Angles subtended by equal chords at the centre are equal.

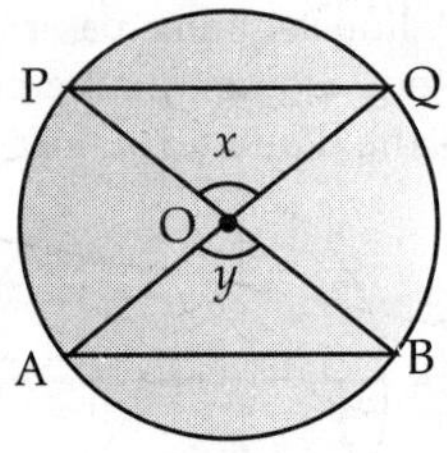

i.e., If AB = PQ, then $\angle x = \angle y$

NOTE: Vice-versa is also true.

If angles subtended at the centre by two chords are equal, then the chords are also equal.

6. The angle subtended by an arc or a chord at the centre is double the angle subtended by the same arc or chord at any point on the circumference of the circle.

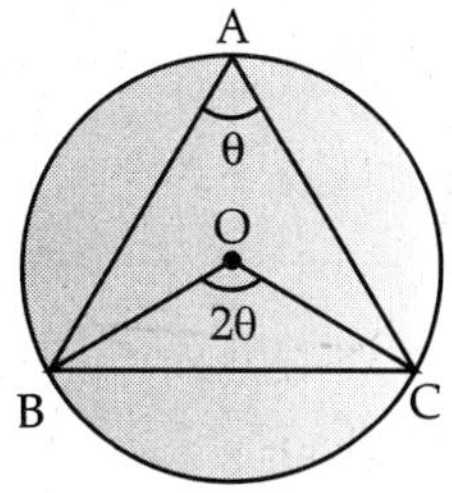

i.e., ∠BOC = 2∠BAC

7. The angle subtended by the diameter is a right angle.

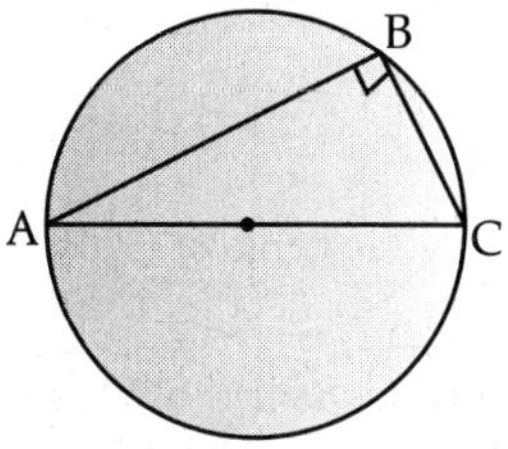

i.e., ∠ABC = 90°

8. Angles formed in the same segment of a circle are equal.

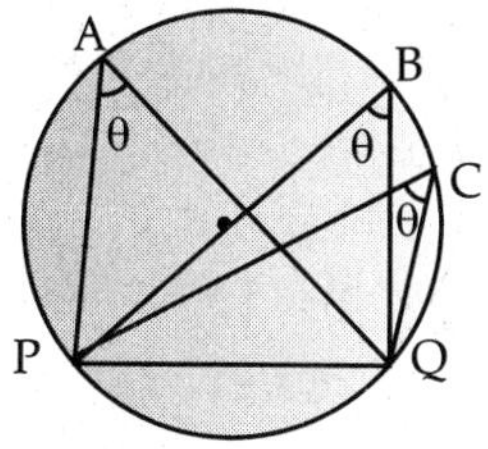

i.e., ∠PAQ = ∠PBQ = ∠PCQ.

9. Opposite angles of a cyclic quadrilateral are suplementary, i.e., 180°.

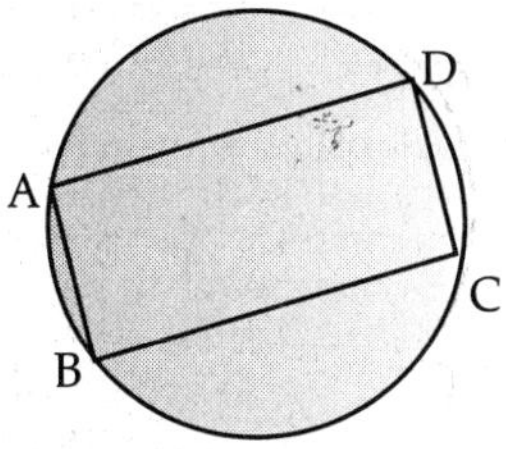

∠A + ∠C = 180°
∠B + ∠D = 180°

10. If two chords of the circle intersect (inside or outside the circle) each other at point A.

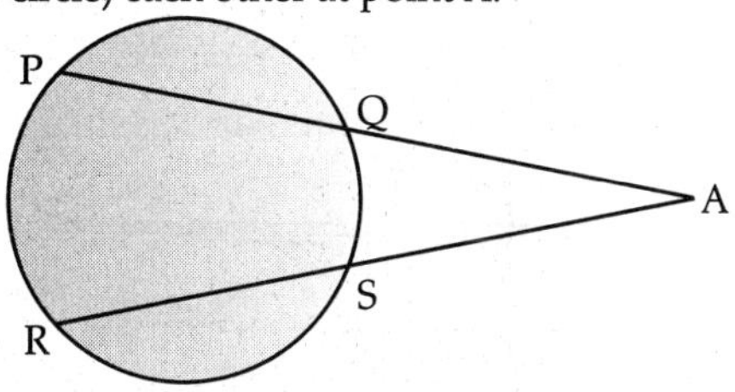

then AQ × AP = AS × AR

11. When a secant and tangent intersect each other externally, then

$PT^2 = PA \times PB$

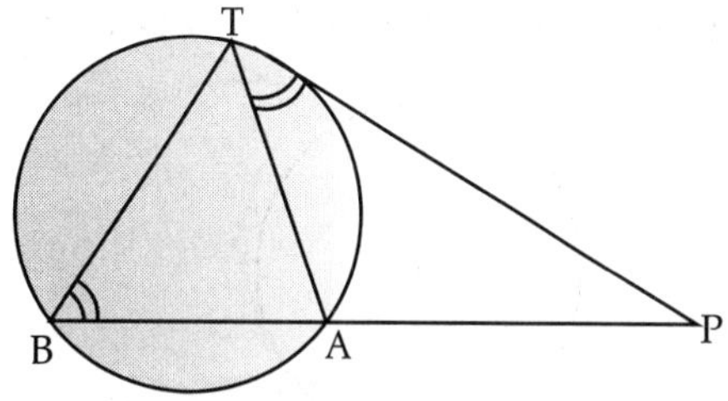

12. If two secants and one tangent intersect externally

$PA \times PB = PC \times PD$

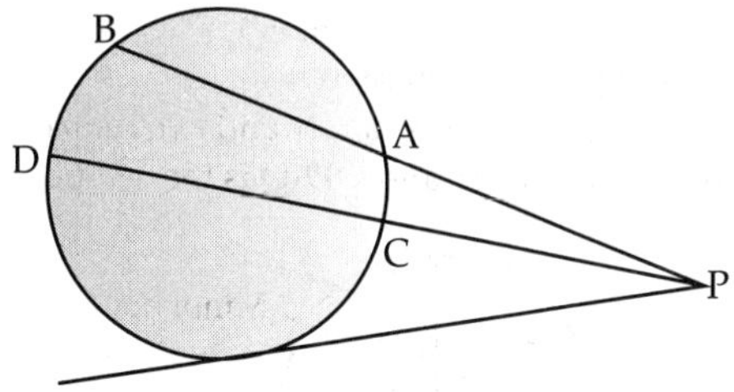

13. If two tangents are drawn from an external point, these tangents are equal in length.

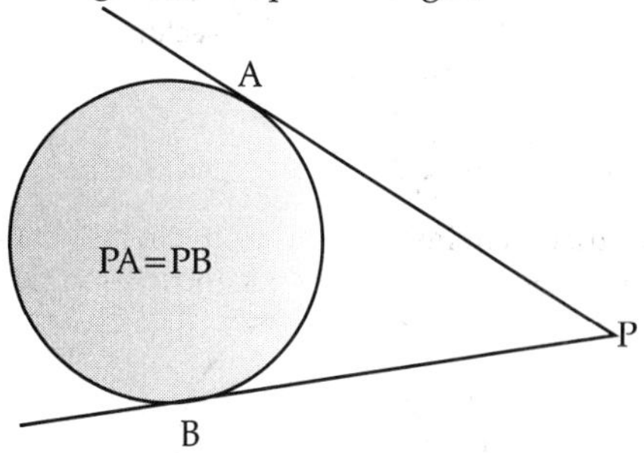

i.e., PA = PB

14. Tangent is ⊥ radius
Here, OM ⊥ PQ

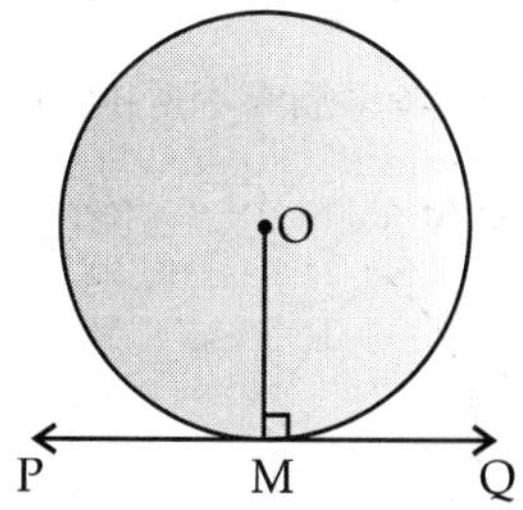

15. When two tangents are drawn from an external point, then
(i) Tangents are equal
(ii) ∠APO = ∠BPO
(iii) ∠POB = ∠POA
(iv) $\frac{PB}{BO} = \frac{BS}{SO}$

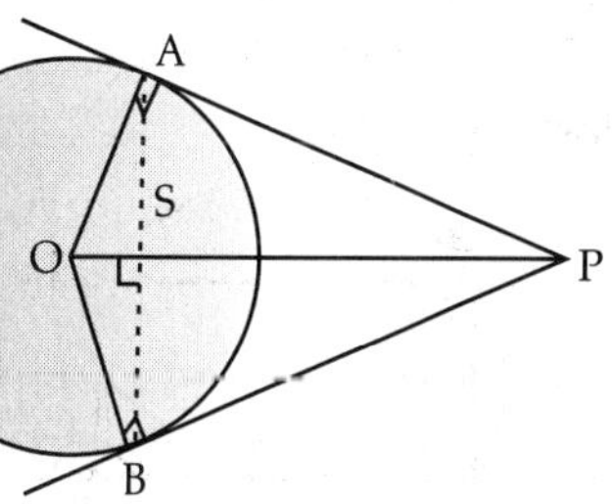

16. Here, PAOB is a quadrilateral.

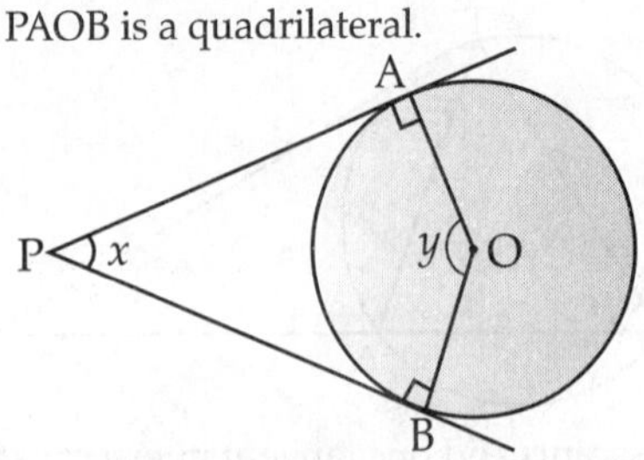

$$x + y = 180°$$

17. If $\angle APB = x$, then

$$\angle AOB = 180 - x$$

$$\angle ACB = 90 - \frac{x}{2}$$

$$\angle ADB = 90 + \frac{x}{2}$$

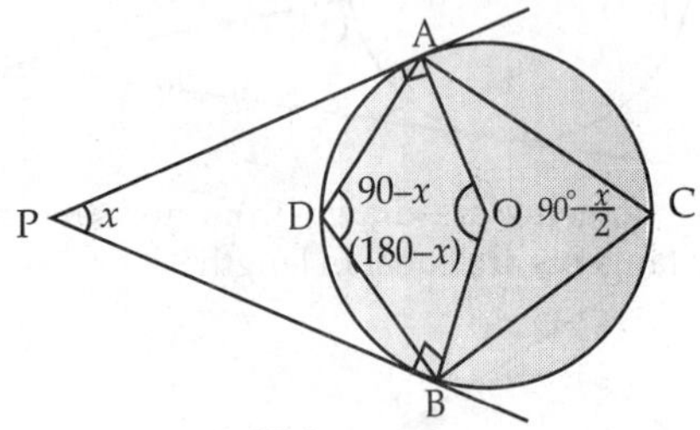

18. If $\angle MPN = x$

then $\angle MCN = 90 - \frac{x}{2}$

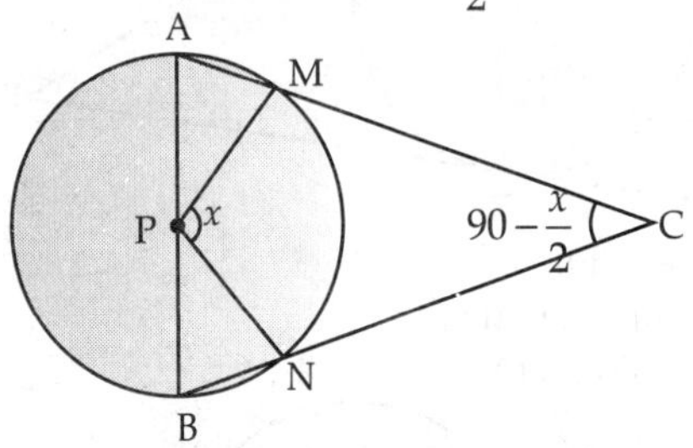

19. A circle touches externally side BC at P. AB and AC are produced at Q and R, respectively.

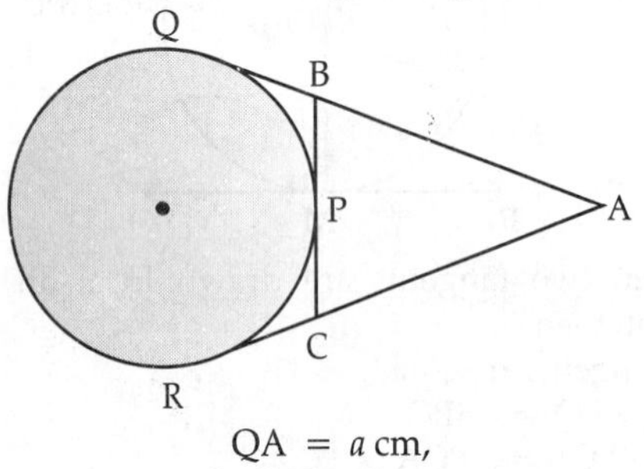

If $QA = a$ cm,

then perimeter of $\Delta ABC = 2a$

20. Sum of opposite sides are equal.

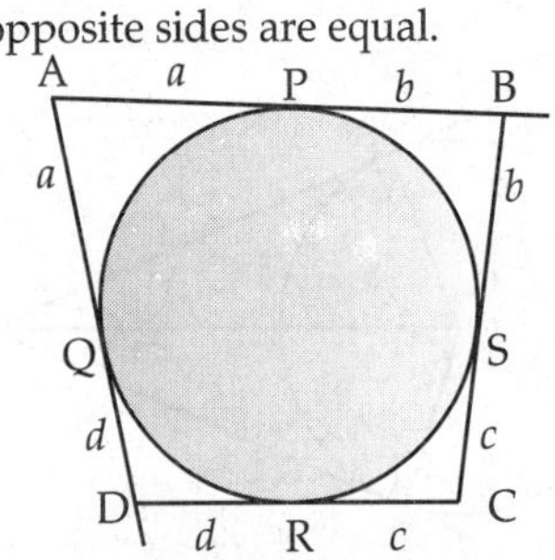

AB + CD = AD + BC

RELATION BETWEEN TWO CIRCLES

- If two circles have equal radii, then they are congruent.
- If circles intersect each other

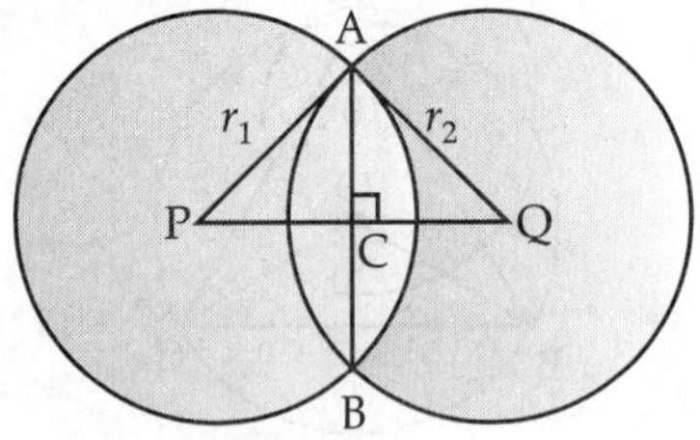

Here, AB is common chord

PQ is distance between centres

$$PQ = PC + CQ$$

$$PQ = \sqrt{r_1^2 - \left(\frac{AB}{2}\right)^2} + \sqrt{r_2^2 - \left(\frac{AB}{2}\right)^2}$$

- If AQ and PA are tangents of C_1 and C_2, respectively

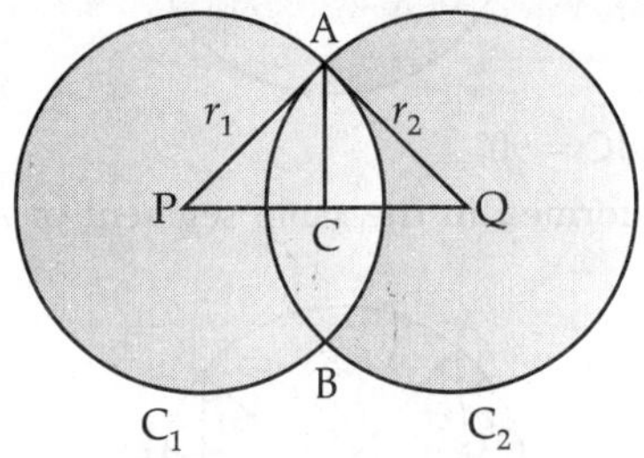

then ΔPAQ is a right angled Δ.

$$\therefore \quad PA \times AQ = PQ \times AC$$

$$AC = \frac{PA \times AQ}{PQ}$$

As we know length of the common chord = 2AC

$$AB = 2AC$$

So
$$AB = \frac{2PA \times AQ}{PQ}$$

COMMON TANGENTS

- Circles touch each other internally.

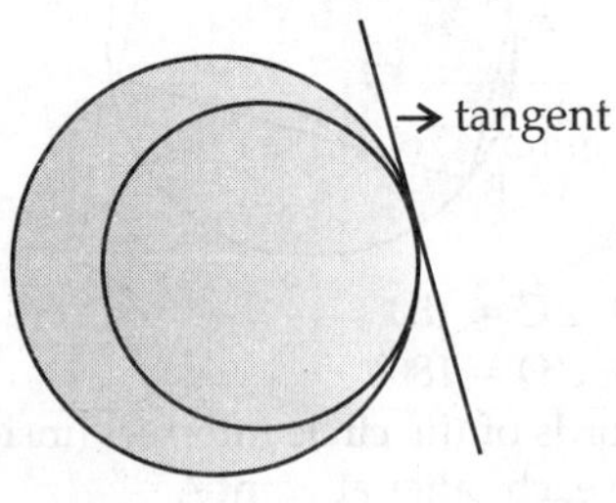

only one tangent is possible

- Circles touch each other externally.

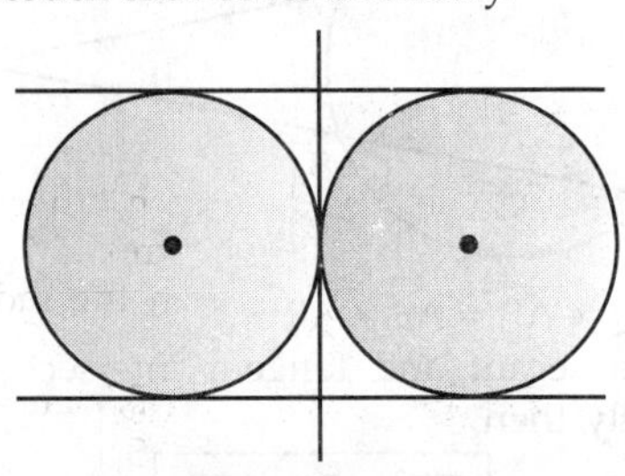

3 tangents are possible

➤ Circles neither touch nor intersect:

Case 1:

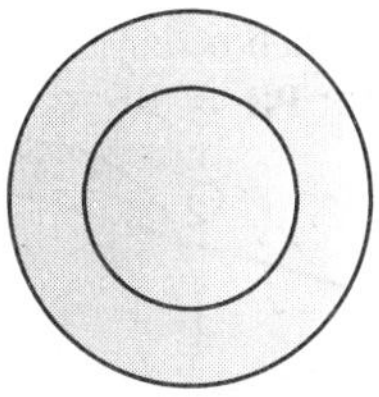

No tangent is possible

Case 2:

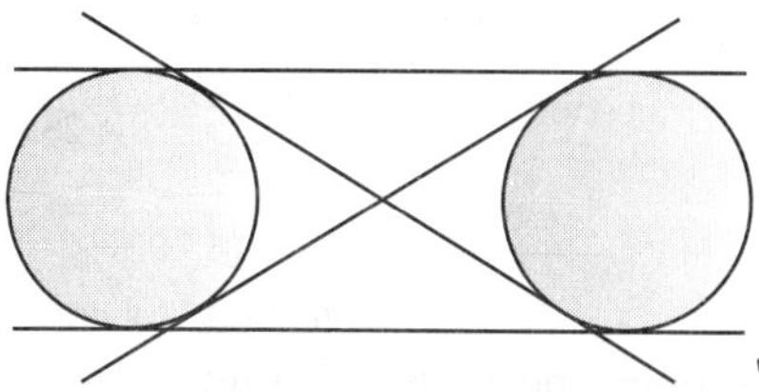

Four tangents are possible

➤ Circles are intersecting each other.

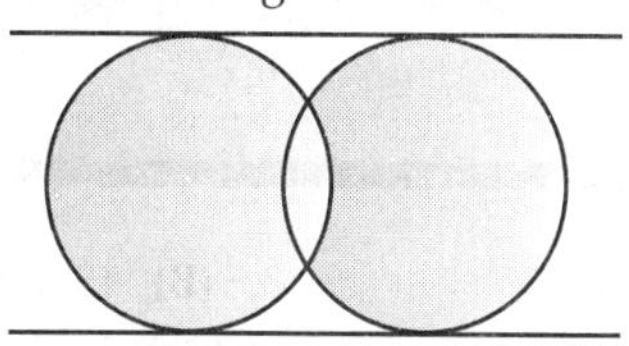

Two tangents are possible

Direct Common Tangent (DCT)

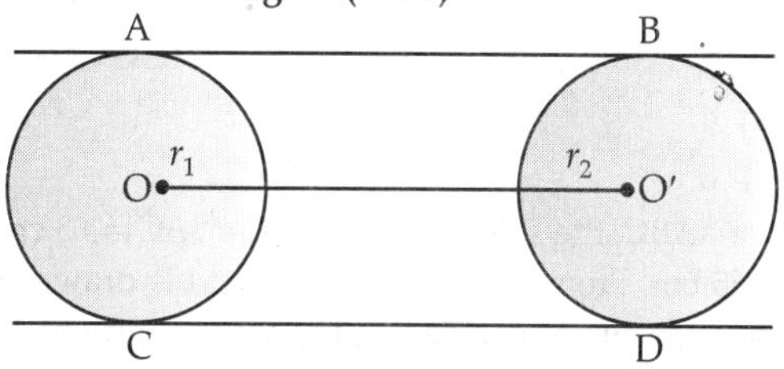

Here, AB and CD are (DCTs)

$$DCT = \sqrt{(\text{Distance between centres})^2 - (r_1 - r_2)^2}$$

$$\boxed{= \sqrt{(OO')^2 - (r_1 - r_2)^2}}$$

Transverse Common Tangent (TCT)

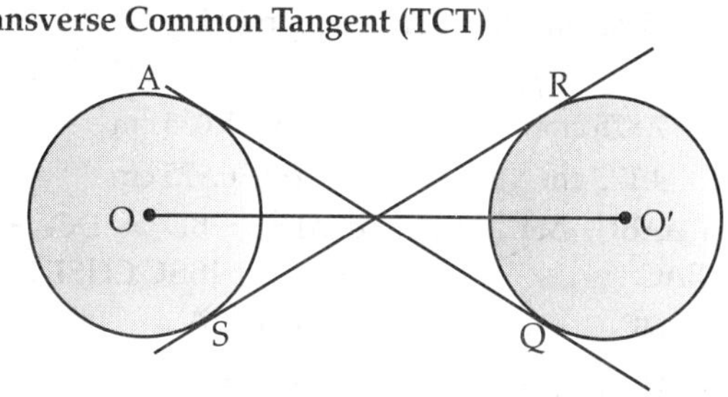

Here, RS and PQ are TCTs.

$$TCT = \sqrt{(OO')^2 - (r_1 + r_2)^2}$$

Example 1: Two circles touch each other externally. The distance between their centres is 7 cm. If the radius of the circle is 4 cm, then the radius of the other circle is:

(a) 4 cm (b) 3.5 cm

(c) 2 (d) 3

Sol. (d)

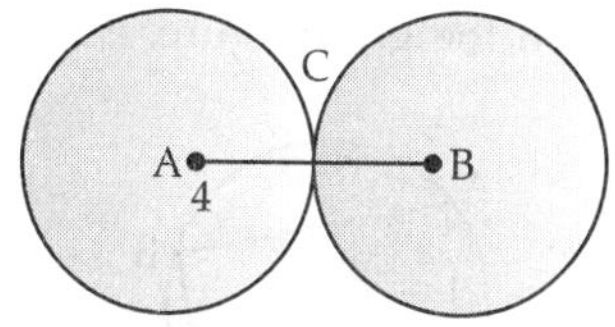

$$\begin{aligned} \text{Distance} &= AC + BC \\ 7 &= 4 + BC \\ BC &= 3 \end{aligned}$$

Hence, option (d) is the correct answer.

Example 2: A chord of length 10 cm subtends an angle 120° at the centre of a circle. The distance of the chord from the centre is:

(a) $5\sqrt{3}$ cm (b) $5\frac{\sqrt{3}}{2}$ cm

(c) $\frac{5}{\sqrt{3}}$ cm (d) 5 cm

Sol. (c) Given AB = 10 cm, ∠ACB = 120°

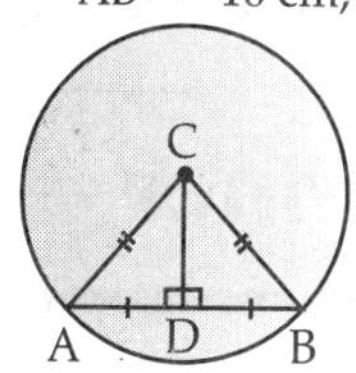

AD ⊥ BC

So, BD = DC = 5 cm

Now ∠CAD = 30°

(Angle sum property in ΔABC)

∠ACD = 60°

(Angle sum property in ΔABC)

In ΔCAD, $\tan 30° = \frac{CD}{AD}$

$$\Rightarrow \quad \frac{1}{\sqrt{3}} = \frac{CD}{5} \Rightarrow CD = \frac{5}{\sqrt{3}}\text{cm}$$

Hence, option (c) is the correct answer.

Example 3: In the given figure BD passes through centre O, AB = 12 and AC = 8. What is the radius of the circle?

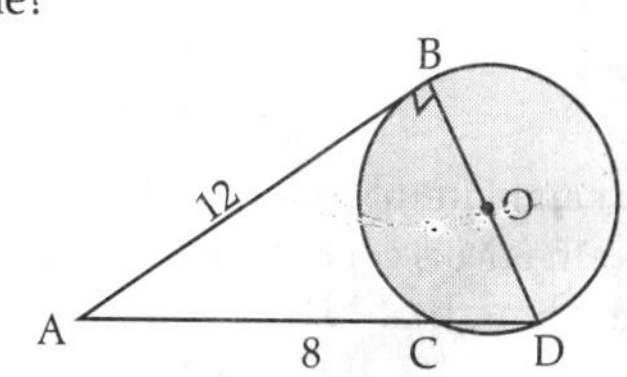

(a) $3\sqrt{2}$ (b) $4\sqrt{3}$

(c) $3\sqrt{5}$ (d) $3\sqrt{3}$

Sol. (c) We know

$AC \times AD = AB^2$ ∵ AB is tangent, AD is secant

$$AD = \frac{12 \times 12}{8} = 18$$

By pythagoras, $BD = \sqrt{AD^2 - AB^2}$

$$= \sqrt{18^2 - 12^2} = 6\sqrt{5}$$

Hence, Radius of circle $= \frac{6\sqrt{5}}{2} = 3\sqrt{5}$

Hence, option (c) is the correct answer.

Example 4: In the given figure, if ∠A = 100°, then ∠C = ?

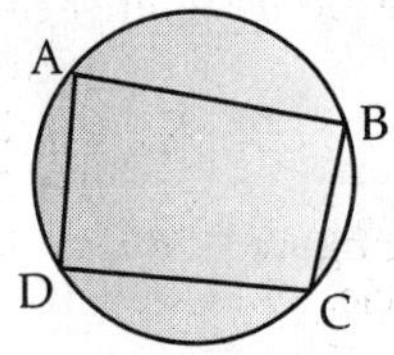

(a) 50° (b) 90°
(c) 80° (d) 100°

Sol. (c) ∠A + ∠C = 180°
(opp. angles of a cyclic quadrilateral)
100° + ∠C = 180°
∠C = 80°

Example 5: In a circle, chords PQ and TS are produced to meet at 'R'. If RQ = 14.4 cm, PQ = 11.2 cm and SR = 12.8 cm, then the length of chord TS is:

(a) 18 cm (b) 14.2 cm
(c) 12.4 cm (d) 16 cm

Sol. (d) We know,
RQ × PR = RS × TR

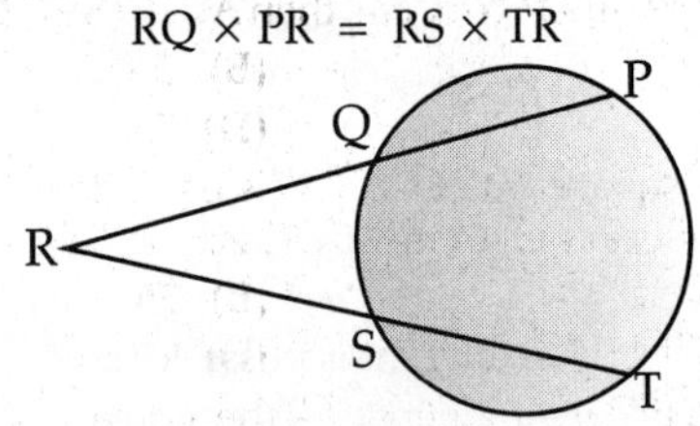

⇒ 14.4 × (14.4+11.2) = 12.8 × TR

⇒ $TR = \frac{14.4 \times 25.6}{12.8} = 28.8$ cm

So, TS = TR – SR
= (28.8 – 12.8) cm = 16 cm

Hence, option no. (d) is the correct answer.

Level 1 Beginner

1. In an equilateral triangle of side 10 cm each, find the ratio of the inradius to the circum-radius of the triangle. **[SSC CHSL 2018]**
(A) 1 : 1 **(B)** 1 : 2
(C) 1 : 3 **(D)** 2 : 1

2. The centroid of an equilateral triangle ABC is 'G'. If AB = 10 cm then length of AG is **[SSC CGL Tier-2 2014]**
(A) $5\sqrt{3}$ **(B)** $\frac{5\sqrt{3}}{3}$
(C) $\frac{10\sqrt{3}}{3}$ **(D)** $10\sqrt{3}$

3. ΔABC is an equilateral triangle and AD⊥BC, where D lies on BC. If AD = $4\sqrt{3}$ cm, then find the perimeter of ΔABC. **[SSC CGL Tier-1 2020]**
(A) 24 **(B)** 21
(C) 30 **(D)** 27

4. ΔPQR is an equilateral triangle. MN is drawn parallel to QR such that M is on PQ and N is on PR. If PN = 6 cm, then the length of MN is: **[SSC CGL Tier-1 2016]**
(A) 3 **(B)** 6
(C) 12 **(D)** 4.5

5. The base and altitude of an isoceles triangle are 10 cm and 12 cm, respectively. Then, the length of each equal side is: **[SSC CGL 2019]**
(A) 8.5 **(B)** 10
(C) 13 **(D)** 7.5

6. A circle is inscribed in the triangle ABC whose sides are given as *AB* = 10, *BC* = 8, *CA* = 12 units as shown in the figure. The value of *AD* × *BF* is :

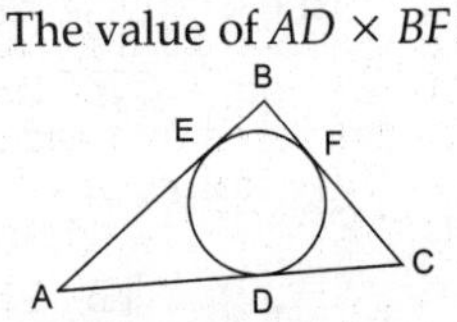

[SSC CHSL 2019]
(A) 21 units **(B)** 15 units
(C) 18 units **(D)** 16 units

7. For a triangle ABC, D,E,F are the mid points of its sides. If area of ΔABC = 24 sq. units then ΔDEF is: **[SSC CGL 2014]**
(A) 4 **(B)** 6
(C) 8 **(D)** 12

8. In a ΔABC, the sides are AB = 16 cm, AC = 63 cm, BC = 65 cm. From A, a straight line AM is drawn up to the midpoint M of side BC. Then, the length of AM is: **[SSC CGL 2019]**
(A) 32.5 cm **(B)** 24.5 cm
(C) 23.5 cm **(D)** 31.5 cm

9. In a circle, AB and DC are two chords. When AB and DC are produced, they meet at P. If PC = 2.8 cm, PB = 3.15 cm an AB = 3.85 cm, then CD = ? **[SSC CHSL 2021]**
(A) 7.875 cm **(B)** 5.075 cm
(C) 4.175 cm **(D)** 6.975 cm

10. In ΔABC, AD ⊥ BC and AD² = BD × DC. Find ∠BAC. **[SSC CHSL 2015]**
(A) 60° **(B)** 75°
(C) 90° **(D)** 45°

11. In ΔABC, ∠A = 90°, AD ⊥ BC at D. If AB = 12 cm and AC = 16 cm, then the length of BD is: **[SSC CGL 2020]**
(A) 8.4 **(B)** 7.2
(C) 6.4 **(D)** 7.8

12. In ΔABC, angle BAC = 90°, if BC = 25 cm, then length of median AD is : **[SSC CPO 2019]**
(A) 24 cm **(B)** 12.5 cm
(C) 14.5 cm **(D)** 10 cm

13. Let $\Delta ABC \sim \Delta RPQ$ and $\dfrac{ar.\Delta ABC}{ar.\Delta PQR} = \dfrac{1}{4}$. If PQ = 4 cm, QR = 6 cm and PR = 7 cm, then AC is: **[SSC CPO 2019]**

(A) 4 **(B)** 2
(C) 3 **(D)** 3.5

14. Inside a square ABCD, ΔBEC is equilateral. If CE and BD intersect at O, then ∠BOC is: **[SSC CGL 2013]**

(A) 60° **(B)** 75°
(C) 90° **(D)** 120°

15. PA and PB are tangents to the circle and O is the centre of the circle. The radius is 5 cm PO is 13 cm. If the area of the triangle PAB is M, then the value of $\sqrt{\dfrac{M}{15}}$ is: **[SSC CHSL 2019]**

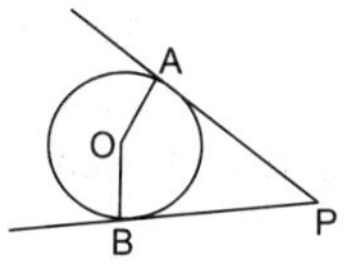

(A) $\dfrac{12}{13}$ **(B)** $\dfrac{24}{13}$
(C) $\sqrt{\dfrac{12}{13}}$ **(D)** $\sqrt{\dfrac{24}{13}}$

16. In a || gm PQRS, if angle P is four times of angle Q, then the measure of ∠R is: **[SSC CGL 2015]**

(A) 36° **(B)** 144°
(C) 130° **(D)** 72°

17. ABCD is a cyclic quadrilateral such that AB is the diameter of the circle circumscribing it and ∠ADC = 150°, then ∠BAC is: **[SSC CGL 2019]**

(A) 60° **(B)** 38°
(C) 50° **(D)** 40°

18. ABCD is a rhombus whose side AB = 4 cm and ∠ABC = 120°, then the length of diagonal BD is equal to: **[SSC CHSL 2011]**

(A) 2 **(B)** 1
(C) 4 **(D)** 3

19. If the parallel sides of a trapezium are 8 cm and 4 cm. M and N are the midpoints of the diagonals of the trapezium, then length of MN is: **[SSC CGL Tier-II 2016]**

(A) 12 cm **(B)** 6 cm
(C) 2 cm **(D)** 1 cm

20. Two circles touch each other externally. The distance between their centre is 7 cm. If the radius of one circle is 4 cm, then the radius of other circle is: **[SSC CGL Tier-1 2013]**

(A) 4 cm **(B)** 2 cm
(C) 3 cm **(D)** 3.5 cm

21. In the adjoining figure, ∠AOC = 140° where O is the centre of the circle. ∠ABC is : **[SSC CPO 2016]**

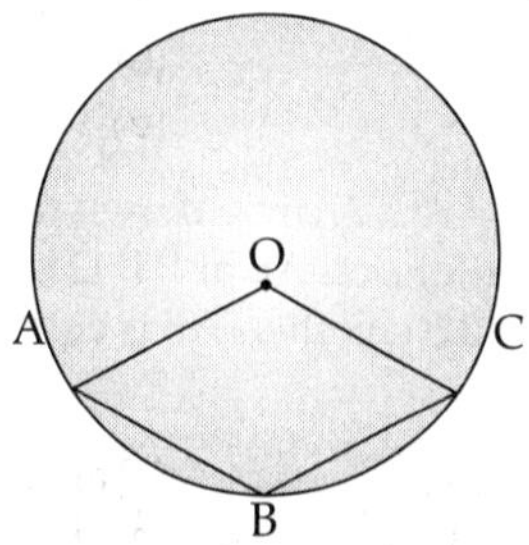

(A) 90° **(B)** 40°
(C) 110° **(D)** 100°

22. In an isosceles triangle ABC, AB - AC and AD is perpendicular to BC. If AD = 12 cm and the perimeter of ΔABC is 36 cm, then the length of BC (in cm) is : **[SSC CHSL 2021]**

(A) 12 **(B)** 5
(C) 13 **(D)** 10

23. Let o be the centre of a circle and AC be the diameter. BD is a chord intersecting AC at E. AD and AB are joined. If ∠BOC = 40° and ∠AOD = 120°, then ∠BEC is equal to: **[SSC CHSL 2021]**

(A) 90° **(B)** 70°
(C) 80° **(D)** 55°

24. In the given figure, a circle touches the quadrilateral ABCD. If AB = $2x + 3$, BC = $3x - 1$, CD = [illegible] 6 and DA = $x + 4$, find the value of x. **[SSC CGL 2017]**

(A) 4.5 **(B)** 6.5
(C) 6 **(D)** 3

25. The circumcentre, incentre, orthocentre and the centroid of a triangle are on a single and same point. The triangle must be: **[SSC CHSL 2019]**

(A) Equilateral triangle **(B)** Isosceles triangle
(C) Right-angled triangle **(D)** Scalene triangle

2 Intermediate
Level

1. The radius of a circle circumscribing the three vertices of an equilateral triangle is 12 cm. Determine the height of the equilateral triangle. **[SSC CHSL 2018]**

(A) 12 **(B)** 18
(C) 14 **(D)** 20

2. In ΔABC, ∠A = 40°, if the bisectors of ∠B and ∠C, meet at a point O, then ∠BOC is equal to: **[SSC CPO 2019]**

(A) 130° **(B)** 90°
(C) 110° **(D)** 70°

3. In ΔABC. Point D and E are on AB and AC, respectively, such that DE is parallel to BC. If AD = 3 cm, BD = 6 cm and AE = 2 cm, then find the length of CE. **[SSC CHSL 2021]**

(A) 6 cm **(B)** 8 cm
(C) 16 cm **(D)** 4 cm

4. In an isosceles triangle having AB = AC and ∠A = 40°. Bisectors PO and OQ of the exterior angles ∠ABD and ∠ACE formed by producing BC on both sides, meet at O. Then, the value of ∠BOC is: **[SSC CGL Tier-2 2016]**

(A) 70° **(B)** 110°
(C) 55° **(D)** 80°

5. The mid points of sides AB and AC of a triangle ABC are, respectively, X and Y. If (BC + XY) = 12 units, then value of (BC – XY). **[SSC CGL 2016]**
   (A) 2 units (B) 6 units
   (C) 4 units (D) 8 units

6. ΔABC is similar to ΔPQR. The area of ΔABC is 64 cm^2, and the area of ΔPQR is 121 cm^2. If QR=15.4 cm, what is the length of BC? **[SSC CHSL 2022]**
   (A) 13.2 cm (B) 15.4 cm
   (C) 11.2 cm (D) 12.3 cm

7. In ΔABC, AB = AC. A circle drawn through B touches AC at D and intersects AB at P. If D is the mid point of AC and AP = 2.5 cm, then AB is equal to: **[SSC CGL 2020]**
   (A) 9 cm (B) 7.5 cm
   (C) 12.5 cm (D) 10 cm

8. In ΔABC, ∠A = 90° and if BM and CN are two medians then, $\frac{BM^2 + CN^2}{BC^2}$ is equal to: **[SSC CHSL 2020]**
   (A) $\frac{3}{5}$ (B) $\frac{5}{4}$
   (C) $\frac{4}{5}$ (D) $\frac{3}{4}$

9. The lengths of the parallel sides of a trapezium are 51 cm and 21 cm, and that of each of the other two sides is 39 cm. What is the area of the trapezium. (in cm^2)? **[SSC CPO 2019]**
   (A) 1206 (B) 1296
   (C) 1152 (D) 1260

10. In ΔABC, F and E are the points on sides AB and AC, respectively, such that FE||BC and FE divides the triangle in two parts of equal area. If AD ⊥ BC and AD intersects FE at G, then GD : AG = ? **[SSC CGL 2019]**
    (A) $\sqrt{2}:1$ (B) $(\sqrt{2}-1):1$
    (C) $2\sqrt{2}:1$ (D) $(\sqrt{2}+1):1$

11. In ΔABC, ∠A is a right angle. The length of AC and BC are 6 cm and 10 cm, respectively. Point D is on AB such that BD = 4 cm. What is the length of CD? **[SSC CGL 2019]**
    (A) $3\sqrt{10}$ (B) $3\sqrt{13}$
    (C) $2\sqrt{13}$ (D) $2\sqrt{10}$

12. In ΔABC, the sides are AB = 16 cm, AC = 63 cm, BC = 65 cm. From A, a straight line AM is drawn up to the midpoint M of a side BC. Then, the length of AM is equal to: **[SSC CGL 2019]**
    (A) 32.5 cm (B) 31.5 cm
    (C) 24.5 cm (D) 23.5 cm

13. PA and PB are tangents to a circle with centre O, from a point P outside the circle, and A and B are points on the circle. If ∠APB = 40°, then ∠OAB is equal to: **[SSC CGL 2019]**
    (A) 50° (B) 26°
    (C) 40° (D) 20°

14. In a circle with centre O and radius 13 cm, a chord AB is drawn. Tangents at A and B intersect at P such ∠APB = 60°. If the distance of AB from the centre O is 5 cm, then what is the length of AP? **[SSC CGL 2018/2021]**
    (A) 22 (B) 24
    (C) 11 (D) 12

15. Points P and Q are on the sides AB and BC, respectively, of a triangle ABC, right angled at B. If AQ = 11 cm, PC = 8 cm and AC = 13 cm, then find the length of PQ. **[SSC CGL 2021]**
    (A) $4\sqrt{7}$ (B) $\sqrt{15}$
    (C) 4.5 (D) 4

16. Two circles of radius 15 cm and 37 cm intersect each other at the points A and B. If the length of the common chord is 24 cm, what is the distance between the centres of the circles? **[SSC CGL 2020]**
    (A) 45 (B) 42
    (C) 44 (D) 40

17. ABCD is a cyclic quadrilateral. AB and DC meet at F, when produced. AD and BC meet at E, when produced. If ∠BAD = 68° and ∠AEB = 27°, then ∠BFC = ? **[SSC CGL 2020]**
    (A) 27° (B) 22°
    (C) 15° (D) 17°

18. Angle subtended by a chord xy on the centre of a circle is 180 degree. If length of this chord is 36 cm, then what will be the radius of this circle? **[SSC CHSL 2023]**
    (A) 24 cm (B) 18 cm
    (C) 27 cm (D) 21 cm

19. Chords AB and CD of a circle intersect externally at P. If CD = 11.6 cm, PD = 6.4 cm, PB = 7.2 cm, then AB is: **[SSC CHSL 2021]**
    (A) 12 (B) 16
    (C) 8.8 (D) 4.8

20. A circle inscribed in a triangle ABC touches its sides AB, BC and AC at the point D, E and F, respectively. If AB = 18 cm, BC = 15 cm and AC = 13 cm, then find the value of AD + BE + CF. **[SSC CHSL 2020]**
    (A) 70 (B) 33
    (C) 23 (D) 20

21. In ΔABC, D is a point on BC such that AD is the bisector of ∠A, AB = 11.7 cm, AC = 7.8 cm and BC = 13 cm. What is the length of DC? **[SSC CGL 2020]**
    (A) 5.2 (B) 6.5
    (C) 7.8 (D) 5.6

22. Two tangents TP and TQ are drawn to a circle with centre O from an external point T. If TP = 7 cm, find the length of TQ. **[SSC CHSL 2022]**
    (A) 7 cm (B) 10.5 cm
    (C) 3.5 cm (D) 14 cm

3 Level Expert

1. If the perimeter of the isoceles right triangle is $8(\sqrt{2}+1)$, then the length of the hypotenuse of the triangle is: [SSC CGL Tier-2 2020]
   (A) 8 cm (B) 12 cm
   (C) 10 cm (D) 24 cm
2. Radii of two circles are 12 cm and 5 cm. Distance between their centres is 25 cm. What is the length of the direct common tangent? [SSC CHSL 2023]
   (A) 21 cm (B) 24 cm
   (C) 22 cm (D) 23 cm
3. The sum of the radius of two circles is 286 cm and the area between the concentric circles is 5033 cm. What are the radii of the two circles? [SSC CHSL 2021]
   (A) 91, 84 (B) 115, 91
   (C) 171, 115 (D) 171, 84
4. In ΔABC, ∠B = 90°, AB = 8 cm, BC = 15 cm. D is a point on BC such that AD bisects ∠A. The length of BD (in cm) is: [SSC CHSL 2021]
   (A) 4.5 (B) 4.8
   (C) 4.2 (D) 3.6
5. Chords AB and CD of a circle are produced to meet at the point P, outside the circle, and AD is the diameter of the circle. If ∠DAP = 36° and ∠APC=30°, then what will be the measure of ∠CBD? [SSC CGL 2021]
   (A) 34° (B) 26°
   (C) 24° (D) 16°
6. Two circles of radii 20 cm and 5 cm, respectively, touch each other externally at the point P. AB is the direct common tangent of these two circles of centres R and S, respectively. The length of AB is equal to : [SSC CGL 2020]
   (A) 15 cm (B) 5 cm
   (C) 10 cm (D) 20 cm
7. In ΔABC, ∠B = 90°. If points D and E are on side BC such that BD = DE = EC, then which of the following is true? [SSC CGL 2020]
   (A) $8AE^2 = 3AC^2 + 5AD^2$
   (B) $8AE^2 = 5AC^2 + 3AD^2$
   (C) $5AE^2 = 2AC^2 + 3AD^2$
   (D) $5AE^2 = 3AC^2 + 2AD^2$
8. Two circles intersect each other such that each passes through the centre of other. Radius of these circles are equal. If the length of common chord is 14√3 cm, then what will be the sum of circumferences of these two circles? [SSC CHSL 2023]
   (A) 88 cm (B) 352 cm
   (C) 176 cm (D) 188 cm
9. In ΔABD, C is the mid point of BD. If AB = 10 cm, AD = 12 cm and AC = 9 cm, then BD = ?[SSC CGL 2019]
   (A) $2\sqrt{41}$ (B) $2\sqrt{10}$
   (C) $\sqrt{41}$ (D) $5\sqrt{41}$
10. In a circle with centre O, ABCD is a cyclic quadrilateral and AC is the diameter. Chords AB and CD are produced to meet at E. If ∠CAE = 34° and ∠E = 30°, then ∠CBD is equal to: [SSC CGL 2019]
    (A) 36° (B) 26°
    (C) 24° (D) 34°
11. AD is the median of Δ ABC. G is the centroid of Δ ABC. If AG = 14 cm, then what is the length of AD? [SSC CHSL 2023]
    (A) 42 cm (B) 28 cm
    (C) 35 cm (D) 21 cm
12. Two regular polygons are such that the ratio between their number of sides is 1 : 2 and the ratio of measures of their interior angles is 3 : 4. Then, the number of sides of each polygon is: [SSC CGL 2016]
    (A) 7, 9 (B) 5, 4
    (C) 5, 10 (D) 12, 15
13. In the given figure, triangle PQR is a right angled Δ at Q. If PQ = 35 cm and QS = 28 cm, then what is the value of SR? [SSC CGL Tier-2 2018]

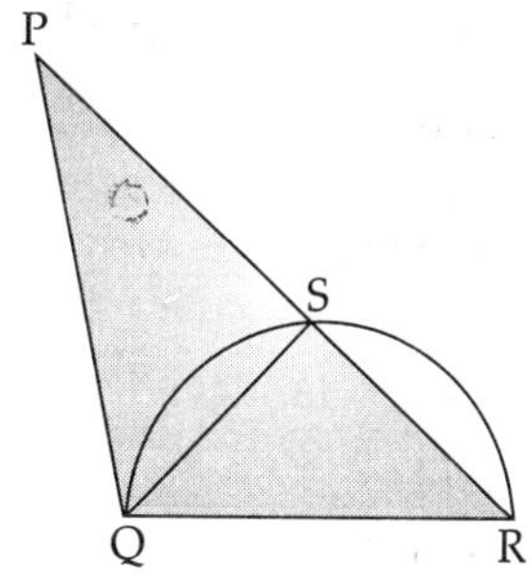

    (A) 35.33 (B) 37.33
    (C) 41.33 (D) 43.33
14. In the given figure, ABC is a right angled triangle. ∠ABC = 90° and ∠ACB = 60°. If the radius of the smaller circle is 2 cm, then what is the radius of the larger circle. [SSC CGL Tier-2 2018]

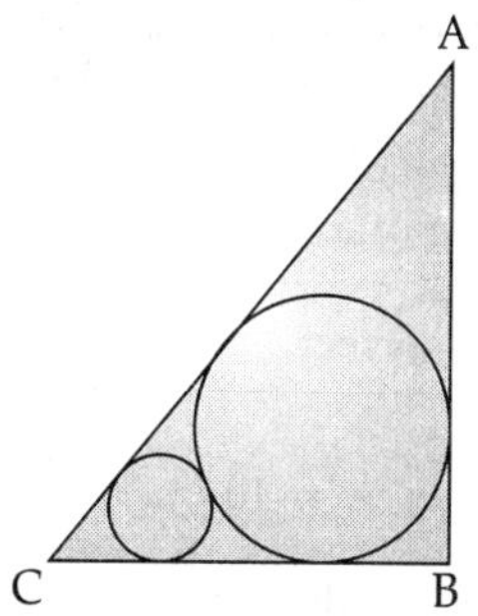

    (A) 4 (B) 6
    (C) 4.5 (D) 7.5
15. A point 'A' is at a distance 26 cm from the centre O of a circle of radius 10 cm. AP and AQ are the tangents to the circle at the point of contacts P and Q. If a tangent BC is drawn at a point R lying on the minor are PQ to intersect AP at B and AQ at C, then the perimeter of ΔABC is: [SSC CHSL 2020]
    (A) 40 (B) 46
    (C) 48 (D) 42

16. The distance between the centres of two equal circles each of radius 4 cm is 17 cm. The length of a transverse tangent is. **[SSC CHSL 2020]**

(A) 15 (B) 16
(C) 14 (D) 19

17. In ΔABC, AB = AC and AL is perpendicular to BC at L. In ΔDEF, DE = DF and DM is $\perp$ EF at M. If area of (ΔABC) : area of Δ(DEF) = 9 : 25, then $\frac{DM + AL}{DM - AL}$ is equal to : **[SSC CGL 2020]**

(A) 6 (B) 4
(C) 3 (D) 5

18. In ΔABC, $\angle C = 90°$ and CD is $\perp$ AB at D. If $\frac{AD}{BD} = \sqrt{K}$, then $\frac{AC}{BC} = ?$ **[SSC CPO 2019]**

(A) $\sqrt{K} : 1$ (B) $2 : 1$
(C) $\sqrt[3]{K}$ (D) $\sqrt[4]{K}$

19. If ΔABC is an equilateral triangle in which D, E, and F are the points on sides BC, AC, and AB, respectively, such that AD $\perp$ BC, BE $\perp$ AC and CF $\perp$ AB, which is the following is true? **[SSC CPO 2019]**

(A) $7AB^2 = 9AD^2$ (B) $2AB^2 = 3AD^2$
(C) $4AC^2 = 5BE^2$ (D) $3AC^2 = 4BE^2$

20. In ΔABC, AM is $\perp$ BC and AN is the bisector of $\angle$A. What is the measure of $\angle$MAN, if $\angle B = 55°$ and $\angle C = 35°$? **[SSC CGL 2019]**

(A) 10° (B) 12°
(C) 15° (D) 5°

ANSWER KEY

Level-1: Beginner

1.	(B)	2.	(C)	3.	(A)	4.	(B)	5.	(C)	6.	(A)	7.	(B)	8.	(A)	9.	(B)	10.	(C)
11.	(B)	12.	(B)	13.	(C)	14.	(B)	15.	(B)	16.	(B)	17.	(A)	18.	(C)	19.	(C)	20.	(C)
21.	(C)	22.	(D)	23.	(C)	24.	(C)	25.	(A)										

Level-2: Intermediate

1.	(B)	2.	(C)	3.	(D)	4.	(A)	5.	(C)	6.	(C)	7.	(D)	8.	(B)	9.	(B)	10.	(B)
11.	(C)	12.	(A)	13.	(D)	14.	(B)	15.	(D)	16.	(D)	17.	(D)	18.	(B)	19.	(C)	20.	(C)
21.	(A)	22.	(A)																

Level-3: Expert

1.	(A)	2.	(B)	3.	(C)	4.	(B)	5.	(C)	6.	(D)	7.	(A)	8.	(C)	9.	(A)	10.	(B)
11.	(D)	12.	(C)	13.	(B)	14.	(B)	15.	(C)	16.	(A)	17.	(B)	18.	(D)	19.	(D)	20.	(A)

Solutions with Detailed Explanation

Level-1: BEGINNER

1. Option (B) is correct.

Explanation:

$$\text{Side} = 10 \text{ cm}$$

$$\text{Inradius of an equilateral } \Delta(r) = \frac{a}{2\sqrt{3}} = \frac{10}{2\sqrt{3}} = \frac{5}{\sqrt{3}}$$

Ex-radius or circumradius of an equilateral triangle

$$R = \frac{a}{\sqrt{3}} = \frac{10}{\sqrt{3}}$$

So, r : R

$$\frac{5}{\sqrt{3}} : \frac{10}{\sqrt{3}} = 1 : 2$$

2. Option (C) is correct.

Explanation: Given,

AB = 10 cm

BD = 5 cm (∵ AD is a median)

ΔADB is a right angled Δ.

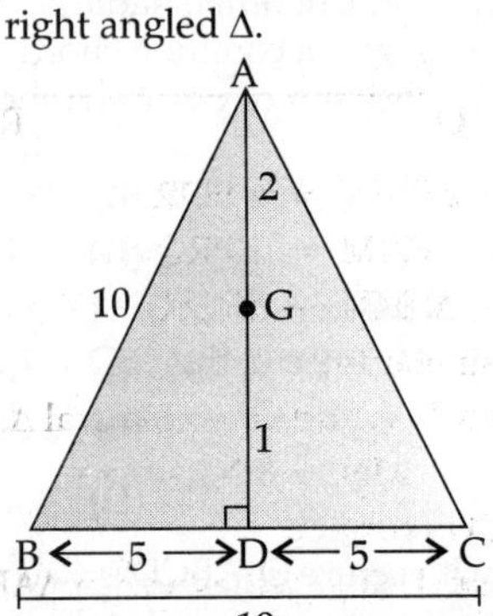

So $\quad AD = \sqrt{AB^2 - BD^2}$

$= \sqrt{10^2 - 5^2} = \sqrt{75} = 5\sqrt{3}$ cm

We know, AG : GD, $\quad$ [AG + GD = AD]

2 : 1

$$AG = \frac{2}{3} \times AD$$

$$= \frac{2}{3} \times 5\sqrt{3} = \frac{10\sqrt{3}}{3}$$

3. Option (A) is correct.

Explanation: AD is the height of ΔABC

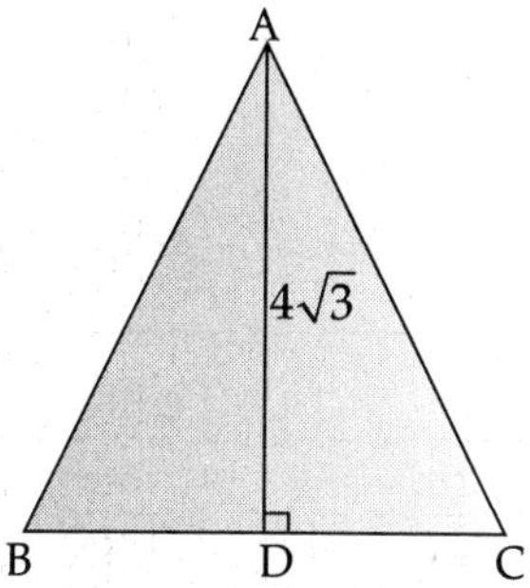

$$AD = \frac{\sqrt{3}}{2} \times \text{side}$$

$$4\sqrt{3} = \frac{\sqrt{3}}{2} \times \text{side}$$

$$\text{side} = \frac{4\sqrt{3} \times 2}{\sqrt{3}} = 8 \text{ cm}$$

Now, perimeter of ΔABC

= AB + BC + AC = 3 × side = 3 × 8 = 24 cm

4. Option (B) is correct.

Explanation: Clearly, MN || QR

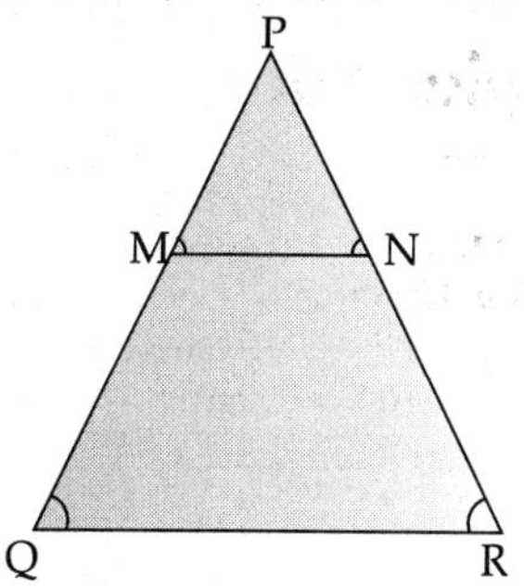

So, $\quad \angle PMN = \angle PQR$

$\angle PNM = \angle PRQ$

$\Delta PMN \sim \Delta PQR$

(By AAA-similarity)

Hence, ΔPMN is also an equilateral Δ.

$\therefore \quad MN = PN = 6$ cm

5. Option (C) is correct.

Explanation: Using pythagoras in ΔADC

$$AC^2 = AD^2 + CD^2$$

$$AC = \sqrt{AD^2 + CD^2}$$

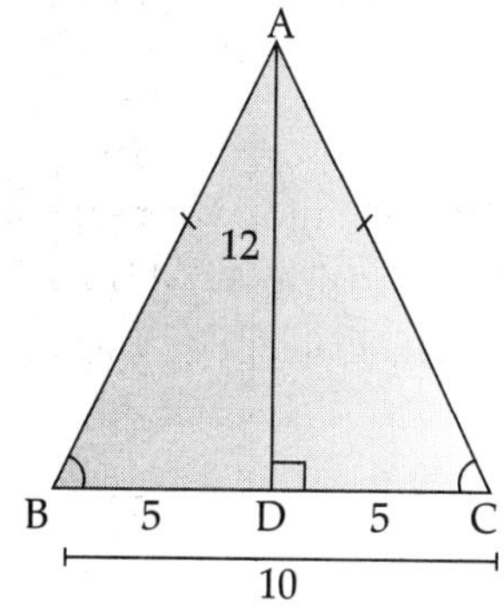

$$= \sqrt{12^2 + 5^2} = \sqrt{144 + 25}$$

$$= \sqrt{169} = 13 \text{ cm}$$

6. Option (A) is correct.

Explanation:

We have,

AB = 10 cm, BC = 8 cm and CA = 12 cm

We know that the length of tangents drawn from an external point to a circle are equal.

Let $\quad$ BE = BF = x unit

And $\quad$ CF = CD = y unit

And $\quad$ AD = AE = z unit

Now $\quad$ AB = AE + BE = $z + x = 10$ $\quad$ ...(1)

BC = BF + CF = $x + y = 8$ $\quad$ ...(2)

AC = AD + CD = $z + y = 12$ $\quad$ ...(3)

By adding equation (1), (2) and (3),

$$2(x + y + z) = 30$$

$\Rightarrow \quad x + y + z = 15$ $\quad$ ...(4)

By equation (4) – equation (2), Z = 7

By equation (4) – equation (3), X = 3

So, AD × BF = $z \times x = 7 \times 3 = 21$

7. Option (B) is correct.

Explanation: We know

$$\text{ar } \Delta DEF = \text{ar} \frac{1}{4} \Delta ABC$$

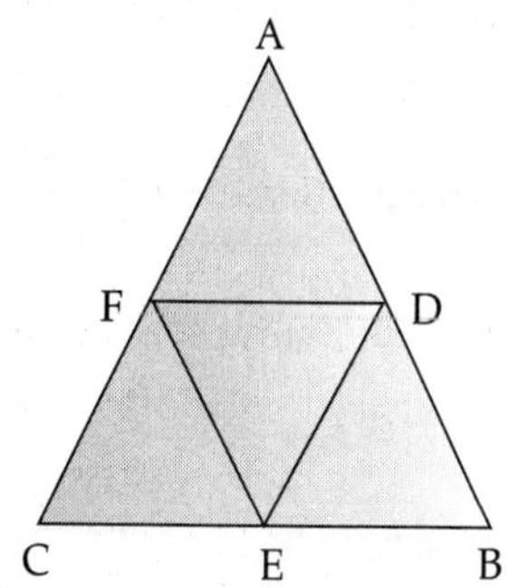

So, $\quad \text{ar } \Delta DEF = \frac{1}{4} \times 24 = 6$ sq. units

8. Option (A) is correct.

Explanation:

Using Apollonius theorem

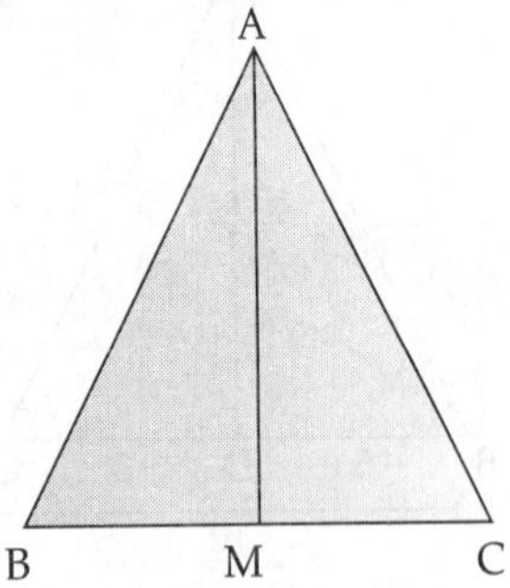

$$AB^2 + AC^2 = 2(AM^2 + BM^2)$$

$$16^2 + 63^2 = 2\left[AM^2 + \left(\frac{65}{2}\right)^2\right]$$

$$256 + 3969 = 2\left[AM^2 + \left(\frac{65}{2}\right)^2\right]$$

$$2112.5 = AM^2 + 1056.25$$

$$AM = \sqrt{1056.25} = 32.5 \text{ cm}$$

9. Option (B) is correct.

Explanation:

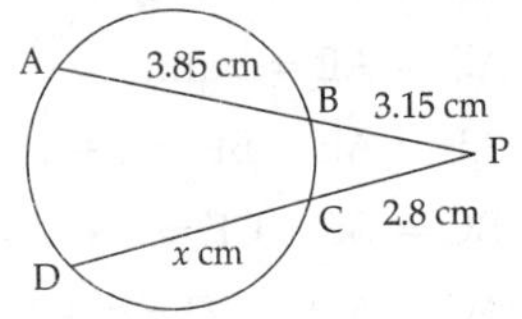

As shown in diagram,

$PC = 2.8$ cm, $PB = 3.15$ cm, $AB = 3.85$ cm

So, $PA = PB + AB = 3.15 + 3.85 = 7$ cm

Let $CD = x$ cm

As we know, $PC \times PD = PB \times PA$

$\Rightarrow \quad 2.8 \times (2.8 + x) = 3.15 \times 7$

$\Rightarrow \quad 2.8 + x = 7.875$

$\Rightarrow \quad x = 5.075$

So, $CD = 5.075$ cm

10. Option (C) is correct.

Explanation:

In rt. angled ΔABD, $AB^2 = AD^2 + BD^2$ ...(1)

In ΔADC, $AC^2 = AD^2 + DC^2$ ...(2)

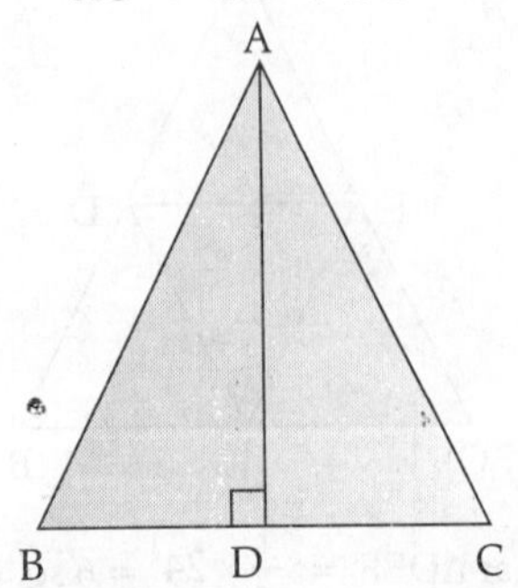

Add (1) and (2)

$$AB^2 + AC^2 = 2AD^2 + BD^2 + CD^2$$

$$AB^2 + AC^2 = 2BD \times CD + BD^2 + CD^2$$

$[\because AD^2 = BD \times CD \text{ (Given)}]$

$\therefore \quad AB^2 + AC^2 = (BD + CD)^2 = BC^2$

$\therefore \quad \angle BAC = 90°$

11. Option (B) is correct.

Explanation:

Here, $\Delta ABC \sim \Delta DBA$

$\therefore \quad AB^2 = BD \times BC$

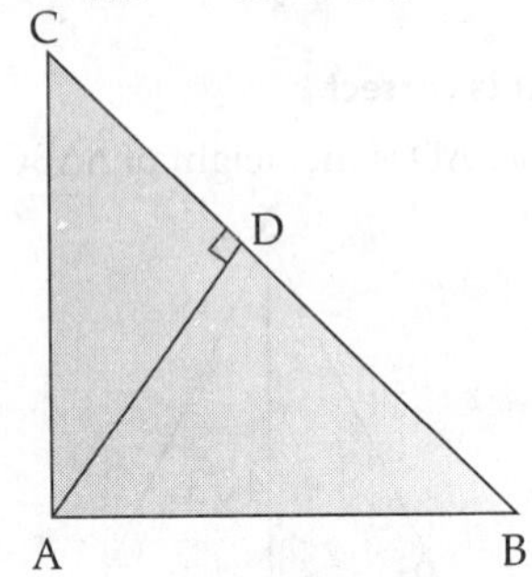

$$12 \times 12 = BD \times 20$$

$$BD = \frac{12 \times 12}{20} \quad \left[\begin{aligned} BC &= \sqrt{AB^2 + AC^2} \\ &= \sqrt{12^2 + 16^2} \\ &= \sqrt{400} = 20 \end{aligned}\right]$$

$$= 7.2 \text{ cm}$$

12. Option (B) is correct.

Explanation:

Here $AD = BD = CD = \boxed{\frac{BC}{2}} = \frac{25}{2}$

$= 12.5$ cm

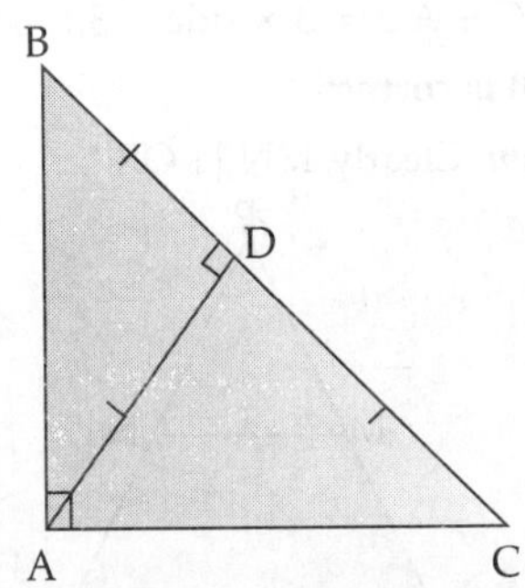

NOTE : The median drawn to the hypotenuse of a right angled triangle divides the triangle into two isosceles triangles.

13. Option (C) is correct.

Explanation:

Given,

$\Delta ABC \sim \Delta RPQ$, $\frac{ar}{ar}$ of $\frac{\Delta ACB}{\Delta PQR} = \frac{1}{4}$

So,

$$\frac{\text{ar. of } \Delta ABC}{\text{ar. of } \Delta PQR} = \frac{AC^2}{RQ^2} = \frac{1}{4}$$

$$\Rightarrow \quad \frac{AC}{RQ} = \sqrt{\frac{1}{4}} = \frac{1}{2}$$

$$\Rightarrow \quad AC = \frac{RQ}{2} = \frac{6}{2} = 3 \text{ cm}$$

14. Option (B) is correct.

Explanation:

We know that

$\angle ABC = 90°$

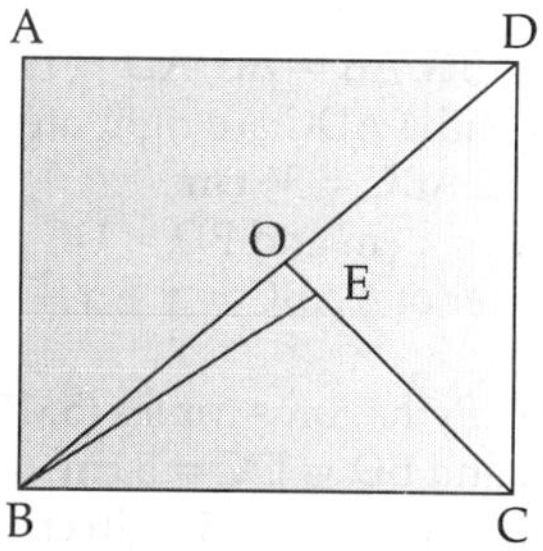

[each angle of a square is 90°]

$\Rightarrow \quad \angle OBC = 45° \quad [\because \angle ABC = 2\angle OBC]$

$\angle OCB = 60°$

[$\because$ each angle of equ Δ is 60°]

$\therefore \quad \angle BOC = 180° - 60° - 45° = 75°$

15. Option (B) is correct.

Explanation: We have,

Radius $\quad OA = OB = 5$ cm and $PO = 13$ cm

$\angle OAP = \angle OBP = 90°$

[the tangent makes an angle of 90° with the radius of circle]

In ΔAOP, by Pythagoras theorem,

$OP^2 = OA^2 + AP^2$

$\Rightarrow \quad 13^2 = 5^2 + AP^2$

$\Rightarrow \quad AP^2 = 169 - 25 = 144 \Rightarrow AP = 12$ cm

And $\quad AP = BP = 12$ cm

[tangents drawn from common point to a circle are equal in length]

Now area of quadrilateral PAOB = area of ΔPAO+ area of ΔPBO $= \frac{1}{2} \times 5 \times 12 + \frac{1}{2} \times 5 \times 12 = 60 \text{ cm}^2$

Let AB intersect PO at N.

Then ON = x cm and NP = $(13 - x)$ cm

area of quadrilateral PAOB = area of ΔOAB + area of ΔPAB

$$\Rightarrow \quad 60 = \frac{1}{2} \times AB \times x + \frac{1}{2} \times AB \times (13 - x)$$

$$\Rightarrow \quad 60 = \frac{1}{2} \times AB(x + 13 - x)$$

$$\Rightarrow \quad AB = \frac{120}{13}$$

Since ON is perpendicular to AB and O is the centre. Then On will bisect AB.

$AN = AB/2$

or $\quad AN = \frac{60}{13}$ cm

In ΔANO, $\quad AO^2 = AN^2 + ON^2$

$$\Rightarrow \quad 52 = \left(\frac{60}{13}\right)^2 + ON^2$$

$$\Rightarrow \quad ON^2 = \frac{625}{169} \Rightarrow ON = \frac{25}{13}$$

Area of $\Delta AOB = \frac{1}{2} \times AB \times ON = \frac{1}{2} \times \frac{120}{13} \times \frac{25}{13} = \frac{1500}{169}$ cm^2

Area of ΔAPB (M) $= 60 - \frac{1500}{169} = \frac{8640}{169}$

So, value of $\sqrt{\frac{M}{15}} = \sqrt{\frac{8640}{169 \times 15}} = \sqrt{\frac{576}{169}} = \frac{24}{13}$

16. Option (B) is correct.

Explanation: We know,

$\angle P + \angle Q = 180° \quad$ [adjacent angles]

$4\angle Q + \angle Q = 180° \quad$ [Given, $\angle P = 4\angle Q$]

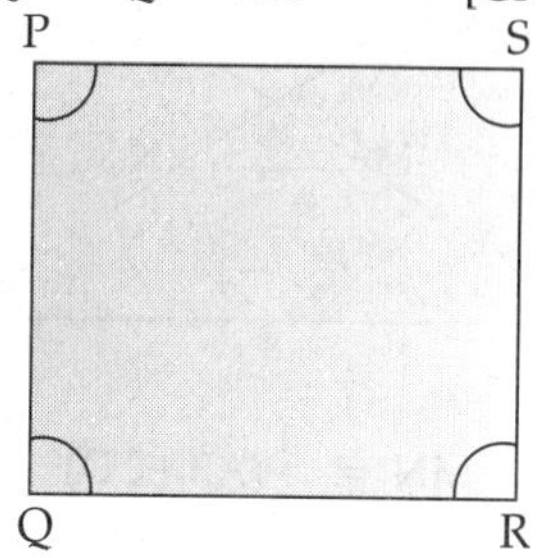

$\angle Q = \frac{180}{5} = 36°$

Again,

$\angle Q + \angle R = 180°$

[adjacent angles of || gm are supplementary, i.e., 180°]

$\angle R = 180° - 36° = 144°$.

17. Option (A) is correct.

Explanation:

Given, $\quad \angle D = 150°$

In quadrilateral ABCD,

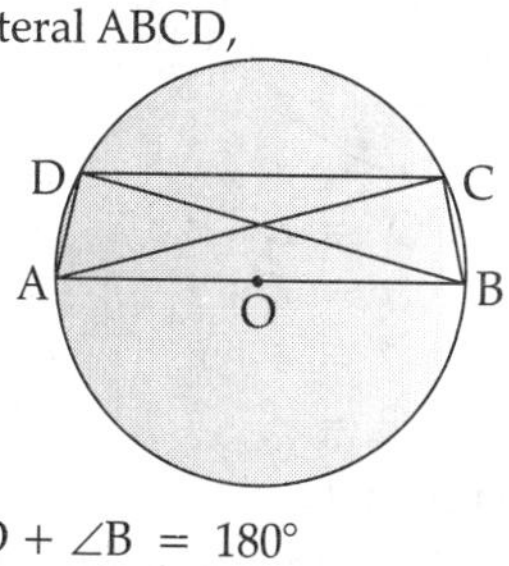

$\angle D + \angle B = 180°$

[sum of opposite angle of cyclic quadrilateral]

$\angle B = 180° - 150° = 30°$.

In ΔABC, $\quad \angle ACB = 90° \quad$ (angle of a semi-circle)

$\therefore \quad \angle BAC = 180 - (90° + 30°)$

$= 180 - 120° = 60°$

18. Option (C) is correct.

Explanation:

In ΔBOC, $\quad \frac{BO}{4} = \cos 60°$

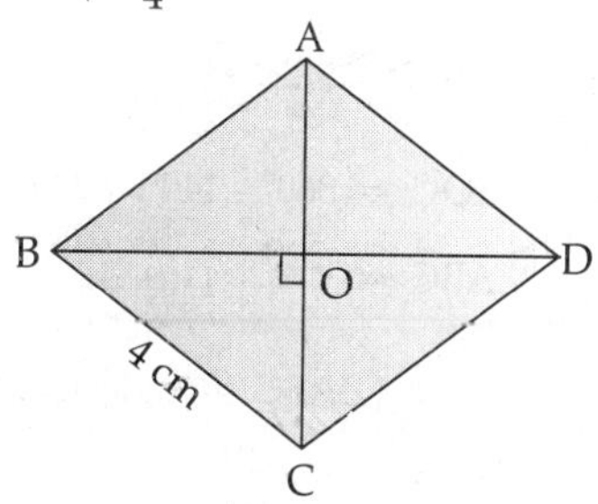

$$\frac{BO}{4} = \frac{1}{2}$$

$$BO = \frac{1}{2} \times 4 = 2\,\text{cm}$$

$\therefore$ $$BD = 2 \times BO$$

[diagonal of a rhombus bisect each other]

$$BD = 2 \times 2 = 4\text{ cm}$$

19. Option (C) is correct.

Explanation:

We know, $MN = \frac{1}{2}$ (difference of two || sides)

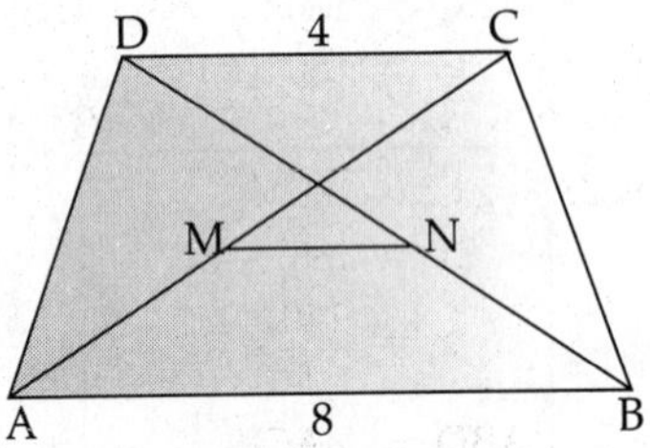

i.e., $$MN = \frac{1}{2}(AB - CD)$$

$$= \frac{1}{2}(8-4) = \frac{1}{2} \times 4 = 2\text{ cm}$$

20. Option (C) is correct.

Explanation: Here, distance between centres = 7 cm

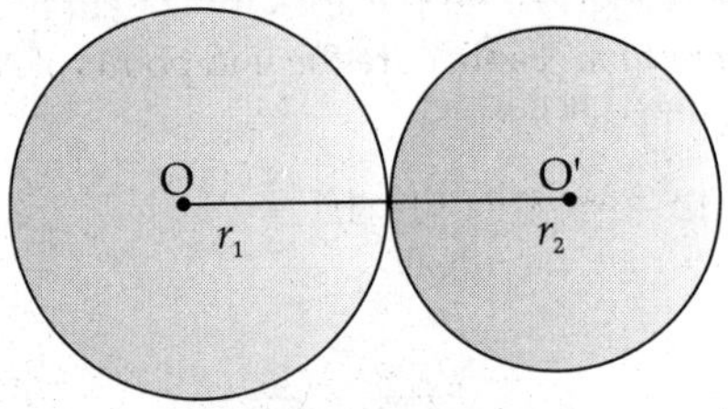

$$OO' = r_1 + r_2$$
$$7 = r_1 + r_2$$
$$7 = 4 + r_2$$
$$3 = r_2$$

21. Option (C) is correct.

Explanation: We know, reflex angle = angle subtended by an arc at the centre.

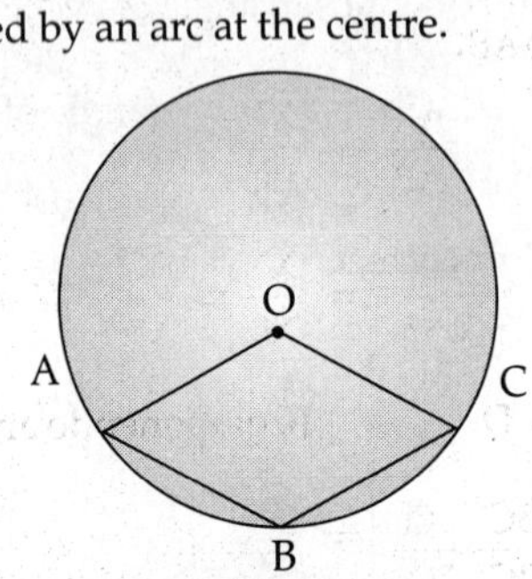

$$\angle AOC = 360° - 140° = 220°$$

$\therefore$ $$\angle ABC = \frac{220}{2} = 110°$$

[$\angle ABC$ = angle at circumference]

22. Option (D) is correct.

Explanation:

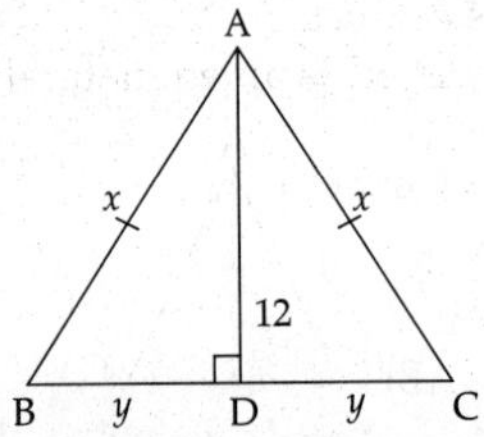

Given: In Δ ABC, AB = AC, AD = 12 cm
And Δ ADB and Δ ADC are right angle triangle.
Perimeter of Δ ABC = 36 cm
Let AB = AC = x cm and BD = DC = y cm
Now perimeter of Δ ABC = $x + x + 2y = 36$
$\Rightarrow x + y = 18$
In Δ ADB, by Pythagoras triples (5, 12, 13),
AB = 13 cm and BD = DC = 5 cm
So, BC = BD + DC = 5 + 5 = 10 cm

23. Option (C) is correct.

Explanation:

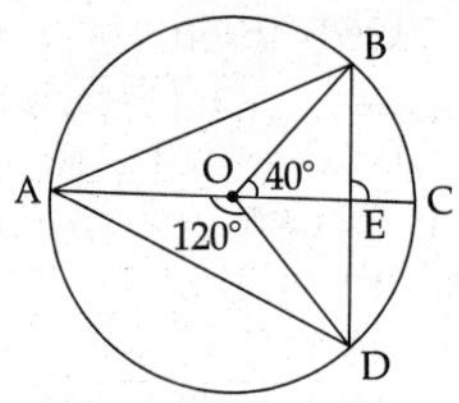

As shown in diagram,
$\angle BOC = 40°$
So, $\angle BOA = 180° - 40° = 140°$
As, angle by arc AB at centre is 140°. So, from same arc angle on the circumference = $\frac{140°}{2} = 70°$

Now $\angle DOC = 360° - (\angle AOB + \angle AOD + \angle BOC)$
$= 360° - (140° + 120° + 40°) = 60°$
As, angle by arc DC at centre is 60°. So, from same arc angle on the circumference = $\frac{60°}{2} = 30°$

Now, $\angle BEC = (180° - (70° + 30°)) = 80°$

24. Option (C) is correct.

Explanation: In this situation,

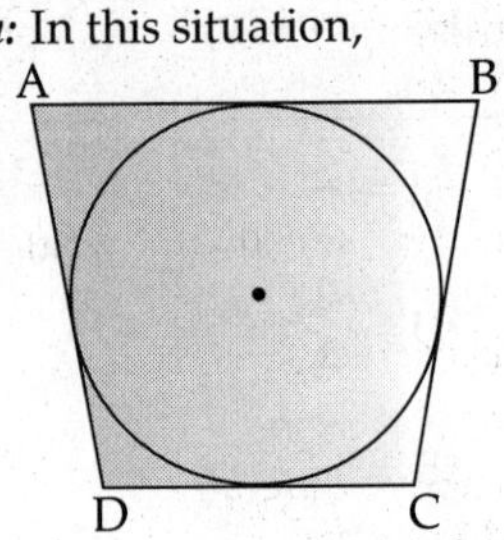

$\therefore$ $$AB + CD = BC + AD \text{ (always)}$$
$$2x + 3 + x + 6 = 3x - 1 + x + 4$$
$$3x + 9 = 4x + 3$$
$$6 = x$$

25. Option (A) is correct.

Explanation:

$\because$ In an equilateral triangle all the centres lie on the same point.

Level-2: INTERMEDIATE

1. **Option (B) is correct.**

Explanation: ΔABC is an equilateral Δ

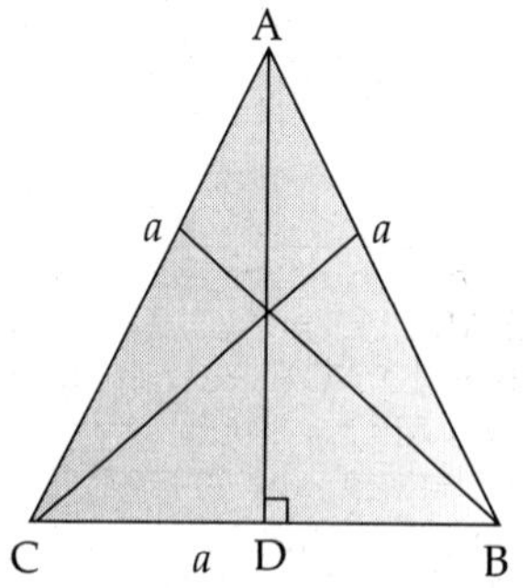

So, circumradius of an eq. $\Delta = \frac{a}{\sqrt{3}} = 12$

$\Rightarrow \quad a = 12\sqrt{3}$

Now, $AD \perp BC$

$\therefore \quad BD = 6\sqrt{3}$

$$\Delta ABD, \quad AD = \sqrt{AB^2 - BD^2}$$
$$= \sqrt{(12\sqrt{3})^2 - (6\sqrt{3})^2}$$
$$= \sqrt{(12\sqrt{3}+6\sqrt{3})(12\sqrt{3}-6\sqrt{3})}$$
$$= \sqrt{18\sqrt{3} \times 6\sqrt{3}}$$
$$= \sqrt{18 \times 18} = 18 \text{ cm}$$

2. **Option (C) is correct.**

Explanation:

Here, $\angle BOC = 90 + \frac{A}{2}$

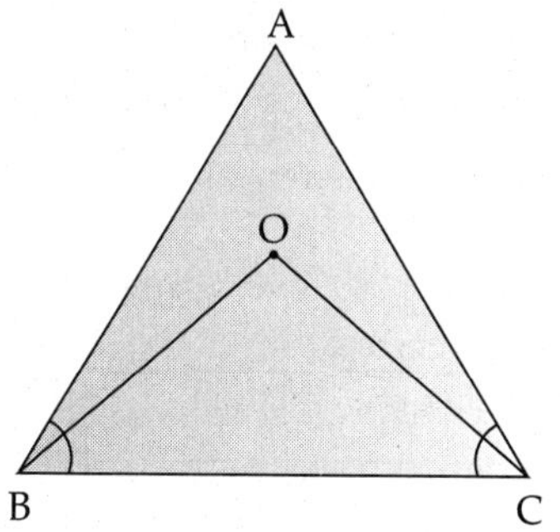

$$= 90 + \frac{40}{2} = 90 + 20 = 110°$$

3. **Option (D) is correct.**

Explanation:

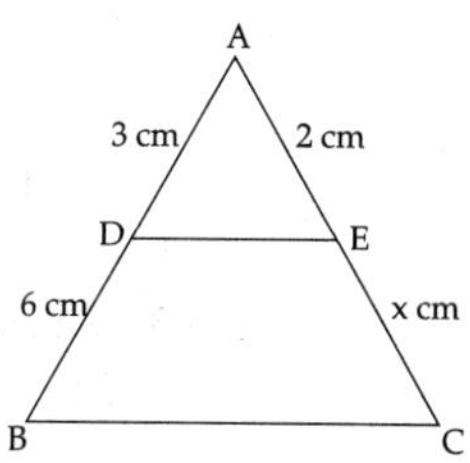

As shown in above diagram,

In ΔABC, $AD = 3$ cm,

$BD = 6$ cm

So, $AB = 6 + 3 = 9$ cm

$AE = 2$ cm,

Let $EC = x$ cm

So, $AC = (2 + x)$ cm

As DE || BC, then by triangle property,

$$\Rightarrow \frac{AB}{AD} = \frac{AC}{AE} \Rightarrow \frac{9}{3} = \frac{2+x}{2} \Rightarrow 18 = 6 + 3x \Rightarrow x = 4$$

So, CE = 4 cm

4. **Option (A) is correct.**

Explanation:

Given, $AB = AC$

$\angle A = 40°$

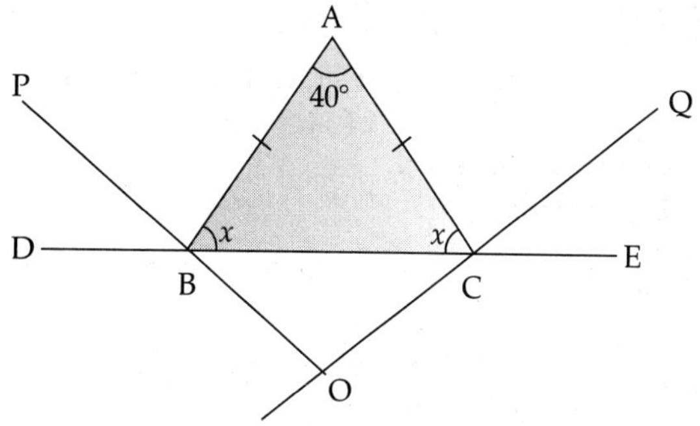

$$\angle B + \angle A + \angle C = 180°$$
$$2x = 180° - 40°$$
$$x = \frac{140}{2} = 70°$$

$\therefore \quad \angle ABD = \angle ACE$

$= 180 - 70 = 110°$ [linear pair]

$\therefore \quad \angle PBD = 55° = \angle CBO$

$\angle QCE = \angle BCO = 55°$

$\therefore \quad \angle BOC = 180° - 2 \times 55°$

$= 180 - 110° = 70°$

5. **Option (C) is correct.**

Explanation: X and Y are the mid points of AB and AC

So, XY || BC

Also, by AA–similarity

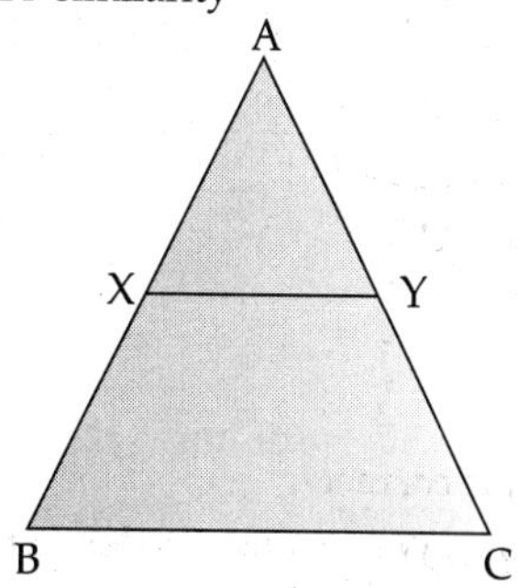

$\Delta AXY \sim \Delta ABC$

$$\therefore \quad \frac{AX}{AB} = \frac{XY}{BC}$$

So $$\frac{AX}{2AX} = \frac{XY}{BC} \Rightarrow \frac{BC}{XY} = 2$$

Using C & D (Componendo and Dividendo)

$$\frac{BC+XY}{BC-XY} = \frac{2+1}{2-1}$$

$$\Rightarrow \quad \frac{12}{BC-XY} = 3$$

$$= \frac{12}{3} = 4 \text{ units.}$$

6. **Option (C) is correct.**

Explanation:

Given that ΔABC and ΔPQR are similar triangle.

$$\text{Ar. } \Delta ABC = 64 \text{ cm}^2$$

$$\text{Ar. } \Delta PQR = 121 \text{ cm}^2$$

$$QR = 15.4 \text{ cm}$$

Using similar triangle property,

$$\Rightarrow \frac{\text{Ar. } \Delta ABC}{\text{Ar. } \Delta PQR} = \left(\frac{BC}{QR}\right)^2$$

$$\Rightarrow \frac{64}{121} = \left(\frac{BC}{15.4}\right)^2$$

$$\Rightarrow BC = 11.2 \text{ cm}$$

7. **Option (D) is correct.**

Explanation: Here AD is tangent, AB is a sucant.

So, $AD^2 = AP \times AB$

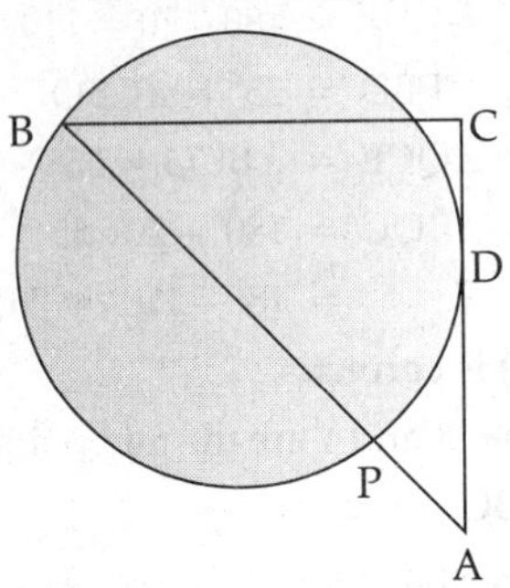

$$AP \times AB = AD^2$$

$$2.5 \times AB = \left(\frac{AB}{2}\right)^2$$

$$\frac{AB}{4} = 2.5$$

$$AB = 10 \text{ cm}$$

8. **Option (B) is correct.**

Explanation: We know that in a rt. angled Δ.

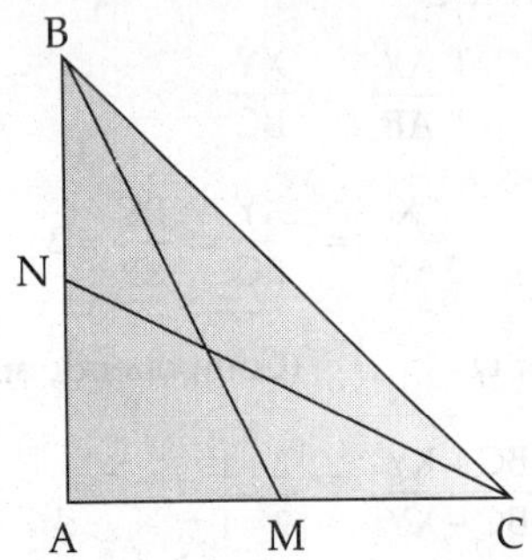

$4(BM^2 + CN^2) = 5BC^2$ always as given in above expression

$$\frac{(BM^2 + CN)^2}{BC^2} = \frac{5}{4}$$

9. **Option (B) is correct.**

Explanation:

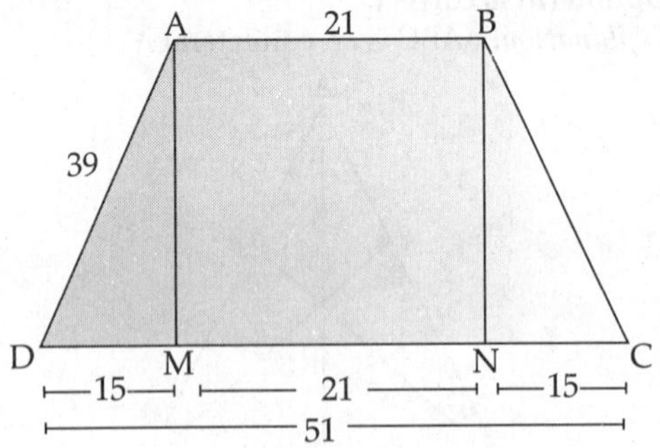

Here AM and BN are heights

∵ In ΔADM,

$$AM = \sqrt{(39)^2 - (15)^2}$$

$$= \sqrt{(39+15)(39-15)}$$

$$= \sqrt{54 \times 24}$$

$$AM = 36$$

Area of a trapezium: $\frac{1}{2}(AB + CD) \times h$

$$= \frac{1}{2} \times 72 \times h$$

$$= \frac{1}{2} \times 72 \times 36 = 1296 \text{ cm}^2$$

10. **Option (B) is correct.**

Explanation: As given EF | BC

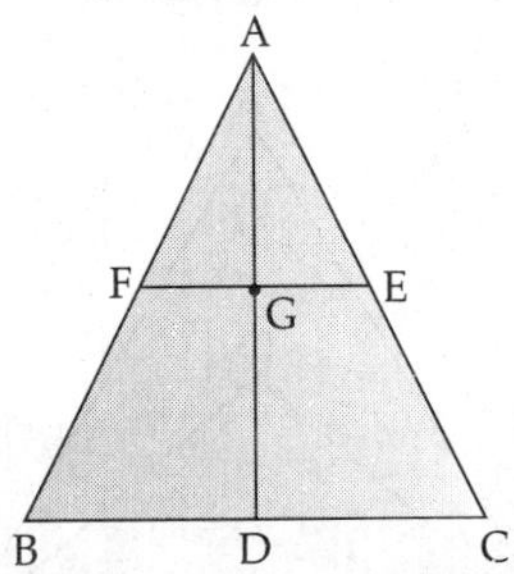

We conclude

$$\sqrt{\frac{ar.\Delta AFE}{ar.\Delta ABC}} = \frac{AG}{AD}$$

G divides a line into 2 : 1.

Let ar. of ΔABC = 2

ar. of ΔAFE = 1

So, $\frac{AG}{AD} = \sqrt{\frac{1}{2}} = \frac{1}{\sqrt{2}}$

$$GD = AD - AG = \sqrt{2} - 1$$

So, $GD : AG = (\sqrt{2} - 1) : 1$

11. Option (C) is correct.

Explanation: Using pythagoras is ΔABC

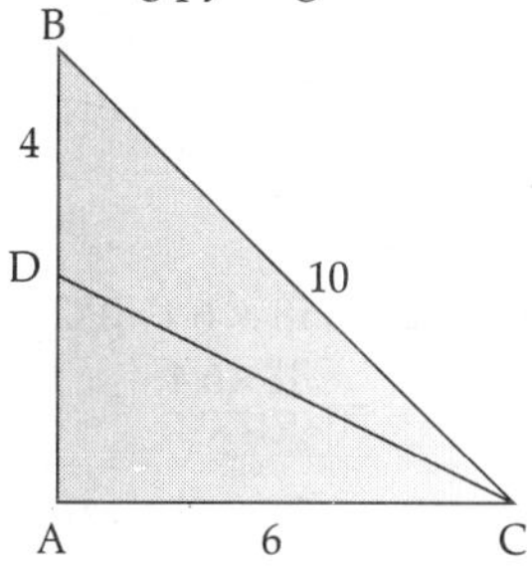

$$AB = \sqrt{10^2 - 6^2} = \sqrt{100-36} = 8$$

Also $AD = AB - BD = 8 - 4 = 4$ cm

Now, in ΔADC

$$DC = \sqrt{AD^2 + AC^2}$$

$$= \sqrt{4^2 + 6^2} = \sqrt{52} = 2\sqrt{13}$$

12. Option (A) is correct.

Explanation: By using Apollonius theorem

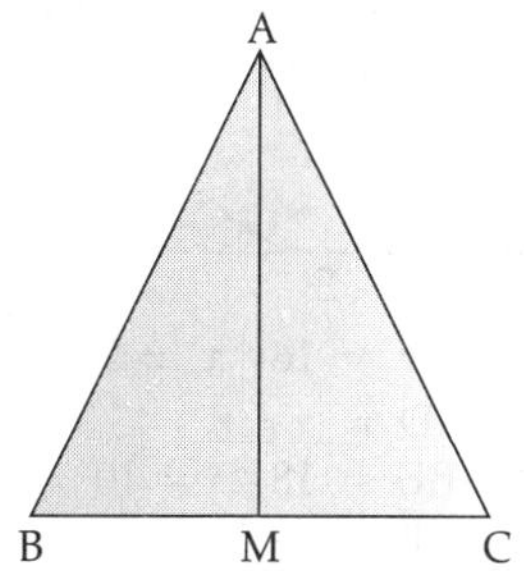

$$AB^2 + AC^2 = 2(AM^2 + BM^2)$$

$$16^2 + 63^2 = 2\left[AM^2 + \left(\frac{65}{2}\right)^2\right]$$

$$256 + 3969 = 2\left[AM^2 + \left(\frac{65}{2}\right)^2\right]$$

$$2112.5 = AM^2 + 1056.25$$

$$AM^2 = 1056.25$$

$$AM = \sqrt{1056.25} = 32.5$$

13. Option (D) is correct.

Explanation:

Given $\angle APB = 40°$, AP, PB are tangents

We know, $OA \perp AP$ and $AB \perp PB$

(angle by radius on tangent is 90°)

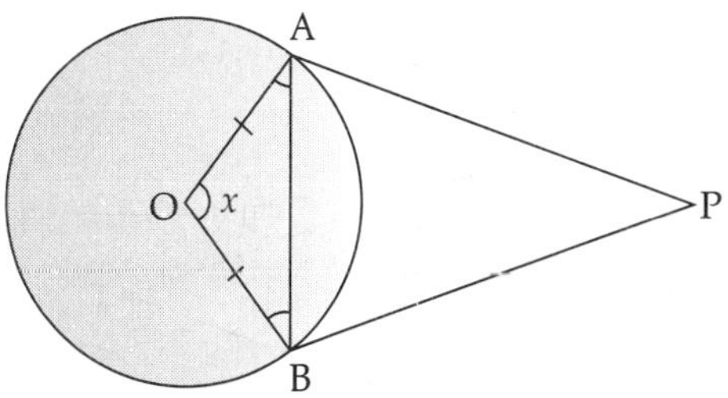

In ΔAPB

$\angle APB + \angle PBO + \angle BOA + \angle OAP$

$= 40° + 90° + x + 90° = 360°$

[sum of all angles of quadrilateral is 360°]

$$x = 360 - 220° = 140°$$

In ΔOAB, $\angle A = \angle B$ [OB = OA] radius

$\Rightarrow x + \angle A + \angle B = 180°$

$\Rightarrow 140° + 2\angle A = 180$

$\Rightarrow \angle A = 20°$

14. Option (B) is correct.

Explanation: Clearly in ΔAOD,

$OD \perp AB$

So, $AD = \sqrt{(13)^2 - (5)^2}$ Using triplet

$AD = 12$

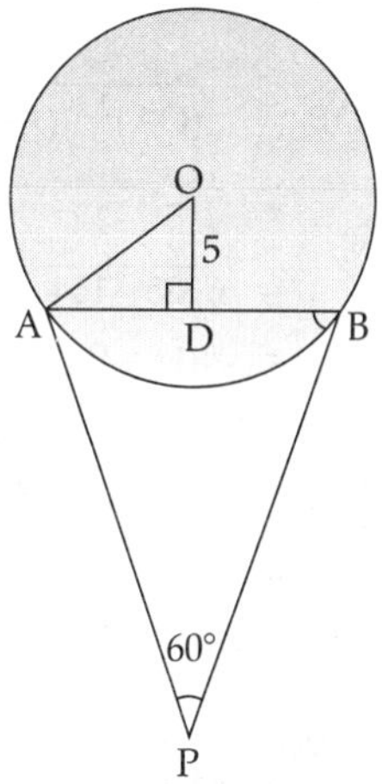

We know $AD = DB$

So $AB = 2AD = 2 \times 12 = 24$

[perpendicular drawn to the chord divides it in equal parts]

So, in ΔAPB

$\angle PAB = \angle ABP = 60°$

[tangent drawn from an external point to a circle are equal]

So, it is an equilateral Δ.

Hence, $AP = AB = 24$ cm

15. Option (D) is correct.

Explanation:

Given, $AQ = 11$, $PC = 8$ cm, $AC = 13$ cm

In a rt. angle triangle

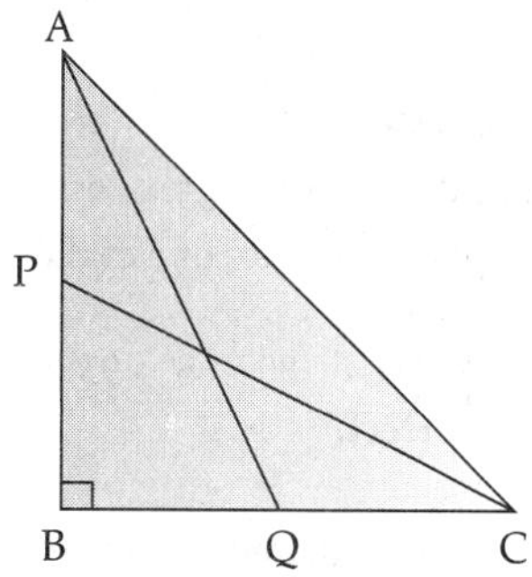

If P and Q are any points on sides AB, BC, respectively then

$$AC^2 + PQ^2 - AQ^2 + PC^2$$

$$169 + PQ^2 = 121 + 64$$

$$PQ^2 = 185 - 169$$

$$PQ = \sqrt{16} = 4$$

16. Option (C) is correct.

Explanation:

Given $OA = 15$ $AO' = 37$

$AB = 24$

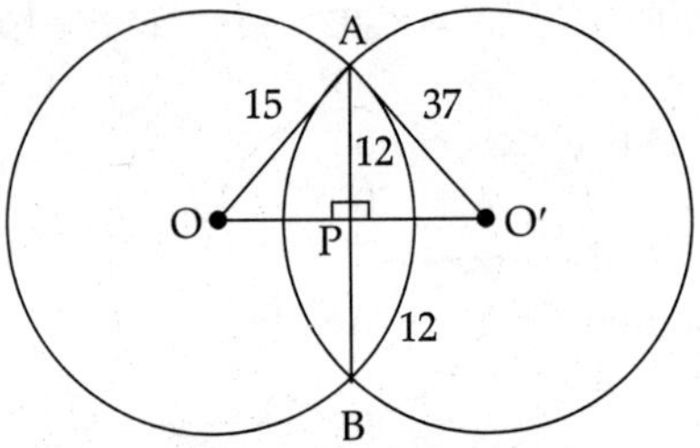

$$PB = AP = \frac{AB}{2} = \frac{24}{2} = 12$$

Now in ΔAOP

$$OP = \sqrt{(OA)^2 - (AP)^2}$$
$$= \sqrt{15^2 - 12^2}$$
$$= \sqrt{225 - 144}$$
$$= \sqrt{81} = 9$$

Again in ΔAO'P

$$O'P = \sqrt{(AO')^2 - (AP)^2}$$
$$= \sqrt{37^2 - 12^2} = 35$$

So, the distance between centres = OP + O'P = 9 + 35 = 44

17. Option (D) is correct.

Explanation:

Given, $\angle BAD = 68°, \angle AEB = 27°, \angle ABE = 85°$ [by angle sum properly in ΔABE]

In cyclic quadrilateral

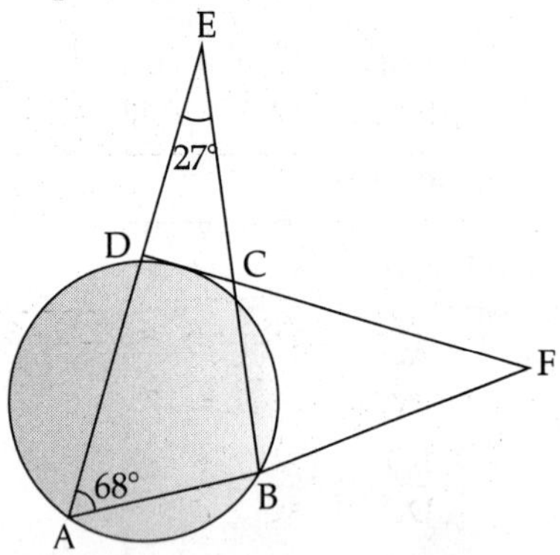

$\angle ADC = 180 - 85° = 95°$

[opposite angles of a cyclic quad. are 180°]

In ΔADF

$\angle AFD = 180 - 68° - 95° = 17°$

18. Option (B) is correct.

Explanation:

We know that only diameter can make an angle of 180° on centre of the circle.

So, according to the question,

Diameter of the circle = 36 cm

So, radius = $\frac{36}{2} = 18$ cm

19. Option (C) is correct.

Explanation: We know that

$$PA \times PB = PC \times PD$$

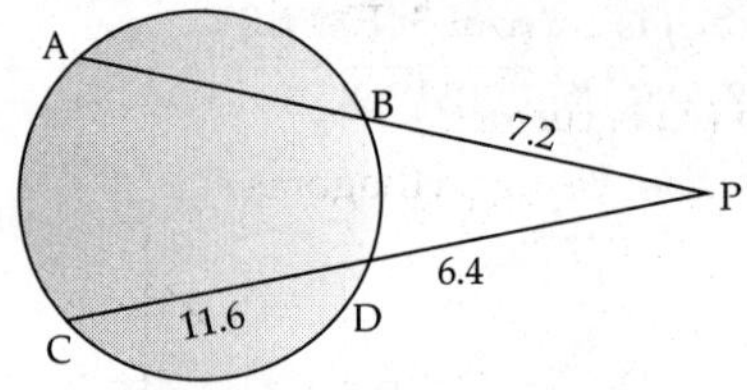

$$PA \times 7.2 = 18 \times 6.4 \quad [PC = 11.6 + 6.4 = 18]$$
$$PA = \frac{18 \times 6.4}{7.2} = 16 \text{ cm}$$
$$AB = PA - PB = 16 - 7.2 = 8.8$$

20. Option (C) is correct.

Explanation:

Given, AB = 18, BC = 15, AC = 13

If a circle is inscribed in Δ, then

AD = AF, BD = BE, FC = EC

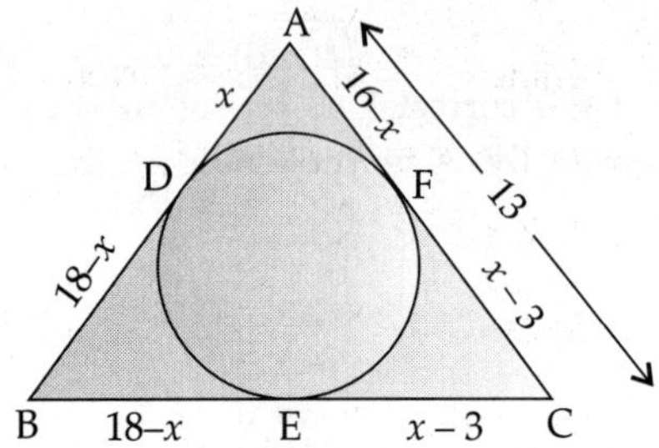

Here $x = 16 - x \Rightarrow 2x = 16, x = 8$

then, $AD = x = 8$

$BE = 18 - x = 10$

$CF = x - 3 = 8 - 3 = 5$

So, AD + DE + CF = 8 + 10 + 5 = 23

21. Option (A) is correct.

Explanation: Given, AD is a angle bisector of 'A'.

According to angle bisector theorem,

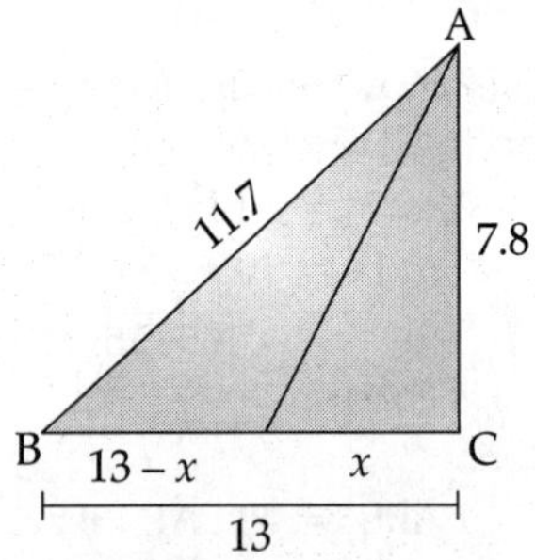

$$\frac{AB}{AC} = \frac{BD}{CD} \Rightarrow \frac{11.7}{7.8} = \frac{13 - x}{x}$$

$\Rightarrow x = 5.2$ cm

22. Option (C) is correct.

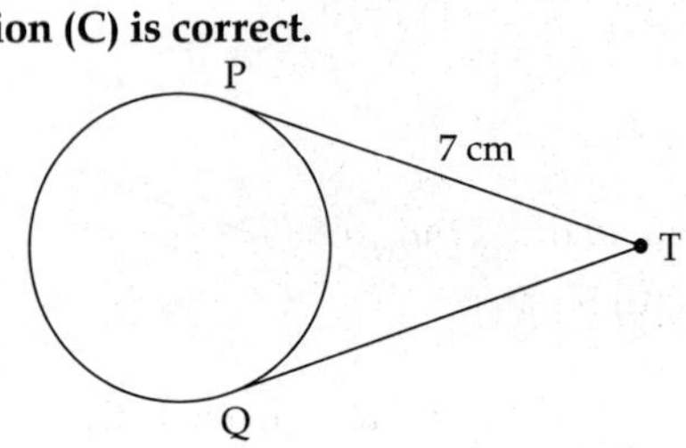

We have, the length of tangents drawn from a point will be of equal length.

So, TP = TQ = 7 cm

Level-3: EXPERT

1. **Option (A) is correct.**

Explanation: Using pythagoras

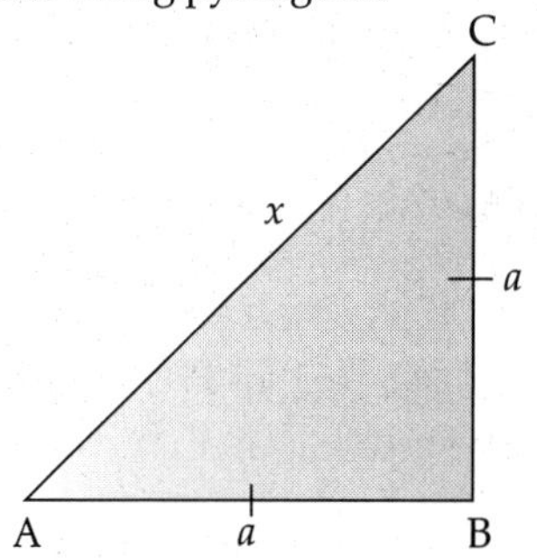

$$x^2 = a^2 + a^2$$

$$x = \sqrt{2a^2} = a\sqrt{2}$$

$$\text{Perimeter} = 8(\sqrt{2}+1) = \text{Given}$$

$$a + a + x = 8(\sqrt{2}+1)$$

$$2a + x = 8(\sqrt{2}+1)$$

$$2a + a\sqrt{2} = 8(\sqrt{2}+1) \quad [\because x = a\sqrt{2}]$$

$$a(\sqrt{2}+2) = 8(\sqrt{2}+1)$$

$$a = \frac{8(\sqrt{2}+1)}{2+\sqrt{2}} \times \frac{(2-\sqrt{2})}{(2-\sqrt{2})}$$

$$a = \frac{8\sqrt{2}}{4-2} = 4\sqrt{2}$$

$\therefore$ Length of AC $= 4\sqrt{2} \times \sqrt{2} = 4 \times 2 = 8$ cm

2. **Option (B) is correct.**

Explanation:

As shown in above diagram,

EC || AB and $\angle$EDC = 90°

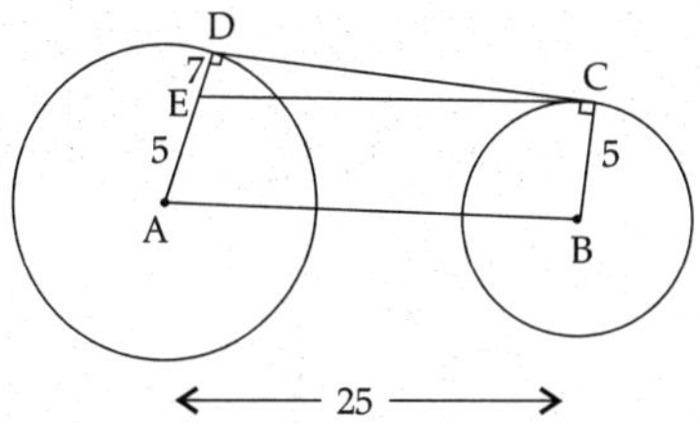

In Δ EDC, using pythagorus theorem,

$$EC^2 = ED^2 + DC^2$$

$\Rightarrow$ $25^2 = 7^2 + DC^2$

$\Rightarrow$ $DC^2 = 625 - 49$

$\Rightarrow$ $DC^2 = 576$

$\Rightarrow$ DC = 24

So, length of direct tangent = 24 cm.

3. **Option (C) is correct.**

Explanation:

Here, R = radius of circle C_1

r = radius of circle C_2

R + r = 286

Area of circle $= \pi r^2$

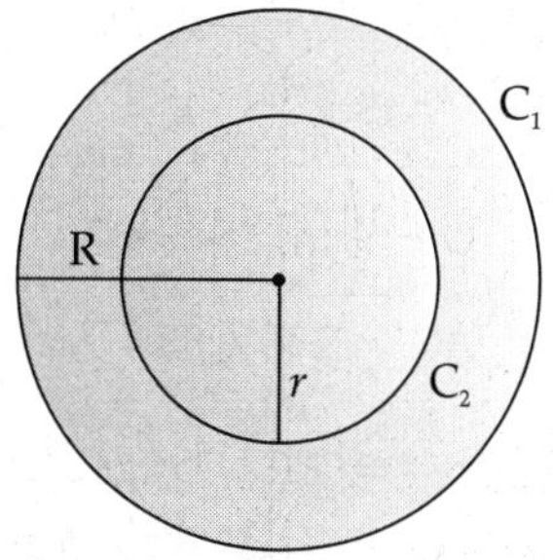

So, $\pi R^2 - \pi r^2 = 50336$

$$\pi(R^2 - r^2) = 50336$$

$$\frac{22}{7}(R+r)(R-r) = 50336$$

$$(R+r)(R-r) = \frac{50336 \times 7}{22}$$

$$(R+r)(R-r) = 2288 \times 7$$

$$(R-r) = \frac{2288}{286} \times 7 = 56$$

$$\therefore (R+r) + (R-r) = 286 + 56 = 342$$

$$R = 171, r = 115$$

4. **Option (B) is correct.**

Explanation: Here AD - angle bisector of $\angle$A.

from ΔABC

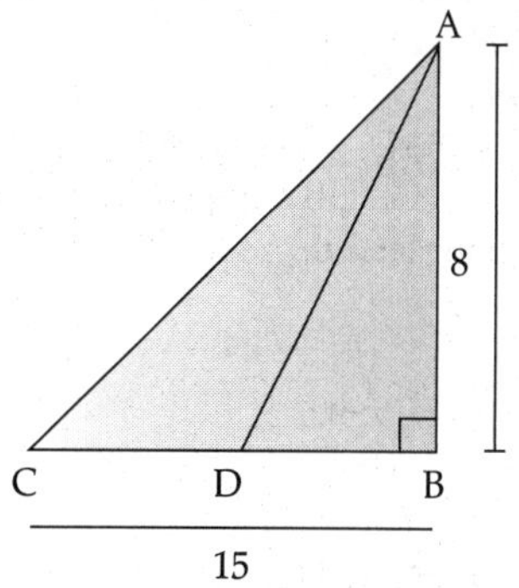

$$AC = \sqrt{15^2 + 8^2} = \sqrt{225 + 64}$$

So, $AC = \sqrt{289} = 17.$

Now, $\frac{BD}{DC} = \frac{AB}{AC} = \frac{8}{17}$

[angle bisector divides the sides of a triangle in the ratio $\frac{AB}{AC} = \frac{BD}{DC}$]

$$BD = \frac{8}{8+17} \times 15 = 4.8$$

5. **Option (C) is correct.**

Explanation:

Here, $\angle$DAP = 36°

$\angle$APC = 30 (Given)

$\angle$ADC = $\angle$DAP + $\angle$DPA

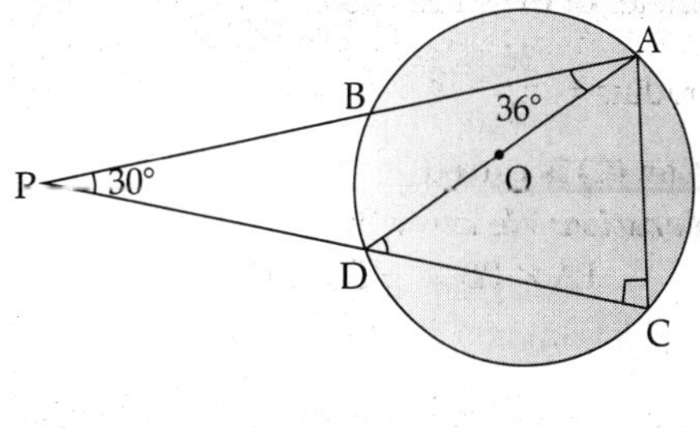

$$\angle ADC = 36° + 30° \text{ [Ex. angle property]}$$
$$\angle ADC = 66°$$
$$\angle ACD = 90° \text{ [angle subtended by a diameter at circumference is 90°]}$$

Now, using angle sum property in ΔACD

$$\angle CAD = 180 - [90 + 66°]$$
$$= 180 - 156 = 24°$$
$$\angle CBD = \angle CAD = 24°$$

[angles at the circumference of the circle by the same chord are equal]

6. **Option (D) is correct.**

Explanation: Here, $r_1 = 5, r_2 = 20$

DCT when only radii are given.

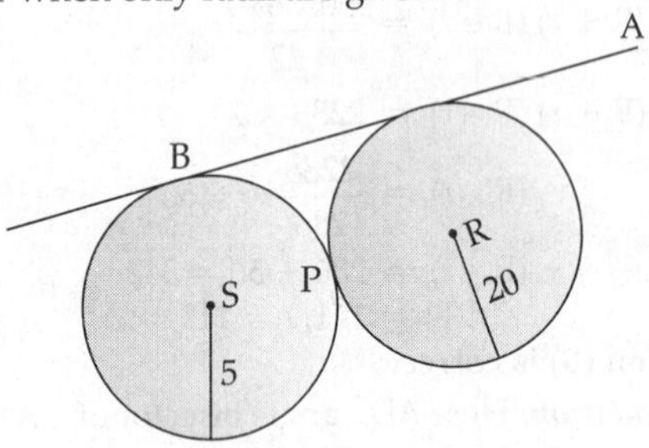

$$DCT = \sqrt{(r_2 + r_1)^2 - (r_2 - r_1)^2}$$
$$AB = \sqrt{(20+5)^2 - (20-5)^2}$$
$$= \sqrt{(25)^2 - (15)^2} = \sqrt{625 - 225}$$
$$= \sqrt{400} = 20 \text{ cm}$$

7. **Option (A) is correct.**

Explanation:

In ΔABC $\angle B = 90°$

Let $AB = 8$ and $BC = 6$ cm

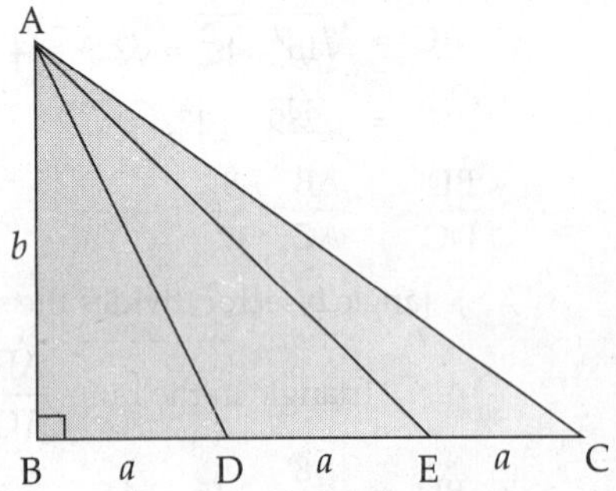

So,
$$AC^2 = b^2 + 9a^2 = 100 \text{ cm}$$
$$AD^2 = b^2 + a^2 = 68 \text{ cm}$$
$$AE^2 = b^2 + 4a^2 = 80 \text{ cm}$$

By hit and trial method

$$8(AE)^2 = 3(AC)^2 + 5(AD)^2$$
$$8(80) = 3(100) + 5(68)$$
$$340 = 300 + 340$$
$$640 = 640$$

8. **Option (C) is correct.**

Explanation:

As shown in diagram, P and Q are the centre of circles and AB is common chord.

In Δ ACQ, using pythagoras theorem,

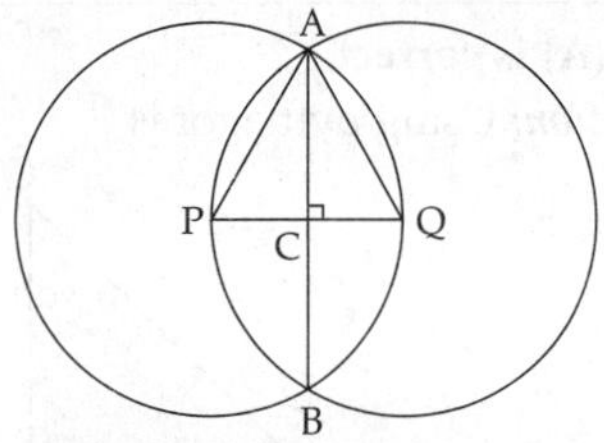

$$AQ^2 = AC^2 + CQ^2$$
$$\Rightarrow \quad r^2 = (7\sqrt{3})^2 + \left(\frac{r}{2}\right)^2$$
$$\Rightarrow \quad r = 14$$

So, circumference of both circles $= 2 \times 2\pi r$

$$= 2 \times 2 \times \frac{22}{7} \times 14 = 176 \text{ cm}$$

9. **Option (A) is correct.**

Explanation: In this type of question, directly sue Apollonius theorem,

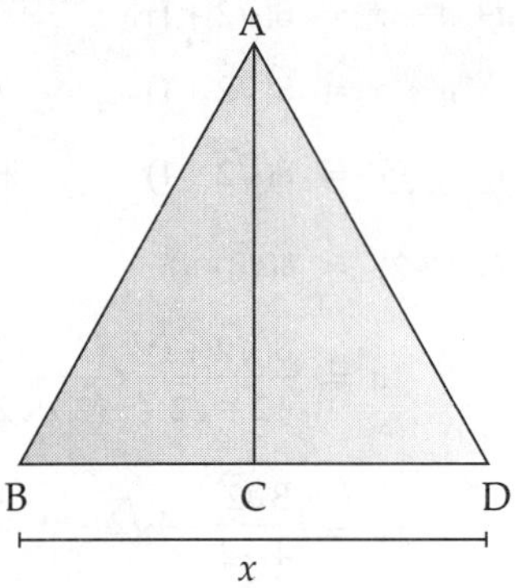

Here, C is the mid point of BD

$\Rightarrow$ AC is the median

$$AC = \frac{\sqrt{2AB^2 + 2AD^2 - BD^2}}{2}$$
$$9 = \frac{\sqrt{2(10)^2 + 2(12)^2 - (x)^2}}{2}$$
$$= \sqrt{200 + 288 - x^2}$$
$$x^2 = (200 + 288) - 324$$
$$x = \sqrt{488 - 324}$$
$$x = \sqrt{184} = 2\sqrt{41}$$

10. **Option (B) is correct.**

Explanation: AC = diameter

Given $\angle CAE = 34°$

$\angle E = 30°$

ABCD is a quadrilateral inscribed in a circle.

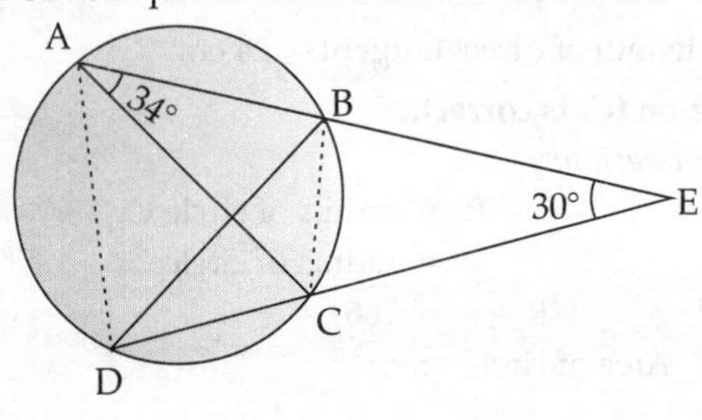

$$\angle ADC = 90° \quad \text{[AC is diameter]}$$

In ΔADE, $\angle DAC = 180° - [90° + 34° + 30°]$ [angle sum property]

$= 180° - [154°] = 26°$

$\angle DAC = \angle DBC = 26°$

[angle made by same chords are equal]

11. Option (D) is correct.

Explanation:

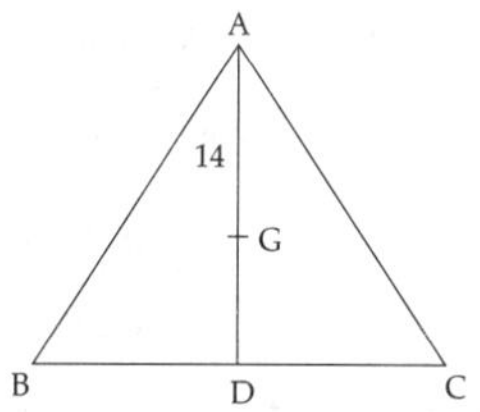

We know that centroid divides each median into segment with ratio of 2 : 1.

So, AG : GD = 2 : 1

Given that AG = 14 cm

$\therefore \quad GD = \frac{14}{2} = 7$ cm.

So, AD = AG + GD = 14 + 7 = 21 cm

12. Option (C) is correct.

Explanation:

No. of side $= x$

Each int. angle $= \frac{2x-4}{x} \times 90°$

So

$$\frac{\left(\frac{2\times x-4}{x}\right)\times 90°}{\frac{2\times 2x-4}{2x}\times 90} = \frac{3}{4}$$

$$\Rightarrow \quad \frac{2x-4}{x} \times \frac{2x}{4x-4} = \frac{3}{4}$$

$$\Rightarrow \quad \frac{4x-8}{x-1} = 3$$

$$\Rightarrow \quad x = 5$$

No. of sides are 5 and 10.

13. Option (B) is correct.

Explanation:

$\angle QSP = 90°$(angle of a semicircle = 90°)

In ΔPQS, $PS = \sqrt{35^2 - 28^2}$

$= \sqrt{(35+28)(35-28)}$

$= \sqrt{63\times 7} = 3 \times 7 = 21$ cm

Now, $\angle PSQ = \angle QSR$

$\angle PQS = \angle R$

So, $\Delta PSQ \sim \Delta QSR$

$QS^2 = PS \times SR$

$\Rightarrow \quad 28 \times 28 = 21 \times SR$

$SR = \frac{28\times 28}{21} = 37.33$

14. Option (B) is correct.

Explanation:

Given, $\angle ABC = 90°$

$\angle ACB = 60°$

DC_1 = radius = 2

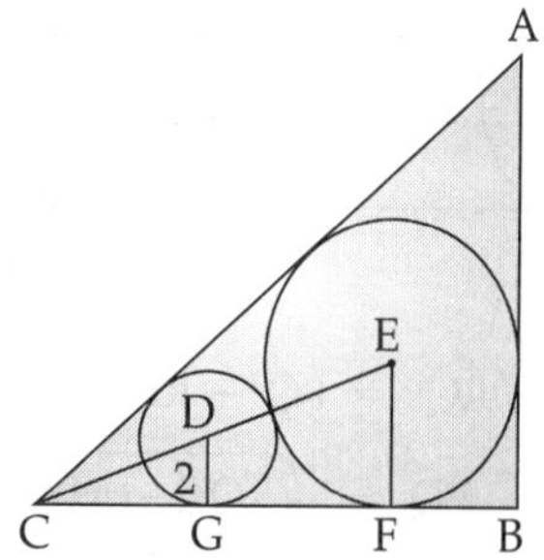

Now, $\sin 30° = \frac{DG}{CD}$

$\frac{1}{2} = \frac{2}{CD}$

$\Rightarrow \quad CD = 4$ cm

$\Delta CDG \sim \Delta CFE$ (by AA similarity rule)

$\therefore \quad \frac{DG}{EF} = \frac{CD}{CE}$

$\Rightarrow \quad \frac{2}{x} = \frac{4}{4+2+x} \quad (x = EF)$

$\Rightarrow \quad \frac{1}{x} = \frac{2}{6+x}$

$\Rightarrow \quad x = 6$ cm

15. Option (C) is correct.

Explanation:

Here, AO = 26

Also radius = PO = OQ = 10 cm

In ΔAPO,

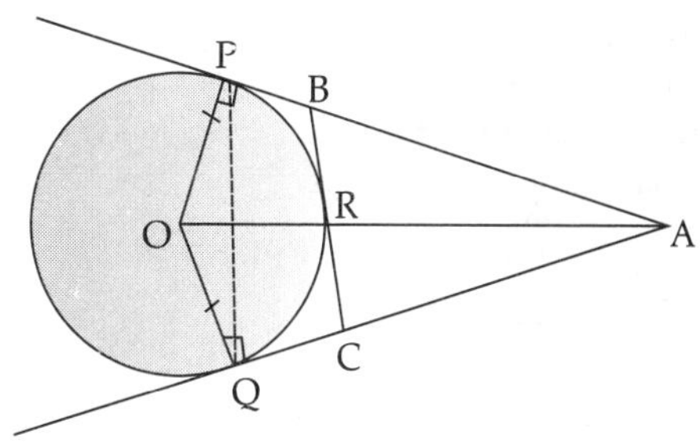

Apply pythagoras

$AP = \sqrt{(AO)^2 - (OP)^2}$

$= \sqrt{26^2 - 10^2} = 24$

AP = AQ = 24 cm

[tangents drawn from an external point to a circle are equal]

Also we know,

AP + AQ = AB + BC + AC

24 + 24 = AB + BC + AC

the perimeter of ΔABC = 24 + 24 = 48 cm.

16. Option (A) is correct.

Explanation: Clearly, ΔRPQ is rt. angle triangle

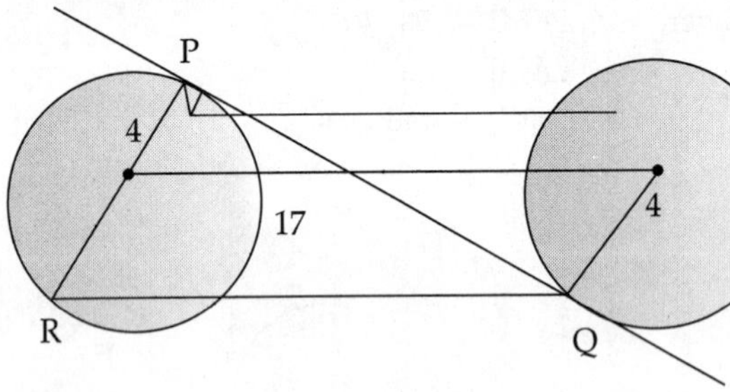

So, $$RQ^2 = PQ^2 + RP^2$$

$$PQ = \sqrt{(RQ)^2 - (RP)^2}$$

$$= \sqrt{(17)^2 - (8)^2} = \sqrt{289 - 84}$$

$$= 15 \text{ cm}$$

17. Option (B) is correct.

Explanation: Ratio of areas of ΔABC and DEF = 9 : 25

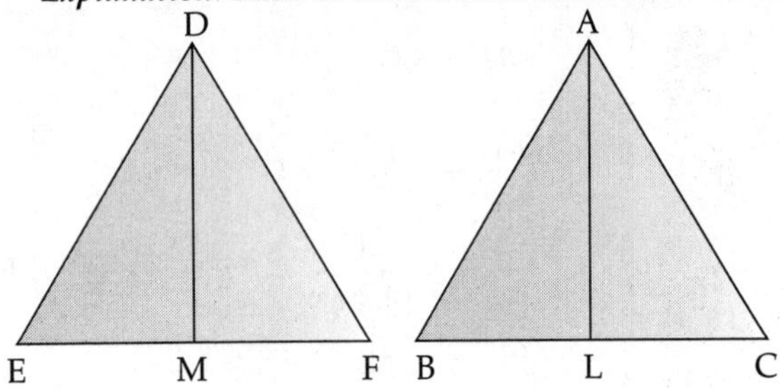

$$\frac{\text{area of } \Delta ABC}{\text{area of } \Delta DEF} = \frac{9}{25} = \left(\frac{AL}{DM}\right)^2$$

$$\frac{AL}{DM} = \sqrt{\frac{9}{25}}$$

$$\Rightarrow \quad \frac{AL}{DM} = \frac{3}{5}$$

Then $$\frac{DM + AL}{DM - AL} = 4 : 1$$

18. Option (D) is correct.

Explanation: In a rt. triangle

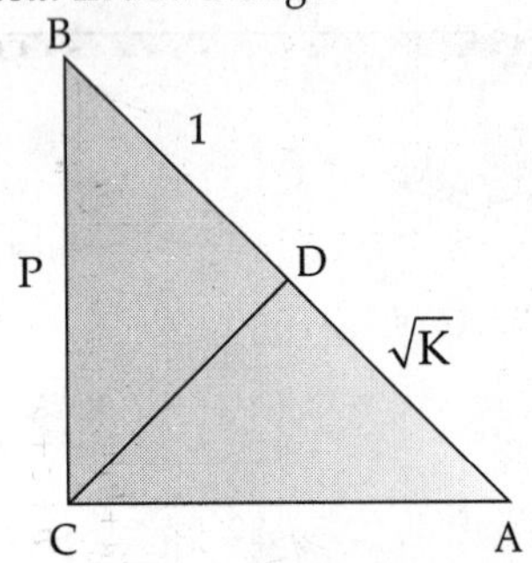

$$CD^2 = AD \times BD$$

$$CD^2 = \sqrt{K}$$

$$CD = \sqrt[4]{K}$$

Again in ΔADC,

$$AC = \sqrt{AD^2 + CD^2}$$

$$AC = \sqrt{K + \sqrt{K}}$$

In ΔBDC, $$BC = \sqrt{(BD)^2 + (CD)^2}$$

$$= \sqrt{1 + \sqrt{K}}$$

$$\therefore \quad \frac{AC}{BC} = \frac{\sqrt{K + \sqrt{K}}}{\sqrt{1 + \sqrt{K}}}$$

$$= \sqrt[4]{K} . \sqrt{\frac{\sqrt{K} + 1}{\sqrt{K} + 1}} = \sqrt[4]{K}$$

19. Option (D) is correct.

Explanation: We know in an equilateral Δ when 3 medians meet, we get this relation:

$\Rightarrow 3\,[AB^2 + BC^2 + AC^2] = 4\,[AD^2 + BE^2 + CF^2]$

Also we know,

$$AB = BC = \angle AC$$

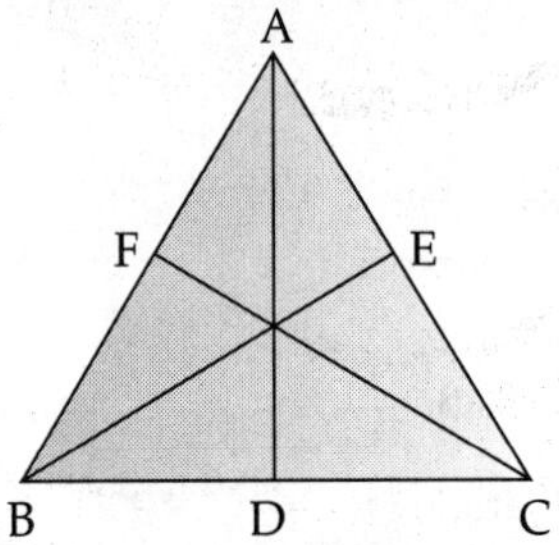

[$\because$ Altitude, median and angle bisector are equal in equilateral triangle]

Put the value in the above relation

$$3\,[3\,AC^2] = 4\,[3\,BE^2]$$

$$3AC^2 = 4BE^2$$

Also, $$\frac{AC^2}{BE^2} = \frac{4}{3}$$

20. Option (A) is correct.

Explanation: Given $AM \perp BC$

AN is angle bisector.

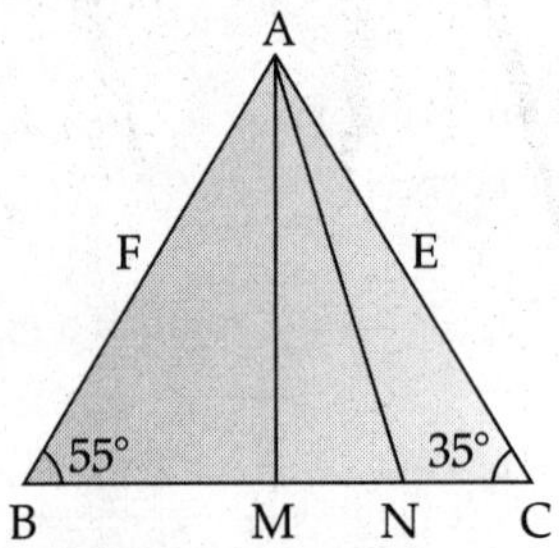

Always remember,

The angle made between a $\perp$ and an angle bisector is

$$\angle MAN = \frac{1}{2}(\angle B - \angle C)$$

$$= \frac{1}{2}(55° - 35°) = 10°$$

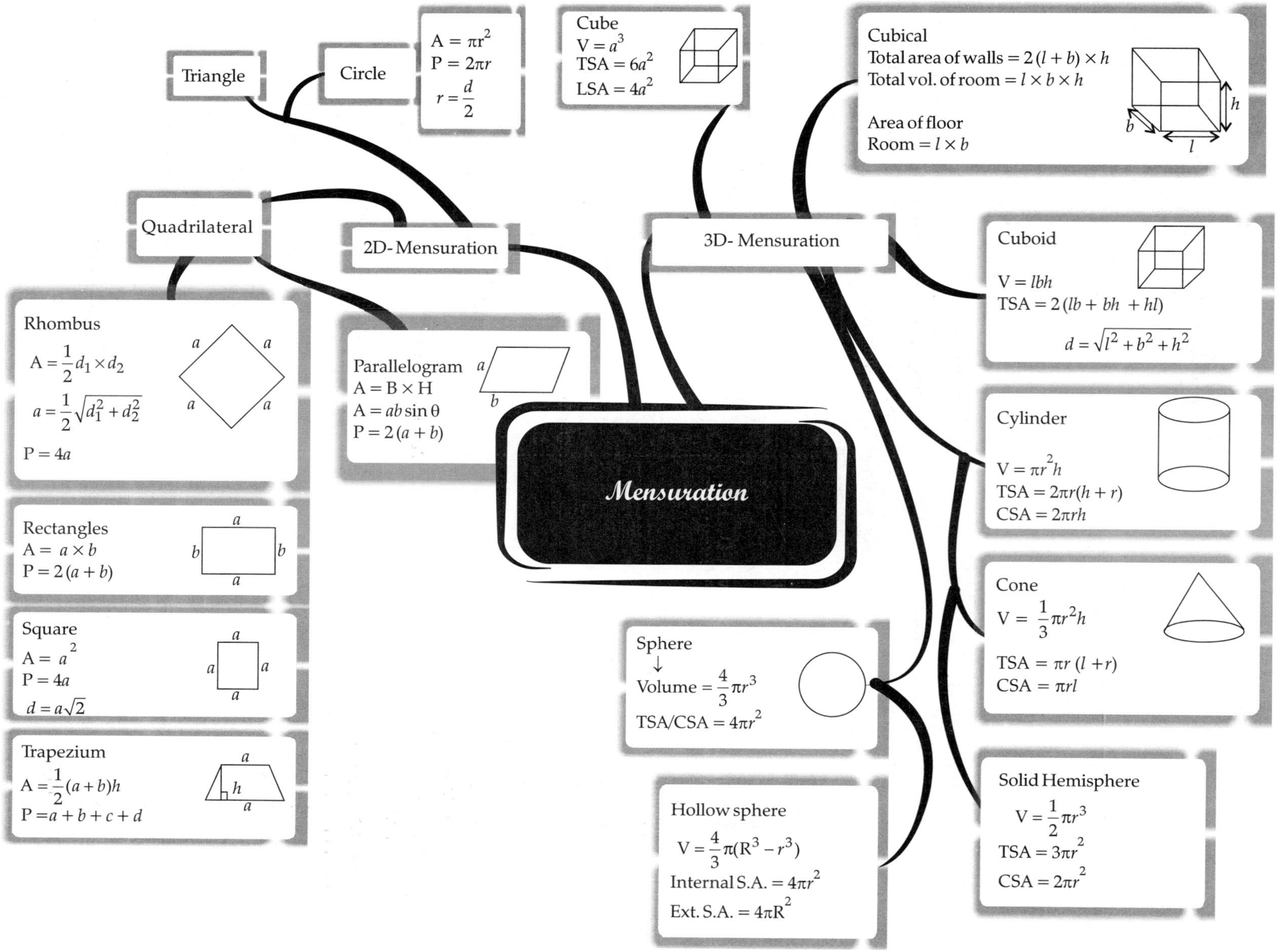
Mensuration
2D-Mensuration
3D- Mensuration
Triangle
Circle
$A = \pi r^2$
$P = 2\pi r$
$r = \frac{d}{2}$
Quadrilateral
Rhombus
$A = \frac{1}{2} d_1 \times d_2$
$a = \frac{1}{2}\sqrt{d_1^2 + d_2^2}$
$P = 4a$
Rectangles
$A = a \times b$
$P = 2(a + b)$
Square
$A = a^2$
$P = 4a$
$d = a\sqrt{2}$
Trapezium
$A = \frac{1}{2}(a + b)h$
$P = a + b + c + d$
Parallelogram
$A = B \times H$
$A = ab \sin\theta$
$P = 2(a + b)$
Cube
$V = a^3$
$TSA = 6a^2$
$LSA = 4a^2$
Cubical
Total area of walls $= 2(l + b) \times h$
Total vol. of room $= l \times b \times h$
Area of floor
Room $= l \times b$
Cuboid
$V = lbh$
$TSA = 2(lb + bh + hl)$
$d = \sqrt{l^2 + b^2 + h^2}$
Cylinder
$V = \pi r^2 h$
$TSA = 2\pi r(h + r)$
$CSA = 2\pi rh$
Cone
$V = \frac{1}{3}\pi r^2 h$
$TSA = \pi r(l + r)$
$CSA = \pi rl$
Sphere
↓
Volume $= \frac{4}{3}\pi r^3$
$TSA/CSA = 4\pi r^2$
Hollow sphere
$V = \frac{4}{3}\pi(R^3 - r^3)$
Internal S.A. $= 4\pi r^2$
Ext. S.A. $= 4\pi R^2$
Solid Hemisphere
$V = \frac{1}{2}\pi r^3$
$TSA = 3\pi r^2$
$CSA = 2\pi r^2$

Chapter 13 Mensuration

LEARNING OBJECTIVES:

- ❖ Basic concepts related to 2-dimensional and 3-dimensional mensuration.
- ❖ Perimeter, area of triangle and circle.
- ❖ Perimeter, area, diagonal and length of side of quadrilateral.
- ❖ Perimeter, area, volume and length of sides of prism and pyramid.
- ❖ Different types of questions asked in various competitive exams.
- ❖ Method of solving questions.

2-D MENSURATION

2-D–TWO DIMENSIONAL

➢ **Classification of 2D**

(1) Triangle
(2) Quadrilateral → Trapezium; → Parallelogram ↓ (1) Rectangle (2) Square (3) Rhombus
(3) Polygon
(4) Circle

➢ **Triangle (Area)**

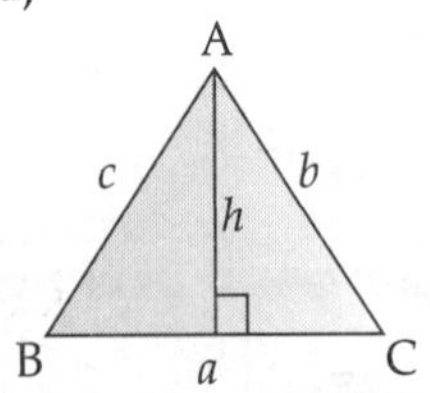

➢ Area of a triangle $= \frac{1}{2} \times \text{base} \times \text{height}$

➢ Area of triangle $= \frac{1}{2}bc\sin A = \frac{1}{2}ac\sin B = \frac{1}{2}ab\sin C$

➢ Area of triangle using Hero's formula

$$\text{Area} = \sqrt{s(s-a)(s-b)(s-c)}$$

where a, b, c are sides

$$\text{semi perimeter } s = \frac{a+b+c}{2}$$

➢ Area of an equilateral $\Delta = \frac{1}{2} \times \text{base} \times \text{height}$

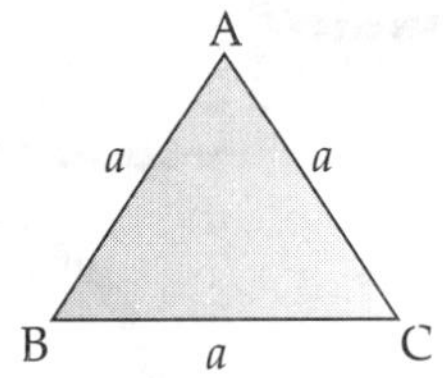

$$= \frac{1}{2}a \times \frac{\sqrt{3}}{2}a = \frac{\sqrt{3}a^2}{4}$$

$$\text{Height} = \frac{\sqrt{3}a}{2}$$

➢ Area of an isosceles triangle

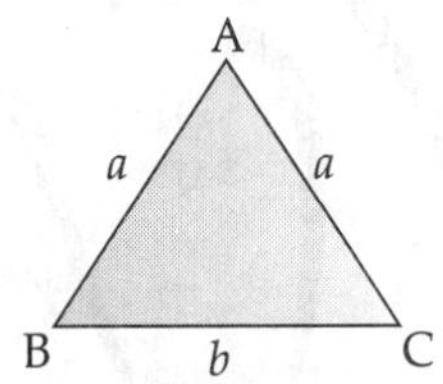

$$A = \frac{1}{4} \times b \times \sqrt{4a^2 - b^2}$$

Here, b = different side
a = similar sides

➢ **Area of similar triangles:** If two triangles are similar, all their corresponding angles are equal and the ratios of their corresponding sides are also equal.

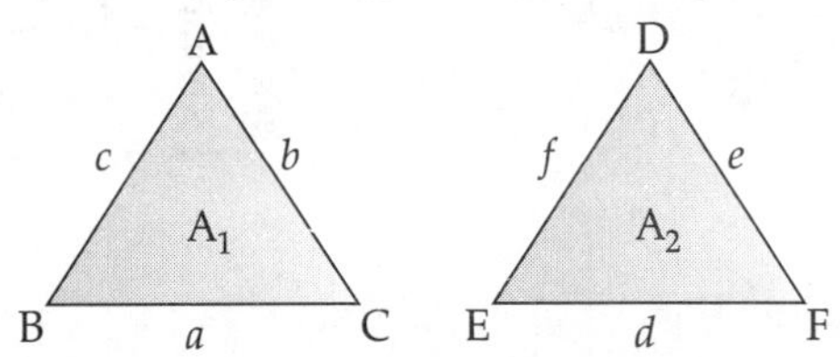

$\Delta ABC \sim \Delta DEF$

$$\frac{A_1}{A_2} = \left(\frac{BC}{EF}\right)^2 = \left(\frac{AC}{DF}\right)^2 = \left(\frac{AB}{DE}\right)^2$$

Example 1: Two triangles ABC and DEF are similar to each other. If AB = 10 cm, DE = 8 cm, then the ratio of the area of triangles ABC and DEF is:

(a) 25 : 16 (b) 64 : 125

(c) 4 : 7 (d) 4 : 5

Sol. (a) Given AB = 10 cm

DE = 8 cm

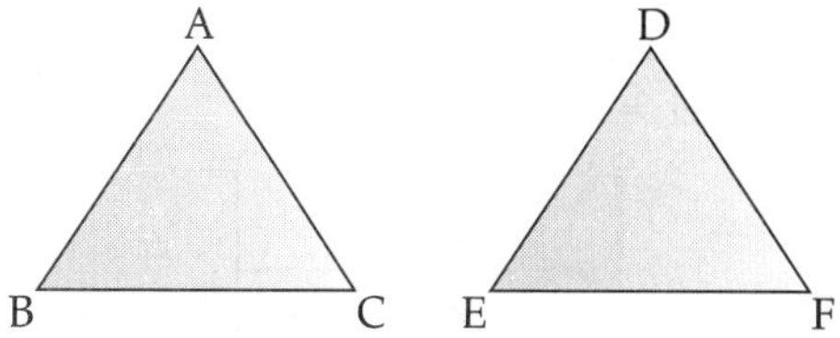

We know $\Delta ABC \sim \Delta DEF$

$$\text{So, } \frac{Ar.(\Delta ABC)}{Ar.(\Delta DEF)} = \left(\frac{AB}{DE}\right)^2 = \left(\frac{10}{8}\right)^2 = \left(\frac{5}{4}\right)^2 = \frac{25}{16}$$

Example 2: The area of two similar triangles ABC and DEF is 20 cm^2 and 45 cm^2, respectively. If AB = 5 cm, then DE is equal to:

(a) 6.5 cm (b) 7.5 cm

(c) 8.5 cm (d) 5.5 cm

Sol. (b) As given, $\Delta ABC \sim \Delta DEF$

$$\therefore \frac{Ar.(\Delta ABC)}{Ar.(\Delta DEF)} = \left(\frac{AB}{DE}\right)^2$$

Let DE = x cm

$$\frac{20}{45} = \left(\frac{5}{x}\right)^2$$

$$\Rightarrow \sqrt{\frac{4}{9}} = \frac{5}{x}$$

$$\Rightarrow \frac{2}{3} = \frac{5}{x}$$

$$\Rightarrow x = \frac{5\times 3}{2} = 7.5 \text{ cm}$$

So, DE = 7.5 cm

Hence, option (b) is the correct answer.

Example 3: The base of a triangle is 15 cm and height is 12 cm. The height of another triangle of double the area having base 20 cm is:

(a) 18 cm (b) 8 cm

(c) 12.5 cm (d) 9 cm

Sol. (a) In 1st triangle, $b = 15, h = 12$

$$A = \frac{1}{2}\times b\times h = \frac{1}{2}\times 15\times 12 = 90$$

In 2nd triangle,

Area = 2 × 90

$$\frac{1}{2}\times b\times h = 180$$

$$\frac{1}{2}\times 20\times h = 180$$

$$h = 18$$

Hence, option (a) is the correct answer.

QUADRILATERALS

➢ A quadrilaterals is a four-sided closed figure. It is denoted as '▱' ABCD.

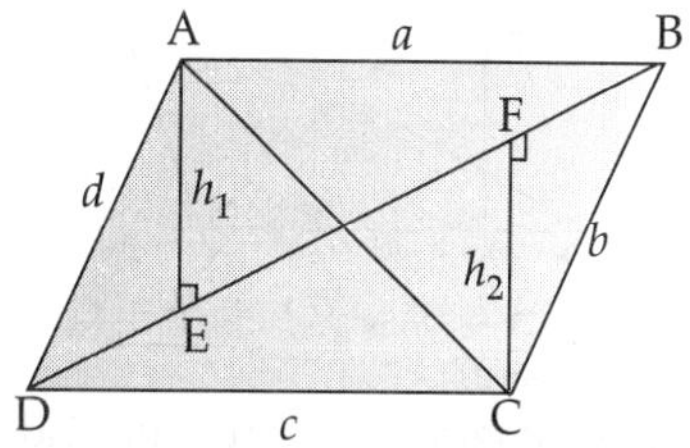

SOME IMPORTANT FACTS

- $\angle A + \angle B + \angle C + \angle D = 360°$

  Sum of all four angles is 360°
- Area of a quadrilateral ABCD = $\frac{1}{2}(BD)(h_1 + h_2)$

  Here, h_1 and h_2 are heights and BD = diagonal

  or Area = $\frac{1}{2}\times d_1 \times d_2 \times \sin\theta$

  where θ is angle between diagonals.

  and d_1 - diagonal, d_2 - diagonal
- If the diagonals intersect at 90°, then

  $$a^2 + c^2 = b^2 + d^2$$

NOTE :

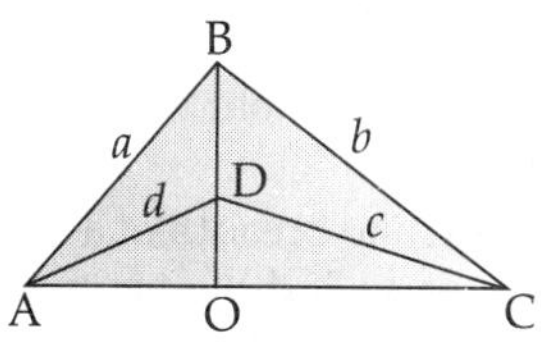

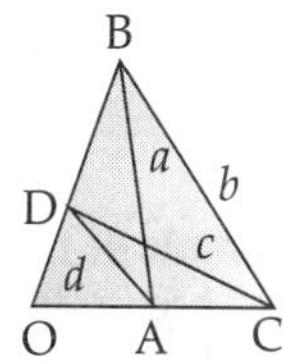

Here also,

$$a^2 + c^2 = b^2 + d^2$$

Quadrilaterals

1. Parallelogram 2. Square 3. Rectangle 4. Rhombus 5. Trapezium

Parallelogram (||gm)

➢ It is a type of quadrilateral which has equal opposite sides and equal opposite angles.

SOME IMPORTANT FACTS

- Opposite sides are equal.

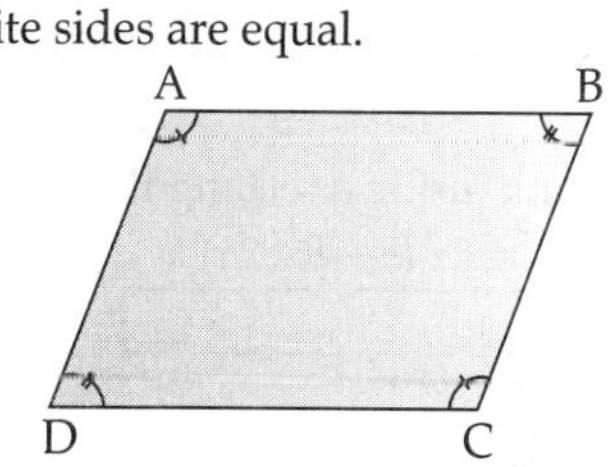

So, AB = DC and AD = BC

- Opposite angles are equal.
  So, $\angle A = \angle C$, $\angle B = \angle D$
- Sum of two adjacent angles is 180°.
  $\angle A + \angle B = 180°$, $\angle A + \angle D = 180°$,
  $\angle D + \angle C = 180°$, $\angle B + \angle C = 180°$
- Diagonals bisect each other. But diagonals need not be equal.

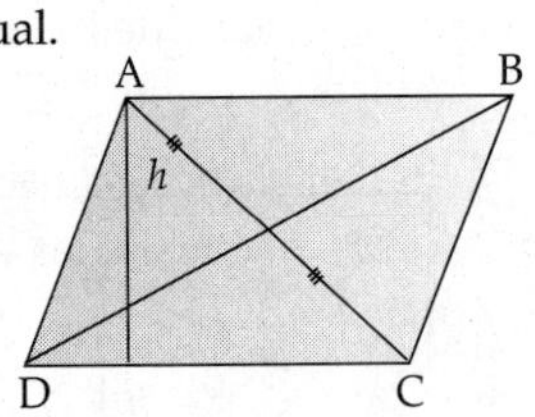

- Area of a ||gm = base × height = CD × h
  or = $l \times b \times \sin\theta$
  where l = length, b = breadth and θ is angle between adjacent sides.
- Each diagonal of a ||gm divides it is two congruent triangles.
  So, ΔABD ≅ ΔBCD
  ΔABC ≅ ΔADC

RECTANGLE

➤ A rectangle is a ||gm with each angle of 90°.
(a) Perimeter = $2(l + b)$
(b) Area = $l \times b$
(c) Both the diagonals are equal.

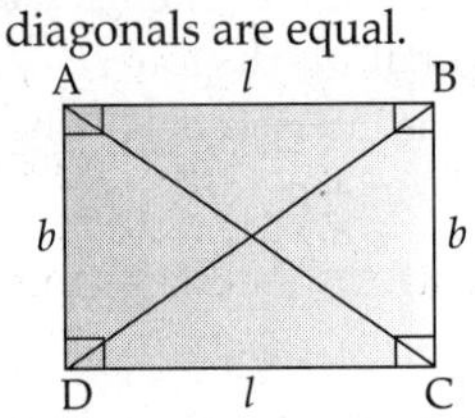

(d) Diagonals bisect each other but not necessarily at 90°.

Example 4: The length and breadth of a rectangular field are in the ratio of 3 : 2. If the perimeter of the field is 80 cm, its breadth (in m) is:

(a) 18 m (b) 16 m
(c) 10 m (d) 24 m

Sol. (b) Let $l = 3x$
$b = 2x$
Perimeter = $2(l + b)$
$80 = 2(3x + 2x)$
$80 = 2(5x)$
$40 = 5x$
$8 = x$

Now, breadth = $b = 2x = 2 \times 8 = 16$
Hence, option (b) is the correct answer.

SOME IMPORTANT POINTS RELATED TO RECTANGLE

- Area of a path inside a rectangular field.
  Area of path = $2x(l + b - 2x)$

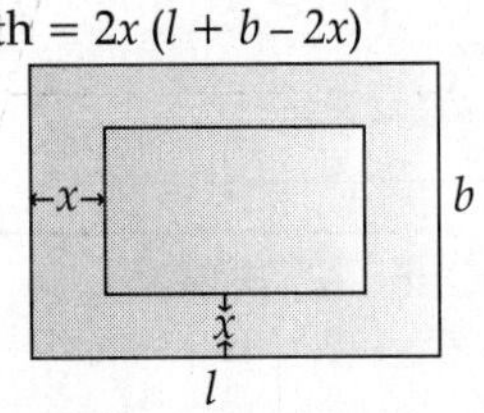

- Perimeter of path = inner peri + outer peri
  $= 4(l + b - 2x)$
- Area and perimeter of the path outside the rectangle
  Area = $2x(l + b + 2x)$
  Perimeter = $4(l + b + 2x)$

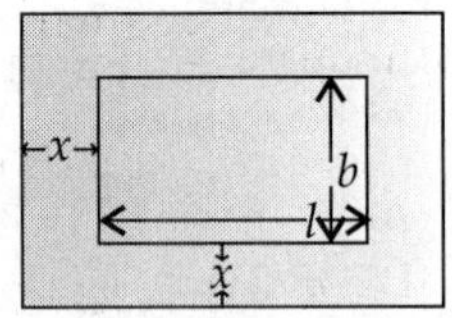

- Area of path mid way = $x(l + b - x)$
  Perimeter = $2(l + b - 2x)$

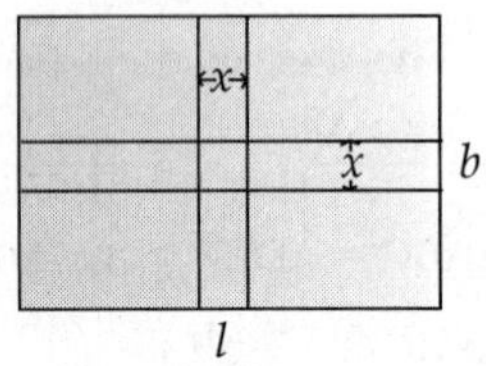

SQUARE

It is a rectangle with equal sides and each angle is 90°.

SOME IMPORTANT FACTS

- All sides are equal.

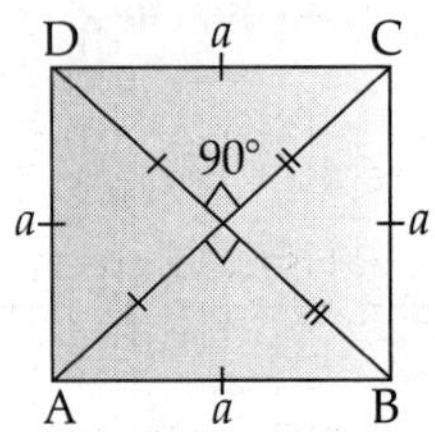

- All angles are equal, i.e., 90° each.
- Every square is a rhombus but vice versa is not possible.
- Perimeter = $4a$
- Area = $(\text{side})^2 = a^2 = \frac{d^2}{2}$ where d is the diagonal
  Diagonal = $a\sqrt{2}$
- Diagonals are equal and bisect each other.
- Diagonals are ⊥ to each other.
- After joining the mid points of adjacent sides, the figure obtained is a square.

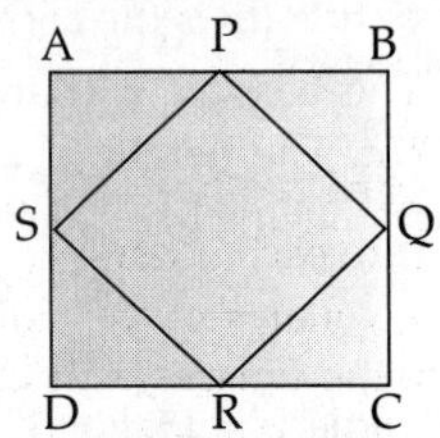

ABCD is a square and PQRS is also a square.

- If the area of a square is x cm², then the area of the circle formed by the same perimeter is = $\frac{4a^2}{\pi}$ cm².

Example 5: The length of a diagonal of a square is $15\sqrt{2}$ cm. Its area is :

(a) 225 (b) 112.5

(c) 450 (d) $\frac{225\sqrt{2}}{2}$

Sol. (a) Area of a square $= \frac{(\text{dia})^2}{2}$

$$= \frac{(15\sqrt{2})^2}{2}$$

$$= \frac{225 \times 2}{2} = 225 \text{ cm}^2$$

Hence, option (a) is the correct answer.

Example 6: The area of the square inscribed in a circle of radius 8 cm is:

(a) 128 (b) 256

(c) 125 (d) 250

Sol. (a) Given, $r = 8$

Dia $= AC = r + r = 16$

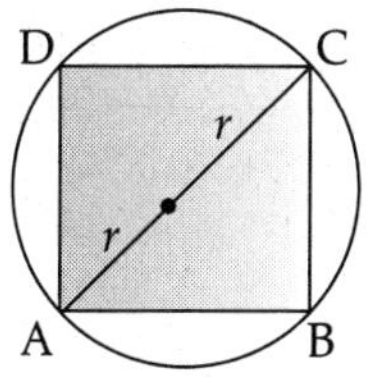

$$\text{Area of square} = \frac{(\text{dia})^2}{2} = \frac{16^2}{2} = \frac{256}{2} = 128 \text{ cm}^2$$

Hence, option (a) is the correct answer.

RHOMBUS

- It is *a* ||gm having all 4 sides equal.

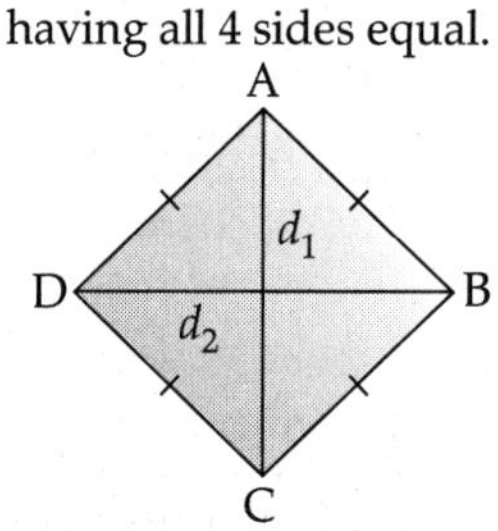

(a) Area $= \frac{1}{2} \times d_1 \times d_2$

(b) Area = (side)^2 × sinθ

(c) Area = base × height

(d) All sides are equal.

(e) Diagonals bisect each other at 90°.

(f) Diagonals are ⊥ to each other.

(g) The sum of the squares of the sides of a rhombus is equal to sum of the squares of its diagonal.

$$d_1^2 + d_2^2 = 4a^2 \qquad \text{where } a = \text{side}$$

(h) Opposite angles are equal.

Example 7: The area of a rhombus is 150 cm^2. The length of one of its diagonals is 10 cm. The length of the other diagonal is:

(a) 25 cm (b) 35 cm

(c) 30 cm (d) 40 cm

Sol. (c) Given, area of rhombus $= \frac{d_1 \times d_2}{2}$

$$150 = \frac{d_1 \times d_2}{2}$$

$$150 = \frac{10 \times d_2}{2}$$

$$10d_2 = 300$$

$$d_2 = 30 \text{ cm}$$

Hence, option (c) is the correct answer.

Example 8: The ratio of the angles ∠A and ∠B of a non-square rhombus ABCD is 4 : 5, then the value of ∠C is :

(a) 45° (b) 50°

(c) 80° (d) 90°

Sol. (c) We know,

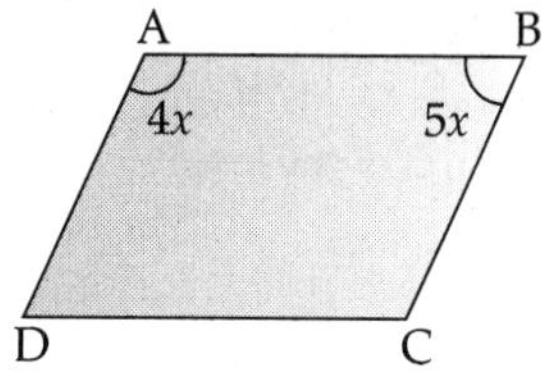

Adjacents are supplementary

So, $4x + 5x = 180°$

$$9x = 180$$

$$x = 20°$$

$$\angle C = \angle A = 4\,(20)$$

[Opposite angles are equal]

$$= 80°$$

Hence, option (c) is the correct answer.

TRAPEZIUM

- It is a quadrilateral with two parallel sides and two non-parallel sides.

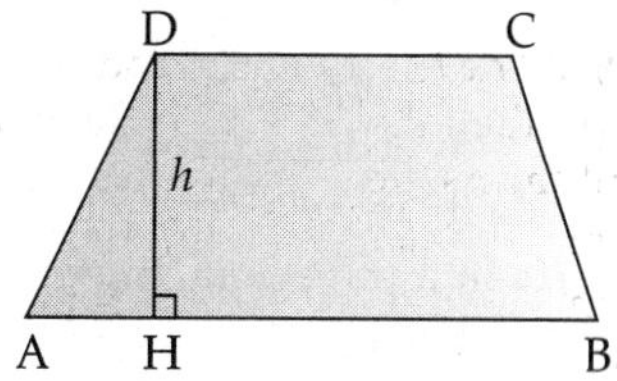

Here, CD and AB are parallel sides.

AD and CB are non-parallel sides.

h is the height.

SOME IMPORTANT FACTS

- Area $= \frac{1}{2} \times$ (sum of parallel sides) × height

$$= \frac{1}{2} \times (AB + CD) \times DH = \frac{1}{2}(AB + CD) \times h$$

- ∠A + ∠D = ∠B + ∠C = 180°

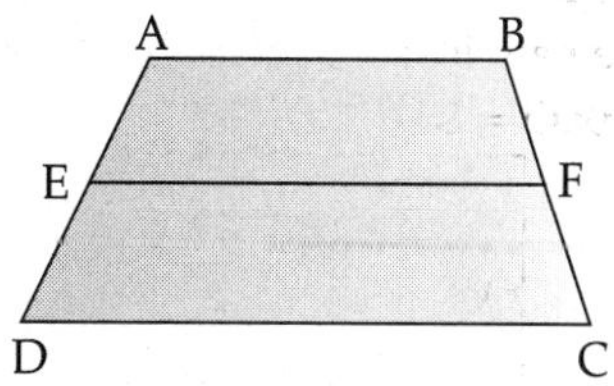

If E and F are mid points, then EF (Median) $= \frac{1}{2}$ (AB + CD) Also, $\frac{AE}{ED} = \frac{BF}{FC}$

- After joining the mid points of adjacent sides of a trapezium, four similar triangles are obtained.

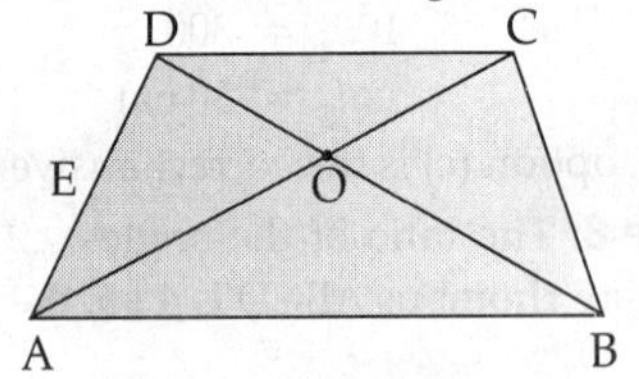

$$\frac{AO}{OC} = \frac{BO}{OD} = \frac{AB}{DC}$$

Example 9: The ratio of the length of the parallel sides of a trapezium is 3 : 2. The shortest distance between them is 15 cm. If the area of the trapezium is 450 cm^2, the sum of the length of the parallel sides is :

(a) 42 (b) 60
(c) 30 (d) 15

Sol. (b)

Ratio = 3 :2

Sides = $3x, 2x$

Shortest distance = height = h = 15

Area = 450 cm^2

$$\text{Area of a trapezium} = \frac{1}{2}(\text{sum of }||\text{sides}) \times h$$

$$450 = \frac{1}{2}(3x + 2x) \times 15$$

$$450 = \frac{1}{2} \times 5x \times 15$$

$$\frac{450 \times 2}{15} = 5x$$

$$60 = 5x$$

$$12 = x$$

Now, $3x + 2x = 5x = 5 \times 12 = 60$

Hence, option (b) is the correct answer.

Example 10: In a trapezium, one diagonal divides the other in the ratio 2 : 9. If the length of the larger of the two parallel sides is 45 cm, then what is the length (is cm) of other parallel side?

(a) 10 (b) 5
(c) 18 (d) 14

Sol. (a) $\frac{AO}{OC} = \frac{2}{9}$ (Given)

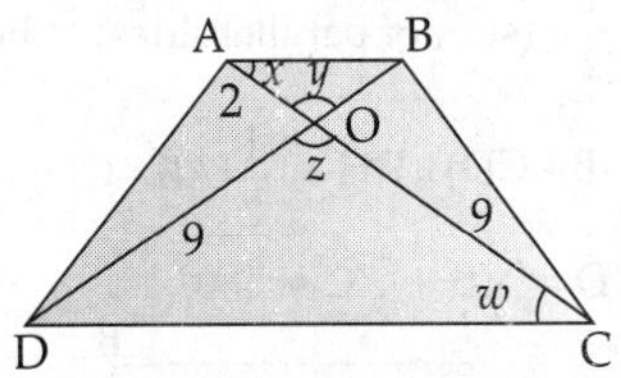

We know AB||CD

$x = w$

$y = z$

$\Delta AOB \sim \Delta COD$

$$\frac{AB}{CD} = \frac{AO}{OC}$$

$$\frac{AB}{45} = \frac{2}{9}$$

AB = 5 × 2 = 10

Hence, option (a) is the correct answer.

CIRCLE

- **Circle:** It is a set of points which are at a constant distance from its centre.

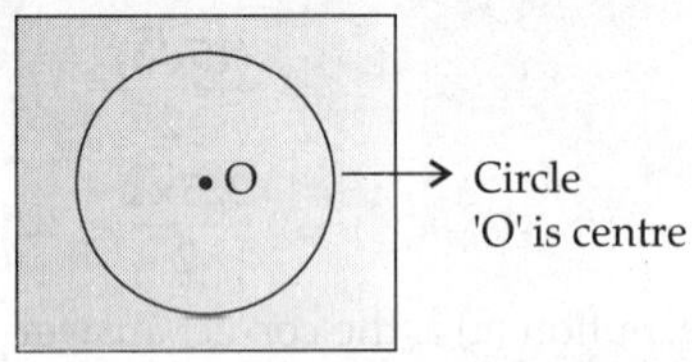

SOME IMPORTANTS TERMS RELATED TO A CIRCLE

- **Diameter:** A line segment passes through the centre and has its endpoints on the circumference of the circle.

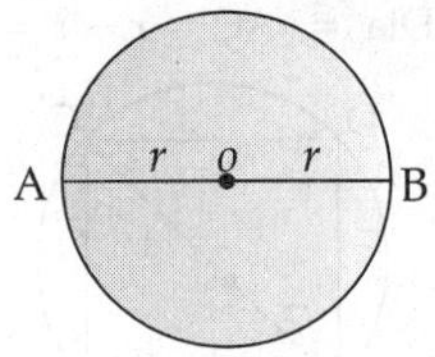

'AB' is the diameter, $d = 2r$

- **Radius:** The distance from the centre to the point on the circumference.

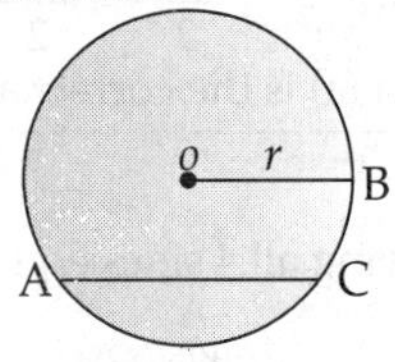

OB = radius

AC = chord

$\therefore r = \frac{d}{2}$

- **Chord:** It is a line segment whose end points lie on the circumference.
- **Secant:** It is a line segment which intersects a circle at two different points.

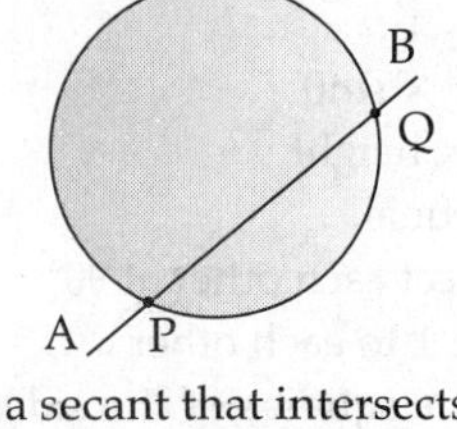

Here, AB is a secant that intersects at P and Q.

Tangent: It is a line that meets the circle only at one point.

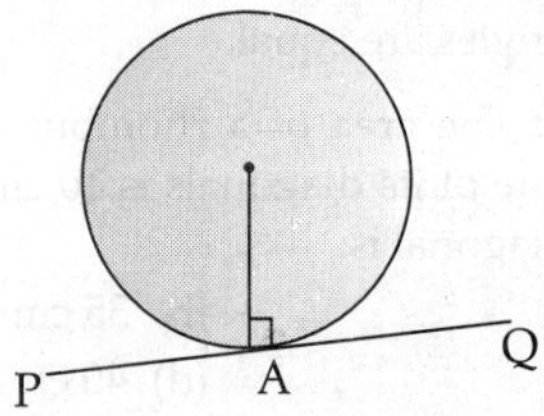

PQ = tangent meeting at point A

Note: Radius is always ⊥ to a tangent.

- **Arc:** It is a part of the circumference.
- **Sector:** Sector is made by an arc and two radius of a circle.

Here, PAQ is the arc

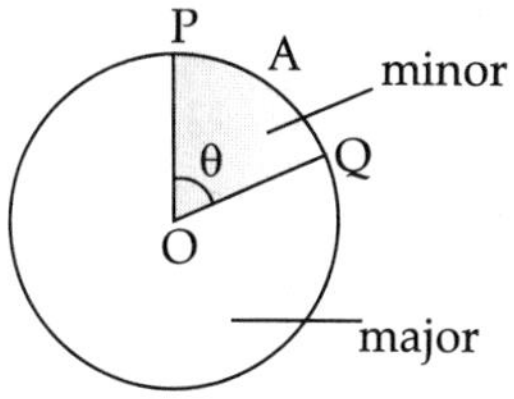

OPAQ is the sector

$$\text{Area of sector} = \frac{\pi r^2 \theta}{360°}$$

- **Concentric circles:** When two circles have the same centre, they are said to be concentric circles.

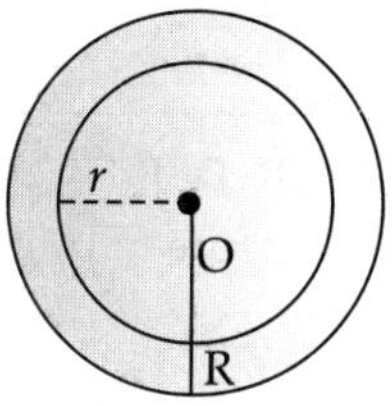

Here, r and R are the radius of two circles with the same centre 'O'.

- **Central angle:** Angle at the centre

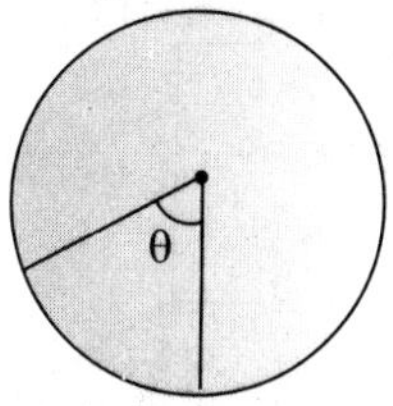

- **Cyclic quadrilaterals:** The quadrilateral which has all four vertices on the circle.

Sum of opposite angles is supplementary

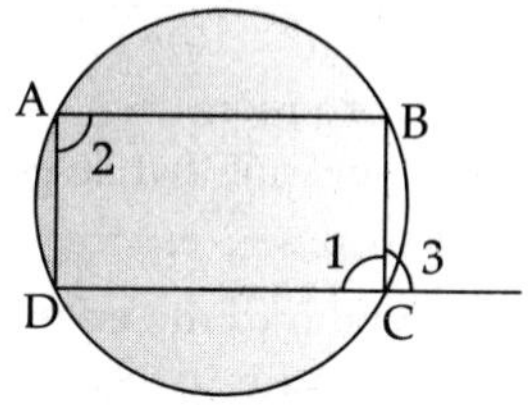

- $\angle 2 + \angle 1 = 180°$, $\angle 1 + \angle 3 = 180°$

$\angle 2 = \angle 3$

∵ In a cyclic quadrilateral,

Ext. angle = Opp. int. angle.

CIRCULAR RING

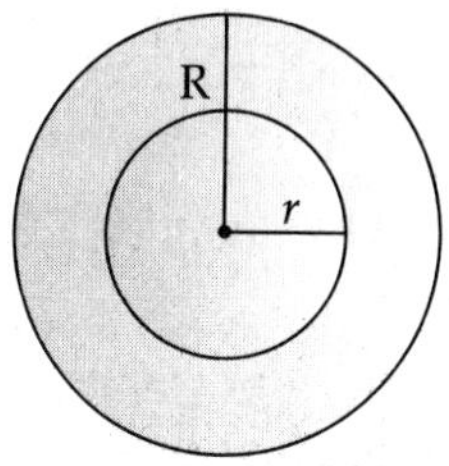

- Here, R = radius of outer ring.

r = radius of inner ring.

Area = $\pi(R^2 - r^2)$

Circumference difference = $2\pi(R - r)$

SOME OTHER POINTS TO REMEMBER

- If the length and breadth of a rectangle, square, or side of any triangle on a polygon is increased by $x\%$, then

$$\% \text{ change in area} = x\left[2 + \frac{x}{100}\right]\% = \left(2x + \frac{x^2}{100}\right)$$

Note: Use –ve sign if side is decreased.

- If the length and breadth of a rectangle inc. by $x\%$ and increase by $y\%$, then

$$\% \text{ change in area} = \left(x + y + \frac{xy}{100}\right)\%$$

3-D MENSURATION

CUBE

- It is a 3-dimensional figure having equal sides in length.
- It has six faces (each face is a square).

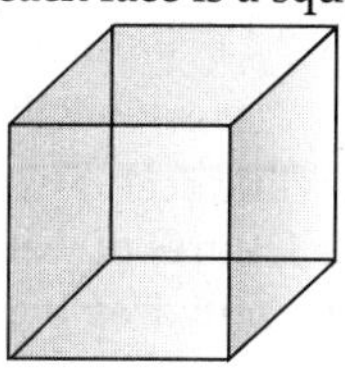

- Let 'a' be the side

Volume of cube = $a \times a \times a = a^3$

Total surface area = $6a^2$

Diagonal of a cube = $a\sqrt{3}$

Face diagonal of a cube = $a\sqrt{2}$

CUBOID

- It is a 3-dimensional figure.
- It has six faces (each face is a rectangle).

➤ Let l = length, b = breadth, h = height

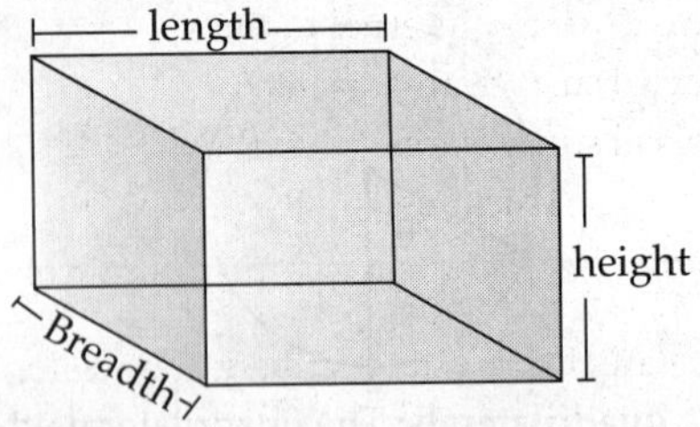

Volume of cuboid $= l \times b \times h$

T.S.A. $= 2(lb + bh + hl)$

Diagonal $= \sqrt{l^2 + b^2 + h^2}$

Area of four walls of a room $= 2 \times (L + B) \times H$

Area of roof and four walls (while painting)

$= 2H(L + B) + LB$

Example 11: The ratio of the edges of a cuboid is 1 : 2 : 3 and its surface area is 88 cm². The volume of cuboid is:

(a) 48 (b) 120

(c) 64 (d) 24

Sol. **(a)** Length $= x$

Breadth $= 2x$

Height $= 3x$

We know,

Surface area of cuboid $= 2(lb + bh + hl)$

$$88 = 2(x \times 2x + 2x \times 3x + 3x \times x)$$
$$= 2[2x^2 + 6x^2 + 3x^2]$$
$$88 = 2(11x^2)$$
$$4 = x^2$$
$$2 = x$$

Volume $= x \times 2x \times 3x$

$= 2 \times 2 \times 2 \times 3 \times 2$

$= 48 \text{ cm}^3$

Hence, option (a) is the correct answer.

Example 12: The area of a floor of a cubical room in 48 sq.m. The length of the longest rod that can be kept in that room is:

(a) 3,850 (b) 2,450

(c) 4,250 (d) 12

Sol. **(d)** Given, area of floor = 48 m²

Longest rod will be equal to diagonal.

We know,

area of floor = area of a square

$$48 = a^2$$
$$4\sqrt{3} = a$$

Now, longest rod or diagonal $= a\sqrt{3}$

$= 4\sqrt{3} \times \sqrt{3} = 12$ m

Hence, option (d) is the correct answer.

Example 13: Find the length of the longest rod that can be placed in a room 16 m long, 12 m broad, $10\frac{2}{3}$ m high.

(a) 68 m (b) 23 m

(c) $22\frac{1}{3}$ m (d) $22\frac{2}{3}$ m

Sol. **(d)** $l = 16$ m

$b = 12$ m

$h = 10\frac{2}{3}\text{m} = \frac{32}{3}\text{m}$

largest rod = diagonal of cuboid/room

$$= \sqrt{l^2 + b^2 + h^2}$$
$$= \sqrt{16^2 + 12^2 + \left(\frac{32}{3}\right)^2}$$
$$= \sqrt{256 + 144 + \frac{1{,}024}{9}}$$
$$= \sqrt{400 + \frac{1{,}024}{9}}$$
$$= \sqrt{\frac{3{,}600 + 1{,}024}{9}}$$
$$= \frac{68}{3} = 22\frac{2}{3}\text{m}$$

RIGHT CIRCULAR CYLINDER

➤ It is a 3-dimensional figure having a circular top and base with height 'h'.

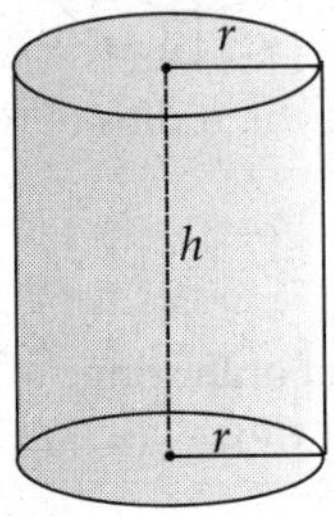

Let r = radius, h = height

Volume of cylinder $= \pi r^2 h$

T.S.A. of cylinder $= 2\pi r(r + h)$

C.S.A. of cylinder $= 2\pi rh$

HOLLOW CYLINDER

➤ Volume of hollow cylinder $= \pi(R^2 - r^2)h$

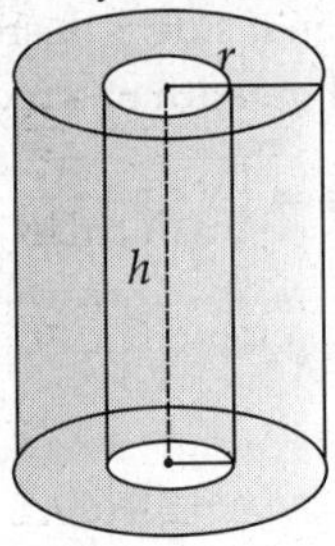

C.S.A. $= 2\pi h(R + r)$

T.S.A. $= 2\pi(R + r)h + 2\pi(R^2 - r^2)$

Here R = External radius

r = internal radius

h = height

Example 14: A cylindrical tank of diameter 35 cm is full of water. If 11 litres of water is drawn off, the water level in tank null drop by:

(a) $11\frac{1}{7}$ (b) $11\frac{3}{7}$

(c) 14 (d) $12\frac{6}{7}$

Sol. **(b)** We know,

$$11 \text{ litres drawn} = \pi r^2 h$$

$$11{,}000 \text{ cm} = \frac{22}{7}\times\frac{35}{2}\times\frac{35}{2}\times h$$

$$h = \frac{100\times 4}{35}$$

$$= \frac{400}{35} = 11\frac{3}{7} \text{ cm}$$

Example 15: The volume of a metal in a cylindrical pipe is 748 cm^3. Its length is 14 cm and external radius is 9 cm. It thickness is:

(a) 11 cm (b) 17 cm

(c) 1 cm (d) 7 cm

Sol. **(c)** It is clear that it is a hollow cylinder

∴ Volume of a hollow cylinder

$$= \frac{22}{7}(R^2 - r^2)\times h$$

$$748 = \frac{22}{7}(9^2 - r^2)\times 14 \qquad \because R = 9$$

$$81 - r^2 = \frac{68}{4}$$

$$81 - r^2 = 17$$

$$r^2 = 64$$

$$r = 8$$

Thus, thickness $= R - r$

$= 9 - 8 = 1$ cm

SPHERE

➤ It is a 3-dimensional figure that is round in shape.

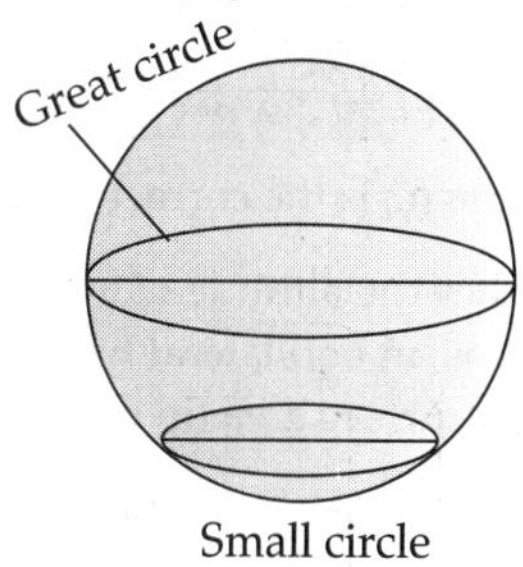

$$\text{Volume of sphere} = \frac{4}{3}\pi r^3$$

$$\text{T.S.A./C.S.A.} = 4\pi r^2$$

HOLLOW SPHERE OR SPHERICAL SPHERE

$$\text{Volume} = \frac{4}{3}\pi(R^3 - r^2)$$

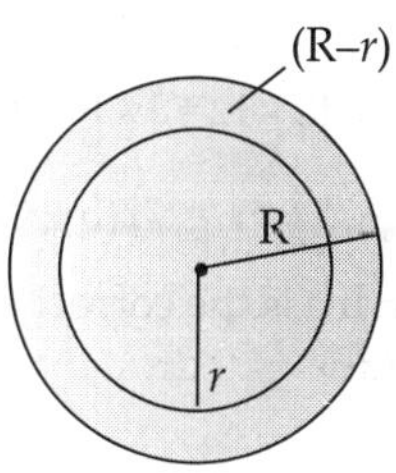

R = external radius

r = internal radius

Internal surface area $= 4\pi r^2$

External surface area $= 4\pi R^2$

Thickness $= R - r$

Example 16: If the surface area and volume of a sphere are S and V, respectively, then value of $\frac{S^3}{\pi V^2}$ is:

(a) 36 units (b) 9 units

(c) 18 units (d) 27 units

Sol. (a) Volume of sphere = V

T.S.A. of sphere = S (Given)

Now,

We know,

T.S.A. of sphere $= 4\pi r^2 = S$

Volume of sphere $= \frac{4}{3}\pi r^3 = V$

So, $$\frac{S^3}{\pi V^2} = \frac{4\times 4\times 4\times \pi^3\times r^6}{\pi\times\frac{4}{3}\times\frac{4}{3}\times\pi^2\times r^6}$$

$$\frac{S^3}{\pi V^2} = 4\times 9 = 36$$

Hence, option (a) is the correct answer.

Example 17: If the radii of two spheres are in the ratio 1 : 4, then their surface area are in the ratio:

(a) 1 : 2 (b) 1 : 4

(c) 1 : 8 (d) 1 : 16

Sol. **(d)** Given $r_1 : r_2$ = 1 : 4, r_1 – radius of S_1, r_2 – radius of S_2

$$\frac{\text{Area}\, S_1}{\text{Area}\, S_2} = \frac{4\pi r_1^2}{4\pi r_2^2}$$

$$= \left(\frac{r_1^2}{r_2^2}\right) = \left(\frac{1}{4}\right)^2 = \frac{1}{16}$$

Hence, option (d) is the correct answer.

HEMISPHERE

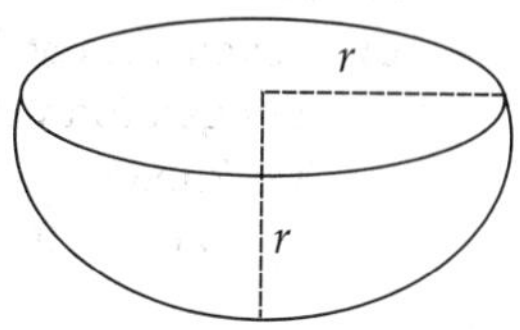

r = radius

➤ Volume $= \frac{2}{3}\pi r^3$

➤ T.S.A. $= 3\pi r^2$

➤ C.S.A. $= 2\pi r^2$

CONE

➤ A cone is a 3-dimensional figure with one circular base, pointed top and a height h.

Let h = height

l = slant height

r = radius

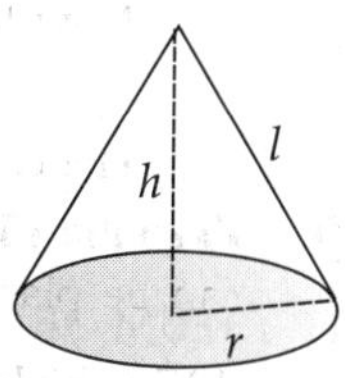

$$\text{Volume} = \frac{1}{3}\times \text{base area}\times\text{height} = \frac{1}{3}\pi r^2 h$$

$$\text{Slant height} = \sqrt{r^2 + h^2}$$

$$\text{C.S.A.} = \pi rl$$
$$\text{T.S.A.} = \pi rl + \pi r^2$$
$$= \pi r^2 + \pi r\sqrt{r^2+h^2}$$

Example 18: The heights of two cones are in the ratio 1 : 3 and the diameters of their base are in the ratio 3 : 5. The ratio of their volume is:

(a) 3 : 25 (b) 4 : 25
(c) 7 : 25 (d) 6 : 25

Sol. (a)

	Diameters	Height
Cone 1	3	1
Cone 2	5	3

$$\frac{\text{Volume of cone 1}}{\text{Volume of cone 2}} = \frac{\frac{1}{3}\pi r_1^2 h_1}{\frac{1}{3}\pi r_2^2 h_2}$$
$$= \frac{r_1^2 h_1}{r_2^2 h_2} = \frac{\left(\frac{3}{2}\right)^2 \times 1}{\left(\frac{5}{2}\right)^2 \times 3}$$
$$= \frac{3}{25}$$

Hence, option (a) is the correct answer.

PYRAMID

$$\text{Volume of a pyramid} = \frac{1}{3} \times \text{base area} \times \text{height}$$
$$\text{Lateral surface area} = \frac{1}{2} \times (\text{perimeter of base}) \times \text{slant } h$$
$$\text{Slant height} = \sqrt{r^2+h^2}$$

TETRAHEDRON

➢ It is a pyramid with a regular triangular base, and bounded by four regular triangular base/faces.

Volume = $\frac{1}{2}\times$ base area × height

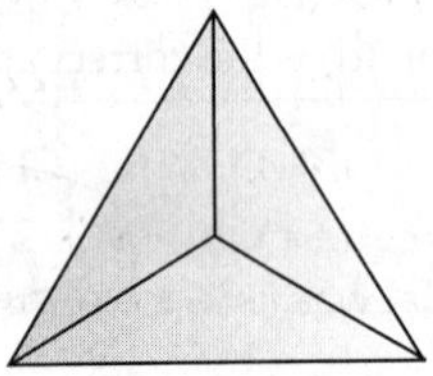

$$V = \frac{\sqrt{2}}{12}a^3$$
$$\text{Total surface area} = 3\times\frac{\sqrt{3}}{4}a^2 + \frac{\sqrt{3}}{4}a^2$$
$$= \sqrt{3}a^2$$

FRUSTUM OF CONE

➢ When a cone is cut by a plane parallel to its base then the lower part is called frustum.

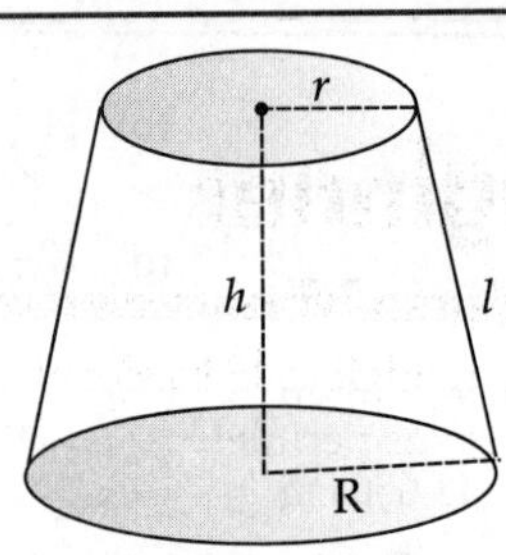

Here, l = slant height
$= \sqrt{h^2+(R-r)^2}$
r = radius of upper part
R = radius of lower part

$$\text{Volume} = \frac{\pi h}{3}(r^2+R^2+rR)$$
$$\text{T.S.A.} = \pi\{(R+r)\,l + R^2 + r^2]$$
$$\text{C.S.A.} = \pi(R+r)\,l$$

PRISM

➢ Volume of prism = area of base × h
➢ Lateral/curved and area = Perimeter of base × height
➢ Total surface area = lateral/ curved area + area of base and top surfaces

Example 19: The base of a right prism is an equilateral triangle of side 8 cm and height of the prism is 10 cm. Then, the volume of the prism is: **[SSC Delhi Police]**

(a) $320\sqrt{3}$ cm^3 (b) $300\sqrt{3}$ cm^3
(c) $160\sqrt{3}$ cm^3 (d) $150\sqrt{3}$ cm^3

Sol. (c) We know, volume of a right prism
= Base area × h

$$V = \frac{\sqrt{3}}{4}a^2 \times h$$
$$= \frac{\sqrt{3}}{4}\times 8\times 8\times 10 = 160\sqrt{3}\text{ cm}^3$$

Hence, option (c) is the correct answer.

Example 20: If the altitude of a right prism is 10 cm and its base is an equilateral triangle of side 12 cm, then its total surface area (in cm^2) is:

(a) $(5+3\sqrt{3})$ (b) $36\sqrt{3}$
(c) 360 (d) $72(5+\sqrt{3})$

Sol. (d) T.S.A. of right prism
= area of (top + bottom) + area of 3 lateral surfaces

$$= 2\left(\frac{\sqrt{3}}{4}\times 12^2\right) + 3(10\times 12)$$
$$= 2\times\frac{\sqrt{3}}{4}\times 12\times 12 + 3\times 10\times 12$$
$$= 36\times 2(\sqrt{3}+5) = 72(5+\sqrt{3})$$

Hence, option (d) is the correct answer.

1 Level Beginner

1. The area of a triangle is 15 sq. cm and the radius of its incircle is 3 cm. Its perimeter is equal to: [SSC CGL 2019]
(A) 12 cm (B) 20 cm (C) 10 cm (D) 5 cm

2. The base of an isosceles triange is 6 cm and its perimeter is 16 cm. Its area is: [SSC CPO 2019]
(A) 11 cm^2 (B) 9 cm^2
(C) 12 cm^2 (D) 10 cm^2

3. If the radius of a sphere is thrice than the radius of a hemisphere, then what will be the respective ratio of their volumes? [SSC CHSL 2023]
(A) 27 : 1 (B) 16 : 1 (C) 54 : 1 (D) 18 : 1

4. In ΔABC, $\angle A = 90°$, AB = 16 cm and AC = 12 cm. D is the midpoint of AC and DE $\perp$ CB at E. What is the area (in cm^2) of ΔCDE? [SSC CPO 2019]
(A) 7.68 (B) 8.64 (C) 5.76 (D) 6.25

5. The lateral surface area of a cylinder is 352 cm^2. If its height is 7 cm, then its volume (in cm^3) is: $\left(\text{Take } \pi = \frac{22}{7}\right)$ [SSC CGL Tier-II 2019]
(A) 1,408 (B) 1,078 (C) 1,243 (D) 891

6. The perimeter of a rhombus is 148 cm and one of its diagonals is 25 cm. The area of the rhombus is: [SSC CHSL 2021]
(A) 840 (B) 700 (C) 875 (D) 770

7. How many solid spheres are made if a metallic cone of radius 12 cm and height 24 cm is melted into sphere of radius 2 cm each? [SSC CHSL 2023]
(A) 105 (B) 101 (C) 108 (D) 103

8. The radius of a circular cone is R and its height is H. The volume of the cone is: [SSC CHSL 2020]
(A) $\frac{\pi R^2 H}{3}$ (B) $\pi R^2 H$
(C) $\pi H^2 R$ (D) $\frac{2}{\pi R^2 H}$

9. If the area of an isosceles right angled triangle is 121 cm^2, find its hypotenuse. [SSC CHSL 2020]
(A) 23 (B) 21 (C) 20 (D) 22

10. The circumference of the circle exceeds its diameter by 60 cm. The area of the circle is : $\left(\text{take } \pi = \frac{22}{7}\right)$ [SSC CPO 2019]
(A) 546.6 cm^2 (B) 346.6 cm^2
(C) 616 cm^2 (D) 1,078 cm^2

11. The side of a hexagon is 4 cm. The side of a square is $4\sqrt{2}$ cm . Find the ratio of their areas: [SSC MTS 2019]
(A) $3\sqrt{3}:2$ (B) $2\sqrt{3}:1$
(C) $\frac{\sqrt{3}}{2}:1$ (D) $3\sqrt{3}:4$

12. If the curved surface area of a cylinder is increased by 20%, and height is decreased by 4%, then the net decrease or increase in the volume will be: [SSC CHSL 2023]
(A) 36% decrease (B) 20% increase
(C) 50% increase (D) 33% decrease

13. If the length of the base and hypotenuse of a right-angled triangle is 9 cm and 41 cm, respectively. What is the area of the triangle ? [SSC MTS 2019]
(A) 190 cm^2 (B) 210 cm^2
(C) 170 cm^2 (D) 180 cm^2

14. What is the ratio between the inradius and the circumradius of a square? [SSC MTS 2019]
(A) $\sqrt{2}:3$ (B) 1:3 (C) $1:\sqrt{2}$ (D) 1:2

15. The sides of a triangular park are 200 m, 210 m, 290 m. The area of the park is: (in hectares) [SSC MTS 2019]
(A) 2.3 (B) 2.4 (C) 2.1 (D) 2.9

16. The volume of a right pyramid is $45\sqrt{3}$ cm^3 and its base is an equilateral triangle with side 6 cm. What is the height of the pyramid. [SSC T2 2019]
(A) 18 (B) 15 (C) 12 (D) 20

17. A rod of 5 cm radius and 52 cm length is converted into a wire of 100 cm length of uniform thickness. The radius of the wire (in cm) is: [SSC CHSL 2023]
(A) $\sqrt{13}$ (B) $\sqrt{15}$ (C) $\sqrt{23}$ (D) $\sqrt{17}$

18. A bicycle wheel has a radius of 42 cm. It makes 40 revolutions in 25 seconds. What is its speed (is kmph), up to one decimal place? [SSC CHSL 2020]
(A) 11.6 (B) 15.2 (C) 9.5 (D) 3.5

19. The volume of a solid hemisphere is 19, 404 cm^3. Its total surface area (is cm^2) is: $\left(\text{Take } \pi = \frac{22}{7}\right)$ [SSC CGL Tier-I 2021]
(A) 3,465 (B) 4,158 (C) 2,772 (D) 2,079

20. A pillar 11 metre in radius is 21 metre high. How much material was used to construct it? [SSC CHSL 2022]
(A) 7,989 (B) 7,996 (C) 7,886 (D) 7,986

21. If the radius of a circle is decreased by 10%, then the area of the circle is decreased by: [SSC Constable GD 2015]
(A) 19% (B) 89% (C) 25% (D) 18%

22. If a right circular cone of height 24 cm has the circumference of its base 42 π cm, then the volume of the cone is (use $\pi = \frac{22}{7}$): [SSC CHSL 2023]
(A) 15211 cm^3 (B) 11088 cm^3
(C) 12034 cm^3 (D) 21011 cm^3

23. The base of a prism is a right-angled triangle with two sides 5 cm and 12 cm. The height of the prism is 10 cm. The total surface area of the prism is: **[SSC CGL Tier-II 2014]**
(A) 330 cm^2 (B) 360 cm^2
(C) 325 cm^2 (D) 300 cm^2

24. The lengths of two diagonals of a rhombus are 8 cm and 15 cm, respectively. Find its area (is cm^2): **[SSC CHSL 2018]**
(A) 90 (B) 30 (C) 120 (D) 60

25. If the slant height and radius of a right circular cone are 28 cm and 21 cm, respectively, then the total surface area of the right circular cone (in cm^2) is:
Take ($\pi = \frac{22}{7}$) **[SSC CHSL 2023]**
(A) 3234 (B) 3342 (C) 3243 (D) 3324

2 Intermediate Level

1. If the radius of sphere is decreased by 10 percent, then volume of sphere will be decreased by what percentage? **[SSC CHSL 2023]**
(A) 32.5% (B) 30.6% (C) 25.6% (D) 27.1%

2. The areas of three adjacent faces of a cuboidal tank are $3m^2$, $12m^2$ and $16m^2$. The capacity of the tank (in litres) is: **[SSC CGL 2020]**
(A) 36,000 (B) 72,000
(C) 48,000 (D) 24,000

3. A rectangle with perimeter 50 cm has its sides is the ratio 1 : 4. What is the perimeter of a square whose area is the same as that of the rectangle? **[SSC CHSL 2021]**
(A) 50 (B) 40 (C) 36 (D) 45

4. The length of each side of a regular hexagon is 10 cm. What is the area of the hexagon? **[SSC CHSL 2022]**
(A) $156\sqrt{3}$ cm^2 (B) $144\sqrt{3}$ cm^2
(C) $148\sqrt{3}$ cm^2 (D) $150\sqrt{3}$ cm^2

5. The base of a solid prism of height 10 cm is a square and its volume is 160 cm^3. What is its total surface area of the prism (in cm^3)? **[SSC CGL Tier-II 2020]**
(A) 200 (B) 192 (C) 180 (D) 176

6. If the length of a rectangle is increased by 40% and the breadth is decreased by 20%, then the area of the rectangle is increased by x%. The value of x is: **[SSC CGL 2020]**
(A) 18 (B) 8 (C) 20 (D) 12

7. A field is in the shape of a trapezium whose parallel sides are 200 m and 400 m long, whereas each of the other two sides is 260 m long. What is the area (in m^2) of the field? **[SSC CPO 2019]**
(A) 72,000 (B) 60,000
(C) 52,000 (D) 48,000

8. The curved surface area and the height of a right circular cylinder are 660 cm^2 and 10 cm respectively. Find its diameter (in cm). **[CHSL 2018]**
(A) 14 (B) 10 (C) 21 (D) 17.5

9. The inner and outer radius of a circular track are 23 m and 29 m. The cost of levelling the track at ₹7/m^2 is: **[SSC CGL 2020]**
(A) ₹3,284 (B) ₹5,300
(C) ₹7,215 (D) ₹6,864

10. A circulr park whose diameter is 210 m has a 5 m wide path running around it (on the outside). What is the area (in m^2) of the path? **[SSC CPO 2019]**
(A) 1100π (B) 1020π (C) 1050π (D) 1075π

11. When the radius of the sphere is increased by 5 cm, its surface area increases by 704 cm^2. The diameter of the original sphere is: $\left(\text{Take } \pi = \frac{22}{7}\right)$ **[SSC CPO 2019]**
(A) 8.2 cm (B) 5.2 cm
(C) 6.8 cm (D) 6.2 cm

12. The ratio of the radius of the base to the height of a solid right circular cylinder is 2 : 3. If its volume is 202.125 cm^3, then its total surface area is: $\left(\text{Take } \pi = \frac{22}{7}\right)$ **[SSC CPO 2020]**
(A) 154 cm^2 (B) 168 cm^2
(C) 115.5 cm^2 (D) 192.5 cm^2

13. The area of the base of a right circular cone is 400 π and its height is 15 cm. The curved surface area of the cone is: **[SSC CGL 2019]**
(A) 480π (B) 500π (C) 400π (D) 560π

14. A spherical metallic shell with 6 cm external radius weighs 6,688 g. What is the thickness of the sheet, if the density of metal is 10.5 g per cm^3? $\left(\pi = \frac{22}{7}\right)$ **[SSC CGL Tier-II 2020]**
(A) 2 cm (B) 3 cm (C) $2\frac{1}{2}$cm (D) 4 cm

15. The internal length, breadth and height of a cuboidal room are 12m, 8m and 10 m, respectively. The total cost (in ₹) of white washing only all four walls of the room at the cost of ₹ 25 per m^2 is: **[SSC CPO 2020]**
(A) 18,000 (B) 1,18,400
(C) 12,600 (D) 10,000

16. The radius of a cylinder is increased by 150% and its height is decreased by 20%. What is the percentage (%) increase in its volume? **[SSC CPO 2019]**
(A) 500% (B) 80% (C) 600% (D) 400%

17. A rectangular sheet of paper which is 88 cm long and 11 cm wide is rolled to form a cylinder of height equal to its width of the paper. What is the volume of the cylinder so formed? **[SSC CPO 2019]**
(A) 7,676 (B) 6,776 (C) 6,546 (D) 6,786

18. N solid metallic spherical balls are melted and recast into a cylindrical rod whose radius is 3 times that of a spherical ball and height is 4 times the radius of a spherical ball. The value of N is: [SSC CGL Mains 2019]

(A) 27 (B) 24 (C) 36 (D) 30

19. In a right circular cylinder, the ratio of the curved surface to the total surface area is 3:7. Find the ratio of the height of the cylinder to the radius of its base. [SSC CHSL 2022]

(A) 3 : 4 (B) 2 : 3 (C) 3 : 2 (D) 4 : 3

20. A solid cylinder has a radius of 9 cm and a height of 25 cm. What is the ratio of its total surface area to its curved surface area? [SSC CHSL 2022]

(A) 9 : 25 (B) 25 : 9 (C) 25 : 34 (D) 34 : 25

21. If the radius of a right circular cylinder is decreased by 20% while its height is increased by 40%, then the percentage change in its volume will be: [SSC CGL Tier-II 2019]

(A) 10.4% dec. (B) 10.4% inc.
(C) 1.04% inc. (D) No effect

22. A cylindrical vessel of diameter 32 cm is partially filled with water. A solid metallic sphere of radius 12 cm is dropped into it. What will be the increase in the level of water is the vessel (in cm): [SSC CGL 2022]

(A) 72 (B) 27 (C) 9 (D) 2.25

23. The height and slant height of a conical vessel are 12 cm and 13 cm, respectively. The capacity of the vessel is: (Use $\pi = 3.14$). [SSC CGL 2022]

(A) 0.314 litres (B) 0.5 litres
(C) 0.523 litres (D) 0.298 litres

3 Level Expert

1. A steel vessel has a base of length 50 cm and breadth 30 cm. Water is poured in the vessel. A cubical box having an edge of 30 cm is immersed completely in the vessel. By how much will the water rise? [SSC CPO 2019]

(A) 9 cm (B) 15 cm (C) 10 cm (D) 12 cm

2. The volume of a wall whose height is 10 times its width and whose length is 8 times its height, is 51.2 m^2. What is the cost in (₹) of painting the wall on one side at the rate of Rs. 100/m^2? [SSC CGL 2021]

(A) 12,800 (B) 13,000
(C) 14,200 (D) 12,500

3. The length of a rectangle is 10 cm more than the side of a square and its breadth is 8 cm less than the side of the square. If the areas of both the rectangle and square are equal, then what will be the perimeter (in cm) of the rectangle? [SSC CGL 2021]

(A) 160 (B) 156 (C) 144 (D) 164

4. A rectangular lawn whose length is twice its breadth is extended by having four semi-circular portions on its sides. What is the total surface area (in m^2) of the lawn if the smaller side of the rectangle is 12 m? (Take $\pi = 3.19$) [SSC CPO 2020]

(A) 853.2 (B) 548.32
(C) 444 (D) 308.64

5. The area of a triangle field whose sides are 65 m, 72 m, and 97 m is equal to the area of a rectangular park whose sides are in the ratio of 5 : 13. What is the perimeter (in m) of the rectangular park? [SSC CHSL 2021]

(A) 108 (B) 180
(C) 216 (D) 144

6. A hemispherical tank full of water is emptied by a pipe at the rate of 7.7 litres per seconds. How much time (in hours) will it take to empty $\frac{2}{3}$ part of the tank if the internal radius of the tank is 10.5 m? [SSC CGL Mains 2020]

(A) $\frac{185}{3}$ (B) $\frac{175}{3}$ (C) $\frac{175}{2}$ (D) $\frac{185}{6}$

7. A solid metallic cuboid of dimensions 18 cm × 36 cm × 72 cm is melted and recast into 8 cubes of the same volume. What is the ratio of the total surface area of the cuboid to the sum of the lateral surface area of all 8 cubes? [SSC CGL Mains 2020]

(A) 2 : 3 (B) 7 : 12 (C) 7 : 8 (D) 4 : 7

8. In a right triangle ABC, AB = AC and perimeter of ΔABC is $8(2+\sqrt{2})$cm. If the length of BC is $\sqrt{2}$ times the length of AB, then find the area of ΔABC. [SSC CGL Mains 2020]

(A) 32 (B) 16 (C) 36 (D) 28

9. A solid cylinder has a radius of 9 cm and a height of 25 cm. What is the ratio of its total surface area to its curved surface area? [SSC CHSL 2022]

(A) 9 : 25 (B) 25 : 9 (C) 25 : 34 (D) 34 : 25

10. A right circular cone of largest volume is cut from a solid wooden hemisphere. The remaining material is what percentage of the volume of the original hemisphere? [SSC CPO 2019]

(A) 75% (B) 50%
(C) 33.33% (D) 66.66%

11. A field roller, in the shape of a cylinder has a diameter of 1 m and length of $1\frac{1}{4}$m. If the speed at which the roller rolls is 14 revolutions per mintue, then maximum (in m^2) that it can roll in 1 hour is: $\left(\text{Take } \pi = \frac{22}{7}\right)$. [SSC CGL Mains 2019]

(A) 1,386 (B) 2,772 (C) 1,337 (D) 3,300

12. How many 25 cm × 11.25 cm × 6 cm bricks will be required to construct an 8 m × 6 m × 22.5 cm wall? (Ignoring other material used) [SSC CHSL 2022]

(A) 7020 (B) 6400 (C) 5800 (D) 6800

13. A solid metallic cuboid measuring 343 cm × 49 cm × 7 cm is melted and converted into cubes with side 7 cm. The sum of the total surface areas (cm^2) of all the cubes is: **[SSC 2019]**

(A) 16,807 **(B)** 12,506
(C) 1,00,842 **(D)** 10,842

14. A reservoir is in the shape of a frustum of a right circular cone. The radii of its circular ends are 4 m and 8 m and its depth is 7 m. How many kilolitre of water can it hold? $\pi = \frac{22}{7}$. **[SSC 2020]**

(A) 821.3 **(B)** 175.7 **(C)** 815.7 **(D)** 79.3

15. The height of a cylinder is two-third of its diameter. It volume is equal to the volume of a sphere whose radius is 4 cm. What is the curved surface area (in cm^2) of the cylinder? **[SSC CPO 2019]**

(A) $\frac{112}{3}\pi$ **(B)** 32π **(C)** $\frac{128}{3}\pi$ **(D)** 40π

16. A sector of radius 10.5 cm with the central angle 120° is folded to form a cone by joining the two bounding radii of the sector. What is the volume (in cm^3) of the cone so formed? **[SSC 2019]**

(A) $\frac{343\sqrt{3}}{6}\pi$ **(B)** $\frac{343\sqrt{2}}{6}\pi$
(C) $\frac{343\sqrt{2}}{12}\pi$ **(D)** $\frac{343\sqrt{3}}{12}\pi$

17. The radius of the base of a cylinderical tank is 4 m. If three times the sum of the areas of its circular faces is twice the area of its curved surface, then the capacity (in kilolitres) of the tank is: **[SSC CGL Tier-II 2022]**

(A) 54π **(B)** 108π **(C)** $144\pi^2$ **(D)** 96π

18. The curved surface area of a right circular cone is 2,310 cm^2 and its radius 21 cm. If its radius is increased by 100% and height is reduced by 50%, then its capacity (in litres) will be? $\left(\text{Take } \pi = \frac{22}{7}\right)$ **[SSC Tier-II 2022]**

(A) 26.7 **(B)** 25.9 **(C)** 27.8 **(D)** 28.2

19. The inner circumference of a circular path enclosed between two concentric circles is 264 m. The uniform width of the circular path is 3 m. What is the area (in m^2, to the nearest whole no.) of the path? Take $\pi = \frac{22}{7}$ **[SSC CGL Tier-I 2022]**

(A) 696 **(B)** 756 **(C)** 820 **(D)** 948

20. In the given figure, PQR is a quadrant whose radius is 7 cm. A circle is inscribed is the quadrant as shown in the figure. What is the area of the circle? **[SSC CGL Tier-II 2018]**

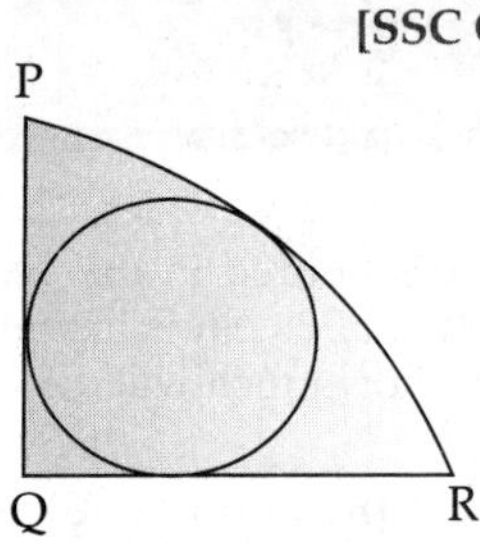

(A) $385 - 221\sqrt{2}$ **(B)** $462 - 308\sqrt{2}$
(C) $308 - 154\sqrt{2}$ **(D)** $154 - 77\sqrt{2}$

ANSWER KEY

Level-1: Beginner

1.	(C)	2.	(C)	3.	(C)	4.	(B)	5.	(A)	6.	(C)	7.	(C)	8.	(A)	9.	(D)	10.	(C)
11.	(D)	12.	(C)	13.	(D)	14.	(C)	15.	(C)	16.	(B)	17.	(A)	18.	(B)	19.	(B)	20.	(D)
21.	(A)	22.	(B)	23.	(B)	24.	(D)	25.	(A)										

Level-2: Intermediate

1.	(D)	2.	(D)	3.	(B)	4.	(D)	5.	(B)	6.	(D)	7.	(A)	8.	(C)	9.	(D)	10.	(D)
11.	(D)	12.	(D)	13.	(B)	14.	(A)	15.	(D)	16.	(D)	17.	(B)	18.	(A)	19.	(A)	20.	(D)
21.	(A)	22.	(C)	23.	(A)														

Level-3: Expert

1.	(B)	2.	(A)	3.	(D)	4.	(A)	5.	(C)	6.	(B)	7.	(C)	8.	(A)	9.	(D)	10.	(B)
11.	(D)	12.	(B)	13.	(C)	14.	(A)	15.	(C)	16.	(C)	17.	(D)	18.	(B)	19.	(C)	20.	(B)

Solutions with Detailed Explanation

Level-1: BEGINNER

1. Option (C) is correct.

Explanation:

Given, Area of $\Delta = 15 \text{ cm}^2$

Inradius = 3 cm

$$\text{Inradius} = \frac{\text{area of } \Delta}{\text{semiperimeter}}$$

$$3 = \frac{15}{s}$$

$$5 = s$$

We know, $\quad$ perimeter $= 2 \times s$

$$= 2 \times 5 = 10 \text{ cm}$$

2. Option (C) is correct.

Explanation: **Method 1**

We know,

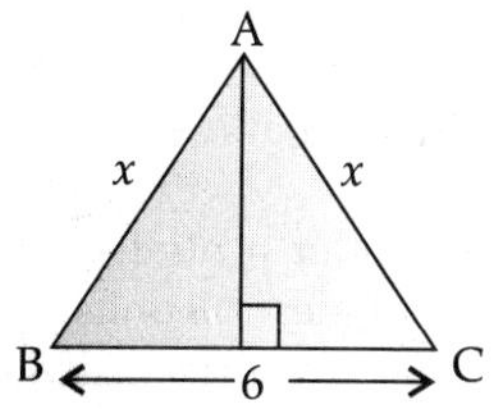

x = common sides

b = different side

In an isosceles triangle, two sides are equal.

So, $\quad x + x + 6 = 16$

$$2x = 10$$

$$x = 5$$

$$\text{Area of an isosceles riangle} = \frac{1}{4} \times b \times \sqrt{4a^2 - b^2}$$

$$= \frac{1}{4} \times 6 \times \sqrt{4(5)^2 - 6^2}$$

$$= \frac{1}{4} \times 6\sqrt{4(25) - 36}$$

$$= \frac{1}{4} \times 6\sqrt{100 - 36}$$

$$= \frac{1}{4} \times 6 \times \sqrt{64}$$

$$= \frac{1}{4} \times 6 \times 8 = 12 \text{ cm}$$

Method 2:

$$x + x + 6 = 16$$

$$2x = 10$$

$$x = 5 \text{ cm}$$

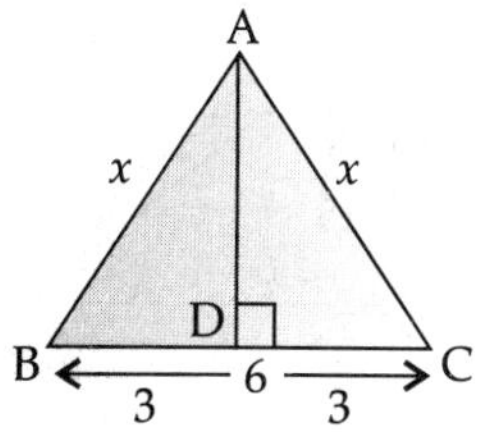

AD is $\perp$ to BC,

$$AD = \sqrt{5^2 - 3^2} = \sqrt{16} = 4$$

$$\text{Area} = \frac{1}{2} \times \text{base} \times \text{height}$$

$$= \frac{1}{2} \times 6 \times 4 = 12 \text{ cm}^2$$

3. Option (C) is correct.

Explanation: Given that the radius of sphere is thrice than the radius of hemisphere.

Let the radius of hemisphere $= x$

Then the radius of sphere $= 3x$

We have, volume of sphere $= \frac{4}{3}\pi r^3$

So, volume of the given sphere $= \frac{4}{3}\pi(3x)^3 = 36\pi x^3$

we have, volume of hemisphere $= \frac{2}{3}\pi r^3$

So, volume of the given hemisphere $= \frac{2}{3}\pi x^3$

$$\text{Required ratio} = \frac{36\pi x^3}{\frac{2}{3}\pi x^3} = \frac{54}{1}$$

4. Option (B) is correct.

Explanation: It is clear that

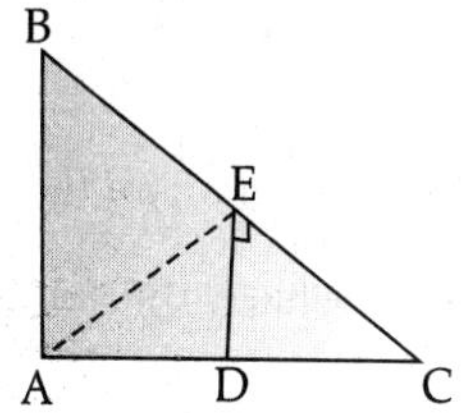

$$\Delta CAB \sim \Delta CED$$

$$\angle CAB = \angle CED = 90°$$

$$\angle C = \angle C$$

$$\angle CBA = \angle CDE$$

$$\text{Now, } \frac{\text{Ar. of } \Delta CED}{\text{Ar. of } \Delta CAB} = \left(\frac{6}{20}\right)^2$$

$$\text{Area of } \Delta DEC = \frac{36 \times 96}{400}$$

$$\text{Ar. } \Delta DEC = 8.64 \text{ cm}^2$$

5. Option (A) is correct.

Explanation:

Given, $\quad h = 7$ cm

L.S.A. $= 352$

Lateral surface area of a cylinder $= 2\pi rh$

$$352 = 2 \times \frac{22}{7} \times r \times 7$$

$$\frac{352}{2 \times 22} = r$$

$$8 = r$$

$$\text{Volume} = \pi r^2 h$$

$$= \frac{22}{7} \times 8 \times 8 \times 7 = 1{,}408 \text{ cm}^3$$

6. Option (C) is correct.

Explanation:

Given $\quad$ Perimeter $= 148$ cm

Diagonal $= 25$

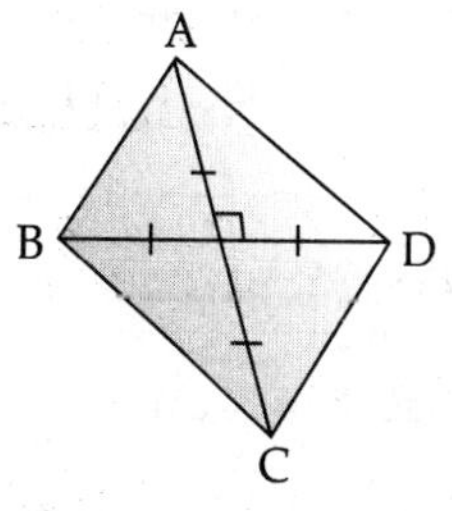

$$\text{Perimeter} = 4 \times \text{side}$$
$$148 = 4 \times \text{side}$$
$$37 = \text{side}$$
$$\text{side}^2 = \frac{d_1^2}{2} + \frac{d_2^2}{2} \text{ (using pythogoras)}$$
$$d_2 = 70$$
$$\text{Area of rhombus} = \frac{1}{2} \times 70 \times 25 = 35 \times 25 = 875$$

7. Option (C) is correct.

Explanation: Radius and height at cone are 12cm and 24cm respectively.

Let number of small sphere made = n

According to question,

$$n \times \frac{4}{3} \times \pi \times 2^3 = \frac{1}{3} \times \pi \times 12^2 \times 24$$
$$\Rightarrow \quad n = \frac{12 \times 12 \times 24}{4 \times 8} = 108$$

8. Option (A) is correct.

Explanation:

$$\text{Radius} = \text{R}$$
$$\text{Height} = \text{H}$$
$$\text{Volume of a cone} = \frac{1}{3}\pi \text{R}^2\text{H}$$

9. Option (D) is correct.

Explanation:

$$\text{Area of } \Delta = \frac{1}{2} \times \text{ base } \times \text{ height}$$

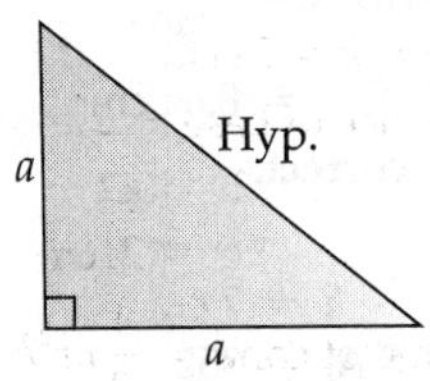

$$121 = \frac{1}{2} \times a \times a$$
$$121 = \frac{1}{2} a^2$$
$$a = 11\sqrt{2}$$
$$\text{Hypotenuse} = \sqrt{2} \times 11\sqrt{2} = 22 \text{ cm}$$

10. Option (C) is correct.

Explanation:

Given, $2\pi r - 2r = 60$
$$2r(\pi - 1) = 60$$
$$2r\left(\frac{22}{7} - 1\right) = 60$$
$$r = 14 \text{ cm}$$
$$\text{Area of circle} = \pi r^2$$
$$= \frac{22}{7} \times 14 \times 14 = 616 \text{ cm}^2$$

11. Option (D) is correct.

Explanation: Given,

$$\text{Side of hexagon} = 4 \text{ cm}$$
$$\text{Side of square} = 4\sqrt{2} \text{ cm}$$

Now,

$$\text{Area of hexagon} = 6 \times \text{ar. of eq. } \Delta$$
$$= 6 \times \frac{\sqrt{3}}{4} a^2$$
$$= 6 \times \frac{\sqrt{3}}{4} \times 4 \times 4 = 24\sqrt{3}$$
$$\text{Area of square} = a^2 = 4\sqrt{2} \times 4\sqrt{2} = 32 \text{ cm}^2$$
$$\therefore \text{ Required ratio} = 24\sqrt{3} : 32 = 3\sqrt{3} : 4$$

12. Option (C) is correct.

Explanation:

Let radius of cylinder = r units

and height of cylinder = h units

$\because$ Increase in curved surface area = 20% and height decreased by 4%

$$\Rightarrow \quad \frac{100+20}{100} \times 2\pi rh = 2\pi r' \times \left[\frac{100-4}{100}\right] h$$
$$\Rightarrow \quad \frac{120}{100} r = \frac{96}{100} r'$$
$$\Rightarrow \quad r' = \frac{5}{4} r = \frac{125}{100} r$$

$\Rightarrow$ Increase in radius is 25%

$\therefore$ Change in volume

$$= \frac{\pi\left(\frac{5}{4}r\right)^2 \times \frac{24}{25}h - \pi r^2 h}{\pi r^2 h} \times 100$$
$$= \left(\frac{25}{16} \times \frac{24}{25} - 1\right) \times 100$$
$$= \frac{8}{16} \times 100\% = 50$$

13. Option (D) is correct.

Explanation:

Given, Base = 9 cm

Hypotenuse = 41 cm

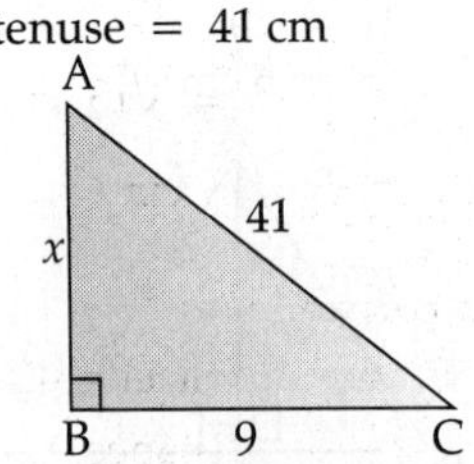

$$x = \sqrt{41^2 - 9^2} = 40 \text{ cm}$$
$$\text{Area} = \frac{1}{2} \times \text{ base } \times \text{ height}$$
$$= \frac{1}{2} \times 9 \times 40 = 180 \text{ cm}^2$$

14. Option (C) is correct.

Explanation: Let side of a square = x

Now, inradius of a square = $\frac{x}{2}$

Also, circum radius of a square = $\frac{x\sqrt{2}}{2}$

$$\text{Required ratio} = \frac{x}{2} : \frac{x\sqrt{2}}{2} = 1 : \sqrt{2}$$

15. Option (C) is correct.

Explanation:

$$\text{Area of D} = \frac{1}{2} \times \text{base} \times \text{height}$$
$$= \frac{1}{2} \times 200 \times 210 = 100 \times 210$$

∵ [200, 210, 290 are triplets. Thus, makes a right angle triangle.]

$$= 21{,}000 \text{ m}^2 = \frac{21{,}000}{10{,}000} \text{ hectares}$$
$$= 2.1 \text{ hectares}$$

16. Option (B) is correct.

Explanation: Volume of pyramid = $45\sqrt{3}$ cm

Base of pyramid = an equilateral triangle

$$\therefore \text{Volume of pyramid} = \frac{1}{3} \times \text{base area} \times \text{height}$$
$$45\sqrt{3} = \frac{1}{3} \times \frac{\sqrt{3}}{4} \times 6 \times 6 \times \text{height}$$
$$\frac{45\sqrt{3} \times 3 \times 4}{\sqrt{3} \times 6 \times 6} = \text{height}$$
$$15 = \text{height}$$

17. Option (A) is correct.

Explanation:

Radius of rod, $r_1 = 5$ cm

Length of rod, $h_1 = 52$ cm

Length of wire, $h_2 = 100$ cm

Radius of rod, $r_2 = x$ cm (Assume)

According to question,

$$\pi r_1^2 h_1 = \pi r_2^2 h_2$$
$$\Rightarrow 5 \times 5 \times 52 = r_2^2 \times 100$$
$$\Rightarrow \frac{52}{4} = x^2$$
$$\Rightarrow x^2 = 13$$
$$\Rightarrow x = \sqrt{13} \text{ cm}$$

Radius of wire, $r_2 = \sqrt{13}$ cm

18. Option (B) is correct.

Explanation: Radius of wheel = 42 cm = 0.42 m

$$\text{Speed} = \frac{\text{distance}}{\text{time}}$$

So, distance in 25 seconds = $2\pi r \times 40$

$$= 2 \times \frac{22}{7} \times 0.42 \times 40 = 105.6 \text{ m}$$
$$\text{Speed (in m/s)} = \frac{105.6}{25} = 4.224 \text{ m/s}$$
$$= 4.224 \times \frac{18}{5} \text{ km/h}$$
$$= 15.2 \text{ km/h}$$

19. Option (B) is correct.

Explanation: Given volume of hemisphere = $\frac{2}{3}\pi r^3$

$$19{,}404 = \frac{2}{3} \times \frac{22}{7} \times r^3$$
$$\frac{19{,}404 \times 7 \times 3}{2 \times 22} = r^3$$
$$r^3 = 9{,}261$$
$$r = \sqrt[3]{9{,}261}$$
$$r = 21$$

Total surface area of hemisphere = $3\pi r^2$

$$= 3 \times \frac{22}{7} \times 21 \times 21 = 4{,}158 \text{ cm}^2$$

20. Option (D) is correct.

Explanation: Radius = 11 m, height = 21

Now,

$$\text{material used} = \text{volume of cylindrical pillar}$$
$$= \pi r^2 h$$
$$= \frac{22}{7} \times 11 \times 11 \times 21 = 7{,}986 \text{ cm}^3$$

21. Option (A) is correct.

Explanation:

$$\text{Use method} = \left(a + b + \frac{ab}{100}\right)\% \text{ here, } a = b$$
$$= 2a + \frac{a^2}{100} = 2(-10)\frac{+(-10)^2}{100}$$
$$= -20 + 100/100 = -20 + 1 = 19\%$$

22. Option (B) is correct.

Explanation:

Let the radius = r cm

Height of cone, h = 24 cm

∵ Circumference of base = $2\pi r = 42\pi$

$$\Rightarrow 2r = 42$$
$$r = 21\text{cm}$$
$$\text{Volume of cone} = \frac{1}{3}\pi r^2 h = \frac{22}{3 \times 7} \times 21 \times 21 \times 24$$
$$= 11088 \text{ cm}^3$$

23. Option (B) is correct.

Explanation:

Base of prism = Right angle triangle

Here, [5, 12, 13] are sides of a right angle triangle.

Now, lateral surface area of prism

= height × perimeter of base.

= $h \times (a + b + c)$

= 10 (5 + 12 + 13)

= 10 (30) = 300 cm^2

Now, T.S.A. of prism = L.S.A. + 2 × area of base

$$= 300 + 2 \times \frac{1}{2} \times 5 \times 12$$
$$= 300 + 30 \times 2 = 360 \text{ cm}^2$$

24. Option (D) is correct.

Explanation: We know,

$$\text{Area of rhombus} = \frac{1}{2} \times d_1 \times d_2$$
$$= \frac{1}{2} \times 15 \times 8 = 60 \text{ cm}^2$$

25. Option (A) is correct.

Explanation:

Slant height of cone, $l = 28$ cm

Radius of cone, $r = 21$ cm

Total surface area of cone

$$= \pi r(r+l) = \frac{22}{7} \times 21(21+28)$$

$$= 22 \times 3 \times 49 = 3234 \text{ cm}^2$$

Level-2: INTERMEDIATE

1. Option (D) is correct.

Explanation:

Given that the radius of sphere is decreased by 10%. Then the percentage change in the volume of sphere will be equivalent to 3 successive decreases of 10% the volume.

Let the initial volume of sphere = 100 unit^3

So, after changing the radius, new volume

$$= 100 \times \frac{90}{100} \times \frac{90}{100} \times \frac{90}{100} = 72.9 \text{ unit}^3$$

Hence, percentage change in the volume

$$= \frac{100-72.9}{100} \times 100 = 27.1\%$$

2. Option (D) is correct.

Explanation: Given,

$$lb = 3, \quad bh = 12, \quad hl = 18$$

∵ Area of rectangle = product of two different sides

Now, $(lbh)^2 = 3 \times 12 \times 16 \Rightarrow lbh = 24$

∴ Volume of cuboid = $l \times b \times h = 24$

Now, $1 \text{ m}^3 = 1{,}000$ l

∴ Total volume = 24,000 l

3. Option (B) is correct.

Explanation: Given, $2(l + b) = 50$ cm

Let sides be $1x$, $4x$.

Now, perimeter = 50 cm

$2(x + 4x) = 50$

$x = 5$

∴ $l = 5, b = 20$

Now, Area = $l \times b = 5 \times 20 = 100$

Area of rectangle = Area of square (Given)

$100 = a^2$

$10 = a$

∴ Perimeter of square = $4a = 4 \times 10 = 40$ cm

4. Option (D) is correct.

Explanation:

Given:

Side of regular hexagon = 10 cm

We have, the area of regular hexagon

$$= \frac{3\sqrt{3}}{2}s^2$$

$$= \frac{3\sqrt{3}}{2} \times 10 \times 10 = 150\sqrt{3} \text{ cm}^2$$

5. Option (B) is correct.

Explanation:

Given, $h = 10$, Volume = 160 cm^3, Base = Square

We know,

Volume of prism = Area of base × Height

$160 = 10 \times$ area of base

$16 =$ area of base

$16 =$ area of square

$16 = a^2$

$4 = a$

T.S.A. of prism = (2 × area of base) + height × (perimeter of base)

$= 2 \times 16 + 10 \times 4 \times 4$

$= 32 + 160 = 192$

6. Option (D) is correct.

Explanation: Using fraction formula $\left(x + y + \frac{xy}{100}\right)$

Overall increase in area $= 40 - 20 + \frac{-20 \times 40}{100}$

$= 20 - 8 = 12\%$ increase

7. Option (A) is correct.

Explanation: Using Pythagoras

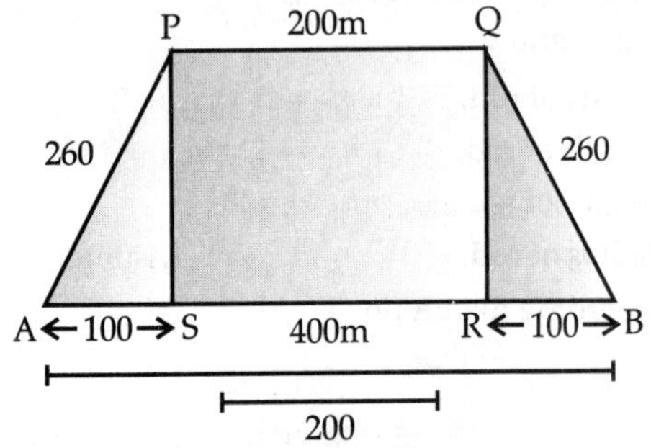

In ΔPAS, $PS = \sqrt{260^2 - 100^2}$

$= \sqrt{360 \times 160}$ ∵ $a^2 - b^2 = (a+b)(a-b)$

$= \sqrt{36 \times 16 \times 100}$

$= 6 \times 4 \times 100 = 240$

Now, area of trapezium $= \frac{1}{2} \times (200 + 400) \times 240$

$= 600 \times 120 = 72{,}000$

8. Option (C) is correct.

Explanation:

Given that C.S.A = 660 cm^2 and $h = 10$ cm

∵ C.S.A of cylinder = $2\pi rh$

$$660 = 2 \times \frac{22}{7} \times r \times 10$$

$$\Rightarrow r = \frac{660 \times 7}{2 \times 22 \times 10} = \frac{21}{22} \text{ cm}$$

$$\therefore \text{Diameter} = \frac{21}{2} \times 2 = 21 \text{ cm}$$

9. Option (D) is correct.

Explanation:

Given, inner radius $(r) = 23$ m

outer radius = 29

Now, area of circular track = $\pi R^2 - \pi r^2$

$= \pi(R^2 - r^2)$

$= \frac{22}{7}(29^2 - 23^2)$

$= \frac{22}{7} \times 6 \times 52$

$\therefore$ Cost of levelling the track = ₹$7 \times \frac{22}{7} \times 6 \times 52$

= ₹22 × 6 × 52 = ₹6,864

10. Option (D) is correct.

Explanation: Given,

$d = 210$ m

$r = 105$ m

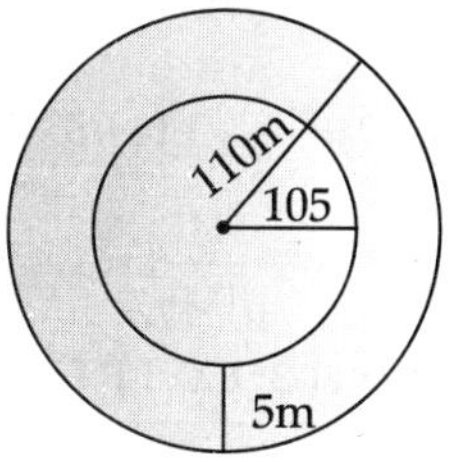

Now Area $= \pi R^2 - \pi r^2$

$= \pi(R^2 - r^2)$

$= \pi(110^2 - 105^2)$

$= \pi(110 - 105)(110 + 105)$

$= \pi(5)(215) = 1{,}075\,\pi$

11. Option (D) is correct.

Explanation:

Area of sphere $= 4\pi r^2$

So, original $= 4\pi r^2$

after increment $= 4\pi(r + 5)^2$

So, $4\pi(r + 5)^2 - 4\pi r^2 = 704$

$4 \times \frac{22}{7} \times (2r + 5) \times 5 = 704$

$2r + 5 = 8 \times \frac{7}{5}$

$2r = 6.2$

$d = 6.2 \qquad \because d = 2r$

12. Option (D) is correct.

Explanation: Given

$r : h$

$2 : 3$

So, $r : 2x, h = 3x$

Volume of cylinder $= \pi r^2 h$

$202.125 = \pi r^2 h$

$\frac{202125}{1000} = \frac{22}{7} \times 4x^2 \times 3x$

$\frac{49}{8} = \frac{8}{7} \times x^3$

$x = \frac{7}{4}$

Now, T.S.A. of cylinder $= 2\pi r(r + h)$

$= 20\pi x^2$

$= 20 \times \frac{22}{7} \times \frac{7}{4} \times \frac{7}{4}$

$= \frac{385}{2} = 192.5 \text{ cm}^2$

13. Option (B) is correct.

Explanation:

Base of cone = Circle

Area of base $= \pi r^2 = 400\pi$

$r = 20$

Slant height (l) $= \sqrt{15^2 + 20^2}$

$= \sqrt{225 + 400} = \sqrt{625} = 25$

$\therefore$ C.S.A. of cone $= \pi r l$

$= \pi \times 20 \times 25 = 500\,\pi$

14. Option (A) is correct.

Explanation: We know,

$D = \frac{\text{Mass}}{\text{volume}}$

$\text{Volume} = \frac{\text{Mass}}{\text{Density}}$

$= \frac{6{,}688}{10.5}$

$\text{Volume} = \frac{4}{3}\pi(R^3 - r^3) \qquad [R = 6] \text{ Given}$

$\frac{6{,}688}{10.5} = \frac{4}{3} \times \frac{22}{7}(216 - r^3)$

$216 - r^3 = 152$

$r = 4$

$\therefore$ Thickness $(R - r) = 6 - 4 = 2$ cm

15. Option (D) is correct.

Explanation: Given

$l = 12$ m

$b = 8$ m

$h = 10$ m

Area of four walls $= 2h(l + b)$

$= 20(20) = 400 \text{ m}^2$

$\therefore$ Cost of white washing = 400 × 25 = ₹ 10,000

16. Option (D) is correct.

Explanation:

Volume of cylinder $= \pi r^2 h$

	Radius	:	height	volume
Initial	2	:	5	20
New	5	:	4	100

So required % $= \frac{100 - 20}{20} \times 100 = 400\%$

17. Option (B) is correct.

Explanation:

Given length of sheet = 88

$2\pi r = 88$ cm

$r = 14$ cm

width of rectangle = height of cylinder

= 11 cm

$\therefore$ Volume of cylinder $= \pi r^2 h$

$= \frac{22}{7} \times 14 \times 14 \times 11$

$= \frac{22}{7} \times 196 \times 11 = 6{,}776 \text{ cm}^3$

18. Option (A) is correct.

Explanation: Radius of cylinder = $3r$

Height of cylinder = $4r$ [Given]

Now, $N = \frac{\pi r^2 h}{\frac{4}{3}\pi r^3} = \frac{\pi(3r)^2(4r)}{\frac{4}{3} \times \pi \times r^3}$

$N = 27$

19. Option (A) is correct.

Explanation:

Given that ratio between curved surface area to total surface area = 3 : 7

We know, curved surface area of a cylinder

$= 2\pi rh$

And the total surface area

$= 2\pi rh + 2\pi r^2 = 2\pi r(h+r)$

So, $\frac{2\pi rh}{2\pi r(h+r)} = \frac{3}{7}$

$\Rightarrow 7h = 3h + 3r$

$\Rightarrow \frac{h}{r} = \frac{3}{4}$

20. Option (D) is correct.

Explanation:

Given,

The radius of solid cylinder = 9 cm

And height = 25 cm

Using total surface area of cylinder = $2\pi rh + 2\pi r^2$

And curved surface area = $2\pi rh$

Required ratio = $\frac{2\pi rh + 2\pi r^2}{2\pi rh} = \frac{h+r}{h} = \frac{25+9}{25} = \frac{34}{25}$

21. Option (A) is correct.

Explanation:

	r	:	h	volume
Initial	5	:	5	125
New	4	:	7	112

Net effect $= \frac{125-112}{125} \times 100$

$= \frac{13}{125} \times 100 = \frac{52}{5}$

= 10.4 % decrease

22. Option (C) is correct.

Explanation:

Diameter of cylinder = 32 cm, r_1= 16 cm

Radius of sphere = 12 cm

$\therefore$ Volume of sphere= $\frac{4}{3}\pi r^3$

$= \frac{4}{3} \times r \times 12 \times 12 \times 12$

$= \pi \times 16 \times 12 \times 12$

$\therefore$ Increase is level of water = h of cylinder

Volume of dispalaced water = volume of sphere ...(1)

Now, volume of cylinder = $\pi r_1^2 h = \pi \times 16 \times 16 \times h$

According to eqn. (1)

$\pi r^2 h = \pi \times 16 \times 12 \times 12$

$16 \times 16h = 16 \times 12 \times 12$

$h = \frac{16 \times 12 \times 12}{16 \times 16} = 9$ cm

23. Option (A) is correct.

Explanation: h = 12 cm

l = 13 cm

$r = \sqrt{l^2 - h^2} = \sqrt{13^2 - 12^2}$

r = 5 cm

Now, Volume $= \frac{1}{3}\pi r^2 h$

$= \frac{1}{3} \times 3.14 \times 5 \times 5 \times 12 = 314 \text{ cm}^3$

$= \frac{314}{1{,}000}$ litre = 0.314 litre

Level-3: EXPERT

1. Option (B) is correct.

Explanation:

Length of base = 60 cm

Breadth = 30 cm

Edge of cube = 30 cm

$\therefore$ Volume of cuboid = a^3

= 30 × 30 × 30 = 2700 cm^3

Now, rise is water level = $\frac{\text{volume of cuboid}}{l \times b}$

$= \frac{2{,}700}{60 \times 30} = 15$ cm

2. Option (A) is correct.

Explanation:

Volume of the wall = $l \times b \times h$

So, let length = $80x$

Breadth = x

Height = $10x$

Now, volume of the wall = $80x \times x \times 10x$

$51.2 = 800x^3$

$51.2 = 800x^3$

$x = 0.4$

$\therefore$ Length of wall = 80 × 0.4 = 32 m

Height of wall = 4 m

Area of the one side of wall = 128 m^2

Cost of painting = 128 × 100 = ₹ 12,800

3. Option (D) is correct.

Explanation:

Side of square = a

Length of rectangle= $a + 10$

Breadth of rectangle= $a - 8$

$\therefore$ Area of square = Area of rectangle

$a \times a = (a + 10)(a - 8)$

$2a - 80 = 0$

$2a = 80$

$a = 40$

$\therefore$ Length = 40 + 10 = 50

Breadth = 40 – 8 = 32

$\therefore$ Perimeter of rectangle = (50 + 32) 2 = 164 cm

4. Option (A) is correct.

Explanation:

Let the breadth = 12

length = 24

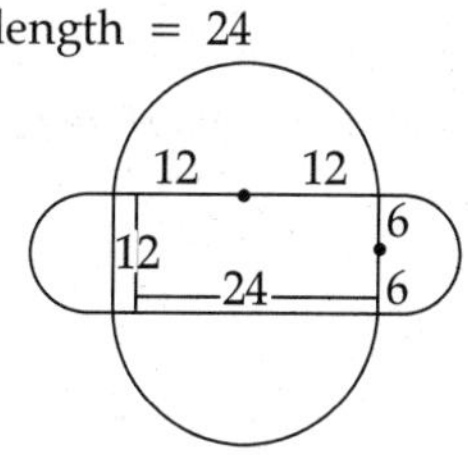

$\therefore$ Area of rectangular field = 24 × 12 = 288

Area of bigger semicircle = $\frac{1}{2}\pi r^2$

$= \frac{1}{2} \times \pi \times 12 \times 12 = 72\pi$

Area of 2 bigger semicircles = 2 × 72π = 144π

Now, Area of 2 smaller circles = $2 \times \frac{1}{2}\pi r^2$

$= \pi r^2 = \pi \times 6 \times 6 = 36\pi$

$\therefore$ Total area of circles = 144π + 36π

= 180π = 565.2

So, total area = 853.2 m²

5. Option (C) is correct.

Explanation: Given: Sides of triangular field are 65 m, 72 m and 97 m.

We have semi perimeter of triangles = $\frac{65+72+97}{2} = 117$ m

Area of triangle

$= \sqrt{(s(s-a)(s-b)(s-c))}$

$= \sqrt{(117(117-65)(117-72)(117-97))}$

$= \sqrt{(117(52)(45)(20))} = 2340 \text{ m}^2$

Let length and breadth of rectangular park are $5x$ and $13x$.

According to the question,

$\Rightarrow \quad 5x \times 13x = 2340$

$\Rightarrow \quad x^2 = 36$

$\Rightarrow \quad x = 6$

So, perimeter of rectangular park

$= 2(5x + 13x) = 36 \times 6 = 216$ m

6. Option (B) is correct.

Explanation:

Volume of hemispherical tank = $\frac{2}{3} \times \pi r^3$

$\therefore$ According to question,

Volume of tank = $\frac{2}{3} \times \pi \times 10.5 \times 10.5 \times 10.5 \times \frac{2}{3}$

= 1,617 m³

So, 1,617 m³ = 1,61,7000 l $\quad \because$ 1 m³ = 1,000 l

So, required time = $\frac{16,17,000}{7.7 \times 3,600}$

$= \frac{1,61,700}{77 \times 36} = \frac{175}{3}$ h

7. Option (C) is correct.

Explanation: $l = 18$

$b = 36$

$h = 72$

Now, volume of cuboid = 18 × 36 × 72 = 46,656 cm³

Volume of one new cube = $\frac{46,656}{8}$

$a^3 = 5,832$ ...(1)

From eq. (1) $a = \sqrt[3]{5,832} = 18$

Now, T.S.A. of cuboid = 2 ($lb + bh + hl$)

= 2 (18 × 36 + 36 × 72 + 72 × 18)

= 9,072

L.S.A. of cube = 8 × 4a^2

= 8 × 4 × 18 × 18 = 10,368

$\therefore$ Ratio required = 10,368 : 9,072 = 7 : 8

8. Option (A) is correct.

Explanation:

Perimeter = Sum of all sides

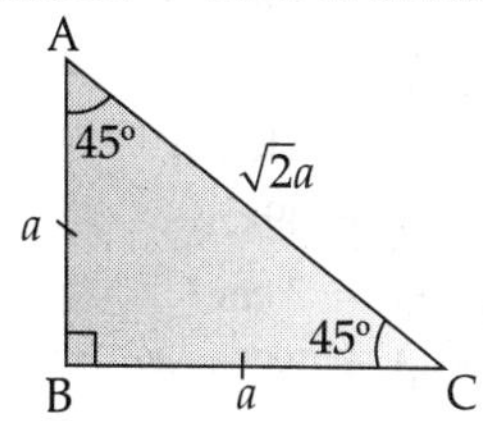

$= x + x + \sqrt{2}x$

$8(2+\sqrt{2}) = x(2+\sqrt{2})$ ...(1)

From Eq. (1) $x = 8$

$\therefore$ Area of ΔABC = $\frac{1}{2} \times 8 \times 8 = 32$ cm²

9. Option (D) is correct.

Explanation:

Given,

The radius of solid cylinder = 9 cm

And height = 25 cm

Using total surface area of cylinder = $2\pi rh + 2\pi r^2$

And curved surface area = $2\pi rh$

Required ratio = $\frac{2\pi rh + 2\pi r^2}{2\pi rh} = \frac{h+r}{h} = \frac{25+9}{25} = \frac{34}{25}$

10. Option (B) is correct.

Explanation: Volume of remaining portion

= Volume of H.S. – Volume of cone

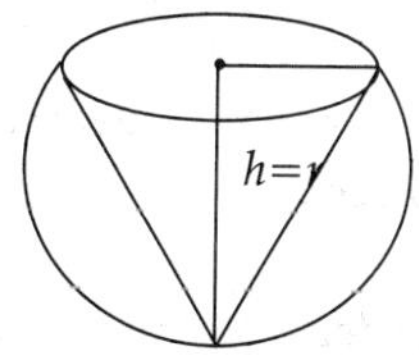

$= \frac{2}{3}\pi r^3 - \frac{1}{3}\pi r^3 = \frac{1}{3}\pi r^3$

$\therefore$ % required = $\frac{\frac{\pi}{3} \times r^3}{\frac{2}{3}\pi r^3} \times 100 = 50\%$

11. Option (D) is correct.

Explanation:

Diameter of cylinder = 1m, $r = \frac{1}{2}, h = \frac{5}{4}$m

Area covered in one revolution = C.S.A. of cylinder

$= 2\pi rh$

$= 2 \times \frac{22}{7} \times \frac{1}{2} \times \frac{5}{4} = \frac{55}{14}$

Revolutions in hour= 60 × 14

Area covered in one hour = $60 \times 14 \times \frac{55}{14}$ = 3,300 m^2

12. Option (B) is correct.

Explanation: Using, volume of cuboid = lbh

Volume of each brick = $25 \times 11.25 \times 6 = 1687.5$ cm^3

And volume of wall

$= (8 \times 100) \times (6 \times 100) \times (22.5) = 1080 \times 10^4$ cm^3

Required number of bricks = $\frac{1080 \times 10^4}{1687.5} = 6400$

13. Option (C) is correct.

Explanation: l = 343 cm

b = 49 cm

h = 7 cm

Volume of cuboid = 343 × 49 × 7

Volume of cube = a^3 = 7 × 7 × 7 = 343 cm^3

Let the no. of cubes = x

∴ $n \times 343 = 343 \times 49 \times 7$

$n = \frac{343 \times 49 \times 7}{343} = 343$

∴ Total surface area = $6a^2 = 6 \times 7^2 = 294$

T.S.A. of 343 cubes = 343 × 294 = 1,00,842 cm^2

14. Option (A) is correct.

Explanation: R = 8, r = 4

So, volume of a frustum of a cone

$= \frac{1}{3}\pi(R^2 + r^2 + rR)h = \frac{1}{3} \times \frac{22}{7} \times (8^2 + 4^2 + 8 \times 4) \times 7$

= 821.3 m^3 = 821.3 kilolitre

15. Option (C) is correct.

Explanation:

Let d = diameter

$h = \frac{2}{3}d$

$h = \frac{2}{3}(2r)$

$\frac{h}{r} = \frac{4}{3}$

Now, vol. of cylinder = vol. sphere

$\pi r^2 h = \frac{4}{3} \times \pi \times 4^3$

$r = 4$

C.S.A. = $2\pi rh = 2\pi \times 4 \times \frac{16}{3} = \frac{128}{3}\pi$

16. Option (C) is correct.

Explanation:

Radius of sector = 10.5 cm

Central angle= 120°

Also, Slant height = radius of sector and

$\frac{\theta}{360} \times$ perimeter of the sector

= perimeter of base of cone

$\frac{120}{360} \times 2\pi \times 10.5 = 2 \times \pi \times r$

⇒ $r = 3.5$

h of cone $= \sqrt{l^2 - r^2}$

$= \sqrt{(10.5)^2 - (3.5)^2} = 7\sqrt{2}$

∴ Volume of the cone = $\frac{1}{3} \times \pi \times 3.5 \times 3.5 \times 7\sqrt{2}$

$= \frac{343\sqrt{2}}{12}\pi$

17. Option (D) is correct.

Explanation: Radius of cylinder = 4 m

According to question,

3 × area of base = 2 × curved surface area

$3 \times 2\pi r^2 = 2 \times 2\pi rh$

$6r = 4h$

$h = \frac{6}{4} \times r = \frac{6}{4} \times 4 = 6$

∴ Volume of tank $= \pi r^2 h$

$= \pi \times 4 \times 4 \times 6$

$= 96\pi$ kilolitres

18. Option (B) is correct.

Explanation:

r of cone = 21

C.S.A. cone = 2,310

We know C.S.A. of a cone = 2,310

$\pi r l = 2{,}310$

$\frac{22}{7} \times 21 \times l = 2{,}310$

$l = \frac{2{,}310 \times 7}{22 \times 21} = 35$ cm

We know, $h = \sqrt{l^2 - r^2} = \sqrt{(35)^2 - (21)^2}$

$= \sqrt{56 \times 14}$

= 28 cm

Now, radius after increament = 42 cm

height after decrement = 14 cm

∴ Volume of cone = $\frac{1}{3} \times \pi \times 42 \times 42 \times 14$

= 25,872 cm^3

$= \frac{25{,}872}{1{,}000}$

= 25.872 = 25.9 approx.

19. Option (C) is correct.

Explanation: Inner cirucmference of path = 264 m

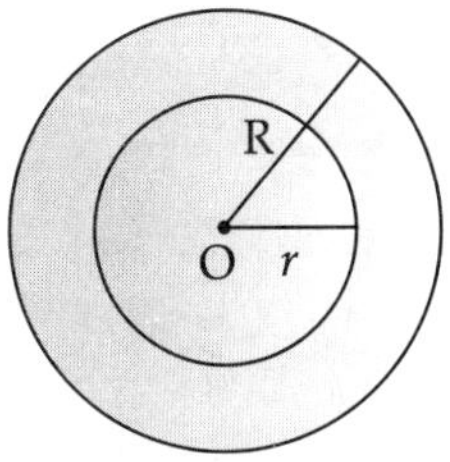

$$\text{Width of path} = 3\text{ m}$$

$$\text{Now, Inner radius} = r\text{ m}$$

$$\Rightarrow \quad 2\pi r = 264$$

$$\Rightarrow \quad 2\times\frac{22}{7}\times r = 264$$

$$r = 42\text{ m}$$

Again, radius of outer radius (r) = $r + 3$

= 42 + 3 = 45 m

$$\therefore \quad \text{Area of path} = \pi R^2 - \pi r^2$$

$$= \pi(R^2 - r^2)$$

$$= \frac{22}{7}(R+r)(R-r)$$

$$= \frac{22}{7}(45+42)(45-42)$$

$$= \frac{5742}{7} = 820.286\text{ m}^2$$

$$= 820\text{ m}^2$$

20. Option (B) is correct.

Explanation: BC = 7 cm (radius of quadrant)

BR = x cm

OR = OP = r cm

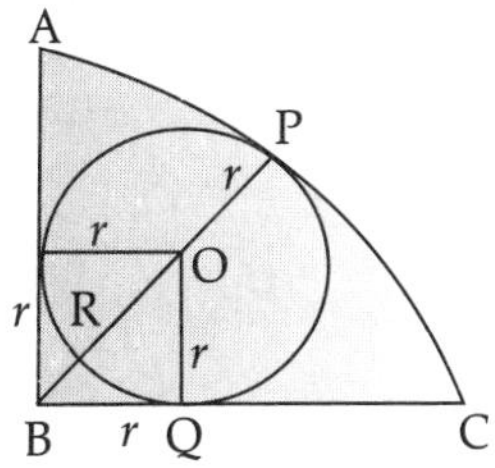

$$\therefore \quad 2r + x = 7 = BP \qquad ...(1)$$

$$OB = \sqrt{BQ^2+OQ^2}$$

$$= \sqrt{r^2+r^2}$$

$$x + r = \sqrt{2r^2}$$

$$x = (\sqrt{2}-1)r$$

Now, from Eq. (1)

$$2r + (\sqrt{2}-1)r = 7$$

$$r = \frac{7}{\sqrt{2}+1}$$

$$r = \frac{7}{\sqrt{2}+1}\frac{\sqrt{2}-1}{\sqrt{2}-1}$$

$$= 7(\sqrt{2}-1)\text{ cm}$$

$$\therefore \quad \text{Area of circle} = \pi r^2$$

$$= \frac{22}{7}\times 7\times 7(\sqrt{2}-1)^2$$

$$= 154(3-2\sqrt{2})\text{cm}^2$$

$$= 154(3-2\sqrt{2})$$

$$= (462-308\sqrt{2})\text{ cm}^2$$

Algebra

$(a+b)^3 = a^3 + b^3 + 3ab\,(a+b)$

$(a-b)^3 = a^3 - b^3 - 3ab\,(a-b)$

$a^3 + b^3 = (a+b)^3 - 3ab\,(a+b) = (a+b)(a^2 - ab + b^2)$

$a^3 - b^3 = (a-b)^3 + 3ab\,(a-b) = (a-b)(a^2 + ab + b^2)$

$(a+b+c)^3 = a^3 + b^3 + c^3 + 3\,(b+c)\,(c+d)\,(a+b)$

$(a+b)^2 = a^2 + 2ab + b^2$

$(a-b)^2 = a^2 - 2ab + b^2$

$(a+b)^2 = (a-b)^2 + 4ab$

$(a-b)^2 = (a+b)^2 - 4ab$

$a^2 - b^2 = (a+b)\,(a-b)$

$a^3 + b^3 + c^3 - 3abc = (a+b+c)\{a^3 + b^3 + c^3 - (ab + bc + ca)\}$

If $a + b + c = 0$ then

$a^3 + b^3 + c^3 = 3abc$

$a^2 + b^2 = (a+b)^2 - 2ab$

$a^2 + b^2 = (a-b)^2 + 2ab$

$(a+b+c)^2 = a^2 + b^2 + c^2 + 2ab + 2ac + 2bc$

$= a^2 + b^2 + c^2 + 2(ab + bc + ca)$

$x + \frac{1}{x} = a,$

$x^3 + \frac{1}{x^3} = a^3 - 3a$

$a^4 + b^4 + a^2b^2 = (a^2 - ab + b^2)\,(a^2 + b^2 + ab)$

$x + \frac{1}{x} = a \qquad x - \frac{1}{x} = b$

$x^2 + \frac{1}{x^2} = a^2 - 2$

$\left(x^2 - \frac{1}{x^2}\right) = \left(x + \frac{1}{x}\right)\left(x - \frac{1}{x}\right) = ab$

$x + \frac{1}{x} = a$

$x - \frac{1}{x} = \sqrt{a^2 - 4}$

$x + \frac{1}{x} = \sqrt{a^2 + 4}$

If $x - \frac{1}{x} = a$

Chapter 14

Algebra

LEARNING OBJECTIVES:

- Detailed identities related to algebra.
- Important results of algebraic expressions.
- $x+\frac{1}{x}=a$ form explained in detail.
- Different types of questions asked in various competitive exams.
- Method of solving questions.

➤ Algebra is that part of mathematics which allows problems and solutions to be represented in the form of mathematical expressions.

➤ **Algebraic Identities [Set-1]**

1. $(a+b)^2 = a^2+b^2+2ab$
2. $(a-b)^2 = a^2+b^2-2ab$
3. $(a+b)^2+(a-b)^2 = 2(a^2+b^2)$
4. $(a+b)^2-(a-b)^2 = 4ab$
5. $(a+b)^2 = (a-b)^2+4ab$
6. $(a-b)^2 = (a+b)^2-4ab$
7. $(a^2-b^2) = (a+b)(a-b)$

Example 1: If $a^2+b^2 = 169$ and $ab = 60$, $(a > b)$ then, find (a^2-b^2).

(a) 149 (b) 129

(c) 119 (d) 139

Sol. (c) Traditional Method:

Given, $a^2+b^2 = 169$, $ab = 60$

We know,

$$a^2-b^2 = (a+b)(a-b) \quad ...(1)$$

Also,

$$(a+b)^2 = a^2+b^2+2ab$$
$$(a+b)^2 = 169+120$$
$$a+b = \sqrt{289} = 17 \quad ...(2)$$

Similarly, $(a-b)^2 = a^2+b^2-2ab$

$$(a-b)^2 = 169-120$$
$$a-b = \sqrt{49} = 7 \quad ...(3)$$
$$\therefore \quad a^2-b^2 = 17\times 7 = 119$$

Value putting method

Given, $a^2+b^2 - 169$, $ab = 60$

Put $a = 12, b = 5$

Now $a^2+b^2 = (12)^2+(5)^2$

$= 144+25 = 169$

$= (a^2+b^2)$ (Given)

Also, $ab = 60$

$12\times 5 = 60$

$60 = 60$

It is clear that both conditions are satisfied.

So, $(a^2-b^2) = 12^2-5^2 = 144-25 = 119.$

Hence, option (c) is the correct answer.

Example 2: If $\frac{x}{y}+\frac{y}{x} = 2, (x, y \neq 0)$, then the value of $(x-y)$ is:

(a) 1 (b) 0

(c) –1 (d) 2

Sol. (b)

$$\frac{x}{y}+\frac{y}{x} = 2$$
$$\frac{x^2+y^2}{xy} = \frac{2}{1}$$

[for $x^2+y^2 = 2$, $xy = 1$]

Now, $(x-y)^2 = x^2+y^2-2xy$

$$(x-y)^2 = 2-2$$
$$x-y = 0$$

Hence, option (b) is the correct answer.

➤ **Algebraic Identities [Set - 2]**

1. $(a+b)^3 = a^3+b^3+3ab(a+b)$
$= a^3+b^3+3a^2b+3ab^2$
2. $(a-b)^3 = a^3-b^3-3ab(a-b)$
$= a^3-b^3-3a^2b+3ab^2$
3. $(a^3+b^3) = (a+b)(a^2+b^2-ab)$
$= (a+b)[(a+b)^2-3ab]$
$= (a+b)[(a-b)^2+ab]$
4. $(a^3-b^3) = (a-b)[(a^2+b^2+ab]$
$= (a-b)[(a+b)^2-ab]$
$= (a-b)[(a-b)^2+3ab]$

5. $(a + b)^3 + (a-b)^3 = 2(a^3 + 3ab^2)$
6. $(a + b)^3 - (a-b)^3 = 2(b^3 + 3a^2b)$

Example 3: If $a^3 - b^3 = 56$ and $(a - b) = 2$, then the value of $a^2 + b^2$ is:

(a) 20 (b) 48
(c) 5 (d) 22

Sol. (a) Given, $a^3 - b^3 = 56, (a - b) = 2$

We know $a^3 - b^3 = (a - b)[(a - b)^2 + 3ab]$

$56 = 2[(2)^2 + 3ab]$

$56 = 8 + 6ab$

$ab = 8$

Now, $a^3 - b^3 = (a^2 + b^2 + ab)(a - b)$

$56 = (a^2 + b^2 + 8)(2)$

$56 = 2(a^2 + b^2) + 16$

$56 - 16 = 2(a^2 + b^2)$

$20 = a^2 + b^2$

By value putting method

Option 'a' is the correct option

Given $a^3 - b^3 = 56, a - b = 2$

Put $a = 4, b = 2$

$4^3 - 2^3 = 56$

$64 - 8 = 56$

$56 = 56$

Now, $a - b = 2$

$4 - 2 = 2$

$2 = 2$

Hence, both conditions are satisfied.

$\therefore$ $a^2 + b^2 = 4^2 + 2^2 = 16 + 4 = 20$

Hence, option (a) is the correct answer i.e., 20.

Example 3: If $a^3 + b^3 = 9$ and $a + b = 3$, then find the value of $\frac{1}{a}+\frac{1}{b}$ is:

(a) $\frac{3}{2}$ (b) $\frac{5}{2}$
(c) –1 (d) $\frac{1}{2}$

Sol. (a) **Traditional method:**

Given $a^3 + b^3 = 9, a + b = 3$

Using $a^3 + b^3 = (a + b)[(a + b)^2 - 3ab]$

$9 = 3[(3)^2 - 3ab]$

$9 = 27 - 9ab$

$9ab = 18$

$ab = 2$

Now, $\frac{1}{a}+\frac{1}{b} = \frac{b+a}{ab}=\frac{3}{2}$

Hence, option (a) is the correct answer. i.e., $\frac{3}{2}$

Example 4: If $a^3 - b^3 = 416$ and $a - b = 8$, then find the value of $(a + b)^2 - ab$.

(a) 42 (b) 38
(c) 32 (d) 52

Sol. (d) Given, $a^3 - b^3 = 416, a - b = 8$

We know $(a^3 - b^3) = (a - b)(a^2 + b^2 + ab)$

$416 = 8[(a + b)^2 - ab]$

$\frac{416}{8} = (a + b)^2 - ab$

$52 = (a + b)^2 - ab$

Hence, option (d) is the correct answer. i.e., 52

➤ **Algebraic Identities [Set - 3]**

1. $(a + b + c)^2 = a^2 + b^2 + c^2 + 2[ab+bc+ca]$
2. $a^3 + b^3 + c^3 - 3abc = (a + b + c)[a^2 + b^2 + c^2 - (ab + bc + ca)]$

$= \frac{1}{2}(a + b + c)[(a - b)^2 + (b - c)^2 + (c - a)^2]$

$= (a + b + c)[(a + b + c)^2 - 3(ab + ca + cb)]$

$= \frac{(a+b+c)\left[3(a^2+b^2+c^2)-(a+b+c)^2\right]}{2}$

REMEMBER

➤ $a^3 + b^3 + c^3 - 3abc = 0, a^3 + b^3 + c^3 = 3abc$

If (i) $a + b + c = 0$ $(a \neq b \neq c)$

or

(ii) $a^2 + b^2 + c^2 - ab + bc - ca = 0$

➤ If $a^3 + b^3 + c^3 - 3abc = 0$, [a, b, c are integers] then $a = b = c$

➤ If $a^2 + b^2 + c^2 - ab - ca - bc = 0$ or $a^2 + b^2 + c^2 = ab + bc + ca$ then $a = b = c$

Example 5: If $a^2 + b^2 + c^2 = ab + bc + ac$, then find the value of $\frac{a+c}{b}$.

(a) 0 (b) 2
(c) 3 (d) 1

Sol. (b) We know,

If $a^2 + b^2 + c^2 = ab + bc + ac$

Then, $a = b = c$

So, $\frac{a+c}{b} = \frac{a+a}{a}=\frac{2a}{a}=2$

Hence, option (b) is the correct answer. i.e., 2

Example 6: If $x \neq 0, y \neq 0, z \neq 0$ and $\frac{1}{x^2}+\frac{1}{y^2}+\frac{1}{z^2}=\frac{1}{xy}+\frac{1}{yz}+\frac{1}{zx}$, then the relation among x, y, z is:

(a) $x + y + z = 0$ (b) $x + y = z$
(c) $\frac{1}{x}+\frac{1}{y}+\frac{1}{z}=0$ (d) $x = y = z$

Sol. (d) Given that $x, y, z \neq 0$

Assume $\frac{1}{x} = a, \frac{1}{y}=b, \frac{1}{z}=c$

$\therefore$ $a^2 + b^2 + c^2 = ab + bc + ca$

$\Rightarrow$ $a = b = c$

$\Rightarrow$ $\frac{1}{x} = \frac{1}{y}=\frac{1}{z}$

Also, $x = y = z$

Hence, option (d) is the correct answer. i.e., $x = y = z$

Example 7: If $x = 5$, $y = 6$ and $z = -11$, then the value of $x^3 + y^3 + z^3$ is:

(a) –890 (b) –990
(c) –970 (d) –890

Sol. (b) Given $x = 5, y = 6, z = -11$

Now, $x + y + z = 5 + 6 - 11 = 0$

It is possible when $[x^3 + y^3 + z^3 - 3xyz = 0]$

So, $x^3 + y^3 + z^3 = 3xyz$
$= 3[(5)(6)(-11)] = -990$

Hence, option 'b' i.e. –990 is the correct answer.

Example 8: If $a + b + c = 15$, $a^2 + b^2 + c^2 = 83$, then $a^3 + b^3 + c^3 - 3abc$ is:

(a) 220 (b) 180
(c) 145 (d) 270

Sol. (b) Method 1:

Given $a + b + c = 15$
$a^2 + b^2 + c^2 = 83$

We know,

$$(a+b+c)^2 = a^2 + b^2 + c^2 + 2(ab + bc + ca)$$
$$(15)^2 = 83 + 2(ab + bc + ca)$$
$$225 - 83 = 2(ab + bc + ca)$$
$$142 = 2[ab + bc + ca]$$
$$71 = [ab + bc + ca]$$

$\therefore a^2 + b^3 + c^3 - 3abc$
$$= (a + b + c)[(a^2 + b^2 + c^2) - (ab + bc + ca)]$$
$$= 15(83 - 71) = 15(12)$$
$$a^3 + b^3 + c^3 - 3abc = 180$$

Hence, option (b) is the correct answer i.e., 180.

Method 2: Option (b) is correct.

We know,

$a^3 + b^3 + c^3 - 3abc$

$$= \frac{[a+b+c][3(a^2+b^2+c^2)-(a+b+c)^2]}{2}$$

$$= \frac{15}{2}[3(83)-(15)^2] = \frac{15}{2}(249-225)$$

$$= \frac{15}{2}(24) = 15 \times 12 = 180$$

Hence, option (b) is the correct answer.

➤ Algebraic Identities [Set-4]

1. $(a^2 + b^2)^2 = a^4 + b^4 + 2a^2b^2$

Also, $(a^2 + b^2)^2 - a^2b^2 = a^4 + b^4 + a^2b^2$

$$\boxed{(a^2 + b^2 + ab)(a^2 + b^2 - ab) = a^4 + b^4 + a^2b^2}$$

2. $a^4 + b^4 = (a^2 + b^2)^2 - 2a^2b^2$

$$= (a^2 + b^2 + \sqrt{2}ab)(a^2 + b^2 - \sqrt{2}ab)$$

3. $(a^2 - b^2)^2 = a^4 + b^4 - 2a^2b^2$

$(a^2 - b^2)^2 - a^2b^2 = a^4 + b^4 - 3a^2b^2$

$$\boxed{(a^2 - b^2 + ab)(a^2 - b^2 - ab) = a^4 + b^4 - 3a^2b^2}$$

[Important]

Example 9: If $a^4 + a^2b^2 + b^4 = 8$, $a^2 + b^2 + ab = 4$ then find ab.

(a) 2 (b) 1
(c) 0 (d) 5

Sol. (b) Method 1: We know that,

$$a^4 + b^4 + a^2b^2 = (a^2 + b^2 + ab)(a^2+b^2-ab)$$

Given,

$$a^4 + b^4 + a^2b^2 = 8$$
$$a^2 + ab + b^2 = 4$$

So, $8 = 4(a^2 + b^2 - ab)$
$2 = a^2 + b^2 - ab$

Now, $a^2 + b^2 + ab = 4$
$a^2 + b^2 - ab = 2$
$\underline{-\quad -\quad +\qquad -}$
$2ab = 2$
$ab = 1$

Hence, option (b) i.e., 1 is the correct answer.

Method 2 : Short method

If $a^4 + b^4 + a^2b^2 = \underset{(x)}{(a^2 + b^2 + ab)}\underset{(y)}{(a^2 + b^2 - ab)}$

Then, $\boxed{ab = \frac{x-y}{2} \quad a^2 + b^2 = \frac{x+y}{2}}$ Always

So,

$$a^4 + b^4 + a^2b^2 = (a^2 + b^2 + ab)(a^2 + b^2 - ab)$$
$$8 = 4(a^2 + b^2 - ab)$$
$$2 = (a^2 + b^2 - ab)$$

So, $ab = \frac{4-2}{2} = 1$

Hence, option (b) is the correct answer.

Example 10: If $x^4 + y^4 + x^2y^2 = 21$, $x^2 + y^2 - xy = 7$, find the value of $\frac{x}{y} + \frac{y}{x}$.

(a) $\frac{-5}{2}$ (b) $\frac{-3}{4}$
(c) $\frac{3}{4}$ (d) $\frac{5}{2}$

Sol. (a) Given

$$x^4 + y^4 + x^2y^2 = 21, x^2 + y^2 - xy = 7$$
$$x^4 + y^4 + x^2y^2 = \underbrace{(x^2+y^2+xy)}_{(a)},\underbrace{(x^2+y^2-xy)}_{(b)} \quad ...(1)$$

$$21 = (x^2 + y^2 + xy)7$$
$$3 = x^2 + y^2 + xy$$

We know, from eq. (1)

$$x \times y = \frac{a-b}{2} = \frac{3-7}{2} = \frac{-4}{2} = -2$$

$$x^2 + y^2 = \frac{a+b}{2} = \frac{3+7}{2} = 5$$

So, $\frac{x}{y} + \frac{y}{x} = \frac{x^2+y^2}{yx} = \frac{-5}{2}$

Hence, option (a) is the correct answer i.e., $\frac{-5}{2}$

CONCEPT-1

(i) If $x+\frac{1}{x} = a$

then, (a) $x^2+\frac{1}{x^2} = a^2-2$ Let $a^2-2 = b$

(b) $x^4+\frac{1}{x^4} = b^2-2$ Let $b^2-2 = c$

(c) $x^8+\frac{1}{x^8} = c^2-2$ and so on

Let $x+\frac{1}{x} = 5$

$x^2+\frac{1}{x^2} = (5)^2-2 = 23$

$x^4+\frac{1}{x^4} = (23)^2-2 = 529-2 = 527$

(ii) If $x+\frac{1}{x} = a$

then, $x^3+\frac{1}{x^3} = a^3-3a$ Let $a^3-3a = b$

$x^9+\frac{1}{x^9} = b^3-3b$

Let $x+\frac{1}{x} = 5$

$x^3+\frac{1}{x^3} = 125-15 = 110$

$x^9+\frac{1}{x^9} = (110)^3-3(110)$

$= 13,31,000-330$

$= 13,30,670$

(iii) If $x+\frac{1}{x} = a$

then $x^5+\frac{1}{x^5} = \left(x^2+\frac{1}{x^2}\right)\left(x^3+\frac{1}{x^3}\right)-\left(x+\frac{1}{x}\right)$

$x^7+\frac{1}{x^7} = \left(x^3+\frac{1}{x^3}\right)\left(x^4+\frac{1}{x^4}\right)-\left(x+\frac{1}{x}\right)$

$x^9+\frac{1}{x^9} = \left(x^4+\frac{1}{x^4}\right)\left(x^5+\frac{1}{x^5}\right)-\left(x+\frac{1}{x}\right)$

Let $x+\frac{1}{x} = 3$

then, $x^5+\frac{1}{x^5} = \left(x^2+\frac{1}{x^2}\right)\left(x^3+\frac{1}{x^3}\right)-\left(x+\frac{1}{x}\right)$

$= 7\times 18-3 = 123$

$x^7+\frac{1}{x^7} = 18\times 47-3 = 843$

$x^9+\frac{1}{x^9} = 47\times 123-3 = 5,778$

(iv) If $x-\frac{1}{x} = a$

then $x^2-\frac{1}{x^2} = \left(x+\frac{1}{x}\right)\left(x-\frac{1}{x}\right)$

$x^3-\frac{1}{x^3} = a^3+3a$

$x^4-\frac{1}{x^4} = \left(x^4-\frac{1}{x^2}\right)\left(x^2+\frac{1}{x^2}\right)$

$x^5-\frac{1}{x^5} = \left(x^2+\frac{1}{x^2}\right)\left(x^3+\frac{1}{x^3}\right)-\left(x-\frac{1}{x}\right)$

$x^6-\frac{1}{x^6} = \left(x^3+\frac{1}{x^3}\right)\left(x^3-\frac{1}{x^3}\right)$

Let $x-\frac{1}{x} = 3$

$\left(x^2-\frac{1}{x^2}\right) = \sqrt{13}\times\sqrt{5} = \sqrt{65}$

$x^3-\frac{1}{x^3} = (3)^3+3(3) = 27+9 = 36$

NOTE:

If $x+\frac{1}{x} = a,$

then $x-\frac{1}{x} = \sqrt{a^2-4}$

If $x-\frac{1}{x} = a,$

then $x+\frac{1}{x} = \sqrt{a^2+4}$

(v) If $x-\frac{1}{x} = a$

then,

(a) $x^2+\frac{1}{x^2} = a^2+2 \Rightarrow b$

(b) $x^4+\frac{1}{x^4} = b^2+2$

Let $x-\frac{1}{x} = 3$

$x^2+\frac{1}{x^2} = 9+2 = 11$

$x^4+\frac{1}{x^4} = 11^2+2 = 121+2 = 123.$

(vi) If $x^4+\frac{1}{x^4} = a,$

then

(i) $x^2+\frac{1}{x^2} = \sqrt{a+2}$

(ii) $x+\frac{1}{x} = \sqrt{b+2};\ b=\sqrt{a+2}$

(iii) $x-\frac{1}{x} = \sqrt{b-2}$

SOME IMPORTANT POINTS OF CONCEPT-1

- If $x+\frac{1}{x}=2$, then $x = 1$

  So, $x^2+\frac{1}{x^2}=x^3+\frac{1}{x^3}=x^4+\frac{1}{x^4}$ ..... = 2 Always
- If $x+\frac{1}{x} = -2$, then $x = -1$
- If $x+\frac{1}{x} = 1$, then $x^3 = -1$
- If $x+\frac{1}{x} = -1$, then $x^3 = 1$
- If $x+\frac{1}{x} = \sqrt{3}$, then $x^3+\frac{1}{x^3} = 0$,

  $\Rightarrow x^6 = -1$ or $x^6 + 1 = 0$

Example 11: If $x+\frac{1}{x}=2$, , then $x^{12}-\frac{1}{x^{12}}=?$

(a) –4 (b) 0
(c) 4 (d) 2

Sol. (b) $x+\frac{1}{x} = 2$, so $x = 1$

$\therefore \quad x^{12}-\frac{1}{x^{12}} = 1-\frac{1}{1} = \frac{0}{1} = 0$

Hence, option (b) is the correct option i.e., 0.

Example 12: If $x+\frac{1}{x}=2$, then $x^{2013}+\frac{1}{x^{2014}}$ is:

(a) 1 (b) 53,554
(c) 0 (d) 2

Sol. (d) $x+\frac{1}{x} = 2, x = 1$ always

So, $x^{2013}+\frac{1}{x^{2014}} = 1 + 1 = 2$

Hence, option (d) is the correct answer.

Example 13: If $x+\frac{1}{x}=2\sqrt{3}$, then the value of $x^3+\frac{1}{x^3}$ is:

(a) $16\sqrt{3}$ (b) $20\sqrt{3}$
(c) $30\sqrt{3}$ (d) $18\sqrt{3}$

Sol. (d) $x+\frac{1}{x} = 2\sqrt{3}$

So, $x^3+\frac{1}{x^3} = (2\sqrt{3})^3-3(2\sqrt{3})$

$= 24\sqrt{3}-6\sqrt{3}=18\sqrt{3}$

Hence, option (d) is correct answer.

Example 14: If $x+\frac{1}{16x}=3$, then $16x^3+\frac{1}{256x^3}=?$

(a) 525 (b) 576
(c) 423 (d) 492

Sol. (c) $x+\frac{1}{16x} = 3$

Multiply both sides by 4

$4x+\frac{1}{4x} = 12$

Now, $64x^3+\frac{1}{64x^3} = 12^3-3(12)$

$= 1{,}728 - 36 = 1{,}692$

Now, divide both sides by 4

$16x^3+\frac{1}{256x^3} = \frac{1{,}692}{4}=423$

Hence, option (c) is the correct answer.

Example 15: If $\frac{a}{b}+\frac{b}{a}=3$, then $\frac{a^6}{b^6}+\frac{b^6}{a^6}=?$

(a) 423 (b) 322
(c) 574 (d) 623

Sol. (b) Here, $\frac{a}{b}+\frac{b}{a}$ is clearly is the reciprocal form.

So, we can apply the reciprocal concept

$\therefore \quad \frac{a}{b}+\frac{b}{a} = 3$

$\frac{a^3}{b^3}+\frac{b^3}{a^3} = (3)^3-3(3) = 18$

$\frac{a^6}{b^6}+\frac{b^6}{a^6} = (18)^2-2 = 324-2 = 322$

Hence, option (b) is the correct answer.

Example 16: If $x=3+\sqrt{8}, x^2+\frac{1}{x^2}=?$

(a) 29 (b) 34
(c) 11 (d) 37

Sol. (b) $x = 3+\sqrt{8}$

$\frac{1}{x} = \frac{1}{3+\sqrt{8}}\times\frac{3-\sqrt{8}}{3-\sqrt{8}}=\frac{3-\sqrt{8}}{(3)^2-(\sqrt{8})^2}$

$\Rightarrow \quad \frac{1}{x} = 3-\sqrt{8}$

So, $x+\frac{1}{x} = 3+\sqrt{8}+3-\sqrt{8} = 6$

$\therefore \quad x^2+\frac{1}{x^2} = (6)^2-2 = 34$

Hence, option (b) is the correct answer.

Example 17: If $a-\frac{1}{a-3}=6$, then $(a-3)^3-\frac{1}{(a-3)^3}$ is:

(a) 23 (b) 47
(c) 36 (d) 54

Sol. (c) $a-\frac{1}{a-3} = 6$

Subtract 3 from both sides

$$(a-3)-\frac{1}{(a-3)} = 6-3$$

$$(a-3)-\frac{1}{(a-3)} = 3$$

$$\therefore \quad (a-3)^3-\frac{1}{(a-3)^3} = (3)^3 + 3(3)$$

$$= 27 + 9 = 36$$

Hence, option (c) is the correct answer.

Example 18: If $2p+\frac{1}{p}=4$, then $p^3+\frac{1}{8p^3}$ is:

(a) 5 (b) 9
(c) 7 (d) 3

Sol. (a) $2p+\frac{1}{p} = 4$

Divide both sides by 2

$$p+\frac{1}{2p} = 2$$

Now, $p^3+\frac{1}{8p^3} = 8-3\times p\times\frac{1}{2p}(2)$

$$p^3+\frac{1}{8p^3} = 8-3$$

$\because a^3+b^3 = (a+b)^3-3ab(a+b)$

$= 5$

Hence, option (a) is the correct answer.

1 Level Beginner

1. If $x+\frac{1}{x}=5$, then $x^3+\frac{1}{x^3}$ is equal to: [SSC CGL 2019]
(A) 110 (B) 130 (C) 125 (D) 145

2. If $x + x^{-1} = 2$, then the value of $x^3 + x^{-3}$ is: [SSC CPO 2019]
(A) 1 (B) 2 (C) $\frac{1}{2}$ (D) 3

3. If $x-\frac{1}{x}=10$, then $x^3-\frac{1}{x^3}$ is equal to: [SSC CHSL 2019]
(A) 800 (B) 760 (C) 1,300 (D) 1,030

4. Expand $(4a + 3b + 2c)^2$ [SSC CGL 2020]
(A) $16a^2 + 9b^2 + 4c^2 + 24ab + 12bc + 16ca$
(B) $16a^2 + 9b^2 + 4c^2 - 24ab - 12bc - 16ca$
(C) $16a^2 - 9b^2 + 4c^2 - 24ab + 12bc - 16ca$
(D) $4a^2 + 3b^2 + 2c^2 + 24ab + 12bc + 16ca$

5. If $\left(y^2+\frac{1}{y^2}\right) = 74$ and $y > 1$, find the value of $\left(y-\frac{1}{y}\right)$. [SSC CHSL 2023]
(A) $6\sqrt{2}$ (B) $-2\sqrt{19}$
(C) $2\sqrt{19}$ (D) $-6\sqrt{2}$

6. If $a + b = 10$ and $\frac{3}{7}$ of $ab = 9$, then the value of $a^3 + b^3$ is: [SSC CHSL 2020]
(A) 370 (B) 360 (C) 270 (D) 350

7. The difference between two numbers is 43 and their product is 50. Find the sum of their squares. [SSC CHSL 2020]
(A) 1,949 (B) 1,948 (C) 1,946 (D) 1,947

8. The coefficient of 'y' in the expansion $(2y-5)^3$ is: [SSC CGL 2020]
(A) 30 (B) 50 (C) 150 (D) –150

9. If $(a-b) = 4$ and $ab = 2$, then (a^3-b^3) is equal to: [SSC CGL 2019]
(A) 88 (B) 92 (C) 84 (D) 80

10. If $\left[5x-\frac{1}{4x}=6\right], x>0$, then find the value of $\left[25x^2-\frac{1}{16x^2}\right]$: [SSC CGL Tier-I 2020]
(A) 36 (B) $6\sqrt{41}$
(C) $\sqrt{246}$ (D) $6\sqrt{31}$

11. If $x^2-8x+1=0$, what is the value of $x^8-3842x^4+1$? [SSC CGL 2022]
(A) –1 (B) 0 (C) 2 (D) 1

12. The reciprocal of $x+\frac{1}{x}=?$ [SSC CGL 2014]
(A) $\frac{x}{x^2+1}$ (B) $\frac{x}{x+1}$
(C) $x-\frac{1}{x}$ (D) $\frac{1}{x}+x$

13. If $4r = h+\sqrt{r^2+h^2}$, then $r:h$ is: [SSC CGL 2016]
(A) 8 : 17 (B) 17 : 8 (C) 8 : 15 (D) 15 : 8

14. If $a + b + c = 15$ and $\frac{1}{a}+\frac{1}{b}+\frac{1}{c}=\frac{71}{abc}$, then $a^3+b^3+c^3-3abc = ?$ [SSC CGL Tier-I 2016]
(A) 200 (B) 180 (C) 220 (D) 160

15. The value of $\sqrt{6-\sqrt{17-2\sqrt{72}}}$ is closest to: [SSC CPO 2019]

(A) 2.4 (B) 2.1 (C) 2.7 (D) 1.7

16. If $ab + bc + ca = 8$ and $a + b + c = 12$, then $(a^2 + b^2 + c^2)$ is equal to: [SSC CPO 2019]

(A) 134 (B) 144 (C) 128 (D) 160

17. If $\left(y-\frac{1}{y}\right)=8$, find the value of $\left(y^2+\frac{1}{y^2}\right)$. [SSC CHSL 2023]

(A) 64 (B) 62 (C) 60 (D) 66

18. If $(a + b) = 6$ and $ab=\frac{16}{3}$, then $a^3 + b^3$ is equal to: [SSC CGL 2019]

(A) 190 (B) 150 (C) 110 (D) 120

19. What will be the third proportional to $\left(\frac{x}{y}+\frac{y}{x}\right)$ and $\sqrt{x^2+y^2}$? [SSC CGL Tier-I 2013]

(A) $3\sqrt{xy}$ (B) $\sqrt{xy}$ (C) $4\sqrt{xy}$ (D) xy

20. If α and β are the roots of equation $x^2 - x + 1 = 0$, then which equation will have roots α^3 and β^3? [SSC CGL 2018]

(A) $x^2 + 2x + 1 = 0$ (B) $x^2 - 2x - 1 = 0$
(C) $x^2 + 3x - 1 = 0$ (D) $x^2 - 3x + 1 = 0$

21. If $x^2 + 9y^2 = 6xy$, then $x : y$ is: [SSC Constable GD]

(A) 1 : 3 (B) 3 : 2 (C) 3 : 1 (D) 2 : 3

22. If $p^4=119-\frac{1}{p^4}$, then the value of $p^3-\frac{1}{p^3}$ is: [SSC CGL 2015]

(A) 29 (B) 32 (C) 36 (D) 18

23. What is the constant term in the expansion of $\left(5x^2-\frac{1}{x}\right)^3$? [SSC CGL 2021]

(A) 5 (B) –15 (C) 15 (D) 75

24. If $x+\frac{1}{x}=\sqrt{3}$, then the value of $x^{18}+x^{12}+x^6+1$ is: [SSC CHSL 2020]

(A) 2 (B) 0 (C) 3 (D) 1

25. If $a + b + c = 5$, $a^2 + b^2 + c^2 = 15$, then find the value of $a^3 + b^3 + c^3 - 3abc - 27$. [SSC CHSL 2023]

(A) 23 (B) 27 (C) 25 (D) 21

26. If $A=\frac{x-1}{x+1}$, then the value of $A-\frac{1}{A}$ is: [SSC CHSL 2020]

(A) $\frac{x^2-1}{-4(2x+1)}$ (B) $\frac{x^2-1}{-4(2x-1)}$

(C) $\frac{-4(2x-1)}{x^2-1}$ (D) $\frac{-4x}{x^2-1}$

Level 2 Intermediate

1. If $\sqrt{x}-\frac{1}{\sqrt{x}}=3\sqrt{2}$, then $x^2+\frac{1}{x^2}=?$ [SSC CGL 2019]

(A) 402 (B) 324 (C) 326 (D) 398

2. If $\sqrt{x}+\frac{1}{\sqrt{x}}=\sqrt{6}$, then $x^2+\frac{1}{x^2}$ is: [SSC CGL 2019]

(A) 18 (B) 14 (C) 16 (D) 12

3. Find the value of:

$$\frac{6.35\times6.35\times6.35+3.65\times3.65\times3.65}{63.5\times63.5+36.5\times36.5-63.5\times36.5}$$ [SSC CPO 2020]

(A) 0.01 (B) 1 (C) 10 (D) 0.1

4. If $a^4 + b^4 + a^2b^2 = 273$ and $a^2 + b^2 - ab = 21$, then one of the values of $\left[\frac{1}{a}+\frac{1}{b}\right]$ is: [SSC CGL 2021]

(A) $-\frac{9}{4}$ (B) $\frac{-3}{4}$ (C) $\frac{9}{8}$ (D) $\frac{3}{2}$

5. If $a + b + c = 0$, then what is the value of $\frac{(b+c)^2}{bc}+\frac{(c+a)^2}{ca}+\frac{(a+b)^2}{ab}$? [SSC CGL 2021]

(A) 1 (B) –3 (C) –1 (D) 3

6. If $x^2 - 4x + 4 = 0$, then the value of $16\left(x^4-\frac{1}{x^4}\right)$ is: [SSC CGL 2020]

(A) $\frac{255}{16}$ (B) 255 (C) $\frac{127}{16}$ (D) 127

7. If $x=\sqrt{5}+2$, then the value of $\frac{2x^2-3x-2}{3x^2-4x-3}$ is: [SSC CGL 2019]

(A) 0.185 (B) 0.525
(C) 0.625 (D) 0.785

8. If $a = 331$, $b = 336$ and $c = -667$, then the value of $a^3 + b^3 + c^3 - 3abc$ is: [SSC CPO 2014]

(A) 1 (B) 6 (C) 3 (D) 0

9. If $x^2 - 3x + 1 = 0$, then the value of $\frac{\left[x^4+\frac{1}{x^2}\right]}{(x^2+5x+1)}$ is: [SSC CGL 2022]

(A) $\frac{27}{8}$ (B) $\frac{9}{4}$ (C) $\frac{5}{2}$ (D) 2

10. Simplify : $\frac{(375+125)^2-(125-375)^2}{375\times375-125\times125}$ [SSC CGL 2021]

(A) $\frac{15}{8}$ (B) $\frac{3}{4}$ (C) $\frac{3}{2}$ (D) $\frac{27}{28}$

11. If $a+b+c=0$, then what is the value of:

$\left(\frac{(b+c)^2}{bc}+\frac{(c+a)^2}{ca}+\frac{(a+b)^2}{ab}\right)\left(\frac{1}{a}+\frac{1}{b}+\frac{1}{c}\right)$?

[SSC CGL 2021]

(A) $\frac{-3}{2}$ (B) $\frac{9}{2}$ (C) $\frac{-1}{6}$ (D) $\frac{3}{2}$

12. If $a^2+b^2+c^2+84=4(a-2b+4c)$, then $\sqrt{ab-bc+ca}$ is equal to : [SSC CPO 2020]

(A) $5\sqrt{10}$ (B) $4\sqrt{10}$
(C) $\sqrt{10}$ (D) $2\sqrt{10}$

13. If $x+3y=6$, what is the value of x^3+27y^3+54xy? [SSC CHSL 2023]

(A) 264 (B) 258 (C) 216 (D) 220

14. If the sum of two nos is 11 and sum of their squares is 65. Then, the sum of their cubes is: [SSC CHSL 2020]

(A) 355 (B) 576 (C) 407 (D) 615

15. If $x+y+z=3$ and $x^2+y^2+z^2=101$, then what is the value of $\sqrt{x^3+y^3+z^3-3xyz}$? [SSC CGL 2020]

(A) 21 (B) 19
(C) 28 (D) 24

16. If $(x-5)^3+(x-6)^3+(x-7)^3=3(x-5)(x-6)(x-7)$, the what is the value of x? [SSC CPO 2019]

(A) 6 (B) 5
(C) 18 (D) 1

17. If $(3x+1)^3+(x-3)^3+(2x-4)^3=6(3x+1)(x-3)(x-2)$, then what is the value of x? [SSC CHSL 2019]

(A) 3 (B) 1
(C) 2 (D) $\frac{-1}{3}$

18. If $a+b+c=6$ and $a^3+b^3+c^3-3abc=126$, then $ab+bc+ca$ is equal to : [SSC CGL 2019]

(A) 5 (B) 6
(C) 12 (D) 8

19. The factors of $a^2-1-2x-x^2$ are ______. [SSC CHSL 2022]

(A) $(a-x-1)(a-x-1)$ (B) $(a+1+x)(a-1-x)$
(C) $(a-x+1)(a-x+1)$ (D) $(a-x+1)(a-x-1)$

20. If $x=\sqrt{1+\frac{\sqrt{3}}{2}}-\sqrt{1-\frac{\sqrt{3}}{2}}$, then the value of $\frac{\sqrt{2}-x}{\sqrt{2}+x}$ is closest to: [SSC CGL Tier-II 2019]

(A) 0.17 (B) 0.12
(C) 1.4 (D) 1.2

21. If $\frac{3(x^2+1)-7x}{3x}=6, x\neq0$, then the value of $\sqrt{x}+\frac{1}{\sqrt{x}}$ is:

(A) $\sqrt{\frac{25}{3}}$ (B) $\sqrt{\frac{11}{3}}$ (C) $\sqrt{\frac{35}{3}}$ (D) $\sqrt{\frac{31}{3}}$

22. If $b+c=ax$, $c+a=by$ and $a+b=cz$, then, $\frac{1}{9}\left[\frac{1}{x+1}+\frac{1}{y+1}+\frac{1}{z+1}\right]$ is: [SSC CGL 2020]

(A) 0 (B) $\frac{1}{3}$ (C) 1 (D) $\frac{1}{9}$

23. If $x^4+\frac{1}{x^4}=194$, $x>0$, then find the value of $x^3+\frac{1}{x^3}+x+\frac{1}{x}$. [SSC CHSL 2023]

(A) 76 (B) 66 (C) 56 (D) 46

24. If $l+m+n=0$, then what will be the value of $\left(\frac{l^2}{mn}+\frac{m^2}{nl}+\frac{n^2}{lm}\right)^2$? [SSC CHSL 2023]

(A) 9 (B) 16 (C) 4 (D) 1

25. If $2x^2-7x+5=0$, then what is the value of $x^2+\frac{25}{4x^2}$? [SSC CGL Tier-II 2020]

(A) $9\frac{1}{2}$ (B) $7\frac{1}{4}$
(C) $9\frac{3}{4}$ (D) 5

26. If $x-\frac{3}{x}=6$, then the value of $\frac{x^4-\frac{27}{x^2}}{x^2-3x-3}$ is: [SSC CGL 2020]

(A) 90 (B) 270
(C) 80 (D) 54

Level 3 Expert

1. If $a^{\frac{1}{3}}+b^{\frac{1}{3}}+c^{\frac{1}{3}}=0$, then $(a+b+c)^6$ is : [SSC CHSL 2019]

(A) $81abc$ (B) $729abc$
(C) $91abc$ (D) $729a^2b^2c^2$

2. If $a^2+\frac{1}{(a-3)^2}-6a=9$, then $(a-3)-\frac{1}{(a-3)}=?$ [SSC CGL 2019]
(A) 5 (B) 4 (C) 2 (D) 3

3. $144x^2-36x+\frac{9}{4}$ can be expressed as the square of ______. [SSC CHSL 2022]
(A) $14x-\frac{3}{2}$ (B) $12x-\frac{9}{4}$
(C) $12x-\frac{3}{2}$ (D) $12x-9$

4. If $\sqrt{x}+\frac{1}{\sqrt{x}}=3$, then $x^2(x^2-47)$ is: [SSC CGL 2020]
(A) 2 (B) –1 (C) 4 (D) 6

5. If $b^2-4b-1=0$, then find the value of $b^2+\frac{1}{b^2}+3b-\frac{3}{b}$. [SSC CHSL 2022]
(A) 32 (B) 30 (C) 18 (D) 24

6. If $a^2+b^2+c^2+27=6(a+b+c)$, then $\sqrt[3]{a^3+b^3-c^3}=?$ [SSC CGL 2019]
(A) 1 (B) 9 (C) 3 (D) 6

7. If $x+y+z=2$, $xy+yz+zx=-11$ and $xyz=-12$, then $\sqrt{x^3+y^3+z^3-2}=?$ [SSC CGL Tier-II 2019]
(A) 12 (B) 9 (C) 8 (D) 6

8. If $P=\frac{x^3+y^3}{(x-y)^2+3xy}$, $Q=\frac{(x+y)^2-3xy}{x^3-y^3}$
$R=\frac{(x+y)^2+(x-y)^2}{x^2-y^2}$, then $(P \div Q)\times R$ is: [SSC CGL 2020]
(A) $2(x^2+y^2)$ (B) $4xy$
(C) x^2+y^2 (D) $2xy$

9. If $2x^2+y^2+8z^2-2\sqrt{2}xy+4\sqrt{2}yz-8zx=(Ax+y+Bz)^2$, then (A^2+B^2-AB) is: [SSC CGL 2020]
(A) 16 (B) 14 (C) 6 (D) 18

10. If $x=\frac{\sqrt{3}}{2}$, then the value of $\frac{\sqrt{1+x}+\sqrt{1-x}}{\sqrt{1+x}-\sqrt{1-x}}=?$ [SSC CHSL 2020]
(A) 3 (B) 2 (C) $\sqrt{3}$ (D) $\sqrt{2}$

11. If $x+\frac{1}{x}=5$, then the value of $\frac{3x}{2x^2+2-5x}$ will be ______. [SSC CHSL 2022]
(A) $\frac{5}{2}$ (B) $\frac{2}{5}$ (C) $\frac{3}{5}$ (D) $\frac{5}{3}$

12. $(2x+y)^3-(x+2y)^3=(x-y)[A(x^2+y^2)+Bxy]$, then $2A-B$ is: [SSC CHSL 2021]
(A) 0 (B) 7 (C) 1 (D) 10

13. If $(56\sqrt{7}x^3-2\sqrt{2}y^3)\div(2\sqrt{7}x-\sqrt{2}y)=Ax^2+By^2-Cxy$, then find the value of $A+B-\sqrt{14}C$. [SSC CGL 2021]
(A) 58 (B) 10 (C) 38 (D) 19

14. If $(16\sqrt{2}x^3+81\sqrt{3}y^3)\div(2\sqrt{2}x+3\sqrt{3}y)=Ax^2+By^2+Cxy$, then, $2A-3B-2\sqrt{6}C$ is: [SSC CGL 2021]
(A) 25 (B) 137 (C) 79 (D) 7

15. If $x^2+4y^2=53$, $x-2y=5$, then x^3-8y^3 is: [SSC CGL 2022]
(A) –85 (B) 335 (C) 155 (D) 85

16. If $x=\sqrt[6]{27}-\sqrt{6\frac{3}{4}}$ and $y=\frac{\sqrt{46}+\sqrt{605}+\sqrt{245}}{\sqrt{80}+\sqrt{125}}$, then the value of x^2+y^2 is: [SSC Tier-II 2019]
(A) $\frac{223}{36}$ (B) $\frac{221}{36}$ (C) $\frac{227}{9}$ (D) $\frac{221}{9}$

17. If $x=a+\frac{1}{a}$ and $y=a-\frac{1}{a}$, then $\sqrt{x^4+y^4-2x^2y^2}$ is: [SSC CGL 2019]
(A) 8 (B) $16a^2$ (C) 4 (D) $\frac{8}{a^2}$

18. The value of $\frac{0.0203\times 2.92}{0.7\times 0.0365\times 2.9}\div\frac{(12.12)^2-(8.12)^2}{(0.25)^2+(0.25)(19.99)}$ [SSC CGL Tier-II 2020]
(A) 0.05 (B) 0.5 (C) 6 (D) 9

19. If $a+b+c=2, \frac{1}{a}+\frac{1}{b}+\frac{1}{c}=0, ac=\frac{4}{b}$ and $a^3+b^3+c^3=28$, find the value of $a^2+b^2+c^2$. [SSC CHSL 2020]
(A) 8 (B) 4 (C) 12 (D) 10

20. If the value of $\frac{3x\sqrt{y}+2y\sqrt{x}}{3x\sqrt{y}-2y\sqrt{x}}-\frac{3x\sqrt{y}-2y\sqrt{x}}{3x\sqrt{y}+2y\sqrt{x}}$ is the same as that of $\sqrt{x}\sqrt{y}$, then which of the following expression between x and y is correct? [SSC CHSL 2020]
(A) $9x-4y=36$ (B) $9x+4y=24$
(C) $9x+4y=36$ (D) $9x-4y=24$

21. If $x^4+\frac{1}{x^4}=14159$, then a possible value of $x+\frac{1}{x}$ is: [SSC CHSL 2022]
(A) 69 (B) 121 (C) 81 (D) 11

22. If $x+y+3=0$, then find the value of $x^3+y^3-9xy+9$. [SSC CGL 2022]
(A) 18 (B) –18 (C) 36 (D) –36

23. The value of $\frac{(a-b)^3+(b-c)^3+(c-a)^3}{(a^2-b^2)^3+(b^2-c^2)^3+(c^2-a^2)^3}$ is: [SSC CHSL 2020]
(A) $ab+bc+ca$ (B) 0
(C) 1 (D) $\frac{1}{(a+b)(b+c)(c+a)}$

24. If $a^2 + c^2 + 17 = 2(a - 8b - 2b^2)$, then value of $a^3 + b^3 + c^3$ is : [SSC Tier-I 2019]
(A) 9 (B) 3 (C) 6 (D) –7

25. If $27x^3 - 64y^3 = (Ax + By)(Cx^2 - Dy^2 + 12xy)$, then the value of 4A + B + 3C + 2D is : [SSC CGL 2022]
(A) –3 (B) 5 (C) 3 (D) –4

ANSWER KEY

Level-1: Beginner

1.	(A)	2.	(B)	3.	(D)	4.	(A)	5.	(A)	6.	(A)	7.	(A)	8.	(C)	9.	(A)	10.	(B)
11.	(B)	12.	(A)	13.	(C)	14.	(B)	15.	(A)	16.	(C)	17.	(D)	18.	(D)	19.	(D)	20.	(A)
21.	(C)	22.	(C)	23.	(C)	24.	(B)	25.	(A)	26.	(D)								

Level-2: Intermediate

1.	(A)	2.	(B)	3.	(D)	4.	(B)	5.	(D)	6.	(B)	7.	(C)	8.	(D)	9.	(B)	10.	(C)
11.	(B)	12.	(D)	13.	(C)	14.	(C)	15.	(A)	16.	(A)	17.	(C)	18.	(A)	19.	(B)	20.	(A)
21.	(D)	22.	(D)	23.	(C)	24.	(A)	25.	(B)	26.	(A)								

Level-3: Expert

1.	(D)	2.	(B)	3.	(C)	4.	(B)	5.	(B)	6.	(C)	7.	(D)	8.	(A)	9.	(B)	10.	(C)
11.	(C)	12.	(C)	13.	(A)	14.	(D)	15.	(B)	16.	(A)	17.	(C)	18.	(A)	19.	(B)	20.	(D)
21.	(D)	22.	(B)	23.	(D)	24.	(D)	25.	(C)										

Solutions with Detailed Explanation

Level-1: BEGINNER

1. Option (A) is correct.

Explanation:

$$x + \frac{1}{x} = 5, \text{ let } 5 = a$$

We know,

$$x^3 + \frac{1}{x^3} = a^3 - 3(a)$$

So, $$x^3 + \frac{1}{x^3} = (5)^3 - 3(5) = 125 - 15 = 110$$

2. Option (B) is correct.

Explanation:

$$x + x^{-1} = 2 \qquad x^{-1} = \frac{1}{x}$$

$$\Rightarrow x + \frac{1}{x} = 2$$

So, $$x^3 + \frac{1}{x^3} = (2)^3 - 3(2) = 8 - 6$$

$$x^3 + \frac{1}{x^3} = 2$$

3. Option (D) is correct.

Explanation:

$$x - \frac{1}{x} = 10$$

Using, $$x^3 - \frac{1}{x^3} = a^3 + 3a$$

$$= (10)^3 + 3(10) = 1000 + 30$$

$$x^3 - \frac{1}{x^3} = 1030$$

4. Option (A) is correct.

Explanation:

$\because \quad (a + b + c)^2 = a^2 + b^2 + c^2 + 2[ab + bc + ca]$

$(4a + 3b + 2c)^2$

$= 16a^2 + 9b^2 + 4c^2 + 2[(4a \times 3b) + (3b \times 2c) + (2c \times 4a)]$

$= 16a^2 + 9b^2 + 4c^2 + 2[12ab + 6bc + 8ac]$

$= 16a^2 + 9b^2 + 4c^2 + 24ab + 12bc + 16ac$

5. Option (A) is correct.

Explanation:

$$y^2 + \frac{1}{y^2} = 74$$

$$\Rightarrow y^2 + \frac{1}{y^2} - 2 \times y \times \frac{1}{y} = 74 - 2$$

$$\Rightarrow \left(y - \frac{1}{y}\right)^2 = 72$$

$$\Rightarrow y - \frac{1}{y} = \sqrt{72} = 6\sqrt{2}$$

6. **Option (A) is correct.**

Explanation:

Given $a + b = 10$

$$\frac{3}{7}\text{ of } ab = 9$$

$$\frac{3}{7} \times ab = 9$$

$$ab = 21$$

We know, $a^3 + b^3 = (a + b)[(a + b)^2 - 3ab]$

$$= 10[(10)^2 - 3(21)]$$

$$= 10[100 - 63] = 10(37)$$

$$a^3 + b^3 = 370$$

7. **Option (A) is correct.**

Explanation:

Given $a - b = 43, ab = 50$

We know, $(a - b)^2 = a^2 + b^2 - 2ab$

$$(43)^2 = a^2 + b^2 - 2(50)$$

$$1849 = a^2 + b^2 - 100$$

$$1949 = a^2 + b^2$$

8. **Option (C) is correct.**

Explanation: $\because [(x-y)^3 = x^3 - y^3 - 3xy(x-y)]$

$$(2y - 5)^3 = (2y)^3 - (5)^3 - 3(2y)(5)(2y - 5)$$

$$= 8y^3 - 125 - 30y(2y - 5)$$

$$= 8y^3 - 125 - 60y^2 + 150y$$

Hence, coefficient of 'y' is 150

9. **Option (A) is correct.**

Explanation:

Given $a - b = 4, ab = 2$

We know, $a^3 - b^3 = (a - b)[(a - b)^2 + 3ab]$

$$= 4[(4)^2 + 3(2)]$$

$$= 4[16 + 6] = 4[22]$$

$$a^3 - b^3 = 88$$

10. **Option (B) is correct.**

Explanation:

Given, $5x - \frac{1}{4x} = 6$

$\Rightarrow$ We know, $(a - b)^2 = (a + b)^2 - 4ab$ ...(1)

So $\left(5x - \frac{1}{4x}\right)^2 = 6^2 = 36$

From eq. (1)

$$\left(5x + \frac{1}{4x}\right)^2 - 4 \times 5x \times \frac{1}{4x} = 36$$

$$\left(5x + \frac{1}{4x}\right)^2 = 36 + 5 = 41$$

$$5x + \frac{1}{4x} = \sqrt{41}$$

So, $25x^2 - \frac{1}{16x^2} = \left(5x - \frac{1}{4x}\right)\left(5x + \frac{1}{4x}\right)$

$$= 6 \times \sqrt{41} = 6\sqrt{41}$$

11. **Option (B) is correct.**

Explanation:

Given equation, $x^2 - 8x + 1 = 0$

Divide the equation by x,

$$\Rightarrow x + \frac{1}{x} = 8$$

Squaring both the sides,

$$\Rightarrow x^2 + \frac{1}{x^2} = 64 - 2 = 62$$

Again, squaring both the sides,

$$\Rightarrow x^4 + \frac{1}{x^4} = 3842$$

$$\Rightarrow x^8 + 1 = 3842x^4$$

$$\Rightarrow x^8 - 3842x^4 + 1 = 0$$

12. **Option (A) is correct.**

Explanation:

$$x + \frac{1}{x} = \frac{x^2 + 1}{x}$$

So, Reciprocal $= \frac{x}{x^2 + 1}$

13. **Option (C) is correct.**

Explanation:

Given, $4r = h + \sqrt{r^2 + h^2}$

$$4r - h = \sqrt{r^2 + h^2}$$

On squaring both sides,

$$(4r - h)^2 = (\sqrt{r^2 + h^2})^2$$

$$16r^2 + h^2 - 8rh = r^2 + h^2$$

$$16r^2 - r^2 = 8rh$$

$$15r = 8h$$

$$\frac{r}{h} = \frac{8}{15}$$

14. **Option (B) is correct.**

Explanation:

Given $a + b + c = 15$

$$\frac{1}{a} + \frac{1}{b} + \frac{1}{c} = \frac{71}{abc}$$

$$\frac{bc + ac + ab}{abc} = \frac{71}{abc}$$

$$ab + bc + ac = 71$$

Now, we know,

$$a^3 + b^3 + c^3 - 3abc = (a + b + c\ [(a + b + c)^2 - 3(ab + bc + ca)]$$

$$= 15[(15)^2 - 3(71)]$$

$$= 15(225 - 213) = 15(12) = 180$$

15. **Option (A) is correct.**

Explanation: Given $\sqrt{6 - \sqrt{17 - 2\sqrt{72}}}$ ....(1)

Take $\sqrt{17 - 2\sqrt{72}}$ and solve

$$\sqrt{17 - 2\sqrt{72}} = \sqrt{9 + 8 - 2\sqrt{8}.\sqrt{9}}$$

$$= \sqrt{(3 - 2\sqrt{2})^2}$$

$$= 3 - 2\sqrt{2}.... \quad ...(2)$$

Now from eq. (1) and (2),

$$= \sqrt{6-3+2\sqrt{2}}$$

$$= \sqrt{3+2\sqrt{2}} = \sqrt{(\sqrt{2}+1)^2}$$

$$= \sqrt{2}+1 = 1.41 + 1 = 2.4$$

16. Option (C) is correct.

Explanation: $ab + bc + ca = 8, a + b + c = 12$

We know,

$$(a + b + c)^2 = a^2 + b^2 + c^2 + 2(ab + bc + ca)$$

$$(12)^2 = a^2 + b^2 + c^2 + 2(8)$$

$$144 - 16 = a^2 + b^2 + c^2$$

$$128 = a^2 + b^2 + c^2$$

17. Option (D) is correct.

Explanation:

$$\because \quad y - \frac{1}{y} = 8$$

$$\Rightarrow \left(y - \frac{1}{y}\right)^2 = 8^2$$

$$\Rightarrow \quad y^2 + \frac{1}{y^2} - 2 \times x \times \frac{1}{y} = 64$$

$$\Rightarrow \quad y^2 + \frac{1}{y^2} - 2 = 64$$

$$\Rightarrow \quad y^2 + \frac{1}{y^2} = 64 + 2 = 66$$

18. Option (D) is correct.

Explanation:

Given $\quad a + b = 6$

$$ab = \frac{16}{3}$$

We know,

$$a^3 + b^3 = (a + b)^3 - 3ab\,(a + b)$$

$$= (6)^3 - 3 \times \frac{16}{3}(6)$$

$$= 216 - 96 = 120$$

19. Option (D) is correct.

Explanation:

Let $\quad a = \frac{x}{y} + \frac{y}{x} = \frac{x^2+y^2}{xy}$

$$b = \sqrt{x^2+y^2}$$

We know, third proportional of a and $b = \frac{b^2}{a}$

So, $\quad \frac{\left(\sqrt{x^2+y^2}\right)^2}{\frac{x^2+y^2}{xy}} = \frac{x^2+y^2}{\frac{x^2+y^2}{xy}} = xy$

20. Option (A) is correct.

Explanation:

Given, $\quad x^2 - x + 1 = 0$

We know, $\quad \alpha = -\omega$ as $\beta = -\omega^2$

$$[1 + \omega + \omega^2 = 0, \omega^3 = 1]$$

$$\therefore \quad \alpha^3 + \beta^3 = -\omega^3 - \omega^6 = -1 - 1 = -2$$

Now, $\quad \alpha^3 \times \beta^3 = -\omega^3 \times -\omega^6 = \omega^9 = 1$

$\therefore$ Required equation is $x^2 + 2x + 1 = 0$

21. Option (C) is correct.

Explanation:

$$x^2 + 9y^2 = 6xy$$

$$x^2 + 9y^2 - 6xy = 0$$

$$(x)^2 + (3y)^2 - 2x3y = 0$$

$$(x - 3y)^2 = 0 \quad \because (a-b)^2 = a^2 + b^2 - 2ab$$

$$x - 3y = 0$$

$$x = 3y$$

$$\frac{x}{y} = \frac{3}{1}$$

$$x : y = 3 : 1$$

22. Option (C) is correct.

Explanation: $\quad p^4 = 119 - \frac{1}{p^4}$

$$p^4 + \frac{1}{p^4} = 119$$

So, $\quad p^2 + \frac{1}{p^2} = \sqrt{119+2} = \sqrt{121} = 11$

$$p - \frac{1}{p} = \sqrt{11-2} = \sqrt{9} = \pm 3$$

Now, we have,

$$p^3 - \frac{1}{p^3} = a^3 + 3a$$

$$= (3)^3 + 3(3) = 27 + 9 = 36$$

23. Option (C) is correct.

Explanation:

We know, $\quad (a - b)^3 = a^3 - b^3 - 3a \times b\,[a - b]$

So, $\quad \left(5x^2 - \frac{1}{x}\right)^3 = 5x^6 - \frac{1}{x^3} - 3 \times 5x^2 \times \frac{1}{x}\left[5x^2 - \frac{1}{x}\right]$

$$= 5x^6 - \frac{1}{x^3} - 15x^3 + 15$$

So, the constant term = 15

24. Option (B) is correct.

Explanation: We know $x^6 = -1$ when $x - \frac{1}{x} = \sqrt{3}$

So, $\quad x^{18} + x^{12} + x^6 + 1$

$\Rightarrow (x^6)^3 + (x^6)^2 + x^6 + 1$

$\Rightarrow (-1)^3 + (-1)^2 + (-1) + 1$

$\Rightarrow -1 + 1 - 1 + 1 = 0$

25. Option (A) is correct.

Explanation:

$a + b + c = 5$ and $a^2 + b^2 + c^2 = 15$

Now, $(a + b + c)^2 = 5^2$

$$a^2 + b^2 + c^2 + 2(ab + bc + ca) = 25$$

$15 + 2(ab + bc + ca) = 25$

$ab + bc + ca = 5 \quad ...(i)$

Now, $a^3 + b^3 + c^3 - 3abc - 27$

$= (a + b + c)\left(a^2 + b^2 + c^2 - ab - bc - ca\right) - 27$

$= 5 \times (15 - 5) - 27 = 50 - 27 = 23$

26. Option (D) is correct.

Explanation:

Given $\quad A = \dfrac{x-1}{x+1}$

So, $\quad A - \dfrac{1}{A} = \dfrac{x-1}{x+1} - \dfrac{x+1}{x-1}$

$= \dfrac{(x-1)^2 - (x+1)^2}{(x+1)(x-1)}$

$= \dfrac{x^2 + 1 - 2x - x^2 - 1 - 2x}{x^2 - 1}$

$\because (a+b)(a-b) = a^2 - b^2$

$A - \dfrac{1}{A} = \dfrac{-4x}{x^2 - 1}$

Level-2: INTERMEDIATE

1. Option (A) is correct.

Explanation:

$\sqrt{x} - \dfrac{1}{\sqrt{x}} = 3\sqrt{2} \rightarrow a$

We know,

$x - \dfrac{1}{x} = a^2 + 2$

$x - \dfrac{1}{x} = (3\sqrt{2})^2 + 2$

$= 18 + 2 = 20 \rightarrow b$

Now, $\quad x^2 + \dfrac{1}{x^2} = b^2 + 2$

$= 20^2 + 2 = 400 + 2 = 402$

2. Option (B) is correct.

Explanation:

$\sqrt{x} + \dfrac{1}{\sqrt{x}} = \sqrt{6}$

Squaring both sides

$x + \dfrac{1}{x} = (\sqrt{6})^2 - 2 = 4$

So, $\quad x^2 + \dfrac{1}{x^2} = (4)^2 - 2 = 16 - 2 = 14$

3. Option (D) is correct.

Explanation:

$$\frac{6.35 \times 6.35 \times 6.35 + 3.65 \times 3.65 \times 3.65}{63.5 \times 63.5 + 36.5 \times 36.5 - 63.5 \times 36.5}$$

Now, to knows decimal, multiply both numerator and denominator by 10^6.

Now, $\quad \dfrac{(635)^3 + (365)^3}{\left[(635)^2 + (365)^2 - 635 \times 365\right] \times 10^4} \quad ...(1)$

By $\quad a^3 + b^3 = (a + b)(a^2 + b^2 - ab)$

So, $\quad \dfrac{a^3 + b^3}{(a^2 + b^2 - ab) \times 10^4} \qquad a = 635, b = 365$

$$\frac{(a+b)(a^2 - ab + b^2)}{(a^2 + b^2 - ab) \times 10^4} = \frac{a+b}{10^4} = \frac{635 + 365}{10,000} = \frac{1,000}{10,000} = 0.1$$

4. Option (B) is correct.

Explanation: Given

$a^4 + b^4 + a^2b^2 = 273, a^2 + b^2 - ab = 21$

We know,

$a^4 + b^4 + a^2b^2 = (a^2 + b^2 + ab)(a^2 + b^2 - ab)$

$273 = \dfrac{13}{x} \times \dfrac{21}{y}$

Now, $\quad a^2 + b^2 + ab = 13 = x \quad (1)$

$a^2 + b^2 - ab = 21 = y \quad (2)$

By solving (1) and (2)

$a^2 + b^2 = 17, ab = -4$

OR we know,

$a^2 + b^2 = \dfrac{x+y}{2} = \dfrac{13+21}{2} = 17$

$ab = \dfrac{x-y}{2} = \dfrac{13-21}{2} = -4$

$\therefore \quad (a + b)^2 = a^2 + b^2 + 2ab$

$(a + b)^2 = 17 - 8$

$a + b = \sqrt{9} = 3$

So, $\quad \dfrac{1}{a} + \dfrac{1}{b} = \dfrac{a+b}{ab} = -\dfrac{3}{4}$

5. Option (D) is correct.

Explanation:

$a + b + c = 0 \quad ...(1)$

Put $\quad a = 1$

$b = 1$

$c = -2$

So, $\quad 1 + 1 - 2 = 0 \quad$ (Condition satisfied)

Now,

$\dfrac{(b+c)^2}{bc} + \dfrac{(c+a)^2}{ca} + \dfrac{(a+b)^2}{ab}$

$= \dfrac{(1-2)^2}{-2} + \dfrac{(-2+1)^2}{-2} + \dfrac{(1+1)^2}{1}$

$= -\dfrac{1}{2} - \dfrac{1}{2} + 4 = \dfrac{-1-1+8}{2} = \dfrac{6}{2} = 3$

6. Option (B) is correct.

Explanation:

Given $\quad x^2 - 4x + 4 = 0$

$(x)^2 + (2)^2 - 2 \times 2x = 0$

$(x - 2)^2 = 0$

So, $\quad x - 2 = 0$

$x = 2$

Now, $16\left[x^4-\frac{1}{x^4}\right]$

$$16\left[2^4-\frac{1}{2^4}\right] = \left[16-\frac{1}{16}\right]\times 16$$

$$= \frac{256-1}{16}\times 16 = 255$$

7. Option (C) is correct.

Explanation:

Given $x = \sqrt{5}+2$

So, $\frac{1}{x} = \sqrt{5}-2$

$$x-\frac{1}{x} = \sqrt{5}+2-(\sqrt{5}-2) = 4$$

Now, $\frac{2x^2-3x-2}{3x^2-4x-3}$

Divide the expression by x

$$= \frac{2x-3-\frac{2}{x}}{3x-4-\frac{3}{x}}$$

$$= \frac{2\left(x-\frac{1}{x}\right)-3}{3\left(x-\frac{1}{x}\right)-4} = \frac{2(4)-3}{3(4)-4}$$

$$= \frac{5}{8} = 0.625$$

8. Option (D) is correct.

Explanation:

Given, $a = 331, b = 336, c = -667$

We know, $a^3+b^3+c^3-3abc$

$= (a+b+c)\,[a^2+b^2+c^2-(ab+bc+ca)]$ ...(1)

$a+b+c = 331+336-667 = 0$

Put this value of $a+b+c$ in eq. (1)

$a^3+b^3+c^3-3abc = 0 \quad [a^2+b^2+c^2-[ab+ca+bc]$

$a^3+b^3+c^3-3abc = 0$

If $a+b+c=0$, then $a^3+b^3+c^3-3abc = 0$ [always]

9. Option (B) is correct.

Explanation:

$$x^2-3x+1 = 0$$

Divide the expression by 'x'

$$x-3+\frac{1}{x} = 0$$

$$x+\frac{1}{x} = 3$$

$$\Rightarrow x^3+\frac{1}{x^3} = (3)^3-3(3) = 18$$

Now, $\frac{x^4+\frac{1}{x^2}}{x^2+5x+1}$

Divide both numerator and denominator by 'x'

$$\frac{x^3+\frac{1}{x^3}}{x+\frac{1}{x}+5} = \frac{18}{3+5} = \frac{18}{8} = \frac{9}{4}$$

10. Option (C) is correct.

Explanation:

$$\frac{(375+125)^2-(125-375)^2}{375\times375-125\times125} \quad ...(1)$$

We know $(a+b)^2-(a-b)^2 = 4ab$

$a^2-b^2 = (a+b)(a-b)$

Using both in eq. (1)

$$\frac{4(125)(375)}{500\times250} = \frac{3}{2}$$

11. Option (B) is correct.

Explanation:

$a+b+c = 0$

Put $a = 1, b = 1, c = -2$

So, $a+b+c = 0$

$1+1-2 = 0$

$0 = 0$ satisfied

Now,

$$\left[\frac{(1-2)^2}{-2}+\frac{(-2+1)^2}{-2}+\frac{(1+1)^2}{1}\right]\left(\frac{1}{1}+\frac{1}{1}+\frac{1}{-2}\right)$$

$$= \left(\frac{-1}{2}\frac{-1}{2}+4\right)\left(2-\frac{1}{2}\right) = (3)\left(\frac{3}{2}\right) = \frac{9}{2}$$

12. Option (D) is correct.

Explanation:

$a^2+b^2+c^2+84 = 4(a-2b+4c)$

$a^2+b^2+c^2+84 = 2(2a-4b+8c)$

Here, $a = \frac{\text{coeff. of } a}{\text{coeff. of } a^2}$, $b = \frac{\text{coeff. of } b}{\text{coeff. of } b^2}$

$c = \frac{\text{coeff. of } c}{\text{coeff. of } c^2}$

$a = 2, b = -4, c = 8$

Now, $\sqrt{ab-bc+ca} = \sqrt{-8+32+16} = \sqrt{40} = 2\sqrt{10}$

13. Option (C) is correct.

Explanation:

$x+3y = 6$ ...(i)

Cube both sides

$\Rightarrow (x+3y)^3 = 6^3$

$\Rightarrow x^3+27y^3+3\times x\times 3y\,(x+3y) = 216$

$\Rightarrow x^3+27y^3+9xy\times 6 = 216$

Using Equation (i)

$\Rightarrow x^3+27y^3+54xy = 216$

14. Option (C) is correct.

Explanation:

$a+b = 11$

$a^2+b^2 = 65,\ a^3+b^3 = ?$

We know $(a + b)^2 = a^2 + b^2 + 2ab$

$(11)^2 = 65 + 2ab$

$121 - 65 = 2ab$

$28 = ab$

Also, $a^3 + b^3 = (a + b)(a^2 + b^2 - ab)$

$= (11)(65 - 28) = (11)(37) = 407$

15. Option (A) is correct.

Explanation: Given

$$x + y + z = 3, x^2 + y^2 + z^2 = 101$$

Method 1 : We know,

$$(x + y + z)^2 = x^2 + y^2 + z^2 + 2(xy + yz + zx)$$

$$(3)^2 = 101 + 2(xy + yz + zx)$$

$$9 = 101 + 2[xy + yz + zx]$$

$$\frac{-92}{2} = xy + yz + zx$$

$$-46 = xy + yz + zx$$

Now, $x^3 + y^3 + z^3 - 3xyz$

$= (x + y + z)[x^2 + y^2 + z^2 - (xy + yz + zx)]$

$= 3[101 + 48] = 3(147)$

$$\sqrt{x^3 + y^3 + z^3 - 3xyz} = \sqrt{441} = 21$$

Method 2 : Use $x^3 + y^3 + z^3 - 3xyz$

$$= \frac{(x+y+z)[3(x^2+y^2+z^2)-(x+y+z)^2]}{2}$$

$$= \frac{3[3(101)-(3)^2]}{2} = \frac{3(303-9)}{2} = 3\left[\frac{294}{2}\right]$$

$= 3(147) = 441$

Now, $\sqrt{x^3 + y^3 + z^3 - 3xyz} = \sqrt{441} = 21$

16. Option (A) is correct.

Explanation:

$(x - 5)^3 + (x - 6)^3 + (x - 7)^3 = 3(x - 5)(x - 6)(x - 7)$

Let $a = x - 5, b = x - 6, c = x - 7$

We know,

$$a^3 + b^3 + c^3 = 3abc, \text{ when } a + b + c = 0$$

So, $(x - 5) + (x - 6) + (x - 7) = 0$

$$3x - 18 = 0$$

$$3x = 18$$

$$x = 6$$

17. Option (C) is correct.

Explanation:

$(3x + 1)^3 + (x - 3)^3 + (2x - 4)^3$

$= 6(3x + 1)(x - 3)(x - 2)$

Let $a = (3x + 1), b = (x - 3), c = (2x - 4)$

We know, $a^3 + b^3 + c^3 = 3abc$, when $a + b + c = 0$

So, $(3x + 1) + (x - 6) + (2x - 7) = 0$

$$6x - 12 = 0$$

$$6x = 12$$

$$x = 2$$

18. Option (A) is correct.

Explanation:

Given $a + b + c = 6$

$$a^3 + b^3 + c^3 - 3abc = 126$$

$$ab + bc + ca = ?$$

We know,

$a^3 + b^3 + c^3 - 3abc$

$= (a + b + c)[(a + b + c)^2 - 3(ab + ca + bc)]$

$$126 = 6[(6)^2 - 3(ab + bc + ca)]$$

$$21 = 36 - 3(ab + bc + ca)$$

$$21 - 36 = -3(ab + bc + ca)$$

$$3(ab + bc + ca) = 15$$

$$ab + bc + ca = 5$$

19. Option (B) is correct.

Explanation:

Given expression,

$$a^2 - 1 - 2x - x^2 = 0$$

$\Rightarrow a^2 - (x^2 + 2x + 1) = 0$

$\Rightarrow a^2 - (x + 1)^2 = 0$

$\Rightarrow (a + x + 1)(a - x - 1) = 0$

[as $a^2 - b^2 = (a + b)(a - b)$]

20. Option (A) is correct.

Explanation:

Given, $x = \sqrt{1+\frac{\sqrt{3}}{2}} - \sqrt{1-\frac{\sqrt{3}}{2}}$

$$= \sqrt{\frac{2+\sqrt{3}}{2}} - \sqrt{\frac{2-\sqrt{3}}{2}}$$

Multiply and divide by 2

$$= \sqrt{\frac{4+2\sqrt{3}}{4}} - \sqrt{\frac{4-2\sqrt{3}}{4}}$$

$$= \sqrt{\left(\frac{\sqrt{3}+1}{2}\right)^2} - \sqrt{\left(\frac{\sqrt{3}-1}{2}\right)^2}$$

$$= \frac{\sqrt{3}+1}{2} - \frac{\sqrt{3}-1}{2} = 1$$

$$x = 1$$

$$\therefore \frac{\sqrt{2}-x}{\sqrt{2}+x} = \frac{\sqrt{2}-1}{\sqrt{2}+1}$$

$$= \frac{\sqrt{2}-1}{\sqrt{2}+1} \times \frac{\sqrt{2}-1}{\sqrt{2}-1}$$

$$= \frac{2+1-2\sqrt{2}}{(\sqrt{2})^2-1} = \frac{3-2\sqrt{2}}{1}$$

$= 3 - 2\sqrt{2} = 0.17$ approx.

21. Option (D) is correct.

Explanation:

$$\frac{3(x^2+1)-7x}{3x} = 6$$

$\Rightarrow 3x^2 + 3 - 7x = 18x$

Divide both sides by x

$$3x + \frac{3}{x} - 7 = 18$$

$$3\left(x+\frac{1}{x}\right) = 25$$

$$x+\frac{1}{x} = \frac{25}{3}$$

Now,

$$\sqrt{x}+\frac{1}{\sqrt{x}} = \sqrt{\frac{25}{3}+2} \qquad \because \text{If } a^2+\frac{1}{a^2}=k,$$

$$= \sqrt{\frac{31}{3}} \qquad \text{then } a+\frac{1}{a} = \sqrt{k+2}$$

22. Option (D) is correct.

Explanation: Given, $b + c = ax, c + a = by, a + b = cz$

Make above expressions in the form of $a + b + c$

$$a + b + c = a + ax$$

$$\Rightarrow \frac{a+b+c}{a} = 1 + x \qquad ...(1)$$

$$a + b + c = b + by$$

$$\Rightarrow \frac{a+b+c}{b} = 1 + y \qquad ...(2)$$

$$a + b + c = c + cz$$

$$\Rightarrow \frac{a+b+c}{a} = 1 + z \qquad ...(3)$$

From eq. (1), (2) and (3)

$$\Rightarrow \frac{1}{9}\left[\frac{1}{x+1}+\frac{1}{y+1}+\frac{1}{z+1}\right] = \frac{1}{9}\left[\frac{a+b+c}{a+b+c}\right] = \frac{1}{9}$$

23. Option (C) is correct.

Explanation:

$$\because x^4+\frac{1}{x^4} = 194$$

$$\Rightarrow (x^2)^2+\left(\frac{1}{x^2}\right)^2+2\times x^2\times\frac{1}{x^2} = 194 + 2 = 196 = 14^2$$

$$\Rightarrow \left(x^2+\frac{1}{x^2}\right)^2 = 14^2$$

$$\Rightarrow x^2+\frac{1}{x^2} = 14$$

$$\Rightarrow x^2+\frac{1}{x^2}+2\times x\times\frac{1}{x} = 14 + 2 = 16 = 4^2$$

$$\Rightarrow x+\frac{1}{x} = 4 \qquad ...(i)$$

$$\text{Now, } x^3+\frac{1}{x^3}+x+\frac{1}{x}$$

$$= \left(x+\frac{1}{x}\right)^3 - 3\left(x+\frac{1}{x}\right) + \left(x+\frac{1}{n}\right)$$

$$= 4^3 - 3\times 4 + 4 + = 64 - 8 = 56$$

24. Option (A) is correct.

Explanation:

$$l + m + n = o$$

$$\Rightarrow l^3+m^3+n^3 = 3lmn \qquad ...(i)$$

$$\text{Now, } \left[\frac{l^2}{mn}+\frac{m^2}{ln}+\frac{n^2}{lm}\right]^2 = \left[\frac{l^3+m^3+n^3}{lmn}\right]^2$$

$$= \left[\frac{3lmn}{lmn}\right]^2 = 3^2$$

[Using equation (i)]

$$= 9$$

25. Option (B) is correct.

Explanation:

$$2x^2 - 7x + 5 = 0$$

$$2x^2 + 5 = 7x \qquad ...(1)$$

Divide the eq. (1) by $2x$.

$$x+\frac{5}{2x} = 3.5$$

Squaring both sides.

$$x^2+\frac{25}{4x^2}+2\times\frac{5}{2x}\times x = 12.25$$

$$x^2+\frac{25}{4x^2} = 7.25 = 7\frac{1}{4}$$

26. Option (A) is correct.

Explanation:

$$x-\frac{3}{x} = 6, \text{ let } a = x, b = \frac{3}{x}$$

We know, $a^3 - b^3 = (a - b)^3 + 3ab\,(a - b)$

$$x^3-\frac{27}{x^3} = 216+3\times x\times\frac{3}{x}(6)$$

$$= 216 + 9 \times 6 = 270$$

$$\text{Now, } \frac{x^4-\frac{27}{x^2}}{x^2-3x-3}$$

Divide numerator and denominator by x.

$$\frac{x^3-\frac{27}{x^3}}{x-3-\frac{3}{x}} = \frac{x^2-\frac{27}{x^3}}{\left(x-\frac{3}{x}\right)-3}$$

$$= \frac{270}{6-3} = \frac{270}{3} = 90$$

Level-3: EXPERT

1. Option (D) is correct.

Explanation: Given

$$a^{\frac{1}{3}}+b^{\frac{1}{3}}+c^{\frac{1}{3}} = 0$$

We know,

$$a + b + c = 0, \text{ then } a^3+b^3+c^3 = 3abc$$

$$\text{So, } \left(a^{\frac{1}{3}}\right)^3+\left(b^{\frac{1}{3}}\right)^3+\left(c^{\frac{1}{3}}\right)^3 = 3.a^{\frac{1}{3}}\times b^{\frac{1}{3}}\times c^{\frac{1}{3}}$$

$$\Rightarrow a + b + c = 3(abc)^{\frac{1}{3}}$$

$$\text{Now, } (a + b + c)^6 = \left[3(abc)^{\frac{1}{3}}\right]^6 = 729\,a^2b^2c^2$$

2. **Option (B) is correct.**

Explanation: Given

$$a^2 + \frac{1}{(a-3)^2} - 6a = 9 \quad ...(1)$$

Now, we know $(a-3)^2 = a^2 - 6a + 9$ ...(2)

From eq. (1)

$$(a^2 - 6a + 9) + \frac{1}{(a-3)^2} = 9 + 9$$

$$(a-3)^2 + \frac{1}{(a-3)^2} = 18$$

Now,

$$(a-3) - \frac{1}{(a-3)} = \sqrt{18-2} = \sqrt{16} = 4$$

3. **Option (C) is correct.**

Explanation:

Given equation $= 144x^2 - 36x + \frac{9}{4}$

$= (12x)^2 - 2 \times 12 \times \frac{3}{2} \times x + \left(\frac{3}{2}\right)^2$

$= \left(12x - \frac{3}{2}\right)^2$ [Using, $(a-b)^2 = a^2 + b^2 - 2ab$]

4. **Option (B) is correct.**

Explanation:

$$\sqrt{x} + \frac{1}{\sqrt{x}} = 3$$

So, $x + \frac{1}{x} = 7$

$$x^2 + \frac{1}{x^2} = \sqrt{7^2 - 2} = 47$$

$$x^2 - 47 = \frac{-1}{x^2} \quad ...(1)$$

Now, $x^2(x^2 - 47)$

From eq. (1)

$$x^2\left(\frac{-1}{x^2}\right) = -1$$

5. **Option (B) is correct.**

Explanation:

Given,

$b^2 - 4b - 1 = 0$

dividing the equation by b,

$$\Rightarrow \quad b - \frac{1}{b} = 4 \quad ...(1)$$

Squaring both sides,

$$\Rightarrow \quad b^2 + \frac{1}{b^2} = 18 \quad ...(2)$$

So, the value of $b^2 + \frac{1}{b^2} + 3b - \frac{3}{b} = 18 + 3(4) = 30$

6. **Option (C) is correct.**

Explanation: Given

$a^2 + b^2 + c^2 + 27 = 6(a + b + c)$

$\Rightarrow a^2 + b^2 + c^2 + 27 - 6a - 6b - 6c = 0$

$\Rightarrow (a^2 + 9 - 6a) + (b^2 + 9 - 6b) + (c^2 + 9 - 6c) = 0$

$\Rightarrow (a-3)^2 + (b-3)^2 + (c-3)^2 = 0$ ...(1)

Eq. (1) is only possible when

$a - 3 = 0 \Rightarrow a = 3$

$b - 3 = 0 \Rightarrow b = 3$

$c - 3 = 0 \Rightarrow c = 3$

So, $a = b = c = 3$

Now,

$$\sqrt[3]{a^3 + b^3 - c^3} = \sqrt{3^3 + 3^3 - 3^3}$$

$$= \sqrt[3]{3^3} = \sqrt[3]{27} = 3$$

7. **Option (D) is correct.**

Explanation:

Given $x + y + z = 2$

$xy + yz + zx = -11$ and $xyz = -12$

$(2)^2 = x^2 + y^2 + z^2 + 2(-11)$

$\because (a+b+c)^2 = a^2 + b^2 + c^2 + 2[ab + bc + ca]$

$(4) = x^2 + y^2 + z^2 - 22$

$26 = x^2 + y^2 + z^2$ ...(1)

Now, $\sqrt{x^3 + y^3 + z^3 - 2} = ?$

We know, $x^3 + y^3 + z^3 - 3xyz = (x + y + z)(x^2 + y^2 + z^2 - xy - zy - zx)$

$x^3 + y^3 + z^3 - 3(-12) = (2)[26 - (-11)]$

$x^3 + y^3 + z^3 + 36 = 2[37]$

$x^3 + y^3 + z^3 = 74 - 36 = 38$

Now, $\sqrt{x^3 + y^3 + z^3 - 2} = \sqrt{38 - 2} = 6$

8. **Option (A) is correct.**

Explanation:

Given $P = \frac{x^3 + y^3}{(x-y)^2 + 3xy}$,

$$Q = \frac{(x+y)^2 - 3xy}{x^3 - y^3}$$

$$R = \frac{(x+y)^2 + (x-y)^2}{x^2 - y^2},$$

So, $(P \div Q) \times R$,

$x^3 - y^3 = (x-y)(x^2 + y^2 + xy)$
$x^3 + y^3 = (x+y)(x^2 + y^2 - xy)$

$$= \left(\frac{x^3 + y^3}{(x-y)^2 + 3xy} \div \frac{(x+y)^2 - 3xy}{x^3 - y^3}\right) \times \frac{(x+y)^2 + (x-y)^2}{x^2 - y^2}$$

$$= \frac{x^3 + y^3}{(x-y)^2 + 3xy} \times \frac{x^3 - y^3}{(x+y)^2 - 3xy} \times \frac{(x+y)^2 + (x-y)^2}{x^2 - y^2}$$

$$= \frac{x^3 + y^3}{x^2 + y^2 + xy} \times \frac{x^3 - y^3}{x^2 + y^2 - xy} \times \frac{2(x^2 + y^2)}{x^2 - y^2}$$

$$= \frac{x^3+y^3}{(x-y)(x^3+y^2+xy)} \times \frac{x^3-y^3}{(x+y)(x^2+y^2-xy)} \times 2(x^2+y^2)$$

$$[\because x^2 - y^2 = (x+y)(x-y)]$$

$$= \frac{x^3+y^3}{x^3-y^3} \times \frac{x^3-y^3}{x^3+y^3} \times 2(x^2+y^2)$$

$= 2(x^2 + y^2)$

9. Option (B) is correct.

Explanation: Given

$$2x^2 + y^2 + 8z^2 - 2\sqrt{2}xy + 4\sqrt{2}yz - 8zx = (Ax + y + Bz)^2$$

So, $(-\sqrt{2}x)^2 + y^2 + (2\sqrt{z})^2 - 2\sqrt{2}xy + 4\sqrt{2}yz - 8zx = (Ax + y + Bz)^2$

Using $(a + b + c)^2 = a^2 + b^2 + c^2 + 2(ab + bc + ca)$

$A = -\sqrt{2}$

$B = 2\sqrt{2}$

$\therefore A^2 + B^2 - AB = (-\sqrt{2})^2 + (2\sqrt{2})^2 - (-\sqrt{2})(2\sqrt{2})$

$= 2 + 8 + 4 = 14$

10. Option (C) is correct.

Explanation: Given

$$x = \frac{\sqrt{3}}{2}$$

Now, $1 + x = 1 + \frac{\sqrt{3}}{2} = \frac{2+\sqrt{3}}{2} = \frac{4+2\sqrt{3}}{4}$

$1 - x = 1 - \frac{\sqrt{3}}{2} = \frac{2-\sqrt{3}}{2} = \frac{4-2\sqrt{3}}{4}$

Now, $\dfrac{\sqrt{\frac{4+2\sqrt{3}}{4}} + \sqrt{\frac{4-2\sqrt{3}}{4}}}{\sqrt{\frac{4+2\sqrt{3}}{4}} - \sqrt{\frac{4-2\sqrt{3}}{4}}}$

NOTE: $4 + 2\sqrt{3} = (\sqrt{3}+1)^2$

$4 - 2\sqrt{3} = (\sqrt{3}-1)^2$

$$= \frac{\sqrt{\frac{(\sqrt{3}+1)^2}{4}} + \sqrt{\frac{(\sqrt{3}-1)^2}{4}}}{\sqrt{\frac{(\sqrt{3}+1)^2}{4}} - \sqrt{\frac{(\sqrt{3}-1)^2}{4}}}$$

$$= \frac{\frac{\sqrt{3}+1}{2} + \frac{\sqrt{3}-1}{2}}{\frac{\sqrt{3}+1}{1} - \frac{\sqrt{3}-1}{2}}$$

$$= \frac{\frac{\sqrt{3}+1+\sqrt{3}-1}{2}}{\frac{\sqrt{3}+1-\sqrt{3}+1}{2}} = \sqrt{3}$$

11. Option (C) is correct.

Explanation:

Given, $x + \frac{1}{x} = 5$

So, the value of $\frac{3x}{2x^2+2-5x}$, $= \frac{3}{2x + \frac{2}{x} - 5}$

[dividing numerator and denominator by x]

$$= \frac{3}{2\left(x+\frac{1}{x}\right)-5} = \frac{3}{2(5)-5} = \frac{3}{5}$$

12. Option (C) is correct.

Explanation: Given

$(2x + y)^3 - (x + 2y)^3 = (x - y)[A(x^2 + y^2) + Bxy]$ ...(1)

In this type of question use,

$a^3 - b^3 = (a - b)(a^2 + ab + b^2)$

Let $a = 2x + y, b = x + 2y$

So, $a - b = (2x + y - x - 2y) = x - y$

$a^2 + b^2 = (2x + y)^2 + (x + 2y)^2$

$= 5x^2 + 5y^2 + 8xy$

$ab = (2x + y)(x + 2y)$

$= 2x^2 + 2y^2 + 5xy$

So, $(2x + y)^3 - (x + 2y)^3$

$= (x - y)[5x^2 + 5y^2 + 8xy + 2y^2 + 2x^2 + 5xy]$

$(2x + y)^3 - (x + 2y)^3 = (x - y)[7x^2 + 7y^2 + 13xy]$ ...(2)

After comparing (1) and (2),

$A = 7, B = 13$

So, $2A - B = 2(7) - 13 = 14 - 13 = 1$

13. Option (A) is correct.

Explanation:

$(56\sqrt{7}x^3 - 2\sqrt{2}y^3) \div (2\sqrt{7}x - \sqrt{2}y) = Ax^2 + By^2 - Cxy$

Now,

$[(2\sqrt{7}x)^3 - (\sqrt{2}y)^3] \div (2\sqrt{7}x - \sqrt{2}y) = Ax^2 + By^2 - Cxy$

Using $\frac{a^3 - b^3}{(a-b)} = a^2 + b^2 + ab$

$28x^2 + 2y^2 + 2\sqrt{14}xy = Ax^2 + By^2 - Cxy$

$A = 28, B = 2, C = -2\sqrt{14}$

$A + B - \sqrt{14}C = 28 + 2 + 28 = 58$

14. Option (D) is correct.

Explanation:

Given $(16\sqrt{2}x^3 + 81\sqrt{3}y^3) \div (2\sqrt{2}x + 3\sqrt{3}y)$

$= Ax^2 + By^2 + Cxy$

$(2\sqrt{2}x)^3 + (3\sqrt{3}y)^3 \div (2\sqrt{2}x + 3\sqrt{3}y)$

$= Ax^2 + By^2 + Cxy$

Now, compare it with $\frac{a^3 + b^3}{a + b} = a^2 + b^2 - ab$

We get $a = 2\sqrt{2}x, b = 3\sqrt{3}y$

$\therefore \quad a^2 + b^2 - ab = 8x^2 + 27y^2 - 6\sqrt{6}xy$

So, $\quad A = 8, B = 27$ and $C = -6\sqrt{6}$

Now, putting these values in $2A - 3B - 2\sqrt{6}C$

$= 16 - 81 + 72 = 7$

15. Option (B) is correct.

Given $x^2 + 4y^2 = 53, x - 2y = 5$

Now, $\quad (x-2y)^2 = x^2 + 4y^2 - 4xy$

$25 = 53 - 4xy$

$xy = 7$

Now, $\quad x^3 - 8y^3 = (x-2y)(x^2 + 4y^2 + 2xy)$

$x^3 - 8y^3 = 5(53 + 14) = 5 \times 67 = 335$

16. Option (A) is correct.

Explanation: $\quad x = \sqrt[6]{27} - \sqrt{6\frac{3}{4}}$

$$x^2 = \left(\sqrt[6]{27} - \sqrt{6\frac{3}{4}}\right)^2$$

$$= \sqrt[3]{27} + \frac{27}{4} - 2 \times \sqrt[6]{27} \times \sqrt{\frac{27}{4}}$$

$$= 3 + \frac{27}{4} - 9 = \frac{3}{4}$$

Now, $\quad y = \dfrac{\sqrt{45} + \sqrt{605} + \sqrt{295}}{\sqrt{80} + \sqrt{125}}$

$$y = \frac{3\sqrt{5} + 11\sqrt{5} + 7\sqrt{5}}{4\sqrt{5} + 5\sqrt{5}} = \frac{21\sqrt{5}}{9\sqrt{5}} = \frac{7}{3}$$

$y^2 = \dfrac{7}{3}$ the whole square $= \dfrac{49}{9}$

$$= x^2 + y^2 = \frac{3}{4} + \frac{49}{9} = \frac{223}{36}$$

17. Option (C) is correct.

Explanation: Always use value putting method in these type of questions.

So, $\quad x = a + \dfrac{1}{a}, y = a - \dfrac{1}{a}$

Let $\quad a = 1$

Then, $x = 1 + 1 = 2, y = 1 - 1 = 0$

$$\therefore \sqrt{x^4 + y^4 - 2x^2y^2} = \sqrt{24 + 0 - 0} = \sqrt{16} = 4$$

18. Option (A) is correct.

Explanation:

$$\frac{0.0203 \times 2.92}{0.7 \times 0.0365 \times 2.9} \div \frac{(12.12)^2 - (8.12)^2}{(0.25)^2 + (0.25)(19.99)}$$

$$= \frac{203 \times 292 \times 10000 \times 100}{7 \times 365 \times 29 \times 10 \times 10000 \times 10}$$

$$\div \frac{(12.12 + 8.12)(12.12 - 8.12)}{0.25 \times 0.25 + 0.25 \times 19.99}$$

$\because \quad a^2 - b^2 = (a-b)(a+b)$

$$= \frac{203 \times 292}{7 \times 365 \times 29} \div \frac{(20.24)4}{0.25(0.25 + 19.99)}$$

$$= \frac{4}{5} \times \frac{20.24 \times 0.25}{20.24 \times 4} = 0.05$$

19. Option (B) is correct.

Explanation:

$$a + b + c = 2, \frac{1}{a} + \frac{1}{b} + \frac{1}{c} = 0, ac = \frac{4}{b}$$

or $\quad abc = 4$

Using $(a+b+c)^2 = a^2 + b^2 + c^2 + 2(ab+bc+ca)$

$(2)^2 = a^2 + b^2 + c^2 + 2(0)$

$4 = a^2 + b^2 + c^2$

$$\because \left[\frac{1}{a} + \frac{1}{b} + \frac{1}{c} = 0 \Rightarrow bc + ab + ca = 0\right]$$

20. Option (D) is correct.

Explanation:

$$\frac{3x\sqrt{y} + 2y\sqrt{x}}{3x\sqrt{y} - 2y\sqrt{x}} - \frac{3x\sqrt{y} - 2y\sqrt{x}}{3x\sqrt{y} + 2y\sqrt{x}} = \sqrt{x}\sqrt{y} \quad \text{[Given]}$$

$$\Rightarrow \frac{(3x\sqrt{y} + 2y\sqrt{x})^2 - (3x\sqrt{y} - 2y\sqrt{x})^2}{(3x\sqrt{y} - 2y\sqrt{x})(3x\sqrt{y} + 2y\sqrt{x})} = \sqrt{x}\sqrt{y}$$

$$\Rightarrow \frac{4(3x\sqrt{y})(2y\sqrt{x})}{9x^2y - 4y^2x} = \sqrt{x}\sqrt{y}$$

$$\Rightarrow \quad 9x - 4y = 24$$

21. Option (D) is correct.

Explanation:

Given, $x^4 + \dfrac{1}{x^4} = 14159$

$$\Rightarrow \left(x^2 + \frac{1}{x^2}\right)^2 = 14159 + 2$$

[using, $(a+b)^2 = a^2 + b^2 + 2ab$]

$$\Rightarrow \left(x^2 + \frac{1}{x^2}\right) = 14161$$

$$\Rightarrow \left(x + \frac{1}{x}\right)^2 = 119 + 2$$

$$\Rightarrow x + \frac{1}{x} = \sqrt{121}$$

$$\Rightarrow x + \frac{1}{x} = 11$$

22. Option (B) is correct.

Explanation:

$x + y + 3 = 0$

$x + y = -3$

Cube both sides

$(x+y)^3 = (-3)^3$

$x^3 + y^3 + 3xy(x+y) = -27$

$x^3 + y^3 + 3xy(-3) = -27$

$x^3 + y^3 - 9xy = -27 \quad \text{...(1)}$

Put value of eq. (1) in

$x^3 + y^3 - 9xy + 9 = -27 + 9 = -18$

23. Option (D) is correct.

Explanation:

$$\frac{(a-b)^3+(b-c)^3+(c-a)^3}{(a^2-b^2)^3+(b^2-c^2)^3+(c^2-a^2)^3}$$

Here, $a - b + b - c + c - a = 0$

and $a^2 - b^2 + b^2 - c^2 + c^2 - a^2 = 0$

So, if $x + y + z = 0$, then $x^3 + y^3 + z^3 = 3xyz$

$$\text{So, } \frac{3(a-b)(b-c)(c-a)}{3(a^2-b^2)(b^2-c^2)(c^2-a^2)}$$

$$= \frac{(a-b)(b-c)(c-a)}{(a+b)(a-b)(b+c)(b-c)(c+a)(c-a)}$$

$$= \frac{1}{(a+b)(b+c)(c+a)}$$

24. Option (D) is correct.

Explanation:

$$a^2 + c^2 + 17 = 2(a - 8b - 2b^2)$$

$$\Rightarrow a^2 + c^2 + 17 = 2a - 16b - 4b^2$$

$$\Rightarrow a^2 - 2a + 4b^2 + 16b + 17 + c^2 = 0$$

$$\Rightarrow a^2 - 2a + 1 + 4b^2 + 16b + 16 + c^2 = 0$$

$$(a-1)^2 + (2b+4)^2 + c^2 = 0$$

$$a - 1 = 0 \Rightarrow a = 1;$$

$$2b + 4 = 0$$

$$b = -2$$

$$c = 0$$

[If $a^2 + b^2 + c^2 = 0$, $a = 0 = b = c$]

$$\therefore a^3 + b^3 + c^3 = 1^3 + (-2)^3 + 0$$

$$= 1 - 8 + 0 = -7$$

25. Option (C) is correct.

Explanation:

$$27x^3 - 64y^3 = (Ax + By)(Cx^2 - Dy^2 + 12xy)$$

Using $a^3 - b^3 = (a - b)(a^2 + b^2 + ab)$

So, $(3x - 4y)(9x^2 + 16y^2 + 12xy)$ ...(i)

$= (Ax - By)(Cx^2 - Dy^2 + 12xy)$ ...(ii)

Comparing (i) and (ii)

$A = 3, B = -4, C = 9, D = -16$

$\therefore 4A + B + 3C + 2D = 4 \times 3 - 4 + 3 \times 9 + 2 \times -16$

$= 12 - 4 + 27 - 32 = 39 - 36 = 3$

■■■

Trignometry

Branch of mathematics that studies relationship between sides of triangles and their angles

Right angled triangle and T-ratios

$\sin\theta - \frac{P}{H}$

$\cos\theta - \frac{B}{H}$

$\tan\theta - \frac{P}{B}$

$\cot\theta - \frac{B}{P}$

$\text{cosec}\,\theta - \frac{H}{P}$

$\sec\theta - \frac{R}{B}$

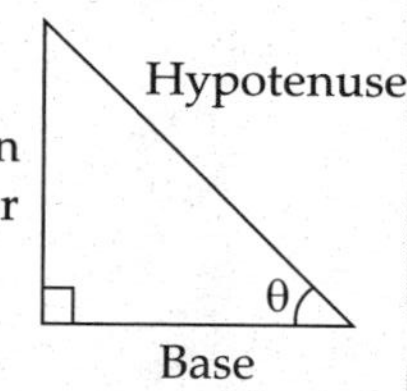

$(\text{Hyp.})^2 = (\text{Pep})^2 + (\text{Base})^2$

Trignometric Identities

$\sin^2\theta + \cos^2\theta = 1$

$\sec^2\theta - \tan^2\theta = 1$

$\text{cosec}^2\theta - \cot^2\theta = 1$

	0°	30°	45°	60°	90°
sinθ	0	$\frac{1}{2}$	$\frac{1}{\sqrt{2}}$	$\frac{\sqrt{3}}{2}$	1
cosθ	1	$\frac{\sqrt{3}}{2}$	$\frac{1}{\sqrt{2}}$	$\frac{1}{2}$	0
tanθ	0	$\frac{1}{\sqrt{3}}$	1	$\sqrt{3}$	∞
cotθ	∞	$\sqrt{3}$	1	$\frac{1}{\sqrt{3}}$	0
secθ	1	$\frac{2}{\sqrt{3}}$	$\sqrt{2}$	2	∞
cosecθ	∞	2	$\sqrt{2}$	$\frac{2}{\sqrt{3}}$	1

Trigonometric ratio of some specific angles

Compound Angles

$\sin(x+y) = \sin x \cos y + \cos x \sin y$

$\sin(x-y) = \sin x \cos y - \cos x \sin y$

$\cos(x+y) = \cos x \cos y + \cos x \sin y$

$\cos(x-y) = \cos x \cos y + \sin x \sin y$

Double Angles

1. $\sin 2x = 2\sin x.\cos x = \frac{2\tan x}{1+\tan^2 x}$
2. $\cos 2x = \cos^1 x - \sin^2 x = 1 - 2\sin^1 x = 2\cos^1 x - 1$
3. $\tan 2x = \frac{2\tan x}{1-\tan^2 x}$

Complementary Angles

$\sin(90° - \theta) = \cos\theta$

$\cos(90° - \theta) = \sin\theta$

$\tan(90° - \theta) = \cot\theta$

$\cot(90° - \theta) = \tan\theta$

$\sec(90° - \theta) = \text{cosec}\,\theta$

$\text{cosec}(90° - \theta) = \sec\theta$

Chapter

15 Trigonometry

LEARNING OBJECTIVES:

- ❖ Trigonometric identities and their use.
- ❖ Various operations of trigonometric ratios.
- ❖ Concepts related to circular measures of angles.
- ❖ Maximum and minimum values of T-ratios.
- ❖ Different types of question asked in various competitive exams.
- ❖ Method of solving questions.

➤ It is a branch of mathematics which involves study of relationship between the sides of triangles and their angles.

$$\boxed{H^2 = B^2 + P^2}$$

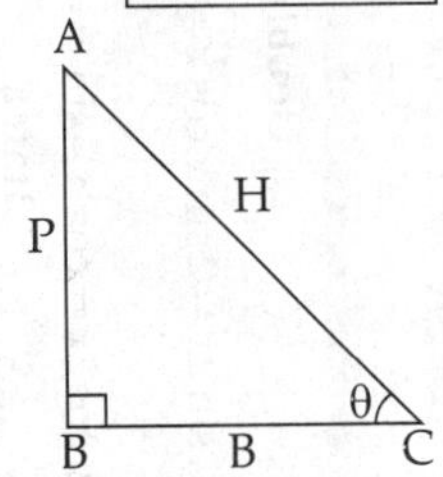

Here, P = Perpendicular

B = Base

H = Hypotenuse (longest side of a rt. angle triangle)

∴ Trignometric ratios are as follows.

1. $\sin\theta = P/H \text{ or } \frac{P}{H}$

$\cos\theta = B/H$

$\tan\theta = P/B$

$\cot\theta = B/P$

$\text{cosec}\theta = H/P$

$\sec\theta = H/B$

2. $\sin\theta = \frac{1}{\text{cosec}\theta}$

$\cos\theta = \frac{1}{\sec\theta}$

$\tan\theta = \frac{1}{\cot\theta} = \frac{\sin\theta}{\cos\theta}$

$\cot\theta = \frac{1}{\tan\theta} = \frac{\cos\theta}{\sin\theta}$

3. $\sin^2\theta + \cos^2\theta = 1$

$\tan^2\theta + 1 = \sec^2\theta$

$1 + \cot^2\theta = \text{cosec}^2\theta$

Example 1: If $\tan\theta = \frac{3}{4}$, find $4\cos\theta - 3\sin\theta$.

(a) $\frac{3}{5}$ (b) $\frac{4}{5}$

(c) $\frac{7}{5}$ (d) $\frac{2}{5}$

Sol. (c) ΔABC is a rt. angle triangle

We know $\tan\theta = \frac{3}{4} = \frac{P}{B}$

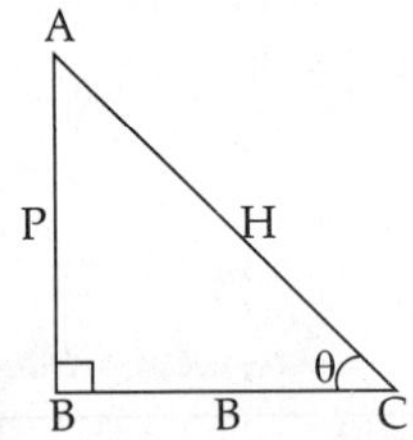

$$\therefore \quad P^2 + B^2 = H^2$$

$$\sqrt{3^2 + 4^2} = H$$

$$5 = H$$

$$\cos\theta = \frac{B}{H} = \frac{4}{5}$$

$$\sin\theta = \frac{P}{H} = \frac{3}{5}$$

Now, $4\cos\theta - 3\sin\theta = 4 \times \frac{4}{5} - 3 \times \frac{3}{5}$

$$= \frac{16}{5} - \frac{9}{5} = \frac{7}{5}$$

Example 2: If $\tan\theta = \frac{8}{15}$, then find $\frac{15\sin\theta - 8\cos\theta}{15\sin\theta + 8\cos\theta}$.

(a) 0 (b) 1
(c) –1 (d) 2

Sol. (a) Method 1: We know,

$$\tan\theta = \frac{8}{15}$$

Using triplet 8, 15 and 17,
P = 8, B = 15, H = 17

So, $\sin\theta = \frac{8}{17}, \cos\theta = \frac{15}{17}$

$$\therefore \frac{15\times\frac{8}{17} - 8\times\frac{15}{17}}{15\times\frac{8}{17} + 8\times\frac{15}{17}} = \frac{120-120}{120+120} = 0$$

Method 2: $\frac{15\sin\theta - 8\cos\theta}{15\sin\theta - 8\cos\theta}$ ...(1)

Divide eq. by $\cos\theta = \frac{15\tan\theta - 8}{15\tan\theta + 8}$

$$= \frac{15\times\frac{8}{15} - 8}{15\times\frac{8}{15} + 8} = 0$$

Method 3: $\tan\theta = \frac{8 - \sin\theta}{15 - \cos\theta}$

$$\left[\because \tan\theta = \frac{\sin\theta}{\cos\theta}\right]$$

$$\therefore \frac{15\sin\theta - 8\cos\theta}{15\sin\theta + 8\cos\theta} = \frac{15\times 8 - 8\times 15}{15\times 8 + 8\times 15}$$

$$\frac{120-120}{120+120} = \frac{0}{240} = 0$$

NOTE: Method 3 is applicable only if values are same in numerator and denominator.

Example $= \frac{15\cos\theta - 8\sin\theta}{15\cos\theta + 8\sin\theta}$

[Here, it is applicable]

But

$\frac{15\cos^2\theta - 8\sin^2\theta}{15\cos\theta + 8\sin\theta}$ × [Here, it is not applicable]

➤ $\sin^2\theta + \cos^2\theta = 1$

or $\sin^2\theta = 1 - \cos^2\theta$

or $\cos^2\theta = 1 - \sin^2\theta$

➤ $1 + \tan^2\theta = \sec^2\theta$

or $\sec^2\theta - \tan^2\theta = 1$

also $(\sec\theta - \tan\theta)(\sec\theta + \tan\theta) = 1$

or $(\sec\theta - \tan\theta) = \frac{1}{(\sec\theta + \tan\theta)}$

or $(\sec\theta + \tan\theta) = \frac{1}{\sec\theta + \tan\theta}$

➤ $1 + \cot^2\theta = \text{cosec}^2\theta$

or $\text{cosec}^2\theta - \cot^2\theta = 1$

also $(\text{cosec}\theta - \cot\theta)(\text{cosec}\theta + \cot\theta) = 1$

Example 3: Find the value of $\frac{\sin A}{1+\cos A} + \frac{\sin A}{1-\cos A}$, $0 < A < 90°$.

(a) 2 sinA (b) 2 cosecA
(c) 2 cosA (d) 2 secA

Sol. (b) Given $\frac{\sin A}{1+\cos A} + \frac{\sin A}{1-\cos A}$

$$= \sin A\left[\frac{1}{1+\cos A} + \frac{1}{1-\cos A}\right]$$

$$= \sin A\left[\frac{(1-\cos A + 1 + \cos A)}{1-\cos^2 A}\right]$$

$$= \sin A\left[\frac{2}{\sin^2 A}\right]$$

$\because 1 - \cos^2 A = \sin^2 A$

$$= 2\times\frac{1}{\sin A} = 2\,\text{cosec}A$$

Example 4: Find the value of

$$\frac{4}{1+\tan^2\theta} + \frac{3}{1+\cot^2\theta} + \sin^2\theta$$

(a) 4 (b) 2
(c) –1 (d) 3

Sol. (a) $\because 1 + \tan^2\theta = \sec^2\theta$ and $1 + \cot^2\theta = \text{cosec}^2\theta$

$$\frac{4}{1+\tan^2\theta} + \frac{3}{1+\cot^2\theta} + \sin^2\theta$$

$$= \frac{4}{\sec^2\theta} + \frac{3}{\text{cosec}^2\theta} + \sin^2\theta$$

$$= 4\cos^2\theta + 3\sin^2\theta + \sin^2\theta = 4\cos^2\theta + 4\sin^2\theta$$

$$= 4(\cos^2\theta + \sin^2\theta) = 4(1) = 4$$

$[\sin^2 a + \cos^2 a = 1]$

➤ $a\sin\theta + b\cos\theta = c$ or $a\sin\theta + b\cos\theta = c$
$a\cos\theta - b\sin\theta = x$ $b\sin\theta - a\cos\theta = x$

In this type of equation,

$$\therefore \boxed{\begin{array}{l} a^2 + b^2 = c^2 + x^2 \\ x = \sqrt{a^2 + b^2 - c^2} \end{array}}$$ [Always]

➤ $a\sin\theta + b\cos\theta = c$

If a, b, c are triplets

Then, $\sin\theta = \frac{a}{c}$

$\cos\theta = \frac{b}{c}$

Example 5: If $12\cos\theta + 9\sin\theta = 15$, then $\cot\theta$ = ?

(a) $\frac{12}{9}$ (b) $\frac{3}{9}$
(c) $\frac{4}{9}$ (d) $\frac{9}{4}$

Sol. (a) $12\cos\theta + 9\sin\theta = 15$

We know 9, 12, 15 is a triplet

$\therefore \quad \cos\theta = \frac{12}{15}, \sin\theta = \frac{9}{15}$

So, $\quad \cot\theta = \frac{\cos\theta}{\sin\theta} = \frac{12}{15} \times \frac{15}{9} = \frac{12}{9}$

Example 6: If $5\cos\theta + 12\sin\theta = 13$, then $\tan\theta = ?$

(a) $\frac{13}{5}$ (b) $\frac{12}{5}$

(c) $\frac{3}{15}$ (d) $\frac{15}{3}$

Sol. (b) $5\cos\theta + 12\sin\theta = 13$

$\Rightarrow \quad (12\sin\theta)^2 = (13 - 5\cos\theta)^2$

$144\sin^2\theta = 169 + 25\cos^2\theta - 130\cos\theta$

$144(1 - \cos^2\theta) = 169 + 25\cos^2\theta - 130\cos\theta$

$169(\cos^2\theta) - 130\cos\theta + 25 = 0$

$(13\cos\theta - 5)^2 = 0$

$\because (a + b)^2 = a^2 + b^2 - 2ab$

$\cos\theta = \frac{5}{13}$

So, $\quad \frac{12}{13} = \sin\theta$

$\therefore \quad \tan\theta = \frac{\sin\theta}{\cos\theta} = \frac{12}{13} \times \frac{13}{5} = \frac{12}{5}$

Shortcut:

As 5, 12 and 13 are pythagoras triplet,

then, $\quad \cos\theta = \frac{5}{13}$

$\sin\theta = \frac{12}{13}$

So, $\quad \tan\theta = \frac{40}{(1+4}$

$= \frac{\left(\frac{12}{13}\right)}{\left(\frac{5}{13}\right)} = \frac{12}{5}$

Example 7: $\sin\theta - \cos\theta = \frac{7}{13}$, $\sin\theta + \cos\theta = ?$ $0 < \theta < 90°$

(a) $\frac{13}{17}$ (b) $\frac{17}{13}$

(c) $\frac{1}{13}$ (d) $\frac{1}{17}$

Sol. (b) Traditional Method: Let $\sin\theta + \cos\theta = x$

Now, $\sin^2\theta + \cos^2\theta - 2\sin\theta\cos\theta = \frac{49}{169}$ ...(1)

$\sin^2\theta + \cos^2\theta + 2\sin\theta\cos\theta = x^2$ ...(2)

Add (1) and (2)

$2 = \frac{49}{169} + x^2$

$[\because \sin^2\theta + \cos^2\theta = 1]$

$\sqrt{2 - \frac{49}{169}} = x$

$\sqrt{\frac{338 - 49}{169}} = x$

$\sqrt{\frac{289}{169}} = x \Rightarrow \frac{17}{13} = x$

SHORT METHOD: We know,

$a\sin\theta - b\cos\theta = c$

$b\sin\theta + a\cos\theta = x$

Then, $\quad x = \sqrt{a^2 + b^2 - c^2}$

So, $a = 1, b = 1, c = \frac{7}{13}$

$\therefore \quad x = \sqrt{1^2 + 1^2 - \left(\frac{7}{13}\right)^2}$

$= \sqrt{1 + 1 - \frac{49}{169}}$

$= \sqrt{\frac{338 - 49}{169}} = \sqrt{\frac{289}{169}}$

$x = \frac{17}{13}$

Example 8: If $\sec\theta + \tan\theta = x$, then $\sin\theta = ?$

(a) $x^2 + 1$ (b) $\frac{x^2+1}{x^2-1}$

(c) $x^2 - 1$ (d) $\frac{x^2-1}{x^2+1}$

Sol. (d) Given, $\sec\theta + \tan\theta = x$

So, $\quad \sec\theta - \tan\theta = \frac{1}{x}$

$\because \left(\sec\theta + \tan\theta = \frac{1}{\sec\theta - \tan\theta}\right)$

By adding above equations,

$2\sec\theta = x + \frac{1}{x}$

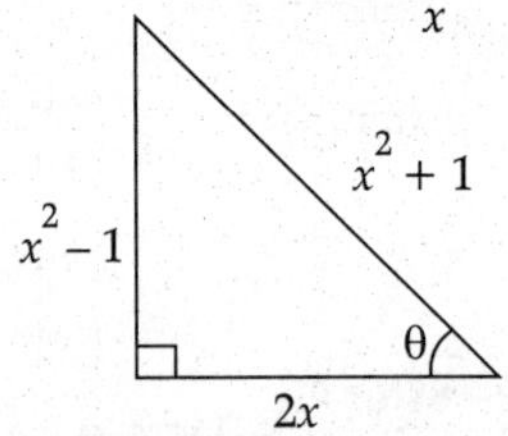

$2\sec\theta = \frac{x^2+1}{x}$

$\sec\theta = \frac{x^2+1}{2x}\left[\begin{matrix}-H \\ -B\end{matrix}\right] \quad \therefore P = x^2 - 1$

Now, $\quad \sin\theta = \frac{x^2-1}{x^2+1}$

NOTE : Always,

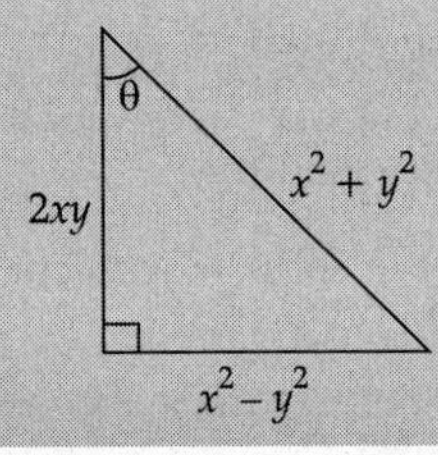

➢ Trignometric ratio value.

	0°	30°	45°	60°	90°
sinθ	0	$\frac{1}{2}$	$\frac{1}{\sqrt{2}}$	$\frac{\sqrt{3}}{2}$	1
cosθ	1	$\frac{\sqrt{3}}{2}$	$\frac{1}{\sqrt{2}}$	$\frac{1}{2}$	0
tanθ	0	$\frac{1}{\sqrt{3}}$	1	$\sqrt{3}$	∞
cotθ	∞	$\sqrt{3}$	1	$\frac{1}{\sqrt{3}}$	0
secθ	1	$\frac{2}{\sqrt{3}}$	$\sqrt{2}$	2	∞
cosecθ	∞	2	$\sqrt{2}$	$\frac{2}{\sqrt{3}}$	1

NOTE :
(a) Value of sin increases as we go forward.
(b) Value of cos decreases as we go forward.

Example 9: If $\tan\theta \cos 60° = \frac{1}{2}$, then θ = ?

(a) 0 (b) 60°
(c) 30° (d) 45°

Sol. (d) $\tan\theta \cos 60° = \frac{1}{2}$

$$\tan\theta \times \frac{1}{2} = \frac{1}{2}$$
$$\tan\theta = 1$$
$$\theta = 45° \qquad \because \tan 45° = 1$$

Example 10: If $x \sin 60°. \tan 30° = \sec 60° . \cot 45°$, then the value of x is:

(a) $2\sqrt{3}$ (b) 2
(c) 4 (d) $4\sqrt{3}$

Sol. (c) $x \sin 60°. \tan 30° = \sec 60° . \cot 45°$

$$x \times \frac{\sqrt{3}}{2} \times \frac{1}{\sqrt{3}} = 2 \times 1$$
$$\frac{x}{2} = 2$$
$$x = 4$$

Hence, the value of x is '4'.

Example 11: $\sqrt{2}\cos(5x + 5°) = \cot 45°$, then x = ?

(a) 9° (b) 7°
(c) 8° (d) 10°

Sol. (c) Given,

$$\sqrt{2}\cos(5x + 5°) = \cot 45°$$
$$\sqrt{2}\cos(5x + 5°) = 1$$
$$\cos(5x + 5°) = \frac{1}{\sqrt{2}}$$
$$5x = 40° \quad [\text{As, } \cos 45° = \frac{1}{\sqrt{2}}]$$
$$x = 8°$$

SOME IMPORTANT RESULTS

➲ $a^2 - b^2 = (a + b)(a - b)$
➲ $a^4 - b^4 = (a^2 + b^2)(a^2 - b^2)$
➲ $a^6 - a^6 = (a^3 + b^3)(a^3 - b^3)$
➲ $a^8 - b^8 = (a^4 + b^4)(a^4 - b^4)$

Now,

➲ $\sin^4\theta - \cos^4\theta = (\sin^2\theta + \cos^2\theta)(\sin^2\theta - \cos^2\theta)$
➲ $\cos^4\theta - \sin^4\theta = (\cos^2\theta + \sin^2\theta)(\cos^2\theta - \sin^2\theta)$
➲ $\sec^4\theta - \tan^4\theta = (\sec^2\theta - \tan^2\theta)(\sec^2\theta + \tan^2\theta)$
➲ $\text{cosec}^4\theta - \cot^4\theta = (\text{cosec}^2\theta + \cot^2\theta)(\text{cosec}^2\theta - \cot^2\theta)$

We know, that $\sin^2\theta + \cos^2\theta = 1$

$\sec^2\theta - \tan^2\theta = 1$

$\text{cosec}^2\theta - \cot^2\theta = 1$

So,

➲ $\cos^4\theta - \sin^4\theta = \cos^2\theta - \sin^2\theta$
➲ $\sin^4\theta - \cos^4\theta = \sin^2\theta - \cos^2\theta$
➲ $\sec^4\theta - \tan^4\theta = \sec^2\theta + \tan^2\theta$
➲ $\text{cosec}^2\theta - \cot^4\theta = \text{cosec}^2\theta + \cot^2\theta$

Example 12: If $\cos^4\theta - \sin^4\theta = \frac{2}{3}$, then $\cos^2\theta - \sin^2\theta$ = ?

(a) $\frac{3}{2}$ (b) 3
(c) 2 (d) $\frac{2}{3}$

Sol. (d) Given,

$$\cos^4\theta - \sin^4\theta = \frac{2}{3}$$

We know,

$$\cos^4\theta - \sin^4\theta = (\cos^2\theta + \sin^2\theta)(\cos^2\theta - \sin^2\theta)$$
$$\frac{2}{3} = 1 \times (\cos^2\theta - \sin^2\theta)$$
$$\therefore \quad \cos^2\theta - \sin^2\theta = \frac{2}{3}$$

Example 13: If $\sin^4\theta + \cos^4\theta = 2\sin^2\theta\cos^2\theta$, θ is an acute angle, then the value of tan θ is:

(a) 2 (b) $\sqrt{2}$
(c) 0 (d) 1

Sol. (d) Given,

$$\sin^4\theta + \cos^4\theta = 2\sin^2\theta\cos^2\theta$$
$$(\sin^2\theta)^2 + (\cos^2\theta)^2 - 2\sin^2\theta\cos^2\theta = 0$$
$$[\text{Using } (a - b)^2 = a^2 + b^2 - 2ab]$$
$$(\sin^2\theta - \cos^2\theta)^2 = 0$$
$$\sin^2\theta - \cos^2\theta = 0$$
$$\sin^2\theta = \cos^2\theta$$
$$\frac{\sin\theta}{\cos\theta} = 1 \Rightarrow \tan\theta = 1$$

➤ **Quadrant Basics**

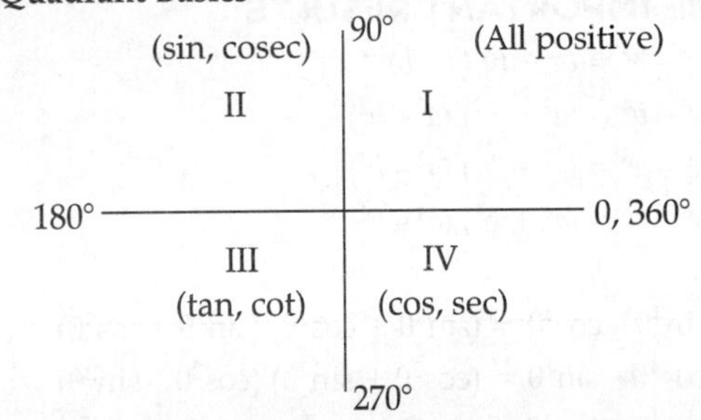

$$\sin x = \cos y,\ x + y = 90°$$
Here, x and y are complementary

or $\sin x.\sec y = 1$

$$\tan x = \cot y,\ x + y = 90°$$

or $\tan x.\tan y = 1$

$$\sec x = \mathrm{cosec}\ y,\ x + y = 90°$$

or $\cos x.\mathrm{cosec}\ y = 1$

Also,
$$\sin(90 - \theta) = \cos\theta,\ \cos(90 - \theta) = \sin\theta$$
$$\tan(90 - \theta) = \cot\theta,\ \cot(90 - \theta) = \tan\theta$$
$$\sec(90 - \theta) = \mathrm{cosec}\theta,$$
$$\mathrm{cosec}\ (90 - \theta) = \sec\theta$$

e.g.,
$$\sin 35° = \cos 55°,\ \cot 40° = \tan 50°$$
$$\cos 48° = \sin 42°,\ \mathrm{cosec} 37° = \sec 53°$$
$$\tan 59° = \cot 31°,\ \sec 41 = \mathrm{cosec}\ 49°$$

Example 14: If θ be acute angle and $\tan(4\theta - 50°) = \cot(50° - \theta)$ then the value of θ is degree is :

(a) 50 (d) 40
(c) 30 (d) 20

Sol. (c) $\tan(4\theta - 50°) = \cot(50° - \theta)$

$$4\theta - \theta = 90$$

[Using $\tan x = \cot y,\ x + y = 90°$]

$$3\theta = 90$$
$$\theta = 30°$$

Example 15: If $\tan 2\theta \tan 4\theta = 1$, then find the value of θ.

(a) 15° (b) 30°
(c) 45° (d) 18°

Sol. (a)
$$\tan 2\theta = \frac{1}{\tan 4\theta}$$
$$\tan 2\theta = \cot 4\theta$$
$$2\theta + 4\theta = 90° \quad [\text{as } x + y = 90°]$$
$$6\theta = 90°$$
$$\theta = 15°$$

Example 16: Find the value of $\dfrac{\cot 30° - \cot 75°}{\tan 15° - \tan 60°}$.

(a) 1 (b) 0
(c) $\sqrt{3} - 1$ (d) –1

Sol. (d) $\dfrac{\cot 30° - \cot 75°}{\tan 15° - \tan 60°}$

$$\frac{\tan 60° - \tan 15°}{\tan 15° - \tan 60°} = \frac{-(\tan 15° - \tan 60°)}{\tan 15° - \tan 60°} = -1$$

Example 17: Find $\sin(630° + \theta)$.

(a) $\cos\theta$ (b) $-\cos\theta$
(c) $\sin\theta$ (d) $-\sin\theta$

Sol. (b)
$$\sin(630° + \theta) = \sin(360 + 270 + \theta)$$
$$= \sin(270 + \theta) = -\cos(\theta)$$

If A + B = 90°, then cot A.cot B = 1
$$\sin^2 A + \sin^2 B = 1$$
$$\cos^2 A + \cos^2 B = 1$$
$$\sin A.\ \sec B = 1$$
$$\cos A\ .\ \mathrm{cosec} B = 1$$
$$\tan A.\ \tan B = 1$$

Example 18: Find the value of $\sin^2 10° + \sin^2 20° + \sin^2 70° + \sin^2 80°$.

(a) 0 (b) 1
(c) 2 (d) –1

Sol. (c) Given,

$$\sin^2 10° + \sin^2 20° + \sin^2 70° + \sin^2 80°$$

$\because \sin^2 A + \sin^2 B = 1$

If A + B = 90

$$= 1 + 1 = 2$$

Example 19: $\sin^2 1 + \sin^2 2 + \sin^2 3 + ... + \sin^2 89$

(a) $44\frac{1}{2}$ (b) $45\frac{1}{2}$
(c) $42\frac{1}{2}$ (d) –44

Sol. (a) Using (if A + B = 90°, $\sin^2 A + \sin^2 B = 90°$]

$$= \sin^2 1 + \sin^2 2 + \sin^2 3 + ... + \sin^2 89$$
$$= 44 + \sin^2 45°$$
$$= 44 + \frac{1}{2} = 44\frac{1}{2}$$

or $\dfrac{\text{total terms}}{2}$ If sin or cos are there in question

statement $= \dfrac{89}{2} = 44\dfrac{1}{2}$

Example 20: Find the value of cot10° cot 20° cot 60° cot 70° cot 80°.

(a) $\frac{1}{\sqrt{3}}$ (b) 0
(c) 2 (d) –2

Sol. (a) cot10° cot 20° cot 60° cot 70° cot 80°

$$= \cot 10° \cot 20° \frac{1}{\sqrt{3}} \tan 20° \tan 10°$$
$$= 1 \times 1 \times \frac{1}{\sqrt{3}} \quad [\because \tan\theta \times \cot\theta = 1]$$
$$= \frac{1}{\sqrt{3}}$$

Or

cot10° cot 20° cot 60° cot 70° cot 80°

$= 1 \times 1 \times \frac{1}{\sqrt{3}}$ $\because$ If A + B = 90°

$\because$ cot A . cot B = 1

$= \frac{1}{\sqrt{3}}$

➢ **Pythagoras theorem**

P	B	H
3	4	5
11	60	61
5	12	13
7	24	25
9	40	41
20	21	29
12	35	37
8	15	17
10	24	26

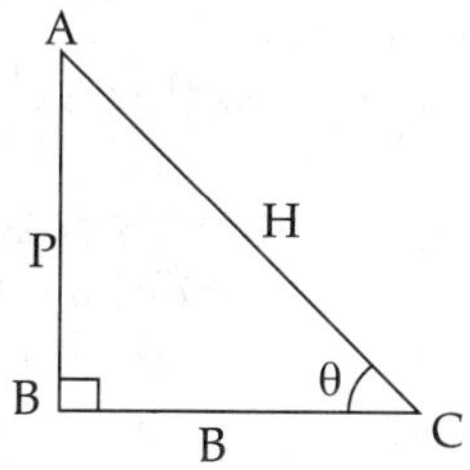

Example 21: If $\sin\theta = \frac{3}{5}$, then the value of $\frac{\tan\theta + \cos\theta}{\cos\theta + \text{cosec}\theta}$ is equal to :

(a) $\frac{29}{60}$ (b) $\frac{31}{60}$

(c) $\frac{34}{60}$ (d) $\frac{37}{60}$

Sol. (b) Given,

P B H

3 4 5

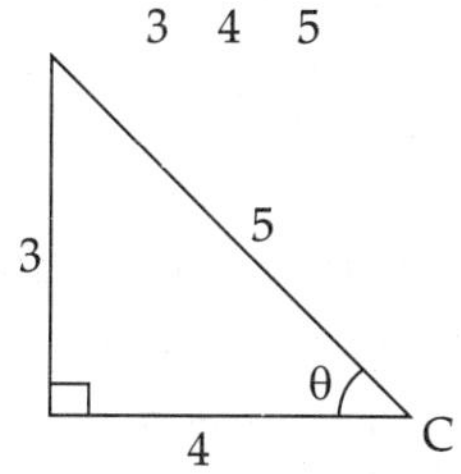

$$\sin\theta = \frac{3 - P}{5 - H}$$

$$\therefore \quad \frac{\tan\theta + \cos\theta}{\cot\theta + \text{cosec}\theta} = \frac{\frac{3}{4} + \frac{4}{5}}{\frac{4}{3} + \frac{5}{3}} = \frac{\frac{15+16}{20}}{\frac{12+15}{9}}$$

$$\Rightarrow \quad \frac{\frac{31}{20}}{\frac{9}{3}} = \frac{31}{60}$$

Example 21: If $\sec\theta - \tan\theta = \frac{1}{\sqrt{3}}$, then the value of $\sec\theta . \tan\theta$ is:

(a) $\frac{4}{\sqrt{3}}$ (b) $\frac{2}{\sqrt{3}}$

(c) $\frac{2}{3}$ (d) $\frac{1}{\sqrt{3}}$

Sol. (c) Given,

$$\sec\theta - \tan\theta = \frac{1}{\sqrt{3}}$$

$$\sec\theta + \tan\theta = \sqrt{3}$$

$$\therefore \quad \sec\theta = \left(\frac{1}{2}\right)\left(\frac{1}{\sqrt{3}} + \sqrt{3}\right)$$

$$= \frac{1+3}{2\sqrt{3}} = \frac{4}{2\sqrt{3}} \begin{matrix} -H \\ -B \end{matrix}$$

$$\tan\theta = \frac{2}{2\sqrt{3}} = \frac{1}{\sqrt{3}} \qquad \begin{matrix} P & B & H \\ 2 & 2\sqrt{3} & 4 \end{matrix}$$

$$\therefore \quad \sec\theta . \tan\theta = \frac{4}{2\sqrt{3}} \times \frac{1}{\sqrt{3}} = \frac{2}{3}$$

SOME IMPORTANT FORMULA

- sin (A + B) = sin A cos B + cos A sin B
- sin (A – B) = sin A cos B – cos A sin B
- cos (A + B) = cos A cos B – sin A sin B
- cos (A – B) = cos A cos B + sin A sin B
- $\tan(A + B) = \frac{\tan A + \tan B}{1 - \tan A \tan B}$
- $\tan(A - B) = \frac{\tan A - \tan B}{1 + \tan A \tan B}$
- $\cot(A + B) = \frac{\cot A \cot B - 1}{\cot B + \cot A}$
- $\cot(A - B) = \frac{\cot A \cot B + 1}{\cot B - \cot A}$
- $2. \sin x \cos y = \sin(x + y) + \sin(x - y)$
- $2. \cos x \sin y = \sin(x + y) - \sin(x - y)$
- $2. \cos x \cos y = \cos(x + y) - \cos(x - y)$
- $-2 \sin x \sin y = \cos(x + y) - \cos(x - y)$
- $\sin C + \sin D = 2\sin\frac{C+D}{2}.\cos\frac{C-D}{2}$
- $\sin C - \sin D = 2\cos\frac{C+D}{2}.\sin\frac{C-D}{2}$
- $\cos C + \cos D = 2\cos\frac{C+D}{2}.\cos\frac{C-D}{2}$
- $\cos C - \cos D = 2\sin\frac{C+D}{2}.\sin\frac{D-C}{2}$
- $\cos C - \cos D = -2\sin\frac{C+D}{2}.\sin\frac{C-D}{2}$

- $\sin(A+B)\times\sin(A-B) = \sin^2 A - \sin^2 B$ or $\cos^2 B - \cos^2 A$
- $\cos(A+B)\times\cos(A-B) = \sin^2 A - \cos^2 B$ or $\sin^2 B - \cos^2 A$
- $\sin\theta \sin(60-\theta)\sin(60+\theta) = \frac{1}{4}\sin 3\theta$
- $\cos\theta\cos(60-\theta)\cos(60+\theta) = \frac{1}{4}\cos 3\theta$
- $\tan\theta\tan(60-\theta)\tan(60+\theta) = \tan 3\theta$

(i) $\sin 2\theta = 2\sin\theta\cos\theta = \dfrac{2\tan\theta}{1+\tan^2\theta}$

(ii) $\cos 2\theta = \cos^2\theta - \sin^2\theta = 1 - 2\sin^2\theta = 2\cos^2\theta - 1$

$= \cos^4\theta - \sin^4\theta = \dfrac{1-\tan^2\theta}{1+\tan^2\theta}$

(iii) $\tan 2\theta = \dfrac{2\tan\theta}{1-\tan^2\theta}$

NOTE:

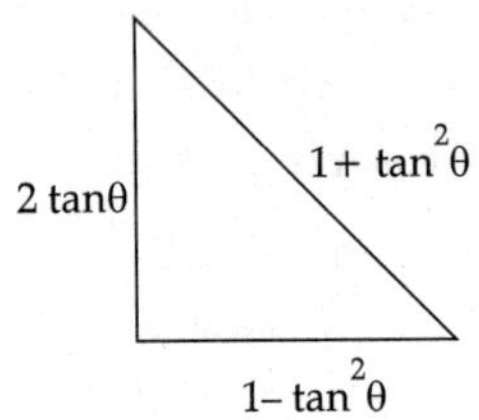

- (i) $\sin 3\theta = 3\sin\theta - 4\sin^3\theta$

  (ii) $\cos 3\theta = 4\cos^3\theta - 3\cos\theta$

  (iii) $\tan 3\theta = \dfrac{3\tan\theta - \tan^3\theta}{1-3\tan^2\theta}$

Example 23: If $2(\cos^2\theta - \sin^2\theta) = 1$ (θ is a positive acute angle), then $\cot\theta$ is equal to:

(a) $\sqrt{3}$ (b) 1

(c) $\frac{1}{\sqrt{3}}$ (d) $-\sqrt{3}$

Sol. (a) $2(\cos^2\theta - \sin^2\theta) = 1$

We know $(\cos^2\theta - \sin^2\theta = \cos 2\theta)$

$\therefore\ 2(\cos 2\theta) = 1$

$\cos 2\theta = \frac{1}{2}$ $\quad \because \cos 60 = \frac{1}{2}$

So, $\cos 2\theta = \cos 60°$

$\theta = 30°$

$\therefore\ \cot 30° = \sqrt{3}$

SOME IMPORTANT CONDITIONS

Condition 1:

$x + \frac{1}{x} = 2$, Here $x = 1$ always

Let $x = \sin\theta$, $\frac{1}{x} = \frac{1}{\sin\theta}$

then, $\sin\theta + \frac{1}{\sin\theta} = 2$

Example 24: If $\tan\theta + \cot\theta = 2$, then value of $\tan^{99}\theta + \cot^{99}\theta$ is:

(a) 0 (b) 2

(c) 1 (d) $\sqrt{2}$

Sol. (b) $\tan\theta + \cot\theta = 2$

$\tan\theta + \frac{1}{\tan\theta} = 2$ $\quad \because \cot\theta = \frac{1}{\tan\theta}$

$\tan\theta = 1$

$\therefore\ \tan^{99}\theta + \frac{1}{\tan^{99}\theta} = 2$

CONDITION 2:

(i) If A + B + C = 180°, then A + B = 180–C

(a) tan A + tan B + tan C = tan A tan B tan C

(b) cot A cot B + cot B cot C + cot C. cot A = 1

(ii) If A + B + C = 90°, A + B = 90 – C

(a) tan A tan B + tan B tan C + tan C tan A = 1

(b) cot A + cot B + cot C = cot A cot B cot C

(iii) If A + B = 45° or 225°

(1 – cot A) (1 – cot B) = 2

Example 25: If A + B + C = 180°, then sin 2A + sin 2B + sin 2C = ?

(a) 4 cosA cos B cos C (b) 4 sin A sin C sin B

(c) 3 sin A sin C sin B (d) 8 sin A sin C sin B

Sol. (b) 2 sin (A + B) cos (A – B) + 2 sin C cos C

⇒ 2 sin (180 – C) cos (A – B) + 2 sin C cos C

⇒ 2 sin C [cos (A – B) + cos C]

⇒ 2 sin C [cos (A – B) + cos (A + B)]

⇒ 2 sin C [2 sin A sin B)

⇒ 4 sinA sin B sin C

Condition 3:

- Question is the form of $\cos\theta + \cos^2\theta = 1$ and $\sin\theta + \sin^2\theta = 1$

Example 26: If $\sin A + \sin^2 A = 1$, then the value of $\cos^2 A + \cos^4 A = ?$

(a) 2 (b) 1

(c) $1\frac{1}{2}$ (d) $1\frac{2}{3}$

Sol. (b) Given, $\sin A + \sin^2 A = 1$

We know $(1 - \sin^2 A = \cos^2 A)$

$\therefore\ \sin A = 1 - \sin^2 A = \cos^2 A$

Now,

$\cos^2 A + \cos^4 A = \sin A + \sin^2 A$

$= 1$ Given

$[\sin A + \sin^2 A = 1]$

SINE AND COSINE FORMULA

➢ **Sine formula**

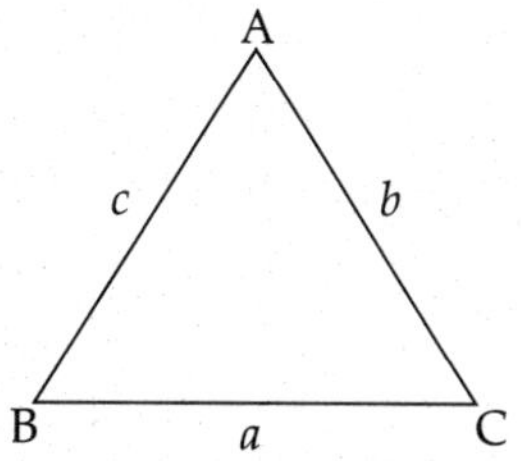

Here, ABC is a triangle with sides a, b and c.

$$\therefore \quad \frac{a}{\sin A} = \frac{b}{\sin B} = \frac{c}{\sin C} = 2R$$

[where R = circumradius]

➢ **Cosine formula**

In ΔABC,

$$\cos A = \frac{b^2 + c^2 - a^2}{2bc}$$

$$\cos B = \frac{a^2 + c^2 - b^2}{2ac}$$

$$\cos C = \frac{a^2 + b^2 - c^2}{2ab}$$

Example 27: If P is the midpoint of side BC of a triangle ABC and AP is perpendicular to AC, then:

(a) $a^2 = b^2 - 3c^2$ (b) $3b^2 = a^2 - c^2$

(c) $a^2 + b^2 = 3c^2$ (d) $2b^2 = a^2 - c^2$

Sol. (b) In ΔAPC

$$\therefore \quad \cos C = \frac{\text{Base}}{\text{hypotenuse}} = \frac{b}{\frac{a}{2}}$$

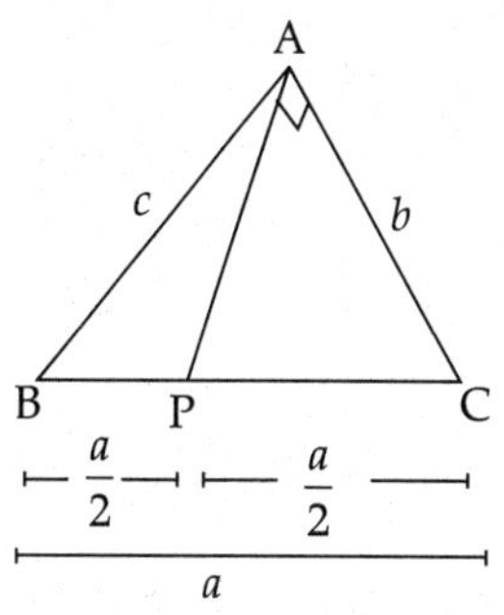

Now, in ΔABC

$$\cos C = \frac{b^2 + a^2 - c^2}{2ab}$$

Now, $$\frac{2b}{a} = \frac{b^2 + a^2 - c^2}{2ab}$$

$$4b^2 = b^2 + a^2 - c^2$$

$$\therefore \quad 3b^2 = a^2 - c^2$$

➢ **Maximum and minimum values.**

(If power is even)	If power is odd
$\sin\theta = [0, 1]$	$(-1, 1)$
$\cos\theta = [0, 1]$	$(-1, 1)$
$\tan\theta = [0, \infty)$	$(-\infty, \infty)$
$\cot\theta = [0, \infty)$	$(-\infty, \infty)$
$\sec\theta = [1, \infty)$	$(-\infty, \infty) - (-1, 1)$
$\text{cosec}\,\theta = [1, \infty)$	$(-\infty, -\infty) - (-1, 1)$

Various types of questions based on max. and min. values

TYPE-1

➢ $a \sin\theta \pm b\cos\theta$

In this case, max. value $\sqrt{a^2 + b^2}$

min. value $-\sqrt{a^2 + b^2}$

$4\sin\theta + 5\cos\theta$

then, max. value $= \sqrt{4^2 + 5^2} = \sqrt{41}$

min. value $= -\sqrt{4^2 + 5^2} = -\sqrt{41}$

TYPE-2

$\Rightarrow a\sin^2\theta + b\cos^2\theta$

In this case, max. value = coeff. which is greater

min. value = coeff. which is smaller

Let $3\sin^2\theta - 5\cos^2\theta$

Here, max. value = 3

min. value = –5

TYPE-3

$\Rightarrow \quad x^2 + \dfrac{1}{x^2}$ or $\tan^2\theta + \cot^2\theta$

$\sin^2\theta + \text{cosec}^2\theta$

$\cos^2\theta + \sec^2\theta$

Here, maximum value = ∞ (always)

minimum value = $2\sqrt{ab}$

Let, $25\tan^2\theta + 36\cot^2\theta$

Here, min$\rightarrow$ $2\sqrt{25 \times 36} = 2 \times 5 \times 6 = 60$

Max $\rightarrow \infty$

TYPE-4

$\Rightarrow \quad a\sec^2\theta + b\,\text{cosec}^2\theta$

Here, max. value $\rightarrow \infty$

min. value $\rightarrow a + b + 2\sqrt{ab}$

Let $4\sec^2\theta + 9\,\text{cosec}^2\theta$

Here, max $\rightarrow \infty$ Ans.

Min. value $\rightarrow 4 + 9 + 2\sqrt{4 \times 9} = 4 + 9 + 2 \times 2 \times 3$

$= 13 + 12 = 25$

TYPE-5

$\Rightarrow \quad a\tan^2\theta + b\,\text{cosec}^2\theta$

Here, min = $b + 2\sqrt{ab}$

max = ∞

Let $9\tan^2\theta + 25\,\text{cosec}^2\theta$

min. $= 25 + 2\sqrt{9 \times 25}$

$= 25 + 2 \times 3 \times 5$

$= 25 + 30 = 55$

TYPE-6

$\Rightarrow \quad a\sec^2\theta + b\cot^2\theta$

Here, min $= a + 2\sqrt{ab}$

max. $= \infty$

Let 16 $\sec^2\theta$ + 25 $\cot^2\theta$

Here, max = ∞

min = $16 + 2\sqrt{16 \times 25}$

= 16 + 2 × 4 × 5 = 56

TYPE-7

⇒ $\sin^n\theta + \cos^n\theta$

Here, if 'n' is even

then, max. = $\frac{1}{2^n}$

min. = 0

and if 'n' is odd

then max = $\frac{1}{2^n}$

min = $\frac{-1}{2^n}$

Let, $\sin^{119}\theta \cdot \cos^{119}\theta$

∴ max = $\frac{1}{2^n} = \frac{1}{2^{119}}$

min = $\frac{-1}{2^n} = \frac{-1}{2^{119}}$

Example 28: Find the min. value of $\sin^2\theta + \cos^2\theta + \sec^2\theta + \text{cosec}^2\theta + \tan^2\theta + \cot^2\theta$.

(a) 3 (b) 5

(c) 1 (d) 7

Sol. (d) Given $\sin^2\theta + \cos^2\theta + \sec^2\theta + \text{cosec}^2\theta + \tan^2\theta + \cot^2\theta$

∴ $\sin^2\theta + \cos^2\theta + \tan^2\theta + \cot^2\theta + \sec^2\theta + \text{cosec}^2\theta$

$= 1 + 2\sqrt{1 \times 1} + 1 + 1 + 2\sqrt{1 \times 1}$

= 1 × 2 + 2 + 2 = 7

Example 29: Find the minimum value of $2\sin^2\theta + 3\cos^2\theta$.

(a) 4 (b) 2

(c) 3 (d) 1

Sol. (b) $2\sin^2\theta + 3\cos^2\theta$

Now

$= 2(\sin^2\theta + \cos^2\theta) + \cos^2\theta$

$= 2(1) + \cos^2\theta$

$= 2 + \cos^2\theta$

= 2 + 0 = 2 $\quad \because (\sin\theta)^2 \le \sin\theta$, $(\cos\theta)^2 \le \cos\theta$

Both are equal at 0° and 90°

CIRCULAR MEASURES OF ANGLES

➢ **Measure of an angle:** It is the amount of rotation from the initial side ot the terminal side.

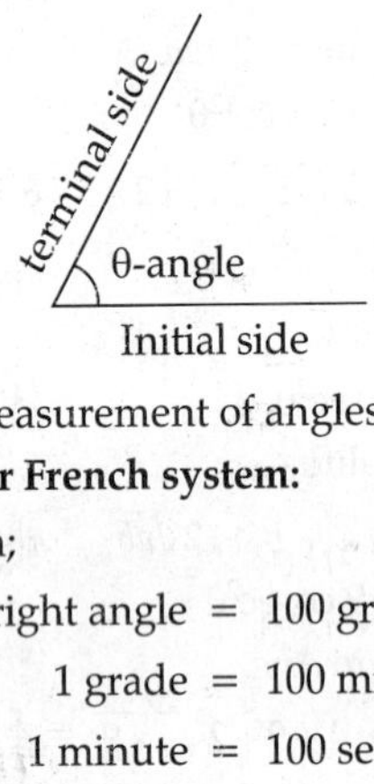

➢ Systems of measurement of angles

1. **Centesimal or French system:**

In this system;

1 right angle = 100 grades = 100^g

1 grade = 100 minute = (100′)

1 minute = 100 seconds = 100″

2. **Sexagonal system:**

In this system;

1 degree = 1° = $\frac{1}{90}$ right angle

1 minute = 1′ = $\frac{1}{60}$ degree

1 second = 1″ = $\frac{1}{60}$ minute

In short; 90° = 1 right angle

60′ = 1°

60″ = 1′

3. **Circular system:**

Here,

Angle (in radian) $\theta = \frac{\text{arc}}{\text{radius}}$

NOTE:

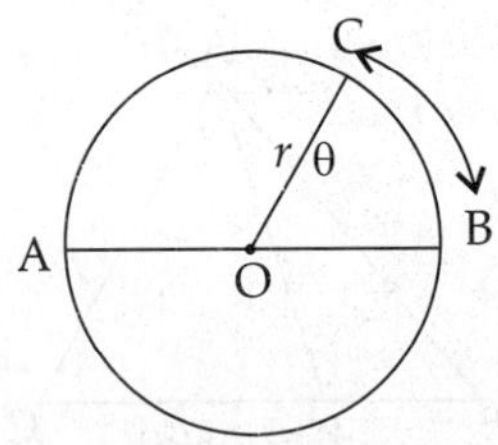

arc BC = radius (OB)

∴ ∠BOC = 1 radian

$1° = \frac{\pi}{180°}$ radian

POINTS TO REMEMBER

- Angle between two consecutive digits is a clock is $30° = \frac{\pi}{6}$ radians.
- The hour hand rotates through an angle of 30°.
- The minute hand rotates through an angle of 6° is one minute.

NOTE :

Degree	Radian
30°	$\frac{\pi}{6}$
45°	$\frac{\pi}{4}$
60°	$\frac{\pi}{3}$
90°	$\frac{\pi}{2}$
120°	$\frac{2\pi}{3}$
135°	$\frac{3\pi}{4}$
150°	$\frac{5\pi}{6}$
180°	π
270°	$\frac{3\pi}{2}$
360°	2π

Example 30: The value of 80° is radian is:

(a) $\left(\frac{2\pi}{9}\right)^c$ (b) $\left(\frac{4\pi}{9}\right)^c$

(c) $\left(\frac{2\pi}{3}\right)^c$ (d) $\left(\frac{4\pi}{3}\right)^c$

Sol. (b) We know, $\pi^c = 180°$

$$\therefore \quad 80° = \left(\frac{\pi}{180}\times 80\right)^c = \left(\frac{4\pi}{9}\right)^c$$

Example 31: Find the degree measures corresponding to $\left(\frac{1}{6}\right)^c$.

(a) 10° (b) 9° 32'

(c) 20° 41' (d) 9°32' 43.6"

Sol. (d) Given $\left(\frac{1}{6}\right)^c = \left(\frac{1}{6}\times\frac{180}{\pi}\right)^\circ$

$$= \left(\frac{1}{6}\times\frac{180}{22}\times 7\right)^\circ = \left(\frac{105}{11}\right)^\circ$$

$$= \left(9\frac{6}{11}\right)^\circ = 9°\left(\frac{6}{11}\times 60\right)'$$

$$= 9°\left(32\frac{8}{11}\right)'$$

$$= 9°32'\left(\frac{8}{11}\times 60\right)$$

$$= 9°32'\ 43.6''$$

Level 1 Beginner

1. What is the value of $\sin^2 45° + \cos^2 45°$? **[SSC CHSL 2020]**

(A) 2 **(B)** –1 **(C)** 0 **(D)** 1

2. If $\cos x = \frac{p}{q}$ and $0° < x < 90°$, then the value of tan x is: **[SSC CHSL 2020]**

(A) $\frac{\sqrt{q^2-p^2}}{q}$ **(B)** $\frac{q}{\sqrt{q^2-p^2}}$

(C) $\frac{p}{\sqrt{p^2-q^2}}$ **(D)** $\frac{\sqrt{q^2-p^2}}{p}$

3. Find value of $\frac{\text{cosec } 31°}{\sec 59°}$. **[SSC CPO 2019]**

(A) 2 **(B)** 1

(C) 3 **(D)** 0

4. If $\tan 15° = 2-\sqrt{3}$, then the value of tan 15° cot 75° + tan 75° cot 15° is: **[SSC CHSL 2023]**

(A) 6 **(B)** 10 **(C)** 8 **(D)** 14

5. Find the value of sin 0° sin 30° sin 45° sin 60° sin 90°. **[SSC CGL 2020]**

(A) 1 **(B)** 0

(C) 4 **(D)** $\frac{\sqrt{6}}{8}$

6. In ΔPRQ, If PQ = 13 cm, PR = 12 cm, then the value of sinθ + tanθ = ? **[SSC CHSL 2019]**

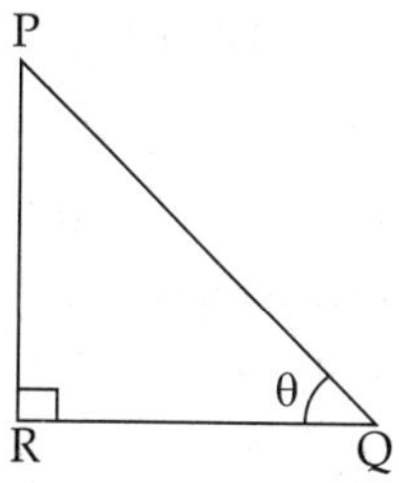

(A) $\frac{213}{5}$ **(B)** $\frac{218}{5}$

(C) $\frac{216}{13}$ **(D)** $\frac{216}{65}$

7. The value of cos 10° cos 30° cos 50° cos 70° cos 90° is : **[SSC CGL 2020]**

(A) 0 **(B)** 5

(C) 1 **(D)** 3

8. The value of $\frac{\tan 30° \text{ cosec } 60° + \tan 60° \sec 30°}{\sin^2 30° + 4\cos^2 45° - \sec^2 60°}$ is: **[SSC CGL 2020]**

(A) $\frac{32}{3}$ **(B)** $\frac{8}{3}$ **(C)** $\frac{32}{99}$ **(D)** $\frac{2}{3}$

9. In right angled triangle ABC, if ∠A = 30°, find the value of 3 sin A – 4 sin³ A. **[SSC CHSL 2023]**

(A) 2 (B) –1 (C) –2 (D) 1

10. If 2 cot θ = 3, then $\frac{\sqrt{13}\cos\theta - 3\tan\theta}{3\tan\theta + \sqrt{13}\sin\theta}$ is:

(A) $\frac{2}{3}$ (B) $\frac{1}{5}$ (C) $\frac{1}{4}$ (D) $\frac{3}{4}$

11. 'If sin ϕ = 5/6, the value of cot ϕ . sin ϕ . cos ϕ is ________. **[SSC CHSL 2023]**

(A) $\frac{6}{5}$ (B) $\frac{25}{36}$ (C) $\frac{5}{6}$ (D) $\frac{11}{36}$

12. If sin 3x = cos (3x – 45°), 0° < 3x < 90°, then x is equal to: **[SSC CPO 2020]**

(A) 35° (B) 22.5° (C) 45° (D) 27.5°

13. If sinθ + cosecθ = $\tan\frac{\pi}{3}$, then the value of (sin³θ + cosec³θ) is equal to: **[SSC CHSL 2021]**

(A) 1 (B) $\frac{1}{2}$ (C) $\frac{3}{2}$ (D) 0

14. Find the value of 'θ', if cos²θ – sin²θ = $\frac{1}{2}$. 0 < θ< 90° **[SSC CPO 2020]**

(A) 40° (B) 90° (C) 30° (D) 45°

15. If $\tan\theta = \frac{4}{3}$, then the value of $\frac{9\sin\theta + 12\cos\theta}{27\cos\theta - 20\sin\theta}$. **[SSC CHSL 2021]**

(A) 36 (B) 18 (C) 100 (D) 72

16. The value of cot²46° – sec²44° + (sin²1° + sin²3° + sin²5° + ... + sin²89°). **[SSC CHSL 2021]**

(A) 22.5 (B) 21.5 (C) 20.5 (D) 23.5

17. If (sinA – cosA) = 0, then what is the value of cot A. **[SSC CHSL 2021]**

(A) 0 (B) 1 (C) $\frac{\pi}{4}$ (D) $\frac{\pi}{6}$

18. If sinθ = 4 cosθ, then the value of sinθ cosθ is: **[SSC CGL 2019]**

(A) $\frac{3}{10}$ (B) $\frac{4}{17}$ (C) $\frac{3}{4}$ (D) $\frac{2}{9}$

19. The value of sin² 38° + sin²52° + sin² 30° – tan² 45° is equal to: **[SSC CGL 2019]**

(A) $\frac{1}{4}$ (B) $\frac{1}{2}$ (C) $\frac{1}{3}$ (D) $\frac{3}{4}$

20. Which among the following is an irrational quantity? **[SSC CGL 2019]**

(A) tan 45° (B) sin 30° (C) tan 30° tan 60° (D) cos 30°

21. Find the value of cos 225°. **[SSC CHSL 2020]**

(A) –0.866 (B) 0.866 (C) –0.7071 (D) 0.7071

22. Find the value of the following. **[SSC CHSL 2022]**

$$\frac{\sin 67°\cos 37° - \sin 37°\cos 67°}{\cos 13°\cos 17° - \sin 13°\sin 17°}$$

(A) $\frac{1}{\sqrt{3}}$ (B) $\frac{4}{\sqrt{3}}$ (C) $\frac{2}{\sqrt{3}}$ (D) 7

23. If θ is an acute angle and sin (θ + 18°) = $\frac{1}{2}$, then the value of θ in circular measure is : **[SSC CGL 2016]**

(A) $\frac{2\pi}{12}$ radians (B) $\frac{3\pi}{13}$ radians (C) $\frac{\pi}{15}$ radians (D) $\frac{\pi}{12}$ radians

24. If cot B = $\frac{12}{5}$, what is the value of sec B? **[SSC CGL 2022]**

(A) $\frac{5}{12}$ (B) $\frac{12}{13}$ (C) $\frac{13}{12}$ (D) $\frac{18}{5}$

25. If $\tan\theta + \frac{1}{\tan\theta} = 2$, then the value of $\left(\tan^2\theta + \frac{1}{\tan^2\theta}\right)$ is, **[SSC CHSL 2022]**

(A) 2 (B) –4 (C) 3 (D) 4

26. If $\sin\theta = \frac{\sqrt{3}}{2}$, and θ is an acute angle, find the vlaue of cos3θ. **[SSC CHSL 2022]**

(A) –1 (B) $\frac{1}{2}$ (C) 0 (D) 1

Level 2 Intermediate

1. If $\sin\theta = \frac{a}{\sqrt{a^2+b^2}}, 0° < \theta < 90°$, then the value of secθ + tanθ is: **[SSC CGL 2019]**

(A) $\frac{\sqrt{a^2+b^2}+a}{b}$ (B) $\frac{\sqrt{a^2+b^2}+b}{2a}$

(C) $\frac{\sqrt{a^2+b^2}+a}{2b}$ (D) $\frac{\sqrt{a^2+b^2}+b}{a}$

2. If, $\sqrt{\frac{1-\cos\theta}{1+\cos\theta}} \times \sqrt{\frac{\text{cosec}\theta - \cot\theta}{\text{cosec}\theta + \cot\theta}} = \frac{1-r}{1+r}$, then the value of r is : **[SSC CHSL 2019]**

(A) sinθ (B) cosecθ (C) sec (D) cosθ

3. The elimination of θ from x cosθ – y sinθ = 2 and x sinθ – y cosθ = 4 will give: **[SSC CGL 2019]**

(A) x² + y² = 20 (B) 3x² – y² = 20 (C) x² – y² = 20 (D) 3x² + y² = 20

4. The value of $\sqrt{\sec^2\theta + \operatorname{cosec}^2\theta} \times \sqrt{\tan^2\theta - \sin^2\theta}$ is equal to: [SSC CGL Tier-I 2019]
(A) $\sin\theta \cos^2\theta$ (B) $\operatorname{cosec}\theta \cos^2\theta$
(C) $\sin\theta \sec^2\theta$ (D) $\operatorname{cosec}\theta \sec^2\theta$

5. In ΔPQR, $\angle\theta = 90°$. If $\tan R = \frac{1}{3}$, then what is the value of $\frac{\sec P(\cos R + \sin P)}{\operatorname{cosec} R(\sin R - \operatorname{cosec} P)}$? [SSC CGL 2021]
(A) $\frac{-2}{7}$ (B) $\frac{-18}{7}$ (C) $\frac{18}{7}$ (D) $\frac{2}{7}$

6. The value of $\frac{\tan(45° - a)}{\cot(45° + a)} - \frac{(\cos 19° + \sin 71°)(\sec 19° + \operatorname{cosec} 71°)}{\tan 12°.\tan 24°.\tan 66°.\tan 78°}$ is: [SSC CGL 2021]
(A) 2 (B) –2 (C) –3 (D) 0

7. If $\frac{\sin^2\theta}{\tan^2\theta - \sin^2\theta} = 5, \theta$ is an acute angle, then the value of $\frac{24\sin^2\theta - 15\sec^2\theta}{6\operatorname{cosec}^2 - 7\cot^2\theta}$ is: [SSC CGL 2021]
(A) 14 (B) –14 (C) –2 (D) 2

8. If A = 2 $(\sin^6\theta + \cos^6\theta)$ – 3 $(\sin^4\theta + \cos^4\theta)$, then the value of 3α such that $\cos\alpha = \sqrt{\frac{3+A}{5+A}}$ is:
(A) 135° (B) 180° (C) 90° (D) 45°

9. The value of $\tan(63° - \theta) - \cot(27° + \theta) + \frac{\operatorname{cosec}^2 70° - \tan^2 20°}{\sec^2 37° - \cot^2 53°}$ is : [SSC CHSL 2020]
(A) 1 (B) 0 (C) 3 (D) 2

10. If A lies in the quadrant and 6 tan A = 5, then the value $\frac{8\sin A - 4\cos A}{\cos A + 2\sin A}$ is : [SSC CGL 2020]
(A) 1 (B) –2 (C) 0 (D) 4

11. The value of $4\left[\frac{(1-\sec A)^2 + (1+\sec A)^2}{1+\sec^2 A}\right]$ is: [SSC CGL 2020]
(A) 8 (B) 4 (C) 1 (D) 2

12. The value of $\frac{\sec^6\theta - \tan^6\theta - 3\sec^2\theta\tan^2\theta + 1}{\cos^4\theta - \sin^4\theta + 2\sin^2\theta + 2}$ is: [SSC CGL 2020]
(A) $\frac{1}{2}$ (B) $\frac{3}{4}$ (C) 1 (D) $\frac{2}{3}$

13. If $\frac{\cos\alpha}{\sin\alpha + \cos\beta} + \frac{\cos\beta}{\sin\beta - \cos\alpha} = \frac{x}{\sin\alpha - \cos\beta} + \frac{\cos\beta}{\sin\beta + \cos\alpha}$, then x is equal to: [SSC CHSL 2019]
(A) $\cos\alpha$ (B) $\cos\beta$ (C) $\sin\alpha$ (D) $\sin\beta$

14. Let $a = \frac{2\sin x}{1 + \sin x + \cos x}$ and $b = \frac{C}{1 + \sin x}$, then $a = b$, if c = ? [SSC CGL 2019]
(A) $1 + \sin x - \cos x$ (B) $1 + \cos x - \sin x$
(C) $1 + \sin x . \cos x$ (D) $1 + \cos x - \sin x$

15. $\left(\frac{1}{\cos\theta} - \frac{1}{\sin\theta}\right) + \frac{1}{\operatorname{cosec}\theta - \cot\theta} - \frac{1}{\sec\theta + \tan\theta} = ?$ [SSC CGL 2019]
(A) $\sec\theta \operatorname{cosec}\theta$ (B) $\sin\theta \tan\theta$
(C) $\operatorname{cosec}\theta \cot\theta$ (D) $\sin\theta \cos\theta$

16. Using formula $\tan\frac{x}{2} = \frac{1 - \cos x}{\sin x}$; find the value of tan 22.5°. [SSC CHSL 2022]
(A) $\sqrt{2} + 1$ (B) $\frac{\sqrt{3} + \sqrt{2}}{2}$
(C) $\frac{\sqrt{3} - \sqrt{2}}{2}$ (D) $\sqrt{2} - 1$

17. What is the value of the expression?
$\frac{[(\sin x + \sin y)(\sin x - \sin y)]}{[(\cos x + \cos y)(\cos y - \cos x)]}$ [SSC CGL Tier-II 2018]
(A) 1 (B) –1 (C) 2 (D) 0

18. What is the value of the expression?
$\frac{\{(\sin 4x + \sin 4y)[\tan(2x - 2y)]\}}{(\sin 4x - \sin 4y)}$ [SSC CGL 2018]
(A) $\tan^2 2x + 2y$ (B) $\tan^2(2x + 2y)$
(C) $\cot(x - y)$ (D) $\tan(2x + 2y)$

19. What is the simplified value of
$\frac{\tan A}{1 - \cot A} + \frac{\cot A}{1 - \tan A} - \frac{2}{\sin 2A}$? [SSC CGL 2017]
(A) 0 (B) –1 (C) 2 (D) 1

20. If $2\operatorname{cosec}^2 A = x$, then the value of x is: [SSC CGL 2017]
(A) $\frac{1}{1 - \operatorname{cosec} A} - \frac{1}{1 + \operatorname{cosec} A}$
(B) $\left(\frac{1}{1 + \cos A}\right) + \left(\frac{1}{1 - \cos A}\right)$
(C) $\left(\frac{1}{1 + \sin A}\right) + \left(\frac{1}{1 - \tan A}\right)$
(D) $\left(\frac{1}{1 - \tan A}\right) - \left(\frac{1}{1 + \sin A}\right)$

21. What is the simplified value of
$\cos^2(90° - \theta) - \left[\frac{\{\cos(90° - \theta)\cos\theta\}}{\cot\theta}\right]$? [SSC CHSL 2022]
(A) 4 (B) 2 (C) 0 (D) 1

22. If 0 be an acute angle and tan 0 + cot θ = 2, then the value of $2\tan^2\theta + \cot^2\theta + \tan^4\theta \cot^4\theta$ is: [SSC CHSL 2023]
(A) 4 (B) 2 (C) 3 (D) 6

23. Find the value of $\frac{\cos A}{1+\sin A}+\frac{1+\sin A}{\cos A}+2$. **[SSC CHSL 2023]**

(A) $1 + 2 \sec A$ (B) $2 - \sec A$
(C) $2 + \sec A$ (D) $2(1 + \sec A)$

Level 3 Expert

1. If $3\tan\theta = 2\sqrt{3}\sin\theta, 0° < \theta < 90°$, then the value of $\frac{\operatorname{cosec}^3 2\theta + \cot^2 2\theta}{\sin^2\theta + \tan^2 2\theta}$ is: **[SSC CGL Tier-II 2022]**

(A) $\frac{20}{27}$ (B) $\frac{20}{39}$ (C) $\frac{4}{13}$ (D) $\frac{4}{3}$

2. If $\sin A = \frac{5}{13}$ and $7\cot B = 24$, then the value of (secA cos B) (cosec B tan A) is: **[SSC CGL Tier-II 2022]**

(A) $\frac{13}{14}$ (B) $\frac{65}{42}$ (C) $\frac{13}{7}$ (D) $\frac{15}{13}$

3. If $\frac{\sec\theta - \tan\theta}{\sec\theta + \tan\theta} = \frac{1}{7}$, θ lies in first quadrant, then the value of $\frac{\operatorname{cosec}\theta + \cot^2\theta}{\operatorname{cosec}\theta - \cot^2\theta}$ is: **[SSC CGL Tier-II 2022]**

(A) $\frac{22}{3}$ (B) $\frac{37}{12}$ (C) $\frac{19}{5}$ (D) $\frac{37}{19}$

4. If A = 30°, what is the value of $\frac{[8\sin A + 11\operatorname{cosec} A - \cot^2 A]}{11\cos^2 A}$? **[SSC CGL Tier-I 2022]**

(A) $4\frac{3}{5}$ (B) $5\frac{1}{5}$ (C) $4\frac{2}{5}$ (D) $3\frac{4}{5}$

5. The value of: **[SSC CGL 2022]**

$$\frac{3(\operatorname{cosec}^2 26° - \tan^2 64°) + [\cot^2 42° - \sec^2 48°]}{\cot(22° - \theta) - \operatorname{cosec}^2(62° + \theta) - \tan(\theta + 68°) + \tan^2(28° - \theta)}$$

is:

(A) 4 (B) –1 (C) –2 (D) 3

6. If sin (A + B) = 1 and cos (A – B) = $\frac{\sqrt{3}}{2}$, A + B ≤ 90° and A > B, then the value of $\frac{5\sin^2 B + 4\tan^2 A}{2\sin B\cos B}$ is: **[SSC CGL 2021]**

(A) 26.5 (B) 18 (C) 16.5 (D) 20

7. If 0° < θ < 90°, the value of $\frac{(1-\sin\theta)(\sec\theta+\tan\theta)\tan\theta}{(\sec\theta+\tan\theta+1)(\cot\theta-\operatorname{cosec}\theta+1)}$ is: **[SSC CHSL 2021]**

(A) $\frac{\cos\theta}{2}$ (B) cosθ (C) $\frac{\sin\theta}{2}$ (D) sinθ

8. The value of $\frac{3\tan^2 60° + \sec^2 30° - \sin^2 45°}{(\cos 15° + \sin 75°)(\sec 15° + \operatorname{cosec} 75°)}$ is: **[SSC CHSL 2021]**

(A) $\frac{13}{12}$ (B) $\frac{65}{24}$ (C) $\frac{5}{12}$ (D) $\frac{59}{24}$

9. If $\cot^2\theta + \cot^4\theta = 2$, then the value of $2\sin^4\theta + \sin^2\theta$ = ? **[SSC CHSL 2021]**

(A) 1 (B) 0 (C) 2 (D) –1

10. If α + β = 90° and α = 2β, then the value of $3\cos^2\alpha - 2\sin^2\beta$ is equal to: **[SSC CGL 2020]**

(A) $\frac{3}{2}$ (B) $\frac{1}{4}$ (C) $\frac{4}{3}$ (D) $\frac{3}{4}$

11. If $\cos(x - y) = \frac{\sqrt{3}}{2}$ and $\sin(x + y) = 1$, where x and y are positive acute angles and $x \ge y$, then x and y are $(0° < (x + y) \le 90°)$ **[SSC CHSL 2022]**

(A) 70°; 20° (B) 50°; 40°
(C) 80°; 10° (D) 60°; 30°

12. If θ is an acute angle and $\sin\theta\cos\theta = 2\cos^3\theta - \frac{1}{4}\cos\theta$, then the value of sin θ is: **[SSC CHSL 2023]**

(A) $\frac{\sqrt{15}-1}{8}$ (B) $\frac{\sqrt{15}-1}{4}$
(C) $\frac{\sqrt{15}+1}{4}$ (D) $\frac{\sqrt{15}-1}{2}$

13. If $\frac{1-\tan A}{1+\tan A} = \frac{\tan 3°\tan 15°\tan 30°\tan 75°\tan 87°}{\tan 27°\tan 39°\tan 51°\tan 60°\tan 63°}$, then the value of cot A = ? **[SSC 2020]**

(A) 4 (B) 1 (C) 2 (D) 3

14. If $x = 4\cos A + 5\sin A$ and $y = 4\sin A - 5\cos A$, then the value of $x^2 + y^2$ is: **[SSC CGL 2020]**

(A) 16 (B) 25 (C) 0 (D) 41

15. If secθ + tanθ = P, 0° < θ < 90°, then $\frac{p^2-1}{p^2+1}$ is: **[SSC 2020]**

(A) sinθ (B) cosecθ
(C) cosθ (D) 2 cosecθ

16. $\sqrt{\frac{\cot\theta+\cos\theta}{\cot\theta-\cos\theta}}$ is equal to: **[SSC CGL Tier-II 2019]**

(A) secθ + tanθ (B) 1 + secθ.tanθ
(C) secθ – tanθ (D) secθ – tanθ

17. The value of $(\tan 29° \cot 61° - \operatorname{cosec}^2 61°) + \cot^2 54° - \sec^2 36° + (\sin^2 1° + \sin^2 3° + \sin^2 5° + ... + \sin^2 89°)$ is: **[SSC CGL Tier-II 2019]**

(A) 21 (B) $20\frac{1}{2}$ (C) $22\frac{1}{2}$ (D) 22

18. The value of $\dfrac{\sec\theta\,(1-\sin\theta)(\sin\theta+\cos\theta)(\sec\theta+\tan\theta)}{\sin\theta\,(1+\tan\theta)+\cos\theta\,(1+\cot\theta)}$

(A) cosecθ secθ **(B)** 2cosθ

(C) 2 sinθ **(D)** sinθ cosθ

19. If secθ + tanθ = p, (p > 1) then $\dfrac{\text{cosec}\theta+1}{\text{cosec}\theta-1}=?$

[SSC CGL Tier-II 2019]

(A) $\dfrac{p+1}{p-1}$ **(B)** $\dfrac{p-1}{p+1}$ **(C)** $2p^2$ **(D)** p^2

20. If $\cos x=\dfrac{-\sqrt{3}}{2}$ and $\pi<x<\dfrac{3\pi}{2}$, then the value of $2\cot^2 x + 3\,\text{cosec}^2 x$ is: [SSC CHSL 2019]

(A) 14 **(B)** 18

(C) 16 **(D)** 8

21. If 5cosθ – 12 sin θ = 0, the value of $\dfrac{2\sin\theta+\cos\theta}{\cos\theta-\sin\theta}$:

[SSC CPO 2019]

(A) $7\frac{1}{3}$ **(B)** $2\frac{44}{35}$ **(C)** $\frac{2}{3}$ **(D)** $1\frac{75}{119}$

22. If $\dfrac{\tan\theta}{1-\cot\theta}+\dfrac{\cot\theta}{1-\tan\theta}=1+k$, then k = ?

[SSC CGL 2019]

(A) cotθ + secθ **(B)** tanθ + secθ

(C) tanθ cosecθ **(D)** cosecθ secθ

23. The minimum value of 8 cosec²θ + 25 sin²θ is:

[SSC CHSL 2020]

(A) $40\sqrt{2}$ **(B)** $20\sqrt{2}$

(C) $30\sqrt{2}$ **(D)** $10\sqrt{2}$

24. If $\dfrac{(\sin\theta-\text{cosec}\theta)(\cos\theta-\sec\theta)}{\tan^2\theta-\sin^2\theta}=r^3$, then r = ?

[SSC CHSL 2019]

(A) sinθ cosθ **(B)** tanθ

(C) cotθ **(D)** cosecθ secθ

25. $\left(\dfrac{\sin\theta-2\sin^3\theta}{2\cos^3\theta-\cos\theta}\right)^2+1, \theta\neq 45°$ is equal to:

[SSC CGL 2019]

(A) sec²θ **(B)** cot²θ

(C) 2tan²θ **(D)** cosec²θ

ANSWER KEY

Level-1: Beginner

1.	(D)	2.	(D)	3.	(B)	4.	(D)	5.	(B)	6.	(D)	7.	(A)	8.	(A)	9.	(D)	10.	(C)
11.	(D)	12.	(B)	13.	(D)	14.	(C)	15.	(D)	16.	(B)	17.	(B)	18.	(B)	19.	(A)	20.	(D)
21.	(C)	22.	(A)	23.	(C)	24.	(C)	25.	(A)	26.	(A)								

Level-2: Intermediate

1.	(A)	2.	(D)	3.	(A)	4.	(C)	5.	(B)	6.	(C)	7.	(B)	8.	(D)	9.	(A)	10.	(A)
11.	(A)	12.	(D)	13.	(A)	14.	(A)	15.	(A)	16.	(D)	17.	(A)	18.	(D)	19.	(D)	20.	(B)
21.	(C)	22.	(A)	23.	(D)														

Level-3: Expert

1.	(B)	2.	(B)	3.	(C)	4.	(A)	5.	(C)	6.	(A)	7.	(C)	8.	(D)	9.	(A)	10.	(B)
11.	(D)	12.	(B)	13.	(C)	14.	(D)	15.	(A)	16.	(A)	17.	(B)	18.	(D)	19.	(D)	20.	(B)
21.	(A)	22.	(D)	23.	(B)	24.	(C)	25.	(A)										

Solutions with Detailed Explanations

Level-1: BEGINNER

1. Option (D) is correct.

Explanation: Given sin²45° + cos²45°

Since, (cos²θ + sin²θ = 1)

∴ sin²45° + cos² 45° – 1

2. Option (D) is correct.

Explanation:

Given, $\cos x = \dfrac{p}{q}$ –Base / –hypotenuse

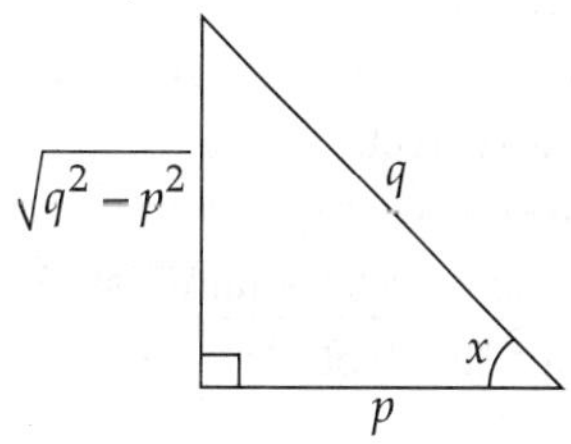

Using pythagoras

$$\text{Perpendicular} = \sqrt{q^2 - p^2}$$

$$\therefore \quad \tan x = \frac{\text{Perpendicular}}{\text{Base}} = \frac{\sqrt{q^2 - p^2}}{p}$$

3. **Option (B) is correct.**

Explanation: Given, $\frac{\text{cosec } 31°}{\sec 59°}$

Now, $\frac{\text{cosec } x}{\sec y} = 1$ when $x + y = 90°$

$$\therefore \quad \frac{\text{cosec } 31°}{\sec 59°} = 1$$

4. **Option (D) is correct.**

Explanation:

$$\because \quad \tan 15° = 2 - \sqrt{3}$$

$$\Rightarrow \quad \cot [90° - 15°] = 2 - \sqrt{3} \quad [\tan\theta = \cot(90 - \theta)]$$

$$\Rightarrow \quad \cot 75° = 2 - \sqrt{3}$$

Now, tan 15° . cot 75° + tan 75° . cot 15°

$$= (2-\sqrt{3})(2-\sqrt{3}) + \frac{1}{\cot 75°} \times \frac{1}{\tan 15°}$$

$$= (4+3-4\sqrt{3}) + \frac{1}{(2-\sqrt{3})(2-\sqrt{3})}$$

$$= 7 - 4\sqrt{3} + \frac{1}{7-4\sqrt{3}}$$

$$= 7 - 4\sqrt{3} + \frac{7+4\sqrt{3}}{49-48}$$

$$= 7 - 4\sqrt{3} + 7 + 4\sqrt{3}$$

$$= 14$$

5. **Option (B) is correct.**

Explanation: Given:

sin0° sin 30° sin 45° sin 60° sin 90°

We know, sin 0° = 0

∴ sin 0° sin 30° sin 45° sin 60° sin 90° = 0

6. **Option (D) is correct.**

Explanation:

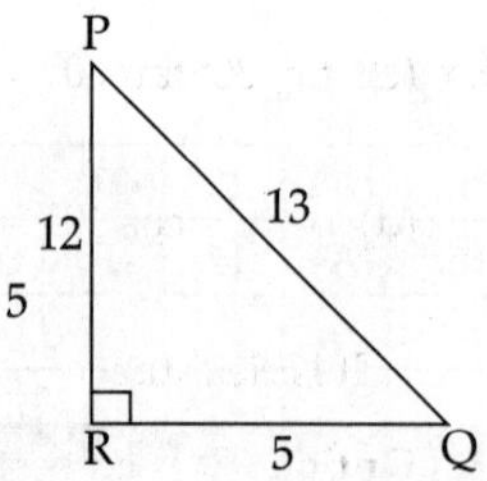

Given PQ = 13 cm

PR = 12 cm

$$\therefore RQ = \sqrt{13^2 - 12^2} = \sqrt{25} = 5$$

Now, sinθ + tanθ

$$\frac{12}{13} + \frac{12}{5} = \frac{60+156}{65} = \frac{216}{65}$$

7. **Option (A) is correct.**

Explanation: Given:

cos10° cos 30° cos 50° cos 70° cos 90° is

We know, cos 90° = 0

∴ cos 10° cos 30° cos 50° cos 70° × 0 = 0

8. **Option (A) is correct.**

Explanation:

$$\text{Given, } \frac{\tan 30° \text{ cosec} 60° + \tan 60° \sec 30°}{\sin^2 30 + 4\cot^2 45° - \sec^2 60°}$$

$$\text{Now, } \frac{\frac{1}{\sqrt{3}} \times \frac{2}{\sqrt{3}} + \sqrt{3} \times \frac{2}{\sqrt{3}}}{\left(\frac{1}{2}\right)^2 + 4(1)^2 - (2)^2}$$

$$= \frac{\frac{1}{\sqrt{3}} \times \frac{2}{\sqrt{3}} + \sqrt{3} \times \frac{2}{\sqrt{3}}}{\frac{1}{4} + 4 - 4} = \frac{\frac{2}{3} + 2}{\frac{1}{4}}$$

$$= \frac{32}{3}$$

9. **Option (D) is correct.**

Explanation:

$$3 \sin A - 4 \sin^3 A = 3 \sin 30° - 4 \sin^3 30°$$

$$[\because \angle A = 30°]$$

$$= 3 \times \frac{1}{2} - 4 \times \left(\frac{1}{2}\right)^3$$

$$= \frac{3}{2} - \frac{1}{2} = 1$$

10. **Option (C) is correct.**

Explanation:

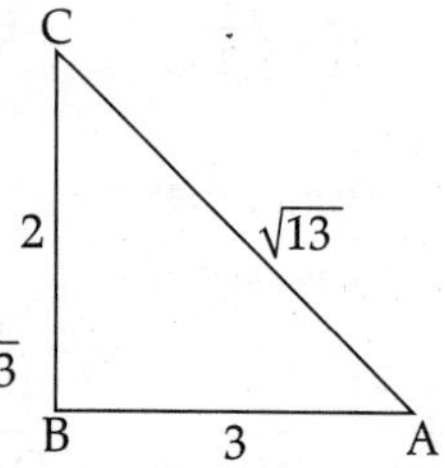

Given 2 cot θ = 3

$$\cot\theta = \frac{3}{2} \begin{matrix} -B \\ -P \end{matrix}$$

Now, H(Hyp) = $\sqrt{3^2 + 2^2} = \sqrt{13}$

$$\therefore \quad \frac{\sqrt{13}\cos\theta - 3\tan\theta}{3\tan\theta + \sqrt{13}\sin\theta}$$

$$= \frac{\sqrt{13} \times \left(\frac{3}{\sqrt{13}}\right) - 3 \times \left(\frac{2}{3}\right)}{3 \times \frac{2}{3} + \sqrt{13}\left(\frac{2}{\sqrt{13}}\right)} = \frac{3-2}{2+2} = \frac{1}{4}$$

11. **Option (D) is correct.**

Explanation:

$$\cot\theta . \sin\theta . \cos\theta = \frac{\cos\theta}{\sin\theta} . \sin\theta . \cos\theta = \cos^2\theta$$

$$= 1 - \sin^2\theta \quad \left[\because \cot\theta = \frac{\cos\theta}{\sin\theta}\right]$$

$$= 1 - \left(\frac{5}{6}\right)^2 \quad [\cos^2\theta = 1 - \sin^2\theta]$$

$$= 1 - \frac{25}{36} = \frac{11}{36}$$

12. **Option (B) is correct.**

Explanation:

Given sin 3*x* = cos (3*x* – 45°)

Now, 3*x* + 3*x* – 45 = 90° If sin*x* = cos*y*, *x* + *y* = 90°

$$6x = 135$$

$$x = \frac{135}{6} = 22.5°$$

13. Option (D) is correct.

Explanation:

$$\text{cosec}\theta + \sin\theta = \tan\frac{\pi}{3} \quad \text{(Given)}$$

$$\text{cosec}\theta + \sin\theta = \sqrt{3} \quad \left(\because \tan\frac{\pi}{3} = \tan 60 = \sqrt{3}\right)$$

$$\therefore \quad \sin\theta + \frac{1}{\sin\theta} = \sqrt{3} = a$$

Now,

$$\sin^3\theta + \text{cosec}^3\theta = \sin^3\theta + \frac{1}{\sin^3\theta}$$

$$= a^3 - 3a$$

$$= (\sqrt{3})^3 - 3\sqrt{3} = 0$$

14. Option (C) is correct.

Explanation: Given $\cos^2\theta - \sin^2\theta = \frac{1}{2}, 0° < \theta < 90°$

Now, $\cos^2\theta - \sin^2\theta = \cos 2\theta$

$$\therefore \quad \cos 2\theta = \frac{1}{2} \quad \because \cos 60° = \frac{1}{2}$$

$$\therefore \quad 2\theta = 60°$$

$$\theta = 30°$$

NOTE: Value putting in method can also be used here.

15. Option (D) is correct.

Explanation:

Given $\tan\theta = \frac{4}{3}$ [Using triplet]

P	B	H
4	3	5

$$\cos\theta = \frac{3}{5}$$

$$\sin\theta = \frac{4}{5}$$

$$\therefore \frac{9\sin\theta + 12\cos\theta}{27\cos\theta - 20\sin\theta} = \frac{9\times\frac{4}{5} + 12\times\frac{3}{5}}{27\times\frac{3}{5} - 20\times\frac{4}{5}}$$

$$= \frac{36+36}{81-80} = 72$$

16. Option (B) is correct.

Explanation:

$\cot^2 46 - \sec^2 44° + (\sin^2 1° + \sin^2 3° + \sin^2 5° + ... + \sin^2 89)$

$= \tan^2 44° - \sec° 44° +$ No. of terms $\div 2$

$$= -1 + \left[\frac{89-1}{2} + 1 \div 2\right]$$

$= -1 + 45 \div 2$

$$\left[\text{because No. of terms} = \frac{\text{last term} - \text{first term}}{\text{Common difference}+1}\right]$$

$= -1 + 22.5 = 21.5$

17. Option (B) is correct.

Explanation: Given, $\sin A - \cos A = 0$

This condition is satisfied when $A = 45°$

$$\sin 45° - \cos 45° = 0$$

$$\frac{1}{\sqrt{2}} - \frac{1}{\sqrt{2}} = 0$$

$$0 = 0$$

$$\therefore \quad A = 45°$$

So, $\cot 45° = 1$

18. Option (B) is correct.

Explanation:

Given $\sin\theta = 4\cos\theta$

So, $\frac{\sin\theta}{\cos\theta} = 4$

$$\Rightarrow \quad \tan\theta = \frac{4}{1}$$

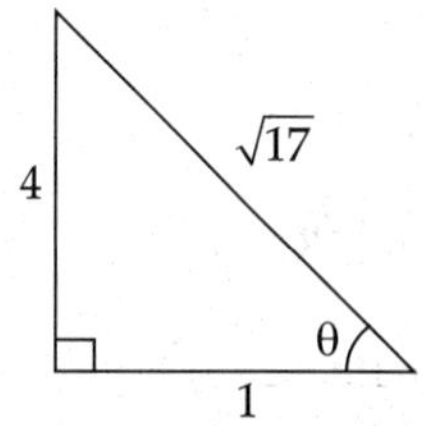

Now, $\sin\theta\cos\theta = \frac{4}{\sqrt{17}} \times \frac{1}{\sqrt{17}}$ Using triplet,

P	B	H
4	1	$\sqrt{17}$

$$= \frac{4}{17}$$

19. Option (A) is correct.

Explanation:

Given, $\sin^2 38° + \sin^2 52° + \sin^2 30° - \tan^2 45°$

$$= 1 + \left(\frac{1}{2}\right)^2 - (1)^2$$

[Using $\sin^2 52° = \cos^2 38°$ and $\sin^2 a + \cos^2 a = 1$]

$$= 1 + \frac{1}{4} - 1 = \frac{5-4}{4} = \frac{1}{4}$$

20. Option (D) is correct.

Explanation: Check option wise

(a) $\tan 45° = 1$

(b) $\sin 30° = \frac{1}{2}$

(c) $\tan 30° \tan 60° = \frac{1}{\sqrt{3}} \times \sqrt{3} = 1$

(d) $\cos 30° = \frac{\sqrt{3}}{2}$

$\therefore$ It is clear that $\frac{\sqrt{3}}{2}$ is an irrational value.

21. Option (C) is correct.

Explanation: $\cos 225°$ (Given)

So, $= \cos(180 + 45°)$

$= -\cos 45°$

$$= -\frac{1}{\sqrt{2}} = -0.7071$$

22. Option (A) is correct.

Explanation: Value of

$$\frac{\sin 67°.\cos 37° - \sin 37°.\cos 67°}{\cos 13°.\cos 17° - \sin 13° \sin 17°} = \frac{\sin(67° - 37°)}{\cos(13° + 17°)}$$

$$= \frac{\sin(30°)}{\cos(30°)} = \tan 30° = \frac{1}{\sqrt{3}}$$

23. Option (C) is correct.

Explanation:

Given, $\sin(\theta + 18^\circ) = \frac{1}{2}$

We know $\sin 30^\circ = \frac{1}{2}$

$\therefore \quad \theta + 18 = 30^\circ$

$\Rightarrow \quad \theta = 12^\circ$

$\therefore \quad 12^\circ = \frac{\pi}{180} \times 12$

$\Rightarrow \quad \frac{\pi}{15}$ radian

24. Option (C) is correct.

Explanation:

$\cot B = \frac{12}{5}$ Using triplet,

P	B	H
5	12	13

$\therefore \quad \sec B = \frac{H}{B} = \frac{13}{12}$

25. Option (A) is correct.

Explanation: Given, $\tan\theta + \frac{1}{\tan\theta} = 2$

In this case, $\tan\theta = 1$ always

So, $\tan^2\theta + \frac{1}{\tan^2\theta} = 2$

26. Option (A) is correct.

Explanation: $\sin\theta = \frac{\sqrt{3}}{2} = \sin 60^\circ$

$\therefore \quad \theta = 60^\circ$

Now, $\cos 3\theta = \cos 180^\circ = -1$

$\because \cos 180^\circ = -1$

Level-2: INTERMEDIATE

1. Option (A) is correct.

Explanation:

Given, $\sin\theta = \frac{a}{\sqrt{a^2+b^2}}$,

$\left[\text{using, } \cos\theta = \sqrt{1-\sin^2\theta}\right]$

$\therefore \quad \cos\theta = \sqrt{1-\left(\frac{a}{\sqrt{a^2+b^2}}\right)^2} = \frac{b}{\sqrt{a^2+b^2}}$

Now, $\sec\theta + \tan\theta$

$\Rightarrow \quad \frac{1}{\cos\theta} + \frac{\sin\theta}{\cos\theta} \Rightarrow \frac{1+\sin\theta}{\cos\theta}$

$\Rightarrow \quad \frac{1+\frac{a}{\sqrt{a^2+b^2}}}{\frac{b}{\sqrt{a^2+b^2}}} \Rightarrow \frac{\sqrt{a^2+b^2}+a}{b}$

2. Option (D) is correct.

Explanation: $\sqrt{\frac{1-\cos\theta}{1+\cos\theta}} \times \sqrt{\frac{\operatorname{cosec}\theta - \cot\theta}{\operatorname{cosec}\theta + \cot\theta}} = \frac{1-r}{1+r}$

Now, solving the above expression

$\Rightarrow$ We know, $\operatorname{cosec}\theta = \frac{1}{\sin\theta}, \cot\theta = \frac{\cos\theta}{\sin\theta}$

Now, $\sqrt{\frac{1-\cos\theta}{1+\cos\theta}} \times \sqrt{\frac{\frac{1}{\sin\theta} - \frac{\cos\theta}{\sin\theta}}{\frac{1}{\sin\theta} + \frac{\cos\theta}{\sin\theta}}} = \frac{1-r}{1+r}$

$\Rightarrow \quad \frac{1-\cos\theta}{1+\cos\theta} = \frac{1-r}{1+r}$

Comparing both sides we get,

$r = \cos\theta$

3. Option (A) is correct.

Explanation: Given, $x\cos\theta - y\sin\theta = 2$

$x\sin\theta - y\cos\theta = 4$

We know in this situation,

$(x^2 + y^2)(\cos^2\theta + \sin^2\theta) = 2^2 + 4^2 \quad \because \cos^2\theta + \sin^2\theta = 1$

$x^2 + y^2 = 4 + 16$

$\therefore \quad x^2 + y^2 = 20$

4. Option (C) is correct.

Explanation:

Given $\sqrt{\sec^2\theta + \operatorname{cosec}^2\theta} \times \sqrt{\tan^2\theta - \sin^2\theta}$

Let $\theta = 45^\circ$

$\Rightarrow \sqrt{\sec^2 45^\circ + \operatorname{cosec}^2 45^\circ} \times \sqrt{\tan^2 45^\circ - \sin^2 45^\circ}$

$\Rightarrow \sqrt{(\sqrt{2})^2 + (\sqrt{2})^2} \times \sqrt{1-\left(\frac{1}{\sqrt{2}}\right)^2}$

$\Rightarrow \sqrt{2}$

Now, compare this value with each option.

$\sin\theta \sec^2\theta = \sin 45^\circ \sec^2 45^\circ$

$= \frac{1}{\sqrt{2}} \times (\sqrt{2})^2$

$= \frac{1}{\sqrt{2}} \times 2$

$= \frac{2}{\sqrt{2}} \times \frac{\sqrt{2}}{\sqrt{2}} = \sqrt{2}$

5. Option (B) is correct.

Explanation:

In ΔPQR, $\tan R = \frac{1}{3}$

$PR = \sqrt{3^2+1^2} = \sqrt{10}$

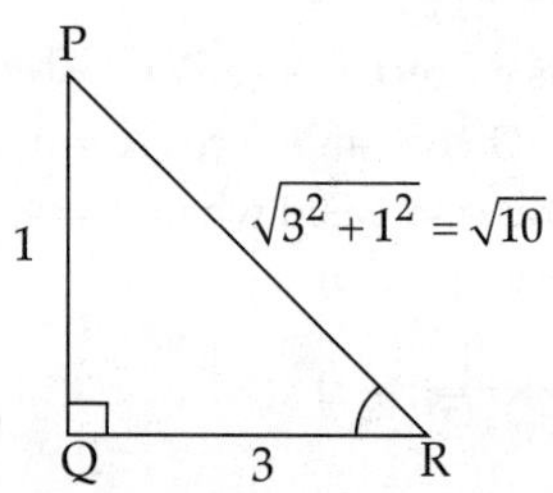

Now $\sec P = \sqrt{10}, \cos R = \frac{3}{\sqrt{10}}$

$\sin P = \frac{3}{\sqrt{10}}$

$\text{cosec}R = \sqrt{10}, \sin R = \frac{1}{\sqrt{10}}$

$\text{cosec}P = \frac{\sqrt{10}}{3}$

Now, $\frac{\sec P(\cos R + \sin P)}{\text{cosec } R(\sin R - \text{cosec } P)}$

$$= \frac{\sqrt{10}\left(\frac{3}{\sqrt{10}} + \frac{3}{\sqrt{10}}\right)}{\sqrt{10}\left(\frac{1}{\sqrt{10}} - \frac{\sqrt{10}}{3}\right)}$$

$$= \frac{\frac{6\sqrt{10}}{\sqrt{10}}}{\frac{3-10}{3}} = \frac{6}{\frac{-7}{3}} = \frac{-18}{7}$$

6. **Option (C) is correct.**

Explanation:

$$\frac{\tan(45° - \alpha)}{\cot(45° + \alpha)} - \frac{(\cos 19° + \sin 71°)(\sec 19° + \text{cosec} 71°)}{\tan 12°.\tan 24°.\tan 66°.\tan 78°}$$

Take, $\alpha = 0$

$$\frac{\tan(45° - 0)}{\cot(45° + 0)} - \frac{(\cos 19° + \sin 71°)(\sec 19° + \text{cosec} 71°)}{\tan 12°.\tan 24°.\tan 66°.\tan 78°}$$

$\Rightarrow \quad 1 - \frac{2\cos 19°.2\sec 19°}{1}$

$\Rightarrow \quad 1 - \frac{2 \times 2}{1}$

$\Rightarrow \quad 1 - 4 = -3$

7. **Option (B) is correct.**

Explanation: Given, $\frac{\sin^2\theta}{\tan^2\theta - \sin^2\theta} = 5$

We known $\tan^2\theta = \frac{\sin^2\theta}{\cos^2\theta}$

$\therefore \quad \frac{\sin^2\theta}{\frac{\sin^2\theta}{\cos^2\theta} - \sin^2\theta} = 5$

$\Rightarrow \frac{\sin^2\theta}{\sin^2\theta\left(\frac{1}{\cos^2\theta} - 1\right)} = 5$

$\Rightarrow \quad \frac{\cos^2\theta}{\sin^2\theta} = \frac{5}{1}$

$\Rightarrow \quad \cot\theta = \frac{\sqrt{5}}{1}$

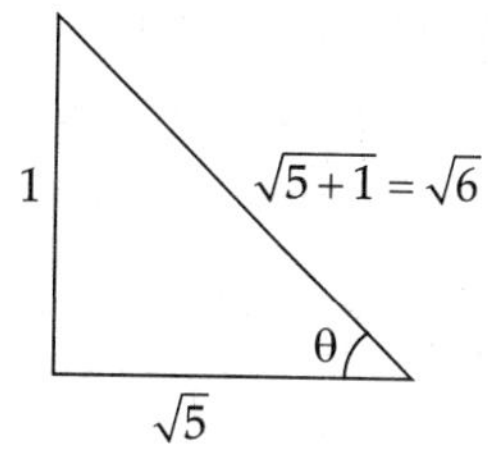

$\therefore \quad \sin\theta = \frac{P}{H} = \frac{1}{\sqrt{6}}$

$\cos\theta = \frac{B}{H} = \frac{\sqrt{5}}{\sqrt{6}}$

Now, $\frac{24\sin^2\theta - 15\sec^2\theta}{6\text{cosec}^2\theta - 7\cot^2\theta}$

$$= \frac{24 \times \left(\frac{1}{\sqrt{6}}\right)^2 - 15 \times \left(\frac{\sqrt{6}}{\sqrt{5}}\right)^2}{6 \times (\sqrt{6})^2 - 7 \times (\sqrt{5})^2}$$

$$= \frac{24 \times \frac{1}{6} - 15 \times \frac{6}{5}}{6 \times 6 - 7 \times 5}$$

$$= \frac{4 - 18}{36 - 35} = -14$$

8. **Option (D) is correct.**

Explanation:

Given, $A = 2(\sin^6\theta + \cos^6\theta) - 3(\sin^4\theta + \cos^4\theta)$

Let $\theta = 0°$ (no condition is given for 'θ')

$\therefore \quad A = 2(0 + (1)^2) - 3(0 + (1)^4)$

$A = 2 - 3 = -1$

$\therefore \quad \cos\alpha = \sqrt{\frac{3+A}{5+A}}$

$\cos\alpha = \sqrt{\frac{3-1}{5-1}} = \sqrt{\frac{2}{4}}$

$\cos\alpha = \frac{1}{\sqrt{2}}$

$\alpha = 45° \qquad \because \cos 45° = \frac{1}{\sqrt{2}}$

9. **Option (A) is correct.**

Explanation: Given,

$$\tan(63° - \theta) - \cot(27° + \theta) + \frac{\text{cosec}^2 70° - \tan^2 20°}{\sec^2 37° - \cot^2 53°}.$$

$$= \tan(63° - \theta) - \tan(63° - \theta) + \frac{\text{cosec}^2 70° - \tan^2 20°}{\sec^2 37° - \cot^2 53°}$$

$$= \tan(63° - \theta) - \tan(63 - \theta) + \frac{\text{cosec}^2 70° - \cot^2 70°}{\sec^2 37° - \tan^2 37°}$$

$= 0 + 1 = 1$

10. **Option (A) is correct.**

Explanation:

$6\tan A = 5 \qquad$ (Given)

$\tan A = \frac{5}{6}$

Now, using pythagoras theorem,

$$\text{Hypotenuse} = \sqrt{5^2+6^2} = \sqrt{61}$$

Now,

$$\frac{8\sin A - 4\cos A}{\cos A + 2\sin A} = \frac{8\times\frac{5}{\sqrt{61}} - 4\times\frac{6}{\sqrt{61}}}{\frac{6}{\sqrt{61}} + 2\times\frac{5}{\sqrt{61}}}$$

$$= \frac{8\times5-4\times6}{6+2\times5}$$

$$= \frac{40-24}{6+10} = \frac{16}{16} = 1$$

11. Option (A) is correct.

Explanation:

$$4\left[\frac{(1-\sec A)^2+(1+\sec A)^2}{1+\sec^2 A}\right]$$

Expand the above expression

$$\Rightarrow 4\left[\frac{1+\sec^2 A - 2\sec A + 1 + \sec^2 A + 2\sec A}{1+\sec^2 A}\right]$$

$$\Rightarrow 4\left[\frac{2+2\sec^2 A}{1+\sec^2 A}\right] = 4\left[\frac{2(1+\sec^2 A)}{(1+\sec^2 A)}\right] = 8$$

12. Option (D) is correct.

Explanation: $\frac{\sec^6\theta - \tan^6\theta - 3\sec^2\theta\tan^2\theta + 1}{\cos^4\theta - \sin^4\theta + 2\sin^2\theta + 2}$

$a^3 - b^3 = (a-b)(a^2+b^2+ab)$

$$\Rightarrow \frac{(\sec^2\theta)^3 - (\tan^2\theta)^3 - 3\sec^2\theta\tan^2\theta + 1}{\cos^4\theta - \sin^4\theta + 2\sin^2\theta + 2}$$

$$\Rightarrow \frac{(\sec^2\theta - \tan^2\theta)(\sec^4\theta + \tan^4\theta + \sec^2\theta\tan^2\theta) - 3\sec^2\theta\tan^2\theta + 1}{(\cos^2\theta - \sin^2\theta)(\cos^2\theta + \sin^2\theta) + 2\sin^2\theta + 2}$$

$$\Rightarrow \frac{(\sec^2\theta - \tan^2\theta)^2 + 1}{\cos^2\theta + \sin^2\theta + 2}$$

$$\Rightarrow \frac{1+1}{3} \Rightarrow \frac{2}{3}$$

13. Option (A) is correct.

Explanation: Let $\alpha = 0, \beta = 45°$

Now, $\frac{\cos 0°}{\sin 0° + \cos 45°} + \frac{\cos 45°}{\sin 45° - \cos 0°} = \frac{x}{\sin 0° - \cos 45°} + \frac{\cos 45°}{\sin 45° + \cos 0°}$

$$\Rightarrow \frac{1}{\frac{1}{\sqrt{2}}} + \frac{1}{\sqrt{2}\left(\frac{1}{\sqrt{2}}-1\right)} = \frac{-x}{\frac{1}{\sqrt{2}}} + \frac{1}{\sqrt{2}\left(\frac{1}{\sqrt{2}}+1\right)}$$

$$\Rightarrow \sqrt{2} + \frac{1}{1-\sqrt{2}} = -\sqrt{2}x + \frac{1}{1+\sqrt{2}}$$

$$\Rightarrow \sqrt{2}(1+x) = 2\sqrt{2}$$

$$\Rightarrow 1 + x = 2$$

$$\Rightarrow x = 1$$

Now, check options

$$\cos\beta = \cos 45 = \frac{1}{\sqrt{2}}$$

$$\cos\alpha = \cos 0° = 1$$

$$\sin\beta = \sin 45° = \frac{1}{\sqrt{2}}$$

14. Option (A) is correct.

Explanation:

Given $a = \frac{2\sin x}{1+\sin x+\cos x}, b = \frac{c}{1+\sin x}$

Let $x = 0°$

$$a = \frac{2\sin 0°}{1+\sin 0° + \cos 0°} = \frac{0}{1+0+1} = 0$$

$$b = \frac{c}{1+\sin 0°} = \frac{c}{1+0} = c$$

$\therefore$ $a = b$, when $c = 0$

Now, check option.

$\Rightarrow 1 + \sin x - \cos x$

$\Rightarrow 1 + \sin 0° - \cos 0°$

$\Rightarrow 1 + 0 - 1 \Rightarrow 0$

15. Option (A) is correct.

Explanation:

Given $\underbrace{\left(\frac{1}{\cos\theta} - \frac{1}{\sin\theta}\right)}_{\downarrow} + \underbrace{\frac{1}{\operatorname{cosec}\theta - \cot\theta}}_{\downarrow} - \underbrace{\frac{1}{\sec\theta + \tan\theta}}_{\downarrow}$

$\Rightarrow (\sec\theta - \operatorname{cosec}\theta) + (\operatorname{cosec}\theta + \cot\theta) - (\sec\theta - \tan\theta)$

$\because \operatorname{cosec}^2\theta - \cot^2\theta = 1$

$\sec^2\theta - \tan^2\theta = 1$

$\therefore \Rightarrow \sec\theta - \operatorname{cosec}\theta + \operatorname{cosec}\theta + \cot\theta - \sec\theta + \tan\theta$

$\Rightarrow \cot\theta + \tan\theta$

$\Rightarrow \frac{\cos\theta}{\sin\theta} + \frac{\sin\theta}{\cos\theta}$

$\Rightarrow \frac{\cos^2\theta + \sin^2\theta}{\sin\theta\cos\theta}$ $\quad\because \cos^2\theta + \sin^2\theta = 1$

$\Rightarrow \frac{1}{\sin\theta\cos\theta}$

$\Rightarrow \sec\theta.\operatorname{cosec}\theta$

16. Option (D) is correct.

Explanation:

Given, $\tan\frac{x}{2} = \frac{1-\cos x}{\sin x}$

Let $x = 45°$ so that $\tan\frac{x}{2} = \tan 22.5°$

Now, $\tan 22.5° = \frac{1-\cos 45°}{\sin 45°}$

$$= \frac{1-\frac{1}{\sqrt{2}}}{\frac{1}{\sqrt{2}}} = \frac{\frac{\sqrt{2}-1}{\sqrt{2}}}{\frac{1}{\sqrt{2}}}$$

$$= \sqrt{2}-1$$

17. Option (A) is correct.

Explanation:

Given $\dfrac{(\sin x+\sin y)(\sin x-\sin y)}{(\cos x+\cos y)(\cos y-\cos x)}$

$\because a^2 - b^2 = (a-b)(a+b)$

$$=\frac{\sin^2 x-\sin^2 y}{\cos^2 y-\cos^2 x}$$

$$=\frac{\sin^2 x-\sin^2 y}{1-\sin^2 y-1+\sin^2 x}$$

$\because \sin^2 x + \cos^2 x = 1$
$\therefore \cos^2 x = 1 - \sin^2 x$

$$=\frac{\sin^2 x-\sin^2 y}{\sin^2 x-\sin^2 y}=1$$

18. Option (D) is correct.

Explanation:

Given, $\dfrac{(\sin 4x+\sin 4y)}{(\sin 4x-\sin 4y)}.\tan(2x-2y)$

$$\Rightarrow \frac{2\sin\left(\frac{4x+4y}{2}\right)\cos\left(\frac{4x-4y}{2}\right)}{2\cos\left(\frac{4x+4y}{2}\right).\sin\left(\frac{4x-4y}{2}\right)}.\tan(2x-2y)$$

$$\Rightarrow \frac{\sin(2x+2y).\cos(2x-2y)}{\cos(2x+2y).\sin(2x-2y)}.\tan(2x-2y)$$

$$\Rightarrow \frac{\tan(2x+2y)}{\tan(2x-2y)}.\tan(2x-2y)$$

$\Rightarrow \tan(2x+2y)$

19. Option (D) is correct.

Explanation: Take the simplest triplet and put the value in the given expression.

Let P B H

3 4 5

Now, $\dfrac{\tan A}{1-\cot A}+\dfrac{\cot A}{1-\tan A}-\dfrac{2}{\sin 2A}$

$\because \sin 2A = 2\sin A.\cos A$

$$\Rightarrow \frac{\frac{3}{4}}{1-\frac{4}{3}}+\frac{\frac{4}{3}}{1-\frac{3}{4}}=\frac{2}{2\times\frac{3}{5}\times\frac{4}{5}}$$

$$\Rightarrow \frac{3}{4}\times\frac{3}{(-1)}+\frac{4}{3}\times\frac{4}{1}-\frac{2}{\frac{24}{25}}$$

$$\Rightarrow \frac{-9}{4}+\frac{16}{3}-\frac{25}{12}\Rightarrow\frac{-27+64-25}{12}=1$$

20. Option (B) is correct.

Explanation:

$$2\operatorname{cosec}^2 A=\frac{2}{\sin^2 A}\qquad \because \operatorname{cosec}A=\frac{1}{\sin A}$$

$$=\frac{2}{1-\cos^2 A}$$

$$=\frac{2}{(1+\cos A)(1-\cos A)}$$

$$=\frac{1}{(1+\cos A)}+\frac{1}{(1-\cos A)}$$

21. Option (C) is correct.

Explanation:

Value of $\cos^2(90-\theta)-\left[\dfrac{\cos(90-\theta)\cos\theta}{\cot\theta}\right]$

$$=\sin^2\theta-\left[\frac{\sin\theta\cos\theta}{\frac{\cos\theta}{\sin\theta}}\right]$$

$$=\sin^2\theta-\sin^2\theta$$

$$=0$$

22. Option (A) is correct.

Explanation: $\because \tan\theta.\cot\theta = 1$

Now, $2\tan^2\theta+\cot^2\theta+\tan^4\theta.\cot^4\theta$

$$=2\tan^2 45^\circ+\cot^2 45^\circ+1$$

$$\left[\begin{array}{l}\because \tan\theta+\cot\theta=2\\ \Rightarrow \tan 45^\circ+\cot 45^\circ=1+1=2\end{array}\right]$$

$$=2\tan^2 45^\circ+\cot^2 45^\circ+1$$

$$=2\times 1^2+1^2+1=4$$

23. Option (D) is correct.

Explanation:

$$\frac{\cos A}{1+\sin A}+\frac{1+\sin A}{\cos A}+2$$

$$=\frac{\cos^2 A+(1+\sin A)^2}{\cos A(1+\sin A)}+2$$

$$=\frac{\cos^2+1+\sin^2 A+2\sin A}{\cos A(1+\sin A)}+2\ \left[\cos^2 A+\sin^2 A=1\right]$$

$$=\frac{1+1+2\sin A}{\cos A(1+\sin A)}+2$$

$$=2\left[\frac{1+\sin A}{\cos A(1+\sin A)}\right]+2$$

$$=\frac{2}{\cos A}+2=2\sec A+2=2[1+\sec A]$$

Level-3: EXPERT

1. Option (B) is correct.

Explanation:

Given, $3\tan\theta = 2\sqrt{3}\sin\theta$

Method 1 : $\dfrac{3\sin\theta}{\cos\theta} = 2\sqrt{3}\sin\theta$

$\Rightarrow 2\sqrt{3}\sin\theta.\cos\theta-3\sin\theta = 0$

$\Rightarrow \sqrt{3}\sin\theta(2\cos\theta-\sqrt{3}) = 0$

$\Rightarrow 2\cos\theta-\sqrt{3} = 0$

But $\sqrt{3}\sin\theta\neq 0$ $\quad\because 0^\circ<\theta<90^\circ$

$\therefore 2\cos\theta = \sqrt{3}$

$\cos\theta = \dfrac{\sqrt{3}}{2}=\cos 30^\circ$ $\quad\because \cos 30^\circ=\dfrac{\sqrt{3}}{2}$

$\therefore \theta = 30^\circ$

Now, $\frac{\text{cosec}^2 60° + \cot^2 60°}{\sin^2 30° + \tan^2 60°} = \frac{\left(\frac{2}{\sqrt{3}}\right)^2 + \left(\frac{1}{\sqrt{3}}\right)^2}{\left(\frac{1}{2}\right)^2 + (\sqrt{3})^2}$

$$= \frac{\frac{4}{3}+\frac{1}{3}}{\frac{1}{4}+3} = \frac{5}{3} \times \frac{4}{13} = \frac{20}{39}$$

Method 2 : Given, $3\tan\theta = 2\sqrt{3}\sin\theta$

Put $\theta = 30°$

$$3 \times \frac{1}{\sqrt{3}} = 2\sqrt{3} \times \frac{1}{2}$$

$$3 \times \frac{1}{\sqrt{3}} \times \frac{\sqrt{3}}{\sqrt{3}} = \sqrt{3}$$

$$\sqrt{3} = \sqrt{3}$$

Condition satisfied:

Now, $\frac{\text{cosec}^2 2\theta + \cot^2\theta}{\sin^2\theta + \tan^2 2\theta}$

$$= \frac{\text{cosec}^2 60° + \cot^2 60°}{\sin^2 30° + \tan^2 60°}$$

$$= \frac{\left(\frac{2}{\sqrt{3}}\right)^2 + \left(\frac{1}{\sqrt{3}}\right)^2}{\left(\frac{1}{2}\right)^2 + (\sqrt{3})^2} = \frac{\frac{4}{3}+\frac{1}{3}}{\frac{1}{4}+3} = \frac{\frac{4+1}{3}}{\frac{1+12}{4}}$$

$$= \frac{5}{3} \times \frac{4}{13} = \frac{20}{39}$$

2. **Option (B) is correct.**

Explanation:

Given $\sin A = \frac{5}{13}$

Using triplet P B H

5 12 13

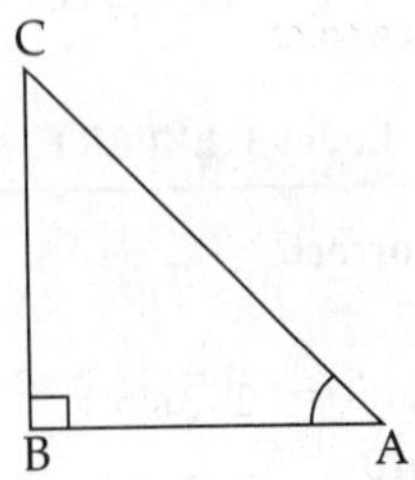

$\therefore$ $\sec A = \frac{13}{12}, \tan A = \frac{5}{12}$

Also, $7\cot B = 24$

$$\cot B = \frac{24}{7} \frac{- B}{- P}$$

Using triplet P B H

7 24 25

$$\cos B = \frac{24}{25}, \text{ cosec} B = \frac{25}{7}$$

Now, (sec A cos B) (cosec B tan A)

$$= \frac{13}{12} \times \frac{24}{25} \times \frac{25}{7} \times \frac{5}{12} = \frac{65}{42}$$

3. **Option (C) is correct.**

Explanation:

Given, $\frac{\sec\theta - \tan\theta}{\sec\theta + \tan\theta} = \frac{1}{7}$

Also, $\frac{\sec\theta + \tan\theta}{\sec\theta - \tan\theta} = \frac{7}{1}$

Use componendo and dividendo

$$\frac{2\sec\theta}{2\tan\theta} = \frac{8}{6}$$

$\Rightarrow \frac{1}{\cos\theta} \times \frac{\cos\theta}{\sin\theta} = \frac{4}{3}$ $\quad \because \sec\theta = \frac{1}{\cos\theta}$

$\Rightarrow \text{cosec}\,\theta = \frac{4}{3}$ $\quad \because \tan\theta = \frac{\sin\theta}{\cos\theta}$

Now, $\text{cosec}^2\theta - 1 = \cot^2\theta$

$$\frac{7}{9} = \cot^2\theta$$

$$\therefore \frac{\text{cosec}\theta + \cot^2\theta}{\text{cosec}\theta - \cot^2\theta} = \frac{\frac{4}{3}+\frac{7}{9}}{\frac{4}{3}-\frac{7}{9}}$$

$$= \frac{19}{9} \times \frac{9}{5} = \frac{19}{5}$$

4. **Option (A) is correct.**

Explanation:

Given, $A = 30°$

$$\therefore \frac{8\sin A + 11\text{cosec}\,A - \cot^2 A}{11\cos^2 A}$$

$$= \frac{8\sin 30° + 11\text{cosec}\,30° - \cot^2 30°}{11\cos 60°}$$

$$= \frac{8 \times \frac{1}{2} + 11 \times 2 - (\sqrt{3})^2}{10 \times \frac{1}{2}}$$

$$= \frac{4+22-3}{5} = \frac{23}{5} = 4\frac{3}{5}$$

5. **Option (C) is correct.**

Explanation: Given,

$$\frac{3(\text{cosec}^2 26° - \tan^2 64°) + (\cot^2 42° - \sec^2 48°)}{\cot(22° - \theta) - \text{cosec}^2(62° + \theta) - \tan(\theta + 68°) + \tan^2(28° - \theta)}$$

$$= \frac{3(\text{cosec}^2 26° - \cot^2 26°) + (\tan^2 48° - \sec^2 48°)}{\tan(68°+\theta) - \tan(68°+\theta) - \text{cosec}^2(62°+\theta) + \cot^2(62°+\theta)}$$

$\because \cot\theta = \tan(90° - \theta)$

$\cot(90 - \theta) = \tan\theta$

$$= \frac{3+(-1)}{-1} = -2$$

$\because \text{cosec}^2\theta - \cot^2\theta = 1$

$\sec^2\theta - \tan^3\theta = 1$

6. Option (A) is correct.

Explanation:

Given, $\sin(A + B) = 1$

We know, $\sin 90° = 1$

$\therefore \quad A + B = 90°$ ...(a)

Also, $\cos(A - B) = \frac{\sqrt{3}}{2}$

$A - B = 30°$ ...(b) $\because \cos 30° = \frac{\sqrt{3}}{2}$

Using eq 'a' and 'b'

$A = 60°, B = 30°$

$$\therefore \frac{5\sin^2 B + 4\tan^2 A}{2\sin B.\cos A} = \frac{5\sin^2 30° + 4\tan^2 60°}{2\sin 30°.\cos 60°}$$

$$= \frac{5\times\frac{1}{4} + 4\times 3}{2\times\frac{1}{2}\times\frac{1}{2}} = \frac{\frac{5}{4}+12}{\frac{1}{2}} = \frac{53}{2} = 26.5$$

7. Option (C) is correct.

Explanation: Given $0° < \theta < 90°$

Let $\theta = 30°$

Now, $\frac{(1-\sin\theta)(\sec\theta+\tan\theta)\tan\theta}{(\sec\theta+\tan\theta+1)(\cot\theta-\text{cosec}\theta+1)}$

$$= \frac{\left(1-\frac{1}{2}\right)\left(\frac{2}{\sqrt{3}}+\frac{1}{\sqrt{3}}\right)\frac{1}{\sqrt{3}}}{\left(\frac{2}{\sqrt{3}}+\frac{1}{\sqrt{3}}+1\right)(\sqrt{3}-2+1)}$$

$$= \frac{\left(\frac{1}{2}\right)\left(\frac{3}{\sqrt{3}}\right)\frac{1}{\sqrt{3}}}{(\sqrt{3}+1)(\sqrt{3}-1)} = \frac{\frac{1}{2}}{(\sqrt{3}+1)(\sqrt{3}-1)}$$

$= \frac{1}{4}$, by taking option (c) $\frac{\sin\theta}{2}$

$$\because \frac{\sin 30°}{2} = \frac{1}{2\times 2} = \frac{1}{4}$$

8. Option (D) is correct.

Explanation:

Given, $\frac{3\tan^2 60° + \sec^2 30° - \sin^2 45°}{(\cos 15° + \sin 75°)(\sec 15° + \text{cosec} 75°)}$ ...(1)

Now, take (cot 15° + sin 75°) (sec 15° + cosec 75°)

$$\Rightarrow (\cos 15° + \sin 75°)\left(\frac{1}{\cos 15°} + \frac{1}{\sin 75°}\right)$$

$$\Rightarrow (\cos 15° + \sin 75°)\frac{(\cos 15° + \sin 75°)}{\sin 75° \cos 15°}$$

$$= \frac{(\cos 15° + \sin 75°)^2}{\cos 15°.\sin 75°}$$

$$= \frac{\sin^2 75° + \cos^2 15° + 2\cos 15°.\sin 75°}{\cos 15°.\sin 75°}$$

$$= \frac{2\sin^2 75° + 2\sin^2 75°}{\sin^2 75°} = \frac{2\sin^2 75°}{\sin^2 75°} + \frac{2\sin^2 75°}{\sin^2 75°}$$

$= 2 + 2 = 4$ ...(2)

Now, put value of eq. (2) is eq (1)

$$\frac{3\times 3 + \frac{4}{3} - \frac{1}{2}}{4} = \frac{59}{6\times 4} = \frac{59}{24}$$

9. Option (A) is correct.

Explanation: Given $\cot^2\theta + \cot^4\theta = 2$

Method 1 : Using value putting method

Put $\theta = 45°$

$\cot^2 45 + \cot^4 45 = 2$

$1 + 1 = 2$

$2 = 2$

Condition satisfied

$\therefore \quad 2\sin^4\theta + \sin^2\theta = 2\sin^4 45° + \sin^2 45$

$$= 2\times\frac{1}{4} + \frac{1}{2} = 1$$

Method 2 : $\cot^2\theta + \cot^4\theta = 2$

$\cot^2\theta(1 + \cot^2\theta) = 2$

$\therefore \quad \cot^2\theta = 2\sin^2\theta$

$\because (1 + \cot^2\theta = \text{cosec}^4\theta)$

Also, $\cot^4\theta = 4\sin^2\theta$

$$\therefore \quad 2\sin^4\theta + \sin^2\theta = \frac{\cot^4\theta}{2} + \frac{\cot^2\theta}{2}$$

$$= \frac{\cot^2\theta + \cot^4\theta}{2} = \frac{2}{2} = 1$$

10. Option (B) is correct.

Explanation:

Given $\alpha + \beta = 90°$

$\alpha = 2\beta$

Clearly $\alpha = 60°, \beta = 30°$

$\therefore$ Put these values in the given expression

$\Rightarrow 3\cos^2\alpha - 2\sin^2\beta$

$\Rightarrow 3\cos^2 60° - 2\sin^2 30$

$$\Rightarrow 3\times\left(\frac{1}{2}\right)^2 - 2\times\left(\frac{1}{2}\right)^2$$

$$\Rightarrow 3\times\frac{1}{4} - 2\times\frac{1}{4} \Rightarrow \frac{1}{4}$$

11. Option (D) is correct.

Explanation:

Given: $\cos(x - y) = \frac{\sqrt{3}}{2}$

$\Rightarrow \quad \cos(x-y) = \cos 30°$

So, $\quad x - y = 30° \quad ...(1)$

Also given, $\quad \sin(x+y) = 1$

$\Rightarrow \quad \sin(x+y) = \sin 90°$

So, $\quad x + y = 90° \quad ...(2)$

By equation (1) and (2),

$x = 60°$ and $y = 30°$

12. Option (B) is correct.

Explanation:

$\because \ \sin\theta.\cos\theta = 2\cos^3\theta - \frac{1}{4}\cos\theta$

$\Rightarrow \sin\theta.\cos\theta = \cos\theta\left[2\cos^2\theta - \frac{1}{4}\right]$

$\Rightarrow \quad \sin\theta = 2\cos^2\theta - \frac{1}{4} = 2(1-\sin^2\theta) - \frac{1}{4}$

$\Rightarrow \quad 4\sin\theta = 8 - 8\sin^2\theta - 1$

$\Rightarrow \quad 8\sin^2\theta + 4\sin\theta - 7 = 0$

$\Rightarrow \quad \sin\theta = \frac{-4 \pm \sqrt{4^2 - 4\times8\times(-7)}}{2\times8}$

$= \frac{-4\pm\sqrt{240}}{16}$

$= \frac{-1\pm\sqrt{15}}{4}$

$\because$ θ is acute angle

$\Rightarrow \quad \sin\theta = \frac{\sqrt{15}-1}{4}$

13. Option (C) is correct.

Explanation: Given,

$$\frac{1-\tan A}{1+\tan A} = \frac{\tan 3°\tan 15°\tan 30°\tan 75°\tan 87°}{\tan 27°\tan 39°\tan 51°\tan 60°\tan 63°}$$

↓ solving this

$$\frac{\tan 3°\tan 15°\tan 30°\cot 15°\cot 3°}{\tan 27°\tan 39°\cot 39°\tan 60°\cot 27°}$$

$\therefore \quad \frac{1-\tan A}{1+\tan A} = \frac{\tan 30°}{\tan 60°} = \frac{\frac{1}{\sqrt{3}}}{\sqrt{3}}$

$$\frac{\frac{1}{\tan A} - \frac{\tan A}{\tan A}}{\frac{1}{\tan A} + \frac{\tan A}{\tan A}} = \frac{1}{3}$$

$\therefore \quad \frac{\cot A - 1}{\cot A + 1} = \frac{1}{3}$

$\Rightarrow \quad 3\cot A - 3 = \cot A + 1$

$\Rightarrow \quad 2\cot A = 4$

$\Rightarrow \quad \cot A = 2$

14. Option (D) is correct.

Explanation:

Given, $\quad x = 4\cos A + 5\sin A$

$y = 4\sin A - 5\cos A$

Now, $(x^2 + y^2)$

$= (4\cos A + 5\sin A)^2 + (4\sin A - 5\cos A)^2$

$= 16\cos^2 A + 25\sin^2 A + 40\cos A\sin A + 16\sin^2 A + 25\cos^2 A - 40\cos A\sin A$

$= 16(\cos^2 A + \sin^2 A) + 25(\sin^2 A + \cos^2 A) = 41$

15. Option (A) is correct.

Explanation: Given,

$\sec\theta + \tan\theta = P \quad ...(1)$

$\sec\theta - \tan\theta = \frac{1}{P} \quad ...(2) \because \sec^2\theta - \tan^2\theta = 1$

$= \sec\theta - \tan\theta = \frac{1}{\sec\theta + \tan\theta}$

On adding (1) and (2)

$P + \frac{1}{P} = 2\sec\theta \Rightarrow P^2 + 1 = 2\sec\theta \times P$

Likewise, $\quad P - \frac{1}{P} = 2\tan\theta \Rightarrow P^2 - 1 = 2\tan\theta \times P$

$\therefore \quad \frac{P^2+1}{P^2-1} = \sin\theta$

16. Option (A) is correct.

Explanation:

Given, $\sqrt{\frac{\cot\theta + \cos\theta}{\cot\theta - \cos\theta}} = \sqrt{\frac{\frac{\cos\theta}{\sin\theta} + \cos\theta}{\frac{\cos\theta}{\sin\theta} - \cos\theta}}$

$= \frac{\sqrt{(1+\sin\theta)\cos\theta}}{\sqrt{(1-\sin\theta)\cos\theta}} = \sqrt{\frac{1+\sin\theta}{1-\sin\theta} \times \frac{1+\sin\theta}{1+\sin\theta}}$

$= \sqrt{\frac{(1+\sin\theta)^2}{(1-\sin^2\theta)}} = \sqrt{\frac{(1+\sin\theta)^2}{\cos^2\theta}}$

$= \frac{(1+\sin\theta)}{\cos\theta} = \sec\theta + \tan\theta$

17. Option (B) is correct.

Explanation:

Solve $(\sin^2 1° + \sin^2 3° + \sin^2 5° + ... + \sin^2 89°)$

$= \frac{\text{no. of terms}}{2}$

$= \frac{45....}{2} \qquad \because n = \frac{89-1}{2} + 1 = 45$

$= 22\frac{1}{2} \quad ...(1)$

Now, $(\tan 29° \cot 61° - \text{cosec}^2 61°) + \cot^2 54° - \sec^2 36° + (\sin^2 1° + \sin^2 3° + \sin^2 5° + ... + \sin^2 89°)$

$\Rightarrow (\cot^2 61° - \text{cosec}^2 61°) + \tan^2 36° - \sec^2 36° + 22\frac{1}{2}$

$\Rightarrow (\cot^2 61 - \text{cosec}^2 61°) + (-1) + 22\frac{1}{2}$

$\because \sec^2\theta - \tan^2\theta = 1$

$\Rightarrow -1 - 1 + 22\frac{1}{2} \qquad \because \text{cosec}^2\theta - \cot^2\theta = 1$

$\Rightarrow 20\frac{1}{2}$

18. Option (D) is correct.

Explanation:

$$\frac{\sec\theta(1-\sin\theta)(\sin\theta+\cos\theta)(\sec\theta+\tan\theta)}{\sin\theta(1+\tan\theta)+\cos\theta(1+\cot\theta)}$$

$$=\frac{\frac{1}{\cos\theta}(1-\sin\theta)(\sin\theta+\cos\theta)\left(\frac{1}{\cos\theta}+\frac{\sin\theta}{\cos\theta}\right)}{\sin\theta\left(1+\frac{\sin\theta}{\cos\theta}\right)+\cos\theta\left(1+\frac{\cos\theta}{\sin\theta}\right)}$$

$$=\frac{\frac{1}{\cos\theta}(1-\sin\theta)(\sin\theta+\cos\theta)\left(\frac{1+\sin\theta}{\cos\theta}\right)}{\sin\theta\left(\frac{\cos\theta+\sin\theta}{\cos\theta}\right)+\cos\theta\left(\frac{\sin\theta+\cos\theta}{\sin\theta}\right)}$$

$$=\frac{\frac{1}{\cos^2\theta}(1-\sin^2\theta)(\sin\theta+\cos\theta)}{\left[\left(\frac{\sin\theta}{\cos\theta}\right)+\left(\frac{\cos\theta}{\sin\theta}\right)\right](\sin\theta+\cos\theta)}$$

$$=\frac{\frac{1}{\cos^2\theta}\times\cos^2\theta}{\frac{\sin^2\theta+\cos^2\theta}{\sin\theta.\cos\theta}}=\sin\theta\,.\,\cos\theta$$

19. Option (D) is correct.

Explanation: Given,

$\sec\theta + \tan\theta = P$ ...(a)

$\therefore \quad \sec\theta - \tan\theta = \frac{1}{P}$ ...(b) $\because \sec^2\theta - \tan^2\theta = 1$

From (a) and (b)

$\Rightarrow \quad P+\frac{1}{P} = 2\sec\theta$

Let $\quad P = 2$

$\sec\theta = \frac{5}{4}$

$\text{cosec}\,\theta = \frac{5}{3}$

Using triplet

P	B	H
3	4	5

$\therefore \quad \frac{\text{cosec}\,\theta+1}{\text{cosec}\,\theta-1} = \frac{\frac{5}{3}+1}{\frac{5}{3}-1} = \frac{\frac{8}{3}}{\frac{2}{3}} = 4$

Check options

$\Rightarrow \quad P^2 = 2^2 = 4$

20. Option (B) is correct.

Explanation:

Given, $\quad \cos x = -\frac{\sqrt{3}}{2}, 180 < x < 270$

$\therefore \quad x = 210$

Now,

$2\cot^2 x + 3\,\text{cosec}^2 x = 2\cot^2 210° + 3\,\text{cosec}^2 210°$

$= 2(\sqrt{3})^2 + 3(-2)^2 = 18$

21. Option (A) is correct.

Explanation: Given

$5\cos\theta - 12\sin\theta = 0$

$5\cos\theta = 12\sin\theta$

$\therefore \quad \frac{5}{12} = \frac{\sin\theta}{\cos\theta}$

$\frac{5}{12} = \tan\theta$

$\therefore \quad \tan\theta = \frac{\text{Perpendicular}}{\text{Base}} = \frac{5}{12}$

$\therefore \quad \text{Hypotenuse} = \sqrt{12^2+5^2} = 13$

So, $\quad \sin\theta = \frac{5}{13}, \cos\theta = \frac{12}{13}$

$\therefore \quad 2\sin\theta + \cos\theta = 2\times\frac{5}{13}+\frac{12}{13}$

$= \frac{10}{13}+\frac{12}{13}$

$= \frac{22}{13}$ ...(1)

Now $\Rightarrow \cos\theta - \sin\theta$

$\Rightarrow \frac{12}{13}-\frac{5}{13}$

$\Rightarrow \frac{7}{13}$ ...(2)

Now, $\quad \frac{2\sin\theta+\cos\theta}{\cos\theta-\sin\theta} = \frac{\frac{22}{13}}{\frac{7}{13}} = \frac{22}{7} = 7\frac{1}{3}$

22. Option (D) is correct.

Explanation:

We know, $\quad \cot\theta = \frac{1}{\tan\theta}$

$\Rightarrow \frac{\tan\theta}{1-\frac{1}{\tan\theta}}+\frac{1}{(1-\tan\theta)(\tan\theta)} = 1+k$

$\Rightarrow \frac{\tan^2\theta}{\tan\theta-1}-\frac{1}{(\tan\theta-1)\tan\theta} = 1+k$

$\Rightarrow \frac{\tan^3\theta-1}{\tan\theta(\tan\theta-1)} = 1+k$

$\Rightarrow \frac{(\tan^2\theta+1+\tan\theta)(\tan\theta-1)}{\tan\theta(\tan\theta-1)} = 1+k$

$\Rightarrow \frac{(\tan^2\theta+1+\tan\theta)}{\tan\theta} = 1+k$

$\Rightarrow \tan\theta + \cot\theta + 1 = k$

$\Rightarrow \tan\theta + \cot\theta = k$

$\therefore \quad \frac{\sin\theta}{\cos\theta}+\frac{\cos\theta}{\sin\theta} = k$

$\frac{\sin^2\theta+\cos^2\theta}{\sin\theta.\cos\theta} = k$

$\Rightarrow \text{cosec}\,\theta\,.\,\sec\theta = k$

23. Option (B) is correct.

Explanation:

Given, $8\,\text{cosec}^3\theta + 25\sin^2\theta$

$$\text{min. value} = 2\sqrt{ab}$$

$$= 2\sqrt{8\times 25} = 20\sqrt{2}$$

24. Option (C) is correct.

Explanation: $\dfrac{(\sin\theta - \text{cosec}\theta)(\cos\theta - \sec\theta)}{\tan^2\theta - \sin^2\theta} = r^3$

Now, put $\theta = 30°$

$$\Rightarrow \frac{(\sin 30° - \text{cosec}30°)(\cos 30° - \sec 30°)}{\tan^2 30° - \sin^2 30°} = r^3$$

$$\Rightarrow \frac{\left(\frac{1}{2}-2\right)\left(\frac{\sqrt{3}}{2}-\frac{2}{\sqrt{3}}\right)}{\left(\frac{1}{\sqrt{3}}\right)^2 - \left(\frac{1}{2}\right)^2} = r^3$$

$$\Rightarrow \frac{\left(-\frac{3}{2}\right)\left(\frac{3-4}{2\sqrt{3}}\right)}{\frac{1}{3}-\frac{1}{4}} = r^3$$

$$\Rightarrow \frac{\left(\frac{3}{4\sqrt{3}}\right)}{\frac{1}{12}} = r^3$$

$$\Rightarrow r^3 = 3\sqrt{3}, \Rightarrow r = \sqrt{3}$$

Now, check options

$$\cot 30° = \sqrt{3} = r$$

$$\therefore r = \cot\theta$$

25. Option (A) is correct.

Explanation:

Given, $\left(\dfrac{\sin\theta - 2\sin^3\theta}{2\cos^3\theta - \cos\theta}\right)^2 + 1$

$$\left[\frac{\sin\theta\,(1-2\sin^2\theta)}{\cos\theta\,(2\cos^2\theta - 1)}\right]^2 + 1$$

We know, $[1 - 2\sin^2\theta = \cos 2\theta = 2\cos^2\theta - 1]$

$$\therefore \left[\frac{\sin\theta.\cos 2\theta}{\cos.\cos 2\theta}\right]^2 + 1$$

$$\tan^2\theta + 1 = \sec^2\theta$$

■■■

Height and Distance

Line of sight
Line drawn from eyes of the observer to the point on the object.

Applications:
- Measuring heights of buildings and towers
- Calculate distance of the shape from sea
- Determining distance between celestral bodies

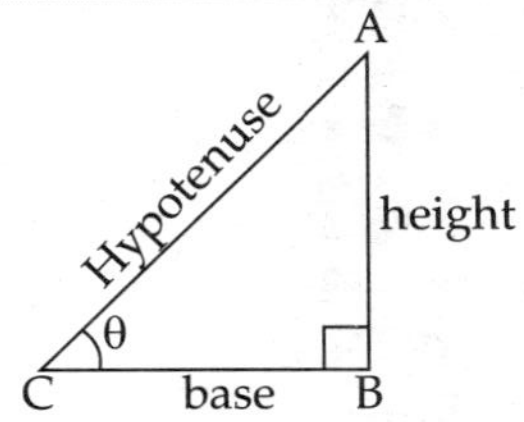

$$\sin\theta = \frac{\text{height}}{\text{hypotenuse}}$$

$$\cos\theta = \frac{\text{base}}{\text{hypotenuse}}$$

$$\tan\theta = \frac{\text{height}}{\text{base}}$$

Angle of elevation
Angle formed by line of sight with horizontal level

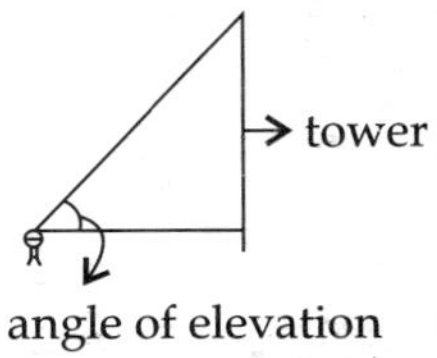

Angle of depression
Angle of the point on the object (below horizontal level) viewed by the observer which is formed by line of sight (with horizontal level.)

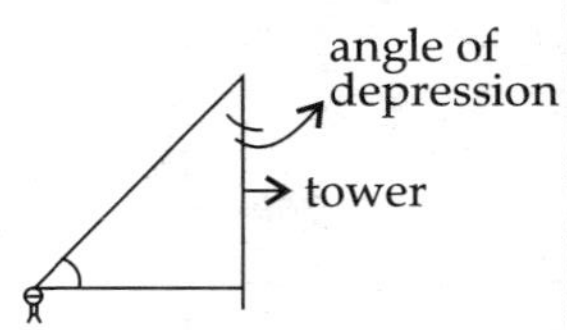

Chapter 16

Height and Distance

LEARNING OBJECTIVES:

- Applications of trigonometry: Angle of elevation and angle of depression.
- Common situation based questions.
- Some direct results.
- Different types of questions asked in various exams.
- Method of solving questions.

➢ The important application of trigonometry is to find the height and distance of a point that are not measurable. It is achieved using trigonometric ratios.

➢ **Angle of Elevation**

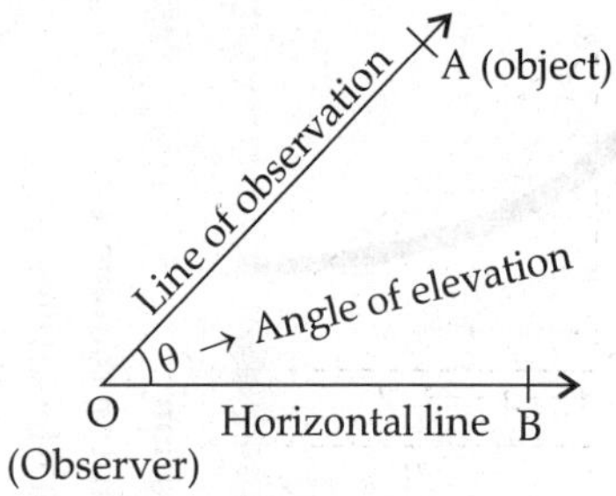

➢ **Angle of Depression**

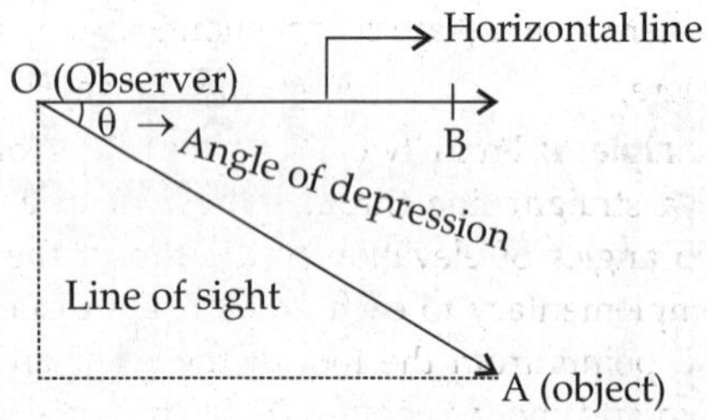

There are some useful concepts or short tricks, by which we will solve all questions of this chapter.

1. If $\theta = 30°$, then

P	B	H
1	$\sqrt{3}$	2

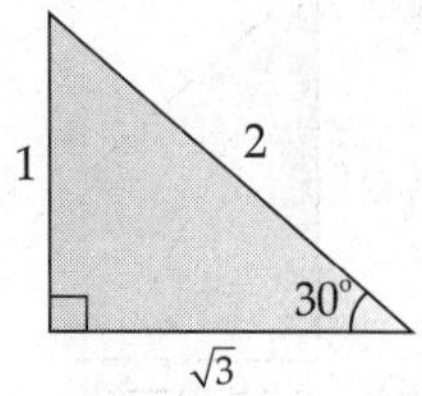

2. If $\theta = 45°$

P	B	H
1	1	$\sqrt{2}$

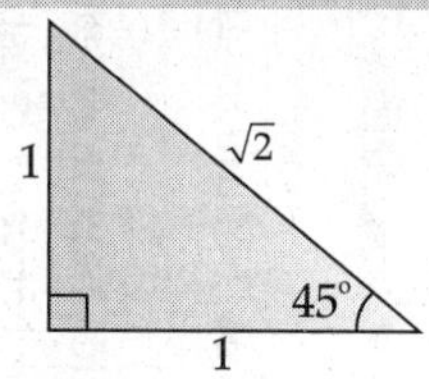

3. If $\theta = 60°$

P	B	H
$\sqrt{3}$	1	2

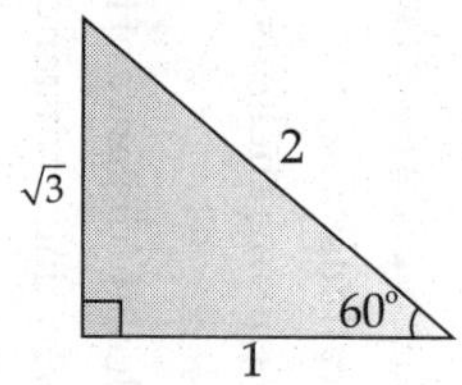

Example 1: The angle of elevation of a tower from a distance 100 m from its foot is 30°. Height of the tower is:

(a) $\frac{100}{\sqrt{3}}$m (b) $50\sqrt{3}$m

(c) $\frac{200}{\sqrt{3}}$m (d) $100\sqrt{3}$m

Sol. (a) BC = 100 m

By using Trick (1),

$\sqrt{3}$ unit = 100 m

$1 = \frac{100}{\sqrt{3}\text{ unit}}$

$\therefore$ AB = 1 unit = $\frac{100}{\sqrt{3}}$ m

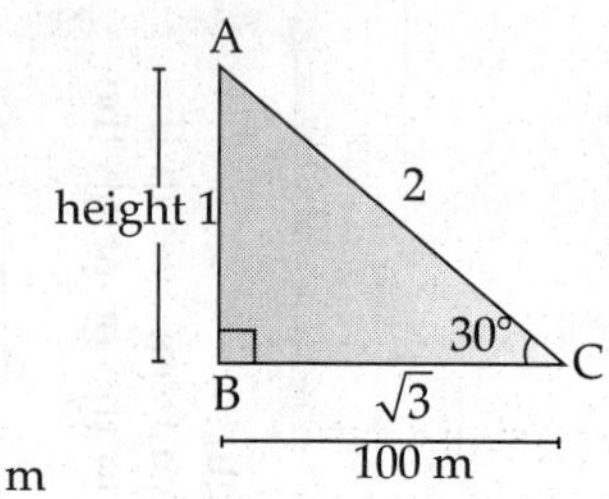

TRADITIONAL METHOD:

Let, $\tan\theta = \frac{AB}{BC}$

$\tan 30° = \frac{x}{100\text{ m}}$

$\Rightarrow \frac{1}{\sqrt{3}} = \frac{x}{100\text{ m}}$

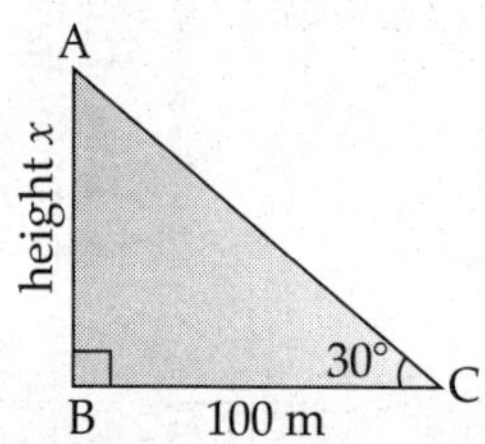

$\therefore \quad x = \frac{100}{\sqrt{3}}\text{m}$

Example 2: The angle of elevation of a ladder leaning against a house is 60° and the foot of ladder is 6.5 m from the house. The length of the ladder is :

(a) 3.25 m (b) 15 m

(c) 13 m (d) $\frac{13}{\sqrt{3}}$m

Sol. (c) Clearly from the figure, BC = 1 = 6.5

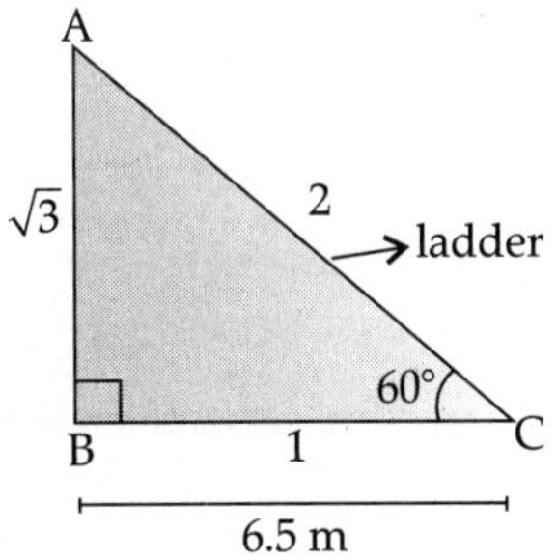

Using Trick (3),
Value of 1 = 6.5
So, value of 2, length of ladder
= 6.5 × 2 = 13 m

➤ Concept used when two angles are given or angles are complementary.

1.

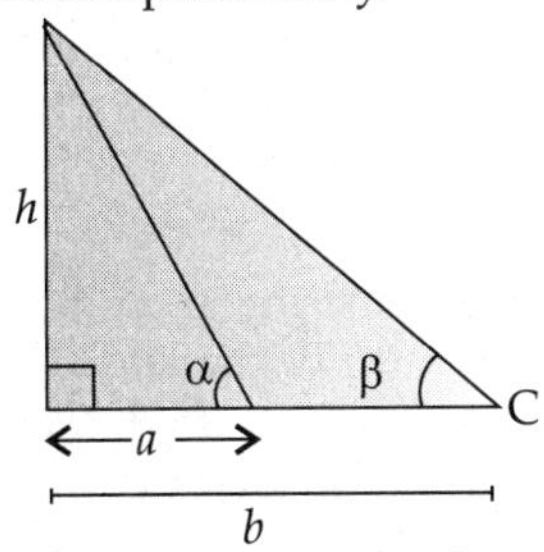

where $\alpha+\beta = 90°$

So, $h = \sqrt{ab}$

2.

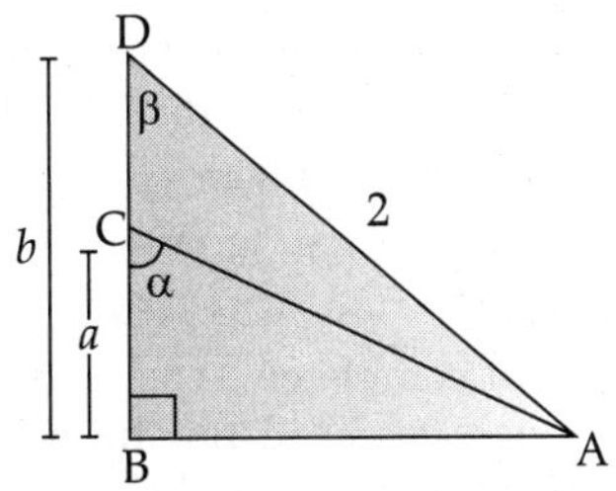

where $\alpha+\beta = 90°$

$AB = \sqrt{ab}$

Using T-ratios

1.

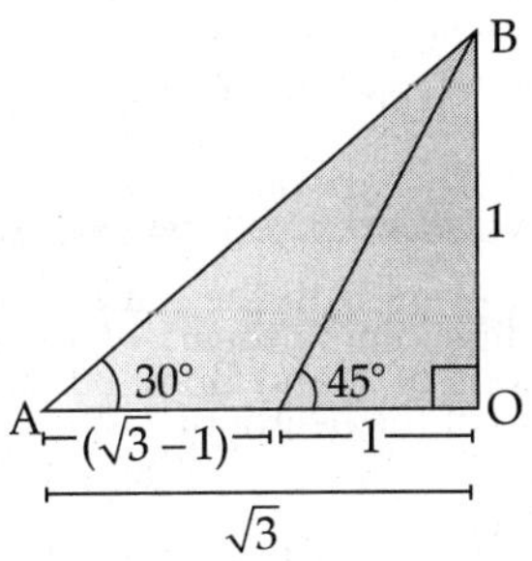

2.

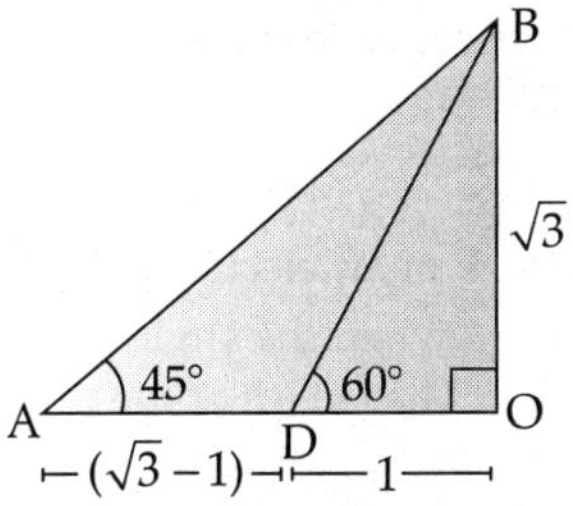

3.

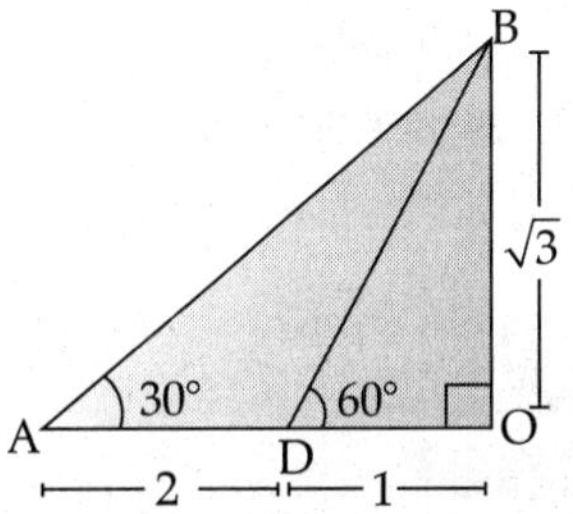

Example 3: The angle of elevation of top of a tower from the point P and Q at distance of 'a' and 'b', respectively from the base of the tower and in the same straight line with it are complementary. The height of the tower is:

(a) ab (b) $\sqrt{ab}$

(c) $\frac{a}{b}$ (d) a^2b

Sol. (b)

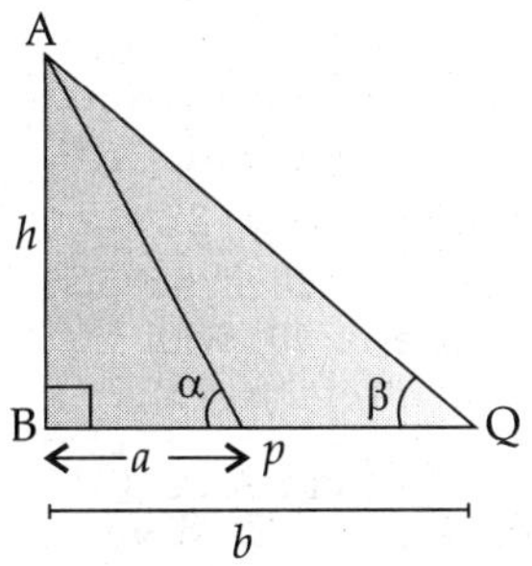

In ΔABC, $BP = a$

$BC = b$

where, α and β are complementary

Here, $h = \sqrt{ab}$ (always)

Example 4: From two points on the ground lying on a straight line through the foot of a pillar, the two angles of elevation of the top of the pillar are complementary to each other. If the distance of the two points from the foot of the pillar are 9 m and 16 m and the two points lie on the same side of the pillar, then the height of the pillar is:

(a) 10 m (b) 7 m

(c) 12 m (d) 5 m

Sol. (c)

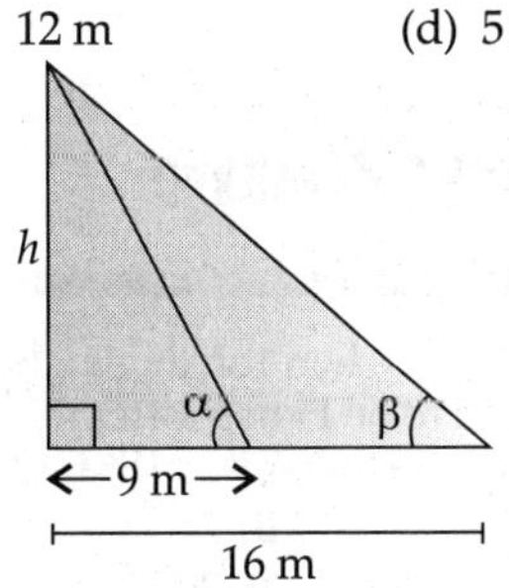

Given, α and β are complementary

So, $h = \sqrt{ab}$

$= \sqrt{9 \times 16} = \sqrt{144} = 12$ m

Example 5: The shadow of an electric pole standing on a ground is 40 m less when the angle of elevation changes from 30° to 45°. The length of the pole is:

(a) $20(\sqrt{3}-1)$m (b) $20(\sqrt{3}+1)$m

(c) 20 m (d) $20\sqrt{3}$ m

Sol. (b) Given, $(\sqrt{3}-1)$ unit → 40 m

So, 1 unit → $\frac{40}{\sqrt{3}-1} \times \frac{\sqrt{3}+1}{\sqrt{3}+1} = 20(\sqrt{3}+1)$

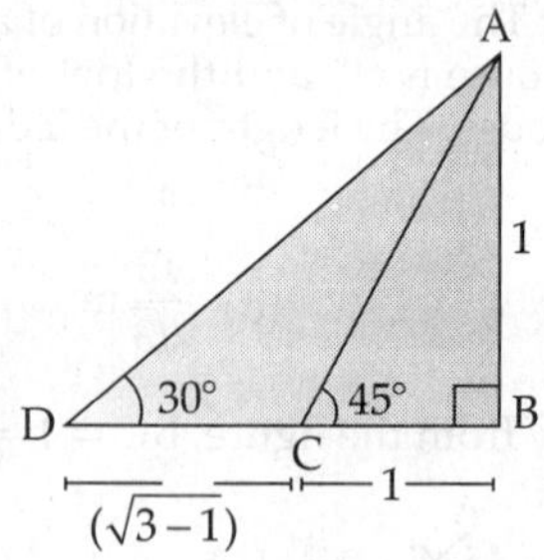

∴ AB = $1 \times 20(\sqrt{3}+1) = 20(\sqrt{3}+1)$

1 Level Beginner

1. The thread of a kite makes angle 60° with the horizontal plane. If the length of the thread be 80 m, then the vertical height of the kite will be: **[SSC Tier-II 2016]**

(A) $\frac{40}{\sqrt{3}}$m **(B)** $40\sqrt{3}$m

(C) 80m **(D)** $80\sqrt{3}$m

2. A 1.6 m tall observer is 45 m away from a tower. The angle of elevation from his eye to the top of the tower is 30°, then the height of the tower is (in metres). **[SSC CGL Tier-I 2016]**

(A) 26.58 **(B)** 27.58 **(C)** 27.98 **(D)** 25.98

3. A kite flying at a height of 120 m is attached to string which makes an angle of 60° with the horizontal. What is the length (in m) of the string? **[SSC CGL 2022]**

(A) $75\sqrt{3}$ **(B)** $90\sqrt{3}$ **(C)** $80\sqrt{3}$ **(D)** $54\sqrt{3}$

4. The string of a kite is 158 m long and it makes an angles of 30° with the horizontal. What is the height (in m) of the kite? Assume there is no stack in the string. **[SSC CHSL 2021]**

(A) 80 **(B)** 99 **(C)** 100 **(D)** 79

5. The angle of depression of a boat from the masthead of a 180 m high ship is 60°. Find the distance of boat from the ship (in m). **[SSC Tier-I 2022]**

(A) $60\sqrt{3}$ **(B)** $120\sqrt{3}$ **(C)** 180 **(D)** 360

6. A ladder 10 m long rests against a vertical wall making an angle of 30° with the wall. How high up (in m) does it reach the wall from the ground? (Take $\sqrt{3} = 1.73$). **[SSC CHSL 2021]**

(A) 5.88 **(B)** 5

(C) 8.56 **(D)** 8.65

7. What is angle of elevation of Sun from the top of a pillar's shadow, when its height is equal to the length of its shadow? **[SSC CPO 2019]**

(A) 45° **(B)** 90°

(C) 30° **(D)** 60°

8. If the height of a pole and the distance between the pole and a man standing nearby are equal, what would be the angle? **[SSC CPO 2019]**

(A) 30° **(B)** 90°

(C) 45° **(D)** 60°

9. Seema flies a kite on a 16 m string at an inclination of 60°. What is the height (h) of the kite above the ground? **[SSC CGL 2020]**

(A) $6\sqrt{3}$ m **(B)** $4\sqrt{3}$ m

(C) $8\sqrt{3}$ m **(D)** $16\sqrt{3}$ m

10. From the top of a light-house at a height 20 m above sea level, the angle of depression of a ship is 30°. The distance of the ship from the foot of the light house is : **[SSC CPO 2014]**

(A) $20\sqrt{3}$ m **(B)** 20m

(C) 30 m **(D)** $30\sqrt{3}$ m

11. A vertical post 15 ft high is broken at a certain height and its upper part, not completely separated, meets the ground at an angle of 30°. Find the height at which the post is broken. **[SSC CHSL DEO 2012]**

(A) 10 ft **(B)** 5ft

(C) $15\sqrt{3}(2-\sqrt{3})$ft **(D)** $5\sqrt{3}$ft

2 Level Intermediate

1. The shadow of a tower when the angle elevation of the Sun is 60° is found to be 15 m shorter than when it is 45°. Then height of the tower is: **[SSC CPO 2019]**

(A) 35.5 m **(B)** 26.5 m

(C) 41.5 m **(D)** 20.5 m

2. Let A and B be two towers with the same base from the mid point of the line joining their feet, the angles of elevation of the tops of A and B are 30° and 45°, respectively. The ratio of the height of A and B is: **[SSC CPO 2020]**

(A) 1 : 3 **(B)** $\sqrt{3}:1$ **(C)** $1:\sqrt{3}$ **(D)** 3 : 1

3. The length of the shadow of the vertical tower on level ground increases by 10 m when the altitude of the Sun changes from 45° to 30°. The height of the tower is: [SSC CGL 2019]

(A) $5\sqrt{3}$ m (B) $10(\sqrt{3}-1)$m

(C) $10\sqrt{3}$ m (D) $5(\sqrt{3}+1)$m

4. The length of the shadow of a vertical pole on the ground is 18 m. If the angle of elevation of the Sun at that time is θ, such that $\cos\theta=\frac{12}{13}$, then what is the height (is m) of the pole? [SSC CPO 2020]

(A) 18 (B) 7.5 (C) 12 (D) 9

5. A straight vertical pole was broken during a cyclone in such a way that its top touches the ground at a distance of $6\sqrt{3}$m from the bottom of the pole and made an angle of 30° with the horizontal. What was the height of the pole? (in m) [SSC CHSL 2021]

(A) $18\sqrt{3}$ (B) 12

(C) 18 (D) $12\sqrt{3}$

6. A girl 1.2 m tall can just see the Sun over a 3.62 m tall which is 2.42 m away from her. The angle of elevation of the Sun is [SSC CPO 2019]

(A) 30° (B) 45° (C) 60° (D) 90°

7. Let A and B be two towers with same base, from the mid point of the line joining their feet, the angles of elevation of the tops of A and B are 30° and 60°, respectively. The ratio of the heights of A and B is: [SSC CPO 2020]

(A) $\sqrt{3}:1$ (B) $2\sqrt{3}:1$ (C) $1:2\sqrt{3}$ (D) 1 : 3

8. The angle of elevation of a pole from two points which are 75 m and 48 m away from its base are α and β, respectively. If α and β are complementary angles, then the height of the tower is [SSC CPO 2019]

(A) 60 m (B) 54.5 m

(C) 50 m (D) 61.5 m

9. When the sun's angle of depression changes from 30° to 60°, the length of the shadow of a tower decreases by 70 m. What is the height of the tower? [SSC CPO 2019]

(A) 65.55 m (B) 45.65 m

(C) 60.55 m (D) 36.55 m

10. As observed from the top of a light house, $120\sqrt{3}$m above the sea level, the angle of depression of a ship sailing towards it from 30° to 60°. The distance travelled by the ship during the period of observation is : [SSC CGL Tier-II 2019]

(A) $240\sqrt{3}$m (B) 240 m

(C) 180 m (D) $180\sqrt{3}$m

11. From a point 12 m above the water level, the angle of elevation of the top of a hill is 60° and the angle of depression of the base of the hill is 30°. What is the height (is m) of the hill? [SSC CPO 2019]

(A) $48\sqrt{3}$ (B) 48

(C) 36 (D) $36\sqrt{3}$

3 Expert Level

1. The angle of elevation of a flying drone from a point on the ground is 60°. After flying for 5 seconds the angle of elevation drops to 30°. If the drone is flying horizontally at a constant height of $1{,}000\sqrt{3}$m, the distance travelled by the drone is: [SSC CPO 2019]

(A) 2,000 m (B) 1,000 m

(C) 3,000 m (D) 4,000 m

2. From the top of house A in a street, the angle of elevation and depression of the top and foot of another house B on the opposite side of the street are 60° and 45°, respectively. If the height of house A is 36 m, then what is the height of house B? (nearest to an integer) [SSC CGL Tier-II 2019]

(A) 93 m (B) 94 m

(C) 98 m (D) 91 m

3. The angle of elevation of the top of a tree from a point on the ground which is 300 m away from the tree is 30°. When the tree grew up, its angle of elevation of the top of it became 60°, from the same point. How much did the tree grow? (nearest to an integer) [SSC CPO 2019]

(A) 346 m (B) 364 m (C) 342 m (D) 384 m

4. A pole of length 7 m is fixed vertically on the top of a tower, the angle of elevation of the top of the pole observed from a point on the ground is 60° and the angle of depression of the same point on the ground from the top of the tower is 45°. The height (in m) of the tower is : [SSC CPO 2019]

(A) $7\sqrt{3}$ (B) $7(2\sqrt{3}-1)$

(C) $\frac{7}{2}(\sqrt{3}-1)$ (D) $\frac{7}{2}(\sqrt{3}+2)$

5. From the top of a hill 240 m high the angle of depression of the top and of the bottom of a pole are 30° and 60°, respectively. The difference (in m) between the height of the pole and its distance from the hill is: [SSC CGL 2019]

(A) $120(\sqrt{3}-1)$ (B) $80(\sqrt{3}-1)$

(C) $120(2-\sqrt{3})$ (D) $80(2-\sqrt{3})$

6. A 22 m long ladder (whose foot is on the ground) leans against a wall making an angle of 60° with the wall. What is the height (in m) of the point where the ladder touches the wall from the ground? [SSC CPO 2020]

(A) 11 (B) $11\sqrt{3}$

(C) $11\sqrt{2}$ (D) $\frac{22\sqrt{2}}{3}$

7. An aeroplane flying horizontally at a height of 3 km above the ground, is observed at a certain point on the Earth to subtend an angle of 60°. After 15 seconds of flight, its angle of elevation is changed to 30°. The speed of the aeroplane (Take, $\sqrt{3} = 1.732$) is: **[SSC CGL Tier-II 2016]**
(A) 230.6 m/sec (B) 230.5 m/sec
(C) 230.93 m/sec (D) 236.25 m/sec

8. The tops of two poles of heights 18 m and 30.5 m are connected by a wire. If the wire makes an angle of 30° with the horizontal, what is the length (in m) of the wire? **[SSC CGL 2022]**
(A) 28 (B) 20 (C) 25 (D) 36

9. Two persons are on either side of a temple, 75 m high, observe the angle of elevation of the top of the temple to be 30° and 60°, respectively. The distance between the two persons is : **[SSC CGL 2016]**
(A) 100 m (B) 173.2 m
(C) 273.2 m (D) 157.7 m

10. As observed from the top of the lighthouse, 45 m high above sea level, the angle of depression of a ship, sailing directly towards it, changes from 30° to 45°. The distance travelled by the ship during the period of observation is : (Correct to one decimal) **[SSC CPO 2019]**
(A) 36.9 m (B) 24.8 m
(C) 33.4 m (D) 32.9 m

11. The angle of elevation of an aeroplane from a point on the ground is 60°. After flying 30 seconds, the angle of elevation changes to 30°. If the aeroplane is flying at a height of 4,500 m, then what is the speed of aeroplane? **[SSC CGL Tier-II 2017]**
(A) $50\sqrt{3}$ m/sec (B) $100\sqrt{3}$ m/sec
(C) $200\sqrt{3}$ m/sec (D) $300\sqrt{3}$ m/sec

12. A pilot in an aeroplane at an altitude of 200 m observes two points lying on either side of a river. If the angles of depression of the two points be 45° and 60°, then the width of the river is: **[SSC CGL 2018]**
(A) $\left(200 - \frac{200}{\sqrt{3}}\right)$ m (B) $\left(200 + \frac{200}{\sqrt{3}}\right)$ m
(C) $400\sqrt{3}$ m (D) $\frac{200}{\sqrt{3}}$ m

ANSWER KEY

Level-1: Beginner

1.	(B)	2.	(B)	3.	(C)	4.	(D)	5.	(A)	6.	(D)	7.	(A)	8.	(C)	9.	(C)	10.	(A)
11.	(B)																		

Level-2: Intermediate

1.	(A)	2.	(C)	3.	(B)	4.	(B)	5.	(C)	6.	(B)	7.	(D)	8.	(A)	9.	(C)	10.	(B)
11.	(B)																		

Level-3: Expert

1.	(A)	2.	(C)	3.	(A)	4.	(C)	5.	(D)	6.	(A)	7.	(C)	8.	(C)	9.	(B)	10.	(D)
11.	(B)	12.	(B)																

Solutions with Detailed Explanations

Level-1: BEGINNER

1. **Option (B) is correct.**

Explanation:

TRADITIONAL METHOD:

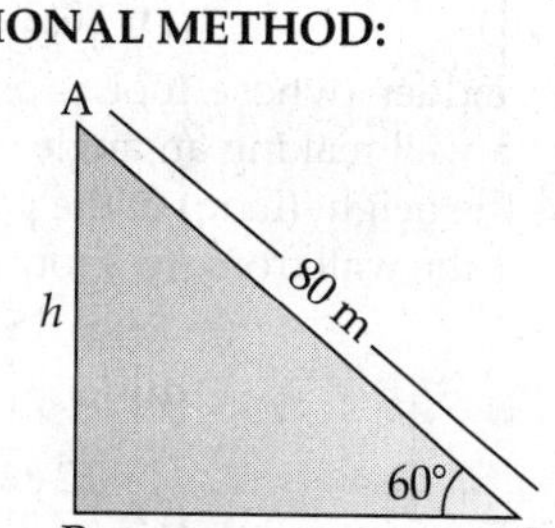

$$\sin 60° = \frac{AB}{AC} \Rightarrow \frac{\sqrt{3}}{2} = \frac{h}{80}$$

$$\therefore \quad h = \frac{\sqrt{3}}{2} \times 80 = 40\sqrt{3}\text{m}$$

SHORTCUT METHOD:

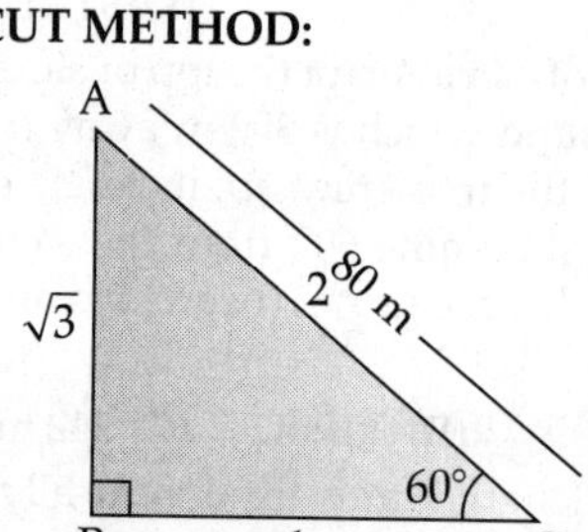

In ΔABC, $\theta = 60^o$

$\therefore$ Trignometric ratio value

$AB = \sqrt{3}, BC = 1, AC = 2$

Now, $AC = 2 \rightarrow 80$

So, $1 \rightarrow 40$

Hence, $AB = \sqrt{3} \times 40 = 40\sqrt{3}$ m

2. **Option (B) is correct.**

Explanation:

$$\tan 30° = \frac{1}{\sqrt{3}}$$

$\therefore$ $AB = 1, BC = \sqrt{3}, AC = 2$

Now, $BC \Rightarrow \sqrt{3} \rightarrow 45$

$\therefore$ $1 \rightarrow \frac{45}{\sqrt{3}} = 15\sqrt{3}$

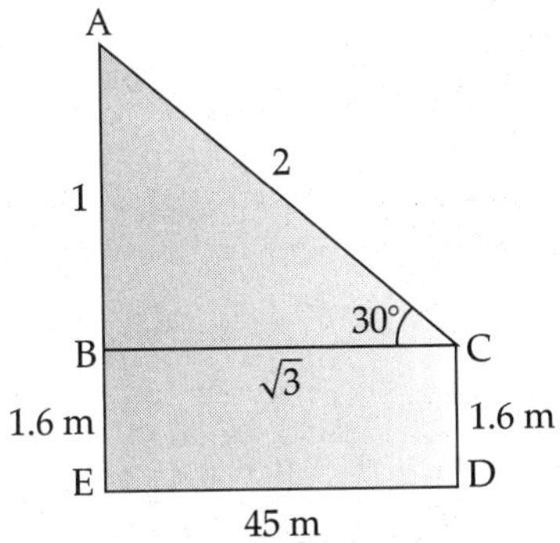

$\therefore$ $AB = 1 \times 15\sqrt{3} = 15\sqrt{3}$ m

Now, height of tower $= 1.6 + 15\sqrt{3}$

$= 1.6 + 15 \times 1.732$

$= 1.6 + 25.98 = 27.58$ m

3. **Option (C) is correct.**

Explanation:

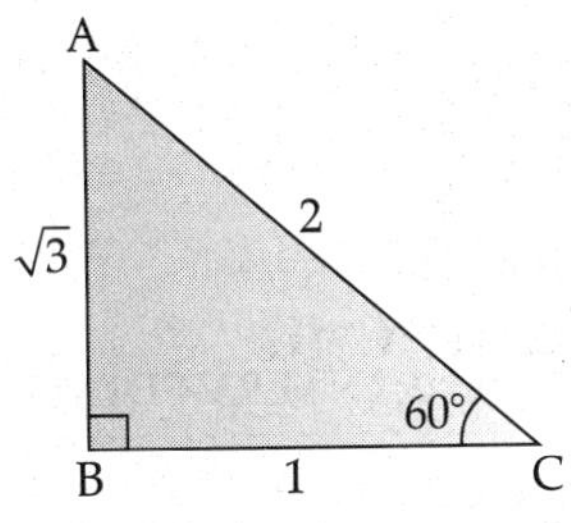

$AB = 120$ m

In ΔABC, $\theta = 60°$

AB	BC	AC
$\sqrt{3}$	1	2
$) 40\sqrt{3}$		$) \times 40\sqrt{3}$
120		$80\sqrt{3}$

So, length of string $= 80\sqrt{3}$ m

TRADITIONAL METHOD:

$$\sin 60° = \frac{AB}{AC}$$

$$\Rightarrow \frac{\sqrt{3}}{2} = \frac{AB}{AC}$$

$$\Rightarrow \frac{\sqrt{3}}{2} = \frac{120}{AC}$$

$$\Rightarrow AC = \frac{120 \times 2}{\sqrt{3}}$$

$$= 80\sqrt{3} \text{ m}$$

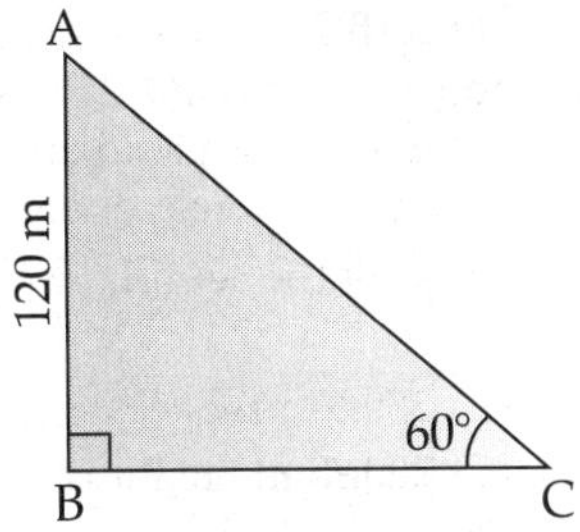

4. **Option (D) is correct.**

Explanation:

In ΔABC, $\theta = 30°$

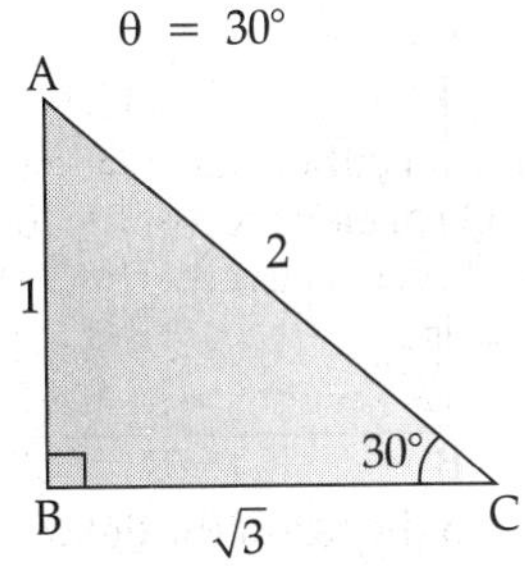

AB	BC	AC
1	$\sqrt{3}$	2
$) \times 79$		$) 79$
79		158 m

So, height of kite = 79 m

5. **Option (A) is correct.**

Explanation:

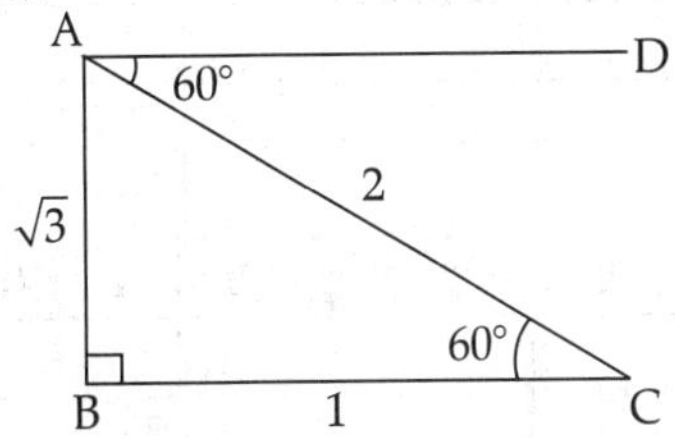

$\angle DAC = \angle ACB = 60°$

$\therefore$ AB = height of masthead

BC = distance of boat from the ship

Now, in ABC

AB	BC	AC
$\sqrt{3}$	1	2
$) \times 60\sqrt{3}$	$) \times 60\sqrt{3}$	
180	$60\sqrt{3}$	

So, the distance of boat from ship $= 60\sqrt{3}$ m

6. **Option (D) is correct.**

Explanation:

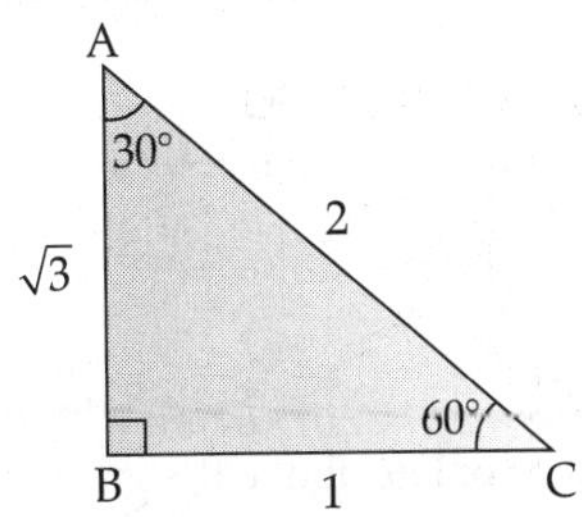

In ΔABC,

AB	BC	AC
$\sqrt{3}$	1	2
$\big)\times 5$		$\big)\times 5$
$5\sqrt{3}$		10

$\therefore$ Required height = $5 \times 1.73 = 8.65$ m

7. **Option (A) is correct.**

Explanation:

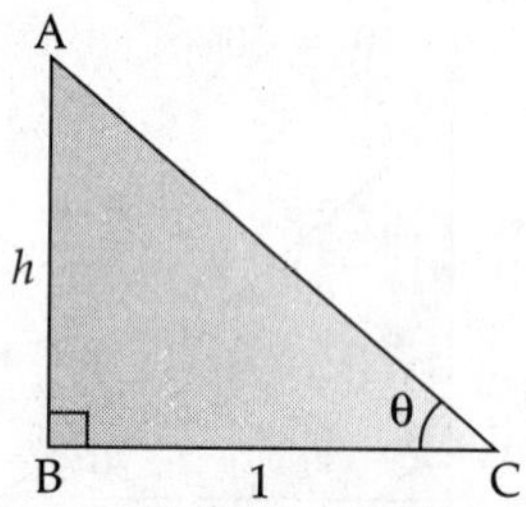

Length of shadow

In ΔABC, Height = Length of shadow

$$\tan\theta = \frac{AB}{BC}$$

$$\Rightarrow \quad \tan\theta = \frac{AB}{AB} = 1$$

$$\Rightarrow \quad \theta = 45°$$

8. **Option (C) is correct.**

Explanation:

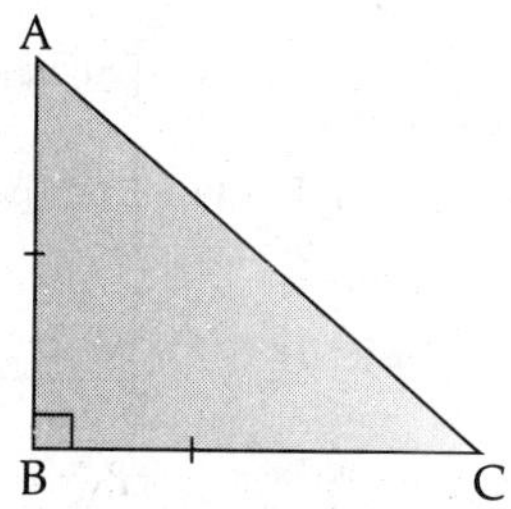

AB = BC (Given)

$$\therefore \quad \tan\theta = \frac{AB}{BC} = \frac{AB}{AB}$$

$$\tan\theta = 1$$

$$\therefore \quad \theta = 45°$$

9. **Option (C) is correct.**

Explanation:

In ΔABC,

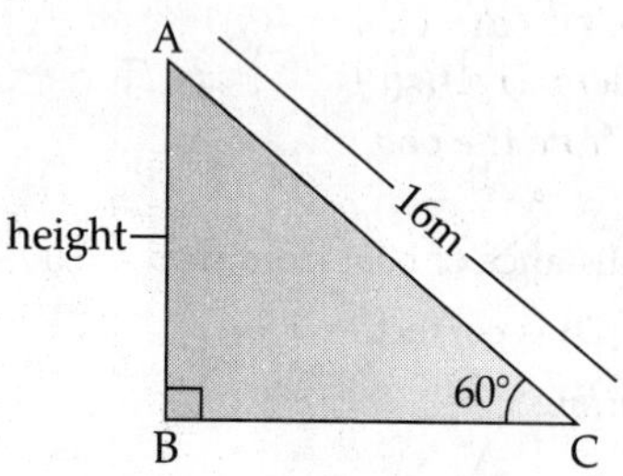

AB	AC	BC
$\sqrt{3}$	2	1
$\big)\times 8$	$\big)\times 8$	
$8\sqrt{3}$	16	

So, the height of kite above the ground = $8\sqrt{3}$ m

10. **Option (A) is correct.**

Explanation:

In ΔABC,

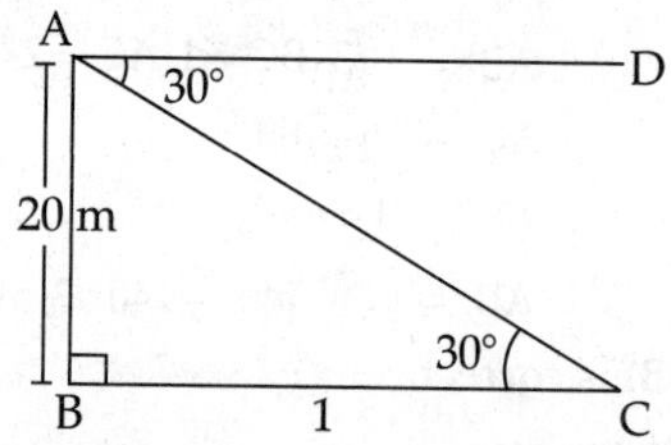

AB	BC	AC
1	$\sqrt{3}$	2
$\big)\times 20$	$\big)\times 20$	
20	$20\sqrt{3}$	

So, distance of the ship from the foot of light house $= 20\sqrt{3}$ m

11. **Option (B) is correct.**

Explanation: In ΔBCD,

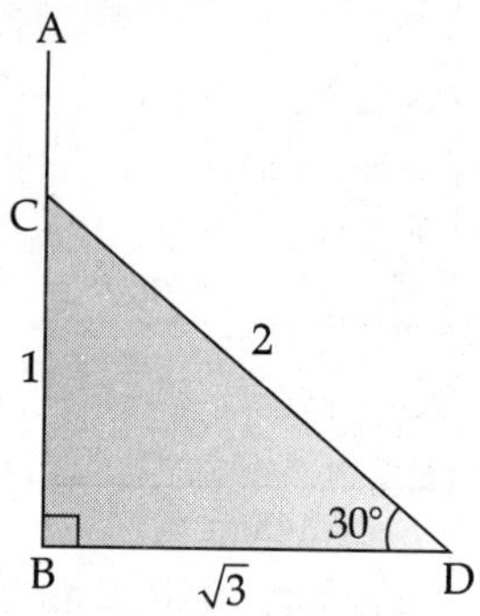

BC : CD : BD

1 : 2 : $\sqrt{3}$

$$\Rightarrow \quad 2BC = CD$$

$$\Rightarrow \quad CD = AC = (AB - BC)$$

$$= 15 - BC$$

So $\quad 2BC = 15 - BC$

$$\Rightarrow \quad 3BC = 15$$

$$\Rightarrow \quad BC = 5 \text{ ft}$$

So, required height = 5 ft

Level-2: INTERMEDIATE

1. **Option (A) is correct.**

Explanation:

In ΔABD

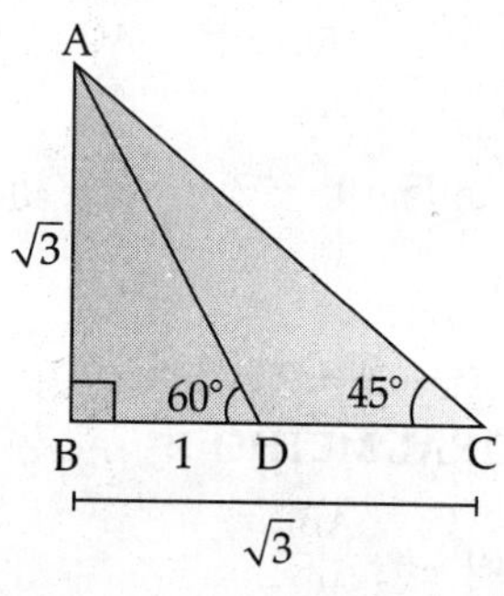

$$\tan 45^\circ = \frac{AB}{BC} = \frac{1}{1}$$

$$\tan 60^\circ = \frac{AB}{BD} = \frac{\sqrt{3}}{1}$$

Balance the values of AB

$$AB = \sqrt{3}, BD = 1, BC = \sqrt{3}$$

According to question

$$BC - BD = \sqrt{3} - 1$$

$$\Rightarrow \quad (\sqrt{3} - 1) \text{ unit} = 15$$

$$1 \text{ unit} = \frac{15}{\sqrt{3} - 1}$$

$\therefore$ Height of the tower AB $= \sqrt{3}$ unit

$$= \sqrt{3} \times \frac{15}{\sqrt{3} - 1}$$

$$= \frac{45 + 15\sqrt{3}}{2} = 35.5 \text{ m}$$

2. **Option (C) is correct.**

Explanation: Given, angle of elevation of A = 30°

Angle of elevation of B = 45°

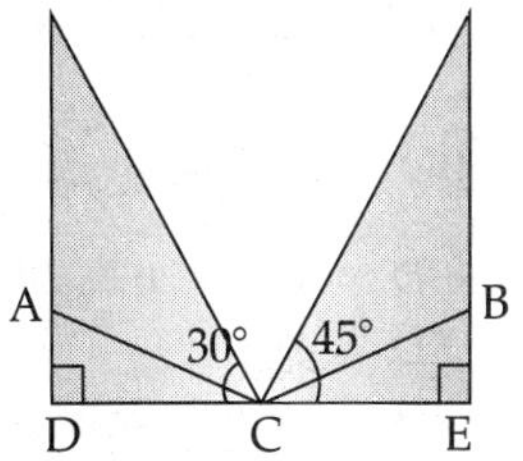

We know, $\tan\theta = \frac{DC}{AC}$ and the angle of elevation is drawn from the midpoint.

So, base for both A and B is equal.

So, height of A : height of B

$$= \tan 30^\circ : \tan 45^\circ = \frac{\frac{1}{\sqrt{3}}}{1} = \frac{1}{\sqrt{3}} = 1 : \sqrt{3}$$

3. **Option (B) is correct.**

Explanation:

Height $= h = AB$

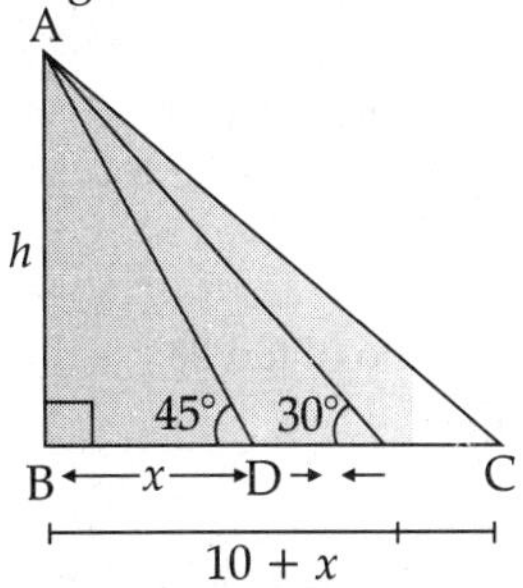

Now, $\tan 45^\circ = \frac{AB}{BD}$

$$\Rightarrow \quad 1 = \frac{h}{BD} \Rightarrow BD = h$$

$$x = h$$

Now, $\tan 30^\circ = \frac{AB}{BC}$

$$\Rightarrow \quad \frac{1}{\sqrt{3}} = \frac{h}{10 + x}$$

$$10 + x = \sqrt{3}h$$

$$10 + h = \sqrt{3}h$$

$$10 = \sqrt{3}h - h$$

$$10 = h(\sqrt{3} - h)$$

$$\frac{10}{\sqrt{3} - 1} = h$$

4. **Option (B) is correct.**

Explanation: Given

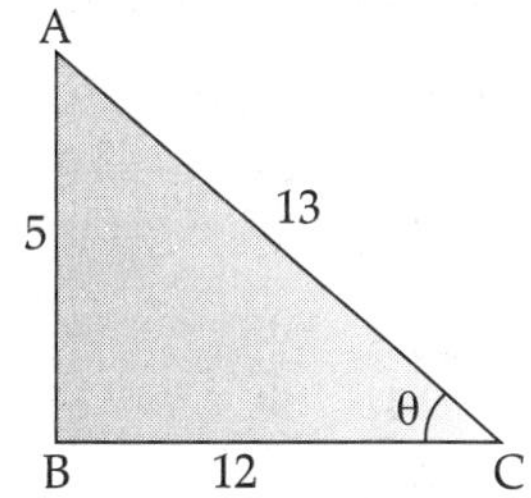

Length of shadow = 18 m

Given, $\cos\theta = \frac{12}{13}$

Using Pythagoras triples,

Now, B P H

12 5 13

$$\therefore \quad BC = \frac{18}{12}$$

So, height $= \frac{18}{12} \times 5 = 7.5 \text{m}$

5. **Option (C) is correct.**

Explanation: Given,

Distance from the bottom $= 6\sqrt{3}$m

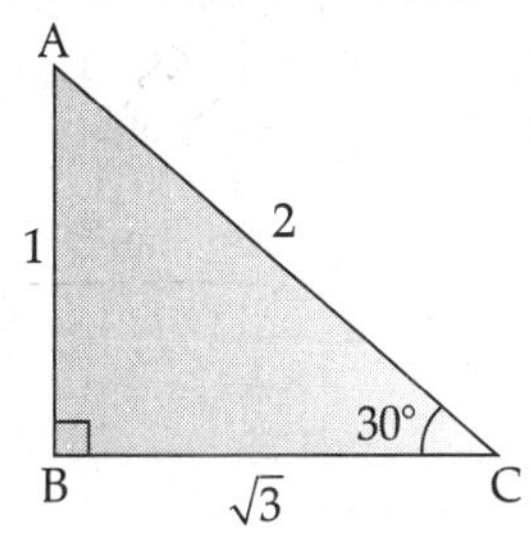

Now, $\tan 30^\circ = \frac{AB}{BC}$

$$\Rightarrow \quad \frac{1}{\sqrt{3}} = \frac{AB}{6\sqrt{3}}$$

$$\Rightarrow \quad 6 \text{ m} = AB$$

Using T-ratios values,

AB	AC	BC
1	2	$\sqrt{3}$
)×6	)×6	
6	12	

Now, total height of the pole = AB + AC
= 6 + 12 = 18 m

6. **Option (B) is correct.**
Explanation: Given,

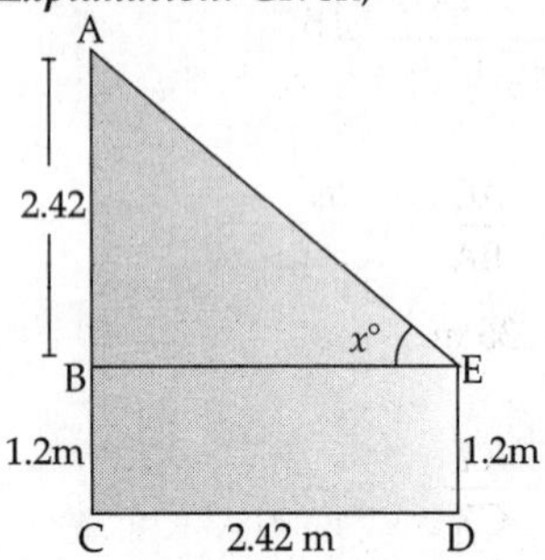

$$DE = 1.2 \text{ m}$$
$$AC = 3.62 \text{ m}, CD = 2.42 \text{ m}$$
$$\therefore \quad AB = 3.62 - 1.2 = 2.42 \text{ m}$$
$$\Rightarrow \quad \tan x = \frac{AB}{BE}$$
$$\therefore \quad \tan x = \frac{2.42}{2.42}$$
$$\Rightarrow \quad \tan x = 1$$
$$\Rightarrow \quad x = 45^\circ \qquad (\because \tan 45^\circ = 1)$$

7. **Option (D) is correct.**
Explanation:

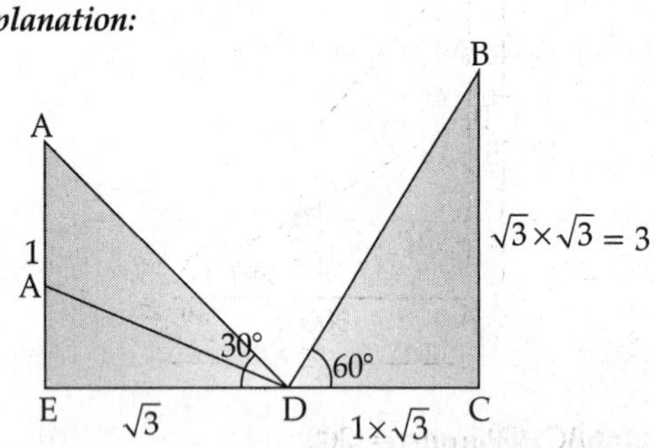

$$\tan\theta = \frac{\text{height}}{\text{base}}$$

Also ED = DC [D is midpoint of EC]

$\therefore$ Height of A : Height of B
= ED.tan30° : DC.tan60°
= tan30 : tan 60
$= \frac{1}{\sqrt{3}} : \sqrt{3}$
= 1 : 3

8. **Option (A) is correct.**
Explanation: Given: α and β are complementary.
$\therefore h^2$ = product of the distance of two parts from the pole, where h is the height of pole.

$$\therefore \quad h = \sqrt{75\times 48}$$
$$h = \sqrt{15\times5\times8\times6}$$
$$h = 4\times3\times5 = 60 \text{ m}$$

9. **Option (C) is correct.**
Explanation: In ΔABD,

$$\tan 60^\circ = \frac{AB}{BD}$$

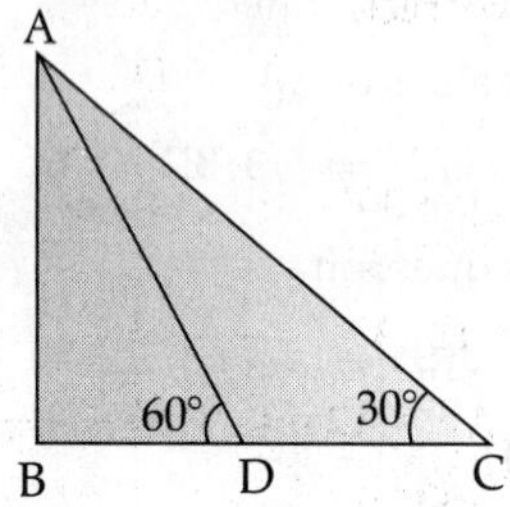

$$\Rightarrow \quad \sqrt{3} = \frac{AB}{BD}$$
$$\Rightarrow \quad \sqrt{3}BD = AB \qquad ...(1)$$

In ΔABC

$$\tan 30^\circ = \frac{AB}{BC}$$
$$\Rightarrow \quad \frac{1}{\sqrt{3}} = \frac{AB}{BC}$$
$$\Rightarrow \quad AB = \frac{BC}{\sqrt{3}}$$
$$\text{Now,} \quad AB = \frac{BD+70}{\sqrt{3}} \qquad [\because BC = BD + 70]$$
$$\Rightarrow \quad \sqrt{3}BD = \frac{BD+70}{\sqrt{3}}$$
$$\Rightarrow \quad 3BD = BD + 70 \Rightarrow 2BD = 70$$
$$\Rightarrow \quad BD = 35 \text{ m}$$

From Eq. (1), $AB = 35\sqrt{3} = 60.55$ m
So, height of the tower = 60.55 m

10. **Option (B) is correct.**
Explanation:

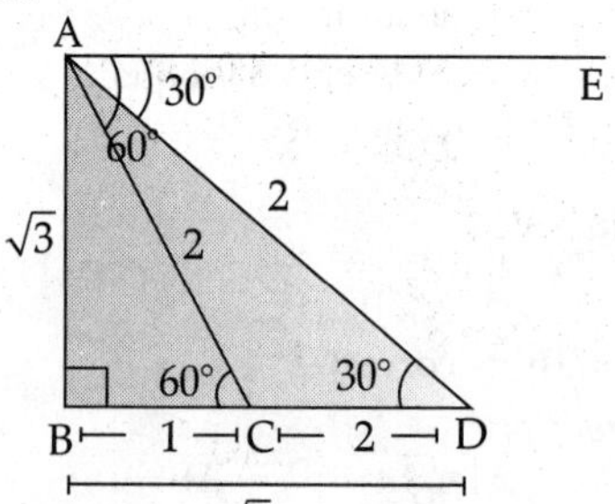

According to T-ratio of tan 60°

AB	BC	AC
$\sqrt{3}$	1	2

...(1)

According to T-ratio of tan 30°

AB	BD	AD
1	$\sqrt{3}$	2

...(2)

After balancing the ratio of AB in Eq. (2) with Eq. (1)

AB	BD	AD
$\sqrt{3}$	3	2
×120		
$120\sqrt{3}$		

As, $CD = BD - BC = 3 - 1 = 2$

Now, $CD = 120 \times 2 = 240$ m

So, required distance = 240 m

11. Option (B) is correct.

Explanation:

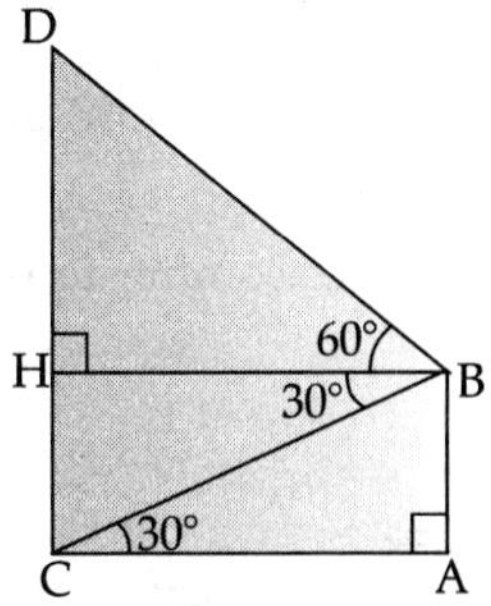

$$\frac{AB}{AC} = \tan 30°$$

$$AC = 12\sqrt{3}$$

[As, AB = 12 m]

$$AC = BH$$

$$\Rightarrow \quad BH = 12\sqrt{3}$$

and $HC = 12$ m

Now, in ΔBHD

$$\tan 60° = \frac{DH}{BH} \Rightarrow \frac{DH}{BH} = \frac{\sqrt{3}}{1}$$

$$\Rightarrow \quad DH = 12\sqrt{3} \times \sqrt{3} = 36 \text{ m}$$

Now, height of the hill = 36 + 12 = 48 m.

Level-3: EXPERT

1. Option (A) is correct.

Explanation:

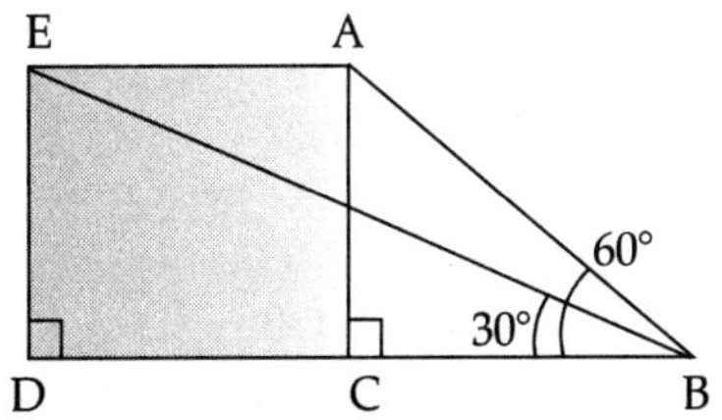

$$ED = 1{,}000\sqrt{3}\text{m} \qquad \text{(Given)}$$

Also, $ED = AC$

Now, in ΔACB,

$$\tan 60° = \frac{AC}{BC}$$

$$\Rightarrow \quad \sqrt{3} = \frac{1{,}000\sqrt{3}}{BC}$$

$$\Rightarrow \quad 1{,}000 \text{ m} = BC$$

Now, in ΔBED,

$$\tan 30° = \frac{ED}{BD}$$

$$\Rightarrow \quad \frac{1}{\sqrt{3}} = \frac{1{,}000\sqrt{3}}{BD}$$

$$\Rightarrow \quad BD = 3{,}000 \text{ m}$$

∴ DC (distance covered) by = 3,000 – 1,000 = 2,000 m

2. Option (C) is correct.

Explanation:

Height = 36 m

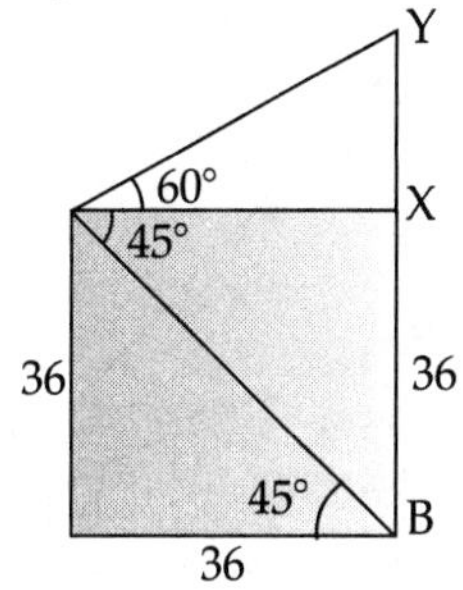

In ΔABC,

$$\tan 45° = \frac{AC}{BA}$$

$$\Rightarrow \quad AB = 36 \text{ m}$$

In ΔCXY,

$$\tan 60° = \frac{XY}{CX}$$

$$\Rightarrow \quad \sqrt{3} = \frac{XY}{36}$$

$$\Rightarrow \quad XY = 36\sqrt{3} \text{ m}$$

Then, height of B = $BY = 36 + 36\sqrt{3}$

= 98.28 m = 98 m

3. Option (A) is correct.

Explanation:

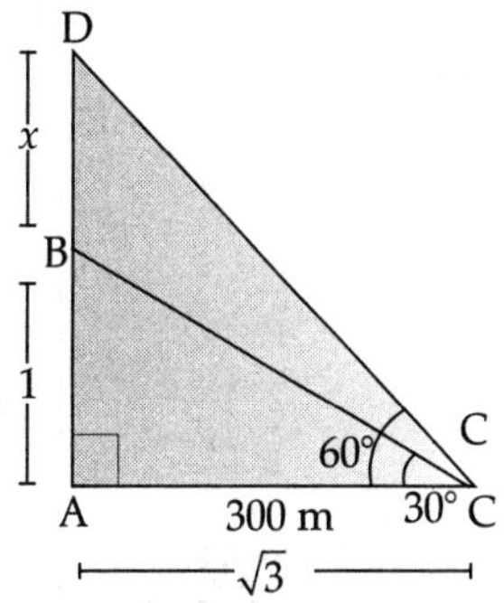

In ΔABC, $\sqrt{3}$ unit = 300

$$\Rightarrow \quad 1 \text{ unit} = 100\sqrt{3}$$

$$\therefore \quad AB = 100\sqrt{3} \text{ m}$$

Now, in ADC, 1 unit = 300

So, $\sqrt{3}$ unit = $300\sqrt{3}$

$$AD = 300\sqrt{3}$$

Also, $AB = 100\sqrt{3}$

$$\therefore \quad BD = AD - AB$$

$$= 300\sqrt{3} - 100\sqrt{3}$$

$$= 200\sqrt{3}$$

$$= 346 \text{ m} \qquad \boxed{\because \sqrt{3} = 1.73}$$

4. Option (C) is correct.

Explanation: Let height of the tower = x m

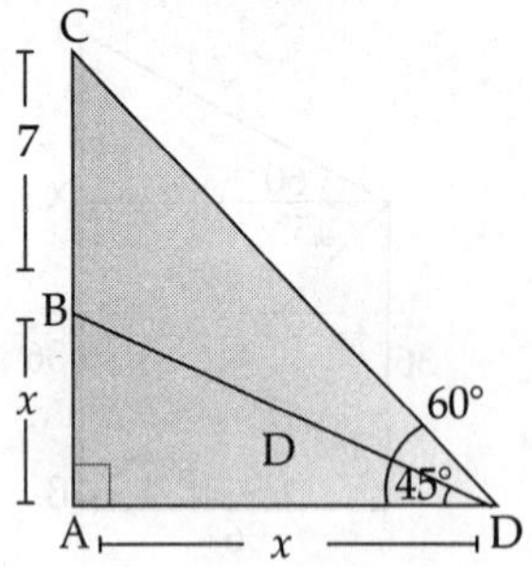

In ΔACD,

$$\frac{7+x}{x} = \tan 60^\circ$$

$$\Rightarrow \quad \sqrt{3}x = 7 + x$$

$$\Rightarrow \quad x = \frac{7}{(\sqrt{3}-1)} = \frac{7(\sqrt{3}-1)}{2} \text{ m}$$

5. Option (D) is correct.

Explanation:

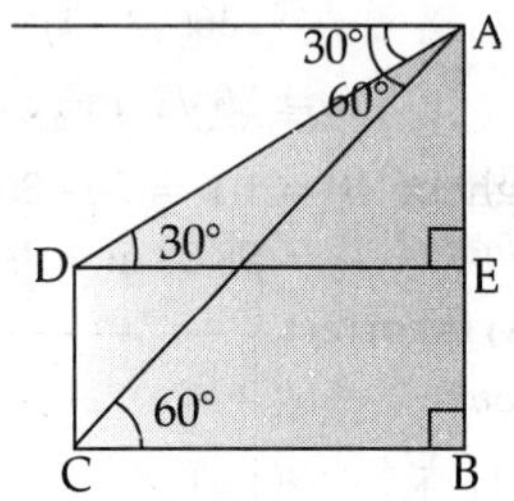

$$\text{Height} = 240 \text{ m} = AB$$

Now, in ΔABC,

$$\tan 60^\circ = \frac{AB}{BC}$$

$$\Rightarrow \quad \sqrt{3} = \frac{240}{BC}$$

$$\Rightarrow \quad BC = 80\sqrt{3} \text{ m}$$

Again, in ΔAED,

$$\tan 30^\circ = \frac{AE}{ED}$$

$$\Rightarrow \quad \frac{1}{\sqrt{3}} = \frac{AE}{80\sqrt{3}}$$

$$\therefore \quad AE = 80 \text{ m}$$

Now $\quad DC = EB = AB - AE$

$$= 240 - 80 = 160 \text{ m}$$

$$\therefore \quad DC - BC = 160 - 80\sqrt{3}$$

$$= 80(2-\sqrt{3}) \text{ m}$$

6. Option (A) is correct.

Explanation: **NOTE :** Angle is made with wall. So,

$$\angle ACB = 90^\circ - 60^\circ = 30^\circ$$

Given: $\quad AC = 22$ m

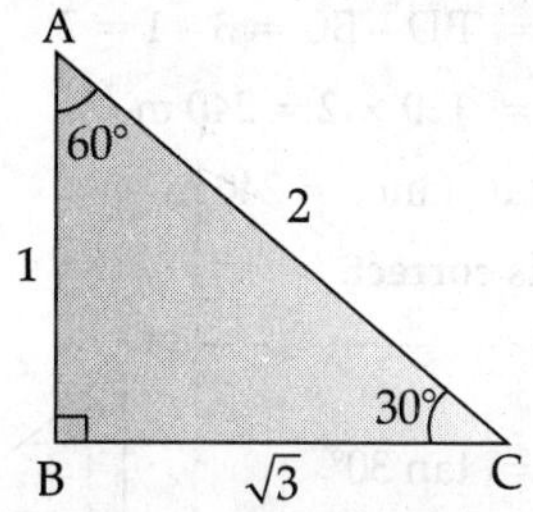

But, according to T-ratio values in ΔABC,

AB	BC	AC
1	$\sqrt{3}$	2
) ×11		) ×11
11 m		22

Required height = 11 m

7. Option (C) is correct.

Explanation:

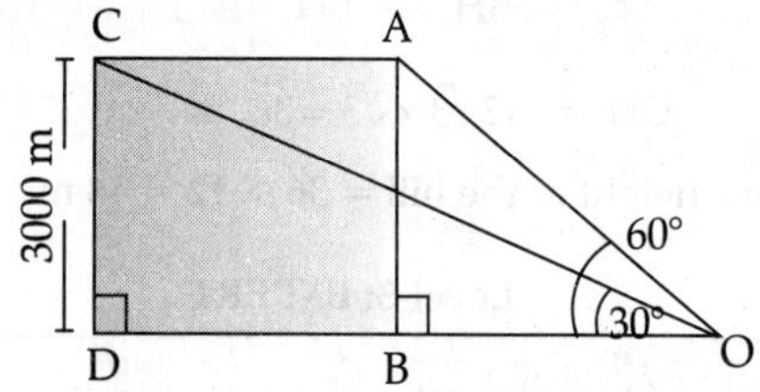

$$\text{Height} = 3{,}000 \text{ m} = CD = AB$$

In ΔOAB,

$$\tan 60^\circ = \frac{AB}{OB}$$

$$\Rightarrow \quad \sqrt{3} = \frac{3{,}000}{OB}$$

$$\Rightarrow \quad OB = \frac{3{,}000}{\sqrt{3}} \text{ m}$$

$$\Rightarrow \quad OB = 1{,}000\sqrt{3}\text{m}$$

Now, in ΔOCD,

$$\tan 30^\circ = \frac{CD}{OD}$$

$$\Rightarrow \quad \frac{1}{\sqrt{3}} = \frac{3{,}000}{OD}$$

$$\Rightarrow \quad OD = 3{,}000\sqrt{3} \text{ m}$$

$$\therefore \quad BD = (3{,}000\sqrt{3} - 1{,}000\sqrt{3}) \text{ m}$$

$$= 2{,}000\sqrt{3} \text{ m}$$

Now, speed of aeroplane

$$= \frac{\text{distance}}{\text{time}}$$

$$= \frac{2{,}000\sqrt{3}}{15} \text{ m / sec}$$

$$= 230.93 \text{ m/sec} \quad [\because \sqrt{3} = 1.732]$$

8. Option (C) is correct.

Explanation:

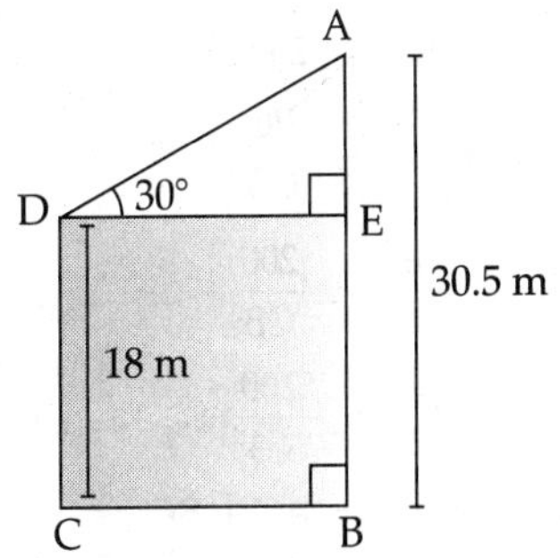

Length of larger pole = 30.5 m = AB

Length of smaller pole = 18 m = CD

Now, AE = AB – BE = AB – CD

= 30.5 – 18 = 12.5 m

Now, length of wire = AD

In ΔADE, $\sin 30° = \frac{AE}{AD}$

$\Rightarrow \quad \frac{1}{2} = \frac{12.5}{AD}$

$\Rightarrow \quad AD = 25$ m

9. Option (B) is correct.

Explanation:

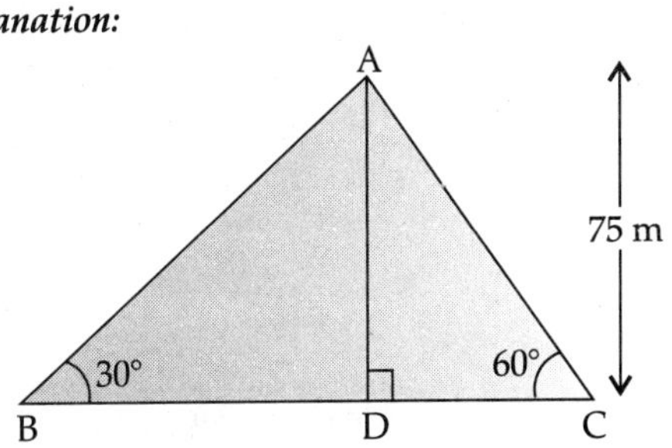

In ΔABD, $\frac{AD}{BD} = \tan 30°$

$\Rightarrow \quad \frac{75}{BD} = \frac{1}{\sqrt{3}}$

$\Rightarrow \quad BD = 75\sqrt{3}$ m

In ΔACD, $\frac{AD}{DC} = \tan 60°$

$\Rightarrow \quad \frac{75}{DC} = \sqrt{3}$

$\Rightarrow \quad DC = 25\sqrt{3}$ m

$\therefore \quad BC = BD + DC$

$= 75\sqrt{3} + 25\sqrt{3}$

$= 100\sqrt{3}$m

= 173.2 m

10. Option (D) is correct.

Explanation:

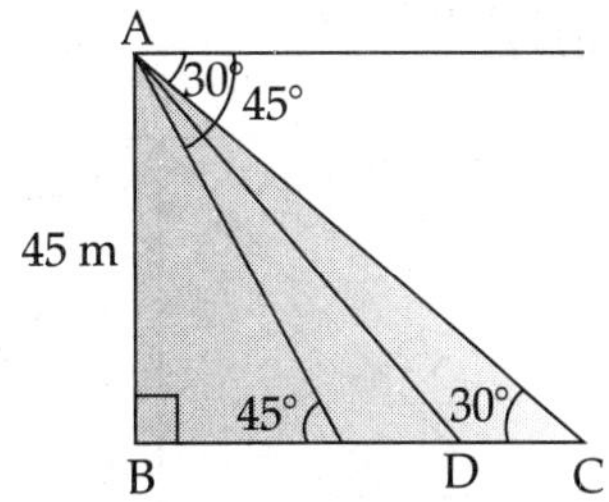

AB = 45 m (Given)

Let CD = x

In triangle ABD,

$\tan 45° = \frac{AB}{BD}$

$\therefore \quad BD = 45$ m

In ΔABC, $\tan 30° = \frac{AB}{BC}$

$\Rightarrow \quad \frac{1}{\sqrt{3}} = \frac{45}{45+x}$

$\Rightarrow \quad 45 + x = 45\sqrt{3}$

$\Rightarrow \quad x = 45(\sqrt{3}-1)$

$x = 32.85 \approx 32.9$ m $\quad [\because \sqrt{3} = 1.73]$

11. Option (B) is correct.

Explanation:

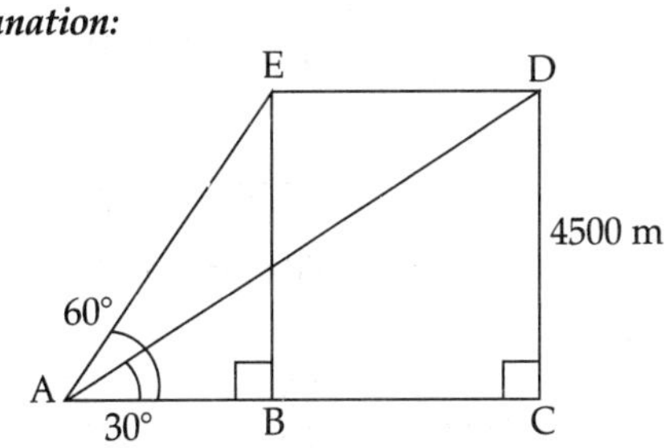

Height = 4,500 m = DC = EB

In ΔAEB, $\tan 60° = \frac{EB}{AB}$

$\therefore \quad AB = \frac{EB}{\tan 60°}$

$\Rightarrow \quad AB = \frac{EB}{\sqrt{3}} = \frac{4,500}{\sqrt{3}} = 1,500\sqrt{3}$ m

In ΔACD, $\tan 30° = \frac{CD}{AC}$

$\Rightarrow \quad \frac{1}{\sqrt{3}} = \frac{4,500}{AC}$

$\Rightarrow \quad AC = 4,500\sqrt{3}$ m

$\therefore \quad BC = AC - AB$

$= 4,500\sqrt{3} - 1,500\sqrt{3}$

$= 3,000\sqrt{3}$ m

Now, speed of aeroplane = $\frac{\text{Distance}}{\text{Time}}$

$= \frac{3,000\sqrt{3}}{30} = 100\sqrt{3}$ m

12. Option (B) is correct.

Explanation:

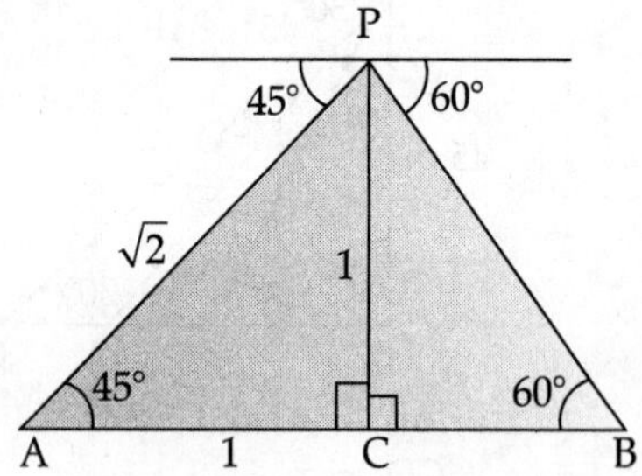

In ΔAPC,

AP	AC	PC
$\sqrt{2}$:	1:	1

$$\tan 45° = \frac{PC}{AC}$$

$$\Rightarrow \quad 1 = \frac{200}{AC}$$

$$\Rightarrow \quad AC = 200 \text{ m}$$

In ΔPCB, $\tan 60° = \frac{PC}{CB}$

$$\Rightarrow \quad \sqrt{3} = \frac{200}{CB}$$

$$\Rightarrow \quad CB = \frac{200}{\sqrt{3}} \text{ m}$$

$\therefore$ Width of river $= AC + BC$

$$= \left(200 + \frac{200}{\sqrt{3}}\right) \text{m}$$

Coordinate Geometry

CARTESIAN PLANE

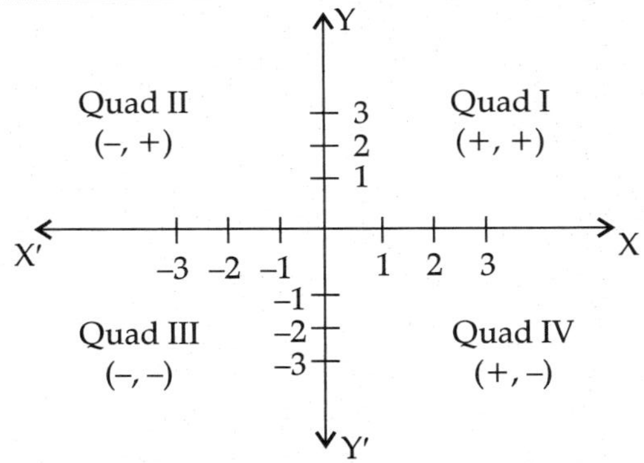

Polar Coordinates of (x, y)

When

$r = \sqrt{x^2 + y^2}$

$P(r\cos\phi, r\sin\phi)$

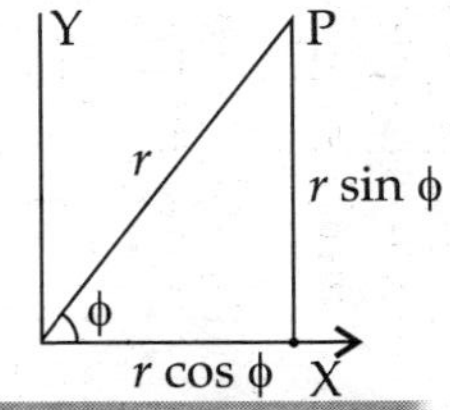

Distance Formula

$$D = \sqrt{(x_2 - x_1)^2 + (y_2 - y_1)^2}$$

Mid-Point Formula

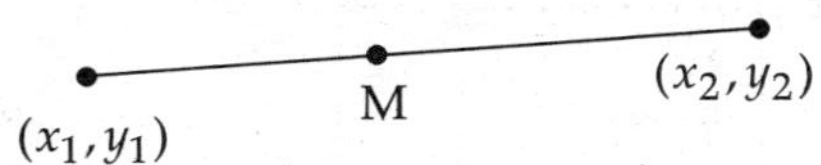

$$M = \left(\frac{x_1 + x_2}{2}, \frac{y_2 + y_1}{2}\right)$$

Area of triangle

$$\text{ar.of } \Delta = \frac{1}{2}[x_1(y_2 - y_3) + x_2(y_3 - y_1) + x_3(y_1 - y_2)]$$

Section formula Internal

$$x = \frac{mx_2 + nx_1}{m + n};$$

$$y = \frac{my_2 + ny_1}{m + n};$$

Section formula External

$$x = \frac{mx_2 - nx_1}{m - n},$$

$$y = \frac{my_2 - ny_1}{m - n}$$

Slope (m)

$m = \tan\theta$

or

$$\text{Slope} = \frac{y_2 - y_1}{x_2 - x_1}$$

Chapter 17

Co-ordinate Geometry

LEARNING OBJECTIVES:

- Basic concepts of cartesian plane.
- Understanding of distance formula, mid-point formula and section formula.
- Slope of line, equation of line.
- Intercept form of equation.
- Point of intersection of two lines.
- Area of triangle and polygons.
- Different types of questions asked in various competitive exams.
- Method of solving questions.

➢ It is a branch of geometry where an ordered pair of numbers known as coordinates is used to define the position of the points on the plane.

➢ **Some basics of co-ordinate geometry.**

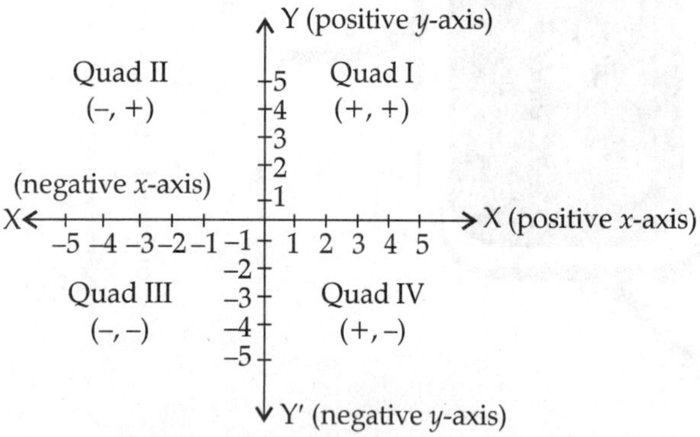

(a) 'X' represents the horizontal line.
(b) 'Y' represents the vertical line.
(c) Horizontal position of a point is determined on X-axis.
(d) Vertical position of a point is determined on Y-axis.
(e) **Origin:** Origin is the intersection point of X and Y axis, (0, 0) and denoted by 'O' (0, 0) are the coordinates of origin.
(f) 'X' coordinate is called 'abscisa'.
(g) 'Y' coordinate is called 'ordinate'.
(h) OY' and OX' are negative directions of X-axis and Y-axis. Similarly, OY and OX are positive directions of X-axis and Y-axis.
(i) The axes divide the plane into four parts that are called quadrants. We call this plane as 'the cartesian plane' or the coordinate plane, or the XY-plane. The axis is called the coordinate axes.

For example:

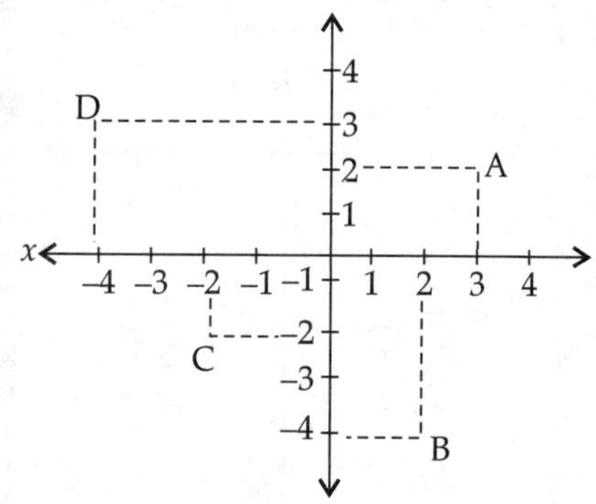

Here, coordinates of the given points are:

	x y
A	(3, 2)
B	(2, –4)
C	(–2, –2)
D	(–4, 3)

Example 1: What is the ordinate of point A (5, 7)?

(a) 5 (b) 6
(c) 7 (d) 8

Sol. (c) We know

A(x, y) — x: abscissa, y: ordinate

∴ A (5, 7) — 5: abscissa, 7: ordinate

∴ ordinate = 7

Example 2: What is the difference of the abscissa and ordinate of the point P(7, –3)?

(a) –7 (b) 4

(c) 10 (d) 4

Sol. (c) Given, P(7, –3)

$\therefore \quad x = 7$

$y = -3$

$\therefore \quad (x - y) = (7 - (-3)) = 10$

POLAR CO-ORDINATE OF A POINT

- When a co-ordinate is written is the form of distance from origin and angle, then it is called the polar form.
- The polar-coordinate of (x, y) will be $(r \cos\phi, r \sin\phi)$

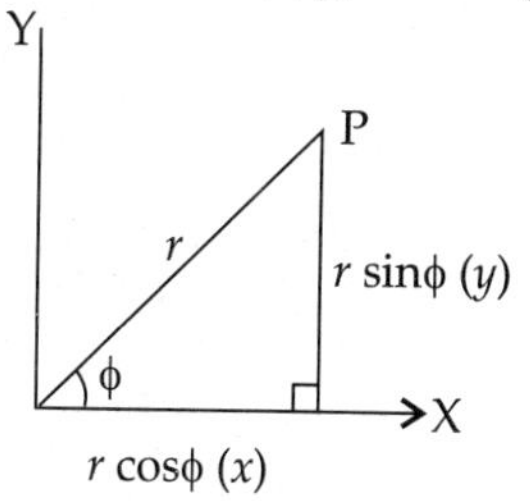

where, $r = \sqrt{x^2 + y^2}$

and $P = (r \cos\phi, r \sin\phi)$

Example 3: What is the polar coordinate of $(1, \sqrt{3})$?

(a) (cos 60°, sin 60°) (b) (cos 45°, sin 45°)

(c) 2 cos 60°, 2 sin 60° (d) cos 30°, sin 30°

Sol. (c) In ΔABC,

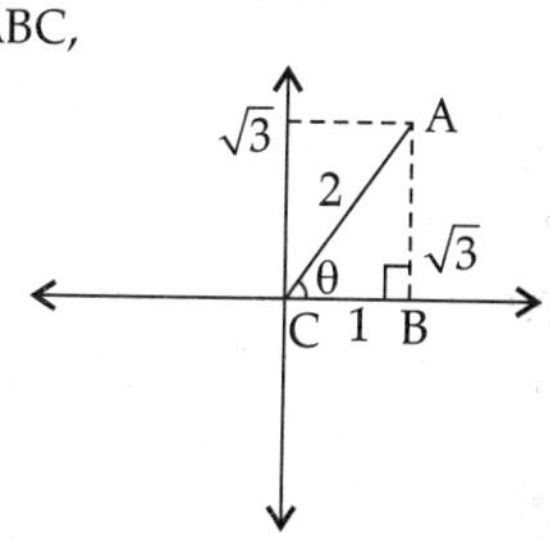

$$r = \sqrt{(\sqrt{3})^2 + (1)^2} = 2$$

Also $\tan\theta = \frac{AB}{BC} = \frac{\sqrt{3}}{1} = \sqrt{3}$

$\therefore \quad \theta = 60°$

Now, $A = (r \cos\theta, r \sin\theta)$

$= (2 \cos 60°, 2 \sin 60°)$

DISTANCE FORMULA

Distance between two points $P(x_1, y_1)$ and $Q(x_2, y_2)$

$$d = \sqrt{(x_2 - x_1)^2 + (y_2 - y_1)^2}$$

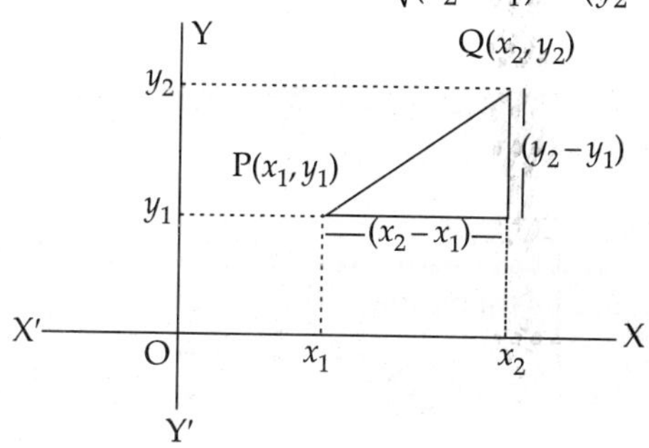

Example 4: Find the distance between points A(2, 5) and B(6, 8).

(a) 4 (b) 5

(c) 2 (d) 3

Sol. (b) We know,

$$d = \sqrt{(x_2 - x_1)^2 + (y_2 - y_1)^2} \quad ...(1)$$

Now, $x_2 = 6, x_1 = 2$

$y_2 = 8, y_1 = 5$

So, $d = \sqrt{(6-2)^2 + (8-5)^2}$

$= \sqrt{16 + 9} = \sqrt{25} = 5$

Example 5: Find the value of x if the distance between points $(x, -1)$ and (3, 2) is 5 cm.

(a) 4 (b) 7

(c) 3 (d) 2

Sol. (b) Points $(x, -1)$, (3, 2), $d = 5$ cm

Here, $x_1 = x, y_1 = -1$

$x_2 = 3, y_2 = 2$

Now, $d = \sqrt{(x_2 - x_1)^2 + (y_2 - y_1)^2}$

$= \sqrt{(3 - x)^2 + (2 - (-1))^2}$

$25 = (3 - x)^2 + 9$

$\sqrt{16} = 3 - x$

∴ We get two equations

$3 - x = +4, \; 3 - x = -4$

$\therefore x = -1, x = 7$

MID-POINT FORMULA

- The midpoint of H of the line segment from $A(x_1, y_1)$ to $B(x_2, y_2) = \left(\frac{x_1 + x_2}{2}, \frac{y_1 + y_2}{2}\right)$

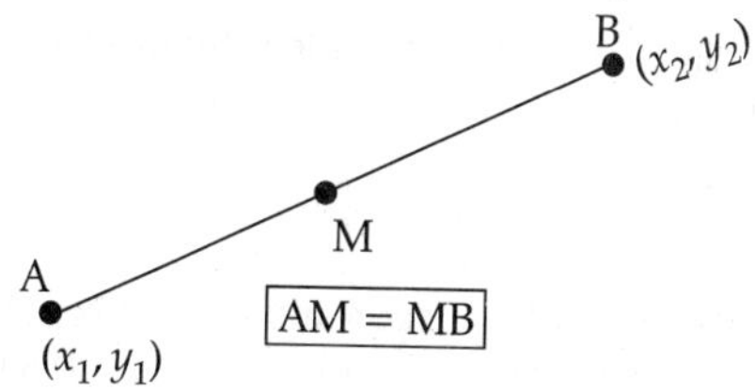

Example 6: If the mid point of join (–8, 13) and $(k, 7)$ is (4, 10), then find the value of k?

(a) 17 (b) 14

(c) 16 (d) 11

Sol. (c) Mid point formula $\left(\frac{x_1 + x_2}{2}, \frac{y_1 + y_2}{2}\right)$

Now, $\frac{-8 + k}{2} = 4$

$-8 + k = 8$

$k = 16$

SECTION FORMULA – INTERNAL

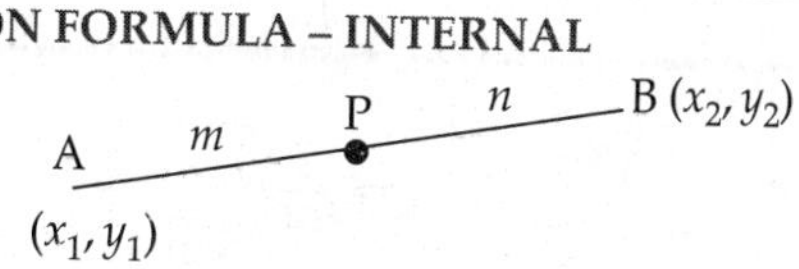

The coordinates of a point P which divides AB internally is the ratio $m : n$

$$x = \frac{mx_2 + nx_1}{m+n},$$

$$y = \frac{my_2 + ny_1}{m+n}$$

Example 7: Find the coordinates of the point which divides the line segment joining the points (2, –3) and (–4, 6) is the ratio 1 : 2 internally.

(a) (3, –5) (b) (4, 3)

(c) (0, 0) (d) (8, 0)

Sol. (c) Points (2, –3), (–4, 6)

$$\therefore \quad x_1 = 2 \; y_1 = -3$$
$$x_2 = -4 \; y_2 = 6$$

Using internal section formula,

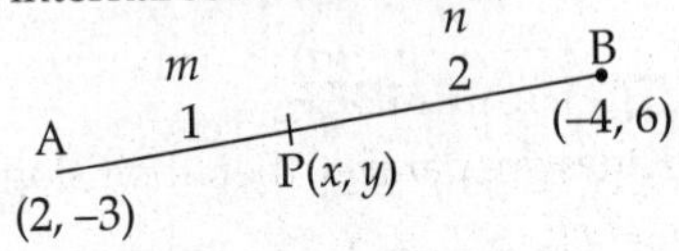

$$x = \frac{mx_2 + nx_1}{m+n}$$

$$= \frac{1(-4)+2(2)}{1+2} = \frac{-4+4}{1+2} = 0$$

$$y = \frac{my_2 + ny_1}{m+n}$$

$$= \frac{1(6)+2(-3)}{1+2} = \frac{6-6}{3} = 0$$

∴ Coordinates of point P are (0, 0)

EXTERNAL SECTION FORMULA

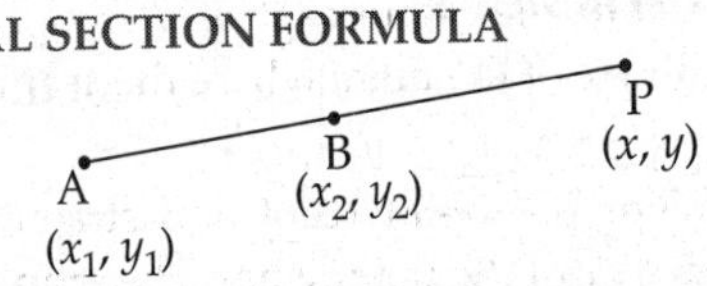

The coordinates of a point P which divides AB externally is the ratio $m : n$

$$x = \frac{mx_2 - nx_1}{m-n}, \; y = \frac{my_2 - ny_1}{m-n}$$

Example 8: Find the coordinates of the point which divides the line segment joining the points (2, 1) and (3, 5) externally in the ratio 2 : 3.

(a) (0, –6) (b) (0, 0)

(c) (0, –7) (d) (3, –5)

Sol. (c) Points (2, 1), (3, 5)

where, $x_1 = 2 \; y_1 = 1$

$x_2 = 3 \; y_2 = 5$

External section formula,

$$x = \frac{mx_2 - nx_1}{m-n}, \quad y = \frac{my_2 - ny_2}{m-n}$$

$$x = \frac{2(3)-3(2)}{2-3}, \quad y = \frac{2(5)-3(1)}{2-3}$$

$$= \frac{6-6}{-1} \quad = \frac{10-3}{-1}$$

$$= 0, \quad = \frac{7}{-1} = -7$$

∴ The coordinates are (0, –7)

Example 9: In which ratio, point P(1, 2) divides the line segment joining (–2, 1) and (7, 4)?

(a) 2 : 1 (b) 3 : 2

(c) 2 : 3 (d) 1 : 2

Sol. (d) Points (–2, 1), and (7, 4)

Dividing point (1, 2)

Let, Ratio = $k : 1$ (always))

Now,

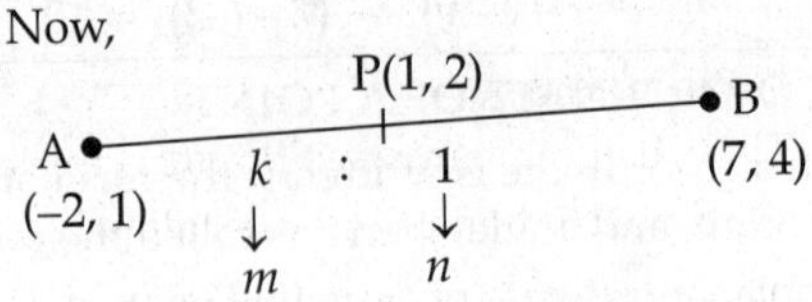

$$x = \frac{mx_2 + nx_1}{m+n}$$

$$\Rightarrow \quad \frac{7k-2}{k+1} = 1$$

$$7k - 2 = k + 1$$

$$6k = 3$$

$$k = \frac{1}{2}$$

∴ Ratio is 1 : 2 (internally)

DIVISION BY AXIS

➤ If two points P (x_1, y_1) and Q (x_2, y_2) are given, then:

(a) X-axis will divide the line joining the points in the ratio = $(-y_1 : y_2)$

(b) Y-axis will divide the line joining the points in the ratio = – $(x_1 : x_2)$

Example 10: In what ratio Y-axis divides the line joining the points (2, 3) and (5, 7)?

(a) 5 : 2 internally (b) 2 : 5 externally

(c) 5 : 1 (internally) (d) 5 : 3 externally

Sol. (c) When Y-axis divides the line joining the points in the ratio = – (x_1, x_2)

$$\therefore \quad x_1 = 2, x_2 = 5$$

Required ratio = – (2 : 5) externally

> **Note :**
> – = External division
> \+ = internal division

AREA OF TRIANGLE

➤ Let ABC is a triangle with vertices (x_1, y_1) (x_2, y_2) (x_3, y_3)

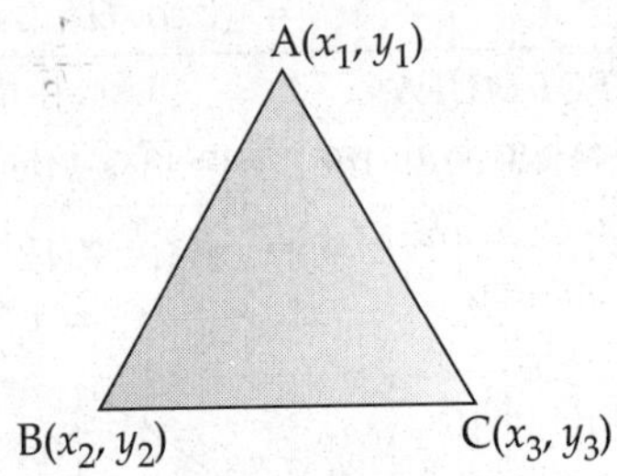

$$\text{Area of } \Delta = \frac{1}{2}[x_1(y_2 - y_3) + x_2(y_3 - y_1) + x_3(y_1 - y_2)]$$

OR use this short method

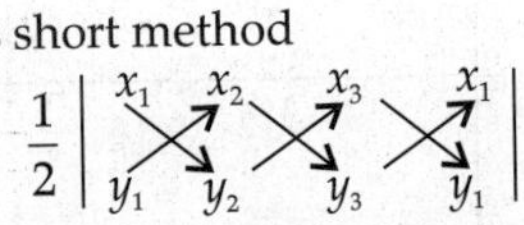

COLLINEAR POINTS

- If 3 or more than three points lie on a single line, then these points are said to be in collinear form.
- To check if points are collinear or not.

1. Using distance formula
   Find PQ, QR, PR
   Then, if sum of any two points is the same as the third point, then points are collinear.
2. Area of triangle must be zero.
3. Slope of PQ = slope of QR

Example 11: Find the value of 'Q' for which the points (1, 2), (3, 4) and (5, –a) are collinear.

(a) –6 (b) –4
(c) –1 (d) –2

Sol. (a) Using slope method

$$m = \frac{y_2 - y_1}{x_2 - x_1}$$

$$\Rightarrow \frac{2}{2} = \frac{(-a-4)}{4}$$

$$\Rightarrow 2 = -a - 4$$

$$-6 = a$$

SLOPE OF LINE

- When a line a makes an angle θ with positive X-axis, then the tangent of that angle is called the slope of line.
- Slope of a line is denoted by m, where, $m = \tan\theta$

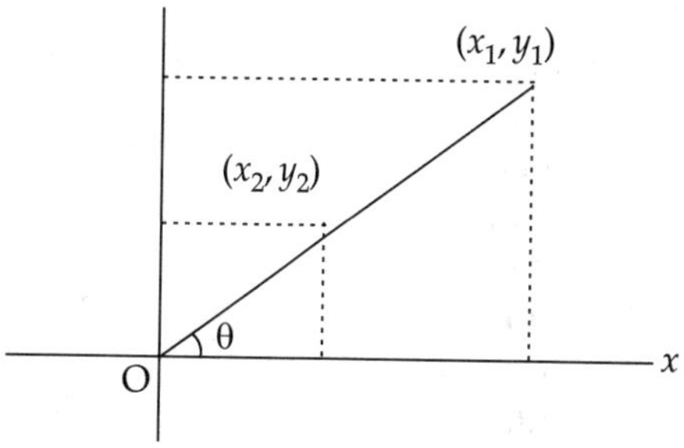

Also, Slope $= \dfrac{y_2 - y_1}{x_2 - x_1}$

Example 12: Find the slope of a line making 30° with X-axis.

(a) $\frac{1}{\sqrt{3}}$ (b) 1
(c) $\frac{1}{\sqrt{2}}$ (d) $\frac{\sqrt{3}}{2}$

Sol. (a) We know $m = \tan\theta$

$$m = \tan 30° = \frac{1}{\sqrt{3}}$$

Example 13: Find the slope of a line which passes through (4, 2) and (7, 6).

(a) $\frac{1}{3}$ (b) $\frac{3}{2}$
(c) $\frac{2}{3}$ (d) $\frac{4}{3}$

Sol. (d) We know, $m \text{ (slope)} = \dfrac{y_2 - y_1}{x_2 - x_1}$

$$= \frac{6-2}{7-3} = \frac{4}{3}$$

POINTS TO REMEMBER

- If two lines are parallel, then their slopes are equal. i.e., $m_1 = m_2$
- If two lines are perpendicular, then the product of their slopes is (–1). i.e., $(m_1 \times m_2 = -1)$

EQUATION OF A STRAIGHT LINE

(1) Slope intercept form (2) Point slope form
(3) Two point form (4) Intercept form
(5) General or normal form.

INTERCEPT FORM OF EQUATION

(a) ***x*-intercept:** The x-intercept of a straight line is the x-coordinate of the point where the graph crosses the X-axis.

(b) ***y*-intercept:** The y-intercept of a straight line is the y-coordinate of the point where the graph crosses the Y-axis.

Here, $\frac{x}{a} + \frac{y}{b} = 1$

$b = y$ intercept $a = x$ intercept

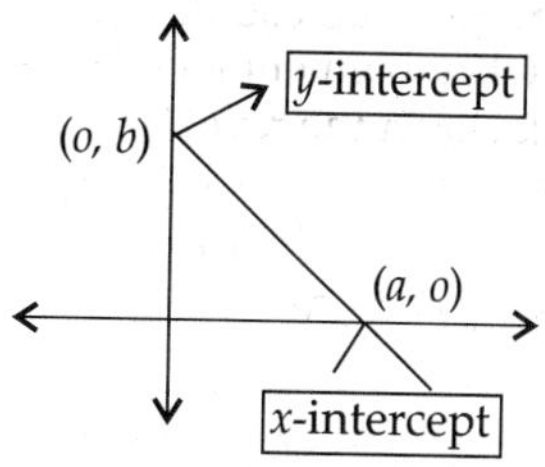

(1) Equation of a line in slope intercept form.

Form of equation $\Rightarrow y = mx + c$

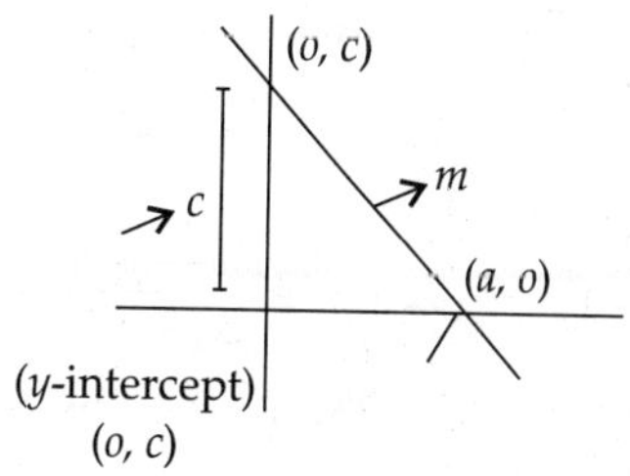

Example 14: Find the equation of a line whose slope is 5 and y intercept is 12.

(a) $y - 5x - 12 = 0$ (b) $5x - y - 12 = 0$

(c) $3x + y - 15 = 0$ (d) $y + 5x + 12 = 0$

Sol. (a) We know,

$$y = mx + c$$
$$y = 5x + 12$$
$$y - 5x - 12 = 0$$

(2) Point slope form: The equation of a straight line passing through a point (x_1, y_1) and whose slope is m is given by.

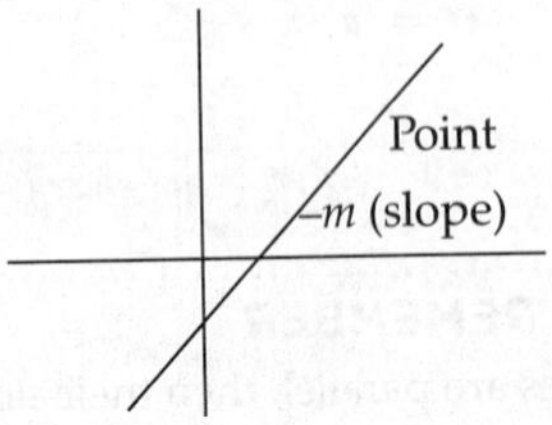

$$y - y_1 = m(x - x_1)$$

where, m = slope of the line

(x_1, y_1) = coordinates of known point

Also, $m = \dfrac{y - y_1}{x - x_1}$

Example 15: Find the equation of a line whose slope is –3 and its passes through point (2, –5).

(a) $x + 3y - 1 = 0$ (b) $3x + y - 1 = 0$

(c) $x + 3y + 1 = 0$ (d) $3x + y + 1 = 0$

Sol. (b) Here, $m = -3$

$y_1 = -5$

$x_1 = 2$

We know, $m = \dfrac{y - y_1}{x - x_1}$

$$\Rightarrow \quad -3 = \frac{y - (-5)}{x - 2}$$
$$\Rightarrow \quad -3x + 6 = y + 5$$
$$y + 3x - 1 = 0$$

or $3x + y - 1 = 0$

(3) Two point form: Equation of a line passing through two points (x_1, y_1) and (x_2, y_2)

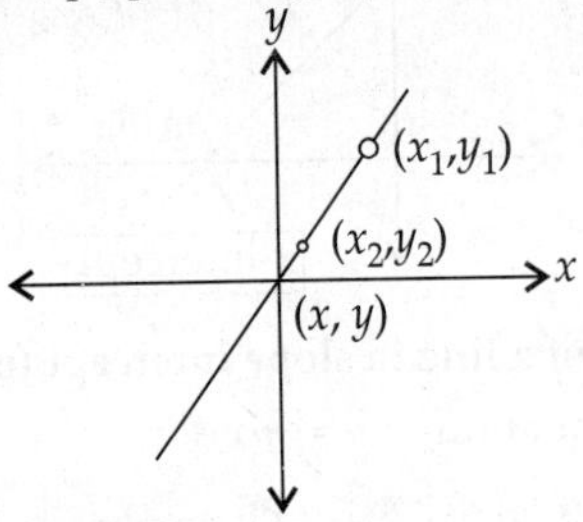

$$(y - y_1) = \frac{y_2 - y_1}{(x_2 - x_1)}(x - x_1)$$

OR

$$(y - y_2) = \frac{y_2 - y_1}{x_2 - x_1}(x - x_2)$$

Here, (x, y) are variables (x_1, y_1) and (x_2, y_2) are two points on the line.

Example 16: The equation of line passing through (4, –2) and (–1, 3) is:

(a) $x + y = 0$ (b) $x + y + 2 = 0$

(c) $x - y = 2$ (d) $x + y = 2$

Sol. (d) Equation of line in two point form

$$y - y_1 = \frac{y_2 - y_1}{x_2 - x_1}(x - x_1)$$
$$\Rightarrow \quad y - (-2) = \frac{(3 - (-2))}{-1 - (4)}(x - 4)$$
$$= y + 2 = \frac{5}{-5}(x - 4)$$
$$y + 2 = -x + 4$$
$$y + x = 2$$

(5) General form of equation of a line

$$ax + by + c = 0$$

POINT OF INTERSECTION OF TWO LINES

Suppose, we have the equations of two intersecting lines as

$$a_1x + b_1y + c_1 = 0 \quad ...(1)$$
$$a_2x + b_2y + c_2 = 0 \quad ...(2)$$

Let the above equations of two intersecting lines intersect at $P(x_1, y_1)$. Then, (x_1, y_1) will satisfy both the equations (1) and (2)

So,

$$a_1x_1 + b_1y_1 + c_1 = 0$$
$$a_2x_1 + b_2y_1 + c_2 = 0$$

Example 17: Two graphs of the equations $3x + y - 5 = 0$ and $2x - y - 5 = 0$ intersect at the point $P(\alpha, \beta)$. What is the value of $(3\alpha + \beta)$?

(a) 5 (b) –4

(c) 4 (d) 3

Sol. (a)

$$3x + y - 5 = 0 \quad ...(1)$$
$$2x - y - 5 = 0 \quad ...(2)$$

On solving (1) and (2),

$$x = 2, y = -1$$

$\therefore \quad (x, y) = (2 - 1)$

$\downarrow \ \downarrow$

$\alpha \ \ \beta$

Now, $3\alpha + \beta = 3 \times 2 + (-1)$

$= 6 - 1 = 5$

Second method : If $a_1x + b_1y + c_1 = 0$

$a_2x + b_2y + c_2 = 0$

Then $x = \dfrac{b_1c_2 - b_2c_1}{b_2a_1 - a_2b_1}$

$y = \dfrac{c_1a_2 - c_2a_1}{b_2a_1 - a_2b_1}$

$$\therefore \quad \alpha = \frac{-5 - 5}{-3 - 2} = \frac{-10}{-5} = 2$$
$$\beta = \frac{-10 - (15)}{-5} = \frac{5}{-5} = -1$$

So, $3\alpha + \beta = 3 \times 2 + (-1)$

$= 6 - 1 = 5$

ANGLE BETWEEN TWO LINES

- If two lines have slopes m_1 and m_2 and θ is the angle between them then,

$$\tan\theta = \left|\frac{m_1 - m_2}{1 + m_1 m_2}\right|$$

- If two lines are parallel, then $m_1 = m_2$
- If two lines are perpendicular then $m_1 \times m_2 = -1$.

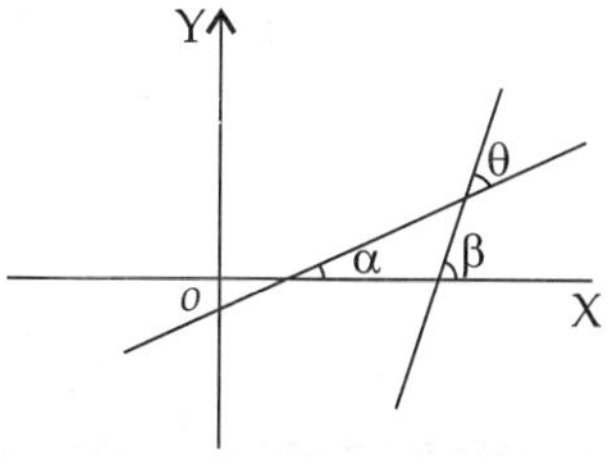

Example 18: If the lines $2y + 4x + 5 = 0$ and $y = 2 + ax$ are parallel, then find the value of a.

(a) –2 (b) –4

(c) 4 (d) 2

Sol. (a) $\because\ 2y + 4x + 5 = 0$

$$2y = -4x + 5$$

$$y = \frac{-4x}{2y} + 5$$

Lines are parallel

$$\therefore \quad m_1 = m_2$$

$$\frac{-4}{2} = a$$

$$-2 = a$$

$$y = mx + c$$

DISTANCE OF A POINT FROM A LINE

- Distance of a point (x_1, y_1) from a line $ax + by + c = 0$

$$d = \left|\frac{ax_1 + by_1 + c}{\sqrt{a^2 + b^2}}\right|$$

Example 19: Find the perpendicular distance of point (2, 3) from the line $3x + 4y + 7 = 0$.

(a) 5 (b) 2

(c) 4 (d) 3

Sol. (a) We know, $d = \left|\frac{ax_1 + by_1 + c}{\sqrt{a^2 + b^2}}\right|$

$$d = \left|\frac{3(2) + 4 \times 3 + 7}{\sqrt{3^2 + 4^2}}\right|$$

$$d = \frac{25}{5} = 5$$

- Distance of a line $ax + by + c = 0$ from given (0, 0)

$$d = \left|\frac{c}{\sqrt{a^2 + b^2}}\right|$$

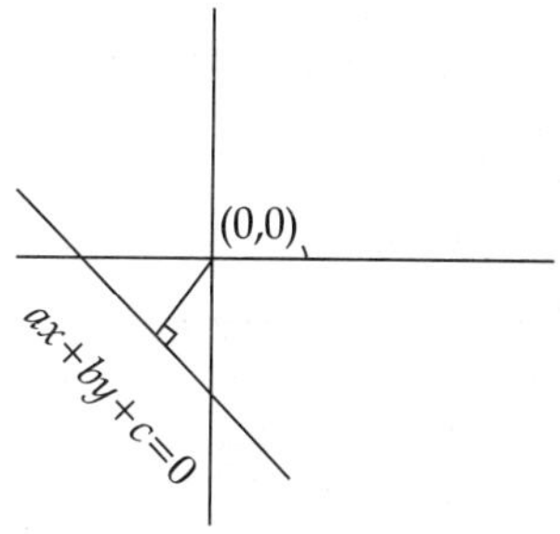

- Distance between two parallel lines:

Let, $ax + by + c_1 = 0$

$ax + by + c_2 = 0$

$$d = \left|\frac{c_1 - c_2}{\sqrt{a^2 + b^2}}\right|$$

CENTRES OF A TRIANGLE

1. **Centroid:** Let (x_1, y_1) (x_2, y_2) and (x_3, y_3) be the vertices of a triangle.

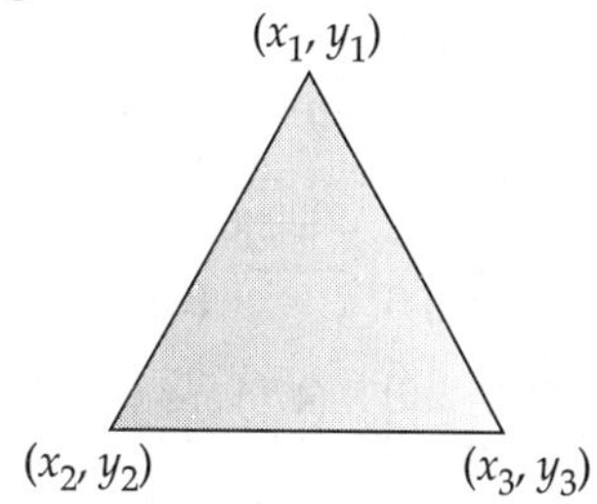

Then, coordinates of centroid

$$= \left(\frac{x_1 + x_2 + x_3}{3}, \frac{y_1 + y_2 + y_3}{3}\right)$$

2. **Incentre**

Incentre $\rightarrow \left[\frac{ax_1 + bx_2 + cx_3}{a + b + c}, \frac{ay_1 + by_1 + cy_3}{a + b + c}\right]$

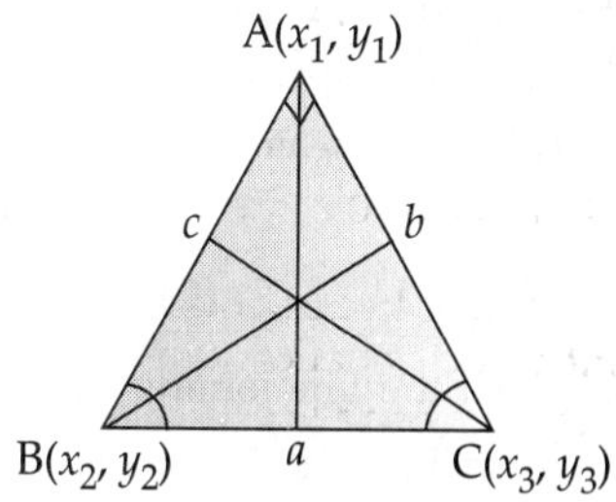

AREA OF POLYGONS

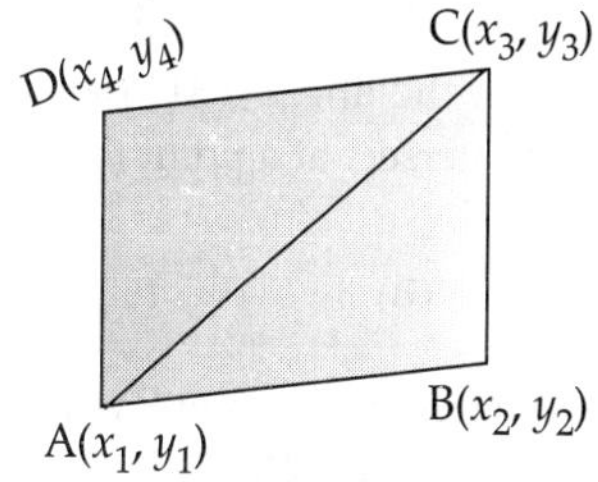

$$= \frac{1}{2}\begin{bmatrix} x_1 & x_2 & x_3 & x_4 & x_1 \\ y_1 & y_2 & y_3 & y_4 & y_1 \end{bmatrix}$$

CIRCLE

Equation of circle

$\Rightarrow \quad x^2 + y^2 = r^2$

$(x - a)^2 + (y - b)^2 = r^2$

$\Rightarrow \quad x^2 + a^2 - 2ax + y^2 + b^2 - 2by = r^2$

$\Rightarrow \quad x^2 + y^2 - 2ax - 2by + a^2 + b^2 - r^2 = 0$

$$x^2 + y^2 + 2gx + 2fy + c = 0$$

$\Rightarrow$ centre $= (-g, -f)$

radius $= \sqrt{g^2 + f^2 - c}$

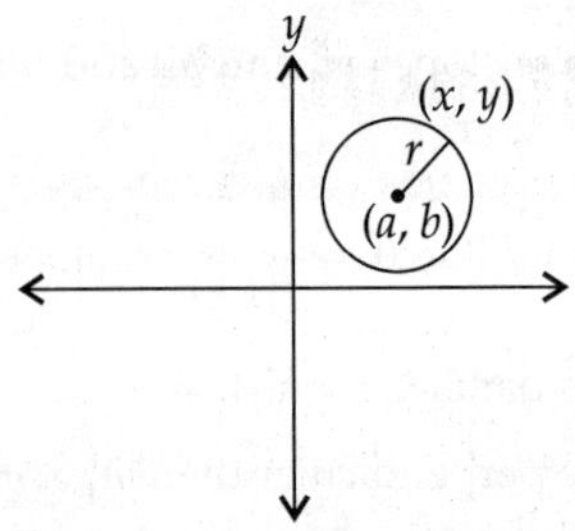

Level 1 Beginner

1. Find the slope of the line passing through the point (2, 8) and (6, 9). **[RRB CBT-II 2018]**
   (A) –5 **(B)** 5 **(C)** –0.25 **(D)** 0.25
2. The slope of line $3x + 7y + 8 = 0$ is: **[RRB CBT-II 2018]**
   (A) 7 **(B)** 3 **(C)** $\frac{3}{7}$ **(D)** $-\frac{3}{7}$
3. If P(3, 5), Q (4, 5) and R (4, 6) are any three points, the angle between PQ and PR is: **[RRB CBT-II 2018]**
   (A) 60° **(B)** 45° **(C)** 30° **(D)** 90°
4. The equation of circle with centre (1, –2) and radius 4 cm is: **[SSC CHSL 2020]**
   (A) $x^2 + y^2 + 2x - 4y = 16$
   (B) $x^2 + y^2 - 2x + 4y = 16$
   (C) $x^2 + y^2 - 2x + 4y = 11$
   (D) $x^2 + y^2 + 2x - 4y = 11$
5. The area of the triangle formed by the graphs of $8x + 3y = 24$, $2x + 8 = y$ and the x-axis is: **[SSC CGL 2020]**
   (A) 15 **(B)** 14 **(C)** 24 **(D)** 28
6. The angle which the line joining the points $(\sqrt{3}, 1)$ and $(\sqrt{15}, \sqrt{5})$ makes with X-axis is: **[RRB CBT-II 2018]**
   (A) 30° **(B)** 45° **(C)** 60 **(D)** 90°
7. The graphs of the linear equations $4x - 2y = 10$ and $4x + ky = 2$ intersect at a point $(a, 4)$. The value of k is equal to :
   (A) –3 **(B)** 3 **(C)** 4 **(D)** –4
8. The co-ordinates of the point P which divides the join of A(3, –2) and B $\left(\frac{11}{2}, \frac{21}{2}\right)$ is the ratio 2 : 3 are: **[RRB CBT-II 2018]**
   (A) $\left(4, \frac{5}{2}\right)$ **(B)** (4, 3) **(C)** (4, 5) **(D)** (6, 4)
9. What is the equation of a circle with centre of origin and radius is 6 cm? **[SSC CHSL 2019]**
   (A) $x^2 + y^2 - x - y = 36$ **(B)** $x^2 + y^2 - x = 36$
   (C) $x^2 + y^2 - y = 36$ **(D)** $x^2 + y^2 - 36 = 0$
10. The distance between two points (a cos α, 0) and (0, a sin α) is : **[RRB NTPC CBT-I 2019]**
    (A) a **(B)** $|a|$
    (C) $|2a|$ **(D)** $2a$
11. If (2, –2) and (5, 2) are two consecutive vertices of a square, then the length of each side of the square will be : **[RRB NTPC 2019]**
    (A) 5 **(B)** $\frac{5}{\sqrt{2}}$
    (C) $5\sqrt{2}$ **(D)** $\sqrt{5}$
12. Find the value of c if the distance between the point (c, 4) and the origin is 5 units. **[RRB CBT-II 2018]**
    (A) 3 **(B)** 0
    (C) None of these **(D)** Both (A) and (B)
13. Find the coordinates of the point which will divide the line joining the point (2, 4) and (7, 9) internally in the ratio 1 : 2. **[RRB NTPC CBT-I 2019]**
    (A) $\left(\frac{5}{3}, \frac{1}{3}\right)$ **(B)** $\left(\frac{3}{8}, \frac{3}{11}\right)$
    (C) $\left(\frac{11}{3}, \frac{17}{3}\right)$ **(D)** $\left(\frac{8}{3}, \frac{11}{3}\right)$
14. Which of the following point lies on the X-axis? **[RRB NTPC CBT-I 2021]**
    (A) (0, 4) **(B)** (2, 0) **(C)** (2, 3) **(D)** (1, 2)
15. Which of the following equations represent a line parallel to Y-axis? **[RRB NTPC CBT-I 2021]**
    (A) $y - 2$ **(B)** $y = 3$
    (C) $2x + y = 0$ **(D)** $x + 3 = 4 - 2x$

2 Level Intermediate

1. Find the equation of a circle whose diameter has end points (4, 3) and (–2, 1). [SSC CHSL 2019]
(A) $x^2 + y^2 - 2x - 4x = 3$ (B) $x^2 + y^2 - 2x - 4y = 5$
(C) $x^2 + y^2 - 6x + 2y = 3$ (D) $x^2 + y^2 - 2x + 4y = 5$

2. The equation of the line pssing through the point of (1, 1) and perpendicular to the line $3x + 4y - 5 = 0$, is: [SSC CBT-II 2018]
(A) $3x + 4y - 7 = 0$ (B) $3x + 4y + k = 0$
(C) $3x - 4y - 1 = 0$ (D) $4x - 3y - 1 = 0$

3. The lines whose equations are $2x - 5y + 7 = 0$ and $8x - 20y + 28 = 0$ are: [SSC CBT-II 2018]
(A) parallel (B) perpendicular
(C) coincident (D) intersecting

4. The points A (1, 2), B (3, 4) and C (4, 1) are the vertices of a triangle which is: [RRB NTPC 2019]
(A) right-angled (B) isosceles
(C) equilateral (D) scalene

5. Find the third vertex of an equilateral triangle whose vertices are (2, 4) and (2, 6). [RRB NTPC 2019]
(A) $(2\sqrt{3}, 5)$ (B) $(2+\sqrt{3}, 5)$
(C) (2, 5) (D) $(\sqrt{3}, 5)$

6. The line passing through (4, 3) and (*y*, 0) is parallel to the line passing through (–1, –2) and (3, 0). Find *y*. [RRB CBT-II 2018]
(A) –1 (B) –2
(C) 2 (D) –5

7. Find the area of a triangle whose vertices are $(a, b + c)$, $(a, b - c)$ are $(-a, c)$. [RRB NTPC 2019]
(A) $2bc$ (B) $2b(a+c)$
(C) $2ac$ (D) $c(a-b)$

8. The graphs of equations $3x + y - 5 = 0$ and $2x - y - 5 = 0$ intersect at the point P(α, β). What is the value of (2α + β)? [SSC CGL 2018]
(A) 4 (B) 3 (C) –4 (D) 5

9. The graph of the equations $5x - 2y + 1 = 0$ and $4y - 3x + 5 = 0$, intersect at the point P(α, β). What is the value of (2α – 3β) ? [SSC CGL 2018]
(A) 6 (B) 4 (C) –3 (D) –4

10. What is the area (in square units) of the triangular region enclosed by the graphs of the equations $x + y = 3$, $2x + 5y = 12$ and the X-axis? [SSC CGL 2018]
(A) 4 (B) –3 (C) 3 (D) 6

11. The equation of a straight line passing through (–2, 5) and (1, 3) is: [RRB NTPC 2021]
(A) $2x + 3y - 11 = 0$ (B) $3x + 2y + 9 = 0$
(C) $2x - 3y - 9 = 0$ (D) $3x - 2y - 11 = 0$

12. What is the area of the triangle formed by the coordinate axes and the line $2x + 3y = 6$? [RRB NTPC 2021]
(A) 2 sq. units (B) 12 sq. units
(C) 3 sq. units (D) 6 sq. units

13. If the radius of the circle $x^2 + y^2 - 6x + 8y + c = 0$ is 6 unit then the value of *c* is : [SSC CGL 2019]
(A) –11 (B) –10 (C) 25 (D) 11

14. The measure of the angle between the graph of the linear equation $35x - 35y + 15 = 0$ and the X-axis is : [RRB NTPC 2021]
(A) 55° (B) 35° (C) 40° (D) 45°

15. Find the value of *k* such that the equations $2x + 3y + 11 = 0$ and $6x + ky + 33 = 0$ represent coincident lines. [RRB NTPC 2021]
(A) 9 (B) 12 (C) 6 (D) 5

3 Level Expert

1. The graph of the equation $x - 7y = -42$, intersects the *y*-axis at P(α, β) and the graph of $6x + y - 15 = 0$, intersects the X-axis at Q(γ, δ). Find the value of α + β + γ + δ ? [SSC CGL 2018]
(A) $\frac{17}{2}$ (B) 6 (C) $\frac{9}{2}$ (D) 5

2. The graphs of the equation $x - 2y + 12 = 0$ intersects $2x + 3y = 11$ at $P(x_1, y_1)$ and the X-axis at $Q(x_2, y_2)$. What is the value of $(x_1 - x_2 + y_1 + y_2)$? [SSC CGL 2018]
(A) –9 (B) –11 (C) 13 (D) 15

3. The graphs of the equations $3x - 20y - 2 = 0$ and $11x - 5y + 61 = 0$ intersect at P(*a*, *b*). What is the value of $(a^2 + b^2 - ab)/(a^2 - b^2 + ab)$? [SSC CGL Tier-II 2019]
(A) $\frac{31}{41}$ (B) $\frac{37}{35}$ (C) $\frac{5}{7}$ (D) $\frac{41}{31}$

4. What is the area of the triangle formed by the graphs of the equations $2x + 5y - 12 = 0$, $x + y = 3$ and $y = 0$? [SSC CGL Tier-II 2019]
(A) 6 (B) 5 (C) 3 (D) 2

5. Find the coordinates of centroid of a triangle formed by the points (2, 5), (3, 9) and (4, 1). [SSC CGL 2019]
(A) (6, 6) (B) (9, 15) (C) (3, 9) (D) (3, 5)

6. If the centroid of the triangle formed by the points (3, 5), (–7, 4), (10, –6) is at the point (*k*, 1), then the value of *k* is: [RRB NTPC 2021]
(A) 3 (B) 1 (C) 2 (D) 4

7. Find the relation between x and y such that the points (x, y) are equidistant from (5, 3) and (4, 6). [RRB NTPC 2021]

(A) $x - 3y = 9$ (B) $x + 3y = 10$
(C) $x + 3y + 9 = 0$ (D) $3y - x = 9$

8. Find the radius of the circle $x^2 + y^2 + 7x + 4y + 9 = 0$. [RRB NTPC 2021]

(A) $\frac{\sqrt{23}}{2}$ (B) $\frac{\sqrt{19}}{2}$ (C) $\frac{\sqrt{29}}{2}$ (D) $\frac{\sqrt{13}}{2}$

9. Find the points of intersection of the line $4x - 3y = 10$ and the circle $x^2 + y^2 - 2x + 4y - 20 = 0$. [RRB NTPC 2021]

(A) (4, 2) and (–2, –6) (B) (2, –3) and (4, 2)
(C) (–2, 3) and (4, 3) (D) (–2, 3) and (4, 2)

10. Find the relation between x and y such that the points (x, y) are equidistant from (6, 2) and (4, 6). [NTPC 2021]

(A) $x + 2y = 3$ (B) $2x - y = 3$
(C) $2x + y = -3$ (D) $x - 2y = -3$

11. If (2, –2) and (5, 2) are two consecutive vertices of a square, then the length of each side of square will be: [NTPC 2021]

(A) 5 units (B) $5\sqrt{2}$ units
(C) $\frac{55}{\sqrt{2}}$ units (D) $\sqrt{5}$ units

12. The system of equations $2x + ky = 11$, $5x - 7y = 5$ has no solutions when k = ? [NTPC 2021]

(A) $\frac{-13}{5}$ (B) $\frac{-14}{5}$ (C) $\frac{-16}{5}$ (D) $\frac{13}{5}$

ANSWER KEY

Level-1: Beginner

1.	(D)	2.	(D)	3.	(B)	4.	(C)	5.	(D)	6.	(A)	7.	(D)	8.	(B)	9.	(D)	10.	(B)
11.	(A)	12.	(A)	13.	(C)	14.	(B)	15.	(D)										

Level-2: Intermediate

1.	(B)	2.	(D)	3.	(A)	4.	(B)	5.	(B)	6.	(B)	7.	(C)	8.	(B)	9.	(B)	10.	(C)
11.	(A)	12.	(C)	13.	(A)	14.	(D)	15.	(A)										

Level-3: Expert

1.	(A)	2.	(D)	3.	(A)	4.	(C)	5.	(D)	6.	(C)	7.	(D)	8.	(C)	9.	(A)	10.	(D)
11.	(A)	12.	(B)																

Solutions with Detailed Explanations

Level-1: BEGINNER

1. **Option (D) is correct.**

Explanation: We know,

$$\text{slope } (m) = \frac{y_2 - y_1}{x_2 - x_1} \quad ...(1)$$

Given points (2, 8) and (6, 9)

Here, $x_1 = 2$, $x_2 = 6$

$y_1 = 8$, $y_2 = 9$

Put those values in equation (1)

$$\therefore \quad m = \frac{9-8}{6-2} = \frac{1}{4} = 0.25$$

2. **Option (D) is correct.**

Explanation: Given equation

$$3x + 7y + 8 = 0$$
$$7y = -3x - 8$$
$$y = \frac{-3}{7}x - \frac{8}{7} \quad ...(1)$$

We know $\quad y = mx + c \quad ...(2)$

Compare the values of equations (1) and (2)

$$m = -\frac{3}{7}$$

3. **Option (B) is correct.**

Explanation: Given

P(3, 5), Q (4, 5), R (4, 6)

$$m(\text{PQ}) = \frac{5-5}{3-4} = 0$$
$$m(\text{PR}) = \frac{6-5}{4-3} = 1$$

$\therefore$ Angle between lines $\Rightarrow \tan\theta = \frac{1-0}{1+0} = \frac{1}{1}$

$$\therefore \quad \theta = 45^{\circ}$$

4. Option (C) is correct.

Explanation:

Given: Radius = 4 cm

Centre = (1, –2)

We know, equation of circle $\Rightarrow (x-a)^2+(y-b)^2=r^2$

$\therefore (x-1)^2+(y+2)^2=(4)^2$

$\Rightarrow \quad x^2+1-2x+y^2+4+4y=16$

$\Rightarrow \quad x^2-2x+y^2+4y=16-5$

$\Rightarrow \quad x^2+y^2-2x+4y=11$

5. Option (D) is correct.

Explanation:

Given, $8x+3y = 24$

$2x+8 = y$

Points of intersection

$8x+3y = 24,\ 2x+8=y$ is (0, 8)

$y = 0,\ 2x+8=y$ is (–4, 0)

$y = 0,\ 8x+3y=24$ is (3, 0)

Using product method,

(0, 8)

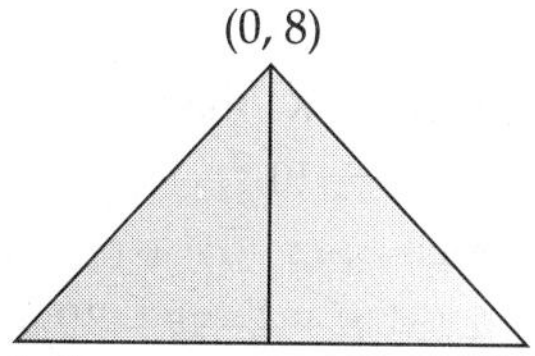

(–4, 0) (3, 0)

$$= \frac{1}{2}|0(0-0)-4(0-8)+3(8-0)|$$

$$= \frac{1}{2}|56| = 28$$

6. Option (A) is correct.

Explanation: Given points $(\sqrt{3},1)$ and $(\sqrt{15},\sqrt{5})$

We know $m = \dfrac{y_2-y_1}{x_2-x_1}$

$$= \frac{\sqrt{5}-1}{\sqrt{15}-\sqrt{3}} = \frac{(\sqrt{5}-1)}{\sqrt{3}(\sqrt{5}-1)}$$

$$m = \frac{1}{\sqrt{3}}$$

We know, $m = \tan\theta$

$$\frac{1}{\sqrt{3}} = \tan\theta$$

$\therefore \quad \theta = 30°$

7. Option (D) is correct.

Explanation: They intersect at $(a, 4)$.

$\therefore \quad y = 4$

So, $4x-(2)(4) = 10$

$x = 4.5$

Now, $4x+ky = 2$

$4(4.5)+k(4) = 2$

$4k = 2-18$

$k = -4$

8. Option (B) is correct.

Explanation: Given, points A (3, –2) and B $\left(\dfrac{11}{2},\dfrac{21}{2}\right)$

We know Ratio = 2 : 3

$$x = \frac{mx_2+nx_1}{m+n}, \qquad y = \frac{my_2+ny_1}{m+n}$$

$$= \frac{11+9}{5} \qquad = \frac{21-6}{5}$$

$$= \frac{20}{5} \qquad = \frac{15}{5}$$

$$\boxed{x=4} \qquad \boxed{y=3}$$

$\therefore$ Coordinates are (4, 3)

9. Option (D) is correct.

Explanation:

Given, Centre = (0, 0) (origin)

Radius = 6

Equation of circle is :

$\therefore (x-a)^2+(y-b)^2 = r^2$

$(x-0)^2+(y-0)^2 = 6^2$

$x^2+y^2 = 36$

$\therefore \quad x^2+y^2-36 = 0$

10. Option (B) is correct.

Explanation: Given $(a\cos\alpha, 0)$ $(0, a\sin\alpha)$

$x_1 = a\cos\alpha \quad y_1 = 0$

$x_2 = 0 \quad y_2 = a\sin\alpha$

Now, by distance formula $= \sqrt{a^2\cos^2\alpha+a^2\sin^2\alpha}$

$$D = \sqrt{a^2\cos^2\alpha+a^2\sin^2\alpha}$$

$$= \sqrt{a^2(\cos^2\alpha+\sin^2\alpha)}$$

$$D = \sqrt{a^2} \qquad \because \cos^2\alpha+\sin^2\alpha=1$$

$$D = |a|$$

11. Option (A) is correct.

Explanation: Two vertices are (2, –2) (5, 2)

As vertices are consecutive, we can apply distance formula

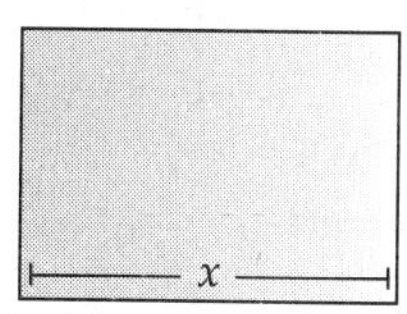

(2, –2) (5, 2)

$$x = d = \sqrt{(x_2-x_1)^2+(y_2-y_1)^2}$$

$$x = \sqrt{(3)^2+(4)^2}$$

$$= \sqrt{9+16} = \sqrt{25}$$

$$x = 5$$

Therefore, each side of square is 5 units.

12. Option (A) is correct.

Explanation: Given point $(c, 4)$, coordinates of origin = (0, 0)

$$\text{Distance} = 5$$

$$\text{Distance formula} = \sqrt{(x_2-x_1)^2+(y_2-y_1)^2}$$

$$5 = \sqrt{c^2+(4)^2}$$

$$5 = \sqrt{c^2+16}$$

$$25 = c^2 + 16$$

$$9 = c^2$$

$$3 = c$$

13. Option (C) is correct.

Explanation: Points joining the line are (2, 4) and (7, 9)

$m : P\ n$

A (x_1, y_1) — (x, y) — B (x_2, y_2)

$$\text{Ratio} = 1:2$$

Internal section formula will be used.

where,

$$x = \frac{mx_2+mx_1}{m+n} \qquad y = \frac{my_2+my_1}{m+n}$$

$$x = \frac{7+4}{3} \qquad y = \frac{9+8}{3}$$

$$x = \frac{11}{3} \qquad y = \frac{17}{3}$$

$\therefore$ Coordinates $(x,y) = \left(\frac{11}{3}, \frac{17}{3}\right)$

14. Option (B) is correct.

Explanation: This type question is solved by plotting given coordinates as graph.

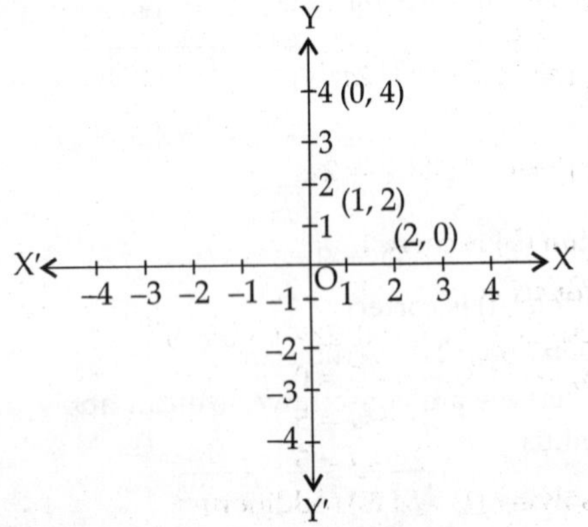

$\therefore$ (2, 0) lies on X-axis

15. Option (D) is correct.

Explanation:

If a line is || to X-axis,

then $\quad y = \pm k$

If a line is || to Y-axis,

then $\quad x = \pm k \quad$ (no coefficient of y)

Checking options

$\Rightarrow \quad x + 3 = 4 - 2x$

[It is in the form of $x = \pm k$, no coefficient of y).

Level-2: INTERMEDIATE

1. Option (B) is correct.

Explanation: Given, diameter end points (4, 3) and (–2, 1)

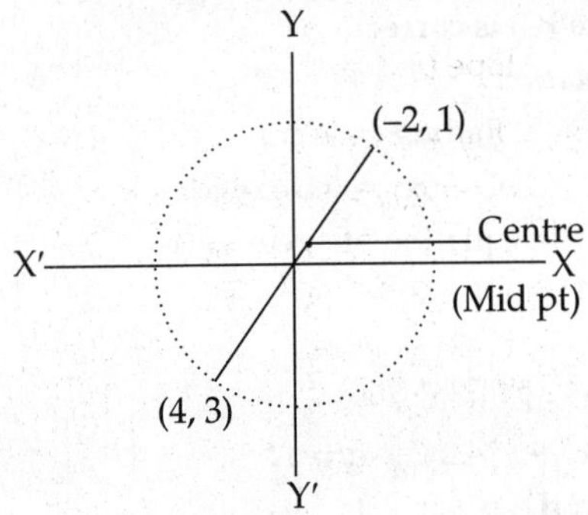

Points of centre (using mid point formula)

$$x = \frac{x_1+x_2}{2} = \frac{4-2}{2} = 1$$

$$y = \frac{y_1+y_2}{2} = \frac{3+1}{2} = 2$$

So, coordinates of centre (1, 2)

Now, using distance formula,

$$D^2 = (-3)^2 + (-1)^2$$

$$D^2 = 10$$

$$\text{Distance} = \text{Radius}$$

$$\therefore \quad R^2 = 10$$

Now, eqn. of circle $\Rightarrow (x-1)^2 + (y-2)^2 = 10$

$$x^2 + 1 - 2x + y^2 + 4 - 4y = 10$$

$$\therefore \quad x^2 + y^2 - 2x - 4y = 5$$

2. Option (D) is correct.

Explanation: Given, point (1, 1)

Eqn, $\quad 3x + 4y - 5 = 0$

So, $\quad 4y = -3x + 5$

$$y = \frac{-3x}{4} + \frac{5}{4}$$

Now, $\quad y = mx + c$

$$\therefore \quad m = \frac{-3}{4} \qquad \text{...(1)}$$

$$m_1 \times m_2 = -1$$

When two lines are $\perp$, then $m_1 \times m_2 = -1$

Now, check options

$$4x - 3y - 1 = 0$$

$$-3y = -4x + 1$$

$$y = \frac{+4x}{3} - \frac{1}{3}$$

$$m_2 = \frac{4}{3} \qquad \text{...(2)}$$

from Eqs. (1) and (2)

It is clear that $m_1 \times m_2 = -1$

3. Option (A) is correct.

Explanation:

Given, $2x - 5y + 7 = 0$, $8x - 20y + 28 = 0$

Now, $\quad 2x - 5y + 7 = 0$

$$5y = 2x + 7$$

$$y = \frac{2}{5}x + \frac{7}{5}$$

So, slope $(m_1) = \frac{2}{5}$ $\because y = mx + c$

Now, $8x - 20y + 28 = 0$

$$20y = 8x + 28$$

$$y = \frac{2}{5}x + \frac{28}{20}$$

$\therefore$ slope $(m_2) = \frac{2}{5}$

$\therefore$ $m_1 = m_2$

$\therefore$ It means lines are parallel.

4. Option (B) is correct.

Explanation: Given, A(1, 2), B (3, 4) and C (4, 1)

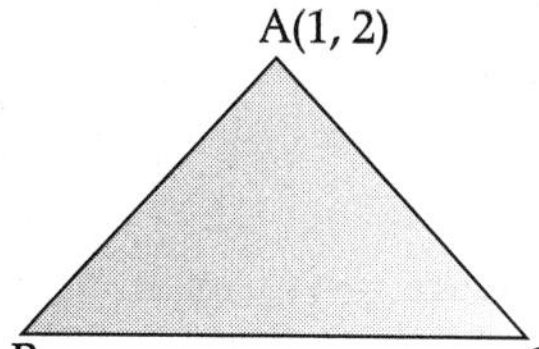

Using distance formula,

$$d = \sqrt{(x_1 - x_2)^2 + (y_1 - y_2)^2}$$

$\therefore$ $AB = \sqrt{(2)^2 + (2)^2} = \sqrt{4+4} = \sqrt{8}$

$BC = \sqrt{(1)^2 + (3)^2} = \sqrt{1+9} = \sqrt{10}$

$CA = \sqrt{9+1} = \sqrt{10}$

It means $BC = CA$

$\therefore$ ABC is an isosceles triangle

5. Option (B) is correct.

Explanation: ABC is an equilateral triangle

$\therefore$ $AB = BC = AC$

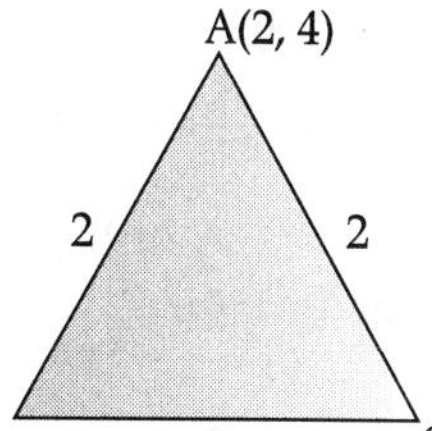

Using distance formula

$AB = \sqrt{4} = 2 = BC = AC$

Now, $BC = \sqrt{(x-2)^2 + (y-6)^2}$

$$2 = \sqrt{(x-2)^2 + (y-6)^2} \quad ...(1)$$

$$AC = \sqrt{(x-2)^2 + (y-4)^2}$$

$$2 = \sqrt{(x-2)^2 + (y-4)^2} \quad ...(2)$$

On comparing (1) and (2)

We get $x = 2+\sqrt{3}$

$y = 5$

$\therefore$ Third vertex $= (2+\sqrt{3}, 5)$

6. Option (B) is correct.

Explanation: We will find the slope of both lines.

Slope of line passing through (4, 3), (*y*, 0)

$$m_1 = \frac{y_2 - y_1}{x_2 - x_1} = \frac{0-3}{y-4} = \frac{-3}{y-4}$$

Slope of line passing through (–1, –2), (3, 0)

$$m_2 = \frac{y_2 - y_1}{x_2 - x_1} = \frac{0-(-2)}{3-(-1)} = \frac{1}{2}$$

We know, if two lines are parallel then,

$$m_1 = m_2$$

$$\frac{-3}{y-4} = \frac{1}{2}$$

$$-6 = y - 4$$

$$y = -2$$

7. Option (C) is correct.

Explanation:

Vertices are: $(a, b + c)$ $(a, b - c)$ $(-a, c)$

$x_1 = a \quad y_1 = b + c$

$x_2 = a \quad y_2 = b - c$

$x_3 = -a \quad y_3 = c$

$\therefore$ Area of triangle

$$= \frac{1}{2}|x_1(y_2 - y_3) + x_2(y_3 - y_1) + x_3(y_1 - y_2)|$$

$$= \frac{1}{2}|a(b-c-c) + a(c-b-c) + (-a)(b+c-(b-c))|$$

$$= \frac{1}{2}|ab - 2ac - ab - 2ac|$$

$$= \frac{1}{2}|-4ac| = |-2ac| = 2ac$$

8. Option (B) is correct.

Explanation:

Given, $3x + y - 5 = 0$, $2x - y - 5 = 0$

Now, $3x + y - 5 = 0$

$3x + y = 5$ ...(1)

and $2x - y = 5$ ...(2)

On solving (1) and (2) (Addition)

$$5x = 10$$

$$x = 2$$

Put value of '*x*' in Eq. (1)

We get, $y = -1$

$\therefore$ Value of $(2\alpha + \beta) = 2 \times 2 + (-1)$ $\because x = \alpha$

$= 4 - 1 = 3$ $y = \beta$

9. Option (B) is correct.

Explanation:

We are given, $5x - 2y + 1 = 0$, $4y - 3x + 5 = 0$

Now, $5x - 2y + 1 = 0$

$5x - 2y = -1$ ...(1)

Similarly, $4y - 3x = -5$ ...(2)

On solving Eqs. (1) and (2)

$$x = -1, y = -2$$

$\therefore$ $P(\alpha, \beta) = (-1, -2)$

$\therefore$ Value of $(2\alpha - 3\beta)$

$$= 2(-1) - (3(-2))$$
$$= -2 + 6 = 4$$

10. Option (C) is correct.

Explanation: $x + y = 3$, $2x + 5y = 12$

Now, $\frac{x}{3} + \frac{y}{3} = 1$ ...(1)

$\frac{x}{6} + \frac{y}{\frac{12}{5}} = 1$ ...(2)

Now, $x + y = 3$ ...(a)

$2x + 5y = 12$ ...(b)

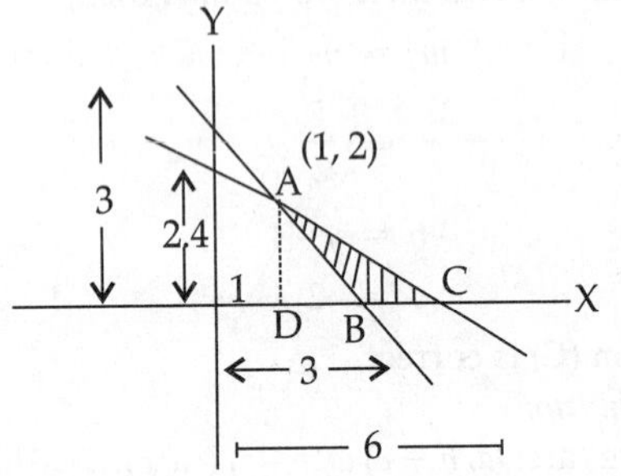

On solving (a) and (b)

$$x = 1, y = 2$$

$\therefore$ Point of intersection = (1, 2)

In ΔABC Area $= \frac{1}{2} \times$ base $\times$ height

$$= \frac{1}{2} \times 3 \times 2 = 3$$

where, AD = 2 = height

BC = OC – OB

= 6 – 3 = 3

11. Option (A) is correct.

Explanation: Given, A(–2, 5), B (1, 3)

(–2, 5) A ———————— B (1, 3)
(x_1, y_1) (x_2, y_2)

We know, $y - y_1 = \left(\frac{y_2 - y_1}{x_2 - x_1}\right)(x - x_1)$

$$y - 5 = \frac{3-5}{1+2}(x+2)$$
$$3y - 15 = -2x - 4$$
$$\Rightarrow 2x + 3y - 11 = 0$$

12. Option (C) is correct.

Explanation:

$$2x + 3y = 6$$

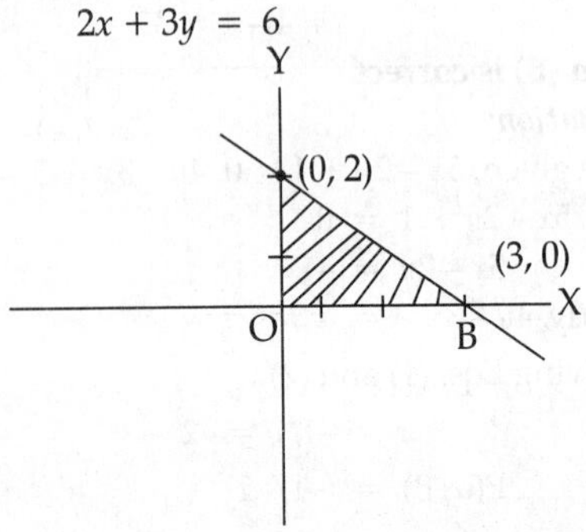

At X-axis, $y = 0$

$\therefore$ $2x = 6$

$x = 3$

At Y-axis, $x = 0$

$\therefore$ $3y = 6$

$y = 6$

Now, in ΔAOB

Area $= \frac{1}{2} \times$ base $\times$ height

$= \frac{1}{2} \times 3 \times 2 = 3$ sq. units

13. Option (A) is correct.

Explanation:

Given $x^2 + y^2 - 6x + 8y + c = 0$ ...(1)

General equation, $x^2 + y^2 + 2gx + 2fy + c = 0$ ...(2)

and

centre $= (-g, -f)$

Also, Radius $= \sqrt{g^2 + f^2 - c}$

Comparing Eq. (2) with (1)

$\therefore$ $2gx = -6x$, $2fy = 8y$

$g = -3$ $f = 4$

Now Radius $= \sqrt{g^2 + f^2 - c}$

$$6 = \sqrt{(-3)^2 + (4)^2 - c}$$
$$36 = 25 - c$$
$$c = 25 - 36 = -11$$

14. Option (D) is correct.

Explanation:

Given, $35x - 35y + 15 = 0$

$ax + by + c = 0$

Slope $(m) = \tan\theta = \left(\frac{-a}{b}\right)$

$$m = \tan\theta = \left(\frac{-35}{-35}\right) = 1$$

$\therefore$ $\theta = 45°$

15. Option (A) is correct.

Explanation:

$2x + 3y + 11 = 0$

$6x + ky + 33 = 0$

For, coincident lines,

$a_1x + b_1y + c_1 = 0$

$a_2x + b_2y + c_2 = 0$

where, $\frac{a_1}{a_2} = \frac{b_1}{b_2} = \frac{c_1}{c_2}$

So, $\frac{a_1}{a_2} = \frac{b_1}{b_2}$

$$\frac{2x}{6x} = \frac{3y}{ky}$$
$$k = 9$$

Level-3: EXPERT

1. **Option (A) is correct.**

Explanation:

$$x - 7y = -42 \quad ...(1)$$

We know at Y-axis, $x = 0$

$$\therefore \quad 0 - 7y = -42$$

$$y = 6$$

$\therefore$ Point of intersection $P(\alpha, \beta) = (0, 6)$

Similarly, at X axis, $y = 0$

$$\therefore \quad 6x + y - 15 = 0$$

$$6x + 0 - 15 = 0$$

$$6x = 15$$

$$x = 2.5$$

$$\therefore \quad Q(\gamma, \delta) = (2.5, 0)$$

$\therefore$ Value of $\alpha + \beta + \gamma + \delta$

$$= 0 + 6 + 2.5 + 0 = 8.5$$

$$= \frac{85}{10} = \frac{17}{2}$$

2. **Option (D) is correct.**

Explanation: Given,

$$2x + 3y = 11 \quad ...(1)$$

$$x - 2y + 12 = 0$$

$$x - 2y = -12 \quad ...(2)$$

Multiply Eq. (2) by 2 and subtract (1) from (2)

$$\therefore \quad y = 5, x = -2$$

Point of intersection $P(x_1, y_1) : (-2, 5)$

Now, at X-axis, $y = 0$

$$\therefore \quad x - 2y + 12 = 0$$

$$x - 0 + 12 = 0$$

$$x = -12$$

$\therefore$ Point of intersection $Q(x_2, y_2) = (-12, 0)$

Now, $x_1 - x_2 + y_1 + y_2 = -2 + 12 + 5 + 0 = 15$

3. **Option (A) is correct.**

Explanation:

$$3x - 20y - 2 = 0 \quad ...(1)$$

$$11x - 5y + 61 = 0 \quad ...(2)$$

Now, $3x - 20y = 2 \quad ...(a)$

$$11x - 5y = -61 \quad ...(b)$$

On solving (a) and (b)

$$\therefore \quad x = -6, y = -1$$

$$\therefore \quad P(a, b) = P(x, y) = (-6, -1)$$

$$\therefore \quad \frac{a^2 + b^2 - ab}{a^2 - b^2 + ab} = \frac{36 + 1 - 6}{36 - 1 + 6} = \frac{31}{41}$$

4. **Option (C) is correct.**

Explanation:

$$2x + 5y - 12 = 0 \quad ...(i)$$

$$x + y = 3 \quad ...(ii)$$

$$y = 0$$

Put value of 'y' in other two equations

(i) $2x_1 + 0 - 12 = 0$

$$x_1 = 6$$

(ii) $x_2 + 0 = 3$

$$x_2 = 3$$

$$\text{Base} = x_1 - x_2$$

$$= 6 - 3 = 3$$

Height = on solving Eqs. (1) and (2)

$$y = 2$$

$$\therefore \quad \text{Area} = \frac{1}{2} \times \text{base} \times \text{height}$$

$$= \frac{1}{2} \times 3 \times 2 = 3$$

5. **Option (D) is correct.**

Explanation: Given coordinates, A(2, 5), B (3, 9), C (4, 1)

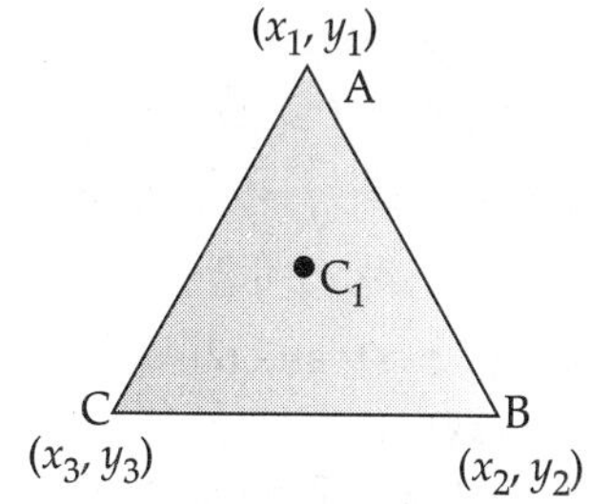

Here, C_1 is the centroid of triangle ΔABC.

We know coordinates of a centroid are determined by,

$$x = \frac{x_1 + x_2 + x_3}{3},$$

$$y = \frac{y_1 + y_2 + y_3}{3}$$

In ΔABC, $x_1 = 2 \quad y_1 = 5$

$$x_2 = 3 \quad y_2 = 9$$

$$x_3 = 4 \quad y_3 = 1$$

Now, $x = \frac{2 + 3 + 4}{3} = \frac{9}{3} = 3$

$$y = \frac{5 + 9 + 1}{3} = \frac{15}{3} = 5$$

$\therefore$ Coordinates of centroid are (3, 5)

6. **Option (C) is correct.**

Explanation: Given, points A(3, 5), B(–7, 4), C(10, –6)

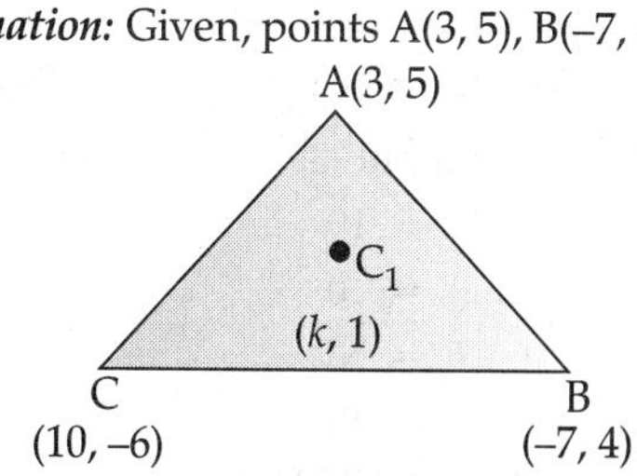

Centroid $(k, 1)$
$\quad\quad\quad\;\; x \;\; y$

We know, $x = \frac{x_1 + x_2 + x_3}{3}$

$$k = \frac{3 - 7 + 10}{3}$$

$$k = \frac{6}{3} = 2$$

7. Option (D) is correct.

Explanation:

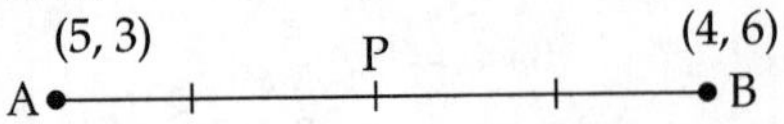

As points (5, 3) and (4, 6) are equidistant from 'P'.

$$\therefore \quad PA = PB$$

$$\sqrt{(x-5)^2+(y-3)^2} = \sqrt{(x-4)^2+(y-6)^2}$$

$$(x-5)^2 + (y-3)^2 = (x-4)^2 + (y-6)^2$$

$$-10x - 6y + 34 = -8x - 12y + 52$$

$$\therefore \quad 2x - 6y + 18 = 0$$

$$\text{So} \quad 3y - x = 9$$

8. Option (C) is correct.

Explanation: General form of equation of circle :

$$\Rightarrow \quad x^2 + y^2 + 2gx + 2fy + c = 0 \quad ...(1)$$

Where, centre $= (-g, -f)$

$$\text{Radius} = \sqrt{g^2+f^2-c}$$

Now, $x^2 + y^2 + 7x + 4y + 9 = 0$ ...(2)

On comparing Eqs. (1) and (2)

$$2gx = 7x$$

$$g = \frac{7}{2}$$

also, $2fy = 4y$

$$f = 2$$

and $c = 9$

Now, radius $= \sqrt{g^2+f^2-c}$

$$r = \sqrt{\left(\frac{7}{2}\right)^2+(2)^2-9}$$

$$= \sqrt{\frac{49}{4}+4-9} = \sqrt{\frac{49}{4}-5}$$

$$r = \sqrt{\frac{49-20}{4}}$$

$$r = \sqrt{\frac{29}{4}} = \frac{\sqrt{29}}{2}$$

9. Option (A) is correct.

Explanation: Always solve with the help of options.

So, equation of line $\Rightarrow 4x - 3y = 10$

Equation of circle $\Rightarrow x^2 + y^2 - 2x + 4y - 20 = 0$

Take option 'A' and put its value in equation of line:

$$\therefore \quad 4x - 3y = 10$$

$$4(4) - 3(2) = 10$$

$$16 - 6 = 10$$

$$10 = 10$$

$$\text{L.H.S.} = \text{R.H.S.}$$

Now, $x^2 + y^2 - 2x + 4y - 20 = 0$

$(-2)^2 + (-6)^2 - (2)(-2) + 4(-6) - 20 = 0$

$4 + 36 + 4 - 24 - 20 = 0$

$$44 - 44 = 0$$

$$0 = 0$$

10. Option (D) is correct.

Explanation: Given coordinates, (6, 2) and (4, 6)

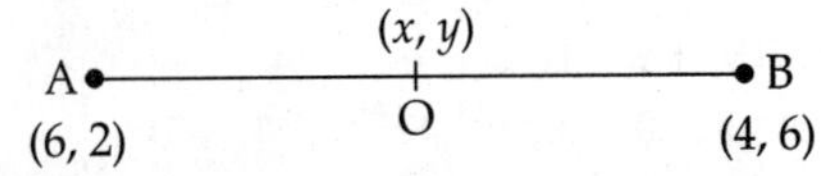

Now, $AO^2 = OB^2$

$$\left(\sqrt{(x-6)^2+(y-2)^2}\right)^2 = (\sqrt{(y-6)^2+(x-4)^2})^2$$

$$(x-6)^2 + (y-2)^2 = (y-6)^2 + (x-4)^2$$

$$x^2 + 36 - 12x + y^2 + 4 - 4y$$

$$= x^2 + 16 - 8x + y^2 + 36 - 12y$$

$$4x - 8y = -12$$

$$x - 2y = -3$$

11. Option (A) is correct.

Explanation: CD is a side of square

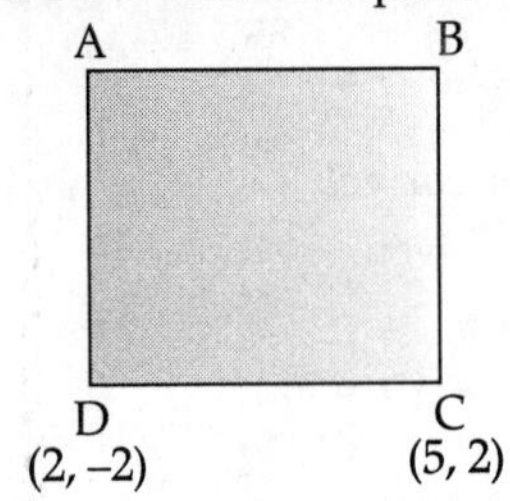

$$CD = \sqrt{(5-2)^2+(2-(-2))^2}$$

$$= \sqrt{(3)^2+(4)^2}$$

$$= \sqrt{9+16} = \sqrt{25} = 5 \text{ units}$$

12. Option (B) is correct.

Explanation:

If $a_1x + b_1y + c_1 = 0$

and $a_2x + b_2y + c_2 = 0$

then, if one solution $= \frac{a_1}{a_2} \neq \frac{b_1}{b_2}$

Many solutions $= \frac{a_1}{a_2} = \frac{b_1}{b_2} = \frac{c_1}{c_2}$

No solution $= \frac{a_1}{a_2} = \frac{b_1}{b_2} \neq \frac{c_1}{c_2}$

Now, according to 'No solution condition'

$$2x + ky = 11$$

$$5x - 7y = 5$$

$$\frac{a_1}{a_2} = \frac{b_1}{b_2}$$

$$\therefore \quad \frac{2}{5} = \frac{k}{-7}$$

$$\frac{-14}{5} = k$$

■■■

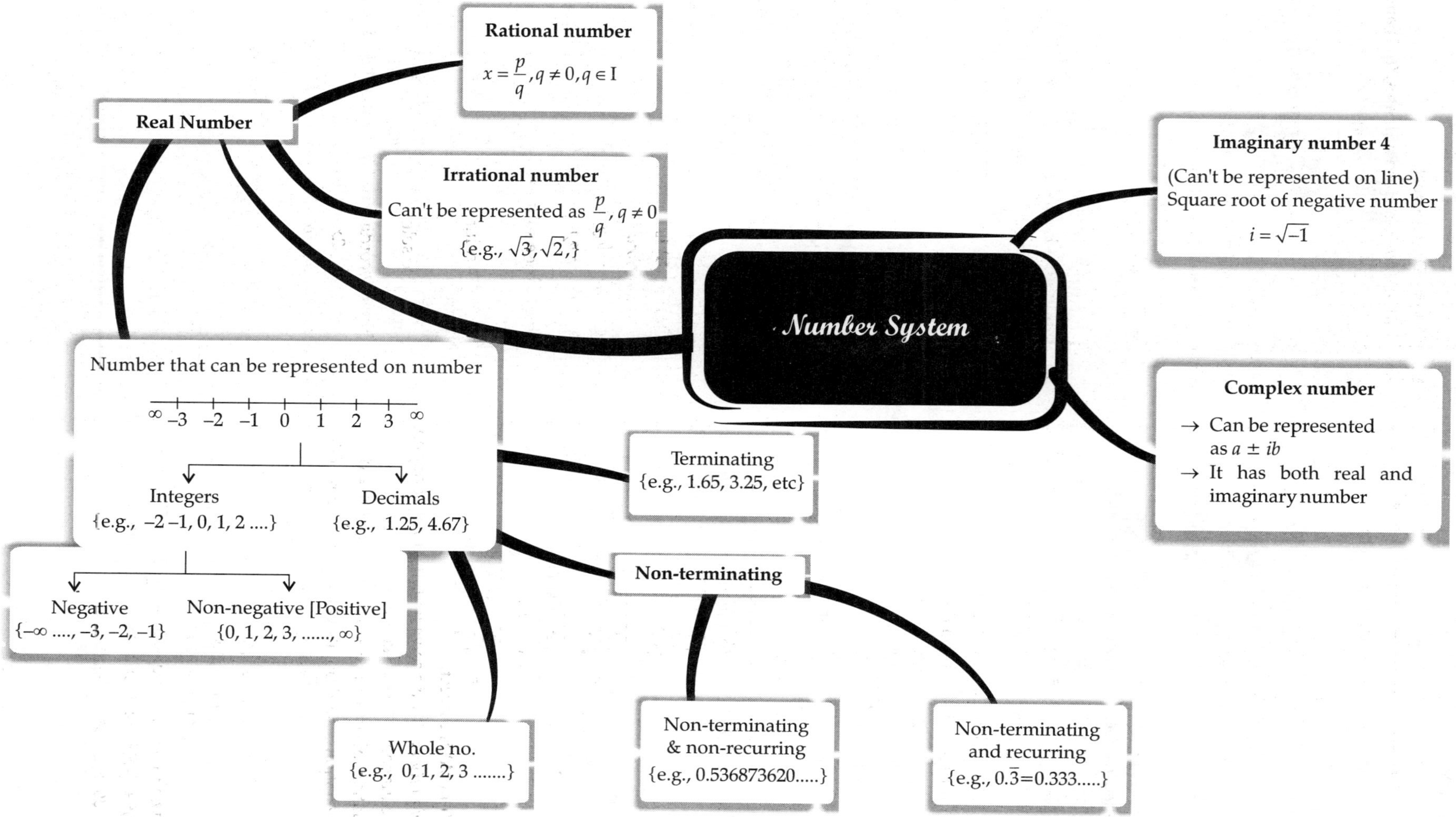
Number System
Real Number
Rational number
$x = \frac{p}{q}, q \neq 0, q \in I$
Irrational number
Can't be represented as $\frac{p}{q}, q \neq 0$
{e.g., $\sqrt{3}, \sqrt{2}$,}
Number that can be represented on number
∞ –3 –2 –1 0 1 2 3 ∞
Integers
{e.g., –2 –1, 0, 1, 2 ....}
Decimals
{e.g., 1.25, 4.67}
Negative
{–∞ ...., –3, –2, –1}
Non-negative [Positive]
{0, 1, 2, 3, ..., ∞}
Whole no.
{e.g., 0, 1, 2, 3 ....}
Terminating
{e.g., 1.65, 3.25, etc}
Non-terminating
Non-terminating
& non-recurring
{e.g., 0.536873620.....}
Non-terminating
and recurring
{e.g., $0.\overline{3}$=0.333.....}
Imaginary number 4
(Can't be represented on line)
Square root of negative number
$i = \sqrt{-1}$
Complex number
→ Can be represented as $a \pm ib$
→ It has both real and imaginary number

Section-3 : Number System

Chapter 18

Number System

LEARNING OBJECTIVES:

- Types of numbers and their representation on number line.
- Number of factors.
- Sum and product of factors.
- Concept related remainder.
- Divisibility rules.
- Different types of questions asked in various competitive exams.
- Methods to solve questions.

SOME BASICS

- **Real Numbers:** Numbers that can be represented on number line.

$-\infty$ .... –5 –4 –3 –2 –1 0 1 2 3 4 .... $+\infty$

- **Imaginary Numbers:** Numbers that cannot be represented on number line or square root of any negative numbers.

  Example: $\sqrt{-7}, \sqrt{-19}, \sqrt{-26}$

  Imaginary number 'iota' $i = \sqrt{-1}$

  $\therefore \quad \sqrt{-7} \times \sqrt{-1} = \sqrt{-7}i$

- **Complex Number:** Number that can be represented in the form of '$a \pm ib$'

  Here, a = real number

  ib = imaginary number

Real Numbers

Integers | Decimal

DECIMAL: Two types

(a) **Terminating decimal:** When number do not get repeated after decimal or a number is completely divisible, it is said to be terminating decimal.

Example: 0.79, 0.258, 0.175, etc.

(b) **Non-terminating decimal:** It exactly the opposite of the terminating decimal.

Example: 0.6666..., 0.45354535...., 0.12345678..., etc.

- **Rational Numbers:** Numbers that can be represented in the form of $\frac{p}{q}$ where $q \neq 0$.

  Example: $\frac{3}{5}, \frac{3}{20}, \frac{811}{25}$, etc.

NOTE: Rational numbers are repeating decimals.

- **Irrational Numbers:** Numbers that can't be represented in the form of $\frac{p}{q}$, where $q \neq 0, p, q \neq N$

  Example: $\sqrt{\pi}, \sqrt{2}, \sqrt{5}, \sqrt{13}$....., etc.

NOTE : All non repeating non-terminating decimals are irrational.

- **Integers:** Integers are those rational numbers where $q = 1$.

  Integers can be negative as well as positive.

- **Whole Numbers:** The set of all positive numbers including '0' is called whole number.

  Whole numbers = {0, 1, 2, 3, 4, 5, 6....}

- **Natural Numbers:** The set of all positive numbers excluding '0'.

  Natural numbers = {1, 2, 3, 4, ...}

- **Even Numbers:** Which are divisible by 2.

  Example: –10, –4, +4, +10, +12 .....

- **Odd Numbers:** Which are not divisible by 2.

  Example: –5, –3, –1, +1, +3, +5, etc.

NOTE: '0' is neither odd nor even.

- **Prime Numbers:** The number which exactly has two factors, i.e., 1 and the number itself.

  Example: {2, 3, 5, 7, 11, 13 ......}

- **Composite Numbers:** The number which has more than two factors.

  Example: Let 16 be the number.

  Factors: 1, 2, 4, 8, 16.

∴ 16 has more than two factors.

Here, it is a composite number.

Note: (a) '1' is neither prime nor composite

(b) Between [1 – 50] → 15 prime numbers

(c) [50 – 100] → 10 prime numbers

∴ between [1 – 100] → 25 prime numbers

- **Relatively prime or co-prime:** 2 numbers that have their HCF as '1'.

  Example: (a) (5, 7) (b) (9, 32)

- **Perfect Number:** If sum of all the factors of a number is equal to that number, then this is called perfect number. (Excluding the number itself)

  Example: Let '6' be the number

  6 → 1, 2, 3, 6

  1 + 2 + 3 = 6

  ∴ '6' is a perfect number

- **Face Value:** It is the number itself that has been asked.

  Example: Let 5269 be the number.

  What is the face value of 5 and 6

  then, face value of 5 = 5

  Face value 6 = 6

- **Place Value:** It depends on the position of that digit in the number. Each position has a value 10 times the places to its right.

  Example: Let '13,467' be the number.

  Now, place value of '4' is 400.

FACTORS

Universal Factor: '1' is known as universal factor.

- **Number of Factors:** Factors of 120: 1, 2, 3, 4, 5, 6, 8, 10, 12, 15, 20, 24, 30, 40, 60, 120

  ∴ 120 has 16 factors.

  In exam, use prime factorisation method.

  Step 1: $120 = 2^3 \times 3^1 \times 5^1$

2	120
2	60
2	30
5	15
3	3
	1

Step 2: Now, add '1' to each power and multiply

∴ 4 × 2 × 2 = 16

∴ No. of factors of 120 are 16.

ODD FACTORS

Step 1: $120 = 2^3 \times 3^1 \times 5^1$

Step 2: Now, add '1' in powers of odd numbers and multiply.

∴ 120 = 2 × 2 = 4

∴ No. of odd factors of 120 are 4.

Even factors = Total factors – odd factors

∴ Even factors of 120 = 16 – 4 = 12

Example 1: Find the number of factors of 720.

(a) 15 (b) 30

(c) 17 (d) 26

Sol. (b) After prime factorisation

$$720 = 2^4 \times 3^2 \times 5^1$$

$$\text{Factors} = 5 \times 3 \times 2 = 30$$

Example 2: Find odd, even and total factors of 480.

(a) 4, 20, 360 (b) 8, 24, 460

(c) 24, 32, 360 (d) 64, 32, 360

Sol. (a) After prime factorisation

$$480 = 2^5 \times 3^1 \times 5^1$$

$$\text{Total factors} = 6 \times 2 \times 2 = 24$$

$$\text{Odd factors} = (1+1)(1+1) = 2 \times 2 = 4$$

$$\text{Even factors} = \text{total} - \text{odd factors} = 24 - 4 = 20$$

Sum and product of factors of any number

$$\text{Sum (N)} = p^a \times q^b \times r^c = \frac{(p^{a+1}-1)(q^{b+1}-1)(r^{c+1}-1)}{(p-1)(q-1)(r-1)}$$

$$\text{Sum (120)} = 2^3 \times 3^1 \times 5^1 = \frac{(2^4-1)(3^2-1)(5^2-1)}{1 \times 2 \times 4} = \frac{15 \times 8 \times 24}{2 \times 4} = 360$$

$$\text{Product} = N^{\frac{f}{2}},$$

where, N = Number itself.

f = Number of factors of that number.

$$\text{Product (120)} = (120)^{\frac{16}{2}} = (120)^8$$

∵ No. of factors of 120 = 16

DIVISIBILITY RULES

- **Divisibility by 2:** If the last digit of a number is even or '0' then that number is divisible by 2.

  Example: 12, 30, 1,000, 2,500, etc.

- **Divisibility by 3:** If the sum of all the digits of a number is divisible by 3, then the number is divisible by 3.

  Example: Let '129' be the number to be divided by 3.

  Sum of digits = 1 + 2 + 9 = 12

  As 12 is divisible by 3, then 129 is divisible by 3.

- **Divisibility by 4:** If the last two digits of a number are divisible by 4, then the given number is divisible by 4.

  Example: Let, 2,804 be the number.

  Now, divide 04 by 4 and it is divisible by 4.

  ∴ 2,804 is divisible by 4.

- **Divisibility by 5:** If the last digit of a number is 5 or 0, then the number is divisible by 5.

  Example: 100, 145, 2005, 1,64,290 etc.

- **Divisibility by 6:** If the number is divisible by 2 and 3 both, then the number is divisible by 6.

  Example: Let '102' be the number

  ∴ 102 is divisible by both 2 and 3

  Hence, 102 is divisible by 6.

- **Divisibility by 7:** If the last digit of a number is double and then subtracted from the rest of the number, and the answer is 0 or is divisible by 7, then the number is divisible by 7.

  Example: '791' $= 79 - (1 \times 2) = 79 - 2$
  $= 77$ which is divisible by 7

  Hence, 791 is also divisible by 7.

- **Divisiblity by 8:** If the last three digits of a number are divisible by 8, then the no. is divisible by 8.

  Example: '30168'

  Last three digit = 168
  $\therefore$ 168 is divisible by 8.
  Hence, 30,168 is divisible by 8.

- **Divisiblity by '9':** If the sum of all digits of a number is divisible by 9, then the number is divisible by 9.

  Example: '7290342'
  Sum = 7 + 2 + 9 + 0 + 3 + 4 + 2
  = 27, which is divisible by 9
  Hence 72,90,342 is divisible by 9.

- **Divisiblity by 10:** If the last digit of a number is '0' then it is divisible 10:

  Example: 120, 1600, 7020, 590230 etc.

- **Divisibility by 11:** If the difference between "sum of digits at even place" and "the sum of digit at odd place" is '0' or is a multiple of 11, then the number is divisible by 11.

  Example:

  7 4 9 9 8

  So, difference = (7 + 9 + 8) – (4 + 9) = 24 – 13 = 11
  Hence, 74,998 is divisible by 11.

  Divisibility by 12: If a number is divisible by 3 and 4 both, then the number is divisibility by 12.

  Example: '3,240'
  3,240 is divisible by both 3 and 4.
  $\therefore$ 3,240 is divisible by 12.

- **Divisibility by 13:** Multiply the last digit by 9 and subtract it from the rest of the number. If the resulted number is divisible by 13. Then, the number is divisible by 13.

  Example: '1,690'
  Now, $9 \times 0 = 0$
  So 169 – 0 = 169 which is divisible by 13
  Hence, 1690 is divisible by 13.

- **Divisibility by 14:** If a number is divisible by 2 and 7 both then that number is divisible by 14, i.e., number is even and osculator 2 is applicable.

  Example: 1456
  So, 1456 is divisible by 2, 7
  Hence, 1456 is divisible by 14.

POINTS TO REMEMBER

- If a is divisible by b then ac is also divisible by b.
- If a is divisible by b and b is divisible by c then a is divisible by c.
- Product of n consecutive numbers is always divisible by $n!$ or $\lfloor n$.
- The square of an odd number when divided by 8 always leaves a remainder 1.
- Square of any natural number can be written in the form of $3n$ or $3n + 1$ or $4n$ or $(4n + 1)$.

SOME IMPORTANT RULES

- If $\frac{a^n}{a-1}$, then remainder will always be 1.
  n = even or odd
- If $\frac{a^{n\to(\text{even number})}}{(a+1)}$, then remainder will be 1.
- If $\frac{a^{n\to(\text{odd number})}}{(a+1)}$, then remainder will be a.
- If n is a single digit number, then in n^3, n will be at unit place. It is valid for the number 0, 1, 4, 5, 6 or 9.
- If n is a single digit number then in n^p, where p is any number (+ve), n will be at unit place. It is valid for 5 and 6.
- If the sum of number and the number formed by reversing the digit is 'a', then the sum of digits of the numbers is $\frac{a}{11}$
- Dividend = (Division × Qutient) + Remainder

  $$\text{Divisor} = \frac{\text{Dividend} - \text{Remainder}}{\text{Quotient}}$$

  $$\text{Quotient} = \frac{\text{Dividend} - \text{Remainder}}{\text{Divisor}}$$

  Remainder = Dividend – (Divisor × Quotient)

LCM AND HCF

- **LCM (Least Common Multiple):** LCM is the least number that is divisible by two or more numbers.

  Example: LCM of 12, 15, 20 = 60
  $\therefore$ 60 is the least number which is divisible by 12, 15, 20

  Method for calculating LCM.

(i) Factor Method

Example: LCM of 3, 5, 6

3	3,5,6
2	1,5,2
5	1,5,1
	1,1,1

LCM = 2 × 3 × 5 = 30

- **HCF (Highest Common Factor):** HCF is the greatest number which divides the given two or more numbers.

  Example: 20, 30, 40
  HCF = 10
  $\because$ 10 is the greatest number that divides 20, 30, 40.

METHOD OF CALCULATING HCF

(i) Factor method

Example: HCF (6, 12, 18)

$6 = 2 \times 3$

$$12 = 2 \times 2 \times 3$$
$$18 = 2 \times 3 \times 3$$
$$\therefore \quad HCF = 2 \times 3 = 6$$

(ii) Division method

Example: HCF (323 and 391)

```
323)391(1
   -323
   ----
    68)323(4
      -272
      ----
       51)68(1
         -51
         ---
         17)51(3
           -51
           ---
             0
```

∴ HCF of 323 and 391 = 17.

Factors and Multiples

(i) Factors: It is the number which perfectly divides the given number.

(ii) Multiple: Multiple is the number which is perfectly divisible by a number.

IMPORTANT POINTS

- LCM of fractions: $\dfrac{\text{LCM of numerators}}{\text{HCF of denominators}}$
- HCF of fractions: $\dfrac{\text{HCF of numerators}}{\text{LCM of denominators}}$
- LCM × HCF = Product of two numbers.
- LCM is always a multiple of HCF of the given numbers.
- **Co-prime numbers:** If HCF of two numbers is 1, they are called co-primes.

Example 3: LCM of $\frac{2}{3}, \frac{4}{9}, \frac{5}{6}$ is:

(a) $\frac{8}{27}$ (b) $\frac{20}{3}$

(c) $\frac{10}{3}$ (d) $\frac{20}{27}$

Sol. (b) $LCM = \dfrac{\text{LCM of 2, 4, 5}}{\text{HCF of 3, 9, 6}} = \dfrac{20}{3}$

Example 4: The HCF and LCM of two numbers are 12 and 240, respectively. If the first number is 24, what is the second number?

(a) 144 (b) 228

(c) 264 (d) 120

Sol. (d) We know:

$$HCF \times LCM = 1^{st} \text{ number} \times 2^{nd} \text{ number}$$
$$\therefore \quad 2^{nd} \text{ number} = \frac{HCF \times LCM}{1^{st} \text{ Number}}$$
$$= \frac{12 \times 240}{24} = 120$$

Example 5: Two numbers are in the ratio 7 : 11. If their HCF is 28, then the difference between the two numbers is:

(a) 196 (b) 128

(c) 308 (d) 112

Sol. (d) Let $7k$ and $11k$ be the numbers.

We know,

$$HCF = 28$$
$$\therefore \quad k = 28$$

Clearly, the numbers are $7 \times 28 = 196$

$$11 \times 28 = 308$$
$$\text{Difference} = 308 - 196 = 112$$

Level 1 Beginner

1. Which of the following is divisible by 3? **[SSC CHSL 2020]**

(A) 6,54,22,589 (B) 45,39,763

(C) 23,62,735 (D) 37,45,932

2. What is the value of $\dfrac{8 \times 5 \div 25}{7 \div 14 \times 2} - \dfrac{14 \div 7 - 5}{7 \div 14 - 25}$? **[SSC CHSL 2023]**

(A) $\frac{362}{245}$ (B) $\frac{115}{245}$

(C) $\frac{306}{245}$ (D) $\frac{106}{245}$

3. The sum of the two numbers is 9 and sum of their inversions is $\frac{1}{2}$, then one of them is: **[RRB NTPC 2019]**

(A) 2 (B) 6

(C) 5 (D) 4

4. 276x1 is divisible by 3. What is the sum of the possible values of 'x'? **[RRB GROUP D 2018]**

(A) 82 (B) 15 (C) 12 (D) 21

5. Calculate the difference between the largest and smallest two-digit prime numbers. **[RRB NTPC 2016]**

(A) 384 (B) 83 (C) 84 (D) 86

6. Which of the following numbers is NOT divisible by 11? **[SSC CHSL 2023]**

(A) 1735624 (B) 752563

(C) 1661308 (D) 1904529

7. Find the smallest 6-digit number, which is a multiple of 18. **[RRB NTPC 2016]**

(A) 10,000 (B) 9,99,900

(C) 1,00,008 (D) 1,00,006

8. In number 16,008, the numeral 6 has a face value: **[SSC CPO 2019]**

(A) 6,000 (B) 6 (C) 60 (D) 600

9. What is the ratio of the mean proportion between 1.2 and 10.8 to the third proportional to 0.2 and 1.2? **[SSC CHSL 2021]**

(A) 1 : 3 (B) 1 : 2 (C) 2 : 1 (D) 3 : 1

10. $2^{25} + 2^{26} + 2^{27}$ is divisible by **[SSC CHSL 2020]**

(A) 5 (B) 6 (C) 9 (D) 7

11. The HCF and LCM of two numbers are 37 and 444, respectively. If the first number is 111, then the other number will be: **[SSC MTS 2019]**

(A) 333 (B) 148 (C) 111 (D) 74

12. The largest three digit number that is exactly divisible by 6, 7 and 8 is: **[SSC MTS 2019]**

(A) 358 (B) 999 (C) 840 (D) 168

13. Two numbers are in the ratio 4 : 7, If the HCF is 26, then the sum of the numbers will be: **[SSC CPO 2019]**

(A) 364 (B) 338 (C) 364 (D) 286

14. The factor of 3,600 is: **[SSC CGL 2019]**

(A) 44 (B) 45 (C) 42 (D) 43

15. When 200 is divided by a positive integer x, the remainder is 8. How many value of x are there? **[SSC CGL 2020]**

(A) 8 (B) 5 (C) 6 (D) 7

16. A fraction is greater than twice its reciprocal by $\frac{7}{15}$. What is the fraction? **[SSC CGL 2017]**

(A) $\frac{5}{3}$ (B) $\frac{3}{5}$ (C) $\frac{3}{4}$ (D) $\frac{4}{5}$

17. If $\frac{1}{2}$ is added to a number and the sum is multiplied by 3, the result is 21. Then the number is: **[SSC CGL 2016]**

(A) 5.5 (B) 6.5 (C) –6.5 (D) 4.5

18. Median of an equilateral triangle is $15\sqrt{3}$ cm. What is the side of this triangle? **[SSC CHSL 2023]**

(A) 24 cm (B) 18 cm
(C) 30 cm (D) 36 cm

19. Which of the following fractions does not lie between $\frac{5}{6}$ and $\frac{8}{15}$? **[SSC CPO 2016]**

(A) $\frac{3}{4}$ (B) $\frac{2}{3}$ (C) $\frac{6}{7}$ (D) $\frac{4}{5}$

20. Which of the following is not divisible by 15? **[SSC CHSL 2022]**

(A) 3,195 (B) 2,995 (C) 2,595 (D) 3,465

21. The average of all the prime and composite numbers upto 100 is: **[SSC MTS 2019]**

(A) 50 (B) 50.5 (C) 49.5 (D) 51

22. The sum of three consecutive odd numbers is always divisibie by **[SSC CPO 2017]**

(A) 9 (B) 21 (C) 3 (D) 15

23. Given n is an integer, what is the remainder when $(6n + 3)^2$ is divided by 9? **[SSC CHSL 2019]**

(A) 2 (B) 1 (C) 0 (D) 3

24. What is the unit digit of 279 + 167 × 342? **[SSC MTS 2017]**

(A) 8 (B) 5 (C) 3 (D) 1

25. How many numbers between 400 and 800 are divisible by 4, 5 and 6? **[SSC Constable (GD) 2013]**

(A) 8 (B) 7 (C) 10 (D) 9

Level 2 Intermediate

1. What is HCF of $\frac{4}{5}, \frac{6}{8}, \frac{8}{25}$? **[SSC CPO 2019]**

(A) $\frac{1}{5}$ (B) $\frac{1}{100}$ (C) $\frac{1}{200}$ (D) $\frac{1}{50}$

2. The largest number of four digits that is exactly divisible by 15, 21 and 30 is: **[SSC CPO 2019]**

(A) 9,870 (B) 9,910 (C) 9,840 (D) 9,830

3. The length, breadth and height of a box is 506 cm, 345 cm and 230 cm, respectively. Give the length of the longest scale, so that the three dimensions of the box can be measured. **[SSC CPO 2019]**

(A) 23 cm (B) 46 cm (C) 30 cm (D) 15 cm

4. An oil merchant has three varieties of oil of volumes 432, 594 and 702, respectively. The number of cans of equal size that would be required to fill the oil separately is: **[SSC CPO 2019]**

(A) 8, 11, 13 (B) 8, 13, 15
(C) 13, 15, 17 (D) 6, 9, 11

5. If $N = 4^{11} + 4^{12} + 4^{13} + 4^{14}$, then how many position factors of N are there? **[SSC CGL Tier-II 2017]**

(A) 92 (B) 48 (C) 56 (D) 51

6. If $N = 3^{14} + 3^{13} - 12$, then what is largest prime factor of N? **[SSC CGL 2017]**

(A) 11 (B) 79 (C) 13 (D) 73

7. The sum of all the positive three digit numbers formed by digits 3, 0 and 7 using each digit only once is: **[SSC CPO 2019]**

(A) 2,010 (B) 1,990
(C) 2,220 (D) 2,110

8. If a nine digit no. $7698x138y$ is divisible by 72, then the value of $\sqrt{4x+y}$ is: **[SSC CGL 2021]**

(A) 8 (B) 6 (C) 5 (D) 9

9. The least number should be added to 10,000 so that it is exactly divisible by 327 is: **[SSC CPO 2019]**

(A) 327 (B) 137 (C) 237 (D) 190

10. If a number is divided by 899, the remainder is 63. If the same number is divided by 29, the remainder will be. **[SSC CHSL 2020]**

(A) 2 (B) 4 (C) 5 (D) 10

11. What is the remainder when $(127^{97} + 97^{97})$ is divided by 32? **[SSC CGL Tier-II 2019]**

(A) 2 (B) 7 (C) 4 (D) 0

12. The least common multiple of two numbers is 252 and highest common factor of them is 12, if the difference between the numbers is 48, then what is the sum of the numbers? [DELHI Police Constable 2020]
(A) 110 (B) 140 (C) 112 (D) 120

13. What is the sum of the digits of the least number, which when divided by 15 and 27 leaves the same remainder 9 in each case and is also completely divisible by 11? [SSC SI (DP) 2019]
(A) 18 (B) 20 (C) 17 (D) 19

14. If a 10-digit number 75462A97B6 is divisible by 72, then the value of $\sqrt{8A-4B}$ is: [SSC CGL Tier-I 2022]
(A) $\sqrt{30}$ (B) $\sqrt{28}$
(C) $\sqrt{27}$ (D) $\sqrt{21}$

15. Which of the following numbers is largest among all?
$0.7, 0.\overline{7}, 0.0\overline{7}, 0.\overline{07}$ [SSC CHSL 2018]
(A) $0.0\overline{7}$ (B) $0.\overline{07}$
(C) $0.\overline{7}$ (D) 0.7

16. Which is the largest of the following fractions?
$\frac{2}{3}, \frac{3}{5}, \frac{8}{11}, \frac{11}{7}$ [SSC CGL Tier-I 2014]
(A) $\frac{2}{3}$ (B) $\frac{11}{17}$ (C) $\frac{3}{5}$ (D) $\frac{8}{11}$

17. What is the sum of all natural numbers beween 1 and 100 which are multiples of 7? [SSC MTS 2017]
(A) 675 (B) 745 (C) 735 (D) 705

18. If x is the remainder when 3^{61284} is divided by 5 and y is the remainder when 4^{96} is divided by 6, then what is the value of $(2x - y)$? [SSC CGL Tier-II 2021]
(A) –2 (B) 2 (C) 4 (D) –4

19. If the difference between two numbers is 5 and the difference between their cubes is 1,850, then the difference between their square is: [SSC CHSL 2021]
(A) $5\sqrt{483}$ (B) $5\sqrt{482}$
(C) $5\sqrt{484}$ (D) $5\sqrt{485}$

20. If a positive integer 'n' is divided by 7, the remainder is 2. Which of the numbers in the options yields a remainder of 0, when it is divided by 7? [SSC CHSL 2020]
(A) $n + 3$ (B) $n + 1$
(C) $n + 2$ (D) $n + 5$

21. Let x be the least number divisible by 16, 24, 30, 36 and 45, and x is also a perfect square. What is the remainder when x is divided by 123? [SSC CPO 2019]
(A) 40 (B) 103 (C) 33 (D) 100

22. A temple has five bells which ring at intervals of 12, 15, 16, 20 and 25 minutes, respectively. If they ring together at midnight, then at what time next ring will they ring together? [SSC MTS 2019]
(A) 8:00 p.m. (B) 7:00 p.m.
(C) 8:30 p.m. (D) 7:30 p.m.

3 Level Expert

1. The product of digits of a 2-digit number is 24. If we add 45 to the number, the new number obtained is a number formed by interchanging the original number? [SSC CHSL 2017]
(A) 45 (B) 83 (C) 54 (D) 38

2. A fraction becomes $\frac{1}{3}$ when 1 is subtracted from both the numerator and the denominator. The same fraction becomes $\frac{1}{2}$ when 1 is added to both the numerator and denominator. The sum of numerator and denominator of the fraction is: [SSC CHSL 2011]
(A) 18 (B) 10 (C) 6 (D) 7

3. Let p, q, r and s be positive natural numbers having three exact factors including 1 and the number itself. If $q > p$ and both are two digit numbers, and $r > s$ and both are one digit numbers, then the value of expression $\frac{p-q-1}{r-s}$ is: [SSC CPO 2020]
(A) $s - 1$ (B) $1 - s$ (C) $s + 1$ (D) $-s-1$

4. What is the sum of digits of the last number which when divided by 15, 18 and 24 leaves the remainder 8 in each case and is also divisible by 13? [SSC CPO 2019]
(A) 16 (B) 17 (C) 18 (D) 15

5. What is the LCM of the HCF of $\frac{2}{3}, \frac{3}{4}$ and LCM of $\frac{5}{6}, \frac{7}{8}$? [SSC MTS 2019]
(A) $\frac{1}{12}$ (B) $\frac{1}{2}$ (C) $\frac{35}{12}$ (D) $\frac{35}{2}$

6. What is the least number of square tiles required to pave the floor of a room 15 m 17 cm long and 9 m 43 cm broad? [SSC MTS 2019]
(A) 830 (B) 840 (C) 841 (D) 851

7. The LCM of two numbers x and y is 204 times their HCF. If their HCF is 12 and the difference between the numbers is 60, then $x + y$ = ? [SSC CGL 2019]
(A) 852 (B) 348 (C) 426 (D) 660

8. Let x and y be the 3-digit numbers such that their difference is 729 and HCF is 81. Find the value of $(x + y)$? [SSC CHSL 2019]
(A) 1,377 (B) 891 (C) 1,053 (D) 1,539

9. If the 6 digit number $x35624$ and $1257y4$, are divisible by 11 and 72, respectively, then what is the value of $(5x - 2y)$? [SSC CGL 2020]
(A) 10 (B) 14 (C) 13 (D) 12

10. When 2388, 4309 and 8151 are divided by a certain 3 digit number, the remainder in each case is the same. The remainder is: [SSC CPO 2019]
(A) 15 (B) 39 (C) 23 (D) 19

11. Let a, b and c be the fractions such that $a < b < c$. If c is divided by a, the result is $\frac{9}{2}$, which exceeds b by $\frac{23}{6}$. If $a + b + c = \frac{19}{12}$, then $(2a + b - c)$ will be equal to: **[SSC CGL Tier-II 2019]**

(A) $\frac{1}{4}$ (B) $\frac{1}{12}$ (C) $\frac{1}{2}$ (D) $\frac{1}{3}$

12. If $\frac{a}{b}=\frac{3}{4}, \frac{b}{c}=\frac{4}{5}$ and $\frac{c}{d}=\frac{5}{6}$, then the sum of the numerator and the denominator (which are coprimes) of $\left(\frac{a}{d}\right)^{10}$ is: **[SSC MTS 2019]**

(A) 513 (B) 2,049 (C) 4,097 (D) 1,025

13. If $x = (164)^{169} + (333)^{337} - (727)^{726}$, then what is the unit digit of x? **[SSC CGL Tier-II 2019]**

(A) 9 (B) 8 (C) 7 (D) 5

14. If six-digit number $5x2y6z$ is divisible by 7, 11 and 13, then the value of $(x - y + 3z)$ is: **[SSC CPO 2020]**

(A) 9 (B) 7 (C) 0 (D) 4

15. When a two-digit, number is multiplied by the sum of its digits, the product is 424. When the number obtained by interchanging its digits is multiplied by the sum of the digits, the result is 280. The sum of the digits of the given number is: **[SSC CGL 2019]**

(A) 7 (B) 18 (C) 8 (D) 6

16. If 5-digit number $535ab$ is divisible by 3, 7 and 11, then what is the value of $(a^2 - b^2 + ab)$? **[SSC CGL Tier-II 2020]**

(A) 89 (B) 95 (C) 83 (D) 77

17. Tanzeem spent $\frac{1}{5}$ of his salary on his friends, $\frac{1}{10}$ of his salary on accommodation and $\frac{1}{4}$ of his salary on savings. If he has ₹ 1,800 left is his wallet, then find the total expenditure on accommodation and savings. **[SSC CHSL 2018]**

(A) ₹ 1,400 (B) ₹ 1,200
(C) ₹ 1,600 (D) ₹ 1,800

18. Three fractions, x, y and z are such that $x > y > z$. When the smallest of them is divided by the greatest of them is divided by the greatest, of the result is $\frac{9}{16}$, which exceeds y by 0.0625. If $x+y+z=1\frac{13}{24}$, then the value of $(x + z)$ is : **[SSC CGL Tier-II 2019]**

(A) $\frac{7}{6}$ (B) $\frac{25}{24}$ (C) 1 (D) $\frac{7}{8}$

19. The sum of the numerator and denominator of positive fraction is 11. If 2 is added to both numerator and denominator, the fraction is increased by $\frac{1}{24}$. The difference of numerator and denominator of the fraction is: **[SSC CHSL 2011]**

(A) 3 (B) 5 (C) 9 (D) 1

20. When an integer is divided by 7, the remainder is 3. What will be the remainder of $6n$ is divided by 7? **[SSC CGL Tier-I 2019]**

(A) 1 (B) 4 (C) 0 (D) 2

ANSWER KEY

Level-1: Beginner

1.	(D)	2.	(D)	3.	(B)	4.	(B)	5.	(D)	6.	(B)	7.	(C)	8.	(B)	9.	(B)	10.	(D)
11.	(B)	12.	(C)	13.	(D)	14.	(B)	15.	(A)	16.	(A)	17.	(B)	18.	(C)	19.	(C)	20.	(B)
21.	(D)	22.	(C)	23.	(C)	24.	(C)	25.	(B)										

Level-2: Intermediate

1.	(B)	2.	(A)	3.	(A)	4.	(A)	5.	(A)	6.	(D)	7.	(D)	8.	(B)	9.	(B)	10.	(C)
11.	(D)	12.	(D)	13.	(A)	14.	(B)	15.	(C)	16.	(D)	17.	(C)	18.	(A)	19.	(D)	20.	(D)
21.	(C)	22.	(A)																

Level-3: Expert

1.	(D)	2.	(B)	3.	(D)	4.	(B)	5.	(D)	6.	(D)	7.	(B)	8.	(C)	9.	(B)	10.	(A)
11.	(A)	12.	(D)	13.	(B)	14.	(B)	15.	(C)	16.	(B)	17.	(A)	18.	(B)	19.	(D)	20.	(B)

Solutions with Detailed Explanations

Level-1: BEGINNER

1. **Option (D) is correct.**
Explanation: We know,
Divisibility rule for 3 states that sum of digits must be divisible by 3.
Now check options.
So, option (D), i.e., 37,45,932
$= 3 + 7 + 4 + 5 + 9 + 3 + 2$
= 33, which is divisible by 3.
∴ 37,45,932 is divisible by 3.

2. **Option (A) is correct.**
Explanation: Value of $\frac{8\times5\div25}{7\div14\times2}-\frac{14\div7-5}{7\div14-25}$

$$=\frac{8\times5\times\frac{1}{25}}{7\times\frac{1}{14}\times2}-\frac{14\times\frac{1}{7}-5}{7\times\frac{1}{14}-25}$$

$$=\frac{\frac{8}{5}}{1}-\frac{2-5}{\frac{1}{2}-25}=\frac{8}{5}-\frac{3\times2}{49}=\frac{362}{245}$$

3. **Option (B) is correct.**
Explanation: Let '*a*' and '*b*' the two numbers.
According to question,

$$a+b = 9 \quad ...(1)$$

$$\frac{1}{a}+\frac{1}{b} = \frac{1}{2}$$

$$\Rightarrow \frac{a+b}{ab} = \frac{1}{2}$$

Take the value of $a + b$ from Eq. (1)

$$\therefore \frac{9}{ab} = \frac{1}{2}$$

$$\Rightarrow ab = 18$$

Now, $(a + b)^2 - (a - b)^2 = 4ab$

$$\Rightarrow 81-(a-b)^2 = 72$$

$$\Rightarrow (a-b)^2 = 9$$

$$\Rightarrow a-b = 3 \quad ...(2)$$

Solving Eqs. (1) and (2)

$$a = 6, b = 3$$

One number is '6', according to the options.

4. **Option (B) is correct.**
Explanation:
Divisibility rule of 3 : Sum of digit is divisible by 3.

$$\therefore 276x1 = \frac{2+7+6+x+1}{3} \quad ...(1)$$

Now, it is clear that '*x*' can be a single digit.
∴ According to Eq. (1),

$$x = 2, 5, 8$$

$$\therefore \text{Sum required} = 2 + 5 + 8 = 15$$

5. **Option (D) is correct.**
Explanation: Smallest two-digit prime number = 11
Largest two-digit prime number = 97
∴ Difference = 97 – 11 = 86

6. **Option (B) is correct.**
Explanation:
Divisibility test for 11:
[Sum of even place digits a number-sum of odd place digits of a number] ÷ 11
= Number must be divisible by 11.
For 1735624:
$(7 + 5 + 2) - (1 + 3 + 6 + 4) = 0$ which is divisible by 11
So, 1735624 is divisible by 11
For 752563:
$(7 + 2 + 6) - (5 + 5 + 3) = 2$ which is not divisible by 11
⇒ 752563 is not divisible by 11

7. **Option (C) is correct.**
Explanation: Smallest 6-digit number = 1,00,000

$$\text{Now, } \frac{1,00,000}{18} = 5,555$$

Now (5,555 + 1) × 18 = 1,00,008

8. **Option (B) is correct.**
Explanation: Face value of 6 is number 16,008 is '6' because face value is the digit itself in the number.

9. **Option (B) is correct.**
Explanation:

$$\text{Mean proportion} = \sqrt{1.2\times10.8} = 3.6$$

$$\text{Third proportion} = \frac{1.2\times1.2}{0.2} = 7.2$$

$$\text{Ratio} = 3.6 : 7.2 = 1 : 2$$

10. **Option (D) is correct.**
Explanation: Given, $2^{25} + 2^{26} + 2^{27}$
$= 2^{25}(1 + 2^1 + 2^2) = 2^{25} \times 7$
∴ Number is divisible by 7

11. **Option (B) is correct.**
Explanation: We know,
LCM × HCF = Product of two numbers
Let '*a*' and '*b*' be the two numbers

$$\therefore 444\times37 = 111\times b$$

$$\Rightarrow \frac{444\times37}{111} = b$$

$$\Rightarrow 148 = b$$

12. **Option (C) is correct.**
Explanation: Largest three-digit number = 999
L.C.M. of 6, 7 and 8 = 168

$$\therefore 168\overline{)999}(5$$
$$\underline{-840}$$
$$159$$

∴ The required largest number = 999 – 159 = 840

13. **Option (D) is correct.**
Explanation:
Given HCF = 26

$$\text{Ratio} = 4:7$$
$$\text{Sum} = \text{HCF}(x + y) = 26(4 + 7) = 26 \times 11 = 286$$

14. Option (B) is correct.

Explanation: After prime factorisation,

$$3,600 = 2^4 \times 3^2 \times 5^2$$
$$\therefore \text{No. of factors} = 5 \times 3 \times 3 = 45$$

15. Option (A) is correct.

Explanation:

According to question,

192 is the number exactly divisible by x.

$\therefore$ Factors 192 = 1, 2, 3, 4, 6, 8, 12, 16, 24, 32, 48, 64, 96, 192

Clearly, $x > 8$

$\therefore$ Required values : 12, 16, 24, 32, 48, 64, 96, 192.

Total eight values of x follows the condition.

16. Option (A) is correct.

Explanation: Let 'x' be the fraction

According to question,

$$x - \frac{2}{x} = \frac{7}{15}$$
$$\Rightarrow \frac{x^2 - 2}{x} = \frac{7}{15}$$
$$\Rightarrow 15x^2 - 30 = 7x$$
$$\Rightarrow 15x^2 - 7x - 30 = 0$$
$$\Rightarrow 15x^2 - 25x + 18x - 30 = 0$$
$$\Rightarrow 5x(3x - 5) + 6(3x - 5) = 0$$
$$\Rightarrow (3x - 5)(5x + 6) = 0$$
$$\therefore x = \frac{5}{3} \text{ or } \frac{-6}{5}$$

17. Option (B) is correct.

Explanation: Let x be the number.

$$\text{So, } \left(x + \frac{1}{2}\right) \times 3 = 21$$
$$\Rightarrow x + \frac{1}{2} = \frac{21}{3}$$
$$\Rightarrow x = 7 - \frac{1}{2} = \frac{13}{2} = 6.5$$

18. Option (C) is correct.

Explanation:

Given that the median of triangle = $15\sqrt{3}$ cm

Using, median = $\frac{\sqrt{3}}{2} \times \text{side}$

$\Rightarrow 15\sqrt{3} = \frac{\sqrt{3}}{2} \times \text{side}$

$\Rightarrow$ side = 30 cm

19. Option (C) is correct.

Explanation: Given, $\frac{5}{6}$ and $\frac{8}{15}$

Now, $\frac{5}{6} = 0.83, \frac{8}{15} = 0.53$

Check options,

So, $\frac{6}{7} = 0.86$

$\therefore 0.53 < 0.83 < 0.86$

20. Option (B) is correct.

Explanation: Check the option using divisibility

Divisibility by 15 = divisibility by 3 and 5

$\therefore$ Divisibility by 5 = unit digit of number be 0 or 5

Divisibility by 3 = Sum of digits must be divisible by 3.

$\therefore$ option 'B', i.e., 2,995 is not divisible by 3.

$\because$ 2,995 = 2 + 9 + 9 + 5 = 25, which is not divisible by 3.

21. Option (D) is correct.

Explanation: According to question,

2, 3, 4, 5 100

$$\therefore \text{Average} = \frac{2+3+4+....100}{99} = \frac{\frac{100(100+1)}{2} - 1}{99} = \frac{\frac{10,000+100}{2} - 1}{99} = \frac{5,050 - 1}{99} = \frac{5,049}{95} = 51$$

22. Option (C) is correct.

Explanation: Let $2x + 1$, $2x + 3$ and $2x + 5$ be the three consecutive odd numbers.

According to question,

$2x + 1 + 2x + 3 + 2x + 5 = 6x + 9$

$= 3(2x + 3)$, which is divisible by 3

23. Option (C) is correct.

Explanation: Given

$$(6n + 3)^2 = 36n^2 + 36n + 9 = 9(4n^2 + 4n + 1)$$

$\therefore$ $9(4n^2 + 4n + 1) \div 9$ leaves no remainder

$\therefore$ Remainder = 0

24. Option (C) is correct.

Explanation: Given, $279 + 167 \times 342$ (279 → 9)

Unit digit → 9 + (7 × 2)

→ 9 + 14

= 9 + 4

= 13 → unit digit

$\therefore$ 3 is the unit digit.

25. Option (B) is correct.

Explanation: Take LCM (4, 5, 6) = 60

Now, $\frac{400}{60} = 6$ (approx.)

$\frac{800}{60} = 13$ (approx.)

$\therefore$ Required answer = 13 – 6 = 7

Level-2: INTERMEDIATE

1. **Option (B) is correct.**

Explanation: Given, $\frac{4}{5}, \frac{6}{8}$ and $\frac{8}{25}$

$$\text{HCF} = \frac{\text{HCF}(4, 6, 8)}{\text{LCM}(5, 8, 25)} = \frac{2}{200} = \frac{1}{100}$$

2. **Option (A) is correct.**

Explanation: We know,

Largest 4 digit number = 9,999

Now, LCM (15, 21, 30) = 210

$$\therefore \quad 210\overline{)9999}\,47$$
$$-840$$
$$1599$$
$$-1470$$
$$129$$

∴ Required number = 9,999 – 129 = 9,870

3. **Option (A) is correct.**

Explanation:

Given, Length = 506 cm

Breadth = 345 cm

Height = 230 cm

Now, required longest scale

= HCF of (506, 345, 230) = 23 cm

4. **Option (A) is correct.**

Explanation: HCF of (432, 594, 702) = 54

Now,

Cans for 1st variety = $\frac{432}{54} = 8$

Cans for 2nd variety = $\frac{594}{54} = 11$

Cans for 3rd variety= $\frac{702}{54} = 13$

5. **Option (A) is correct.**

Explanation:

Given, $N = 4^{11} + + 4^{12} + 4^{13} + 4^{14}$

Now, $= 4^{11}(1 + 4 + 16 + 64) = 4^{11}(85)$

$= 4^{11}(85) = (2^2)^{11}(85)$

$= 2^{22} \times 5^1 \times 17^1$

Now, add '1' to each power and multiply powers factors = 23 × 2 × 2 = 92

6. **Option (D) is correct.**

Explanation: $N = 3^{14} + 3^{13} - 12$

$= 3^{13}(3 + 1) - 12$

$= 3^{13}(4) - 12$

$= 3 \times 4(3^{12} - 1)$

$= 12(3^6 - 1)(3^6 + 1)$

$= 12 \times 728 \times 730$

$= 4 \times 3 \times 26 \times 28 \times 73 \times 10$ ....(1)

From (1) it is clear 73 is the prime factor of N.

7. **Option (D) is correct.**

Explanation: Given digits are 3, 0 and 7

three-digit numbers that can be formed are as follows:

(a) 307 (b) 370 (c) 730 (d) 703

So, sum = 307 + 370 + 730 + 703 = 2,110

8. **Option (B) is correct.**

Explanation: Given, $7698x138y$ is divisible by 72.

So, it must be divisible by 8 and 9

∴ divisibility by 8 = $7698x138y$

Here, $38y$ must be divisible by 8.

So, $y = 4$

∴ Divisibility by 9 = $7 + 6 + 9 + 8 + x + 1 + 3 + 8 + 4$

$= 46 + x$

Here, $46 + x$ must be divisible by 9.

So, $x = 8$

∴ $\sqrt{4x + y} = \sqrt{4 \times 8 + 4} = \sqrt{36} = 6.$

9. **Option (B) is correct.**

Explanation:

$$327\overline{)10000}(30$$
$$9810$$
$$190 \text{ -Remainder}$$

Now, required number = 327 – 190 = 137

10. **Option (C) is correct.**

Explanation: $N = 899q + 63$

According to question,

$$\frac{899q + 63}{29}$$

Here $899(q)$ is completely divisible by 29.

∴ Required remainder = $\frac{63}{29} = 5$

11. **Option (D) is correct.**

Explanation: We know,

If n is odd, $(a + b)$ is the factor of $(a^n + b^n)$

So, 127 + 97 = 224 (factor)

∴ 224 ÷ 32 = 7

So, there is no remainder.

i.e., remainder = 0

12. **Option (D) is correct.**

Explanation: Let the numbers be a, b

We know, $a \times b$ = LCM × HCF

$a - b$ = 48 (Given)

Now, $a + b = \sqrt{(a - b)^2 + 4ab}$

$= \sqrt{(48)^2 + 4 \times 252 \times 12}$

$= \sqrt{2,304 + 12,096}$

$= \sqrt{14,400} = 120$

∴ Sum of numebrs = 120

13. **Option (A) is correct.**

Explanation:

LCM (15, 27) = 135

So, N (required no.)= $135x + 9$

N is divisible by 11.

Now, $135x + 9 = 12 \times 11x + 3x + 9$

$\therefore$ $3x + 9$ must be divisible by 11.

So, $x = 8$

Number $= 135 \times 8 + 9$

$= 1{,}089$

Required sum $= 1 + 0 + 8 + 9 = 18$

14. Option (B) is correct.

Explanation: 75462A97B6 is divisible by 72

$\therefore$ it is also divisible by 8×9

Divisibility by 8: Last three-digits must be divisible by 8.

i.e., $7B6 \div 8$

It is possible when B = 3 or 7.

Divisibility by 9: Sum of digits i.e., 53 + A when B = 7 must be divisible by 9.

When, $A = 1, 54 \div 9 = 6$

So, $A = 1, B = 7$

Now, $\sqrt{8A - 4B} = \sqrt{8 - 4 \times 7} = \sqrt{-20}$

When $B = 3$

Sum of digits, i.e., 49 + A is divisible by 9 for A = 5

$\therefore$ $A = 5, B = 3$

$\therefore$ $\sqrt{8A - 4B} = \sqrt{8 \times 5 - 4 \times 3}$

$= \sqrt{40 - 12} = \sqrt{28}$

$\therefore$ According to the options, $\sqrt{28}$ is answer.

15. Option (C) is correct.

Explanation: Given, $0.7, 0.\overline{7}, 0.07, 0.\overline{07}$

Now, calculate value of each.

$0.\overline{7} = 0.77....$

$0.0\overline{7} = \frac{7}{90} = 0.077 ....$

$0.\overline{07} = 0.0707 ....$

$\therefore 0.\overline{07} < 0.0\overline{7} < 0.7 < 0.\overline{7}$

So, the largest number $= 0.\overline{7}$

16. Option (D) is correct.

Explanation:

Given, $\frac{2}{3}, \frac{3}{5}, \frac{8}{11}, \frac{11}{17}$

$\frac{2}{3} = 0.67$

$\frac{3}{5} = 0.6$

$\frac{8}{11} = 0.73$

$\frac{11}{17} = 0.65$

Clearly, 0.73, i.e., $\frac{8}{11}$ is largest among all.

17. Option (C) is correct.

Explanation: Find multiple of 7 between 1 and 100

$= 7, 14, 21, ..., 98$

Now, sum $= 7 + 14 + 21 + ... + 98$

$= 7\,[1 + 2 + ... + 14]$

$= \frac{7 \times 14(14+1)}{2}$ $\left[\because \text{Sum} = \frac{n(n+1)}{2}\right]$

$= \frac{7 \times 14 \times 15}{2} = 735$

18. Option (A) is correct.

Explanation: According to question,

$3^{61284} = (3^4)^{15321}$

So, $3^4 = 81$

Now, $81 \div 5$ gives 1 as remainder

$\therefore$ $(1)^{15321} = 1$

So, remainder when 3^{61284} is divided by 5 = x = 1

Now $(4)^{96} \div 6$ gives remainder 4.

$\therefore$ $y = 4$

Now, $(2x - y) = 2(1) - 4 = -2$

19. Option (D) is correct.

Explanation: Let a and b be the two numbers

According to question,

$a - b = 5$

Squaring both sides

$a^2 - 2ab + b^2 = 25$ ...(1)

Also, $a^3 - b^3 = 1{,}850$

$\therefore$ $(a - b)(a^2 + ab + b^2) = 1{,}850$

$5(a^2 + ab + b^2) = 1{,}850$

$a^2 + ab + b^2 = 370$ ...(2)

Add Eq. (1) and 2 × (2)

$3a^2 + 3b^2 = 765$

$a^2 + b^2 = 255$ and $ab = 115$

$a^2 + b^2 + 2ab = 485$

$a + b = \sqrt{485}$

So, $(a + b)(a - b) = 5\sqrt{485}$

20. Option (D) is correct.

Explanation: We know,

Dividend = (Divisor × Quotient) + Remainder

$n = 7 \times \text{quotient} + 2$

$\therefore$ If we add 5 to 'n', it becomes divisible by 7.

$\therefore$ $n + 5 = 7 \times \text{quotient} + 2 + 5$

$= 7 \times \text{quotient} + 7$

Now, $n + 5$ is divisible by 7.

21. Option (C) is correct.

Explanation:

LCM (16, 24, 30, 36 and 45) $= 9 \times 5 \times 4^2 = 720$

$720 \times 5 = 3{,}600$ = perfect square

$\therefore$ $x = 3{,}600$

$\therefore$ When $3{,}600 \div 123$

We get remainder $= 33$

22. Option (A) is correct.

Explanation: Given intervals, 12, 15, 16, 20 and 25

LCM (12, 15, 16, 20 and 25) = 1200 minutes or 20 hours.

$\therefore$ They will ring together at 12:00 a.m. + 20 hours = 8:00 p.m.

Level-3: EXPERT

1. Option (D) is correct.

Explanation: Let p and q be the two numbers.

As given in the question,

$$pq = 24 \quad ...(a)$$

Also, $10p + q + 45 = 10q + p$

$\Rightarrow 10q + p - 10p - q = 45$

$\Rightarrow \quad 9q - 9p = 45$

$\Rightarrow \quad q - p = 5 \quad ...(b)$

$\therefore \quad (p + q)^2 = (q - p)^2 + 4pq$

$= (5)^2 + 4 \times 24$

$= 25 + 96$

$(p + q)^2 = 121$

$\therefore \quad p + q = 11 \quad ...(c)$

Adding (b) and (c),

$q - p + p + q = 16$

$\Rightarrow \quad 2q = 16$

$\Rightarrow \quad q = 8$

$\because \quad pq = 24$

$\Rightarrow \quad 8p = 24$

$\Rightarrow \quad p = 3$

$\therefore$ Required answer $= 10p + q$

$= 10 \times 3 + 8 = 38.$

2. **Option (B) is correct.**

Explanation: Let the fraction be $\frac{p}{q}$.

$\therefore \quad \frac{p-1}{q-1} = \frac{1}{3}$

$\Rightarrow \quad 3p - 3 = q - 1$

$\Rightarrow \quad 3p - q = 2 \quad ...(1)$

Also, $\quad \frac{p+1}{q+1} = \frac{1}{2}$

$\Rightarrow \quad 2p + 2 = q + 1$

$\Rightarrow \quad 2p - q = -1 \quad ...(2)$

Subtracting Eq. (2) from (1),

$3p - q - (2p - q) = 2 - (-1)$

$\Rightarrow 3p - q - 2p + q = 2 + 1$

$\Rightarrow \quad p = 3$

Put value of p in Eq. (1)

$3 \times 3 - q = 2$

$\Rightarrow \quad q = 9 - 2 = 7$

$\therefore \quad p + q = 3 + 7 = 10.$

3. **Option (D) is correct.**

Explanation: According to question,

4, 9, 25 and 49 are the numbers with exactly 3 factors.

Given that $q > p$ and both are two digit numbers

Clearly, $\quad q = 49$

$p = 25$

Also, $r > s$ and both are one-digit numbers

Clearly, $\quad r = 9,$

$s = 4$

$\therefore \quad \frac{p-q-1}{r-s} = \frac{25-49-1}{9-4}$

$= \frac{-24-1}{5} = \frac{-25}{5}$

$= -5 = -s - 1$

4. **Option (B) is correct.**

Explanation: According to question,

Take LCM of 15, 18 and 24, i.e., 360

Number that is required $= 360k + 8$

If this is to be divisible by 13, then $(9k + 8)$ should also be divisible by 13.

$\therefore$ If $k = 2$, then $(9k + 8)$ is divisible by 13.

Clearly, the required no. $= 728$

$\therefore \quad$ Sum of digits $= 7 + 2 + 8 = 17$

5. **Option (D) is correct.**

Explanation:

According to question,

$$\text{HCF of } \left(\frac{2}{3}, \frac{3}{4}\right) = \frac{\text{HCF }(2, 3)}{\text{LCM }(3, 4)} = \frac{1}{12}$$

$$\text{Now LCM of } \left(\frac{5}{6}, \frac{7}{8}\right) = \frac{\text{LCM }(5, 7)}{\text{HCF }(6, 8)} = \frac{35}{2}$$

$$\therefore \text{ LCM of } \left(\frac{1}{12}, \frac{35}{2}\right) = \frac{\text{LCM }(1, 35)}{\text{HCF }(12, 2)} = \frac{35}{2}$$

6. **Option (D) is correct.**

Explanation: Length of the room = 15 m 17 cm

= 1,500 cm + 17 cm = 1,517 cm

Breadth of the room = 9 m 43 cm

= 900 cm + 43 cm = 943 cm

Now, HCF of 1,517 and 943 = 41

$\therefore$ Required no. of tiles $= \frac{1{,}517 \times 943}{41 \times 41} = 851$

7. **Option (B) is correct.**

Explanation: According to question,

HCF $= 12$, LCM $= 12 \times 204$

Now, $\quad x - y = 60 \Rightarrow x = 60 + y$

Also, $\quad x \times y = 12 \times (12 \times 204)$

$\Rightarrow \quad (60 + y) \times y = 12 \times (12 \times 204)$

$\Rightarrow \quad 60y + y^2 - 144 \times 204 = 0$

$\Rightarrow \quad y^2 + 204y - 144y - 144 \times 204 = 0$

$\Rightarrow \quad (y + 204)(y - 144) = 0$

$\Rightarrow \quad y = 144, x = 144 + 60 = 204$

$\therefore \quad$ Sum required $= x + y$

$= 204 + 144 = 348$

8. **Option (C) is correct.**

Explanation: As per given in the question

$x - y = 729$

HCF $= 81$

Let $81a$ and $81b$ be the numbers

$\therefore \quad 81a - 81b = 729$

$a - b = 9$

So, $81a < 1{,}000$

$a < 12.34$

$\therefore$ a could be 10, 11 and 12

and b could be 1, 2 and 3

If $81b > 100$

$b > 1.23$

$\therefore$ b could be 2 and 3.

a could be 11 and 12

Possible pairs of x and y = (891, 162) or (972, 243)

HCF of (972, 243) $= 243$

$\therefore$ Required pair is (891, 162)

Also, $x + y = 891 + 162 = 1,053$

9. Option (B) is correct.

Explanation: According to question,

Divisible by 11 $= x35624$

$\Rightarrow (x + 5 + 2) - (3 + 6 + 4) = 0$ or $11 \Rightarrow x = 6$

Now divisibility by 72 for $1257y4$

$\therefore$ $1257y4$ is divisible by 9 and 8

Now, $1257y4 \div 9$

$\therefore$ $1 + 2 + 5 + 7 + y + 4$ must be divisible by 9 and possible value of y is 8.

Also, 784 is divisible by 8 when $y = 8$

$\therefore \quad 5x - 2y = 30 - 16 = 14$

10. Option (A) is correct.

Explanation: According to question,

Remainder should be equal in each case

$\therefore$ Divisor $=$ HCF [(4,309 – 2,388), (8,151 – 4,309)]

$=$ HCF [1921, 3842] $= 1921$

$\therefore$ Factors of 1921 $= 113 \times 17$

113)2388(21	113)4309(38	113)8151(72
226	339	791
128	919	241
113	904	226
15	15	15

11. Option (A) is correct.

Explanation: According to question,

$$a + b + c = \frac{19}{12} \quad \text{...(a)}$$

Also, $$\frac{c}{a} = \frac{9}{2}$$

Assume, $c = 9$ unit and $a = 2$ unit

As stated is the question,

$$b = \frac{9}{2} - \frac{23}{6} = \frac{2}{3}$$

Put this value in Eq. (a)

$$\Rightarrow \quad a + c = \frac{19}{12} - \frac{2}{3} = \frac{11}{12}$$

$$\therefore \quad (9 + 2) \text{ unit} = \frac{11}{12}$$

$$1 \text{ unit} = \frac{1}{12}$$

$$\therefore \quad 9 \text{ unit} = \frac{1}{12} \times 9 = \frac{3}{4}$$

Also, $$2 \text{ unit} = \frac{1}{12} \times 2 = \frac{1}{6}$$

$$\therefore \quad (2a + b - c) = 2\left(\frac{1}{6}\right) + \frac{2}{3} - \frac{3}{4}$$

$$= \frac{1}{3} + \frac{2}{3} - \frac{3}{4} = \frac{1}{4}$$

12. Option (D) is correct.

Explanation:

Given, $$\frac{a}{b} = \frac{3}{4}, \quad \frac{b}{c} = \frac{4}{5}, \quad \frac{c}{d} = \frac{5}{6}$$

or $a : b : c : d$

3 : 4

4 : 5

5 : 6

$$\therefore \quad a : b : c : d = 3 : 4 : 5 : 6$$

$$\Rightarrow \quad \left(\frac{a}{d}\right)^{10} = \left(\frac{3}{6}\right)^{10}$$

$$\left(\frac{a}{d}\right)^{10} = \left(\frac{1}{2}\right)^{10} = 1,024$$

$$\therefore \quad \text{Sum} = 1,024 + 1 = 1,025$$

13. Option (B) is correct.

Explanation: Given,

$$x = (164)^{169} + (333)^{337} - (727)^{726}$$

Unit digit of $(164)^{169} = 4^1 = 4$

Unit digit of $(333)^{337} = 3^1 = 3$

Unit digit of $(727)^{726} = 7^2 = 9$

Unit digit of $x = 4 + 3 - 9$

$= -2$ it is not possible

$\therefore$ Required unit digit $= 10 + (-2) = 8$.

14. Option (B) is correct.

Explanation: $7 \times 11 \times 13 = 1,001$

$\therefore$ The number is also divisible by 1,001

and we know, if a number is divisible by 1,001 then its first three digits repeat.

$\therefore$ If $5x2y6z$ is divisible by 1001

then its first three digits should repeat.

$\therefore$ The numbers is 5,62,562

Clearly, $x = 6, y = 5, z = 2$

$\therefore \quad x - y + 3z = 6 - 5 + 6 = 7$

15. Option (C) is correct.

Explanation: Let $(10p + q)$ be the number

According to question,

$$(10p + q)(p + q) = 424 \quad \text{...(1)}$$

Also,

$$(10q + p)(p + q) = 280 \quad \text{...(2)}$$

Now, (1) $\div$ (2)

$$\Rightarrow \quad \frac{(10p+q)}{(10q+p)} = \frac{424}{280}$$

$$\Rightarrow \quad \frac{(10p+q)}{(10q+p)} = \frac{53}{35}$$

$$\Rightarrow \quad 350p + 35q = 530q + 53p$$

$$\Rightarrow \quad 297p = 495q$$

$$\Rightarrow \quad \frac{p}{q} = \frac{5}{3}$$

Using the value is equations

$$(10q + p)(p + q) = [\{10(3) + 5\}(5 + 3)] = 280$$

$\therefore$ Sum of desired values $= 5 + 3$

16. **Option (B) is correct.**
Explanation: LCM (3, 7, 11) = 231
∴ Largest possible value of 535 *ab* is 53,599

$$\begin{array}{r} 232 \\ 231\overline{)53599} \\ -462 \\ \hline 739 \\ -693 \\ \hline 469 \\ -462 \\ \hline 7 \end{array} \text{— Remainder}$$

$$\therefore \quad \text{Number} = 53{,}599 - 7 = 53{,}592$$
$$\therefore \quad a = 9, b = 2$$
$$\therefore \quad (a^2 - b^2 + ab) = 9^2 - 2^2 + 9 \times 2 = 81 - 4 + 18 = 95$$

17. **Option (A) is correct.**
Explanation: Given,

$$\text{Expenditure on friends} = \frac{1}{5}$$
$$\text{Expenditure on accomodation} = \frac{1}{10}$$
$$\text{Saving} = \frac{1}{4}$$
$$\text{Total part} = \frac{1}{5}+\frac{1}{10}+\frac{1}{4} = \frac{11}{20}$$
$$\text{Remaining} = 1-\frac{11}{20} = \frac{9^{th}}{20}\text{ part}$$

∴ Part of expenditure on accommodation and savings

$$= \frac{1}{10}+\frac{1}{4} = \frac{2+5}{20} = \frac{7^{th}}{20}\text{ part}$$

$$\text{Given,} \quad \frac{9^{th}\text{ part}}{20} = 1{,}800$$
$$\therefore \quad \frac{7^{th}\text{ part}}{20} = \frac{1{,}800}{9}\times 7 = ₹\,1{,}400$$

18. **Option (B) is correct.**
Explanation: As per the details given

$$x > y > z$$
$$\text{So,} \quad \frac{z}{x} = \frac{9}{16}$$
$$\text{Also,} \quad \frac{z}{x} - y = 0.0625$$
$$\Rightarrow \quad \frac{9}{16} - y = 0.0625$$
$$\therefore \quad y = \frac{9}{16} - 0.0625 = 0.5$$
$$\text{So,} \quad x + y + z = 1\frac{13}{24}$$
$$\Rightarrow \quad x + 0.5 + z = \frac{37}{24}$$
$$\Rightarrow \quad x + z = \frac{37}{24} - 0.5 = \frac{37-12}{24} = \frac{25}{24}$$

19. **Option (D) is correct.**
Explanation: Let the numerator be P, then denominator = 11 – P

$$\text{Now,} \quad \text{fraction} = \frac{P}{11-P}$$
$$\text{Also,} \quad \frac{P+2}{11-P+2} = \frac{P}{11-P}+\frac{1}{24}$$
$$\Rightarrow \frac{P+2}{13-P}-\frac{P}{11-P} = \frac{1}{24}$$
$$\Rightarrow \frac{11P - P^2 + 22 - 2P - 13P + P^2}{(13-P)(11-P)} = \frac{1}{24}$$
$$\Rightarrow \frac{22-4P}{(13-P)(11-P)} = \frac{1}{24}$$
$$\Rightarrow 528 - 96P = 143 - 24P + P^2$$
$$\Rightarrow P^2 + 72P - 385 = 0$$
$$\Rightarrow P^2 + 77P - 5P - 385 = 0$$
$$\Rightarrow (P-5)(P+77) = 0$$
$$\therefore \quad P = 5$$
$$\therefore \quad \text{Denominator} = 11 - 5 = 6$$
$$\text{So,} \quad \text{difference} = 6 - 5 = 1$$

20. **Option (B) is correct.**
Explanation:

$$\text{Let,} \quad n = 7k + 3$$
$$\Rightarrow \quad 6n = 6(7k+3)$$
$$\Rightarrow \quad 6n = 42k + 18$$
$$\Rightarrow \quad 6n = 42k + 14 + 4$$
$$\Rightarrow \quad 6n = 7(6k+2) + 4$$

When $6n$ is divided by 7 then remainder = 4

Power, Surds and Indices

Surds

- Quadration: Surd of order 2 is called quadratic surd i.e. $\sqrt{a}$
- Cubic: Surd of order 3 is called cubic surd i.e. $3\sqrt{a}$
- Quadratic or biquadratic surd: surd of order 4 is known as quartic surd
- Mixed Surds: A surd having a rational factor other than unity

Important Laws of Surds

1. $\sqrt[n]{a} = (a)^{\frac{1}{n}}$
2. $\sqrt[n]{ab} = \sqrt[n]{a}.\sqrt[n]{b}$
3. $\sqrt{a} \times \sqrt{a} = a^{\frac{1}{2}} \times a^{\frac{1}{2}} = a$
4. $\sqrt[m]{\frac{a}{b}} = \frac{\sqrt[m]{a}}{\sqrt[m]{b}} = \left(\frac{a}{b}\right)^{\frac{1}{m}}$
5. $\sqrt[m]{\sqrt[n]{a}} = \sqrt[mn]{a}$
6. $\sqrt{a^2 b} = a\sqrt{b}$
7. $(\sqrt[n]{a})^m = (a)^{m/n} = (am)^{\frac{1}{n}}$

Laws of Exponents

Power of same base

1. $a^m \times a^n = a^{m+n}$
2. $\frac{a^m}{a^n} = a^{m-n}$

Power with same exponent

1. $a^m \times b^m = (ab)^m$
2. $\frac{a^n}{b^n} = \left(\frac{a}{b}\right)^n$

Power of power

1. $(a^m)^n = a^{mn}$
2. $(a^m)^{\frac{1}{n}} = a^{\frac{m}{n}}$
3. $\left[(a^m)^n\right]^P = a^{mnP}$

Miscellaneous

1. $a^{-m} = \frac{1}{a^m}$
2. $a^m = \frac{1}{a^{-m}}$
3. $a^0 = 1$

Chapter 19

Power, Indices and Surds

LEARNING OBJECTIVES:

- Review properties of numbers.
- State the rules of indices.
- Simplify expressions involving indices.
- Define relevant vocabulary relating to calculating surds.

➢ **Indices:** It is the power or exponent that is raised to a number or a variable.

Example : 6^2

Here, 6 – base

2 – power or index of six

RULES RELATED TO INDICES

1. $a^n = a \times a \times a \times .... \times a$ (n times)

where a = base

n = power or exponent or index.

2. $a^m \times a^n = a^{m+n}$

3. $a^m \times a^n \times a^p = a^{m+n+p}$

4. (i) $\frac{a^m}{a^n} = a^{m-n}$ if $m > n$

(ii) $\frac{a^m}{a^n} = \frac{1}{a^{n-m}}$ if $n > m$

(iii) $\frac{a^m}{a^n} = 1$ if $m = n$

5. $a^x \times b^x \times c^x = (abc)^x$

6. (i) $a^{-m} = \frac{1}{a^m}$

(ii) $a^m = \frac{1}{a^{-m}}$

7. (i) $(a^m)^n = (a^n)^m$

(ii) $(a^m)^{\frac{1}{n}} = a^{\frac{m}{n}}$

(iii) $\{(a^m)^n\}^p = a^{mnp}$

8. $(ab)^n = a^n b^n$

9. (i) $\left(\frac{a}{b}\right)^m = \frac{a^m}{b^m}$

(ii) $\left(\frac{a}{b}\right)^{-m} = \left(\frac{b}{a}\right)^m$

10. $(-b)^n = \begin{cases} b^n, & \text{When } n \text{ is even} \\ -b^n & \text{When } n \text{ is odd} \end{cases}$

11. NOTE: (a) $a^{m^n} \neq (a^m)^n$

as $a^{mn} = a^{m+m+m+m.........n \text{ times}}$

$(a^m)^n = a^{mn}$

(b) $a^{\frac{1}{mn}} \neq (a^m)^{\frac{1}{n}}$

(c) $a^{m^{n^p}} \neq [(a^m)^n]^p$

12. If $a^m = a^n$

then, $m = n$

also,

if $a^m = b^m$, then $a = b$

13. If index of any number is '0', the value of the number is '1'.

$x^0 = 1, 6^0 = 1, (6000)^0 = 1$

➢ **Surds:** An expression that has a square root, cube root or other root symbol. Surds are used to write irrational number precisely.

Example: $\sqrt[n]{a}, \sqrt[3]{9}$

where n – is a positive integer

a – rational number

$\sqrt[n]{a}$ – irrational number.

1. **Quadritic Surd:** A surd of order 2 (i.e., $\sqrt{a}$) is called quadratic surd.

Example: $\sqrt{3} = 3^{\frac{1}{2}}$ is a quadratic surd.

But $\sqrt{4} = 2$ is a rational number, thus it is not a quadratic surd or surd.

2. **Cubic surd:** A surd of order 3 (i.e., $\sqrt[3]{a}$) is called a cubic surd.

   Example: $\sqrt[3]{5}$ is a cubic surd.

   But $\sqrt[3]{8}=2$ is a rational number. Thus $\sqrt[3]{8}$ is not a surd.

3. **Quartic or biquadratic surd:** A surd of order 4 is known as a quadratic or biquadratic surd.

> **NOTE:**
> Each surd can be represented on the number line.

4. $\sqrt[n]{a} = (a)^{\frac{1}{n}}$

5. $\sqrt[n]{ab} = \sqrt[n]{a}\cdot\sqrt[n]{b}$

6. $\sqrt{a}\times\sqrt{a} = a^{\frac{1}{2}}\times a^{\frac{1}{2}} = a$

7. $\sqrt{a}\times\sqrt{b} = \sqrt{ab}$

   Also, $x\cdot\sqrt[n]{a}\times y\cdot\sqrt[m]{b} = xy\sqrt[n]{a}.\sqrt[m]{b} = xy\sqrt[mn]{a^m b^m}$

8. $\sqrt[n]{\frac{a}{b}} = \frac{\sqrt[n]{a}}{\sqrt[n]{b}} = \left(\frac{a}{b}\right)^{\frac{1}{n}}$

9. $\sqrt[m]{\sqrt[n]{a}} = \sqrt[mn]{a}$

10. $\sqrt{a^2 b} = a\sqrt{b}$

11. $\left(\sqrt[n]{a}\right)^m = (a)^{m/n} = (a^m)^{\frac{1}{n}}$

12. $(\sqrt{a}+\sqrt{b})^2 = a+b+2\sqrt{ab}$

13. $(\sqrt{a}-\sqrt{b})^2 = a+b-2\sqrt{ab}$

14. $(\sqrt{a}+\sqrt{b})\times(\sqrt{a}-\sqrt{b}) = a-b$

    where a and b are positive rational numbers.

15. **Mixed surds:** A surd that has a rational coefficient other than unity is called a mixed surd.

16. **Similar or like surds:** Surds having same irrational factors are called "similar or like surd".

17. **Unlike surds:** Surds having no-common irrational factors are called "unlike surds".

18. **Pure surd:** The surd whose factor is 1 and other factor is an irrational number, then that type of surd is called pure surd or the surd which is completely under radical sign.

19. If $x = \sqrt{y\sqrt{y\sqrt{y\ldots..}}}$ n times, then $y^{\left(1-\frac{1}{2^n}\right)}$

Example 1: The value of $(256)^{0.16}\times(256)^{0.09}$ is:

(a) 4 (b) 64
(c) 16 (d) 256.25

Sol. (a) Now,

$$(256)^{0.16}\times(256)^{0.09} = (256)^{0.16+0.09}$$
$$[\because m^a\times m^b = m^{a+b}]$$
$$= ((4)^4)^{0.25}$$
$$= (4)^{4\times\frac{1}{4}} = 4^1 = 4$$

Example 2: $(256)^{0.16}\times(4)^{0.36}$ is equal to:

(a) 4 (b) 64
(c) 16 (d) 256.25

Sol. (a) $(256)^{0.16}\times(4)^{0.36} = (4^4)^{0.16}\times(4)^{0.36}$

$$= (4)^{0.64}\times 4^{0.36} = (4)^{0.64+0.36}$$
$$= 4^1 = 4$$

Example 3: If $(125)^{\frac{2}{3}}\times(625)^{\frac{-1}{4}} = 5^x$; then value of x is

(a) 2 (b) 1
(c) 3 (d) 4

Sol. (b) $(125)^{\frac{2}{3}}\times(625)^{\frac{-1}{4}} = 5^x \Rightarrow (5^3)^{\frac{2}{3}}\times(5^4)^{\frac{-1}{4}} = 5^x$

$\Rightarrow$ $5^2\times 5^{-1} = 5^x$

$\Rightarrow$ $5^1 = 5^x$

$\therefore$ $x = 1$

Example 4: The sum of the square of 2 numbers is 146 and the square root of one of them is $\sqrt{5}$. The cube of the other number is:

(a) 1331 (b) 1221
(c) 1111 (d) 1441

Sol. (a) Let a and b be the nos.

According to question,

$$a^2+b^2 = 146$$
$$b^2 = 146-a^2 \quad ...(1)$$

Now, $\sqrt{a} = \sqrt{5}$

$$a^2 = 25 \quad ...(2)$$

Put the value of (2) in (1)

$\therefore$ $b^2 = 146-25$

$b^2 = 121$

So, $b = 11$

$\therefore$ Cube of other no. $= 11^3 = 1331$

Example 5: Find that value of $\sqrt{11.981+7\sqrt{1.2996}}$ is closest to:

(a) 4.9 (b) 4.5
(c) 4.1 (d) 5.1

Sol. (b) $\sqrt{11.981+7\sqrt{1.2996}} = \sqrt{11.981+7\sqrt{(1.14)^2}}$

$$= \sqrt{11.981+7(1.14)}$$
$$= \sqrt{11+0.98+7+0.98+0.001}$$
$$= \sqrt{18+1.96+0.001}$$
$$= \sqrt{19.961}$$

Checking options,

$$(4.5)^2 = 20.25$$

$\therefore$ $\sqrt{19.961}$ is very close to 20.25

Example 6: Simplify:

$$\sqrt{8+\sqrt{57+\sqrt{38+\sqrt{108+\sqrt{169}}}}} = ?$$

(a) 8 (b) 6
(c) 10 (d) 4

Sol. (d) Given, $\sqrt{8+\sqrt{57+\sqrt{38+\sqrt{108+\sqrt{169}}}}}$

$$= \sqrt{8+\sqrt{57+\sqrt{38+\sqrt{108+13}}}}$$
$$= \sqrt{8+\sqrt{57+\sqrt{38+11}}} = \sqrt{8+\sqrt{57+7}}$$
$$= \sqrt{8+8} = \sqrt{16} = 4$$

1 Level Beginner

1. $3\sqrt{1-\frac{127}{343}}$ is equal to: [SSC CGL 2011]
(A) $1-\frac{1}{7}$ (B) $\frac{5}{9}$ (C) $1-\frac{2}{7}$ (D) $\frac{4}{7}$

2. What must be added to the expression $16a^2 - 12a$ to make it a perfect square? [SSC CGL 2013]
(A) $\frac{11}{2}$ (B) $\frac{9}{4}$ (C) $\frac{13}{2}$ (D) 16

3. If $\sqrt[3]{3^n} = 27$, then the value of n is: [SSC CHSL 2012]
(A) 9 (B) 6 (C) 1 (D) 3

4. What is the largest four digit number which is a perfect square? [CAPF ASI & Delhi Police 2017]
(A) 9704 (B) 9999 (C) 9801 (D) 9901

5. Find the value of $\sqrt{30+\sqrt{30+\sqrt{30....\infty}}}$ [SSC CGL 2020]
(A) $3\sqrt{10}$ (B) 6 (C) 7 (D) 5

6. Find the value of $\sqrt{5\sqrt{5\sqrt{5\sqrt{5}}}}$. [SSC CHSL 2018]
(A) $5^{\frac{1}{16}}$ (B) $5^{\frac{15}{32}}$ (C) $5^{\frac{1}{32}}$ (D) $5^{\frac{15}{16}}$

7. If $x=\frac{1}{\sqrt{2}+1}$ then $(x + 1)$ equals to: [SSC CGL 2015]
(A) $\sqrt{2}$ (B) $\sqrt{2}+1$
(C) $\sqrt{2}-1$ (D) 2

8. What is the positive square root of $(19+4\sqrt{21})$? [SSC CGL 2018]
(A) $\sqrt{7}+2\sqrt{3}$ (B) $\sqrt{2}+3\sqrt{7}$
(C) $\sqrt{3}+2\sqrt{7}$ (D) $\sqrt{7}+3\sqrt{3}$

9. If $x^{\frac{1}{4}}+x^{\frac{-1}{4}}=2$, then what is the value of $x^{81}+\frac{1}{x^{81}}$? [SSC CHSL 2017]
(A) 0 (B) –2 (C) 2 (D) 1

10. Among the following numbers $\sqrt{2}, \sqrt[3]{9}, \sqrt[4]{16}, \sqrt[5]{32}$, the greatest one is: [SSC CHSL 2011]
(A) $\sqrt[3]{9}$ (B) $\sqrt{2}$ (C) $\sqrt[5]{32}$ (D) $\sqrt[4]{16}$

11. If $\sqrt{1+\frac{x}{144}}=\frac{13}{12}$, when x equals to: [SSC CGL 2016]
(A) 13 (B) 27 (C) 25 (D) 1

12. If $\sqrt{y}=\sqrt{4}-\sqrt{6}$, then find the value of $(y^2 - 20y + 12)$. [SSC CHSL 2018]
(A) 8 (B) 10 (C) 12 (D) 4

13. Find the value of $\sqrt[3]{\frac{4913}{2197}}$: [SSC CHSL 2018]
(A) $\frac{13}{17}$ (B) $\frac{13}{7}$ (C) $\frac{17}{7}$ (D) $\frac{17}{13}$

14. If $a=7-4\sqrt{3}$, the value of $a^{\frac{1}{2}}+\frac{1}{a^{\frac{1}{2}}}$ is [SSC FCI Assistant 2013]
(A) 4 (B) $3\sqrt{3}$ (C) $2\sqrt{3}$ (D) 7

15. What is the value of $\left[\sqrt{529}+\sqrt{5.29}+\sqrt{0.0529}\right]$? [SSC CHSL 2018]
(A) 25.323 (B) 25.53 (C) 23.253 (D) 23.53

16. What is the value of 'x' if $\sqrt{(2+7x)}=\sqrt{3x+4}$? [SSC CHSL 2018]
(A) 1.5 (B) 1 (C) 2 (D) 0.5

17. Evaluate: $\frac{(12.5)^3+(7.5)^3}{(12.5)^2+(7.5)^2-12.5\times 7.5}$ [SSC CHSL 2020]
(A) 15 (B) 30 (C) 25 (D) 20

18. If $6^{\sqrt[4]{x}}+8^{\sqrt[4]{x}}=10^{\sqrt[4]{x}}$, then the value of x is : [SSC CHSL 2019]
(A) 8 (B) 2 (C) 16 (D) 4

19. If $N=\left(\frac{\sqrt{6}-\sqrt{5}}{\sqrt{6}+\sqrt{5}}\right)$, then what is the value of $\left(N+\frac{1}{N}\right)$? [SSC CAPFs ASI & Delhi Police 2017]
(A) 11 (B) 22 (C) 10 (D) 12

20. If $x=\sqrt{15\sqrt{15\sqrt{15\sqrt{15......\infty}}}}$ and $x > 0$, find the value of $(x^2 + 4)$. [SSC CHSL 2018]
(A) 125 (B) 179 (C) 229 (D) 200

21. If $9\sqrt{x}=\sqrt{12}+\sqrt{147}$, then x = ? [SSC CHSL 2014]
(A) 3 (B) 5 (C) 2 (D) 4

22. What is x, if $x^3 = 1.5^3 - 0.9^3 - 2.43$? [SSC CPO 2016]
(A) –0.5 (B) –1.6 (C) 0.6 (D) –0.7

23. If $x+\sqrt{5}=5+\sqrt{y}$ and x, y are the integers, then the value of $\frac{\sqrt{x}+y}{x+\sqrt{y}}$ is : [SSC CGL Tier-I 2016]
(A) 2 (B) $\sqrt{5}$ (C) 5 (D) 1

24. If $x=(0.25)^{\frac{1}{2}}, y=(0.4)^2, z=(0.216)^{\frac{1}{3}}$, then: [SSC CGL Tier-I 2016]
(A) $x > y > z$ (B) $y > x > z$
(C) $z > x > y$ (D) $x > z > y$

25. If $2+x\sqrt{3}=\frac{1}{2+\sqrt{3}}$, then the simplest value x is : [SSC CGL Tier-I 2015]
(A) 1 (B) –1 (C) –2 (D) 2

2 Level Intermediate

1. If $\sqrt{5329} = 73$, then the value of $\sqrt{5329} + \sqrt{53.29} + \sqrt{0.5329} + \sqrt{0.005329} + \sqrt{0.00005329}$ is: **[SSC CGL Tier-II 2015]**
(A) 81.1003 **(B)** 81.0113
(C) 81.1103 **(D)** 81.1013

2. If x, y are rational numbers and $\frac{5+\sqrt{11}}{3-2\sqrt{11}} = x + y\sqrt{11}$. The value of x, y is: **[SSC GD Constable 2015]**
(A) $x = \frac{-14}{7}, y = \frac{-13}{26}$ **(B)** $x = \frac{9}{13}, y = \frac{11}{17}$
(C) $x = \frac{-37}{35}, y = \frac{-37}{35}$ **(D)** $x = \frac{-37}{35}, x = \frac{-13}{35}$

3. If $x = \sqrt{\frac{2+\sqrt{3}}{2-\sqrt{3}}}$, then what is the value of $(x^2 + x - 9)$? **[SSC CGL Tier-I 2017]**
(A) $3\sqrt{3}$ **(B)** 0 **(C)** $5\sqrt{3}$ **(D)** $3\sqrt{2}$

4. If $x = 5 + 2\sqrt{6}$, then what is the value of $\left(\sqrt{x} + \frac{1}{\sqrt{x}}\right)$? **[SSC CAPFs Exam 2017]**
(A) $2\sqrt{3}$ **(B)** $3\sqrt{2}$ **(C)** $6\sqrt{2}$ **(D)** $2\sqrt{6}$

5. If $5^{\sqrt{3x}} + 12^{\sqrt{3x}} = 13^{\sqrt{3x}}$, then the value of x is: **[SSC CHSL 2019]**
(A) 4 **(B)** 1 **(C)** 8 **(D)** 2

6. The value of $\frac{\sqrt{72} \times \sqrt{363} \times \sqrt{175}}{\sqrt{32} \times \sqrt{147} \times \sqrt{252}}$ is: **[SSC CHSL 2013]**
(A) $\frac{45}{56}$ **(B)** $\frac{45}{28}$ **(C)** $\frac{55}{28}$ **(D)** $\frac{55}{42}$

7. If the numbers $\sqrt[3]{9}, \sqrt[4]{20}, \sqrt[6]{25}$ are arranged is ascending order, then the right arrangement is :
(A) $\sqrt[6]{25}, \sqrt[4]{20}, \sqrt[3]{9}$ **(B)** $\sqrt[3]{4} < \sqrt[4]{20} < \sqrt[6]{5}$
(C) $\sqrt[4]{20} < \sqrt[6]{20} < \sqrt[3]{9}$ **(D)** $\sqrt[6]{25} < \sqrt[3]{9} < \sqrt[4]{20}$

8. If $x = \sqrt{1+\frac{\sqrt{3}}{2}} - \sqrt{1-\frac{\sqrt{3}}{2}}$, then the value of $\frac{\sqrt{3}-x}{\sqrt{3}+x}$, (correct to two decimal places) is: **[SSC CGL Tier-II 2022]**
(A) 0.17 **(B)** 0.25 **(C)** 0.19 **(D)** 0.27

9. Find the value of x is $\sqrt[3]{15625} - \sqrt{x} = 4$. **[SSC CHSL 2020]**
(A) 343 **(B)** 625 **(C)** 81 **(D)** 441

10. If $\sqrt{x} - \sqrt{y} = 1, \sqrt{x} + \sqrt{y} = 17$ then $\sqrt{xy} = ?$ **[SSC CHSL 2016]**
(A) 32 **(B)** $\sqrt{72}$ **(C)** $\sqrt{32}$ **(D)** 72

11. If $P = 7 + 4\sqrt{3}$ and $PQ = 1$ then what is the value of $\frac{1}{P^2} + \frac{1}{Q^2} = ?$ **[SSC CGL 2018]**
(A) 182 **(B)** 196 **(C)** 194 **(D)** 206

12. The value of $\frac{1}{\sqrt{2}+1} + \frac{1}{\sqrt{3}+\sqrt{2}} + \frac{1}{\sqrt{4}+\sqrt{3}} + \ldots + \frac{1}{\sqrt{100}+\sqrt{99}}$ is **[SSC MTS 2011]**
(A) 9 **(B)** $\sqrt{99}$ **(C)** $\sqrt{99} - 1$ **(D)** 1

13. The simplified value of $(\sqrt{6} + \sqrt{10} - \sqrt{21} - \sqrt{35})(\sqrt{6} - \sqrt{10} + \sqrt{21} - \sqrt{35})$ is: **[SSC CPO 2014]**
(A) 10 **(B)** 11 **(C)** 12 **(D)** 13

14. What is the simplified value of $(3 + 1)(3^2 + 1)(3^4 + 1)(3^8 + 1)(3^{16} + 1)$? **[SSC CPO 2017]**
(A) $\frac{(3^{32}-1)}{2}$ **(B)** $\frac{(3^{16}-1)}{2}$
(C) $\frac{(3^{128}-1)}{2}$ **(D)** $\frac{(3^{64}-1)}{2}$

15. What value of 'P' will satisfy the equation?
$\frac{P}{\sqrt{540}} = \frac{\sqrt{240}}{P}$? **[SSC CHSL 2018]**
(A) 10 **(B)** 6
(C) $\sqrt{10}$ **(D)** $6\sqrt{10}$

16. If $N = \frac{(\sqrt{8}+\sqrt{6})}{(\sqrt{8}-\sqrt{6})}$, then what is the value of $N - \frac{1}{N}$? **[SSC CPO 2017]**
(A) 14 **(B)** 7 **(C)** $8\sqrt{3}$ **(D)** 0

17. Let $x = \left(\frac{\sqrt{1875}}{\sqrt{3888}} \div \frac{\sqrt{1200}}{\sqrt{768}}\right) \times \frac{\sqrt{175}}{\sqrt{1792}}$. Then $\sqrt{x}$ is equal to : **[SSC CGL 2020]**
(A) $\frac{4}{9}$ **(B)** $\frac{5}{12}$ **(C)** $\frac{5}{9}$ **(D)** $\frac{7}{12}$

18. The value of $\frac{1}{4-\sqrt{15}} - \frac{1}{\sqrt{15}-\sqrt{14}} + \frac{1}{\sqrt{14}-\sqrt{13}} - \frac{1}{\sqrt{13}-\sqrt{12}} + \frac{1}{\sqrt{12}-\sqrt{11}} - \frac{1}{\sqrt{11}-\sqrt{10}} + \frac{1}{\sqrt{10}-3} - \frac{1}{3-\sqrt{8}}$ **[SSC CGL Tier-II 2022]**
(A) $4 + 2\sqrt{2}$ **(B)** $2 + 2\sqrt{2}$
(C) $4 - 2\sqrt{2}$ **(D)** $2 - 2\sqrt{2}$

19. If $\frac{4}{1+\sqrt{2}+\sqrt{3}} = a + b\sqrt{2} + c\sqrt{3} - d\sqrt{6}$ where a, b, c, d are natural numbers, then the value of $a + b + c + d$ is: [SSC CHSL 2020]

(A) 2 (B) 4 (C) 1 (D) 0

20. If $\sqrt{10-2\sqrt{21}} + \sqrt{8+2\sqrt{15}} = \sqrt{a} + \sqrt{b}$, where a and b are positive integers, then the value of $\sqrt{ab}$ is closest to : [SSC CGL Tier-II 2019]

(A) 5.9 (B) 6.8 (C) 7.2 (D) 4.6

3 Level Expert

1. If $\frac{8+2\sqrt{3}}{3\sqrt{3}+5} = a\sqrt{3} - b$, then the value of $a + b$ is equal to : [SSC CGL Tier-II 2020]

(A) 15 (B) 18 (C) 15 (D) 24

2. What is the value of

$$\sqrt{1+\frac{1}{2^2}+\frac{1}{3^2}} + \sqrt{1+\frac{1}{3^2}+\frac{1}{4^2}} + \sqrt{1+\frac{1}{4^2}+\frac{1}{5^2}} = ?$$

[SSC CPO 2017]

(A) $\frac{4}{3}$ (B) $\frac{7}{3}$ (C) $\frac{33}{10}$ (D) $\frac{18}{5}$

3. If $a = \frac{\sqrt{3}+\sqrt{2}}{\sqrt{3}-\sqrt{2}}$ and $b = \frac{\sqrt{3}-\sqrt{2}}{\sqrt{3}+\sqrt{2}}$, then what is the value of $(a^2 + b^2 - ab)$? [SSC CGL Tier-II 2018]

(A) $(2\sqrt{3})+2$ (B) $(4\sqrt{6})+1$

(C) 98 (D) 97

4. If $2^x = 3^y = 6^{-z}$ then $\left(\frac{1}{x}+\frac{1}{y}+\frac{1}{z}\right)$ is equal to: [SSC CHSL 2011]

(A) $\frac{-1}{2}$ (B) 0

(C) 1 (D) $\frac{3}{2}$

5. If $\frac{1}{4-\sqrt{8}} + \frac{3+2\sqrt{2}}{3-2\sqrt{2}} - \frac{3-2\sqrt{2}}{3+2\sqrt{2}} = a + b\sqrt{2}$, then what is the value of $(3a + 4b)$? [SSC CGL Tier-II 2020]

(A) $98\frac{1}{2}$ (B) 97

(C) 98 (D) $99\frac{1}{2}$

6. The value of $\frac{(0.13)^2+(0.21)^2}{(0.39)^2+81(0.07)^2} \div \frac{(2.4)^4+3\times(11.52)+9}{(2.4)^6+6(2.4)^4+3\times(17.28)}$ lies between: [SSC CPO 2019]

(A) 0.5 and 0.6 (B) 0.7 and 0.8

(C) 0.4 and 0.5 (D) 0.6 and 0.7

7. If $\frac{\sqrt{a+2b}+\sqrt{a-2b}}{\sqrt{a+2b}-\sqrt{a-2b}} = \sqrt{3}$, then $a : b$ is equal to: [SSC CPO 2019]

(A) $4:\sqrt{3}$ (B) $\sqrt{3}:4$

(C) $2:\sqrt{3}$ (D) $\sqrt{3}:2$

8. If $4x = \sqrt{5}+2$, then the value of $\left(x - \frac{1}{16x}\right)$ is: [SSC CPO 2016]

(A) $\sqrt{2}+1$ (B) $\sqrt{2}-1$ (C) 1 (D) $\sqrt{2}$

9. If $\frac{10}{7}(1 - 2.43 \times 10^{-3}) = 1.417 + x$, then x is equal to: [SSC CHSL 2019]

(A) 0.417 (B) 0.0417 (C) 0.81 (D) 0.0081

10. If $3a = 4b = 6c$ and $a + b + c = 27\sqrt{29}$ then $\sqrt{a^2+b^2+c^2}$ is equal to: [SSC CGL Tier-I 2016]

(A) 82 (B) 87 (C) 83 (D) $3\sqrt{29}$

11. The value of $\frac{(243)^{\frac{n}{5}} \times 3^{2n+1}}{9^n \times 3^{n-1}}$ is : [SSC CGL 2014]

(A) 9 (B) 6 (C) 12 (D) 3

12. If $3\sqrt{3}x^3 - 2\sqrt{2}y^3 = (\sqrt{3}x - \sqrt{2}y)(Ax^2 + By^2 + Cxy)$, then the value of $(A \times B) \div C$ [SSC CGL 2019]

(A) $6\sqrt{3}$ (B) $6\sqrt{6}$ (C) $\sqrt{6}$ (D) $\sqrt{3}$

13. The mean of $1^3, 2^3, 3^3, 4^3, 5^3, 6^3, 7^3$ is: [SSC CGL 2015]

(A) 20 (B) 56 (C) 28 (D) 112

14. If $x = \frac{\sqrt{5}-\sqrt{3}}{\sqrt{5}+\sqrt{3}}$, and y is the reciprocal of x, then what is the value of $(x^3 + y^3)$? [SSC CGL Tier-II 2019]

(A) 504 (B) 488

(C) 472 (D) 476

15. Let $x = \sqrt[6]{27} - \sqrt{6\frac{3}{4}}$ and $y = \frac{\sqrt{45}+\sqrt{605}+\sqrt{245}}{\sqrt{80}+\sqrt{125}}$ then the value of $(x^2 + y^2)$ is : [SSC CGL Tier-II 2019]

(A) $\frac{227}{9}$ (B) $\frac{221}{36}$

(C) $\frac{221}{9}$ (D) $\frac{223}{36}$

16. If $\frac{22\sqrt{2}}{4\sqrt{2}-\sqrt{3+\sqrt{5}}} = a+\sqrt{5}b$, with $a, b > 0$ then what is the value of $(ab) : (a + b)$? [SSC CGL Tier-II 2021]
(A) 7 : 4 (B) 4 : 7 (C) 7 : 8 (D) 8 : 7

17. Find the value of $(70^3 + 20^3 - 90^3)$: [SSC CGL Tier-I 2021]
(A) 378000 (B) –378000
(C) 30000 (D) 0

18. If $P^4 = 4354 - \frac{1}{P^4}$, then the value of $\left(P^3 - \frac{1}{P^3}\right)$ can be: [SSC CHSL 2022]
(A) 436 (B) 416 (C) 516 (D) 536

19. If $(a + b + 4)\{ab + 4(a + b)\} - 4ab = 0$, and $a \neq -4$, $b \neq -4$, then, $\left[\frac{1}{(a+b+4)^{117}} - 2^{-234}\right]$ is equal to: [SSC CHSL 2019]
(A) 0 (B) $\frac{1}{-2^{234}}$ (C) $\frac{1}{2^{117}}$ (D) $\frac{1}{4^{117}}$

20. If $\sqrt{x}+\frac{1}{\sqrt{x}}=3$, then the value of $x^3+\frac{1}{x^3}$ is: [SSC CGL Tier-II 2020]
(A) 324 (B) 322 (C) 326 (D) 422

ANSWER KEY

Level-1: Beginner

1.	(A)	2.	(B)	3.	(A)	4.	(C)	5.	(B)	6.	(D)	7.	(A)	8.	(A)	9.	(C)	10.	(A)
11.	(C)	12.	(A)	13.	(D)	14.	(A)	15.	(B)	16.	(D)	17.	(D)	18.	(C)	19.	(B)	20.	(C)
21.	(A)	22.	(C)	23.	(D)	24.	(C)	25.	(B)										

Level-2: Intermediate

1.	(C)	2.	(D)	3.	(C)	4.	(A)	5.	(C)	6.	(C)	7.	(D)	8.	(D)	9.	(D)	10.	(D)
11.	(C)	12.	(A)	13.	(A)	14.	(A)	15.	(D)	16.	(C)	17.	(B)	18.	(C)	19.	(B)	20.	(A)

Level-3: Expert

1.	(B)	2.	(C)	3.	(D)	4.	(B)	5.	(A)	6.	(D)	7.	(A)	8.	(C)	9.	(D)	10.	(B)
11.	(A)	12.	(C)	13.	(D)	14.	(B)	15.	(D)	16.	(C)	17.	(B)	18.	(D)	19.	(A)	20.	(B)

Solutions with Detailed Explanations

Level-1: BEGINNER

1. **Option (A) is correct.**

Explanation:

Given, $\sqrt[3]{1-\frac{127}{343}} = \sqrt[3]{\frac{343-127}{343}}$

$= \sqrt[3]{\frac{216}{343}}$

$= \frac{6}{7}$ [$\because 6^3 = 216$, $7^3 = 343$]

i.e., $1-\frac{1}{7}$

2. **Option (B) is correct.**

Explanation:

Given, $16a^2 - 12a$

Using, $a^2 + b^2 - 2ab = (a - b)^2$ ...(1)

Clearly, $16a^2 - 12a = (4a)^2 - 2\times 4a \times \frac{3}{2}$ ...(2)

Now on comparing (1) and (2)

On adding $\left(\frac{3}{2}\right)^2$, the expression become a perfect square.

$\therefore \left(\frac{3}{2}\right)^2 = \frac{9}{4}$

3. **Option (A) is correct.**

Explanation:

Given, $\sqrt[3]{3^n} = 27$

$(3^n)^{\frac{1}{3}} = 27$ [$27 = 3^3$]

$(3)^{\frac{n}{3}} = 27$

$$(3)^{\frac{n}{3}} = 3^3$$

$$\frac{n}{3} = 3 \qquad [\because \text{ if } a^m = a^n \text{ then } m = n]$$

$$n = 9$$

4. Option (C) is correct.

Explanation: We know, largest 4-digit no = 9999

Now,

+9	
9	9999
	81
189	1899
9	1701
	198

$\therefore \quad 9999 - 198 = 9801 \rightarrow$ Required 4-digit number

5. Option (B) is correct.

Explanation: $\sqrt{30+\sqrt{30+\sqrt{30.......}}}$

Step 1: Co-prime factors of 30 = $n\,(n + 1)$

i.e., $5(5 + 1) = 5 \times 6$

Step 2: We know

$$\sqrt{x+\sqrt{x+\sqrt{x.....}}} = n+1 = 6.$$

6. Option (D) is correct.

Explanation: Given, $\sqrt{5\sqrt{5\sqrt{5\sqrt{5}}}}$

Using, $\sqrt{a\sqrt{a\sqrt{a\sqrt{a.....n}}}} = a^{\left(1-\frac{1}{2^n}\right)}$, n = no. of terms

$$\therefore \quad \sqrt{5\sqrt{5\sqrt{5\sqrt{5}}}} = 5^{\left(1-\frac{1}{2^4}\right)} = 5^{\left(1-\frac{1}{16}\right)} = 5^{\left(\frac{15}{16}\right)}$$

7. Option (A) is correct.

Explanation:

Given, $x = \dfrac{1}{\sqrt{2}+1}$

After rationalising

$$x = \frac{1}{\sqrt{2}+1} \times \frac{\sqrt{2}-1}{\sqrt{2}-1}$$

$$= \frac{\sqrt{2}-1}{2-1} = \sqrt{2}-1$$

$\therefore$ Required value, $(x + 1) = \sqrt{2}-1+1 = \sqrt{2}$

8. Option (A) is correct.

Explanation: Given, $19+4\sqrt{21}$

$$\text{Square root} = \sqrt{19+4\sqrt{21}} = \sqrt{7+12+4\times\sqrt{21}}$$

$$= \sqrt{(\sqrt{7})^2+(2\sqrt{3})^2+2\times\sqrt{7}\times 2\sqrt{3}}$$

$[\because (a + b)^2 = a^2 + b^2 + 2ab]$

$$= \sqrt{(\sqrt{7}+2\sqrt{3})^2} = \sqrt{7}+2\sqrt{3}$$

9. Option (C) is correct.

Explanation:

Given, $x^{\frac{1}{4}} + x^{\frac{-1}{4}} = 2$

$$\therefore \quad x^{\frac{1}{4}} + \frac{1}{x^{\frac{1}{4}}} = 2$$

So, $x^{81} + \dfrac{1}{x^{81}} = 1+\dfrac{1}{1} = 2 \qquad [\because \text{ if } x+\frac{1}{x}=2$ then $x = 1]$

10. Option (A) is correct.

Explanation: Given number:

$\sqrt{2}, \sqrt[3]{9}, \sqrt[4]{16}, \sqrt[5]{32}$

$\Rightarrow \quad (2)^{1/2}, (3)^{2/3}, (2)^{4/4}, (2)^{5/5}$

$\Rightarrow \quad 2^{1/2}, 3^{2/3}, 2^1, 2^1$

Multiply all powers by 6

$\Rightarrow \quad 2^{1/2 \times 6}, 3^{2/3 \times 6}, 2^{1 \times 6}, 2^{1 \times 6}$

$\Rightarrow \quad 2^3, 3^4, 2^6, 2^6$

$\Rightarrow \quad 8, 81, 64, 64$

So, 81 is largest number.

or $\sqrt[3]{9}$ is largest in given numbers.

So, option (A) is correct.

11. Option (C) is correct.

Explanation: Given,

$$\sqrt{1+\frac{x}{144}} = \frac{13}{12}$$

Squaring both sides

$$1+\frac{x}{144} = \left(\frac{13}{12}\right)^2$$

$$\frac{x}{144} = \frac{169}{144}-1$$

$$x = 25$$

12. Option (A) is correct.

Explanation: Expression,

$$\sqrt{y} = \sqrt{4}-\sqrt{6}$$

Squaring both sides,

$$y = 4+6-2\sqrt{24} = 10-2\sqrt{24}$$

Now, $y^2 - 20y + 12 = y^2 - 2 \times y \times 10 + 100 - 88$

$= (y - 10)^2 - 88$

$= (10-2\sqrt{24}-10)^2 - 88$

$= 4 \times 24 - 88$

$= 96 - 88 = 8.$

13. Option (D) is correct.

Explanation: Given, $\sqrt[3]{\dfrac{4913}{2197}}$

Now, $\dfrac{\sqrt[3]{4917}}{\sqrt[3]{2197}} = \sqrt[3]{\dfrac{17\times17\times17}{13\times13\times13}} = \dfrac{17}{13}$

14. Option (A) is correct.

Explanation:

Given, $a = 7-4\sqrt{3}$

$$\frac{1}{a} = \frac{1}{7-4\sqrt{3}} \times \frac{7+4\sqrt{3}}{7+4\sqrt{3}} = 7+4\sqrt{3}$$

Now using

$$\left(\sqrt{a}+\frac{1}{\sqrt{a}}\right)^2 = a+\frac{1}{a}+2$$

$$= 7-4\sqrt{3}+7+4\sqrt{3}+2 = 16$$

$$\sqrt{a}+\frac{1}{\sqrt{a}} = 4$$

15. Option (B) is correct.

Explanation: $\sqrt{529}+\sqrt{5.29}+\sqrt{0.0529}$

= 23 + 2.3 + 0.23 = 25.53

16. Option (D) is correct.

Explanation:

$$\sqrt{2+7x} = \sqrt{3x+4}$$

On squaring both sides:

$$2 + 7x = 3x + 4$$

$$7x - 3x = 2$$

$$x = \frac{2}{4} = \frac{1}{2} = 0.5$$

17. Option (D) is correct.

Explanation: We know,

$$\frac{a^3+b^3}{a^2+b^2-ab} = \frac{(a+b)(a^2+b^2-ab)}{a^2+b^2-ab}$$

$$= (a + b) \quad ...(1)$$

In given expression, $a = 12.5$, $b = 7.5$

$$\frac{(12.5)^3+(7.5)^3}{(12.5)^2+(7.5)^2-12.5\times 7.5} = \frac{a^3+b^3}{a^2+b^2-ab}$$

$$= a + b$$

$$= 12.5 + 7.5 = 20$$

18. Option (C) is correct.

Explanation: Given, $6^{\sqrt[4]{x}}+8^{\sqrt[4]{x}} = 10^{\sqrt[4]{x}}$

We know, 6, 8, 10 is a triplet

$$\therefore \quad \sqrt[4]{x} = 2$$

$$x^{\frac{1}{4}} = 2$$

$$\left(x^{\frac{1}{4}}\right)^4 = 2^4$$

$$x = 16$$

19. Option (B) is correct.

Explanation:

Given, $N = \dfrac{\sqrt{6}-\sqrt{5}}{\sqrt{6}+\sqrt{5}}$

After rationalisation

$$= \frac{\sqrt{6}-\sqrt{5}}{\sqrt{6}+\sqrt{5}} \times \frac{\sqrt{6}-\sqrt{5}}{\sqrt{6}-\sqrt{5}}$$

$$= \frac{(\sqrt{6}-\sqrt{5})^2}{(\sqrt{6})^2-(\sqrt{5})^2}$$

$$= \frac{6+5-2\sqrt{30}}{6-5} = 11-2\sqrt{30}$$

$$\therefore \quad \frac{1}{N} = 11+2\sqrt{30}$$

$$\therefore \quad N+\frac{1}{N} = 11\text{-}2\sqrt{30}+11+2\sqrt{30} = 22$$

20. Option (C) is correct.

Explanation:

Given $x = \sqrt{15\sqrt{15\sqrt{15\sqrt{15...\infty}}}}$

$x = 15$ [$\because$ When $x = \sqrt{x\sqrt{x\sqrt{x}...\infty}}$ then $x = n$]

Now, $x^2 + 4 = (15)^2 + 4 = 225 + 4 = 229$

21. Option (A) is correct.

Explanation:

Given, $9\sqrt{x} = \sqrt{12}+\sqrt{147}$

Write above expression in its simplest form

$$\therefore \quad 9\sqrt{x} = 2\sqrt{3}+7\sqrt{3}$$

$$9\sqrt{x} = \sqrt{3}(2+7)$$

$$9\sqrt{x} = \sqrt{3}(9)$$

$$\therefore \quad x = 3$$

22. Option (C) is correct.

Explanation:

Given, $x^3 = 1.5^3 - 0.9^3 - 2.43$

Using, $(a-b)^3 = a^3 - b^3 - 3ab(a-b)$

$= (1.5)^3 - (0.9)^3 - 3 \times 1.5 \times 0.9\,(1.5 - 0.9)$

$= (1.5 - 0.9)^3 = (0.6)^3$

$\therefore \quad x = 0.6$

23. Option (D) is correct.

Explanation:

Given, $x+\sqrt{5} = 5+\sqrt{y}$

on comparing both side of above equation,

$$x = 5, y = 5$$

$$\therefore \quad \frac{\sqrt{x}+y}{x+\sqrt{y}} = \frac{\sqrt{5}+5}{5+\sqrt{5}} = 1$$

24. Option (C) is correct.

Explanation: Solve each variable:

$$\therefore \quad x = (0.25)^{\frac{1}{2}} = 0.5$$

$$y = (0.4)^2 = 0.16$$

$$z = (0.216)^{\frac{1}{3}} = (0.6^3)^{\frac{1}{3}} = 0.6$$

$\therefore$ Clearly $z > x > y$

25. Option (B) is correct.

Explanation:

Given, $2+x\sqrt{3} = \frac{1}{2+\sqrt{3}}$

On rationalising $= \frac{1}{2+\sqrt{3}} \times \frac{2-\sqrt{3}}{2-\sqrt{3}}$

$\Rightarrow \quad 2+x\sqrt{3} = 2-\sqrt{3}$

$x\sqrt{3} = -\sqrt{3}$

$x = -1$

Level-2: INTERMEDIATE

1. Option (C) is correct.

Explanation:

Given, $\sqrt{5329} = 73$

$\sqrt{53.29} = 7.3$

$\sqrt{0.5329} = 0.73$

$\sqrt{0.005329} = 0.073$

$\sqrt{0.00005329} = 0.0073$

$\therefore \sqrt{5329} + \sqrt{53.29} + \sqrt{0.5329} + \sqrt{0.005329} + \sqrt{0.00005329}$

$= 73 + 7.3 + 0.73 + 0.073 + 0.0073$

$= 81.1103$

2. Option (D) is correct.

Explanation:

Given, $\frac{5+\sqrt{11}}{3-2\sqrt{11}} = x+y\sqrt{11}$

On rationalising:

$\Rightarrow -\left(\frac{5+\sqrt{11}}{2\sqrt{11}-3}\right)\times\left(\frac{2\sqrt{11}+3}{2\sqrt{11}+3}\right) = x+y\sqrt{11}$

$\Rightarrow \frac{-(15+10\sqrt{11}+3\sqrt{11}+22)}{44-9} = x+y\sqrt{11}$

$\Rightarrow -\left(\frac{+37+13\sqrt{11}}{35}\right) = x+y\sqrt{11}$

$\Rightarrow \frac{-37}{35}-\frac{13}{35}\sqrt{11} = x+y\sqrt{11}$

$x = \frac{-37}{35}, y = \frac{-13}{35}$

3. Option (C) is correct.

Explanation:

Given, $x = \sqrt{\frac{2+\sqrt{3}}{2-\sqrt{3}}}$

Squaring both sides

$x^2 = \frac{2+\sqrt{3}}{2-\sqrt{3}}$

Now, on rationalising above equation

$x^2 = \frac{2+\sqrt{3}}{2-\sqrt{3}} \times \frac{2+\sqrt{3}}{2+\sqrt{3}}$

$x^2 = \frac{(2+\sqrt{3})^2}{4-3}$

$x^2 = 4+3+4\sqrt{3}$

$\therefore \quad x = \sqrt{4+3+2\times 2\times\sqrt{3}}$

$x = \sqrt{(2+\sqrt{3})^2}$

$x = 2+\sqrt{3}$

Now, $x^2 + x - 9 = 7+4\sqrt{3}+2+\sqrt{3}-9 = 5\sqrt{3}$

4. Option (A) is correct.

Explanation:

Given, $x = 5+2\sqrt{6}$ ...(1)

$\frac{1}{x} = \frac{1}{5+2\sqrt{6}}$

$= \frac{5-2\sqrt{6}}{5-2\sqrt{6}} \times \frac{1}{5+2\sqrt{6}}$

$= \frac{5-2\sqrt{6}}{(5+2\sqrt{6})(5-2\sqrt{6})}$

$= \frac{5-2\sqrt{6}}{25-24}$

$\frac{1}{x} = 5-2\sqrt{6}$ ...(2)

Now, $\left(\sqrt{x}+\frac{1}{\sqrt{x}}\right)^2 = x+\frac{1}{x}+2$ ...(3)

Putting values from eq. (1) and (2) in eq. (3),

$= 5+2\sqrt{6}+5-2\sqrt{6}+2$

So, $\left(\sqrt{x}+\frac{1}{\sqrt{x}}\right)^2 = 12$

$\therefore \quad \sqrt{x}+\frac{1}{\sqrt{x}} = \sqrt{12} = 2\sqrt{3}$

5. Option (C) is correct.

Explanation: Given, $5^{\sqrt[3]{x}} + 12^{\sqrt[3]{x}} = 13^{\sqrt[3]{x}}$

Using triplet,

$5^2 + 12^2 = 13^2$

$\therefore \quad \sqrt[3]{x} = 2$

Now, $x^{\frac{1}{3}} = 2$

$\Rightarrow \quad \left(x^{\frac{1}{3}}\right)^3 = 2^3$

$\Rightarrow \quad x = 8$

6. Option (C) is correct.

Explanation: Given, $\frac{\sqrt{72}\times\sqrt{363}\times\sqrt{175}}{\sqrt{32}\times\sqrt{147}\times\sqrt{252}}$

$= \frac{\sqrt{2\times2\times2\times3\times3}\times\sqrt{3\times11\times11}\times\sqrt{5\times5\times7}}{\sqrt{2\times2\times2\times2\times2}\times\sqrt{7\times7\times3}\times\sqrt{2\times2\times3\times3\times7}}$

$$= \frac{6\sqrt{2} \times 11\sqrt{3} \times 5\sqrt{7}}{4\sqrt{2} \times 7\sqrt{3} \times 6\sqrt{7}}$$

$$= \frac{6 \times 11 \times 5}{4 \times 7 \times 6} = \frac{55}{28}$$

7. **Option (D) is correct.**

Explanation: In this type of question, always make each surd of same order.

$\therefore$ LCM of 3, 4 and 6 = 12

$$\therefore \quad \sqrt[3]{9} = 9^{\frac{1}{3}}, (9)^{\frac{4}{12}} = (9^4)^{\frac{1}{12}} = \sqrt[12]{9^4}$$

$$= \sqrt[12]{6561}$$

$$\sqrt[4]{20} = \sqrt[12]{20^3} = \sqrt[12]{8000}$$

$$\sqrt[6]{25} = \sqrt[12]{25^2} = \sqrt[12]{625}$$

So, $\sqrt[12]{625} < \sqrt[12]{6561} < \sqrt[12]{8000}$

$\therefore \sqrt[6]{25} < \sqrt[3]{9} < \sqrt[4]{20}$

8. **Option (D) is correct.**

Explanation: Given,

$$x = \sqrt{1+\frac{\sqrt{3}}{2}} - \sqrt{1-\frac{\sqrt{3}}{2}}$$

$$= \sqrt{\frac{2+\sqrt{3}}{2}} - \sqrt{\frac{2-\sqrt{3}}{2}}$$

Now, multiply numerator and denominator by $\sqrt{2}$

$$= \sqrt{\frac{4+2\sqrt{3}}{4}} - \sqrt{\frac{4-2\sqrt{3}}{4}}$$

$$= \sqrt{\frac{3+1+2\sqrt{3}}{4}} - \sqrt{\frac{3+1-2\sqrt{3}}{4}}$$

$$= \frac{\sqrt{(\sqrt{3})^2 + 2\times\sqrt{3}\times 1 + (1)^2}}{2} - \frac{\sqrt{(\sqrt{3})^2 + (1)^2 - 2\times\sqrt{3}\times 1}}{2}$$

$$= \sqrt{\frac{(\sqrt{3}+1)^2}{2}} - \sqrt{\frac{(\sqrt{3}-1)^2}{2}} = \frac{\sqrt{3}+1-\sqrt{3}+1}{2}$$

$$\therefore \quad x = 1$$

Now, $$\frac{\sqrt{3}-x}{\sqrt{3}+x} = \frac{\sqrt{3}-x}{\sqrt{3}+x} \times \frac{\sqrt{3}-x}{\sqrt{3}-x}$$

$$= \frac{4-2\sqrt{3}}{2}$$

$$= 2-\sqrt{3} = 2-1.732$$

$$= 0.268 \approx 0.27$$

9. **Option (D) is correct.**

Explanation: Expression, $\sqrt[3]{15625} - \sqrt{x} = 4$

$$25 - \sqrt{x} = 4$$

$$25 - 4 = \sqrt{x}$$

$$21 = \sqrt{x}$$

$$(21)^2 = x$$

$$441 = x$$

10. **Option (D) is correct.**

Explanation:

Given, $\sqrt{x} - \sqrt{y} = 1$

$$\sqrt{x} + \sqrt{y} = 17$$

$$\therefore (\sqrt{x}+\sqrt{y})^2 - (\sqrt{x}-\sqrt{y})^2 = 4\sqrt{xy}$$

$$17^2 - 1 = 4\sqrt{xy}$$

$$289 - 1 = 4\sqrt{xy}$$

$$288 = 4\sqrt{xy}$$

$$\frac{288}{4} = \sqrt{xy}$$

$$72 = \sqrt{xy}$$

11. **Option (C) is correct.**

Explanation:

Given, $P = 7 + 4\sqrt{3}$

$$PQ = 1$$

$$\therefore \quad Q = \frac{1}{P} = \frac{1}{7+4\sqrt{3}}$$

$$= \frac{1}{7+4\sqrt{3}} \times \frac{7-4\sqrt{3}}{(7-4\sqrt{3})}$$

$$= \frac{7-4\sqrt{3}}{(7+4\sqrt{3})(7-4\sqrt{3})}$$

$$= \frac{7-4\sqrt{3}}{49-48} = 7-4\sqrt{3}$$

$$\therefore \quad \frac{1}{P} = 7-4\sqrt{3}$$

$$\therefore \quad \frac{1}{Q} = \frac{1}{7-4\sqrt{3}}$$

$$= \frac{1}{7-4\sqrt{3}} \times \frac{7+4\sqrt{3}}{7+4\sqrt{3}}$$

$$= \frac{7+4\sqrt{3}}{(7-4\sqrt{3})(7+4\sqrt{3})}$$

$$\frac{1}{Q} = 7+4\sqrt{3}$$

$$\therefore \quad \frac{1}{P^2} + \frac{1}{Q^2} = (7-4\sqrt{3})^2 + (7+4\sqrt{3})^2$$

$$= 2\left[(7)^2 + (4\sqrt{3})^2\right]$$

$$= 2(49 + 48) = 2 \times 97 = 194$$

12. **Option (A) is correct.**

Explanation:

Expression,

$$\frac{1}{\sqrt{2}+1} + \frac{1}{\sqrt{3}+\sqrt{2}} + \frac{1}{\sqrt{4}+\sqrt{3}} + \ldots + \frac{1}{\sqrt{100}+\sqrt{99}}$$

After rationalisation,

$$= \sqrt{2} - 1 + \sqrt{3} - \sqrt{2} + \sqrt{4} - \sqrt{3} + \ldots + \sqrt{99} - \sqrt{98} + \sqrt{100} - \sqrt{99}$$

$$= \sqrt{100} - 1 = 10 - 1 = 9$$

13. Option (A) is correct.

Explanation: Given,

$(\sqrt{6}+\sqrt{10}-\sqrt{21}-\sqrt{35})(\sqrt{6}-\sqrt{10}+\sqrt{21}-\sqrt{35})$

Now,

$= [(\sqrt{6}-\sqrt{35})+(\sqrt{10}-\sqrt{21})]\{(\sqrt{6}-\sqrt{35})-(\sqrt{10}-\sqrt{21})\}$

$= (\sqrt{6}-\sqrt{35})^2-(\sqrt{10}-\sqrt{21})^2$

$= (6+35-2\sqrt{210})-(10+21-2\sqrt{210})$

$= 41-2\sqrt{210}-31+2\sqrt{210}$

$= 41 - 31 = 10$

14. Option (A) is correct.

Explanation: Given,

$(3 + 1)(3^2 + 1)(3^4 + 1)(3^8 + 1)(3^{16} + 1)$

Multiply and divide by (3 – 1):

$$= \frac{(3-1)(3+1)(3^2+1)(3^4+1)(3^8+1)(3^{16}+1)}{(3-1)}$$

$$= \frac{(3^2-1)(3^2+1)(3^4+1)(3^8+1)(3^{16}+1)}{2}$$

$$= \frac{(3^8-1)(3^8+1)(3^{16}+1)}{2}$$

$$\frac{(3^{16}-1)(3^{16}+1)}{2} \Rightarrow \frac{3^{32}-1}{2}$$

15. Option (D) is correct.

Explanation: Expression

$$\frac{P}{\sqrt{540}} = \frac{\sqrt{240}}{P}$$

Now,

$$P^2 = \sqrt{540}\times\sqrt{240}$$

$$P^2 = \sqrt{2\times3\times3\times3}\times\sqrt{10}\times\sqrt{2\times2\times2\times3}\times\sqrt{10}$$

$$P^2 = 2\times2\times3\times3\times10$$

$$\therefore \quad P = \sqrt{2\times2\times3\times3\times10}$$

$$= 2\times3\times\sqrt{10} = 6\sqrt{10}$$

16. Option (C) is correct.

Explanation: Expression,

$$N = \frac{\sqrt{8}+\sqrt{6}}{\sqrt{8}-\sqrt{6}}$$

$$N = \frac{\sqrt{8}+\sqrt{6}}{\sqrt{8}-\sqrt{6}}\times\frac{\sqrt{8}+\sqrt{6}}{\sqrt{8}+\sqrt{6}}$$

$$= \frac{8+6+2\sqrt{48}}{8-6} = \frac{14+2\times4\sqrt{3}}{2}$$

$$= \frac{2(7+4\sqrt{3})}{2} = 7+4\sqrt{3}$$

So, $\frac{1}{N} = 7-4\sqrt{3}$

Now, $N-\frac{1}{N} = (7+4\sqrt{3})-(7-4\sqrt{3})$

$$= 7+4\sqrt{3}-7+4\sqrt{3} = 8\sqrt{3}$$

17. Option (B) is correct.

Explanation: Given,

$$x = \left(\frac{\sqrt{1875}}{\sqrt{3888}}\div\frac{\sqrt{1200}}{\sqrt{768}}\right)\times\frac{\sqrt{175}}{\sqrt{1792}}$$

$$= \frac{\sqrt{1875}}{\sqrt{3888}}\times\frac{\sqrt{768}}{\sqrt{1200}}\times\frac{\sqrt{175}}{1792}$$

$$= \frac{\sqrt{5\times5\times5\times5\times3}\times\sqrt{16\times16\times3}\times\sqrt{5\times5\times7}}{\sqrt{2\times2\times2\times2\times9\times9\times3}\times\sqrt{2\times2\times3\times10\times10}\times\sqrt{8\times8\times7\times4}}$$

$$= \frac{25\sqrt{3}\times16\sqrt{3}\times5\sqrt{7}}{36\sqrt{3}\times20\sqrt{3}\times16\sqrt{7}}$$

$$x = \frac{25}{36\times4}$$

$$\therefore \quad \sqrt{x} = \sqrt{\frac{25}{36\times4}}$$

$$\sqrt{x} = \sqrt{\frac{25}{144}}$$

$$\sqrt{x} = \frac{5}{12}$$

18. Option (C) is correct.

Explanation: $\frac{1}{4-\sqrt{15}}$

Rationalising the denominator:

$$= \frac{1}{4-\sqrt{15}}\times\frac{4+\sqrt{15}}{4+\sqrt{15}} = 4+\sqrt{15}$$

Likewise, after rationalising each expression we get:

$= (4+\sqrt{15})-(\sqrt{15}+\sqrt{14})+(\sqrt{14}+\sqrt{13})-(\sqrt{13}+\sqrt{12})+$
$(\sqrt{12}+\sqrt{11})-(\sqrt{11}+\sqrt{10})+(\sqrt{10}+3)-(3+\sqrt{8})$

$= 4+\sqrt{15}-\sqrt{15}-\sqrt{14}+\sqrt{14}+\sqrt{13}-\sqrt{13}-\sqrt{12}+$
$\sqrt{12}+\sqrt{11}-\sqrt{11}-\sqrt{10}+\sqrt{10}+3-3-\sqrt{8}$

$= 4-\sqrt{8} = 4-2\sqrt{2}$

19. Option (B) is correct.

Explanation:

$$\frac{4}{1+\sqrt{2}+\sqrt{3}} = a+b\sqrt{2}+c\sqrt{3}-d\sqrt{6}$$

Taking left side expression and rationalising

$$\frac{4}{(1+\sqrt{2})+\sqrt{3}}\times\frac{((1+\sqrt{2})-\sqrt{3})}{((1+\sqrt{2})-\sqrt{3})}$$

$$= \frac{4(1+\sqrt{2}-\sqrt{3})}{\{(1+\sqrt{2})+\sqrt{3}\}\{(1+\sqrt{2})-\sqrt{3}\}}$$

$$= \frac{4(1+\sqrt{2}-\sqrt{3})}{(1+\sqrt{2})^2-(\sqrt{3})^2} = \frac{4(1+\sqrt{2}-\sqrt{3})}{1+2+2\sqrt{2}-3}$$

$$= \frac{4(1+\sqrt{2}-\sqrt{3})}{2\sqrt{2}}\times\frac{\sqrt{2}}{\sqrt{2}} = \frac{4\sqrt{2}(1+\sqrt{2}-\sqrt{3})}{4}$$

$$= \sqrt{2}(1+\sqrt{2}-\sqrt{3}) = \sqrt{2}+2-\sqrt{6}$$

$$\therefore \quad 2+\sqrt{2}-\sqrt{6} = a+b\sqrt{2}+c\sqrt{3}-d\sqrt{6}$$

On comparing the corresponding coefficients

$a = 2, b = 1, c = 0, d = 1$

$\therefore \quad a + b + c + d = 2 + 1 + 1 = 4$

20. Option (A) is correct.

Explanation:

$$\sqrt{10-2\sqrt{21}}+\sqrt{8+2\sqrt{15}} = \sqrt{a}+\sqrt{b}$$

On comparing,

$$\sqrt{10-2\sqrt{21}} = \sqrt{a}$$

$$\sqrt{10-2\times\sqrt{7}\times\sqrt{3}} = \sqrt{a}$$

$$\sqrt{7+3-2\sqrt{7}\times\sqrt{3}} = \sqrt{a}$$

$$\Rightarrow \sqrt{(\sqrt{7}-\sqrt{3})^2} = \sqrt{a}$$

$$\sqrt{7}-\sqrt{3} = \sqrt{a} \quad ...(1)$$

Likewise,

$$\sqrt{8+2\sqrt{15}} = \sqrt{b}$$

$$\sqrt{5}+\sqrt{3} = \sqrt{b}$$

$$\therefore \quad \sqrt{a}+\sqrt{b} = \sqrt{7}-\sqrt{3}+\sqrt{5}+\sqrt{3}$$

$$= \sqrt{7}+\sqrt{5}$$

Squaring both sides

$$a+b+2\sqrt{ab} = 7+5+2\sqrt{7\times5}$$

$$= 12+2\sqrt{35}$$

So, $\sqrt{ab} = \sqrt{35} = 5.9$

Level-3: EXPERT

1. Option (B) is correct.

Explanation:

$$\frac{8+2\sqrt{3}}{3\sqrt{3}+5} = a\sqrt{3}-b$$

$$8+2\sqrt{3} = (3\sqrt{3}+5)(a\sqrt{3}-b)$$

$$8+2\sqrt{3} = 9a+5a\sqrt{3}-3b\sqrt{3}-5b$$

$$8+2\sqrt{3} = (9a-5b)+(5a-3b)\sqrt{3}$$

On comparing both sides

$$9a-5b = 8 \quad ...(1)$$

$$5a-3b = 2 \quad ...(2)$$

After solving eq. (1) and (2)

We get, $a = 7, b = 11$

$\therefore \quad a + b = 7 + 11 = 18$

2. Option (C) is correct.

Explanation: Expession given,

$$\sqrt{1+\frac{1}{2^2}+\frac{1}{3^2}}+\sqrt{1+\frac{1}{3^2}+\frac{1}{4^2}}+\sqrt{1+\frac{1}{4^2}+\frac{1}{5^2}}$$

$$\because \sqrt{1+\frac{1}{n^2}+\frac{1}{(n+1)^2}} = \frac{n(n+1)+1}{n(n+1)}$$

So,

$$= \frac{2\times3+1}{2\times3}+\frac{3\times4+1}{3\times4}+\frac{4\times5+1}{3\times4}$$

$$= \frac{7}{6}+\frac{13}{12}+\frac{21}{20}$$

$$= (1+1+1)+\left(\frac{1}{6}+\frac{1}{12}+\frac{1}{20}\right)$$

$$= 3+\left(\frac{10+5+3}{60}\right)$$

$$= 3+\frac{18}{60} = \frac{33}{10}$$

3. Option (D) is correct.

Explanation:

Given, $a = \dfrac{\sqrt{3}+\sqrt{2}}{\sqrt{3}-\sqrt{2}}$

Rationalisation the denominator

$$= \frac{\sqrt{3}+\sqrt{2}}{\sqrt{3}-\sqrt{2}}\times\frac{\sqrt{3}+\sqrt{2}}{\sqrt{3}+\sqrt{2}}$$

$$= \frac{3+2+2\sqrt{6}}{3-2} = 5+2\sqrt{6}$$

$$a = 5+2\sqrt{6} \quad ...(1)$$

Similarly, $b = \dfrac{\sqrt{3}-\sqrt{2}}{\sqrt{3}+\sqrt{2}}$

After rationalisation

$$b = 5-2\sqrt{6}$$

$$\therefore \quad a-b = (5+2\sqrt{6})-(5-2\sqrt{6}) = 4\sqrt{6}$$

Also $ab = (5+2\sqrt{6})(5-2\sqrt{6})$

$$= (5)^2-(2\sqrt{6})^2$$

$$= 25 - 24 = 1.$$

We know,

$$a^2 + b^2 - ab = (a - b)^2 + ab$$

$$= (4\sqrt{6})^2+1 = 96 + 1 = 97$$

4. Option (B) is correct.

Explanation:

Let, $2^x = 3^y = 6^{-z} = k$

$\therefore \quad 2 = k^{\frac{1}{x}},$

$3 = k^{\frac{1}{y}},$

and $6 = k^{-\frac{1}{z}}$

Now, $k^{\frac{1}{x}}\times k^{\frac{1}{y}} = k^{\frac{-1}{z}} \quad [\because 2\times3 = 6]$

$$k^{\frac{1}{x}+\frac{1}{y}} = k^{\frac{-1}{z}}$$

$$\frac{1}{x}+\frac{1}{y} = \frac{-1}{z}$$

$$\therefore \quad \frac{1}{x}+\frac{1}{y}+\frac{1}{z} = 0$$

5. **Option (A) is correct.**
Explanation: Expression

$$\frac{1}{4-\sqrt{8}}+\frac{3+2\sqrt{2}}{3-2\sqrt{2}}-\frac{3-2\sqrt{2}}{3+2\sqrt{2}} = a+b\sqrt{2}$$

Solving it further

$$\frac{1}{4-2\sqrt{2}}+\frac{(3+2\sqrt{2})^2-(3-2\sqrt{2})^2}{3^2-(2\sqrt{2})^2} = a+b\sqrt{2}$$

$$\frac{1}{4-2\sqrt{2}}+\frac{4\times3\times2\sqrt{2}}{1} = a+b\sqrt{2}$$

$[\because (a+b)^2-(a-b)^2 = 4ab]$

$$\frac{1}{4-2\sqrt{2}}\times\frac{4+2\sqrt{2}}{4+2\sqrt{2}}+24\sqrt{2} = a+b\sqrt{2}$$

$$\frac{4+2\sqrt{2}}{8}+24\sqrt{2} = a+b\sqrt{2}$$

$$\frac{1}{2}+\frac{97\sqrt{2}}{4} = a+b\sqrt{2}$$

$$\therefore \quad a = \frac{1}{2}, b = \frac{97}{4}$$

So, $3a+4b = \frac{3}{2}+97 = \frac{3+194}{2}$

$$= \frac{197}{2} = 98\frac{1}{2}$$

6. **Option (D) is correct.**
Explanation:

$$\frac{(0.13)^2+(0.21)^2}{(0.39)^2+81(0.07)^2}\div\frac{(2.4)^4+3\times(11.52)+9}{(2.4)^6+6(2.4)^4+3\times(17.28)}$$

$$= \frac{0.0169+0.0441}{0.1521+0.3969}\div\frac{(2.4)^4+3(11.52)+9}{(2.4)^6+6(2.4)^4+3\times17.28}$$

$$= \frac{0.061}{0.549}\div\frac{(2.4)^2+3(11.52)+9}{(2.4)^2[(2.4)^4+3\times(11.52)+9]}$$

$$= \frac{1}{9}\div\frac{1}{5.76} = \frac{1}{9}\times 5.76 = 0.64$$

$\therefore \quad 0.6 < 0.64 < 0.7$

7. **Option (A) is correct.**
Explanation: Expression

$$\frac{\sqrt{a+2b}+\sqrt{a-2b}}{\sqrt{a+2b}-\sqrt{a-2b}} = \frac{\sqrt{3}}{1}$$

Applying componendo and dividendo,

$$\frac{\sqrt{a+2b}}{\sqrt{a-2b}} = \frac{\sqrt{3}+1}{\sqrt{3}-1}$$

Square both sides

$$\left(\frac{\sqrt{a+2b}}{\sqrt{a-2b}}\right)^2 = \frac{(\sqrt{3}+1)^2}{(\sqrt{3}-1)^2}$$

$$\frac{a+2b}{a-2b} = \frac{3+2\sqrt{3}+1}{3-2\sqrt{3}+1}$$

$$\frac{a+2b}{a-2b} = \frac{2+\sqrt{3}}{2-\sqrt{3}} \qquad ...(1)$$

Again apply 'C' and 'D' to expression (1)

$$\frac{2a}{4b} = \frac{4}{2\sqrt{3}}$$

$$\frac{a}{2b} = \frac{2}{\sqrt{3}}$$

So, $\frac{a}{b} = \frac{4}{\sqrt{3}}$ or $4:\sqrt{3}$

8. **Option (C) is correct.**
Explanation:

$$4x = \sqrt{5}+2$$

Multiply above expression by 4

$$16x = 4(\sqrt{5}+2)$$

$$16x = 4\sqrt{5}+8$$

So $\frac{1}{16x} = \frac{1}{4\sqrt{5}+8}$

$$\frac{1}{16x} = \frac{4\sqrt{5}-8}{(4\sqrt{5}+8)(4\sqrt{5}-8)}$$

$$= \frac{4\sqrt{5}-8}{80-64} = \frac{4\sqrt{5}-8}{16}$$

$$\frac{1}{16x} = \frac{\sqrt{5}-2}{4}$$

So, required

$$x-\frac{1}{16x} = \frac{\sqrt{5}+2}{4}-\frac{\sqrt{5}-2}{4}$$

$$= \frac{\sqrt{5}+2-\sqrt{5}+2}{4} = \frac{4}{4} = 1.$$

9. **Option (D) is correct.**
Explanation: Given,

$$\frac{10}{7}(1-2.43\times10^{-3}) = 1.417+x$$

$$\frac{10}{7}(1-0.00243) = 1.417+x$$

$$\frac{10}{7}(0.99757) = 1.417+x$$

$$\therefore \quad 1.4251 = 1.417+x$$

$$x = 1.4251-1.417$$

$$x = 0.0081$$

10. Option (B) is correct.

Explanation:

Given, $3a = 4b = 6c$

Now $a : b : c$

$\frac{1}{3}\times 12 : \frac{1}{4}\times 12 : \frac{1}{6}\times 12$

$\Rightarrow a : b : c = 4 : 3 : 2$

$\therefore 4x + 3x + 2x = 27\sqrt{29}$

$9x = 27\sqrt{29}$

$x = 3\sqrt{29}$

Now, $\sqrt{a^2+b^2+c^2} = \sqrt{(4x)^2+(3x)^2+(2x)^2}$

$= \sqrt{16x^2+9x^2+4x^2}$

$= \sqrt{29x^2} = \sqrt{29}x$

$= \sqrt{29}\times 3\sqrt{29}$

$= 29 \times 3 = 87$

11. Option (A) is correct.

Explanation: Given,

$$\frac{(243)^{\frac{n}{5}}\times 3^{2n+1}}{9^n \times 3^{n-1}} = \frac{(3^5)^{\frac{n}{5}}\times 3^{2n+1}}{(3^2)^n\times 3^{n-1}}$$

$$= \frac{(3)^{5\times\frac{n}{5}}\times 3^{2n+1}}{3^{2n}\times 3^{n-1}} = \frac{3^{3n+1}}{3^{3n-1}}$$

$$= 3^{3n+1-3n+1} = 3^2 = 9$$

12. Option (C) is correct.

Explanation: Given,

$$\underbrace{3\sqrt{3}x^3 - 2\sqrt{2}y^3}_{\text{Part-1}} = \underbrace{(\sqrt{3}x-\sqrt{2}y)(Ax^2+By^2+Cxy)}_{\text{Part-2}}$$

Taking L.H.S. $= 3\sqrt{3}x^3 - 2\sqrt{2}y^3$

$= (\sqrt{3}x)^3 - (\sqrt{2}y)^3$

$= (\sqrt{3}x-\sqrt{2}y)[(\sqrt{3}x)^2+(\sqrt{2}y)^2+\sqrt{3}x\times\sqrt{2}y]$

$= (\sqrt{3}x-\sqrt{2}y)[3x^2+2y^2+\sqrt{6}xy]$ ...(1)

Now, $(\sqrt{3}x-\sqrt{2}y)(3x^2+2y^2+\sqrt{6}xy)$

$= (\sqrt{3}x-\sqrt{2}y)(Ax^2+By^2+Cxy)$

$3x^2+2y^2+\sqrt{6}xy = Ax^2+By^2+Cxy$

$\therefore A = 3, B = 2, C = \sqrt{6}$

$\therefore (A \times B) \div C = 3\times 2\div\sqrt{6}$

$= 6\times\frac{1}{\sqrt{6}} = \sqrt{6}$

13. Option (D) is correct.

Explanation: Given, $1^3, 2^3, 3^3, 4^3, 5^3, 6^3, 7^3$

We know, sum of the cubes of first n natural number

$= \left(\frac{n(n+1)}{2}\right)^2$

So, average a mean $= \frac{n(n+1)^2}{4}$

$= \frac{7(7+1)^2}{4} = \frac{7(8)^2}{4} = 112.$

14. Option (B) is correct.

Explanation:

Given, $x = \frac{\sqrt{5}-\sqrt{3}}{\sqrt{5}+\sqrt{3}}$

After rationalising the denominator

$x = 4-\sqrt{15}$

Also, $y = \frac{1}{x} = \frac{1}{4-\sqrt{15}}$

$= \frac{1}{4-\sqrt{15}}\times\frac{4+\sqrt{15}}{4+\sqrt{15}} = 4+\sqrt{15}$

$\therefore x+\frac{1}{x} = 4-\sqrt{15}+4+\sqrt{15} = 8$

$\therefore (x^3+y^3) = x^3+\frac{1}{x^3}$

$= \left(x+\frac{1}{x}\right)^3 - 3x\times\frac{1}{x}\left(x+\frac{1}{x}\right)$

$= 8^3 - 3\times 8 = 512 - 24 = 488$

15. Option (D) is correct.

Explanation:

Given, $x = \sqrt[6]{27} - \sqrt{6\frac{3}{4}}$,

$y = \frac{\sqrt{45}+\sqrt{605}+\sqrt{245}}{\sqrt{80}+\sqrt{125}}$

$x = \sqrt[6]{27} - \sqrt{\frac{27}{4}} = (27)^{\frac{1}{6}} - \frac{3\sqrt{3}}{2}$

$= (3^3)^{\frac{1}{6}} - \frac{3\sqrt{3}}{2} = \sqrt{3} - \frac{3\sqrt{3}}{2}$

$= \frac{2\sqrt{3}-3\sqrt{3}}{2} = \frac{-\sqrt{3}}{2}$

So, $y = \frac{\sqrt{45}+\sqrt{605}+\sqrt{245}}{\sqrt{80}+\sqrt{125}}$

$= \frac{3\sqrt{5}+11\sqrt{5}+7\sqrt{5}}{4\sqrt{5}+5\sqrt{5}}$

$= \frac{21\sqrt{5}}{9\sqrt{5}} = \frac{7}{3}$

Now, $x^2+y^2 = \left(\frac{-\sqrt{3}}{2}\right)^2 + \left(\frac{7}{3}\right)^2 = \frac{3}{4}+\frac{49}{9}$

$= \frac{27+196}{36} = \frac{223}{36}$

16. Option (C) is correct.

Explanation:

$$\text{Given, } \frac{22\sqrt{2}}{4\sqrt{2}-\sqrt{3+\sqrt{5}}} = a+\sqrt{5}b$$

$$\frac{22\sqrt{2}\times\sqrt{2}}{4\sqrt{2}\times\sqrt{2}-\sqrt{6+2\sqrt{5}}} = a+\sqrt{5}b$$

$$\frac{44}{8-\sqrt{(\sqrt{5})^2+(1)^2+2\times\sqrt{5}\times 1}} = a+\sqrt{5}b$$

$$\Rightarrow \frac{44}{8-\sqrt{(\sqrt{5}+1)^2}} = a+\sqrt{5}b$$

$$\Rightarrow \frac{44}{8-(\sqrt{5}+1)} = a+\sqrt{5}b$$

$$\Rightarrow \frac{44}{8-\sqrt{5}-1} = a+\sqrt{5}b$$

$$\Rightarrow \frac{44}{7-\sqrt{5}} = a+\sqrt{5}b$$

After rationalising the denominator of L.H.S.

$$\frac{44(7+\sqrt{5})}{44} = a+\sqrt{5}b$$

$$7+\sqrt{5} = a+\sqrt{5}b$$

$\therefore$ $a = 7, b = 1$

So, $ab : a+b$

$7 : 8$

17. Option (B) is correct.

Explanation: Given, $(70^3 + 20^3 - 90^3)$

Let, $x = 70, y = 20, z = -90$

We know, if $(x + y + z) = 0$

then, $x^3 + y^3 + z^3 = 3xyz$

In given expression

$x + y + z = 0$

$70 + 20 - 90 = 0$

$\therefore\ 70^3 + 20^3 - 90^3 = 3 \times 70 \times 20 \times (-90) = -378000$

18. Option (D) is correct.

Explanation:

Given, $P^4 = 4354 - \frac{1}{P^4}$

$\therefore\ P^4 + \frac{1}{P^4} = 4354$

$$P^2 + \frac{1}{P^2} = \sqrt{4354+2} = \sqrt{4356}$$

So, $P^2 + \frac{1}{P^2} = 66$ ...(1)

$$P - \frac{1}{P} = \sqrt{66-2} = \sqrt{64}$$

$\therefore\ P - \frac{1}{P} = 8$

We know,

$$P^3 - \frac{1}{P^3} = \left(P-\frac{1}{P}\right)^3 + 3\left(P-\frac{1}{P}\right)$$

$\therefore\ P^3 - \frac{1}{P^3} = (8)^3 + 3(8)$

$= 512 + 24 = 536$

19. Option (A) is correct.

Explanation: Given,

$(a + b + 4)\,[ab + 4\,(a + b)] - 4ab = 0$

$a^2b + ab^2 + 4(a^2 + b^2) + 8ab + 16\,(a + b) = 0$

$ab\,(a + b) + 4\,(a^2 + b^2 + 2ab) + 16\,(a + b) = 0$

$ab\,(a + b) + 4\,(a + b)^2 + 16\,(a + b) = 0$

$(a + b)\,[ab + 4\,(a + b) + 16] = 0$

So, $a + b = 0$

$$\therefore \left\{\frac{1}{(a+b+4)^{117}} - 2^{-234}\right\} = \left\{\frac{1}{(0+4)^{117}} - 2^{-234}\right\}$$

$$= \left\{\frac{1}{(2^2)^{117}} - \frac{1}{2^{234}}\right\} = \left\{\frac{1}{2^{234}} - \frac{1}{2^{234}}\right\} = 0$$

20. Option (B) is correct.

Explanation:

Given, $\sqrt{x} + \frac{1}{\sqrt{x}} = 3$ ...(1)

We know,

$$x + \frac{1}{x} = 3^2 - 2$$

$$x + \frac{1}{x} = 9 - 2$$

$\therefore\ x + \frac{1}{x} = 7$

Now, $x^3 + \frac{1}{x^3} = \left(x+\frac{1}{x}\right)^3 - 3\left(x+\frac{1}{x}\right)$

$= 7^3 - 3(7) = 343 - 21 = 322$

■■■

Simplification

VBODMAS – It is a sequence in which an expression is solved.

- V – Vineculium
- B – Brackets
- O – of
- D – Division
- M – Multiplication
- A – Addition
- S – Subtraction

Important Identities

1. $(a+b)^2 = a^2 + b^2 + 2ab$
2. $(a-b)^2 = a^2 + b^2 - 2ab$
3. $a^2 - b^2 = (a-b)(a+b)$
4. $(a+b+c)^2 = a^2 + b^2 + c^2 + 2(ab + bc + ca)$
5. $(a-b)^2 + (a+b)^2 = 2(a^2 + b^2)$
6. $(a+b)^2 - (a-b)^2 = 4ab$

Types of Brackets

1. Line/Bar → '—'
2. Open brackets → '( )'
3. Curly Brackets → '{ }'
4. Square brackets → '[ ]' or closed brackets

Important Rules

1. $\sqrt{a^4 \times b^4 \times c^4} = a^2b^2c^2$
2. $\sqrt{a^n \times b^m} = a^{\frac{n}{2}} \times b^{\frac{m}{2}}$
3. $\frac{\sqrt{a}}{\sqrt{b}} = \sqrt{\frac{a}{b}}$
4. $\sqrt{a} \times \sqrt{b} = \sqrt{ab}$
5. $\frac{a^2 - b^2}{a - b} = a + b$,

   or $\frac{a^2 - b^2}{a + b} = a - b$
6. $\frac{a^3 + b^3}{a^2 - ab + b^2} = a + b$
7. $\frac{a^3 - b^3}{a^2 + ab + b^2} = a - b$
8. $\frac{(a+b)^2 + (a-b)^2}{a^2 + b^2} = 2$

Chapter

20 Simplification

LEARNING OBJECTIVES:

- Concept of VBODMAS.
- Concept related to bar.
- Important identities used in simplification.
- Important square roots and cube roots.
- Methods for calculating cube and square roots.
- Different types of questions asked in various competitive exams.
- Method of solving questions.

➢ **VBODMAS:** This is the sequence in which an expression is simplified.

VBODMAS

V – Vineculum (line brackets)/Bar
B – Brackets
O – of
D – Division
M – Multiplication
A – Addition
S – Subtraction

TYPES OF BRACKETS

(i) Line bar = '–'
(ii) Open brackets = '( )'
(iii) Curly brackets = '{ }'
(iv) Square or closed brackets = '[ ]'

Example 1: The value of $\frac{3 \div \{5 - 5 \div (6-7) \times 8 + 9\}}{4 + 4 \times 4 \div 4 \text{ of } 4}$

(a) $\frac{1}{18}$ (b) $\frac{1}{45}$

(c) $\frac{1}{3}$ (d) $\frac{1}{90}$

Sol. (d) Given,

$$= \frac{3 \div \{5 - 5 \div (6-7) \times 8 + 9\}}{4 + 4 \times 4 \div 4 \text{ of } 4}$$

$$= \frac{3 \div \{5 - 5 \div (-1) \times 8 + 9\}}{4 + 4 \times 4 \div 16}$$

$$= \frac{3 \div \{5 + 5 \times 8 + 9\}}{4+1} = \frac{3 \div 54}{5} = \frac{3}{54 \times 5} = \frac{1}{90}$$

Example 2: Find the value of $225 - [42 - \{25 - (18 - \overline{18+13}\}]$.

(a) 221 (b) 223

(c) 244 (d) 222

Sol. (a) Given, $225 - [42 - \{25 - (18 - \overline{18+13}\}]$

Using ,VBODMAS $= 225 - [42 - \{25 - (18 - 31)\}]$

$= 225 - [42 - \{25 + 13\}]$

$= 225 - [42 - 38]$

$= 225 - 4 = 221$

IMPORTANT IDENTITIES

- $(a + b)^2 = a^2 + b^2 + 2ab$
- $(a - b)^2 = a^2 + b^2 - 2ab$
- $(a^2 - b^2) = (a + b)(a - b)$
- $(a + b)^3 = a^3 + b^3 + 3ab(a + b)$
  $= a^3 + b^3 + 3a^2b + 3ab^2$
- $(a - b)^3 = a^3 - b^3 - 3ab(a - b)$
  $= a^3 - b^3 - 3a^2b + 3ab^2$
- $(a^3 + b^3) = (a + b)(a^2 - ab + b^2)$
- $(a^3 - b^3) = (a - b)(a^2 + ab + b^2)$
- $a^3 + b^3 + c^3 - 3abc = (a + b + c)(a^2 + b^2 + c^2 - ab - bc - ca)$
  $= \frac{1}{2}(a+b+c)[(a-b)^2 + (b-c)^2 + (c-a)^2]$
  Also, if $(a + b + c) = 0$
  then $a^3 + b^3 + c^3 - 3abc = 0$
  $a^3 + b^3 + c^3 = 3abc$

Example 3: $\dfrac{0.0347 \times 0.0347 \times 0.0347 + (0.9653)^3}{(0.0347)^2 - (0.0347)(0.9653) + (0.9653)^2}$

(a) 1 (b) 1.0009
(c) 0.9306 (d) 1.0050

Sol. (a) Given, $\dfrac{0.0347 \times 0.0347 \times 0.0347 + (0.9653)^3}{(0.0347)^2 - (0.0347)(0.9653) + (0.9653)^2}$

Let $0.0347 = a$, and $0.9653 = b$

$$\therefore \quad = \frac{a^3 + b^3}{a^2 - ab + b^2}$$

$$= \frac{(a+b)(a^2 - ab + b^2)}{a^2 - ab + b^2}$$

$$= a + b = 0.0347 + 0.9653 = 1$$

Example 4: Solve the following: $113 \times 87 = ?$

(a) 10026 (b) 9831
(c) 10000 (d) 10169

Sol. (b) Given $113 \times 87 = (100 + 13)(100 - 13)$

$= (100)^2 - (13)^2$

$\because a^2 - b^2 = (a + b)(a - b)$

$= 10000 - 169 = 9831$

SQUARE ROOTS AND CUBE ROOTS

➢ **Methods for calculating square root**

(i) Square root by factorisation

Square root of 3600

$$3600 = 2 \times 2 \times 2 \times 2 \times 3 \times 3 \times 5 \times 5$$

$$\sqrt{3600} = \sqrt{2 \times 2 \times 2 \times 2 \times 3 \times 3 \times 5 \times 5}$$

$$= 2 \times 2 \times 3 \times 5 = 60$$

(ii) Square root by division method.

Square root of 2304

	48
4	$\overline{23}\,\overline{04}$
+4	16
88	704
	704
	×

$\therefore \quad \sqrt{2304} = 48$

➢ Square roots

$\sqrt{0} = 0$ $\quad \sqrt{1} = 1$

$\sqrt{2} = 1.414$ $\quad \sqrt{3} = 1.732$

$\sqrt{4} = 2$ $\quad \sqrt{25} = 5$

$\sqrt{9} = 3$ $\quad \sqrt{49} = 7$

$\sqrt{36} = 6$ $\quad \sqrt{81} = 9$

$\sqrt{64} = 8$ $\quad \sqrt{121} = 11$

$\sqrt{100} = 10$ $\quad \sqrt{169} = 13$

$\sqrt{144} = 12$ $\quad \sqrt{225} = 15$

$\sqrt{196} = 14$ $\quad \sqrt{289} = 17$

$\sqrt{256} = 16$ $\quad \sqrt{361} = 19$

$\sqrt{324} = 18$ $\quad \sqrt{441} = 21$

$\sqrt{400} = 20$

➢ **Method for calculating cube root.**

(i) Cube root by factorisation

Cube root of 1331

$$1331 = 11 \times 11 \times 11$$

$$\sqrt[3]{1331} = \sqrt[3]{11 \times 11 \times 11} = 11$$

➢ Cube roots

$\sqrt[3]{1} = 1$ $\quad \sqrt[3]{8} = 2$

$\sqrt[3]{27} = 3$ $\quad \sqrt[3]{64} = 4$

$\sqrt[3]{125} = 5$ $\quad \sqrt[3]{216} = 6$

$\sqrt[3]{343} = 7$ $\quad \sqrt[3]{512} = 8$

$\sqrt[3]{729} = 9$ $\quad \sqrt[3]{1000} = 10$

$\sqrt[3]{1331} = 11$ $\quad \sqrt[3]{1728} = 12$

$\sqrt[3]{2197} = 13$ $\quad \sqrt[3]{2744} = 14$

$\sqrt[3]{3375} = 15$ $\quad \sqrt[3]{4096} = 16$

$\sqrt[3]{4913} = 17$ $\quad \sqrt[3]{5832} = 18$

$\sqrt[3]{6859} = 19$ $\quad \sqrt[3]{8000} = 20$

DIVISIBILITY RULES

1. **Divisibility by 2:** If the last digit of a number is even or '0', then that number is divisible by 2.
   Example: 12, 30, 1000, 2500, etc.
2. **Divisibility by 3:** If the sum of all the digits of a number is divisible by 3, then the number is divisible by 3.
   Example: Let '129' be the no. to be divided by 3.
   Sum of digits = 1 + 2 + 9 = 12
   As 12 is divisible by 3, then 129 is divisible by3.
3. **Divisibility by 4:** If the last two digits of a number are divisible by 4, then the given number is divisible by 4.
   Example: Let 2804 be the number .
   Now, divide 04 by 4 and it is divisible by 4.
   ∴ 2804 is divisible by 4.
4. **Divisibility by 5:** If the last digit of a number is 5 or 0, then the number is divisible by 5.
   Example: 100, 145, 2005, 164290, etc.
5. **Divisibility by 6:** If the number is divisible by 2 and 3 both, then the number is divisible by 6.
   Example: Let '102' be the number.
   ∴ 102 is divisible by both 2 and 3
   Hence, 102 is divisible by 6.
6. **Divisibility by 7:** If the last digit of a number is doubled and then subtracted from the rest of the number, and the answer is 0 or is divisible by 7, then the number is divisible by 7.
   Example: '791' = 79 – (1 × 2) = 79 – 2
   = 77 which is divisible by 7

Hence, 791 is also divisible by 7.

7. **Divisibility by 8:** If the last three digits of a number are divisible by 8, then the number is divisible by 8.
Example: '30168'
Last three digits = 168 ÷ 8
∴ 168 is divisible by 8 = 21
Hence, 30168 is divisible by 8.

8. **Divisibility by 9:** If the sum of all digits of a number is divisible by 9, then the number is divisible by 9.
Example: '7290342'
Sum = 7 + 2 + 9 + 0 + 3 + 4 + 2
= 27, which is divisible by 9.
Hence, 7290342 is divisible by 9.

9. **Divisibility by 10:** If the last digit of a number is '0', then it is divisible 10.
Example: 120, 1600, 7020, 590230, etc.

10. **Divisibility by 11:** If the difference between 'Sum of digits at even place' and 'the sum of digit at odd place' is '0' or is a multiple of 11, then the number is divisible by 11.
Example: 7 4 9 9 8
Sum of digits at odd place = (7 + 9 + 8 – (4 + 9))
= 24 – 13 = 11
Hence 74998 is divisible by 11.

11. **Divisibility by 12:** If a number is divisible by 3 and 4 both, then the number is divisible by 12.
Example : '3240'
3240 is divisible by both 3 and 4.
∴ 3240 is also divisible by 12.

12. **Divisibility by 13:** Multiply the last digit by 9 and subtract it from the rest of the number. If the resulted number is divisible by 13. Then, the number is divisible by 13.
Example: '1690'
Now, 9 × 0 = 0
So, 169 – 0 = 169 which is divisible by 13.
Hence, 169 is divisible by 13.

13. **Divisibility by 14:** If a number is divisible by 2 and 7 both, then that number is divisible by 14, i.e., number is even and divisible by 7.
Example : 1456
So, 1456 is divisible by 2, 7.
Hence, 1456 is divisible by 14.

POINTS TO REMEMBER

- If a is divisible by b, then ac is also divisible by b.
- If a is divisible by b and b is divisible by c, then a is divisible by c.
- Product of n consecutive numbers is always divisible by $n!$ or $\angle n$.
- The square of an odd number when divided by 8 always leaves a remainder 1.
- Square of any natural number can be written in the form of $3n$ or $3n + 1$ or $4n$ or $(4n + 1)$.

SOME IMPORTANT RULES

- If $\frac{a^n}{a-1}$, then remainder will always be 1
n = even or odd
- If $\frac{a^{n\to\text{(even number)}}}{(a+1)}$, then remainder will be 1.
- If $\frac{a^{n\to\text{(odd number)}}}{(a+1)}$, then remainder will be a.
- If n is a single digit number, then in n^3, n will be at unit place. It is valid for the number 0, 1, 4, 5, 6 or 9.
- If n is a single digit number, then is n^p, where p is any number (+ve), n will be at unit place. It is valid for 5 and 6.
- If the sum of a number and the number formed by reversing the digit is 'a', then the sum of digits of the numbers is $\frac{a}{11}$.
- Dividend = (Divisor × Quotient) + Remainder

$$\text{Divisor} = \frac{\text{Dividend} - \text{Remainder}}{\text{Quotient}}$$

$$\text{Quotient} = \frac{\text{Dividend} - \text{Remainder}}{\text{Divisor}}$$

Remainder = Dividend – (Divisor × Quotient)

1 Level Beginner

1. Find the cube root of 287496. **[SSC CHSL 2018]**
(A) 46 (B) 56 (C) 64 (D) 66

2. $1+\frac{1}{1+\frac{1}{5}}=?$ **[SSC Constable GD 2011]**
(A) $\frac{13}{6}$ (B) $\frac{11}{6}$
(C) $\frac{15}{6}$ (D) $\frac{12}{5}$

3. What is the value of $\frac{\frac{1}{3}\div\frac{1}{3}\times\frac{1}{3}}{\frac{1}{3}\times\frac{1}{3}\div\frac{1}{3}}$? **[SSC Delhi Police 2017]**
(A) 3 (B) $\frac{1}{3}$
(C) $\frac{1}{2}$ (D) 1

4. If $\left(\frac{-1}{2}\right)\times(x-5)+3=-\frac{5}{2}$, then what is the value of x? [SSC CGL 2017]

(A) –4 (B) 4 (C) 16 (D) –6

5. What is the sum of the largest and the smallest of the given fractions?
$\frac{6}{5}, \frac{11}{15}, \frac{4}{7}, \frac{5}{13}$ [SSC CHSL 2023]

(A) $\frac{97}{65}$ (B) $\frac{61}{65}$ (C) $\frac{94}{65}$ (D) $\frac{103}{65}$

6. The value of
$2 \times 3 \div 2$ of $3 \times 2 \div (4 + 4 \times 4 \div 4$ of $4 - 4 \div 4 \times 4)$ is: [SSC CGL 2019]

(A) 1 (B) 4 (C) 2 (D) 8

7. The value of $99\frac{95}{99}\times 99-95$ is: [SSC MTS 2019]

(A) 9887 (B) 9999 (C) 9801 (D) 9993

8. Solve the following $\frac{4}{3}\div\frac{1}{6}\times 2-1=?$ [SSC CGL 2020]

(A) 3 (B) 8 (C) –2 (D) 15

9. The value of $\dfrac{40-\frac{3}{4}\text{ of }32}{37-\frac{3}{4}\text{ of }(34-6)}$ is: [SSC CPO 2020]

(A) 1 (B) 0
(C) $\frac{-1}{2}$ (D) $\frac{1}{2}$

10. Find the value of 'a' using the concept of BODMAS.
$42 \div 2 + a \times 3 - 22 = 8$ [SSC CHSL 2022]

(A) 6 (B) 4 (C) 3 (D) 5

11. Find the sum of 6 + 8 + 10 + 12 + ... + 40. [SSC CGL 2020]

(A) 424 (B) 1600 (C) 400 (D) 414

12. Simplify the following expression.
$(2.19)^2 + 2\,(2.19)\,(3.81) + (3.81)^2$ [SSC CHSL 2022]

(A) 12 (B) 216 (C) 6 (D) 36

13. Find the value of
$8 + [16 - \{7 + 4 - (9 \text{ of } 3 + 6 - 4 \times 7)\}]$. [SSC CGL 2022]

(A) 23 (B) 18 (C) 21 (D) 18

14. Simplify: $9 - [10 - \{20 - (15 - \overline{9-3})\}]$ [SSC CHSL 2022]

(A) 12 (B) 7 (C) 8 (D) 10

15. The value of $4-\dfrac{5}{1+\dfrac{1}{3+\dfrac{1}{2+\frac{1}{4}}}}$ is: [SSC CGL 2015]

(A) $\frac{1}{64}$ (B) $\frac{1}{8}$
(C) $\frac{1}{16}$ (D) $\frac{1}{32}$

16. The least number which must be added to 1728 to make it a perfect square is: [SSC CGL Tier-I 2014]

(A) 32 (B) 36 (C) 60 (D) 38

17. Number of digits in the square root of 62478078 is: [SSC CGL 2013]

(A) 5 (B) 4 (C) 3 (D) 6

18. What is the difference of the largest and smallest of the given fractions? [SSC CHSL 2023]
$\frac{5}{11}, \frac{5}{7}, \frac{3}{8}, \frac{6}{13}$

(A) $\frac{17}{56}$ (B) $\frac{19}{56}$ (C) $\frac{1}{7}$ (D) $\frac{23}{56}$

18. What is the value of $(a^2 + b^2 + 4c^2 - ab - 2bc - 2ca)(a + b + 2c)$? [SSC CHSL 2023]

(A) $a^3 + b^3 + 8c^3 - 8abc$ (B) $a^3 + b^3 + 6c^3 - 4abc$
(C) $4a^3 + b^3 + 8c^3 - 9abc$ (D) $a^3 + b^3 + 8c^3 - 6abc$

19. What is the least number that should be added to the product $11 \times 12 \times 13 \times 14$ to make it a perfect square? [SSC CHSL 2018]

(A) 311 (B) 1 (C) 0 (D) 5

20. The least number which when divides 37044, gives the result a perfect cube is: [SSC CGL Tier-I 2016]

(A) 4 (B) 14 (C) 21 (D) 2

21. Find the value of x in $\sqrt[3]{15625}-\sqrt{x}=4$. [SSC CHSL 2020]

(A) 343 (B) 342 (C) 441 (D) 81

22. If A = 2 ÷ 3 × 4, B = 3 of 4 + (7 – 2) and C = 4 + 5 – 6, then what is the value of A + B + C? [SSC MTS 2019]

(A) $\frac{79}{3}$ (B) $\frac{85}{3}$
(C) $\frac{68}{3}$ (D) $\frac{59}{3}$

23. $\frac{3}{4}+\frac{5}{2}\left[\frac{1}{4}\times\left(\frac{8}{5}-\frac{4}{3}\right)\right]$ is equal to: [SSC CPO 2019]

(A) $\frac{1}{4}$ (B) $\frac{11}{12}$
(C) $\frac{1}{5}$ (D) $\frac{13}{24}$

24. What is the value of $\dfrac{\left[\frac{1}{9}\div\frac{1}{9}\text{ of }\frac{1}{9}\right]\times\frac{1}{9}}{\frac{1}{9}+\frac{1}{9}\times\frac{1}{9}}$? [SSC CHSL 2021]

(A) $9\frac{1}{10}$ (B) $9\frac{1}{81}$
(C) $8\frac{1}{81}$ (D) $8\frac{1}{10}$

25. The value of $\frac{284}{5}\div\left[\left(\frac{4}{5}\right)\times(15+35)-11\frac{3}{5}\right]$ is: [SSC CHSL 2021]

(A) 10 (B) 0 (C) 3 (D) 2

2 Level Intermediate

1. Find the sum of $\left(1-\frac{1}{n+1}\right)+\left(1-\frac{2}{n+1}\right)+\left(1-\frac{3}{n+1}\right)+....\left(1-\frac{n}{n+1}\right)$ [SSC CGL Tier-II 2013]

(A) $\frac{1}{2}n$ (B) $(n + 1)$
(C) n (D) $\frac{1}{2}(n+1)$

2. If $2 = x + \cfrac{1}{1+\cfrac{1}{5+\cfrac{1}{2}}}$, then the value of x is equal to: [SSC CGL Tier-II 2020]

(A) 1 (B) $\frac{14}{13}$ (C) $\frac{15}{13}$ (D) $\frac{13}{15}$

3. The value of $\frac{7+8\times8\div8 \text{ of } 8+8\div8\times4 \text{ of } 4}{4\div4 \text{ of } 4+4\times4\div4-4\div4 \text{ of } 2}$ [SSC CGL Tier-II 2019]

(A) 7.8 (B) 4.6 (C) 8.7 (D) 6.4

4. The value of $\frac{\frac{1}{3}+\left[4\frac{3}{4}-\left(3\frac{1}{6}-2\frac{1}{3}\right)\right]}{\left(\frac{1}{5}\text{ of }\frac{1}{5}\div\frac{1}{5}\right)\div\left(\frac{1}{5}\div\frac{1}{5}\times\frac{1}{5}\right)}$ lies between:

(A) 4.2 and 4.4 (B) 10.2 and 10.8
(C) 0.4 and 0.9 (D) 8.2 and 8.8

5. Find the value of $\left(\frac{9^3+9^4+9^5+9^6+9^7}{9^1+9^2+9^3+9^4+9^5}\right)^{\frac{1}{2}}$ [SSC CHSL 2022]

(A) 729 (B) 3 (C) 9 (D) 81

6. If the following interchanges are made in signs and numbers, which equation would be correct?
Interchange: signs ÷ and –
Numbers: 15 and 5 [SSC CHSL 2020]

(A) 4 × 30 – 15 ÷ 5 + 12 = 21
(B) 4 × 30 – 15 ÷ 5 + 12 = 27
(C) 4 × 30 – 5 ÷ 15 + 14 = 21
(D) 12 × 30 – 15 ÷ 5 + 4 = 37

7. Simplify $(x - y + z)^2 - (x - y - z)^2$ [SSC CGL 2021]

(A) $2xz + 2yz$ (B) $4xz - 4yz$
(C) $4xz + 4yz$ (D) $4xz + 4yz$

8. The value of $\left(\frac{5}{2}\div1\frac{7}{8}\right)\div\left(9\frac{4}{3}\div11\frac{1}{3}\text{ of }\frac{1}{8}\right)\text{ of }\frac{4}{3}\times5\frac{1}{3}-\frac{9}{8}\div\frac{3}{4}$ is: [SSC CHSL 2021]

(A) $\frac{22}{10}$ (B) $\frac{1}{5}$ (C) $\frac{-4}{5}$ (D) $\frac{-7}{10}$

9. What is the value of x if it is given that
$4\left(2\left(\frac{3}{4}\text{ of } 24-1\right)+3(7\div x)-5\times8+1\right)=20^2$? [SSC CHSL 2021]

(A) 0.2 (B) 0.75 (C) 0.4 (D) 0.625

10. Simplify the following:
$4\frac{4}{5}\div\left[2\frac{1}{5}-\frac{1}{2}\left\{1\frac{1}{4}-\left(\frac{1}{4}-\frac{1}{5}\right)\right\}\right]$ [SSC CHSL 2020]

(A) 4 (B) 2 (C) 3 (D) 1

11. The value of $\left(2\frac{6}{7}\text{of}\,4\frac{1}{5}\div\frac{2}{3}\right)\times1\frac{1}{9}\div\left(\frac{3}{4}\times2\frac{2}{3}\text{ of }\frac{1}{2}\div\frac{1}{4}\right)$ is: [SSC CGL 2019]

(A) $\frac{1}{8}$ (B) 8 (C) $\frac{1}{5}$ (D) 5

12. If $(\sqrt{2}+\sqrt{5}-\sqrt{3})\times k=-12$, then what will be the value of k? [SSC CGL Tier-II 2019]

(A) $2+\sqrt{5}+\sqrt{3}$
(B) $(\sqrt{2}+\sqrt{5}-\sqrt{3})(2+\sqrt{5})$
(C) $(\sqrt{2}+\sqrt{5}+\sqrt{3})(2-\sqrt{5})$
(D) $(\sqrt{2}+\sqrt{5}+\sqrt{3})(2-\sqrt{10})$

13. Solve (0.125 × 0.01) ÷ (0.5 × 0.005).[SSC CHSL 2023]

(A) 0.6 (B) 0.5 (C) 0.8 (D) 0.7

14. If '+' means '÷', '×' means '+"; ' ÷' means '–' and '–' means '×', then the value of 18 + 3 – 5 × 6 ÷ 4 is: [SSC CHSL 2010]

(A) 15.5 (B) 13.5 (C) 32 (D) 30

15. The value of $\frac{4}{5}\div3\frac{1}{4}\text{ of }\frac{8}{13}-\frac{\frac{-1}{5}-\frac{1}{8}}{\frac{1}{5}+\frac{1}{8}}\times5\frac{1}{5}+\frac{5}{6}$ is: [SSC CHSL 2020]

(A) $\frac{7}{30}$ (B) $\frac{1}{30}$ (C) $\frac{1}{15}$ (D) $\frac{2}{15}$

16. The value of $5-\frac{8+2\sqrt{15}}{4}-\frac{1}{8+2\sqrt{15}}$ is equal to: [SSC CGL 2019]

(A) 1 (B) $\frac{2}{3}$ (C) $\frac{1}{2}$ (D) $\frac{1}{4}$

17. Simplify the given expression. [SSC CHSL 2023]
$$\frac{(381+119)^2+(381-119)^2}{(381)^2+(119)^2}$$

(A) –1 (B) –2 (C) 1 (D) 2

18. What is the product of two consecutive even numbers, the difference of whose squares is 84? **[Delhi Police Constable 2020]**

(A) 400 **(B)** 528 **(C)** 440 **(D)** 360

19. The square root of $33 - 4\sqrt{35}$ is: **[SSC CGL 2013]**

(A) $\pm(\sqrt{7} + 2\sqrt{5})$ **(B)** $\pm(2\sqrt{7} + \sqrt{5})$

(C) $\pm(2\sqrt{7} - \sqrt{5})$ **(D)** $\pm(2\sqrt{7} + \sqrt{5})$

20. If $\dfrac{1}{x + \dfrac{1}{y + \dfrac{2}{z + \dfrac{1}{4}}}} = \dfrac{29}{79}$, where x, y and z are natural numbers, then the value of $(2x + 3y - z)$ is : **[SSC CGL 2020]**

(A) 4 **(B)** 2

(C) 12 **(D)** 0

21. The value of $(2.\overline{4} \times 0.\overline{6} \times 3 \times 0.1\overline{6}) \times [0.\overline{27} \times (0.8\overline{3} \div 0.1\overline{6}]$ is: **[SSC CGL 2020]**

(A) $1.\overline{1}$ **(B)** $1.\overline{11}$ **(C)** $1.\overline{36}$ **(D)** $1.\overline{814}$

22. The value of $11.\overline{4} + 22.5\overline{67} - 33.5\overline{9}$ is: **[SSC CGL 2022]**

(A) $4.\overline{12}$ **(B)** $40.\overline{12}$

(C) $0.4\overline{12}$ **(D)** $0.04\overline{12}$

23. The value of $\dfrac{1}{4} + \dfrac{[(20.35)^2 - (8.35)^2 \times 0.0175]}{(1.05)^2 + (1.05)(27.65)}$ is: **[SSC CGL 2022]**

(A) $\dfrac{7}{20}$ **(B)** $\dfrac{3}{10}$ **(C)** $\dfrac{3}{20}$ **(D)** $\dfrac{9}{20}$

24. The simplified value of

$\dfrac{2}{3} \div \left\{\dfrac{3}{7} \text{ of } \dfrac{14}{5} \times 1\dfrac{2}{3} - \left(3\dfrac{1}{2} - 2\dfrac{1}{6}\right)\right\}$ is : **[SSC CHSL 2019]**

(A) $\dfrac{2}{3}$ **(B)** 2 **(C)** 1 **(D)** $\dfrac{1}{3}$

25. Simplify the following:

18 × [24 ÷ 70 × {25 × 49 ÷ (5 × 7)}] **[SSC CHSL 2023]**

(A) 218 **(B)** 216 **(C)** 215 **(D)** 220

3 Level Expert

1. $\sqrt{\dfrac{4\frac{1}{7} - 2\frac{1}{4}}{3\frac{1}{2} + 1\frac{1}{7}} \div \dfrac{1}{2 + \dfrac{1}{2 + \dfrac{1}{5 - \frac{1}{5}}}}}$ is equal : **[SSC CHSL 2020]**

(A) 4 **(B)** 3 **(C)** 2 **(D)** 1

2. A student was asked to find the value of $9\dfrac{4}{9} \div 11\dfrac{1}{3}$ of $\dfrac{1}{6} + \left(1\dfrac{1}{3} \times 1\dfrac{4}{5} \div \dfrac{3}{5}\right) \times 2\dfrac{1}{6}$ of $\dfrac{2}{3} \div \dfrac{4}{3}$ of $\dfrac{2}{3}$.

His answer was $19\dfrac{1}{4}$. What is the difference between his answer and the correct answer? **[SSC CGL Tier-II 2018]**

(A) $6\dfrac{2}{3}$ **(B)** $7\dfrac{1}{2}$ **(C)** $6\dfrac{1}{3}$ **(D)** $7\dfrac{3}{4}$

3. What is the value of

$1\dfrac{1}{8} \div \left(4\dfrac{1}{4} \div \dfrac{3}{5} \text{ of } 8\dfrac{1}{2}\right) - \dfrac{2}{5} \times 1\dfrac{1}{3} \div \dfrac{4}{5}$ of $1\dfrac{2}{3} + \dfrac{11}{20}$? **[SSC CGL 2020]**

(A) $1\dfrac{1}{2}$ **(B)** $1\dfrac{1}{4}$ **(C)** $3\dfrac{1}{2}$ **(D)** $3\dfrac{1}{8}$

4. If $\left(n^r - tn + \dfrac{1}{4}\right)$ is a perfect square, than the values of t are : **[SSC CGL Tier-I 2013]**

(A) 1, 2 **(B)** ± 1 **(C)** 2, 3 **(D)** ± 2

5. If $\left[4 - \dfrac{5}{1 + \dfrac{1}{3 + \dfrac{1}{2 + \frac{1}{4}}}}\right]$ th part of a journey takes 10 minutes, then to complete $\dfrac{3}{5}$ th of that journey it will take: **[SSC CHSL 2013]**

(A) 48 minutes **(B)** 45 minutes

(C) 88 minutes **(D)** 36 minutes

6. Let $x = \dfrac{5\frac{3}{4} - \frac{3}{7} \times 15\frac{3}{4} + 2\frac{2}{35} + 1\frac{11}{25}}{\frac{3}{4} \div 5\frac{1}{4} + 5\frac{3}{5} \div 3\frac{4}{15}}$. When y is added to x, the result is $\dfrac{7}{13}$. What is the value of y? **[SSC CGL Tier-II 2022]**

(A) $\dfrac{9}{13}$ **(B)** $\dfrac{2}{13}$

(C) $\dfrac{4}{13}$ **(D)** $\dfrac{1}{13}$

7. The value of $\left[\dfrac{4}{7} \text{ of } 2\dfrac{4}{5} \times 1\dfrac{2}{3} - \left(3\dfrac{1}{2} - 2\dfrac{1}{6}\right)\right]$

$\div \left(3\dfrac{1}{5} \div 4\dfrac{1}{2} \text{ of } 5\dfrac{1}{3}\right)$ is: **[SSC CGL Tier-II 2020]**

(A) $7\dfrac{1}{2}$ **(B)** 10 **(C)** 15 **(D)** $1\dfrac{1}{3}$

8. The value of $\frac{4}{21} \div \frac{3}{7}$ of $\frac{1}{2} - \frac{1}{2} \times 1\frac{2}{3} +$ $\left(0.\overline{89} \div 0.\overline{98} \times 7\frac{1}{3}\right) \div 2\frac{2}{2}$ is:

[Delhi Police Constable 2020]

(A) $\frac{25}{18}$ **(B)** $\frac{49}{18}$ **(C)** $\frac{32}{9}$ **(D)** $\frac{7}{9}$

9. The value of

$\frac{(2.53)^3 + (2.47)^3}{25.3 \times 25.3 - 624.91 + 24.7 \times 24.7}$ is 5×10^k, where the value of k is: **[SSC CGL 2022]**

(A) –1 **(B)** 1 **(C)** 2 **(D)** –2

10. What is the simplified value $\left(1 - \frac{1}{4 - \frac{2}{1 + \frac{1}{\frac{1}{3} + 2}}}\right) \times \frac{15}{16}$ $\div \frac{2}{3}$ of $2\frac{1}{4} - \frac{3+4}{3^3 + 4^3}$ **[SSC CPO 2019]**

(A) $\frac{8}{13}$ **(B)** $\frac{6}{13}$ **(C)** $\frac{4}{13}$ **(D)** $\frac{5}{13}$

11. Find the value:

$\left(1 + \frac{3}{4}\right) \times \frac{3}{21}$ of $5\frac{1}{3} \div \frac{128}{49} + \frac{2}{3} \times \frac{7}{11} \times \frac{121}{49} \div \left(\frac{15}{14} - \frac{2}{7}\right)$?

[SSC MTS 2019]

(A) $\frac{62}{29}$ **(B)** $\frac{69}{25}$ **(C)** $\frac{59}{32}$ **(D)** $\frac{57}{41}$

12. The value of

$\frac{(0.13)^2 + (0.21)^2}{(0.39)^2 + 81(0.07)^2} \div \frac{(2.4) + 3 \times (11.52) + 4}{(2.4)^6 + 6(2.4)^4 + 3 \times (17.2)}$ lies between: **[SSC CPO 2019]**

(A) 0.6 to 0.7 **(B)** 0.4 to 0.5
(C) 0.1 to 0.2 **(D)** 0.8 to 0.9

13. What will come at place of x_1 $(x < 10)$ for

$\frac{(132 \div 12 \times x - 3 \times 3)}{5^2 - 6 \times 4 + x^2} = 1$? **[SSC CHSL 2020]**

(A) 1 **(B)** 3 **(C)** 4 **(D)** 2

14. What is the value of $\frac{8 \times 5 \div 25}{7 \div 14 \times 2} - \frac{14 \div 7 - 5}{7 \div 14 - 25}$?

[SSC CHSL 2023]

(A) $\frac{362}{245}$ **(B)** $\frac{115}{245}$
(C) $\frac{306}{245}$ **(D)** $\frac{106}{245}$

15. The value of 56 ÷ [12 + 9 ÷ 3 – {8 + (18 of 2 ÷ 9) – (40 ÷ 5 of 2)}] + $\frac{27 + \frac{2}{5} \text{ of } 75}{5 + \frac{2}{5} \times (58 - 37)}$ is: **[SSC CHSL 2021]**

(A) –11 **(B)** 8 **(C)** 11 **(D)** –8

16. Find the value of the given expression.

$\frac{\left(4\frac{1}{3} + 3\frac{1}{3} \times 1\frac{4}{5} \div 3\frac{3}{4} \times \left(1\frac{1}{2} + 1\frac{1}{3}\right)\right)}{\left(\frac{2}{3} \div \frac{5}{6} \times \frac{2}{3}\right)}$ **[SSC CHSL 2023]**

(A) $11\frac{3}{8}$ **(B)** $10\frac{1}{8}$ **(C)** $14\frac{3}{8}$ **(D)** $16\frac{5}{8}$

17. The value of

$\left(1\frac{1}{8} \div \frac{3}{4}\right) \div \left(\left(\frac{1}{2} \text{ of } 1\frac{1}{2}\right) \div \left(3\frac{1}{2} - 1\frac{1}{4}\right) \text{ of } \left(\frac{3}{4} - \frac{3}{4} \div 2\frac{1}{4}\right)\right.$

of $\frac{3}{4}$ is: **[SSC CHSL 2021]**

(A) 6 **(B)** 12 **(C)** 9 **(D)** 18

18. Simplify the given expression.

$(2x - 3y)^3 - 18xy(2x - 3y)$ **[SSC CHSL 2021]**

(A) $8x^3 - 27y^3$
(B) $8x^3 + 108xy^2 - 72x^2y$
(C) $3x^3 - 27y^3 - 36x^2y - 54xy^2$
(D) $8x^3 - 27y^3 - 72x^2y + 108xy^2$

19. A student was asked to find the value of

$\frac{\left(2\frac{1}{3} + 2\frac{1}{2} - \frac{1}{6}\right) \div 2\frac{1}{3} \times 5\frac{2}{3} \div 1\frac{2}{3} \text{ of } 4\frac{1}{4}}{3\frac{1}{5} \div 4\frac{1}{2} \text{ of } 5\frac{1}{3} + 5\frac{1}{3} \times \frac{3}{4} \div 2\frac{2}{3}}$. His answer was $\frac{6}{7}$. What is the difference between the correct answer and his answer? **[SSC CPO 2019]**

(A) $\frac{6}{49}$ **(B)** $\frac{11}{49}$ **(C)** $\frac{5}{14}$ **(D)** $\frac{9}{14}$

20. A student was asked to find the value of

$9\frac{4}{9} \div 11\frac{1}{3}$ of $\frac{1}{6} + \left(1\frac{1}{3} \times 1\frac{4}{5} \div \frac{3}{5}\right) \times 2\frac{1}{6}$ of $\frac{2}{3} \div \frac{4}{3}$ of $\frac{2}{3}$. His answer was $19\frac{7}{4}$. What is the difference between his answer and the correct answer?

[SSC CGL Tier-II 2019]

(A) $6\frac{1}{3}$ **(B)** $9\frac{1}{4}$ **(C)** $6\frac{2}{3}$ **(D)** $11\frac{3}{4}$

21. The value of

$\frac{5 - 2 \div 4[5 - (3 - 4)] + 5 \times 4 \div 2 \text{ of } 4}{4 + 4 \div 8 \text{ of } 2 \times (8 - 5) \times 2 \div 3 - 8 \div 2 \text{ of } 8}$ is:

[SSC CPO 2019]

(A) $\frac{89}{4}$ **(B)** $\frac{15}{32}$ **(C)** $\frac{9}{4}$ **(D)** $\frac{9}{8}$

22. $\frac{6.75 \times 6.75 - 4.25 \times 4.25 \times 4.25}{67.5 \times 67.5 + 42.5 \times 42.5 + 67.5 \times 42.5}$ is equal to:

[SSC CPO 2019]

(A) 0.25 **(B)** 2.5 **(C)** 0.025 **(D)** 0.025

23. The value of $\dfrac{0.72\times0.72\times0.72-0.39\times0.39\times0.39}{0.72\times0.72+0.72\times0.39+0.39\times0.39}$ is:

[SSC CPO 2019]

(A) 0.33 **(B)** 0.45 **(C)** 0.36 **(D)** 0.39

24. The value of $\dfrac{(4.6)^4+(5.4)^4+(24.84)^2}{(4.6)^2+(5.4)^2+(24.84)}$ is :

[SSC CGL Tier-II 2019]

(A) 24.24 **(B)** 24.42 **(C)** 25.48 **(D)** 25.42

ANSWER KEY

Level-1: Beginner

1.	(D)	2.	(B)	3.	(D)	4.	(C)	5.	(D)	6.	(C)	7.	(C)	8.	(D)	9.	(A)	10.	(C)
11.	(D)	12.	(D)	13.	(B)	14.	(D)	15.	(B)	16.	(B)	17.	(B)	18.	(B)	19.	(D)	20.	(B)
21.	(A)	22.	(C)	23.	(C)	24.	(B)	25.	(D)	26.	(D)								

Level-2: Intermediate

1.	(A)	2.	(C)	3.	(D)	4.	(A)	5.	(C)	6.	(A)	7.	(B)	8.	(D)	9.	(A)	10.	(C)
11.	(B)	12.	(D)	13.	(B)	14.	(C)	15.	(B)	16.	(A)	17.	(D)	18.	(C)	19.	(C)	20.	(B)
21.	(A)	22.	(C)	23.	(D)	24.	(C)	25.	(B)										

Level-3: Expert

1.	(D)	2.	(D)	3.	(A)	4.	(B)	5.	(A)	6.	(C)	7.	(B)	8.	(B)	9.	(D)	10.	(C)
11.	(C)	12.	(A)	13.	(A)	14.	(A)	15.	(C)	16.	(D)	17.	(D)	18.	(D)	19.	(A)	20.	(B)
21.	(D)	22.	(D)	23.	(A)	24.	(C)												

Solutions with Detailed Explanations

Level-1: BEGINNER

1. Option (D) is correct.

Explanation: Given number 287496

Now, $287496 = 2\times2\times2\times3\times3\times3\times11\times11\times11$

$$\text{Cube root} = \sqrt[3]{2\times2\times2\times3\times3\times3\times11\times11\times11} = 2\times3\times11 = 66$$

2. Option (B) is correct.

Explanation: $1+\dfrac{1}{1+\dfrac{1}{5}} = 1+\dfrac{1}{\dfrac{6}{5}} = 1+\dfrac{5}{6} = \dfrac{11}{6}$

3. Option (D) is correct.

Explanation: Given

$$\frac{\frac{1}{3}\div\frac{1}{3}\times\frac{1}{3}}{\frac{1}{3}\times\frac{1}{3}\div\frac{1}{3}} = \frac{\frac{1}{3}\times3\times\frac{1}{3}}{\frac{1}{3}\times\frac{1}{3}\times3} = 1$$

4. Option (C) is correct.

Explanation: Given,

$$\frac{-1}{2}\times(x-5)+3 = \frac{-5}{2}$$

$$\frac{-x}{2}+\frac{5}{2}+3 = \frac{-5}{2}$$

$$\frac{x}{2} = \frac{5}{2}+\frac{5}{2}+3$$

$$\frac{x}{2} = 5+3 = 8$$

$$\frac{x}{2} = 8$$

$$x = 2\times8 = 16$$

5. Option (D) is correct.

Explanation: We have,

$$\frac{6}{5}=1.2,\ \frac{11}{15}=0.7333,\ \frac{4}{7}=0.571,\ \frac{5}{13}=0.384$$

So, sum of largest and smallest fraction

$$= \frac{6}{5}+\frac{5}{13} = \frac{103}{65}$$

6. Option (C) is correct.

Explanation: $2\times3\div2$ of $3\times2\div(4+4\times4\div4$ of $4-4\div4\times4)$

Using 'BODMAS'

$$= 2\times3\div(2\times3)\times2\div\left[4+4\times4\div16-\frac{4\times4}{4}\right]$$

$$= \frac{2\times3\times2}{2\times3}\div\left[4+4\times\frac{4}{16}-4\right]$$

$$= \frac{2\times3\times2}{2\times3}\div[4+1-4] = 2\div1 = 2$$

7. **Option (C) is correct.**

Explanation: $99\frac{95}{99}\times 99-95 = \left(99+\frac{95}{99}\right)\times 99-95$

$= 99\times 99+\frac{95}{99}\times 99-95$

$= 99 \times 99 + 95 - 95 = 99 \times 99 = 9801$

8. **Option (D) is correct.**

Explanation: $\frac{4}{3}\div\frac{1}{6}\times 2-1$

Using 'BODMAS'

$= \frac{4}{3}\times 6\times 2-1 = 16-1 = 15$

9. **Option (A) is correct.**

Explanation: $\dfrac{40-\frac{3}{4}\text{ of }32}{37-\frac{3}{4}\text{ of }(34-6)}$

$= \dfrac{40-\frac{3}{4}\times 32}{37-\frac{3}{4}\text{ of }(34-6)} = \dfrac{40-24}{37-\frac{3}{4}\text{ of }28}$

$= \dfrac{16}{37-\frac{3}{4}\times 28} = \dfrac{16}{37-21}=\dfrac{16}{16}=1$

10. **Option (C) is correct.**
Explanation: Expression
$42 \div 2 + a \times 3 - 22 = 8$
$\Rightarrow\quad 21 + 3a - 22 = 8$
$\Rightarrow\quad 21 + 3a = 30$
$\Rightarrow\quad 3a = 9$
$a = 3$

11. **Option (D) is correct.**
Explanation: $6 + 8 + 10 + 12 + \ldots + 40$
$= 2\,[3 + 4 + 5 + 6 + \ldots\ldots 20]$
$= 2\,[1 + 2 + 3 + 4 + 5 + 6 + \ldots 20 - (1 + 2)]$
$= 2\left[\frac{20(20+1)}{2}-3\right]$ $\because$ Sum of n natural nos. $= \frac{n(n-1)}{2}$
$= 2\,(210 - 3) = 2 \times 207 = 414$

12. **Option (D) is correct.**
Explanation: Given $(2.19)^2 + 2\,(2.19)\,(3.81) + (3.81)^2$
Clearly, the above expression is in the form of
$a^2 + 2ab + b^2$
So, $a = 2.19, b = 3.81$
Also, $(a + b)^2 = a^2 + 2ab + b^2$
$\therefore\quad (a + b)^2 = (2.19 + 3.81)^2$
$= (6)^2 = 36$

13. **Option (B) is correct.**
Explanation: Given,
$8 + [16 - \{7 + 4 - (9 \text{ of } 3 + 6 - 4 \times 7)\}]$
Using 'BODMAS'.
$= 8 + [16 - \{7 + 4 - (27 + 6 - 28)\}]$
$= 8+[16 - \{11 - (27 + 6 - 28)\}]$
$= 8 + [16 - \{11 - 5\}]$
$= 8 + [16 - 6] = 8 + 10 = 18$

14. **Option (D) is correct.**
Explanation: Given
$9-[10-\{20-(15-\overline{9-3})\}]$
$= 9-[10-\{20-(15-6)\}]$
$= 9-[10-\{20-9\}]$
$= 9-[10-11] = 9-(-1)$
$= 9 + 1 = 10$

15. **Option (B) is correct.**
Explanation: Given,

$$4-\cfrac{5}{1+\cfrac{1}{3+\cfrac{1}{2+\cfrac{1}{4}}}} = 4-\cfrac{5}{1+\cfrac{1}{3+\cfrac{1}{\frac{(8+1)}{4}}}}$$

$$= 4-\cfrac{5}{1+\cfrac{1}{3+\cfrac{4}{9}}}$$

$$= 4-\cfrac{5}{1+\cfrac{1}{\frac{27+4}{9}}}$$

$$= 4-\cfrac{5}{1+\cfrac{9}{31}}$$

$$= 4-\frac{5\times 31}{40}=\frac{1}{8}$$

16. **Option (B) is correct.**
Explanation: Find a nearby square to 1728
i.e., $42 \times 42 = 1764$
$\therefore\quad 1764 - 1728 = 36$
$\therefore$ 36 is the required number

17. **Option (B) is correct.**
Explanation: $\sqrt{62478078} \approx 7904$
$\therefore$ No. of digits = 4

18. **Option (B) is correct.**
Explanation:
Given numbers are $\frac{5}{11}, \frac{5}{7}, \frac{3}{8}, \frac{6}{13}$.

$\Rightarrow \frac{5}{11} = 0.4545$

$\Rightarrow \frac{5}{7} = 0.714$

$\Rightarrow \frac{3}{8} = 0.375$

$\Rightarrow \frac{6}{13} = 0.4615$

So, the difference between largest and smallest number $= \frac{5}{7} - \frac{3}{8} = \frac{19}{56}$

19. Option (D) is correct.

Explanation: We have, $a^3 + b^3 + c^3 - 3abc = (a + b + c)(a^2 + b^2 + c^2 - ab - bc - ca)$

So, the value of $(a + b + 2c)(a^2 + b^2 + 4c^2 - ab - 2bc - 2ca) = a^3 + b^3 + 8c^3 - 6abc$

20. Option (B) is correct.

Explanation: Product of $11 \times 12 \times 13 \times 14 = 24024$

Also $\sqrt{24025} = 155$

$\therefore 24024 + 1 = 24025$

$\therefore$ Add 1 to 24024 to make it a perfect square.

21. Option (A) is correct.

Explanation: $37044 = 3 \times 3 \times 3 \times 7 \times 7 \times 7 \times 2 \times 2$

$= 3^3 \times 7^3 \times 2^2$

So, $2 \times 2 = 4$ is the required number.

22. Option (C) is correct.

Explanation: We know,

$$\sqrt[3]{15625} - \sqrt{x} = 4$$

$$25 - 4 = \sqrt{x}$$

$$21 = \sqrt{x}$$

$$441 = x$$

23. Option (C) is correct.

Explanation: $A = 2 \div 3 \times 4 = \frac{2}{3} \times 4 = \frac{8}{3}$

$B = 3 \times 4 + (7 - 2) = 12 + 5 = 17$

$C = 4 + 5 - 6 = 3$

$\therefore A + B + C = \frac{8}{3} + 17 + 3 = \frac{8}{3} + 20$

$= \frac{8 + 60}{3} = \frac{68}{3}$

24. Option (B) is correct.

Explanation:

Expression

$$= \frac{3}{4} + \frac{5}{2}\left[\frac{1}{4} \times \left(\frac{8}{5} - \frac{4}{3}\right)\right]$$

$$= \frac{3}{4} + \frac{5}{2}\left[\frac{1}{4} \times \left(\frac{4}{15}\right)\right]$$

$$= \frac{3}{4} + \frac{1}{6} = \frac{11}{12}$$

25. Option (D) is correct.

Explanation: $\dfrac{\left[\frac{1}{9} \div \frac{1}{9} \text{ of } \frac{1}{9}\right] \times \frac{1}{9}}{\frac{1}{9} + \frac{1}{9} \times \frac{1}{9}}$

$$= \frac{\left[\frac{1}{9} \div \frac{1}{81}\right] \times \frac{1}{9}}{\frac{1}{9} + \frac{1}{81}} = \frac{81}{10} = 8\frac{1}{10}$$

26. Option (D) is correct.

Explanation: $\frac{284}{5} \div \left[\left(\frac{4}{5}\right) \times (15 + 35) - 11\frac{3}{5}\right]$

Using BODMAS,

$$= \frac{284}{5} \div \left[\frac{4}{5} \times 50 - \frac{58}{5}\right] = \frac{285}{5} \div \left[40 - \frac{58}{5}\right]$$

$$= \frac{284}{5} \div \frac{142}{5} = \frac{284}{5} \times \frac{5}{142} = 2$$

Level-2: INTERMEDIATE

1. Option (A) is correct.

Explanation:

$$\left(1 - \frac{1}{n+1}\right) + \left(1 - \frac{2}{n+1}\right) + \left(1 - \frac{3}{n+1}\right) + \ldots + \left(1 - \frac{n}{n+1}\right)$$

$$= n - \left[\frac{1}{n+1} + \frac{2}{n+1} + \frac{3}{n+1} + \ldots + \frac{n}{n+1}\right]$$

$$= n - \frac{1 + 2 + 3 + \ldots + n}{n+1}$$

$$= n - \frac{n(n+1)}{2(n+1)} = n - \frac{n}{2}$$

$$= \frac{n}{2} = \frac{1}{2}n$$

2. Option (C) is correct.

Explanation: Given,

$$2 = x + \cfrac{1}{1 + \cfrac{1}{5 + \cfrac{1}{2}}}$$

$$\Rightarrow 2 = x + \cfrac{1}{1 + \cfrac{2}{11}}$$

$$2 = x + \frac{11}{13}$$

$$\Rightarrow 26 = 13x + 11$$

$$\Rightarrow x = \frac{15}{13}$$

3. Option (D) is correct.

Explanation: Expression

$$\frac{7 + 8 \times 8 \div 8 \text{ of } 8 + 8 \div 8 \times 4 \text{ of } 4}{4 \div 4 \text{ of } 4 + 4 \times 4 \div 4 - 4 \div 4 \text{ of } 2}$$

Using BODMAS rule,

$$= \frac{7+8\times 8\div 64+8\div 8\times 16}{4\div 16+4\times 4\div 4-4\div 8}$$

$$= \frac{7+1+16}{\frac{1}{4}+4-\frac{1}{2}} = \frac{24}{\frac{1+16-2}{4}}$$

$$= \frac{24\times 4}{15} = \frac{96}{15} = 6.4$$

4. **Option (A) is correct.**

Explanation:

$$\text{Expression } \frac{\frac{1}{3}+\left[4\frac{3}{4}-\left(3\frac{1}{6}-2\frac{1}{3}\right)\right]}{\left(\frac{1}{5}\text{ of }\frac{1}{5}\div\frac{1}{5}\right)\div\left(\frac{1}{5}\div\frac{1}{5}\times\frac{1}{5}\right)}$$

$$= \frac{\frac{1}{3}+\left[4\frac{3}{4}-\left(\frac{19}{6}-\frac{14}{6}\right)\right]}{\left(\frac{1}{5}\times\frac{1}{5}\times 5\right)\div\left(\frac{1}{5}\times 5\times\frac{1}{5}\right)} = \frac{\frac{1}{3}+\left[\frac{19}{4}-\frac{5}{6}\right]}{1}$$

$$= \frac{\frac{1}{3}+\frac{57-10}{12}}{1} = \frac{\frac{1}{3}+\frac{47}{12}}{1} = \frac{51}{12} = 4.25$$

5. **Option (C) is correct.**

Explanation: Given $\left[\frac{9^3+9^4+9^5+9^6+9^7}{9^1+9^2+9^3+9^4+9^5}\right]^{\frac{1}{2}}$

$$= \left[\frac{9^2(9^1+9^2+9^3+9^4+9^5)}{9^1+9^2+9^3+9^4+9^5}\right]^{\frac{1}{2}} = (9^2)^{\frac{1}{2}} = 9$$

6. **Option (A) is correct.**

Explanation:

$4 \times 30 - 15 \div 5 + 12 = 21$

After interchange

$4 \times 30 \div 5 - 15 + 12 = 21$

$4 \times 6 - 15 + 12 = 21$

$24 - 15 + 12 = 21$

$9 + 12 = 21$

$21 = 21$

7. **Option (B) is correct.**

Explanation: Given, $(x-y+z)^2-(x-y-z)^2$

Solving above algebraic identities,

$\Rightarrow x^2+y^2+z^2-2xy-2yz+2xz-x^2-y^2-z^2 + 2xy-2yz+2xz$

$\Rightarrow \quad 4xz-4yz$

8. **Option (D) is correct.**

Explanation:

$$\left(2\frac{1}{2}\div 1\frac{7}{8}\right)\div\left(9\frac{4}{9}\div 11\frac{1}{3}\text{ of }\frac{1}{8}\right)\text{ of }\frac{4}{3}\times 5\frac{1}{3}-\frac{9}{8}\div\frac{3}{4}$$

Using BODMAS

$$\Rightarrow \left(\frac{5}{2}\div\frac{15}{8}\right)\div\left(\frac{85}{9}\div\frac{34}{3}\text{ of }\frac{1}{8}\right)\text{ of }\frac{4}{3}\times\frac{16}{3}-\frac{9}{8}\div\frac{3}{4}$$

$$\Rightarrow \left(\frac{4}{3}\right)\div\left(\frac{85}{9}\div\frac{34}{24}\right)\text{ of }\frac{4}{3}\times\frac{16}{3}-\frac{3}{2}$$

$$\Rightarrow \left(\frac{4}{3}\right)\div\left(\frac{20}{3}\right)\text{ of }\frac{4}{3}\times\frac{16}{3}-\frac{3}{2} \Rightarrow \left(\frac{4}{3}\right)\div\left(\frac{80}{9}\right)\times\frac{16}{3}-\frac{3}{2}$$

$$\Rightarrow \left(\frac{3}{20}\right)\times\frac{16}{3}-\frac{3}{2} \Rightarrow \frac{4}{5}-\frac{3}{2} \Rightarrow \frac{-7}{10}$$

9. **Option (A) is correct.**

Explanation:

$$4\left\{2\left(\frac{3}{4}\text{ of }24-1\right)+3(7\div x)-5\times 8+1\right\} = 20^2$$

$$\therefore\ 4\left\{2\left(\frac{3}{4}\times 24-1\right)+3\left(\frac{7}{x}\right)-5\times 8+1\right\} = 400$$

$$4\left\{2(17)+\frac{21}{x}-39\right\} = 400$$

$$34+\frac{21}{x}-39 = 100$$

$$\frac{21}{x} = 105$$

$$\therefore \quad x = \frac{21}{105} = 0.2$$

10. **Option (C) is correct.**

Explanation: $4\frac{4}{5}\div\left[2\frac{1}{5}-\frac{1}{2}\left\{1\frac{1}{4}-\left(\frac{1}{4}-\frac{1}{5}\right)\right\}\right]$

$$= \frac{24}{5}\div\left[\frac{11}{5}-\frac{1}{2}\left\{\frac{5}{4}-\frac{1}{20}\right\}\right]$$

$$= \frac{24}{5}\div\left[\frac{11}{5}-\frac{1}{2}\times\frac{6}{5}\right]$$

$$= \frac{24}{5}\div\frac{8}{5} = \frac{24}{5}\times\frac{5}{8} = 3$$

11. **Option (D) is correct.**

Explanation:

$$\left(2\frac{6}{7}\text{ of }4\frac{1}{5}\div\frac{2}{3}\right)\times 1\frac{1}{9}\div\left(\frac{3}{4}\times 2\frac{2}{3}\text{ of }\frac{1}{2}\div\frac{1}{4}\right)$$

$$= \left(\frac{20}{7}\text{ of }\frac{21}{5}\div\frac{2}{3}\right)\times\frac{10}{9}\div\left(\frac{3}{4}\times\frac{8}{3}\text{ of }\frac{1}{2}\div\frac{1}{4}\right)$$

$$= \left(\frac{20}{7}\times\frac{21}{5}\div\frac{2}{3}\right)\times\frac{10}{9}\div\left(\frac{3}{4}\times\frac{8}{3}\times\frac{1}{2}\div\frac{1}{4}\right)$$

$$= \left(12\div\frac{2}{3}\right)\times\frac{10}{9}\div\left(\frac{3}{4}\times\frac{16}{3}\right)$$

$$= 18\times\frac{10}{9}\div 4 = 5$$

12. Option (D) is correct.

Explanation: Given,

$$(\sqrt{2}+\sqrt{5}-\sqrt{3})\times k = -12$$

So, $$k = \frac{-12}{(\sqrt{2}+\sqrt{5}-\sqrt{3})}$$

Rationalise the denominator,

$$\therefore \frac{-12}{(\sqrt{2}+\sqrt{5}-\sqrt{3})}\times\frac{(\sqrt{2}+\sqrt{5}+\sqrt{3})}{(\sqrt{2}+\sqrt{5}+\sqrt{3})}$$

$$= \frac{-12(\sqrt{2}+\sqrt{5}+\sqrt{3})}{(\sqrt{2}+\sqrt{5})^2-(\sqrt{3})^2}$$

$$\because a^2-b^2 = (a-b)(a+b)$$

$$= \frac{-12(\sqrt{2}+\sqrt{5}+\sqrt{3})}{4+2\sqrt{10}}$$

$$= \frac{-6(\sqrt{2}+\sqrt{5}+\sqrt{3})}{2+\sqrt{10}}$$

$$= \frac{-6(\sqrt{2}+\sqrt{5}+\sqrt{3})}{2+\sqrt{10}}\times\frac{\sqrt{10}-2}{\sqrt{10}-2}$$

$$= \frac{-6(\sqrt{2}+\sqrt{5}+\sqrt{3})(\sqrt{10}-2)}{6}$$

$$= (\sqrt{2}+\sqrt{5}+\sqrt{3})(2-\sqrt{10})$$

13. Option (B) is correct.

Explanation: $\dfrac{0.125\times 0.01}{0.5\times 0.005} = 0.5$

14. Option (C) is correct.

Explanation: Expression $18 + 3 - 5 \times 6 \div 4$

After interchanging the signs,

$= 18 \div 3 \times 5 + 6 - 4$

$= \dfrac{18}{3}\times 5+6-4$

$= 6 \times 5 + 6 - 4 = 30 + 6 - 4 = 36 - 4 = 32$

15. Option (B) is correct.

Explanation: Given,

$$\frac{4}{5}\div 3\frac{1}{4} \text{ of } \frac{8}{13}-\frac{\frac{1}{5}-\frac{1}{8}}{\frac{1}{5}+\frac{1}{8}}\times 5\frac{1}{5}+\frac{5}{6}$$

$$= \frac{4}{5}\div\frac{13}{4} \text{ of } \frac{8}{13}-\frac{3}{18}\times 5\frac{1}{5}+\frac{5}{6}$$

$$= \frac{4}{5}\div 2-\frac{3}{18}\times\frac{26}{5}+\frac{5}{6}$$

$$= \frac{2}{5}-\frac{6}{5}+\frac{5}{6}=\frac{12-36+125}{30} = \frac{1}{30}$$

16. Option (A) is correct.

Explanation: Given,

$$5-\frac{8+2\sqrt{15}}{4}-\frac{1}{8+2\sqrt{15}}$$

$$= 5-\frac{8+2\sqrt{15}}{4}-\frac{1}{8+2\sqrt{15}}\times\frac{8-2\sqrt{15}}{8-2\sqrt{15}}$$

$$= 5-\frac{8+2\sqrt{15}}{4}-\frac{8-2\sqrt{15}}{(8)^2-(2\sqrt{15})^2}$$

$$= 5-\frac{8+2\sqrt{15}}{4}-\frac{8-2\sqrt{15}}{64-60} = 5-\frac{16}{4}=1$$

17. Option (D) is correct.

Explanation:

$$\frac{(381+119)^2+(381+119)^2}{(381)^2+(119)^2}$$

$$= \frac{(381)^2+(119)^2+2\times381\times119+(381)^2+(119)^2-2\times381\times119}{(381)^2+(119)^2}$$

$$= \frac{2\left[(381)^2+(119)\right]^2}{(381)^2+(119)^2} = 2$$

18. Option (C) is correct.

Explanation: Let x and $x + 2$ be the two consecutive even numbers.

Now,

$$(x+2)^2-(x)^2 = 84$$
$$x^2+4+4x-x^2 = 84$$
$$4x+4 = 84$$
$$x = 20$$

$\therefore$ Required product $= x(x + 2)$

$= 20(20 + 2)$

$= 20 \times 22 = 440$

19. Option (C) is correct.

Explanation: Given,

$$33-4\sqrt{35} = 33-2\times2\sqrt{5\times7}$$
$$= 33-2\times2\sqrt{7}\times\sqrt{5}$$
$$= 28+5-2\times2\sqrt{7}\times\sqrt{5}$$
$$= (2\sqrt{7})^2+(\sqrt{5})^2-2\times2\sqrt{7}\times5$$
$$= (2\sqrt{7}-\sqrt{5})^2$$

So, $$\sqrt{33-4\sqrt{35}} = \sqrt{(2\sqrt{7}-\sqrt{5})^2}$$
$$= \pm(2\sqrt{7}-\sqrt{5})$$

20. Option (B) is correct.

Explanation:

$$\frac{1}{x+\cfrac{1}{y+\cfrac{2}{z+\cfrac{1}{4}}}} = \frac{29}{79}$$

$$\frac{1}{x+\cfrac{1}{y+\cfrac{2}{z+\cfrac{1}{4}}}} = \frac{1}{\cfrac{79}{29}}$$

$$\frac{1}{x+\cfrac{1}{y+\cfrac{2}{z+\cfrac{1}{4}}}} = \frac{1}{2+\cfrac{21}{29}}$$

$$\frac{1}{x+\cfrac{1}{y+\cfrac{2}{z+\cfrac{1}{4}}}} = \frac{1}{2+\cfrac{1}{\cfrac{29}{21}}}$$

$$\frac{1}{x+\cfrac{1}{y+\cfrac{2}{z+\cfrac{1}{4}}}} = \frac{1}{2+\cfrac{1}{1+\cfrac{8}{21}}}$$

$$\frac{1}{x+\cfrac{1}{y+\cfrac{2}{z+\cfrac{1}{4}}}} = \frac{1}{2+\cfrac{1}{1+\cfrac{21}{4}}}$$

$\therefore \quad x = 2, y = 1, z+\frac{1}{4}=\frac{21}{4} \Rightarrow z=5$

Now, $2x + 3y - z = 2 \times 2 + 3 \times 1 - 5 = 7 - 5 = 2$

21. Option (A) is correct.

Explanation: Given,

$$(2.\overline{4} \times 0.\overline{6} \times 3 \times 0.\overline{16}) \times [0.\overline{27} \times (0.8\overline{3} \div 0.1\overline{6})]$$

$$= \left(2\frac{4}{9} \times \frac{6}{9} \times 3 \times \frac{16-1}{90}\right) \times \left[\frac{27}{99} \times \left(\frac{(83-8)}{90} \div \frac{(16-1)}{90}\right)\right]$$

$$= \frac{22}{5} \times \frac{6}{9} \times 3 \times \frac{15}{90} \times \frac{27}{99} \times \frac{75}{90} \times \frac{90}{15} = \frac{10}{9} = 1.\overline{1}$$

22. Option (C) is correct.

Explanation: Given

$$11.\overline{4} + 22.5\overline{67} - 33.5\overline{9}$$

$$= 11 + 0.\overline{4} + 22 + 0.5\overline{67} - 33 - 0.5\overline{9}$$

$$= 0.\overline{4} + 0.5\overline{67} - 0.5\overline{9}$$

$$= 0.4\overline{44} + 0.5\overline{67} - 0.5\overline{99}$$

$$= 1.0\overline{11} - 0.59\overline{9} = 0.4\overline{12}$$

23. Option (D) is correct.

Explanation: $\dfrac{1}{4} + \dfrac{[(20.35)^2 - (8.35)^2] \times 0.175}{(1.05)^2 + 1.05 \times 27.65}$

$$= \frac{1}{4} + \frac{[(20.35+8.35)(20.35-8.35) \times 0.0175]}{1.05(1.05+27.65)}$$

$$= \frac{1}{4} + \frac{28.7 \times 12 \times 0.0175}{1.05 \times 28.7}$$

$$= \frac{1}{4} + \frac{12 \times 175}{105 \times 100}$$

$$= \frac{1}{4} + \frac{1}{5} = \frac{9}{20}$$

24. Option (C) is correct.

Explanation: Expression

$$\Rightarrow \frac{2}{3} \div \left\{\frac{3}{7} \text{ of } \frac{14}{5} \times 1\frac{2}{3} - \left(3\frac{1}{2} - 2\frac{1}{6}\right)\right\} \text{ is}$$

$$= \frac{2}{3} \div \left\{\frac{6}{5} \times \frac{5}{3} - \left(\frac{7}{2} - \frac{13}{6}\right)\right\} = \frac{2}{3} \div \left\{2 - \left(\frac{21-13}{6}\right)\right\}$$

$$= \frac{2}{3} \div \left\{2 - \frac{8}{6}\right\} = \frac{2}{3} \div \left\{\frac{12-8}{6}\right\} = \frac{2}{3} \times \frac{6}{4} = 1$$

25. Option (B) is correct.

Explanation: $18 \times [24 \div 70 \times \{25 \times 49 \div (5 \times 7)\}]$

$= 18 \times [24 \div 70 \times \{25 \times 49 \div 35\}]$

$= 18 \times [24 \div 70 \times (35)]$

$= 18 \times \left[\frac{24}{70} \times 35\right] = 18 \times 12 = 216$

Level-3: EXPERT

1. Option (D) is correct.

Explanation:

Given, $\sqrt{\dfrac{4\frac{1}{7} - 2\frac{1}{4}}{3\frac{1}{2} + 1\frac{1}{7}} + \cfrac{1}{2+\cfrac{1}{2+\cfrac{1}{5-\cfrac{1}{5}}}}}$

$$\frac{4\frac{1}{7} - 2\frac{1}{4}}{3\frac{1}{2} + 1\frac{1}{7}} = \frac{\frac{29}{7} - \frac{9}{4}}{\frac{7}{2} + \frac{8}{7}}$$

$$= \frac{53}{28} \times \frac{14}{65} = \frac{53}{130}$$

Now, $\dfrac{1}{2+\cfrac{1}{2+\cfrac{1}{5-\cfrac{1}{5}}}} = \dfrac{1}{2+\cfrac{1}{2+\cfrac{1}{\cfrac{25-1}{5}}}}$

$$= \frac{1}{2+\cfrac{1}{\cfrac{48+5}{24}}} = \frac{1}{2+\cfrac{24}{53}}$$

$$\frac{1}{\cfrac{106+24}{53}} = \frac{53}{130}$$

$\therefore$ Required answer $= \sqrt{\dfrac{53}{130} \div \dfrac{53}{130}} = 1$

2. Option (D) is correct.

Explanation: According to question,

$$9\frac{4}{9} \div 11\frac{1}{3} \text{ of } \frac{1}{6} + \left(1\frac{1}{3} \times 1\frac{4}{5} \div \frac{3}{5}\right) \times 2\frac{1}{6} \text{ of } \frac{2}{3} \div \frac{4}{3} \text{ of } \frac{2}{3}$$

$$=\frac{85}{9}\div\left(\frac{34}{3}\times\frac{1}{6}\right)+\left(\frac{4}{3}\times\frac{9}{5}\times\frac{5}{3}\right)\times\left(\frac{13}{6}\times\frac{2}{3}\right)\div\left(\frac{4}{3}\times\frac{2}{3}\right)$$

$$=\frac{85}{9}\div\frac{17}{9}+4\times\frac{13}{9}\times\frac{9}{8}$$

$$=\frac{85}{9}\times\frac{9}{17}+\frac{13}{2}=5+\frac{13}{2}=\frac{23}{2}$$

Now, students answer $= 19\frac{1}{4}=\frac{77}{4}$

So, difference $= \frac{77}{4}-\frac{23}{2}$

$$=\frac{77-46}{4}=\frac{31}{4}=7\frac{3}{4}$$

3. **Option (A) is correct.**

Explanation:

$$1\frac{1}{8}\div\left(4\frac{1}{4}\div\frac{3}{5}\text{ of }8\frac{1}{2}\right)-\frac{2}{5}\times1\frac{1}{3}\div\frac{4}{5}\text{ of }1\frac{2}{3}+\frac{11}{20}$$

$$=\frac{9}{8}\div\left(\frac{17}{4}\div\frac{3}{5}\text{of}\frac{17}{2}\right)-\frac{2}{5}\times\frac{4}{3}\div\frac{4}{5}\text{ of }\frac{5}{3}+\frac{11}{20}$$

$$=\frac{9}{8}\div\left(\frac{17}{4}\div\frac{3}{5}\times\frac{17}{2}\right)-\frac{2}{5}\times\frac{4}{3}\div\frac{4}{3}+\frac{11}{20}$$

$$=\frac{9}{8}\div\left(\frac{17}{4}\times\frac{10}{3\times17}\right)-\frac{2}{5}\times\frac{4}{3}\times\frac{3}{4}+\frac{11}{20}$$

$$=\frac{9}{8}\div\frac{5}{6}-\frac{2}{5}+\frac{11}{20}=\frac{9}{8}\times\frac{6}{5}-\frac{2}{5}+\frac{11}{20}$$

$$=\frac{27}{20}-\frac{2}{5}+\frac{11}{20}=\frac{38}{20}-\frac{2}{5}=\frac{38-8}{20}=\frac{30}{20}=\frac{3}{2}=1\frac{1}{2}$$

4. **Option (B) is correct.**

Explanation: As, $n^r - tn + \frac{1}{4}$ is a perfect square.

$$r = 2 \text{ and } t = \pm 1$$

$$n^2-n+\frac{1}{4} = n^2-2.n.\frac{1}{2}+\frac{1}{4}$$

$$=\left(n-\frac{1}{2}\right)^n$$

$$\therefore\quad n^2+n+\frac{1}{4} = n^2+2.n.\frac{1}{2}+\frac{1}{4}=\left(n+\frac{1}{2}\right)^2$$

5. **Option (A) is correct.**

Explanation:

$$4-\cfrac{5}{1+\cfrac{1}{3+\cfrac{1}{\frac{9}{4}}}} = 4-\cfrac{5}{1+\cfrac{1}{3+\frac{4}{9}}}$$

$$=4-\cfrac{5}{1+\cfrac{1}{\frac{27+4}{9}}}=4-\frac{5}{\frac{40}{31}}=4-\frac{5\times31}{40}=4-\frac{31}{8}=\frac{1}{8}$$

$\because$ Time taken is completing $\frac{1}{8}$ part = 10 minutes

$\therefore$ Time taken is completing $\frac{3}{5}$ part $= 10\times8\times\frac{3}{5}$

= 48 minutes

6. **Option (C) is correct.**

Explanation: Given

$$x=\frac{5\frac{3}{4}-\frac{3}{7}\times15\frac{3}{4}+2\frac{2}{35}\div1\frac{11}{25}}{\frac{3}{4}\div5\frac{1}{4}+5\frac{3}{5}\div3\frac{4}{15}}$$

$$=\frac{\frac{23}{4}-\frac{3}{7}\times\frac{63}{4}+\frac{72}{35}\div\frac{36}{25}}{\frac{3}{4}\div\frac{21}{4}+\frac{28}{5}\div\frac{49}{15}}=\frac{\frac{23}{4}-\frac{27}{4}+\frac{72}{35}\times\frac{25}{36}}{\frac{3}{4}\times\frac{4}{21}+\frac{28}{5}\times\frac{15}{49}}$$

$$=\frac{\frac{23}{4}-\frac{27}{4}+\frac{10}{7}}{\frac{1}{7}+\frac{12}{7}}=\frac{\frac{10}{7}-1}{\frac{12}{7}}=\frac{3}{7}\times\frac{7}{13}=\frac{3}{13}$$

$$\because\quad x+y=\frac{7}{13}$$

$$\Rightarrow\quad \frac{3}{13}+y=\frac{7}{13}$$

$$y=\frac{7}{13}-\frac{3}{13}=\frac{4}{13}$$

7. **Option (B) is correct.**

Explanation: Given

$$\left[\frac{4}{7}\text{ of }2\frac{4}{5}\times1\frac{2}{3}-\left(3\frac{1}{2}-2\frac{1}{6}\right)\right]\div\left(3\frac{1}{5}\div4\frac{1}{2}\text{of}5\frac{1}{3}\right)$$

$$=\left[\frac{4}{7}\times\frac{14}{5}\times\frac{5}{3}-\left(\frac{7}{2}-\frac{13}{6}\right)\right]\div\left(\frac{16}{5}\div\left(\frac{9}{2}\times\frac{16}{3}\right)\right)$$

$$=\left(\frac{8}{3}-\frac{8}{6}\right)\div\left[\frac{16}{5}\div24\right]$$

$$=\frac{8}{6}\div\left(\frac{16}{5}\times\frac{1}{24}\right)=\frac{8}{6}\div\frac{2}{15}=\frac{8}{6}\times\frac{15}{2}=10$$

8. **Option (B) is correct.**

Explanation: Given,

$$\frac{4}{21}\div\frac{3}{7}\text{ of }\frac{1}{2}-\frac{1}{2}\times1\frac{2}{3}+(0.\overline{89}\div0.9\overline{8}\times7\frac{1}{3})\div2\frac{2}{2}$$

$$=\frac{4}{21}\div\frac{3}{14}-\frac{1}{2}\times\frac{5}{3}+\left(\frac{89}{99}\div\frac{98-9}{90}\times\frac{22}{3}\right)\div\frac{5}{2}$$

$$=\frac{4}{21}\div\frac{3}{14}-\frac{5}{6}+\left(\frac{89}{99}\times\frac{90}{89}\times\frac{22}{3}\right)\div\frac{5}{2}$$

$$=\frac{8}{9}-\frac{5}{6}+\frac{20}{3}\times\frac{2}{5}=\frac{8}{9}-\frac{5}{6}+\frac{8}{3}$$

$$=\frac{32-30+96}{36}=\frac{98}{36}=\frac{49}{18}$$

9. Option (D) is correct.

Explanation:

$$\frac{(2.53)^3+(2.47)^3}{25.3\times 25.3-624.91+24.7\times 24.7}$$

Let $a = 2.53, b = 2.47$

So, $25.3 = 10a$ and $24.7 = 10b$

According to question,

$$= \frac{a^3+b^3}{100(a^2-ab+b^2)} = \frac{(a+b)(a^2-ab+b^2)}{100(a^2-ab+b^2)}$$

$$= \frac{a+b}{100} = \frac{2.53+2.47}{100} = \frac{5}{100}$$

$$\therefore \quad \frac{5}{100} = 5\times 10^k$$

So, $10^{-2} = 10^k$

$\therefore \quad k = -2$

10. Option (C) is correct.

Explanation:

$$\left(1-\cfrac{1}{4-\cfrac{2}{1+\cfrac{1}{\cfrac{1}{3}+2}}}\right)\times\frac{15}{16}\div\frac{2}{3}\text{ of }2\frac{1}{4}-\frac{3+4}{3^3+4^3}$$

$$= 1-\cfrac{1}{4-\cfrac{2}{1-\cfrac{1}{\cfrac{7}{3}}}}\times\frac{15}{16}\div\left(\frac{2}{3}\times\frac{9}{4}\right)-\frac{7}{27+64}$$

$$= 1-\cfrac{1}{4-\cfrac{2}{1+\cfrac{3}{7}}}\times\frac{15}{16}\div\frac{3}{2}-\frac{7}{91}$$

$$= 1-\cfrac{1}{4-\cfrac{2}{\cfrac{7+3}{7}}}\times\frac{15}{16}\times\frac{2}{3}-\frac{7}{91} = 1-\cfrac{1}{4-\cfrac{14}{10}}\times\frac{5}{8}-\frac{7}{91}$$

$$= 1-\cfrac{1}{4-\cfrac{7}{5}}\times\frac{5}{8}-\frac{1}{13} = 1-\cfrac{1}{\cfrac{20-7}{5}}\times\frac{5}{8}-\frac{1}{13}$$

$$= \frac{13-5}{13}\times\frac{5}{8}-\frac{1}{13} = \frac{8}{13}\times\frac{5}{8}-\frac{1}{13}=\frac{4}{13}$$

11. Option (C) is correct.

Explanation: Given,

$$\left(1+\frac{3}{4}\right)\times\frac{3}{21}\text{ of }5\frac{1}{3}\div\frac{128}{49}+\frac{2}{3}\times\frac{7}{11}\times\frac{121}{49}\div\left(\frac{15}{14}-\frac{2}{7}\right)$$

$$=\frac{7}{4}\times\frac{3}{21}\times\frac{16}{3}\times\frac{49}{128}+\frac{2}{3}\times\frac{7}{11}\times\frac{121}{49}\div\left(\frac{15-4}{14}\right)$$

$$=\frac{7}{4}\times\frac{7}{24}+\frac{2}{3}\times\frac{7}{11}\times\frac{121}{49}\times\frac{14}{11}$$

$$=\frac{7}{4}\times\frac{7}{24}+\frac{2}{3}\times\frac{7}{11}\times\frac{22}{7} = \frac{49}{96}+\frac{4}{3}=\frac{59}{32}$$

12. Option (A) is correct.

Explanation: Given,

$$\frac{(0.13)^2+(0.21)^2}{(0.39)^2+81(0.07)^2}\div\frac{(2.4)^4+3\times(11.52)+9}{(2.4)^6+6(2.4)^4+3\times(17.28)}$$

Take first term and solve:

$$\frac{(0.13)^2+(0.21)^2}{(0.39)^2+81(0.07)^2} = \frac{(0.13)^2+(0.21)^2}{(3\times 0.13)^2+9(0.07\times 3)^2}$$

$$= \frac{1(0.13)^2+(0.21)^2}{9[(0.13)^2+(0.21)^2]}$$

$$= \frac{1}{9} \quad \text{...(1)}$$

Take second term and solve.

$$\frac{(2.4)^4+3\times(11.52)+9}{(2.4)^6+6(2.4)^4+3\times(17.28)}$$

$$= \frac{(5.76)^2+3\times(11.52)+9}{(5.76)^3+6(5.76)^2+3\times 3\times 5.76}$$

$$= \frac{(5.76)^2+3\times 2\times 5.76+9}{5.76[(5.76)^2+3\times 2\times 5.76+9}$$

$$= \frac{1}{5.76} \quad \text{...(2)}$$

Now, from (1) and (2)

$$\frac{1}{9}\div\frac{1}{5.76} = \frac{5.76}{9} = 0.64$$

Thus, 0.64 lies between 0.6 and 0.7

13. Option (A) is correct.

Explanation: Given,

$$\frac{132\div 12\times x-3\times 3}{5^2-6\times 4+x^2} = 1$$

$$\Rightarrow \quad \frac{(11\times x-9)}{25-24+x^2} = 1$$

$$\frac{11\times x-9}{1+x^2} = 1$$

$$11\times x-9 = 1+x^2$$

$$x^2-11x+10 = 0$$

$$(x-1)(x-10) = 0$$

$$x = 1, 10$$

$$x = 1$$

$\therefore$ 1 satisfies the condition.

14. Option (A) is correct.

Explanation: Value of $\frac{8\times 5\div 25}{7\div 14\times 2}-\frac{14\div 7-5}{7\div 14-25}$

$$= \frac{8\times 5\times\frac{1}{25}}{7\times\frac{1}{14}\times 2}-\frac{14\times\frac{1}{7}-5}{7\times\frac{1}{14}-25}$$

$$= \frac{\frac{8}{5}}{1} - \frac{2-5}{\frac{1}{2}-25} = \frac{8}{5} - \frac{3\times 2}{49} = \frac{362}{245}$$

15. Option (C) is correct.

Explanation: Given,

$$56 \div [12 + 9 \div 3 - \{8 + (18 \text{ of } 2 \div 9) - (40 \div 5 \text{ of } 2)\}] + \frac{27 + \frac{2}{5} \text{ of } 75}{5 + \frac{2}{5} \times (58-37)}$$

$$= 56 \div [12 + 9 \div 3 - \{8 + (36 \div 9) - (40 \div 10)\}]1 + \frac{27+30}{5+\frac{2}{3}\times(21)}$$

$$= 56 \div [12 + 3 - \{8 + 4\}] + \frac{30}{5+14}$$

$$\Rightarrow \quad 56 \div [15 - 8] + \frac{57}{19} = 8 + 3 = 11$$

16. Option (D) is correct.

Explanation:

$$\frac{\left[4\frac{1}{3} + 3\frac{1}{3} \times 1\frac{4}{5} \div 3\frac{3}{4} \times \left(1\frac{1}{2} + 1\frac{1}{3}\right)\right]}{\left(\frac{2}{3} \div \frac{5}{6} \times \frac{2}{3}\right)}$$

$$= \frac{\left[\frac{13}{3} + \frac{10}{3} \times \frac{9}{5} \div \frac{15}{4} \times \left(\frac{3}{2} + \frac{4}{3}\right)\right]}{\frac{2}{3} \times \frac{6}{5} \times \frac{2}{3}}$$

$$= \frac{\left[\frac{13}{3} + \frac{10}{3} \times \frac{9}{5} \times \frac{4}{15} \times \frac{17}{6}\right]}{\frac{8}{15}}$$

$$= \frac{\left[\frac{13}{3} + \frac{68}{15}\right]}{\frac{8}{15}} = \frac{\frac{65+68}{15}}{\frac{8}{15}}$$

$$= \frac{133}{8} = 16\frac{5}{8}$$

17. Option (D) is correct.

Explanation:

$$\left(1\frac{1}{8} \div \frac{3}{4}\right) \div \left[\left(\frac{1}{2} \text{ of } 1\frac{1}{2}\right) \div \left(3\frac{1}{2} - 1\frac{1}{4}\right) \text{ of } \frac{3}{4} - \frac{3}{4} \div 2\frac{1}{4}\right] \text{ of } \frac{3}{4}$$

$$= \left(\frac{9}{8} \div \frac{3}{4}\right) \div \left[\left(\frac{1}{2} \text{of } \frac{3}{2}\right) \div \left(\frac{7}{2} - \frac{5}{4}\right) \text{ of } \frac{3}{4} - \frac{3}{4} \div \frac{9}{4}\right] \text{ of } \frac{3}{4}$$

$$= \left(\frac{9}{8} \times \frac{3}{4}\right) \div \left[\left(\frac{3}{4}\right) \div \left(\frac{14}{4} - \frac{5}{4}\right) \text{ of } \frac{3}{4} - \frac{3}{4} \times \frac{4}{9}\right] \text{ of } \frac{3}{4}$$

$$= \left(\frac{3}{2}\right) \div \left[\left(\frac{3}{4}\right) \div \left(\frac{9}{4}\right) \text{ of } \frac{3}{4} - \frac{1}{3}\right] \text{ of } \frac{3}{4}$$

$$= \frac{3}{2} \div \left[\frac{3}{4} \div \frac{27}{16} - \frac{1}{3}\right] \text{ of } \frac{3}{4} = \frac{3}{2} \div \left[\frac{3}{4} \times \frac{16}{27} - \frac{1}{3}\right] \text{ of } \frac{3}{4}$$

$$= \frac{3}{2} \div \left[\frac{4}{5} - \frac{3}{9}\right] \text{ of } \frac{3}{4} = \frac{3}{2} \div \left[\frac{1}{5}\right] \text{ of } \frac{3}{4}$$

$$= \frac{3}{2} \div \frac{1}{12} = 18$$

18. Option (D) is correct.

Explanation: Expression,

$(2x - 3y)^3 - 18xy\,(2x - 3y)$

Using identity $(a - b)^3 = a^3 - b^3 - 3ab\,(a - b)$

$= 8x^3 - 27y^3 - 36x^2y + 54xy^2 - 36x^2y + 54xy^3$

$= 8x^3 - 27y^3 - 72x^2y + 108xy^2$

19. Option (A) is correct.

Explanation: Given,

$$\frac{\left(2\frac{1}{3} + 2\frac{1}{2} - \frac{1}{6}\right) \div 2\frac{1}{3} \times 5\frac{2}{3} \div 1\frac{2}{3} \text{ of } 4\frac{1}{4}}{3\frac{1}{5} \div 4\frac{1}{2} \text{ of } 5\frac{1}{3} + 5\frac{1}{3} \times \frac{3}{4} \div 2\frac{2}{3}}$$

$$= \frac{\left(\frac{7}{3} + \frac{5}{2} - \frac{1}{6}\right) \div \frac{7}{3} \times \frac{17}{3} \div \frac{5}{3} \text{ of } \frac{17}{4}}{\frac{16}{5} \div \frac{9}{2} \text{ of } \frac{16}{3} + \frac{16}{3} \times \frac{3}{4} \div \frac{8}{3}}$$

$$= \frac{\frac{14}{3} \times \frac{3}{7} \times \frac{17}{3} \times \frac{12}{85}}{\frac{16}{5} \times \frac{1}{24} + \frac{16}{3} \times \frac{9}{32}} = \frac{\frac{8}{5}}{\frac{2}{15} + \frac{3}{2}} = \frac{\frac{8}{5}}{\frac{49}{30}}$$

$$= \frac{8}{5} \times \frac{30}{49} = \frac{48}{49}$$

But students answer $= \frac{6}{7}$

$\therefore$ Difference required $= \frac{48}{49} - \frac{6}{7} = \frac{48-42}{49} = \frac{6}{49}$

20. Option (B) is correct.

Explanation: According to question,

$$9\frac{4}{9} \div 11\frac{1}{3} \text{ of } \frac{1}{6} + \left(1\frac{1}{3} \times 1\frac{4}{5} \div \frac{3}{5}\right) \times 2\frac{1}{6} \times \frac{2}{3} \div \frac{4}{3} \text{ of } \frac{2}{3}$$

$$= \frac{85}{9} \div \left(\frac{34}{3} \times \frac{1}{6}\right) + \left(\frac{4}{3} \times \frac{9}{5} \times \frac{5}{3}\right) \times \left(\frac{13}{6} \times \frac{2}{3}\right) \div \left(\frac{4}{3} \times \frac{2}{3}\right)$$

$$= \frac{85}{9} \times \frac{9}{17} + \frac{13}{2} = 5 + \frac{13}{2} = \frac{23}{2}$$

But, student's answer $= 19\frac{7}{4} = \frac{83}{4}$

$\therefore$ Required answer $= \frac{83}{4} - \frac{23}{2}$

$$= \frac{83-46}{4} = \frac{37}{4}$$

$$= 9\frac{1}{4}$$

21. Option (D) is correct.

Explanation: Given,

$$\frac{5 - 2 \div 4 \times [5 - (3-4)] + 5 \times 4 \div 2 \text{of } 4}{4 + 4 \div 8 \text{ of } 2 \times (8-5) \times 2 \div 3 - 8 \div 2 \text{ of } 8}$$

Using BODMAS,

$$= \frac{5-2\div 4\times[6]+20\div 8}{4+4\div 16\times 3\times 2\div 3-\frac{1}{2}}$$

$$= \frac{5-\frac{1}{2}\times 6+5\times\frac{1}{2}}{4+4\div 16\times 3\times 2\div 3-\frac{1}{2}} = \frac{\frac{9}{2}}{4} = \frac{9}{8}$$

22. Option (D) is correct.

Explanation: Given,

$$\frac{6.75\times 6.75\times 6.75-4.25\times 4.25\times 4.25}{67.5\times 67.5+42.5\times 42.5+67.5\times 42.5}$$

Let $6.75 = x, 4.25 = y$

So, $67.5 = 10x, 42.5 = 10y$

$$\therefore \quad = \frac{x^3-y^3}{100(x^2+y^2+xy)}$$

$$= \frac{(x-y)(x^2+y^2+xy)}{100(x^2+y^2+xy)}$$

$$= \frac{x-y}{100} = \frac{6.75-4.25}{100}$$

$$= \frac{2.5}{100} = 0.025$$

23. Option (A) is correct.

Explanation: $\dfrac{0.72\times 0.72\times 0.72-0.39\times 0.39\times 0.39}{0.72\times 0.72+0.72\times 0.39+0.39\times 0.39}$

Let $a = 0.72, b = 0.39$

$$= \frac{a^3-b^3}{a^2+b^2+ab}$$

$$= \frac{(a-b)(a^2+b^2+ab)}{a^2+b^2+ab}$$

$$= a-b = 0.72-0.39 = 0.33$$

24. Option (C) is correct.

Explanation: Given,

$$\frac{(4.6)^4+(5.4)^4+(24.84)^2}{(4.6)^2+(5.4)^2+(24.84)}$$

$$= \frac{[(4.6)^2+(5.4)^2]^2-2\{(4.6)^2(5.4)^2\}+(24.84)^2}{(4.6)^2+(5.4)^2+24.84}$$

$$= \frac{[\{(4.6)^2+(5.4)^2\}-(24.84)][\{(4.6)^2+(5.4)^2\}+(24.84)]}{(4.6)^2+(5.4)^2+24.84}$$

$= (4.6)^2 + (5.4)^2 - 24.84$

$= 21.16 + 29.16 - 24.84$

$= 50.32 - 24.84 = 25.48$

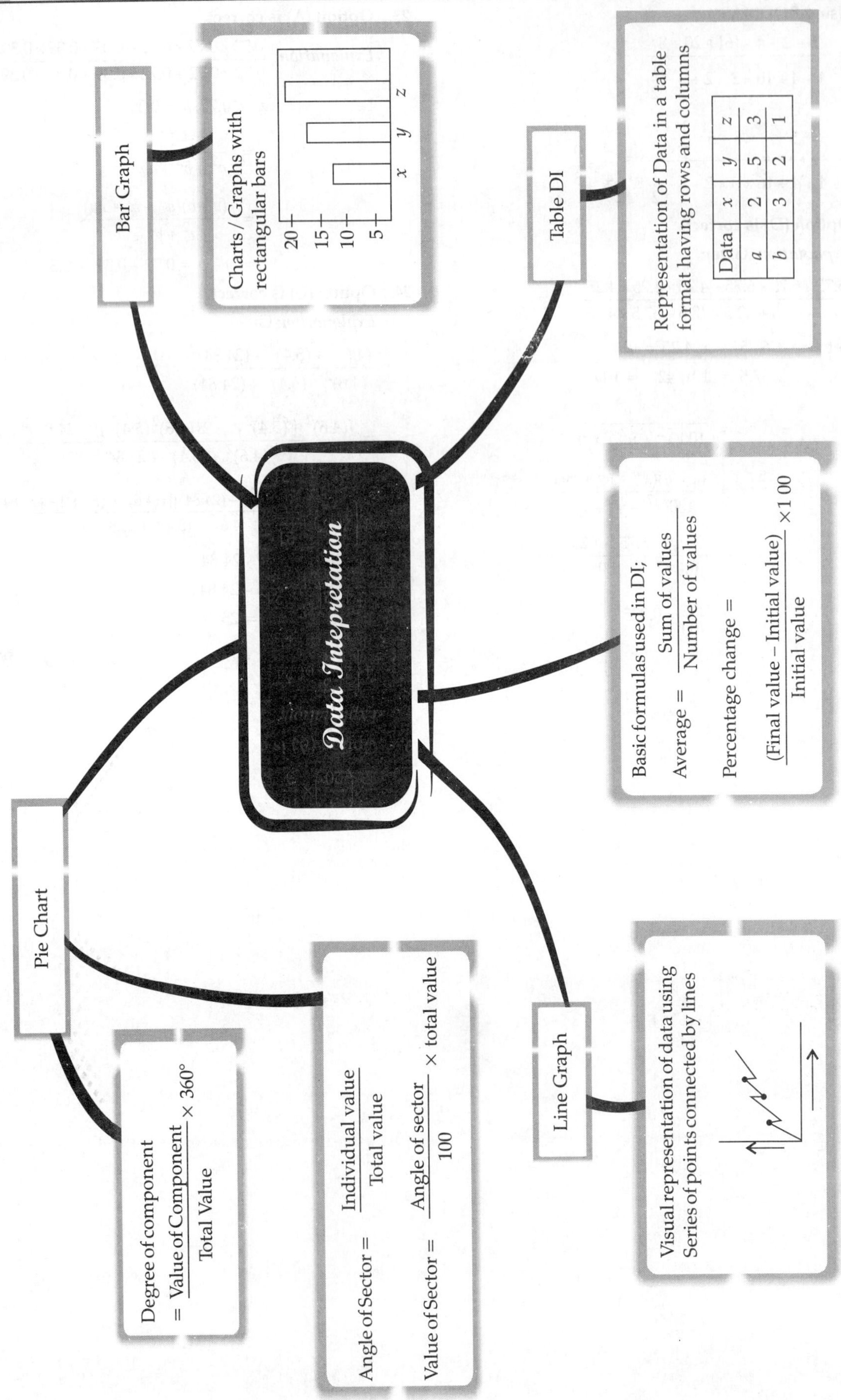
Data Intepretation
Bar Graph
Charts / Graphs with rectangular bars
20 15 10 5
x y z
Table DI
Representation of Data in a table format having rows and columns
Data x y z
a 2 5 3
b 3 2 1
Basic formulas used in DI;
Average = Sum of values / Number of values
Percentage change = (Final value – Initial value) / Initial value ×1 00
Line Graph
Visual representation of data using Series of points connected by lines
Pie Chart
Degree of component = Value of Component / Total Value × 360°
Angle of Sector = Individual value / Total value
Value of Sector = Angle of sector / 100 × total value

Section-4 : Data Interpretation

Chapter 21

Bar and Line Graph

LEARNING OBJECTIVES:

- ❖ Understanding the basic concept.
- ❖ Interpreting data.
- ❖ Identifying trends.
- ❖ Comparing data.
- ❖ Methods to solve questions asked in various competitive exams.

BAR GRAPH

A bar graph represents data using rectangular bars that vary in height or length according to the value being represented. The horizontal axis of a bar graph usually represents the categories being compared, while the vertical axis represents the numerical values.

- ➢ **Finding the range:** To find the range of a set of data represented in a bar graph, subtract the minimum value from the maximum value. For example, if a bar graph shows the number of goals scored by a team in each game of a season, the range would be the difference between the highest number of goals scored and the lowest.
- ➢ **Finding the mean/average:** To find the mean of a set of data represented in a bar graph, add up all the values and divide by the total number of values. For example, if a bar graph shows the number of books read by each student in a class, the mean would be the total number of books read divided by the number of students.
- ➢ **Comparing data:** Bar graphs can be used to compare data by looking at the relative heights or lengths of the bars. When comparing two or more sets of data, it is important to ensure that the bars are drawn to the same scale.
- ➢ **Interpreting data:** To interpret data from a bar graph, look for patterns or trends in the data. For example, if a bar graph shows the sales of different products over a period of time, it may be possible to identify which products are more popular at certain times of the year.
- ➢ **Reading bar graphs:** When reading a bar graph, it is important to pay attention to the scale used on the vertical axis. If the scale is not evenly spaced, it can be misleading and make it difficult to compare the data accurately.
- ➢ **Percentage calculation:** To calculate the percentage of a particular value in a bar graph, divide the value by the total and multiply by 100. For example, if a bar graph shows the number of students in a school who play different sports, and there are 100 students in total, to find the percentage of students who play basketball, divide the number of basketball players by 100 and multiply by 100.

SOME TIPS TO SOLVE QUESTIONS RELATED TO BAR GRAPHS

- ➲ To find the total or sum of values represented in a bar graph, add the heights of all the bars.
- ➲ To find the average or mean value of the data represented in a bar graph, add the heights of all the bars and divide by the number of bars.
- ➲ To find the percentage of a particular value in a bar graph, divide the height of the bar representing that value by the total height of all the bars and multiply by 100.
- ➲ To find the difference between two values represented in a bar graph, subtract the heights of the bars representing those values.
- ➲ To find the ratio of two values represented in a bar graph, divide the heights of the bars representing those values.
- ➲ To compare two or more sets of data represented in a bar graph, make sure the bars are drawn to the same scale, and then compare the heights of the bars.
- ➲ To find the range of a set of data represented in a bar graph, subtract the height of the smallest bar from the height of the largest bar.
- ➲ To find the mode of a set of data represented in a bar graph, identify the value(s) with the highest bar(s).

- To find the median of a set of data represented in a bar graph, identify the middle bar(s) and find the average of their heights if there are two middle bars.

LINE GRAPH

A line graph is a visual representation of data that uses a series of points connected by straight lines. The horizontal axis of a line graph usually represents time or some other quantitative variable, while the vertical axis represents the numerical values being compared.

IMPORTANT TERMS AND FORMULAS

- **Mean/average:** The mean, also known as the average, is calculated by adding up all the values in a set of data and then dividing by the number of values. The formula for calculating the mean is:
  Mean = (Sum of values) / (Number of values)
- **Median:** The median is the middle value in a set of data when the values are arranged in order from smallest to largest. If there is an even number of values, the median is the average of the two middle values.
- **Mode:** The mode is the most common value in a set of data.
- **Range:** The range is the difference between the largest and smallest values in a set of data. The formula for calculating the range is:
  Range = (Largest value) – (Smallest value)
- **Per cent change:** Per cent change is a measure of the change in a value over time. The formula for calculating per cent change is:
  Per cent change = [(New value – Old value) / Old value] × 100%
- **Proportions and percentages:** Proportions and percentages are used to express a part of a whole. A proportion is the part divided by the whole, while a percentage is the proportion multiplied by 100. The formulas for calculating proportions and percentages are:
  Proportion = (Part) / (Whole)
  Percentage = (Proportion) × 100%
- **Ratios:** Ratios are used to compare two or more quantities. The ratio of two values is calculated by dividing one value by the other. For example, if the ratio of the number of boys to the number of girls in a class is 2 : 3, this means that there are two boys for every three girls.

Directions: The bar graph given below shows the sales of the (in thousand number) from six branches of publishing company during two consecutive years 2000–2001.

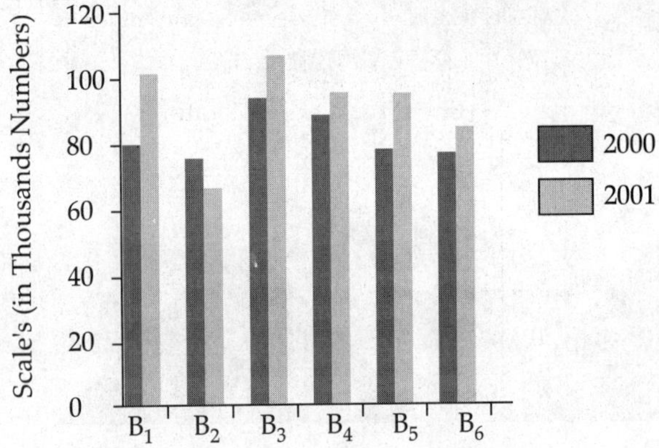

Example 1: Sales of books (in thousands numbers) from six branches B_1, B_2, B_3, B_4, B_5 and B_6 of a publishing company in 2000 and 2001. What is the ratio of the total sales of branch B_2 for both years to the total sales of branch B_4 for both year?

(a) 4 : 5 (b) 7 : 9
(c) 8 : 5 (d) 10 : 1

Sol. (b) Required ratio:

$$\frac{\text{Total sales of branch } B_2 \text{ for both years}}{\text{Total sales of branch } B_4 \text{ for both year}}$$

$$= \frac{75+65}{85+95} = \frac{140}{180} = \frac{7}{9} = 7:9$$

Example 2: Total sales of branch B_6 for both years is what percent of the total sales of branch B_3 for both the years?

(a) 73.17 (b) 75.3
(c) 80.23 (d) 85.7

Sol. (a) Total sales of branch B_6 for both years
= 70 + 80 = 150
Total sales of branch B_3 for both years
= 95 + 110 = 205

$$\text{Required \%} = \frac{150}{205} \times 100 = 73.17$$

Example 3: What is the average sales of all branches (in thousands number) for the year 2000?

(a) 73 (b) 77
(c) 80 (d) 87

Sol. (c) Total sales of all the six branches (in thousands) for the year 2000
= 80 + 75 + 95 + 85 + 75 + 70 = 480
Average sales of all the six branches in thousand, the year 2000 = $\frac{480}{8} = 80$

Example 4: Total sales branches B_1, B_3 and B_5 together for both the year (in thousands number) is?

(a) 250 (b) 315
(c) 435 (d) 560

Sol. (d) Total sales of branches B_1, B_3 and B_5 for both years (in thousands number)
= (80 + 105) + (95 + 110) + (75 + 95) = 560

Directions: Study the following graph carefully and answer the question given below:

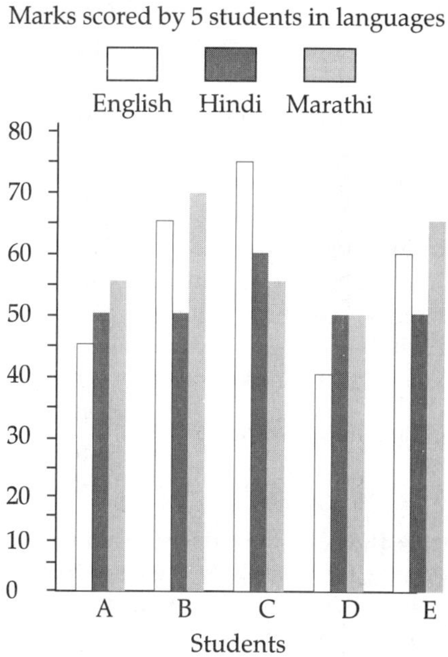

Example 1: What is the difference between the total marks obtained by B and the total marks obtained by C?

(a) 2 marks (b) 5 marks
(c) 8 marks (d) 18 marks

Sol. (b) ∴ Total marks obtain by C = 75 + 60 + 55
= 190

Total marks obtain by B = 65 + 50 + 70 = 185

Difference = 190 – 185 = 5 marks

Example 2: What is C's overall approximate percentage?

(a) 56 (b) 60
(c) 63 (d) 70

Sol. (c) Total marks of C = 190

Maximum marks = 300

$$\text{Percentage} = \frac{190}{300} \times 100 = 63.3 = 63\%$$

Example 3: Which of the following statements is true?

(a) A's overall percentage is 50%
(b) B and D had the same score in Hindi
(c) E scored the highest total marks.
(d) All students scored maximum marks in Hindi

Sol. (a) By observation, the bar graph and solving method A's overall percentage is 50.

Example 4: What is respective ratio of D's marks in English to B's marks in English?

(a) 5 : 14 (b) 6 : 13
(c) 7 : 12 (d) 8 : 13

Sol. (d) D's marks : B's marks

40 : 65

8 : 13

Example 5: What are approximate average marks obtained by D?

(a) 38 (b) 47
(c) 50 (d) 54

Sol. (b) Total marks of D in three subjects = 140

No. of subjects = 3

$$\text{Average} = \frac{140}{3} = 46.6 = 47$$

Directions: The following chart represents demand and production for 5 companies A, B, C, D and E on the basis of the given answer the question.

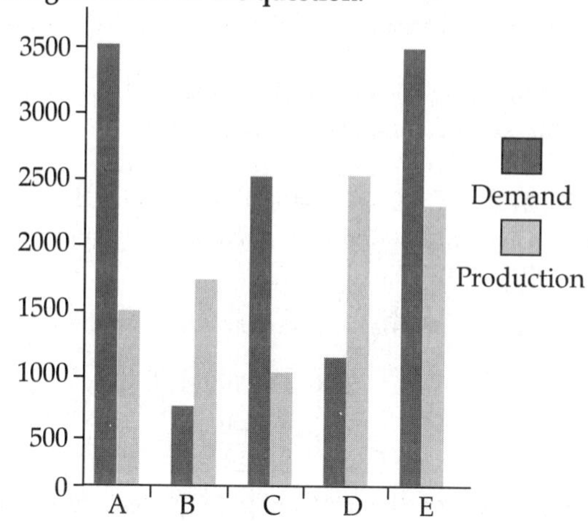

Example 1: If company A desires to meet the demand by purchasing surplus production of company then the most suitable company is:

(a) A (b) B
(c) C (d) D
(e) E

Sol. (d) Difference between demand and production of company A = 3,000 – 1,500 = 1,500

Difference between production and demand of company D = 2,700 – 1,200 = 1,500

So, company D is most suitable company.

Example 2: The difference betwen average demand and average production of the five companies taken together is

(a) 130 (b) 280
(c) 480 (d) 620

Sol. (b) Total production of the five companies

1,500 + 1,800 + 1,000 + 2,700 + 2,200 = 9,200

Total demand of the five companies

3,000 + 600 + 2,500 + 1,200 + 3,300 = 10,600

$$\text{Required difference} = \frac{1}{5}(10,600 - 9,200)$$

$$= \frac{1}{5} \times 1,400 = 280$$

Example 3: The ratio of the number of companies having more demand to those having more production than production than demand is:

(a) 1 : 2 (b) 2 : 2
(c) 3 : 2 (d) 4 : 1

Sol. (c) Number of companies having more demand than production = 3

Number of companies having more production than demand = 2

Required ratio = 3 : 2

Example 4: If the production of company D is h times of the production of the company A then h equals to:

(a) 1.2 (b) 1.5
(c) 1.8 (d) 2.5

Sol. (c) Production of company D = 2,700
Production of company A = 1,500

$$h = \frac{\text{Production of company D}}{\text{Production of company A}} = \frac{2{,}700}{1{,}500}$$

$$= \frac{9}{5} = 1.8$$

Example 5: If X% of demand for company C equals demand for company B. Then X equals:

(a) 4 (b) 20
(c) 24 (d) 60

Sol. (c) Given X% of demand for company C = Demand for company B

$$\Rightarrow \quad \frac{2{,}500 \times X}{100} = 600$$

$$25X = 600$$

$$X = \frac{600}{25} = 24$$

Directions: Study the following graph carefully and answer the question that follows.

Number of students (in thousands) who opted for three different specialisations during the given five years in a university.

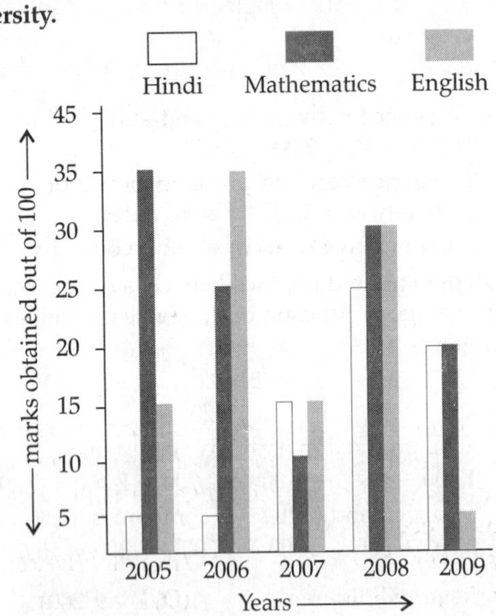

Example 1: Out of the total number of students who opted for the given three subjects in the year 2009, 38% were girls. How many boys opted for Mathematics in the some year?

(a) 1,312 (b) 1,322
(c) 1,332 (d) Cannot be determined

Sol. (d) Number of students who opted for the given three subjects in the year 2009 is

= (20,000 + 20,000 + 5,000) = 45,000

Number of girls = 38% of 45,000

$$= 45{,}000 \times \frac{38}{100} = 17{,}100$$

Out of these the number of boys who opt for Mathematics cannot be found.

Example 2: If the total number of students in the university in the year 2007 was 4,55,030 the total number of students who opted for the given three subjects was approximately what per cent of the total students?

(a) 5 (b) 9
(c) 12 (d) 19

Sol. (b) In 2007, we have

Total number of students = 4,55,030

Number of those choosing the given three subjects

= (15,000 + 10,000 + 15,000) = 40,000

$$\text{Required percentage} = \left(\frac{40{,}000}{4{,}55{,}030} \times 100\right)\%$$

= 8.79% = 9%

Example 3: What is the ratio of the number of student who opted for English in the year 2006 and 2008 together to the number of students who opted for Hindi in the year 2005 and 2009 together?

(a) 11 : 2 (b) 11 : 5
(c) 11 : 7 (d) 11 : 9

Sol. (b) Ratio of the number who opted for English in 2006 and 2008 to the number who opted for Hindi in 2005 and 2009

= (25 + 30) : (5 + 20) = 55 : 25 = 11 : 5

Example 4: What is the total number of students who opted for Hindi and Mathematics in the year 2006, 2007 and 2009 together?

(a) 97,000 (b) 96,000
(c) 85,000 (d) 95,000

Sol. (d) Number of students who opt Hindi and Mathematics 2006, 2007 and 2009

= [(5 + 35) + (15 + 15) + (20 + 5)] thousands
= 95,000

Example 5: The total number of students who opted for Mathematics in the year 2005 and 2008 together is approximately what per cent of the total numbers of students who opted for all three subjects in the same year?

(a) 28 (b) 32
(c) 42 (d) 52

Sol. (b) No. of students opting Maths in 2005 and 2008

= (15,000 + 30,000) = 45,000

No. of students opting for three subjects in 2005 and 2008

= [(5 + 35 + 15) + (25 + 30 + 30) thousands]
= [55,000 + 85,000] = 1,40,000

$$\text{Required \%} = \left(\frac{45{,}000}{1{,}40{,}000} \times 100\right)\% = \frac{225}{7}\%$$

= 32% (nearly)

Level 1 Beginner

Directions (Qs. 1–5): Study the following graph carefully and answer the questions that follow?

The graph given below represents the number of users of broadband services A and B across 5 cities P, Q, R, S and T.

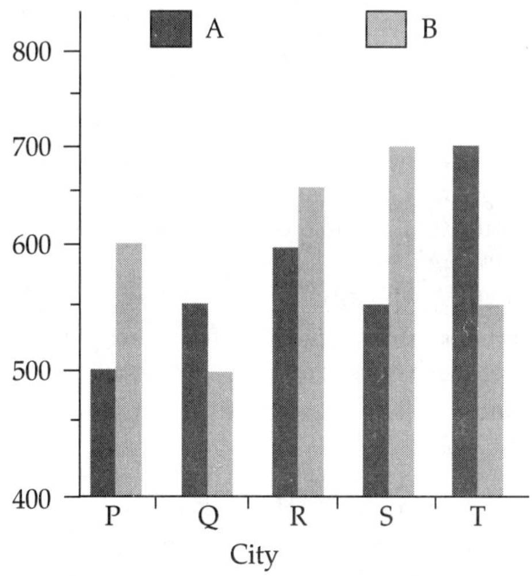

1. What is the total number of users of brand B across all five cities together?
   (A) 2,700 (B) 3,000
   (C) 3,100 (D) 2,900
   (E) 3,200
2. The number of users of brand A in city T is what per cent of the number of users of brand B in city Q?
   (A) 150 (B) 110
   (C) 140 (D) 160
   (E) 120
3. What is the average number of user of brand A across all five cities together?
   (A) 560 (B) 570
   (C) 580 (D) 590
   (E) 550
4. What is the difference between the total number of users of the brand A and B together in city R and the total number of user of brand A and B together in city P?
   (A) 170 (B) 140
   (C) 130 (D) 160
   (E) 150
5. What is the respective ratio of the number of user of brand A in city P to the number of users of brand B in city S?
   (A) 5 : 7 (B) 4 : 7
   (C) 2 : 5 (D) 3 : 4
   (E) 5 : 6

Direction (Qs. 6–10): Study the following bar graph carefully to answer the question:

Marks obtained by five students in Physics and Chemistry.

[SSC CLERK 2012]

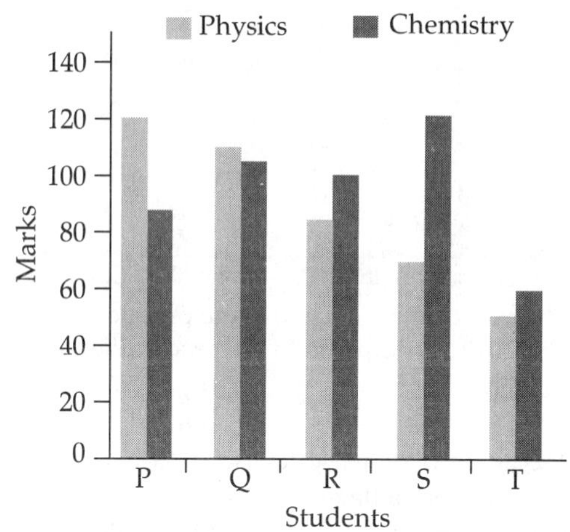

6. Marks obtained by S in Chemistry in what per cent of the total marks obtained by all the studetns in chemistry?
   (A) 25 (B) 28.5
   (C) 35 (D) 31.5
   (E) 22
7. If the marks obtained by T in Physics were increased by 14% of the original marks, what would be his new approximate percentage in Physics if maximum marks in physics were 140?
   (A) 57 (B) 32
   (C) 38 (D) 48
   (E) 41
8. Fill in the blank space in order to make the sentence correct as per given information. Total marks obtained by T in both the subjects together is more then the marks obtained by __________.
   (A) Q in Chemistry (B) R in Physics
   (C) S in Chemistry (D) P in Physics
   (E) R in both subjects together
9. What is the respective ratio between the total marks obtained by P in Physics and Chemistry together to the total marks obtained by T in Physics and Chemistry together?
   (A) 3 : 2 (B) 4 : 3
   (C) 5 : 3 (D) 2 : 1
   (E) None of these
10. What is the respective ratio between the total marks obtained by Q and S together in Chemistry to the total marks obtained by P and R together in Physics?
    (A) 23 : 25 (B) 23 : 21
    (C) 17 : 19 (D) 17 : 23
    (E) None of these

Direction (Qs. 11–15): Production of three different flavors soft drinks X, Y, and Z for a period of six years has been expressed in the follow graph. Study the graph and answer the questions.

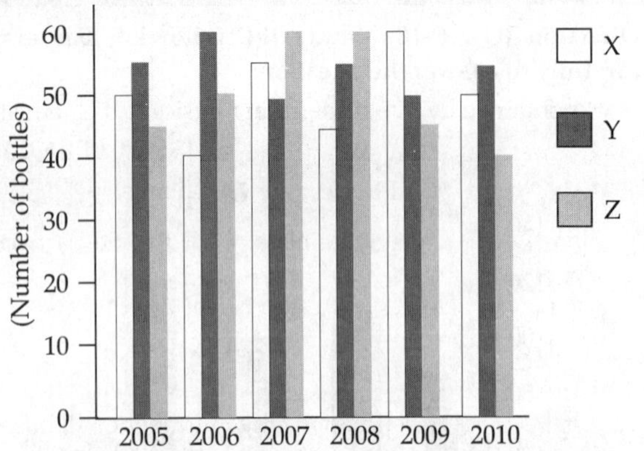

11. The approximate decline in the production of flavour Z in 2010 as compared to the production in 2008 is:
(A) 33% (B) 22.5%
(C) 42% (D) 25%

12. The average annual production was maximum in the given period of flavour:
(A) Y only (B) Z only
(C) X and Z (D) X only

13. What per cent of the total production of falvour X in 2005 and 2006 combined in the total production of flavour Z in 2007 and 2008 combined?
(A) 102.25 (B) 115.57
(C) 133.33 (D) 96.67

14. The percentage of rise/fall in production from the previous year in maximum for the flavour Y in which year?
(A) 2007 (B) 2008 (C) 2009 (D) 2006

15. The difference (in lakh bottles) between the average production of flavour X in 2005, 2006, 2007 and the average production of flavour Y in 2008, 2009 and 2010 is:
(A) 2.4 (B) 0.5 (C) 1.5 (D) 5

Direction (Qs. 16–19): The bar charge represents the number of first year B.com students in St. Xavier's college using different companies smart phones.

The bar graph representing the number of students using different smart phones.

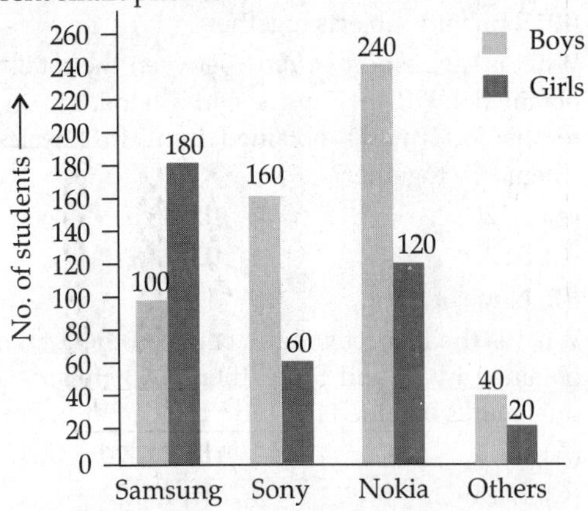

Different smart phone companies

16. The ratio of the number of boys to the number of girls using the smart phones of Samsung and Sony together is:
(A) 13 : 12 (B) 12 : 13
(C) 14 : 11 (D) 11 : 14

17. What is the percentage of boys who use the smart phones of Samsung?
(A) 16.52% (B) 17.52%
(C) 18.52% (D) 15.52%

18. What is percentage of girls who use the smart phones of Nokia?
(A) 33.58% (B) 32.58%
(C) 30.58% (D) 31.58%

19. The difference between the total number of students using smart phones of samsung combined together and the total number of student using phone of Sony taken together is
(A) 20 (B) 60 (C) 80 (D) 40

Direction (Qs. 20–24): Study the following graph carefully to answer these questions.

Producting (in lakhs tons) of six units of a company in 2001 and 2002.

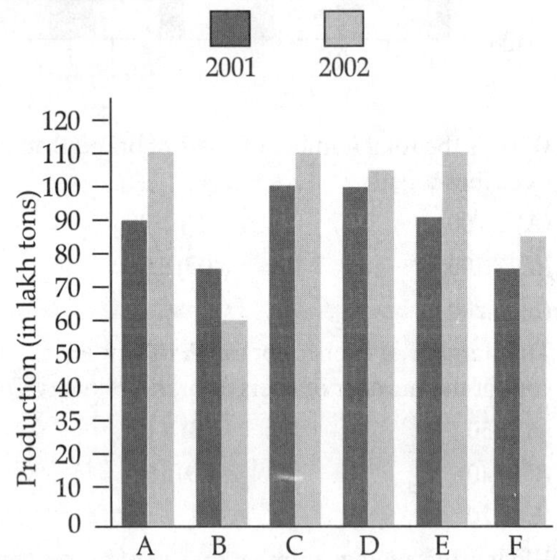

20. What is the average production of all the units (in lakh tons) for the year 2002?
(A) 89 (B) 92
(C) 87 (D) 95
(E) None of these

21. Average production of three units A, B and C in 2001 is what per cent of the average production of units D, E and F in the 2002?
(A) 109.43 (B) 90.37
(C) 91.38 (D) 106.43
(E) None of these

22. What is the ratio of total production for two years together for unit B to that for C?
(A) 17 : 13 (B) 13 : 17
(C) 11 : 13 (D) 19 : 13
(E) None of these

23. Total of production for two years together by unit F is what per cent of the total production of the two years together by unit D?

(A) 79.40 (B) 78.49
(C) 78.47 (D) 79.29
(E) None of these

24. What is the total production of units C, D and E together for both the year? (in lakh tones)
(A) 495 (B) 595
(C) 545 (D) 515
(E) None of these

Directions (Qs. 25–29): Given bar graph shows the data of two types of school buses X and Y for three schools A, B and C. Study the chart carefully and answer the following questions.

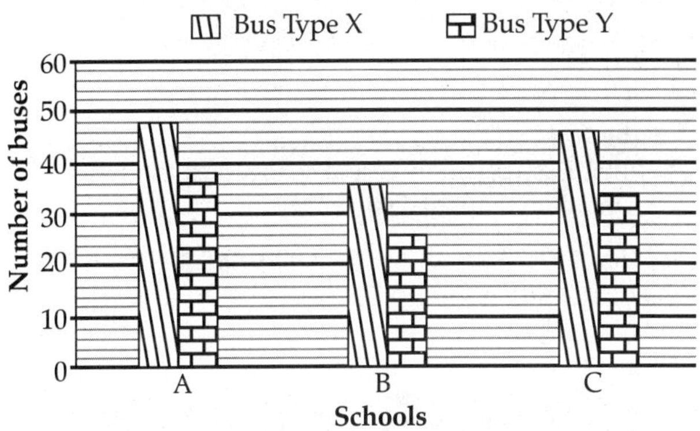

25. What is the average number of X type buses from school B and school C together?
(A) 40 (B) 70
(C) 30 (D) 59
(E) 54

26. X type buses from school A are how much more than that of X type buses from school B?
(A) $55\frac{3}{19}\%$ (B) 25%
(C) $5\frac{3}{9}\%$ (D) $45\frac{5}{6}\%$
(E) $33\frac{1}{3}\%$

27. What is the average number of all the buses from school B?
(A) 43 (B) 39
(C) 31 (D) 54
(E) 59

28. What is the difference of average number of all buses from school A and average number of all buses from school C?
(A) 16 (B) 4
(C) 8 (D) 24
(E) 12

29. Which school has maximum number of buses?
(A) School B (B) School C
(C) School A and School C
(D) School A and School B
(E) School A

2 Level Intermediate

Direction (Qs. 1–4): Study the following graph which show income and expenditure of a company over the years 2005-2009 and answer the questions:

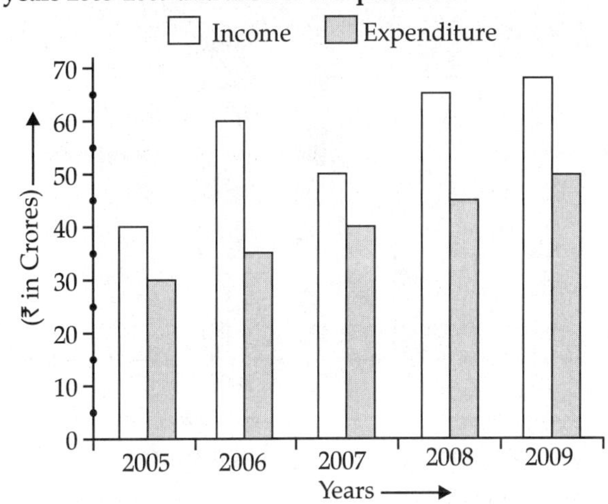

1. The difference in profit (₹ in crore) of the company during 2006 and 2007 is:
(A) 10 (B) 15
(C) 20 (D) 25

2. In how many year was the income of the company less than the average income of the give years?
(A) 4 (B) 3
(C) 2 (D) 1

3. The percentage increase in expenditure of the company from 2007 to 2008 is:
(A) 20% (B) 25%
(C) 30 (D) 35%

4. Profit of the company was maximum in the year
(A) 2009 (B) 2008
(C) 2006 (D) 2005

Direction (Qs. 5–9): Study the following graph and table carefully and answer the questions given below:

Time taken to travel (in hours) by six vehicles on two different days.

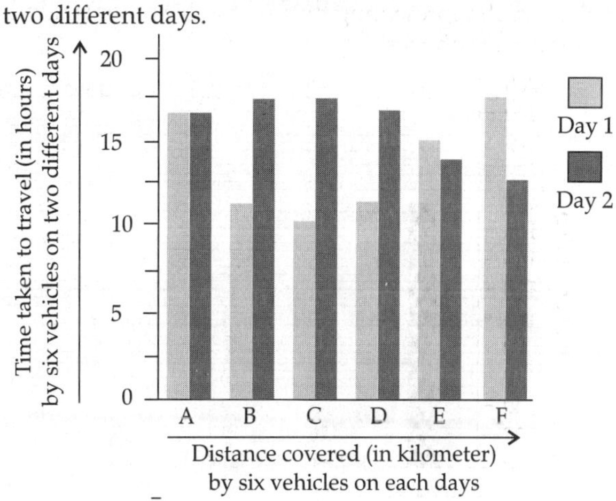

Vehicle	Day 1	Day 2
A	832	864
B	516	774
C	693	810
D	552	765
E	935	546
F	703	636

[IBPS PO 2012]

5. Which one of the following vehicles travelled a the same speed on both the days?
(A) Vehicle A (B) Vehicle C
(C) Vehicle F (D) Vehicle B
(E) None of these

6. What was the difference between the speed of Vehicle A on day 1 and the speed of Vehicle C on the same day?
(A) 7 km/h (B) 12 km/h
(C) 11 km/h (D) 8 km/h
(E) None of these

7. What was the speed of Vehicle C on day 2 in term of metres per second?
(A) 15.3 (B) 12.8
(C) 11.5 (D) 13.8
(E) None of these

8. The distance travelled by Vehicle F on day 2 was approximately what per cent of the distance travelled by it on day 1?
(A) 80 (B) 65
(C) 85 (D) 95
(E) 90

9. What is the respective ratio between the speed of Vehicle D and Vehicle E on day 2?
(A) 15 : 13 (B) 17 : 13
(C) 13 : 11 (D) 17 : 14
(E) None of these

Directions (Qs. 10–14): Line graph given below shows number of passengers travelling in five (A, B, C, D and E) different compartment of a trains. Read the data carefully and answer the questions.

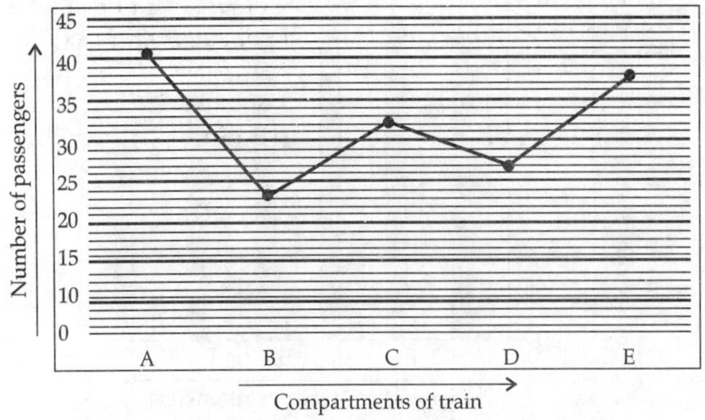

10. Total passengers in E are what per cent less than total passengers in A?
(A) $6\frac{1}{4}\%$ (B) $8\frac{1}{3}\%$
(C) $6\frac{1}{3}\%$ (D) $6\frac{2}{3}\%$
(E) 5%

11. Find average number of passengers in A, C and E?
(A) 32 (B) 30
(C) 36 (D) 33
(E) 27

12. Find the ratio of total passengers in B to that of in D?
(A) 7 : 9 (B) 9 : 10
(C) 11 : 9 (D) 9 : 13
(E) 9 : 11

13. Total passengers in C and E together are what per cent more than total passengers in A?
(A) $33\frac{1}{3}\%$ (B) $66\frac{2}{3}\%$
(C) $66\frac{1}{3}\%$ (D) 50%
(E) 60%

14. Find total number of passengers traveling in B, C and D together?
(A) 69 (B) 65
(C) 67 (D) 63
(E) 71

Direction (Qs. 15–16): The pass percentage for an examination in the adjoying bar diagram for males and females separately for four years, study the diagram and answer the questions.

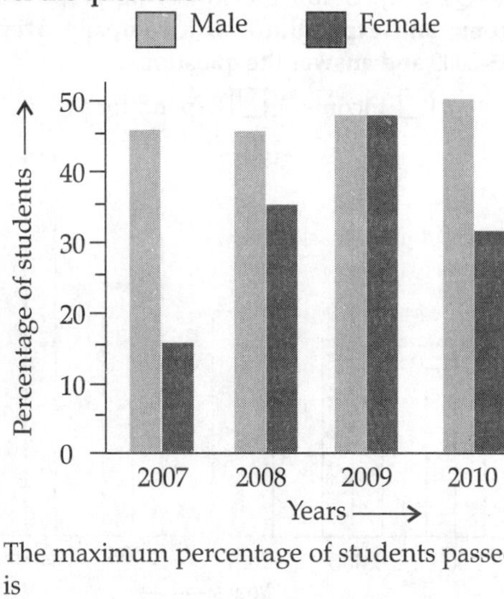

15. The maximum percentage of students passed in year is
(A) 2007 (B) 2008
(C) 2009 (D) 2010

16. The year in which the difference of pass percentage between male and female is maximum.
(A) 2010 (B) 2009
(C) 2008 (D) 2007

Direction (Qs. 17–20): Study the graphs carefully and answer the questions:

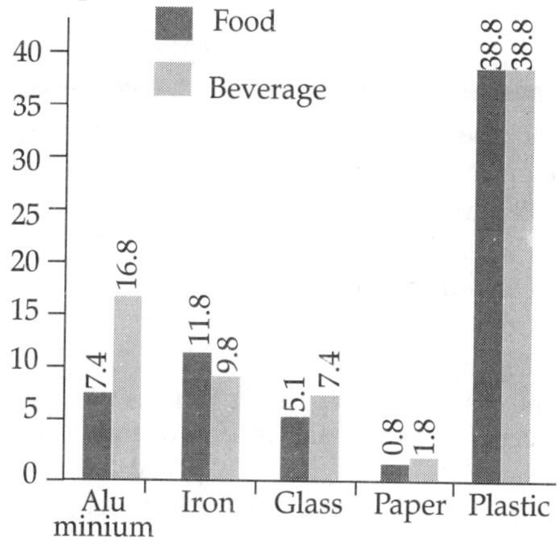

17. What per cent of the total glass packing material was used for packing food items?

(A) 40.8 (B) 41.8
(C) 40.7 (D) 41.0
(E) None of these

18. Approximately how much per cent more plastic was used than iron for packing food item?

(A) 32 (B) 320
(C) 33 (D) 325
(E) 225

19. In the case of which one of the following packing materials used for packing food item and beverages respectively the ratio is 4 : 9?

(A) Glass (B) Paper
(C) Aluminium (D) Iron
(E) None of these

20. What is the ratio between the glass and aluminium packing materials used for packing beverages?

(A) 17 : 56 (B) 56 : 17
(C) 84 : 37 (D) 37 : 84
(E) None of these

21. The number of patients in four different categories in three hospitals A, B and C are given below.

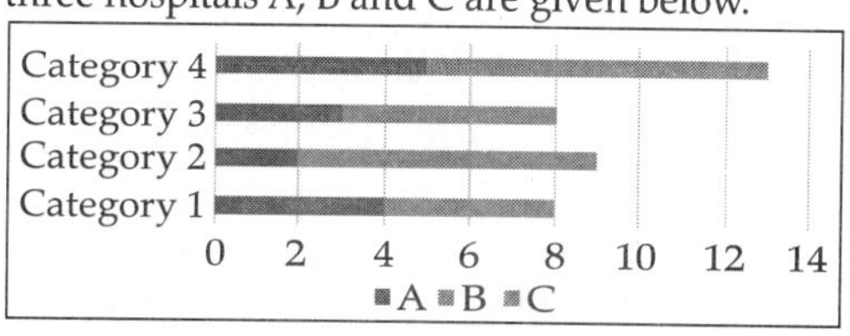

The total number of patients in three hospitals A, B and C, respectively, are: [SSC CHSL 2023]

(A) 12, 14, 12 (B) 12, 12, 14
(C) 14, 12, 12 (D) 14, 13, 12

22. The following bar graph gives the details of income and expenditure of five companies A, B, C, D, C (in crores of rupees)

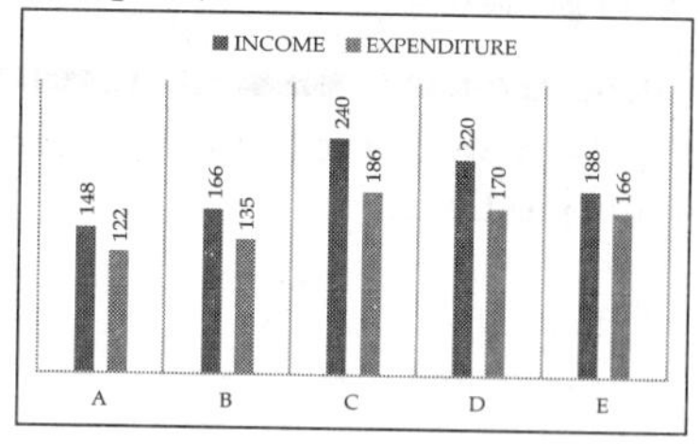

The profit percentage $\left(\frac{\text{Income} - \text{Expenditure}}{\text{Expenditure}} \times 100\right)$ is highest for the company: [SSC CHSL 2023]

(A) D (B) E (C) A (D) C

23. The following bar graph shows the incomes and expenditures (in million rupees) of three companies in the year 2020. Study the graph and answer the question that follows.

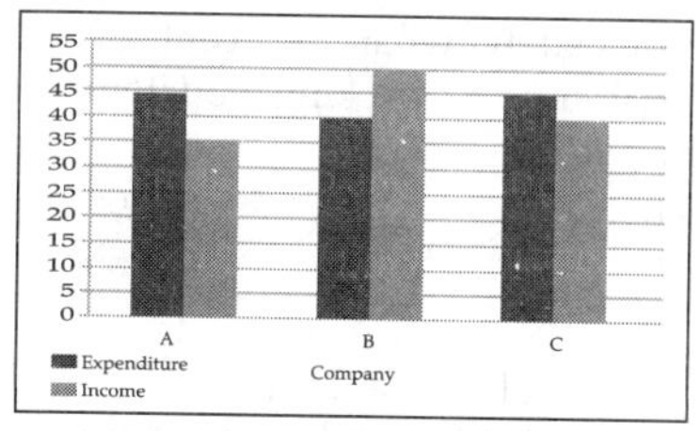

Which company earned the maximum percentage profit (Profit is calculated on expenditure) in the year 2020, and by what percentage? [SSC CHSL 2023]

(A) Company A, by 18% (B) Company B, by 20%
(C) Company B, by 25% (D) Company C, by 15%

24. The following bar graph indicates the sales of various items in a shop for one day. Study the bar graph carefully and answer the question that follows.

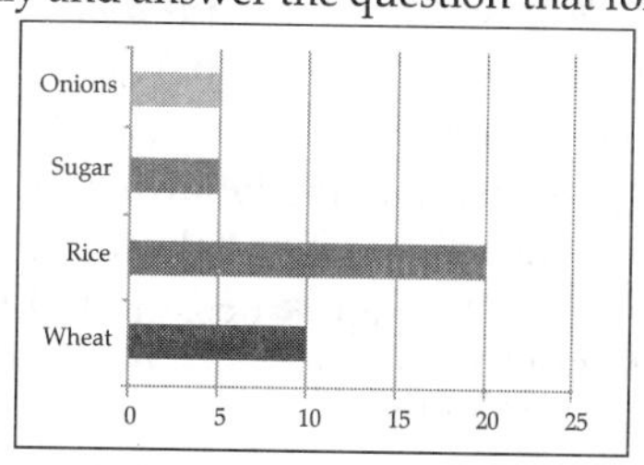

Find the ratio between the sale of wheat and rice and also the ratio between the sale of sugar and onions, respectively. [SSC CHSL 2023]

(A) 1 : 2 and 1 : 1 (B) 1 : 1 and 2 : 1
(C) 2 : 1 and 1 : 2 (D) 1 : 1 and 1 : 1

3 Level Expert

Direction (Qs. 1–3): Study the following graph carefully and answer the questions:

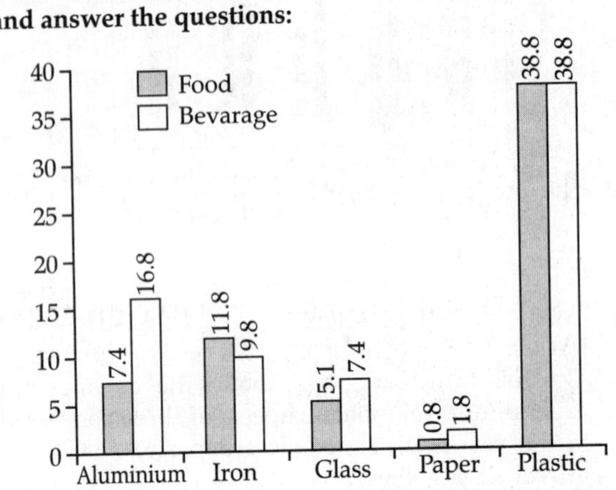

1. Approximately what per cent of all the packing materials used for packing food items was contributed by plastic?
   (A) 60 (B) 65
   (C) 70 (D) 55
   (E) 50
2. Approximately what per cent of all the packing materials used for packing food item and beverages was contributed by plastic and aluminium together?
   (A) 60 (B) 70
   (C) 80 (D) 55
   (E) 75
3. What per cent of all the packing materials used for packing beverages was contributed by paper? Find the answer up to two decimal places.
   (A) 2.42 (B) 3.41
   (C) 2.41 (D) 3.42
   (E) None of these

Direction (Qs. 4–8): Study the following graph carefully and answer the questions given below:

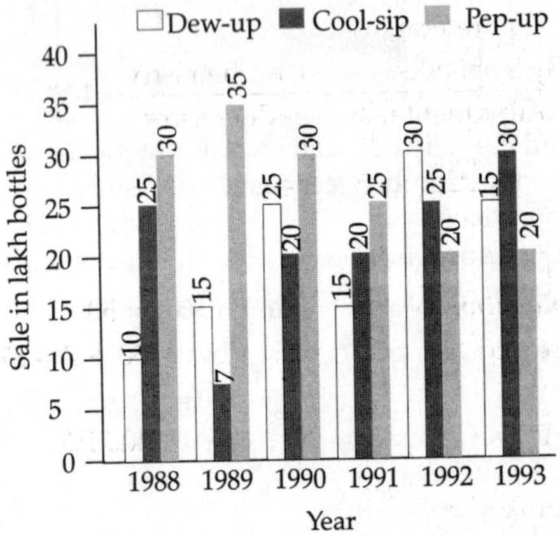

4. In which year was the sale of 'pep-up' the maximum?
   (A) 1990 (B) 1991
   (C) 1992 (D) 1993
   (E) None of these
5. In the case of which soft drink was the average annual sale maximum in the period?
   (A) Pep-up only
   (B) Cool-sip only
   (C) Dew-drop only
   (D) Cool-sip and Dew-drop
   (E) Pep-up Dew drop
6. In the case of cool-sip drink. What is the approximate per cent increase in sale in 1992 over its sale in 1991?
   (A) Less 20 (B) 20–25
   (C) 25 (D) 31–35
   (E) 36–41
7. In the year 1990, what was the difference between the number of 'Pep-up' and cool-sip bottles sold?
   (A) 50,00,000 (B) 5,00,000
   (C) 50,000 (D) 5,000
   (E) 10,00,000
8. What was the approximate per cent drop in sale of pep-up in 1990 over its sale in 1989?
   (A) 5 (B) 12
   (C) 14 (D) 20
   (E) None of these

Direction (Qs. 9–13): Study the following graph carefully and answer the questions given below:

Per cent profit earned by two companies A and B over the year 1991 to 1997.

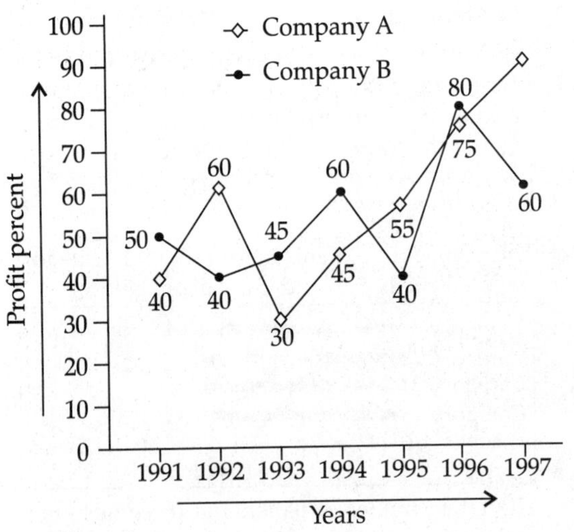

9. Investment of company 'B' in 1997 is more by 40% than that in the previous year income in 1997. What was the per cent of the ivnestment in 1996?
   (A) 280% (B) 252%
   (C) 242% (D) 52%
   (E) None of these
10. Average investment of company 'A' over the year was ₹26 lakhs. What was its average income over the year?
    (A) ₹ 40.56 lakhs (B) ₹ 41.60 lakhs
    (C) ₹50.26 lakhs (D) Data inadequate
    (E) None of these

11. Income of company 'A' in 1995 was ₹21.7 lakh. What was the investment?
(A) ₹ 14.5 lakhs (B) ₹ 15.4 lakhs
(C) ₹ 15.8 lakhs (D) ₹ 14.6 lakhs
(E) None of these

12. Income of company 'A' in 1995 is equal to the investment of company 'B' in 1996. What is the ratio of the investment of company 'A' in 1995 to the investment of company 'B' in 1996 ?
(A) 31 : 36 (B) 31 : 20
(C) 20 : 31 (D) Data inadequate
(E) None of these

13. Investment of company 'B' in 1993 was ₹ 15,40,000. What was the income in that year?
(A) ₹ 23.33 lakhs (B) ₹ 22.33 lakhs
(C) ₹ 22.23 lakhs (D) ₹ 23.23 lakhs
(E) None of these

ANSWER KEY

Level-1: Beginner

1.	(B)	2.	(C)	3.	(C)	4.	(E)	5.	(A)	6.	(A)	7.	(E)	8.	(B)	9.	(D)	10.	(B)
11.	(A)	12.	(A)	13.	(C)	14.	(A)	15.	(D)	16.	(A)	17.	(C)	18.	(D)	19.	(B)	20.	(D)
21.	(C)	22.	(E)	23.	(A)	24.	(B)	25.	(A)	26.	(E)	27.	(C)	28.	(B)	29.	(B)		

Level-2: Intermediate

1.	(B)	2.	(C)	3.	(B)	4.	(C)	5.	(D)	6.	(C)	7.	(E)	8.	(E)	9.	(B)	10.	(B)
11.	(A)	12.	(E)	13.	(B)	14.	(C)	15.	(C)	16.	(D)	17.	(A)	18.	(E)	19.	(B)	20.	(D)
21.	(C)	22.	(A)	23.	(C)	24.	(A)												

Level-3: Expert

1.	(A)	2.	(E)	3.	(C)	4.	(E)	5.	(A)	6.	(C)	7.	(E)	8.	(C)	9.	(B)	10.	(D)
11.	(E)	12.	(C)	13.	(B)														

Solutions with Detailed Explanations

Level-1 : BEGINNER

1. **Option (B) is correct.**
Explanation: Total number of users of brand B across all five cities together
$= 500 + 600 + 700 + 650 + 550 = 3{,}000$

2. **Option (C) is correct.**
Explanation:
$$700 = z\% \text{ of } 500$$
$$\Rightarrow \quad 700 = \frac{z \times 500}{100} \Rightarrow 700 = z \times 5$$
$$\Rightarrow \quad z = \frac{700}{5} = 140$$

3. **Option (C) is correct.**
Explanation: The average number of users of brand A all five cities together
$$\frac{500+550+600+550+700}{5} = \frac{2{,}900}{5} = 580$$

4. **Option (E) is correct.**
Explanation: Difference between the total number of users of brand A and brand B in city R and city P
$= 1{,}250 - 1{,}100 = 150$

5. **Option (A) is correct.**
Explanation: The respectively ratio brand A in city P to brand B in city S $= 500 : 700 = 5 : 7$

6. **Option (A) is correct.**
Explanation: All students marks in Chemistry
$= 110 + 100 + 90 + 120 + 160 = 480$
So, required ratio
$$= \frac{\text{By S obtained marks in Chemistry}}{\text{All student marks in Chemistry}} \times 100$$
$$\Rightarrow \quad \frac{120}{480} \times 100 = 25\%$$

7. **Option (E) is correct.**
Explanation: Marks of T in Physics = 50
increased 14% marks, new score = 50 + 7 = 57
$$\text{Physics new\%} = \frac{57}{140} \times 100 = 40.71\%$$
Approximate % is 41%.

8. **Option (B) is correct.**
Explanation: Both subject obtained marks by T
$= 50 + 60 = 110$
Obtained marks by R in Physics = 80

9. **Option (D) is correct.**
Explanation: By P marks in Physics and Chemistry both = 130 + 90 = 220
By T, obtained marks in both Physics and Chemistry = 50 + 60 = 110
Ratio P : T = 220 : 110 = 2 : 1

10. **Option (B) is correct.**
Explanation:
By P and R together in Physics = 130 + 80 = 210
By Q and S together in Chemistry = 110 + 120 = 230
Ratio Q and S : P and R
230 : 210 = 23 : 21
Hence (B) is right.

11. **Option (A) is correct.**
Decrease % of flavour z in 2010 as in 2008

$$= \frac{60-40}{60} \times 100$$

$$= \frac{20}{60} \times 100 = \frac{1}{3} \times 100 = 33\frac{1}{3}\%$$

Approximate 33%.

12. **Option (A) is correct.**
Explanation:

Flavour	Annual Average Production	Bottles
X	$\frac{1}{6} \times 300$	50 lakh
Y	$\frac{1}{6} \times 325$	$54\frac{1}{6}$ lakh
Z	$\frac{1}{6} \times 300$	50 lakh

Hence, the average annual production was maximum in the given period of flavour Y.

13. **Option (C) is correct.**
Explanation:
Flavour X in 2005 and 2006 = 90
Flavour Z in 2007 and 2008 = 120

$$\text{Percentage} = \frac{120}{90} \times 100$$

$$= \frac{1,200}{9} = 133.3$$

14. **Option (A) is correct.**
Explanation: Percentage rise/fall in production flavour Y

$$\text{In year, } 2007 = \frac{60-50}{60} \times 100 = \frac{10}{60} \times 100$$

= 16% decrease

$$\text{In year, } 2008 = \frac{55-50}{50} \times 100 = \frac{5}{50} \times 100$$

= 10% increase

$$\text{In year, } 2009 = \frac{55-50}{55} \times 100 = \frac{5}{55} \times 100$$

= 9% decrease

15. **Option (D) is correct.**
Explanation: Required difference (in lakhs bottles) between the average production of flavour X and Y in:

$$= \frac{1}{3}\ [(55 + 50 + 55) - (55 + 40 + 50)]$$

$$= \frac{1}{3}(160-145) = \frac{1}{3} \times 15 = 5 \text{ lakhs bottle}$$

16. **Option (A) is correct.**
Explanation: Ratio of number of boys and girls using the Samsung and Sony smart phones
(100 + 160) : (180 + 60)
260 : 240
13 : 12

17. **Option (C) is correct.**
Explanation: Percentage of boys using the samsung phones

$$= \frac{100}{100+240+40+160} \times 100 = \frac{100}{540} \times 100$$

$$= \frac{1,000}{54} = 18.52\%$$

18. **Option (D) is correct.**
Explanation: Percentage of girls using the phones of Nokia:

$$\frac{120}{180+120+60+20} \times 100 = \frac{100}{380} \times 100$$

$$= \frac{1,000}{38} = 31.58\%$$

19. **Option (B) is correct.**
Explanation: Girls and boys using samsung = 100 + 180 = 280
Girls and boys using sony = 160 + 60 = 220
Difference = 280 – 220 = 60

20. **Option (D) is correct.**
Explanation:
Average production of all untis (in lakhs tons) is

$$2002 = \frac{110+60+110+100+105+85}{6}$$

$$= \frac{570}{6} = 95 \text{ lakhs tons}$$

21. **Option (C) is correct.**
Explanation: Units A, B and C in 2001 average production

$$= \frac{90+75+100}{3} = \frac{265}{3}$$

Unit, D, E and F in 2002 average production

$$= \frac{100+105+85}{3} = \frac{290}{3}$$

$$\text{Average in \%} = \frac{265 \times 3}{3 \times 290} \times 100$$

$$= \frac{265}{290} \times 100 = 91.38\%$$

22. **Option (E) is correct.**
Explanation: 2001 and 2002 both year unit B's production
= 75 + 60 = 135 lakhs tons
2001 and 2002 both year unit C's production
= 110 + 110 = 210 lakhs tons
Ratio B : C = 135 : 210 = 9 : 14

23. **Option (A) is correct.**
Explanation:
Unit F total production in both year
= 70 + 85 = 155 lakhs tons
Unit D total production in both year
= 95 + 100 = 195 lakhs tons

$$\% \text{ required is} = \frac{155}{195} \times 100 = 79.49\%$$

24. **Option (B) is correct.**
Explanation: Total production of unit C, D and E together for both years (in lakhs tons)
= 100 + 110 + 95 + 100 + 85 + 105 = 595 lakhs tons

25. **Option (A) is correct.**
Explanation: X type buses from school B = 36
Y type buses from school C = 44

$$\text{Hence, required average} = \frac{36+44}{2} = \frac{80}{2} = 40$$

26. **Option (E) is correct.**
Explanation:
X type buses from school B = 36
Y type buses from school A = 48

$$\text{Hence, required percentage} = \frac{(48-36)}{36} \times 100$$

$$= 33\frac{1}{3}\%$$

27. **Option (C) is correct.**
Explanation: X type buses from B = 36
Y type buses from A = 26
total number of buses from B = 36 + 26 = 62

$$\text{Hence required average} = \frac{62}{2} = 31$$

28. **Option (B) is correct.**
Explanation: X type buses from A = 48
Y type buses from A = 38

$$\text{Average number of buses from A} = \frac{48+38}{2}$$

$$= \frac{86}{2} = 43$$

X type buses from C = 44
Y type buses from C = 34

$$\text{Average number of buses from C} = \frac{44+34}{2}$$

$$= \frac{78}{2} = 39$$

Hence, required difference = 43 – 39 = 4

29. **Option (B) is correct.**
Explanation:
Number of buses of A = 48 + 38 = 86
Number of buses of B = 36 + 26 = 62
Number of buses of C = 46 + 34 = 80

Level-2: INTERMEDIATE

1. **Option (B) is correct.**
Explanation:
Year 2006 profit (in crore ₹) = 60 – 35 = 25
Year 2007 profit (in crore ₹) = 50 – 40 = 10
Difference in profit = 25 – 10 = ₹15 crore

2. **Option (C) is correct.**
Explanation: Average Income of company given years

$$= \frac{40+60+50+65+70}{5} = \frac{285}{5} = ₹\ 57 \text{ crore}$$

Average less then 2 year.

3. **Option (B) is correct.**
Explanation: Increase in expenditure of the company % in 2007 to 2008

$$= \frac{50-40}{40} \times 100 = \frac{10}{40} \times 100 = 25\%$$

4. **Option (C) is correct.**
Explanation: Maximum profit of the company in the year 2006.
[It is clear from bar graph.]

5. **Option (D) is correct.**
Explanation: Vehicle B is travelled at the same speed 43 km/h in Day 1 and Day 2

$$\text{Day 1} = \frac{516}{12} = 43\text{km/h} \text{] Same}$$

$$\text{Day 2} = \frac{774}{18} = 43\text{km/h} \text{] Same}$$

6. **Option (C) is correct.**
Explanation:

$$\text{Day 1 speed of Vehicle A} = \frac{832}{16} = 52 \text{ kmph}$$

$$\text{Day 1 speed of Vehicle C} = \frac{693}{11} = 63 \text{ kmph}$$

Difference speed = 63 – 52 = 11 km/h.

7. **Option (E) is correct.**
Explanation:

$$\text{Vehicle C speed of Day 2} = \frac{810}{18} = 45 \text{ km/h}$$

$$\text{Convert of m/s} = 45 \times \frac{5}{18} = 12.5 \text{ m/s}$$

8. **Option (E) is correct.**
Explanation: Distance travelled by Vehicle F on both days

$$= \frac{\text{Day 2 travelled distance}}{\text{Day 1 travelled distance}}$$

$$= \frac{636}{703} \times 100 = \frac{63,600}{703} = 90\% \text{ (approximate)}$$

approximate = 90%

9. **Option (B) is correct.**
Explanation: Vehicle D speed on day 2 = 51
Vehicle E speed on day 2 = 39
Required ratio of Vehicle D and Vehicle E on Day 2
= 51 : 39 = 17 : 13

10. Option (B) is correct.

Explanation: Total passengers in A = 36

Total passengers in E = 33

Hence, percentage of passengers in E less than A

$$= \frac{(36-33)}{36} \times 100 = \frac{3}{36} \times 100 = 8\frac{1}{3}\%$$

11. Option (A) is correct.

Explanation: Total passengers in A = 36

Total passengers in C = 27

Total passengers in E = 33

Hence, average number of passengers in A, C and E

$$= \frac{36+27+33}{3} = 32$$

12. Option (E) is correct.

Explanation: Total number of passengers in B = 18

Total number of passengers in D = 22

Hence, required ratio, i.e., B : D = 18 : 22 = 9 : 11

13. Option (B) is correct.

Explanation:

Total passengers in C = 27

Total passengers in E = 33

Total number of passengers in C and E together

= 27 + 33 = 60

Number of passengers in A = 36

Hence, required percentage $= \frac{(60-36)}{36} \times 100$

$$= \frac{24}{36} \times 100 = 66\frac{2}{3}\%$$

14. Option (C) is correct.

Explanation: Number of passengers in B = 18

Number of passengers in C = 27

Number of passengers in D = 22

Hence, total number of passengers in B, C and D together

= 18 + 27 + 22 = 67

15. Option (C) is correct.

Explanation: Check the graph carefully. It shows that the year 2009 has the maximum percentage of students.

16. Option (D) is correct.

Explanation: By observing graph shows this difference of pass% between girls and boys is maximum in year 2007.

17. Option (A) is correct.

Explanation: Total glass packing material = 5.1

Packing food item = 12.5

$$\text{Per cent is} = \frac{5.1}{12.5} \times 100$$

$$= \frac{5{,}100}{125} = 40.8\%$$

18. Option (E) is correct.

Explanation: Difference of plastic and iron used for fan packing food = 38.8 – 11.8

$$\text{So, required\%} = \frac{27}{11.8} \times 100$$

$$= \frac{2{,}700}{11.8} = 225\% \text{ approximate}$$

19. Option (B) is correct.

Explanation: Observe the graph.

20. Option (D) is correct.

Explanation: Ratio between the glass and aluminium used for packing

7.4 : 16.8

74 : 168

37 : 84

21. Option (C) is correct.

Explanation: Total number of patients in the hospital A

= 5 + 3 + 2 + 4 = 14

Total number of patients in the hospital B

= 3 + 2 + 5 + 2 = 12

Total number of patients in the hospital C

= 5+3+2+2 = 12

22. Option (A) is correct.

Explanation:

$$\text{Profit \% of A} = \frac{148-122}{122} \times 100 = 21.31\%$$

$$\text{Profit \% of B} = \frac{166-135}{135}\ 100 = 22.95\%$$

$$\text{Profit \% of C} = \frac{240-186}{186}\ 100 = 29.03\%$$

$$\text{Profit \% of D} = \frac{220-170}{170}\ 100 = 29.41\%$$

$$\text{Profit \% of E} = \frac{188-166}{166}\ 100 = 13.25\%$$

Clearly company D has maximum profit.

23. Option (C) is correct.

Explanation: Clearly expenditure is more than the income in company A and C.

∴ Profit is earned by only company B.

∴ Profit percentage of company B

$$= \left[\frac{50-40}{40}\right] \times 100\% = 25\%$$

24. Option (A) is correct.

Explanation:

$$\text{Ratio between the sale of wheat and rice} = \frac{10}{20} = 1:2$$

$$\text{Ratio between the sale of sugar and onion} = \frac{5}{5} = 1:1$$

Level-3: EXPERT

1. Option (A) is correct.

Explanation: All packing materials contributed by

Plastic = 38.8

All = 63.9

$$\text{\% Required} = \frac{38.8}{63.9} \times 100 = 60\% \text{ approx.}$$

2. **Option (E) is correct.**

Explanation: All packing material contributed = 101.80

Plastic and Aluminium = 138.50

Percentage by required = $\frac{101.80}{138.50} \times 100$ = 75% approx

3. **Option (C) is correct.**

Explanation:

All packing material = 74.6

Paper = 1.8

$$\% \text{ Required} = \frac{1.8}{74.6} \times 100 = 2.4\%$$

4. **Option (E) is correct.**

Explanation: Pep-up was sold maximum in 1989 year. By observing the graph.

5. **Option (A) is correct.**

Explanation:

The average annual sale of all product is

$$\text{Dew up} = \frac{10+15+25+15+30+25}{6}$$

$$= \frac{120}{6} = 20 \text{ lakhs}$$

$$\text{Cool- sip} = \frac{25+7+20+20+25+30}{6}$$

$$= \frac{127}{6} = 21.16 \text{ lakhs}$$

$$\text{Pep-up} = \frac{30+35+30+25+20+20}{6}$$

$$= \frac{160}{6} = 26.66 \text{ lakhs maximum}$$

6. **Option (C) is correct.**

Explanation:

Cool-sip increased % in sale 1992 over its 1991 sale

$$= \frac{25-20}{20} \times 100 = \frac{5}{20} \times 100 = 25\%$$

7. **Option (E) is correct.**

Explanation:

Pep-up sold bottles in year 1990 = 30 lakhs bottle

Cool-sip sold bottles in 1990 = 20 lakhs bottles

Difference = 30 – 20 = 10 lakhs bottles

8. **Option (C) is correct.**

Explanation:

Droped % is sale pep-up in given years

$$= \frac{35-30}{35} \times 100 = \frac{5}{35} \times 100 = 14\% \text{ approx.}$$

9. **Option (B) is correct.**

Explanation: Suppose the invested of company B = r lakhs in 1996

$\therefore$ 1997 investment by B = ₹ $\frac{7}{5}r$

1997 income of company = $\frac{9}{5} \times \frac{7}{5} r = \frac{63}{25} r$

$$\therefore \% = \frac{63}{25} \times 100 = 252\%$$

10. **Option (D) is correct.**

Explanation: Each year investment has not been given for question. So, data inadequate.

11. **Option (E) is correct.**

Explanation: Income of company A in 1995 = 21.7 lakhs

So, investment in 1995 = $21.7 \times \frac{100}{155}$ = 14 lakhs

12. **Option (C) is correct.**

Explanation: Income of company A in 1995 = Investment of company B in 1996 = r

$$\therefore \quad \frac{r \times \frac{100}{155}}{r} = \frac{100}{155} = 100 : 155 = 20 : 31$$

13. **Option (B) is correct.**

Explanation:

Investment of company B = 15,40,000

Income company B in 1993 = 15,40,000 × $\frac{145}{100}$

= ₹ 22.33 lakhs

Chapter 22

Pie Chart

LEARNING OBJECTIVES:

- Understanding basic concept.
- Comparing data.
- Creating pie chart.
- Identifying percentage.
- Methods to solve questions asked in previous year exams.

➢ **Concept:** A pie chart is a circular graph that is divided into sectors, each representing a proportion of the whole. The size of each sector is determined by the value it represents in relation to the total value.

➢ **Formula:** To calculate the percentage of each sector in a pie chart, use the following formula:

Percentage of sector = (Value of sector/Total value) × 100

To calculate the angle of each sector in a pie chart, use the following formula:

Angle of sector = (Value of sector/Total value) × 360°

Example: Suppose a pie chart represents the distribution of expenses for a company, and the total expense is ₹ 1,00,000. The pie chart shows that 30% of the expenses are for salaries, 20% for rent, 25% for utilities and the remaining for miscellaneous expenses.

To find the value of each sector, we can use the following formula:

Value of sector = (Percentage of sector/100%) × Total value

For example, the value of the salaries sector would be:

Value of salaries = (30%/100%) × ₹ 1,00,000 = ₹ 30,000

Using this formula, we can calculate the value of each sector and use it to answer questions about the data represented in the pie chart.

Direction (Qs. 1–2): Study the following pie chart and answer the following question.

Various expenditures incured by a publishing company for publishing a book in 2014 are given below.

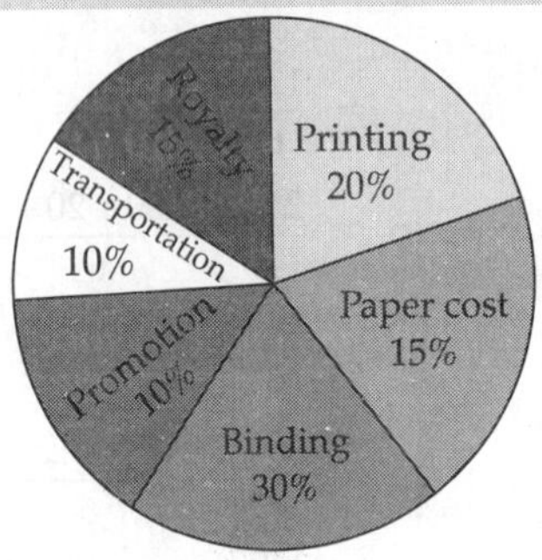

Example 1: Royalty of book is less than the printing cost by:

(a) 20% (b) 25%

(c) 5% (d) $33\frac{1}{3}\%$

Sol. (c) Printing of book = 20%, royalty of book = 15%

∴ Royalty of book is less than the printing cost of 5%.

Example 2: Price of a book is 20% above cost price. If the marked price is ₹ 180, then the cost of paper, a single copy in ₹, is:

(a) 42 (b) 44.25

(c) 36 (d) 22.50

Sol. (d) Cost price + $\frac{20}{100}$ × cost price = 180

$\Rightarrow \frac{6}{5}$ cost price = 180

$\Rightarrow$ CP = ₹ 150

Cost of paper = 15% of CP

= $\frac{15}{100} \times 150$ = ₹ 22.50

Directions (Qs. 3–6): Study the following chart and answer the questions given below:

Percentage wise distribution of employees in six different professions

Total number of employees = 26,800

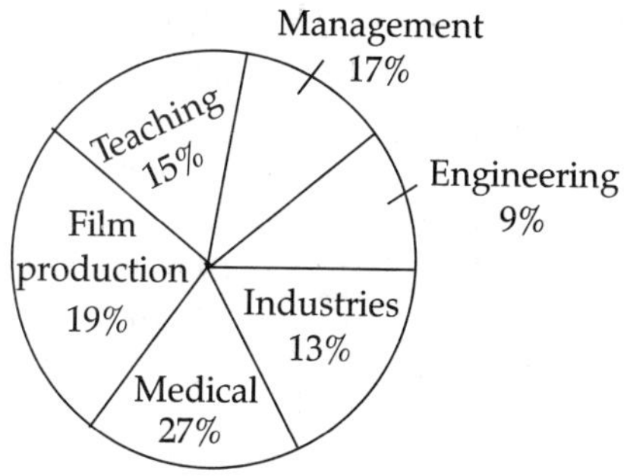

[SBI PO 2013]

Example 3: What is the difference between the total number of employees in teaching and medical profession together and the number of employees in management profession?

(a) 6,770 **(b)** 7,700
(c) 6,700 **(d)** 7,770
(e) 7,670

Sol. (c) Number of employees in teaching and medical = 42%
Management employees = 17%
Difference = 42 – 17 = 25%

So, required value $= \dfrac{26,800 \times 25}{100} = 6,700$

Example 4: In management profession, three-fourth of the number of exployees are females. What is the number of male employees in management profession?

(a) 1,239 **(b)** 1,143
(c) 1,156 **(d)** 1,289
(e) 1,139

Sol. (e) In management, $\frac{3}{4}$ employees are females

$\therefore$ $\frac{1}{4}$ employees in management are males

So, number of male employees

$= \dfrac{26,800 \times 17}{100} \times \dfrac{1}{4} = 1,139$

Example 5: 25% of the employees from film production profession went on a strike. What is the number of employees from film production who have not participated in the strike?

(a) 3271 **(b)** 3819
(c) 3948 **(d)** 1273
(e) 1246

Sol. (b) On strike in film production = 25%
Not on strike employees = 75%
Number of employees not on strike

$\dfrac{26,800 \times 19}{100} \times \dfrac{75}{100} = 268 \times 19 \times \dfrac{3}{4} = 3,819$

Example 6: What is the total number of employees in engineering profession and industries together?

(a) 5,698 **(b)** 5,884
(c) 5,687 **(d)** 5,896
(e) 5,487

Sol. (d) Total number of employees in engineering and industries together = 9 + 13 = 22%

Hence, $\dfrac{26,800 \times 22}{100} = 268 \times 22 = 5,896$

1 Level Beginner

Directions (Qs. 1–3): The following graph shows the expenditure incurred in bringing a book by magazine producer. Study the graph and answer the questions.

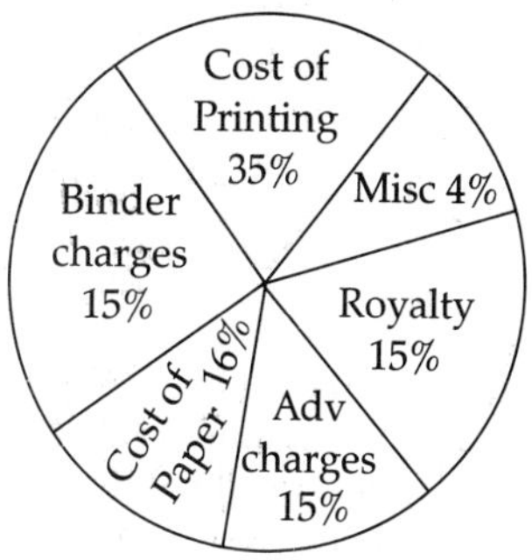

[SSC CGL 2013]

1. What should be the central angle of the sector for the cost of the paper?
   (A) 57.6° **(B)** 54.4°
   (C) 56.7° **(D)** 54.8°
2. If the miscellaneous charge is ₹ 6,000, the cost of paper is:
   (A) ₹ 12,000 **(B)** ₹ 18,000
   (C) ₹ 15,000 **(D)** ₹ 24,000
3. If 5500 copies are published, miscellaneous expenditures amount to ₹ 1,848. Find the cost price of 1 copy.
   (A) ₹ 10.40 **(B)** ₹ 9.40
   (C) ₹ 12.40 **(D)** ₹ 8.40

Directions (Qs. 4–8): The pie chart given below shows the distribution of workforce by occupational category for country X in 1981 and 1995. Study the pie chart and answer the questions.

1981

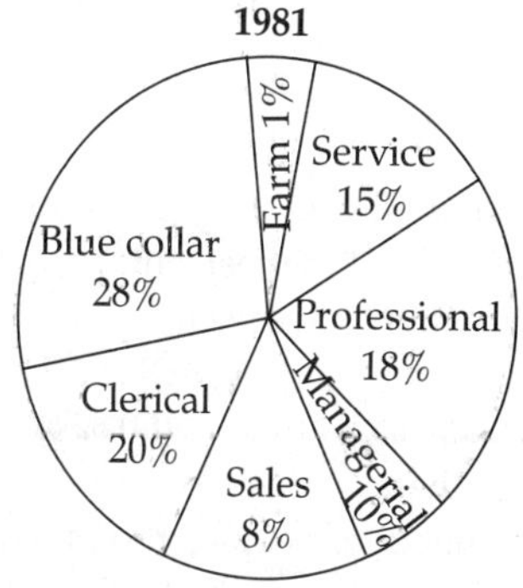

Total workforce = 150 million

1995

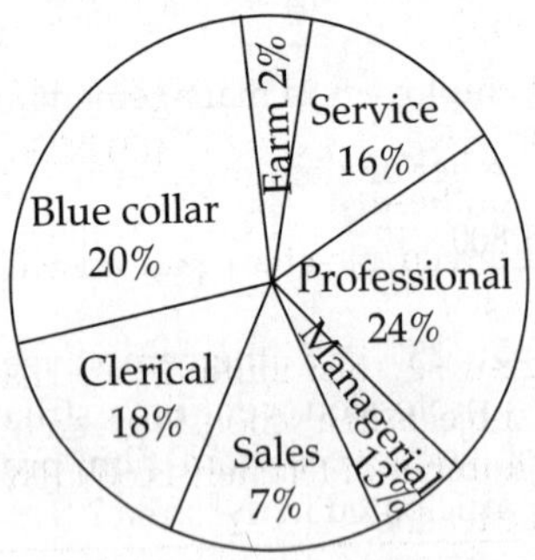

Total workforce = 175 million

[SSC Sub Inspector 2012]

4. In 1981, the number of service worker in the workforce in millions was:
(A) 15.0 (B) 20.5 (C) 22.5 (D) 28.0

5. In 1981, the number of categories which comprised more than 25 million workers each is:
(A) two (B) three (C) four (D) five

6. The ratio of the number of workers in the professional category in 1981 to the number of such workers in 1995 is:
(A) 4 : 9 (B) 5 : 14 (C) 9 : 14 (D) 14 : 9

7. To increase in the number of clerical workers in the work force of the country X from 1981 to 1995 (in millions) is:
(A) 0.75 (B) 1.5 (C) 0.5 (D) 1.25

8. The percentage decrease in the number of blue collar workers in the workforce of the country X from 1981 to 1995 is:
(A) $42\frac{1}{2}$ (B) 35 (C) 20 (D) $16\frac{2}{3}$

Directions (Qs. 9–13): Read the following chart and answer the questions given below.

The following pie chart shows the preference of musical instruments of 60,000 people surveyed over the whole India.

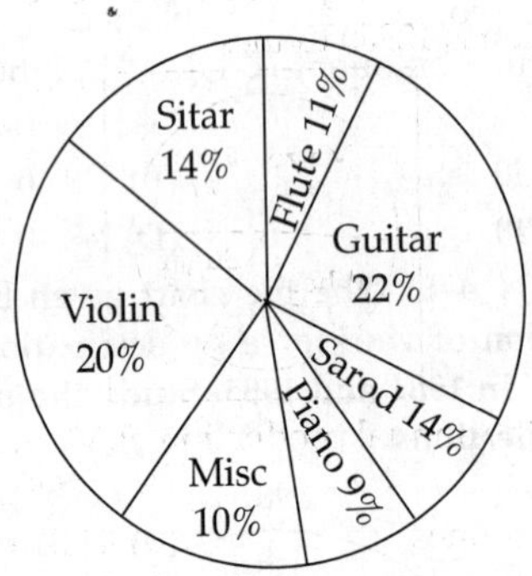

[SSC Clerk 2014]

9. If 2,100 people be less from the number of people who prefer Flute, the percentage of people who prefer Flute would have been:
(A) 9.5% (B) 6.5%
(C) 7.5% (D) 8.5%
(E) None of these

10. The total number of people who prefer either Sarod or Guitar is greater than the total number of people who prefer either Violin or Sitar by:
(A) 1,200 (B) 1,600
(C) 1,100 (D) 1,400
(E) None of these

11. The number of people who prefer the musical instrument Sarod is:
(A) 7,400 (B) 8,400
(C) 6,400 (D) 8,600
(E) None of these

12. If $16\frac{2}{3}\%$ of the people who prefer Piano would go with the people who prefer Flute the percentage of the people who prefer Flute would have been:
(A) 13.5% (B) 14.5%
(C) 15.5% (D) 12.5%
(E) None of these

13. The number of people who prefer Guitar is greater than the total number of people who prefer either Flute or Piano by:
(A) 1,200 (B) 1,100
(C) 1,300 (D) 1,400
(E) None of these

Directions (Qs. 14–18): These questions are based on the following data. The distribution of appeared and qualified aspirants in a competitive examination from different states.

Total appeared aspirants – 45,000

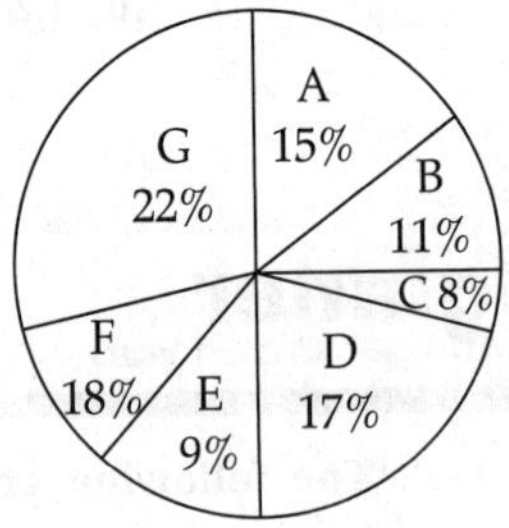

Total qualified aspirants – 9,000

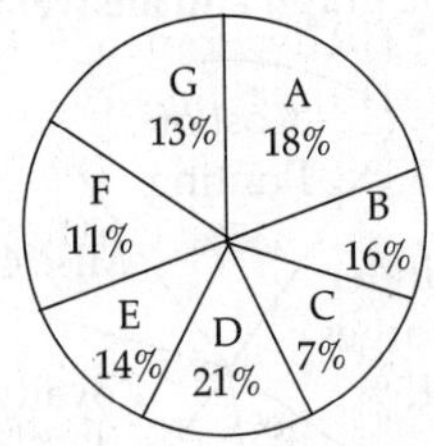

14. What is the ratio of the number of appeared aspirants from states C and E together to that of the appeared aspirants from states A and F together?
(A) 17 : 33 (B) 11 : 13 (C) 13 : 27
(D) 17 : 27 (E) None of these

15. In which state the % of qualified aspirants to appeared aspirants is the least?
(A) C (B) F (C) D
(D) E (E) G

16. What is the difference in the number of qualified aspirants in states D and G?
(A) 690 (B) 670 (C) 780
(D) 720 (E) None of these

17. What is the percentage of qualified aspirants with respect to appeared aspirants from states B and C taken together (rounded off to two decimal places)?
(A) 23.11% (B) 24.21% (C) 21.24%
(D) 23% (E) None of these

18. What is the ratio between number of candidates qualified from states B and D together and the number of candidates appeared from states C, respectively?
(A) 8 : 37 (B) 11 : 12 (C) 37 : 40
(D) 7 : 37 (E) None of these

Directions (Qs. 19–23): Study the following pie chart carefully to answer the questions.

Degree-wise break up of employees working in various departments of an organisation and the ratio of men to women.

Total number of employees = 3,250

Respective ratio of men and woman in each department

Department	Men	Women
Production	4	1
HR	12	13
IT	7	3
Marketing	3	2
Accounts	6	7

[IBPS PO 2013]

19. What is the number of men working in the marketing department?
(A) 462 (B) 452 (C) 418
(D) 424 (E) 429

20. What is the respective ratio of the number of women working in the HR department to the number of men working in the IT department?
(A) 11 : 12 (B) 17 : 29
(C) 13 : 28 (D) 12 : 35
(E) None of these

21. The number of men working in the production department of the organisation forms what percentage of the total number of employees working in that department?
(A) 88% (B) 90%
(C) 75% (D) 65%
(E) 80%

22. The number of women working in the IT department of the organisation forms is what % of total number of employees in the organisation from all department together?
(A) 3.2% (B) 4.8%
(C) 6.3% (D) 5.6%
(E) None of these

23. What is the total number of men working in the organisation?
(A) 2,198 (B) 2,147
(C) 2,073 (D) 2,236
(E) None of these

24. Study the given pie-chart and answer the question that follows.

Percentage-wise distribution of teachers in six different subjects in a school is given in the pie-chart. The total number of teachers is 600. The ratio of male and female teachers is 3 : 1.

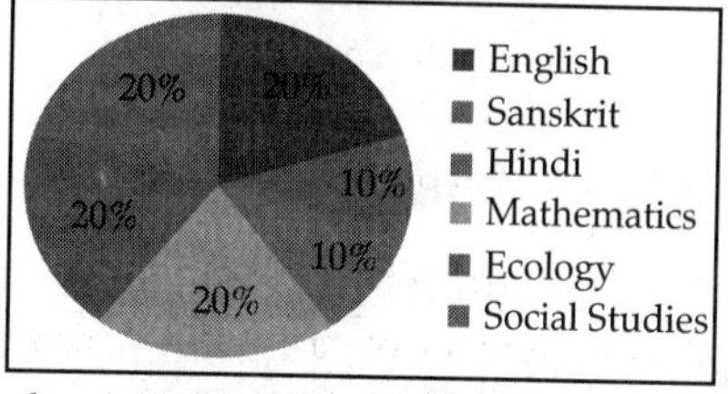

Find the ratio of teachers in English, Sanskrit and Hindi to teachers in Mathematics, Biology and Social Studies. **[SSC CHSL 2023]**
(A) 2 : 5 (B) 1 : 2 (C) 2 : 3 (D) 1 : 5

25. The sales of an item of a company in 4-quarters are given below.

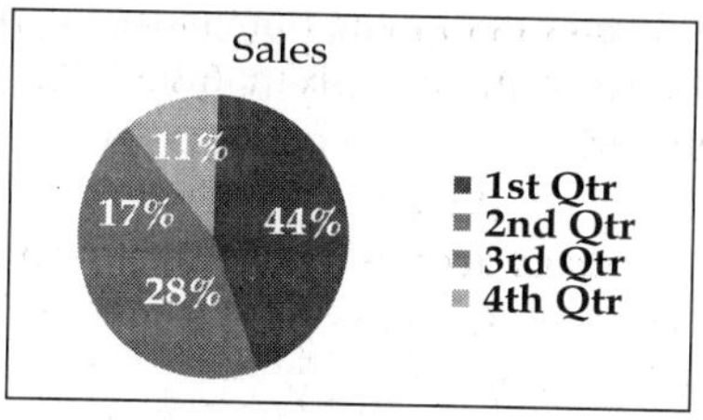

If the difference in sales of item in 3rd quarter and 4th quarter is 36. then the total sale of the 1st quarter is ________. **[SSC CHSL 2023]**
(A) 250 (B) 256 (C) 264 (D) 260

26. The annual agricultural production (in tonnes) of an Indian state is given in the pie chart. The total production is 12960 tonnes.

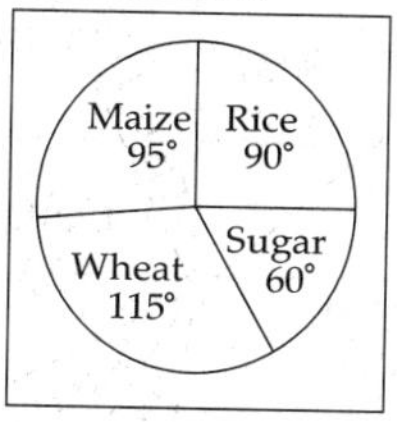

What is the annual production of Maize? **[SSC CHSL 2023]**
(A) 3240 tonnes (B) 4140 tonnes
(C) 3420 tonnes (D) 2160 tonnes

27. The following pie chart shows the percentage distribution of the expenditure incurred in publishing a book.

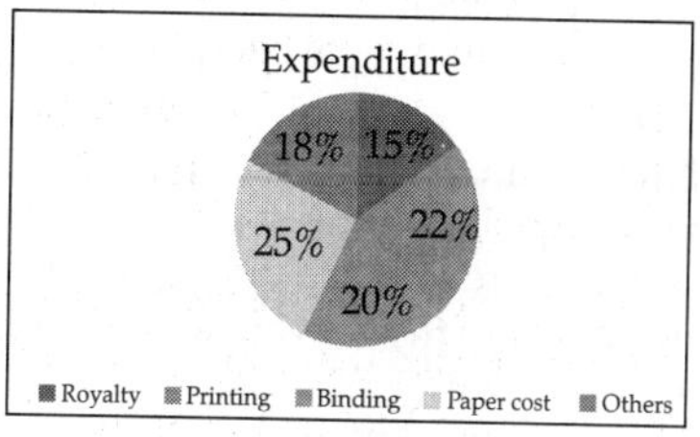

Find the paper cost, if the royalty is ₹ 22,500.

[SSC CHSL 2023]

(A) ₹32,500 (B) ₹37,500
(C) ₹30,000 (D) ₹33,000

28. Study the given pie-chart and table and answer the question that follows.
The pie-chart shows the percentage distribution of age groups of visitors to a park in a month.

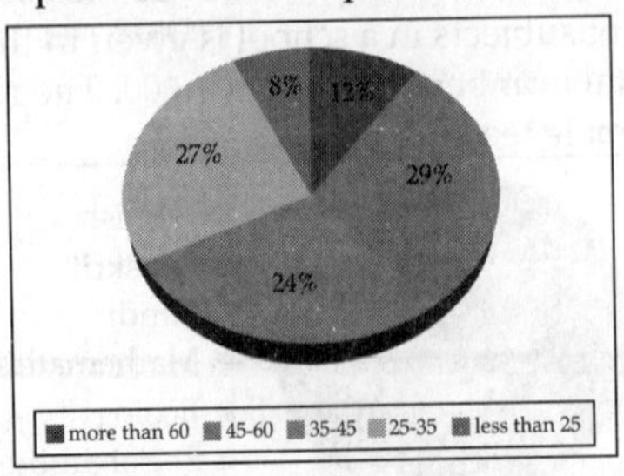

The table shows the male, female distribution of the visitors in terms of the percentage.

Age	Male Percentage	Female Percentage
More than 60	58	42
45-60	80	20
35-45	81	19
25-35	60	40
Less than 25	45	55

If 2000 male visitors and 1500 female visitors were there in all, then the ratio of the number of male visitors in the age group 25-35, to the female visitors of the age group 45-60 is: [SSC CHSL 2023]

(A) 71:45 (B) 57:41
(C) 63:47 (D) 81:29

Level 2 Intermediate

Directions (Qs. 1–5): Study the following pie chart carefully to answer the questions.

Percentage distribution of the number of mobile phones sold by a shopkeeper during six months

Total number of mobile phones sold = 45,000

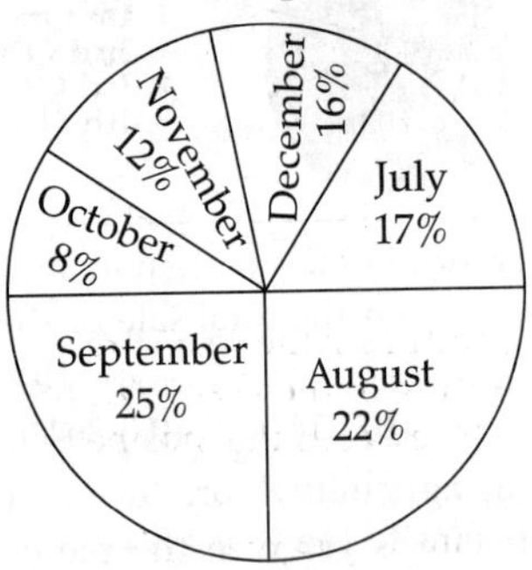

The respective ratio between the number of mobile phones sold by company A and company B during six months.

Month	Ratio
July	8 : 7
August	4 : 5
September	3 : 2
October	7 : 5
November	7 : 8
December	7 : 9

[IBPS PO 2012]

1. What is the respective ratio between the number of mobile phones sold by company B in July and those sold during December.
(A) 119 : 145 (B) 116 : 135
(C) 119 : 135 (D) 119 : 130
(E) None of these

2. If 35% of mobile phone sold by company A during November were sold at a discount, how many mobile phones of company A were sold during that month without discount?
(A) 882 (B) 1,635
(C) 1,638 (D) 885
(E) None of these

3. If the shopkeeper earned a profit of ₹ 433 on each mobile phone sold by company B during October, what was his total profit during the same month?
(A) ₹ 6,49,900 (B) ₹ 6,45,900
(C) ₹ 6,49,400 (D) ₹ 6,49,500
(E) None of these

4. The number of mobile phones sold by company A during July is approximately what percentage of the number of phones sold by company A during December?
(A) 110 (B) 140 (C) 150
(D) 105 (E) 130

5. What is the total number of mobile phones sold by company B during August and September together?
(A) 10,000 (B) 15,000
(C) 10,500 (D) 9,500
(E) None of these

Directions (Qs. 6–10): Study the following pie chart and answer the questions given below:

Preference of students among six beverages in terms of degree of angle in the pie chart.

Total number of students = 6,800

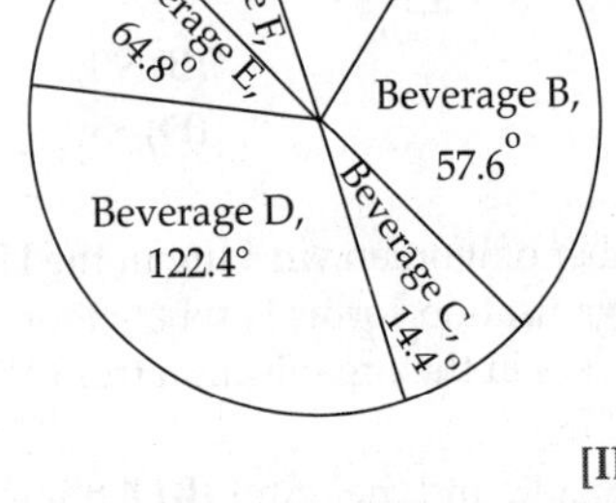

[IBPS PO 2011]

6. The number of students who prefer beverage C are approximately what per cent of number of students who prefer beverage D?

(A) 7 (B) 12 (C) 18
(D) 22 (E) 29

7. How many students prefer beverage B and beverage E together?
(A) 2,312 (B) 2,313 (C) 2,315
(D) 2,318 (E) None of these

8. What is the difference between the total number of students who prefer beverage A and C together and the total number of students who prefer beverage D and F together?
(A) 959 (B) 955 (C) 952
(D) 954 (E) None of these

9. The number of students who prefer beverage E and F together are what percentage of the total number of students?
(A) 18 (B) 14 (C) 26
(D) 24 (E) None of these

10. What is the respective ratio between the number of students who prefer beverage F and the number of students who prefer beverage A?
(A) 3 : 11 (B) 3 : 13
(C) 6 : 11 (D) 5 : 11
(E) None of these

3 Level Expert

Direction (Qs. 1–5): Study the pie chart and table carefully to answer the questions that follow:

Pie chart showing percentage-wise distribution of cars in four different states.

Total cars = 700

Distribution of cars

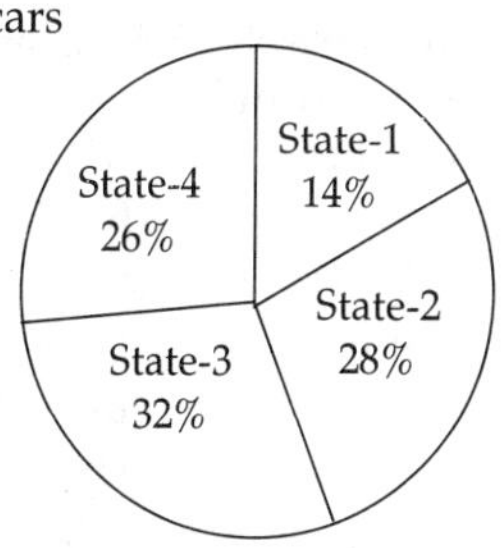

Table showing ratio between diesel and petrol engine cars which are distributed among four different states.

State	Diesel engine cars	Petrol engine cars
State 1	3	4
State 2	5	9
State 3	5	3
State 4	1	1

[SBI PO 2013]

1. What is the differrence between the number of diesel engine cars in State 2 and the number of petrol engine cars in State 4?
(A) 159 (B) 21 (C) 28
(D) 34 (E) 161

2. The number of petrol engine cars in State 3 is what per cent more than the no. of diesel engine cars in State 1?
(A) 100 (B) 200 (C) 300
(D) 125 (E) 225

3. If 25% of diesel engine cars in State 3 are AC and remaining cars are non-AC, what is the number of diesel cars in State 3 which are non-AC?
(A) 75 (B) 45 (C) 95
(D) 105 (E) 35

4. What is the difference between the total number of cars in State 3 and the number of petrol engine cars in State 2?
(A) 96 (B) 106 (C) 112
(D) 102 (E) 98

5. What is the average number of petrol engine cars in the states together?
(A) 86.75 (B) 89.25 (C) 89.75
(D) 86.25 (E) 88.75

Direction (Qs. 6–10): The following pie chart represents the profits earned by a certain company in seven consecutive years. Study the pie chart carefully and answer the questions.

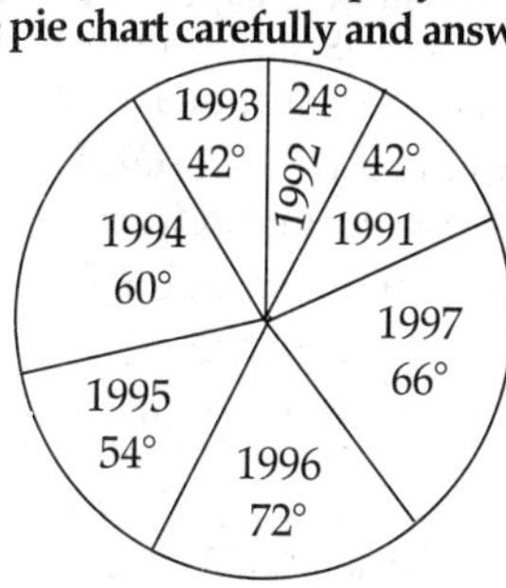

[SSC CGL 2012]

6. If the expenditure in the year 1993 was 30% more than the expenditure in the year 1991, then the income in the year 1993 exceeds the income in the year 1991 by 30% of:
(A) the income in the year 1991.
(B) the expenditure in the year 1993.
(C) the income in the year 1993.
(D) the expenditure in the year 1991.

7. If X% of the total of profits earned in all the given years is the same as the profit earned in the year 1994, then X is:
(A) $16\frac{2}{3}$ (B) $33\frac{1}{3}$ (C) $12\frac{1}{2}$ (D) $11\frac{2}{3}$

8. The ratios of expenditures and income in the year 1992, 1994 and 1996 are given to be 6 : 5 : 8 and 2 : 3 : 4, respectively. The ratio of the income in the year 1996 to the total expenditure in the years 1992 and 1994 is:
(A) 40 : 11 (B) 10 : 7
(C) 20 : 11 (D) 20 : 13

9. The year in which the profit is nearest to the average of the profits earned in all the given years is:
(A) 1991 (B) 1995 (C) 1993 (D) 1994

10. If the income in the year 1997 was 5 times the expenditure made in the same year, then the ratio of the profit earned in the year 1991 to the expenditure in the year 1997 was:
(A) 11 : 28 (B) 44 : 7
(C) 28 : 11 (D) 7 : 44

Directions (Qs. 11–15): The following pie chart shows the monthly expenditure of a family on food, house rent, clothing, education, fuel and miscellaneous.

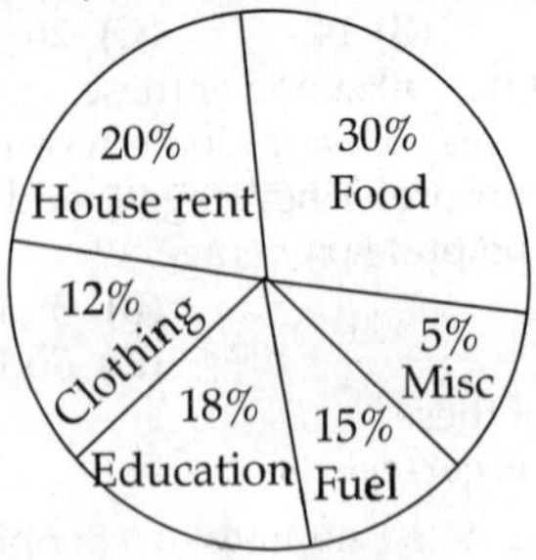

[SSC Sub Inspector 2014]

11. If the expenditure for food is ₹9,000, then the expenditure for education is:
(A) ₹5,000 (B) ₹5,200
(C) ₹5,400 (D) ₹6,000

12. The central angle of the sector for the expenditure for fuel is: (in degrees)
(A) 50.4 (B) 54 (C) 57.6 (D) 72

13. If the expenditure on fuel is 3,000, then the total expenditure excluding expenditure on house rent and education is:
(A) ₹11,600 (B) ₹12,000
(C) ₹12,400 (D) ₹12,500

14. If the percentage of expenditure on food is X% of the total percentage of expenditure on clothing, education and fuel, then X equals to:
(A) 66 (B) $66\frac{1}{3}$ (C) $66\frac{2}{3}$ (D) 67

15. Total percentage of expenditure on house rent, clothing and fuel is greater than the percentage of expenditure on food by:
(A) 16 (B) 18 (C) 17 (D) 20

Directions (Qs. 16–20): Read the graph and answer the questions that follow.

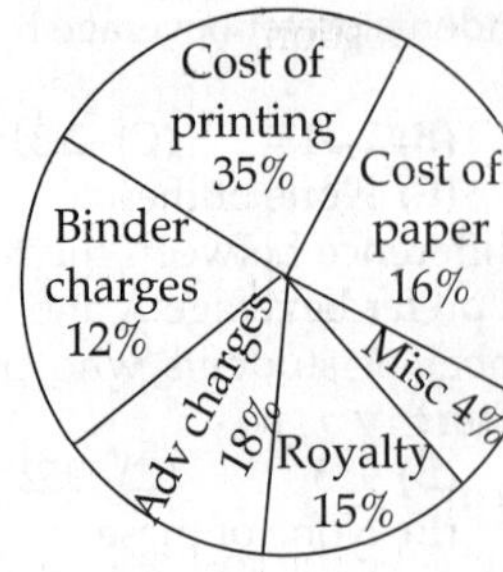

[SSC 10+2 2012]

16. The central angle of the sector for the cost of paper is:
(A) 22.5° (B) 16°
(C) 54.8° (D) 57.6°

17. Royalty on books is less than the advertisement charges by:
(A) 3% (B) 25%
(C) 20% (D) $16\frac{2}{3}\%$

18. If 5,500 copies are published miscellaneous expenditure amount to ₹1,848 and published profit is 25%, then the marked price of each copy is:
(A) ₹12.50 (B) ₹10.50
(C) ₹10 (D) ₹8.40

19. If the cost of printing is ₹17,500, the royalty is:
(A) ₹8,750 (B) ₹6,300
(C) ₹7,500 (D) ₹3,150

20. If the miscellaneous charges is ₹6,000, the advertisement charges are:
(A) ₹27,000 (B) ₹90,000
(C) ₹12,000 (D) ₹1,333.33

ANSWER KEY

Level-1: Beginner

1.	(A)	2.	(D)	3.	(D)	4.	(C)	5.	(B)	6.	(C)	7.	(B)	8.	(C)	9.	(C)	10.	(A)
11.	(B)	12.	(D)	13.	(A)	14.	(A)	15.	(E)	16.	(D)	17.	(B)	18.	(C)	19.	(E)	20.	(C)
21.	(E)	22.	(B)	23.	(B)	24.	(C)	25.	(C)	26.	(C)	27.	(B)	28.	(D)				

Level-2: Intermediate

1.	(C)	2.	(C)	3.	(D)	4.	(E)	5.	(A)	6.	(B)	7.	(A)	8.	(C)	9.	(D)	10.	(A)

Level-3: Expert

1.	(B)	2.	(A)	3.	(D)	4.	(E)	5.	(B)	6.	(D)	7.	(A)	8.	(C)	9.	(B)	10.	(C)
11.	(C)	12.	(B)	13.	(C)	14.	(C)	15.	(C)	16.	(D)	17.	(D)	18.	(B)	19.	(C)	20.	(A)

Solutions with detailed explanations

Level-1 : BEGINNER

1. Option (A) is correct.

Explanation: Cost of paper % = 16%

Central angle for the cost of paper

$$= \frac{16}{100} \times 360° = 57.6°$$

2. **Option (D) is correct.**

Explanation: Let the cost of paper = t

According to the question,

$$\frac{\text{Cost of paper}}{\text{Miscellaneous charges}} = \frac{16\%}{4\%}$$

$$\Rightarrow \quad \frac{t}{6{,}000} = \frac{16}{4} \Rightarrow x = \frac{16 \times 6{,}000}{4}$$

$= 4 \times 6{,}000 =$ ₹ 24,000

3. **Option (D) is correct.**

Explanation: Let X be the cost price of 1 copy

5,500 copies cost price = 5,500X

4% of (5,500 X) = 1,848

$\Rightarrow$ 4/100 × 5,500 X = 1,848

$$\Rightarrow \quad X = \frac{1{,}848 \times 100}{5{,}500 \times 4} = \frac{1{,}848}{55 \times 4} = ₹\,8.40$$

4. **Option (C) is correct.**

Explanation: Number of service workers in 1981 = 15% of 150

$= \frac{15}{100} \times \frac{150}{1}$ = 22.5 millions

5. **Option (B) is correct.**

Explanation: In 1981, number of categories more than 25 million workers, i.e., more than 16% of 150.

Observe the pie chart that shows more than is 16% = Professional, clerical, Blue collar, i.e., 3

6. **Option (C) is correct.**

Explanation:

According to the question, the required ratio Professional 1981 : Professional 1995,

18% of 150 : 24% of 175

$= \frac{18}{100} \times 150 : \frac{24}{100} \times 175$

$= 27 : 42$

$= 9 : 14$

7. **Option (B) is correct.**

Explanation:

Clerical % country X in 1981 = 20% of 150

$= \frac{20}{100} \times 150 = 30$

Clerical% country X in 1995 = 18% of 175

$= \frac{18}{100} \times 175 = 31.5$

Hence, increased is 31.5 – 30 = 1.5 million

8. **Option (C) is correct.**

Explanation: Blue collar workers in 1981

= 28% of 150

$= \frac{28}{100} \times 150 = 42$

Blue collar workers in 1995 = 20% of 175

$= \frac{20}{100} \times 175 = 35$

So, Decreased% $= \frac{42 - 35}{35} \times 100 = \frac{7}{35} \times 100 = 20\%$

9. **Option (C) is correct.**

Explanation: Number of people who prefer Flute = 11% of 60,000

$= \frac{11}{100} \times 60{,}000 = 6{,}600$

2,100 people be less than from prefer Flute

= 6,600 – 2,100 = 4,500

% required $= \frac{4{,}500}{60{,}000} \times 100 = \frac{45}{6} = 7.5\%$

10. **Option (A) is correct.**

Explanation: Total number of people who prefer Violin or Sitar $= \frac{20}{100} \times 60{,}000 + \frac{14}{100} \times 60{,}000$

= 12,000 + 8,400 = 20,400

Total number of people who prefer Sarod or Guitar

$= \frac{14}{100} \times 60{,}000 + \frac{22}{100} \times 60{,}000$

= 8,400 + 13,200 = 21,600

Difference = 21,600 – 20,400 = 1,200

11. **Option (B) is correct.**

Explanation:

Number of people who prefer the Sarod is

$= \frac{14}{100} \times 60{,}000$ = 14 × 600 = 8,400

12. **Option (D) is correct.**

Explanation: Number of people who prefer piano

$= \frac{9}{100} \times 60000 = 5400$

So, $16\frac{2}{3}\%$ of 5400 $= \frac{50}{3} \times \frac{5400}{100} = 900$

Now, new number of people who prefer flute

$= \frac{11}{100} \times 60000 + 900 = 6600 + 900 = 7500$

Required% $= \frac{7500}{60000} \times 100 = 12.5\%$

13. **Option (A) is correct.**

Explanation: Number of people who prefer guitar

$= \frac{10}{100} \times 60{,}000 = 13{,}200$

Number of people who prefer citar flute or piano

$= \frac{11}{100} \times 60{,}000 + \frac{9}{100} \times 60{,}000$

= 6,600 + 5,400 = 12,000

So, difference = 13,200 – 12,000 = 1,200

14. **Option (A) is correct.**

Explanation: Number of appeared aspirants from states C and E together = (8 + 9)% of 45,000

$= \frac{15}{100} \times 45{,}000 = 7650$

Number of appeared aspirants from states A and F together = (15 + 18)% of 45,000

$= \frac{33}{100} \times 45{,}000 = 14{,}850$

$\therefore$ Ratio = 7650 : 14850 = 17 : 33

15. Option (E) is correct.

Explanation: The percentage of qualified aspirant from C

$= \frac{9{,}000 \times 7\%}{45{,}000 \times 8\%} \times 100 = 17.5\%$

% of qualified aspirants from D

$= \frac{9{,}000 \times 21\%}{45{,}000 \times 17\%} \times 100 = 24.70\%$

% of qualified aspirants from E

$= \frac{9{,}000 \times 14\%}{45{,}000 \times 9\%} \times 100 = 31.11\%$

% of qualified aspirants from F

$= \frac{9{,}000 \times 11\%}{45{,}000 \times 18\%} \times 100 = 12.22\%$

% of qualified aspirants from G

$= \frac{9{,}000 \times 13\%}{45{,}000 \times 22\%} \times 100 = 11.82\%$

So, least % is from state G.

16. Option (D) is correct.

Explanation: Difference between the number of qualified aspirants in state D and state G

$= 9{,}000 \times (21 - 13)\% = 9{,}000 \times \frac{8}{100} = 720$

17. Option (B) is correct.

Explanation: The percentage of qualified aspirants from state B and C taken together

$= \frac{9{,}000(16+7) \times 100}{45{,}000 \times (11+8)} = 24.21\%$

18. Option (C) is correct.

Explanation: Qualified number of candidates state

$(B + D) = 9{,}000 \times \frac{(16+21)}{100} = 90 \times 37 = 3{,}330$

State C appeared candidates $= 45{,}000 \times \frac{8}{100}$

$= 450 \times 8 = 3{,}600$

Ratio required = 3,330 : 3,600 = 37 : 40

19. Option (E) is correct.

Explanation: The number of men working in the marketing department $= 3{,}250 \times \frac{79.2}{360°} \times \frac{3}{5} = 429$

20. Option (C) is correct.

Explanation: Ratio between the of women working in HR department: Number of men working in IT department

$= 3{,}250 \times \frac{36°}{360°} \times \frac{13}{25} : 3{,}250 \times \frac{57.6°}{360°} \times \frac{7}{10} = 13 : 28$

21. Option (E) is correct.

Explanation: Number of men in the production department = 988

Total number of employees in production department = 1,235

% required $= \frac{988}{1{,}235} \times 100 = 80\%$

22. Option (B) is correct.

Explanation: Total number of employees = 3,250

Working women in IT department

$= 3{,}250 \times \frac{57.6°}{360} \times \frac{3}{10} = 156$

% required $= \frac{156}{3{,}250} \times 100 = 4.8\%$

23. Option (B) is correct.

Explanation: Total number of men in the organisation,

Accounts: $3{,}250 \times \frac{50.4^o}{360^o} \times \frac{6}{13} = 210$

Marketing: $3{,}250 \times \frac{79.2^o}{360^o} \times \frac{3}{5} = 429$

IT: $3{,}250 \times \frac{51.6^o}{360^o} \times \frac{7}{10} = 364$

HR: $3{,}250 \times \frac{36^o}{360^o} \times \frac{12}{25} = 156$

Production: $3{,}250 \times \frac{136.8^o}{360^o} \times \frac{4}{5} = 988$

Total number of men working in the organisation

= 210 + 429 + 364 + 156 + 988 = 2,147

24. Option (C) is correct.

Explanation: Percentage of teachers in English, Sanskrit and Hindi = 20% + 10% + 10% = 40%

Percentage of teachers in Mathematics, Biology and Social studies = 20% + 20% + 20% = 60%

$\therefore$ Required ratio $= \frac{40}{60} = 2:3$

25. Option (C) is correct.

Explanation: Let total sales of item = x

Difference in sales of 3rd quarter and 4th quarter = 36

According to the question,

$\Rightarrow \frac{17-11}{100} \times x = 36$

$\Rightarrow x = 600$

$\therefore$ Total sale of the 1st quarter $= \frac{44}{100} \times 600$

$= 264$

26. Option (C) is correct.

Explanation: Total production = 12960

Annual production of maize $= \frac{95}{360} \times 12960$

= 3420 tonnes.

27. Option (B) is correct.

Explanation: Let total expenditure = ₹x

$\therefore$ Expenditure on royalty = $\frac{15}{100}x = 22500$

$\Rightarrow \quad x = \frac{2250000}{15}$

$\Rightarrow \quad x = ₹150000$

Expenditure on paper = $\frac{25}{100} \times 150000 = ₹37500$

28. Option (D) is correct.

Explanation: Total visitors = 2000 + 1500 = 3500

Number of male visitors in age group 25–35 years

$= \frac{27}{100} \times \frac{60}{100} \times 3500$

Number of female visitors in age group 45–60 years

$= \frac{29}{100} \times \frac{20}{100} \times 3500$

$\therefore$ Request ratio $= \frac{\frac{27}{100} \times \frac{60}{100} \times 3500}{\frac{29}{100} \times \frac{20}{100} \times 3500}$

$= \frac{81}{29} = 81:29$

Level-2: INTERMEDIATE

(1-5):

	Total mobiles sold	Company A	Company B
July	7,650	4,080	3,570
Aug	9,900	4,400	5,500
Sep	11,250	6,750	4,500
Oct	3,600	2,100	1,500
Nov	5,400	2,520	2,880
Dec	7,200	3,150	4,050

1. **Option (C) is correct.**

Explanation: Company B sold mobiles in July = 3,570

Company B sold mobiles in December = 4,050

Ratio between = 3,570 : 4,050 = 119 : 135

2. **Option (C) is correct.**

Explanation: Mobiles sold in November by company A = 2,520

Number of mobiles sold on discount

$= \frac{35}{100} \times 2520 = 882$

Total mobiles sold without discount

= 2,520 – 882 = 1,638

3. **Option (D) is correct.**

Explanation: Company B sold the mobile phones in October = 1,500

Total profit during the month = (433 × 1,500)

= ₹ 6,49,500

4. **Option (E) is correct.**

Explanation: Required percentage = $\frac{4,080}{3,150} \times 100$

= 129.5 = 130% approx.

5. **Option (A) is correct.**

Explanation:

Company B sold phones in August = 5,500

Company B sold phones in September = 4,500

Total = 10,000

6. **Option (B) is correct.**

Explanation: Required percentage

$= \frac{\text{Beverage C}}{\text{Beverage D}} \times 100$

$= \frac{14.4}{122.4} \times 100$

= 11.76 = 12% approx

7. **Option (A) is correct.**

Explanation: Total number of students prefer beverages B and E together

$= \frac{57.6^\circ + 64.8^\circ}{360^\circ} \times 6,800 = \frac{122.4^\circ}{360^\circ} \times 6,800 = 2,312$

8. **Option (C) is correct.**

Explanation: Difference = Total number of people who prefer beverage A and C together – Total number of people who prefer beverage D and F together

$= \frac{(122.4^\circ + 21.6^\circ) - (79.2^\circ + 14.4^\circ)}{360^\circ} \times 6,800$

$= \frac{144^\circ - 93.6^\circ}{360^\circ} \times 6,800 = 952$

9. **Option (D) is correct.**

Explanation:

Required % $= \frac{64.8^\circ + 21.6^\circ}{360}$

$= \frac{86.4}{360^\circ} \times 100 = 24\%$

10. **Option (A) is correct.**

Explanation:

Ratio between number of students who prefer beverage F : beverage A = 21.6° : 79.2° = 3 : 11

Level-3: EXPERT

(1-5):

TOTAL CARS

State	Diesel Cars	Petrol Cars	Total Cars
1	42	56	98
2	70	126	196
3	140	84	224
4	91	91	182

1. **Option (B) is correct.**

Explanation: Difference = Number of petrol cars in state 4 – Number of diesel cars in state 2 = 91 – 70 = 21

2. **Option (A) is correct.**
Explanation:
State 3, petrol cars = 84
State 1, diesel car = 42
$$\text{Required\%} = \frac{84-42}{42} \times 100 = 100\%$$

3. **Option (D) is correct.**
Explanation:
$$\text{Number of non-AC cars in state 3} = \frac{140 \times 75}{100} = 105$$

4. **Option (E) is correct.**
Explanation: Difference between total cars in state 3 – petrol cars in state 2 = 224 – 126 = 98

5. **Option (B) is correct.**
Explanation: All states together average of petrol cars
$$= \frac{56+126+84+91}{4} = \frac{357}{4} = 89.25$$

6. **Option (D) is correct.**
Explanation: According to the question, observing the graph option (D) is right.

7. **Option (A) is correct.**
Explanation:
$$X\% \text{ of } 360 = 6$$
$$\Rightarrow X = \frac{60 \times 100}{360} = 16\frac{2}{3}$$
$$\Rightarrow X = 16.\frac{2}{3}\%$$

8. **Option (C) is correct.**
Explanation: Observe the graph; hence (C) is right.

9. **Option (B) is correct.**
Explanation: Average of the 1995 year
$$= \frac{11.67+6.67+16.67+16.67+15+20+18.33}{7}$$
= 14.28% = 15% approx. in 1995

10. **Option (C) is correct.**
Explanation: Observe the graph pie chart.

11. **Option (C) is correct.**
Explanation:
$$\text{Expenditure for education} = \frac{9{,}000 \times 18}{30} = ₹5{,}400$$

12. **Option (B) is correct.**
Explanation: The sector of the central angle the fuel
$$\text{expenditure} = \frac{360}{100} \times 15 = 54°$$

13. **Option (C) is correct.**
Explanation: Education and excluding rent expenditure
$$= \frac{3{,}000}{15} \times (100-20-18) = 200 \times 62 = ₹\,12{,}400$$

14. **Option (C) is correct.**
Explanation:
$$30 = \frac{X}{100} \times 45$$
$$\Rightarrow X = \frac{200}{3} = 66\frac{2}{3}$$

15. **Option (C) is correct.**
Explanation: Difference = (20 + 12 + 15) – 30 = 47 – 30 = 17%

16. **Option (D) is correct.**
Explanation: The central angle of the sector for the:
$$\text{Cost of paper} = \frac{\theta}{360°} \times 100 = 16°$$
$$\theta = \frac{16}{100} \times 360 = \frac{576}{10} = 57.6°$$

17. **Option (D) is correct.**
Explanation: Difference in % value
$$= \frac{18-15}{18} \times 100 = \frac{3}{18} \times 100 = 16\frac{2}{3}\%$$

18. **Option (B) is correct.**
Explanation: 4% of the total expenditure for publication 5,500 copies = 1,848
$$\text{Total cost of copies} = \frac{1{,}848 \times 100}{4} = 46{,}200$$
$$\text{per copy} = \frac{46{,}200}{5{,}500} = ₹\,8.40$$
Hence each copy price = 8.40 + 2.10 = ₹ 10.50

19. **Option (C) is correct.**
Explanation:
35% cost printing = 17,500
$$\text{Royalty 15\%} = \frac{17500}{35} \times 15 = ₹\,7{,}500$$

20. **Option (A) is correct.**
Explanation: Total expenditure miscellaneous charge 4% = 6,000
Advertising charge = 18%
$$\text{So, required value } \frac{6{,}000}{4} \times 18 = ₹\,27{,}000$$

■■■

Chapter 23

Data Tabulation

LEARNING OBJECTIVES:

- ❖ Understanding basic concept.
- ❖ Interpreting data.
- ❖ Identifying tools.
- ❖ Comparing data.
- ❖ Enhancing time management skill.

IMPORTANT TERMS AND FORMULAS

- **Mean/Average:** The mean, also known as the average, is calculated by adding up all the values in a set of data and then dividing by the number of values. The formula for calculating the mean is:
Mean = (Sum of values) / (Number of values)
- **Median:** The median is the middle value in a set of data when the values are arranged in order from smallest to largest. If there is an even number of values, the median is the average of the two middle values.
- **Mode:** The mode is the most common value in a set of data.
- **Range:** The range is the difference between the largest and smallest values in a set of data. The formula for calculating the range is:
Range = (Largest value) – (Smallest value)
- **Per cent change:** Per cent change is a measure of the change in a value over time. The formula for calculating per cent change is:
Per cent change
= [(New value – Old value) / Old value] × 100%
- **Proportions and per centages:** Proportions and per centages are used to express a part of a whole. A proportion is the part divided by the whole, while a per centage is the proportion multiplied by 100. The formulas for calculating proportions and per centages are:
Proportion = (Part) / (Whole)
Per centage = (Proportion) × 100%
- **Ratios:** Ratios are used to compare two or more quantities. The ratio of two values is calculated by dividing one value by the other. For example, if the ratio of the number of boys to the number of girls in a class is 2:3, this means that there are two boys for every three girls.

TIPS FOR SOLVING QUESTIONS RELATED TO TABLE DATA

- ➢ **Read the title and labels carefully:** The title and labels on the table provide important information about the data being presented. Read them carefully before starting to answer the questions.
- ➢ **Look for patterns and trends:** Examine the data in the table to identify any patterns or trends.
For example, are there any values that stand out as being particularly high or low? Are there any values that are increasing or decreasing over time?
- ➢ **Pay attention to units and scales:** Make sure you understand the units and scales used in the table. For example, if the table shows data in thousands or millions, be sure to adjust your calculations accordingly.
- ➢ **Estimate where possible:** In some cases, you may be able to estimate the value of a particular cell in the table. Use this technique when you are running short of time, but make sure that your estimate is reasonable.
- ➢ **Use formulas and calculations:** Use the formulas and calculations mentioned in the previous answer to help you analyse and interpret the data in the table. For example, you may need to calculate the mean, median, mode, range, per cent change, proportions, per centages, or ratios to answer the questions.

Directions: Study the following and answer carefully.

Following chart shows the number of students in different universities.

Total number of students = 1,20,000

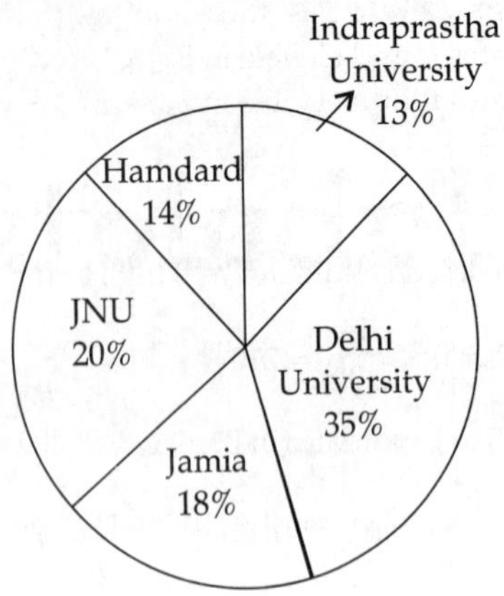

Percentage of listener of different FM channels in national capital region

University	FM Channels				
	Radio Mirchi	Radio City	Red FM	FM Gold	Rainbow
Indraprastha	76%	72%	46%	54%	48%
Hamdard	63%	64%	59%	47%	53%
JNU	52%	65%	64%	51%	54%
DU	82%	44%	32%	35%	45%
Jamia	75%	32%	36%	52%	64%

[SBI PO 2011]

Example 1: How many students of JNU listen to radio city?

(a) 15,200 (b) 14,400
(c) 15,600 (d) 14,600
(e) None of these

Sol. (c) Number of students (of JNU) listening to radio city $= 1,20,000 \times \frac{20}{100} \times \frac{65}{100} = 15,600$

Example 2: The number of Inderprastha students listening to FM rainbow is what per centage of the Jamia students listening FM Gold?

(a) 65 (b) 56
(c) 66.66% (d) 58
(e) None of these

Sol. (c) The number of Inderprastha students listening to FM rainbow = 1,20,000 × 13% × 48%

The number of students of Jamia listening to FM Gold

= 1,20,000 × 18% × 52%

Required percentage

$$= \frac{1,20,000 \times 13\% \times 48\%}{1,20,000 \times 18\% \times 52\%} \times 100 = 66.66\%$$

Example 3: From which of the following university the number of students listening Red FM is minimum

(a) Inderprastha (b) Jamia
(c) JNU (d) DU
(e) Hamdard

Sol. (a) Hence (a) is correct.

Example 4: How many students of Indraprastha and Jamia together listen to Red FM?

(a) 12,562 (b) 12,872
(c) 14,952 (d) 14,272
(e) None of these

Sol. (c) The number of students of Indraprastha listening Red FM:

$$1,20,000 \times \frac{13}{100} \times \frac{46}{100} = 12 \times 598$$

The number of students Jamia listening to Red FM:

$$1,20,000 \times \frac{18}{100} \times \frac{36}{100} = 12 \times 648$$

Total : (12 × 598) + (12 × 648) = 12 × 1246 = 14,952

Directions: The table shows production of different five years and different cars production in five years by a company (in thousand).

Car→ Years ↓	A	B	C	D	E
2012	54	43	46	33	47
2013	58	54	50	35	43
2014	60	56	63	48	53
2015	63	63	73	45	48
2016	55	67	77	49	22

Example 1: The total production of type E cars in 2012 and 2013 is approximately what per cent more than the average production of type A cars during the year 2012 to 2016 ?

(a) 53.8% (b) 55.2%
(c) 52.2% (d) 56.4%

Sol. (b) The total production type E cars in 2012 and 2013 = 47 + 43 = 90

Type A cars during 2012 to 2016 average

$$= \frac{54 + 58 + 60 + 63 + 55}{5} = 58$$

$$\text{Required } \% = \frac{90 - 58}{58} \times 100 = 55.2$$

Example 2: The total production of all type of cars except type B in 2012 is what per cent less than the total production of all types car in 2016 ?

(a) 33.3% (b) 25.8%
(c) 26.7% (d) 42%

Sol. (a) 2012 → Total production of all type except type B = 180

2016 →Total production of all type cars = 270

$$\text{Required } \% = \frac{270 - 180}{270} \times 100$$

$$= \frac{90}{270} \times 100 = 33\frac{1}{3}\%$$

Example 3: If the data related to the production of type D car is represented by a pie chart than the central angle of the sector representing the production of cars in 2013 will be :

(a) 84° (b) 75°
(c) 60° (d) 77°

Sol. (c) D cars production = 210

Type D in 2013 = 35

$$\text{Required angle} = \frac{35}{210} \times 360 = 60°$$

Example 4: What is the ratio of the total production of type E car in 2014 and type C car in 2016 taken together to the total production of type B car in 2014 and type D cars in 2013 taken together?

(a) 9 : 8 (b) 10 : 7
(c) 11 : 8 (d) 11 : 5

Sol. (b) Total production of car E in 2014 + type C car in 2016 = 53 + 77 = 130

Car B total production in 2014 + 2013 type D car = 56 + 35 = 91

Required ratio = 130 : 91 = 10 : 7

Directions: The table shows the number of candidates appearing in the interview for a past in six banks (H, I, J, K, L, M) and the per centage of candidates found eligible [SSC MTS 2012]

Banks	Candidates appearing	% of candidates qualifying
H	1,500	14
I	2,200	26
J	3,000	17
K	980	20
L	1,200	28
M	2,500	21

Example 1: The number of candidates found (not eligible in Bank K is approximately what per cent of the number of candidates found not eligible in Bank I?

(a) 42 (b) 48
(c) 44 (d) 51

Sol. (b) Not qualify in Bank K $= 980 \times \frac{80}{100}$

$= 98 \times 8 = 784$

Not qualify in Bank I $= 2,200 \times \frac{74}{100}$

$= 22 \times 74 = 1,628$

Required% $\frac{784}{1,628} \times 100 = 48.16\%$

$= 48\%$ approximately

Example 2: What was the average number of candidates appeared in the interview for Banks H, J and L taken together?

(a) 1,900 (b) 1,500
(c) 1,800 (d) 2,000

Sol. (a) According to the question,

$$\text{Required average} = \frac{1,500 + 3,000 + 1,200}{3}$$

$$= \frac{5,700}{3} = 1,900$$

Example 3: What is the ratio of the number of candidates found eligible in Bank H to the number of candidates found eligible in Bank L?

(a) 2 : 5 (b) 3 : 7
(c) 5 : 8 (d) 5 : 6

Sol. (c) Qualified candidates in Bank H

$= 1,500 \times \frac{14}{100} = 210$

Qualified candidates in Bank L $= 1,200 \times \frac{28}{100} = 336$

Required ratio = Bank H : Bank L

= 210 : 336 = 5 : 8

Directions: The table shows income, expenditure of a person for 3 years (in thousands): [SSC CPO 2019]

Year	Income	Expenditure	Saving
2000	110	103	+7
2001	223	214	+9
2002	243	197	+46
2003	189	232	–43

Example 1: In the given table if a person inverted his serving every year at 8% simple interest, how much interest earned of the end of 2003?

(a) 7.46 (b) 6.80
(c) 4.96 (d) 5.52

Sol. (b) Required interest

$$= \left(7 \times \frac{8}{100} \times 3\right) + \left(9 \times \frac{8}{100} \times 2\right) + \left(46 \times \frac{8}{100} \times 1\right)$$

= (1.68 + 1.44 + 3.68) thousands

= 6.80 thousands.

Example 2: What is per centage of expenditure on income in the year 2002? (round off)

(a) ₹85% (b) ₹78%
(c) ₹82% (d) ₹81%

Sol. (d) Percentage of expenditure on income (2002)

$$= \frac{197}{243} \times 100 = 81.06\% = 81\% \text{ (approx.)}$$

Example 3: If a person reduced his expenditure by 10% how much would the total saving increased?

(a) ₹69.8 (b) ₹83
(c) ₹74.6 (d) ₹78.2

Sol. (c) Required value

$$= \left(103 \times \frac{10}{100}\right) + \left(214 \times \frac{10}{100}\right) + \left(197 \times \frac{10}{100}\right) + \left(232 \times \frac{10}{100}\right)$$

= 10.3 + 21.4 + 19.7 + 23.2 = ₹74.6

Level 1 Beginner

Directions (Qs. 1–5): Study the table carefully to answer the questions that follow.

Per centage of marks obtained by different students in different subjects of MBA

Students	Subjects (Maximum Marks)					
	Strategic Management	Brand Management	Compension Management	Consumer Behaviour	Service Marketing	Training and Development
	150	100	150	125	75	50
Anushka	66	75	88	56	56	90
Archit	82	76	84	96	92	88
Arpan	76	66	78	88	72	70
Garvita	90	88	96	76	84	86
Gunit	64	70	68	72	68	74
Pranita	48	56	50	64	64	58

[IBPS PO 2011]

1. How many marks did Anushka get in all the subjects together?
(A) 369 (B) 463
(C) 558 (D) 496
(E) None of these

2. Who scored the highest total marks in all the subjects together?
(A) Archit (B) Gunit
(C) Pranita (D) Garvita
(E) Arpan

3. Marks obtained by Garvita in Brand Management are what per centage of marks obtained by Archit in the same subject? (round off of two digits after the decimal)
(A) 86.36 (B) 101.71
(C) 115.79 (D) 133.33
(E) None of these

4. How many students have scored the highest marks in more than one subject?
(A) Three (B) Two
(C) One (D) None
(E) None of these

5. What are the average marks obtained by all students together in Compensation Management?
(A) 116 (B) 120
(C) 123 (D) 131
(E) None of these

Directions (Qs. 6–10): Study the following table carefully and answer the questions given below.

Number of people taking fresh loan from different banks over the years and the per centage of defaulters amongst them each year.

Year	Bank				
	P	Q	R	S	T
2004	27,361	26,345	25,467	28,246	30,164
2005	32,081	27,456	32,461	29,435	35128
2006	25,361	28,637	32,652	29,565	32,443
2007	23,654	29,045	32,561	28,314	36,152
2008	36,125	30,467	25,495	23,764	35,463
2009	35,465	31,963	27,649	24,356	33,214
2010	34,135	31,974	28,283	26,553	31,264

Approximate per centage of defaulters among them

Year	Bank				
	P	Q	R	S	T
2004	12	9	15	13	19
2005	24	8	17	20	23
2006	22	13	16	21	25
2007	18	11	18	22	19
2008	12	10	13	23	18
2009	11	20	11	22	21
2010	9	21	12	21	23

[IBPS PO 2013]

6. Approximately how many people taking a loan from Bank S in the year 2006 were defaulters?
(A) 6,490 (B) 6,210
(C) 5,020 (D) 6,550
(E) 5,580

7. Approximately what was the difference between the number of defaulters of Bank Q in the year 2004 and 2005?
(A) 175 (B) 125
(C) 190 (D) 205
(E) 140

8. In which of the following year was the number of defaulters of Bank R the maximum among the given year?
(A) 2005 (B) 2006
(C) 2007 (D) 2010
(E) None of these

9. In which of the following year was the difference in number of people taking loan from Bank P from the previous year the highest?
(A) 2008 (B) 2006
(C) 2007 (D) 2005
(E) None of these

10. Approximately what was the total number of defaulters of Bank T in the years 2007 and 2008 together?
(A) 14,110 (B) 13,620
(C) 13,250 (D) 14,670
(E) 15,330

Directions (Qs. 11–15): Study the table carefully to answer the questions that follow.

Number of people visiting six different super markets and the per centage of men, women and children visiting there super markets.

Name of the super market	Total number of people	Percentage of		
		Men	Women	Children
A	34,560	35	55	10
B	65,900	37	43	20
C	45,640	35	45	20
D	55,500	41	26	33
E	42,350	6	70	24
F	59,650	24	62	14

[IBPS PO 2011]

11. What is the respective ratio of number of women visiting super-markets A to those visiting super-market C?
(A) 35 : 37 (B) 245 : 316
(C) 352 : 377 (D) 1041 : 1156
(E) None of these

12. Number of men visiting super-market D from approximately what per cent of the total number people visiting all the super markets together?
(A) 11 (B) 5.5
(C) 13 (D) 9
(E) 7.5

13. Number of children visiting super maket C is what per cent the number of children visiting super market F?
(A) 91.49 (B) 49.85
(C) 121.71 (D) 109.30
(E) None of these

14. What is the total number of children visiting super markets B and D together?
(A) 18,515 (B) 28,479
(C) 31,495 (D) 22,308
(E) None of these

15. What is the average number of women visiting all the super markets together?
(A) 24,823.5 (B) 22,388.5
(C) 26,432.5 (D) 20,988.5
(E) None of these

Direction (Qs. 16–20): Study the table carefully to answer the questions that follow:

Math	Temperature									
	Bhuj		Sydney		Ontario		Kabul		Beijing	
	Max.	Min	Max.	Min	Max.	Min	Max.	Min	Max.	Min
1st September	24	14	12	2	5	1	34	23	12	9
1st October	35	21	5	–1	15	6	37	30	9	3
1st November	19	8	11	3	4	0	45	36	15	1
1st December	9	2	–5	–9	–11	–7	31	–3	2	–3
1st January	–4	–7	11	–13	–14	–19	20	11	5	–13

[SBI PO 2013]

16. What is the difference between the maximum temperature of Ontario on 1st November and the minimum temperature of Bhuj on 1st January?
(A) 3°C (B) 18°C
(C) 15°C (D) 9°C
(E) 11°C

17. In which month respectively the maximum temperature of Kabul is second highest and minimum temperature of Sydney is highest?
(A) 1st October and 1st January
(B) 1st October and 1st November
(C) 1st December and 1st January
(D) 1st September and 1st January
(E) 1st December and 1st September

18. In which month (on 1st day) is the difference between maximum temperature and minimum temperature of Bhuj second highest?
(A) 1st September (B) 1st October
(C) 1st November (D) 1st December
(E) 1st January

19. What is the average maximum temperature of Beijing over all months together?
(A) 8.4°C (B) 9.6°C
(C) 7.6°C (D) 8.6°C
(E) 9.2°C

20. What is the respective ratio between the minimum temperature of Beijing on 1st September and the maximum temperature of Ontario 1st October?

(A) 3 : 4 (B) 3 : 5
(C) 4 : 5 (D) 1 : 5
(E) 1 : 4

21. Study the table given below and answer the question that follows.

The table below shows the total number of students studying different subjects in a college and the percentage of boys and girls.

Subject	Number of Students	Percentage of Girls	Percentage of Boys
Hindi	110	60	40
English	70	50	50
Physics	50	30	70
Chemistry	40	80	20
Mathematics	80	20	80
Computers	90	40	60

What is the total number of students in all the subjects? [SSC CHSL 2023]

(A) 200 (B) 240
(C) 420 (D) 440

22. Study the following table carefully and answer the question that follows.

State/Year	1994	1995	1996	1997	1998
Maharashtra	723	840	900	920	925
Kerala	1035	940	1200	1400	1500
Karnataka	750	600	830	575	900
West Bengal	500	550	450	600	525
Delhi	1500	1625	1700	1475	1800
Andhra Pradesh	800	840	875	925	785
Total	**5308**	**5395**	**5955**	**5895**	**6435**

In the case of which state/UT was there a continuous increase in the number of students over the given years? [SSC CHSL 2023]

(A) Andhra Pradesh (B) Maharashtra
(C) Karnataka (D) West Bengal

23. The following table shows the month-wise temperature of four cities from January to May 2022 (in degree Celsius).

Months	Hyderabad	Bangalore	Pune	Kolkata
January	26°	22°	24°	25°
February	27°	24°	25°	26°
March	34°	30°	32°	32°
April	37°	32°	35°	34°
May	42°	36°	40°	40°

Which city recorded the maximum temperature in all five months compared with the other cities? [SSC CHSL 2023]

(A) Pune (B) Bangalore
(C) Hyderabad (D) Kolkata

24. Study the given table and answer the question that follows.

The table indicates the number of students studying in three disciplines in four different colleges.

Disciplines	Colleges			
	A	B	C	D
Commerce	520	550	515	690
Management	212	234	289	390
Agriculture	234	567	456	876

Which college has the minimum number of students in Commerce? [SSC CHSL 2023]

(A) A (B) B (C) C (D) D

2 Level Intermediate

Direction (Qs. 1–5): Study the table carefully to answer the questions that follow:

Monthly Bill (in rupees) of landline phone, electricity, laundry and mobile phone paid by three different people in five different months. [SBI PO 2013]

Month	Monthly Bills											
	Landline Phone			Electricity			Laundry			Mobile Phone		
	Ravi	Dev	Manu	Ravi	Dev	Manu	Ravi	Dev	Manu	Ravi	Dev	Manu
March	234	190	113	145	245	315	93	323	65	144	234	345
April	124	234	321	270	220	135	151	134	35	164	221	325
May	156	432	211	86	150	98	232	442	132	143	532	332
June	87	123	124	124	150	116	213	324	184	245	134	125
July	221	104	156	235	103	131	413	532	143	324	432	543

1. What is the total amount of bill paid by Dev in the month of June for all the four commodities?

(A) ₹ 608/- (B) ₹763/- (C) ₹731/-
(D) ₹683/- (E) ₹674/-

2. What is the average electricity bill paid by Manu over all the five months together?
(A) ₹183/- (B) ₹149/- (C) ₹159/-
(D) ₹178/- (E) ₹164/-

3. What is the difference between the mobile phone bill paid by Ravi in the month of May and the laundry bill paid by Dev in the month of March?
(A) ₹180/- (B) ₹176/- (C) ₹190/-
(D) ₹167/- (E) ₹196/-

4. In which month respectively did Manu pay the second highest mobile phone bill and the lowest electricity bill?
(A) April and June (B) March and June
(C) April and May (D) March and May
(E) July and May

5. What is the respective ratio between the electricity bill paid by Manu in the month of April and the mobile phone bill paid by Ravi in the month of June?
(A) 27 : 49 (B) 27 : 65
(C) 34 : 49 (D) 135 : 184
(E) 13 : 24

Direction (Qs. 6–10): Study the following carefully and answer the questions that follow.
Plan of Public sector under various plans sectorwise expenditure out of that total expenditure (in million).

[IBPS PO 2013]

Plan	I	II	III	IV	V	VI
Public sector plan expenditure	19,600	46,720	85,770	2E + 05	4E + 05	97,500
Social Service	4,180	7,440	12,960	24,620	63,720	14,035
Education	1,530	2,730	5,890	7,860	13,360	25,240
Health	980	2,140	2,260	3,370	7,610	18,210
Family Planning	–	20	250	2,780	4,220	10,100
Housing and Urban Source	330	800	1,280	2,470	11,500	24,880
Water supply and Sanitation	–	–	1,060	4,740	10,920	39,220
Social welfare and related area	1,340	1,750	2,220	3,400	15,410	22,700

6. In various plans in the ratio of expenditure on Public sector which of the following graphs explain best the expenditure on water supply and sanitation?

(A)
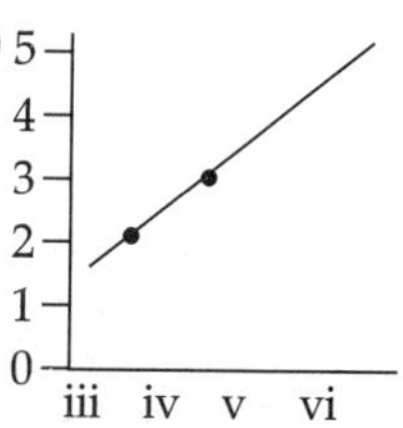

(B)
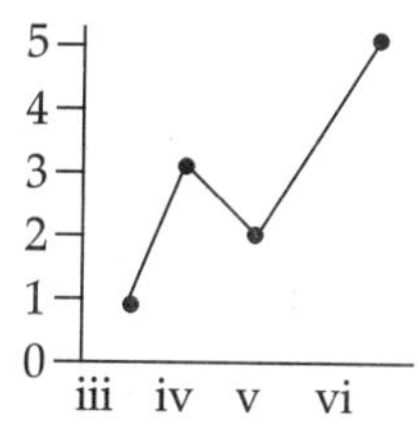

(C)
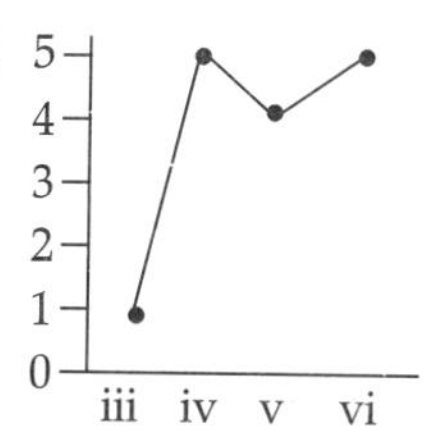

(D)
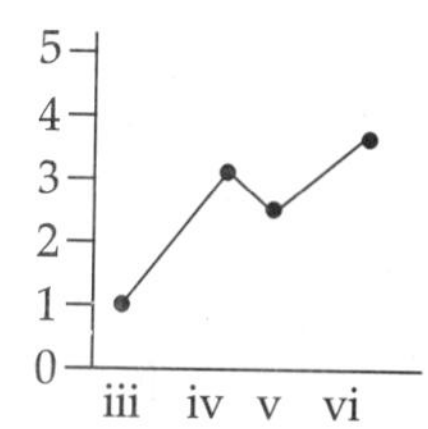

(E) None of these

7. The ratio of public sector expenditure to the expenditure on the social services was highest in which plan?
(A) I (B) VI
(C) V (D) II
(E) None of these

8. In the successive plans in the ratio of public sector expenditure there was a continuous decrease in which sector?
(A) In no sector (B) Health
(C) Education (D) Social
(E) Social welfare and related areas

9. For plan VI out of public sector expenditure what per cent of expenditure is on housing and urban service?
(A) 0.35 (B) 0.5
(C) 25.5 (D) 2.5
(E) 20.5

10. For all the given plans, what was the difference in expenditure of education and health?
(A) ₹22,04,00,000 (B) ₹ 22,40,00,000
(C) ₹22,04,00,00,000 (D) ₹ 2,20,40,00,00,000
(E) None of these

Direction (Qs. 11–15): Study the following table following carefully and answer the questions that follow.
The distribution of marks (out of 150) obtained by 180 students in each of the five subjects.

Marks→ Sub.↓	0–29	30–59	60–89	90–119	120–150
Maths	22	47	74	25	12
Science	39	38	67	22	14
Hindi	19	59	47	36	19
English	24	41	58	34	23
Geography	42	32	52	41	13
Average of five subjects	27	45	60	31	17

[SBI PO 2011]

11. If for passing, the student has to obtain minimum 60% marks in the average of five subjects, how many students will pass?
(A) 108 (B) 58
(C) 48 (D) 72
(E) None of these

12. How many students will pass in Geography if minimum passing marks is 40%?
(A) 74 (B) 106
(C) 96 (D) Can't say
(E) None of these

13. How many students have obtained 60 or more marks in at least one of the five subjects?
(A) 111 (B) 103
(C) 108 (D) 106
(E) None of these

14. If the criteria for distinction is minimum 75% marks in Maths, how many students will get distinction?
(A) 37 (B) 27
(C) 12 (D) Can't say
(E) None of these

15. The number of students who obtained more than or equal to 40% marks in Science is what per cent less than that of those who scored less than 60% in Hindi?
(A) 17.60% (B) 15.40%
(C) 19.80% (D) 24.30%
(E) None of these

Direction (Qs. 16–19): The following table shows the productions of food grains (in millions tons) in a state for the period 1999–2000 to 2003–2004. Read the table and answer the questions.

Year	Wheat	Rice	Barley	Other
1999–2000	680	270	250	450
2000–2001	800	420	440	300
2001–2002	680	350	320	460
2002–2003	720	400	380	500
2003–2004	820	560	410	690

[SSC Sub Inspector 2013]

16. In 2002–2003, the per centage increase in the production of barley as compared to the previous year was.
(A) 14.20 (B) 17.85 (C) 18.75 (D) 7.90

17. During the period 1999-2000 to 2003-2004, x per cent of the total production is production of wheat. The value is x is
(A) 12.6 (B) 37.8 (C) 37.4 (D) 20.2

18. In year 2003–2004, the per cent increase in production was maximum over the previous year for:
(A) Rice (B) Barley
(C) Other cereals (D) Wheat

19. The difference of average production of rice and the average production of barley over the years is :
(A) 50 (B) 60 (C) 80 (D) 40

20. The table below shows the laptop sold on different days by different wholesalers. Study the table and answer the questions that follow.

	Monday	Tuesday	Wednesday	Thursday	Friday
Wholesaler 1	22	20	14	24	10
Wholesaler 2	46	45	06	14	8
Wholesaler 3	18	40	07	15	19
Wholesaler 4	23	30	32	06	26

Laptop sold by wholesaler 1 and wholesaler 2 together on Thursday is what percent of laptop sold by wholesalers 3 on Friday? **[SSC CHSL 2023]**
(A) 200% (B) 150% (C) 100% (D) 50%

21. Study the table given below and answer the question that follows.
The table below shows the total number of students studying different subjects in a college and the percentage of boys and girls. **[SSC CHSL 2023]**

Subject	Number of Students	Percentage of Girls	Percentage of Boys
Hindi	110	60	40
English	70	50	50
Physics	50	30	70
Chemistry	40	80	20
Mathematics	80	20	80
Computers	90	40	60

What is the ratio of the total number of girls in all the subjects to that of boys in all the subjects?
(A) 5 : 6 (B) 7 : 9 (C) 6 : 7 (D) 2 : 3

Level 3 Expert

Direction (Qs. 1–5): Study the following table carefully and answer the questions given below it:

Area and population of different states

State	Area (in sq. kilometres)	Population (in lakhs)
A	6,230	1,122
B	2,540	838
C	8,135	649
D	7,436	572
E	4,893	711
F	3,718	286
G	4,297	860

[SBI PO 2011]

1. Among the given states, in case of how many states the area of that state was more than 15 per cent of the total areas taken together?
(A) One (B) Three
(C) Two (D) Can't say
(E) None of these

2. For which two states the density of population is approximately equal?
(A) No state (B) A and G
(C) D and F (D) C and F
(E) None of these

3. Approximately how much more is the density of population of state B in comparison to that of state A?
(A) 15,000 (B) 18,000
(C) 13,000 (D) 14,000
(E) 17,000

4. In case of how many states the density of population was more than 12 thousand?
(A) Two (B) Five
(C) Three (D) Four
(E) None of these

5. What is the approximate ratio of the areas of state B to the areas of state A and G together.
(A) 1 : 3 (B) 1 : 4
(C) 1 : 5 (D) 1 : 7
(E) None

Direction (Qs. 6–10): Study the following table to answer the given questions:

Each company produces two types of steel. In Table I the total production (in lakh tonnes) of both type of steel together of six companies over the years is given. In Table II the ratio of production of two types A and B (A : B) is given over the years.

[SBI PO 2011]

Table I

Year→ Com↓	1997	1998	1999	2000	2001	2002	Total
BS	424	390	258	756	319	427	2,574
T.S.	3,395	663	812	598	663	782	3,857.5
SBI	532	576	364	936	595	665	3,668
MPI	620	850	876	1,045	1,247	1296	5,961
ES	612	806	627	406	874	760	4,085
LTS	840	836	776	748	384.72	816	4,400.72
Total	33,675	4,121	3713	4,489	4,109.72	4,746	24,546.22

Table II

Year→ Com↓	1997	1998	1999	2000	2001	2002
BS	3 : 5	8 : 7	1 : 2	4 : 5	6 : 5	5 : 2
T.S.	1 : 25	9 : 8	13 : 15	7 : 6	6 : 7	14 : 9
SBI	13 : 15	7 : 9	1 : 3	11 : 7	10 : 7	62 : 71
MPI	41 : 59	17 : 8	100 : 119	53 : 42	24 : 25	7 : 9
ES	2 : 7	12 : 19	6 : 5	3 : 11	10 : 13	19 : 21
LTS	13 : 11	21 : 23	5 : 3	4 : 7	1 : 1.29	7 : 5

6. The production of steel A by company MPI in 1999 is approximately what per cent of production 2001?
(A) 51% (B) 53%
(C) 55% (D) 60%
(E) 64%

7. In 2001 in how many companies production of A style steel is more than that of B type steel?
(A) No company (B) Two
(C) Three
(D) Cannot be determined
(E) None of these

8. For how many companies did the production of steel increase every year and the production of steel decrease every year together from that of the previous year?
(A) No company (B) One
(C) Two (D) Three
(E) None of these

9. Production of T.S. increases by 10% in 2003 and production of SBI decreases by 10% in 2003 in comparison to 2002. If the ratio of production remains the same in 2002. Find the ratio of production of A type to B type steel for both the companies together.
(A) 7026 : 6561 (B) 6561 : 8026
(C) 5226 : 4281 (D) 6066 : 6561
(E) None of these

10. If the profit ratio per unit tonne of steel A and B is 3 : 4 for company BS, what is the actual profit ratio of the company BS for the year 1998 for steel A and B?
(A) 6 : 7
(B) 3 : 4
(C) 8 : 7
(D) Can't be determined
(E) None of these

Direction (Qs. 11–15): Study the table carefully the question that follow. **[SBI PO 2013]**

Station Name	Arrival Time	Departure time	Half time	Distance travelled from origin in km	No. of passengers boarding the train at each station
Dader	Starting point	12.05 a.m.	-	0 km	437
Varsai Road	12:53 a.m.	12.56 a.m.	5 min	42 km	378
Surat	4:15 a.m.	4.20 a.m.	5 min	257 km	458
Vadodara	6:05 a.m.	6:10 a.m.	5 min	386 km	239
Anand Jn	6:43 a.m.	6:45 a.m.	2 min	422 Km	290
Nadiad Jn	7:01 a.m.	7:03 a.m.	2 min	440 km	132
Ahmedabad	8:00 a.m.	8:20 a.m.	20 min	486 km	306
Bhuj	5:40 pm	ending point	-	977 km	None

11. What is the distance travelled by the train from Surat to Nadiad Jn?
(A) 176 km (B) 188 km
(C) 183 km (D) 193 km
(E) 159 km

12. How much time does the train take to reach Ahmedabad after departing from Anand Jn (including half time)
(A) 1 h 59 min (B) 1 h 17 min
(C) 1 h 47 min (D) 1 h 45 min
(E) 1 h 15 min

13. What is the respective ratio between the number of passengers boarding from Varsai Road to from Ahmedabad in the train?
(A) 21 : 17 (B) 13 : 9
(C) 21 : 19 (D) 15 : 13
(E) 13 : 15

14. If half time (stopping time) of the train at Vadodara is decreased by 2 minutes and increased by 23 minutes at Ahmedabad. At what will the train reach Bhuj?
(A) 6.10 a.m. (B) 6.01 p.m.
(C) 6.05 a.m. (D) 6.50 a.m.
(E) 6.07 p.m.

15. Distance between which two stations is second lowest?
(A) Nadiad Jn to Ahmedabad
(B) Anand Jn to Nadiad Jn
(C) Dadar Jn to Vadodara
(D) Anand Jn to Vadodara
(E) Vasai Road to Surat

Directions (Qs. 16–20): Study the table carefully and answer the question that follow:

Number of pages printed by 6 printes in 5 different weeks.

Printer→ Week↓	A	B	C	D	E	F
1st	664	618	628	552	638	419
2nd	569	441	519	438	621	537
3rd	440	614	503	527	541	742
4th	256	563	347	651	412	321
5th	717	429	598	582	519	693

[IBPS Clerk 2013]

16. What is the respective ratio between the number of pages printed by printer B in 2nd week and the number of pages printed by printer F in 5th week?
(A) 4 : 9 (B) 11 : 13
(C) 9 : 13 (D) 7 : 11
(E) 9 : 11

17. What is the average number of pages printed by all the given printer's in 4th week?
(A) 375 (B) 425
(C) 415 (D) 430
(E) 390

18. Which of the following printer printed maximum number of pages in all the given weeks together?
(A) Printer A (B) Printer E
(C) Printer D (D) Printer C
(E) Printer F

19. Number of pages printed by printer A in 3rd week is what per cent of the total number of pages printed by printer D in all the given weeks?
(A) 22 (B) 18
(C) 12 (D) 14
(E) 16

20. What is the difference between the total number of pages printed by printer E in 1st, 2nd and 4th week together and total number of pages printed by printer C in all the given weeks together?
(A) 952 (B) 878
(C) 924 (D) 934
(E) 918

ANSWER KEY

Level-1: Beginner

1.	(B)	2.	(D)	3.	(C)	4.	(B)	5.	(A)	6.	(B)	7.	(A)	8.	(C)	9.	(A)	10.	(C)

11.	(E)	12.	(E)	13.	(D)	14.	(C)	15.	(A)	16.	(E)	17.	(B)	18.	(C)	19.	(D)	20.	(B)
21.	(D)	22.	(B)	23.	(C)	24.	(C)												

Level-2: Intermediate

1.	(C)	2.	(C)	3.	(A)	4.	(D)	5.	(A)	6.	(A)	7.	(B)	8.	(A)	9.	(C)	10.	(C)
11.	(C)	12.	(B)	13.	(E)	14.	(D)	15.	(A)	16.	(C)	17.	(C)	18.	(A)	19.	(D)	20.	(A)
21.	(A)																		

Level-3: Expert

1.	(B)	2.	(C)	3.	(A)	4.	(D)	5.	(B)	6.	(E)	7.	(B)	8.	(A)	9.	(E)	10.	(A)
11.	(C)	12.	(B)	13.	(A)	14.	(B)	15.	(D)	16.	(D)	17.	(B)	18.	(C)	19.	(E)	20.	(C)

Solutions with Detailed Explanations

Level-1 : BEGINNER

1. **Option (B) is correct.**
Explanation: Total marks obtained by Anushka

$$= 150 \times \frac{66}{100} + 100 \times \frac{75}{100} + 150 \times \frac{88}{100} + 125 \times \frac{56}{100} + 75 \times \frac{56}{100} + 50 \times \frac{90}{100}$$

= 99 + 75 + 132 + 70 + 42 + 45 = 463

2. **Option (D) is correct.**
Explanation: Marks obtained by Arpan
= 114 + 66 + 117 + 110 + 54 + 35 = 496
Marks obtained by Archit
= 123 + 76 + 126 + 120 + 69 + 44 = 558
Marks obtained by Garvita
= 135 + 88 + 144 + 95 + 63 + 43 = 568
Marks obtained by Gunit
= 96 + 70 + 102 + 90 + 51 + 37 = 446
Marks obtained by Pranita
= 72 + 56 + 75 + 80 + 48 + 29 = 360
Garvita scored the highest total marks in all the subjects together.

3. **Option (C) is correct.**
Explanation:

$$\text{Archit obtained marks percentage} = \frac{88}{76} \times 100$$

= 115.79%

4. **Option (B) is correct.**
Explanation: Archit consumer behaviours and service, marketing and Garvita strategic management, brand management and compansation management.
Hence two students are right.

5. **Option (A) is correct.**
Explanation:
Average of all students together marks obtained in compensation management:

$$= \frac{(88+84+78+96+68+50) \times 150}{100 \times 6}$$

$$= \frac{464 \times 150}{600} = 116$$

6. **Option (B) is correct.**
Explanation:
Required number of people = 21% of 2,9565

$$= \frac{21}{100} \times 29{,}565 = 6{,}208.65 = 6{,}210 \text{ (approx.)}$$

7. **Option (A) is correct.**
Explanation:

$$\text{Required difference} = \frac{9}{100} \times \frac{26{,}345}{1} - \frac{8}{100} \times 27{,}456$$

= 2,371.05 – 2,196.48 = 174.57 = 175 (approx.)

8. **Option (C) is correct.**
Explanation: Number of defaulters of Bank R in the

$$\text{year } 2004 = \frac{15}{100} \times 25{,}467 = 3{,}820.05$$

$$\text{In } 2005 = \frac{17}{100} \times 32{,}461 = 5{,}518.37$$

$$\text{In } 2006 = \frac{16}{100} \times 32{,}652 = 5{,}224.32$$

$$\text{In } 2007 = \frac{18}{100} \times 32{,}561 = 5{,}860.98$$

$$\text{In } 2008 = \frac{13}{100} \times 25{,}495 = 3{,}314.35$$

$$\text{In } 2009 = \frac{11}{100} \times 27{,}649 = 3{,}041.39$$

$$\text{In } 2010 = \frac{12}{100} \times 28{,}283 = 3{,}393.96$$

9. **Option (A) is correct.**
Explanation: Number of people taking loan from Bank P previous year - in Present year,
In 2008 = 36,125 – 23,654 = 12,471

10. **Option (C) is correct.**
Explanation: Number of defaulters → 19% × 36,152 + 18% of 35,463

$= 6{,}868.88 + 6{,}383.34 = 13{,}252.22$

$= 13{,}250$ (approximate)

11. **Option (E) is correct.**

Explanation: Ratio of women visiting super market A to those visiting super market C,

$$= 34{,}560 \times \frac{55}{100} : 45{,}640 \times \frac{45}{100}$$

$= 19{,}008 : 20{,}538 = 1{,}056 : 1{,}441$

12. **Option (E) is correct.**

Explanation: Required% =

$$\frac{55{,}500 \times \frac{41}{100}}{34{,}560 + 65{,}900 + 45{,}640 + 55{,}500 + 42{,}350 + 59{,}650} \times 100$$

$$= \frac{22{,}755}{3{,}03{,}600} \times 100$$

$= 7.495\% = 7.5\%$ (approx.)

13. **Option (D) is correct.**

Explanation: Required percentage

$$= \left(45{,}640 \times \frac{20}{100} \div 59{,}650 \times \frac{14}{100}\right) \times 100$$

$$= \frac{9{,}128}{8{,}351} \times \frac{100}{1} = 109.30\%$$

14. **Option (C) is correct.**

Explanation: Total number of children visiting super market B and D together

$$= \frac{65{,}900 \times 20}{100} + 55{,}500 \times \frac{33}{100}$$

$= 13{,}180 + 18{,}315 = 31{,}495$

15. **Option (A) is correct.**

Explanation: Average number of women visiting all the supermarket:

$$= \frac{19{,}008 + 28{,}337 + 20{,}538 + 14{,}430 + 29{,}645 + 36{,}983}{6}$$

$$= \frac{1{,}48{,}941}{6} = 24{,}823.5$$

16. **Option (E) is correct.**

Explanation:

Maximum temperature of Ontario on 1st Nov. = 4°C

Minimum temperature of Bhun on 1st Jan. = –7°C

Difference = 4 – (–7) = 11°C

17. **Option (B) is correct.**

Explanation: We observe the table and find the answer easily. So (B) is the right answer.

18. **Option (C) is correct.**

Explanation: Difference between maximum and minimum temperature of Bhuj:

Sep. = 10°C

Oct. = 14°C

Nov. = 11°C

Dec. = 7°C

Jan. = 3°C

19. **Option (D) is correct.**

Explanation: Over all the months average maximum temperature of Beijing $= \frac{43}{5} = 8.6°C$

20. **Option (B) is correct.**

Explanation: Ratio between minimum temperature of Beijing on 1st September and maximum temperature of Ontario on 1st October

$= 9 : 15 = 3 : 5$

21. **Option (D) is correct.**

Explanation: From the table, total number of students

$= 110 + 70 + 50 + 40 + 80 + 90 = 440$

22. **Option (B) is correct.**

Explanation: It is clear from the table that only Maharashtra has a continuous increase in number of students.

23. **Option (C) is correct.**

Explanation: Clearly, Hyderabad recorded the maximum temperature in May.

24. **Option (C) is correct.**

Explanation: From the given data, college C has the minimum number of students in commerce.

Level-2: INTERMEDIATE

1. **Option (C) is correct.**

Explanation: Total amount of bill paid by Dev in the month of June for all the four commodities

= 123 + 150 + 324 + 134 = ₹731

2. **Option (C) is correct.**

Explanation: Electricity bill paid by Manu in average over all five months = (315 + 135 + 98 + 116 + 131)/5

$= \frac{795}{5} =$ ₹159/-

3. **Option (A) is correct.**

Explanation: Mobile phone bill paid by Ravi in the month of May = ₹143

Dav paid loundry bill in March = ₹323

Difference = 323 – 143 = ₹180/-

4. **Option (D) is correct.**

Explanation: March and May is the right answer from table.

5. **Option (A) is correct.**

Explanation: Manu paid electricity bill in April = ₹135

Ravi paid mobile bill in June = ₹245

Ratio = 135 : 245 = 27 : 49

6. **Option (A) is correct.**

Explanation: Observe the table that expenditure on water supply and sanitations increasing plan.

So, this information in option (A) is represent in best way of it.

7. **Option (B) is correct.**

Explanation: From table, we saw the ratio of public sector expenditure to the total expenditure is maximum in plan VI.

8. Option (A) is correct.

Explanation: According to the table, in the all sectors there is no continously decrease.

9. Option (C) is correct.

Explanation: Per cent of expenditures on housing and urban service

$= \frac{24,880}{97,500} \times 100 = 2.5\% = 25.5\%$

10. Option (C) is correct.

Explanation: For all the given plans, total expenditure of education

= 1,530 + 2,730 + 5,890 + 7,860 + 13,360 + 25,240

= 56,610 millions

For all the given plans, total expenditure of health

= 980 + 2,140 + 2,260 + 3,370 + 7,610 + 18,210

= 34,570 millions

Required difference = (56,610 – 34,570)

= 22,040 millions = 22,04,00,00,000/-

11. Option (C) is correct.

Explanation:

$60\% \text{ of } 150 = \frac{60}{100} \times 150 = 90$ marks

Observe table and find 90 or more that 90 marks

Required number of students = 31 + 17 = 48

12. Option (B) is correct.

Explanation: $40\% \text{ of } 150 = \frac{160}{16} \times 150 = 60$

Required number of students = 52 + 41 + 13 = 106

13. Option (E) is correct.

Explanation: (E) is right option from table.

14. Option (D) is correct.

Explanation: Criteria for distinction is 75% minimum. Student get distinction can't be decided from the given table exactly.

15. Option (A) is correct.

Explanation: Number of student more than 40% in Science = 67 + 22 + 14 = 103

Number of students less than 60% in Hindi

= 19 + 59 + 47 = 125

So, required % $= \frac{125 - 103}{125} = \frac{22}{125} \times 100 = 17.60\%$

16. Option (C) is correct.

Explanation: Increase percentage production of barley as compared in 2002 – 2003

$= \frac{380 - 320}{320} \times 100 = 18.75\%$

17. Option (C) is correct.

Explanation: Total production of wheat, rice, barley and other = 3,700 + 2,000 + 1,800 + 2,400 = 9,900 in million tonnes

Required percentage $= \frac{3,700}{9,900} \times 100 = 37.4\%$

18. Option (A) is correct.

Explanation: Percentage increase in the production of,

Rice = 14

Wheat = 100

Other cereals = 190

Barley = 30

So, Rice is right answer .

19. Option (D) is correct.

Explanation: Difference of average over the years of Rice – Barley

$= \frac{2,000}{5} - \frac{1,800}{5}$

= 400 – 360 = 40 million tonnes.

20. Option (A) is correct.

Explanation: Laptop sold by wholesaler 1 and wholesaler 2 together on thursday = 24 + 14 = 38

Laptop sold by the wholesaler 3 on friday = 19

Required percentage $= \frac{38}{19} \times 100\% = 200\%$

21. Option (A) is correct.

Explanation: Total number of girls

$= \frac{60}{100} \times 110 + \frac{50}{100} \times 70 + \frac{30}{100} \times 50 + \frac{80}{100} \times 40 + \frac{20}{100} \times 80 + \frac{40}{100} \times 90 = 200$

∴ Total number of boys

= 110 + 70 + 50 + 40 + 80 + 90 – 200

= 240

Required ratio $= \frac{200}{240} = \frac{5}{6} = 5:6$

Level-3: EXPERT

1. Option (B) is correct.

Explanation: Among the given states the area of A, C and D was more than 15 per cent of the total areas taken together.

2. Option (C) is correct.

Explanation: From the given table, State D and F have equal density of population.

3. Option (A) is correct.

Explanation: Required difference of State B – State A = 33 – 18 = 15 thousand

4. Option (D) is correct.

Explanation: Density of population is more than 12 thousand in states as given below.

State A, B, E and G = 4 states.

5. Option (B) is correct.

Explanation: Required ratio = State B : State A and G

= 2,540 : (6,230 + 4,297)

= 2,540 : 10,527

= 1 : 4.1 (approx.)

6. **Option (E) is correct.**

Explanation: Required percentage = $\dfrac{876\left(\dfrac{100}{219}\right)}{1247\left(\dfrac{24}{49}\right)} \times 100$

= 65% approximately.

7. **Option (B) is correct.**

Explanation: Observe the Table II find the ratio that only BS and SBI have production of A style steel is more than that of B type steel.

8. **Option (A) is correct.**

Explanation: We can observe from the table that "No company" is the correct option.

9. **Option (E) is correct.**

Explanation: In 2003 T.S. total production = 860.2

Indeed, SBI total production = 598.5

A type steel total = 523.6 + 279 = 802.6

B type steel total production = 336.6 + 319.5 = 656.1

A type steel : B type steel

= 802.6 : 656.1 (Both side × 10)

= 8,026 : 6,561

10. **Option (A) is correct.**

Explanation: According to the question,

Required ratio = $\dfrac{3}{4}\times\dfrac{8}{7} = \dfrac{6}{7} = 6:7$

11. **Option (C) is correct.**

Explanation: Train from Surat to Nadiad Jn., covered distance = 440 – 257 = 183 kms

12. **Option (B) is correct.**

Explanation: Taken total time

= 1 h 15 min + 2 min = 1 hr. 17 min

13. **Option (A) is correct.**

Explanation: Number of passengers boarding from Vasai : from Ahmedabad

= 378 : 306 = 21 : 17

14. **Option (B) is correct.**

Explanation:

Increased total time = (23 – 2) = 21 min.

Time when train reached at Bhuj = 5:40 p.m. + 21 min

= 6:01 p.m.

15. **Option (D) is correct.**

Explanation: View the table, second lowest distance between Anand Jn. and Vadodra.

16. **Option (D) is correct.**

Explanation: Pages printed by printer B in 2nd week: Pages printed by F in 5th week

= 441 : 693 = 7 : 11

17. **Option (B) is correct.**

Explanation: Required average

$= \dfrac{321+412+651+347+563+256}{6} = 425$

18. **Option (C) is correct.**

Explanation: Total print up to 5th week by,

A = 2,646, B = 2,665, C = 2,595

D = 2,750, E = 2,731, F = 2,712

So, printer D printed maximum number of pages.

19. **Option (E) is correct.**

Explanation: According to question

Required % = $\dfrac{\text{Printer A in } 3^{rd} \text{ week}}{\text{Printer D in } 1^{st} \text{ to } 5^{th} \text{ week}} \times 100$

$= \dfrac{440}{2750}\times 100 = 16\%$

20. **Option (C) is correct.**

Explanation: Difference between total printed pages by printer C all week and printer E in 1st, 2nd and 4th week = 2,595 – (638 + 621 + 412) = 924

■■■

Chapter

24 Caselets

LEARNING OBJECTIVES:

- ❖ Understanding the problem.
- ❖ Identifying relevant data.
- ❖ Analysing and interpreting data.
- ❖ Solving problems.
- ❖ Methods to solve questions asked in previous years' exams.

➢ **Concept:** A caselet is a short passage or scenario that presents a problem or situation. The passage may include data, facts, or figures that are relevant to the problem or situation. Candidates are then asked to answer questions based on the information provided in the caselet.

➢ **Formula:** Caselet questions may involve different types of mathematical formulas, depending on the nature of the problem. Some common formulas that may be helpful for answering caselet questions include:

Percentage change formula: Percentage change = [(New value – Old value)/Old value] × 100%

This formula can be used to calculate the percentage increase or decrease in a value over time. For example, if a company's profits increased from ₹. 1,00,000 last year to ₹ 1,20,000 this year, the percentage increase would be:

Percentage increase = [(₹ 1,20,000 - ₹ 1,00,000)/₹ 1,00,000] × 100% = 20%

Average = (Sum of values)/Number of values

This formula can be used to calculate the average or mean value of a set of numbers. For example, if a company's sales for the first five months of the year were ₹ 10,000, ₹ 12,000, ₹ 8,000, ₹ 14,000, and ₹ 16,000, the average sales would be:

Average sales = (₹ 10,000 + ₹ 12,000 + ₹ 8,000 + ₹ 14,000 + ₹ 16,000)/5 = ₹ 12,000

Directions (Qs. 1-3): Read the given information carefully and answer the questions that follow.

SHORT QUESTION SECTION

I. Each question is of 5 marks.

II. Candidates have to attempt at least 7 out of every 9 questions.

LONG QUESTION SECTION

I. Each question has 10 marks.

II. Candidates have to attempt at least 7 out of 9 questions.

Example 1: If C did a spelling mistake in the ratio of 5 : 3 in long question section. Then, find marks obtained by him in short question if he did no spelling mistake and word mistake.

(a) 170 (b) 150
(c) 155 (d) 160
(e) 180

Sol. (d) Total marks obtained in long section by

10Y (5 × 0.5 + 3 × 0.75) = 150.5

for x = 2% will have

integral value 16 and Y < 18

So, total marks obtained by him 32 × 5 = 160

Example 2: A did 25% more spelling mistakes in long questions than that and part of 16 long question and obtained 135 marks in it, then find how among questions are wrong in short questions.

(a) 1 (b) 2
(c) 3 (d) 4
(e) 5

Sol. (b) Let spelling errors made by A in short questions be $4x$. Then, number of spelling errors in long section $= 5x$

$$16 \times 10 - 5 \times 0.5 = 135$$

$$x = 10$$

Let number of questions corrected in short question

$$a \times 5 - 40 \times 0.5 = 160 \Rightarrow a \Rightarrow 36$$

A has attempted 38 short questions

So, wrong questions = 2

Example 3: B did 43 spelling errors and 18 full word errors in short section while total number of spellings errors done by D is equal to the number of questions answered correctly by B. Find number of marks obtained by D in both section if he corrects 40 short questions.

(a) 318 (b) 322
(c) 329 (d) 309
(e) 315

Sol. (b) Total questions answered correctly by

$B = 42 + 14 = 56$

Spelling errors done by D in short section = 32
Spelling errors done by D in long questions = 24
So, D $(15 \times 10 - 24 \times 0.5) + (40 \times 5 - 32 \times 0.5)$
$= 322$

Level 1 Beginner

Directions (Qs. 1–5): Study the following information carefully to answer the questions that follow.

There are two trains A and B. Both trains have four different types of coaches viz. General coaches, sleeper coaches, first class coaches and AC coaches. In train A, there are 700 passengers. Train B has 30% more passengers than train A. 20% of the passengers of train A are in general coaches. One-fourth of the total number of passengers of train A are in AC coaches. 23% of passengers of train A are in sleeper class coaches. Remaining passengers of train A are in first class coaches. Total number of passenger in AC coaches in both trains together is 480.30% of the number of passengers of train B is in sleeper class coaches. 10% of the total number of passengers of train B are in first class coaches. Remaining passengers of train B are in general class coaches. **[IBPS PO 2013]**

1. What is the ratio of the of passengers in first class coaches of train A to the all the number of passengers in sleeper class coaches of train B?
   (A) 13 : 7 (B) 7 : 13
   (C) 32 : 39 (D) Data inadequate
   (E) None of these
2. What is the total number of passengers in the general coaches of train A and the AC coaches of train B together?
   (A) 449 (B) 459
   (C) 435 (D) 445
   (E) None of these
3. What is the difference between the number of passengers in the AC coaches of train A and total number of passengers in sleeper class coaches and first class coaches together of train B?
   (A) 169 (B) 178
   (C) 189 (D) 179
   (E) None of these
4. Total number of passengers in general class coaches in both trains together is approximately what per cent of total number of passengers in train B?
   (A) 35% (B) 42%
   (C) 45% (D) 38%
   (E) 31%
5. If the cost of per ticket of first class coach ticket is ₹450, what total amount will be generated from first class coaches of train A?
   (A) ₹ 1,00,080 (B) ₹ 1,08,000
   (C) ₹ 1,00,800 (D) ₹ 10,800
   (E) None of these

Directions (Qs. 6–8): Study the following information carefully to answer the questions that follow.

In a team, there are 240 members (males and females). Two-third of them are males. Fifteen per cent of males are graduates. Remaining males are not graduate. Three-fourth of the females are graduates. Remaining females are non-graduates. **[SBI PO 2013]**

6. What is the difference between the number of females who are not graduates and the number of males who are graduates?
   (A) 2 (B) 24
   (C) 4 (D) 116
   (E) 36
7. What is the sum of the number of females who are graduates and the number of males who are non-graduates?
   (A) 184 (B) 96
   (C) 156 (D) 84
   (E) 196
8. What is the ratio between the total number of males and the number of females who are non graduates?
   (A) 6 : 1 (B) 8 : 1
   (C) 8 : 3 (D) 5 : 2
   (E) 7 : 2

Directions (Qs. 9–13): Study the following information carefully to answer the questions that follow.

The premises of a bank are to be renovated in terms of floaring. Certain areas are to be floored either with marble or wood. All rooms/halls and pantry are rectangular. The area to be renovated comprises a hall for customer transaction measuring 23 m by 29 m, branch manager's room measuring 13 m by 17 m and a pantry measuring 14 m by 13 m, a record keeping cum server room measuring 21 m by 13 m and locker room measuring 29 m by 21 m. The total area of the bank is 2000 sq. m. The cost of wooden flooring is ₹170 per square metres and the cost of marble flooring is ₹190 per square metre. The locker area record keeping cum server room and pantry are to be floored with marble. The branch manager's room and the hall for a customer transaction are to be floored with wood. No other area is to be renovated in terms of flooring. **[IBPS PO 2012]**

9. What is the respective ratio of the total cost of wooden flooring to the total cost of marble flooring?
   (A) 1,879 : 2,527 (B) 1,887 : 2,386
   (C) 1,887 : 2,527 (D) 1,887 : 2,351
   (E) 1,829 : 2,527

10. If the four walls and ceiling of the branch manager's room (the height of the room is 12 metres) are to be painted at the cost of ₹ 190 per square metre, how much will be the total cost of renovation of the branch manager's room, including the cost of flooring.
(A) ₹ 1,36,800 (B) ₹ 2,16,660
(C) ₹ 1,78,790 (D) ₹ 2,11,940
(E) None of these

11. If the remaining area of the bank is to be carpeted at the rate of ₹110 per square metre, how much will be the increment in the total cost of renovation of the bank premise?
(A) ₹ 5,820/- (B) ₹ 4,848/-
(C) ₹ 3,689/- (D) ₹ 6,890/-
(E) ₹ 5,280/-

12. What is the percentage area of the bank that is not be renovated?
(A) 2.2% (B) 2.4%
(C) 4.2% (D) 4.4%
(E) None of these

13. What is the total cost of renovation of the hall for customer transaction and the locker area?
(A) ₹ 2,29,100/- (B) ₹ 2,30,206/-
(C) ₹ 2,16,920/- (D) ₹ 2,42,440/-
(E) None of these

Directions (Qs. 14–19): Read the data carefully and answer the questions.

There are 3 colleges A, B, C offering 3 courses Mechanical, Engineering (ME), Chemical Engineering (CE) and Electrical Engineering (EE).

College A: Number of students in ME is 40 less than that of EE and the number of students in CE is 50% more than that of ME.

College B: Number of students in EE is 20 less than that of EE in college and number of students in CE is 340 which is 40 more than that of CE in college A. Number of students in EE is $22\frac{2}{9}\%$ more than that of ME.

College C: Number of students in ME is 40% less than that of ME in college A. Number of students in CE is 40 less than that of ME.

Total students in EE in all colleges together are 780.

[IBPS Clerk Mains 2019]

14. How many students are in college C?
(A) 620 (B) 740
(C) 560 (D) 680
(E) 520

15. If 10% students of ME course from college A shifted to CE course in college C, then what is the difference between the total number of students in CE in college C now and average of students in ME in all colleges now?
(A) 60 (B) 380
(C) 260 (D) 80
(E) 180

16. Number of students in EE in college B are what per cent more/less than number of students in ME in college?
(A) 75% (B) $87\frac{1}{3}\%$
(C) $83\frac{1}{3}\%$ (D) $66\frac{2}{3}\%$
(E) 50%

17. What is the ratio of the total number of students in ME and CE together in college A to the total number of students in CE and EE together in college B?
(A) 23 : 27 (B) 25 : 28
(C) 26 : 25 (D) 25 : 26
(E) 27 : 28

18. What is difference between the average of total number of students in EE in all colleges and average of total number of students in CE is all colleges?
(A) 30 (B) 60
(C) 40 (D) 20
(E) 50

19. Total students in college C are what per cent of total students in college A? **[SSC CGL 2021]**
(A) 79% (B) 70%
(C) 100% (D) 73%
(E) 85%

Directions (Qs. 20–24): Given data shows number of total number of male and female employees in three companies in a seminar. Read the data carefully and answer the questions that follow.

In the annual seminar of three companies A, B and C, some male and females employees expressed their companies. Average number of female employees who represent A and B is 420. Total number of male employees in A and B is 1620. Number of female employees is $\frac{2}{3}$rd and $\frac{2}{5}$th of male employees in A and B, respectively. Total number of female employees who represent C are 25% more than total number of female employees who represent A and total male number of employees who represent C are $33\frac{1}{3}\%$ more than the total number of female employees who represent B. **[IBPS PO 2020]**

20. Total number of employees who represent A is what per cent more than the total number of male employees who represent B?
(A) $33\frac{1}{3}\%$ (B) $30\frac{1}{2}\%$
(C) $27\frac{1}{3}\%$ (D) $29\frac{1}{3}\%$
(E) $39\frac{1}{5}\%$

21. If 25% of total number of female employees and 20% of total number of male employees who represent B and C together have MBA degrees, then find the total number of employees who do not have MBA degree?
(A) 1,624 (B) 1,424
(C) 1,824 (D) 1,648
(E) 1,244

22. Find the ratio between the total number of male employees who represent B and C together to the total number of female employees who represent A and C together.

(A) 23 : 13 (B) 23 : 14
(C) 23 : 18 (D) 23 : 12
(E) 23 : 20

23. Find the difference between the total number of male employees who represent C and total number of female employees who represent B.
(A) 120 (B) 140
(C) 100 (D) 160
(E) 180

24. Find the average number of females in B and C.
(A) 480 (B) 420
(C) 520 (D) 540
(E) 600

2 Intermediate Level

Direction (Qs. 1–5): There are 450 coupons which can be used in pedicure and hair cutting. The ratio between males to females who use their coupons in hair cutting is 13:7. Number of males who use their coupons in pedicure is 72 more than the number of females who use their coupons in hair cutting. Total number of males who use their coupons in pedicure and hair cutting together is 174 more then the total number of females who use their coupons in pedicure and hair cutting together.

[IBPS PO Prelim]

1. Males who use **their** coupon in pedicure is what per cent of the males who use their coupons in hair cutting.
(A) 200% (B) 100% (C) 0%
(D) 150% (E) None of these

2. Find the ratio between the total number of persons who use their coupons in pedicure to the total number of persons who use their coupons in hair cutting.
(A) 52 : 23 (B) 7 : 8 (C) 8 : 9
(D) 8 : 7 (E) None of these

3. Females who use their coupon in pedicure:
(A) 15 (B) 45 (C) 30
(D) 60 (E) None of these

4. If 25% of males who use thier coupons on hair cutting belong to city A, then find the number of males who use their coupons in hair cutting who do not belong to city A.
(A) 135 (B) 108 (C) 126
(D) 117 (E) None of these

5. Ratio between males who use their coupons in pedicure to that of Spa is 4:5 while the ratio between females who use their coupons in hair cutting to that of Spa is 6 : 11. Find the total number of people who use their coupons in Spa.
(A) 349 (B) 481 (C) 300
(D) 440 (E) None of these

Directions (Qs. 6–10): Study the following information carefully to answer the questions that follow.

A company is the producer of the bottles and sells bottles though a distributor on a condition that on selling the stock of every 50 bottles, he will get ₹ 1,000 as commission. The distributor is responsible to sell all those bottles to retailers. If he marks the bottles at the price which is 30% above the production cost and allows a discount of Y%. He sells total of X bottles which is 40 less than the total received stock by him.

Total production price of the whole stock of bottles received by him to sell to retailers is ₹ 7.8 lakhs. The commission received by the distributor is ₹ 7,000 and he made a profit of ₹ 1.4 lakhs on selling the bottles.

[IBPS Clerk Mains 2018]

6. What is value of Y?
(A) $9\frac{9}{12}\%$ (B) $7\frac{9}{13}\%$
(C) $5\frac{9}{12}\%$ (D) $8\frac{9}{13}\%$
(E) None of these

7. What will be ratio of Y : (X + 40)?
(A) 10 : 511 (B) 10 : 503
(C) 10 : 513 (D) 10 : 507
(E) 10 : 509

8. Instead of Y, employees allow 10% discount on one bottle, then what is the percentage profit of the distributor?
(A) 17% (B) 15%
(C) 12% (D) 10%
(E) 19%

9. If the company added the given commission in cost price and it gives a stock of $(x + 450)$ bottles to another distributor who sold all the stock, then find new cost price of one bottle.
(A) ₹ 2,200 (B) ₹ 2,020
(C) ₹ 2,040 (D) ₹ 2,060
(E) ₹ 2,080

10. If the distributor allowed two successive discounts of 5% and 12.5% on marked price, then find the profit made by the distributor on selling of one bottle.
(A) ₹ 161.25 (B) ₹ 162.25
(C) ₹ 172.25 (D) ₹ 176.25
(E) ₹ 174.25

Directions (Qs. 11–15): Data given below shows the number of units of electricity consumed by Fans, lights and other appliances in three different houses. Study the data carefully and answer the following questions:

House A: Total number of units consumed in House 'A' is 250 units out of which 120 units are consumed by other appliances. Units consumed by fans are 30 less than units consumed by lights.

House B: Units consumed by lights in House 'A' and House 'B' are same. Units consumed by fans in House 'B' are 60% more than that of fans in House 'A'.

House C: Total units consumed by lights in all the three houses are 200 units and units consumed by fans and lights are the same in House C. Units consumed by other appliances are 125% more than that by fans in this house. Total units consumed by other appliances in all three houses are 320 units. **[SBI Clerk Mains 2018]**

11. Number of units consumed by lights in House 'B' is what per cent more than the the units consumed by lights in House 'C'?

(A) 100% **(B)** 200%
(C) 120% **(D)** 50%
(E) 150%

12. Average number of units consumed by other appliances in House 'B' and Houses 'C', 'D' is 110 units. Find the units consumed by other appliances in House 'D'.

(A) 110 units **(B)** 140 units
(C) 130 units **(D)** 120 units
(E) None of these

13. Find the total number of units consumed in House 'A' and 'C' together.

(A) 420 units **(B)** 410 units
(C) 430 units **(D)** 400 units
(E) None of these

14. Find the difference between units consumed by other appliances in House 'B' and House 'C'.

(A) 10 units **(B)** 20 units
(C) 30 units **(D)** 40 units
(E) None of these

15. Total units consumed by fans and lights together in House 'C' is what per cent less than the total units consumed by lights and other appliances together in House 'A'?

(A) 20% **(B)** 40% **(C)** 50%
(D) 60% **(E)** 80%

3 Level Expert

Directions (Qs. 1–5): Study the passage given below and answer the following questions.

There are 3 cities: Delhi, Dhaka and Bangkok. Total distance between Delhi–Dhaka, Dhaka–Bangkok and Delhi–Bangkok is 19,800 km. Distance between Dhaka–Bangkok is 80% of the distance between Delhi–Bangkok and the ratio of distance between Delhi–Dhaka to the distance between Bangkok–Dhaka is 27:32. Fares of 3 different flight operators (A, B and C) on 3 routes (Delhi–Dhaka, Dhaka–Bangkok and Delhi–Bangkok) are:

Delhi–Dhaka: Fare of C is 25% more than that of B and fare of A is ₹ 2,700 less than that of B. Ratio of fare of A to that of C is 3 : 5.

Delhi–Bangkok: Average fare of A and B is ₹ 20,000 and fare of C is ₹ 8,000 more than the average fare of A and B. Average fare of B and C is ₹ 26,000.

Dhaka–Bangkok: Fare of B is ₹ 16,000 and the ratio of fare of A to that of B to that of C is 6 : 5 : 8.

[SBI Clerk Main 2018]

1. If Veer wants to travel from Delhi–Dhaka and then Dhaka–Bangkok without changing the flight operator, then which flight operator would be the cheapest option among A, B and C for Veer?

(A) A **(B)** B
(C) C **(D)** Either A or B
(E) Either D or C

2. If Deepak is travelling from Dhaka–Bangkok and Bangkok–Delhi from C, then what is the amount paid by Deepak per km for the entire trip?

(A) ₹ 3.11/ km **(B)** ₹ 3.98/ km
(C) ₹. 3.42/ km **(D)** ₹ 3.72/ km
(E) ₹. 3.01/ km

3. For which of the following trip, the fare will be maximum?

(A) A, Delhi–Bangkok **(B)** C, Delhi–Dhaka
(C) B, Dhaka–Bangkok **(D)** A, Dhaka–Bangkok
(E) B, Delhi–Dhaka

4. On Dhaka-Bangkok route, which flight operator is charging the lowest fare per km?

(A) A **(B)** B
(C) C **(D)** Either B or C
(E) Cannot be determined

5. Find average fare of A, B and C on Delhi–Dhaka route.

(A) ₹ 12,000 **(B)** ₹ 11,500
(C) ₹ 10,400 **(D)** ₹ 11,200
(E) ₹ 10,800

Directions (Qs. 6–10): Read the following information carefully to answer the questions that follow.

There are four Hostels A, B, C, D

In Hostel A: Number of boys are 120 and number of girls are 30% more than that of number of girls in Hostel B.

In Hostel B: Number of boys are double than that of number of girls.

In Hostel C: Number of boys are 100 more than that of boys in hostel A and total number of boys and girls in C is 1000.

In Hostel D: Number of boys are 182 more than the number of boys in hostel A. Average number of girls of hostel A and that of hostel D is 223. Number of boys in hostel D are 98 less than that of boys in hostel B.

[IBPS PO Prelims 2020]

6. Difference between number of boys and girls in hostel D is what per cent of difference between boys and girls in hostel B?

(A) 53% **(B)** 58%
(C) 63% **(D)** 60%
(E) 57.5%

7. Find the difference between the total number of boys and girls together in hostel A and that in hostel D.

(A) 108 **(B)** 118 **(C)** 112
(D) 98 **(E)** 128

8. Find the ratio of total number of boys and girls together in hostel B to that of hostel C.

(A) 3 : 5 (B) 2 : 5 (C) 3 : 4
(D) 4 : 5 (E) 6 : 5

9. If 20 boys from each hostel left their hostel, then find the average of the remaining number of boys in all the hostels.

(A) 239.5 (B) 235 (C) 250.5
(D) 240.5 (E) 245.5

10. Total number of boys in hostel A and that of girls in hostel C is what per cent more than the number of boys in hostel B?

(A) 100% (B) 125% (C) 150%
(D) 137.5% (E) 175%

Directions (Qs. 11–12): Read the following information carefully to answer the questions that follow.

A and B started a business by investing ₹ 6,000 & 12,000, respectively. A left business after 'X' months and at same time, C joined B with ₹ 7,000. At the end of year, the ratio of their profit share (A : B : C) is 18 : 48 : Z. **[IBPS PO Mains 2019]**

11. Find 'X'.

(A) 8 (B) 6
(C) 9 (D) 7
(E) 10

12. Find value of Z.

(A) 27 (B) 18
(C) 24 (D) 21
(E) 15

Directions (Qs. 13–17): The data given below shows the information of number of students in Class A, B and C which are divided in three groups X, Y and Z.

Class A: Total number of students are 90. 30 students are in group X. The ratio of number of students in group Y and Z is 1 : 2.

Class B: Total number of students is 80. The ratio of number of students in groups X, Y and Z is 8:5:3.

Class C: The number of students in group Y are half of that in group X. The number of students in group X of class C are 20 more than that in group X of class A. Number of students in group Z of class C are 20% less than that in group X of the same class. **[SBI Clerk Prelims 2021]**

13. What is the total number of students in group Y of all the classes?

(A) 95 (B) 70
(C) 120 (D) 80
(E) 60

14. Number of students in group X of class B are what per cent of number of students in group Y of class C?

(A) 160% (B) 80%
(C) 100% (D) 150%
(E) 75%

15. There are total 34 girls in class A. If 12 girls are in group X, then find the number of boys in group Y and Z together in class A.

(A) 38 (B) 34
(C) 30 (D) 32
(E) 36

16. Total number of students in group X is how much more or less than that in group Z?

(A) 20 (B) 25
(C) 15 (D) 50
(E) 35

17. Find the respective ratio between average students in group X in class A and B to total number of students in class C.

(A) 12 : 17 (B) 7 : 23
(C) 4 : 21 (D) 7 : 12
(E) 11 : 16

Directions (Qs. 18–20): Study the following information carefully and answer the given questions for information that is related and in sequence.

I. **Bag X:** There are total 30 red and green balls. Probability of choosing a red and green ball out of total is $\frac{40}{87}$. Number of red balls in bag is (A).

II. Number of green balls are taken and after painting them red, they are placed back into the bag X.

III. Probability of choosing two green balls from the bag X is $\frac{7}{29}$.

IV. **Bag Y:** All balls from bag X are taken and placed into bag Y. If [C] number of green balls are withdrawn from the bag and [C – 5] number of red balls are added to the bag, then the probability of choosing two red balls from the bag is $\frac{2}{5}$.

[SBI PO Mains 2019]

18. Find the value of A.

(A) 10 (B) 15
(C) 12 (D) 18
(E) 20

19. Find the probability of choosing [B – 3] green balls from X [(consider the initial number of red and green balls in the bag].

(A) $\frac{35}{87}$ (B) $\frac{12}{29}$
(C) $\frac{40}{87}$ (D) $\frac{38}{87}$
(E) $\frac{34}{87}$

20. Find the value of C.

(A) 5 (B) 6
(C) 4 (D) 7
(E) 3

Directions (Qs. 21–23): Read the given information carefully and answer the following questions.

An apple pie of radius R cm was cut into X identical pieces, area of each piece was 0.77 cm^2. But later on, it was found that 50% of the pie was rotten, so the remaining 50% was cut into (X – 3) pieces with area of 0.616 cm^2 of each piece. **[SBI PO Mains 2019]**

21. Find out the value of X.

(A) 10 (B) 12
(C) 8 (D) 6
(E) None of these

22. Find out the circumference of the original pie.

(A) $\frac{44}{25}$ cm (B) $\frac{88}{25}$ cm
(C) $\frac{176}{25}$ cm (D) $\frac{132}{25}$ cm
(E) None of these

23. If initially, the entire pie would have been cut into $(x + 3)$ identical pieces, then what would have been the area of each piece?

(A) 0.64 cm^2 **(B)** 0.56 cm^2
(C) 0.28 cm^2 **(D)** 0.42 cm^2
(E) None of these

ANSWER KEY

Level-1: Beginner

1.	(C)	2.	(D)	3.	(C)	4.	(B)	5.	(C)	6.	(C)	7.	(E)	8.	(B)	9.	(C)	10.	(C)
11.	(A)	12.	(B)	13.	(A)	14.	(E)	15.	(A)	16.	(C)	17.	(B)	18.	(D)	19.	(B)	20.	(A)
21.	(C)	22.	(C)	23.	(A)	24.	(A)												

Level-2: Intermediate

1.	(E)	2.	(B)	3.	(E)	4.	(D)	5.	(A)	6.	(B)	7.	(D)	8.	(A)	9.	(B)	10.	(A)
11.	(A)	12.	(C)	13.	(A)	14.	(B)	15.	(D)										

Level-3: Expert

1.	(B)	2.	(D)	3.	(D)	4.	(B)	5.	(E)	6.	(B)	7.	(A)	8.	(A)	9.	(D)	10.	(B)
11.	(C)	12.	(D)	13.	(B)	14.	(A)	15.	(A)	16.	(B)	17.	(B)	18.	(A)	19.	(D)	20.	(B)
21.	(C)	22.	(E)	23.	(B)														

Solutions with Detailed Explanations

Level-1 : BEGINNER

1. **Option (C) is correct.**

   Explanation: Number of passengers in first class coaches of train A = 224

   Number of passengers in sleeper class coaches of train B = 273

   $\therefore$ Required ratio $= \frac{224}{273} = \frac{7\times32}{7\times39} = 32 : 39$

2. **Option (D) is correct.**

   Explanation: Passengers in general coaches of train = 140

   Passenger in the AC coaches of train B = 305

   Total no. = 140 + 305 = 445

3. **Option (C) is correct.**

   Explanation: The number of passengers in AC coaches of train A = 175

   Total number of passengers in sleeper class coaches and first class coaches together of train B = (273 + 91) = 364

   $\therefore$ Difference = 364 – 175 = 189

4. **Option (B) is correct.**

   Explanation: Passengers in general class coaches of train A and B = 140 + 241 = 381

   Total passengers in train B = 910

   Required percentage $= \frac{381}{910}\times 100 = 41.8\% = 42\%$

5. **Option (C) is correct.**

   Explanation: The cost of the ticket of first class coach = ₹450

   Number of passengers in first class coaches of train A = 224

   Total amount = 450 × 224 = ₹ 1,00,800

6. **Option (C) is correct.**

   Explanation: Difference between number of non-graduate females and number of graduate males = 24 – 20 = 4

7. **Option (E) is correct.**

   Explanation: Sum of graduate females and non-graduate males 60 + 136 = 196

8. **Option (B) is correct.**

   Explanation: Ratio between total number of males and number of non-graduate females = 160 : 20 = 8 : 1

9. **Option (C) is correct.**

   Explanation: Area of customer transaction room

   23 m × 29 m = 667 sq. m

   Area of branch manager's room

   = 13 m × 17 m = 221 sq. m

   Area of pantry room = 14 m × 13 m = 182 sq. m

   Area of server room = 21 m × 13 m = 273 sq. m

   Area of locker room = 29 m × 21 m = 609 sq. m

   Total cost of wooden flooring = ₹[(170 × (667 + 221)]

   = 888 × 170

   Total cost of marble flooring

   = ₹[(190 × (182 + 273 + 609)]

   = ₹(190 × 1064)

   Req. ratio = 888 × 170 : 1,064 × 190

   = 1,887 : 2,527

10. **Option (C) is correct.**
Explanation: Area of 4 walls and ceiling of branch manager's room
= 2 (lh + bh) + lb = 2 [17 ×12 +13 × 12] + 13 × 17
= 941 sq cm.
So, total cost of renovation = 941 × 190 = ₹ 1,78,790

11. **Option (A) is correct.**
Explanation: Total area of bank is 2,000 sq. cm
Total area of bank to be renovated = 1,952 sq. cm
Remaining area = 2,000 – 1,952 = 48 sq. m
Total cost of remaining area to be carpeted at the rate of ₹110/sq. m = ₹(48 × 110) = ₹ 5,280

12. **Option (B) is correct.**
Explanation: Required percentage area
$= \frac{\text{Area of bank not renovated}}{\text{Total area of bank}}$
$= \frac{48}{2,000} \times 100 = 2.4\%$

13. **Option (A) is correct.**
Explanation: Total cost of hall of customer transaction
= (170 × 667) = ₹1,13,390
Total cost of locker area = ₹(190 × 609) = ₹1,15,710
Total cost of customer transaction hall + Locker area
= (1,13,390 + 1,15,710) = ₹2,29,100

(14-19).

14. **Option (E) is correct.**
Explanation:
College A: Let number of students in ME = $2x$
Students in EE = $2x + 40$
Students in CE = $340 = 40 + 3x$
Students in ME = $\frac{9}{11}(2x + 20)$
Students in ME = $1.2x$
Students in CE = $1.2x – 40$
Students in EE = $780 – (2x + 40 + 2x + 20)$
= $720 – 4x$
⇒ $x = 100$
Students in college C = 520

15. **Option (A) is correct.**
Explanation: Students who shifted to CE in college C from ME in college A = 20
Student in CE in college C now = 80 + 20 = 100
Average students in ME in all classes
$= \frac{180 + 180 + 120}{3} = 160$
Required difference = 160 – 100 = 60

16. **Option (C) is correct.**
Explanation: Required% = $\frac{220 - 120}{120} \times 100 = 83\frac{1}{3}\%$

17. **Option (B) is correct.**
Explanation: Required ratio = (200 + 300) : (340 + 220)
= 500 : 560 = 25 : 28

18. **Option (D) is correct.**
Explanation: Required difference
$= \frac{240 + 220 + 320}{3} - \frac{300 + 340 + 80}{3} = 20$

19. **Option (B) is correct.**
Explanation: Required% = $\frac{520}{740} \times 100$ = 70% (approx.)

(20-24).
Make a table to solve the questions

Companies	Male	Females
A	720	480
B	900	360
C	480	600

20. **Option (A) is correct.**
Total employees who represent A = 720 + 480 = 1,200
Required% = $\frac{1,200 - 900}{900} \times 100 = 33\frac{1}{3}\%$

21. **Option (C) is correct.**
Explanation: Total employees who represent B and C is who do not have MBA degrees
$= (900 + 480) \times \frac{80}{100} = (360 + 600) \times \frac{75}{100}$
= 1,104 + 720 = 1,824

22. **Option (C) is correct.**
Explanation: Required ratio = $\frac{(900 + 480)}{(480 + 600)}$ = 23 : 18

23. **Option (A) is correct.**
Explanation: Required difference = 480 – 360 = 120

24. **Option (A) is correct.**
Explanation: Required average = $\frac{360 + 600}{2}$ = 480

Level-2: INTERMEDIATE

(1-5).

Pedicure		Hour	Cutting
Males	Females	Males	Females
156	54	156	84

1. **Option (E) is correct.**
Explanation: Required% = $\frac{156}{156} \times 100$ = 100%

2. **Option (B) is correct.**
Explanation: Required ratio = $\frac{156 + 54}{156 + 84} = \frac{210}{240} = \frac{7}{8}$

3. **Option (E) is correct.**
Explanation: Required difference = 54

4. **Option (D) is correct.**
Explanation: Number of males who use their coupons in hair cutting which does not belong to city A
$= 156 \times \frac{75}{100} = 117$

5. **Option (A) is correct.**
Explanation:
Males who use their coupons in spa = $156 \times \frac{5}{4} = 195$
Females who use their coupons in spa = $84 \times \frac{11}{6} = 154$

Total number of people who use their coupons in Spa
= 195 + 154 = 349

6. **Option (B) is correct.**

Explanation: $Y = \frac{200}{2,600} \times 100 = 7\frac{9}{13}\%$

7. **Option (D) is correct.**

Explanation: Required ratio = $\frac{100}{\frac{13}{390}}$

$= \frac{100}{13 \times 390} = 10 : 507$

88. **Option (A) is correct.**

Explanation: New selling price of one bottle

$= 2,600 \times \frac{90}{100} = ₹\ 2,340$

Profit percentage = [(2,340 – 2,000)/2,000] × 100
= 17%

9. **Option (B) is correct.**

Explanation: Stock sold by another distributor
= (350 + 450) = 800

Commission received by another distributor

$= \frac{800}{50} \times 1000 = ₹16,000$

New cost price of one bottle

$= 2,000 + \frac{16,000}{800} = ₹2,020$

10. **Option (A) is correct.**

Explanation:

Selling price $= 2,600 \times \frac{95}{100} \times \frac{7}{8} = ₹\ 2,161.25$

(11-15).

Required profit = 2,161.25 – 2,000 = ₹ 161.25

Units consumed	Fans	Lights	Other appliances
House A	50	80	120
House B	80	80	110
House C	40	40	90

11. **Option (A) is correct.**

Explanation: Percentage in according to question,

$= \frac{80 - 40}{40} \times 100 = \frac{40}{40} \times 100 = 100\%$

12. **Option (C) is correct.**

Explanation: Consumed by other appliances in Houses B, C and D together = 110 × 3 = 330 units

Units consumed by other appliances in House D
= 330 – 110 – 90 = 130 units

13. **Option (A) is correct.**

Explanation: Total units consumed by House A and C together = 50 + 80 + 120 + 40 + 40 + 90 = 420 units

14. **Option (B) is correct.**

Explanation: Other appliances in House B – other appliances in House C = 110 – 90 = 20 units

15. **Option (D) is correct.**

Explanation: Required % according to the question

$= \frac{200 - 80}{200} = \frac{120}{200} \times 100 = 60\%$

Level-3: EXPERT

(1-5).

Routes	Distance (in km)	A's fare (in ₹)	B's fare (in ₹)	C's fare (in ₹)
Delhi–Dhaka	5,400	8,100	10,800	13,500
Delhi–Bangkok	8,000	16,000	24,000	28,000
Dhaka–Bangkok	6,400	19,200	16,000	25,600

1. **Option (B) is correct.**

Explanation: Total fare, if Veer uses trip by A
= 8,100 + 19,200 = ₹ 27,300

Total fare, if Veer uses B for his trip
= 10,800 + 16,000 = ₹ 26,800

Total fare, if Veer uses C for his trip
= 13,500 + 25,600 = ₹ 39,100

So, the cheapest flight operator is B.

2. **Option (D) is correct.**

Explanation:

Total fare paid = 25,600 + 28,000 = ₹ 53,600

Amount per km $= \frac{53,600}{6,400 + 8,000} = \frac{53,600}{14,400}$

= ₹. 3.72 / km

3. **Option (D) is correct.**

Explanation: A, Delhi–Bangkok

Fares = 40,000 – 24,000 = ₹ 16,000

C, Delhi–Dhaka

Fares = 40,000 – 24,500 = ₹ 13,500

B, Dhaka–Bangkok = ₹ 16,000

A, Dhaka–Bangkok = ₹ 19,200

B, Delhi–Dhaka = ₹ 10,800

So, maximum fares is (A Dhaka–Bangkok).

4. **Option (B) is correct.**

Explanation:

A, per km fare $= \left(\frac{19,200}{6,400}\right) = ₹\ 3/\text{km}$

B, per km fare $= \frac{16000}{6400} = ₹\ 2.5/\text{km}$

C, of per km fare $= \frac{25600}{6400} = ₹\ 4/\text{km}$

B is charging lowest fare per km.

5. **Option (E) is correct.**

Explanation: According to the question,

Average required $= \frac{8,100 + 10,800 + 13,500}{3}$

$= \frac{32,400}{3} = \text{Rs } 10,800$

(6–10).

Hostels	Boys	Girls
A	120	260
B	400	200
C	220	780
D	302	186

6. **Option (B) is correct.**
Explanation: Required percentage
$= \frac{302-186}{400-200} = \frac{116}{200} \times 100 = \frac{116}{2} = 58\%$

7. **Option (A) is correct.**
Explanation:
Difference (girls + boys) Hostel D – (girls + boys) Hostel A = (302 + 186) – (120 + 260) = 488 – 380 = 108

8. **Option (A) is correct.**
Explanation: According to the question,
Required ratio = 600 : 1,000 = 3 : 5

9. **Option (D) is correct.**
Explanation: According to the question,
$= \frac{100+380+200+282}{4} = \frac{962}{4} = 240.5$

10. **Option (B) is correct.**
Explanation: Required Percentage
$= \frac{(120+780)-400}{400} \times 100$
$= \frac{900-400}{400} \times 100 = \frac{500}{400} \times 100 = 125\%$

11. **Option (C) is correct.**
Explanation: Profit divided = A : B : C
= (6,000 × x) : (12,000 × 12) : (7,000 × x)
= $6x$: 144 : $7x$ = 18 : 48 : z
$\Rightarrow \quad \frac{6x}{144} = \frac{18}{48}$
$\Rightarrow \quad x = 9$ months
and $\quad \frac{144}{7x} = \frac{48}{z}$
z = 21 months

12. **Option (D) is correct.**
Explanation: According to the question, z = 21

(13–17).

	Group X	Group Y	Group Z	Total
A	30	20	40	90
B	40	25	15	80
C	50	25	40	115
Total	120	70	95	285

13. **Option (B) is correct.**
Explanation: Total students of all classes in Group Y = 70

14. **Option (A) is correct.**
Explanation: Percentage required = $\frac{40}{25} \times 100 = 160\%$

15. **Option (A) is correct.**
Explanation: Total number of girls in Groups Y and Z together = 34 – 12 = 22
Number of boys together in group Y and Z in class A = (90 – 30) – 22 = 38

16. **Option (B) is correct.**
Explanation: Difference = 120 – 95 = 25

17. **Option (B) is correct.**
Explanation: Average = $\frac{40+30}{2} = \frac{70}{2} = 35$
Ratio = 35 : 115 = 7 : 23

(18-20). Let number of green balls = a
So, number of red balls = $3a - a$
According to question
$\frac{{}^{a}C_1 \times {}^{(30-a)}C_1}{{}^{30}C_2} = \frac{40}{87}$
$a \times (30 - a) = 200$
$a = 10$ or 20 but $a \neq 20$

18. **Option (A) is correct.**
Explanation: Value of A = 10

19. **Option (D) is correct.**
Explanation: Probability of choosing (B – 3) green balls from X bag (according to the question)
$B = \frac{20C_2}{30C_2} = \frac{38}{87}$

20. **Option (B) is correct.**
Explanation: According to question
$\frac{(10+C)C_2}{25C_2} = \frac{2}{5} = C = 6, -25$
But $\quad C \neq -25$
Hence, $\quad C = 6$

21. **Option (C) is correct.**
Explanation: R is the radius of original pie
According to question,
$(x - 3) \times 0.616 \times 2 = x \times 0.77 \Rightarrow x = 8$

22. **Option (E) is correct.**
Explanation: Original pie radius = R cm
Area of pie = $0.77 \times 8\ cm^2$
Required in question $= \pi R^2 = 8 \times 0.77 \Rightarrow R = \frac{7}{5}$ cm
Circumference = $2 \times \frac{22}{7} \times \frac{7}{5} = 8.8$ cm

23. **Option (B) is correct.**
Explanation: Total area of pie = $0.77 \times 8\ cm^2$
Area of one piece of pie = $\frac{0.77 \times 8}{11} = 0.56\ cm^2$

Permutations and Combinations

Permutation - Different ways in which a set of objects can be arranged or ordered

Combination - Different ways in which a set of objects can be selected or chosen

To calculate number of combinations of 'n' objects taken 'r' at a time;

$$^{n}C_{r} = \frac{n!}{r!(n-r)!}$$

Formula to calculate number of permutations of 'n' objects taken 'r' at a time;

$$^{n}P_{r} = \frac{n!}{(n-r)!}$$

! = factorial, it means product of all positive integers up to and including that number

e.g., $5! = 5 \times 4 \times 3 \times 2 \times 1 = 120$

Permutation v/s Combination

- Permutation involve order, combination do not.
- Permutation have more possible outcomes than combination
- Number of permutations $\geq$ Number of combination

$0! = 1$

$^{n}C_{n} = 1$

$^{n}C_{(n-1)} = n$

$^{n}P_{n} = n!$

$^{n}C_{1} = 1$

$^{n}P_{1} = n$

Section-5 : Modern Mathematics

Chapter 25

Permutations and Combinations

LEARNING OBJECTIVES:

- Identify the difference between permutation and combination.
- Understand methods to calculate permutations.
- Understand methods to solve questions related to combinations.
- Solve real-life word problems based on permutations and combinations.
- Apply the concept of probability.
- Solve previous year questions asked in various competitive exams.

PERMUTATIONS

- Permutations refer to the different ways in which a set of objects can be arranged or ordered. The order of arrangement matters in permutations.

  For example, consider the letters "A", "B", and "C". The possible permutations of these letters are:

  ABC, ACB, BAC, BCA, CAB, CBA

  The formula to calculate the number of permutations of "n" objects taken "r" at a time is:

$$^nP_r = \frac{n!}{(n-r)!}$$

  where "!" means factorial, which is the product of all positive integers up to and including that number.

  For example, if we have 6 books and want to arrange 3 of them on a shelf, the number of permutations would be:

$$^6P_3 = \frac{6!}{(6-3)!} = \frac{6!}{3!} = 6 \times 5 \times 4 = 120$$

  Therefore, there are 120 different ways to arrange 3 books out of 6 on a shelf.

COMBINATIONS

- Combinations refer to the different ways in which a set of objects can be selected or chosen, without regard to their order.

  For example, consider the letters "A", "B", and "C". The possible combinations of these letters are:

  ABC, ACB, BAC, BCA, CAB, CBA

  Notice that the same combinations were listed as permutations, but in a different order. The order does not matter in combinations.

  The formula to calculate the number of combinations of "n" objects taken "r" at a time is:

$$^nC_r = \frac{n!}{(r!(n-r)!)}$$

  For example, if we have 6 books and want to select 3 of them to read, the number of combinations would be:

$$^6C_3 = \frac{6!}{(3!(6-3)!)} = \frac{6!}{(3!3!)} = 20$$

  Therefore, there are 20 different combinations of 3 books out of 6 that we can choose to read.

SOME KEY POINTS TO REMEMBER

- Permutations involve order, while combinations do not.
- Permutations have more possible outcomes than combinations.
- The number of permutations is always greater than or equal to the number of combinations for the same set of objects.

SOME IMPORTANT CONCEPTS

- **Permutations:** A permutation is an arrangement of objects in a particular order. For example, if you have 3 alphabets and arrange them in a particular order, you can create 6 different permutations: ABC, ACB, BAC, BCA, CAB, CBA. The number of permutations of n distinct objects taken r at a time is given by the formula $^nP_r = n!/(n-r)!$. Here, n is the total number of objects and r is the number of objects being arranged.
- **Factorial:** The factorial of a non-negative integer n, denoted by $n!$, is the product of all positive integers up to n. For example, $5! = 5 \times 4 \times 3 \times 2 \times 1 = 120$.
- **Combinations:** A combination is a selection of objects without regard to order. For example, if you have 3 alphabets and want to select 2 of them, you can create 3 different combinations: AB, AC, BC. The number of combinations of n distinct objects taken r at a time is given by the formula $^nC_r = n!/(r!(n-r)!)$. Here, n is the total number of objects and r is the number of objects being selected.

- **Permutations with repetitions:** When objects can be repeated in a permutation, the formula to calculate the number of permutations is n^r, where n is the total number of objects and r is the number of objects being arranged.
- **Combinations with repetitions:** When objects can be repeated in a combination, the formula to calculate the number of combinations is $^{(n+r-1)}C_{(r-1)}$, where n is the total number of objects and r is the number of objects being selected.
- **Circular permutations:** A circular permutation is a permutation where the order of the objects matters, but the starting point does not. For example, if you have 4 objects and arrange them in a circle, you can create 6 different circular permutations: ABCD, BCDA, CDAB, DABC, and DCBA. The number of circular permutations of n distinct objects is $(n - 1)!$
- **Permutations and combinations with identical objects:** When there are identical objects, the number of permutations or combinations may change. For example, if you have 3 identical balls and want to arrange them in a particular order, there is only 1 permutation: AAA. The number of permutations of n objects where p_1 are identical, p_2 are identical, ..., p_k are identical is $n! / (p_1! \times p_2! \times ... \times p_k!)$ The number of combinations of n objects where p1 are identical, p_2 are identical, ..., p_k are identical is $(n + p_1 + p_2 + ... + p_k - 1)\ C\ (p_1 + p_2 + ... + p_k - 1)$.

Example 1: A committee of 5 people is to be chosen from a group of 10 people. In how many ways can this be done?

(a) 25 (b) 50
(c) 252 (d) 500

Sol. (c) The number of ways of choosing r objects from n distinct objects is given by the formula,

$^nC_r = \frac{n!}{(r!(n-r)!)}$. Here, $n = 10$ and $r = 5$.

Therefore, the number of ways of choosing 5 people from a group of 10 people is:

$$^{10}C_5 = \frac{10!}{(5!(10-5)!)} = 252$$

Therefore, the answer is (c) 252.

Example 2: A pizza shop offers 4 different toppings for its pizzas. If a customer can choose exactly 3 toppings, how many different pizza combinations are possible?

(a) 4 (b) 10
(c) 16 (d) 24

Sol. (a) The number of ways of choosing r objects from n distinct objects is given by the formula

$$^nC_r = \frac{n!}{(r!(n-r)!)}$$

Here, $n = 4$ and $r = 3$.

Therefore, the number of ways of choosing 3 toppings out of 4 is:

$$^4C_3 = \frac{4!}{(3!(4-3)!)} = 4$$

Therefore, the answer is option (a).

Example 3: A combination lock has 4 dials, each labelled with the digits 0–9. How many possible combinations are there?

(a) 10,000 (b) 1,000
(c) 100 (d) 10

Sol. (a) Since each dial has 10 possible digits, there are 10 choices for the first dial, 10 choices for the second dial, and so on. Therefore, the total number of possible combinations is:

$$10 \times 10 \times 10 \times 10 = 10{,}000$$

Therefore, the answer is (a) 10,000.

Example 4: A group of 8 people are going to ride in a car that can seat 5 people. In how many ways can the people be chosen to ride in the car?

(a) 56 (b) 1,680
(c) 56,320 (d) 40,320

Sol. (a) The number of ways of choosing r objects from n distinct objects is given by the formula,

$$^nC_r = \frac{n!}{(r!(n-r)!)}$$

Here, $n = 8$ and $r = 5$.

Therefore, the number of ways of choosing 5 people out of 8 is:

$$^8C_5 = \frac{8!}{(5!(8-5)!)} = 56$$

Level 1 Beginner

1. How many different 5-letter words (with or without meaning) can be constructed using all the letters of the word 'DELHI'. So that each word has to start with 'D" and end with 'I'? [UPSC 2020]

(A) 24 (B) 18 (C) 12 (D) 6

2. The number of parallelograms that can be formed form a set of four parallel lines intersecting another set of four parallel lines is: [UPSC 2019]

(A) 18 (B) 24 (C) 32 (D) 36

3. How many triplets (x, y, z) satisfy the equation $x + y + z = 6$, where x, y and z are natural numbers? [UPSC 2019]

(A) 4 (B) 5 (C) 9 (D) 10

4. While writing all the numbers from 700 to 1,000, how many numbers occur in which the digit at hundred's place is greater than the digit at ten's place, and the digit at ten's place is greater than the digit at unit's place? [UPSC 2018]

(A) 61 (B) 64 (C) 85 (D) 91

5. A bag contains 20 balls, 8 green, 7 white and 5 red. What is the minimum number of balls that must be picked up from the bag blind folded (without replacing any of it) to be assured of picking at least one ball of each colour? [UPSC 2017]
(A) 17 (B) 16 (C) 13 (D) 11

6. Which of the following words can be written in 120 differrent ways? [IBPS Clerk 2012]
(A) STABLE (B) STILL
(C) WATER (D) DARE

7. Find the numbers between 300 and 3,000 that can be formed with the digits 0, 1, 2, 3, 4 and 5, no digits being repeated. [SBI PO 2011]
(A) 180 (B) 160 (C) 240 (D) 60

8. In how many different ways can be letters of the word 'CREAM' be arranged? [SBI Clerk 2012]
(A) 720 (B) 120 (C) 360 (D) 504

9. How many different sums can be formed with the denomination ₹ 50, ₹ 100, ₹ 200, ₹ 500 and ₹ 2,000 taking at least three denominations at a time? [UPSC 2020]
(A) 16 (B) 15 (C) 14 (D) 10

10. One page is torn from a booklet whose pages are numbered in the usual manner starting from the first page as 1. The sum of the numbers on the remaining pages is 195. The page contains which of the following numbers? [UPSC 2020]
(A) 5, 6 (B) 7, 8 (C) 9, 10 (D) 11, 12

2 Level Intermediate

1. A printer numbers the pages of a book starting with 1 and uses 3,089 digits in all. How many pages does the book have? [UPSC 2019]
(A) 1,040 (B) 1,048 (C) 1,049 (D) 1,050

2. For a sports meet, a winner's stand comprising three wooden blocks is in the following form.
There are six different colours available to choose from and each of three wooden blocks is to be painted such that no two of them has the same colour. In how many different ways can be winners' stand be painted? [UPSC 2018]
(A) 120 (B) 81 (C) 66 (D) 36

3. In how many different ways can the numbers '256974' be arranged using each digit only once in each arrangement, such that the digits 6 and 5 are at the extreme ends in each arrangement? [IBPS PO 2013]
(A) 48 (B) 720 (C) 36 (D) 360

4. In how many different ways can the letters of the word 'ABACUS' be arranged such that the vowels always appears together?
(A) $5! \times 3!$ (B) $3! \times 3!$
(C) $\frac{3! \times 3!}{2!}$ (D) $\frac{4! \times 3!}{2!}$

5. Two girls and 4 boys are to be seated in a row in such a way that the girls do not sit together. In how many different ways can it be done? [SPI PO 2002]
(A) 720 (B) 480 (C) 360 (D) 240

3 Level Expert

Directions (Qs. 1 & 2): A committee of five members is to be formed out of 3 trainees, 4 professors and 6 research associates. In how many different ways can this be done if: [SBI PO 2010]

1. The committee should have all 4 professors and 1 research associate or all 3 trainees and 2 professors:
(A) 12 (B) 13
(C) 24 (D) 52

2. The committee should have 2 trainees and 3 research associates:
(A) 15 (B) 45
(C) 60 (D) 9

3. In how many different ways can the letters of the word 'MIRACLE' be arranged? [SBI PO 2008]
(A) 720 (B) 5,040
(C) 2,520 (D) 40,320

4. How many five-digit prime numbers can be formed using 1, 2, 3, 4 and 5 without repetition? [UPSC 2020]
(A) 0 (B) 1
(C) 9 (D) 10

5. Suppose you have money in three denominations ₹ 1, ₹ 10 and ₹ 50. In how many ways can you pay a bill of ₹ 107? [UPSC 2019]
(A) 16 (B) 17
(C) 18 (D) 19

6. Each face of a cube can be painted in black or white colours. In how many ways can the cube be painted? [UPSC 2019]
(A) 9 (B) 10
(C) 11 (D) 12

7. How many diagonals can be drawn by joining the vertices of an octagon? [UPSC 2018]
(A) 20 (B) 24
(C) 28 (D) 64

ANSWER KEY

Level-1: Beginner

1.	(D)	2.	(D)	3.	(D)	4.	(C)	5.	(B)	6.	(C)	7.	(A)	8.	(B)	9.	(A)	10.	(B)

Level-2: Intermediate

1.	(C)	2.	(A)	3.	(A)	4.	(D)	5.	(B)										

Level-3: Expert

1.	(A)	2.	(C)	3.	(B)	4.	(A)	5.	(C)	6.	(D)	7.	(A)						

Solutions with Detailed Explanation

Level-1: BEGINNER

1. Option (D) is correct.

Explanation:

D _ _ _ I
E,L,H

These 3 letters (E, H, I) can be arranged in 3! ways

$$3! = 3 \times 2 \times 1 = 6$$

[as position D and I is fixed]

2. Option (D) is correct.

Explanation: Total number of parallelograms

$$= {}^4C_2 \times {}^4C_2$$

$$= \frac{4!}{2! \times (4-2)!} \times \frac{4!}{2!(4-2)!} = 36$$

3. Option (D) is correct.

Explanation:

$$x + y + z = 6$$

Here $n = 6$ [n = no. of similar objects distributed among r persons]

Total numbers = 3 (x, y, z)

So $r = 3$

Hence, Triplets $= {}^{(6-1)}C_{(3-1)}$

$${}^5C_2 = \frac{5!}{2! \times 3!} \quad \left[\text{Using } {}^nC_r = \frac{n!}{(n-r)!r!}\right]$$

$$= \frac{5 \times 4 \times 3 \times 2 \times 1}{2 \times 1 \times 3 \times 2 \times 1} = \frac{20}{2} = 10$$

4. Option (C) is correct.

Explanation:

I. Numbers from 700 to 800 which satisfy the conditions given in question are
710, 720, 721, 730, 731, 732, 740, 741, 742, 743, 750, 751, 752, 753, 754, 760, 761, 762, 763, 764, 765
= 21 numbers

II. Numbers from 801 to 900 which satisfied the condition given in question
⇒ 801 to 879 [Same group as in I]
Other numbers = 870, 871, 872, 873, 874, 875, 876
Total numbers = 21 + 7 = 28

III. Numbers from 901 to 1,000
901 to 969 [Same as previous group]
Other numbers = 970, 971, 972, 973, 974, 975, 976, 980, 981, 982, 983, 984, 985, 986, 987
Total numbers = 21 + 15 = 36
Hence, total number which satisfy the condition given in question = 21 + 28 + 36 = 85

5. Option (B) is correct.

Explanation: 8 green + 7 white balls; if we pick 15 balls, then it is possible to have two colours and if we pick 1 more ball, it will be confirmed that we got all colours.

Hence, 16 is the correct choice.

6. Option (C) is correct.

Explanation: For 120 different ways, we need 5 letter words, in which all the letters are different.

Hence, WATER is correct choice.

7. Option (A) is correct.

Explanation:

I. Three-digit numbers

3/4/5		
↓ 3 ways	↓ 5 ways	↓ 4 ways

larger than 300

No. of ways = $3 \times 5 \times 4 = 60$

II. Four-digit numbers

1/2			
↓ 2 ways	↓ 5 ways	↓ 4 ways	↓ 3 ways

No. of ways = $2 \times 5 \times 4 \times 3 = 120$

Hence, total numbers = 120 + 60 = 180

8. Option (B) is correct.

Explanation:

C R E A M
1 2 3 4 5

= 5!

⇒ $5 \times 4 \times 3 \times 2 \times 1 = 120$ ways

9. **Option (A) is correct.**
Explanation:
$$3 \text{ out of } 5 = {}^5C_3 = 10 \text{ ways}$$
$$4 \text{ out of } 5 = {}^5C_4 = 5 \text{ ways}$$
$$5 \text{ out of } 5 = {}^5C_5 = 1 \text{ ways}$$
Hence, total no of ways = 10 + 5 + 1 = 16

10. **Option (B) is correct.**
Explanation: According to question,
Remaining page sum = 195
Let sum of no. of pages = x
So, total sum = 195 + x
$$195 + x = \frac{n}{2}(n+1)$$
[We know that the number of page starts from 1]
Checking for n = 20
$$195 + x = \frac{20}{2}(20+1)$$
$$195 + x = 210$$
$$x = 15$$
Hence, option (B) only give sum of 15, i.e., (7, 8)

Level-2: INTERMEDIATE

1. **Option (C) is correct.**
Explanation: From 1 to 9 = 9 digit
From 10 to 99 = 2 × 90 = 180 digit
From 100 to 999 = 3 × 900 = 2,700
So total digits used = 9 + 180 + 2,700 = 2,889
Remaining = 200
$$\text{No. of pages having 4 digits} = \frac{200}{4} = 50$$
Hence, required no. = 999 + 50 = 1,049

2. **Option (A) is correct.**
Explanation:
No. of colours = 6
Colours to be chosen = 3
$$\text{Using, } {}^nP_r = \frac{n!}{(n-r)!}$$
$$= {}^6P_3 \Rightarrow \frac{6!}{(6-3)!}$$
$$= 6 \times 5 \times 4 = 120$$

3. **Option (A) is correct.**
Explanation: I[st] situation

6					5

2, 9, 7 only 4 can be fill in 4 empty spaces
So, 4 × 3 × 2 × 1 = 24 ways
IInd situation

					6

...o. can be filled in 4 blank spaces
... 1 = 24 ways
... = 24 + 24 = 48

Explanation: No. of vowels in ABACUS = 3
When we take vowel together then, no. of letters = 4

A	B	A	B	C	S

But 3 vowels can be arranged in 3 different ways with repetition of vowel A
$$\text{Hence, no. of ways} = \frac{4! \times 3!}{2!}$$

5. **Option (B) is correct.**
Explanation: Arrangement of 4 boys = ${}^4P_4 = 4!$
g b g b g b g b g
Arrangement of 2 girls in 5 spaces = ${}^5P_2$ ways
Hence, total no. of ways in which girls don't sit together = $4! \times {}^5P_2 = 4 \times 3 \times 2 \times 5 \times 4 = 480$

Level-3: EXPERT

1. **Option (A) is correct.**
Explanation: 4 professors and 1 research fellow
= ${}^4C_4 \times {}^6C_1$ ways = 1 × 6
or
3 trainees and 2 professors
= ${}^3C_3 \times {}^4C_2$ ways = 1 × 6
Hence, total ways = 6 + 6 = 12

2. **Option (C) is correct.**
Explanation: Selecting 2 trainees out of 3 and 3 research associates out of 6 = ${}^3C_2 \times {}^6C_3 = 60$

3. **Option (B) is correct.**
Explanation: MIRACLE has all 7 different letters
Hence, no. of ways of arrangement = 7!
= 7 × 6 × 5 × 4 × 3 × 2 × 1 = 5,040

4. **Option (A) is correct.**
Explanation: No prime number can be formed using 1, 2, 3, 4 and 5 because sum of 1, 2, 3, 4 and 5 is divisible by 3.
Hence, 0 is correct choice.

5. **Option (C) is correct.**
Explanation:
50 + 50 + 7 = 107 → 1 way
Using one 50, five 10 and one 7
Maximum of 5 tens ⇒ 5 + 1 = 6 ways
No. 50 using 10 tens and 7 one 7 = 10 + 1 = 11 ways
Hence, total number of ways = 1 + 6 + 11 = 18

6. **Option (D) is correct.**
Explanation: Possibilities of each face in black is 6 and each face in white is 6.
So, total number of ways = 6 + 6 = 12

7. **Option (A) is correct.**
Explanation: Using, number of diagonals in a polygon:
$$= n \times \frac{(n-3)}{2} \quad [n = \text{no. of sides}]$$
$$= 8 \times \frac{(8-3)}{2} = 8 \times \frac{5}{2}$$
= 20 diagonals.

Probability

Deals with study of random events

$$P(E) = \frac{\text{No. of favourable outcomes}}{\text{Total no. of outcomes}}$$

Experiment:

Action resulting in multiple outcomes

Sample Space – Set of all possibilities

Event – Subset of Sample space

Events

Certain Event – Sure to happen

Impossible Event – Cannot happen and zero probability

Independent Events – No event affect other $P(A \text{ and } B) = P(A) \times P(B)$

Applications:

- Permutation – Combination
- Dice based questions
- Coins based questions
- Card based questions

Dice

- Probability of getting a number $= \frac{1}{6}$ [one dice rolled]
- When two dice rolled $P(\text{sum}) = \frac{\text{no. of ways to get the sum}}{\text{total number of outcomes}}$

Coins

1. When a fair coin tossed, probability of particular outcome $= \frac{1}{2}$
2. When two dice rolled $P(\text{Combination}) = \frac{\text{No. of ways to get combination}}{\text{Total no. of outcomes}}$

Cards

- Probability of getting a card $\frac{1}{52}$ [a deck of card]

26 red colour cards, 26 black colour cards, 12 face cards (6 red, 6 black) 4 Queens, 4 Kings, 4 Jocker in each deck

Chapter 26

Probability

LEARNING OBJECTIVES:

- Solve questions related to coins, dice and cards.
- Understand the method to calculate the probability of different types of events.
- Solve questions asked in various competitive exams.

- Deals with study of random events. Probability can be used to solve problems related to various topics such as permutations and combinations, dice, cards, coins, etc.

IMPORTANT TERMS

- **Experiment:** Any action that can result in multiple outcomes is called an experiment.
- **Sample space:** The set of all possible outcomes of an experiment is called sample space.
- **Event:** Any subset of the sample space is called an event.
- **Probability:** Probability of an event is defined as the ratio of number of favourable outcomes to the total number of possible outcomes.

$$P(E) = \frac{\text{No. of favourable outcomes}}{\text{Total no. of outcomes}}$$

Type of Events:

- **Certain Event:** An event that is sure to happen has a probability of 1.
- **Impossibe Event:** An event that cannot happen has a probability of 0.
- **Equally Likely Events:** When all the outcomes of an experiment are equally likely, the probability of each outcome is given by:

  $P(E) = \frac{1}{N}$ where N = no. of possible outcomes
- **Mutually Exclusive Events:** When two events have no outcomes, they are called mutually exclusive events. The probability of union of mutually exclusive events is given by:

  P (A or B) = P(A) + P(B)
- **Independent Events:** Two events are independent if the occurrence of one event does not affect the occurrence of the other event. The probability of the intersection of independent events is given by:

  $$P(A \text{ and } B) = P(A) \times P(B)$$
- **Dependent Events:** Two events are dependent if the occurrence of one event affects the occurrence of the other event. The probability of the intersection of dependent events is given by:

  P (A and B) = P(A) × P (B/A)

Dice

- When a fair dice is rolled once, the probability of getting a particular number is $\frac{1}{6}$.
- When two fair dice are rolled together, the probability of getting a particular sum is given by:

  $$P(\text{sum}) = \frac{\text{no. of ways to get the sum}}{\text{total number of outcomes}}$$

Cards

- When a card is drawn from a standard deck of 52 cards, the probability of getting a particular card is $\frac{1}{52}$.
- When two cards are drawn from a standard deck of 52 cards without replacement, the probability of getting a particular combination is given by,

  $$P(\text{combination}) = \frac{\text{no. of ways to get the combination}}{\text{total number of outcomes}}$$

Coins

- When a fair coin is flipped once, the probability of getting a particular outcome (head or tail) is $\frac{1}{2}$.
- When two fair coins are flipped together, the probability of getting a particular combination is given by:

  $$P(\text{combination}) = \frac{\text{no. of ways to get the combination}}{\text{total number of outcomes}}$$

1 Level Beginner

1. Two digits out of 1, 2, 3, 4, 5 are chosen at random and multiplied together. What is the probability that the last digit in the product appears as 0? [NDA-I 2022]
(A) $\frac{1}{10}$ (B) $\frac{1}{5}$ (C) $\frac{2}{5}$ (D) $\frac{4}{5}$

Directions (Qs. 2–4): The incidence of suffering from a disease among workers in an industry has a chance of $33\frac{1}{3}\%$. Consider the above data for next three questions that follow: [NDA-I 2022]

2. What is the probability that exactly 3 out of 6 workers suffers from a disease?
(A) $\frac{80}{729}$ (B) $\frac{10}{81}$ (C) $\frac{10}{243}$ (D) $\frac{160}{729}$

3. What is the probability that no one out of 6 workers suffers from a disease?
(A) $\frac{665}{729}$ (B) $\frac{64}{729}$ (C) $\frac{4}{243}$ (D) $\frac{1}{729}$

4. What is probability that at least one out of 6 workers suffers from a disease?
(A) $\frac{728}{729}$ (B) $\frac{665}{729}$ (C) $\frac{653}{729}$ (D) $\frac{596}{729}$

5. A card is drawn from a well-shuffled ordinary deck of 52 cards. What is the probability that it is an ace? [NDA-I 2017]
(A) $\frac{1}{13}$ (B) $\frac{2}{13}$ (C) $\frac{3}{13}$ (D) $\frac{1}{52}$

6. If three dice are rolled under the condition that no two dice show the same face, then what is the probability that one of the three is having the number 6? [NDA 2020]
(A) $\frac{5}{6}$ (B) $\frac{5}{9}$ (C) $\frac{1}{2}$ (D) $\frac{5}{12}$

7. What is the probability that February of a leap year selected at random, will have five Sundays? [NDA 2020]
(A) $\frac{1}{5}$ (B) $\frac{1}{7}$ (C) $\frac{2}{7}$ (D) 1

2 Level Intermediate

1. A committee of 3 is to be formed from a group of 2 boys and 2 girls. What is the probability that the committee consists of 2 boys and 1 girl? [NDA 2020]
(A) 2/3 (B) 1/4 (C) 3/4 (D) 1/2

2. A husband and wife appears in an interview for two vacancies for the same post. The probability of husband's selection is 1/7 and that of wife's selection is 1/5. If the events are independent, the the probability of which one of the following is 11/35? [NDA 2020]
(A) Atleast one of them will be selected
(B) Only one of them will be selected
(C) None of them will be selected
(D) Both of them will be selected

3. In a lottery of 10 tickets numbered 1 to 10, two tickets are drawn simultaneously. What is probability that both the tickets drawn have prime numbers? [NDA 2020]
(A) $\frac{1}{15}$ (B) $\frac{1}{2}$ (C) $\frac{2}{15}$ (D) $\frac{1}{5}$

4. A dealer has a stock of 15 gold coins out of which 6 are counterfeits. A person randomly picks 4 of the 15 gold coins. What is probability that all the coins picked will be counterfeit? [NDA 2020]
(A) $\frac{1}{91}$ (B) $\frac{4}{91}$ (C) $\frac{6}{91}$ (D) $\frac{15}{91}$

5. A coin is tossed three times. What is probability of getting head and tail alternately? [NDA 2016]
(A) $\frac{1}{8}$ (B) $\frac{1}{4}$ (C) $\frac{1}{2}$ (D) $\frac{3}{4}$

6. A card is drawn from a well-shuffled deck of 52 cards. What is probability that it is a queen of spade? [NDA-I 2016]
(A) $\frac{1}{52}$ (B) $\frac{1}{13}$ (C) $\frac{1}{4}$ (D) $\frac{1}{8}$

7. If two dice are thrown, then what is the probability of that the sum on the two faces is greater than or equal to 4? [NDA 2016]
(A) $\frac{13}{18}$ (B) $\frac{5}{6}$ (C) $\frac{11}{12}$ (D) $\frac{35}{36}$

3 Level Expert

1. What is the probability of 5 Sundays in the month of December? [NDA 2016]
(A) $\frac{1}{7}$ (B) $\frac{2}{7}$
(C) $\frac{3}{7}$ (D) None of these

2. A fair coins tossed 100 times. What is the probability of getting tails an odd number of times? [NDA 2016]
(A) $\frac{1}{2}$ (B) $\frac{3}{8}$
(C) $\frac{1}{4}$ (D) $\frac{1}{8}$

3. The probability that a student will solve question A and B are 0.4 and 0.5, respectively. What is the probability that he solves at least one of the two question? **[NDA 2018]**
(A) 0.6 (B) 0.7 (C) 0.8 (D) 0.9

4. Two fair dice are rolled. What is the probability of getting a sum of 7? **[NDA 2018]**
(A) $\frac{1}{36}$ (B) $\frac{1}{6}$ (C) $\frac{7}{12}$ (D) $\frac{5}{12}$

5. One bag contains 3 white and 2 black balls. Another bag contains 5 white and 3 black balls. If a bag is chosen at random and a ball is drawn from it, what is the chance that it is white? **[NDA 2018]**
(A) $\frac{3}{8}$ (B) $\frac{49}{80}$ (C) $\frac{8}{13}$ (D) $\frac{1}{2}$

6. A committee of three has to be chosen from a group of 4 men and 5 women. If the selection is made at random, what is probability that exactly two members are men? **[NDA 2018]**
(A) $\frac{5}{14}$ (B) $\frac{1}{21}$ (C) $\frac{3}{14}$ (D) $\frac{8}{21}$

7. A committee of 3 members is to be selected out of 3 men and 2 women. What is probability that the committee has at least one woman? **[SBI Clerk Mains 2016]**
(A) $\frac{1}{10}$ (B) $\frac{9}{20}$
(C) $\frac{9}{10}$ (D) None of these

8. Two boxes contain 4 and 16 balls, respectively. Two balls in the first box and four in the second are black. If a box is chosen randomly and two balls are drawn at random from it, what is the probability that at least one ball is black if no ball is replaced? **[SBI Clerk Mains 2018]**
(A) $\frac{11}{20}$ (B) $\frac{43}{120}$ (C) $\frac{77}{120}$ (D) $\frac{9}{120}$

9. When 2 cards are drawn randomly from a pack of cards, then find the probability of getting 1 ace card? **[SBI Clerk Mains 2019]**
(A) $\frac{209}{221}$ (B) $\frac{10}{13}$ (C) $\frac{220}{221}$ (D) $\frac{1}{13}$

10. In a box, there are 6 blue balls, 'x' red balls and 10 green balls. Probability of choosing one red ball from the given box is $\frac{1}{3}$. Then, find the sum of red and blue balls in the box. **[SBI PO 2018]**
(A) 20 (B) 12 (C) 14 (D) 18

11. A bag has seven red, four white and three green balls while another bag has five red, six yellow and three blue balls. A bag is selected at random and a ball is drawn out of it. Then, find the probability that the ball drawn is red. **[SBI PO 2020]**
(A) $\frac{1}{7}$ (B) $\frac{3}{7}$ (C) $\frac{2}{7}$ (D) $\frac{6}{7}$

12. In a bag which contains 40 balls, there are 18 red balls, some green and blue balls. If two balls are picked at random, then the probability of the first ball being red and second being green is $\frac{3}{26}$. Find the number of blue balls in the bag. **[IBPS Clerk Mains 2018]**
(A) 16 (B) 12 (C) 10 (D) None

ANSWER KEY

Level-1: Beginner

1.	(B)	2.	(D)	3.	(B)	4.	(B)	5.	(A)	6.	(C)	7.	(B)

Level-2: Intermediate

1.	(D)	2.	(A)	3.	(C)	4.	(A)	5.	(B)	6.	(A)	7.	(C)

Level-3: Expert

1.	(C)	2.	(A)	3.	(B)	4.	(B)	5.	(B)	6.	(A)	7.	(C)	8.	(C)	9.	(D)	10.	(C)
11.	(B)	12.	(B)																

Solutions with Detailed Explanation

Level-1: BEGINNER

1. **Option (B) is correct.**
Explanation:

Given digits = 1, 2, 3, 4, 5

We can choose two digits in ${}^5C_2$ ways

$$n(S) = {}^5C_2 = 10$$

If the last digit = 0

So, required outcomes must be {(2, 5) (4, 5)}

$$n(E) = 2$$

Hence, probability which is required $\frac{n(E)}{n(S)} = \frac{2}{10} = \frac{1}{5}$

2. **Option (D) is correct.**
Explanation: Using binomial distribution

$$P(x) = {}^nC_x p^x q^n$$

Probability when exactly 3 out of 6 workers suffer from disease P ($x = 3$)

$$= {}^6C_3 \left(\frac{1}{3}\right)^3 \left(\frac{2}{3}\right)^{6-3}$$

$$= \frac{6!}{3!3!}\frac{2^3}{3^6} \qquad \left[\text{Here } P = \frac{1}{3}\right.$$

$$= \frac{160}{729} \qquad \left.q = 1 - \frac{1}{3} = \frac{2}{3}\right]$$

Hence, $\frac{160}{729}$ is required answer.

3. **Option (B) is correct.**
Explanation: Using binomial distribution

$$P(x) = {}^nC_x p^x q^{n-x} \left[p = \frac{1}{3}, q = 1 - \frac{1}{3} = \frac{2}{3}\right]$$

When no one suffer from disease P($x = 0$)

$$= {}^6C_0 \left(\frac{1}{3}\right)^0 \left(\frac{2}{3}\right)^{6-0} = \frac{64}{729}$$

Hence, required answer $= \frac{64}{729}$

4. **Option (B) is correct.**
Explanation: Using binomial distribution:

$$p(x) = {}^nC_x p^x q^{n-x}$$

P(A) = probability when no one out of 6 suffers

$= \frac{64}{729}$ [from question 3]

Assuming P(B) = Probability when at least one out of 6 suffers from disease.

As we know,

$$P(A) + P(B) = 1$$

$$P(B) = 1 - P(A) = 1 - \frac{64}{729} = \frac{665}{729}$$

Hence, $\frac{665}{729}$ is required answer.

5. **Option (A) is correct.**
Explanation: Required probability

$$= \frac{\text{No. of aces in the deck}}{\text{Total no. of cards}} = \frac{4}{52} = \frac{1}{13}$$

Hence, $\frac{1}{13}$ is required answer.

6. **Option (C) is correct.**
Explanation: Sample space $= 6^3 = 216$
E = Event that all faces have different numbers
$n(E) = 6 \times 5 \times 4 = 120$
A = Event of getting no. 6 on one of the face
$n(A) = (1 \times 5 \times 4) + (1 \times 5 \times 4) + (1 \times 5 \times 4) = 60$
$n(EPA) = 60$

$$\text{Hence, required probability} = \frac{P(E \cap A)}{P(E)} = \frac{\frac{60}{216}}{\frac{120}{216}} = \frac{1}{2}$$

7. **Option (B) is correct.**
Explanation: There are 4 weeks and 1 day in leap year of February.
This one day can be any 7 days of week.
So, total outcomes = 7
Favourable outcomes which is Sunday = 1
Hence, required probability = 1/7

Level-2: INTERMEDIATE

1. **Option (D) is correct.**
Explanation: Assuming

$$\text{Two boys} = b_1b_2$$
$$\text{Two girls} = g_1g_2$$
$$\text{Sample space} = S$$
$$= (b_1b_2g_1)\,(b_1b_2g_2)\,(g_1g_2b_1)\,(g_1g_2b_2)$$
$$= 4$$

E = event that consists of 2 boys and 1 girl

$$= \{b_1b_2g_1, b_1b_2g_2\} = 2$$

$$\text{Hence, required probability} = \frac{2}{4} = \frac{1}{2}$$

2. **Option (A) is correct.**
Explanation: Checking option (A)
P (a^+ least one out of them will be selected)
= 1 – P (none of them selected)
P (none of them selected) = [1 – P (Husband selected)] × [1 – P (Wife selected)]

$$= \left[1 - \frac{1}{7}\right] \times \left[1 - \frac{1}{5}\right] = \frac{24}{35}$$

Hence, probability of at least one of them selected

$$= 1 - \frac{24}{35} = \frac{11}{35}$$

3. **Option (C) is correct.**
Explanation: Prime nos. (between 1 and 10) = 4
Total tickets in first draw = 10

$$\text{Probability of getting prime no.} = \frac{4}{10} = \frac{2}{5}$$

In second draw
Remaining prime nos. = 3
Remaining tickets = 9
Probability of getting prime ticket in second draw

$$= \frac{3}{9} = \frac{1}{3}$$

Hence, probability of getting both prime tickets

$$= \frac{2}{5} \times \frac{1}{3} = \frac{2}{15}$$

4. **Option (A) is correct.**
Explanation: Total gold coins = 15
Counterfeits = 6
Hence, probability of getting all 4 coins counterfiet

$$= \frac{{}^6C_4}{{}^{15}C_4} = \frac{\frac{6}{2} \times \frac{5}{1}}{\frac{15 \times 14 \times 13 \times 12}{4 \times 3 \times 2 \times 1}} = \frac{1}{7 \times 13} = \frac{1}{91}$$

5. **Option (B) is correct.**
Explanation: Total possibilities $= 2^3 = 8$
favourable cases = 2 [HTH, THT]

$$\text{Hence, required probability} = \frac{2}{8} = \frac{1}{4}$$

6. **Option (A) is correct.**
Explanation: Total cards = 52
Queen of spade = 1

$$\text{Hence, required probability} = \frac{1}{52}$$

7. **Option (C) is correct.**
Explanation: Assuming 'A' be no. on the first dice, 'B' on the second dice
$(A + B) \geq = 4$
Total no. of possible outcomes = $6^2 = 36$
Possibile outcomes when sum is lower than 4
= (1, 1) (1, 2) and (2, 1) = 3
So, probability when sum is lower than 4 = $\frac{3}{36} = \frac{1}{12}$
Hence, probability when sum is 4 or more than
4 = 1 – 1/12 = 11/12

Level-3: EXPERT

1. **Option (C) is correct.**
Explanation: In December = 31 days
4 weeks + 3 days
So, we have to get any Sunday in these extra 3 days.
Possible outcomes in there 3 days = 7 (Monday, Tuesday, Wednesday, Thursday, Friday, Saturday, Sunday)
Hence, required probability = $\frac{3}{7}$

2. **Option (A) is correct.**
Explanation: Assuming T = event of getting tail
Required probability
= P(T = 1) + P (T = 3) + ... + P(T = 99)
$$= {}^{100}C_1\left(\frac{1}{2}\right)\left(\frac{1}{2}\right)^{99} + \ldots + {}^{100}C_{99}\left(\frac{1}{2}\right)^{100}$$
$$= \frac{\frac{2^{100}}{2}}{2^{100}} = \frac{2^{99}}{2^{100}} = \frac{1}{2}$$
Hence, 1/2 is required probability.

3. **Option (B) is correct.**
Explanation: P(A) = 0.4
P(B) = 0.5
Probability of solving at least one of two $(A \cup B)$
$= 1 - P(\overline{A \cup B}) = 1 - \{P(\bar{A}) \times P(\bar{B})\}$
$= 1 - \{(1 - 0.4) \times (1 - 0.5)\} = 1 - 0.3 = 0.7$

4. **Option (B) is correct.**
Explanation: Possible outcomes = $6^2 = 36$
Favourable outcomes = 6
(1, 6) (2, 5) (3, 4) (4, 3) (6, 1) (5, 2)
Hence, required probability = $\frac{6}{36} = \frac{1}{6}$

5. **Option (B) is correct.**
Explanation:
Probability of getting white ball from bag 1 = $\frac{3}{5}$
Probability of getting white ball from bag 2= $\frac{5}{8}$
Using, total probability law
$$P(A) = P(E_1)\,P(A/E_1) + P(E_2)\,P(A/E_2)$$
$$= \left(\frac{1}{2}\times\frac{3}{5}\right) + \left(\frac{1}{2}\right)\times\left(\frac{5}{8}\right)$$
$$= \frac{24+25}{80} = \frac{49}{80}$$

6. **Option (A) is correct.**
Explanation: Total number = 4 + 5 = 9
Choosing 3 out of 9 = ${}^9C_3 = 84$
Assuming A = event where two are men
$n(A) = {}^4C_2 \times {}^5C_1 = 30$
Hence, required probability = $\frac{30}{84} = \frac{5}{14}$

7. **Option (C) is correct.**
Explanation: $n(S) = {}^5C_3$
$= \frac{5\times4}{2\times1} = 10$ [3 out of total five]
Case 1: 1 woman and 2 men = ${}^2C_1 \times {}^3C_2$
Case 2: 2 women and 1 man = ${}^2C_2 \times {}^3C_1$
$n(E) = ({}^2C_1 \times {}^3C_2) + ({}^2C_2 \times {}^3C_1)$
$= (2 \times 3) + (1 \times 3) = 9$
Hence, P(E) = 9/10

8. **Option (C) is correct.**
Explanation: First box
$$\frac{1}{2}\times\left(\frac{2}{3}\times\frac{2}{4}+\frac{2}{4}\times\frac{2}{3}+\frac{2}{4}\times\frac{1}{3}\right) = \frac{5}{12}$$
Probability [at least one black ball from 2nd box]
$$= \frac{1}{2}\times\left(\frac{4}{16}\times\frac{12}{15}+\frac{12}{16}\times\frac{4}{15}+\frac{4}{16}\times\frac{3}{15}\right) = \frac{27}{120}$$
Hence, required probability = $\frac{5}{12} + \frac{27}{120} = \frac{77}{120}$

9. **Option (Bonus) is correct.**
Explanation: Favourable cases = ${}^4C_1 \times {}^{48}C_1$
[Total 4 aces in 52 cards]
No. of possible outcomes = ${}^{52}C_2$
Hence, required probability = $\frac{{}^4C_1 \times {}^{48}C_1}{{}^{52}C_2} = \frac{16}{221}$

10. **Option (C) is correct.**
Explanation: Balls in box = 10 + 6 + x = 16 + x
Probability (getting red ball) = $\frac{x}{x+16}$
Now, as given in the question
$$\frac{x}{x+16} = \frac{1}{3}$$
$$x = 8$$
Hence, sum of red and blue balls = 8 + 6 = 14

11. **Option (B) is correct.**
Explanation:
Probability [choosing one bag out of two) = $\frac{1}{2}$
Hence, required probability
$= \frac{1}{2}$ [red ball from bag 1 + red ball from bag 2]
$$= \frac{1}{2}\left[\frac{7}{14}+\frac{5}{14}\right] = \frac{3}{7}$$

12. **Option (B) is correct.**
Explanation:
Total balls = 40
Red = 18
So Green = x
Blue = $22 - x$
Now, probability of first ball being red and second green = $\frac{18}{40}\times\frac{x}{39} = \frac{3}{26}$
$x = 10$
Hence, blue balls = $22 - x = 22 - 10 = 12$

Set Theory

Set: Collection of objects such as number, letter, etc.

Type of sets

1. Empty set/null sell:
   Does not contain any element
2. Subset of sets:
   – If all the elements of set 'B' present in set 'S'.
   $B = \{2, 4\}$ $S = \{1, 2, 3, 4\}$
3. Equal sets:
   – Contains same elements.
4. Universal sets:
   – contains all the elements and denoted by 'U'.
5. Power set:
   – set of all subsets of set.

Venn Diagrams

Union of sets:

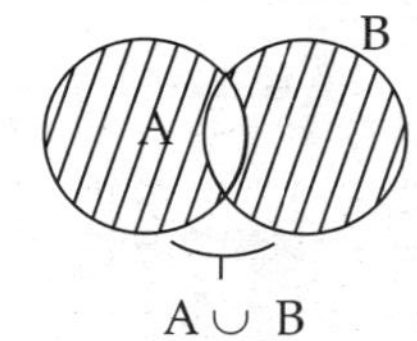

Intersection of sets:

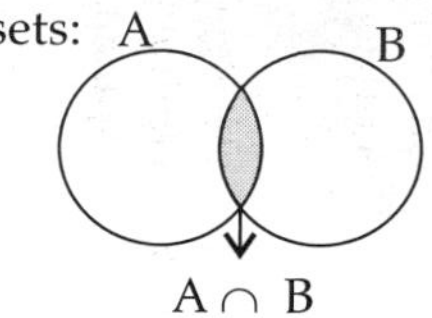

Union $(A \cup B)$

$A = \{2, 4\}$

$B = \{1, 3, 5\}$

$A \cup B = \{1, 2, 3, 4, 5\}$

Intersection $(A \cap B)$

$A = \{2, 4\}$

$B = \{1, 2, 3, 4\}$

$A \cap B = \{2, 4\}$

Some Basic Formulas

$n(A \cap B) = n(A) + n(B) - n(A \cap B)$

$n(A \cup B \cup C) = n(A) + n(B) + n(C) - n(A \cap B) - n(B \cap C) - n(C \cap A) + n(A \cap B \cap C)$

Chapter 27

Set Theory

LEARNING OBJECTIVES:

- Concept of sets.
- Different set of operations such as union, intersection, complement, etc.
- Set identities and their properties.
- Application to probability.
- Uses in real world problems.
- Different types of questions asked in previous year papers of competitive exams.

- Set theory is a fundamental mathematical concept that deals with the study of sets and their properties.

  In mathematics, a set is a collection of distinct objects, which are called elements or members of the set. These objects can be anything, such as numbers, letters, shapes, or even other sets.

  Sets are fundamental in mathematics and have many applications in different fields, including algebra, geometry, statistics and computer science. They are used to define functions, relations and operations, and are an essential tool for studying the properties of numbers and other mathematical objects.

- **Set notation:** A set is a collection of distinct objects or elements. Sets can be represented using curly brackets {}. For example, the set of all even numbers less than 10 can be represented as {2, 4, 6, 8}. The elements of a set can be listed either individually or using a rule. For example, the set of all prime numbers less than 20 can be represented as {2, 3, 5, 7, 11, 13, 17, 19}.

DIFFERENT TYPES OF SETS

In set theory, there are several different types of sets based on their properties and elements.

Here are some common types of sets:

- **Finite set:** A set that contains a finite number of elements is called a finite set. For example, the set of all prime numbers less than 10 is a finite set {2, 3, 5, 7}.
- **Infinite set:** A set that contains an infinite number of elements is called an infinite set.

  For example, the set of all natural numbers is an infinite set {1, 2, 3, 4, ...}.
- **Empty set:** A set that contains no elements is called an empty set or null set. The empty set is denoted by {} or Ø.
- **Singleton set:** A set that contains exactly one element is called a singleton set. For example, the set {2} is a singleton set.
- **Equal set:** Two sets are said to be equal if they have the same elements, regardless of the order in which they are listed. For example, {2, 4, 6} = {4, 2, 6}.
- **Subset:** A set A is said to be a subset of another set B if every element in A is also in B. The subset is denoted by $A \subseteq B$. For example, {2, 4} is a subset of {2, 3, 4, 5}.
- **Proper subset:** A set A is said to be a proper subset of another set B if A is a subset of B, but A is not equal to B. The proper subset is denoted by $A \subset B$. For example, {2, 4} is a proper subset of {2, 3, 4, 5}, but {2, 3, 4, 5} is not a proper subset of itself.
- **Power set:** The power set of a set A is the set of all subsets of A, including the empty set and A itself. The power set of A is denoted by P(A). For example, if A = {1, 2}, then P(A) = {{}, {1}, {2}, {1, 2}}.
- **Universal set:** The universal set is a set that contains all possible elements that can be considered for a given problem. It is denoted by U. For example, in a probability problem, the universal set may be the set of all possible outcomes.
- **Set operations:** Set operations are used to manipulate and compare sets. The most common set operations are union, intersection and complement.
- **Union of sets:** In set theory, union of collection of sets is a set containing every element from those sets, i.e., if there are two sets A and B, then their union contains elements which are in A, in B, or both A and B. It is denoted by '$\cup$'. If we have two sets A and B then their union is denoted as $A \cup B$ and is called A union B. Mathematically, $A \cup B = \{x : x \in A \text{ or } x \in B\}$. For example,

  A = {1, 3} and B = {3, 4, 5}, then

  $A \cup B = \{1, 3, 4, 5\}$
- **Intersection of sets:** Intersection of collection of sets containing elements that are common to all the sets, i.e., if A and B are two sets, then their intersection is the set containing elements that are commonly

present in both of them. It is denoted by symbol '$\cap$'. Mathematically, $A \cap B = \{x : x \in A \text{ and } x \in B\}$. For example,

$A = \{1, 3\}$ and $B = \{3, 4, 5\}$, then

$A \cap B = \{3\}$

➢ **Difference of sets:** If A and B are two sets, then their difference (A – B) is a set containing elements that are only present in A and not in B. Mathematically, $A - B = \{x : x \in A \text{ and } x \notin B\}$ and $B - A = \{x : x \in B \text{ and } x \notin A\}$.

For example,

$A = \{1, 3\}$ and $B = \{3, 4, 5\}$, then

$A - B = \{1\}$, and $B - A = \{4, 5\}$

- **Complement:** The complement of a set A with respect to a universal set U is the set of all elements in U that are not in A. The complement of set A is denoted by A'. For example, if U is the set of all integers and A is the set of even integers, then A' is the set of odd integers.

➢ **Examples:** Here are some examples of questions related to set theory:

Example 1: Let $A = \{2, 4, 6\}$ and $B = \{3, 6, 9\}$. Find $A \cup B$ and $A \cap B$.

Sol. $A \cup B = \{2, 3, 4, 6, 9\}$ $A \cap B = \{6\}$

Example 2: Let U be the set of all letters in the English alphabet, and let A be the set of vowels. Write the complement of set A.

Sol. The set of consonants is the complement of set A with respect to U.

Example 3: In a class of 50 students, 30 students play football and 20 students play cricket. If 10 students play both football and cricket, how many students play neither football nor cricket?

Sol. Let F be the set of students who play football, and let C be the set of students who play cricket.

Then, $|F| = 30$, $|C| = 20$, and $|F \cap C| = 10$.

Using the formula $|F \cup C| = |F| + |C| - |F \cap C|$, we get: $|F \cup C| = 30 + 20 - 10 = 40$

Therefore, the number of students who play neither football nor cricket is $50 - 40 = 10$.

VENN DIAGRAMS

A venn diagram is a diagram that shows all possible logical relations between a finite collection of sets. They can be used to depict two sets, three sets, 4 sets or more.

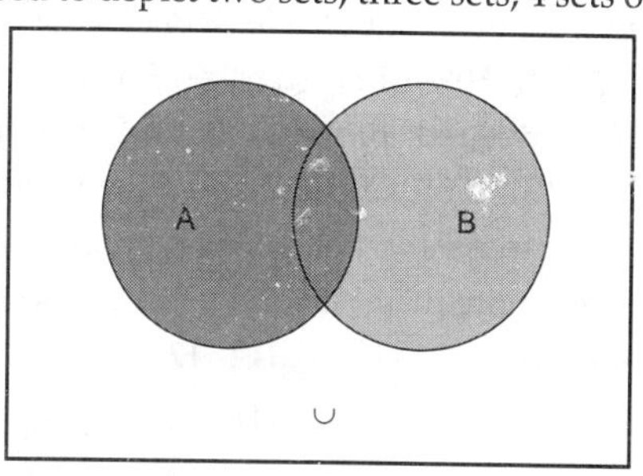

A two set Venn diagram is given alongside.

This diagram is called Venn Diagram where there are two sets A and B and U is the universal set.

$\cup \rightarrow$ Union

$\in \rightarrow$ Belongs to

➢ **Union of Sets**

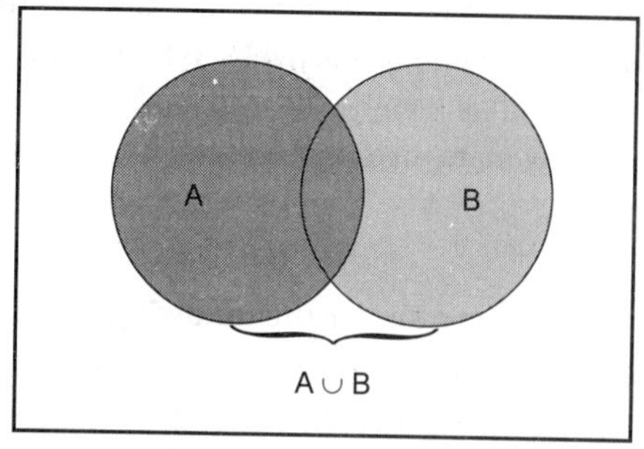

➢ **Intersection of sets**

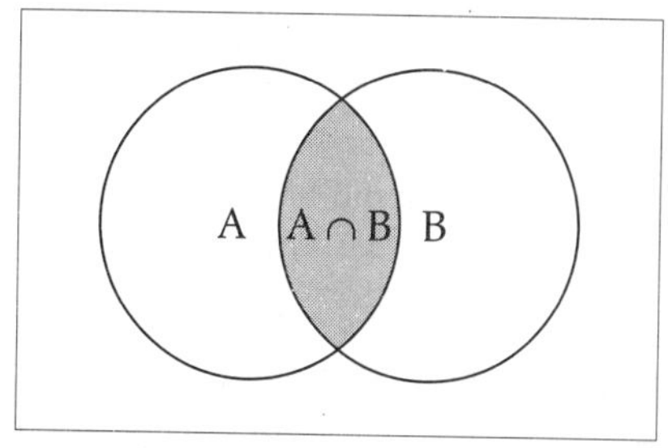

➢ **Complement of A set**

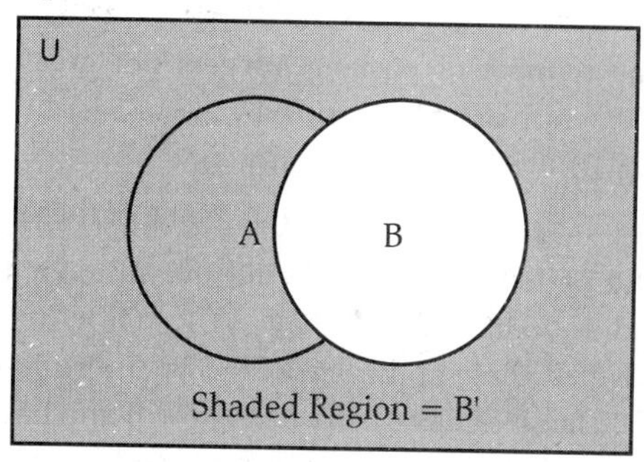

➢ **Venn Diagram for 3 sets:** Let A, B and C be three sets and U be the universal set, then the Venn diagram for 3 sets can be constructed as follows:

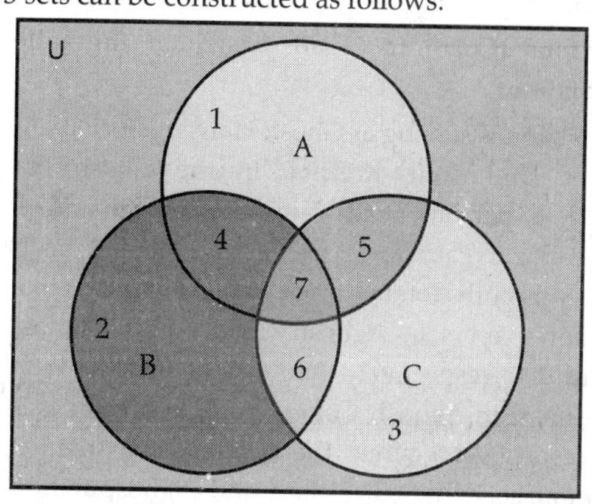

SOME BASIC FORMULA FOR VENN DIAGRAM:

- $n(A \cap B) = n(A) + n(B) - n(A \cap B)$
- $n(A \cup B \cup C) = n(A) + n(B) + n(C) - n(A \cap B) - n(B \cap C) - n(B \cap C) + n(A \cap B \cap C)$

Level 1 Beginner

1. There are 3 clubs A, B and C in a town with 40, 50 and 60 members, respectively. While 10 people are members of all 3 clubs, 70 are members in only one club. How many belong to exactly two clubs?
   (A) 20 (B) 25
   (C) 50 (D) 70

Directions (Qs. 2 and 3): Use the following information:

Eighty five children went to an amusement park where they could ride on the merry-go-round, roller coaster and Ferris wheel. It was known that 20 of them took all three rides, and 55 of them took at least two of the three rides. Each ride costs ₹1, and the total receipt of the amusement park was ₹145.

2. How many children did not try any of the rides?
   (A) 5 (B) 10
   (C) 15 (D) 20
3. How many children took exactly one ride?
   (A) 5 (B) 10
   (C) 15 (D) 20
4. The number of positive integers not greater than 100, which are not divisible by 2, 3 or 5 is:
   (A) 26 (B) 18
   (C) 31 (D) None of these
5. Out of 100 families in the neighbourhood, 45 own radios, 75 have TVs, 25 have VCRs. Only 10 families have all three and each VCR owner also has a TV. If 25 families have radio only, how many have only TV?
   (A) 30 (B) 35
   (C) 40 (D) 45

Directions (Qs. 6 to 8) are based on the following information:

Ghosh babu is staying at Ghosh Housing Society, Aghosh Colony, Dighospur, Kolkata. In the Ghosh Housing Society, 6 persons read daily Ganashakti and 4 read Anand Bazar Patrika; in his colony, there is no person who reads both. Total number of persons who read these two newspapers in Aghosh Colony and Dighospur is 52 and 200, respectively. Number of persons who read Ganashakti in Aghosh Colony and Dighospur is 33 and 121, respectively; while the persons who read Anand Bazar Patrika in Aghosh Colony and Dighospur are 32 and 117, respectively.

6. Number of persons in Dighospur who read only Ganashakti is:
   (A) 121 (B) 83
   (C) 79 (D) 127
7. Number of persons in Aghosh Colony who read both of these newspapers is:
   (A) 13 (B) 20
   (C) 19 (D) 14
8. Number of persons in Aghosh Colony who read only one paper:
   (A) 29 (B) 19
   (C) 39 (D) 20

Directions (Qs. 9 to 11): Answer the questions based on the following information:

A survey of 200 people in a community who watched at least one of the three channels — BBC, CNN and DD — showed that 80% of the people watched DD, 22% watched BBC and 15% watched CNN.

9. What is the maximum percentage of people who can watch all the three channels?
   (A) 12.5%
   (B) 8.5%
   (C) 15%
   (D) Data insufficient
10. If 5% of people watched DD and CNN, 10% watched DD and BBC, then what percentage of people watched BBC and CNN only?
    (A) 2%
    (B) 5%
    (C) 8.5%
    (D) Cannot be determined
11. Referring to the previous question, what percentage of people watched all the three channels?
    (A) 3.5%
    (B) 0%
    (C) 8.5%
    (D) Cannot be determined
12. In a survey of political preferences, 78% of those asked were in favour of at least one of the proposals: I, II and III. 50% of those asked favoured proposal I, 30% favoured proposal II and 20% favoured proposal III. If 5% of those asked favoured all three of the proposals, what percentage of those asked favoured more than one of the three proposals?
    (A) 10 (B) 12
    (C) 17 (D) 22

Level 2 Intermediate

Direction (Q. 1): based on the following information:

A and B are two sets (e.g., A = mothers, B = women). The elements that could belong to both the sets (e.g., women who are mothers) are given by the set C = A.B. The elements which could belong to either A or B, or both, is indicated by the set $D = A \cup B$. A set that does not contain any element is known as a null set, represented by ϕ (e.g., if none of the women in the set B is a mother, then C = A.B is a null set, or $C = \phi$).

Let 'V' signifies the set of all vertebrates; 'M' the set of all mammals; 'D' dogs; 'F' fish; 'A' Alsatian and 'P', a dog named Pluto.

1. Given that X = M.D is such that X = D, which of the following is true?
   (A) All dogs are mammals.
   (B) Some dogs are mammals.
   (C) $X = \phi$
   (D) All mammals are dogs.

Directions (Qs. 2 and 3): Answer the questions on the basis of the information given below.

New Age Consultants have three consultants Gyani, Medha and Buddhi. The sum of the number of projects handled by Gyani and Buddhi individually is equal to the number of projects in which Medha is involved. All three consultants are involved together in 6 projects. Gyani works with Medha in 14 projects. Buddhi has 2 projects with Medha but without Gyani and 3 projects with Gyani but without Medha. The total number of projects for New Age Consultants is one less than twice the number of projects in which more than one consultant is involved.

2. What is the number of projects in which Gyani alone is involved?
   (A) Uniquely equal to zero.
   (B) Uniquely equal to 1.
   (C) Uniquely equal to 4.
   (D) Cannot be determined uniquely.

3. What is the number of projects in which Medha alone is involved?
   (A) Uniquely equal to zero.
   (B) Uniquely equal to 1.
   (C) Uniquely equal to 4.
   (D) Cannot be determined uniquely.

4. A survey on a sample of 25 new cars being sold at a local auto dealer was conducted to see which of the three popular options – air conditioning, radio and power windows – were already installed. The survey found 15 had air conditioning, 2 had air conditioning and power windows but no radios, 12 had radio, 6 had air conditioning and radio but no power windows, 11 had power windows, 4 had radio and power windows, 3 had all three options. What is the number of cars that had none of the options?
   (A) 4 **(B)** 3
   (C) 1 **(D)** 2

Level 3 Expert

1. Three Englishmen and three Frenchmen work for the same company. Each of them knows a secret not known to others. They need to exchange these secrets over person-to-person phone calls so that eventually each person knows all six secrets. None of the Frenchmen knows English and only one Englishman knows French. What is the minimum number of phone calls needed for the above purpose?
   (A) 5 **(B)** 10
   (C) 9 **(D)** 15

2. A survey was conducted of 100 people to find out whether they had read recent issues of Golmal, a monthly magazine. The summarised information regarding readership in 3 months is given below:

Only September:	18
September but not August:	23
September and July:	8
September:	28
July:	48
July and August:	10
None of the three months:	24

   What is the number of surveyed people who have read exactly two consecutive issues (out of the three)?
   (A) 7 **(B)** 9
   (C) 12 **(D)** 14

3. Each of 74 students in a class studies at least one of the three subjects H, E and P. Ten students study all three subjects, while twenty study H and E, but not P. Every student who studies P also studies H or E or both. If the number of students studying H equals that studying E, then the number of students studying H is:
   (A) 50 **(B)** 52
   (C) 54 **(D)** 55

4. If among 200 students, 105 like pizzas and 134 like burgers, then the number of students who like only burgers can possibly be:
   (A) 23 **(B)** 26
   (C) 96 **(D)** 93

5. A club has 256 members out of which 144 can play football, 123 can play tennis and 132 can play cricket. Moreover, 58 members can play both football and tennis, 25 can play both cricket and tennis, while 63 can play both football and cricket. If every member can play at least one game, then the number of members who can play only tennis is:

(A) 38 (B) 32
(C) 45 (D) 43

6. Students in a college have to choose at least two subjects from chemistry, mathematics and physics. The number of students choosing all three subjects is 18, choosing mathematics as one of their subjects is 23 and choosing physics as one of their subjects is 25. The smallest possible number of students who could choose chemistry as one of their subjects is:

(A) 20 (B) 19
(C) 22 (D) 21

ANSWER KEY

Level-1: Beginner

1.	(B)	2.	(C)	3.	(C)	4.	(A)	5.	(C)	6.	(B)	7.	(A)	8.	(C)	9.	(B)	10.	(A)
11.	(D)	12.	(C)																

Level-2: Intermediate

1.	(A)	2.	(D)	3.	(B)	4.	(D)												

Level-3: Expert

1.	(C)	2.	(B)	3.	(B)	4.	(D)	5.	(D)	6.	(A)								

Solutions with Detailed Explanations

Level-1: BEGINNER

1. **Option (B) is correct.**

Explanation: As we know,

$$a + b + c = \text{T} \quad \text{...(i)}$$
$$a + 2b + 3c = \text{RT} \quad \text{...(ii)}$$

a = members of exactly one set = 70
b = members of exactly two sets
c = members of exactly 3 sets = 10
T = Total members
RT = Repeated number of total members
$= (40 + 50 + 60) = 150$

Solving eq. (i) and (ii) by using the values we get
$b = 25$

Hence, required answer is 25.

2. **Option (C) is correct.**

Explanation: 55 took at leat 2 rides where 20 took all the three

So, $(55 - 20) = 35$ took exactly 2 rides

As given, total number of rides taken = 145

$$a + b + c = \text{T} \quad \text{...(1)}$$
$$a + 2b + 3c = \text{RT} \quad \text{...(2)}$$
[where $b = 35, c = 20$, RT = 145)

Solving, Eqs. (1) and (2) we get $a = 15$, T = 70

So, 15 took only 1 ride, 70 at last 1 of 3 rides
$85 - 70 = 15$ did not take any ride

3. **Option (C) is correct.**

Explanation: Referring to the common explanation given in solution of 2nd question, 15 children took only one ride.

4. **Option (A) is correct.**

Explanation:

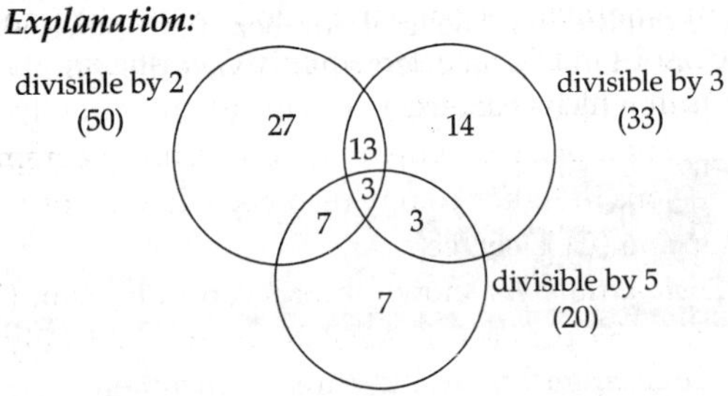

Divisible by 2 = 50 numbers
Divisible by 3 = 33 numbers
Divisible by 5 = 20 numbers
Divisible by 2, 3 and 5 = 3 numbers
Divisible by 2 and 5 (only) = 7 numbers
Divisible by 5 and 3 (only) = 3 numbers
Divisible by 2 and 5 (only) = 13 numbers
So, numbers divisible by 2 only = 27
Numbers divisible by 3 only = 14
Numbers divisible by 5 only = 7
So, 27 + 13 + 14 + 7 + 3 + 3 + 7 = 74 numbers are divisible by one or more.
Hence, only 26 numbers are not divisible by any of them.

5. **Option (C) is correct.**

Explanation: As given in the question, i.e., it can conclude that all 100 own at least a TV or Radio.
75 own TV, 45 Radio

So, total number who own both TV and Radio

$= (75 + 45) - 100 = 20$

[10 own all three]

So, people who have only TV and Radio = 10

Hence, people who have only TV = 75 – 10 – 10 – 15 = 40

Sol. 6–8.

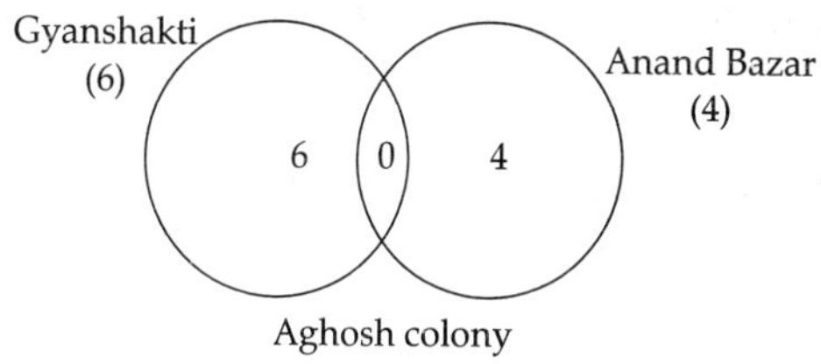

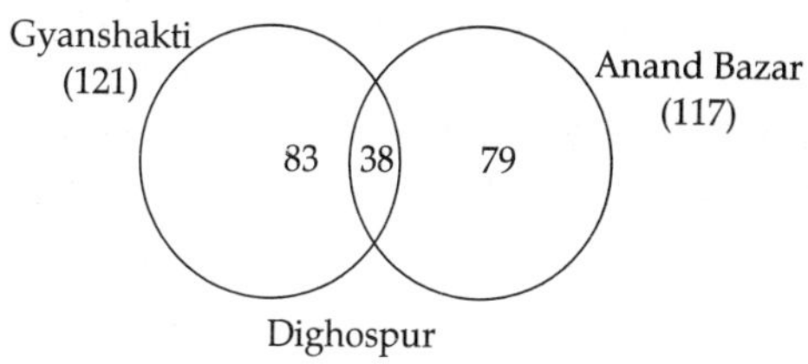

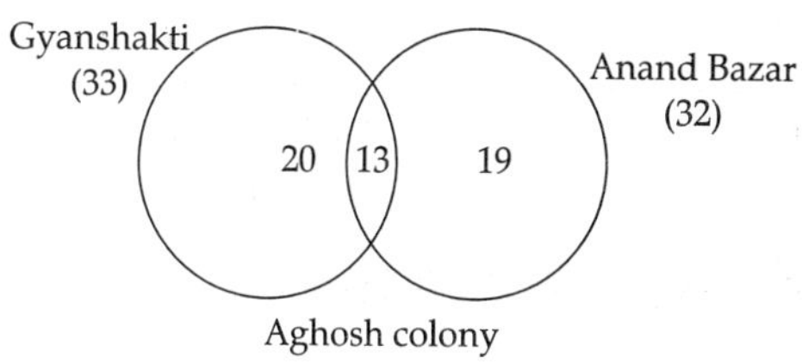

6. **Option (B) i s correct.**

Explanation: As shown in 2nd venn diagram, 83 persons in Dighospur read only Ganashakti.

7. **Option (A) is correct.**

Explanation: As shown in 3rd venn diagram, 13 persons in Aghos colony read both news paper.

8. **Option (C) is correct.**

Explanation: As shown in 3rd venn diagram, (20 + 19) or 39 persons in Aghosh colony read only one news paper.

Sol. 9–11.

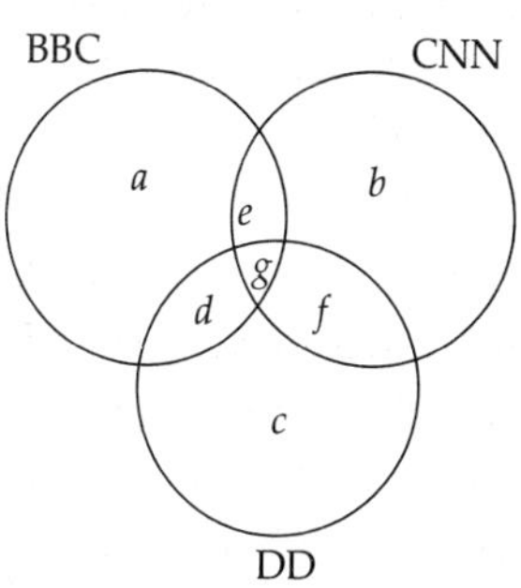

As given, $a + b + c + d + e + f + g = 200$ ...(1)

80% of 200 = 160 [who watch DD] ...(2)

22% of 200 = 44 [BBC] ...(3)

15% of 200 = 30 [CNN] ...(4)

(2) + (3) + (4) = 234

i.e., $a + b + c + 2d + 2e + 2f + 3g = 234$ ...(5)

Subtracting eq. (1) from eq. (5)

$d+e+f+g+g = 34$ ...(6)

9. **Option (B) is correct.**

Explanation: Maximum value of $g = \frac{34}{2} = 17$

[Putting $d = e = f = 0$]

Hence, required percentge $= \frac{17}{200} \times 100 = 8.5\%$

10. **Option (A) is correct.**

Explanation:

5% ard DD and CNN viewers ...(7)

$f + g = 10$ ...(7)

10% are DD and BBC viewers

$d + g = 20$ ...(8)

From (6), (7) and (8)

$e = 4$

Hence, required percentage $= \frac{4}{200} \times 100 = 2\%$

11. **Option (D) is correct.**

Explanation: From (6)

$(d + g + f) + g + g = 34$

$d + f + g + g = 30$

So, we cannot find the value of d and f, the value of 'g' cannot be determined.

12. **Option (C) is correct.**

Explanation:

$x + y + z = 78$ ...(i)

$x + 2y + 3z = 100$ ...(ii)

$y + 2z = 22$ ...(ii – i)

Here, x = who favoured one proposal

y = who favoured two proposal

z = who favoured three proposals

Since, $z = 5, y = 12$

Hence the required percentage $= y + z$

$= 12 + 5 = 17\%$

Level-2: INTERMEDIATE

13. **Option (A) is correct.**

Explanation: Given,

$X = M \cap D = D$ D = Dogs

So, $D \subset M$ M = Mammals

Thus, all dogs are mammals

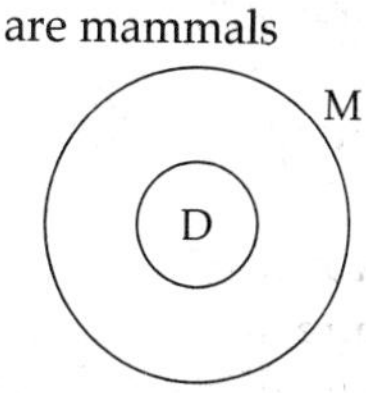

Sol. 14–15. a = Projects only Gyani is involved

g = Projects only Buddhi is involved

c = Projects only Medha is involved

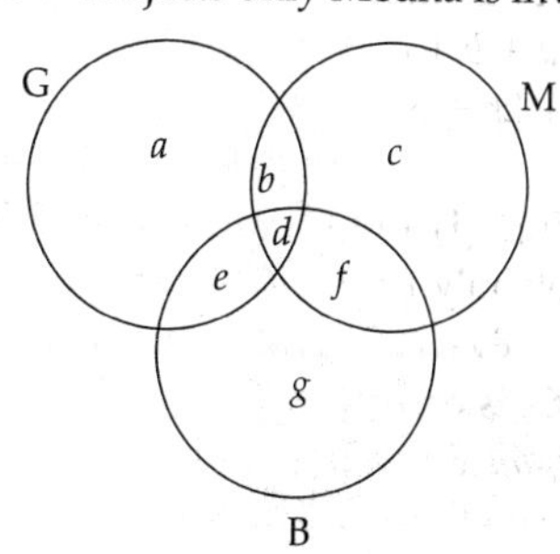

$$d = 6 \text{ and } b + d = 14 \quad \text{[Given]}$$

$$\therefore \quad b = 8, e = 3 \text{ and } f = 2$$

$$a + g = b + d + f + c$$

$$a - c + g = 16 \quad ...(i)$$

Projects which involve more than 1 consultant

$$= 6 + 8 + 2 + 3 = 19$$

$$\therefore \quad \text{Total projects} = 2 \times 19 - 1 = 37$$

$$a + b + c + d + e + f + g$$

$$= 2b + 2d + 2e + 2f \quad ...(i)$$

$$\therefore \quad a + c = g = 19 - 1 = 18 \quad ...(ii)$$

From (ii) and (i) $c = 1, a + g = 17$

14. Option (D) is correct.

Explanation: From common explanation

15. Option (B) is correct.

Explanation: From common explanation

16. Option (D) is correct.

Explanation:

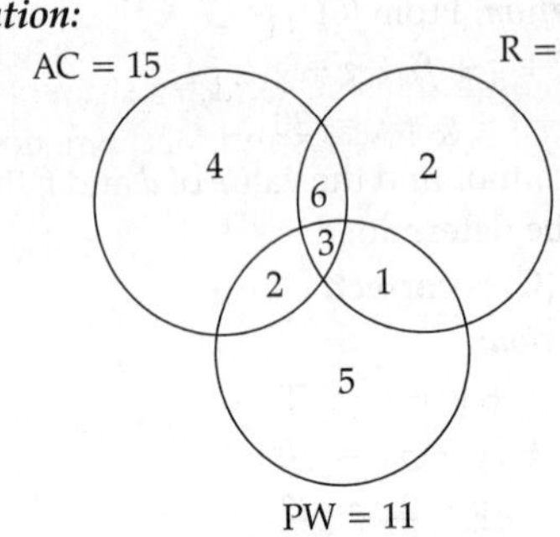

From Venn diagram, adding all values

$\Rightarrow 15 + 5 + 1 + 2 = 23$ cars

Hence, $25 - 23 = 2$ cars don't have any options.

Level-3: EXPERT

17. Option (C) is correct.

Explanation: Frenchmen: D_1, D_2, D_3

Englishmen: B_1, B_2, B_3

1st round of call [Assuming B, knows French)

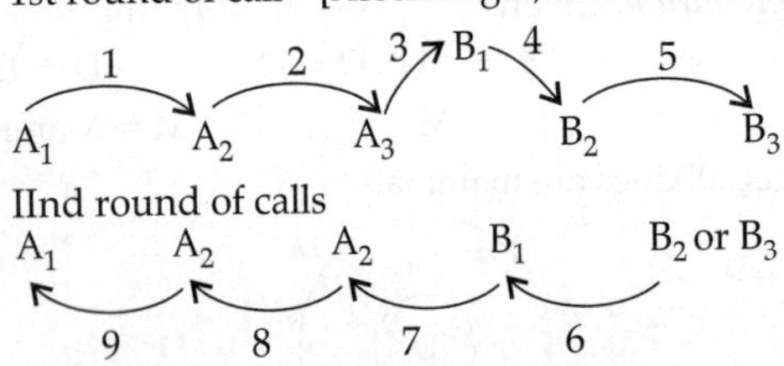

In the 6th call, B_1 knows all the secrets.

Hence, after 9th call, everyone will know all the secrets.

18. Option (B) is correct.

Explanation:

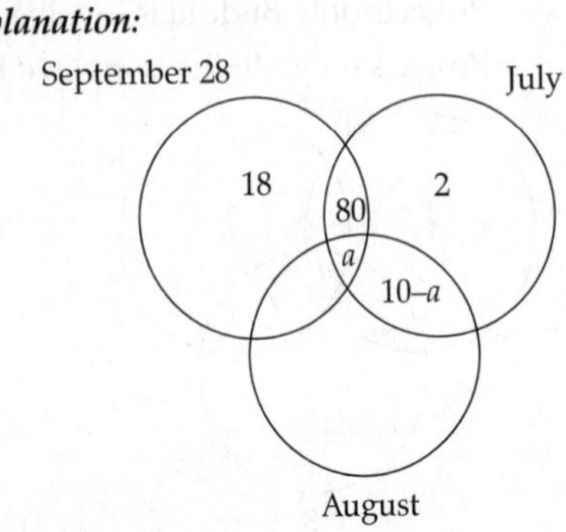

$$100 - 24 = 76 \quad \text{[Read at least one issue]}$$

If 'a' people read all there then $(8 - x)$ read only September and July issue

23 read September and August issue.

$$18 + 8 - a = 23$$

$$a = 3$$

As readers of September issue = 28

$[28 - (8 - 3) - 3 - 18] = 2$ readers of only August and September issue

July and August have 10 readers, then

$$10 - 3 = 7$$

read only July and August issues

Hence, readers who read exactly two consecutive issues $= 7 + 2 = 9$

19. Option (B) is correct.

Explanation: Assuming, students of only H = a

Students of only E = 6

Students of only H and P = x

Students of only E and P = y

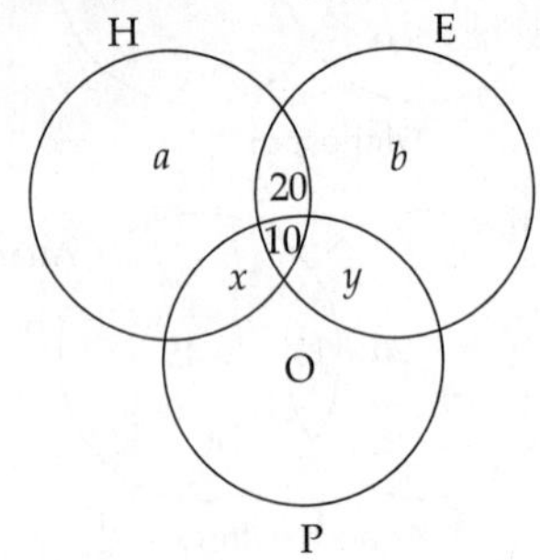

Given, Only P students = 10

Students of H and E but not P = 20

Also given,

No. of students of H = No. of students of E

$$\Rightarrow a + x + 20 + 10 = b + y + 20 + 10$$

$$a + x = b + y$$

Therefore,

$$a + x + 20 + 10 + e + y = 74$$

$$a + x + b + y = 44$$

$$a + x + a + x = 44$$

$$a + x = 22$$

Hence, no. of students studying H

$= a + x + 20 + 10 = 22 + 20 + 10 = 52$

20. Option (D) is correct.

Explanation: Assuming no. of studying liking both = a who like none = b

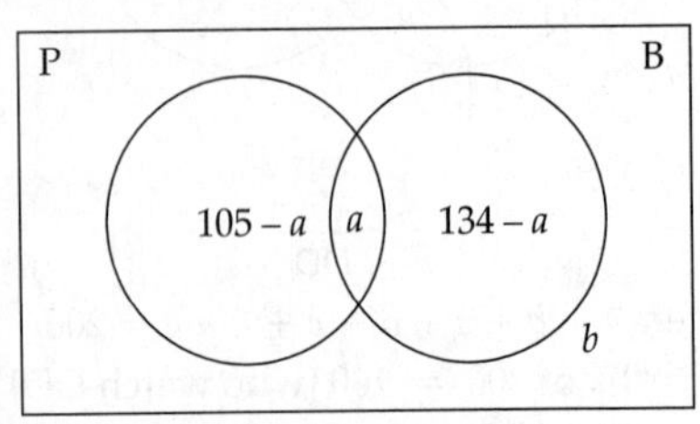

from Venn Diagram

$105 - a + a + 134 - a + b = 200a - b = 39$

$\therefore$ possible values of (a, b) are :

(39, 0) (40, 1).... (105, 66)

Hence, number of students who like only burgers lies in $[134 - 105, 134 - 39] \Rightarrow 29, 95$

21. Option (D) is correct.

Explanation: Assuming number of players of all three games = a

Given, all players play at least one game.

So, union of three sets = 256

$256 = 144 + 123 + 132 - 58 + 25 + 63 + a \Rightarrow a = 3$

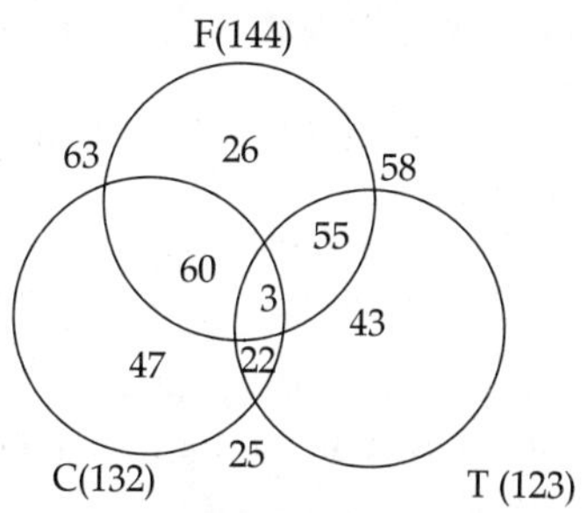

Hence, it is clear from Venn diagram that players who play only tennis = 43

22. Option (A) is correct.

Explanation: Given, P = O, M = O, C = O

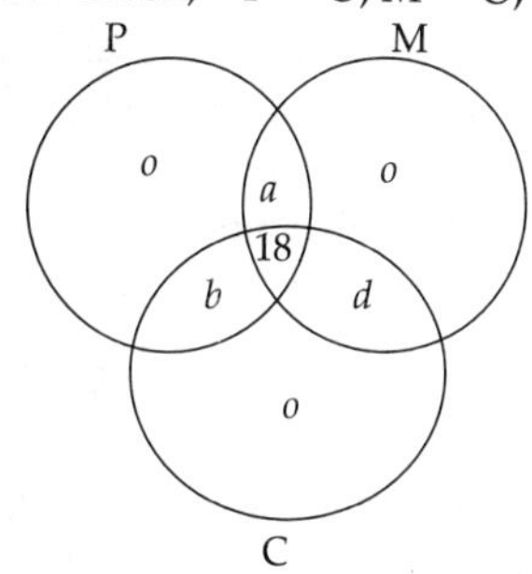

P = Physics students

M = Mathematics students

C = Chemistry students

Assuming, only P and M = a

only P and C = b

only M and C = d

Hence, to minimise Chemistry students, we have to maximise only Physics and Mathematics which is 5.

Writing Your Notes

Just in case you have forgotten today, takedown your notes!
But why is it so important?

Tools for the hands are tools for the brain writes Hetty Roessingh.
Handwritten notes are a powerful tool for encrypting embodied cognition and in turn supporting the brain's capacity for recuperation of information. If that sounds so scientific then in simple words: Writing notes by hand help you in:

- Increasing your comprehension
- Strengthening your memory
- Igniting your creativity
- Engaging your mind
- Increasing your attention span

Are these reasons enough to get you started?

1. ....
2. ....
3. ....
4. ....
5. ....
6. ....
7. ....
8. ....
9. ....
10. ....
11. ....
12. ....
13. ....
14. ....
15. ....
16. ....
17. ....
18. ....
19. ....
20. ....